FUN

NEW SERIES

VOL II

LONDON:

PUBLISHED (FOR THE PROPRIETORS) BY THOMAS BAKER,

80, FLEET STREET, E.C.

The Dictionary of
19th Century British
BOOK ILLUSTRATORS
and CARICATURISTS

Simon Houfe

ANTIQUE COLLECTORS' CLUB

In Memory of my Friend
Margaret Ann Elton
1915-1995

ISBN 1 85149 193 7

First edition 1978
Revised 1981, 1996

British Library Cataloguing-in-Publication Data
A catalogue record for this book is available from the British Library

Printed in England by the Antique Collectors' Club Ltd.
5 Church Street, Woodbridge, Suffolk
on Consort Royal Satin paper
supplied by the Donside Paper Company, Aberdeen, Scotland

Frontispiece: EDMUND DULAC 1882-1953. 'Beauty and the Beast'. Original drawing for *Fairy Tales* by
Sir Arthur Quiller-Couch, 1910. Pen, ink and watercolour, dated 1910   Victoria and Albert Museum

Title page: KATE GREENAWAY 1846-1901. From an illustration for *Under the Window,* 1878, by Kate Greenaway

Antique Collectors' Club

The Antique Collectors' Club was formed in 1966 and now has a five figure membership spread throughout the world. It publishes the only independently run monthly antiques magazine, *Antique Collecting*, which caters for those collectors who are interested in widening their knowledge of antiques, both by greater awareness of quality and by discussion of the factors which influence the price that is likely to be asked. The Antique Collectors' Club pioneered the provision of information on prices for collectors and the magazine still leads in the provision of detailed articles on a variety of subjects.

It was in response to the enormous demand for information on 'what to pay' that the price guide series was introduced in 1968 with the first edition of *The Price Guide to Antique Furniture* (completely revised 1978 and 1989), a book which broke new ground by illustrating the more common types of antique furniture, the sort that collectors could buy in shops and at auctions rather than the rare museum pieces which had previously been used (and still to a large extent are used) to make up the limited amount of illustrations in books published by commercial publishers. Many other price guides have followed, all copiously illustrated, and greatly appreciated by collectors for the valuable information they contain, quite apart from prices. The Antique Collectors' Club also publishes other books on antiques (including horology and art), garden history and architecture, and a full book list is available.

Club membership, open to all collectors, costs little. Members receive free of charge *Antique Collecting*, the Club's magazine (published ten times a year), which contains well-illustrated articles dealing with the practical aspects of collecting not normally dealt with by magazines. Prices, features of value, investment potential, fakes and forgeries are all given prominence in the magazine.

Among other facilities available to members are private buying and selling facilities, the longest list of 'For Sales' of any antiques magazine, an annual ceramics conference and the opportunity to meet other collectors at their local antique collectors' clubs. There are over eighty in Britain and more than a dozen overseas. Members may also buy the Club's publications at special pre-publication prices.

As its motto implies, the Club is an organisation designed to help collectors get the most out of their hobby: it is informal and friendly and gives enormous enjoyment to all concerned.

For Collectors —By Collectors —About Collecting

The Antique Collectors' Club, 5 Church Street, Woodbridge, Suffolk IP12 1DS

Acknowledgements

It is nearly twenty years since I began to prepare the first edition of this book and many of the people who assisted me with the work have retired and in some cases died. I always received kindness and courtesy from the late Rodney Searight, whose collection was bequeathed to the Victoria and Albert Museum, from the late Ronald Marshall of the Stone Gallery and from the late Lady Mander. Mr Grant Uden supplied me with many additional names until his death a few years ago.

In more recent times, I have received help from Michael Broadbent, the Keene scholar, who has shown great interest in my work and from Philip Athill of Abbott & Holder, Mike Heseltine of Sotheby's, Robin de Beaumont and Paul Goldman. I have continued to benefit from the great knowledge of both Jeremy Maas and John Christian.

Numerous foundations and art galleries that helped me in 1978 were mentioned in the preface to the first edition. It would be tedious to list them all again, but I would just like to add, the curator of Leighton House, Ms Julia Findlater, Mrs Shirley Nicholson of Linley Sambourne House and Dr Chris Beetles of Ryder Street, St James's, who generously allowed me to reproduce drawings from his gallery.

I have also received great help from Diana McMillan of Antique Collectors' Club, who has skilfully inserted new names and new information into the book.

Simon Houfe

ANNIE FRENCH fl.1900-1925. 'A Garlanded Wedding.' Pen and watercolour. Signed   Private Collection

Contents

THOMAS ROWLANDSON 1756-1827. 'Dr Syntax and The Gypsies.' Illustration to *The Tour of Dr Syntax in Search of the Picturesque*, 1812. Hand-coloured engraving

Introduction

The years between the late Georgian period and the outbreak of the First World War were revolutionary ones for the art of the book. In no single century, before our own, could such wide ranging developments and industrial advances have been envisaged. At the close of the eighteenth century, the illustrated book was the preserve of a small and highly privileged section of society who could afford to pay high prices for copper plate engravings bringing to life their novels, poetry and travel literature. Book illustrators were no longer under the sole patronage of the aristocracy, a large middle class readership demanded its burlesques to be illustrated by Thomas Rowlandson or Isaac Cruikshank and its topography to appear in aquatint plates by the Daniells or Samuel Howett, a vast and shadowy section of society being catered for by the crude woodcuts of street literature. Within a generation or two, new techniques and the advent of steam presses had changed the landscape – popular literature was possible for everyone, popular education was put forward by such democrats as Charles Knight and the Chambers family and illustrated magazines began to proliferate.

The contrast between the nineteenth century and the eighteenth century can be clearly seen from the listings in Hammelmann and Boase's pioneering *Book Illustrators in Eighteenth Century England*, published in 1975, and the first edition of this *Dictionary*, published in 1978. The former had barely 170 artists included whereas the latter listed several thousand. One can understand from this that between 1800 and 1914, illustrated literature became general literature and therefore the choice of these years becomes a more logical one, the first age of a mass readership.

The Regency period, although not as prolific as the Victorian period, produced some of the greatest artists of the book, from the individual imagination of William Blake to the sumptuous productions of Ackermann's *Oxford* and *Cambridge* and Pugin and Rowlandson's *Microcosm* of 1808. The colour plate book, which was a rarity in 1800, streamed out by the 1820s filling the shelves with volumes of caricature, architecture, botany, decoration and foreign travel. The copper engraving was succeeded by the steel engraving and the lithograph and, by the 1840s, by the facsimile wood engraving which had a great vogue for thirty years and reached perfection in this country.

From the 1850s to the 1860s, British publishers enjoyed a golden age of the illustrated book that was never repeated, except for a brief interlude in the 1890s. For a decade, nearly every major British artist contributed to illustration, notably the Pre-Raphaelite group of Holman Hunt, Millais, Rossetti, Burne-Jones, Morris and their confrères. Book illustration, that had been looked upon as a minor art form by earlier generations, almost as a craft, was suddenly raised to the status of serious painting. At this time it was not considered beneath the notice of academicians or professors, John Ruskin wrote about it and such Olympian figures as Lord Leighton made drawings for novels. Other artists who stood rather aloof from the exhibitions and galleries, such as James McNeil Whistler, also contributed illustrations to magazines.

The impetus and business sense of the Victorians, which made such publications as the *Illustrated London News,* the *Graphic* and *Punch* the success that they were, complemented at the end of the century by huge technical advances. Photographic reproduction, photogravure, the half-tone and the line block enabled black and white artists to achieve new peaks of refinement. Aubrey Beardsley was among that generation of black and white artists who arrived at the right moment and capitalised so brilliantly on the new art. Colour reproduction, which had had several false starts in the middle of the century, was brought to a high point by printers such as Edmund Evans and in the wood block colour prints of Walter Crane's *Toy Books* for Messrs. Routledge. By the 1900s, the superbly illustrated child's book, with its full page colour illustrations by Thomson, Rackham, Dulac and their colleagues, was a normal part of the Edwardian Christmas. After 1914 it was to be swept away in a more cost-conscious society, as was the adult illustrated novel which had survived from Dickens and Trollope to Jerome K. Jerome and Anstey. The children's book remained the last haven of the professional book illustrator, and still does.

The fact that this book deals with British artists and illustrators does not mean that the international aspect is ignored. The tremendous cross-fertilisation between Britain and the Continent resulted in important influences from Paris and Germany in the middle of the nineteenth century. British caricature was softened by the influence of the domestic satire of France in the 1840s and established the tradition of social illustration in this country characterised by Leech, Keene and George Du Maurier. In the 1890s the poster art of Paris (where so many of this country's illustrators were trained) profoundly affected the illustration of the Beggarstaff Brothers, Dudley Hardy and Phil May. One has only to look at the albums produced by Toulouse-Lautrec to recognise them as the near relations of the albums produced by William Nicholson. I have included the names of British illustrators who worked mostly abroad but have also included the names of foreign illustrators whose work appeared regularly in British publications, such as Gavarni, Eugène Lami and Maurice Bonvoisin, known as 'Mars'.

I have tried in this reference book to include as many of the minor figures and more fugitive illustrators as possible. The period was one of great amateur participation, not only did *Punch* or *Fun* publish amateur work, but many private individuals took up the current illustrating fashion – lithography in the 1830s, etching in the 1870s and wood engraving in the 1890s – to produce their own books.

Artists that overlap the rather arbitrary dates of the volume have been given the benefit of the doubt. I have tended to include from the eighteenth century only those artists the bulk of whose work falls on this side of 1800. Similarly, there are a number of artists whose professional careers began before 1914 but whose reputation now rests on books illustrated at a later date. I have included all their books up to 1915 and any books afterwards that seem to be relevant. More detailed references can usually be found in Mr Horne's volume.

This new edition has about 150 new names and many of the existing entries have been amended or updated to include new books, exhibitions or additional material. The original edition of the *Dictionary* (1978), revised in 1981, contained introductory chapters on the art of illustration. Although these are not included, it is hoped to refashion them into a book on the collecting and understanding of book illustration, which would be a suitable companion to the *Dictionary.*

Simon Houfe
Ampthill, 1996

(ISAAC) ROBERT CRUIKSHANK 1786-1856. Drawing for a caricature print, c.1815

A Century of Illustration

In his autobiography, the writer Leigh Hunt (1784-1859) expressed his feelings about the illustrated books of his day. "How I loved these little sixpenny numbers", he wrote, "containing whole poets. I doted on their size; I doted on their type, on their ornaments, on their wrappers containing lists of other poets, and on the engravings from Kirk."[1] Hunt's life actually spanned a revolution in book illustration, from the days of the small illustrated poets when he was a child in 1800 to the vast range of illustrated literature available under the Victorians. He was fortunate that his childhood coincided with a more accessible children's literature,

WILLIAM HEATH (PAUL PRY) 1795-1840. 'Where Are You Going My Pretty Maid?' Hand-coloured engraving, c.1825

a growing school of British illustration and great advances in printing technique. The years before 1800 had seen some remarkable illustrated books, but the advance of a native talent had been patchy.

From 1700, the art of book illustration had been dominated by foreign draughtsmen and engravers, most of them *émigrés* from political upheavals in France, where standards of design were recognisably higher than in this country. The leading publishers employed them gratefully, but the publishers themselves were partly printers and partly booksellers, as well as commissioning new work, and not the best judges of fine art. Among the firms to establish great reputations were those of Jacob Tonson, Robert Dodsley and John Baskerville, specialising variously in portrait frontispieces, full page illustrations and fine typefaces. Tonson encouraged the French artist, Hubert François Gravelot to come to this country and it was Gravelot who established a rococo style of book illustration and a school of artists who worked in it. He illustrated *Dryden* in 1735 and *Shakespeare* in 1740 with a sophistication and technical ability not seen before. He was involved in the continuation of the first teaching institution in the country, the St Martin's Lane Academy and was influential on such figures as Thomas Gainsborough, Francis Hayman and Samuel Wale, the last two being prolific illustrators.

From the 1740s a vigorous tradition was established through the works of William Hogarth, although the artist himself preferred the separately issued print to the tedium of book illustration. In his print series he set his own agenda and created his own texts, providing a 'dumb show' that could be read from the engraved page. This set a valuable precedent for the next hundred years where readers came to expect moral ideas in the illustration of their books.

Political satire was a very potent force from the 1750s, the crude copies of Italian *caricatura* practised by amateurs, gradually becoming the withering and malicious plates of James Gillray (1757-1815), Isaac Cruikshank (1756-1811), and Thomas Rowlandson (1756-1827). Social satire also had its place in the country humour of the semi-amateur George Woodward (1760-1809) and the hunting squire Henry William Bunbury (1750-1811). The advancement of this art was clearly helped by the considerable political liberty and climate of free speech, even at such crucial times as the American War of Independence and the French Revolution. This was in great contrast to the French caricaturists of the Revolution, who had no base on which to build and whose productions were crude and backward-looking in the extreme.[2]

Two early eighteenth century books, *Gulliver's Travels*, 1719 and *Robinson Crusoe*, 1726 had been extensively illustrated through numerous editions and given a taste for the illustration of fantastic tales. With the coming of the literary novel, albeit in the form of letters, Richardson's *Pamela*, 1740 and Fielding's *Joseph Andrews*, 1742, a genre was established that had to be illustrated. A small, widely dispersed readership, which was unable to see stage plays, had always demanded printed plays. There seem to be more printed versions of plays during the eighteenth century than at any other time, and the play readers were probably the same people who became novel readers. For this reason, the illustrations tended to be dramatic and histrionic, frozen scenes or tableaux from a theatre performance and very similar to the 'stills' painted by such artists as Samuel de Wilde. Many artists who went on to succeed as history painters began as book illustrators, among them Tresham, Hamilton, Opie, Fuseli, Smirke, Westall and Northcote, working in this theatrical style. It is noticeable that some of the most popular illustrated volumes were theatre books, Bell's *The British Theatre,* for example, as well as the grander and more serious Boydell *Shakespeare,* published in nine volumes in 1802. The most popular pseudo-sciences of the period were physiognomy and craniology, both of which had a bearing on caricature and illustration. Johann Casper Lavater's *Essays On Physiognomy* had been translated into English before 1797 and both systems were studiously observed in Regency and early Victorian Britain.

The romantic movement in poetry and the picturesque movement in painting and landscape gardening had also spawned a new type of book. Architectural books, itineraries and albums of country seats became extremely popular and were produced to a very high standard of finish and design. Works such as Thomas Pennant's *Tour,* 1772, *A Tour In Wales and a Journey to Snowdon,* 1778-81, *A Journey From London to Chester,* 1782 and others, had specially commissioned views by the artist who travelled with him. *The Seats of the Nobility & Gentry* by W. Watts, 1779, *Angus's Views,* 1787, Harrison & Co's *Picturesque Views,* 1788 and many others, culminated in the mammoth *Beauties of England and Wales* by John Britton (1771-1857), starting in 1801 and falling well within our period.

All these books were for a strictly limited well-to-do audience, few books but religious tracts and perhaps *The Pilgrim's Progress* coming within the grasp of ordinary people, always supposing that they could read. The literature of the street was in ballads and broadsides, commemorating gruesome or heroic events or popular songs, often illustrated by primitive woodcuts. The magazines were few in number and by their titles, *The London Magazine, The European Magazine* were directed at an urban readership; their illustrations were usually limited to fashion plates and the occasional view.

Children's books before 1790 were strictly didactic and not particularly appetising for infant minds. The famous firm of Newbery of St Paul's Church Yard was more adventurous, publishing the celebrated *Mother Goose's Tales*, 1765 and *Goody Two-Shoes*, 1766. Nevertheless, it was to be the new century before great strides were made in juvenile literature, with such classics as *The Swiss Family Robinson*, 1814.

Practically all of the great innovations came after 1800. Before this date, books were illustrated by engraved copper plates, occasionally by etchings, only the most sumptuous being coloured. After the turn of the century one is into the world of lithography, aquatint and eventually steel engraving, one has entered the era of professional fine art publishers, a greatly enlarged market, and the growth of magazines capable of taking illustrations. The issuing of caricatures (eventually grouped into books) becomes an almost daily occurrence, satirical publications abound and the illustrating of novels becomes common.

The wars in Europe between 1795 and 1815 made foreign travel very difficult, except for a short respite in 1802. This halted the great illustrated books on Continental art and topography that had poured from the presses in the wake of the neoclassical revival. Particularly striking was the *Hamilton Vases*, published first by D'Hancarville, 1766-67, and later by Tischbein, 1791-95. British publishers continued to re-issue French books, but increasingly the interest was in British landscape and buildings, fired by the picturesque movement and the poets. The Revd. William Gilpin of Boldre, Hants (1724-1804) was an important figure as an amateur artist and a theoretician. His stream of books on landscape, *The Tour of the Lakes* and *Scottish Tour*, 1789, *Remarks on Forest Scenery*, 1791, *Three Essays*, 1792, and *Western Tour*, 1798, taught people to look at nature from the painterly point of view. More important, his aquatint illustrations were generalised topography and advanced the idea that illustration did not have to be slavishly accurate, but pleasing.

The more architectural approach to buildings and history was provided by an *émigré* from Saxony, Rudolph Ackermann (1764-1834). He set up his business in central London in 1813, producing lavish coloured plate books on medieval and contemporary architecture, costume, interior decoration and fashionable taste.[3] These included the celebrated *Microcosm of London*, 1808, where the artist A.C. Pugin was employed to draw the architecture and Thomas Rowlandson was to people each plate with figures. It was the sort of brilliant combination that Ackermann was best at inventing and he went on to produce *The History of The Abbey of Westminster*, 1812 and the *University of Oxford*, 1814 and *Cambridge*, 1815. For these huge volumes he employed a dazzling team of topographical artists, Thomas Uwins, George Shepherd, Frederick Mackenzie, Nash and Westall. The plates were engraved on copper and coloured by hand in one of Ackermann's colouring workshops. His crowning achievement was perhaps in producing *The History of the Royal Residences* by W.H. Pyne in 1829, the interiors aquatinted in brown, olive, green or red, before being finished by hand. Ackermann's *Repository of Arts* was a forerunner of art magazines and appeared between 1809 and 1828. From 1817, Ackermann was using the new process of lithography in his magazine.

Perhaps the most successful of the Ackermann ventures was the long series of books, illustrated by Thomas Rowlandson, from William Combe's *Dr Syntax*, 1812-1821. They perfectly fit into the Regency love of travelogues and also of

JOHN BUONAROTTI PAPWORTH 1775-1847, 'An Alcove', illustration for his book *Hints On Ornamental Gardening*, 1823

WALTER FITCH fl.1827-1892. 'Flowering Cactus' an original drawing in watercolour for Curtis's *Botanical Magazine*, c.1835   Woburn Collection

ROBERT JOHN THORNTON 1768-1837. 'Roses', from his own *Temple of British Flora or Garden of Nature*, 1805. Engraved by R. Earlom

The KING of BROBDINGNAG and GULLIVER

RICHARD WESTALL, RA 1765-1836. 'Aeneas Triumphing over Turnus.' Original drawing for illustration to *The Aeneid*, c.1800.   Victoria & Albert Museum

JAMES GILLRAY 1757-1815. 'The King of Brobdingnag and Gulliver.' Political caricature issued in July 1803. Hand-coloured engraving

humorous adventures, but it has to be said Rowlandson's plates are more eighteenth century than nineteenth century in flavour.

Lithography had been introduced to this country by Aloys Senefelder (1771-1834) in 1807. J.T. Smith's *Antiquities of Westminster*, 1807, was the first book in this country to have a lithographic plate inserted. The lithographic stone was more durable than metal, gave a more personal autograph image to the page and came closest to watercolour drawing. It was improved by C.J. Hullmandel (1789-1850) who, with the artists Cattermole and J.D. Harding, produced the litho-tint with even more pleasing effects.

Following the Napoleonic Wars, books of foreign travel abounded, lavishly illustrated but directed at a much more popular market than at the close of the previous century. Ackermann published costume books of Russia, China and Austria and illustrated accounts of the recent campaigns. Artists of high calibre such as J.M.W. Turner (1775-1851), William Clarkson Stanfield (1793-1867) and David Roberts (1796-1864) were persuaded to issue specially commissioned album books of travel and topography at home and abroad. Guide books were more heavily illustrated and popular series developed, using the steel plate from which thousands of impressions could be taken.

The Regency and the reign of George IV, 1820-30, was a period of great social change – the industrial revolution was beginning to bite and the middle classes were more dominant. Most towns now had circulating libraries and literary and scientific institutes, provincial presses were being established and at the same time some provincial newspapers. There was a growing perception that every publication, from botanical magazines to religious tracts and working class literature, should be illustrated.

This moral enlightenment was in great contrast to George IV's court which was extravagant, lax and spendthrift. It was wickedly pilloried by the generation of caricaturists who had succeeded Gillray and his friends. The new men included George Cruikshank (1792-1878), William Heath (1795-1840), Robert Seymour (1798-1836) and Charles Williams (fl.1797-1830). They caricatured the politicians, but increasingly came to focus on the peccadilloes of the King and his royal entourage. Great play was made with the King's marital problems with his estranged wife Queen Caroline, who happily for the King but sadly for the caricaturists, died in 1821. Williams in particular was able to make great sport of the King's delight in fat mistresses and in the gaudy appearance of his chinoiserie residence at the Royal Pavilion, Brighton. This tendency to satirise social rather than political foibles was an increasing movement during the 1820s and really made way for the softer humour of the Victorians.

By 1830, the Georgian concept of caricatures issued separately as events occurred was beginning to go out of fashion. As early as 1818, *The New Bon Ton Magazine or Telescope of The Times* had attempted to group caricature material together in a volume, mostly by Lewis Marks. William Heath copied the French idea of caricature magazines and launched *The Northern Looking-Glass*, 1825-26 and *The Looking-Glass*, 1830, in a folio format, neither of which were very successful. One caricaturist, John Doyle (1797-1868), known as 'HB', continued to issue separate caricature sheets in lithography, coloured and plain. They were also sold as volumes with a key to the plates, but have not stood the test of time very well, being mannered, two-dimensional and weightless.

Many of the great caricaturists of the 1820s were moving into the book in the 1830s. George Cruikshank, whose wit and brilliance had made the Regency laugh, became the illustrator of his own books and magazines. *Cruikshank's Comic Almanack* thrived between 1835 and 1853, similarly Thomas Hood's *Comic Album*, 1830 to 1838 was occasionally illustrated by Cruikshank. The artist illustrated one important work by Charles Dickens, *Oliver Twist* in 1838, but preferred to choose his own texts. It was in fact the illustrator Robert Seymour, who had built his reputation as a single print caricaturist, whose work suggested the idea of *Pickwick Papers* to the publishers. Scenes of comic sportsmen had always been popular, since the days of Robert Dighton in the eighteenth century, and Seymour's drawings were to be strung together by a suitable story. Charles Dickens was asked to do the text and the book became a classic after its first appearance in 1836. Seymour's death meant that he was superseded as illustrator by H.K. Browne, 'Phiz', who remained the novelist's chief exponent for many years. These books were always issued in parts before they were issued in volume form as 'three deckers'. The position of the illustrator was therefore always crucial in providing continuity and in acting as a link between the instalments. Just as the author was expected to produce a climax to each monthly episode, so the illustrator was encouraged to provide a dramatic visual crescendo! H.K. Browne's illustrations, like most of those of his contemporaries, were engravings in the caricature tradition. They were made up of small exaggerated figures that perfectly complemented the earlier Dickens' novels. Dickens had many imitators, but so did Browne, artists like Thomas Onwhyn and Watts Phillips, who had the vivacity as humorous artists but not the skill as draughtsmen.

Other artists, such as John Leech (1817-1864) and Daniel Maclise (1806-1870) illustrated Dickens' Christmas Books, issued between 1843 and 1848. The most famous of these was of course *A Christmas Carol*, 1840, including John Leech's memorable images of Ebenezer Scrooge, Marley's Ghost and the Last of the Spirits. Dickens' stories and Leech's engravings almost created the Victorian Christmas, endowing it with a sort of mystique that was to last throughout the nineteenth century into our own day and create hundreds of seasonal illustrated books. *A Christmas Carol* was followed by *The Cricket on The Hearth*, 1845-46, *The Battle of Life*, 1846-47 and *The Haunted Man*, 1847-48. None of these books had quite the success of the first, but they are extremely attractive productions in their bright red cloth covers with delicate gilding.

The design of many of these volumes was very attractive and the whole decade of the 1840s was a period of high standards in book illustration. It is more usual to think of the later decades of the 1860s or 1890s as the apogee of the Victorian pictured book, but from about 1843, the balance of illustration, decoration and printing was beautifully integrated. In 1841, John Murray's published an edition of *Lockhart's Spanish Ballads* with illustrations by William Allan, David Roberts, William Simson, Henry Warren, C.E. Aubrey and William Harvey. These were all well established names but the greatest contribution was by an unknown younger man, Owen Jones (1809-1874), who was credited with the ornamental borders and vignettes. The colour printing, sophisticated for its date, was undertaken by the firm of Vizetelly of Fleet Street and was crisp enough and clear enough in register to do justice to Jones's fascinating Moorish designs. Jones designed the cover and endpapers, but his *tour de force* was in the decorative half-titles and coloured

POLLY . *Stop a moment, Roddy , stop a moment, stop ,*
Before you take a little pop, take a little **drop***.*

Act . III. Scene II.

SIR JOHN TENNIEL 1820-1914. Illustration for the *Book of Beauty,* c.1840

RICHARD DOYLE 1824-1883. Illustration for a children's book, c.1860

Seven little Soldier Boys were playing funny tricks,
One, just in fun, let off his gun, and then there were but **6**.

Anonymous illustrator. Illustration to *Ten Little Soldier Boys*. One of a series of Warne's Juvenile Drolleries, c.1870

A group of illustrated covers from Routledge's books in the 1870s, designed by HARRISON WEIR, EDWARD LEAR and RANDLOPH CALDECOTT

DANTE GABRIEL ROSSETTI 1828-1882. 'St. Cecilia.' Design for Moxon's *Tennyson*, 1856-57. Signed with mongram. Pen and brown ink, 37/8in x 31/4in (9.8cm x 8.3cm)

Birmingham City Art Gallery

NEVER a word ſpak' bonnie Jeanie Roole,
But---" Shepherd let us gang : "
An' never mair, at a gloamin' buchte
Wad ſhe ſing another ſang.

JOSEPH CRAWHALL Senior 1821-1896. Illustration to *The Gloamin' buchte*, 1883. Woodcuts coloured by hand

frontispieces that occur throughout the volume. The monochrome and sometimes two colour borders in a variety of tints surround each poem in the book and they are supplemented by vignette illustrations by the other artists. Although six artists are involved, the book has a unity of design which is very pleasing to the eye. This was definitely a gift-book, one of a new genre of the early Victorian period, designed more for the table than the library. Its origins are probably more Continental than anything else and it resembles some of the books produced in France in the Troubadour Style.

Owen Jones's remarkable talent for design was to continue with his *Alhambra*, 1836-42, *The Grammar of Ornament*, 1856 and *The Victoria Psalter*, 1861. Jones helped to supervise the decorations of the Great Exhibition in 1851 and represented the new spirit that saw the decorative arts and book art as equal to the fine arts, not simply a lesser hand-maid. During this period, Government Schools of Design were established up and down the country and the Art Unions, which made original engraved work more accessible to the general public, also established a magazine, *The Art Union*, later *The Art Journal*.

An equally important book of a few years later was *Moore's Irish Melodies*, published by Longman & Co in 1846. This had an even greater unity than the *Spanish Ballads* because it was the work of one artist alone, Daniel Maclise RA (1806-1870). Here, the full page vignettes incorporated the texts of the poems in rich, luxuriant and rather sensuous borders of flowers, treillage, leaves and figures. Nothing quite like it had been experienced before in this country, but the influence was once more Continental, only German this time, rather than French. Artists and illustrators of the Munich School had used this technique from the 1830s and the intense decorative atmosphere was garnered from the Nazarene painters, German exiles who had worked in Rome. The intricate pencil work of Maclise was worked up into toned engravings by the German artist F.E. Becker, setting a style that was to be influential for several years. The young artist John Tenniel worked in this manner, and so did Charles Keene as a young man. Maclise produced dozens of these drawings for the book, which are little masterpieces, but which were sold after his death for a few shillings each.

Another important contributor to this period was H. Noel Humphreys (1810-1879) who designed illuminated gift-books based on medieval manuscripts. Although they were not illustrated books in the strictest sense, they were widely copied and illumination became a popular pastime. Among the best of his chromo-lithographic works were *The Miracles...*,1848 and *A Record of the Black Prince*, 1849. Works by exceptional designers like Humphreys were accompanied by a welter of lesser gift-books, albums, annuals and keepsakes, all trying to rival each other with insipid steel engravings and tinted prints. Very few of them had specially commissioned illustrations but more usually engraved works after Royal Academy pictures or plates of celebrated beauties. A few, like *Heath's Picturesque Annual*, employed well-known painters like Clarkson Stanfield or Samuel Prout to contribute landscapes of Italy, Spain and Switzerland for a select public.

The Birth of *Punch*

The years 1841-42 were important in the history of illustration because they saw the birth of two British institutions, *Punch* and *The Illustrated London News*, one of which is still happily with us. This was a watershed for illustrated journalism, proving once and for all that journals with pictures were a necessary as well as a possible part of Victorian life. Until this date, the illustrated magazines had been ephemeral and localised, few advancing beyond a year or two of publication, fewer still available anywhere except London or the big cities. Both these new titles were to become national and weekly. The technical innovations in steam-powered printing made large print runs possible, the increasing rail network meant that they could be distributed with ease. W.H. Smith's bought up the sole rights of railway bookstalls in 1848 and the first outlet was opened on Euston Station on 1st November that year. The firm had identified a new public that wished to be seduced into the reading habit while they travelled and yellow back books had on their covers 'For the Fireside, Steamboat or The Rail'.

Punch was born from a succession of ideas floated by men in the literary and printing world. Such characters as Thackeray, the novelist, Ebenezer Landells, the printer and Henry Mayhew, the journalist, felt that a satirical magazine on the French model was viable in London. After several false starts and changes of printer, *Punch* finally settled down under the ownership of Messrs Bradbury & Evans and with the playwright, versifier and columnist, Mark Lemon, as editor. At first, it was not distinguishable from many other caricature weeklies, although its literary content was always stronger. The main contributors were radical in politics as well as young in years and the magazine had a healthily disreputable image for its first three or four years of life. The illustrations were confined to small humorous wood engravings, the occasional pictured joke and a full page wood engraving making some political statement, often anti-government or anti-French, sometimes anti-monarchist.

Punch brought the word 'cartoon' into the vocabulary at this time. Originally an artistic term to describe a pencil study for a painting or the outlines of a mural work, *Punch* adopted it in 1843 to illustrate mock suggestions for murals at the new Palace of Westminster. These large satirical cuts had always been called 'Pencillings' but after the Westminster competition they were referred to as 'cartoons' and cartoons they remained.

The magazine was also paving the way towards a new type of humour in line, the comedy of manners. As the older caricaturists like George Cruikshank moved into book illustration, so the younger men moved into social satire. This style of domestic humour had come from France, where a repressive régime under King Louis-Philippe had controlled all overtly political lampooning. French novelists like Honoré de Balzac had mirrored French bourgeois life and the more cosmopolitan members of the *Punch* team, W.M. Thackeray, Richard Doyle and John Leech, copied their style. W.M. Thackeray, who was both writer and draughtsman, invented improbable servants like 'Jeames' who kept a diary which was published week by week in 1845. A similar series was 'The Snobs of England', 1846-47, which gave Thackeray ample opportunity to move up and down the social scale. The savagery of the Regency was going out of fashion and these men did much to temper it and tame it for a family audience.

The most important figure in this gradual sobering of *Punch* was John Leech (1817-1864). Leech was a true Londoner, the son of a coffee-house keeper on Ludgate Hill, who grew up amid the sights and sounds of a great capital. His capacity to observe and note down the fashions and foibles of his time made him

WALTER CRANE 1845-1915. 'I Saw Three Ships.' Illustration for a book of Nursery Rhymes

invaluable as a chronicler. He had intended to study medicine, but a family bankruptcy pushed him towards the only career with which he was instinctively attuned, that of a humorous draughtsman. He had little formal training, although he did study briefly in Paris, and was one of the few *Punch* artists of the mid-century who had worked with lithography. He was a better draughtsman by far than his friend Thackeray and his portrayal of character and ordinary middle class life were masterly. He had no strong political leanings and his few attempts at political cartoons were feeble and insipid. This was fortunate, for all his energies could be concentrated on the social vagaries of the average Londoner.

Leech was a family man and the trials and tribulations of the householder were translated into his work, the worries of smoking chimneys, noisy neighbours,

Right. CHARLES ROBINSON 1870-1937. 'The unseen clouds of the dew…' for Shelley's *The Sensitive Plant*, 1911. Watercolour

Chris Beetles, St James's Ltd

Below left. FREDERICK CAYLEY ROBINSON 1862-1927. 'And Now Thou Art Cursed', illustration for *The Book of Genesis*, 1914

Below right. ALAN ELSDEN ODLE 1888-1948. 'Gulliver stands to his full height.' Original drawing for a projected edition of *Gulliver's Travels*, c.1912. Pencil and watercolour, 22½in x 15½in (57.2cm x 39.4cm).

Author's Collection

drunken cooks and rude servants all enlivened the pages of *Punch*. Leech carried his readers with him in his vigorous designs, they felt they were part of his family and sympathised with his characters. Like succeeding *Punch* men, Leech evolved a cast of characters who gained instant recognition and popularity – 'The Brook Green Volunteer', who caricatured the territorial soldiers of the day, Tom Noddy, the fearless horseman, and Mr Briggs, the intrepid but unfortunate sportsman! All of the *Punch* illustrations were reproduced by wood engraving, a softer and more intimate medium than the old copper or steel engravings, greatly enhancing the gentler approach of satire in the 1840s and 1850s. The rise of the wood engraving is dealt with later in this introduction.

Punch published extra editions to its weekly output, a *Punch Almanack* for many years, increasing its circulation to 90,000. This supplement, with a calendar format and about a dozen pages of engravings, was mostly illustrated by Leech, the headpiece of each month representing hunting, shooting, fishing or whatever was appropriate for the season. By the 1850s, Leech's strength as a hunting draughtsman was more appreciated, he was not as great an artist as Landseer or Grant or such a good anatomist as Tenniel, but he had the feel for horses and their riders, he could conjure up a landscape, a water-jump or a hedge without making a single study in a sketch-book. This skill was recognised in 1851, when Leech began to make his memorable series of drawings for R.S. Surtees' novels.

His name had been put forward in 1843, but it was only as the artist rose in stature as a sporting draughtsman that the publishers became keen. *Mr Sponge's Sporting Tour* was published in 1852, the books were unusual in Leech's *oeuvre* having coloured steel engravings rather than his more usual wood engravings, although the text was interspersed with smaller wood engravings. Like the Dickens' volumes, they were issued in parts, making the skill of the illustrator in carrying the story forward and linking the numbers absolutely crucial. It proved to be one of the most perfect Victorian partnerships, Leech captured brilliantly the confidence trickster sportsman Soapy Sponge and his female equivalent, Lucy Glitters. In *Handley Cross*, 1853, Leech got his pencil round the corpulent form of Mr Jorrocks and these successes were followed by *Ask Mama*, 1858 and *Mr Facey Romford's Hounds*, 1864. The images of these Victorian personalities are quintessentially Leech's although they were Surtees' creations. This series greatly increased Leech's fame and can hardly have done *Punch* any harm, particularly as Bradbury & Evans were the publishers of both! Leech had few pupils, but quite a number of followers; every Victorian novel with scenes of country life, squires, yokels, infant prodigies and hen-pecked husbands, owes something to him. His spirit, if not his technique, was carried forward into the later draughtsmen of *Punch* such as Cecil Aldin, G.D. Armour and Lionel Edwards.

The other star of early *Punch* was Richard 'Dicky' Doyle (1824-1883). Doyle was the son of the Regency caricaturist 'HB', already mentioned, and three other members of his family were artists. Doyle produced illustrated albums for his family while still a boy and then collaborated with John Leech at the age of eighteen. Whereas Leech's strengths were in the characterisation of humorous situations, Doyle's were in fantasy and imagination, where his meticulous detail was enhanced by a strong decorative ability. He was invaluable to *Punch* for his headpieces, initial letters and *Almanack* contributions. In particular, he was a genius in unshaded line work, a style ultimately derived from Regency line engravings, and one of his *Punch* covers in this manner was used for 110 years! Two notable album books in this style were *Manners & Customs of Ye Englishe*, 1849 and *Birds Eye Views of Society*, 1864, where part of the attraction was the crowded pages and the patchwork of narrative detail. Doyle contributed to three of Dickens' Christmas books and was the sole illustrator of W.M. Thackeray's important novel, *The Newcomens*, 1844-55. Even in this book, Doyle's work is more linear than his contemporaries', but a great deal more assured than in the earlier novels that Thackeray illustrated himself.

Doyle was a devout Roman Catholic and it was the increasingly Anti-Papist attacks by *Punch*, during the controversies of 1850, that forced his resignation from the magazine. Fortunately, he developed a separate career as an illustrator of children's books and as a fairy artist in the 1860s to 1880s. His essentially innocent view of the world and his delight in childhood and child's literature made him the ideal depictor of legend and myth. Rodney Engen, Doyle's most recent biographer, has written – "His character was universally admired for its shy, self-effacing qualities; he had a childish wit and an ability to tell a story and hold his audience in rapt attention. But his artistic ambitions were plagued by a nervous fastidiousness which caused even his best laid plans to suffer – not for lack of ideas but single-minded dedication to complete a project. Even as a child he had been an easy prey to tempting diversions which hindered his progress. And now, as he accepted a number of different book commissions, especially from the Dalziel Brothers, his work and his reputation suffered the same fate."[4] His work was therefore rather unequal, although some of his fairy books, such as Thackeray's *Rebecca & Rowena*, 1850 and Ruskin's *King of the Golden River*, 1851, have never been surpassed. With the age of colour printing, Doyle's work reached its height in the production of *In Fairyland*, published by Longman in 1871 with poems by William Allingham. Doyle was captivated, one might say obsessed, by this fairy world which occupies an important place in Victorian art. Apart from the liberation that it gave to the children's book, it has a more disturbing aspect as an escape for Victorian fantasists, trapped by a moral code and an increasingly regimented society where they could not express their innermost feelings.

Punch also published *Pocket Books* for about thirty years, leather-bound diaries with folding coloured frontispieces, engraved on steel after designs by John Leech and later Charles Keene. These often took the form of satirical comments on dress, the fashionable appearance of the crinoline, the advent of bloomers and the society 'marriage mart'. The magazine was extremely strong on these social subjects, but after the departure of Doyle, less well represented in fantasy work.

Fortunately, the proprietors still had the services of Tenniel, a better pencil artist than Leech, who could work on political cartoons and more imaginative themes. John Tenniel (1820-1914) had made his name as a book illustrator in the 1840s, a fine figure artist with a special talent for animals. Apart from the political pages, which included excellent portraits by him of Disraeli, Gladstone and even the Queen, he drew some marvellous title-pages, initial letters and spreads for the *Almanack*. A particularly striking example of this in 1855 became the formative thought for his *Alice* illustrations, a decade later. It was really in Lewis Carroll's masterpieces that his true stature was realised.

GEORGE SAMUEL ELGOOD 1851-1943. 'Bowls in a castle garden.' Original drawing for illustration. Watercolour, signed and dated 1887

Lattimore Collection

The Illustrated London News

Popular demand also required a current affairs magazine, bringing news of the Empire, industry, inventions and royal occasions to the breakfast table, and *The Illustrated London News* was created to meet it. Herbert Ingram, a Nottingham businessman with a nose for profitable ventures, suggested the idea of an illustrated weekly to the printer Henry Vizetelly. Ingram's original ambition was a rather sensational news-sheet with descriptions of murders, disasters and police cases, but this was gradually abandoned for more objective news coverage.

The first issue appeared on 14th May 1842 when there were just sixteen pages with thirty-two woodcuts, within a year the circulation was 66,000.

As no similar newspaper (it was really a newspaper) had existed before, its staff and organisation were the creations of Ingram and Vizetelly, both of a similar generation, the hard-headed capitalist and the experimental printer. Two well known literary hacks were appointed as editor and sub-editor and the artist John Gilbert was appointed as chief illustrator. It was very soon realised that a paper that covered so much, from Parliamentary reports to obituaries, art exhibitions, banquets and foreign events, needed a whole team of artists and reporters. Ingram performed miracles of publicity and through influence and luck managed to get his representatives into the front line of revolutions, such as that in France in 1848, and into the private apartments of royal and presidential palaces. Artists made lightning sketches of events as they happened and these were posted back to London, transferred to the woodblock by specially trained artists and then split into four to be engraved by four different engravers. The speed of the operation was of the greatest importance so that the completed engraving could be chased up and printed only a day or two after the events

EDMUND DULAC 1882-1953. 'Croquet',
1918   Chris Beetles, St James's Ltd

HENRY MATTHEW BROCK 1875-1960. Illustration for a
book on T. De Quincy, c.1910   Chris Beetles, St James's Ltd

ARTHUR RACKHAM 1867-1939. 'All Stood Amazed', illustration for *Rip Van Winkle* by Washington Irving, 1905. Ink
and watercolour
                                              Chris Beetles, St James's Ltd

depicted. This might seem rather a long lapse of time by today's standards, but to a readership that was used to news that was many days old, delivered at the speed of a mail coach, Ingram's expedition was marvellous!

A good example of where the magazine was going is provided by the volume for 1847, just prior to the readership's peak of 100,000. The magazine opened in January with a rather traditional article on the tercentenary celebrations of Trinity College, Cambridge, well illustrated with architectural views, followed by less serious subjects such as skating in Hyde Park and the onslaught of the famous London fogs! The decorative element, always important in the *News*, was left to William Harvey, veteran wood-engraver and illustrator, who produced a full page of Britannias and cornucopias representing the coming months. Later that month there were pages on new church architecture, always well represented, and a half-page of Louis-Philippe at the Chamber of Deputies "drawn and engraved at Paris" – cross-border reporting was now excellent. Interestingly enough, the Empire was not neglected and subscribers had views of the New Zealand War and Elephant Ploughing in India. Industry and new inventions were keenly awaited and detailed drawings of the machinery and vats at Messrs Barclay & Perkins Brewery would have whetted many appetites. One of the chief problems of 1847 was the Irish Famine and one might expect the *News* to treat the subject with a certain detachment. This was not the case and the illustrated reports by James Mahony of destitution and starvation at Skibbereen were harrowing and truthful. This instant reporting must have appeared very shocking to complacent British readers, but like the development of photography, had an important effect in moulding public opinion and keeping issues before Parliament.

The *News* readership was not specifically urban and there was much of interest in the paper for countrymen, particularly farmers. Great attention was given to poultry and the illustration of their various breeds by the artist J.W. Archer, and an equal amount to the Newton Abbot Ploughing Matches and the field at Tattenham Corner for the Derby Meeting by Harrison Weir. All the furniture for the new House of Lords designed by A.W. Pugin was engraved on a full page in May and the Paris fashions, presumably re-drawn from French magazines such as *Les Modes,* appeared month by month. Disasters were very good value for a paper that could produce the scenes only hours after they occurred, so readers in June had a representation of the Chester railway accident with the Dee bridge damaged, the lines buckled and the railway carriages lying submerged in the river. This would presumably have been sent in by a local artist who realised the value of his sketch to a national paper. The proprietors were able to call on specialist artists outside their team, when 'Jack' the Zoological Society's elephant died on 6th June 1847, the magazine sent George Landseer in to draw the great beast for its pages.

In July 1847, the Royal Agricultural Society of England's meeting at Northampton was rewarded with a full page illustration by Sir John Gilbert, a *tour de force* of decoration with a vignette of the town and a still life of farming implements. Gilbert, reputedly the highest paid illustrator of his time, could always be relied on for great patriotic plates. *Punch* refused to employ him, the editor remarking "We do not require Rubens on *Punch!*" Strangely enough, Gilbert's High Victorian style, so valued by his contemporaries, has never regained its popularity among collectors of illustrated work. Perhaps with such luminaries as Gilbert around, the *News* seldom indulged in caricature, leaving that to its more pedestrian brethren, but in July 1847, it did feature a series of 'types' drawn by Kenny Meadows in anticipation of the election. They make an odd contrast with the obsequies at the death of O'Connell in August and the detailed description of Brunel's new iron steamship the *Great Britain* on the 21st of that month.

Queen Victoria was depicted in nearly every issue and the appearance of the sovereign and her activities must have been more familiar to the nation than at any previous time in its history. The royal visit to Scotland in August was recorded stage by stage, every detail of the Queen's journey chronicled in large engravings and letterpress, the Highland Games at Laggan, the reception by the Scottish people and the return in the Royal Yacht to Fleetwood harbour. The return of the Court to Windsor in October was heralded by pages of Castle views with great attention paid to the interiors, where the taste of the young Queen and the Prince Consort was beginning to make itself felt. Art allied to the Royal Family was a great success in this case, even more so when the *News* was able to illustrate the baptismal shield presented to the Prince of Wales by the King of Prussia and executed by G. Hossauer, Goldsmith to the Court. Opposite to this was a coy engraving of "The Prince of Wales in His Birthday Suit" a somewhat odd phraseology to modern eyes! Aristocratic marriages received almost as much attention as royal parties, the marriage of the Marquis of Kildare at Trentham in October was covered by panoramas of the house and gardens, a glimpse inside the church and carefully rendered engraving of the bridal cake! *The Illustrated London News* did not have a monopoly on such things, but as there was only one other illustrated magazine capable of mounting similar stories, it worked very much like one. "Numerous other publishers brought out periodicals whose names were already forgotten before the century was over; while the presses of *The Illustrated London News*, whose excellent paper came from Ingram's own mill, rolled on majestically."[5]

Anything maritime was regarded as a potential commercial triumph, so the departure of Sir Harry Smith's expedition to the Cape of Good Hope was given the same coverage as a romantic view of barges in the Thames estuary. The explorer's departure was executed by an anonymous artist, as it was regarded as a news item, but the peaceful scene of shrimping hatch-boats was by Edward Duncan (1803-1882), the eminent member of the Watercolour Society, because it was high art.

After the Royal Family and shipping, railways probably received most attention. 1847 was just after the great railway mania, but the pride and satisfaction in the progress of steam is self-evident in every engraved line. The East Anglian Railway was given a tremendous inaugural coverage in October 1847 with views of the Ouse viaduct and the new station at Ely. The former was described as a "stupendous Bridge" where the train was stopped for passengers to "examine its peculiar construction". Although this double-page spread was treated as topographical art rather than engineering, there is no mention of the artist, although the engraver's name, "Smyth", is visible on the block.

Like *Punch*, the *News* made great efforts at Christmas to employ well-known artists who might encourage new readers into the fold through almanacks and special numbers. Gilbert was an essential element to the festive season, so was Leech during the 1850s and Keene at a later date.

The illusion that Victorian Britain was insular and self-contained is soon dispelled by these pages, where the editorial and its pictures run from bridge openings in Hungary to typhoons in the South China seas and political

CHARLES ROBINSON 1870-1937. 'Old King Cole', frontispiece to *The Annals of Fairyland* by J.M. Gibbon, 1901. Ink and watercolour

Chris Beetles, St James's Ltd

CLAUD LOVAT FRASER 1890-1921. 'Eighteenth Century Interior', a design for a theatre programme, 1921. Colour wash   Private Collection

LOUISE WRIGHT 1875-. 'Afternoon dresses' (above); 'Day dress' (right) 1914. Fashion illustrations   Private Collection

demonstrations in Switzerland. The thirst for knowledge was immense and the well oiled presses and smooth distribution from "198 Strand, in the Parish of St Clement Danes" fed that appetite. Ingram became a millionaire and the authors and artists associated with him used the paper as a step-ladder to greater things.

The Illustrated London News actually came of age, seven years later, with the start of the Crimean War. This gave a paper that had steadily built up its circulation a unique opportunity to report a major national event for the public. There had been no national call to arms since the Napoleonic Wars, scarcely within living memory, and the poets, painters and sculptors were stirred and with them the giants of the illustrated press. The paper was twice the size that it had been in 1847 and the war had double the coverage. Large maps appeared of the Black Sea in January 1854 in what was termed "this interesting crisis" and topographical pictures were obtained from books. As the campaign developed, artists were sent out to the Bosphorous to act as interpreters of the scenes, their sketches being sent home to be transcribed for publishing at 198 Strand. Surprisingly, naval officers with graphic skills, employed by the Admiralty, had permission to publish them in the paper. Panoramic views, notably Lieutenant O'Reilly's section of the Battle of Siope in February 1854, gave a good strategic summary of the seat of war. Ingram had already sent his artist Samuel Read (later head of the *News* art department) to Constantinople to sketch. His drawings were returned to London and probably prepared for the press by the young Charles Keene (1823-1891), later to make his name on *Punch*. The preparations of the Allies were equally well recorded, with plates of the Ocean French Fleet leaving Brest and the installation of French army kitchens in the east. A musical score, 'Raise High the Flag!', appeared in the paper for nearly the first time, the tune by Sir Henry Bishop, the pictures engraved by Dalziel's. All this was paralleled by an unusual fascination with Russia, its Court and its Czar as the enemy of the British and French. The pounding of Odessa was depicted with jubilation, while portraits of Omer Pacha were treated with almost religious adulation. The juxtapositions of the famous British regiments alongside the Turks in oriental dress was a feast for the Victorians' love of the exotic and romantic.

The turn of the year and the grind of the war are certainly reflected in the pages of *The Illustrated London News*, as the excitement of the call to arms degenerated into bad organisation, heavy casualties and privations among the allied troops based at Scutari. A leading article above an illustration of the Commissariat Camp on July 28th 1855, is headed "Public Disquietude". The dramatic pages of the Fall of Sebastopol on the 29th September 1855 are a prelude to the editor's promise of a "week by week" coverage of "Splendid Pictures" received from "Our Correspondents and Artists". The increasingly gloomy reports of such influential correspondents as Russell of *The Times*, clearly had an effect on altering public opinion, but so too did the careful drawings of the artists whose literal reporting must have contributed to the war weariness at home. The arrival of photography was to challenge illustration, but not at this early date and not at a time when the artists were independent of coercive editorial control.

During the next fifty years, the magazine was to exercise an important role in the Empire and at home. Controlled by successive members of the Ingram family, it maintained a balanced policy of reporting and a high quality of illustration. Its pages were a complete analysis of Victorian Britain and its studio was a nurturing place for many artists, among them William Simpson RI, Matt Morgan and Samuel Begg. In 1869, *The Graphic*, a publication of William Luson Thomas, appeared as the only challenger to the *News*. This had a vigorous and rather radical team of artists in its early days and from 1870 to 1875 its illustrative work was more interesting than its rival's. Social realist artists such as A. Boyd Houghton, Luke Fildes and H. Von Herkomer cut their teeth in its pages and roving work included Houghton's famous tour of the United States which tackled America with a certain scepticism and antipathy.

The Wood Engraved Page

We have already seen that both *Punch* and *The Illustrated London News* relied on the medium of wood engraving for all their illustrated work. This was a considerable change from the practices at the beginning of the century and it was a gradual and deliberate evolution.

The story really begins at Newcastle-upon-Tyne at the end of the eighteenth century, where the engraver Thomas Bewick (1753-1828) developed the despised art of wood engraving into a fine art. Bewick was trained as a copper plate engraver in the Georgian tradition, but a chance commission, after he had served his apprenticeship, led him into work on the boxwood block with the appropriate graving tools. Bewick was a countryman and an observer of nature as well as a very skilful artist, and he used all these talents to transform his art from mere hack-work to illustrations of the greatest refinement. He could see that the tight-grained edges of the boxwood block were capable of producing superb, small engravings with the subtleties of the pen and a great deal more softness and mood. Wood engraving was not just to be the province of the jobbing printer who made crude blocks for the penny chapbooks sold on street corners, it was to become an important aspect of the romantic movement.

Bewick's main work in the closing years of the eighteenth century was for natural history books, Trip's *History of Beasts and Birds*, 1779; *A General History of Quadrupeds*, 1785-1790; *A History of British Birds*, 1797-1804; *Fables of Aesop*, 1818 and finally *British Fishes*, which was never completed. Bewick's watercolours of his natural history subjects were surprisingly accurate and intensely observed.[6] But from the point of view of the history of illustration, it was his tiny narrative vignette illustrations that were of the greatest importance. In numerous headings and tailpieces, Bewick gave his readers glimpses of country life, not necessarily directly related to the text of *Quadruped*s or *Birds*, but enlivening them with humour and spirit. These silvery-grey images are among the gems of early nineteenth century printing in which hedgerows, ponds and cottages, peopled by tiny figures, are rendered with astonishing beauty.

Bewick was in the position of a leading master wood-engraver in the 1820s and was able to train up a number of apprentices, such as John Jackson, William Harvey, John Thurston and Charles Thomson, most of whom moved south and were ready to give the lead when the revival of the boxwood block came in the 1840s. Bewick was of course an artist, as well as an interpreter of other men's ideas, and much of the genius of his work is in its personality and spontaneity. As the technique was more accepted in the 1830s, particularly for illustrating small educational books, the individual touch was lost and the craft became a serviceable and mundane tool of universal knowledge. There was a distinct divide between the Bewick trained engravers like William Harvey, who designed for and worked upon the woodblock themselves, and a host of competent engravers who translated other artists' work for the page.

In their important book *A Treatise On Wood Engraving*, 1838, William Andrew Chatto and John Jackson (Bewick's pupil) trace the history of the art from early times. In the 1861 edition of the book, Chatto records the division in the ranks that had taken place in the last twenty years: "When, with the age of Bewick, wood engraving began to reassume its importance for book illustration, both designing and engraving were generally designed by the same hand; but, in the present day, the professions are becoming too important to be joined, and those who, like William Harvey, Samuel Williams, and others, commenced by practising both, now recognising the modern policy of a division of labour, confine themselves with few exceptions to one."[7] He goes on to say that his object in the book "so far as designs are concerned, is almost limited to those draughtsmen who habitually draw on wood, for it is unnecessary to say that every drawing or painting may be transferred to wood by the practical operator." The two professions of the artist illustrator and the facsimile wood-engraver therefore emerge in the 1840s and continue as such for the next forty years. Chatto does not make the same distinctions as we would with our modern concepts of originality in art. For him, the two professions served each other and the burgeoning appetite for Victorian illustrated journalism; the artist was not more significant because he was creative or the wood-engraver less significant because he was interpretive. Chatto lists the artists who could both draw on the woodblock and engrave, they include the following: J.W. Archer, the antiquarian artist; C.H. Bennett, humorous artist; J.R. Clayton, who did figure subjects; John Franklin, a noted romantic figure draughtsman; F.W. Hulme, the landscapist; Noel Humphreys, the ornamental artist; Owen Jones, celebrated for his Spanish designs; Charles Keene of *Punch*; M.J. Lawless, a prolific illustrator; Thomas Macquoid, who contributed ornamental borders to *The Illustrated London News*; H.K. Browne, the illustrator of Dickens; F.W. Topham, who drew scenes of Irish character and J.B. Zwecker, the animal artist.

He also lists painters who occasionally draw on wood. These are twenty-four in number and include E.H. Corbould, a figure and architectural artist; J.C. Horsley, a Royal Academician and figure painter; W. Holman Hunt, the Pre-Raphaelite religious painter; J.E. Millais, working extensively for the publishers in the 1860s and David Roberts, the landscape and scene painter.

Chatto went on to explain the absence of many illustrators who could draw on the woodblock in this way: "Considering the number of wood engravings that are yearly executed in this country, it is rather surprising that there should hitherto have been so few persons capable of making a good drawing on wood. Till within the last few years, it might be said that there was probably not more than one artist in the kingdom possessing a knowledge of design who professionally devoted himself to making drawings on the block for wood engravers. Whenever a good design is wanted, there are still but few persons to whom the English wood engraver can apply with the certainty of obtaining it; for though some of our most distinguished painters have occasionally furnished designs to be engraved on wood, it has mostly been a matter of especial favour to an individual who had an interest in the work in which such designs were to appear…The truth is, that a taste for correct drawing has hitherto not been sufficiently cultivated in England; our artists are painters before they can draw; and hence, comparatively few can make a good design on wood. They require the aid of positive colours to deceive the eye, and prevent it from resting upon the defects of their drawing. It is therefore of great importance that a wood engraver should have some knowledge of drawing himself, in order that he may be able to correct many of the defects that are to be found in the commoner kind of subjects sent to him to be engraved."[8]

These were the sort of problems that faced the new breed of facsimile wood engravers whose businesses had appeared in the 1840s to meet the growing demand for illustrated books and periodicals. The woodblock was a cheaper, more durable and more convenient way of producing illustrations for the mass market and as presses became more mechanised, the blocks could be chased in to the letterpress easily, compared with the cumbersome printing of copper or steel plates. A number of engraving workshops opened in London in the 1840s and, bearing in mind what Chatto has said about wood engravers having to have "some knowledge of drawing", it was not surprising that they became ateliers for apprentices. Among these were the firms of Whymper Brothers, Ebenezer Landells, Orrin Smith, Joseph Swain and Horace Harral. It is not possible to deal with every one of these in detail, but the most famous of them were to be the Brothers Dalziel, who continued unabated until 1890, until, that is, facsimile wood engraving itself came to an end. The Dalziel family, like so many other wood engravers, was Northumbrian in origin and had been trained in the tradition of Thomas Bewick.

The four Dalziel Brothers were George Dalziel (1815-1902), Edward Dalziel (1817-1905), John Dalziel (1822-1869) and Thomas Dalziel (1823-1908). They were the children of a Northumbrian farmer, who became an amateur painter, and of his twelve children, six became artists of one sort or another. George and Edward Dalziel trained under Ebenezer Landells, a Bewick pupil, and arrived in London as early as 1835, where they were befriended by William Harvey.

Dalziel's were well established by 1850, when they engraved William Harvey's *The Pilgrim's Progress*, but it was in the later 1850s that they leapt to prominence. Their magisterial and slightly bitter tome, *The Dalziel Brothers, A Record of Work 1840 to 1890*, published in their extreme old age, shows the gradual increase in prominent books and prominent artists. In 1851 they engraved two important Richard Doyle titles, *Jack The Giant Killer* and *An Overland Journey to the Great Exhibition*, one of Doyle's famous panorama books (scores of figures coloured by hand), that must have been hideously difficult to engrave, let alone print! These were followed by *The Salamandrine* and *Longfellow's Poems* for Sir John Gilbert in 1852 and 1856 and *Beattie's Minstrel* for Birket Foster in 1858. After this, the fashion was for them to concentrate on gift books illustrated by various artists and having a less coherent appearance. The success of these ventures encouraged them to go more wholeheartedly into the trade in 1857, when they established their own printing presses at 53 High Street, Camden Town as The Camden Press. At this point Dalziel's were commissioning their own works as 'Dalziel's Fine Art Books', although the results were issued under the imprint of existing publishers like Routledge and Warne and the elaborate bindings were ordered from specialist firms. Thomas Dalziel remained slightly detached from his brothers, was an aspiring artist and ran an atelier within the firm to train young men. Several of his sons went on to be professional painters.[9]

The prelude to the Dalziel's Fine Art Books in the 1860s had been set by two memorable books a few years earlier with which they were loosely associated, Allingham's *The Music Master*, 1855 and *Moxon's Tennyson*, 1857. In the first, the Pre-Raphaelite group of painters appeared together for nearly the first time as illustrators and in the second, a rather more diverse collection of artists made that division between the old and new style readily apparent. *The Music Master* or *Day and Night Songs* brought D.G. Rossetti into the Dalziels' clientele for the first time. It was a classic case of the imaginative artist, untrained for the graving block, coming into confrontation with the professional facsimile wood engravers. As Chatto is already quoted as saying, British artists thought in terms of paint rather than black and white and tried to paint on the block or at least, in Rossetti's case, create effects that were not transmittable into engraved line. The *Moxon Tennyson* also brought together Rossetti, Holman Hunt and Millais as well as the older generation of Stanfield and Mulready, who began to look dated. The Dalziels found Millais professional and Rossetti much less so, but they were generous in their recollections of this epoch-making volume. "This edition", they wrote in 1901, "will always be known as 'Moxon's Tennyson', and will stand out as a landmark in the history of book illustration. In the work of the younger men engaged on it, beyond the extreme beauty of their designs, there was an evidence of earnestness to search after truth that went so deep into nature as to give the work a stamp of superiority; and this advance in art – for it was an advance we endeavoured to follow and promote to the best of our power."[10]

The Dalziel Brothers reached their peak in the early 1860s with the Christmas gift books which followed one after the other in quick succession. They were *Pictures of English Landscape*, 1862, a demonstration of Birket Foster's powers; *Parables of Our Lord*, magnificently illustrated by Millais in 1863; *Home Thoughts and Home Scenes*, 1865, a charming album of Boyd Houghton's best interiors; *A Round of Days*, 1867, and *Wayside Poesies*, 1869. The two last volumes were a medley of artistic work, particularly using the rural talents of the young trio Fred Walker, George Pinwell and J.W. North. The Brothers enjoyed a good relationship with Millais and notable triumphs were in his drawings for the Trollope novels, *Orley Farm*, 1861, *Framley Parsonage*, 1862, *The Small House at Allington*, 1862, *Phineas Finn*, 1869. Throughout this decade, illustration was at a very high level and the Dalziels were able to draw on a remarkable group of artists. Their own productions included *Dalziel's Arabian Nights*, 1864 with many contributions from Thomas B.G. Dalziel, and *Dalziel's Goldsmith*, 1865, a somewhat disappointing work. Their output of sensitively illustrated books continued well into the 1870s with Christina Rossetti's *Sing Song*, 1872, illustrated by Arthur Hughes. A major project of the 1860s, *Dalziel's Bible Gallery*, with most of the leading artists contributing, did not actually appear until 1880, when the heyday of wood engraving was coming to an end and with it the reign of the Dalziels. With an insatiable desire for colour printed books and a hankering after new techniques, Victorian readers wanted to move onwards. The Dalziels, who had created a style and a name, were too set in their ways and were unwilling to adapt their great name to innovations. The firm went bankrupt in 1893 and the Brothers were bitter about the many illustrators they had aided, who ignored them in their time of need.

During this productive period, illustration was highly prized as an art for the first time and many serious painters, like Frederick Leighton, Edward Poynter and

Burne-Jones, undertook book work. This might be accounted for by a slight slump in the art market after 1857, but also by the large number of quality magazines then demanding illustrations. The younger artists whom the Dalziels assisted used the humbler art of illustration to climb the artistic ladder to greater things. Some never made it, but for other illustrators who had endured the grind, the rewards were very great. Myles Birket Foster (1825-1899), who was the most popular landscape illustrator of his time, purchased an estate in Surrey and became the focus for an artistic community. After the 1860s, he scarcely undertook any illustration, preferring to concentrate on watercolours for exhibition.

Children's Books

At the same time that Dalziel's was producing handsome gift books for adults, there was a revolution in children's book making. This was partly due to the advent of chromo-lithography for cheaper books in the 1860s, although the bright colours and oily pages were not particularly pleasing to anyone with a critical eye. More important was a break with the didactic and 'improving' books that had been the diet of children for generations, even the popular *Peter Parley Picture Books* of the 1840s had been about good, clever children who were instructed by their betters! The books of Felix Summerly (Henry Cole) did much to improve the design and to make the contents more palatable. The appearance of books that were fun and could be enjoyed was quite new and the leading lights in this fresh approach were Edward Lear (1812-1888) and Lewis Carroll (1832-1898). Lear had been a private tutor to the children of the Earl of Derby and had drawn humorous pictures for them which he made into albums. A rather sad and repressed man, his isolation and subjectivity gave him insights into the world of childhood that few adults retain. Although his comic drawings and verses were intended for a private audience, their gradual emergence into public gave him a fame and a success that he could never have dreamed would take place. A skilled landscape painter and an illustrator of travel books, his celebrity today still rests on these engaging and insubstantial albums of grotesques. The fact that these tiny sketches were zany and iconoclastic gave them an instant popularity with children, who continued to delight in them for a hundred years. Dalziel's engraved one of the first, *Lear's Book of Nonsense*, 1870. From this followed *Nonsense Songs, Stories, Botany and Alphabets*, 1871, *More Nonsense Pictures, Rhymes, Botany Etc*, 1872, *Laughable Lyrics*, 1877 and a posthumous *Nonsense Songs and Stories*, 1895. So prolific was Lear, that fresh drawings and poems are still turning up in private collections. Lear's genius was that he could draw with the eye of a child, and as a natural historian and scientist could give things a semblance of logic and still turn them on their head! This was exactly the case with the Revd. C.L. Dodgson, alias Lewis Carroll, whose talents as an artist made him an unerring critic of any illustrators of his own works. The author found the ideal illustrator when Sir John Tenniel of *Punch* was asked to illustrate his *Alice In Wonderland* in 1864, published in 1865. This was followed by *Through The Looking Glass* in 1872, Tenniel's wit and adult allusions staying close to Carroll's text. It could be said that of the two authors, Carroll rather than Lear attracted an adult audience as well as a child audience, but they both unleashed Victorian children from a strait-jacket of conformity.

Edmund Evans was a colour printer who had originally trained under the Bewick pupil, Landells. He had been experimenting with colour in the early 1860s and had a very good appreciation of book design as well as the technicalities of colour printing. He wished to produce children's books in full colour and sell at a low price, a very ambitious scheme at the time. The publishers Smith Elder introduced Evans to a young artist, Walter Crane (1845-1915), and this provided the germ for a series of Toy Books. Routledge's were already printing coloured Toy Books by various artists and these and the Crane books were in direct competition with the unattractive productions of Kronheim. The books were usually printed on a tinted paper with a key colour block and two other colours, so that the range was limited. Crane was a decorator rather than an illustrator and the pages have a rather static feel to them like tiles or embroideries, or even the Japanese prints from which some of them were derived. Crane was influenced by a number of movements, Pre-Raphaelitism, Aestheticism and Japonisme, all of which appear in his languorous figures and stylised foliage. This sudden burst of colour in the windows of bookshops must have been a revelation and one that it is difficult to appreciate today. The titles (all of which were undated) include the following, *The Railroad Alphabet* and *The Farmyard Alphabet*, probably 1865; *The Old Courtier*, 1867; *Annie and Jack in London* and *One, Two, Buckle My Shoe*, 1869; *The Little Pig Went To Market*, 1869; *Cinderella* and *Valentine and Orson*, 1873; *Old Mother Hubbard*, 1872; *Little Red Riding Hood*, 1873; *The Sleeping Beauty*, 1876 – the dates are approximate. Three other Crane books for children were more elaborate, more expensive, but equally striking, *The Baby's Opera*, 1877, *The Baby's Bouquet*, 1878 and *The Baby's Aesop*, 1887.

It was only in 1878 that Edmund Evans enlisted another artist in his series of children's books, this time Randolph Caldecott (1846-1886) whose work was less 'arty' than Crane's and whose lack of training gave his figures a certain unaffected charm. He had been employed for some years on *The Graphic*, but two books set in a Georgian atmosphere, *Old Christmas*, 1874 and *Bracebridge Hall*, 1877 were the starting point for a series of picture books for Edmund Evans. These Caldecott Toy Books were more elaborate than their predecessors, contained no back-to-back printing, were on better quality paper and marketed at one shilling each. There were nine coloured illustrations in each, backed up by twenty line drawings. Evans issued two a year at Christmas time between 1878 and 1885, the later ones selling 100,000 copies.

Caldecott was more at home in the Regency period than in any other, and although he occasionally ventured into contemporary subjects, they never had the immediate success of his never-never land of ladies in bonnets, gentlemen in beavers and dairy maids in the high waists of 1800. He can be credited with having invented the pictured letter as a narrative form for magazines and stories. He was a very convincing draughtsman of horses and dogs and his eye for detail was exact. He had more of an innate sense of the balance of a page than Crane and the text and pictures mixed together more naturally. The best Caldecott titles are *The House That Jack Built* and *John Gilpin*, 1878; *The Mad Dog, The Babes in the Wood, Sing a Song for Sixpence*, and *The Three Jovial Huntsmen*, 1880; *The Queen of Hearts* and *The Farmer's Boy*, 1880; *The Milkmaid*, 1882; *Ride a Cock Horse*, 1884 and *The Great Panjandrum*, 1885. These works and many others began a fashion for Georgian costumed illustration in pastel colours that continued up until the First World War.

The third illustrator to make a mark in children's books through the medium of Edmund Evans was a lady, Kate Greenaway (1846-1901). Greenaway was an illustrator of sentimental child subjects set in the same general epoch as those of Caldecott, but rather lacking his robustness. They are very sugary for today's tastes, but they exactly fitted the Victorians' wish for the coy and the frail. Part of their success may well have been due to the high praise they received from the leading critic of the day, John Ruskin, as the Victorians were extremely susceptible to such writers.

Kate Greenaway came from a family of professional engravers and studied at both Heatherley's and the Slade School. This fact would hardly seem apparent from the poor anatomy and slightness of the figures in her extant sketches. By 1868 she was working commercially for a number of companies, including Messrs Marcus Ward, on Christmas cards and valentines. Her connection with Edmund Evans' colour printing work started in 1878. The list of her works in this partnership was long and distinguished, including *Under The Window*, 1878; *A Day in a Child's Life* and *Mother Goose*, 1881; *Little Ann*, 1883; *The Language of Flowers*, 1884; *Marigold Garden*, 1885; *A Apple Pie*, 1886 and *Kate Greenaway's Alphabet*, probably 1885. These were her best known books, but other delightful contributions can be found in *Little Folks, Every Girl's Annual, Girl's Own Paper* and other periodicals of the 1880s. A feature of the 'eighties was the number of little magazines that appeared to serve the juvenile library. Some of the early commentators considered that Greenaway's success had more to do with Evans' talent as a printer than with her skills as an artist. This is hard, her work is more dated than that of her contemporaries, but she established a style of pert insouciance that lived on into the children's books of the 'twenties.

The 1890s represent that logical break in reproductive methods that brought new ideas and a new set of artists into children's books as well as into other branches of the art. Photo-engraving, the line block and the half-tone gave draughtsmen the chance to reproduce their actual lines and shading on the page. It was as personal as the lithograph had been, but capable of greater contrasts and greater play with the white areas of the paper than ever before. The great master of the new style was Aubrey Beardsley (1872-1898) and his mannerism and ornamentation revolutionised book art until 1914. Beardsley had arrived at the very moment when the possibilities for black and white art could be realised, the processes were right, the magazines were right and the artistic public of the 'nineties was right. His earliest works such as the *Morte d'Arthur*, 1893-94, were in the Pre-Raphaelite tradition of William Morris, but this was very soon superseded by Beardsley's own inimitable style of patterned pages, stippling and dramatic uses of light and shade. His greatest impact was in the wealth of works done for the two magazines with which he was associated, *The Yellow Book*, 1894-95 and *The Savoy*, 1896-98. It seems scarcely believable that an artist could have achieved so much before his tragically early death at the age of twenty-six.

The Edwardian years were in some ways as great a contrast to the 1890s as the 1890s had themselves been to the Victorian epoch. The decadence of that last decade was replaced by a less self-conscious style, lavish without being aesthetic. The advent of good colour printing, which had been hesitant in the 'nineties, gave birth after 1900 to a series of grand giftbooks from most of the leading publishers. The artists who benefited most from this new freedom were Hugh Thomson (1860-

1920); Arthur Rackham (1867-1939); the Brock Brothers, C.E. Brock (1870-1938) and H.M. Brock (1875-1960); and Edmund Dulac (1882-1953). Thomson produced a series of remarkable costume classics before 1914, notably *The Merry Wives of Windsor*, 1910; *The School For Scandal*, 1911 and *Quality Street*, 1913. Rackham was more celebrated and more varied in subject, important works being *Rip Van Winkle*, 1905 and *Peter Pan in Kensington Gardens*, 1906. Dulac was the most Continental of this group (he was born in France) with his *The Sleeping Beauty*, 1912, *Princess Badoura*, 1913 and *Sinbad the Sailor*, 1914.

Notes
1. Leigh Hunt, *Autobiography*, 1860, p.70.
2. Antoine de Baecque, *La Caricature Revolutionaire*, 1988.
3. John Ford, *Ackermann 1783-1983*.
4. R. Engen, *Richard Doyle & His Family*, V&A Museum, 1984, p.16.
5. C. Hibbert, *The Illustrated London News, Social History of Victorian Britain*, 1975, p.14.
6. D. Croal Thomson, *The Watercolours of Thomas Bewick*, Barbizon House, 1930.
7. Chatto & Jackson, *A Treatise On Wood Engraving*, 1861, p.549.
8. Ibid., p.610.
9. *The Dalziel Family of Painters & Illustrators*, Sotheby's, 16th May 1978.
10. *The Dalziel Brothers*, 1901, p.83.

KATE GREENAWAY 1846-1901. From an illustration for *Under the Window*, 1878, by Kate Greenaway

Abbreviations
used in this Dictionary

ABMR	*Antiquarian Book Monthly Review*
AJ	*Art Journal*
AL	*Life* by Major J.R. Abbey
ARWS	Associate of the RWS
Ashmolean	Ashmolean Museum, Oxford
AT	*Travel* by Major J.R. Abbey
B	Birmingham
Barber	Barber Institute, Birmingham
BI	British Institution
Bibl.	Bibliography
BM	British Museum
CL	*Country Life*
Colls:	Examples of the artist's work can be found at the listed places
Colnahgi	Colnaghi's Gallery, London
Contrib:	Contributed illustrations to the listed publications
D	Dulwich Gallery
Dulwich	Dulwich College Picture Gallery
Exhib:	Exhibited paintings at the listed places
FAS	Fine Art Society
Free Society	Free Society of Artists
FRGS	Fellow of the Royal Geographical Society
FRS	Fellow of the Royal Society
FSA	Fellow of the Society of Antiquaries
FZS	Fellow of the Zoological Society
G	Glasgow
GG	Grosvenor Gallery
Greenwich	National Maritime Museum
ICS	Indian Civil Service
Illus:	Illustrated the listed books
ILN	*Illustrated London News*
L	Liverpool
Leicester Gall.	Leicester Galleries, London
Liverpool	Walker Art Gallery, Liverpool
London Salon	Allied Artists' Association
M	Manchester
Manchester	City Art Gallery, Manchester
Mellon	Mellon Collection, Richmond, Virginia
Mercury Gall.	Mercury Gallery, London
NEA	New English Art Club
New. Gall.	New Gallery
NG	National Gallery

NG, Ireland	National Gallery, Ireland
NG, Scotland	National Gallery, Scotland
NPG	National Portrait Gallery, London
NWS	New Watercolour Society
OM	Order of Merit
OWS	Old Watercolour Society
P	Royal Society of Portrait Painters
Paris	Paris Salon
Paris, 1900	Universal Exhibition
PRA	President of the Royal Academy
PRWS	President of the RWS
Publ:	Published but did not illustrate the listed books
RA	Royal Academy
RBA	Royal Society of British Artists
RCA	Royal College of Art
RCam.A	Royal Cambrian Society
RE	Royal Society of Painters & Etchers
RHA	Royal Hibernian Academy
RI	Royal Institute of Painters in Watercolours
RIBA	Royal Institute of British Architects
RMS	Royal Miniature Society
ROI	Royal Institute of Oil Painters
Royal Coll.	Royal Collection
RSA	Royal Scottish Academy
RSW	Royal Scottish Society of Painters in Watercolours
RWA	Royal West of England Academy
RWS	Royal Society of Painters in Watercolours
SA	Society of Artists
Soc. of Antiq.	Society of Antiquaries
SWA	Society of Women Artists
Tate	Tate Gallery, Millbank, London
Tooth	Tooth's Gallery, London
V & AM	Victoria & Albert Museum
Walker's	Walker's Gallery, London
Witt Photo	Witt Photographic Library, Courtauld Institute of Art, London

EDWIN AUSTIN ABBEY RA 1852-1911. Study for illustration to Oliver Goldsmith's *She Stoops to Conquer*, 1901. Pen and ink (detail). Signed and dated 1885   Victoria and Albert Museum

ABBEY, Edwin Austin   RA ARWS   1852-1911
Black and white artist and illustrator. Born in Philadelphia, 1 April 1852, and was educated at the Pennsylvania Academy of Fine Arts. After studying with a wood engraver, he began work with *Harper's* in New York in 1871 and was sent by them to England in 1878. With the exception of a brief visit to the United States, Abbey made his home in England from that date and became a very prolific draughtsman and illustrator. Specialising in costume and figure subjects, he established a reputation for fineness of execution and accuracy of detail; he was an important link with American drawing for British artists and was influential in introducing the taste for 18th century subjects and themes. He exhibited his first oil painting at the RA in 1890, was elected an Associate in 1901 and Academician in 1902. He worked in his later years at his home in Fairford, Gloucestershire, and died 2 August 1911.
Illus: *Herrick's Poems [1882]; The Rivals [1885]; Sketching Rambles in Holland [1885]; Old Songs [1889]; The Quiet Life [1890]; Comedies of Shakespeare [1896]; She Stoops to Conquer [1901].*
Contrib: *Scribner's Monthly, St. Nicholas [1875-1881]; The Graphic [1880, 1883]; Longfellow's Portfolio [1887]; The Scarlet Runner [1899-1900].*
Exhib: RA; FAS, 1888, 1895.
Colls: Ashmolean, V & AM.
Bibl: The work of EAA, *The Artist*, Sept. 1900, pp.169-181 illus.; E.V. Lucas, *Life and Work of EAA*, 1921; R.E.D. Sketchley, *Eng. Bk. Illus.* 1903, pp.36, 64, 87, 144.
See illustration.

ABSOLON, John   RI   1815-1895
Painter and illustrator. Born in Lambeth, May 1815, and studied under an Italian, Ferrigi, earning his living as a portrait painter. He then acted as an assistant to Grieve, the theatrical scene-painter, for about four years, before going to Paris in 1835. He remained there some years and returned there again for a year in 1839, practising as a miniaturist. In 1850 he assisted T. Grieve and Telbin with their diorama 'The Route of the Overland Mail to India'. He went to the Continent about 1858, visiting Italy and Switzerland. He became a member of the New Water Colour Society in 1835, resigning in 1858 and rejoining in 1861 to become Treasurer. He made drawings of the battlefields of Crécy and Agincourt which were published by Graves, 1860. He died 26 June 1895.

Absolon stands midway between the illustrators of the old tradition like Mulready and the new generation of the 1860s. He was most successful in figure drawing and particularly so in his contemporary genre subjects and his illustrations to children's books, outlined and with very little shadow.
Illus: *Aunt Carry's Ballads For Children [Mrs. Norton 1847]; Peter Parsey's Annual [1849].*
Contrib: *L'Allegro and Il Penseroso [Art Union, 1848] and The Traveller [Art Union, 1851]; Recollections of The Great Exhibition [1851]; Beattie and Collins Poems [1854]; Goldsmith's Poetical Works; Lockhart's Spanish Ballads; Longfellow's poems [1856]; Rhymes and Roundelayes [1858]; The Home Affections [C. Mackay, 1858]; Favourite English Poems [1859]; Churchman's Family Magazine [1864].*

Exhib: BI; NW; RA; RBA.
Colls: Ashmolean; BM; Leeds; V & AM.
Bibl: Chatto and Jackson, *Treatise on Wood Engraving*, 1861, p.576.

ACKLAND, F.
Black and white artist contributing humorous figure subjects to *Fun*, 1901.

ACKROYD, Miss L.   fl.1910-1932
Watercolourist, illustrator of children's books and designer of Christmas cards, working in Stockport. She made bright drawings in the style of John Hassall.
Exhib: RBA, 1928-32.

ACLAND, Hugh Dyke   1791-1834
Amateur artist and landscape illustrator. He was the son of Sir Thomas Dyke Acland, 9th Bt. He made the drawings for *Illustrations of the Vaudois*, 1831, which were engraved by Finden.

ADAM, Emil   1843-
Sporting painter and caricaturist. Born at Munich 20 May 1843, he was principally a painter of horses and came to London in 1885, where he was an instant success among the sporting fraternity. He contributed one cartoon to *Vanity Fair*, 1909.
Colls: Jockey Club.

ADAMS, H. Isabel
Decorative illustrator contributing to *The Yellow Book*, 1896.

ADAMS, W. Dacres   1864-
Landscape painter and occasional illustrator. Born Oxford, 1864, and educated at Radley and Exeter College, Oxford. Studied at the Birmingham School and at the Herkomer School, Bushey, before working in Munich. His most important illustrated work is *A Book of Beggars*, published by Heinemann about 1912-13, strongly influenced by the Beggarstaff Brothers. Worked at Lechlade, 1889-91, and Dorchester, Oxon, 1902-3.
Exhib: FAS, 1924, 1925, 1927; G; L, Paris, 1937-9; RA, 1892.
Bibl: *Studio*, Vol. 4, p. xlvi 7 xlvii, 1894.

ADAMSON, Sydney   fl.1892-1914
Painter and illustrator. Born in Dundee and working in London for the principal magazines in the 1890s. He designed a book cover for

The Idler in 1895 and exhibited at the RA in 1908 and at Liverpool in 1914, at which time he was residing in Paris.
Contrib: *Fun [1892]; The Sphere [1894]; The Yellow Book [1894]; The Pall Mall Magazine; Illustrated Bits; The Idler; The Minister.*
Colls: V & AM.

ADCOCK, Frederick   **fl.1913**
Topographical artist and brother of Arthur St. John Adcock, essayist and novelist, for whom he illustrated *The Booklover's London*, c.1913.

ADCOCK, George H.   **fl.1827-1832**
Engraver and illustrator working in London. Best known as an engraver of portraits but also engraved an edition of *The Compleat Angler* after G. Hassell and *The Works of Sir Walter Scott*, 1832.
Exhib: RBA, 1827.

AIKMAN, George W.   **ARSA**   **1831-1905**
Painter and engraver. Born in 1831 and began work as an engraver on leaving Edinburgh Royal High School. For many years he was engaged on engraving portraits for *The Encyclopaedia Britannica*, but also executed portraits, landscapes and etchings. The Victoria and Albert Museum has a series of architectural studies of Edinburgh for an unidentified book. Died 8 January 1905.
Illus: *A Round of The Links [J. Smart, 1893]; The Midlothian Esks, [T. Chapman and J. Strathesk, 1895].*
Exhib: L; RA; RHA from 1874; regularly at RSA.
Colls: V & AM.

AIREY, F.W.   **RN**
Amateur artist contributing drawings of China to *The Graphic*, 1901.

CECIL ALDIN 1870-1935. A Street Scene in Larissa, ink and wash drawing from sketches supplied by H.C. Seppings Wright for *The Illustrated London News*, 1897   Victoria and Albert Museum

ALANDY, Sydney
Figure artist contributing to *Punch*, 1901.

ALBERT, Charles Augustus Emmanuel, HRH Prince 1819-1861
Consort of Queen Victoria, amateur etcher and draughtsman. Born at Rosenau, 26 August 1819, and married at St. James's Palace 10 February 1840. Prince Albert was an important patron of the arts during the mid-Victorian era, was largely responsible for the idea of the Great Exhibition of 1851 and established at Court a taste for idealistic German art. He is included here as the illustrator of his home country, Gotha. Sketches by him were engraved for *The Illustrated London News* and published in 1845.
Colls: BM; Windsor.

ALBERT, V.   **fl.1890-1899**
Fashion Illustrator in watercolour, working for *The English Illustrated Magazine*, 1896-99 and *The Lady's Pictorial*, 1890.
Colls: V & AM.

ALDER, W. Brooke
Wash and pen and ink artists contributing to *The English Illustrated Magazine*, 1899.
Colls: V & AM.

ALDIN, Cecil Charles Windsor   **1870-1935**
Sporting artist and humorous illustrator. Born at Slough, 28 April, 1870, and educated at Eastbourne College before studying anatomy at South Kensington and animal painting under Frank W. Calderon. He published his first drawing in *The Graphic* in 1891, but continued to do much straight reporting work for the magazines before gaining a reputation for humorous hunting subjects. Aldin's activities as a countryman (he was MFH of the South Berkshire Foxhounds and a member of the Hunter's Improvement Society) enabled him to draw the funny side of horsemanship from inside that exclusive group. His brightly coloured books, the illustrations simply outlined, were the staple diet of country houses between the wars. His ability was in putting the spirit of an incident on to paper rather than the accuracy of it, in this he shared something with both Leech and Caldecott who clearly influenced him. He was the ideal illustrator for *Pickwick* and *Handley Cross*, which were issued in 1910 and 1912 respectively. He died 6 January 1935.
Illus: *Everyday Characters [W.M. Praed, 1896]; Two Well-Worn Shoe Stories [1899]; The Fallowfield Hunt [1899-1900]; A Dog Day [1902]; Cecil Aldin's Picture Books [c.1908]; White-Ear and Peter [N Heiberg, 1911]; 12 Hunting Countries [1912-13]; The Romance of the Road [1928].*
Contrib: *Sporting and Dramatic News [1892]; Good Works; The Ludgate Monthly; The Boys Own Paper [1892]; Pall Mall Budget – Kipling's Jungle Stories [1894-5]; The Sketch [1894]; ILN [1892-1911 (X)]; Pick-Me-Up [1897]; Black and White [1899], English Illustrated Magazine [1893-97]; Lady's Pictorial; The Gentlewoman; The Queen; The Windsor Magazine; Pearson's Magazine; Punch.*
Exhib. FAS, 1899, 1935.
Colls: V & AM.
Bibl: *CA, Time I Was Dead*, 1934; *Mr. Punch With Horse and Hound*, New Punch Library, 1930.
See illustration.

ALDRIDGE, Sydney
Illustrator. Contributed to *The Royal Magazine* and *The Windmill*, 1899.

ALEXANDER, Captain James Edward
Amateur artist, illustrated his own *Travels to The Seat of War in the East*, 1830, AT 229.

ALEXANDER, William   **1766-1816**
Travelling draughtsman and illustrator. Born at Maidstone in 1766, he became a pupil of W. Pars and J.C. Ibbetson before entering the RA Schools. He went to China in 1792, with Lord Macartney's embassy and his drawings of this were published in G. Staunton's official account, 1797. The sketches for this are in the British Museum. He was Professor of Drawing at the Military College, Great Marlow, 1802-8, and Keeper of Prints and Drawings at the

Go breeze that sweeps the orange grove.

Happy's the love that meets return.

I wanderd once at break of day

He wood, he won her simple heart.

How imperfect is expression.

P. Alken Delt.

HENRY ALKEN 1784-1851. Hand coloured engravings to *Illustrations to Popular Songs*, 1826

British Museum from 1808. He died at Maidstone 23 July 1816.
Illus: *View of the Headlands, Islands etc. of China [1798]; The Costumes of the Russian Empire [1803]; The Costumes of China [1805, AT 534]; Engravings From The Egyptian Antiquities in the BM [1805]: Picturesque Representations of the Dress and Manners of the Austrians [1813]; Picturesque Representations of the Dress and Manners of the Russians [1814]; Picturesque Representations of the Dress and Manners of the Chinese [1814]; Picturesque Representations of the Dress and Manners of the Turks [1814].*
Contrib: *Travels in China [Sir J. Barrow, 1804]; Voyage to Cochin China [Sir J. Barrow, 1806]; Architectural Antiquities [J. Britton, 1804-14].*
Colls: Ashmolean; BM; Fitzwilliam; Leeds; Maidstone; V & AM.

ALFORD, W.
Architectural draughtsman, employed on *The Illustrated London News*, 1888-89.

ALKEN, Henry Thomas   **1785-1851**
Sporting artist, engraver and illustrator. Born in London in 1784 into a family which became celebrated for its sporting artists and engravers. He is said to have worked as a trainer for the Duke of Beaufort, before studying under J.T. Barker Beaumont, the miniaturist, and he exhibited miniatures at the RA in 1801-02. He moved to Melton Mowbray in 1810 to train horses and eke out a livelihood in decorating trays with hunting scenes. His success really began when he issued prints under the name of 'Ben Tally Ho' in 1813 and he was at his most prolific in the 1820s and 1830s. His work was less interesting after that date and he died in poverty on 8

April, 1851. His son H.G. Alken copied his father's work extensively.

Alken's illustrations and separate prints are lively and very colourful and are closer to the 18th century caricature than to the 18th century sporting print. He enlarged Gillray's idea that the mishaps of hunting could be depicted in the same format as scenes of the chase and his publisher was significantly Thomas M'Lean of 'The Repository of Wit and Humour'. Shaw Sparrow considers that he was most influential in creating a medium in which Phiz, Leech and Caldecott could flourish. His *Sketchbook*, 1823 and *Scrapbook*, 1824, with their pages crammed with nearly related but separated incidents, may have influenced strip stories in the Victorian magazines. His drawings are most often seen in soft pencil with colour washes.
Illus: *The Beauties and Defects in the Figure of the Horse comparatively delineated [1816]; National Sports of Great Britain [1821]; Humorous Specimens of Riding [1821]; Symptoms [1822]; Sketchbook [1823]; Sporting Scrapbook [1824]; Shakespeare's Seven Ages [1824]; Flowers From Nature [1824]; A Touch of the Fine Arts [1824]; Humorous Illustrations of Popular Songs [1826]; Don Quixote [1831]; Life and Death of John Mytton [1837]; Jorrocks Jaunts and Jollities [1837]; The Sporting Review [1842-46; The Art and Practice of Etching [1849].*
Colls: BM; Fitzwilliam; Leeds; Leicester; V & AM.
Bibl: W.S. Sparrow, *British Sporting Artists*, 1922, with full bibliography, p.209; W.S. Sparrow, *HA*, 1927; A. Noakes, *The World of HA*, 1952; Arts Council, *British Sporting Painting 1650-1850*, 1974.
See illustration.

WILLIAM DOUGLAS ALMOND RI 1868-1916. The Gas Workers' Strike. Chalk drawing for *The Illustrated London News*, January 4, 1890
Victoria and Albert Museum

ALLEN, James   **fl .1881**
Figure draughtsman probably working on children's books. A series of pen, ink and watercolour drawings, signed and dated 1881, are in the Victoria and Albert Museum.

ALLEN, Olive   **fl.1900-1908**
Illustrator of children's books. Student at the Liverpool School, 1900. Illustrated *Grandmother's Favourites: Holiday House*, C. Sinclair, 1908, in a pretty and whimsical Regency style.
Exhib: Walker AG, 1900.
Bibl: *Studio*, Vol.20, 1900, p.196; *Studio*, Winter No.1900-01, p.78 illus.

ALLEN, Walter James   **fl.1859-1891**
Genre painter and illustrator. He specialised in comic animals, humanised dogs and children. His work appears in *The Churchman's Family Magazine*, 1864 and in *The Illustrated London News*, 1888-91.
Exhib: RA and other exhibitions 1859-61.

ALLEN, Rear-Admiral William   **1793-1864**
Amateur artist. Lieutenant, 1815, commander, 1836, captain, 1842, rear-admiral, 1862. A highly decorated officer who took part in the Niger expeditions of 1832 and 1841-42.
Illus: *Fernando Po [1838, AT 283]; Picturesque Views of the River Niger [1840, AT 284]; The Dead Sea [1855, AT 365].*
Exhib: RA and RBA, landscapes, 1828-47.

ALLINGHAM, Helen   **RWS**   **1848-1926**
Watercolourist and illustrator. Born on 26 September 1848, the daughter of Dr. A.H. Paterson, M.D. She attended the Birmingham School of Design and the Royal Academy Schools from 1867, where she was influenced by the work of Fred Walker. She visited Italy in 1868 but between that time and 1874, drew extensively for the

magazines. In 1874 she married the Irish poet, William Allingham, one of the earliest encouragers of the Pre-Raphaelites, and was elected ARWS in 1875 and RWS in 1890. Her scope as an illustrator was in cottage and rural life with some portraits. An early success was for the serial *Far From the Madding Crowd* by Thomas Hardy in *The Cornhill Magazine*, 1874. She died at Haslemere in 1926.
Illus: *A Flat Iron for a Farthing [Mrs. Ewing, 1872]; Jan of the Windmill [Mrs. Ewing, 1876]; Gentle and Simple [M.A. Paul, 1897]; Happy England [M.B. Huish, 1903]; The Homes of Tennyson [c.1905]; the Cottage Homes of England [1909].*
Contrib: *Once A Week [1868]; London Society [1870]; Cassells Magazine [1870]; The Graphic [1870-74]; ILN [1871-98].*
Exhib: FAS, 1886, 1887, 1889, 1891, 1894, 1898, 1901, 1904, 1908, 1913; RA; RWS.
Colls: BM; Manchester; V & AM.
Bibl: H.B. Huish, *Happy England as Painted by H.A.*, 1903; J. Maas, *Victorian Painters*, 1970, p.231; Arts Council, *English Influences on Van Gogh*, 1974-75, p.53.

ALLINGHAM, Wallace J.   **fl.1898-1907**
Illustrator of stories for *The Illustrated London News*, 1898.
Exhib: RA, 1902.

ALLINSON, Adrian or Alfred Paul   **ROI RBA**   **1890-1959**
Painter, sculptor and caricaturist. Born 9 January 1890. Educated at Wrekin and studied at Slade School, becoming scenic designer to the Beecham Opera Company. Taught painting and drawing at Westminster School of Art and designed posters. He contributed occasional caricatures to magazines, always in black and white with great economy of line, a good example is that to *The Gypsy*, 1915, of G.K. Chesterton.
Exhib: FAS, 1919, 1939; London Salon, 1913; NEA, 1911-16; RA.
Colls: V & AM.

ALLINSON, G.W.
Figure artist, contributing to *Punch*, 1912.

ALLISON, R. Gordon
Topographical illustrator, working for Ingram publications, 1898.
Colls: V & AM.

ALLOM, Thomas   **1804-1872**
Architect and topographical illustrator. Born in London, 13 March 1804, and articled to the architect, Francis Goodwin in 1819. He was a founder member of the RIBA and was associated with Sir Charles Barry on various buildings. He carried out some of his own designs for buildings in the London area and died at Barnes on 21 October 1872. Works are mostly meticulous and in sepia washes.
Illus: *Devonshire Illustrated [1829]; Cumberland and Westmoreland, Scotland Illustrated, The Counties of Chester, Derby and Nottingham [c. 1836]; France Illustrated [G.N. Wright, 1840]; China in a Series of Views [Rev. G.N. Wright, 1843]; China, Its Scenery, Architecture, Social Habits, Illustrated [c.1843]; Constantinople and Its Environs [1843].*
Contrib: *ILN [1851].*
Colls: BM; Chester; Fitzwilliam; G; Newcastle AG; V & AM.

ALLON, Arthur
Architectural illustrator, working for *The Illustrated London News* for which he supplied drawings of The Crystal Palace, 1851.

ALMA TADEMA, Sir Laurence   **1836-1912**
Painter. Born at Dronryp, Netherlands, on 8 January 1836. He studied at the Antwerp Academy and under Baron Leys, but settled in London in 1870 and very soon became one of the Victorian Olympians, living in a lavish house in St. Johns Wood and having a wide circle of students and admirers. He became an ARA in 1873 and an RA in 1879 as well as Member of the OWS in 1875. Alma Tadema was knighted in 1899, received the OM in 1905 and many other honours. His reputation, which suffered a decline after his death, has had a revival in recent years mainly due to the taste for slick and highly coloured classical subjects of which he was a master. He arrived too late in this country to benefit from the great period of illustration, but a few examples from the 1880s exist, most notably an India proof of Findusi's *Epic of Kings*, 1882 in the Victoria and Albert Museum.
Colls: BM; Manchester; V & AM.
Bibl: P.C. Standing, *Sir L A-T* 1905; J Maas, *Victorian Painters,* 1970, pp.181-183.

ALMA TADEMA, Laura Theresa, Lady   **1852-1909**
Artist and occasional illustrator. Born in 1852, the daughter of G.N. Epps, she was a pupil of Sir Laurence before she married him in 1871. She specialised in scenes of childhood, dressed up in the same classical guise as those of her husband.
Contrib: *The English Illustrated Magazine [1889, Vol. VII, p. 625].*
Exhib: FAS, 1910.
Colls: V & AM.

ALMOND, William Douglas   RI RBA   **1868-1916**
Illustrator. Born in London, 28 April 1868, he was educated at King's College and became a Member of the Langham Sketching Club. He joined the staff of *The Illustrated London News* in 1887 and during the next decade did most of his best work for it while acting as an occasional contributor to other periodicals. He was designated 'Special Artist for Character Subjects' in 1891 and it is in social realism that his great strength lies. He was clearly influenced by the earlier generation of realists, Herkomer, Fildes and Holl, but his medium was chalk, adapted to new processes, and more lively than the old engravings. Almond's studies of the workhouses, sweat shops and hospitals of Victorian London have never been surpassed and it is strange that he has never received due recognition. He was also a topographical artist, but these works, like his watercolours, are much weaker in handling. RI, 1897.
Illus: *Sally Dows [Bret Harte, 1897].*
Contrib: *ILN [1887-1894]; Good Words [1891-2]; The Sphere [1894]; Good Cheer [1894]; English Illustrated Magazine [1894-99]; Penny Illustrated Paper; Cassells Family Magazine; The Idler; The*

G. AMATO fl. 1894-1901. The Assassination of the King of Italy at Monza, wash drawing for *The Illustrated London News*, 1900

Pall Mall Magazine; The Windsor Magazine; The Strand Magazine.
Exhib: Paris, 1900; RA; RBA; RI; ROI.
Colls: V & AM.
See illustration.

ALTSON, Abbey   RBA   **fl.1892-1925**
Painter and illustrator. Working at Swiss Cottage, London, 1902, and at Bedford Park, London, 1903-25. Worked for *The Illustrated London News*, 1897; *The Pall Mall Magazine; The Windsor Magazine.* His drawings are very clear and photographic.
Exhib: G; Salon, 1892-93; RA.

AMATO, G   **fl.1894-1901**
Special artist for *The Illustrated London News*, 1894-1901, for *The Graphic*, 1901 and for *L'Illustration*. Amato appears to have been a travelling artist for these papers, in Russia, 1894, in Crete, 1896 and in Rome, 1901. He specialised in royal events and did wash drawings in a mechanical, photographic and dull style.
Colls: V & AM.
See illustration.

AMBROSE, Charles   **fl.1908-1914**
Figure artist, contributing to *Country Life*, 1908-14.

AMES, Mrs. Ernest   **c.1900**
Illustrated her husband's book on the Raj, *Really and Truly*, c.1900. Large colour plates.

ANASTASI, Auguste Paul Charles   **1820-1889**
French landscape painter. He was a pupil of Delacroix, Corot and Delaroche and specialised in views of Normandy, Holland and Rome. He abandoned painting due to blindness. Vizetelly says that he worked for *The Illustrated London News* in its early years.

ANTON VAN ANROOY RI b.1870. Illustration for 'The Observant Friar' by F. H. Melville, wash drawing published in *The English Illustrated Magazine*, 1900

ANDERSON, Martin   **see 'CYNICUS'**

ANDRÉ, R.   **fl.1880-1907**
Illustrator of children's books. Worked at Bushey, Hertfordshire, 1890-1907. Designed covers for *Old Fashioned Fairy Tales*, Mrs. Ewing, c.1880 and the same author's *Grandmother's Spring* and *Master Fritz*, 1885.
Illus: *Old Fashioned Fairy Tales [Mrs. Ewing, c.1880]; The Cruise of the Walnut Shell [Dean, 1881]; Grandmother's Thimble [Warne, 1882]; Pictures and Stories [Warne, 1882]; Up stream [Low, 1884]; Grandmother's Spring [Mrs. Ewing, 1885]; Master Fritz [Mrs. Ewing]; Our Garden [Mrs. Ewing, c.1885]; A Lilliputian Opera [Day, 1885]; The Oak Leaf Library [Warne, n.d.]; Mrs. Ewing's Verse Books [SPCK, n.d.]; A Week Spent in a Glass Pond [Darton, n.d.].*
Bibl: Gleeson White, *Children's Books and Their Illustators; Studio Special No.*, 1897-98.

ANDREWES, Miss D.
Illustrator of children's books. Working at Folkestone, 1902-07. Drew illustrations for *The Little Maid Who Danced To Every Mood*, 1908, with Agnes Stringer.

ANDREWS, Mrs. E.A.   **see CUBITT, Miss Edith Alice**

ANDREWS, George Henry   **RWS FRGS**   **1816-1898**
Marine painter and illustrator. Born at Lambeth in 1816 and trained as an engineer. Principal naval artist to *The Illustrated London News*, 1856-1860 and to *The Illustrated Times*, 1859. Worked for *The Graphic*, 1870. OWS, 1878. Died 31 December 1898.
Illus: *Operations at the Pyramids of Gizeh [H. Vyse, 1840]; English*

Landscape and Views [J.C. Anderson, 1883].
Exhib: BI; OWS, 1840-50; RA, 1850-93; RBA.
Colls: Cardiff; Greenwich; V & AM.
Bibl: Chatto and Jackson, *Treatise on Wood Engraving*, 1861, p.598.

ANELAY, Henry   **1817-1883**
Landscape painter and illustrator. Born at Hull in 1817 and lived at Sydenham from 1848. He was first of all a portrait illustrator and provided numerous plates for *The Illustrated London News*, 1843-55 and may have been sent to Constantinople for the paper in 1853. He exhibited in London from 1845 and at the RA, 1858-73.
Contrib: *London [edited by Charles Knight, 1840]; Illustrated London Magazine [1853-54]: The British Workman [1855]; The Band of Hope Review [1861]; Sandford and Merton; Merrie Days of England; Favourite English Poems; Uncle Tom's Cabin [1852].*
Bibl: Chatto and Jackson, *Treatise on Wood Engraving*, 1861, p.575.

ANGAS, George French   **1822-1886**
Topographical illustrator. Born in Durham, 1822, the son of one of the founders of South Australia. He studied anatomical drawing and lithography in London and in 1841 travelled to Malta and Sicily, issuing the result of the journey in 1842. He went to Australia in 1843 and became director of the Sydney Museum in 1851. Returned to England, 1873, and published a book of poems, 1874.
Illus: *The New Zealanders Illustrated [1846-47, AT 588]; Savage Life and Scenes in Australia and New Zealand [1847]; Description of the Barossa Range [1849, AT 580]; The Kafirs Illustrated [1849, AT 339]; Gold Fields of Ophir [1851, AT 582]; Gold Regions of Australia [1851, AT 583]; South Australia Illustrated [1846-47].*
Exhib: RA; RBA, 1843-74.
Colls: BM; Sydney.

ANGUS, Miss Christine   **fl.1899-1900**
Children's book illustrator. Student at City and Guilds, 1899, and at Liverpool, 1900. Her work shows a slight Greenaway influence. There is no record of published books.
Exhib: Walker AG, Liverpool, 1900.
Bibl: *The Studio*, Vol.17, 1899, p.188 and Vol.20, 1900, p.196.

ANNISON, Edward S.
Illustrator of stories for *The Graphic*, 1912.

ANROOY, Anton van   **RI**   **1870-**
Born in Holland, but came to England at an early age and spent all his working life here. Principally a painter. Signs V. Anrooy or V.A.
Contrib: *The Dome [1897]; The Parade [1897]; The English Illustrated Magazine [1899]; The ILN [1901].*
Exhib: Brighton; Liverpool; RA; RI.
Colls: V & AM.
See illustration.

ANSDELL, Richard   **RA**   **1815-1885**
Animal and sporting painter and illustrator. He was born at Liverpool in 1815 and was educated at the Blue Coat School and the Liverpool Academy. He practised in his native city but moved to London in 1847 and became one of the most successful Victorian sporting artists, collaborating on huge canvases with artists such as T. Creswick and W.P. Frith. ARA, 1861 and RA, 1870. He is a rare illustrator but contributed a few spirited designs to books.
Contrib: *The Illustrated Times [1855-56]; Cassell's Illustrated Family Paper [1857]; Once a Week [1867]; Rhymes and Roundelayes [1858].*
Exhib: RA from 1840; BI from 1846.
Bibl: Chatto & Jackson, *Treatise on Wood Engraving*, 1861, p.598.

ANSTED, H.
Architectural illustrator. Worked during 1827 on *Britton's Cathedrals* 1832-36. He exhibited architetural subjects at the RA, 1826.

ANSTED, William Alexander
Landscape draughtsman, illustrator and etcher, working at Chiswick from 1888-99. He was one of a number of late Victorian artists who specialised in popular and inexpensive travel books.

GEORGE DENHOLM ARMOUR 1864-1949. Illustration for *Punch*, pen and ink. The Point to Point Season. Yokel (to persevering sportsman who in spite of several falls is doggedly completing the Course) "'Urry up mister or the next race'll be catchin' you up!"

Author's Collection

Illus: *Rivers of Devon [1893]. The Riviera [1894]; The Coast of Devon [1895]; Episcopal Palaces of England [1895]; The Master of The Musicians [1896]; London Riverside Churches [1897]; English Cathedral Series [1897-98]; The Romance of our Ancient Churches [1899]; Life of Johnson [1899].*
Contrib: *Good Words* [1894].
Bibl: R.E.D. Sketchley, *English Book Illus.*, 1903, pp.50, 132.

APE   See PELLEGRINI, C.

APE JUNIOR   fl.1910-1911
Pseudonym of caricaturist working for *Vanity Fair*, 1910-11.
Colls: V & AM.

ARCHER, John Wykeham   ARWS   1808-1864
Watercolourist and topographical illustrator. Born at Newcastle-upon-Tyne, 2 August 1808, coming to London in 1820 to serve his apprenticeship with John Scott, the animal engraver. He worked as an engraver in Newcastle in partnership with William Collard and then in Edinburgh. Finally in 1831 he returned to London to work for W. and E. Finden. He slowly abandoned engraving for watercolour, although he did a great number of wood engravings in the 1840s and carried out many drawings of old buildings for topographical works. He became an ARWS in 1842, and died in London, 25 May 1864.
Illus: *The Castles and Abbeys of England [W.Beattie, 1844].*
Contrib: *Winkle's Illustrations of the Cathedral Churches [1836-37]; London [Charles Knight, 1841]; ILN [1847-49 (animals)]; Household Song [1861]; Vestiges of Old London; Douglas Jerrold's Magazine; William Twopenny's Magazine.*
Exhib: NWS, 1842-64.
Colls: BM; V & AM.
Bibl: Chatto and Jackson, *Treatise on Wood Engraving*, 1861, p.599.

ARIS, Ernest Alfred   1883-
Watercolour artist and illustrator. Born 22 April 1883 and studied at the Bradford College of Art and the RCA; diploma at Bradford, 1900. Art master ICS School, 1909-12. His works were widely reproduced in America, Canada and Australia and he did much commercial work.

Contributed children's illustrations to *The Graphic*, 1910.
Exhib: RA; RBA; RI; RWS.
Bibl: *Who's Who in Art, 1964.*

ARMFIELD, Maxwell   RBA   1882-1972
Painter, watercolourist and etcher. Born at Ringwood in 1882, studied at the Birmingham School and in Paris under Collin, Prinet, and Dauchez. Armfield wrote and lectured extensively. As well as painting, he published *The Hanging Garden* 1914, and *White Horses* and some books on technique. Among his illustrated books are *The Confessions of St. Augustine*, E.B. Pusey, 1909 (12 col. pls.); *Sylvia's Travels*, C. Armfield, 1911 (animal vignettes of and col. pls.); *An Artist in Italy*, 1926 (16 illus.).
Exhib: B, from 1902; FAS, 1970, 1971, 1973; L; NAC, from 1907; RA; RHA; RWA; Salon from 1905.
Bibl: *Modern Book Illustrators*, Studio, 1914.
See Horne.

ARMITAGE, Edward   RA   1817-1896
Historical and religious painter and illustrator. Born in London in 1817 and in 1835 went to the École des Beaux-Arts in Paris to study with Paul Delaroche. Entered the Houses of Parliament competition and in 1847 his prize-winning painting 'The Battle of Meeanee' was purchased by Queen Victoria. He visited Russia during the Crimean War and painted military subjects on his return. He became an ARA in 1867, RA in 1872, and was Lecturer on Painting at the RA, 1875.
Contrib: *Lyra Germanica [1861]; Pupils of St. John The Divine [1867-68]; Dalziel's Bible Gallery [1880].*
Exhib: G; L; RA, from 1848-93; Salon, 1842.
Colls: BM; Royal Collection.
Bibl: J.P. Richter, *Pictures and Drawings of EA*, 1897.

ARMOUR, George Denholm   OBE   1864-1949
Black and white artist and illustrator. Born in Lanarkshire, 30 January 1864, and was educated at St. Andrews University, Edinburgh School of Art and the RSA, from 1880 to 1888. He worked in London from about 1890 as a painter and illustrator but only achieved wide recognition after his appearance in *Punch*, 1894. During the First World War,

Armour commanded the depot of the Army Remount Service and served in Salonica, 1917 to 1919, being awarded the OBE in that year.

His drawings are almost exclusively of sporting and country subjects and many of them derived their humour from the Leech tradition. Armour's penwork was impeccable and he could seldom be faulted on his drawing of the horse. An unusual subject, a bullfight in the Victoria and Albert Museum, is reminiscent of J. Crawhall, of whose drawings Armour had a collection. Nevertheless, the artist was criticised by Seaman of *Punch* for being too repetitive and of not introducing enough motor cars into his subjects!

Illus: *Handley Cross [1908]; Foxiana [L. Bell, Country Life, 1929]; Humour in the Hunting Field [1928]; Sport and There's the Humour of It [1935].*
Contrib: *The Graphic [1892]; The Pall Mall Budget [1893]; Pick-Me-Up [1896]; The New Budget [1895]; The Unicorn [1895]; The Pall Mall Magazine [1897]; The Longbow [1898]; The Butterfly [1899]; Sporting and Dramatic News; The Windsor Magazine; Judge [New York]; Country Life [1909, 1914].*
Exhib: FAS, 1924; Leicester Gall.; RSA; RWA.
Colls: Glasgow; *Punch*; V & AM.
Bibl: R.G.G. Price, *A History of Punch*, 1955, pp. 176, 205-206.
See illustration.

ARMOUR, Jessie Lamont
Student at Armstrong College, Newcastle, producing designs for illustration in Birmingham School style. No record of published books.
Bibl: *The Studio*, Vol 44, 1908, p.275 illus.

ARMSTEAD, Henry Hugh   RA   1828-1905
Sculptor and occasional illustrator. Born in London, 18 June 1828, and studied at the RA Schools. ARA, 1875, and RA, 1879. He was a prolific sculptor as well as a wood engraver and chaser; he carved the south and east panels of the podium of the Albert Memorial and part of the frieze of the Albert Hall. He was a frequent exhibitor of busts and reliefs at the RA from 1851. His illustrations, especially his religious subjects, were rather hard and Germanic, his modern genre subjects could be delightful with a good sense of composition. He died 4 December 1905.
Contrib: *Eliza Cook's Poems [1856]; Good Works [1861]; Sacred Poetry [1862]; Churchman's Family Magazine [1863]; Touches of Nature [1866]; Dalziel's Bible Gallery [1880]; Art Pictures from the Old Testament [1897].*

ARMSTRONG, Francis Abel William Taylor RBA RWA
1849-1920
Landscape painter. Armstrong was born at Malmesbury, 15 February 1849, and although trained for a business career eventually devoted himself entirely to art. He drew for *The Art Journal* and *Portfolio*. He practised in Bristol and died there on 1 December 1920.
Contrib: *Lorna Doone [De Luxe Edition, 1883]*; an unrecorded edition of Mathew Arnold's Poems, n.d.
Exhib: Berlin; Cologne; FAS, 1923; Paris; RBA; RWA.
Colls: V & AM.

ARMYTAGE, J. Charles   fl.1863-1874
Figure artist and illustrator. He contributed to *The Cornhill Magazine* and did architectural subjects – perhaps for books.
Colls: V & AM.

ARNALD, George ARA   1766-1841
Landscape painter and topographer. He was born at Farndish, Bedfordshire in 1766 and showed great aptitude for drawing from an early age. He was educated at Houghton Regis and encouraged by members of the local gentry to become an artist. He became a pupil of William Pether and, like his master, developed a talent for seascapes and moonlight scenes. He went on tours of North Wales with John Varley in 1798 and 1799 and was later patronised by Sir George Beaumont. Elected an ARA in 1810, Arnald failed to gain the status of a full academician and became increasingly embittered. His greatest success was the winning of a prize for painting 'The Battle of the Nile' and for undertaking commissions for the Duke of Gloucester. Arnald travelled on the Continent and in Ireland making landscapes, and was an occasional etcher. He died at Pentonville, 21 November 1841.

Illus: *The Border Antiquities of England and Scotland [Walter Scott, 1814-17]; Picturesque Scenery on the Meuse [1835, AT 95]; History and Topography of Essex [1836].*
Exhib: RA, 1788.
Colls: BM; Greenwich Hospital; V & AM.
Bibl: Simon Houfe, 'The Bedfordshire Prodigy', *Bedfordshire Magazine*, Spring 1990, pp. 135-141.

ARUNDALE, Francis Vyvyan Jago   1807-1853
Architect and draughtsman. He was born in 1807 and became a pupil of A. Pugin (q.v.) and accompanied him to Normandy. He studied at the RA Schools in 1829 and in 1831 he went out to Egypt to assist Robert Hay in his archaeological works, later assisting Bonomi and Catherwood, 1831-40. Arundale made many fine architectural studies, many of which were exhibited in London on his return, but his books were not a financial success. He married the daughter of H.W. Pickersgill, RA and died in 1854, probably as the result of a disease contracted in the Egyptian tombs.
Illus: *Illustrations of Jerusalem and Mt. Sinai [1837]; Operations Carried on at The Pyramids of Giza, 1837 [Howard Vyse, 1840].*
Contrib: *Specimens of the Architectural Antiquities of Normandy [1826-28]; Britton's Union of Architecture [1827, AL 7].*
Exhib: BI; RA.
Colls: Searight Coll. at V & AM.

ASHLEY, Alfred   fl.1841-1853
Landscape artist and illustrator. Ashley was a draughtsman and etcher of figure subjects working in the style of 'Phiz' but less certain in his drawing and more scratchy in his line. He published *The Art of Engraving*, 1849.
Contrib: *Punch [1841]; Christmas Shadows [1850]; Old London Bridge [G.H. Rodwell, c.1850].*
Exhib: London, 1850-53.

ASHTON, G. Rossi   fl.1875-1901
Australian artist and illustrator. He appears to have worked in Australia till about 1885 and was for some time a colleague of Phil May on *The Sydney Bulletin*. Came to England and did prolific humorous work for the magazines.
Contrib: *The Graphic [1875, 1885 (Australia)]; Daily Graphic [1890-95]; Lika Joko [1896]; Pearson's Magazine [1896]; St. James's Budget [1898]; Fun [1901]; Illustrated Bits; The Pall Mall Magazine; The Sketch.*

ASSUS
Illustrator of Turkish subjects in popular press, 1912.

ASTZ
Pseudonym of unidentified cancaturist, *Vanity Fair*, 1913.

ATKINSON, Captain George Franklin   1822-1859
Son of the artist James Atkinson. Officer in the Bengal Engineers and amateur artist. He was present at the Indian Mutiny and supplied sketches for *The Illustrated London News*, 1857. Published *The Campaign in India*, 1859, AT 486; *Curry and Rice*, 1860, AT 487.

ATKINSON, John Augustus   OWS   c.1775-c.1833
Painter, etcher and illustrator. Born in London about 1775, he was taken to Russia by his uncle, James Walker, in 1784 and was patronised by the Empress Catherine and the Emperor Paul. He returned to London in 1801 and published books on costume and manners of Russia. Atkinson was an accomplished caricaturist and a battle painter, and he visited the site of the Battle of Waterloo in 1815 as a topographer. He was a Member of the OWS from 1808 to 1812. He remained in London until about 1818 but little is known of his subsequent life.
Illus: *Hudibras [1797 (Russian edition)]; Miseries of Human Life [1807]; A Picturesque Representation of the Costumes of Great Britain [1807]; The Art of the Cutter (caricatures) [1808, AL 295]; A Picturesque Representation of ... the Russians [1812]; Voyage Round the World [1813, AT 1]; Foreign Field Sports [1814, AT 2]; Anecdotes [E. Orme, 1819, AL 376].*
Exhib: BI; OWS; RA, 1803-33; RBA.
Colls: BM; Dublin; Greenwich; Manchester; St. Petersburg; V & AM.

ATKINSON, John Priestman   **fl.1864-1894**
Humorous black and white artist. Official in General Railway Manager's office, Derby, 1864. Began to draw for *The Derby Ram* and later turned completely to art, studying in Paris and becoming a close friend of Harry Furniss. He was a regular contributor to *Punch* under the name 'Dumb Crambo Junior'. Specialised in comic genre subjects. Signs with monogram JPA.
Illus: *Thackeray's The Great Hoggarty Diamond, Paris Sketch Book, Ballads, [1894].*
Contrib: *ILN [1881, 1884]; The Cornhill Magazine [1883]; Moonshine [1892]; The St. James's Budget; The Backslider.*
Colls: V & AM.
Bibl: M.H. Spielmann, *The History of Punch,* 1895, pp.524-525.

ATKINSON, Thomas Witlam   **c.1799-1861**
Architect, traveller and topographer. Born at Cawthorne, Yorkshire, of poor parents and began life as bricklayer and stone carver. In 1827 he settled in London and in 1834 moved to Manchester where he went into partnership with the architect, A.B. Clayton. He designed a number of churches and other buildings in the Manchester area and in 1844 he left England for Hamburg and St. Petersburg, where he abandoned architecture for the life of a painter and traveller. He visited Egypt and Greece and made an extensive tour through Russia, 1848 to 1853.
Illus: *Gothic Ornaments Selected from the different Cathedrals [1829]; Oriental and Western Siberia [1858, AT 530]; Travels in Upper and Lower Amoor [1860].*
Exhib: RA, 1830-42.
Bibl: *Art Journal,* October 1861; *Builder,* XIX, 1861, p.590; H.M. Colvin, *Biog. Dict. Eng. Architects,* 1954, p.47.

ATTWELL, Emily A.
Student competitor in *The Studio* book illustration competitions. Working from address in the Mile End Road, London E.
Bibl: *The Studio,* Vol.10, 1897, illus; and Vol. 12, 1897, illus.

ATTWELL, Mabel Lucie (Mrs. H.C. Earnshaw)   **1879-1964**
Artist and illustrator, author of children's stories and verse. She was born in London 4 June 1879 and was educated at the Cooper's Company School. She studied art at the Regent Street Art School and at Heatherley's. In 1908 she married Harold Earnshaw (q.v.), the illustrator, and in 1925 she was elected SWA. She illustrated works by Charles Kingsley, Hans Andersen, Grimm, Lewis Carroll and J.M. Barrie.
Exhib: SWA, 1924.
See Horne.

AULT, Norman   **1880-1950**
Writer and illustrator. Born 17 December 1880 and attended West Bromwich Art School, 1895 to 1900. On leaving he obtained work with *The Strand* and other magazines and collaborated with his artist wife on children's books. He specialised in costume, architecture, furniture and landscape, giving great attention to period details. He worked for the children's annuals *Chatterbox* and *Sunday.* Did little for books after 1920. Close friend of H.R. Millar.
Illus: *Sammy and the Snarleywink [1904]; The Rhyme Book [1906]; The Podgy Book [1907]* (all with his wife). *The Mabinogion [Lady Guest, 1902]; The Story of an Old Fashioned Doll [J. Connolly, 1905]; Alice in Wonderland [1907]; England's Story for Children [M.B. Williams, 1908]; The Lays of Ancient Rome [T.B. Macaulay, 1911]; Tennyson, The Children's Poets [1913]; The Seven Champions of Christendom [F.J.H. Darton, 1913]; Caravan Tales [W. Hauff, n.d.]; The Shepherd of the Ocean [G.I. Whitham, 1914]; New Tales of Old Times [W.E. Sparkes, 1914]; Chambers Dramatic History Readers [W. Hislop, 1914-15]; Life in Ancient Britain [1920]; Dreamland Shores [1920]; The Poet's Life of Christ [1922].*
Bibl: *The Artist,* c.1900.
See also **LOCKHART, Lena**

AUSTIN, Henry
Topographical illustrator contributing to *The Pall Mall Budget,* c.1890.

AUSTIN, Samuel OWS   **1796-1834**
Watercolourist and topographer. He was born at Liverpool in 1796 and after working as a bank clerk, he took lessons from Peter de Wint. He was a founder member of the SBA and was elected AOWS in 1827 and OWS on his deathbed in 1834. He painted extensively in Lancashire and North Wales but also in Belgium, Holland and Normandy.
Illus: *Views in the East [Elliott, 1833].*
Contrib: *Lancashire Illustrated [1829].*
Exhib: OWS; RA; RBA.
Colls: Ashmolean; Fitzwilliam; Liverpool; Manchester.

AVRIL, Édouard Henri (called Paul)   **1849-1928**
Painter and illustrator. Born in Algiers, 21 March 1849, and studied under Pils and P. Lehmann in Paris. He exhibited at the Salon 1878 to 1884. Avril is included here because he illustrated three lavish books by Octave Uzanne, which were published in England. They are *The Fan,* 1884; *The Sunshade,* 1883, and *The Mirror of the World,* 1890. All the drawings are more French than English and are extremely eclectic and ill-assorted; they make an interesting comparison with contemporary English black and white work.

AYLING, Florence
Book decorator in the William Morris style. She contributed headings to *The English Illustrated Magazine,* 1888.

BACON, John Henry Frederick ARA   **1865-1914**
Portrait painter and illustrator. Painted the Coronation Portrait of
King George V and Queen Mary, 1912. ARA, 1903. MVO, 1913.
Died in London, 24 January 1914.
Illus: *Things Will Take a Turn [B. Harraden, 1894]; The
Ravensworth Scholarship [H. Clarke, 1895]; The King's Empire
[1906]; Celtic Myth and Legend [C. Squire, 1912].*
Contrib: *The Girl's Own Paper [1890-1900]; Black & White [1891-
96]; The Quiver [1892]; The Ludgate Monthly [1895]; Cassell's
Family Magazine [1896-97]; The Windsor Magazine.*
Colls: BM.

BADEN-POWELL, Robert, 1st Baron OM   **1857-1941**
General, Founder of the Scout Movement, sculptor and illustrator.
Born 22 February 1857 and after attending Charterhouse, joined the
13 Hussars, 1876; served in India, Afghanistan and South Africa,
Assistant Military Secretary in South Africa, 1887-89 and Malta,
1890-93. At the Defence of Mafeking, 1899-1900. Major-General,
1900. Lieutenant-General, 1908. CB, 1900; KCB, 1909; KCVO,
1909; Baronet, 1922. Like many army officers of his generation,
Baden-Powell was a talented artist and sculptor. He contributed
sketches to *The Graphic* from South Africa in 1891 and from Ashanti
to *The Daily Graphic*, 1895. A further sketch of scouting appeared in
The Graphic in 1910. Died in Kenya, 1941.
Publ: *Pig-sticking or Hog-hunting [1889]; Reconnaisance and
Scouting [1890]; Vedette [1890]; Cavalry Instruction [1895]; The
Downfall of Prempeh [1896]; The Matabele Campaign [1896]; Aids to
Scouting [1899]; Sport in War [1900]; Sketches in Mafeking and E.
Africa [1907]; Scouting for Boys [1908]; Indian Memories [1915].*
Exhib: RA, 1907.
Bibl: A.C.R. Carter, *The Work of War Artists in South Africa*, 1900,
pp.16, 26.

BAINES, T. FRGS
Illustrator of wildlife. Contributed to *Nature and Art*, 1866.

BAINES, Thomas   **1822-1875**
Artist, explorer and illustrator. Travelled with the British Army
during the Kafir war, 1848-51, and accompanied expeditions to
North-West Australia, Victoria Falls, the Tati goldfields and the
Zambesi under Livingstone. His drawings of African travel appeared
in *The Illustrated London News*, 1869.

BAIRNSFATHER, Bruce   **1888-1959**
Illustrator, cartoonist and journalist. Born at Murree, India, in July
1888, the son of an army officer. He attended the United Service
College and served with the Warwickshire Militia from 1911 to
1914. At the outbreak of war that year he returned to the Royal
Warwickshire Regiment and served in France until December 1916.
Bairnsfather was already becoming known to the public by his
humorous sketches of trench life in the pages of *The Tatler* and other
magazines. An amateur artist who worked in the poster style
developed by Hassall and others, his individual view of the Front, its
cockney humour, its unheroic fortitude and chauvinism, was exactly
right for the grim period after the Somme. His pipe-smoking tommy
'Old Bill' typified British determination with his 'If you know of a
better 'ole go to it!' Bairnsfather was Official War Artist to the U.S.

RONALD E. BALFOUR 1896-1941. Drawing for illustration to
Omar Khayyam, published by Messrs. Constable, 1920. Pen and ink
Victoria and Albert Museum

Army Europe in the Second World War, 1942-44.
Publ: *Fragments From France [6 Vols]; The Better 'Ole, Bullets and
Billets; From Mud to Mufti; Old Bill; Wide Canvas [1939]; Old Bill
Stands By [1939]; Old Bill Does It Again [1940]; Jeeps and Jests
[1943]; No Kiddin' [1944]; C'est Pour La France; Back to Blighty.*
Coll: Imperial War Mus.
See Horne.

BAKER, Annie
Artist working at Egremont, Cheshire, and exhibiting at Liverpool,
1890. She contributed to *The English Illustrated Magazine*, 1888.

BAKER, Colonel Bernard Granville   **fl.1911-1930**
Military painter and illustrator. He worked in London and Beccles,
Suffolk and illustrated his own *The Danube with Pen and Pencil*, 1911.
Exhib: L.

BAKER, Sir Samuel White   **1821-1893**
Traveller and sportsman. Went to Ceylon in 1846 and remained until
1848. He established an English colony at Newera Eliya and
travelled in Asia Minor, 1860-61; Abyssinia, 1861-62; Khartoum,
1862, and to the White Nile in 1864. He received the Gold Medal of
the Royal Geographical Society and was knighted in 1866; FRS,
1869. He published in 1855 *Eight Years Wanderings in Ceylon*, AT
415, with his own sketches.

BAKEWELL, Robert
Illustrated *Travels in the Tarentaise [1823 (coloured aquatints)*, AT 56].

BALCOMB, J.T.
Illustrator specialising in scientific and biological drawings. He worked regularly for *The Illustrated London News*, 1876-83.

BALFOUR, Maxwell   fl.1896-1907
Painter and draughtsman. Working from an address in Cheyne Walk, Chelsea, 1901-02. He contributed to *The Quarto*, 1896, and exhibited at the NEAC, 1901-02.

BALFOUR, Ronald E.   1896-1941
Balfour appears to have been working as a book illustrator between about 1910 and 1925. In 1920 he illustrated an edition of *The Rubaiyat of Omar Khayyam* for Messrs. Constable. He frequently designs in pencil in an early art deco style and signs with monogram REB.
Colls: V & AM.
See illustration.

BALKIN, Lance
Portrait illustrator, working for *The Graphic*, 1887.

BALL, Alec C.
Illustrator of social realism for *The Graphic*, 1902-05 and 1906-10.

BALL, Fred H.   fl. 1899-1925
Black and white and decorative artist for books. Working in Nottingham, 1899, and at Mapperley, Notts., 1914-25. His style is based on that of the French poster artists and much influenced by designers such as Alphonse Mucha.
Exhib: RA, 1913.
Bibl: *The Studio*, Vol. 15, 1899, p.68 illus; pp.144, 295 illus; and Vol. 63, 1914, pp.62-63; *Modern Book Illustrators and Their Work*, Studio, 1914, illus.

BALL, Wilfrid Williams   1853-1917
Illustrator, watercolourist and etcher. Born in London 4 January 1853. He was from a Lincolnshire family, settled in London, and was placed with a firm of accountants, devoting his spare time to painting and etching and studying at Heatherley's. In 1877 he gave up the City for professional painting, working from Putney, where he came into contact with Whistler undertaking his Thames views. He was a member of the Society of Painter Etchers from 1881 and a member of the Hogarth and Arts Clubs. His work was mainly topographical and landscape and it took him on tours abroad to Italy, 1877; Holland, 1889; Germany, 1890; Egypt, 1893. After 1895 he worked at Lymington and died at Khartoum on 14 February 1917 while working in a civil capacity for the army.
Illus: *Hampshire, Sussex [Varley, 1905].*
Contrib: *The Yellow Book [1895].*
Exhib: FAS, 1899, 1904, 1909, 1912, 1915, 1917; Leicester Gall.; New Gall.; RA, 1877-1903; RE.
Colls: V & AM.

BALMER, Clinton   fl.1900-1922
He was probably born in Liverpool and studied under Augustus John, who was teaching at the university, 1901-02. He was befriended by the writer Gordon Bottomley, who became his chief patron. For him he illustrated his poems *The Gate of Smaragdas*, 1904. He decorated a lunette in Toxteth Library in 1904 and emigrated to New York after the First World War.
Coll: Carlisle.
Bibl: Gordon Bottomley, *Poet and Painter*, 1955; *The Last Romantics*, catalogue of exhibition, Barbican Gallery, 1989-90, pp.170-171.

BANNERMAN, Helen   1862-1946
Illustrator of children's stories. She was born in Edinburgh and educated at St Andrew's University and in Germany and Italy. After some years of travel, she married an army doctor and spent thirty years in India at Madras and Bombay. In 1898 she wrote a story for her children *Little Black Sambo*, which was mailed to English friends and discovered by E.V. Lucas; it was published in 1899. Her books are now not politically unfashionable.
Illus: *Little Black Sambo [1899]; Little Black Mingo [1901]; Little Black Quibba [1902]; The Story of Little Degchie-Head [1903]; Pat and the Spider [1904]; The Story of The Teasing Monkey [1906]; The Story of Little Black Quasha [1908]; The Story of Little Black Bobtail*

FREDERICK BARNARD 1846-1896. One of a series of 'London Sketches' in pen and ink for George R. Sims' *How The Poor Live*, 1883   Victoria and Albert Museum

[1909]; Sambo and The Twins [1937]; Little White Squibba [1966].
Bibl: Elizabeth Hay, *Sambo Sahib: The Story of Helen Bannerman*, 1981.

BANNISTER, F.
Figure artist. He contributed to *The Strand Magazine*, 1892.

BARBER, C. Burton   1845-1894
Sporting and animal painter. Born in 1845 and worked latterly at Regents Park, London. He became a Member of the ROI in 1883.
Contrib: *The Graphic [1882-86 (dogs)].*
Exhib: FAS, 1895; G; L; M; RA; ROI; Tooth.

BARBER, T. or J.
Engraver. He engraved views of Scotland and illustrated *Picturesque Illustrations of The Isle of Wight*, c.1830.

BARCLAY, Edgar   1842-1913
Landscape painter and illustrator. He studied in Dresden, 1861, and in Rome, 1874-75. He seems to have specialised in figure drawing and in illustrating stories of eastern life. Practised from Haverstock Hill, Hampstead, and died there in 1913.
Illus: *Orpheus and Eurydice [H.D. Barclay, 1877]; Mountain Life in Algeria [1882].*
Contrib: *English Illustrated Magazine [1888-91]; The Graphic [1899]; The Picturesque Mediterranean [1891].*
Exhib: G; L; M; New Gall; OWS; RA.

BARNARD, Frederick   1846-1896
Illustrator. Born in St. Martin's-le-Grand, London, 26 May 1846. He studied at Heatherley's in Newman Street in 1863 and at Paris under

ROBERT BARNES 1840-1895. A Welsh seller of lace, Llandudno, pen and ink for an unidentified magazine illustration

Author's Collection

Bonnat. Barnard exhibited at the RA from 1866 to 1887, although he freely admitted that he never had the same confidence in oil as in black and white work. He began contributing the latter to *The Illustrated London News* in 1863 and remained until his death one of its most prolific artists. His forte was genre subjects and social realism which brought him the admiration of the young Vincent Van Gogh during his English years. He exhibited at the Paris Exhibition of 1878 and at home contributed to *Punch* and Furniss's *Lika Joko*. His Dickens illustrations are powerful, but his best work is perhaps the London sketches of *How The Poor Live* by George R. Sims, published in 1883, and also engraved for *The Pictorial Times*. His superb character drawing has only one fault, that it tends to be humorous when it is not required to be; the figures in the Paris Commune sketches of 1870, *Illustrated London News*, are a case in point.

Barnard was suffocated or burnt to death at Wimbledon on 28 September 1896. His work is usually in pen and ink, sometimes in chalk or wash, signed: F.B.

Illus: *Dickens Household Edition [1871-79], Barnaby Rudge, Bleak House, Sketches by Boz, etc.; Episodes of Fiction [1870]; All Sorts and Conditions of Men [Walter Besant]; The Four George's [Thackeray, 1894]; Armorel of Lyonesse [1890].*
Contrib: *ILN [1863-96]; Punch [1864, 1884]; The Broadway [1867-74]; Cassell's Illustrated Readings [1867-68]; London Society [1868]; Cassell's Family Magazine [1868]; Once A Week [1869]; Good Words [1869 and 1891-92]; Good Words For The Young [1869]; Fun [1869]; Judy [1887-90]; Boys Own Paper [1890]; Black and White [1891]; Chums [1892]; Sporting and Dramatic News [1893]; Lika Joko [1894]; The Penny Illustrated Paper; Cassell's Saturday Journal.*
Exhib: Paris, 1878; RA from 1866.
Colls: V & AM.
Bibl: *Exhibition of English Humorous Art*, Royal Institute of Painters in Watercolours Gallery, June 1889.
See illustration.

BARNARD, George
Illustrator and drawing master. A pupil of J. D. Harding, he was a regular exhibitor at London galleries from 1832 to 1884 and became

art master at Rugby in 1870. He published a number of books on technique, *Handbook of Foliage and Foreground Drawing*, 1853; *The Theory and Practice of Landscape Painting in Water Colours*, 1855; *Drawing From Nature*, 1856; *Barnard's Trees*, 1868.
Illus: *The Brunnens of Nassau and The River Lahn [1843, AT 61]; A Lady's Tour Round Monte Rosa [Cole, 1859, AT 59]; Two Months in the Highlands, Orcadia and Skye [Charles Richard Weld, 1860].*
Contrib: *ILN [1858].*

BARNES, G.E.
Illustrator. Working for *The Broadway*, c.1867-74 and exhibiting at the RBA, 1866. Specialised in architecture.

BARNES, Robert   ARWS   1840-1895
Painter and illustrator. Worked first at Berkhamsted and later from Ormonde House, Cliveden Place, Brighton. Barnes was among the best of the second rank of illustrators of the 1860s; his drawing was always excellent if it lacks the originality of a Walker or a Pinwell. His range was very much theirs, because he was at his best in rural genre subjects and one of his most important commissions was to illustrate the first serialisation of 'The Mayor of Casterbridge' in *The Graphic*, January to June, 1886. He was elected ARWS in 1876.
Illus: *Sybil and Her Live Snowball [1866]; Gray's Elegy [1868]; A Prisoner of War [G. Norway, 1894].*
Contrib: *London Society [1862]; Churchman's Family Magazine [1863]; Once A Week [1864]; Cornhill [1864, 1869-70, 1884]; The Leisure Hour [1864]; British Workman [1865]; The Band of Hope Review [1865-66]; The Sunday Magazine [1865-66, 1869]; The Sunday at Home [1866]; Touches of Nature by Eminent Artists [1866]; The Quiver [1867-69]; Idyllic Pictures [1867]; Golden Hours [1868]; Christian Lyrics [1868]; Taylor's Original Poems [1868]; Good Words [1869, 1891], Cassell's Magazine [1870]; ILN [1872-77]; The Graphic [1880, 1885-89]; Cassell's Family Magazine [1890]; Our Life Illustrated by Pen and Pencil [1865]; The Months Illustrated With Pen and Pencil [1864]; Pictures of English Life [1865]; Foxe's Book of Martyrs [1865].*
Contrib: *Good Words [1891]; The Quiver [1880, 1892].*
Colls: V & AM; Dorset County Museum.
Bibl: F. Reid, *Illustrators of The Sixties*, 1928, pp 256-258.
See illustration (above).

BARNETT, R.C.   fl.1798-1831
Painter of landscape and draughtsman. Worked in London and exhibited there at the RA and BI, 1798 to 1821. Published at Manchester in 1831, *The Beauties of Antiquity*.
Colls: Ashmolean.

BARRAUD, Allan F.   fl.1880-1908
Landscape painter, etcher and illustrator, working at Watford.
Contrib: *The Quiver [1880].*
Exhib: L; RA; RBA; ROI.

BARRAUD, Francis   -1924
Painter of portraits and genre subjects. Son of Henry Barraud, artist, and nephew of William Barraud, the sporting artist He studied at the RA Schools, where he won the silver medal, and afterwards at Heatherley's, the Beaux-Arts, Antwerp. Barraud worked from the St. John's Wood area of London and was a frequent contributor to exhibitions. His most celebrated work is probably the original advertisement of 'His Master's Voice'. He died 29 August 1924.
Contrib: *The Graphic [Christmas, 1912].*
Exhib: M; RA; RBA; RI; ROI; RWA.
Colls: Liverpool.
Bibl: *Who Was Who, 1916-28.*

BARRETT, C.R.B.   fl.1889-1930
Topographical illustrator.
Illus: *The Tower [1889]; Essex Highways, Byways and Waterways [1892-93]; The Trinity House of Deptford Strand [1893]; Barrett's Illustrated Guides [1892-93]; Somersetshire [1894]; Shelley's Visit to France [C.J. Elton, 1894]; Charterhouse in Pen and Ink [1895]; Surrey [1895]; Battles and Battlefields of England [1896].*
Bibl: R.E.D. Sketchley, *English Book Illustration*, 1903, pp.47,48, 132.

BARRIAS, Felix J. 1822-1907
Distinguished French academic painter who won the *grand prix de Rome* in 1844. He contributed sketches of Italy to *The Illustrated London News*, 1847.

BARRIBAL, W.H. fl. 1907-1925
Portrait illustrator He worked through London agents from 1914 to 1925.
Contrib: *ILN, Christmas [1907]; The Graphic [1911].*

BARROW
Wood engraver and illustrator, working in a rather crude and old fashioned style in the second quarter of the 19th century. His chief interest lies in W. J. Linton's claim that he was Charles Dickens's uncle. Charles Knight says much the same: 'His uncle, Mr. Barrow, was the conductor of *The Mirror of Parliament* and sometimes meeting him at the printing-office of Mr. Clowes, he would tell me of his clever young relative...' *Passages of a Working Life*, 1865, Vol 3, p 37.
Illus: *Gulliver's Travels [1864].*
Contrib: *ILN [1843, Queen Victoria's visit to the Midland counties].*

BARROW, Sir John 1764-1848
Amateur draughtsman. Traveller, secretary of the Admiralty and Founder of the Royal Geographical Society. He contributed to the *Encyclopaedia Britannica* and wrote his autobiography.
Illus: *A Voyage to Cochinchina [1806, AT 514].*

BARTLETT, William Henry 1809-1854
Topographical illustrator. Born in Kentish Town in 1809 and was apprenticed to the topographer, J. Britton. He travelled on the Continent in about 1830 and made visits to Syria, Egypt, Palestine and America. He died on board ship on his last tour, 1854.
Illus: *Britton's Cathedral Antiquities [1832-36]; Switzerland [1833 with W. Beattie]; The History of Essex [1836]; Picturesque Antiquities of English Cities, Scotland Illustrated [1838]; American Scenery [1839-40, AT 651]; Canadian Scenery [1842]; The Danube [1844]; Walks About Jerusalem [1845]; Forty Days in the Desert [1848]; The Nile-Boat or Glimpses of Egypt [1849]; The Overland Route [1850], Footsteps of our Lord and his Apostles in Syria, Greece and Italy [1851]; Pictures From Sicily [1852]; The Pilgrim Fathers [1853]; Scripture Sites and Scenes [1854].*
Exhib: NWS, 1831-33; RA.
Colls: BM; Fitzwilliam; Leeds; V & AM.
Bibl: W. Beattie, *Brief Memoir of WHB*, 1855; J. Britton, *A Brief Biography of WHB*, 1855.

BARTLETT, William H. ROI 1858-
Painter. Born in 1858 and studied at the École des Beaux-Arts under Gerome and then with Bouguereau and Fleury. Exhibited at Paris in 1889 and received a silver medal and the Legion of Honour. He published various photogravures and his work was reproduced in *The Art Journal*, 1894-97. His rare illustrations are strongly drawn with the use of thick black ink.
Contrib: *ILN [1887, Vol. XC p.595].*
Exhib: B; FAS, 1892; G; L; M; New Gall; RA; RI; ROI; RWA.
Colls: Auckland; Bradford; Brighton; Leeds; Liverpool; Reading Savage Club; V & AM.

BARTON, Rose M. RWS 1856-1929
Watercolourist. She was born in Rochestown, Co. Tipperary, the daughter of a solicitor and received drawing lessons in Brussels. She later studied under the Belgian artist, Henri Gervex. She was elected an associate of the Old Watercolour Society in 1893 and became the first woman member of the RWS in 1911. An important collection of her work for the book *Familiar London* was sold from Lord Iveagh's collection at Elveden Hall on 21 May 1984.
Illus: *Picturesque Dublin Old and New [1898]; Familiar London [1904].*
Exhib: GG; RA; RBA; RWS from 1889.

BATEMAN, Henry Mayo 1887-1970
Comic artist in black and white and caricaturist. Born at Sutton Forest, New South Wales, Australia, 15 February 1887. Returned to England as a child and was educated at Forest Hill House School and at the Westminster and New Cross Art Schools. At a very young age, Bateman was encouraged to go ahead with his career by Phil May and was in the studio of Charles Van Havenmaet for several years before starting to draw for reproduction in 1906. Bateman's inimitable style of humour and line only developed after 1911, when, as he put it, he 'went mad on paper' and drew people how they felt rather than how they looked. His vigorous wholly visual approach was closer to the German work of *Simplicissimus* and Caran D'Ache than to anything in England. His infuriated colonels, gauche little men and haughty dames, spring out of the page with an extraordinary freshness. His art was an infusion to the stuffy pages of *Punch*, which had been laughing at social indiscretions rather than with them. Bateman was a master at giving inanimate objects palpable personality, the complete disintegration of a street in 'Love at First Sight' or the ricocheting chandeliers and twisting columns of 'The Man Who Asked for a Double Whisky in the Grand Pump Room at Bath'. Bateman revolutionised humorous art in Great Britain, making it spontaneous, hilarious and economical. Despite this his success and his failure is in stereotypes, he seldom moved away from Mr. Doolittle's 'middle-class morality' and the sequence of the *faux pas*. He contributed to almost all the leading weekly and monthly journals and designed several theatrical posters. In later life he was obsessed by Inland Revenue officials, an eccentricity in which he is not alone, and caricatured them mercilessly. Died in Gozo.
Illus: *Scraps [1903]; The Royal Magazine; The Tatler [1904]; London Opinion [1913]; Punch [1915]; The Graphic [1915]; Burlesques [1916]; After Dinner Stories [George Robey, 1920]; A Book of Drawings [1921]; Suburbia [1922]; More Drawings [1922]; Life [1923]; Adventures at Golf [1923]; Reed's The Complete Limerick Book [1924]; A Mixture [1924]; Our Modern Youth [Desmond Coke, 1924]; Colonels [1925]; Reed's Nonsense Verses [1925]; Bateman and I in Filmland [Dudley Clark, 1926]; Further Nonsense Verses and Prose [1926]; The Art of Drawing [1926]; Rebound [1927]; Brought Forward [1931]; Bateman's*

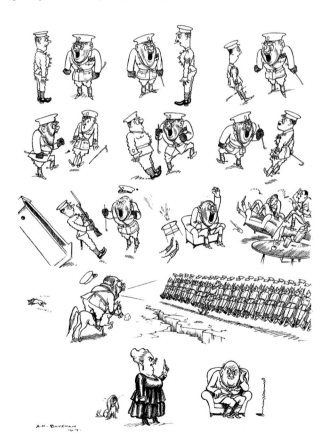

HENRY MAYO BATEMAN 1887-1970. 'The C.O. – A Man's Man', pen and ink illustration for *Punch*, signed and dated 1917
Author's Collection

JOHN D. BATTEN 1860-1932. Illustration of 'The Hunter Finds His Wife' for *The Swan Maiden*, pen and ink, c.1895

Author's Collection

Booklets [1931]; Fly-Fishing For Duffers [1934]; Considered Trifles [1934]; The Art of Caricature [1936]; H.M. Bateman By Himself [1937]; Spinning for Duffers [1939]; On The Move in England [1940]; Art Ain't All Paint [1944]; Walton's Delight [1953]; The Evening Rise [1960].
Exhib: FAS, 1962; Leicester Galleries, 1919, 1921, 1936, 1974.
Colls: Annabels; Author; Guards Club; V & AM.
Bibl: Michael Bateman, *The Man Who Drew The Twentieth Century; The drawings and Cartoons of HMB*, 1969; John Jensen, *The Man Who and Other Drawings*, HMB, Eyre Methuen, 1975.
See illustration.

BATEMAN, James   **1814-1849**
Sporting artist and illustrator. Born in London in 1814 and exhibited at the RA, BI, RBA, 1840-50. Contributed to *The Sporting Review*, 1842-46. Died at Holloway, 24 March 1849.

BATEMAN, Robert
Painter of figures. Exhibited at the RA and Grosvenor Gallery, 1866-89 and illustrated *Art in the House*, 1876.

BATES, Dewey   **1851-1899**
Landscape painter and illustrator. He was born in Philadelphia, USA, in 1851, but settled in England by 1880 and died at Rye, Sussex in 1899.
Contrib: *The English Illustrated Magazine [1887 (figs.), 1888-91 (land.)].*
Exhib: L; M; P; RA; RBA; RI; ROI.

BATES, Frederick D.
Illustrator for *The Sketch*, 1895. Worked from Grosvenor Chambers, Deansgate, Manchester, and specialised in chalk drawings of northern subjects. He signs his work F.D. Bates.
Colls: V & AM.

BATTEN, John Dixon   **1860-1932**
Painter and illustrator. Born at Plymouth, 8 October 1860. He studied at the Slade School under Alphonse Legros and began exhibiting pictures at the RA, New Gallery and Grosvenor Gallery in 1886. Batten was probably the best of that group of illustrators who took mythology as the keynote for their work and assisted such popularisers of it as Andrew Lang. His drawings derive partly from the German woodcuts that were admired by Pre-Raphaelites and partly from the arts and crafts book decoration of Morris and his followers. Batten was closely associated with the later Pre-Raphaelites and in particular with the amateur, George Howard, later Earl of Carlisle. Pennell considered that 'he has a keen appreciation of humour, and is very intelligent in his handling'. Batten took his inspiration from Celtic, Norse and even Indian legend and fairytales, his penmanship has close affinities with the Birmingham School.
Illus: *English Fairy Tales [1890]; Celtic Fairy Tales [1892]; Fairy Tales From The Arabian Nights [1893]; Indian Fairy Tales [1893]; More Celtic Fairy Tales [1894]; More English Fairy Tales [1894]; More Fairy Tales From the Arabian Nights [1895]; A Masque of Dead Florentines [1895]; The Book of Wonder Voyages [1896]; The Saga of the Sea Swallow [1896]; Dante's Inferno [1933].*
Colls: Author; V & AM.
Bibl: J. Pennell, *Pen Drawing and Pen Draughtsmen*, 1894, p.316; *Studio*, Winter No. 1900-01, p.58 illus.; R.E.D. Sketchley, *English Book Illus.*, 1903, pp.109, 110, 158; *Modern Book Illustrators and Their Work*, Studio, 1914; B. Peppin, *Fantasy Book Illus.*, 1975; *The Last Romantics*, Barbican Gallery cat., 1989, p.199., p.185 illus.
See illustration.

BATTY, Lieutenant-Colonel Robert   **FRS**   **1789-1848**
Topographer and illustrator. He was the son of a surgeon who was also a landscape painter and was educated at Caius College, Cambridge. He entered the Grenadier Guards in 1813 and served in the Peninsular War and at Waterloo, where he was wounded. He spent the remainder of his life in travel and published numerous books illustrated from his own drawings.
At the Mentmore sale in May 1977, the unprecedented price of £40,000 was paid for more than sixty original drawings for Batty's *Hanoverian and Saxon Scenery*, 1829.
Illus: *A Sketch of the Late Campaign in the Netherlands [1815]; An Historical Sketch of the Campaign of 1815 [1820]; French Scenery [1822]; Campaign of the Left Wing of the Allied Army ... [1823]; Welsh Scenery [1823]; German Scenery [1823]; Scenery of the Rhine, Belgium and Holland [1826]; Hanoverian and Saxon Scenery [1829]; Six Views of Brussels [1830]; A Family Tour Through South Holland [1831]; Select Views of the Principal Cities of Europe [1832]; The Mutiny and Piratical Seizure of H.M.S. Bounty [1876].*
Exhib: RA, 1813-48.
Colls: Gibraltar Mus.; Nat. Mus., Wales; Wolverhampton.

BAUERLE, Miss Amelia R.E.
Illustrator of children's books and decorator. Working from Willesden, 1894-1907.
Illus: *Happy-go-lucky [1894]; A Mere Pug [1897]; Allegories [1898]; Sir Constant [1899]; Glimpses from Wonderland [1900]; Tennyson's The Day Dream [1901].*
Contrib: *The English Illustrated Magazine [1895-97] The Yellow Book [1897].*
Exhib: L; RE; RI.
Bibl: R.E.D. Sketchley, *English Book Illus.*, 1903, p.14.

BAUGNIET, Charles   **1814-1886**
Painter, lithographer, engraver and illustrator. Born at Brussels, 27 February 1814, and after studying at The Brussels Academy he became a very successful portrait painter and illustrator. He settled in London for some time after 1841 and had wide popularity, publishing a portrait of the Prince Consort. He contributed to *The Illustrated London News*, 1851. Died at Sèvres, 5 July 1886.
Exhib: BI, 1847-70; RA.
Colls: BM; Brussels.

BAUMER, Lewis C.E.   **1870-1963**
Pastellist and illustrator. Born 8 August 1870, educated at University College School and studied at St. John's Wood Art School and Royal

Academy School. Baumer is chiefly remembered for his black and white work during the 1920s and 1930s and he was a prolific contributor to *Punch* and other weekly magazines. He also painted portraits and flower pieces in oils, pastel and watercolour, was a member of the Pastel Society, the Royal Institute of Painters in Watercolours and regularly exhibited with them. All Baumer's drawings are beautifully executed in pen, even if they lack contrast, and are in natural succession to Du Maurier, the humour lying in the letter-press rather than in the line; he is the classic suburban artist. Earlier Baumer drawings are often tinted and in softer line than his later work, all reveal an affinity with 18th century French drawings which he admired. He illustrated a number of children's books between the Wars.

Illus: *Jumbles [1897]; Hoodie [Mrs. Molesworth, 1897]. Elsie's Magician [1897]; The Baby Philosopher [1898]; The Story of The Treasure Seekers [E. Nesbit, 1899]; Henny and others [Mrs. Molesworth, 1898-1900].*

Contrib: *The Queen [1892]; The Pall Mall Magazine [1893]; Pall Mall Budget [1894]; The New Budget [1895]. The Unicorn [1895]; Pick-Me-Up [1895]; The English Illustrated Magazine [1896-97]; The Sketch [1896-1901]; St. James's Budget [1898]; Illustrated Bits; The Idler; The Minister; The Royal Magazine; The Graphic [1910-11]; Punch [1912].*

Exhib: FAS, 1913, 1924; Liverpool; RA; RBA, 1892-93; RI.

Colls: Author: V & AM.

Bibl: *Studio*, Vol.30, 1902, pp.233-239; R.E.D. Sketchley, *English Book Illus.*, 1903. pp.99, 159; R.G.G. Price, *A History of Punch*, 1955, pp.206-207.

BAXTER, William Giles   **1856-1888**
Caricaturist. He was born of English parents in the south of Ireland, where his father had a small business. The venture was not successful and the family moved to America but later returned to England where the father died, leaving the widow in difficult circumstances. The young Baxter was apprenticed to a Manchester architect, but at the end of his indentures decided to give it up in favour of black and white work. His first attempt was produced at the age of twenty-one, a series of lithographed pictures entitled *Buxton Sketches*. Early in 1879, he established a satirical weekly in Manchester called *Comus*, later changed to *Momus*, which featured among other things a remarkable series of life-size heads, 'Studies From Dickens'. This weekly was not long-lived and Baxter moved to London and with an artist friend concentrated on designing humorous and political Christmas cards. At this point, he met Charles H. Ross, newspaper proprietor and amateur cartoonist, who had started a journal *Ally Sloper's Half Holiday*, loosely written round an imaginary character 'Ally Sloper'. Baxter was able to take Ross's rather feeble drawings and turn them into the lovable but monstrous 'Sloper', who soon became a Victorian legend. He had added to Ross's spindly and bottle-nosed 'Sloper', the props of battered hat, enormous brolly and shaggy dog which were to go with him for a generation and make him instantly recognisable.

Baxter's penwork and detailing, the inheritance from the architectural days, were meticulous, his studies of politicians, frequently introduced, brilliant. His great importance was that he foreshadowed 20th century cartoons, sustaining his public issue after issue with, in Pennell's words, 'a mystic and symbolic meaning ... only to be comprehended by his constant followers'. Pennell adds that he was the most original caricaturist of his period and it was a sad day for British illustration when, after the first few numbers of a new publication, *Choodle*, Baxter died of consumption on 2 June 1888. He signs his work W.G. Baxter or WB (monogram).

Illus: *Comus or Momus [1879]; Ally Sloper's Half Holiday.*

Contrib: *Judy [1886]; The Graphic [1887-88]; Choodle [1888]; C.H. Ross's Variety Paper [1887-88].*

Colls: V & AM.

Bibl: *The Star*, July 1888; *The Graphic*, 4 August 1888, p.114 illus.; J. Pennell, *Modern Illus.*, 1903; J. Pennell, *Pen Drawing*, 1895; J. Thorpe, 'A Great Comic Draughtsman', *Print Colls. Quart.*, 1938.

BAYARD, Émile Antoine   **1837-1891**
Painter and draughtsman. Born at La Ferté-sous-Jouarre on 2 November 1837. He was a pupil of Cogniet and worked for most of the major French magazines including *Journal pour rire*,

L'Illustration, Journal des Voyages, Bibliothèque rose. In England he worked for *The Illustrated London News*, 1889 and *Cassell's Magazine*, 1887.

Exhib: Paris, 1853-61.

Colls: Pontoise; Rouen; Saintes; Saint-Étienne; V & AM.

BAYES, Alfred Walter   **RE RWS**   **1832-1909**
Painter and draughtsman. Bayes was a second generation Pre-Raphaelite follower and specialised in illustrating fairy stories and children's books. He was killed by a motor cab in 1909.

Illus: *What the Moon Saw [1866-67]; Original Poems [Taylor, 1868]; Old Fashioned Fairy Tales [Mrs. Ewing, c.1880].*

Contrib: *Golden Light [1864]; London Society [1865]; The Sunday Magazine [1866]; A Round of Days [1866]; Cassell's Illustrated Readings, 1867; The Boys' Own Magazine; Aunt Judy's Magazine.*

Exhib: B; BI, 1859-67; G; L; M; RA; RBA, 1861-; RE; RHA; RI, 1890-1902; ROI; RWS.

BAYLE, Gertrude E.
Artist working in Margate, contributor to *The Studio* title page competition.

Bibl: *The Studio*, Vol.8, 1896, p.253 illus.

BAYNES, Philip
Humorous illustrator, specialising in comic strips. *The Graphic*, 1910. Also contributed to *Punch*, 1914.

BEACH, Ernest George   **1865-**
Portrait and landscape painter and lithographer. He lectured on art and worked in Holland, Belgium and France.

Contrib: *The English Illustrated Magazine [1890-91, 1897 (topography)]; The Strand [1891].*

Exhib: G; L; NEA; RA; RI; ROI.

BEALE, Evelyn   **fl.1906-1925**
Illustrator of children's books, watercolourist, working in Edinburgh in 1907 and at Glasgow, 1925.

Illus: *The Apple Pie [Jack, 1908].*

Exhib: G; RSA, 1906-24.

BEARD, Dan-Carter   **1850-**
American illustrator, who succeeded C. Dana Gibson as President of the Society of Illustrators, U.S. He studied under Sartrain and Carroll Beckwith at the Art Students' League, New York, and is included here as the illustrator of English editions of Mark Twain's works, notably *A Connecticut Yankee At the Court of King Arthur*, 1889 and *Tom Sawyer Abroad*, 1894.

BEARD, Frank-Thomas or Francis   **1842-1905**
American illustrator. He was born in Cincinnatti on 6 February 1842 and became one of the most celebrated illustrators of the American Civil War and a Director of *Illustration* and a frequent contributor to *Harper's Weekly*; he is included here as an occasional artist for *The Illustrated London News*.

BEARDSLEY, Aubrey Vincent   **1872-1898**
Book illustrator, caricaturist, poster-designer and novelist. Born at Brighton on 21 August 1872 and was educated at Brighton Grammar School. A close-knit family group consisting of a weak father, a dominant mother and a much-loved sister, gave Beardsley that strange love-hate relationship with women which tinges his pictures and gives his sexual allegiances a weird character. He was ailing at school, unable to play games, but developed his own aloof arrogance as a witty and spirited caricaturist. Beardsley's circumstances allowed for no formal training and on leaving school he became a clerk to the Guardian Life Insurance Company in London. He began to admire the prints of the Italian Renaissance and among contemporaries the work of Burne-Jones (q.v.). This led to a meeting with the painter and some encouragement resulting in his attending evening classes at the Westminster School of Art. A visit to Paris in 1892 brought him into contact with the mainstream of French art and the posters of Lautrec. Later the same year, he received a windfall commission from Messrs. Dent to illustrate their new edition of Malory's *Le Morte d'Arthur*, the job that gave him independence to

work wholly as an artist. Lewis Hind, the architect of *The Studio*, was so impressed by the artist's work that he asked Pennell to write about him in the first number of it, 1894, publicity that immediately placed him in the front rank.

From 1894 to 1896, Beardsley was in his hey-day, these were the years of *The Yellow Book*, *The Rape of the Lock* and *The Lysistrata of Aristophane*s, and Wilde's *Salome*. Beardsley's identification with Wilde in the public mind was such that he was damaged by the Wilde scandal of 1895 and lost his art-editorship with *The Yellow Book*. But it was temporary, and in the following year he began on *The Savoy*, a successor publication run by Arthur Symons and was engaged on illustrations to *Mademoiselle de Maupin* and *Volpone*. From 1895, Beardsley's early diagnosed tuberculosis worsened, bringing discomfort and lassitude. After advice from London specialists, he was moved to Mentone where he died on 16 March 1898 at the age of twenty-five.

Beardsley's influence stretches a long way beyond his short life, its linear effects were to recur in architecture, textiles, in the applied arts right up to the 1920s and in a host of major and minor book illustrators' work. He received inspiration from various sources, Japanese prints, the Italian masters, the Pre-Raphaelites, 18th century books, but he remained quintessentially just Beardsley. He was the high priest of aesthetic black and white art, arriving at the moment when half-tone and photogravure were perfected, stretching them to the limit. It was part of the tension in the designs that made them at once astounding and repellant, the menacing presences of

AUBREY VINCENT BEARDSLEY 1872-1898. Frontispiece to Walt Rudding's *An Evil Motherhood*, 1896

androgynous figures, the sickly appearance of over-ripe rococo decoration and the melancholy of Harlequin, give his work its disturbing eroticism. In an interview he said, 'If I am not grotesque I am nothing', *The Idler*, Vol.11, p.198.

His various styles can be divided into three groups; an entirely linear style like that of a bas-relief with black and white contrast, a dotted effect as in *The Rape of the Lock* and the later mannerism of *Mademoiselle de Maupin,* where line and wash are used with intermediate tones. Apart from his international reputation, Beardsley united book decoration and illustration in this country and gave it credibility with serious artists of the *avant-garde*.

Illus: *Past and Present [Brighton School magazine, 1887-89]; Evelina [cov.]; Malory's Le Morte d'Arthur [1893-94]; Bons Mots [1893-94]; Pastor Sang [1893 (frontis.)]; The Wonderful History of Virgilius the Sorcerer of Rome [1893]; Keynotes series [1893-96 (frontis., cov. & tail)]; Young Ofeg's Ditties [Hansson, 1895 (tail)]; Lucian's True History [1894]; Pagan Papers [Kenneth Grahame, 1894]; Salome [Oscar Wilde, 1894]; The Barbarous Britishers [1895 (frontis. and tail)]; Plays [John Davidson, 1894 (frontis.)]; The Cambridge ABC [1894 (frontis.)]; Baron Verdegris [J. Quilp, 1894]; Today [1894]; The Works of EA Poe [1894-95]; Earl Lavender [John Davidson, 1895]; Sappho [1895]; The Thread and the Path [1895 (frontis.)]; A London Garland [1896]; The Rape of the Lock [1896]; The Life and Times of Madame Du Barry [1896]; Verses [Ernest Dowson, 1896]; A Book of Bargains [Vincent O'Sullivan, 1896]; The Parade [1897]; The Pierrot of the Minute [1897]; Scenes of Parisian Life [1897]; The Souvenirs of Leonard [1897]; Mademoiselle de Maupin [1898]; A History of Dancing [1898]; Volpone [Ben Johnson, 1898 (illus., cov. & frontis.)]; The London Yearbook [1898].*

AUBREY VINCENT BEARDSLEY 1872-1898. 'L'Education Sentimentale'. Illustration to *The Yellow Book*, Vol.1, April 1894, p.55

Contrib: *Pall Mall Budget [1893]; The Studio [1893-95]; Pall Mall Magazine [1893]; the Idler [1894].*
Posthumous books: *The Early work of Aubrey Beardsley [1899]; The Second Book of Fifty Drawings by Aubrey Beardsley [1899]; The Later Work of Aubrey Beardsley [1901]; Five Drawings Illustrative of Lucian and Juvenal [1906]; A Portfolio of Aubrey Beardsley's Drawings [1907]; The Uncollected Work of Aubrey Beardsley [1925].*
Colls: Ashmolean; Barber Institute, Birmingham; Brighton, BM; Cecil Higgins Art Gallery, Bedford; Fitzwilliam, NPG; Reading Lib.; Sheffield; Tate; V & AM.
Bibl: *The Studio,* Vol.1, No. 1, 1893; Vol.13, 1898, pp.252-263; Robert Ross, *AB*, 1909; A.E. Gallantin, *AB Catalogue of Drawings and Bibliography*, 1945; Brian Reade, *B*, Studio Vista, 1967; B. Reade and F. Dickinson, *AB, Exhibition at the V & AM*, 1966; *The Last Romantics*, Barbican Gallery catalogue, 1989, p.98; Malcolm Easton, *Aubrey and the Dying Lady*, A Beardsley Riddle, 1972.
See illustrations.

BEATRICE, H.R.H. The Princess   1857-1944
Youngest child of Queen Victoria, born 14 April 1857, and married 1885 H.R.H. Prince Henry of Battenberg. She was an amateur artist and produced *A Birthday Book Designed by Her Royal Highness The Princess Beatrice*, London, 1881. This has borders of flowers, insects and berries in colour lithography from her designs. She died 26 October 1944.

BEAUCÉ, Jean-Adophe   1818-1875
Military painter. He was born at Paris on 2 August 1818 and went on many military expeditions to Algeria, Syria and Mexico and was present at the siege of Metz. He contributed to *The Illustrated London News*, 1859-60 and 1862, including sketches of Garibaldi. Died at Boulogne, 13 July 1875.

BEAUMONT, J. Herbert
Amateur bookplate designer, working at Hessle, East Yorkshire.
Bibl: *The Studio*, Vol. 10, 1897, p.274, illus.

BECK, T.
Illustrator, contributing to *Good Words for the Young*, 1872.

BECKEN, A.L.
Contributor to *The Ladies Pictorial*, 1895.

BEDE
Pseudonym of caricaturist contributing two cartoons to *Vanity Fair*, 1905-06.
Bibl: Roy T. Matthews and Peter Mellini, *In Vanity Fair*, 1982.

BEDE, Cuthbert (The Rev. Edward Bradley)   1827-1889
Author and illustrator. Born at Kidderminster in 1827 and was educated at University College, Durham, 1848, taking a licenciate in theology, 1849, ordained 1850. He held various Midland curacies before becoming Vicar of Denton, Peterborough, from 1859-71. He was subsequently in the livings of Stretton, Oakham, 1871-83 and Lenton with Harby, 1883-89. He learnt wood engraving from George Cruikshank (q.v.) but remained very much the amateur, illustrating his own books, *Mr. Verdant Green* and others in a jolly and careless style. He was one of the first humorous illustrators to satirise photography. He died at Lavington in 1889.
Illus: *The Adventures of Mr. Verdant Green, an Oxford Freshman [1853-56]; Little Mr. Bouncer [c.1877 (child's book)].*
Contrib: *Bentley's Miscellany [1846]; Punch [1847-56]; ILN [1851 and 1856]; The Month [1852]; The Illustrated London Magazine [1855]; Churchman's Family Magazine [1863].*
Colls: BM.
Bibl: M.H. Spielmann, *The History of Punch*, 1895, pp.191-195.

BEDFORD, Francis Donkin   1864-1954
Illustrator. He was born in London in 1864 and trained as an architect at South Kensington and the RA Schools. He was articled to the church architect, Sir Arthur Blomfield RA, but turned his attention to illustration in the 1880s and gained a wide popularity in the realm of children's books and as a landscape illustrator. He practised in the Kensington area until 1914 and was working at Wimbledon in 1925.

AUBREY VINCENT BEARDSLEY. 'The Fourth Tableau of Das Rheingold'

Illus: *Old Country Life [1890]; The Deserts of Southern France [1894]; The Battle of the Frogs and Mice [1894]; Old English Fairy Tales [1895]; A Book of Nursery Rhymes [1897]; The Vicar of Wakefeld [1898]; Henry Esmond [1898]; A Book of Verses For Children [E.V. Lucas, 1898]; The Book of Shops [E.V. Lucas, 1899]; Four and Twenty Tailors [E.V. Lucas, 1900]; The Original Poems of Taylor and O'Keefe [1903]; Two are Company [Louise Field, 1905]; Old Fashioned Tales [E.V. Lucas, 1905]; A Night of Wonder [1906]; Forgotten Tales of Long Ago [E.V. Lucas, 1906]; Runaways and Castaways [E.V. Lucas, 1908]; Maggie, A Day Dream [Lady Algernon Percy, 1908]; Anne's Terrible Good Nature [E.V. Lucas, 1908 (cover)]; Peter Pan and Wendy [J.M. Barrie, 1911]; The Magic Fishbone [C. Dickens, 1921]; Billie Barnicole [G. Macdonald, 1923]; At the Back of the North Wind [G. Macdonald, 1924]; The Princess and the Goblin [G. Macdonald, 1926]; A Cricket on the Hearth [C. Dickens, 1927]; Count Billy [G. Macdonald, 1928]; A Christmas Carol [C. Dickens, 1931].*
Contrib: *Examples of Ornament [Bell & Daldy, 1853 (decorations)].*
Exhib: RA, 1892.
Bibl: R.E.D. Sketchley, *English Book Illus.*, 1903, p.106, 159; B. Peppin, *Fantasy Book Illustration*, 1975, p.185, illus.

BEDWELL, Frederick LeB.
Assistant Pay-Master on H.M.S. *Actaeon*, coast of China survey, 1862. Accompanied H.M.S. *Nassau* on Admiralty Survey of South America, 1869, contributed sketches to *The Illustrated London News*.

BEECH, Thomas
Contributing to *Cassell's Illustrated Family Paper*, 1857 (portraits); Belgravia, 1868 (figs.).

BEECHEY, Henry W.   FSA   1870-
Painter and explorer. He was the brother of Sir William Beechey and

SIR MAX BEERBOHM 1872-1956. 'Sir Henry Irving'. Signed. Ink and wash
The Garrick Club

BEERBOHM, Sir Max   1872-1956

Caricaturist, novelist and broadcaster. Born in London on 24 August 1872, the youngest son of Julius E. Beerbohm and younger brother of Sir Beerbohm Tree, the actor. Educated at Charterhouse and Merton College, Oxford, the young Max was already cutting a figure in his undergraduate days as a wit, caricaturist and man-about-town. He referred to Oxford as 'the little city of learning and laughter' and this admirably sums up his attitude to life and to his art; he remained the perpetual impish undergraduate, cocking a snook at society and the philistines but never with very heavy artillery. From the circle of Oxford aesthetes, Max graduated to that of the Café Royal and Will Rothenstein, Oscar Wilde and Lord Alfred Douglas. But he remained on the edge of these groups like a good caricaturist, portraying his friends with an elfin touch and setting a seal on the 1890s as much as Beardsley (q.v.) or May (q.v.). Max was a great admirer of the cartoons of Carlo Pellegrini (q.v.), for *Vanity Fair* and his own drawings are extensions of the type known as *portraits chargés*. He introduced his figures into situations, real or imagined, which gave an extra dimension to the cartoons as well as making them more literary than their prototypes. Max's range was wide but among his favourite targets were Edward, Prince of Wales, Rudyard Kipling, H.G. Wells, Edmund Gosse and the Rothschilds. They were usually drawn with pen, ink and wash, sometimes with a little colour added and always with a fastidious eye for detail. Max's talent was a small and brilliant one which he used with great care and the same miniature scale and perfection is found in his books, a stream of which appeared between 1896 and 1946. From 1910, the year in which he married, Max lived the life of an exile in Italy, his subjects and sources of inspiration remaining totally Edwardian to the end of his days. He died on 19 May 1956 at Rapallo.

Publ: *The Works of Max Beerbohm [1896]; Caricatures of Twenty-Five Gentlemen [1896]; More [1899]; Second Childhood of John*

SAMUEL BEGG fl.1886-1916. The Gordon Highlanders embarking for South Africa, published in *The Illustrated London News*, 1899. Grey wash heightened with white
Victoria and Albert Museum

became Consul-General at Cairo, 1816. He explored the Nile with his brother, G.D. Beechey, and surveyed the coastline from Tripoli to Derna, 1821-22. He was elected FSA in 1825 and is believed to have died in New Zealand.
Illus: *Expedition to Explore The Northern Coast of Africa [1828, AT 305].*
Exhib: Sea pieces at RA and BI, 1829-38.

BEER, John-Axel-Richard   1853-1906

Illustrator. He was born at Stockholm on 18 January 1853, but went to America as a young man in 1869 and stayed there for five years. He travelled to Russia and worked as an artist at the Imperial Court, eventually settling in London where he worked for the principal magazines. Beer was an excellent figure artist, at his best in free pen and wash sketches with effective atmospheric backgrounds.
Contrib: *Journal Illustré de Leipzig; The Graphic [1886 (horses)]; Black and White [1891]; The Sporting and Dramatic News [1894]; ILN [1900].*
Colls: V & AM.

Bull [1901], Poets' Corner [1904]; Book of Caricatures [1907]; Yet Again [1909]; Zuleika Dobson [1910]; A Christmas Garland [1912]; Fifty Caricatures [1913]; Seven Men [1919]; And Even Now [1921]; A Survey [1921]; Rossetti and His Circle [1922]; Things New and Old [1923]; Observations [1925]; The Dreadful Dragon of Hay Hill [Lytton Strachey]; Mainly on the Air [1946].
Contrib: *Pick-Me-Up [1894]; The Yellow Book [1894-96]; The Unicorn [1895]; The Savoy [1896], Vanity Fair [1896 and 1905-06]; Eureka [1897]; The Parade [1897]; The Page [1899]; The Butterfly; The Idler; The Sketch; The Strand; The Pall Mall Budget; John Bull [1903].*
Exhib: Leicester Galleries, 1925.
Colls: Ashmolean; Garrick Club; V & AM.
Bibl: S.N. Behrman, *Portrait of Max*, 1960; David Cecil, *Max a Biography*, 1964; R. Hart Davis, *Catalogue of the Works of MB*, 1972; R. Hart Davis, *The Letters of MB 1892-1956*, 1988.
See illustration.

BEEVER, W.A.
Topographer. He contributed to *Public Works of Great Britain*, 1838, AL 410.

BEGG, Samuel   **fl.1886-1916**
Illustrator and sculptor working in Bedford Park. A prolific contributor to *The Illustrated London News* in the late Victorian and Edwardian periods. Begg seems to have preferred military subjects but also drew sport and the theatre. In many ways he represents the worst features of later illustration, technical perfection in representing almost photographic scenes with heavy use of body-colour but no imagination.
Contrib: *ILN [1887-1916]; Black and White [1892]; Cassell's Family Magazine [1895-96]; The Sporting and Dramatic News [1896].*
Exhib: RA, 1886-91, sculpture.
Colls: V & AM.
See illustration.

BEHNES, William   **1794-1864**
Sculptor, He was born in London in 1794 and studied in Dublin and at the RA Schools, He exhibited portraits at the RA from 1815-18 but then abandoned painting for sculpture, being commissioned to do many political and royal celebrities, In 1837 he became Sculptor in Ordinary to The Queen but this brought him little new work and he died in abject poverty in 1864, The Victoria and Albert Museum has a pencil drawing of *The Seven Ages of Man*, prepared for *The Saturday Magazine*, December 1832.
Bibl: R. Gunnis, *Dict. of British Sculptors, 1660-1851*, pp.45-48,

BELCHER, George Frederick Arthur RA   **1875-1947**
Black and white artist, Born in 1875, Belcher was educated at the Edward VI School, Berkhamsted, and at Gloucester School of Art, His *forté* was in charcoal drawing which he made very much his own in the *Punch* of the inter-war years, He was described by Kenneth Bird as 'Phil May in chalk' and R.G.G. Price says that he was 'A Regency buck in manner and a close observer of the appearance of low life by vocation'. Belcher's low life was different from May's in that it was more rural and less barbed, his favourite characters were the charladies, gossips and workmen whose speech he mimicked so perfectly in his humorous touching figures. An early writer on Belcher in *The Studio* calls his humour 'intrinsic' adding that he had found charcoal the most sympathetic and responsive medium for rendering the subtleties of his models. His backgrounds are carefully observed but wholly atmospheric and a decided break with traditional *Punch* methods. His ability was recognised when he became an ARA in 1931 and an RA in 1945, a highly unusual distinction for an illustrator, He died in 1947.
Illus: *Portfolio of London Types and Characters [1922]; Members and Boxers of the National Sporting Club; Odd Fish [1923]; Potted Char; Taken From Life by George Belcher.*
Contrib: *Punch; The Tatler; The Graphic.*
Exhib: FAS, 1924; Leicester Gall.; RA from 1924.
Bibl: *The Studio*, Vol. 52, 1911, pp.84-94 illus.; R.G.G. Price, *A History of Punch*, 1957, p.214.
See illustration.

GEORGE BELCHER 1875-1947. Illustration for *The Tatler* c.1920, charcoal heightened with white. "Shall I open the other egg sir?" "Certainly not, open the window!"   Victoria and Albert Museum

BELL, J.   **fl.1874-1891**
Special artist for *The Illustrated London News*, Russo-Turkish War and Constantinople, 1874-78, and Mombassa, 1890. He illustrated George Macdonald's *Phantastes*, Chatto, 1894.

BELL, Lilian Russell   **fl.1899-1933**
Painter and illustrator at Wallesey, Cheshire and in London from 1910. She illustrated with Alice B. Woodward (q.v.), *The Golden Ship and Other Tales Translated from the Swahili*, for the Universities Mission, 1900.
Exhib: L.

BELL, Robert Anning   RA   **1863-1933**
Sculptor, illustrator, designer of mosaics and stained glass artist. Born in London and educated at University College School and then at Westminster School of Art under Fred Brown and at the RA Schools. He later studied under Aimé Morot and visited Italy where he took part in exhibitions. Bell was associated with the Arts and Crafts Society and was Master of the Art Workers' Guild. He taught at Glasgow 1914 and was Professor of Design at the RCA, 1918-24. Outside his numerous illustrations, Bell's best work is probably his mosaic in the Houses of Parliament and his tympanum over the west door of Westminster Cathedral.

Bell's early work as an illustrator lies heavily on the Crane style, rather long and angular figures without shading contained in decorative borders. All his work is reminiscent of the woodcut and its two-dimensional quality perhaps results from the large amount of work undertaken in stained glass. He was elected ARA in 1914 and RA in 1922. Died 27 November 1933.
Illus: *Jack the Giant Killer, The Sleeping Beauty, Cinderella, Beauty and the Beast [1894]; After Sunset [G.R. Thomson, 1894 (title and cov.)]; White Poppies [M. Kendall, 1894]; A Midsummer Night's*

ROBERT ANNING BELL RA 1863-1933. 'Ophelia', illustration probably for *Lamb's Tales from Shakespeare*, 1899, pen and watercolour   Victoria and Albert Museum

Dream [1895]; The Riddle [1895]; Verspertilia [R.M. Watson, 1896]; An Altar Book [B. Updike, Boston, 1897]; Poems by John Keats [1897]; English Lyrics from Spenser to Milton [1898]; The Pilgrim's Progress [1898]; The Milan [1898]; The Christian Year [1898]; Lamb's Tales From Shakespeare [1899]; The Tempest [1901]; The Odes of John Keats [1901]; Grimm's Household Tales [1901]; Isabella and St. Agnes Eve [1902]; Poems by Shelley [1902]; Rubaiyat of Omar Khayyam [1902]; Shakespeare's Heroines [A.B. Jameson 1905]; Palgrave's Golden Treasury [1907]; English Fairy Tales [E. Rhys, 1913].
Contrib: *English Illustrated Magazine [1891-94]; The Yellow Book [1894-95]; Pall Mall Magazine.*
Exhib: B; FAS, 1907, 1934; G; L; NEA from 1888; RA from 1885; RHA; RSA; RWA; RWS.
Colls: V & AM.
Bibl: *Studio*, Winter No. 1900-01, p.21, illus.; *Modern Book Illustrators and Their Work*, Studio, 1914; R.E.D. Sketchley, *English Book Illus.* 1903, pp.7, 121; *Who Was Who 1929-40*; *The Last Romantics*, Barbican Gallery catalogue, 1989, pp.154-155.
See illustration.

BELLEW, Frank Henry Temple   **1828-1888**
Humorous illustrator specialising in outline drawings. Born at Cawnpore in 1828. He emigrated to the United States and from there contributed comic genre subjects to *Punch*, 1857-62. He also illustrated more serious subjects of American character and the Civil War for *The Illustrated Times*, 1861. One of the first people to write authoritatively on John Leech. He died at New York in 1888, his son became 'Chip', cartoonist of *New York Life*.
Contrib: *The Compliments of the Season [Piers Shafton, 1849 (one illus.)].*
Bibl: Simon Houfe, *Leech,* 1984.

BENDIXEN, Siegfried Detler   **1786-1864**
Painter. engraver and lithographer. He was born at Kiel on 25 November 1786 and studied under the Italian artist J.A. Pallivia at Enkendorf. He then travelled to Italy in 1808, to Dresden in 1810 and to Munich and Paris in 1811. Returning to Hamburg in 1813, he opened an art school there in 1815, finally settling in London in 1832. Bendixen produced *Preceptive Illustrations of the Bible*, in about 1840, a child's book of rather 'wooden' colour lithographs.
Exhib: BI; NWS, 1833-64; RA; RBA.

BENHAM, Jane E. (Mrs. Hay)   **fl.1850-1862**
Painter and illustrator. She was a close friend of the artist daughter of William and Mary Howitt and of Miss Jessie Meriton White, a Garibaldi supporter. She studied for some years with the latter under Kaulbach at Munich, and then travelled in Italy. Vizetelly, who says that she married and lived in Paris, describes her as 'a grave and enthusiastic young lady'. There is little doubt that she was an interesting one, her few illustrations, notably those for *Longfellow's Evangeline*, 1850, show German influence, but also a familiarity with Blake, unusual for the date.
Illus: *Evangeline, A Tale of Arcadie by Longfellow [1850 (with Birket Foster and John Gilbert)]; Longfellow's Golden Legend [1854]; Beattie and Collins' Poems [1854].* (Vizetelly records a further illustrated edition of Longfellow.)
Exhib: RA, 1848-49; other exhibitions 1859-62.
See illustration.

BENNETT, Charles Henry   **1829-1867**
Illustrator and caricaturist. Apparently untrained but was already contributing to the illustrated press by 1855 with cuts in *Diogenes* and *The Comic Times*. He worked for *Comic News* between 1863 and 1865 and achieved wide popularity with his 'Shadows' and 'Studies in Darwinesque Development' for Vizetelly's *Illustrated Times*. He joined *Punch* in 1865 but only contributed for two years before his death. He was sponsored by Charles Kingsley in producing illustrations for Bunyan and commanded the respect of a wide group of literary men. But his caricature portraits with big heads and tiny bodies were in the style of an earlier humour. White criticised his Bunyan figures for over characterization.

Bennett was a poor businessman and left his family in distress. *Punch* staged a benefit night at Manchester for them in 1867 under the superintendence of Sir Arthur Sullivan. His earliest work is signed with an owl and later an owl with a 'B' in its beak for a phonetic pun on Bennett.
Illus: *The Fables of Aesop [1857]; Proverbs with Pictures [1858-59]; Pilgrim's Progress [1859]; Fairy Tales of Science [1959]; Quarles Emblems [1860]; Nine Lives of a Cat [1860]; Stories little Breeches Told [1862]; London People [c.1864]; Mr. Wind and Madam Rain [c.1864]; Lemon's Fairy Tales; The Sorrowful Ending of Noodledo [1865].*
Contrib: *ILN [1857 & 1866]; The Illustrated Times [1856]; The Cornhill Magazine [1861]; The Welcome Guest [1860]; Good Words [1861]; London Society [1862-65]; Every Boys Magazine [1864-65]; Beeton's Annuals [1866]; Poets Wit and Humour [n.d.].*
Bibl: Gleeson White, *English Illus.* 1895; M.H. Spielmann, *The History of Punch,* 1895; Chatto & Jackson, *Treatise on Wood Engraving,* 1861.

BENNETT, Fred
Contributor of vigorous and well drawn illustrations to *Chums*, first quarter of the twentieth century.

BENNETT, Harriet M.   **fl.1882-1892**
Watercolour painter, working at Forest Hill, London. She specialised in eighteenth century figure subjects and contributed to *A Book of Poems and Pastorals*, c.1885.
Exhib: Dudley Gall.; RA; RI.

JANE E. BENHAM, MRS HAY fl.1850-1862. Cover illustration for H.W. Longfellow's *Evangeline – A Tale of Arcadie*, 1850

BENNITT, Colonel Ward
Amateur illustrator; officer in the 6th Inniskilling Dragoons who contributed social cartoons and initial letters to *Punch*, 1875.

BENSON
Working at Plymouth and contributing to *The Illustrated London News*, 1844.

BENSON, Miss Mary K.   fl. 1879-1907
Artist and decorator of books. Working in Hertford, 1879-90, at Dublin, 1890-1902 and in Bath in 1907. She drew a headpiece for *The Quarto*, 1896, and exhibited at the RA, RBA and RHA. She was the sister of Charlotte E. Benson, the artist, 1846-1893.

BENSON, Robert
Traveller and topographer. Published *Sketches of Corsica*, 1825, AT 76.

BENWELL, Joseph Austin
Painter, watercolourist and illustrator working in Kensington. He specialised in Eastern subjects but sometimes illustrated modern genre subjects with less assurance. He travelled to India and China prior to 1856 and to Egypt and Palestine, 1865-66. Mrs. Benwell was also an artist.
Illus: *Our Indian Army [by Capper].*
Contrib: *The Welcome Guest [1860]; The Cornhill Magazine [1860]; ILN [1863-64].*
Exhib: NW, 1865-86; RA; RBA.

BÉRARD, Evremond de   fl.1852-1863
French landscape painter, born at Guadeloupe and exhibited at the Salon in 1852. He contributed illustrations of Madagascar to *The Illustrated London News*, 1863.

BERESFORD, Captain G.D.
Illustrated *Scenes in Southern Albania*, 1855, AT 46.

BERKELEY, Stanley   fl.1878-1907
Painter and illustrator of animals. Berkeley was a regular contributor to magazines in the 1880s and 1890s, either in fancy pictures or for serials. His work shows a heavy use of bodycolour but, though sentimental in character, is seldom ill drawn. He worked at Esher, 1890-1902, and at Surbiton to 1907; his wife Edith Berkeley was also an artist.
Contrib: *ILN [1882-96]; The Graphic [1886]; Black and White [1891]; The Sporting and Dramatic News [1896]; The Sketch [1896]; The Boys Own Paper; Chums.*
Exhib: B, 1889; L, 1889; NWS; RA, 1878-92; RBA.
Colls: V & AM.

BEWICK, Robert Elliot   1788-1849
Engraver and illustrator. Born at Newcastle in 1788, the only son of Thomas Bewick (q.v.), the reviver of English wood engraving. He went into partnership with his father in 1812 and assisted him with the illustrations for *Aesop's Fables*, 1818, and on the uncompleted *History of British Fishes*. Sketches by him for the latter book, as well as some illustrations for *British Birds*, 1826, are in the BM. He died at Newcastle.

BEWICK, Thomas   1753-1828
Called the 'restorer of wood engraving in England'. Born at Cherryburn House, Ovingham, Northumberland, 10 August 1753 and was apprenticed to Ralph Beilby, the Newcastle-upon-Tyne copper plate engraver. The young Bewick found his work with Beilby unrewarding because it gave him little opportunity to develop as an artist, but he did find that wood engraving was more expressive. After working in London in 1776, he returned to Newcastle and in partnership with Beilby assembled material for a *History of Quadrupeds*, 1790, entirely illustrated by wood engravings. This was followed by a celebrated print of 'The Chillingham Bull' and his most famous work, *British Birds*, 1797 and 1804. Bewick died at 19 West Street, Gateshead, on 8 November 1828 and was buried at Ovingham.

Bewick's career runs parallel to the rise of the romantic school in painting and poetry. He was the first person to translate wood engraving from the crudities of the broadsheets to a fine art and the first person to recognise that naturalism was the vehicle rather than the enemy of book illustration. His first edition of *Quadrupeds* contained tailpieces borrowed from continental sources, but later editions and subsequent books had vignettes which in originality and observation are among his masterpieces. His miniature landscapes, his foliage, houses and animals are drawn with accuracy and his country folk with a humour and gentle truth. Chatto and Jackson,

THOMAS BEWICK 1753-1828. Vignette wood engraving from *A History of British Birds*, 1816

THE COMMON BUZZARD,

OR PUTTOCK.

THOMAS BEWICK 1753-1828. The Common Buzzard or Puttock, wood engraving from *A History of British Birds*, 1816

THE DOMESTIC COCK.

THOMAS BEWICK 1753-1828. The Domestic Cock, wood engraving from *A History of British Birds*, 1816

THOMAS BEWICK 1753-1828. Tailpiece wood engraving from *A History of British Birds*, 1816

who were writing in 1838, only a decade after his death, express this well: 'Bewick was truly a *countryman...* for though no person was capable of closer application to his art within doors, he loved to spend his hours of relaxation in the open air, studying the character of beasts and birds in their natural state; and diligently noting those little incidents and traits of country life which give so great an interest to many of his tailpieces.' *Treatise on Wood Engraving*, p.479. Bewick was a believer in a clean line and did not like cross-

hatching, he liked to cut on the block from dark to light which was an innovation from old practice. His influence established Newcastle as the centre of wood engraving and he had a number of pupils; these include, John Bewick, Robert Johnson, Charlton Nesbit, Luke Clennel, and William Harvey (qq.v.).
Illus: *History of Quadrupeds [1790]; History of Birds [1797 and 1804]; Select Fables [1784]; Gay's Fables [1779]; Aesop's Fables [1818]; A Tour Through Sweden.*
Exhib: FAS, 1880.
Colls: BM (large collection); Newcastle; V & AM; Northumberland Nat. Hist. Soc.
Bibl: F.G. Stephens, *TB Notes on a Collection of Drawings and Woodcuts*, 1881; D.C. Thomson, *The Life and Works of TB*, 1882; D.C. Thomson, *The Watercolour Drawings of TB*, 1930.
See illustrations.

BEWLEY, Miss
Landscape illustrator for *Good Words*, 1880.

BIDDARD, C.
Contributor of social subjects to *Punch*, 1902.

BIDDULPH, Major-General Sir Michael Anthony Shrapnel GCB 1823-1904
Soldier and artist. Born at Cleeve Court, Somerset, 1823. Major, 1854, and Colonel, 1874. Served throughout the Crimean War and was at the Siege of Sebastopol. Groom in Waiting to H.M. Queen Victoria and Keeper of the Regalia. Died 23 July 1904.
Illus: *Norway [Forester, 1849].*
Contrib: *ILN, [1880].*
Exhib: RA, 1889-90.

BILLINGS, Robert William   1815-1874
Landscape painter and architectural illustrator. Born in London in 1815. Worked at Bath, 1834-37. Died at Putney, 4 November 1874. H.M. Colvin suggests that he was a member of the Billings family, who were builders in Reading.
Illus: *Britton's Cathedrals [1832-36 (vignettes)]; Architectural*

Illustrations... of Carlisle Cathedral [1840]; Architectural Illustrations... of Durham Cathedral [1843]; Architectural Illustrations... of Kettering Church [1843]; Baronial Antiquities of Scotland [1848-52].
Exhib: RA, 1845-72.
Colls: Bath AG.

BILLINGHURST, Percy J.   **fl.1899-1900**
Illustrator, designer of bookplates. RA Schools, 1897. There is no biographical information about this talented animal draughtsman who did clever pen drawings in elaborate frames for children's books around 1900.
Illus: *A Hundred Fables of Aesop [1899]; A Hundred Fables of La Fontaine [1900]; A Hundred Anecdotes of Animals [Lane, 1901].*
Bibl: 'P.J. Billinghurst Designer and Illustrator', *The Studio*, Vol.14, 1898, pp.181-186, illus; *The Studio*, Winter No. 1900-01, p.49, illus.; R.E.D. Sketchley, *English Book Illus.*, 1903, pp.117, 160.

BILSBIE, Charles
Contributor of cockney figures to *Punch*, 1906. His style is broadly based on that of Phil May (q.v.).

BINGHAM, The Hon. Albert Yelverton   **1840-1907**
Landscape painter. He was born on 11 February 1840, the third son of Denis, 3rd Baron Clanmorris and was D.L. for County Mayo. He died on 31 March 1907.
Illus: *The Voyage of The Sunbeam [Lady Brassey, 1891].*
Exhib: RA, 1878.

BINT
Contributed one cartoon to *Vanity Fair*, 1893.
Bibl: Roy T. Matthews and Peter Mellini, *In Vanity Fair*, 1982.

BIRCH, Charles Bell   **ARA**   **1832-1893**
Sculptor and illustrator. Born in London September 1832 and studied at the RA Schools and in Berlin with Rauch, later becoming assistant to J.H. Foley, RA. His only illustrated work is *Lara, a Tale of Lord Byron*, Art Union of London Album, 1879. This is very hard and teutonic and quite out-moded for its date. Some further unidentified illustrations are at the Victoria and Albert Museum. ARA 1880.
Contrib: *Cassell's Illustrated Family Readings*, 1897.

BIRCH, Reginald
Illustrator of *Little Lord Fauntleroy* by Frances Hodgson Burnett, 1886, and *The One I Knew Best of All*, by the same author. 1894.

BIRD, John Alexander H.   **1846-**
Painter of animals and illustrator. He specialised in horse subjects and exhibited at the RA, RI and Canadian Academy. He contributed to *Dark Blue*, 1871-73.

BIRD, W.
Pseudonym in *Punch* of Jack B. Yeats (q.v.).

BIRKENRUTH, Adolph   **1861-1940**
Illustrator. Born at Grahamstown, South Africa, 28 November 1861. He was educated at University College School, at Frankfurt and studied art in Paris. He settled in London by 1883 and from 1890 was a prolific contributor to the magazines, illustrating work by 'Q' and Walter Besant. Birkenruth handled plain chalk with greater mastery than he handled his washes and was more at home in social realism than in anecdotal subjects. He died on 15 September 1940. Signs with monogram AB.
Illus: *The Rebel Queen [Walter Besant, 1894].*
Contrib: *Black & White [1892]; ILN [1892-99]; The Pall Mall Budget [1893]; The Butterfly [1893]; English Illustrated Magazine [1893-96]; The Sphere [1894]; Pick-Me-Up [1894]; The New Budget [1895]; The English Illustrated Magazine [1895]; The Idler.*
Exhib: Grafton Gall; L; RA from 1883; RBA; RI; ROI; RWS.
Colls: V & AM.
See illustration.

BLACKBURN, Mrs. J. (née Wedderburn)   **1823-1909**
An important animal and bird illustrator. The daughter of an influential

ADOLPH BIRKENRUTH 1861-1940. 'A Hopper's Wife', black chalk and wash drawing for a story in *The English Illustrated Magazine*, March 1895   Victoria and Albert Museum

Scottish family, she showed an early ability for drawing animals and birds. She was influenced by the naturalism of Bewick's woodcuts and on a visit to London in 1840 became acquainted with Mulready and Landseer, the latter telling her that he had nothing to teach her about drawing. She married Professor Hugh Blackburn, Professor of Mathematics in the University of Glasgow and continued to paint and illustrate until the 1890s. She died at Edinburgh in 1909.

Mrs. Blackburn was strongly influenced by the Pre-Raphaelites and admired by both Millais and Ruskin. In a letter of 1861, George Du Maurier wrote '...look at Mrs. Blackburn, who has monopolised the large page of Good Words, and is decidedly well paid for it too and courted much more for her talent than she ever could be for the title she possesses in common with some 2 or 500 other ladies'. *The Young George Du Maurier*, p.84.
Publ: *Scenes from Animal Life and Character [1858]; Birds Drawn from Nature [1862]; A Few Words About Drawing For Beginners [1893]; Birds from Moidart [1895].*
Illus: *The Instructive Picture Book [A. White, 1859]; Songs and Fables [W.J.M. Rankins, 1874]; Illustrations of Scripture by an animal painter, with notes by a naturalist [James Wilson, Edinburgh, 1855].*
Contrib: *Good Words [1861].*
Exhib: RA from 1863.
Colls: BM.
Bibl: Ray, G.N., *The Letters and Private Papers of W.M. Thackeray*, 1946, Vol.3, p.422.

BLACKWOOD, Lady Alicia
Lithographer and amateur illustrator. She published *Scutari, Bosphorus, Crimea*, 1857, at Bristol, AT 242, and exhibited landscapes at the RA from Box Wood, 1878-80.

WILLIAM BLAKE 1757-1827. 'The Whirlwind of Lovers' from *Dante's Inferno*, Canto V, 1824-27. Line engraving.   Author's Collection

BLAIKIE, F.
Contributor of silhouette cartoons to *Punch*, 1904.

BLAIKLEY, Alexander   **1816-1903**
Portrait painter. Born in Glasgow in 1816 and exhibited at the BI, RA
and RBA, 1842-67. He was a contributor to *The Illustrated London
News*, 1856.

BLAIKLEY, Ernest   **1885-**
Painter and etcher. He was born in London on 11 April 1885 and was
educated at University College School, London, before studying art
at the Slade School. He became Keeper of Pictures at the Imperial
War Museum, 1919.
Illus: *The Artist's London [n.d.].*
Contrib: *Punch [1906].*
Exhib: RA; RBA; RI; RSA.

BLAKE, William   **1757-1827**
Engraver, poet, painter and mystic. Born in London at 28 Broad
Street, Golden Square, on 28 November 1757, the son of a hosier. He
joined William Pars's Drawing School at the age of ten and was
writing poetry at fourteen. He was apprenticed to the engraver James
Basire and made drawings of London churches for engraving,
entering the RA Schools as an engraving student in 1779, and
exhibiting there from 1780. From that date onwards he was engaged
in commercial engraving to supplement his meagre income. This
included plates after other artists in numerous publications like *The
Wits' Magazine*, 1784; *Harrison's Novelists Magazine,
Wollstonecraft's Works*, 1791 and various work by the minor author,
William Hayley, 1800-09. He illustrated Lavater's *Essays on
Physiognomy*. 1789; Young's *Night Thoughts*, 1793-1800; *Leonora*,
1796; *Hayley's Ballads*, 1805; Malkin's *A Father's Memories of His*

Child, 1806; *Thornton's Virgil*, 1821, and wood engravings for
Phillips *Pastorals*, 1820-21.
   Blake's most powerful and individual contribution to illustration
was in his *Prophetic Books*. Blake used his own printing method of
relief etching for these, though some are intaglio etched, and then he
or Mrs. Blake coloured the figures in imitation of drawings. As
Bland says, 'Blake's calligraphy embraces the whole page borders,
figures, and words without distinction. The verse flows into the
borders and the figures encroach on the verse. In this Blake goes
back to the very earliest manuscripts of the Middle Ages before there
was a division between scribe and illuminator and before the attempt
was made to add a third dimension to the page'. The dating and
printing of these mystic books, text and design, is very complex and
can best be understood by reference to *A Bibliography of William
Blake* by Sir Geoffrey Keynes, 1921, and the subsequent Blake
studies by this author. They are as follows – *Songs of Innocence*,
1789; *Visions of the Daughters of Albion*, 1793-95; *The Gates of
Paradise*, 1793; *The Argument*, 1793; *The Book of Thel*, 1789-94:
Songs of Experience, 1794; *The Book of Urizen*, 1794; *Europe: A
Prophecy*, 1794; *America: A Prophecy*, 1793; *Milton*, 1804;
Jerusalem, 1804-18; *The Marriage of Heaven and Hell*, 1815-21;
Paradise Lost, 1806; *Paradise Regained*; *The Song of Los*; *The Book
of Ahania*; *Dante's Inferno* (incomplete); *The Illustrations of The
Book of Job* (incomplete), 1825.
   Blake was very influential but not until late in life. From 1818, he
gathered round him a group of disciples including John Linnell,
Samuel Palmer, Edward Calvert, George Richmond and F.O. Finch.
To the Victorians he was a more substantial poet that artist, Ruskin
admired his figures but not his colour, though David and William
Bell Scott owe much to him (qq.v.). It was only at the end of the
century that the growth of the private presses singled him out for
praise as the precursor of the book as a total work of art.

Exhib: London, 1809.
Colls: Bedford; BM; Fitzwilliam; Leeds; Manchester; Tate; V & AM.
Bibl: W.B. Scott, *WB Etchings From His Works*, 1878; R.L. Binyon, *The Art of WB*, 1906; G.K. Chesterton, *WB*, 1920; W. Gaunt, *Arrows of Desire*, 1956; D. Bland, *A History of Book Illus.*, 1958, pp.242-246. M. Butlin, *Catalogue Tate Gallery*, 1978.
See illustration.

BLAMPIED, Edmund   RE RBA   1886-
Artist and caricaturist. Born in Jersey of a Jersey family, 30 March 1886. As a schoolboy he worked on farms and studied their animals, especially horses, eventually going on to study at the Lambeth School of Art. He exhibited book illustrations in the National Competition, 1905-06 and won an L.C.C scholarship. Blampied was a witty and fluid pen artist but concentrated on painting as a career. He took up etching in 1913, becoming an Associate of the RE in 1920, and RBA, 1938. He lived in Jersey throughout the Occupation and designed the liberation stamps, 1945.
Illus: *Peter Pan [Hodder, 1939]*.
Contrib: *Art Workers' Quarterly [Aug. 1908]; The Graphic [1915]*.
Exhib: Leicester Gall., 1923; Salon.
Colls: V & AM.
Bibl: *Print Collectors' Quarterly*, Vol.13, No.1, 1926, pp.69-96; Vol.19, No.4, 1932, pp.298-319.
See Horne.

BLANCHARD, F.L.
Marine painter. Contributor to *The Graphic*, 1905.

BLANCHARD, Ph.   fl.1853-1860
Figure illustrator. He was chiefly employed on French illustrated papers according to Vizetelly. He contributed French subjects to *The Illustrated London News*, 1853.

BLATCHFORD, Montagu
Amateur cartoonist. By profession a carpet designer. Blatchford lived in Halifax and contributed cartoons to *Punch* in the style of Linley Sambourne from 1876-81.

BLAYLOCK, T. Todd   fl.1897-1925
Artist and illustrator. Studied at Poole School of Art and exhibited at National Competition 1897. Worked in London in 1907 and at Poole, 1914-25. Exhibited at RA, 1906-13.
Bibl: *The Studio*, Vol 11, 1897, p.260, illus.

BLOMFIELD, Sir Reginald   RA FSA   1856-1942
Architect, historian and draughtsman. Born in Kent on 20 December 1856 and was educated at Haileybury and Exeter College, Oxford. Architect of many domestic and civil schemes and gardens. RIBA Gold Medal. RA 1914, ARA 1905, PRIBA 1912-14. Knighted 1919. Blomfield was an authority on French architecture and on architectural draughtsmanship of which he was an accomplished exponent.
Publ: *The Formal Garden in England [1892]; A History of Renaissance Architecture in England [1897]; A Short History of Renaissance Architecture in England [1900]; Studies in Architecture [1906]; The Mistress Art [1908]. History of French Architecture 1494-1661 [1911]; Architectural Drawing and Draughtsmen [1912]; History of French Architecture 1661-1774 [1920]; The Touchstone of Architecture [1925].*
Contrib: *The English Illustrated Magazine [1888-90]*.
Colls: RIBA; V & AM.

BLORE, Edward   FRS FSA   1787-1879
Architect and architectural draughtsman. Born in Rutland, 1787, the son of Thomas Blore, FSA. He lived as a youth in Stamford and developed a passion for Gothic architecture and a talent for drawing it. An introduction to Sir Walter Scott resulted in the chance commission to rebuild Abbotsford in the Gothic style. He had a very large practice in the early Victorian period, was a 'special architect' to William IV and Queen Victoria and as such completed Buckingham Palace, 1831-37. Surveyor of Westminster Abbey, 1827-49.
Illus: *History of Rutland [T. Blore 1811]; History of Durham [Surtees, 1816-40]; Northamptonshire [Baker, 1822-41]; Hertford-shire [Clutterbuck, 1815-27]; Britton's Cathedrals [1832-36]: The Provincial Antiquities and Picturesque Scenery of Scotland; The Monumental Remains of Noble and Eminent Persons [1824]; Essay on Gothic Architecture [Sir J. Hall, 1813].*
Exhib: RA, 1813-36.
Colls: BM; RIBA; Soc. of Antiq.; V & AM.
Bibl: H.M. Colvin, *Biographical Dict. of English Architects*, pp.78-82.

BLOW, Detmar   FRIBA   1867-1939
Artist and architect. He was born on 24 November 1867 and was educated at Hawtrey's. He was a major domestic architect in the first quarter of the century, and specialised in the restoration of old buildings. He died 7 February 1939.
Contrib: *The English Illustrated Magazine [with E.H. New, 1891-92]*.
Exhib: RA, 1924.

BLUM, Robert Frederick   1857-1903
American illustrator who worked for *Scribner's Magazine*. Contributed pen, pencil and wash drawings to *Japonica*, Sir E. Arnold, 1892. Exhibited figures at the RA, 1888.

BLYTH, S.R.
Contributed figures in a posterish style with thick lines to *Fun*, 1900.

BOEHM, Wofgang   fl.1850-1863
Painter and engraver and brother of Sir Edgar Boehm, the sculptor. Boehm prepared in about 1860 (paper watermarked 1858) a series of large scale drawings in ink and outline for Tennyson's *Idylls of The King*. They appear to have been prepared for the Art Union, but it is doubtful if they were ever published.
Exhib: RA; BI.

BOGLE, W. Lockhart   -1900
Portrait painter and illustrator. Born in the Highlands and studied at Glasgow University followed by seven years apprenticeship to a lawyer. Abandoned law for painting and studied in Düsseldorf, specialising on his return in Highland subjects and subjects associated with Scottish history. Bogle was also an accomplished archaeologist and a champion wrestler. Died 20 May 1900. He signed his work 'Lockhart Bogle' or 'LB'.
Contrib: *ILN [1886-89]; The Graphic [1882-89]; Good Words [1891-94]*.
Exhib: New Gall; RA, 1886-93.
Colls: V & AM.

BOND, A.L.
Illustrator. Nothing is known of this draughtsman who illustrated *The Miller's Daughter* by Alfred Tennyson in about 1855. This book contains fine vignette and page designs with large trees and flowers in juxtaposition with small landscape and in ornamental borders. It is possible that the artist was 'J.L.' Bond, a Welsh landscape painter.
Illus: *Three Gems in a Setting (n.d.)*.

BOND, H.
Draughtsman. He designed the frontispiece for *The Surrey Tourist or Excursions Through Surrey*, 1821, with H. Gastineau.

BONE, Herbert Alfred   fl.1882-1907
Craftsman designer and illustrator. Working in Dulwich, 1902-07. Exhibited at the RA, RBA, RI, 1874-92, and contributed to *The Quiver*, 1882.

BONE, Sir Muirhead   1876-1953
Etcher, draughtsman and painter. Born in Glasgow on 23 March 1876, the son of a journalist, he studied at the evening classes of the Glasgow School of Art. He moved to London in 1902 and in 1903 married Gertrude Dodd, the sister of Francis Dodd. Bone was a member of the New English Art Club from 1902, having exhibited there from 1898 and was a member of the Society of 12. He made extensive tours with his wife, she providing the text for a number of books illustrated by her husband. Bone did a great deal of his best work as Official Artist on the Western Front and with the Fleet,

1916-18; in the Second World War he was Official War Artist to the Admiralty, 1940-43. He was a Trustee of The National Gallery, 1941-48 and of The Tate Gallery.

Bone's early training as an architect's pupil led him to study buildings, and it is the structure and form of towns, cities and streets which appear most often in his work. But he was very far from being a mere topographer; his Western Front, best seen in the large paper edition of 1917, brings the contrasts and the anonymity of that First World War to life in chalk and pencil. Bone was particularly good at observing vast industrial activity and in showing myriad figures from above, a sort of Piranesi in reverse.

Illus: *Glasgow in 1901 [1901]; Children's Children [1908]; Glasgow, Fifty Drawings [1911]; The Front Line [1916]; Merchant Men at Arms [1919]: The London Perambulator [1925]; Days in Old Spain [1938]; London Echoing [1948]; Merchant Men Rearmed [1949]; The English and Their Country [1951]; Come to Oxford [1952].*

Contrib: *The Yellow Book [1897].*

Exhib: Colnaghi, 1930; FAS, 1953, 1974, 1975; G; L; Mercury Gall., 1974; NEA; RA; RSA.

Colls: V & AM.

Bibl: Campbell Dodgson, *Etchings and Dry Points of MB.*

BOOT, William Henry James   RBA RI   1848-1918
Landscape painter and illustrator. Born at Nottingham in 1848, he studied at the Derby School of Art. Moved to London and practised in Hampstead, devoting himself in his early years almost exclusively to illustration. He was Art Editor of *The Strand Magazine*, 1895-1915, and a contributor to the first numbers of *The Graphic.* He published two technical books, *Trees and How to Paint Them*, 1883, and *Tree Painting in Watercolours*, 1886. He became a member of the RBA in 1884 and was Vice-President, 1895-1915. He died on 8 September 1918.

Illus: *Picturesque Europe; British Battles; Our Village; Our Own Country; British Ballads; Royal River; Rivers of England; Greater London; Picturesque Mediterranean [1891].*

Contrib: *The Graphic [1870-81]; ILN [1884-86]; Good Words [1890]; The Quiver [1890]; Boys' Own Paper; The Art Journal; The Magazine of Art.*

Exhib: B; RA, 1874-84; RBA, 1889-1913; RHA; RI; RWA.

Colls: Derby.

Bibl: *Who Was Who 1916-28.*

BOOTH, J.L.C.
Black and white artist contributing to *Punch*, 1896-1906. He usually draws hunting subjects and sometimes signs 'JC Booth'.

BOSSOLI, Carlo   1815-1884
Painter and draughtsman. Born at Davesco, near Lugano, in 1815 and specialised in military and political subjects, many of which were undertaken in pen and ink. He travelled to Russia. Sweden, Spain and England, where he was made a painter to Queen Victoria, finally settling at Turin.

Illus: *Views on the Railway Between Turin and Genoa [1853 AT 176]; The War in Italy [1859-60 AT 177].*

BOSTOCK, John   fl . 1826-1859
Portrait painter. He made a number of drawings for the Annuals, especially *The Chaplet*, c.1840. He exhibited at the RA, RBA, BI and Old Watercolour Society, 1826-69, at first from Regent's Park, later from Manchester and Kensington.

BOTHAMS, Walter   fl.1882-1925
Landscape painter and illustrator of rural life. Working in London, 1882, Salisbury, 1885-1902 and Malvern, 1903-25. He contributed to *The Illustrated London News*, 1883-84 and 1894 (fishing and architecture).

Exhib: RA; RBA, 1882-91.

BOUCHER, William H.   -1906
Illustrator. Cartoonist of *Judy*, 1868-87 in succession to J. Proctor (q.v.). Associate of the RWS. Died 5 March 1906.

Exhib: RA, 1888-91.

Bibl: Dalziel, *A Record of Work*, 1901, p.318.

BOUGH, Samuel   RSA   1822-1878
Landscape painter and illustrator. Born at Carlisle on 8 January 1822 and learnt engraving under Thomas Allom, in London. He was for some years in the Civil Service although he continued to associate with artists and in 1845 went to Manchester as scene painter to the Theatre Royal. This was followed by periods at the Princess Theatre, Glasgow, 1848, and the Adelphi Theatre, Edinburgh, 1849. An argumentative and individualistic man who became a well-established Edinburgh character and a popular landscape painter. ARSA 1856, and RSA, 1875. He died in Edinburgh, 19 November 1878.

Illus: *Poems and Songs [Robert Burns 1875]; Edinburgh, Picturesque Notes [R.L. Stevenson 1879].*

Exhib: RA, 1856-76; RSA.

Colls: Aberdeen; BM; Dundee; Fitzwilliam; Glasgow; Manchester; NG, Scotland; V& AM.

Bibl: S. Gilpin, *SB*, 1905.

BOUGHTON, George Henry   RA RI   1833-1905
Painter and illustrator. Born near Norwich on 4 December 1833, the son of a farmer. The family emigrated to the United States in 1839 and Boughton was brought up at Albany where he taught himself to paint. He returned to England in 1853, studying art in London and then went back to the States to practise as a landscape painter. He remained in New York, 1854-59, and then left for France to study under Édouard Frère. He finally settled in London in 1862 and became a regular exhibitor at the RA, being elected ARA, 1879 and RA, 1896.

Boughton established himself as a popular Victorian illustrator who specialised in strongly historical costume subjects with a decidedly literary setting. Van Gogh admired these when they appeared in *The Illustrated London News* and the artist's articles on Holland in *Harper's Magazine*, 1883. Boughton's figures derive a great deal from Fred Walker, but his historical revivalism is very much his own. He died 10 January 1905.

Illus: *Rip Van Winkle; Legend of Sleepy Hollow [Washington Irving, 1893]; The Trial of Sir Jasper [1878].*

Contrib: *ILN [1870-82]; Good Words [1878]; The Pall Mall Magazine.*

Exhib: B; BI; FAS, 1894; G; GG; L; M; New York, 1857; NW; RA from 1862.

Colls: Ashmolean; V & AM.

BOURNE, James   fl.1800-1810
Topographer. He exhibited at the RA, 1800-09, and published *Interesting Views of the Lakes of Cumberland, Westmorland and Lancashire*, n.d.

BOURNE, John Cooke   1814-1896
Topographer and illustrator. Although little is known of this artist, he was solely responsible for one of the most heroic illustrating achievements of the early Victorian period, the publication of two volumes on railway construction. Bourne's *Drawings of the London and Birmingham Railway*, 1839, with its 35 tinted lithographic plates on 30 leaves, united art and industry with the lithograph. *The History and Description of the Great Western Railway* followed in 1846, with 43 tinted lithographs on 34 leaves with three maps. The series provides a unique insight into Victorian engineering stage by stage but, more than that, the artist's role is a new one. 'The revelation of the book is, not surprisingly, of an artist relatively unknown … with his action pictures of the building of the London and Birmingham Railway … He apparently foresaw the up-and-down and roundabout viewpoint of the cinema lens for he looks as up to date as Vertov and the most advanced of his documentaries.' John Grierson, *Scotsman*, 18 May 1968. Bourne stood unsuccessfully for election to the New Watercolour Society between 1866 and 1877 and exhibited there and at the RA and RBA. He visited Russia in about 1864.

In general the drawings resemble the work of Prout and J.D. Harding, his figures in particular being large, vigorous and very detailed in the preparatory sketches. He drew on stone for Hay's *Views in Kairo*, 1840, AT 270, and for *The Illustrated London News*, 1860.

Colls: BM; Elton Collection, Ironbridge.

BOW, Charles
Contributor to *The Illustrated London News*, 1855.

BOWERS, Miss Georgina (Mrs Bowers-Edwards) fl.1866-1880
Punch's second woman cartoonist. She supplied initials, vignettes and social subjects for the magazine from 1866-76. A keen hunting woman, she lived at Holywell House, St. Albans and was first encouraged to draw by John Leech. She exhibited in London, 1878-80. Christmas cards signed 'GB' are almost certainly from her hand.
Illus: *Canters in Crampshire [c 1880]; Mr Crop's Harriers [c.1880]; A Month in the Midlands; Hollybush Hall, Notes from a Hunting Box (Not) In the Shires; Hunting in Hard times [all c.1880]; Across Country by Wanderer [1882].*
Contrib: *Once a Week [1866]; London Society [1867].*

BOWLER, Thomas William   -1869
Landscape painter and illustrator. Born in the Vale of Aylesbury and lived in Brighton from where he exhibited at the RA and the RBA, 1857-60. In about 1860 he left for South Africa where he became an astronomer at the Cape of Good Hope. He drew many landscapes and drawings of the Cape Town area and contributed some to *The Illustrated London News* in 1860. He died in 1869.
Colls: Cape Town.

BOWLEY, A.L.
Book decorator. Contributing ornament to children's stories in *The English Illustrated Magazine*, 1895-97.

BOWMAN, T.G.   fl.1866-67
Domestic artist. Contributor to *Cassell's Illustrated Readings*, 1867.
Exhib: BI.

BOWRING, W. Arminger   fl.1902-1922
Portrait and figure painter. He worked in London and was elected ROI in 1922.
Contrib: *Punch [1902-05 (children)].*
Exhib: L; P; RA; ROI.

BOYD, Alexander Stuart   1854-1930
Illustrator. Born in Glasgow on 7 February 1854; practised in his home city until about 1890, contributing humorous drawings to *Quiz* and *The Bailie of Glasgow* under the pseudonym of 'Twym'. After moving to London, Boyd worked at St. John's Wood and drew most of the leading magazines of the day. His parliamentary subjects were always very accurate and Spielmann considered that the drawings were 'executed with great care and with singular appreciation of the value of his blacks'. His wife, Mary Stuart Boyd, was a writer and they collaborated on a number of books. He emigrated to New Zealand after 1914 and died near Auckland on 21 August 1930.
Illus: *Peter Stonnor [Blatherwick, 1884]; The Birthday Book of Solomon Grundy [Roberts, 1884]; Novel Notes [J.K. Jerome, 1893]; At the Rising of the Moon [Mathew, 1893]; Ghetto Tragedies [Zangwill, 1894]; A Protegée of Jack Hamlin's [Bret Harte, 1894]; The Bell Ringer of Angels [Bret Harte, 1894]; John Inglefield [J.K. Jerome, 1894]; The Sketchbook of the North [1896]; Rabbi Saunderson [1898]; Lowden Sabbath Morn [R.L. Stevenson, 1898]; Days of Auld Lang Syne [1898]; Gillian the Dreamer and Horace in Homespun [1900]; Our Stolen Summer [1900]; A Versailles Christmas-Tide [1901]; The Fortunate Isles [Mrs. Boyd]; Wee Macgregor and Jess and Co. [Bell]; Cottars Saturday Night [Burns]; Hamewith [Murray].*
Contrib: *Good Words [1890]; The Idler [1892]; Sunday Magazine [1894]; Black and White [1897]; The Graphic [1901-04]; Daily Graphic [1911]; Punch [1896-]; The Pall Mall Magazine; Pictures from Punch [Vol. VI, 1896].*
Exhib: G, 1889-1906; RA, 1884-87 and 1913; RSA, 1889-1913; RSW.
Colls: Author; G; V & AM.
Bibl: M.H. Spielmann, *The History of Punch*, 1895, p.567.
See illustration.

BOYLE, The Hon. Mrs. Richard   'E.V.B.'   1825-1916
Illustrator of poetry and children's books. Born Eleanor Vere

ALEXANDER STUART BOYD 1854-1930. A page of sketches in pen and ink for *Immediate Parliament*, 1898

Gordon, youngest daughter of Alexander Gordon of Ellon Castle, Aberdeenshire, she married in 1845, the Hon. and Rev. Richard Boyle, MA, Chaplain in Ordinary to Queen Victoria, Vicar of Marston Bigott, Somerset. She received advice from Boxall and Eastlake and was admired as an illustrator by some of the Pre-Raphaelites. Her delightful little books appeared at intervals from 1853 to 1908 and are full of wide-eyed love of nature and a quirky charm of their own. Her inspiration is often in the work of Holman Hunt or Millais and her decorations and mystical pictures come directly from Arthur Hughes or are softened fantasies from Doyle (qq.v.). Her *May Queen* of 1861 is her most successful work, her *Story Without An End*, 1868, perhaps her most famous. At the close of her career, a writer to *The Bookman*, October 1908, p.54, said 'E.V.B. is an aesthete of Ruskin's school, a lover of beautiful things, of what is decent and quiet and old, of gardens, of nature in selections, and of art'. She is indeed the only woman illustrator of competence to emerge before the 1860s. She lived at Maidenhead in middle life and died on 30 July 1916. Signs with monogram.
Illus: *A Children's Summer [1853]; Child's Play [1858]; The May Queen [1861]; Woodland Gossip [1864]; The Story Without An End [1868 (coloured pls.)]; Andersen's Fairy Tales [1872]; Beauty and The Beast [1875]; The Magic Valley [1877]; The New Child's Play [1880]; A Book of Heavenly Birthdays [1894]; Seven Gardens and a Palace [1900]; The Peacock's Pleasaunce [1908].*
Contrib: *ILN [Christmas, 1863].*
Exhib: Dudley Gallery; Grosvenor Gallery, 1878-81.
Bibl: B. Peppin, *Fantasy Book Illus.*, 1975. pp.8, 11, 57, 60 illus.; *Ancient Monuments Society*, New Series, Vol.26, 1982, pp.94-145.
See illustration.

THE HON. MRS RICHARD BOYLE 'E.V.B.' 1825-1916. Illustration for Alfred, Lord Tennyson's *The May Queen*, 1861

BOYS, Thomas Shotter   **1803-1874**
Painter and lithographer. He was born at Pentonville on 2 January 1803 and articled to G. Cooke, the engraver. In 1825 he went to Paris where he worked for French publishers and met R.P. Bonington. This was the most important influence of his life, for the precocious young painter persuaded him to abandon engraving for watercolours and lithography. Boys grasped the importance of tinted lithographs and the fact that 'painting on stone' was the way to bring the effect of watercolours to the widest public. His masterpiece in this medium was *Picturesque Architecture in Paris, Ghent, Antwerp and Rouen*, 1839, AT 23, which was published at eight guineas. This was followed by *Original Views of London As It Is*, 1842, hand tinted this time and only a small number coloured.

Boys was the most sensitive colourist of the mid-Victorian topographers, his rendering of sunlight on massive buildings and his patches of local rich colour put him almost on a level with Bonington. But he was not successful and spent the latter part of his life on hack work, illustrating Blackie's *History of England*, and etching plates for Ruskin's *Modern Painters* or preparing lithographs for the *Stones of Venice*. He died at St. John's Wood on October 10, 1874.
Exhib: NWS, 1832-73; RA, 1847-48; RBA, 1824-58.
Colls: Ashmolean; Bedford; BM; Fitzwilliam; Liverpool; Mellon, Richmond, Virginia; Newcastle; V & AM.
Bibl: E.B. Chancellor, *Original Views of London*, 1926; *Walker's Quarterly*, XVIII, 1926; E.B. Chancellor, *Picturesque Architecture in Paris*, 1928; J. Roundell, *TSB*, 1974; M. Hardie, *Watercolour Paint. in Brit.*, 1967, Vol. III, pp.183-185, illus.
See illustration.

BRACEBRIDGE, Mrs. Selina   née Mills   **-1874**
Watercolourist and traveller. She was born at Bisterne, Hampshire and became a pupil of Samuel Prout (q.v.). Her journeys included visits to Italy in 1824, Italy and Germany in 1825 and the Near East in about 1833. She was in Sweden in 1840 and in the Pyrenees in 1842. She was a friend and sponsor of Florence Nightingale at Scutari and may have been an acquaintance of Edward Lear, who owned a sketchbook of hers, now in the Victoria and Albert Museum. Her style is like that of both Lear and W. Page and although her work was usually lithographed by others, she was apparently an amateur lithographer. She died in 1874.
Publ: *Panoramic Sketch of Athens [1836]*.
Contrib: *Finden's Landscape Illustrations of the Bible [1837-38]*.
Colls: Searight Coll; V & AM.

BRADDELL, Kyo
Contributor of two cartoons to *Vanity Fair*, 1891-92. The name is given in Puttick & Simpson's sale catalogue, 17 March 1916.

BRADDYLL, Lt.-Colonel Thomas Richard Gale   **1776-1862**
Amateur caricaturist. Presumably the owner of Conishead Priory near Ulverston, Lancs. He was the originator of Gillray's famous caricature of *Gulliver and the King of Brobdingnag*, 1803.
Bibl: M.D. George, *English Political Caricature*, 1959, pp.69, 72, 83, 261.

BRADFORD, Rev. W.
Church of England clergyman of St. John's College, Oxford. He illustrated his own *Sketches of the Country, Character and Costume in Portugal and Spain*, 1809-10, AT 135.

BRADLEY, Basil   RWS   **1842-1904**
Sporting painter and illustrator. He studied at the Manchester School of Art and was a consistent exhibitor in London and provincial shows. He became chief equestrian artist to *The Graphic* in 1869 and his spirited pen did much to enliven its earliest and best years. He became an Associate of the RWS in 1867 and a full Member in 1881.

He travelled to New South Wales.
Contrib: *Once a Week [1866]; Cassell's Magazine [1867]: The Graphic [1869-76].*
Exhib: B; M; RA; RBA; RWS.
Colls: BM; Manchester; Sydney.

BRADLEY, Cuthbert   fl.1885-1907
Equestrian illustrator. Working at Folkingham, Lincolnshire. in about 1907. Contributed to *Moonshine*, 1885. *The Graphic*, 1904 and *The Boys' Own Paper.*

BRADLEY, C.H.
Illustrator and decorative artist. He contributed initials, and social subjects to *Punch*, 1852-60, in a weak and watered-down Tenniel style. His monogram is easily mistaken for that of C.H. Bennett (q.v.).

BRADLEY, Miss Gertrude M.   fl. 1893-1902
Illustrator of children's books. She worked at Brocton, Staffordshire and produced colourful story-books and fairy tales.
Illus: *Songs for Somebody [1893]; The Red Hen and Other Fairy Tales [1893]; New Pictures in Old Frames [1894]; Just Forty Winks [1897]; Tom Unlimited [1897]; Nursery Rhymes [1897-98]; Puff-Puff [1899]; Pillow-Stories [1901].*
Bibl: R.E.D. Sketchley, *English Book Illus.*, 1902, pp.106, 160.

BRADLEY, William H.   1868-
American illustrator, working at New York. He was Art Director of *Colliers Magazine, Metropolitan* and *The Century*. His work is one of the best examples of the Beardsley manner exported to the United States. Pennell, writing in 1895 says: 'The decorative or decadent craze has also reached America and its most amusing representative so far, is W.H. Bradley.' *Modern Illustration*, p.124. He was a talented poster designer and is included here as an artist working for John Lane and exhibiting in this country.
Illus: *Fringilla [R.D. Blackmore, Cleveland, 1895]; The Romance of Zion Chapel [Le Gallienne, 1898]; War is Kind [Stephen Crane, New York, 1899]; Peter Poodle; Toy Maker to The King [1906]; The Wonderbox Stories [1916]; Launcelot and The Ladies [1927].*

BRADSHAW, Percy Venner   fl.1905-1949
Illustrator, writer and art teacher. He was born in London and after being educated at Askes School, he studied art at Goldsmiths and Birkbeck Colleges. He was an illustrator for the magazines for many years before developing an art correspondence course and founding the Press Art School at Tudor Hall, Forest Hill, in 1905. He issued portfolios on *The Art of the Illustrator* from 1915-16 in 20 parts, boxed in 'royal' boxes with his instructions pasted to the cover. These included Rountree, E.J.Sullivan and F.H. Townsend who were among his friends; he had a large private collection of their work.
Publ: *Art in Advertising [1925]; They Make Us Smile [1942]; I Wish I Could Paint [1945]; The Magic of Line [1949].*
Contrib: *The Boys' Own Paper [c.1890].*

BRAGER, Jean Baptiste Henri Durand   1814-1879
Marine painter and illustrator. Born at Dol, France, on 21 May 1814, and studied with Eugène Isabey. The artist was very adventurous and a keen traveller and ranged through most of Europe and Africa (including Algeria and Senegal), in search of subjects. He attended the expedition that brought back the Emperor Napoleon's body to France and published his drawings. Died at Paris in 1879.
Illus: *La Marine française; La Marine du commerce; Études de marine; Types et physionomie des armeés d'Orient.*
Contrib: *The Illustrated Times [1859 (Piedmont campaign), 1860 (Palermo)].*

BRANDARD, Robert   1805-1862
Landscape painter and engraver. Born at Birmingham in 1805, and came to London for a year in 1824 to study with E. Goodall. He was really a professional engraver and in this capacity worked on Turner's *Picturesque Views in England and Wales*, 1838, and engraved work by Stanfield and Callcott. He drew some illustrations for Knight's *London*, 1841-42. Worked mostly in Islington.
Exhib: BI, 1835-58; OW; RA; RBA, 1831-47.
Colls: Leicester; Manchester; V & AM.

THOMAS SHOTTER BOYS 1803-1874. St Paul's from Ludgate Hill, a study for *Original Views of London*, 1842. Ink and wash. 15½in. x 10¼in. (39.4cm x 26cm)   Private Collection

BRANDLING, Henry Charles   fl.1847-1861
Watercolour painter and occasional illustrator. He was an Associate of the Old Watercolour Society from 1853-57, and exhibited at the RA from 1847-50. In 1848, he published *Views in the North of France*, tinted lithographs, AT 98, and in 1851, illustrated W. Wilkie Collins' *Rambles beyond Railways*; sepia sketches for the latter were on the art market in London, 1976. Gleeson White records his illustrations to *The Merchant of Venice*, 1860.
Bibl: Chatto & Jackson, *Treatise on Wood Engraving*, 1861, p.599.

BRANGWYN, Sir Frank RA   1867-1956
Born at Bruges in 1867, the son of a Welsh architect. Brangwyn was an all round figure, being painter, designer, etcher, lithographer and book illustrator, but basically self-taught. He worked with William Morris (q.v.) at Merton Abbey before going to sea, then travelled extensively in Asia Minor, 1888, Algeria and Morocco, 1889, South Africa, 1891, and in the same year to Spain with Arthur Melville (q.v.). This is reflected in the very colourful mural and stained glass work which he undertook for town-halls and public buildings. His choice of subjects is in the tradition of the Newlyn School, but some of his wilder schemes are reminiscent of the northern symbolism of Ensor. In illustration, Brangwyn's range was equally wide; he gave full play to the Edwardian love of colour plate books of travel or romance but could hold his own with the best black and white work, preferring chalk to pen, but sometimes powerfully using black and white contrasts. He became an ARA in 1904, and an RA in 1919. He was knighted in 1941 and died in 1956. There are two museums devoted entirely to his work, that at Bruges, opened in 1936, and

SIR FRANK BRANGWYN RA 1867-1956. 'The Story of Gulmar'. Illustration for *The Arabian Nights*, 1896

SIR FRANK BRANGWYN RA 1867-1956. Illustration for *The Arabian Nights*, Gibbings Edition, 1896   Victoria and Albert Museum

another at Orange in the South of France.

Illus: *The Life of Admiral Lord Collingwood [1890]; The Captured Cruiser [Hyne, 1892]; The Exemplary Novels of Cervantes; The Wreck of the Golden Fleece [1893]; The Cruise of the Midge [1894]; Tales of Our Coast [1896]; Arabian Nights [1896]; Don Quixote [1898]; Tom Cringle's Log [Scott, 1898]; Bread Upon the Waters [Kipling]; Devil and the Deep Blue Sea [Kipling]; Eothen [A.W. Kinglake]; The Book of Bridges [W. Shaw Sparrow, 1915]; Omar Khayyam [1920].*

Contrib: *The Graphic [1891-1904]; Pall Mall Budget [1891]; The Idler; The Pall Mall Magazine; The Acorn [1905-6].*

Exhib: FSA, 1908, 1910,1912,1915, 1916, 1924, 1948, 1952, 1958, 1967; G; New Gall.; RA from 1885; RE; RWA.

Colls: BM; Fitzwilliam; Glasgow; V & AM; Witt Photo.

Bibl: W. Shaw Sparrow *FB and His Work*, 1910; H. Furst, *The Decorative Art of FB*, 1924; *The Artist*, May 1897, pp.193-200, illus.; Rodney Brangwyn, *FB*, 1978.

See illustrations.

BRANSON, Paul   **1885-**

American painter and illustrator, born in Washington in 1885. He illustrated Methuen's 1913 edition of The *Wind in The Willows*. This came in for adverse criticism at the time. 'The author tells the story of some obviously "fairy tale" animals, but in depicting the various characters with so much fidelity to nature … the artist seems to us to have entirely missed the spirit of this delightful romance.' *The Studio*, Vol.60, p.249.

BRANSTON, F.W.

Comic illustrator and watercolourist. Contributor to *Hoods Comic Annual*, 1830, exhibited at RBA, 1833, from address at the Old Mint, Tower of London.

BREDIN, E.G.

Army officer and amateur artist. Lieutenant, Royal Regiment of Artillery, 1847; acting Major 1855; Crimean War Medal. Contributed sketches of the Crimea to *The Illustrated London News*, 1854-58.

Contrib: *Cassell's Illustrated Family Paper*, 1853.

BRENNAN, Alfred

Decorative illustrator to *The Artist*, August 1897.

BRENTNALL, T.H.

Contributed to the *Illustrated London News*, 1887.

BRETON, William H.

Naval officer and amateur artist. Lieutenant RN, 1827; Reserve, 1862. He published *Excursions in New South Wales*, 1833, AT 575; *Scandinavian Sketches*, 1835, AT 255.

BREWER, Henry Charles   RI   1866-1943

Landscape painter and architectural illustrator. He was the son of H.W. Brewer (q.v.), and studied at the Westminster School of Art. He specialised in views of Spain, Venice and Tangier, all of which he visited. He practised in West London, 1902-25.

Contrib: *The Graphic [1887-1910].*

Exhib: FAS, 1908,1911,1932; L; RA; RI; RWA.

BREWER, Henry William   -1903

Architectural illustrator specialising in panoramic views. He was born and educated at Oxford, though living most of his working life in North Kensington. He exhibited at the RA from 1858, and was in 1869 an unsuccessful candidate for the NWS. After his death in 1903, H.C. Brewer (q.v.) moved into his house.

ELEANOR FORTESCUE BRICKDALE 1871-1945. 'The World's Travesties'. Signed and dated 1900. 14in x 16¼in (35.6cm x 41.3cm)

Illus: *Old London Illustrated* [for the *Builder*, c.1895].
Contrib: *The Graphic [1870-1901]; English Illustrated Magazine [1887]; The Daily Graphic [1890]; The Pall Mall Magazine [1894-98]; The Girl's Own Paper [1897-98]; The Dome [1897-99].*
Colls: V & AM.
Bibl: *Art Journal.*

BREWER, J. Alphege
Possibly another son of H.W. Brewer (q.v.), practising at Acton, about 1925. Contributor to *The Graphic*, 1910, architectural subjects, and exhibited with the Royal Cambrian Academy, 1924.

BREWER, W.H.
Watercolourist. There are two drawings in the Victoria and Albert Museum, one for *Master Humphreys Clock* by Charles Dickens, 1840, and the other of fairies, the first signed 'W.H. Brewer delt'.

BREWTNALL, Edward Frederick   RWS   1846-1902
Landscape painter and illustrator. He was an early contributor to *The Graphic*, supplying narrative pictures to that magazine and *The Illustrated London News*. He was a member of the RBA from 1882-86, having exhibited there from 1868, and a member of the RWS from 1883. He died at Bedford Park on 15 November, 1902. He signs his work 'EFB'.
Illus: *The Oceans Highway.*
Contrib: *Once a Week [1867]; Good Words For The Young [1869]; The Graphic [1870-74 and 1889]; Punch [1870]; The Illustrated London News [1873-74 and 1892]; Dalziel's Bible Gallery [1880]; Cassell's Family Magazine; English Illustrated Magazine [1887]; The Quiver [1890]; Black and White [1891]; Pall Mall Magazine [1892].*
Exhib: RA; RBA; RWS from 1875.
Colls: Sheffield; V & AM; Warrington.

BRIAULT, Sydney Graham   1887-1955
Portrait painter and illustrator. He studied at the Regent Street Polytechnic, London, 1900 and at the St. Martin's School of Art.
Contrib: *Punch [1914].*
Exhib: RA.

BRICKDALE, Eleanor Fortescue   RWS   1871-1945
Illustrator, painter and designer. She was born in 1871, the daughter of a barrister and studied at the Crystal Palace School of Art, the RA Schools and with Byam Shaw. She won a prize for the best decoration of a public building in 1896 and began to exhibit at the RA the same year. She represents the last phase of Pre-Raphaelitism, her highly detailed and meaningful little pictures are crammed with medievalism and moral sentiment. She was the ideal illustrator of legend and particularly for those expensive coloured gift books of the 1900s where her bright colours and haughty figures were set off to advantage on the ample pages. She was also a talented stained glass artist and designed windows for Bristol Cathedral. Her work was sometimes criticised for its confusion of black to white making outlines difficult to see and occasionally on scale 'piggies the size of white rats need a good deal of ingenious defence'. *The Studio*, Vol.13, pp.103-108. ARWS, 1902; RWS, 1919.
Illus: *A Cotswold Village [J.A. Gibbs, 1898]; Ivanhoe [1899]; Tennyson's Poems [1905]; Child's Life of Christ [M. Dearmer, 1906]; Pippa Passes [R. Browning, 1908]; Dramatis Personae [R. Browning, 1909]; Beautiful Flowers [Wright, 1909]; Tennyson's Idylls of the King [1911]; Story of Saint Elizabeth of Hungary [W. Canton, 1912]; The Gathering of Brother Hilarius [M. Fairless, 1913]; The Book of Old English Songs and Ballads [1915]; The Golden Book of Famous Women [1920]; Fleur and Blanchefleur [1922]; Palgrave's Golden Treasury [1924]; Christmas Carols [1925]; A Diary of an Eighteenth-century Garden [D.C. Calthrop,*

Sang to him instead of the cruelty of Barbara Allen

C E Brock 1906

CHARLES EDMUND BROCK RI 1870-1938. Illustration for an 18th century story, pen and ink, signed and dated 1906

1926]; The Gentle Art [D.C. Calthrop, 1927].
Exhib: Leighton House, 1904; L; RA; RWS.
Colls: Birmingham; Leeds.
Bibl: *The Studio*, Winter No., 1900-01 p.71 illus.; *Modern Book Illustrators and Their Work*, Studio, 1914, illus.; M. Hardie *Watercolour Paint. in Brit.* Vol. III, 1968, pp.130-131; G.L. Taylor, *EFB Centenary Exhibition*, Ashmolean, 1972-73.
See illustration.

BRIDGENS, Richard H.   **fl.1818-1838**
Architect, practising in Liverpool, 1818, and later in London, in the gothic style. He published and illustrated *Manners and Costumes of France, Switzerland and Italy*, 1821, AT 21; *Sefton Church…*, 1822; *West India Scenery*, 1836, AT 680; *Furniture with Candelabra and Interior Decorations…*, 1838.
Exhib: RA, 1813-26, architecture.
Bibl: H.M. Colvin, *Biog. Dict. of Eng. Architects*, 1954, p.97.

BRIERLY, Sir Oswald Walters RWS   **1817-1894**
Marine painter. He was born in Chester in 1817, the son of a doctor, and studied at Sass's School and at Plymouth. In 1841 he made a voyage round the world, but settled in New Zealand for a time and then visited Australia and North and South America. He accompanied the British Fleet to the Baltic on the outbreak of the Crimean War in 1854, and then proceeded to the Black Sea, making drawings that were later published in two books. He travelled with various members of the Royal Family on tours, notably to Norway, 1867-68, and to the Crimea again in 1868. He was elected ARWS in 1872, and RWS in 1890. He became Marine Painter to the Queen in 1874 and was knighted in 1885.
Illus: *A Visit to the Indian Archipelago in HM Ship Meander [Capt. the Hon. H. Keppel 1853, 2 vols.]; Marine and Coast Sketches of the Black Sea [1856, AT 240]; The English and French Fleets in the Baltic [1858].*
Contrib: *ILN [1851, 1854 (Crimea); 1855 (Finland)].*
Exhib: Pall Mall Gallery, 1887.

BRIGHT, Henry Barnabus   **1824-1876**
The origins of this fascinating artist are unknown, but by December 1846, he was living at 33 George Street, Lambeth and married to Rachel Ratcliff. There were eight children of the marriage, two sons becoming artists. By 1871 Bright was living at Vine Cottage, The Oval, Kennington and sent pictures to the Royal Academy from there. Bright appears to have been an eccentric and isolated figure working in an obsessive way in the style of Cruikshank and Doyle. He used their ideas of a fantasy world to create one of his own, inhabited by frogs. These humanised frogs, painted with incredible detail and skill, represented the social and political ills of the day. On the 12th June 1992, Christie's sold three pencil, watercolour and gouache works by this rare artist. These included the densely packed 'The Batrachomyomachia – The Battle between the Frogs and the Mice', 1871, 'An Allegory of Contemporary Events', 1873 and 'The Frog Bandits', 1876. They represent various allegories of the Franco-German War of 1870 over which Bright evidently had strong views. The scale and detail of these works probably accounts for the artist's small output and rarity. It is suggested that these complex pictures include allusions to Darwinism and animal rights as well as politics.

Bright's son, Henry Bright of Thames Ditton, was a watercolourist of fanciful bird subjects and has often been confused with his father.
Exhib: RA, 1871.
Bibl: *Country Life*, 29 Nov., 1956; Christie's, 12 June 1992, Lots 88-90.

BRIGHTWELL, L.R.   **fl.1914-1938**
Animal painter and etcher. He studied at the Lambeth School of Art and at the Zoological Gardens.
Contrib: *Punch [1914 (figs.)].*
Exhib: L.

BRINE
An early cartoonist for *Punch*. He studied in Paris and in London at the same time as T. Woolner (q.v.) and A. Elmore (q.v.), and worked closely with A.S. Henning (q.v.). He is believed to have taught Birket Foster figure drawing.

BRISCOE, Arthur John Trevor   **1873-**
Painter and engraver. He was born at Birkenhead on 25 February 1873 but spent most of his life in East Anglia. Exhibited at the NEA 1896 and 1900 and at the RA. His one attempt at illustration is 'The Mother', published in *The Quarto*, 1896, showing both the influence of Japan and the Birmingham School illustrators.
Exhib: FAS, 1926, 1928, 1930, 1934, 1936, 1940, 1943.

BRISCOE, Ernest Edward   **1882-**
Watercolourist and illustrator. He was born on 5 March 1882 and exhibited at the RA and RI from Caterham. He illustrated *By Ways of London*, 1928, and specialised in drawings of old houses.

BRITTAIN, I.G.
Contributor of agricultural subjects to *The Strand Magazine*, 1891. This may be identified with Miss Isabel Brittain of Scarborough who exhibited at Dowdeswell Galleries that year.

HENRY MATTHEW BROCK RI 1875-1960.
Illustration for 'Mrs Bellamy's Diamonds', c.1905,
pen and ink   Author's Collection

BRITTEN, William Edward Frank   **fl.1873-1901**
Genre painter and illustrator. Britten was working in London from
about 1873, the year in which he began to exhibit at the RBA. He
was not a prolific illustrator but an eclectic one, his designs ranging
from Victorian classicism to smokey Pre-Raphaelite chalk drawings.
He excelled as a decorative artist, placing his subjects in elaborate
frames, the Shaftesbury Tribute in *The Graphic* of 1885 is a good
example. He was still working in Pimlico in 1890.
Illus: *Carols of the Year, Algernon Swinburne; The Elf Errant*
[1895]; Undine [Baron de la Motte Fouqué, 1896]; The Early
Poems of Alfred Lord Tennyson [1901].
Contrib: *The Graphic [1885-86].*
Colls: V & AM.

BRITTON, John   FSA   **1771-1857**
Architectural draughtsman and antiquary. He was born at Kingston
St. Michael, Wiltshire in 1771 and after being apprenticed to a
publican, became a hop merchant and ballad writer. He joined forces
with Edward Brayley in 1801 to produce their first book, *The*
Beauties of Wiltshire, the first of a giant series which was to set the
seal on romantic topographical guides for a generation. Britton gave
up his interest in the project after Volume VII but was supplying
illustrations for his successor J.C. Smith in 1814. A poor
draughtsman, Britton was a brilliant self-made and irrepressible
editor. For his works he gathered illustrative artists together calling
them 'scientific artists' and showed a definite feel for book-making,
highlighted by his use of Whittingham as his printer. He died in 1857
having published his mammoth *Autobiography*, 1850.
Publ: *Architectural Antiquities of Great Britain [1805-14];*
Cathedral Antiquities of England [1814-35]; Specimens of Gothic
Architecture [1823-25]; The Architectural Antiquities of Normandy
[1825]; Dictionary of Architecture and Archaeology of The Middle
Ages [1829]; Public Buildings of London [1825-28]; History ... of
the ... Palace ... of Westminster [1834-36, with Brayley];
Architectural Description of Windsor [1842].
Exhib: RA, 1799-1819.
Colls: Ashmolean; BM; Devizes.
Bibl: RIBA, *Papers*, 1856-57; *AJ* February 1857; J. Mordaunt Crook
'John Britton and the Genesis of the Gothic Revival'; *Concerning*
Architecture, Penguin, 1968, pp. 98-119.

BROCK, Charles Edmund   RI   **1870-1938**
Book illustrator and portrait painter. Born at Cambridge in February
1870 and spent the whole of his working life there. Educated at the
Cambridge School and in the studio of Henry Wiles, sculptor. Like
his younger brother, H.M. Brock (q.v.), his métier was in the
illustration of period books, the worlds of Jane Austen, Charles

Lamb, Oliver Goldsmith and Daniel Defoe, but also of Scott's
classics and the stories of Whyte-Melville. His career began in
earnest in the middle 1890s and he continued to produce a regular
output until his death in 1938. In general his pen drawings have a
lighter touch than his brother's and are softer in their contrasts, the
finished watercolours have an all over pastel hue which to the
present writer is less successful than the black and white work.
    The Brocks worked closely together in the same studio and gained
stimulation from each other. One of their influences was
undoubtedly the work of Hugh Thomson (q.v.), but their accuracy in
period settings was greater than his, they collected Georgian
furniture and clothing to study from. He became RI, 1908; and died
at Cambridge 28 February 1938.
    A full Bibliography of illustrated books is found in *The Brocks, A*
Family of Cambridge Artists and Illustrators, by C.M. Kelly, 1975.
Contrib: *Good Cheer [1894]; Sunday Magazine [1894]; Good*
Words [1895-96]; Punch [1901-10]; Fun [1901]; The Graphic
[1901-10]; ILN [1912]; Tucks Annuals; Blackie's Annuals.
Exhib: L; RA, from 1906; RI.
Bibl: *The Studio*, Winter No. 1900-01 p.37 illus.; *Modern Book*
Illustrators and Their Work, Studio, 1914 illus.; C.M. Kelly, op. cit.
See illustration.

BROCK, Henry Matthew RI   **1875-1960**
Book illustrator and landscape painter. Born at Cambridge 11 July
1875, the younger brother of C.E. Brock (q.v.). He was educated at
Cambridge Higher Grade School and at the Cambridge School of Art
before joining his brother's studio. He married in 1912 his cousin,
Doris Joan Pegram, sister of Fred Pegram (q.v.). There is little
difference in the careers of the two brothers, except that H.M.'s was
longer and in many respects more varied, he painted landscapes and
was more gifted as a humorous artist. Although meticulous in
signing their drawings, H.M.'s can usually be told apart by their
thicker ink lines and bolder handling. He was elected RI in 1906 and
died at Cambridge in 1960.
    A full Bibliography of illustrated books is found in *The Brocks, A*
Family of Cambridge Artists and Illustrators, by C.M. Kelly, 1975.
Contrib: *Cassell's Family Magazine [1896-97]; The Quiver [1897-*
98]; Good News [1898]; The Captain; C.B. Fry's Magazine; Chums
Annual; Blackie's Annuals; The Strand Magazine; Fun [1901]; The
Graphic [1901]; Punch [1905-40, 415 drawings]; The Sphere
[c.1912].
Exhib: B; L; RA, 1901-1906; RI.
Colls: V & AM; Witt Photo.
Bibl: *Modern Book Illustrators and Their Work*, Studio, 1914 illus.,
C.M. Kelly, op. cit.
See illustration.

BROCK, Richard Henry   fl.1902-1925
Landscape painter and illustrator. Brother of C.M. and H.M. Brock (qq.v.). He practised at Cambridge in the family studio but concentrated more on the illustrations of boys' annuals.
Contrib: *Punch* [1916-17]: *Chatterbox and Prize Annuals* [1908-25]; *Blackie's Boys' Annuals*.
Exhib: L; M; RA, 1901-13; RI.
Bibl: C.M. Kelly, op. cit.

BROMLEY, Clough W.   fl.1880-1904
Landscape and flower painter, engraver and illustrator. He worked in London and contributed pastorals, architecture and decoration to *The English Illustrated Magazine*, 1885-87, 1896.
Exhib: B; L; M; RA; RBA; RHA; RI; ROI.

BROMLEY, Valentine Walter   1848-1877
Painter and illustrator. Born in London in 1848 and exhibited at London exhibitions, 1865-77. He married Miss A.L.M. Atkinson, the landscape painter and was assistant on *The Illustrated London News*, 1873. He travelled to the United States in 1875, illustrating Lord Dunraven's *The Great Divide* and died at Fellows Green, near Harpenden in 1877. Member of RBA, 1871.
Contrib: *The Graphic* [1872-73]; *ILN* [1873-79]; *Punch* [1876].
Exhib: NWS; RA; RBA, 1867-74.
Colls: Shipley; Witt Photo.

BROOK, Ricardo
Illustrator of comic genre. He contributed to *Punch*, 1914.

BROOKE, Sir Arthur De Capel, Bt.   1791-1858
Amateur artist, son of Sir R. De Capel Brooke, he travelled in Europe and published several books illustrated by himself. These included *A Winter in Lapland and Sweden*, 1827; *Winter Sketches in Lapland*, 1827; *Sketches in Spain and Morocco*, 1837.

BROOKE, E. Adveno
Topographer exhibiting at the RA, BI and RBA, 1844-64, from addresses in Islington and Shepherd's Bush. He illustrated *The Book of South Wales* by Mr. and Mrs. S.C. Hall, 1861.

BROOKE, Leonard Leslie   1863-1940
Painter and illustrator. Born at Birkenhead and educated there before being trained in the RA Schools, Armitage medal, 1888. Brooke's talent lay in the illustration of children's books, his figure drawing is strong, characterised by cross hatching and he is capable of considerable humour. He is best remembered as the illustrator of *Mrs. Molesworth's Works*, 1891-97. He died at Hampstead, 1 May 1940.
Illus: *Miriam's Ambition* [1889]; *Thorndyke Manor* [1890]; *The Secret of the Old House* [1890]; *The Light Princess* [G. Macdonald 1890]; *Brownies and Rose Leaves* [1892]; *Bab* [1892]; *Marian* [1892]; *A Hit and a Miss* [1893]; *Moonbeams and Brownies* [1894]; *Penelope and The Others* [1896]; *School in Fairyland* [1896]; *Mrs. Molesworth's Works* [1891-97]; *Pippa Passes* [Robert Browning, 1898]; *A Spring Song* [1898]; *The Pelican Chorus* [E. Lear, 1900]; *The Jumblies* [E. Lear, 1900]; *Johnny Crow's Garden* [1903]; *The Book of Gilly* [Emily Lawless, 1908]; *Johnny Crow's New Garden* [1835].
Contrib: *The Strand* [1891]; *English Illustrated Magazine* [1896]; *The Parade* [1897].
Exhib: B; L; M; New Gall.; NWS, 1887-1901; RA.
Colls: Manchester.
Bibl: *The Studio*, Winter No. 1900-01, p.74 illus.; R.E.D. Sketchley, *English Book Illus.*, 1902, pp.99, 160; *Who Was Who*, 1929-40.

BROOKE, William Henry   1772-1860
Illustrator and caricaturist. Born in 1772, the nephew of Henry Brooke, the historical painter. He exhibited portraits and figure subjects at the RA, 1810-26, but is best known as an illustrator in the style of Stothard. His comic cuts are in the manner of William Heath (q.v.). He practised first in Soho, moving to the Adelphi and finally to Bloomsbury. He died at Chichester in 1860.
Illus: *Moore's Irish Melodies* [1822]; *Hone's Every Day Book* [1826-27]; *The Fairy Mythology* [T. Keightley, 1828]; *Greek and Roman Mythology* [T. Keightley, 1831]; *Walton's Angler; The

Humorist [W.H. Harrison, 1832]; *Antiquarian Etching Club; The Golden Goose Book* [1905]; *Singing Time* [Somervell, c.1910].
Contrib: *Satirist* [1812-14]; *Britton's Cathedrals* [1832-36, figures only].
Colls: BM; V & AM.

BROOKES, Warwick   1808-1882
Designer and illustrator. Born at Salford in 1808 and was one of the first pupils of the new School of Design established at Manchester in 1838. He then became a leading figure among the group of artists in the North-West who wished to study from the life and came together as The United Society of Manchester Artists. Brookes made a considerable local reputation and after the Manchester Exhibition of 1857, received encouragement from the Prince Consort and made yearly visits to London. He was head designer of the Rossendale Printing Company from 1840-66.
Illus: *Marjorie Fleming* [J. Brown. 1884]; *WB's Pencil Pictures of Child Life* [T. Letherbrow, 1889].
Contrib: *A Round of Days* [1866, heads].
Colls: BM.
Bibl: *Apollo*, 1994.

BROOKSHAW, George   fl.1818-1819
Flower painter and drawing-master. He illustrated his own *New Treatise*, 1818, AL 96 and *Groups*, 1819, AL 97.

BROUGH, Robert ARSA   1872-1905
Painter. Born at Invergordon, Ross, in 1872 and was educated in Aberdeen and Glasgow. Studied at Aberdeen Art School and at the RSA, Edinburgh and later in Paris. In Edinburgh he gained the Watters medal and Chalmers bursary. His first London success was with his portrait of W.D. Ross of *Black & White* shown at the New Gallery. He died 22 January 1905.
Contrib: *The Evergreen* [1896].
Exhib: Dresden, 1901; G; L; Munich, 1897; New Gall.; Paris, 1900; RA, 1897; RSA.

BROUGH, Robert Barnabas   1828-1860
Journalist, author and comic draughtsman. He is believed to have practised as a portrait painter in Manchester, before founding the *Liverpool Lion*, a weekly satirical newspaper. He collaborated with his brother William Brough in writing burlesques for the London theatre. Spielmann said that he 'will be remembered for his clever illustrations to most of *Punch*'s rivals of his time, as well as his creation of "Billie Barlow" – the "Ally Sloper" of the day...' G.A. Sala says he worked on *The Man in The Moon*.
Bibl: Spielmann, *History of Punch*, 1895, p.360.

BROWN, A.
Contributed architectural subjects to *Illustrated London News*, 1847.

BROWN, Major Cecil MA RBS   1867-
Equestrian artist and sculptor. Born at Ayr, 1867 and educated at Harrow and Oxford. He designed the medal for the International Medical Congress, London, 1913, and served in the First World War, 1914-18. Art master at Bedford School, 1925.
Illus: *The Horse in Art and Nature.*
Contrib: *ILN* [1896].
Exhib: Paris Salon; RA from 1895.

BROWN, Ford Madox   1821-1893
Painter and occasional illustrator. He was born in Calais in 1821 and studied art in Belgium and Rome. He came into contact with the newly formed Pre-Raphaelite Brotherhood in 1848, when he took D.G. Rossetti (q.v.) as a pupil. Brown remained on the edge of the group, but his contact with them was mutually beneficial; it is particularly marked in his illustrative work where an earnestness and attention to detail is predominant. In 1857, he spent three days in a mortuary getting accurate information on the decomposition of the body for a woodcut illustration measuring 3¾in. x 5in! Perhaps his finest works were the two illustrations for Rossetti's poem 'Down Stream' which combine technical mastery and an objective view of love and nature. Brown taught at the Camden Town Working Men's College from 1854 and was a designer for Morris, Faulkner and Co.,

1861-74. He signs his name 'FMB' or 'FMB/89'.
Illus: *The Feather [1892].*
Contrib: *Willmott's Poets of the Nineteenth Century [1857]; Lyra Germanica [1868]; Once A Week [1869]; Dark Blue [1871]; Dalziel's Bible Gallery [1880-81]; The Builder [1887]; Brown Owl [1891, title and illus.]; Dramas in Miniature [Mathilde Blind, 1897].*
Exhib: BI, 1841-67; RA.
Colls: Ashmolean; Bedford; BM; Manchester; V & AM.
Bibl: B.M. Hueffer, *Memoir of MB*, 1896; W.M. Rosetti, *Pre-Raphaelite Diaries and Letters*, 1900 (FMB's diary); Gleeson White, *English Illustration, The Sixties*, 1906; B. Reid, *Illustrators of The Sixties*, 1928, pp.48-50; J. Maas, *Victorian Painters*, 1969, pp.131-132; *The Pre-Raphaelites*, Tate Gallery catalogue, 1984; Leslie Parris (Editor), *Pre-Raphaelite Papers*, 1984.

BROWN, Isaac L.
Draughtsman. Contributor to *London Society*, 1868.

BROWN, James
He was the creator of the comic strip 'McNab of that Ilk' and contributed to *Ally Sloper's Half Holiday* and *Judy*, 1886-87.

BROWN, John
Architect and County Surveyor of Norfolk. Contributed a church genre subject to *The Illustrated Times*, Christmas, 1856. He exhibited at the RA, 1820-44.

BROWN, J.D. or J.B.
Contributor to *Good Words*, 1860. Exhibited at the RBA, 1862.

BROWN, J.R.   fl.1872-1890
Illustrator. Working at Sefton Park, Liverpool and contributing regularly to *The Graphic*, 1874-77 and 1885-88. The artist has a wide range, tackling comic and genre subjects as well as social realism. Among his best work here is 'Common Lodging House', 1888. There is a fine grey wash drawing by this artist of Prince Imperial's College for *The Graphic*, 1872, in the souvenir albums of the Royal Library, Windsor.
Exhib: L, 1889.

BROWN, M.
Landscape illustrator for *The Illustrated London News*, 1888. Presumably the same as artist practising in Edinburgh and exhibiting at the RSA, 1889.

BROWN, Oliver Madox
Painter. Son of Ford Madox Brown (q.v.). He illustrated, with his father, Moxon's edition of the *Poetical Works of Lord Byron*, 1870.

BROWN, T.R.J.
Illustrator working exclusively for *Ally Sloper's Half Holiday*, c.1890.

BROWN, Thomas   fl. 1842-1856
Painter, sculptor and illustrator. He worked at Pentonville and exhibited at the RA and BI from 1842-55. He illustrated *The Complete Poetical Works of William Cowper*, for Gall & Anglis, Edinburgh, n.d., c.1840.
Colls: Witt Photo.

BROWN, Thomas Austen ARSA   1857-1924
Painter of genre and landscape, illustrator. Born at Edinburgh, 18 September 1859 and was educated there. He was an RA exhibitor from 1885 and a Member of the RI, 1888-99 and a member of The National Portrait Society. He exhibited abroad at Munich, Dresden and Barcelona and won many medals. He died at Boulogne.

Brown has a very individual style both in his watercolours and in the coloured woodcuts he undertook. The figures are sketchy and undefined, the buildings wavy in soft tints. He signs his name with a monogrammed TAB.
Illus: *Bits of Old Chelsea [1922, lithographs].*
Contrib: *ILN [1899].*
Exhib: FAS, 1900,1903; NWS; RA; RSA.
Colls: BM; V & AM.
Bibl: *Who Was Who, 1916-28.*

BROWN, W.
Illustrator of *The Comic Album*, and contributor to *Punch*, 1844. The same artist may be William Brown exhibiting at the RBA from 1825-33 with an address in Chelsea.

BROWNE, Gordon Frederick   RI   1858-1932
Painter and illustrator. Born at Banstead, Surrey. the younger son of H.K. Browne, 'Phiz' (q.v.). He was educated privately and then studied art at Heatherley's, following his father into book illustration as a profession. From about 1880, Browne illustrated a truly amazing quantity of boys' stories, tales and novels, among them works by Defoe, Swift, Bunyan, Scott, R.L. Stevenson, Andrew Lang, and E.F. Benson. In many ways he was the superior of his father as a figure draughtsman, but although very prolific never reached the latter's stature, principally because he had no one writer to collaborate with. He was clearly an artist who pleased editors and in this way there is a sameness about his work which dulls it; characters look much alike whether they are Besant's or Henty's! He was elected RI in 1896 and died 27 May 1932. He signs his name 'GB'.
Illus: *Stories of Old Renown [Ascott R. Hope, 1883]; A Waif of the Sea [Kate Wood, 1884]; Miss Fenwick's Failures [Esme Stuart, 1885]; Thrown on the World [Edwin Hodder, 1885]; Winnie's Secret [Kate Wood, 1885]; Robinson Crusoe [Daniel Defoe, 1885]; Kirke's Mill [Mrs Robert O'Reilly, 1885]; The Champion of Odin [J.F. Hodgetts, 1885]; 'That Child' [1885]; Christmas Angel [E.L. Farjeon, 1885]; The Legend of St Juvenis [George Halse, 1886]; Mary's Meadow [J.H. Ewing, 1886]; Fritz and Eric [John C. Hutcheson, 1886]; Melchior's Dream [J.H. Ewing, 1886]; The Hermit's Apprentice [Ascott R. Hope, 1886]; Gulliver's Travels [Jonathan Swift, 1886]; Gordon Browne's Series of Old Fairy Tales [1886-87]; Rip Van Winkle [Washington Irving, 1887]; Devon Boys [G. Manville Fenn, 1887]; The Log of the 'Flying Fish' [Harry Collingwod, 1887]; Down the Snow-stairs [Alice Corkran, 1887]; Dandelion Clocks [J.H. Ewing, 1887]; The Peace-Egg [J.H. Ewing, 1887]; The Seven Wise Scholars [Ascott R. Hope, 1887]; Chirp and Chatter [Alice Banks, 1888]; The Henry Irving Shakespeare [6 vols., 1888]; Snap-dragons [J.H. Ewing, 1888]; A Golden Age [Ismay Thorn, 1888]; Fairy Tales by the Countess d'Aulnoy [1888]; Harold The Boy Earl [J.F. Hodgetts, 1888]; Claimed at Last [Sibella B. Edgcumb, 1888]; Great Uncle Hoot-Toot [Mrs Molesworth, 1889]; The Origin of Plum Pudding [Frank Hudson, 1889]; Prince Prigio [Andrew Lang, 1889]; A Flock of Four [Ismay Thorn, 1889]; A Apple Pie [1890]; Syd Belton [G. Manville Fenn, 1891]; Great Grandmamma [G.M. Synge, 1891]; Master Rockafellar's Voyage [W. Clarke Russell, 1891]; The Red Grange [Mrs Molesworth, 1891]; A Pinch of Experience [L.B. Walford, 1892]; The Doctor of the 'Juliet' [H. Collingwood, 1892]; A Young Mutineer [L.T. Meade, 1893]; Graeme and Cyril [Barry Pain, 1893]; The Two Dorothys [Mrs Herbert Martin, 1893]; One in Charity [Silas K. Hocking, 1893]; The Book of Good Counsels [Hitopadesa, 1893]; Stevenson's Island Nights Entertainments [1893]; Grimm's Fairy Tales [1894]; National Rhymes of the Nursery [1894]; Beryl [G.M. Synge, 1894]; Prince Booboo and little Smuts [Harry Jones, 1896]; Sintram and His Companions Undine [1896]; The Surprising Adventures of Sir Toady Lion [S.R. Crockett, 1897]; An African Millionaire [Grant Allen, 1897]; Dr. Jolliboy's ABC [1898]; Butterfly Ballads and Stories in Rhyme [Helen Atteridge, 1898]; Paleface and Redskin [F. Anstey, 1898]; Paul Carab Cornishman [Charles Lee, 1898]; Man's Meadow, F. Anstey's Stories For Boys and Girls [Mrs Ewing, 1898, covers and illus.]; Stories from Froissart [1899]; Macbeth [1899]; Miss Cayley's Adventures [Grant Allen, 1899]; The Story of the Treasure Seekers; Eric or Little By Little [F.W. Farrar, 1899]; Hilda Wade [Grant Allen, 1900]; St Winifred's [F.W. Farrar, 1900]; Daddy's Girl [L.T. Meade, 1901]; A Book of Discoveries [J. Masefield, 1910].*
Contrib: *ILN [1881-87, 1891-98]; The Quiver [1890]; Black & White [1891]; Good Words [1891-97]; Chums [1892]; The Captain; Lika Joko [1894]; The New Budget [1895]; The Sporting and Dramatic News [1899]; Cassell's Saturday Journal; Cassell's Family Magazine; The Boy's Own Paper; The Girl's Own Paper; The Pall Mall Magazine; The Sunday Strand [1906].*
Exhib: L; RA, 1886; RBA; RI, 1890-1925; RWA.
Colls: Author; BM; Doncaster; Hove; V & AM.
Bibl: R.E.D. Sketchley, *English Book Illus.*, 1903, pp.161-164 (this contains a full bibliography to 1901); *The Studio*, Winter No. 1900-01, p.27, illus.

HABLOT KNIGHT BROWNE 'PHIZ' 1815-1882. 'Sarah Gamp' from Dickens' *Martin Chuzzlewit*, 1844.

BROWNE, Hablot Knight   'Phiz'   1815-1882

Watercolourist, book illustrator and humorous artist. He was born at Kennington in 1815 and after being educated in Suffolk was apprenticed to Finden, the engraver, subsequently opening a studio of his own and attending the St. Martin's Lane School. He was the artist who most benefited from the untimely death of Robert Seymour (q.v.), when he succeeded him as Dickens' illustrator for *Pickwick Papers*, 1836. The same year he had produced the illustrations for another Dickens work, *Sunday As It Is*, and he was to continue to do so with the major novels, until unseated by more modern illustrators in the 1860s. Browne's draughtsmanship was in the tradition of the Regency, verging on caricature, scratchy in execution and not always very assured in the penwork. His work would not perhaps have remained so stereotyped and old fashioned if he had not stuck to plates when the whole world was enjoying the woodblock. By the time that *Little Dorrit* appeared in 1857 he was moving towards a greater naturalism. Dickens seems to have found the artist companionable and took him on two trips to collect material. He became paralysed in 1867 and moved to Brighton in 1880, where he died in 1882. Browne's studio was sold by Sotheby, Wilkinson & Hodge, 5 December 1887.

Illus: *Sunday under Three Heads* [Dickens, 1836]; *Posthumous Papers of the Pickwick Club* [Dickens, 1836-37]; *Sketches of Young Ladies by 'Quiz'* [1837]; *Sketches in London* [Grant, 1838]; *A Paper of Tobacco* [1839]; *Nicholas Nickleby* [Dickens, 1839]; *Harry Lorrequer* [C. Lever, 1839]; *Master Humphrey's Clock – Old Curiosity Shop and Barnaby Rudge* [Dickens, 1840-41]; *Legendary Tales of the Highlands* [1841]; *Charles O'Malley* [C. Lever, 1841]; *Peter Priggins* [1841]; *Rambling Recollections* [Maxwell, 1842]; *Jack Hinton* [C. Lever, 1842-43]; *Irish Peasantry* [W. Carleton, 1843-44]; *Martin Chuzzlewhit* [Dickens, 1844]; *Tom Burke* [C. Lever, 1844]; *St. Patrick's Eve* [C. Lever, 1845]; *Tales of the Train*

[C. Lever, 1845]; Nuts and Nutcrackers [1845]; The O'Donoghue [C. Lever, 1845]; Fiddle-Faddle's Sentimental Tour [1845]; Fanny the Little Milliner [1846]; The Commissioner [1846]; Teetotalism [1846]; Dombey and Son [Dickens, 1846-48]; The Knight of Gwynne [C. Lever, 1847]; The Fortunes of Colonel Torlogh O'Brien [1847]; Irish Diamonds [1847]; Old St. Paul's [W.H. Ainsworth, 1847]; Pottleton Legacy [Albert Smith, 1849]; David Copperfield [Dickens, 1849-50]; Roland Cashel [C. Lever, 1849-50]: Sketches of Cantabs [Albert Smith, 1850]; The Illustrated Byron [1850]; The Daltons [C. Lever, 1850-52]; Ghost Stories [1851]; Lewis Arundel [Frank Smedley, 1852]; Bleak House [Dickens, 1852-53]; Letters Left at the Pastrycooks [Horace Mayhew, 1853]; Crichton [W.H. Ainsworth]; Christmas Day [1854]; The Water Lily [H. Myrtle, 1854]; The Dodd Family Abroad [C. Lever, 1854]; Harry Coverdale's Courtship [Frank Smedley, 1854]; Martins of Cro' Martin [C. Lever, 1856]; Home Pictures [1856]; Little Dorrit [Dickens, 1855-57]; Spendthrift, Mervyn Clitheroe [W.H. Ainsworth, 1857-58]; Davenpot Dunn [C. Lever, 1859]; The Minister's Wooing [H.B. Stowe, 1859]; Tale of Two Cities [Dickens, 1859]; Ovingdean Grange [W.H. Ainsworth, 1860]; Twigs for Nests [1860]; One of Them [C. Lever, 1861]; Puck on Pegasus [C. Pennell, 1861]; Barrington [1862-63]; Tom Moody's Tales [Mark Lemon, 1864]; Facey Romford's Hounds [1864]; Luttrell of Arran [C. Lever, 1865]; Ballads and Songs of Brittany [1865]; Can You Forgive Her? [A. Trollope, 1866]; Dame Perkins and Her Mare [1866]; Phiz's Funny Alphabet [1883].

Contrib: *New Sporting Magazine* [1839]; *London Magazine* [1840]; *Punch* [1842-44, 1861-69]; *The Great Gun* [1844]; *ILN* [1844-61]; *Ainsworth's Magazine* [1844]; *The Illuminated Magazine* [1845]; *The Union Magazine* [1846]; *Life* [1850]; *Illustrated London Magazine* [1853-55]; *The Illustrated Times* [1855-56]; *New Monthly Magazine*; *Only a Week*; *Tinsley's Magazine*; *London Society*; *St. James's Magazine*; *Illustrated Gazette*; *Sporting Times*; *Judy*; *The Welcome Guest*.

Exhib: BI, 1843-67; FAS, 1883; RA; RBA, 1865-86.

Colls: BM; Dickens House, Doughty Street, London; Manchester; V & AM.

Bibl: Chatto & Jackson, *Treatise on Wood Engraving*, 1861, p.559; F.G. Kitton, *Phiz a Memoir*, 1882; D.C. Thomson, *Life and Labour of HKB*, 1884; S. M. Ellis, *Mainly Victorian*, 1924.
See illustrations.

BROWNE, J. Stewart

Social realism artist and illustrator. He illustrated *One Dinner a Week*, 1884, reprinted 1987.

BROWNE, N. Robert

Humorous illustrator for *Fun*, 1901.

BROWNE, Philip of Shrewsbury   fl.1824-1868

Landscape and sporting artist. A series of his illustrations to *The Vicar of Wakefield* and *Henry VI* were on the London art market in 1986.

Coll: Ashmolean.

Bibl: H. Mallalieu, *The Dictionary of British Watercolour Artists up to 1920*, 1976.

BROWNE, Tom RI   1872-1910

Painter and black and white artist. Born at Nottingham in 1872 into a working class family and after attending the National School, left at the age of eleven to work in the city's Lace Market. Browne had a talent for sketching which led to his being apprenticed to a firm of lithographers in 1886 where he remained until 1893. He had been doing commercial illustration from 1889 and in 1895 settled in London, where he exhibited at the RA in 1897.

Browne was one of the artists, among whom can be counted Beardsley and Phil May, who were young enough to be free of the constraints of wood engraving by hand. They appreciated at once the possibilities of photographic engraving and reproduction and developed their style accordingly. Browne's was a linear style with wide hatching and often a rather obvious contrast of areas of black and white. His stage-door Johnnies and bottle-nosed footmen sometimes have the feeling of May (q.v.) but rarely his subtlety. Browne's humour was more earthy than that of *Punch* and he used

HABLOT KNIGHT BROWNE 'PHIZ' 1815-1882. Illustration of a beach scene for un-identified book, pen and ink   Victoria and Albert Museum

convicts and vicars and fat ladies with less discrimination than May and seems to make little social comment. He was, however, enormously popular in mid-Edwardian England and had his own *Tom Browne's Comic Annual*. He made a trip to Korea in 1909 and the drawings completed show a greater range than one would expect and an incredible facility with pure pencil line. He died 16 March 1910.
Illus: *Tom Browne's Comic Annual; Tom Browne's Cycle Sketch Book; The Khaki Alphabet Book; Night Side of London.*
Contrib: *The Graphic [1898-1911]; Pick-Me-Up [1898]; Eureka [1897]; Black and White [1899]; Moonshine [1900]; Chums; Fun [1901]; Pearson's Magazine; The Royal Magazine; The Sketch [1899]; Punch [1900].*
Exhib: FAS, 1899.
Colls: V & AM.
Bibl: *TB, RI Brush, Pen and Pencil,* c.1905.
See illustration.

BROWNE, Walter
Illustrator. Son of H.K. Browne and brother of G.F. Browne (qq.v.). He contributed to *Punch*, 1875, and then worked on *Fun*, finally devoting himself to news drawing and some book illustration.
Exhib: RBA, 1865.

BROWNING, Amy Kathleen   1881-1978
Figure and flower painter and occasional illustrator. She was born on 31 March 1881 at Little Brammingham Hall near Luton. Worked as an artist on her father's farm at Pulloxhill, Bedfordshire. She attended the Royal College of Art from 1899-1904 where she became a friend of Sylvia Pankhurst. She made a reputation for interior paintings in an impressionistic manner, two of wich were bought by the French Government, 1913. She married the painter T.C. Dugdale RA (q.v.) in 1916. She contributed illustrations to the

suffragette magazine *The Women's Dreadnought*, 1917. ROI, 1916, Royal Soc. of Portrait Painters, 1954.
Exhib: FAS; G; NA; P; RA; ROI; RSA.
Bibl: Joanna Dunham, *AMKB, an Impressionist in the Women's Movement*, 1995.

TOM BROWNE RI 1872-1910. A Dispute with a Servant. Illustration for unidentified periodical. Pen and ink and crayon
Author's Collection

ROBERT BROWNING SENIOR 1782-1866. Amateur caricature in pen and ink

Gordon Collection

BROWNING, Robert, Snr.   **1782-1866**
Father of the poet, amateur caricaturist and draughtsman. For many
years a clerk in the Bank of England, he left an album of 172
caricatures, heads, figure and groups, now in the Victoria and Albert
Museum Library.
Bibl: F.G. Kitton, 'RB The Elder as a Caricaturist', *Art Journal*,
1896, pp.55-58.
See illustration.

BROWNLIE, R.A. 'R.A.B.'   **-1897**
Illustrator and landscape painter. Born in England but worked for
most of his life in Scotland, principally in Glasgow. He was a
talented caricaturist, contributing spirited cartoons to many
magazines. He was influenced by Phil May (q.v.), excelled in
cockney subjects which he treated either with broad grey washes or
in a more linear posterish style. He died at Edinburgh in 1897.
Contrib: *The Sketch [1893-95]; St. Paul's; Judy [1893]; The Pall Mall
Magazine [1893]; The English Illustrated Magazine [1894-96].*
Exhib: G; L; NEA; RSA; RSW.
Colls: V & AM.

BRUCKMAN, William L.   **1866-**
Landscape painter. Born at the Hague and worked in London and
Essex, 1904 to 1917. He contributed illustrations to *The Dome*, 1898.
Exhib: FAS, 1913.

BRUHL, Louis Burleigh RBA   **1861-1942**
Landscape painter. He was born on 29 July 1861, and was trained in
Vienna; President of the British Watercolour Society. He died on 29
January 1942.
Illus: *Essex [Hope Moncreiff, c. 1905 (colour)].*
Exhib: RA, 1889-1924.

BRUNDAGE, Francis
Illustrated *Tales From Tennyson* by Nora Chesson, Tuck, c.1900. A
rather sugary artist not improved by chromo-lithography.

BRUNELLESCHI
Pseudonym of contributor to *The Illustrated London News*, 1913,
colour plates in the style of Poiret.

BRUNTON, William S.   **fl.1859-1871**
Illustrator. He was of Irish extraction and was a founder member of
the Savage Club. Dalziel refers to 'Billy Brunton' as 'a constant
contributor of comic sketches dealing with passing events of
everyday life'. He has an unusual sign-manual of arrow-pierced

hearts, or monogram 'WB'.
Contrib: *Punch [1859]; The Illustrated Times [1861 (military), and
1866 (comic)]; London Society [1863, 1865, 1868]; Fun [1865];
Tinsley's Magazine [1867]; Cassell's Illustrated Readings [1867];
The Broadway [1867-74]; Moonshine, [1871].*
Colls: V & AM.
Bibl: Dalziel, *A Record of Work*, 1901, p.314.

BRYAN, Alfred   **1852-1899**
Caricaturist and illustrator. Born in 1852 and worked chiefly for *The
Sporting and Dramatic News* where he did weekly cartoons as 'our
Captious Critic'. He worked also for *Entracte, The Hornet* and *Judy*,
1890, but is best remembered as chief cartoonist of *Moonshine*.
Colls: Brighton Art Gallery.

BRYANT, Joshua
Landscape artist and topographer, exhibiting at the RA and BI, 1798-
1810, from address in Oxford Street, London. He travelled widely in
France and illustrated Thornton's *A Sporting Tour Through France*,
1806, AT 84.

BRYDEN, Robert RE   **1865-1939**
Wood engraver, etcher and sculptor. He worked in Glasgow after
studying at the RCA, RA Schools and in Belgium, France, Italy,
Spain and Egypt. ARE, 1891; RE, 1899. Died 22 August 1939.
Publ: *Etchings of Ayrshire Castles [3 Vols, 1899, 1908, 1910];
Etchings in Italy [1894]; A Series of Burns Etchings [1894]; Etchings
in Spain [1896]; Auld Ayr and Some Ayr Characters [1897]; Woodcuts
of Men of Letters of the 19th century [1899]; Workers, or Wanting
Crafts [1912]; Edinburgh Etchings [1913]; Glasgow Etchings [1914];
Ayrshire Monuments [1915]; Twenty Etched Portraits From Life
[1916]; Ayr Etchings [1922]; Parables of Our Lord [1924],*
Contrib: *The Dome [1900].*
Exhib: G; L; RA; RE; RSA.

BUCHANAN, Fred
Humorous draughtsman, working for *Fun* 1900, *The Graphic*, 1906
and *The Strand*. He was a member of the Strand Club in 1906.
Contrib: *Punch*, 1902 and 1908.

BUCHEL, Charles A.   **1872-1950**
Portrait painter who made some illustrations of theatrical events and
some posters. He practised in Hampstead, 1902-14, and in St. John's
Wood, 1925.
Exhib: G; L; RA; RBA; ROI; RWA.
Colls: Witt Photo.

BUCK, Adam 1759-1833

Portrait and miniature painter. He was born at Cork in 1759, the son of a silversmith, and acquired a considerable reputation before coming to England in about 1795. Buck's drawings with watercolour finish over pencil, and the face usually given a miniature-like treatment, epitomise slick Regency neo-classicism. His engravings are often of family virtues 'Affection', etc., and frequently include Greek revival ornament and are very decorative. The drawings are much rarer and desirable.
Illus: *Sentimental Journey [Sterne, n.d]; Paintings on Greek Vases [100 pls., 1812].*
Exhib: BI; RA; RBA.
Colls: Ashmolean; BM; Fitzwilliam.

BUCKLAND, Arthur Herbert RBA 1870-

Painter and illustrator. He was born at Taunton on 22 January 1870, and studied at the RCA and at Julian's, Paris, 1894. He subsequently worked in London and Barnet, 1911-25. RBA, 1894.
Illus: *Anne's Terrible Good Nature [E.V. Lucas, 1908].*
Contrib: *The Pall Mall Magazine; The Windsor Magazine; ILN [1898 and 1907]; The Quiver [1900].*
Exhib. RA; RBA; RI; ROI.
Colls: Witt Photo.

BUCKLER, John Chessel 1793-1894

Architect and topographical draughtsman. Born in 1793, the eldest son of John Buckler, FSA, the architect. Buckler was an antiquary like his father and his architectural practice was of houses in the gothic style. His meticulous drawings belong more to the 18th than to the 19th century.
Illus: *Views of Cathedral Churches in Ireland [1822]; Observations on the Original Architecture of St. Mary Magdalen, Oxford...[1823]; Sixty Views Of Endowed Grammar Schools [1827]; An Historical and Descriptive Account of the Royal Palace of Eltham [1828]; Remarks Upon Wayside Chapels [1843]; History of the Architecture of the Abbey Church of St. Albans [1847]; Description of Lincoln Cathedral [1866].*
Contrib: *Oxford Almanac [1816, 1817, 1820].*
Exhib: OWS; RA; RBA.
Colls: Ashmolean; BM; Bristol; Manchester; Norwich.
Bibl: H.M. Colvin, *Biog. Dict. of English Architects*, 1954, p.106.

BUCKLEY, Walter

Illustrator of Sir H.M. Stanley's *My Dark Companions*, 1893.

BUCKMAN, Edwin 1841-1930

Watercolourist and illustrator. Born on 25 January 1841 and, after being educated at King Edward's School, Birmingham, he acquired the rudiments of drawing at the Birmingham Art School. Buckman was one of the original staff of *The Graphic* and contributed to its reputation as a paper of social concern. His drawings of the poor and neglected in Victorian society and his illustrations of the Paris Commune are amongst the strongest works of their kind. Van Gogh admired his work in his London years and wrote of it as 'drawn especially broadly and boldly and in a whole-hearted manner'. He was later drawing master to Her Majesty Queen Alexandra. ARWS, 1877. He died 15 October 1930.
Contrib: *The Graphic [1869-71 and 1889]; ILN [1871-76].*
Exhib: RA to 1877; RWS.
Bibl: *English Influences on Van Gogh*, Arts Council, 1974-75, p.51.

BUCKMAN, W.R.

Illustrator contributing to *Good Words*, 1868, and *Cassell's Magazine*, 1870.

BULCOCK, Percy 1877-1914

Illustrator specialising in ink drawing. Working at Burnley, 1899, and Liverpool, 1907.
Illus: *Blessed Damozel [Rossetti (Lane), 1900].*
Contrib: *The Dome [1899].*
Bibl: R.E.D. Sketchley, *English Book Illus.*, 1903, p.14, 122.

BULL, René -1942

Illustrator and special artist. He was born in Ireland and went to Paris to study engineering, but left this for art work in London, 1892. After working for various magazines, he was appointed 'special' for *Black and White*, 1896, attending the Armenian massacres and the Graeco-Turkish War as artist. He made trips for the paper to the North-West Frontier and to the Atbara and Omdurman campaigns. He served in the First World War in RNVR, 1916, and RAF, 1917.

Bull was one of the most versatile specials because his stature as an artist was above average. Not only an accurate reporter, he was a talented comic draughtsman and a brilliant illustrator of fairy stories. His most successful humorous sketches were in strip cartoon form and were the nearest things in England to the subtle line of Caran D'Ache.
Illus: *Fables [J. de la Fontaine, 1905 (with C. Moore Park, q.v.)]; Uncle Remus [J.C. Harris, 1906]; The Arabian Nights [1912]; The Russian Ballet [A.E. Johnson, 1913]; Rubaiyat of Omar Khayyam [1913]; Carmen [P. Merimée, 1916]; Gulliver's Travels [J. Swift, 1928].*
Contrib: *Black & White [1892]; Chums [1892]; Pall Mall Budget [1893]; ILN [1893]; St. Paul's [1894]; Lika Joko [1894]; English Illustrated Magazine [1894-96] Pick-Me-Up; The New Budget [1895]; The Sketch [1895-1918] The Ludgate Monthly [c.1896]; The Bystander [1904]; Punch [1906-07].*
Colls: V & AM; Witt Photo.
Bibl: *Modern Book Illustrators and Their Work*, Studio, 1914, illus; B. Peppin, *Fantasy Book Illustration*, 1975, p.186 illus.

BULTEEL, Lady Elizabeth 1798-1880

Amateur illustrator. Daughter of the 2nd Earl Grey, and wife of John Crocker Bulteel of Flete and Lyneham, Devon. She produced several books for her grandchildren, illustrated by herself, one small volume being printed.

BUNBURY, Sir Henry Edward 1778-1860

Soldier, military historian and amateur caricaturist, he was the son of Henry William Bunbury, 1750-1811, the amateur caricaturist who published numerous satires at the end of the 18th century. His work strongly reflects the influence of his father.

BUNDY, Edgar ARA 1862-1922

Historical painter and illustrator. He was born at Brighton in 1862 and was largely self-taught. RI, 1891; RBA, 1891; ROI, 1892; ARA, 1915. One of his paintings acquired for the Chantrey Bequest, 1905. He died 10 January 1922.
Contrib: *The Graphic [1899].*
Exhib: B; G; L; RA, from 1881; RBA; RI; ROI.

BURCHELL, William John 1782-1863

Explorer, naturalist and artist. Born in 1782, he worked as a botanist at St. Helena, 1805-10, and then moved to Cape Town to study Cape-Dutch and travel in South Africa, 1811-15. He later explored the interior of Brazil, 1825-29, collecting plants and specimens.
Illus: *Travels in the Interior of Southern Africa [1822-24, AT 327].*
Exhib: RA, l805-20.

BURGES, William ARA FRIBA 1827-1881

Architect. One of the most original Victorian designers, combining a brilliant understanding of structure with a wild imagination. He was the son of a wealthy engineer and in early middle age met Lord Bute who became his enthusiastic and faithful patron. For this eccentric peer he created Cardiff Castle and Castell Cock, both of which have such an air of gothic fantasy that they might easily be three dimensional extensions of *Moxon's Tennyson*! Burges is included here because of his powerful and exciting ink drawing in the Victoria and Albert Museum of 'St. Simeon Stylites'. This masterpiece inspired by rather than for literature, is signed and dated 1861, and is totally in the spirit of the grandest 1860s illustration with German woodcuts as its inspiration. ARA, 1881.
Exhib: RA, l860-80.

BURGESS, Arthur James Wetherall RI 1879-1956

Marine artist and illustrator. Born at Bombola, New South Wales, 6 January 1879, and settled in England in 1901. He studied shipping in the Royal Dockyards and became Art Editor of *Brassey's Naval and Shipping Annual*, 1922-30. He contributed to many illustrated papers, particularly *The Graphic*, 1910. RI, 1916; ROI, 1913.
Exhib: B; G; L; RA, from 1904; RBA; RI; ROI.
Colls: New South Wales, Nat. Gall.

SIR EDWARD COLEY BURNE-JONES RA 1833-1898. Pencil drawing for the frontispiece of *Syr Percyvelle of Gales,* published by William Morris at the Kelmscott Press, 1895

Victoria and Albert Museum

SIR EDWARD COLEY BURNE-JONES RA 1833-1898. Frontispiece for *Syr Percyvelle of Gales*, published by William Morris at the Kelmscott Press, 1895. Wood engraving from the previous drawing   Victoria and Albert Museum

BURGESS, Ella
Illustrated P. Hay Hunter's *My Ducats and My Daughter,* 1894.

BURGESS, Ethel K   **fl.1896-1907**
Figure painter, illustrator, designer of bookplates. She was resident in Camberwell in 1896 and was a student at the Lambeth School in 1900, winning a first prize in the Gilbert Sketching Club. She was a good pen artist, basing her style on the rugged contrasts of the Newlyn School and capable of interesting period designs for children's books.
Exhib: L, 1901-07; RA.
Bibl: *The Artist*, 1897, pp.7-9 illus.; *The Studio*, Vol.10, 1897, p.113, bk. pl; Vol.20, 1900, pp.191-195 illus.

BURGESS, H.G.
American artist, working as an illustrator in Boston in about 1907. He contributed illustrations to *The Illustrated London News*, 1896-97; *English Illustrated Magazine*, 1897; *Cassell's Family Magazine*, 1898; *Pearson's Magazine*.
Colls: V & AM.

BURGESS, Philip L.
Contrib: *Punch*, 1907.

BURGESS, Walter William   **-1908**
Etcher. He was elected RE in 1883 and, in 1894, published *Bits of Old Chelsea*, illustrated by himself.

BURLEIGH, Averil Mary   **-1949**
Painter and illustrator She studied at Brighton School of Art and seems to have worked all her life in Sussex; she married the painter C.H.H. Burleigh. Her mannered medievalism is rather like that of E.F. Brickdale (q.v.), and she tackled the same sort of subjects, the works of Shakespeare and Keats. ARWS, 1939.
Exhib: FAS, 1925, 1934; GG, Arts & Crafts Exhib., 1913; RA; RI; RWS.
Bibl: *The Studio*, Vol.58, 1913.
See Horne.

BURNE-JONES, Sir Edward Coley Bt.RA   **1833-1898**
Artist, book illustrator, caricaturist and writer of illustrated letters. Born at Birmingham 28 August 1833 and after being educated at King Edward's School, Birmingham, went up to Oxford in 1833. There he met William Morris (q.v.), and in the succeeding year became influenced by the paintings of Rossetti and the writings of Ruskin, whom he met in 1856. Burne-Jones' position as a quasi-member of the Pre-Raphaelite group and his development as a major subject and decorative painter are not of primary importance here; his work as an illustrator falls into three categories. In 1857, he illustrated *The Fairy Family* for his friend Maclaren, rather conventional designs and typical of the romantic school of the 1840s. In the 1860s he contributed a few illustrations to the magazines that were thriving on the revival in wood engraving. In the last years of his life, 1892 to 1898, he had a fruitful partnership with the Kelmscott Press in designing for books of high

typographic quality. His influence in the latter venture lasted well into the 1900s in private press work. ARA, 1885; ARWS, 1886. Baronet, 1894.

Illus: *Good Words [1862-63]; Parables from Nature [1865]; Dalziel's Bible Gallery [1880-81]*; design for title to one of Ruskin's lectures, 1865 *(not used)*; *King Poppy [Lytton, (title and frontis.)]; The Queen Who Flew: A Fairy Tale [Hueffer, 1894 (title and frontis.)]; The High History of The Holy Grail [1898]; The Beginning of the World [1903]; Letters to Katie [1925]; The Little Holland House Album [The Dalrymple Press, 1981, Ed. by John Christian]; The Fairy Family [Archibald Maclaren, The Dalrymple Press, 1985, Ed. by John Christian]; Letters to Katie [B.M. 1988, Ed. by John Christian]*.
Kelmscott Press Books: *A Dream of John Ball [frontis.]; A King's Lesson [1892 (frontis.)]; The Golden Legend [1892 (woodcuts)]; The Order of Chivalry [1893 (frontis.)]; The Wood Beyond the World [frontis.]; Sir Pereccyvelle of Gales [1895 (frontis.)]; The Life and Death of Jason, The Well at the World's End [1896]; The Works of Geoffrey Chaucer [1896]; Sire Degrevaunt [1897]; Syr Ysambrace [1897]; Love is Enough [1897]; The Story of Sigurd the Volsung [1898]*.

Exhib: FAS, 1876; GG; New Gall; OWS; RA.
Colls: Ashmolean; Bedford; Birmingham; Fitzwilliam; Manchester; V & AM.
Bibl: M. Bell, *Sir E B-J*, 1898; M. Harrison and B. Waters, *B-J*, 1973; *B-J*, Cat. of Exhibition, Arts Council 1975 (J. Christian); *The Pre-Raphaelites*, Tate Gallery catalogue, 1984.
See illustrations.

BURNE-JONES, Sir Philip Bt.   1862-1926
Portrait painter. He was born on 2 October 1861, the only son of Sir E.C. Burne-Jones Bt. (q.v.). He was educated at Marlborough College and University College, Oxford. He died 21 June 1926.
Illus: *The Little Iliad [Maurice Hewlett, 1915]*.
Exhib: B: G; L: M; P; RA; ROI; RSA.

BURNEY, Edward Francis   1760-1848
Illustrator and caricaturist. Born at Worcester in 1760, the son of Dr. Burney, the composer, and brother of the novelist Fanny Burney. He studied at the RA Schools and exhibited there from 1780 both book illustrations and portraits. Among his earlier works were a set of illustrations for his sister's novel *Evelina*. But Burney's general run of illustrations give no indication of the inventive mind that lies behind his large caricature subjects 'An Elegant Establishment for Young Ladies', 'The Waltz', etc. These superbly finished compositions of many figures are in direct succession to Hogarth, especially from their theatrical and literary standpoint. An album of drawings sold at Christie's on 5 March 1974 gave some indication of the artist's scope, including religious, classical, poetic and comic subjects. The smaller decorative subjects are not uncommon, he excelled in small groups, head and tail pieces.
Illus: *Buffon's Natural History [1791]; The Copper Plate Magazine [1792-1803]; Ireland's Avon [1795]; The Pleasures of Hope [Thomas Campbell, 1806]; Burney's Theatrical Portraits; Sporting Magazine [frontis.]; The New Doll [c.1825]*.
Contrib: *Le Souvenir or Pocket Tablet [1809-40]*.
Colls: BM; V & AM; Witt Photo.
Bibl: Iolo Williams, *Early English Watercolours*, 1952. pp. 132-133; M. Hardie, *Watercolour Paint. in Brit.* Vol.I, 1966, pp.152-153.

BURNS, Cecil Lawrence   c.1863-1929
Portrait and genre painter. He studied under Herkomer (q.v.), and at the RA, becoming the Principal of Camberwell School of Arts and Crafts, 1897, and Principal of Bombay School of Art in 1899. He was curator of the Victoria and Albert Museum, Bombay, 1902-1918. He became a Member of the NEA, 1887 and RBA, 1899. He died 16 July 1929.
Illus: *Belle Dame Sans Merci [n.d.]*.
Exhib: L; M; NEA; RA; RBA; ROI.
Bibl: *The Studio*, Vol.6, 1896, illus.

BURNS, John Inder
Contributor to *Punch*, 1909 (golf).

BURNS, M.J.
Marine artist. Contributed illustrations to *The Graphic*, 1910.

SIR EDWARD COLEY BURNE-JONES RA 1833-1898. Caricature of William Morris, the poet and designer, in a wooden bath tub

BURNS, Robert   ARSA   1869-1941
Figure and portrait painter. He was born at Edinburgh in 1869 and after studying at South Kensington and in Paris, 1890-92, worked for the whole of his life in the city. Burns was specially successful with crowded figure subjects built up densely as in a medieval tapestry; a sketch-book of such subjects of Border legend was sold at Sotheby's in April 1976. The artist was President of the Society of Scottish Artists, ARSA, 1902, resigned 1920, and Director of Painting at Edinburgh College of Art, 1914.
Illus: *The Evergreen [1895]*.
Exhib: B; G; L; M; RA; RHA; RSA; RSW.

BURTON, E.J.
Contributor to *Punch*, 1847-49.

BURTON, Sir Frederick William   RHA RWS   1816-1900
Painter. He was born at Corofin House, County Clare, on 8 April 1816, the son of an amateur landscape painter. In 1828 he went to Dublin and studied under the Brocas brothers, attracting the attention of George Petrie, the landscape painter and archaeologist. He studied in Munich from 1851-58 although he continued to exhibit in London. He was elected ARHA in 1837 and RHA in 1839; ARWS, 1854 and RWS, 1855, Hon Member, 1886. Burton was immensely successful as a miniature painter and watercolourist and became Director of the National Gallery in 1874, receiving a knighthood on his retirement twenty years later. He died at Kensington, 16 March 1900.
Contrib: *ILN, [1896]*.
Exhib: G; RA from 1842; RHA.
Colls: Ashmolean; BM; Nat. Gall., Ireland; V & AM.

BURTON, Sir Richard Francis   1821-1890
Scholar, explorer, translator and artist. Born in 1821 and was educated at Trinity College, Oxford, 1840. He followed an army career from 1842, was an assistant on the Sind survey but abandoned this for a wandering life studying Moslem beliefs and customs. He explored Somaliland in 1854, the Nile in 1856-59, and travelled in North America, 1860. Burton served in the Crimean War, but from 1861 was in the diplomatic service as British Consul in Fernando Po, Santos, Damascus and finally Trieste, 1872. He was made a KCMG in 1885, but his fame really rests on his knowledge of Asiatic languages and his

translation of classics like *The Book of The Sword*, 1884 and *The Arabian Nights*, 1885-88.
Illus: *Falconry in the Valley of the Indus [1852, AT 479]; Personal Narrative of a Pilgrimage to El-Medinah and Meccah [1855-56, AT 368].*

BURTON, William Paton   **1828-1883**
Landscape painter. Born in Madras in 1828, the son of an Indian army officer. He was educated in Edinburgh and, proposing to take up architecture as a career, entered the office of David Bryce. He left Bryce for a life of landscape painting in oils and watercolours and travelled on the Continent and in Egypt in search of subjects. He died on 31 December 1883, near Aberdeen.
Contrib: *Willmott's Sacred Poetry of the 16th, 17th and 18th Centuries [1862]; Legends and Lyrics [1865]; The Postman's Bag [J. de Liefde, 1865]; Golden Thoughts From Golden Fountains [1867].*
Colls: Aberdeen; BM; Manchester; V & AM; Witt Photo.

BURTON, William Shakespeare   **1830-1916**
A minor Pre-Raphaelite who exhibited the 'Wounded Cavalier' at the RA in 1856. He studied at the RA Schools and won the gold medal there in 1851. His only known illustration is for *Once a Week*, 1865.
Exhib: RA; RI.

BURY, Rev. Edward John   MA   1790-1832
Amateur artist. He was the son of Edward Bury of Walthamstow, Essex, and was educated at University College, Oxford, BA, 1811, MA, 1817. He was Rector of Lichfield, Hants from 1814 and married in 1818, the Lady Charlotte Campbell, daughter of the 5th Duke of Argyll, and died in May 1832. He illustrated his wife's *The Three Great Sanctuaries of Tuscany*, 1833.
Bibl: *Alumni Oxonienses 1715-1886.*

BURY, Thomas Talbot   **1811-1877**
Architect and artist. He was born in London and became a pupil of Pugin in 1824 although left him to set up his own practice in 1830. He was one of the draughtsmen of Pugin's *Paris*, 1831.
Illus: *Coloured Views on the Liverpool and Manchester Railway [1833 AL 400]; Six Coloured Views on the London and Birmingham Railway [AL 401].*
Publ: *Remains of Ecclesiastical Woodwork [1847]; Rudimentary Architecture [1849].*
Colls: BM; Manchester.

BURY, Viscount   See KEPPEL, William Coutts

BUSBY, Thomas Lord
Figure artist. He exhibited portraits at the RA from 1804-1837. He illustrated *Costumes of the Lower Orders in Paris*, c.1820, AT 107; *Costumes of the Lower Orders of The Metropolis*, 24 plates, 1818.

BUSHBY, Lady Frances   **1838-1925**
Amateur flower artist. She was born in 1838, the daughter of the 6th Earl of Guildford and wife of the Recorder of Colchester. In 1866 she illustrated *Early Rising by a Late Philosopher*, for private circulation.

BUSHNELL, A.
Contributed illustration to *Good Words*, 1861.

BUSK, Captain Hans
Amateur artist, he presented a lifeboat to the town of Ryde, Isle of Wight, in 1869.
Illus: *Maiden-Hours and Maiden Wiles, Designed by Beaujolais [Sotheran, 1869].*

BUSS, R.W.   **1804-1875**
Painter and illustrator. He was born in London in 1804, the son of R.W. Buss, engraver and enameller. He studied drawing under George Clint, ARA, but began his career as an illustrator by working for Charles Knight. He was particularly closely associated with Knight in producing the *Penny Magazine* and an oil by him in the Victoria and Albert Museum shows the interior of the magazine office with a wood engraver at work. Buss's greatest test was to produce etched work of sufficient quality for use in *Pickwick*, 1836, but he failed in this and was succeeded by H.K. Browne (q.v.). He was Editor of *The Fine Art Almanack* and wrote a book *The Principles of Caricature*, 1874. He died at Camden Town, 1875.
Illus: *London [Knight, 1841]; Old England; Chaucer; Widow Barnaby [Frances Trollope, 1839]; Peter Simple [Marryat]; Jacob Faithful [Marryat, 1834]; The Court of King James II [Ainsworth].*
Exhib: BI; RA; RBA, 1826-1859.
Colls: BM; Fitzwilliam; V & AM.
Bibl: Alfred G. Buss, *Notes and Queries*, April 24, 1875; G. Everitt, *English Caricaturists*, 1893, pp.363-366.

BUTLER, Arthur G.   FZS
Illustrator of birds and insects. Contributed to *Nature and Art*, 1866.

BUTLER, Lady (Elizabeth) née Thompson   RI   1846-1933
Battle painter and illustrator. She was born in Lausanne in 1846 and studied at South Kensington, Florence and Rome. She was the sister of Alice Meynell, the poetess, and married in 1877 Lt-General Sir William F. Butler. Although she specialised in military and equestrian subjects, she did an extensive amount of black and white work and illustrated her sister's poems. She died 2 October 1933.
Illus: *Poems [Alice Meynell]; Ballads [Thackeray]; Campaigns of the Cataracts [W.F. Butler]; Letters From the Holy Land [1905]; From Sketch-Book and Diary [c. 1905].*
Contrib: *Merry England; The Graphic [1873 and 1889].*
Exhib: B; FAS, 1877; G; L; M; RA from 1873.
Colls: BM.
Bibl: *An Autobiography*, 1923; 'The Pallas of Pall Mall', *History Today*, Feb. 1982.

BUXTON, Dudley
Contributor of half-tone comic sporting subjects to *Punch*, 1904.

BYFIELD, Mary   **1795-1871**
Wood engraver. She worked nearly all her life for the Chiswick Press and cut some of the finest frontispieces and decorations, based on sixteenth century originals. These include the page illustrations to the Pickering 1853 edition of *Queen Elizabeth's Prayer Book* and Nicolas's *History of The Orders of Knighthood*, 1842.
Bibl: R. McLean, *Victorian Book Design and Colour Printing*, 1972.

BYLES, W. Housman   RBA   fl.1890-1925
Landscape and figure painter, practising in London, 1903, and at West Hamprett, Chichester, 1907-25. Byles contributed illustrations to *The Pall Mall Magazine* and *The Sketch* in the 1890s. RBA, 1901.
Exhib: B; L; New Gall; RA; RBA; ROI.

BYRNE, Claude
Painter working at Rathmines, Dublin. He contributed illustrations of Irish distress to *The Illustrated London News*, 1886, and exhibited at the RHA, 1884.

BYRNE, E.R.
Contributed marine subjects to *The Graphic*, 1873.

CADENHEAD, James   ARSA RSW   1858-1927

Landscape painter and illustrator. Born at Aberdeen in 1858 and studied at the RSA School and then in Paris under Duran. He was elected ARSA in 1902 and RSA in 1921 and was a founder member of the NEAC, 1889. Cadenhead was a talented printmaker and in his few book illustrations the influence of the Japanese print on his work is very striking. He signs his work ©

Illus: *Pixie [Mrs. G. Ford, 1891]; Master Rex [Mrs. G. Ford, 1891]; Hell's Piper [ballad by Riccardo Stephens, n.d.].*

Contrib: *The Evergreen [1894-96].*

Exhib: G; L; M; NEA, 1899-1900; RSA from 1880.

Bibl: *The Studio,* Vol.10, 1897, p.67 illus.; Vol.55, 1912, pp.10-20 illus.

CADOGAN, Lady Honoria   1813-1904

A very talented amateur watercolourist. She was the daughter of the 3rd Earl of Cadogan, travelled on the Continent and visited many country houses which she rendered in brilliant interior and exterior views. An album of her work was exhibited at the World of Watercolours in January 1992. She published a book of engravings in 1844 in aid of the Chelsea Infant School.

Exhib: RBA, 1869.

Bibl: H. Mallalieu, *Country Life,* 16 Jan. 1992.

CALDECOTT, Randolph RI   1846-1886

Watercolourist and illustrator. Born at Chester on 22 March 1846, the son of an accountant and was educated at the King's School. He became a bank clerk at Whitchurch and Manchester, but had greater success as a draughtsman for local periodicals, 1868-69. His wish to reach a wider public was only realised in 1871, when sketches by him were published in *London Society*; this was his real debut and in the next decade he became the most popular illustrator of children's books of the period published by Edmund Evans, and second only to Kate Greenaway (q.v.). Caldecott shared with Kate Greenaway a love of the past and especially the last days of the 18th century before industrialization. A keen sportsman, Caldecott's world is always rural, pretty and untroubled, a landscape of manor houses, hunts and skating parties loosely hung round a story. His costume subjects for *The Graphic*, often in the form of letters, are better than his contemporary cartoons and he is an artist who comes across more vividly in colour than in black and white.

Caldecott was a very finished artist, but his illustrations lack the humour of Leech and indeed of the period he depicts. His flat colour and slick outlines were to have many successors, in particular Phil May (q.v.), and Cecil Aldin (q.v.), his spiritual follower being Hugh Thomson (q.v.). Caldecott's promising career was cut short by illness and he died at St. Augustine, Florida, where he was seeking a cure on 12 February 1886.

Illus. and Contrib: *Will o'the Wisp [1867]; The Sphinx [1867]; London Society [1871-72]; Punch [1872 and 1883]; The Harz Mountains [1872]; Frank Mildmay [1873]; The Graphic [1873-86]; Pictorial World [1874]; Old Christmas and Bracebridge Hall [Washington Irving, 1876]; North Italian Folk [1878]; The House That Jack Built and John Gilpin [1878]; Elegy on a Mad Dog and The Babes in the Wood [1879]; Aunt Judy's Magazine [1879], Jackanapes, Daddy Darwin's Dovecote [1879]; Three Jovial Huntsmen, Sing a Song of Sixpence [1880], Breton Folk [1880]; What The Blackbird Said [1880]; The Queen of Hearts, The Farmer's Boy [1881]; Hey Diddle Diddle, Baby Bunting [1882]; Greystoke Hall [1882]; The Fox Jumps Over The Parson's Gate, A Frog He Would [1883]; A Sketch Book, Some Of Aesop's Fables [1883]; Come Lasses and Lads, Ride a Cock Horse [1884]; The English Illustrated Magazine [1884-86 (initials)]; Mrs. Mary Blaize, The Great Panjandrum [1885]; The Complete Collection of Pictures and Sons [1887]; The Complete...Contributions; The Boys' Own Paper.*

RANDOLPH CALDECOTT RI 1846-1886. Illustration to *Banbury Cross*, c.1880

RANDOLPH CALDECOTT RI 1846-1886. 'Cupid in Society'. Outline drawing in pen and ink
Jeffrey Gordon Collection

Exhib: RA, 1872-85.
Colls: Ashmolean; Bedford; BM; Fitzwilliam; V & AM; Walsall.
Bibl: Henry Blackburn, *RC, A Personal Memoir*, 1886; *The Artist*, June 1898, pp.65-69 illus.; M.G. Davis, *RC*, 1946; R.K. Engen, *RC*, 1976. See illustrations.

CALDER, Scott
Amateur illustrator working at Chelsea. Winner of book illustration competition, *The Studio*, Vol.8, 1896, p.184, illus.

CALDERON, William Frank ROI   **1865-1943**
Figure, landscape and sporting painter. Born in 1865, son of P.H. Calderon. He studied at the Slade School and became founder and Principal of the School of Animal Painting, St. Mary Abbots Place, Kensington, 1894-1916. Calderon worked in London 1883-90 and then in Midhurst, 1889, and finally at Charmouth. Dorset. He was elected ROI in 1891 and married the daughter of H.H. Armstead RA (q.v.).
Illus: *Reynard The Fox [Macmillan's 1895]*.
Contrib: *Black and White [1891]*.
Exhib: B; G; L; M; New Gall; RA; RBA; RHA; ROI.

CALDWELL, Edmund
Animal painter. He worked in Swanley and Guildford, 1887-90 and in Haverstock Hill, London, 1902-25. He contributed to *The Sporting and Dramatic News*.
Illus: *The Encyclopaedia of Sport by the Earl of Suffolk and Berkshire [Hedley Peck and F.G. Afialo, 1897]*.
Exhib: L; M; RA, 1880; RBA, 1881-83; RHA; RI; ROI.

CALKIN, Lance ROI   **1859-1936**
Portrait painter. Born 22 June 1859 and studied at South Kensington, Slade and RA Schools. He painted all the leading Edwardian figures including King Edward VII, Captain Scott and Joseph Chamberlain. He was elected RBA in 1884 and ROI in 1895. He died 10 October 1936.
Contrib: *The Graphic [1887-89 (portraits) and 1901-02 (genre)]*.
Exhib: B; G; L; M; New Gall.; RA; RBA; ROI.
Bibl: *Who Was Who 1929-40*.

CALLAWAY, Rev. William Frederick
Amateur cartoonist. He was a Baptist minister at York and contributed to *Punch*, 1855. He exhibited at the RA, BI, and at other exhibitions 1855-61. He supplied jokes to Charles Keene (q.v.) of *Punch*.
Bibl: Layard, *Life and Letters of CK*, 1893, p.205.

CALLOW, William   **1812-1908**
Watercolourist. He was born at Greenwich in 1812 and his first art employment was in colouring prints for the Fielding brothers. He went

to Paris in 1829 to help in engraving views of the city for a book, remaining there with a group of English artists until 1841. He was intimate with Turner and Bonington and shared a studio with T.S. Boys (q.v.) but his book illustrating is limited to the one work, Charles Heath's *Picturesque Annual: Versailles*, 1839, compiled in the years 1829-36. RWS, 1848. He died at Great Missenden, 20 February, 1908.
Bibl: *Autobiography*, edited by H.M. Cundall, 1908; *Walker's Quarterly*, 1927 XXII; M. Hardie, *Watercolour Paint. in Brit.*, Vol.III, 1968, pp.35-42.

CALOR, Tom
Figure artist. He contributed to *Punch*, 1914.

CALTHROP, Dion Clayton   **1878-1937**
Artist, writer and stage designer. Born on 2 May 1878, son of John Clayton, the actor. Educated at St. Paul's School and studied art at St. John's Wood, Paris, with Julian's and Colarossi's. In early life he did a good deal of commercial work for magazines but then concentrated entirely on illustrating his own books. He served with the RNVR during the First World War and died 7 March 1937.
Illus: *History of English Costume; King Peter; Guide to Fairyland; The Dance of Love; Everybody's Secret; Tinsel and Gold; The Charm of Gardens; Perpetua; St. Quin; A Trap to Catch A Dream; Bread and Butterflies; A Bit of a Time; Beginners Please; All For the Love of A Lady; English Dress*.
Contrib: *The Dome [1897]; The Quartier Latin [1898]; Pick-Me-Up [1899]; The Idler; The Butterfly [1899]; The Connoisseur [1910 (décor)]*.
Exhib: RA; ROI, 1900-03.
Bibl: *Modern Book Illustrators and Their Work*, Studio, 1914 illus; *My Own Trumpet*, 1935 (autobiography); *Who Was Who 1929-40*.

CALVERT, Edith L.   **fl. 1886-1907**
Flower painter and illustrator. Working in London 1893-1907.
Illus: *Baby's Lays [Elkin Mathews, 1897]; More Baby's Lays [Elkin Mathews, 1898]; Sweetbriar [Dorothea Gore, 1905]*.
Contrib: *The Quarto [1898]*.
Exhib: RBA; SWA, 1886-93.
Bibl: R.E.D. Sketchley, *English Book Illus.*, 1903, pp.102, 165.

CALVERT, Frederick   **d.c.1845**
Illustrator and draughtsman from Cork. He was a drawing master and exhibited at the Dublin Society and the Hibernian Society until 1815.
Publ: *Rural Scenery [c.1825 AL 104]; Amateur Draughtsman [1825 AL 105]; Studies of Foreign and English Landscape [1824]; Picturesque Views in Staffordshire and Shropshire [W. West, 1830];*

Pigot's Coloured Views – The Isle of Wight [1847]; The Interior of Tintern Abbey; Lessons in Landscape Colouring.
Contrib: *Archaeological Journal.*
Colls: Ashmolean; Derby; V & AM.

CALVERT, Rev. W MA   **1819-1880**
Pembroke College, Cambridge, 1838; BA, 1842; MA, 1853; Rector of St. Antholin's, London from 1849 and a canon of St. Paul's. He was later vicar of Kentish Town from 1858 to 1880 and died at Ventnor, Isle of Wight that year. Designed decorations and borders for his own *The Wife's Manual*, 1854 in a German gothic style, published by Longman Brown. He also published *Pneuma or the Wandering Soul.*

CAMERON, Sir David Young   RA   **1865-1945**
Painter and etcher. Born at Glasgow in 1865 and was educated at Glasgow Academy and studied at the Glasgow School of Art and at Edinburgh. Cameron was one of the outstanding group of print-makers who rose to fame before the First World War. He excelled in landscape but also did excellent illustrative work and even bookplates; his oils and watercolours are sensitive interpretations of his native Scotland, but the earlier work is purer. He served as War Artist for the Canadian Government, 1917, and in 1919 taught at the British School at Rome. He became ARA, 1911; RA, 1920 and RSA, 1918. He was knighted in 1924.
Illus: *Old Glasgow Exhibition [1894 (title)]; Charterhouse Old and New [1895]; Scholar Gipsies [John Buchan, 1896]; An Elegy and Other Poems [R.L. Stevenson, 1896 (title)]; Story of the Tweed [Sir Herbert Maxwell, 1905]; The Compleat Angler [1902].*
Portfolios: *The Clyde Set [1890]; North Holland [1892]; North Italy [1896]; The London Set [1900]; Paris Etchings [1904]; Etchings in Belgium [1907].*
Contrib: *Good Words [1891-92]; Black and White [1892]; The Ludgate Monthly [1895]; The Quarto [1896]; The Yellow Book [1896 (cover)].*
Exhib: Antwerp; Brussels, 1895; Chicago, 1893; Munich, 1905; NEA; Paris, 1900; RA; RE; ROI.
Colls: BM; V & AM.
Bibl: *The Studio*, Winter No. 1900-01, pp.34-35, illus.; R.E.D. Sketchley, *English Book Illus.*, 1903, pp.41, 64, 133; F. Rinder, *An Illustrated Catalogue of...Etched Work*, 1912; *Modern Book Illustrators and Their Work*, Studio. 1914; *Print Collectors' Quarterly*, Vol.11, No.1, 1924, pp.44-68.

CAMERON, Hugh   RSA RSW   **1835-1918**
Portrait and genre painter. He was born at Edinburgh in 1835 and studied at the Trustees Academy. He worked partly at Edinburgh and partly at Largs, travelling on the Continent. ARSA, 1859 and RSA, 1869; RSW, 1878.
Contrib: *Pen and Pencil Pictures From the Poets [Nimmo, 1866]; Idyllic Pictures [Cassell, 1867]; Good Words.*
Exhib: GG; RA; RBA.

CAMERON, John
Etcher and dry-point artist. He was working at Inverness in 1917 and at Corstorphine, 1918-25. A coloured illustration by this artist for *Treasure Island* is in Witt Photo Library.
Exhib: B; G; L; RHA; RSA.

CAMERON, Katharine (Mrs. Kay)   RSW ARE   1874-1965
Painter and etcher. Born in Glasgow, daughter of the Rev. Robert Cameron and sister of Sir D.Y. Cameron (q.v.). She was educated in Glasgow and studied at Glasgow School of Art and in Paris at Colarossi's. She was a prolific illustrator of children's books, giving full vent to her gift for flower studies, and in 1928 she married Arthur Kay, HRSA. RSW, 1897 and ARE, 1920.
Illus: *In Fairyland [Loucy Chisholm, 1904]; The Enchanted Land [Loucy Chisholm, 1906]; Celtic Tales [Loucy Chisholm, 1910]; Stories of King Arthur's Knights [M. Macgregor, 1905]; Legends & Stories of Italy [Amy Steedman, 1909]; Aucassin & Nicolette [1908]; The Flowers of Love [Philip Thomas, 1916]; In A City Garden [James Aitken, 1913]; Where the Bee Sucks [Iolo Williams, 1929]; Haunting Edinburgh [Fiona Grierson, 1929]; Iain The Happy Puppy [K. Cameron, 1934]; The Water Babies [Kingsley n.d.].*
Contrib: *The Yellow Book*   [1897].
Exhib: Berlin; L; Leipzig; RA; RSA; Venice.
Bibl: H. Wright, 'The Etchings of KC', *International Studio*, 1975.

CAMPBELL, John E.
Illustrator of the boys' story *Wulnoth the Wanderer*, H. Escott Inman, 1908.
Illus: *Brothers and Sisters [Seeley Service c.1910]; The Dog Crusoe [Ballantyne, 1910]; Daring Deeds of Famous Pirates [Keble Chatterton, 1917]; Benjamin Franklin [Seeley Service c.1920]; Barbrook Grubb Path Finder [N. Davidson, 1924].*
Contrib: *Nash's Pall Magazine [c.1920].*

CAMPBELL, John P. (Seaghan MacCathmhaoill)   fl.1904-1912
Illustrator of Celtic legends. He illustrated *Celtic Romances; Irish Songs; The Tain, Four Irish Songs*, all c.1909-1912. His penwork is reminiscent of wood engraving and his figures usually have a strange bending posture as if floating. No biographical details are known.
Colls: Witt Photo.
Bibl: *An Illustrator of Celtic Romance*, The Studio, Vol.48, 1909, pp.37-43; *Modern Book Illustrators and their Work*, Studio, 1914.

CAMPION, George Bryant   NWS   **1796-1870**
Painter, topographical artist and lithographer. He specialised in military subjects and was for some time a drawing master at the Royal Military Academy, Woolwich. He emigrated to Munich where he died in April 1870. NWS, 1834. Wrote *The Adventures of a Chamois Hunter.*
Illus: *Virtue's View in Kent [1830].*
Exhib: NWS; RBA, 1829-31.
Colls: Ashmolean; BM; Witt Photo.

RANDOLPH CALDECOTT RI 'Three Jovial Huntsmen'

CANZIANI, Estella Louisa Michaela RBA   1887-1964
Portrait painter and illustrator. Daughter of the painter Louisa Starr, was born 12 January 1887 and studied with Sir Arthur Cope at Watson Nichol's School and at the RA Schools. RBA, 1930.
Illus: *Round About Three Palace Green [1939]; Costumes Traditions and Songs of Savoy; Piedmont; Through The Appenines and the Lands of the Abruzzi; Songs of Childhood [Walter de la Mare]; Oxford in Brush and Pen; The Lord's Minstrel [C.M.D. Jones, 1927]; Good Adventure [E. Vipont, 1931].*
Exhib: L; New Gall, 1906; RBA; RI, 1913-; RSA; SWA.
Colls: V & AM.

CAPON, William   1757-1827
Topographical artist and architect. He was born at Norwich in 1757, the son of a painter. At a young age he began to paint portraits but, on moving to London, he showed an aptitude for architecture and was apprenticed to Novozielski as scene painter at Ranelagh Gardens and the Italian Opera. Capon acted as scene painter to Kemble at Drury Lane, 1794, and was generally associated with his productions. He was able to establish a small architectural practice and in 1804 was accredited architectural draughtsman to the Duke of York. He died at Westminster in 1827.
Contrib: *Britton's Beauties of England and Wales [1808, 1815].*
Exhib: BI; RA; RBA, 1788-1827.
Colls: Bath; BM; Witt Photo.
Bibl: H.M Colvin, *Biog. Dict. of English Architects*, 1954, p.121; *Views of Westminster by William Capon*, London Topographical Society, 1923-24.

CARAN D'ACHE (Emanuel Poirée)   1858-1909
French caricaturist. Born in Moscow in 1858 and studied there before settling in Paris. He first came to fame as cartoonist on *Chronique Parisienne*, but also with shadow pictures in *Chat Noir*. He was particularly popular for his silhouette caricatures and for his historical jokes; a vogue for both of these caught on in England, largely due to his influence. Caran D'Ache contributed in his fluid outline to *Figaro, L'Illustration, La Revue Illustrée* and drew for his own books, *Comédie du Jour, Comédie de Notre Temps, Les Courses dans L'Antiquité, Carnet de Cheques, The Discovery of Russia.* He played a leading part in the Dreyfus affair and started the magazine *Ps'itt.* Died in Paris in 1909.
Contrib: *The Graphic [1887]; Pick Me Up [1889]; Punch [1894]; English Illustrated Magazine [1896].*
Exhib: FAS, 1898.
Bibl: J. Pennell, *Pen Drawing and Pen Draughtsmen*, 1894, p.112 illus.

CARLILE, Lieutenant W.O.   RA
Contributor to *The Illustrated London News*, 1873.

CARLISLE, The 9th Earl of   See HOWARD, George

CARMICHAEL, John Wilson   1800-1868
Marine painter and illustrator. Born at Newcastle-upon-Tyne in 1800 and went to sea at an early age, later being apprenticed to a shipbuilder and employed in drawing and designing. He was really a water-colourist, but from 1825 experimented with oils and became a regular exhibitor in London. He moved to London in 1845 and was employed by *The Illustrated London News* to make drawings in the Baltic during the Crimean War, 1853-56. He left London in 1862, due to illness and settled at Scarborough where he died on 2 May 1868.
Publ: *The Art of Marine Painting in Watercolours [1859]: The Art of Marine Painting in Oil Colours [1864].*
Contrib: *Views on the Newcastle and Carlisle Railway [1839]; Howitt's Visits to Remarkable Places [1841].*
Colls: BM; Greenwich; Newcastle; V & AM.

CARMICHAEL, Stewart of Dundee   1867-
Portrait painter, decorator and architect. He studied at Dundee, Antwerp, Brussels and Paris, before practising in Dundee. He produced three designs in 1899, 'The Unhappy Queen', 'The Players of the Jews Harp' and 'Disinherited', which show strong Beardsley influence and may have been intended for a book.
Contrib: *The Dome [1900].*
Exhib: G; L; RSA.
Colls: Witt Photo.

CARNEGIE, Rook
Artist for *The Graphic* in Romania, 1910.

CARPENTER, William   1818-1899
Painter and etcher of oriental subjects. He was born in London in 1818, the son of Mrs. M.S. Carpenter, the portrait painter. He spent most of his life in India, sketching the country's manners and customs and an exhibition of these works was held at South Kensington in 1881. He contributed to *The Illustrated London News*, 1857-59, his Indian scenes being among the first reproduced in colour for the magazine.

CARR, David   1847-1920
Figure and bird painter. Born in London, 1847 and was educated at King's College, London. He was articled as a pupil engineer to W.H. Barlow, CE, Consulting Engineer to The Midland Railway, and worked there in civil engineering. He left this career and became an art student for three years at the Slade School under Alphonse Legros, finally going to Paris, 1881. Carr's interests were wide ranging and as well as practising as a painter in Campden Hill, Kensington, 1890-1902, and at Bedford Park, 1902-14, he designed several country houses in the West of England. He died 25 September 1920.
Contrib: *The Pall Mall Gazette; The England Illustrated Magazine [1884-87 (birds and landscapes)].*
Exhib: B; GG; L; M; New Gall; NWS; RA from 1875; RBA from 1875; RI.
Colls: Witt Photo.
Bibl: *Who Was Who, 1916-28.*

CARR, Ellis
Illustrator of *Climbing in the British Isles*, Alan Wright, 1894. He exhibited at the ROI, 1884. He illustrated *Whittington and His Cat – The story of Sir Richard Whittington, Written and Illustrated...*, 1871, in a very linear medieval style.

CARR, Mrs. Geraldine   fl.1896-1916
Sculptor and painter on enamel. She worked in London and supplied a decorative headpiece to *The Quarto*, 1896.
Exhib: L, 1901-16; RA.

CARR, Sir John   1772-1832
Miscellaneous writer, minor poet and illustrator. Carr was a gentleman of private means, who travelled for his health and was knighted in 1806. He was pilloried by Lord Byron in a cancelled passage of *English Bards and Scotch Reviewers*, 1809.
Publ: *The Stranger in France; A Tour From Devonshire to Paris; A Northern Summer [1805]; A Tour Through Holland [1807, AT 216]; Caledonian Sketches [1808].*
Illus: *Descriptive Travels...in...Spain [1811, AT 144].*
Colls: BM.

CARRICK, J. Mulcaster   fl.1854-1878
Painter and illustrator. An extremely interesting minor Pre-Raphaelite who specialised in landscape painting. He illustrated *The Home Affections*, Charles Mackay, 1858, contributing four drawings, and in 1865 designed some for *Legends and Lyrics* by A.A. Proctor. At least one illustration 'An Episode From Life' was turned into an oil painting. Carrick uses great contrasts of light and shade, dappling the backs and clothing of his figures in sunlight, minutely hatching in the shadow.
Exhib: BI, 1854; RBA, 1856; RI.
Colls: Witt Photo.

CARROLL, Lewis see DODGSON, Charles

CARSE, Alexander 'Old Carse'   fl.1796-1838
Scottish genre painter. He was probably born in Edinburgh, where he worked as a young man before going to London in 1812. There he exhibited at the RA and BI, 1812-20, before returning to Scotland for the last twenty years of his life. He designed title pages and vignettes for editions of Burns and Schiller, c.1830.
Colls: BM; Witt Photo.

CARTER, David Broadfoot   fl.1905-1910
Illustrator and designer. He studied at Glasgow School of Art and

GEORGE CATTERMOLE 1800-1868. 'Little Nell's Grave at Tong Church, Staffordshire'. Watercolour heightened with white. 14⅝in x 19⅜in (37.1cm x 49.2cm)
Victoria and Albert Museum

afterwards in Paris, before settling in London as a professional lithographer. He undertook comic illustrations for books in strong pen line.
Exhib: G.
Colls: Witt Photo.

CARTER, Frederick   ARE   1885-1967
Painter and etcher. He was born near Bradford in 1885 and studied in Paris and at the Académie Royale des Beaux-Arts, Antwerp. On his return to England he worked for poster printers, but went back to study at the Polytechnic, and won gold medals for book illustrations. He studied etching under Sir Frank Short (q.v.), ARE, 1910 and 1922.
Illus: *The Wandering Jew; The Dragon of the Alchemists; Eighteen Drawings; The Dragon of Revelation; D.H. Lawrence and The Body Mystical; Symbols of Revelation; Introduction and Drawings for Byron's Manfred; Florentine Nights [Heine]; decorations for Cyril Tourneur's works.*
Contrib: *various magazines about 1916.*
Exhib: L; NEA; RA; RE; ROI.
Colls: Witt Photo.

CARTER, Owen Browne   1806-1859
Topographical draughtsman and architect. He worked mainly at Winchester but travelled to Egypt in about 1829-30.
Publ: *Picturesque Memorials of Winchester [1830]; Some Account of the Church at Bishopstone [1845].*
Illus: *Illustrations of Cairo [Robert Hay, 1840].*
Exhib: RA, 1847-49.
Colls: BM.

CARTER, Reginald Arthur Lay   1886-
Black and white artist contributing humorous illustrations to magazines, c.1910-13.
Colls: V & AM.

CARTER, Rubens Charles   1877-1905
Painter and comic draughtsman. Born at Clifton in 1877 and studied at the Bristol School of Art. He worked for numerous magazines, his cartoons being in the style of Tom Browne (q.v.).
Illus: *Punch [1900]; Pick-Me-Up [1899].*
Contrib: *Punch, [1900-03].*
Colls: BM; Witt Photo.

CARTER, Samuel John   ROI   1835-1892
Animal painter and illustrator. Born at Swaffham, Norfolk in 1835 and studied in Norwich. For many years he was the principal animal illustrator for *The Illustrated London News*, contributing many fine

drawings of cattle, sheep and horse shows all over Britain. ROI, 1883.
Contrib: *ILN [1867-89]; The Graphic [1886].*
Exhib: BI, 1863-66; GG; RA; RBA, 1861-68; ROI.

CARTER, Z.A.
Contributor of 'Edwin and Angelina' social subjects to *Punch*, 1900.

CASELLA, Miss Julia
Sculptor. Contributing illustration to *The Graphic*, 1880, and exhibiting at Grosvenor Gallery, 1885.

CASTAIGNE, A.   fl.1902-1910
Illustrator of royal events and social subjects for *The Graphic*, 1902-03 and 1905-10.

CATCHPOLE, Frederic T.   fl.1897-1940
Landscape and figure painter. Worked in Chelsea and was elected RBA in 1913. He was drawing for *Judy* in 1890.
Contrib: *Pick Me Up [1899].*
Exhib: GG; L; NEA, 1904; RA; RBA, 1914-25; RI.

CATHERWOOD, Frederick   1799-1854
Architect and topographer. He was born in London in 1799 and became a pupil of the architect, Michael Meredith. He travelled in Italy, Greece and Egypt from 1821-25 and again in 1831 up the Nile Valley to record its antiquities. He settled in New York after 1836 and made a celebrated voyage to South America with J.L. Stephens in 1839, the results appearing in *View of Ancient Monuments in Central America, Chiapas and Yucatan*, 1844. Lost on the steamer *Arctic*, 1854.
Exhib: RA, 1820-31.
Bibl: H.M. Colvin, *Biog. Dict. of English Architects*, 1954, p.129.

CATTERMOLE, Charles   1832-1900
Watercolourist. Born in 1832, nephew of George Cattermole (q.v.). He was elected RI, 1870; RBA, 1876 and ROI, 1883. He illustrated a number of books and died 21 August 1900.
Exhib: BI, 1858-93; RBA; RI.

CATTERMOLE, George   1800-1868
Watercolourist and illustrator of romance. He was born at Dickleburgh, Norfolk in 1800, the youngest brother of the Rev. R. Cattermole (q.v.). He worked first as an architectural draughtsman, contributing largely to Britton's *English Cathedrals*, 1832-36. By the 1830s his emphasis was changing from historic buildings to historic incidents in which figures played a more important part than their backgrounds. Cattermole established a vogue for the swash-buckling 17th century where duels and sieges took place in accurate surroundings and alluring watercolours. His drawings were probably due to a mammoth

GEORGE CATTERMOLE 1800-1868. Interior of a castle with figures. Watercolour and body colour. 6½in x 8½in (16.5cm x 21.6cm)
Author's Collection

edition of Scott which he undertook, *Poetical and Prose Works of Sir W. Scott* and *Landscape Illustrations of the Works of Sir W. Scott*, 1833. He had a great sense of history, his costumes were accurate and the figures drawn in with vivid spontaneous pen lines; sometimes individual illustrations were re-drawn as finished watercolours.

Cattermole enjoyed enormous success, especially after illustrating *Barnaby Rudge* and *The Old Curiosity Shop* in Dickens's *Master Humphreys Clock*, 1841. Dickens was an intimate friend, called him 'Kittenmoles' and through him and others, the artist became part of the Kensington Gore set and a Member of the Garrick Club. Although he refused a knighthood in 1839 and was frequently patronised by Queen Victoria, his later life was clouded by unsuccessful attempts to establish himself as an oil painter. AOWS, 1822, and after a lapse, OWS, 1833. He died in London in 1868.
Illus: *Roscoe's North Wales [1836]; Cattermole's Historical Annual: The Great Civil War [R. Cattermole, 1841-45]; Cattermole's Portfolio [1845].*
Contrib: *Heaths Gallery [1836-38].*
Exhib: BI, 1827; OWS; RA, 1819-.
Colls: Ashmolean; BM; Glasgow; Leeds; Manchester; V & AM.
Bibl: OWS Club, IX, 1932; M. Hardie, *Watercol. Paint. in Brit.* Vol.III, 1968, pp.88-91.
See illustrations.

CATTERMOLE, The Rev. Richard   **c.1795-1896**
Topographical artist. The eldest brother of George Cattermole (q.v.), studied under John Britton and drew nine illustrations for *Pyne's Royal Residences*, 1819, and *The Cathedral Antiquities of Great Britain*, 1814-35. He went up to Christ's College, Cambridge and took a BD in 1831, entering holy orders. He was minister of the South Lambeth Chapel from 1844 and Vicar of Little Marlow from 1849. He compiled the *Historical Annual*, illustrated by his brother and wrote *The Book of the Cartoons of Raphael*, 1837. He died at Boulogne-sur-mer, 1858.
Exhib: OWS, 1814-18.

CATTERSON, Albert   **fl.1895-1896**
Illustrator. He specialised in coloured crayon drawings of sentimental subjects in a pretty posterish style. His work appears chiefly in *The Sketch*, 1895-96. He signs his work Bert Catterson.
Colls: V & AM.

CAWSE, John   **1779-1862**
Portrait painter and caricaturist. He published political caricatures with an anti-Foxite bias between 1799 and 1801. He was also a very talented personal caricaturist and the British Museum has a fine one by him of Joseph Witon, RA. Published *The Art of Oil Painting*, 1840.
Exhib: OWS; RA, 1801-45.
Bibl: M.D. George, *English Political Caricature*, 1959, Vol.II, p.261.
Colls: Witt Photo.

CECIONI, Adriano   **1838-1886**
Italian sculptor and caricaturist. He contributed twenty-six cartoons to *Vanity Fair*, 1872.

CHALON, Alfred Edward RA   **1780-1860**
Portrait and history painter, caricaturist. He was born in Geneva in 1780, the son of a Huguenot refugee and the younger brother of J.J. Chalon (q.v.). The family moved to Kensington and the two brothers lived and worked there for the rest of their lives. He studied at the RA Schools, 1797, and began exhibiting at the RA in 1801. After working in Ireland, Chalon established himself as a fashionable painter of beauties and actresses, many of the portraits appearing in the albums of the period. He became Painter in Watercolours to Queen Victoria and it is his portrait of the Queen that appeared on many early issues of Colonial stamps. Chalon was a Member of the Association of Artists in Watercolours, 1807-08, and founded The Sketching Society in 1808. His caricatures in brown wash were done for private circulation only. He was elected ARA in 1812 and RA, 1816. He died at Campden Hill, Kensington, 3 October 1860 and was buried at Highgate.
Illus: *Gallery of Graces [1832-34]; Portraits of Children of the Nobility [L. Fairlie, 1838]; The Belle of a Season [M. Gardiner, 1840]; A Memoir of Thomas Uwins [S. Uwins, 1858].*
Contrib: *Heath's Gallery [1836, 1838]; The Chaplet [1840]; ILN [1843].*
Exhib: BI, 1807-38; RA, 1810-60.
Colls: Ashmolean; BM; Leeds; NPG; Nottingham; V & AM; Witt Photo.
Bibl: *Art Journal*, January, 1862; M. Hardie, *Watercol. Paint in Brit.*, Vol.II, 1967, p.149.

CHALON, John James   **RA OWS**   **1778-1854**
Landscape painter, genre painter and caricaturist. He was born in Geneva in 1778, the son of a Huguenot refugee and came to England with his family and younger brother A.E. Chalon (q.v.). He studied at the RA Schools, 1796, after giving up a commercial career and exhibited there from 1800. He travelled widely in the south and west of England making sketches and, after a visit to Paris in 1819-20, published a set of lithographs of the city, 1822. Associate of the OWS, 1805, and Member, 1807. He was elected ARA in 1827 and RA, 1841. Like his brother he practised caricature and had more success with it in a spirited and free style of wash. The Laing Art Gallery, Newcastle has a more conventional series of classical book illustrations in sepia, showing the influence of The Sketching Society which he helped to found in 1808. He died at Campden Hill, Kensington, 14 November 1854, and was buried at Highgate.
Illus: *Scenes in Paris [1820-22, AT 108].*
Exhib: BI, 1808-43; OWS; RA, 1800-54.
Colls: BM; Maidstone; Newcastle; V & AM.
Bibl: *Art Journal*, January, 1855; M. Hardie, *Watercol. Paint. in Brit.*, Vol.II, 1967, pp.149-150.

'CHAM' Comte Amédée Charles Henri De Noé   **1819-1879**
French draughtsman and caricaturist. He was born in Paris on 26 January 1819, and was intended to study at the École Polytechnique. After several failures, he turned his talent for drawing into a career and began work under the caricaturist Charlet and with Paul Delaroche. He quickly became one of the leading lithographic caricaturists and published his first series in 1839. A friend of W.M. Thackeray, Cham was persuaded to complete some blocks overnight for Mark Lemon and these appeared in *Punch* in 1859. He died in September 1879.

CHAMBERLAIN, D.   **fl.1887-1914**
Watercolourist and illustrator. Working in Glasgow from 1887 to 1914 and exhibiting there and at the RSW. This artist drew in the late *art nouveau* style of the Glasgow School and won the chapter heading competition in *The Studio*, Vol.12, 1898, illus.

CHAPMAN, C.H.   **1879-1969?**
Comic illustrator. He was the principal illustrator of the 'Billy Bunter' stories from 1912 when he first met their author, Frank Richards. He was the first artist to give all the Greyfriars boys a distinctive character in the pen drawings, working closely to Richards' texts, but choosing

his own subjects. He lived near Reading and died at the age of ninety.
Bibl: W.O. Lofts and D.J. Adley, *The World of Frank Richards*, 1975.
See Horne.

CHAPMAN, Captain E.F.
Amateur illustrator. He travelled to Asia on the Yakund Expedition, 1874, and his sketches appeared in *The Illustrated London News*.

CHAPMAN, George R.   **fl.1863-1890**
Portrait painter who did some illustrations. He exhibited at the RA, 1863-74, and illustrated his own *The Epic of Hades*, c.1890. He also published a book *Songs of Two Worlds*.
Colls: Witt Photo.

CHARLES, William   **-1830**
A caricaturist who worked in England, 1803-04, and drew anti-British satires during the Anglo-American War of 1812. He died in Philadelphia in 1820.
Bibl: M.D. George, *English Political Caricature*, Vol.II, 1959, p.261.

CHARLTON, C. Hedley
Illustrator. He contributed drawings of children in a poster style to *Punch*, 1908.

CHARLTON, Edward William RE   **1859-1925**
Landscape painter. Working at Ringwood, Hants., 1890-99 and at Lymington, Hants., 1899-1925. ARE, 1892 and RE, 1907.
Contrib: *English Illustrated Magazine [1891-02].*
Exhib: L; RA; RE; ROI; RWA.
Bibl: *The Studio*, Winter No. 1900-01, pp.56-57 illus.

CHARLTON, Miss Gertrude
Portrait painter and illustrator of children's books. She worked in Chelsea, 1899-1902, and illustrated her own *Excellent Jane*, 1899. She exhibited at the NEA, 1901.

CHARLTON, John   **1849-1917**
Animal and battle painter and illustrator. He was born at Bamburgh, Northumberland in 1849 and after working in a bookshop, studied at the Newcastle School of Art under W.B. Scott (q.v.). He then went to South Kensington and worked for some time under J.D. Watson (q.v.), thereby forming an important link beween the 1860s illustrators and those of the 1890s. He was at his best when drawing scenes from high life, particularly hunting subjects and royal occasions. He settled permanently in London in 1874 and his connection with *The Graphic* dates from two years later. His work for the magazine on the Egyptian Campaign of 1882 turned his attention to battle scenes, and he became one of the leading exponents of military paintings. He died in London, 5 November 1917. RBA, 1882 and ROI, 1887.
Illus: *Twelve Packs of Hounds [1891]; Red Deer [H.A. Macpherson, 1896].*
Contrib: *The Graphic [1876-95].*
Exhib: B; G; L; M; New Gall.; RA; RBA, 1871- ; ROI; RSA.
Colls: Newcastle, V & AM; Witt Photo.

CHARTRAN, Théobald   **1849-1907**
Portrait painter. He was born at Besançon in 1849 and had a distinguished career painting state portraits and elaborate mural schemes. He exhibited regularly in Paris from 1872 and at the RA from 1881. He contributed several cartoons to *Vanity Fair*, 1878-88.

CHASE, Phyllis
This artist made jacket designs for Enid Blyton's early book *Child Whispers*, 1922.
Contrib: *English Illustrated Magazine [1896-97].*

CHASEMORE, Archibald   **fl.1868-1901**
A regular cartoonist for *Judy*, 1875-89. He was a contributor to *Punch* 1868-79, and supplied jokes for his friend Charles Keene (q.v.) to draw. His own work was in very finished pen and ink but tending to be rather stiff. His political subjects are amusing and

collectable. Contributed to *Pick-Me-Up*, 1901; *Ally Sloper's Half Holiday; The Boys' Own Paper*.
Contrib: *Judy's Annual [1885]; Pictorial World.*

CHATTERTON, Henrietta Georgina Marcia, Lady   1806-1876
Writer and artist. She married in 1824 Sir William Abraham Chatterton of County Cork, but lived in England from 1852. On his death she married Edward Heneage Dering in 1859. She published poems and travels, 1837-76.
Illus: *The Pyrenees with Excursions into Spain [1843, AT 211].*

CHEESEMAN, Thomas Gedge   **fl.1890-1925**
Painter of domestic subjects. He worked at Highbury, 1890, and at Battersea, 1908-25. Exhibiting at the RA, 1890-91 and ROI. He contributed to *The Cornhill Magazine*, 1885.

CHÉRET, Jules   **1836-1933**
Illustrator and designer of posters. He was born in Paris on 31 May 1836 and after working for a printer in France, he was apprenticed in 1856 to a lithographer in England, specialising in colour work. He remained in England until 1866, when he returned to France to found his own colour lithographic works. He adapted Japanese form and line to his art and was the first person to present Sarah Bernhardt in his celebrated poster 'La Biche Au Bois' in 1867. He became a key figure in the birth of pictorial advertising and was a major exhibitor at the Paris Exhibition of 1900. He became blind in later life and died at Nice in 1933. In 1867 Chéret produced a series of valentines entitled 'Animated Flowers' which were produced by Rimmell. They were published in *Nature and Art*, 1867.
Lit: Davray, Henry, *XIXth Century French Posters*, 1944.
Contrib: *Nature and Art [1867].*

CHESTERTON, Gilbert Keith   **1874-1936**
Author, novelist and critic. He was born at Campden Hill in 1874 and studied at the Slade School. Before he established himself as a novelist, Chesterton reviewed art books for *The Bookman*. He was a competent amateur artist and his chalks of humorous subjects have considerable charm.
Colls: Witt Photo.
Bibl: Maisie Ward, *GKC*, 1944; D. Baker, *GKC A Biography*, 1973; J. Sullivan, *GKC 1874-1974*, N. Book League, 1974.

CHESWORTH, Frank
Prolific illustrator in the 1890s.
Contrib: *The Sketch [1894]; The New Budget [1895]; The Sporting and Dramatic News [1895]; Pick-Me-Up [1896]; Illustrated Bits; The Pall Mall Magazine.*

CHINNER, J.A.
Amateur illustrator. He contributed to *Punch*, 1908.

CHRISTIAN, W.F.D.
Illustrator contributing to *The Cambridge Portfolio*, 1840.

CHRISTIE, James Elder   **1847-1914**
Figure and portrait painter. He studied at Paisley School of Art and South Kensington. Visited Paris and worked in London, 1880-94, and at Glasgow, 1894-1914. He became a Member of the NEA in 1887.
Illus: *Susy [Bret Harte, 1897].*
Exhib: B; G; GG; L; M; NEA; New Gall.; RA; RSA.

CLARK, A.H.
He drew the designs for *Illustrations of Don Quixote*, 1819.

CLARK, Christopher   **1875-**
Painter of military subjects and illustrator. He was born 1 March 1875 and was self-taught. He drew frequently for magazines from c.1900 and was also a poster artist. He served in the RNVR, 1917-19. RI, 1905.
Illus: *Lorna Doone [R.D. Blackmore, 1912]; Tales of the Great War [Sir H. Newbolt, 1916].*
Exhib: L; RA; RI.
Colls: Witt Photo.

JOSEPH BENWELL CLARK b.1857. Illustration to *The Surprising Adventures of Baron Munchausen*, 1895. Ink and chinese white. Signed with initials and dated 1894. 6in x 5in (15.2cm x 12.7cm)

Victoria and Albert Museum

CLARK, John Heaviside 'Waterloo Clark'   **c.1771-1863**
Landscape painter and book illustrator. He worked in London between 1802 and 1832, but died in Edinburgh in 1863. He earned his nickname from the series of sketches that he undertook immediately after the Battle of Waterloo.
Illus: *Foreign Field Sports [1814, AT 2].*
Publ: *Practical Essay On The Art of Colouring and Painting Landscapes [1807]; Practical Illustrations of Gilpin's Day [1814].*
Exhib: RA, 1801-32.
Colls: Glasgow.

CLARK, Joseph   **1834-1926**
Painter and illustrator. He was born at Cerne Abbas in Dorset in 1834 and was educated there by the Rev. William Barnes. He studied art at Leigh's School and was a student at the RA Schools. Two of his pictures were bought by the Chantrey Bequest and many were engraved. He died at Ramsgate 4 July 1926.
Contrib: *Passages From Modern English Poets [1862].*
Exhib: NWS; RA, 1857-1925; RBA, RI.
Colls: Tate.
Bibl: *Who Was Who, 1916-28.*

CLARK, Joseph Benwell   **1857-**
Painter, draughtsman and illustrator. He was the nephew of Joseph Clark (q.v.) and specialised in interiors and animal painting. He was a pupil of Alphonse Legros and although much of his output is unremarkable, he was responsible for a handful of exceptional book illustrations in the 1890s. In 1895, he drew the pictures for a Lawrence and Bullen edition of *The Surprising Adventures of Baron Munchausen*, pen and ink work in a bold and woodcutty style, very advanced and imaginative. The publishers clearly thought highly of his

work, for he is one of the supporting illustrators in *Lucian's True History*, 1894, where Beardsley was the star. He worked for most of his life in North London, sometimes in conjunction with V.M. Hamilton.
Illus: *Ali-Baba [1896]; Sinbad the Sailor [1896].*
Contrib: *Judy [1889-90 (strip cartoons)]; ILN, [1891].*
Exhib: GG; RA; RBA, 1876-91.
Colls: V & AM.
See illustration.

CLARKE, Albert T.   **fl.1889-1891**
Illustrator of figure subjects, working in The Vale, Chelsea.
Contrib: *Pick Me Up, 1889.*
Exhib: RI.

CLARKE, Arthur   **-c.1912**
One of the original illustrators of 'Billy Bunter'. He succeeded Hutton Mitchell (q.v.), as artist on *The Magnet* and died about 1912. He also worked for *The Gem*.
Bibl: W.O. Lofts and D.J. Adley, *The World of Frank Richards*, 1975.

CLARKE, Edward Francis C.   **fl.1867-1887**
Painter, architect and illustrator. He practised in London and exhibited there 1872-1887.
Contrib: *The Churchman's Shilling Magazine [1867]: Dark Blue [1871-73].*
Exhib: L; NWS; RBA, 1882-84; RI; RSA.

CLARKE, Harry   **1890-1931**
Illustrator and decorative artist. Born in Dublin in 1890 and was apprenticed to his father, head of a large firm of stained glass artists in 1906. Attended the Dublin Metropolitan School of Art, 1910-13, and was awarded three gold medals and one which took him to the Île-de-France. On his return he set up an independent stained glass workshop in Dublin and carried out a great deal of work in Ireland, England and abroad. As a book illustrator. he was one of the most successful followers of Beardsley, capturing a great deal of the latter's sinister atmosphere, although his finish was less polished. He died of tuberculosis in Switzerland in 1931. RHA, 1915.
Illus: *Fairy Tales [Hans Christian Andersen 1916]; Tales of Mystery and Imagination [Edgar Alan Poe, 1919]; The Years at The Spring [Lettice D'O Walters, 1920]; The Fairy Tales of Charles Perrault [1922]; Faust [Goethe, 1925]; Selected Poems [A.C Swinburne, 1928] The Playboy of the Western World [J.M. Synge].*
Exhib: RHA; St. George's Gall.
Colls: V & AM; Witt Photo.
Bibl: *Modern Book Illustrators and their Work*, Studio. 1914; B. Peppin, *Fantasy Book Illustration*, 1975, pp.21-22, 186 illus.; cat. of exhibition 'HC', Douglas Hyde Gallery, Trinity College, Dublin, 1979; Bowe, N.G., 'The Miniature Stained Glass Panels of HC', *Apollo*, Feb. 1982, pp.111-113; N.G. Bowe, *HC*, 1983; *The Last Romantics*, cat. of Barbican Gall. exhibition, 1989, p.180.
See Horne.
See illustration.

CLARKE, Joseph Clayton   'Kyd'   **1856/7-1937**
Illustrator, designer of postcards, cigarette cards and fore-edge painter, specialising principally in Dickens's characters. He was born in 1856/7 and is thought to have spent his childhood in Birmingham. Worked for *Punch* for one day! Worked as a freelance artist till 1900 and a fore-edge painter after 1912. He was an eccentric and profligate man and died at Hampstead, 8 August 1937.
Illus: *The Characters of Charles Dickens [1889]; Some Well Known Characters from the Works of Dickens [Raphael Tuck, 1892].*
Contrib: *Fleet Street Magazine [1887]; Fun [1890-92]; The Star.*
Exhib: Sawyer Gallery, 9-30 April 1980.
Colls: Witt Photo.
Bibl: Sawyer, Chas J., *'Kyd' Joseph Clayton Clarke, A Preliminary Study of His Life and Work*, 1980.

CLARKE, Miss Maud V.
Horse painter. Contributor to *English Illustrated Magazine*, 1887, *The Illustrated London News*, 1889, and *The Sporting and Dramatic News*, 1890.

CLARKE-HALL, Edna, Lady   **1879-1979**
She was born on 29 June 1879 and entered the Slade School by 1895, becoming a close friend of Augustus John, McEvoy, Orpen, Rutherston and Matthew Smith. She married Sir William Clarke-Hall in 1899 and moved to a farmhouse at Upminster, Essex for the rest of her life. She prepared a large number of drawings to illustrate *Wuthering Heights*, but it appears that they were never used. A retrospective exhibition was held at the Tate Gallery in August, 1979.
Exhib: G; NEA.
Bibl: 'Drawings and Memories', Christopher Neve, *Country Life*, 2 Aug. 1979.

CLAUSEN, Sir George   **RA RWS**   **1852-1944**
Landscape painter and painter of rural life. He was born in London in 1852, the son of a Danish sculptor and was much influenced by continental art and the French School in particular. Member of the NEA, 1888; he was elected ARA in 1895 and RA in 1908, having exhibited there since 1876. Clausen was Professor of Painting at the RA, 1903-06, and Director of the Schools. He was knighted in 1927. RWS, 1898. He provided a single illustration for *The Quarto*, 1897.
Exhib: L; M; RA; RWS.
Colls: Bedford; BM; Fitzwilliam; Manchester; V & AM.

CLAXTON, Adelaide (Mrs. George Turner)   **fl.1858-c.1905**
Illustrator. The younger daughter of Marshall C. Claxton (q.v.), who was the first artist to take an exhibition of pictures to Australia. She accompanied her father there and afterwards to Ceylon, and India, 1860. Vizetelly says she 'satirized the social follies' and her pictures had great popularity, but the drawing was often very stiff and the proportions of the figures poor.
Illus: *A Shillingsworth of Sugar Plums [1867]; Brainy Odds & Ends [1900]*.
Contrib: *ILN [1858]; The Illustrated Times [1859-66]; London Society [1862-65, 1870]; Judy [1871-79]; Sidelights on English Society [Grenville Murray, 1881]*.
Exhib: RA; RBA, 1865-76; SWA, 1880-89.
Colls: V & AM.

CLAXTON, Florence A. (Mrs. Farrington)   **fl.1855-1879**
Illustrator. She was the eldest daughter of Marshall C. Claxton (q.v.), and sister of Adelaide Claxton (q.v.). Accompanied her father to Australia, Ceylon and India and made sketches of the last two countries which were later published. She was a more serious artist than her sister and specialised in historical drawings and the illustration of romantic stories rather than purely humorous subjects. Her work is, however, often poor in composition and coarse in execution.
Publ: *The Adventures of a Woman in Search of Her Rights [c.1865 (oblong octavo)]*.
Contrib: *The Illustrated Times [1855-67]; ILN [1860]; London Society [1862]; The Churchman's Family Magazine [1863]; Good Words [1864]*.
Exhib: RA; RBA, 1865-73; SWA, 1896.
Colls: V & AM.

CLAXTON, Marshall C.   **1811-1881**
Historical painter and illustrator. He was born at Bolton in 1811 and was a pupil of John Jackson RA. He entered the RA Schools in 1831, won a medal in the Painting School, 1832, and a Society of Arts Gold Medal in 1835. He travelled to Australia in the 1850s with the idea of starting an art school and exhibiting pictures, the first man to do so. He returned through Ceylon and India and made sketches of life and scenery there. He signs his work
Contrib: *ILN [1852-58]; The Illustrated Times [1859]; The Churchman's Family Magazine [1863]*.
Exhib: BI, 1833-67; RA; RBA, 1832-75.
Colls: V & AM (Designs for an edition of *Pilgrim's Progress*).

CLAYTON, Benjamin
Illustrator of military scenes. Contributed to *The Illustrated Times*, 1856-60.

CLAYTON, Eleanor 'Ellen' Creathorne   **c.1846-**
Novelist and illustrator. She was born in Dublin and after studying at

HARRY CLARKE 1890-1931. Tailpiece for Goethe's *Faust*, G.G. Harrap, 1925, limited edition

the British Museum began to contribute humorous drawings to magazines. She undertook the designing of calendars, valentines, etc. in the 1870s.
Illus: *Miss Milly Moss [1862]*.

CLAYTON, John R.
Wood engraver and draughtsman, specialising in figure subjects. He was a High Victorian artist whose greatest claim to fame is that he was consulted by D.G. Rossetti (q.v.) about the wood engravings for the *Moxon, Tennyson*, 1857.
Contrib: *Ernest Maltravers [Lytton, 1851 (frontis.)]; Alice [Lytton, 1852 (frontis.)]; George Herbert's Poetical Works [1856]; Pilgrim's Progress [1856]; Course of Time [1857]; Poets of the Nineteenth Century [1857]; Dramatic Scenes and Other Poems [1857]; Lays of the Holy Land [1858]; The Home Affections [1858]; Krummacher's Parables [1858]; Architectural Sketches From the Continent [R. Norman Shaw 1858 (border of frontis.)]; English Poets Illustrated by the Junior Etching Club [1862]; Barry Cornwall's Poems*.
Colls: V & AM; Witt Photo.
Bibl: Chatto & Jackson, *Treatise on Wood Engraving* 1861, p.599; Forrest Reid, *Illustrators of the Sixties*, 1928, pp.32-36.

CLEAVER, Dudley
Contributor to *The Penny Illustrated Paper*, c.1890.

CLEAVER, F.R.
Illustrator of genre subjects for *The Illustrated London News*, 1889.

CLEAVER, Ralph   **fl.1893-1926**
Black and white artist. He was employed on many illustrated papers in the 1890s but regularly on *The Graphic* and *Daily Graphic* from 1906. He served in the RNVR throughout the First World War. Cleaver specialised in naval and military subjects, but also drew theatrical performances and cartoons. He enlivened his straight magazine reportage by introducing comic elements, and his drawing is always clear.
Illus: *Mating of Clopinda [James Bank, 1909]*.
Contrib: *Judy [1893]; ILN [1895-1901]; The St. James's Budget; The Gentlewoman; Penny Illustrated Paper; The Temple Magazine; The Royal Magazine; Punch [1900]*.
Colls: V & AM.
Bibl: *The Studio*, Winter No, 1900-01, p.84 illus.

CLEAVER, Reginald Thomas   **-1954**
Black and white artist. He was employed on *The Graphic* staff from about 1893 and worked for that paper and *The Daily Graphic* until

REGINALD THOMAS CLEAVER d.1954. Study of a seated woman for an illustration in *Punch*, c.1900. Pencil and grey wash. 9½in x 6¾in (24.1cm x 17.1cm)　　　Author's Collection

1910. Spielmann calls his drawing 'somewhat hard but of great beauty in its own line', but this hardness wore off to make Cleaver, according to Thorp, the most important *Graphic* artist of the Edwardian era. His studies for drawings, where washes are subtly added to sensitive pencil lines, are among the most beautiful of their type. Cleaver was a marvellous portrayer of women and of the social scene as numerous *Punch* cuts testify.
Contrib: *The Graphic* [1893-1910]; *Punch* [1894-1930].
Colls: Author; V & AM.
Bibl: Spielmann, *The History of 'Punch'*, 1895, pp.9l. 565; J. Pennell, *Pen Drawing and Pen Draughtsmen*, 1894, pp.330-331: J. Pennell, *Modern Illustration*, 1895, p.106; *The Studio,* Winter No., 1900-01 p.84 illus.; *Mr. Punch With Horse and Hound*, New Punch Library, c. 1930, p.115.
See illustration.

CLEGG, Ada
Book decorator. Contributing to *The English Illustrated Magazine*, 1896-97.

CLEGHORN, John　　　　　　　　　　　　**fl. 1840-1880**
Painter of landscapes, wood carver and sculptor. He exhibited in London from 1840-80.
Contrib: *Winkle's Illustrations to the Cathedral Churches* [1836-37]; *Knight's London* [1842].

CLENNELL, Luke　　　　　　　　　　　　**1781-1840**
Wood engraver, illustrator and watercolourist. He was born at Ugham, near Morpeth, on 8 April 1781, the son of a farmer. Although started in trade, Clennell was apprenticed in 1797 to Thomas Bewick (q.v.), and became one of his best pupils. He left

Newcastle in 1804 and on becoming a wood engraver in London, was awarded the golden palette of the Society of Arts in 1806 and 1809. Chatto records that, 'Clennell who drew beautifully in watercolours, made many of the drawings for the Border Antiquities; and the encouragement that he received as a designer and painter made him resolve to entirely abandon wood engraving.' He became an Associate of the OWS in 1812 and won the 150 guinea premium offered by the BI for the best sketch of 'The Decisive Charge of the Life Guards at Waterloo'; it was published in 1821. In April 1817 he became insane and, although he continued to make small sketches and write poems, his professional career was at an end. Clennell died in Newcastle Lunatic Asylum, 9 February 1840.

Clennell brought to book illustration some of the freedom which was associated with the Bewick School and the naturalness of head and tailpieces which characterised it. Good examples are his engravings after Stothard in *Poems by Samuel Rogers*, 1814. He designed some bookplates and in surviving designs looks backwards to French illustration and forwards to the insouciant charm of Kate Greenaway.
Contrib: *La Belle Assemblée or Fashionable Companion* [1805-06]; *Ackermann's Religious Emblems* [1809]; *Britton's Beauties of England and Wales* [1814]; *Border Antiquities of England and Scotland* [1814-17]; *The Antiquarian Itinerary* [1818].
Exhib: OWS, RA.
Colls: BM; Greenwich; Newcastle; V & AM.
Bibl: Chatto & Jackson, *Treatise on Wood Engraving*, 1861 pp.521-527.
See illustration.

CLIFFORD, Harry P.　　RBA　　　　　　fl.1895-1938
Black and white artist, specialising in architectural subjects. He worked in Kensington, 1902-25, and exhibited at many exhibitions. RBA, 1898.
Exhib: B; L; RA; RBA; RI.
Bibl: *The Studio*, Winter No., 1900-01, p.68, illus.

CLIFFORD, Maurice
Figure artist. Working in Bedford Park, London and winner of *The Studio* tailpiece competition Vol.12, 1897-98, illus.
Exhib: L; M; RA; ROI, 1890-95.

CLINT, George　　ARA　　　　　　　　　1770-1854
Portrait painter and engraver. He was born in London in 1770 and after working as a decorator and a miniature painter, he began to paint personalities from the London stage. He was an ARA from 1821 to 1836.
Contrib: *The British Theatrical Gallery* [1825 AL 418].
Exhib: BI; OWS; RA; RBA.
Colls: BM.

CLUTTON, Henry　　　　　　　　　　　　**1819-1893**
Architect. He was a pupil of Edward Blore and a friend of William Burges (q.v.). With Burges he won the first place in the Lille Cathedral Competition, and in the course of a long career designed many schools, houses and churches.
Illus: *Remarks...On The Domestic Architecture of France* [1853 (tinted liths.) AT 100].

COBB, Ruth
Figure artist. She contributed to *Punch*, 1914.

COCK, Eianley
Perhaps E.C. Loveland Cock, recorded in *The Years Art*, 1909-30. He contributed a cartoon to *Vanity Fair*, 1913.
Bibl: Roy T. Matthews and Peter Mellini, *In Vanity Fair*, 1982.

COCKERELL, Charles Robert　RA　　　　1788-1863
Architect, draughtsman and etcher. He was the son of Samuel Pepys Cockerell, the architect, and was educated at Westminster. After studying with his father, he went on a prolonged tour of Greece, Asia Minor and Sicily, 1810-17, discovering the frieze of the Temple of Apollo at Phigaleia, 181l. He was the leading exponent of Victorian classical architecture, designing the Taylor Buildings at Oxford, 1841-52. RA, 1836; Professor of Architecture at RA, 1840-57.

LUKE CLENNELL 1781-1840. Fashion illustration for *La Belle Assemblée*, c.1905-06. Watercolour

Victoria and Albert Museum

Publ: *The Antiquities of Athens etc. [1830]; The Temple of Jupiter Olympus at Agrigentum [1830]; The Iconography of the West Front of Wells Cathedral [1851]; The Temples of Jupiter Panhellenus etc. [1860].*
Illus: *Ancient Marbles in the British Museum [1820-30 (frontis.)]; Travels in Sicily, Greece and Albania [Rev. T.S. Hughes, 1820, AT 203].*
Exhib: RA, 1818-58.
Colls: BM, RIBA, V & AM.
Bibl: A.E. Richardson, *Monumental Classic Architecture in Great Britain and Ireland*, 1914; David Watkin, *CRC*, 1975.

COHEN, Ellen Gertrude   fl.1884-1905
Figure painter and illustrator. She worked in London and contributed to *The English Illustrated Magazine*, 1890-94.
Exhib: B; L; M; P; RA; RBA; RI; ROI; SWA.

COÏDÉ   See TISSOT, J.J.

COKE, Thomas William   Earl of Leicester   1752-1842
'Mr. Coke of Holkam', created 1st Earl of Leicester, 1837. He was a talented caricaturist in the style of Ghezzi, but his drawings were only for private circulation.
Colls: Windsor.

COLE, C.W.   fl. 1884-1905
Humorous artist. He contributed comic genre subjects to *The Graphic*, 1884-85, and collaborated with C.J. Staniland (q.v.) in views of Japan in the same magazine, 1887.

COLE, Herbert   1867-1930
Draughtsman, illustrator and engraver, designer of bookplates. He was the son of a teacher and born in the West Country in 1867, although the family moved shortly afterwards to Manchester. He attended the Manchester School of Art from 1887 and worked as an illustrator from 1898, but was always subject to poor health. He was living at Walthamstow in 1900 and at Peckham by 1901, where he taught costume illustration at the Camberwell School of Art. He was strongly influenced by the Pre-Raphaelites, as is evident from his books for John Lane and Dent around 1900. In 1905 he moved to Eynsford, Kent and in 1908 to Kemsing. Cole's heyday was in the years before 1914 when there was still a place for romantically illustrated fiction and legend. He was capable of either an imaginative and flamboyant *art nouveau* style or comic illustrations in the manner of Charles Keene (q.v.). Cole combined a fluid pen style with sensuous colouring and his work was always inventive, if it lacks the dramatic force of a Rackham or a Harry Clarke. His work was admired by E.J. Sullivan and the artist was a close friend of the poet Richard Church. In 1924, Cole and his wife left for Australia to join thir son and daughter-in-law, but on his return in 1931, Cole died on 12 September that year. His son, Philip Cole, was also an illustrator.
Illus: *Trivia and Other Poems [J. Gay, 1899]; Women Love and Flowers [Herrick, 1899]; Gulliver's Travels [Swift, 1900]; Shakespeare's Sonnets [1900]; The Rime of the Ancient Mariner [Coleridge, 1900]; An Elizabethan Garland [1900]; Wit and Humour [Hazlitt, 1901]; Persian Love Songs [1901]; Leaves from the Diary of Samuel Pepys [1901]; The Nut Brown Maid [1901]; Christmas at the Mermaid [1901]; A Ballad on a Wedding [1901]; Caleb Williams [W. Godwin, 1904]; The Rubaiyat of Omar Khayyam [1905]; Songs and Lyrics from the Dramatists [1905, title and frontis.]; Fairy Gold [E. Rhys, 1906, 1911, 1913, 1927]; The Dragon Volant [Le Fanu, 1907]; Sonnets From the Portuguese [Browning, 1907-08]; The Village of Eynsford [1908]; Froissart's Chronicles [1908-09]; The Heart of England [E. Thomas, 1909]; The Story of Bayard [C. Hare, 1911]; The Sunset of the Heroes [W.M.L. Hutchinson, 1911 & 1926]; The Book of Simple Delights [Raymond, 1912]; A Child's Book of Warriors [W. Canton, 1912]; An Introduction to the Period Styles of England and France [H. Cole, 1918]; The Song of Hiawatha [1921, port]; The De Coverley Papers [1920]; Black Beauty [1920, port]; Stories from Hakluyt [1921, port]; The Canterbury Pilgrims [1923, port]; The Rise of the Romantic School in France [n.d.].*
Contrib: *The Pall Mall Magazine [1898]; Fun [1901].*
Exhib: RA, 1898 and 1900.
Colls: V & AM; Witt Photo.

Such was the dirge the violet-crowned Muses sang over the son of Thetis

HERBERT COLE 1867-1930. 'Sunset of the Heroes'. An illustration for a book published by W.M.L. Hutchinson in 1911. Pen and ink with watercolour. 12⅛in x 8⅜in (30.8cm x 21.3cm)

Victoria and Albert Museum

Bibl: R.E.D. Sketchley, *English Book Illustration*, 1903, pp.13-14, 122; J.P. Cole, *A Brief Survey of the Life and The Work of the Artist HC*, privately printed, July 1985.
See illustration.

COLEMAN, Edmund Thomas   **fl.1839-1877**
Landscape painter and topographer. He specialised in alpine scenery.
Illus: *Sketches on the Danube [1838 AT 79]; Scenes From The Snow Fields [1859 AT 68].*
Exhib: BI, 1852-59; RA; RBA, 1850-1877.

COLEMAN, William Stephen   **1829-1904**
Landscape and figure painter and illustrator. He was born at Horsham, Sussex in 1829, the son of a physician. He was a keen naturalist and this led him to the arts and the illustration of books. He illustrated the Rev. J.G. Wood's natural history books and worked in oil, pastel and etching. His landscapes are idealised and romantic although his scientific work is accurate. In later life he became associated with Minton's Art Pottery Studio for which he designed. He was on the committee of the Dudley Gallery until 1881 and died on 22 March 1904 at St. John's Wood.
Illus: *Our Woodlands, Heaths and Hedges [1859]; British Butterflies [1860].*
Contrib: *The Illustrated Times [1856]; ILN [1857] The Book of The Thames [S.C. Hall, 1859]; The Book of South Wales [Mr. and Mrs. S.C. Hall, 1861]; Mary Howitt's Tales; The Field.*
Exhib: 1866-79; RBA, 1875.
Colls: Blackpool; Glasgow; V & AM; Witt Photo.

COLEMAN-SMITH, Pamela   **fl.1899-1917**
Painter and illustrator of children's books. She was working at

Knightsbridge, London, 1907 and exhibited at the SWA and the Baillie Gallery, 1905-17. She illustrated *Widdicombe Fair* in a limited edition, 1899, the drawings done in stumpy black outline in the style of the Beggarstaff Brothers. She edited and published the Anglo-Irish periodical *The Green Sheaf* 1903-04 (13 nos.) with hand coloured illustrations and work by Gordon Craig, A.E., Cecil French and Jack B. Yeats (q.v.).

COLES, E.
Contributor to *Fun*, 1900.

COLLIER, The Hon. John   **1850-1934**
Figure, portrait and landscape painter. He was born in London, 27 January 1850, son of 1st Baron Monkswell. He was educated at Eton and the Slade School and then under E.J. Poynter (q.v.), and J.P. Laurens, Paris. He married successively two of the daughters of T.H. Huxley.

Although a very popular artist in the grand manner, Collier was a rare illustrator and reveals himself to be a weak pen artist. He illustrated Thomas Hardy's 'The Trumpet Major' for *Good Words* in 1880, which was not successful and in 1894 tackled *Thackeray's Ballads* in the Cheap Illustrated Edition, *English Illustrated Magazine*, 1890-91. He published various manuals on oil painting. Died 11 April 1934.
Exhib: GG; RA; RBA.
Colls: Blackburn; Sydney; V & AM.
Bibl: E.C.F. Collier, *A Victorian Diarist, Monkswell. 1873-95*, 1944.

COLLINGS, Arthur Henry   **-1947**
Portrait and figure painter. He worked in North London, 1902-25, and won a gold medal at Paris Salon 1907. RBA, 1897; RI, 1913.
Contrib: *The Lady's Pictorial [1895].*
Exhib: L; RA; RBA: RI; ROI.

COLLINGS, J.P. or T.P.
Illustrator, specialising in ornament and works of art, contributing to *The Graphic*, 1875-1889.

COLLINGWOOD, Professor William Gershom   **MA FSA**
1854-1932
Landscape painter and illustrator. He was born in 1854, the son of W. Collingwood, RWS, and was educated at Liverpool College and at University College, Oxford. He then attended the Slade School under Legros and followed a career in art teaching. He was Professor of Fine Art, University College, Reading and President of the Cumberland and Westmorland Antiquarian Society and President of the Lake Artists Society. He published a number of books but made a special study of Scandinavian art and lore. He illustrated *The Elder or Poetic Edda: The Mythological Poems*, by Olive Bray, in 1909. These are very beautiful Norse designs, based on the sculpture of Pre-Norman monuments in the north of England. He lived much of his life in the Lake District and died at Coniston on 1 October 1932.
Exhib: G; L; M; New Gall; RA; RBA; RI.
Bibl: *Who Was Who 1929-1940.*

COLLINS, Charles Allston   **1828-1873**
Pre-Raphaelite painter and brother of Wilkie Collins and son-in-law of Charles Dickens. He studied at the RA Schools and worked with Millais and was thus drawn into the Pre-Raphaelite circle. His output was small and imbued with tremendous religious sentiment as well as Pre-Raphaelite colouring and exactitude. He wrote articles for *Good Words* and *All The Year Round* and exhibited at the RA from 1847 to 1855, when he finally abandoned painting. He designed the wrapper of the first American edition of Dickens's *Edwin Drood*, 1870.
Colls: Ashmolean; BM.
Bibl: J. Maas, *Victorian Painters*, 1969, p.127.

COLLINS, William Wiehe   **1862-1951**
Painter of architecture and military subjects. He was the son of an army doctor and was educated at Epsom College, followed by study at Lambeth School of Art and at Julian's, Paris. He was in the RNVR, 1914-18, in the Dardanelles and in Egypt, which furnished him with material for pictures. He lived at Wareham, Dorset, 1903-25, and died at Bridgwater, Somerset, 1951. RI, 1898.

Publ: *The Cathedral Cities of England [1905]; Cathedral Cities of Spain [1909]; Cathedral Cities of Italy [1911]; The Green Roads of England.*
Contrib: *Black and White [1891].*
Exhib: FAS, 1901.

COLOMB, Wellington
Landscape painter who exhibited at the RA and RBA, 1865-70. He contributed an illustration to *Good Words*, 1864.

COLVILLE, Charles John, 11th Baron and 1st Viscount Colville of Culros   **1818-1903**
Amateur caricaturist, son of General Sir Charles Colville, married daughter of the 2nd Lord Carrington. His sketches are in an album of 1860-70 in the Royal Library, Windsor. He signs with two intersecting half moons and dots.

COLVILLE, Sir William James KCVO   **1827-1903**
Amateur caricaturist. He was the son of General Sir Charles Colville and brother of Lord Colville (q.v.). He married Lady Georgina, daughter of the Duke of Manchester, and became HM Master of Ceremonies in 1893. His military caricatures, dating from 1866-87, are in the Royal Library, Windsor.

COMPTON, Edward Theodore   **1849-**
Painter and alpinist. Lived most of his life in Austria and Germany but exhibited regularly in London. He was interned during the First World War, but continued to work near the Italian frontier.
Illus: *A Mendip Valley [T. Compton, 1892]; Germany [J.F. Dickie, 1912]; Germany [G.W. Bullet, 1930].*
Contrib: *The Picturesque Mediterranean [Cassell, 1891].*

CONCANEN, Alfred   **1835-1886**
Music cover illustrator. He was born in London in 1835 of Irish descent and began designing covers for music in 1859. He was the most prolific of these artists and the best, giving his subjects great verve and clarity and specialising in what Ronald Pearsall has called 'London out-of-doors' subjects.
Illus: *Carols of Cockayne [H.S. Leigh, 1874]; Low Life Deeps [J. Greenwood, 1874]; The Queen of Hearts [Wilkie Collins, 1875]; The Wilds of London [J. Greenwood, 1876].*
Contrib: *Illustrated Sporting and Dramatic News.*
Bibl: Ronald Pearsall, *Victorian Sheet Music Covers*, 1972.

CONDER, Charles Edward   **1868-1909**
Landscape painter and designer of fans. He was born in London in 1868 and spent much of his early life in India. He was educated at Eastbourne and then spent five years in Australia as a civil servant, 1885. While there he worked for the *Illustrated Sydney News* and attended Melbourne School of Art. In 1890 he went to Paris and studied at Julian's, becoming an Associate of the Société Nationale des Beaux Arts, 1893. He settled in London in 1897 and was elected to the NEAC in 1901. He died at Virginia Water in 1909.
Illus: *La Fille Aux Yeux D'Or [Balzac, 1898].*
Contrib: *The Yellow Book [1895]; The Savoy [1896]; The Page [1899].*
Des: *Impressionist Exhibition* [1899 (cover)]; invitation card for Conder Exhibition, Paris, Dec. 1901.
Colls: Bedford; BM; Fitzwilliam; Leeds; Manchester; V & AM; Witt Photo.
Bibl: J. Rothenstein, *The Life and Death of Conder*, 1938; Simon Houfe, *Fin de Siècle*, 1992, p.177.

CONDY, Nicholas Matthew   **1818-1851**
Marine painter. He was the son of Nicholas Condy, 1793-1857, the painter, and taught art at Plymouth.
Illus: *Four Views [1843, AL 332]; Yachting Cruise [Fiona Rose Condy, 1852, AL 333].*
Publ: *Cotehele...the seat of the Earl of Mount Edgecumbe [1850].*
Contrib: *ILN [1845-50 (naval subjects)].*

CONNARD, Philip RA CVO   **1875-1958**
Painter and illustrator. He was born at Southport in 1875 and after being educated at the National Schools, he studied at Julian's in Paris.

Settling in Fulham in 1901, he became Art Master at the Lambeth School of Art and concentrated on book illustration. These works, principally for John Lane, were in a late Pre-Raphaelite style in the manner of Laurence Houseman (q.v.). Elected to the NEAC in 1909; ARA, 1918, and RA, 1925. Keeper of the RA, 1945-49; ARWS, 1933.
Illus: *Flowers of Parnassus [Browning, Lane, 1900]; Marpessa [Stephen Phillips, 1900 (frontis.)].*
Contrib: *The Idler; The Dome [1899-1900]; The Quartier Latin [1898].*
Exhib: G; L; M; NEA, from 1901; RA; RHA; ROI; RSA; RSW; RWS.
Colls: Aberdeen; Bradford; Cardiff; Dublin; Manchester; Southport; Tate.
Bibl: R.D. Sketchley, *English Book Illus.*, 1903, pp.13-14, 122.

CONNELL, M. Christine   **fl.1885-1907**
Painter of domestic subjects. She worked in Chelsea and Chiswick and contributed decorative subjects to *The English Illustrated Magazine*, 1896, and *The Sketch*, 1897.
Exhib: L; M; New Gall.; RA; RBA; ROI; SWA.
Colls: V & AM.

CONNOR, Arthur Bentley   **fl.1903-1925**
Portrait painter. He worked in London, 1903, in Penarth, 1915, and Weston-super-Mare from 1918-1925. He illustrated *Highways and Byways in Hampshire*.
Exhib: P; RA.

COODE, Miss Helen Hoppner   **fl.1859-1882**
Illustrator and watercolourist. She worked at Notting Hill, London, and Guildford, Surrey, and specialised in figure subjects. They are often brittle little drawings with large heads and rather weightless. She was the first woman cartoonist to work for *Punch*, 1859-61 and contributed small illustrations to *Once a Week* 1859. She signs her her work ⟨HGH⟩
Exhib: BI, 1859-66; M; RA; RBA, 1876-81.

COOK, Elizabeth
Contributed panorama of Sebastopol to *Cassell's Illustrated Family Paper*, 1853.

COOK, Richard   RA   **1784-1857**
Painter and book illustrator. He was born in London in 1784 and entered the RA Schools in 1800. He specialised in historical scenes and illustrated numerous works from poetry and classical literature. His handling of the drawings typifies the beautiful ink and grey wash approach which was a legacy from the 18th century but which often lacked punch. The BM has a fine album of his studies for *The Lady of the Lake* by Sir Walter Scott, published in 1811. He became ARA in 1816 and RA in 1822, after which date he ceased to paint.
Illus: *Inchbald's British Theatre [1802]; Young's Night Thoughts [1804]; The Pastoral Care [1808]; The Idler [1810]; Park's British Poets; Miller's Shakespeare etc.*
Exhib: BI, 1807-26; RA, 1808-22.
Colls: BM; Swansea; V & AM; Witt Photo.

COOKE, Arthur Claude   **1867-1951**
Figure, animal and landscape painter and illustrator. He was born at Luton, Bedfordshire, in 1867, the son of a solicitor and educated at Bedford School. He was trained at the St. John's Wood Art School and at the RA Schools, 1886 and again in 1889. Bronze medal, Crystal Palace, 1894. He seems to have returned to Bedfordshire for rural subjects in the 1890s but by the end of the decade had moved back to London with a studio at Haverstock Hill. He exhibited mostly historical or subject pictures at the Royal Academy, but his best work is often small scale and rural, studies that were often transferred for illustration. He moved to Radlett, Herts. in 1925 and remained there until his death. His studio was sold in about 1980, and a retrospective exhibition was held at Luton Art Gallery, Oct.-Nov. 1991.
Contrib: *The Lady's Pictorial [c.1895]; Sporting and Dramatic News [1904]; The Quiver [1906]; Pearson's Magazine [1914-16].*
Exhib: B; L; RA; RBA; ROI.
Bibl: *Arthur Claude Cooke*, illustrated catalogue of an exhibition at Oscar and Peter Johnson, London SW1, Oct.-Nov. 1981; Houfe, Simon, 'Lured by Rural Roots', *Country Life*, 21 March, 1991.
Colls: Durban; Luton.

WILLIAM CUBITT COOKE 1866-1951. 'Mystery of the Balkans'. An illustration for *The English Illustrated Magazine*, Vol.16, 1896. Pen and grey wash. Signed and dated 1890. 7¾in x 5¼in (19.7cm x 13.3cm)

Victoria and Albert Museum

COOKE, Edward William   RA FRS   1811-1880
Marine watercolourist, topographer and illustrator. He was born at Pentonville on 27 March 1811, the son of George Cooke (q.v.), the engraver. He was making wood engravings of plants by the age of nine, some of which were used in J.C. Loudon's *Encyclopaedia of Plants*, 1829, and Loddidge's *Botanical Cabinet*, 1817-33. He married the latter's daughter but after meeting Clarkson Stanfield (q.v.) in 1825, began to draw boats for him and to study shipping. Cooke travelled extensively in Europe, visiting Normandy in 1830 and Belgium and Holland between 1832 and 1844. He went further afield to Italy, 1845-46, and Spain and North Africa. His watercolours are rare but his fine pencil studies and leaves from his sketch-book, showing picturesque groups of fishermen, crowds and shore-lines, are quite common. He became ARA in 1851 and RA in 1864, dying at Groombridge, Kent, on 4 January 1880.
Illus: *Coast Sketches: British Coast [1826-30]; Fifty Plates of Shipping and Craft [1829]; Finden's Ports, Harbours and Watering Places [1840].*
Contrib: *Good Words [1863].*
Exhib: BI, 1835-67; RA; RBA, 1835-38, 1876.
Colls: BM; G; Greenwich; Leeds; Salford; Sheffield; V & AM.
Bibl: M. Hardie, *Watercol. Paint. in Brit*, Vol.III, 1968, p.79.

COOKE, George   1781-1834
Topographical illustrator and engraver. Born in London in 1781 and engraved many works after Turner, Callcott and his son E.W. Cooke (q.v.). Died at Barnes in 1834.
Illus. or contrib: *Britton's Beauties [1803-13]; Pinkerton's Voyages and Travels; The Thames [1811]; The Southern Coast of*

England [Surtees, 1816-40]; Hertfordshire [R. Clutterbuck, 1815-27];Italy [J. Hakewill, 1818-20]; D'Oyly and Mant's Bible; The Botanical Cabinet [1817-1833]; London and Its Vicinity [1826-28].
Exhib: RBA.
Colls: BM.

COOKE, William Bernard   1778-1855
Topographical illustrator and engraver. Elder brother of George Cooke (q.v.). He was a pupil of W. Angus, the topographer, and assisted his brother in publishing *The Thames*, 1811, and *The Southern Coast of England*, 1814-26.
Illus: *A New Picture of The Isle of Wight [1808]; Britton's Beauties [1808-16].*
Colls: Witt Photo.

COOKE, William Cubitt   1866-1951
Watercolourist and book illustrator. He was born in London in 1866 and was educated at the Cowper Street Schools, City Road. At the age of sixteen he was apprenticed to a chromolithographer, but taught himself drawing and painting. He went later to Heatherley's and the Westminster School of Art. Cooke had his first black and white drawing published in 1892 and this was followed by a steady stream, some for short stories with an eastern flavour and some for period novels. He was a very competent figure artist indeed, although his compositions lack great individuality.
Illus: *Evelina and Cecilia [Fanny Burney, 1893]; The Man of Feeling [Mackenzie, 1893]; My Study Fire [1893]; The Vicar of Wakefeld [1893]; Reveries of a Bachelor [1894]; The Master Beggars [1897]; The Singer of Marly [1897], The Temple Dickens [1899]; Novels of Jane Austen [1894]; British Ballads [1894]; By Stroke of Sword [1897]; John Halifax; [1898].*
Contrib: *The Quiver [c.1895]; The Idler; The Pall Mall Magazine; The English Illustrated Magazine [1896-98]; The Windsor Magazine.*
Exhib: RA, from 1893; RBA, from 1890; RI.
Colls: V & AM.
Bibl: R.E.D. Sketchley, *English Illus.*, 1903, pp.84, 149.
See illustration.

COOPER, Abraham   RA   1787-1868
Sporting artist. He was largely self-taught although he had some drawing lessons from Ben Marshall. His inclusion here rests solely on some compositions that appeared in *The Sporting Magazine* and the frontispiece that he designed for *A Treatise on Greyhounds*, 1819. ARA, 1817 and RA, 1820.
Exhib: BI and RA, 1812-1869.
Colls: BM; Witt Photo.

COOPER, Alfred W.   fl.1850-1901
He was the son of Abraham Cooper RA (q.v.) and a close friend of Charles Keene (q.v.), with whom he served in the Volunteers. Illustrator of domestic subjects. One of the best of the second rank of 1860s artists about whom little is known. He was living in North London, 1853-54, and had moved to Twickenham by 1866, where he seems to have worked for the rest of his life. Cooper's earlier drawings are his best. Those in sepia ink or black ink in the Laing Art Gallery, Newcastle, come closest in feeling to Millais and are dated 1857-59. His published work begins with *Good Words*, 1861, and this and succeeding work such as 'On The Hills', *Churchman's Family Magazine*, 1863, retain the quality of line and show an affinity with Fred Walker's rustic illustrations. His later domestic and high life drawings are contrived and the use of gesture is overplayed and almost ludicrous. An early ink drawing by this artist would be very desirable and very rare. He signs his early drawings, which are very rare, ꙮ and his later drawings *AWC*
Illus: *Une Culotte [Digby 1894]; Walton's Compleat Angler [n.d.].*
Contrib: *Good Words [1861]; London Society [1862-68]; Churchman's Family Magazine [1863]; Tinsley's Magazine [1868]; Dark Blue [1871]: The British Workman; Aunt Judy's Magazine; The Graphic [1870].*
Exhib: B; BI, 1853-66; RA; RBA, 1852-80; RI; ROI.
Colls: Newcastle; V & AM.
Bibl: Gleeson White, *English Illustration: The Sixties*, 1897.

COOPER, Florence   **fl.1886-1935**
Miniature painter. She illustrated with James Cadenhead (q.v.), two children's books, *Master Rex* and *Pixie* by Mrs. G. Ford, 1890-91.
Exhib: L; New Gall.; P; RA; RI; RMS; SWA.

COOPER, Frederick Charles
Landscape painter and archaeological illustrator. He went to Nineveh in 1849 to work for H.A. Layard, and drew for the latter's *Nineveh and Babylon*, 1853.

COOPER, J.D.
Figure illustrator, contributing to *Good Words*, 1874.

COOPER, Will
Contributor to *Fun*, 1900.

COPE, Charles West   **RA**   **1811-1890**
Historical painter, watercolourist and illustrator. He was born at Leeds, 28 July 1811, and was educated at Leeds Grammar School. He went to London in 1826 and studied at Sass's School in 1827 followed by some time at the RA Schools, 1828. He travelled to Paris, 1831, and to Italy, 1833-35, and again in 1845. He won a premium in the Houses of Parliament frescoes competition in 1843 and was an authority on Renaissance frescoes. He was a founder member of the Etching Club and was elected ARA in 1843 and RA in 1848. He represented the Academy at Philadelphia in 1876. Cope died at Bournemouth on 21 August 1890.
Contrib: *The Deserted Village [Goldsmith, Etching Club, 1841]; Songs of Shakespeare [Etching Club, 1843]; Poems and Pictures [1846]; Sacred Allegories [1856]; Poems and Songs [Burns, 1858]; Favourite English Poems [1858-59]; A Book of Favourite Modern Ballads [1859]; The Churchman's Family Magazine [1863]; Cassell's Sacred Poems [1867]; Excelsior Ballads; Burns Poems; The Poetry of Thomas Moore.*
Exhib: BI and RA, 1833-82.
Colls: BM; Leicester; Liverpool; Melbourne; Preston.
Bibl: Chatto & Jackson, *Treatise on Wood Engraving*, 1861, p.598; C.H. Cope, *Reminiscences of CWC*, Art Journal, 1869; J. Maas, *Victorian Painters*, 1969, pp.28, 216, 238.

COPPING, Harold   **1863-1932**
Illustrator. He studied at the RA Schools and won the Landseer scholarship to Paris. He travelled to Palestine, Egypt and Canada, finally settling at Sevenoaks in 1902 and remaining there till his death, designing children's books and illustrating scriptural stories. He died 1 July 1932.
Illus: *Hard Lines [1894]; A Newnham Friendship; Toy Book; Mrs. Wiggs of the Cabbage Patch [A.H. Rice, 1908]; Canadian Pictures; The Gospel in the Old Testament; Scenes from the Life of St. Paul; Scripture Picture Books; The 'Copping' Bible.*
Contrib: *The Girls' Own Paper [1890-1900]; The Temple Magazine [1896]; English Illustrated Magazine [1897]; Black & White [1899]; The Windsor Magazine; The Royal Magazine.*

CORBAUX, Louisa   **NWS**   **1808-**
Painter and lithographer. She was the elder sister of Fanny Corbaux (q.v.) and specialised in pictures of animals and children. She collaborated with her sister in gift books and annuals. NWS, 1837.
Illus: *Pearls of the East, Beauties From Lalla Rookh [Tilt, 1837].*
Exhib: RBA, 1828-50.
Colls: BM.

CORBAUX, Marie Françoise Catherine Doetter 'Fanny' NWS
         1812-1883
Watercolourist and illustrator. Born in 1812, she was recognised as an infant prodigy, and won silver medals at the Society of Arts in 1827 and 1830. She was a writer on oriental subjects and a biblical scholar but is best known for her illustrations to gift books. She was granted a Civil List pension in recognition of her work and died at Brighton 1 February 1883. NWS, 1839.
Illus: *Pearls of the East, Beauties From Lalla Rookh [Tilt, 1837 'drawn on stone by Louisa Corbaux']; Cousin Natalia's Tales [T. Moore, 1841].*

HENRY CORBOULD 1787-1844. Original pen and wash illustration

Contrib: *Heath's Gallery [1836]; Finden's Byron Beauties; Le Souvenir [1848].*
Exhib: NWS; RBA, 1828-40.
Colls: BM; National Trust, Calke Abbey (portraits).
Bibl: R. Maclean, *Victorian Book Design*, 1972, pp.26, 28, 53.

CORBOULD, Aster Chantrey RBA   **-1920**
Sporting artist and illustrator. He studied with his uncle Charles Keene (q.v.) who introduced him to *Punch*, in which magazine much of his work was afterwards published. Corbould was at his best in illustration when horses were involved, but his range did include social and military drawings and cartoons. His sketches appear to lose a great deal in the printing. Sheets of sepia illustrations, on the market in 1976, had the clarity of penwork and finesse of Keene, but on the magazine page they look coarse. Elected to RBA, 1893. He signs his work ⟨signature⟩
Illus: *The Sword of Damocles [frontis.].*
Contrib: *Punch [1871-1902]; The Graphic [1873-89]; ILN [1876 (acting Special Artist, Servia)]; Cornhill Magazine [1883]; Daily Graphic; Black & White [1891]; St. Paul's [1894]; Lika Joko [1894]; The New Budget [1895]; The St. James's Budget [1898].*
Exhib: B; L; RA; RBA; RHA; RI; ROI.
Colls: V & AM.
Bibl: R.G.G. Price, *A History of Punch*, 1957 p.120; *Mr. Punch With Horse and Hound*, New Punch Library, c.1930.

CORBOULD, Edward Henry   **RI**   **1815-1905**
Painter, sculptor and illustrator. He was born in London 5 December 1815 and became a pupil of his father, Henry Corbould (q.v.), also a very prolific illustrator. He studied at Sass's and at the RA Schools. In 1851 he was appointed drawing master to the children of Queen Victoria, retaining the post until 1872. His illustration drawings are all in the conventional monochrome washes of the period with fine ink detail, many of them bear the stamp of the artist's studio sale. RI, 1838.
Illus: *Lalla Rookh [1839]; Scott's Works, 1825.*
Contrib: *The Sporting Review [1842-46]; L'Allegro and Il Penseroso [Art Union, 1848]; The Traveller [Goldsmith Art Union, 1851]; Tupper's Proverbial Philosophy [1854]; ILN [1856 (decor.), 1866]; Willmott's Poets of the Nineteenth Century [1857]; Merrie Days of England [1858-59]; London Society [1863]; The Churchman's Family Magazine [1863]; Cassell's Magazine [1870]; Favourite Modern Ballads; Burns Poems; Poetry of Thomas Moore; Barry Cornwall's Poems; Thornbury's Legendary Ballads [1876].*
Exhib: BI, 1846; GG; NWS; RA; RBA, 1835-42
Colls: Ashmolean; BM; Soane; V & AM.
Bibl: Chatto & Jackson, *Treatise on Wood Engraving* 1861, p.598.

CORBOULD, Henry   **1787-1844**
Illustrator, third son of Richard Corbould (q.v.), and father of E.H. Corbould (q.v.). Born at Robertsbridge in 1787, he studied with his father, later becoming a student at the RA Schools under H. Fuseli. He was a close friend of the leading neo-classical artists, Flaxman, Stothard, West and Chantrey, some of whose works he drew. J.

RICHARD CORBOULD 1757-1831. 'Pamela giving up her parcel of papers to her Master'. An illustration for Richardson's *Pamela*, c.1805. Oval vignette in ink and watercolour with decoration.

Britton says that he was 'extensively employed by publishers to make drawings for engraving; and the number of his designs, which adorn many books, amount to several hundreds. He was one of the sufferers from an accident on the Eastern Counties Railway, when the train, falling off a lofty embankment, involved passengers in a smash…he was killed…' *Autobiography* Vol. II, p.172. He spent thirty years on drawings for *Ancient Marbles*, published after his death. He illustrated the marbles at Woburn and Petworth.
Illus: *Paradise Lost [1796]; Rasselas [1810]; Swiss Family Robinson [1814]; Rosara's Chain [Lefanu, 1815]; Letters of Lady R. Russell [1826]; Cecilia [Burney, 1825].*
Contrib: Heath's Gallery [1836-37].
Colls: BM; Leeds; V & AM.
See illustration.

CORBOULD, Richard   1757-1831
Painter of oils and watercolours, miniaturist, enamellist, portraitist. He was born in London in 1757 and most of his life was employed in the illustration of books, principally the series of miniature classics produced by Cooke, 1795-1800. His drawings were either in muted watercolours or monochrome washes, very gem-like and often within decorative frames or feigned ovals. Their quality is usually higher than those by the other members of the Corbould family. Much of his best work falls earlier than the scope of this book, but a selection of work

is given below. He died at Highgate, 1831.
Illus: *The Adventurer; Tom Jones; Thoughts in Prison; Howlett's Views in the County of Lincoln [1800]; Broome's Works; Adventures of a Guinea.*
Contrib: *The Copper Plate Magazine [1792-94].*
Exhib: BI, 1806-17; Free Soc.; RA.
Colls: BM; V & AM.
Bibl: Hammelmann & Boase, *Book Illustrators in Eighteenth Century England*, 1975, pp.27-28.
See illustration.

CORDINER, Rev. James   1775-1836
Traveller and topographer. Son of the Rev. Charles Cordiner of Banff. M.A., Aberdeen, 1793. Army chaplain at Madras, 1797, and at Colombo, 1798-1804. He was minister of St. Paul's Episcopal Church at Aberdeen, 1807-34.
Illus: *A Description of Ceylon [1807, AT 409]; A Voyage to India [1820].*

CORNILLIET, Jules   1830-1886
History painter. He was born at Versailles in 1830 and studied with Ary Scheffer and H. Vernet. Exhibited at the Salon from 1857. He contributed drawings of the Franco-Italian campaign to *The Illustrated London News*, 1859.

COTMAN, Frederick George   **RI ROI**   1850-1920
Landscape and genre painter in watercolour and oil. He was born in Ipswich and was a nephew of J.S. Cotman (q.v.). After being educated at Ipswich, he went to the RA Schools in 1868, winning the gold medal for historical painting, 1873. He accompanied the Duke of Westminster on a Mediterranean tour and was employed to make watercolours of the places visited. His illustrative work is very rare but boldly handled in quite large scale, using a great deal of sepia and bodycolour. He became RI in 1882, ROI, 1883, and died at Felixstowe on 16 July 1920.
Contrib: *ILN [1876 and 1880]; The Yellow Book [1895].*
Exhib: B; FAS, 1893; G; L; M; Paris, 1889; RA; RBA; RI; ROI; RSA.
Colls: Norwich; V & AM.
Bibl: *The Studio*, Vol. 47, 1909, p 167.

COTMAN, John Sell   1782-1842
Painter and etcher, a principal figure of the Norwich School of painters, he is included here as an architectural illustrator. After spending his boyhood in Norwich, he went to London and learnt a good deal about the world of engraving and publishing, acting as a colourer of aquatints for Rudolph Ackermann of the Strand. He collected material for a volume of Norfolk antiquities and visited Normandy in 1817, 1818 and 1820 for a similar project. He produced one hundred etchings for the latter, often arduous work but showing his own individual view of the subject. The 1820s were clouded by mental anxiety and financial problems, but in 1834 Cotman was appointed drawing master at King's College, London, a post he held until his death in 1842.
Illus: *Miscellaneous Etchings of Architectural Antiquities in Yorkshire [1812]; Architectural Antiquities of Norfolk [1812-17]; Sepulchral Brasses in Norfolk [1813-16]; Architectural Antiquities of Normandy [1822]; Sepulchral Brasses of Norfolk & Suffolk; Liber Studiorum; Britton's Cathedrals [183-36]; Eight Original Etchings [n.d.].*
Exhib: BI, 1810-27; OWS; RA; RBA, 1838.
Colls: Ashmolean; BM; Glasgow; Manchester; Norwich; V & AM.
Bibl: S.D. Kitson, *Life of JSC*, 1937; M. Hardie, *Watercol. Paint. in Brit.* Vol. II, 1967, pp.72-96.
See illustration.

COTTON, Lieutenant J.S.
Amateur caricaturist. He illustrated *The New Tale of a Tub* by F.W.N. Bayley, 1841, in lithography.

COULDERY, Thomas W.   fl.1877-1898
Domestic painter and illustrator. He was working in London in 1882, at Pulborough and Chichester, Sussex, 1890-93, and at Brighton in 1897.
Illus: *A Woman Hater [Charles Reade, 1877].*
Contrib: *ILN [1888, 1894]; Cassell's Family Magazine; English Illustrated Magazine [1891-94].*
Exhib: B; L; M; RA; RBA; RI.
Colls: Sydney.

COWELL, G.H. Sydney   **fl.1884-1907**
Domestic painter and illustrator of urban genre, sculptor. He worked
in London and specialised in drawings for school stories and boys'
and girls' novels. His work is competent but not exciting.
Illus: *A Peep Behind The Scenes [Mrs. O.F Walton]; Every Inch a*
Briton [1901].
Contrib: *ILN [1889-92]; The Quiver [1890]; The English*
Illustrated Magazine [1891-92, 1896]; The Idler [1892]; The
Sporting and Dramatic News [1893]; The New Budget [1895];
Pearson's Magazine [1896]; The Temple [1896]; The Minister
[1895]; The Girls' Own Paper; The St. James's Budget; Cassell's
Family Magazine; The Pall Mall Magazine; The Windsor Magazine.
Exhib: B; M; RA; RBA; ROI.

COWHAM, Hilda Gertrude (Mrs. Edgar Lander)   **1873-1964**
Artist, author and book illustrator. She was born in 1873 and after
being educated at Wimbledon College, attended the Lambeth School
of Art. Miss Cowham had drawings published while she was still at
school in *Pick-Me-Up* and *The Queen*. She later became a prolific
contributor to magazines, designed posters and made dolls. Her
claim to be the first woman to draw for *Punch* is quite incorrect, that
honour going to Helen Coode (q.v.).
     Her drawings in pencil and ink for children's books are very
decorative and whimsy. She usually signs: H. Cowham.
Illus: *Fiddlesticks; Our Generals; Blacklegs; Curly Locks and Long*
Legs; Kitty in Fairyland.
Contrib: *The Sketch [1894-95]; Moonshine [1896]; The Royal*
Magazine [1901]; The Graphic [1902-05, 1908, 1912 (Christmas
supps.)]; The Sphere; The Tatler.
Exhib: G; L; RA; RWS; SWA; Walker's.
Colls: V & AM.
Bibl: *The Studio*, Vol.3, p.xvii, 1894, illus.

COWPER, Frank Cadogan   RA RWS   **1877-1958**
Portrait and subject painter. He was born on 16 October 1877 at
Wicken Rectory, Northamptonshire, and was educated at Cranleigh.
He studied first at the St. John's Wood Art School, 1896, then at the
RA Schools, 1897-1902, and worked for six months in the studio of
E.A. Abbey, RA (q.v.). Cowper did numerous portraits but
specialised in subject pictures of romantic type: 'French Aristocrat',
'Venetian Ladies' etc., etc. He was also responsible for painting
panels and altar-pieces. He worked in London but died in Cirencester
in 1958. ARA, 1907; RA, 1934; RP, 1921; RWS, 1911.
Contrib: *The Idler; The Graphic, 1906.*
Exhib: B; G; GG; L; M; P; RA; ROI; RWS.
Bibl: *The Last Romantics*, Barbican Gallery cat., 1989, p.134.

COWPER, Max   **fl.1892-1911**
Figure painter and illustrator. He was working in Dundee in 1893, in
Edinburgh in 1894 and in London from 1901. Cowper made
illustrations for a large number of magazines, his ink drawing is very
good and his grey wash drawings are delicate, but he sometimes
swamps his fine line with wash.
Contrib: *Fun [1892-93]; St. Pauls [1894]; The Rambler [1897];*
The Longbow [1898]; Pick-Me-Up; Illustrated Bits; The Quiver
[1899]; The Idler; The Pall Mall Magazine; The Minister; The
Strand Magazine.
Exhib: G; L; RA; RSA.
Colls: V & AM; Witt Photo.

COX, David OWS   **1783-1859**
Landscape painter and watercolourist. He was born at Deritend,
Birmingham in 1783 and began as a scene painter for the
Birmingham Theatre. He moved to London in 1804 and in the next
decade became highly influential as a drawing-master and
practitioner. He travelled abroad between 1826 and 1832 and
developed as a colourist and in his later years as a forerunner of
impressionism. He is included here for his one recorded work of
illustration *A Treatise on The Aeropleustic Art by means of Kites*,
1851, AL 395. He died at Harborne on 7 June 1859.
Publ: *Treatise on Landscape Painting and Effect in Watercolour*
[1814]; Progressive Lessons on Landscape for Young Beginners
[1816]; A Series of Progressive Lessons [c.1816]; The Young Artist's
Companion [1825]; A Treatise on the Aeropleustic Art or Navigation

JOHN SELL COTMAN 1782-1842. Woman at a well. An etching
for *Eight Original Etchings   by The Late John Sell Cotman*,
Norwich, n.d. 9¼in x 6½in (24.8cm x 16.5cm).   Author's Collection

in the Air by means of Kites [1851, AL 395].
Exhib: BI; OWS; RA; RBA.
Colls: Ashmolean; BM; Birmingham; Nottingham; V & AM.
Bibl: Trenchard Cox, *DC*, 1947.

COX, Everard Morant   **fl.1878-1891**
Black and white illustrator, working in London and producing comic
genre and sporting subjects for the magazines.
Contrib: *ILN [1883-84, 1888, 1891]; Punch [1883].*
Exhib: RA, 1884-85.

CRAFT, Percy Robert   RBA   **1856-1934**
Landscape and coastal painter. He studied at Heatherley's and at the
Slade School under Legros and Poynter, where he was a gold and
silver medallist. He worked in London until 1910 with a brief spell
at Penzance in 1890. He was elected RBA, 1898, and died in London
26 November 1934.
Contrib: *ILN [1883 (Cornwall)].*
Exhib: B; G; L; M; New Gall.; RA; RBA; RE; ROI; RSA.

CRAFTY
Pseudonym of cartoonist to *The Graphic*, 1871.

CRAIG, Edward Gordon   **1872-1966**
Designer, woodcut artist and propagandist for simplicity in the theatre.
He was born 16 January 1872, the son of E.W. Godwin, 1833-1886,
the Victorian architect, and Ellen Terry, 1847-1928, the actress.
Although much of Craig's energy was concentrated on theatre design,
he was a dynamic and original illustrator and typographer. After being
educated at Heidelberg and Bradfield, he went on the stage for a short

EDWARD GORDON CRAIG 1872-1966. 'The Trumpeter'.
Illustration to *The Venture An Annual of Art and Literature*, 1903

period. After moving to Uxbridge, he came under the influence of William Nicholson (q.v.) and James Pryde (q.v.), then living at Denham, and he was taught the rudiments of wood engraving by them. This contact proved a turning point and he immersed himself in Renaissance wood engravings and the study of architecture of the same period. The years 1893-98 saw the production of a number of splendid bold and chunky woodcuts, particularly character studies of Irving and Ellen Terry. Craig designed and produced *The Page* at The Sign of the Rose, Hackbridge, from 1898-1901. He was his own editor, illustrator and publisher for *The Mask* and *The Marionette*. In later years he produced numerous stage sets in Britain and Europe and wrote extensively.

Publ: *The Page [1898-1901]; The Art of The Theatre [1905]; The Mask [Florence 1908-29]; On The Art of The Theatre [1911]; Towards a New Theatre [1913]; The Theatre Advancing [1921]; Scene [1923]; Woodcuts and Some Words [1924]; Books and Theatres [1925]; A Production [1926, 1930]; Fourteen Notes [1931]; Ellen Terry and Her Secret Self [1931].*
Contrib: *The Minister; The Dome [1898-99]; Book of Penny Toys [1899]; The Venture [1903]; The Splendid Wayfaring [Haldane Macfall, 1913].*
Exhib: G; RHA.
Colls: BM; V & AM; Witt Photo.
Bibl: *Print Collectors' Quarterly*, Vol.9, No.4, 1922, pp.406-432; *EGC Cat. of Exhibition*, V & AM, 1967; *EGC Bibliography* (Ifan Kyrle Fletcher); Craig, E.C., *Index to the Story of My Days*, 1956.
See illustration.

CRAIG, Frank   1874-1918
Black and white illustrator. He was born at Abbey, Kent, on 27 February 1874 and studied at the RA Schools. He began working on *The Graphic* in 1895, succeeding Gulich as collaborator with William Hatherell (q.v.). He was sent by *The Graphic* as Special Artist in the South African War, 1900. About 1910 Craig moved to the United States to work closely with *Harper's*, returning in 1912. He was confirmed as a consumptive in 1914 and left England for

Madeira, never getting further than Cintra, Portugal, where he died in 1918. Craig was an accomplished illustrator of stories, using grey wash drawings to powerful effect and drawing in with the brush. He illustrated some of George Gissing's work, some of Rudyard Kipling's and a little of Arnold Bennett, who disliked his style. One of his paintings was purchased for the Chantrey Bequest in 1906.
Contrib: *The English Illustrated Magazine [1894-95]; The Graphic [1895-1910]; The Quiver [1894-1900]; The Temple [1896]; Cassell's Family Magazine [1898]; The Pall Mall Magazine; The Sketch; The Strand Magazine.*
Exhib: G, L, M; RA; RBA, 1892-94. ROI; RSA.
Colls: Author; V & AM.
Bibl: A.C.R. Carter, *The Work of War Artists in South Africa*, Art Journal, 1900; *The Art Journal*, 1906, p.881; *The Studio*, Vol.38, 1906, pp.4-11; Arnold Bennett, *Letters to J.B. Pinker*, Vol. 1, 1966, pp.168-169 (Edited by J. Hepburn); *FC 1874-1918*, Maas Gallery catalogue, 1987.
See illustration.

CRAIG, William Marshall   c.1765-c.1834
Illustrator, drawing master, painter of portraits. He was living in Manchester in 1788 and practising as a drawing master, exhibiting miniatures and landscapes at various exhibitions. He was established in London from 1790 and there became Water-colour Painter to the Queen in 1812 and Court Painter to the Duke of York in 1820. He may have travelled to Russia in 1814 and he gave lectures at the BI.

Craig's output as an illustrator was considerable, all his work was done in the meticulous neo-classic style of drawing favoured for books, charming but not individual. His work is occasionally seen on the market.
Illus: *A Wreath For The Brow of Youth [1804]; Trades of London [1804, AL 271]; Scripture Illustrated [1806]; An Essay on Transparent Prints [1807]; The Economy of Human Life [1808]; Cowper's Poems [1813]; Foxe's Book of Martyrs.*
Contrib: *Britton's Beauties [1803-12]; Inchbald's British Theatre; Bell's British Theatre; Britton's Gallery of Contemporary Portraits.*
Exhib: BI, 1806-20; RA, 1788-1827; RBA, 1826-28.
Colls: Nottingham; V & AM.
Bibl: I. Williams, *Early English Watercolours*, 1952, pp.134-135, illus.

CRAMPTON, Sir John Twistleton Wickham Fiennes 1805-1886
Amateur artist and caricaturist. He was born in 1805, the son of Sir Philip Crampton and entered the Diplomatic service, acting as

FRANK CRAIG 1874-1918. 'A Group of Diners'. Illustration for unidentified story. Ink and grey wash. Signed and dated 1895. 7¼in x 8½in (18.4cm x 21.6cm)   Author's Collection

WALTER CRANE RWS 1845-1915. 'They saw a Knight in dangerous distresse'. An illustration for Spenser's *Faerie Queen*, Book V, 1896. Pen and ink. Signed with monogram. 9⅝in x 7⅝in (24.4cm x 19.4cm)

Victoria and Albert Museum

Secretary of the Legation at Berne, 1844 and Washington, 1845. He was recalled in 1856 after his attempts to recruit American citizens for the Crimea and became Minister at Hanover, 1857, and St. Petersburg, 1858. He finally retired in 1869 and died at Bushey Park, Co. Wicklow in 1886. His ink drawings of figures are very competent although they have a decidedly Georgian look to them.
Colls: BM.
Bibl: *Agnew...Exhib. of Watercolours*, Jan-Feb. 1975.

CRANE, T.
Designer. He was the elder brother of Walter Crane (q.v.), and was art director of the firm of Marcus Ward and Co. He designed ornament for Christmas cards, calendars and children's books, the figure work being by Mrs. Houghton of Warrington. He decorated *At Home*, in the style of Kate Greenaway, 1881 and *Abroad* the same year with Ellen E. Houghton (q.v.).
Bibl: W. Crane, *An Artist's Reminiscences*, 1907.

CRANE, Walter   RWS   **1845-1915**
Painter, decorator, designer, book illustrator, writer and socialist. He was born in Liverpool on 15 August 1845 and was self-taught as an artist before being apprenticed in London to W.J. Linton (q.v.) in 1857. From this technical background, Crane was able to develop a much greater craftsmanship in the art of the book than any other contemporary artist. He had the great strength of being principally an illustrator and not merely a painter who illustrated books. In the following years he studied early printed books, medieval illuminations, Japanese prints and the work of the Pre-Raphaelites in order to adapt them to his own linear patterns. His children's books are the most famous and are characterised by strong outlines, flat tints and solid blacks, all ideally suited to colour wood engraving and the *Picture Books* produced for Messrs. Routledge by Edmund Evans. From 1867, Crane was associated with the Dalziels and in the years following his marriage in 1871, he travelled widely in Italy, later to Greece, Bohemia and the United States. The Paris Commune

103

Simple Honesty
shows in vain
A fashion few
seek to robe in,
while the poor
SHEPHERD'S·PURSE
is ta'en
By rascally
RAGGED·ROBIN.

WALTER CRANE RWS 1845-1915. 'Simple Honesty'. An illustration to *A Floral Fantasy Set Forth in Verses*, 1899. Pen and watercolour. 10in x 14⅝in (25.4cm x 37.1cm)

Victoria and Albert Museum

had a powerful influence on him in 1871 and after it he became associated with William Morris (q.v.) and with the socialist cause.

Crane was associated as well with every project in art education, he was examiner in Design to the Board of Education, to London County Council and the Scottish Board of Education. He taught design at Manchester, 1893-96, was Art Director at Reading College, 1898, and Principal of the RCA, 1898-99. He was first President of the Arts and Crafts Exhibition Society, 1888, and a Master of the Art Workers' Guild. Although direct followers are hard to pin down, Crane was widely influential and the Crane style appears in the Art School work of the 1890s and 1900s. He died at Kensington 14 March 1915.

Publ: *The Basis of Design [1898]; Line and Form [1900]; Of The Decorative Illustration of Books [1901].*

Illus: *Children's Sayings [1862]; Stories of Old [1862]; The New Forest [1863]; Stories From Memel [1863]; True Pathetic History of Poor Match [1863]; Goody Platts and Her Two Cats [1864]; Toy Books [1865-76]; Broken in Harness [Lemon, 1865]; Wait For The End [1866]; Miss Mackenzie [Trollope, 1866]; Poetry of Nature [1868]; Legendary Ballads [Roberts, 1868]; King Gab's Story Nag [1869]; Magic of Kindness [1869]; Merrie Heart [1870]; Labour Stands on Golden Feet [1870]; Mrs. Molesworth's stories from 1875; Songs of Many Seasons [1876]; Baby's Opera [1877]; The Baby's Bouquet [1879]; Grimm's Fairy Tales [1882]; Aesop's Fables [1886]; Flora's Feast [1889]; Queen Summer [1891]; The Old Garden [Margaret Deland, 1893]; Hawthorne's Wonder Book For Girls and Boys [1892]; Spenser's Mutabilitie [1896]; Spenser's Faerie Queene [1897]; Bluebeard's Picture Book [1899]; Don Quixote Retold [Judge Parry, 1900]; Last Essays of Elia [1901].*

Contrib: *Entertaining Things [1861]; London Society [1862]; Good Words [1863]; Once a Week [1863-65]; Every Boy's Magazine [1864-65]; Punch [1866]; The Argosy [1868-69]; Churchman's*

Shilling Magazine [1868]; English Illustrated Magazine [1883-88]; Black & White [1891]; The Quarto [1898]; The Art Journal [cover]; The Graphic [Christmas cover]; Pears Magazine.

Exhib: Dudley; FAS, 1891; RI; RWS.

Colls: Ashmolean; Bedford; BM; Fitzwilliam; Glasgow; V & AM.

Bibl: Walter Crane, *An Artist's Reminiscences*, 1907; *The Studio*, Winter No., 1900-01, p.53, illus.; *WC 1845-1915, Artist, Designer and Socialist*, Whitworth Art Gallery, 1989.

See illustrations.

CRAVEN, The Hon. Richard Keppel   **1779-1851**
Artist and traveller. He was the third son of William, 2nd Earl of Craven and settled at Naples in 1805. The plates in his books are signed 'Sketched by the Hon K Craven.'

Illus: *Italian Scenes: A Series of Interesting Delineations of Remarkable Views, and of the most Celebrated Remains of Antiquity, 1825* and *Excursions in the Abbruzzi, 1838.*

CRAVEN, The Hon. Willy   **1835-1906**
Amateur caricaturist. The nephew of the 2nd Earl of Craven. He was married to the daughter of the 4th Earl of Hardwicke whose sisters and brother had posts at Queen Victoria's court. This accounts for his work being at the Royal Library, Windsor.

CRAWHALL, Joseph   **1821-1896**
Illustrator of chapbooks and ballads. He was born at Newcastle in 1821 and ran a family ropery business. Living in a city which was famous for its wood engravers and still basking in the glory of Thomas Bewick (q.v.), Crawhall enjoyed the spirit of book making and began to assemble material from various sources, writing, illustrating and putting the book together himself. The result is a unique kind of production, part archaism, part bibliomania and part wit. The crude woodcuts, coloured by hand, are in sympathy with the rough paper and the earthy ballads printed below them. Crawhall attempted to bring back the personality to books, dead since industrialisation.

He was a friend of Charles Keene and supplied many of his *Punch* jokes for the artist to work up. He was secretary of the Newcastle Arts Club.

Illus: *The Compleatest Angling Booke that ever was writ [1859]; Ye loving ballad of Lorde Bateman...[1860]; A Collection of Right Merrie Garlands...[1864]; Chaplets from Coquetside [1873]; Northumbrian Small Pipe Tunes [1877]; Border Notes and Mixty-Maxty [1880]; Chap-Book Chaplets [1883]; Olde Tayles...[1883]; Etc.*

Colls: BM; Glasgow.

Bibl: Charles S. Felver, *JC The Newcastle Wood Engraver 1821-96*, 1972 (complete bibliography); Simon Houfe, 'Extracting the Honey', *A.B.M.R.*, Feb. 1984, pp.44-49.

See illustration (colour).

CRAWHALL, Joseph E.   RSW   **1861-1913**
Animal painter. The son of Joseph Crawhall (q.v.) and one of the most distinguished artists connected with the Glasgow School. His sketches of animals in action are particularly fine. He was a contributor to *The Pall Mall Magazine*.

Colls: Burrell; V & AM.

Bibl: A.J.C. Bury, *The Man and The Artist*, 1958; Vivien Hamilton, *JC 1861-1913 One of the Glasgow Boys*, 1990.

CRAWSHAW, J.E.
Amateur artist. He contributed drawings of comic machines to *Punch*, 1906.

CREALOCK, Lieutenant-General Henry Hope   **1831-1891**
Amateur artist. He was educated at Rugby and joined the Army in 1848, serving in the Crimea and China, 1857-58, the Indian Mutiny, New Brunswick, 1865, and Zululand, 1879. He was promoted Lieutenant-Colonel in 1861 and Lieutenant-General in 1884.

Illus: *Wolf-Hunting and Wild Sport in Lower Brittany [1875]; Katerfelto [G.J.W. Melville, 1875]; Sport [W.D.B. Davenport, 1885].*

Contrib: *The Illustrated Times [1855].*

Colls: BM.

CRESWICK, Thomas   RA   1811-1869
Landscape painter and illustrator. He was born at Sheffield in 1811 and studied at Birmingham with Joseph Vincent Barber before settling in London in 1828. His métier was the English landscape in high summer, his compositions are always good, many of them were done in collaboration with animal painters such as Ansdell and Goodall or figure painters like Phillip and Frith. He was an early member of the Etching Club and he was commended by Ruskin, rare distinction, for a book illustration to 'Nut Brown Maid' in the *Book of English Ballads*. ARA, 1842 and RA, 1851. He died in 1869 and was buried at Kensal Green.
Illus: *Walton's Compleat Angler; Works of Goldsmith.*
Contrib: *Deserted Village [Goldsmith, Etching Club, 1841]; Gray's Elegy [Etching Club, 1847]; L'Allegro [Etching Club, 1849]; Songs and Ballads of Shakespeare [Etching Club, 1853]; Moxon's Tennyson [1857]; Favourite English Poems of the Last Two Centuries [1858-59]; Early English Poems [1863]; The Churchman's Family Magazine [1863].*
Exhib: BI, 1829-30; RA, 1828-
Colls: BM; Glasgow; Manchester.
Bibl: Chatto & Jackson, *Treatise on Wood Engraving*, 1861, pp.588-589.

CRIDDLE, Mrs. Henry née Mary Ann Alabaster   1805-1880
Watercolourist and illustrator. The daughter of an amateur caricaturist, she took lessons from Sir George Hayter from 1824-26 and concentrated on oil painting until 1846. She then devoted her time to watercolours and became an AOWS in 1849.
Illus: *The Children's Garden [A. and M.E. Catlow, 1865].*
Exhib: BI; OWS; RA, 1830-1879; RBA,
Bibl: Mallalieu.

CRISP, Frank E.F.   -1915
Artist working in St. John's Wood, who probably died on active service. He illustrated Edward Hutton's *The Cities of Romagna and The Marches*, 1913, with 12 colour plates.
Exhib: L; RA; RSA.

CROMBIE, Benjamin William   1803-1847
Draughtsman, engraver and caricaturist. He was born in Edinburgh and published a set of caricatures for *Modern Athenians*, 1839, in a style akin to that of Dighton.
Colls: Edinburgh.
Bibl: Veth, *Comic Art in England*, 1930, p.41, illus.

CROMBIE, Charles   fl.1904-1912
Cartoonist in black and white and watercolour. He worked for *The Bystander*, 1904, *The Graphic*, 1906, comic illustrations, and *The Illustrated London News* and *Graphic*, Christmas numbers, 1911 and 1912.
Colls: Witt Photo.

CROPSEY, Jasper F.   1823-1900
American painter established in England. He worked in New York 1845-62 and then travelled to Turkey. He was a founder member of the Academy in New York, 1851, before settling in London in 1857.
Illus: *The Poetical Works of E.A. Poe [1857]; The Poetry of Thomas Moore [n.d].*
Bibl: Chatto & Jackson, *Treatise on Wood Engraving*, 1861, p.598.

CROSS, A. Campbell   fl.1895-1898
Illustrator, working in Chelsea for the magazines. His drawings are usually in black chalk with colour washes and are in a late Pre-Raphaelite style.
Contrib: *The Sketch [1895-98]; The Idler; The Quartier Latin [1896]; The Quarto [1896-97].*
Exhib: RA, 1897.
Colls: V & AM.

CROSS, Stanley
Black and white artist. He contributed to *Punch*, 1914 and specialised in drawings of hen-pecked husbands.

J.A. CROWE. 'The Trenches Before Sebastopol', 1855

CROW
Comic illustrator to *Judy*, 1889.

CROWE, Eyre   ARA   1824-1910
Painter and illustrator. He was born in London on 3 October 1824, the son of Eyre Evans-Crowe, the historian. He studied with William Darley and at the Atelier Delaroche in Paris as well as at the RA Schools, 1844. He was secretary to his cousin W.M. Thackeray and lived in the United States, 1852-57. He was elected ARA in 1875 and died in London, 12 December 1910. He was an occasional caricaturist.
Illus: *With Thackeray in America [1893]; Haunts and Homes of W.M. Thackeray.*
Contrib: *ILN [1856-61].*
Exhib: BI, 1850, 1861; RA; RBA, 1854, 1856.
Colls: V & AM.

CROWE, J.A.
Artist. Described by *The Illustrated London News* as their 'Correspondent' in the Crimea, 1855-56.
See illustration.

CROWLEY, Nicholas J.   RHA   1813-1857
Portrait painter. He was born in 1813, probably in Ireland, and lived and worked for the whole of his life in Dublin, visiting England briefly in 1838. He was elected RHA, 1838, and died in 1857.
Contrib: *ILN [1853-54].*
Exhib: BI, 1839-57; RA, 1835- ; RBA, 1836.
Colls: NG, Ireland.

CROWQUILL, Alfred
pseudonym of Alfred Henry Forrestier   1804-1872
Writer and comic artist, caricaturist and illustrator. Born in London in 1804 and already contributing caricatures to the publishers by the age of eighteen. He worked for John Timbs on *The Hive* and *The Mirror*, before becoming associated with *Punch* from its earliest days, after its predecessor *Charivari* had foundered. Crowquill wrote extensively for *The New Monthly* and *Bentley's* magazines and was more widely regarded as a literary man than as an artist. Nevertheless his drawings are incisive and charming and have an element of fantasy at a time when grotesqueness was more usual. He left *Punch* in 1844 and found a highly successful career from the 1850s onwards as an illustrator of children's books. In his early career he sometimes drew social satires that were engraved by George Cruikshank (q.v.). His best work is found when he uses fine ink lines and pastel colours on toned paper.
He signs his work 𝄐
Illus: *Ups and Downs [1823]; Paternal Pride [1825]; Despondency and Jealousy [1825]; Der Freyschutz Travestied, Alfred Crowquill's Sketch Book, Absurdities in Prose and Verse [1827]; Goethe's Faust [1834]; Pickwick Abroad [(wrapper) 1939]; Pickwickian Sketches, Bunn's Vauxhall Papers [1841]; Sea Pie [1842]; Dr. Syntax Tour in*

ALFRED CROWQUILL (A.H. Forrestier) 1804-1872. Title page design for *Music On The Waves, A Set of Songs by The Honble Mrs Norton*. Ink and watercolour. Signed. 12¼in x 8¼in (13.1cm x 21cm)
Victoria and Albert Museum

Search of the Picturesque [1844]; Comic Arithmetic [1844]; Woman's Love [1846]; Wanderings of a Pen and Pencil [1846]; A Peep at Brighton [1848, AL]; A Good-natured Hint about California [1849]; The Excitement [1849]; Pictorial Grammar, Pictorial Arithmetic; Gold [1850]; Familiar Fables [c.1850]; The Guards and the Line [Col. Hort, 1851]; A Bundle of Crowquills Dropped by Alfred Crowquill [1854]; Fun [1854]; Griffel Swillendrunken [1856]; Aunt Mavor's Nursery Tales [1855]; Little Pilgrim [1856]; Little Plays For Little Actors [1856]; Fairy Tales [1857]; Merry Pictures [1857]; Bon Gaultier Ballads [with Leech and Doyle, 1857]; A New Story Book [1858]; Fairy Tales [C. Bede, 1858]; Baron Munchausen [1858]; Twyll Owlglass [1859]; Honesty and Cunning [1859]; Kindness and Cruelty [1859]; The Red Cap [1859]; Paul Prendergast [1859]; Strange Surprising Adventures of the Venerable Gooros Simple [1861]; Fairy Footsteps [1861]; Chambers Book of Days; Pickwick Abroad [G.W. Reynolds]; The Boys and The Giant [1870]; The Cunning Fox [1870]; Dick Doolittle [1870]; Little Tiny's Picture Book [1871]; Guide to the Watering Places.
Contrib: *Punch [1842-44]; ILN [1844-70]; The Illustrated Times [1859].*
Exhib: RA, 1845-46.
Colls: Author; V & AM.
Bibl: G. Everitt, *English Caricaturists*, 1893, pp.368-371; M.H. Spielmann, *The History of Punch*, 1895, pp.449-450.
See illustrations.

CROWTHER, T.S.C. fl.1891-1902
Illustrator. His work is characterised by a very thin pen line.
Contrib: *The Daily Graphic; The Windsor Magazine; The Temple Magazine; The Idler; The English Illustrated Magazine [1891-92]; The Graphic [1902].*

CRUIKSHANK, George, Snr. 1792-1878
Artist, etcher and polemicist on temperance, caricaturist. Born at Duke Street, Bloomsbury, on 27 September 1792, the second son of the caricaturist, Isaac Cruikshank. He worked with his father from an early age, engraving lottery tickets and chapbooks, his first published design appearing in 1806. From his father's death in about 1810, he developed as the foremost political caricaturist of the Regency, both spiritually and physically taking over the place of the insane Gillray at

ALFRED CROWQUILL (A.H. Forrestier) 1804-1872. A page from the artist's Ramsgate sketchbook.
Pen and ink. Signed and dated 1857. 6¾in x 9¼in (17.1cm x 25.5cm)
Author's Collection

GEORGE CRUIKSHANK, Snr. 1792-1878. Lady Caroline Lamb at Billingsgate market, about 1820. Pen and ink. 5in x 8¼in (12.7cm x 21cm)

JOHN BULL IN THE COUNCIL CHAMBER

GEORGE CRUIKSHANK, Snr. 1792-1878. 'John Bull in the Council Chamber'

Mrs. Humphrey's establishment. As early as 1820 when the caricature boom was still at its zenith, Cruikshank had begun contributing to ephemeral journals like *The Wits' Magazine* and was establishing himself as a book illustrator. His first major work in this medium was the Regency best-seller, *Life in London*, by Pierce Egan. This was followed by similar publications, including *Life in Paris*, and then a number of smaller books which became little more than vehicles for his own lively drawings. By the 1830s he was the leading illustrator and was engaged on works by Charles Dickens, Harrison Ainsworth and Sir Walter Scott. At the same time yearly almanacks were issued from 1835 to 1853 under the artist's name and these were succeeded by *George Cruikshank's Magazine*, 1853-54.

Cruikshank's conversion to the teetotal cause in the late 1840s gave him a fresh zest for life at exactly the moment when his fame was starting to diminish. The next thirty years witnessed an incredible activity from his pen, mostly for the Temperance League and including his mammoth 'The Worship of Bacchus', the vast unmanageable canvas which took him three years to complete and is now relegated to the cellars of the Tate Gallery. This frenzied picture, with its hundreds of tiny figure groups in various stages of dissipation says a great deal about the artist. Strongly inventive and with a keen eye for the absurd and the pathetic, he had delusions of grandeur which were unsuited to his small scale genius. Although Ruskin gave him fulsome praise for his children's books, the vigour of his line and the bombast of his humour belonged to the 18th century rather than the 19th.

Cruikshank died at Mornington Crescent on 1 February 1878 and

PERCY CRUIKSHANK fl.1853-54. 'Sunday Evening at the Red cross Gin Shop, Barbican'. Illustration for *Sunday Scenes in London and the Suburbs*, May 1854. Lithograph

was buried at Kensal Green; his body was later removed to St. Paul's at the instigation of the temperance lobby rather than for his acknowledged importance as an artist.

Finished drawings by Cruikshank are rare, the most common items met with are pencil studies in small scale on white paper, the major figures drawn over in ink in preparation for the completed work.

Illus: *Nelson's Funeral Car [1806, first illus]; Life in London [1820]; Life in Paris [1822]; Peter Sclemihl [1824]; Greenwich Hospital [1826]; Phrenological Illustrations [1826]; Illustrations of Time [1827]; Punch and Judy, Scraps and Sketches [1828]; Three Courses and a Dessert [1830]; Hogarth Moralized, Roscoe's Moralists Library [1831]; Salis Populi Suprema Lex [1832]: Sundays in London [1833]; Cruikshankiana [1835]; My Sketchbook; Comic Almanack [1835-53]; Sketches by Boz [Dickens, 1836]; Waverley Novels [1836-38]; Oliver Twist [Dickens]; Jack Sheppard, Guy Fawkes [1838]; The Tower of London [Ainsworth, 1840]; George Cruikshank's Omnibus [1841]; The Bachelor's Own Book, Arthur O'Leary [1844]; George Cruikshank's Table Book, Maxwell's Irish Rebellion [1845]; Outline of Society [1846]; The Bottle [1847]; The Drunkard's Children [1848]; 1851 or The Adventures of Mr. and Mrs. Sandboys [1851]; Uncle Tom's Cabin [1852], George Cruikshank's Fairy Library [1853-54]; The New Political House That Jack Built [1854]; Life of Falstaff [1857]; A Pop Gun Fired Off [1860]; The British Bee Hive [1867]; Our Gutter Children [1868]; The Brownies and Other Tales [Mrs. J.H. Ewing, 1871]; The Trial of Sir Jasper [1873]; Peeps at Life [1875]; The Rose and The Lily [1877].*

Contrib: *Bentley's Miscellany [1837-43]; Ainsworth's Magazine [1842]; Cassell's Illustrated Family Paper [1853]; British Workman [1855]; Ingoldsby Legends [1864]; Cassell's Illustrated Family Readings [1867]; Belgravia [1868]; The Illustrated Times; ILN [1877].*

Exhib: BI, 1833-60; RA.

Colls: BM (large collection); Manchester; Tate; V & AM.

Bibl: Chatto & Jackson, *Treatise on Wood Engraving*, 1861, pp.595-596; Marchmont, Frederick, *The Three Cruikshanks, A Biographical Catalogue*, 1897; J. Grego, *C's Watercolours*, 1904; R. McLean, *GC*, 1949; William Feaver, *GC*, Arts Council, 1974; Jones, W., *George Cruikshank His Life and London*, 1978; Wardroper, J., *GC*, exhibition catalogue, St. John's Gate, 1992; Patten, Robert L., *George Cruikshank's Life, Times, And Art Vol. 1: 1792-1835* (Lutterworth), 1992.

See illustrations.

CRUIKSHANK, George, Jnr.   fl.1866-1894
Son of Percy Cruikshank (q.v.). His drawings are very weak imitations of his uncle, he contributed to magazines in the 1870s and 1880s and usually signs George Cruikshank Junior.

Contrib: *Beeton's Annuals [1866]; London Society [1866, 1874]; Aunt Judy's Magazine [1866-71]; ILN [1882]; The Sphere [1894].*

Colls: V & AM.

CRUIKSHANK, (Isaac) Robert   1786-1856
Caricaturist, illustrator and miniature painter. He was born in 1786, the eldest son of Isaac Cruikshank and brother of George Cruikshank,

Snr. (q.v.). He served as midshipman with the East India Company until 1814, setting up as a miniature painter in London and changing to etching and caricatures in 1816. Between then and 1825 he attained almost as wide a popularity as his brother, issuing caricatures on the follies of fashion, the foibles of military life and those of the stage. He achieved great success with the illustrations for *Life in London*, the book adapted from the play which he had himself designed at the Adelphi Theatre, He also provided lively and well-executed illustrations for *The English Spy*, but after the 1820s he dropped out of favour and published slovenly uneven work. Everitt considers that the new forms of caricature adapted by HB and others killed his not very original talent. He died in poverty, 13 March 1856.

Illus: *Age of Intellect [J. Moore, 1819]; Lessons of Thrift [1820]; Nightingale's Memoirs of Queen Caroline [1820]; Radical Chiefs [1821]; Life in London [1821]; The Commercial Tourist [1822]; Annals of Sporting and Fancy Gazette [1822-25]; Ramsey's New Dictionary of Anecdote [1822]; My Cousin in the Army [1822]; Westmacott's Points of Misery [1823]; Spirit of the Public Journals [1823-24]; Life and Exploits of Don Quixote [1824]; Bernard Blackmantle's English Spy [1825]; Westmacott's Punster's Pocket Book [1826]; London Characters [1827]; Grimm's Fairy Tales [1827]; Thompson's Life of Allen [1828]; Smeeton's Doings in London [1828]; British Dance of Death [1828, frontis.]; Spirit of the Age [1828]; Universal Songster [1828]; London Oddities [1828]; The Finish to the Adventures of Tom, Jerry and Logick [1828]. Etc.*

Exhib: RA, 1811-17.

Colls: BM; V & AM.

Bibl: G. Everitt, *English Caricaturists*, 1893, pp.89-124; W. Bates, *GC the Artist, the Humorist and The Man, with some account of his brother Robert*, 1878.

See illustration (colour).

CRUIKSHANK, Percy   fl.1853-1854
The son of (Isaac) Robert Cruikshank (q.v.). Worked with his uncle and father and illustrated *Sunday Scenes in London and the Suburbs*, twelve illustrations on stone, May 1854.

Colls: BM.

See illustration.

CUBITT, Miss Edith Alice (Mrs. Andrews)   fl.1898-1940
Flower painter and illustrator. She studied at the New Cross Art School and won the prize for black and white illustrations at the National Competition, South Kensington, 1898. She attended Goldsmith's College in 1909. She was working in London in 1900 and at Kent in 1909 and 1931.

Illus: *A Book of Nursery Rhymes, Ernest Nister, c.1900.*

Exhib: B; L; RA; RI.

CUCUEL, Edward   1875-
American painter and illustrator. He was born in San Francisco in 1875, but worked in Switzerland and Germany, 1924.

Contrib: *ILN [1905].*

Exhib: L; Salon, Paris.

CUITT, George   1779-1854
Topographical illustrator and etcher. He was the son of George Cuitt 1743-1814, the landscape painter, and was born at Richmond, Yorks. in 1779. He followed his father as a painter, but specialised in etchings of buildings, ruins and landscapes in a dramatic Italianate style. He taught drawing at Richmond, then at Chester from 1804 to 1820 and it is that city with which he is usually associated. Cuitt was the only artist of his generation to apply the romantic view of buildings to practical illustration as in guides and histories, his crowded streets and small figures are influenced by Piranesi. Cuitt's books, which are very desirable, cannot be obtained easily, but his separate plates from these can be found. He died at Masham, 1854.

Illus: *Six Etchings of Saxon and Other Buildings Remaining of Chester [1810-11]; Six Etchings of Old Buildings in Chester; Six Etchings of Picturesque Buildings in Chester [1810-11]; A History of Chester [1815]; Yorkshire Abbeys [1822-25]; Twenty-four Etchings of Select Parts of Yorkshire [1834]; Wanderings and Pencillings Among Ruins of the Olden Times [1848].*

Colls: BM; Leeds; Newcastle; V & AM; Witt Photo.

See illustration.

GEORGE CUITT 1779-1854. Chester, 1815

CULLIN, Isaac   **fl.1881-1894**
Figure and portrait painter. He exhibited at the RA and Liverpool, 1881-89, and drew sporting subjects for *The Illustrated London News*, 1893-94.

CUNEO, Cyrus Cincinnato   **ROI**   **1879-1916**
Painter and illustrator. He was born in San Francisco of Italian parents and came to Paris to study under Girardo, Prenet and Whistler, 1900. Settled in London in 1902 and died there in 1916. He became ROI in 1908. His illustrative work is unusual in often being in oil on board.
Illus: *The Lost Column [C. Gilson, 1908 (boys' novel)].*
Contrib: *The Pall Mall Magazine; The Strand Magazine [1906]; ILN [1908-12].*
Exhib: G; L; RA; RHA; ROI.
Colls: V & AM.

CUPPLES, G.
Contributed to *Good Words For The Young*, 1872.

CURTIS, Dora   **fl.1899-1905**
Figure painter and illustrator. She designed bookplates, one of which appeared in *The Quarto*, 1896, and exhibited at the NEA, 1899-1901.
Illus: *Stories of King Arthur and The Round Table [Dent, 1905].*

CUTHBERT, E.S.
Contributing illustrations of Arabia to *The English Illustrated Magazine*, 1887.

CUTTS, H.W.
Contributed rural subjects to the *Illustrated London News*, 1887. This could be a misreading for the Liverpool landscape artist J. Cutts, active 1885-86.

'CYNICUS' Pseudonym of Martin Anderson
Political and social cartoonist, designer of postcards. Anderson seems to have originated from Dundee and produced satirical books,

in limited editions from an address at 57 Drury Lane, London. The sketches are inventive if not very masterly in the drawing, according to Thorpe they were popular at the time.
Illus: *The Satires of Cynicus [1892]; The Humours of Cynicus [1892]; The Fatal Smile A Fairy Tale [1892]; Cartoons Social and Political [1893]; Symbols and Metaphors [n.d.].*
Colls: Gordon,
See illustration.

CYNICUS (Martin Anderson). Political cartoon possibly for *The Satires*, 1890. Pen and ink   Jeffrey Gordon Collection

D, H.P.
Unidentified illustrator for *Fun*, 1887.

DA COSTA, John ROI
1867-1931

Portrait painter and illustrator. He was born in 1867 and after being educated in Southampton, studied art in Paris for three years. He did most of his illustrative work in the 1890s before becoming a fashionable portrait painter, elected ROI 1905 and RP 1912. He was living at Newlyn in 1880 and in London 1898-1931, except for a

brief period at Clanfield, Oxon, 1908. He died 26 May 1931.
Contrib: *The Yellow Book; The Quarto [1896]; Eureka [1901]; The Graphic [1901].*
Exhib: G; GG; L; M; New Gall.; Paris, 1907; P; RA; RHA; ROI; RSA.

DADD, Frank RI
1851-1929

Black and white artist and figure illustrator. He was born in London on 28 March 1851 and educated at South Kensington and the RA Schools before starting work as an illustrator in about 1872. Dadd did much work for the magazines, particularly drawing for boys' adventure stories; he joined the staff of *The Graphic* in 1884. His style is very photographic with heavy application of bodycolour and clever uses of grey wash, but it is technically excellent and very accurate in detail. He became RI, 1884 and ROI, 1888 and in 1908 one of his pictures was purchased by the Chantrey Bequest. Dadd was a cousin of Kate Greenaway (q.v.), and his brother married her sister. He died at Teignmouth, Devon, 7 March 1929. Dadd's pictures and drawings are models of Edwardian eloquence, if not of high art.
Illus: *Lead Kindly Light [J.H. Newman, 1887]; Dick O' the Fens [G.M. Fenn, 1888].*
Contrib: *Cornhill Magazine [1870-79]; The Graphic [1876-1910]; ILN [1878-84]; The Quiver [1882]; Boys' Own Paper; The Windsor Magazine.*
Exhib: B; G; L; M; RA, 1905; RI; ROI.
Colls: Author; BM; Exeter.
Bibl: *Who Was Who 1924-40.*
See illustrations.

FRANK DADD RI 1851-1929. 'He's an absent minded beggar but he heard his country call'. Illustration for a magazine during the Boer War, c.1900

FRANK DADD RI 1851-1929. 'A duel'. Illustration for unidentified serial story. Ink and wash with Chinese white. Signed. 5½in x 7in (14cm x 17.8cm)   Author's Collection

DADD, Philip J.S.   -1916

Painter and illustrator, killed in action 1916. There are two pen and ink drawings by this artist of war subjects in the Victoria and Albert Museum, one dated 1899. He worked in Hornsey and exhibited at the RA, RI, ROI and Liverpool, 1905-14. He signs his work 'PD'.

DADD, Richard   1817-1886

Painter, draughtsman and illustrator. He was born at Chatham, the son of a tradesman and after being educated there, studied art at William Dadson's Academy. In 1834 his family moved to London and the young Dadd became friendly with notable artists, including David Roberts (q.v.) and Clarkson Stanfield (q.v.). He entered the RA Schools on their recommendation in 1837 and he specialised in the painting of fancy pictures in which fairies took a principal role. In 1840 he won the medal for life drawing at the RA and began to exhibit regularly in London.

Dadd was fortunate to be encouraged by Sir Thomas Phillips, the art connoisseur, and was taken on an extensive European tour by him in 1842, visiting Italy, Greece and the Middle East. On this expedition he first showed unusual behaviour and delusions about the Pope and his patron, Sir Thomas, whom he was convinced were devils. Although he was clearly insane by his return, the symptoms were not recognised until, on August 28 1843, he brutally murdered his father in Cobham Park, Kent. He immediately fled to France, but was arrested and returned to this country in 1844 and confined in Bethlem Hospital. He was encouraged to continue painting in the asylum and Dr. W.C. Hood, who became physician at Bethlem in 1853, became a collector and admirer of his work. He was moved to Broadmoor in 1864 where he died in 1886. Dadd's work is interesting because of his isolation from the art world for so many years. His watercolours show a microscopic observation of detail and a fresh and rather disturbing use of colour. Some of his drawings might be compared to those of the Pre-Raphaelites, particularly the more intense visions of Millais and Rossetti in the early 1850s. Dadd's work as an illustrator was short-lived. He drew for *The Book of British Ballads*, 1842, contributing vignettes of 'Robin Goodfellow' and made a frontispiece for *The Kentish Coronal* 1840, which is remarkably bold for its date.

Exhib: BI, 1839; RA; RBA, 1837.
Colls: Bedford; BM; Fitzwilliam; Newcastle; V & AM.
Bibl: D. Greysmith, *RD*, 1973. Tate Gallery RD Exhibition catalogue, 1974.

DADD, Stephen T.   fl.1879-1914

Figure painter and illustrator. He worked at Brockley, South London, and contributed domestic and animal subjects to magazines.
Contrib: *The Graphic [1882-91, 1901]; ILN [1889]; Daily Graphic [1890]; The Quiver [1890]; Sporting and Dramatic News [1890]; Black and White [1891]; The Rambler [1897]; Chums; Cassell's Family Magazine.*
Exhib: L; M; NWS, 1879-92; RBA; RI.

DALE, Lawrence

Amateur artist. He contributed to *Punch*, 1909.

DALTON, F.T.

'Dalton' who contributed cartoons to *Vanity Fair*, 1895-1900.
Bibl: Roy T. Matthews & Peter Mellini, *In Vanity Fair*, 1982.

DALZIEL, Edward   1817-1905

Engraver on wood and illustrator. He was born at Wooler, Northumberland, on 5 December 1817, the fifth son of Alexander Dalziel and brother of E. and T.B. Dalziel (qq.v.). He was in business at first, but spent much of his spare time studying art, finally joining his brother George in London in 1839 as a wood engraver. He formed part of the firm of Dalziel for over fifty years. Edward was the brother who took on the role of illustrator more earnestly than the rest of his family; he studied at the Clipstone St. Academy alongside Charles Keene (q.v.), and Sir John Tenniel (q.v.) and exhibited from time to time at the RA. He collaborated with his brother on their book, *The Brothers Dalziel, A Record of Work, 1840-1890*, and died 25 March 1905.
Illus: *The Hermit [Thomas Parnell].*
Contrib: *Bryant's Poems [1857]; Dramatic Scenes [1857]; Poets of the Nineteenth Century [1857]; The Home Affections [Mackay 1858]; Dalziel's Arabian Nights [1865]; A Round of Days [1866]; The Spirit of Praise [1866]: Ballad Stories of the Affections [1866]; Golden Thoughts from Golden Fountains [1867]; North Coast [1868]; National Nursery Rhymes [1870]; The Graphic [1873-74]; Dalziel's Bible Gallery [1881].*
Bibl: The Brothers Dalziel, *A Record of Work 1840-90*, 1901; Gleeson White, *English Illustration The Sixties*, 1897; F. Reid, *Illustrators of the Sixties,* 1928. pp.252-258, illus.; Simon Houfe, *The Dalziel Family*, Sotheby's Belgravia, 1978.

EDWARD GURDON DALZIEL 1849-1889. Illustration for *The Uncommercial Traveller*, Dickens' Household Edition, 1870

DALZIEL, (E.) Gilbert   **1852-1930**
2nd son of Edward Dalziel (q.v.). Studied at South Kensington and at the Slade and with Dalziel Brothers. Living at Hampstead in 1882. Editor of *Judy* and *Ally Sloper's Half Holiday*.
Exhib: D.
Bibl: *The Dalziel Family*, Sotheby's Belgravia, 1978.

DALZIEL, Edward Gurdon   **1849-1889**
Illustrator. He was born in 1849 and was the eldest son of Edward Dalziel (q.v.). For some years he was a contributor to *Fun*, 1878-80, choosing subjects of country life and manners, with figures in the tradition of Pinwell and Walker. In *The Brothers Dalziel* he is described as 'a young artist full of promise and great ability. Had he given continued attention to his oil painting he must undoubtedly have taken a very high position. He exhibited many pictures at the Royal Academy, the Grosvenor and other galleries, but the allurement of black and white became too much for him, and he laid aside his brush for the pencil.' *A Record of Work*, 1901, p. 10. His work in this medium was much admired by Sir John Gilbert, but he died at the comparatively early age of thirty-nine in 1889.
Contrib: *The Uncommercial Traveller [Dickens' Household Edition, 1871]*.
Exhib: NWS, 1865-87; RA; RBA.
See illustration.

DALZIEL, Thomas Bolton Gilchrist Septimus   **1823-1906**
Illustrator and wood engraver. He was born at Wooler, Northumberland, in 1823, the son of Alexander Dalziel, painter. He joined his brothers George, Edward and John in the London engraving business in 1860. He was the only one of the brothers to be a noted draughtsman, he was a more accomplished figure artist than Edward, and he contributed to a number of books that were either augmented or financed by the firm. He was a fine landscape illustrator and some of his best work is in Dalziel's Arabian Nights.
Contrib: *Dramatic Scenes [1857]; Bryant's Poems [1857]; Poets of*

the Nineteenth Century [1857]; Gertrude of Wyoming [1857]; The Home Affections [Mackay 1858]; Lays of the Holy Land [1858]; The Pilgrim's Progress [1863]; The Golden Harp [1864]; The Churchman's Family Magazine [1864]; The Sunday Magazine [1866-68]; Dalziel's Arabian Nights [1865]; The Arabian Nights [1866]; A Round of Days [1866]; Ballad Stories of the Affections [1866]; The Spirit of Praise [1866]; Jean Ingelow's Poems [1867]; Golden Thoughts From Golden Fountains [1867]; North Coast [1865]; National Nursery Rhymes [1870]; Christmas Carols [1871]; Dalziel's Bible Gallery [1881]; Art Pictures From The Old Testament [1891 etc.].
Exhib: BI, 1858; RA; RBA, 1846, 1866.
Bibl: *The Brothers Dalziel - A Record of Work 1840-1890*, 1901; F. Reid, *Illustrators of the Sixties*, 1928, pp.251-252; Simon Houfe, *The Dalziel Family*, Sotheby's Belgravia, 1978.

DANCE, Sir Nathaniel, Bt. RA   **1734-1811**
Caricaturist. He was the eldest son of George Dance, the architect, and was born in London in 1734. He showed a talent for painting from an early age and studied with Francis Hayman, followed by nearly nine years in Italy, where he met and fell in love with Angelica Kauffmann. On his return to England he married a wealthy widow and enjoyed a comfortable life in which he was able to devote his time to politics, eventually being given a baronetcy as MP for East Grinstead. Dance was known in his day as a history and portrait painter and as a founder member of the RA. but ironically is best remembered now for the brilliant caricatures done for his own amusement and for private circulation.
His style of pen drawing is close to Rowlandson (q.v.) in outline and like Hogarth in subject manner. Although it is very much in the tradition of Lord Townshend, it is softer in touch.
Exhib: RA.
Colls: NPG; Witt Photo.

DANIELL, Samuel   **c.1775-1811**
Watercolourist and illustrator. He was born in 1775, the brother of William and the nephew of Thomas Daniell (qq.v.). He studied under Medland and travelled in Africa as secretary and draughtsman for the Bechuanaland mission, 1801. He returned to England in 1804 and travelled to Ceylon; in the following year he died of illness contracted there in the swamps.
Illus: *African Scenery and Animals [1804-05, AT 32]; Barrow's Travels Into The Interior of Southern Africa [1806, AT 322]; The Scenery Animals and Native Inhabitants of Ceylon [1808]; Scenery of Southern Africa [1820, AT 326]*.
Exhib: RA, 1792-1812.
Colls: V & AM.
Bibl: Iolo Williams, *Early English Watercolours*, 1952, p.58 illus.

DANIELL, Thomas   RA   **1749-1840**
Landscape painter. He was born at Kingston-upon-Thames in 1749, the son of an innkeeper. After being apprenticed to a coach painter, he began to work for Thomas Catton RA, and entered the RA Schools in 1773. During this period he worked as a landscapist in the English Shires, but in 1785 he made the journey that was to alter the course of his career, by travelling to India with his nephew, William (q.v.). He worked in Calcutta, 1788-89, then toured North India, returning to Calcutta in 1791. In 1792 they undertook a tour of Southern India and Ceylon, returning to Bombay in 1793 and leaving for home later the same year.
Much of Daniell's subsequent career was taken up with completing and publishing his Indian work. His drawings and watercolours are careful topographer's work, the colours more like tints than full-blooded watercolours. He became ARA in 1796 and RA in 1797. He was a Fellow of the Royal Society and of the Asiatic Society. He died at Kensington on 19 March 1840.
Illus. (with W. Daniell): *Oriental Scenery [1795-1808]; A Picturesque Voyage to India by the Way of China [1810]*.
Illus: *Views in Calcutta [1786-88, AT 492]*.
Exhib: RA, 1772-84.
Colls: BM; Fitzwilliam; India Office Library; V & AM.
Bibl: T. Sutton, *The Daniells*, 1954; M. Shellim, *The Daniells in Indias*, 1970; *Walker's Quarterly*, Vol.35-36, 1932; M. Archer, *Cat. of Drawings in the India Office Library*.

DANIELL, William   RA   1769-1837
Landscape painter and topographer. He was born in 1769 and was trained as his uncle, William Daniell's assistant and accompanied him to India, 1785-94 (q.v.). On his return, Daniell concentrated on making topographical drawings and watercolours, specialising at first in Indian scenery and later in English and Scottish views. He was a very fine aquatinter and engraver and engraved most of the prints for his uncle and family from 1808. His greatest success was probably his *Voyage Round Great Britain*, produced in the years 1813 to 1823 and published 1814-25. He produced some of his best watercolours for this work, although many of the studies for the prints are in sepia wash. Daniell was an early follower of Turner in wiping out highlights in his watercolours but otherwise belonged to the older tradition of watercolours. He died at New Camden Town on 16 August 1837. ARA 1807, and RA 1822.
Illus: *Oriental Scenery [1795-1808, 1812-16, AT 432]; Interesting Selections from Animated Nature [1807-12]; A Picturesque Voyage to India by the Way of China [1810]; A Familiar Treatise on Perspective [1810]; Views in Bootan [1813, AT 434]; A Voyage Round Great Britain [1814-25]; Illustrations of the Island of Staffa [1818, after S. Daniell]; Sketches of the Native Tribes...of Southern Africa [1820]; Views of Windsor, Eton and Virginia Water [1827-30]; The Oriental Annual [1838]; A Brief History of Ancient and Modern India [Blagdon, 1802-05].*
Exhib: BI, 1807-36; RA from 1795.
Colls: Bedford; BM; Fitzwilliam; Greenwich; India Office; V & AM.
Bibl: T. Sutton, *The Daniells*, 1954; M. Shellim, *The Daniells in India*, 1970; M. Archer, *Catalogue of Drawings in the India Office Library*.

DANIELS, George   1854-c.1917
Landscape painter, miniaturist, stained glass artist. He probably undertook some illustrations and a period subject dated '28 February 1874' is in the Victoria and Albert Museum.
Exhib: RA, 1884-93.

DARBYSHIRE, J.A.   fl.1886-1893
Figure illustrator, working in the Manchester area at Flixton and Prestwick. His work is rather exaggerated and weak in drawing.
Exhib: M, 1886-93.
Colls: V & AM.

DARLEY, J. Felix   RBA ACA   -1932
Landscape and figure painter and illustrator. He contributed many competent landscape subjects to books in the 1860s and was elected RBA in 1901. He worked in London from 1886 and at Addlestone, Surrey, from 1898. He died at Woking on 17 October 1932.
Contrib: *The Poetical Works of Edgar Allan Poe [1857]; Poets of the West; London Society [1863].*
Exhib: B; L; RBA; ROI.
Bibl: Chatto & Jackson, *Treatise On Wood Engraving*, 1861, p.599.

DARRÉ, G.   fl.1883-1889
French illustrator. He worked extensively for Parisian satirical publications, including *Charivari, Journal Amusant, Le Grelot, Le Carillon*. He illustrated a *Histoire de France* before coming to London in 1883. There he found work on *Punch*, 1888-89, and some work on *Judy*, 1889. After that date he abandoned illustration for commercial work in black and white.

DAUBENY, Hesketh
Contributing illustrations of comic animals to *Punch*, 1907.

DAVENPORT, W.
Topographer. He illustrated a *Life of Ali Pasha*, 1823, AT 206.

DAVEY, George
Illustrator and contributor to *Fun*, 1901, working in West Hampstead, London, 1901-2.

DAVEY, H.F.
Topographer. Working in Newcastle-upon-Tyne and contributing drawings to *The Illustrated London News*, 1887.

DAVID, S.
Illustrator of the 1822 edition of *Walton's Compleat Angler*.

DAVIDSON, Alexander   RSW   1838-1887
Painter and illustrator who studied in Glasgow. He exhibited at the RA and at the RBA, 1873-92. He made drawings for an edition of Scott's *Waverley Novels*.

DAVIDSON, Thomas   fl.1880-1908
Painter of history and genre. He worked in Hampstead from 1880 and specialised in figure subjects. He contributed the latter to *Good Words*, 1880.
Contrib: *The Quiver [1880].*
Exhib: B; G; L; M; RA; RBA; RHA; ROI.

DAVIEL, Leon   fl. 1893-1930
Portrait painter, wood engraver and illustrator. In his earlier years he specialised in figure subjects for the magazines, 1897-1907; he worked in Chelsea, 1914-25.
Contrib: *Good Words [1897]; Black and White [1900]; Pearson's Magazine; The Temple Magazine; The Illustrated London News [1907, Christmas].*
Exhib: NEA, 1912; New Gall; P; RA; ROI.

DAVIES, Edgar W   fl.1893-1910
Historical, mythical and architectural draughtsman. He was working in Manchester in 1893 and subsequently in London. He designed book covers and made studies of foreign towns, possibly with a view to illustration. An important group of his drawings in a late Pre-Raphaelite style were sold at Sotheby's Belgravia on 24 January 1978.
Exhib: B; L; M; New Gall.; RA; RBA.

DAVIES, Scrope
Figure artist. Contributed to *The English Illustrated Magazine*, 1897; *The Dome*, 1899.

DAVIS, A.L.   fl. 1899-1925
Figure painter. Probably the same artist who lived at Hither Green, Kent, from 1914-25 and exhibited at the RA, 1914. He contributed to Newnes edition of *The Arabian Nights*, 1899.

DAVIS, G.H.
Marine illustrator, contributing naval subjects to *The Graphic*, 1910.

DAVIS, Joseph Bernard   1861-
Painter of landscapes, genre and portraits, and illustrator. He was born at Bowness, Windermere, in 1861, and worked in London, 1890-1911, and from then until 1925 at Gerrards Cross, Bucks. He was a fairly regular illustrator in the 1890s and excelled in robust genre scenes, such as 'Bank Holiday at the Welsh Harp' for *The Graphic*.
Contrib: *The Temple Magazine [1896]; The Quiver [1900]; The Graphic [1903]; The Ludgate Monthly; The Pall Mall Magazine; The Windsor Magazine; The Royal Magazine.*
Exhib: B; G; L; NWS; RA; RBA; RCA; RI; ROI; RSA.
Colls: Witt Photo.

DAVIS, Louis   RWS   1861-1941
Book decorator and illustrator. He worked at Ewelme, Pinner, 1897-1925, and designed borders and bookplates in the style of Morris and Burne-Jones. From 1886-87 he was designing decoration in the form of stylised birds for *The English Illustrated Magazine*, and in 1891-92 contributed topographical work. His drawings are delightful period pieces. He was elected ARWS, 1898.
Illus: *Good Night [Dolly Radford, 1895].*
Contrib: *The Quest [1895].*
Exhib: L; New Gall.; RWS.

DAVIS, Lucien   RI   1860-
Artist and illustrator. He was born at Liverpool in 1860, the son of William Davis, the Liverpool artist. He was educated at St. Francis Xavier's College, Liverpool, and entered the RA Schools in 1877 where he won several prizes. He began his career as an illustrator with Cassell's publications in 1878, but had his first important

drawings published in *The Graphic*, 1880-81. He joined the staff of *The Illustrated London News* in 1885 and remained for the next twenty years as one of its chief artists, specialising in social subjects and in work for the Christmas numbers. He was described in the magazine in 1892 as 'singularly successful in representing the sheen of a silk or satin dress'; certainly his figures are rarely seen out of the ballroom or the drawing room! Davis was elected RI in 1893. Art Master, St. Ignatius College, London. His two brothers, W.P. and Valentine Davis, were also artists.
Illus: *Willow the King [1899 (child's book)]; Cricket, Lawn Tennis* and *Billiards* in the Badminton Library editions.
Contrib: *The Graphic [1880-81]; ILN [1885-1905]; The English Illustrated Magazine [1885]; Fun [1886-87]; The Quiver [1890]; Cassell's Family Magazine.*
Exhib: G; L; M; Paris, 1900; P; RA.
Colls: V & AM; Witt Photo.

DAVIS, Norman
Contributed illustrations to *Illustrated London News*, 1891.

DAVIS, Vaughan
Animal artist. Illustrated Cassell's *The Book of the Dog*, c.1870.

DAVY, C.   fl. 1833-1846
Architectural draughtsman. He contributed to *Public Works of Great Britain*, 1838, AL 410.
Exhib: RA.

DAWSON, Alfred   fl. 1860-1889
Landscape painter. He worked at Chertsey as painter and etcher and exhibited at London exhibitions from 1860. He made illustrations for a history of Dorset and contributed to *The Portfolio*, 1884-92.
Exhib: B; RA; RBA; RE; ROI.
Colls: V & AM; Witt Photo.

DAWSON, Charles Frederick   fl.1909-1933
Painter and designer. He studied at Shipley School of Art and then in Bradford, Manchester and Newlyn, Cornwall. He was for some years headmaster of the Bingley, Nelson and Accrington Schools of Art.
Contrib: *The Page [1899].*
Exhib: L; M; RA.

DEAN, Christopher
Draughtsman, illustrator and book decorator. He was born in Glasgow and worked there until 1895, settling in Marlow, Bucks., in 1898 and in Chelsea from 1925. He designed illustrations and book covers in a bold Celtic style, using distinctive interlaced borders to the page plates.
Designs for: *Hans Sachs His Life and Work [c.1910]; The Odes of Anacreon [c.1910].*
Exhib: G and RSA, 1895-99.
Bibl: *The Studio* Vol.12, 1898, pp.183-187, illus. Winter No. 1900-01, p.64, illus.

DEAN, Frank   **RBA**   **1865-**
Painter of genre and illustrator. He was born near Leeds in 1865 and studied at the Slade School under Legros and then at Paris with Lefevbre and Boulanger, 1882-86. He was a close friend of A.S. Hartrick (q.v.) and joined the staff of *The Graphic* with him in 1890, he later shared a flat with E.J. Sullivan (q.v.). Dean travelled to the Middle East and India in search of subjects and worked at Headingley near Leeds from 1914. He was elected RBA, 1895.
Exhib: L; M; NEA; New Gall.; RA, from 1887; RBA; RCA; RI; ROI; RSA.
Bibl: A.S. Hartrick, *Painters Pilgrimage Through Fifty Years*, 1939.

DEANE, William Wood   **OWS**   **1825-1873**
Painter, watercolourist and draughtsman. He was born in Liverpool Road, Islington, on 22 March 1825, the son of J.W. Wood, amateur watercolourist. He began his career in architecture, but gradually abandoned this for painting. He attended the RA Schools in 1844, where he won a silver medal and travelled to Italy, 1850-52. He was an intimate friend of F.W. Topham (q.v.) and visited Spain with him in 1866; he married the sister of Professor George Aitchison, ARA, the

architect. He was elected ARIBA, 1848, Associate of the NWS, 1862, and Member, 1867, resigning in 1870 to join the OWS. He was a prolific painter of views of France, Spain and Venice, very colourful and moody compositions. He died at Hampstead, 18 January 1873.
Contrib: *The Illustrated Times [Naples, 1856].*
Exhib : BI, 1859-64; OWS; NWS; RA ; RBA, 1857-66.
Colls: V & AM; Wakefield.
Bibl: M. Hardie, *Watercol. Paint. in Britain*, Vol.3, 1968, p.21 illus.

DEAR, Mary E.   fl.1848-1867
Portrait and genre painter and illustrator. She worked in London and exhibited at various exhibitions through Messrs. Colnaghi, Pall Mall East; by 1867 she was working from Rottingdean, Sussex. Her figure drawing is always of high quality.
Illus: *The Scarlet Letter [Nathaniel Hawthorne, 1859].*
Contrib: *The Illustrated Times [1855, Christmas]; The Art Journal [c.1865 (a series of Seasons)].*
Exhib: RA; RBA, 1848-67.

DEARMER, Mrs. Percy (née Mabel White)   **1872-1915**
Writer, dramatist and illustrator. She was born on 22 March 1872 and studied art at the Herkomer School, Bushey. In 1892 she married the Rev. Percy Dearmer, Editor of the *English Hymnal*, and became one of the most popular illustrators of children's books, many of them written by herself and printed in bright colours. She was also engaged in poster work before her death and died at Primrose Hill, London, 10 July 1915.
Illus: *Wymps and Other Fairy Tales [Evelyn Sharp 1897]; Roundabout Rhymes [1898]; The Book of Penny Toys [1899]; The Noah's Ark Geography [1900]; The Seven Young Goslings [Laurence Housman, 1900]; Other Side of the Sun, Fairy Tales [1900, with Nellie Syrett].*
Contrib: *The Yellow Book [1896 (cover), 1897]; The Savoy [1896]; The Parade [1897].*

DE GRIMM see GRIMM

DE HAENEN, F.   fl.1896-1910
War artist and illustrator. He was a Frenchman, working for the magazine, *L'Illustration*, and contributing to *The Illustrated London News*, 1896. He went to South Africa as correspondent for *The Graphic*, in 1900 and continued to work for the journal until 1910.
Illus: *Russia [A & C Black].*

DE KATOW, Paul   **1834-1897**
Battle painter and illustrator. He was born in Strasbourg on 17 October 1834 and became a pupil of Delacroix; he exhibited regularly at the Salon, 1839-82, and was war correspondent of *Gaulois* in 1870. He drew illustrations of the Siege of Paris for *The Illustrated London News*, 1870, and contributed to *The Graphic*, 1872.
Exhib: RBA, 1872-73.

DE LA BERE, Stephen Baghot   **RI**   **1877-1927**
Figure and landscape painter and illustrator. He was educated at Folkestone and Ilkley, Yorks., and studied at Westminster School of Art. His earliest drawings, dated 1903, are in a poster style reminiscent of John Hassall. He worked in Kensington for most of his life, but at Bishop's Stortford, 1913-14. He was elected RI in 1908. De La Bere was an occasional illustrator, capable of very fine pen and ink work, he died in 1927.
Illus: *Lazarillo de Tomes [Hurtado de Mendoza, n.d].*
Contrib: *ILN [1911].*
Exhib: FAS, 1912; L; RA; RI; RWA.

DE LACEY, Charles John   fl. 1885-1925
Landscape and naval artist and illustrator. He worked for *The Illustrated London News*, 1895-1900, and was Special Artist with the Russian Fleet, 1897. He later worked for *The Graphic* and acted as Special for the Admiralty and the Port of London Authority.
Illus: *A Book About Ships [A.O. Cooke 1914]; Our Wonderful Navy [J.S. Margerison, 1919].*
Contrib: *The Pall Mall Magazine.*
Exhib: L; M; RA; RBA, 1885-1918.

DELAMOTTE, E.
Contributed decorative initials to *The Illustrated London Magazine*, 1855.

DELAMOTTE, T.G.
Illustrator of comic anthropomorphic head and tailpieces for *The Compliments of the Season* by Piers Shafton, 1849.

DELAMOTTE, William Alfred   **1775-1863**
Watercolourist and draughtsman. He was born at Weymouth 2 August 1775 and, through the interest of George III, was placed under Benjamin West in 1794. He studied in the life classes of the RA Schools and eventually settled in the Oxford area as a drawing master and topographer. In 1803, he gained the official appointment of drawing master to the Royal Military Academy, Great Marlow, and two years later, became an early member of the OWS. Our view of Regency Oxford and the Thames valley is generally taken through his soft pencil drawings with colour washes, many of which were engraved for books. He died at St. Giles's Field, Oxford, 13 February 1863.
Illus: *Thirty etchings of rural subjects [1816]; Illustrations of Virginia Water [1828]; Memorials of Oxford [J. Ingram 1837]; Original views of Oxford [1843 (liths)]; Windsor Castle [W.H. Ainsworth, 1843]; An Historical Sketch...Hospital of St. Bartholomew [1844]; Smokers and Smoking [G.T. Fisher, 1845]; Journey to India [Broughton, 1847, AT 522].*
Contrib: *Britton's Beauties of England and Wales [1813].*
Exhib: BI, 1808-46; OWS, 1806-8; RA; RBA, 1829-31.
Colls: Ashmolean; BM; Fitzwilliam; Manchester; V & AM.
Bibl: Iolo Williams, *Early English Watercolours*, 1952, p.63, illus.

DELFICO, Melchiorre   **1825-1895**
Draughtsman, musician and caricaturist. He was born at Teramo in 1825 and became well known in Italy for his caricature albums of celebrated people. He died in Naples in 1895. In 1872-73, he contributed eight cartoons to *Vanity Fair*.

DELL, John H.   **1830-1888**
Painter of rustic subjects and animals. He worked in the London area and had addresses at various times in Hammersmith, Chertsey and New Malden. He was noted for the accuracy of his work and his masterpiece in book illustration was *Nature Pictures*, published in 1878 consisting of thirty plates in which were shown, as Gleeson White put it, 'years of patient painstaking labour on the part of artist and engraver'.
Exhib: B; BI, 1851-67; M; RBA, 1851-86.

DE MARTINO, Commendatore Eduardo   **MVO 1834-1912**
Marine artist and illustrator. Born at Meta, near Naples, in 1834 and trained at Naples Naval College for a career in the Italian Navy where he remained until 1867. He then travelled to Brazil and was engaged by the Emperor to make official sketches of the Paraguayan War. Settling in England in 1875, he was made Marine Painter in Ordinary to Queen Victoria and the Royal Yacht Squadron, MVO, 1898. He accompanied the Duke of York on his royal tour in 1901. He died at St. John's Wood, 21 May 1912.
Contrib: *The Graphic [1896-1905].*
Coll: Royal Library, Windsor.
Exhib: GG; L.

DE MONTMORENCY, Lily   **fl.1895-1904**
Landscape and figure artist. She was working in Streatham in 1895, and at Bushey, 1898, where she may have attended the Herkomer School. She was elected ASWA in 1898.
Illus: *Little Tales of Long Ago [1903 (child's book)].*
Contrib: *The Parade [1897 (initials)].*
Exhib: L; RA; SWA.
Bibl: Simon Houfe, *Fin de Siècle*, 1992, illus.

DE MORGAN, William   **1839-1917**
Artist, author and potter. He was born in 1839, and educated at University College and at the RA Schools, 1859. He came under the influence of the Pre-Raphaelite circle and experimented with stained glass and tile processes, founding a pottery at Chelsea in 1871. He is best remembered today for his re-discovery of coloured lustre, a craft

he put to good use in making large chargers and vases. He was associated with William Morris (q.v.) in the Merton Abbey venture, 1882-88, and then on his own at Fulham. He retired in 1905 to Florence and became well-known as a novelist. He died in 1917.
De Morgan was a witty draughtsman of comic sketches and illustrated a book for children, *On a Pincushion and Other Fairy Tales*, 1877. His humorous drawings occasionally come on the market.

DE PARYS or DE PARIS, Alphonse G.   **fl.1902-1933**
Figure painter and illustrator. He contributed to *The Graphic*, 1902-03, mostly crowded social subjects and in particular the Coronation of King Edward VII. He worked in Kensington.

D'EPINAY see EPINAY

DEROY, Isidore Laurent   **1797-1886**
Architectural illustrator. He was well-known in France as a painter and lithographer and exhibited at the Salon. He drew views of churches and castles for some English publications, notably *The Illustrated London News* (Vizetelly).

DERRICK, Thomas C.   **1885-1954**
Artist in stained glass, mural painter and cartoonist. He was born in Bristol in 1885, and was educated at Didcot and studied at the RCA. He was instructor in decorative painting at the RCA for five years, but was best known as a cartoonist contributing to *Punch* and *Time and Tide*. His slick chalk drawings, more like the medium of advertising than the stateliness of *Punch*, typify the 1930s, but probably seemed very untypical at the time. His work was never straight reporting, but a synthesis and abstraction of an event. R.G.G. Price says, 'Reality was patterned and a social point that would be dull presented in a unitary setting gained enormously by being presented rhythmically and decoratively…' *A History of Punch*, 1955, p.283, illus. Derrick married the daughter of Sir George Clausen, RA (q.v.).
Publ: *The Prodigal Son and Other Parables: The Nine Nines [Hilaire Belloc]; Everyman [(72 wood engravings) 1930].*
Exhib: FAS, 1910; G; NEA; RA.

DETMOLD, Charles Maurice   ARE   **1883-1908**
Animal painter, illustrator and etcher. He was born on 21 November 1883, the twin brother of E.J. Detmold (q.v.), with whom he collaborated. He studied animals in the Zoological Gardens with his brother and exhibited watercolours from the age of fourteen. He was strongly influenced by Japanese art and produced, with his brother, a portfolio of etchings of birds and animals of unusual technical ability in 1898. He committed suicide in 1908. Elected RE, 1905.
Illus: *Pictures From Birdland; The Jungle Book [Rudyard Kipling, 1908].*
Exhib: FAS, 1900; G; NEA, 1899; RE; RI, 1897-
Bibl: *Print Collectors' Quarterly*, Vol.9, No.4, 1922, pp.373-405.

DETMOLD, Edward Julius   **1883-1957**
Animal painter, illustrator and etcher. The twin brother of C.M. Detmold (q.v.). He worked with his brother making sketches at the Zoological Gardens and exhibited with him from the age of fourteen. He was strongly influenced by Japanese art but also by the woodcuts of Dürer and became one of the best Edwardian animal illustrators. His sense of composition and the decorative placing of the animal in its natural habitat was much more subtle than the natural history painters or for example A. Thorburn (q.v.). E.J. Detmold's range was considerable and he published a number of books of fantasy drawing in the early 1920s which show a vivid imagination, fine drawing and warm colouring. Detmold settled at Montgomery in Wales and died there in 1957. He was elected RE in 1905. Exhibition at the Keyser Gallery, Oct. 1979.
Illus: *Pictures From Birdland [1899 (with C.M.D.)]; Sixteen Illustrations of subjects from Kipling's 'Jungle Book' [1903 (with C.M.D.)]; The Jungle Book [R. Kipling, 1908]; The Fables of Aesop [1909]; The Life of the Bee [M. Maeterlinck, 1911]; Birds and Beasts [C. Lemmonier, 1911]; The Book of Baby Beasts [F.E. Dugdale, 1911]; The Book of Baby Birds [F.E. Dugdale, 1912]; Hours of Gladness [M. Maeterlinck, 1912]; The Book of Baby Pets [F.E. Dugdale, 1915]; The Book of Baby Dogs [Charles J. Kaberry,*

EDWARD JULIUS DETMOLD 1883-1957. 'Dormice among brambles'. Illustration for a publication of Messrs. Dent, 19⅞in x 13¾in (50.5cm x 34.9cm)
Victoria and Albert Museum

1915]; *Our Little Neighbours, Animals of the Farm and Woodland* [1921]; *Rainbow Houses* [A.V. Hall, 1923]; *Tales From the Thousand and One Nights* [1924].
Contrib: *ILN* [1912, Christmas].
Exhib: FAS, 1900; G; GG; L; M; NEA, 1899; RA; RBA; RHA; RI; ROI.
Colls: BM; Fitzwilliam; V & AM.
Bibl: 'A Note on Mr. Edward J. Detmold's Drawings and Etchings of Animal Life', *The Studio*, Vol.51, 1911, pp.289-296, illus; *Print Collectors' Quarterly*, Vol.9, No.4, 1922, pp.373-405; B. Peppin, *Fantasy Book Illustration*, 1975, p.186, illus.; *The Field*, Sept. 1979. See illustration.

DEVAMBEZ, André Victor Édouard   1867-1943
French book illustrator. He was born in Paris in 1867, and studied with Constant and Lefevbre, winning the *prix de Rome* in 1890. He illustrated many books by French authors, including *La Fête à Coqueville*, Émile Zola, and *Le Condamnes a mort*, Claude Farrere. He contributed to *The Illustrated London News*, 1912-13.

DEWAR, William Jesmond   fl.1890-1903
Figure artist and illustrator. A competent black and white artist in pen who uses bold hatching and outline in the manner of C.D. Gibson (q.v.).
Contrib: *Moonshine* [1885]; *Illustrated Bits* [1890]; *Pick-Me-Up* [1894]; *Black & White* [1896-99]; *The Ludgate Monthly* [1896]; *The Rambler* [1897]; *The Temple Magazine*; *Pearson's Magazine*.
Exhib: RA, 1903.

DE WILDE, Samuel   'Paul'   1748-1832
Dramatic portrait painter and illustrator. He was brought to England when a child by his widowed mother and apprenticed to a wood carver in Soho. His earliest works are a series of etchings and mezzotints after Steen, Van Loo, Reynolds, Vernet and Wright which were published under the pseudonym of 'Paul', 1770-77. From 1795, De Wilde was almost totally absorbed in theatrical portraiture, producing a long series of scenes with actors in character, mostly in oil but also in watercolour. He was also a political caricaturist and contributed anonymous plates to the Tory *Satirist*, 1807-08.
The Victoria and Albert Museum has a series of wash drawings of decorative designs for frontispieces, presumably dating from De Wilde's early years in illustration, c.1770; the Garrick Club has the finest collection of his theatrical portraits. He died 19 January 1832.
Contrib: *The Theatrical Inquisitor [1813]*.
Exhib: BI, 1812; RA, 1782; SA, 1776.
Colls: Ashmolean; BM; Richmond, Virginia; V & AM.
Bibl: M.D. George, *English Political Caricature*, Vol. 2, 1959, p.106; Iolo Williams, *Early English Watercolours*, 1952, pp.148-149, illus.

DIBDIN, Thomas Colman   1810-1893
Painter and illustrator. He was born at Betchworth, Surrey on 22 October 1810, the son of Thomas Dibdin, the dramatist and probably the grandson of Charles Dibdin, the actor-dramatist. He began work as a clerk in the GPO at the age of seventeen, but after eleven years left it to paint. Dibdin travelled in Northern France, Germany and Belgium drawing their old towns and picturesque buildings. In later life he claimed to be the inventor of chromo-lithography. He died at Sydenham on 26 December 1893.
Publ: *Progressive Lessons in Water Colour Painting [1848]*.
Illus: *Heman's Works [1839]; Bacon's Oriental Annual; Rock Cut Temples of India [Ferguson ,1845, AT 467]*.
Exhib: BI, 1832-50; NWS; RA; RBA, 1831-83.
Colls: Ashmolean; BM; Nottingham; Sydney; V & AM.

DICKES, William   fl.1841-1883
Illustrator, engraver and publisher. He was a prolific illustrator in the 1840s but turned his attention to publishing and was chief manager of the Abbotsford Edition of Sir Walter Scott's Works. Chatto records in 1861 that 'Mr. Dickes' attention is now turned to Colour-Printing'. He was living at Loughborough Park, London in 1881.
Illus: *Masterman Ready [Captain Marryat, 1841]; London [Charles Knight, 1841] Glaucus or Wonders of the Shore [Charles Kingsley, 1855 (frontis)]*.
Contrib: *ILN [1843]*.
Exhib: RA, etc, 1843-81.
Bibl: Chatto & Jackson, *Treatise on Wood Engraving*, 1861, p.599; M.H. Spielmann, *The History of Punch*, 1895, p.248.

DICKINSON, F.C.   fl.1898-1906
Black and white artist and watercolourist. He contributed to *The*

SIR FRANCIS BERNARD DICKSEE PRA RI HRSA 1853-1928. 'An elderly couple'. Drawing for unidentified illustration, c.1873-80. Pencil
Victoria and Albert Museum

RICHARD DIGHTON 1795-1880. 'The King and Noblemen before the stag is turn'd out'. Vignette illustration. Ink and watercolour. Signed: Dighton del

Quarto, 1898, and *The Graphic*, 1899-1906. He does quite strong watercolours of figure subjects and may have illustrated an edition of Hans Andersen.

DICKINSON, J. Reed   **fl.1867-1895**
Figure and portrait painter working in Regent's Park and Hammersmith.
Exhib: Dudley; L; M; RA, 1867-81; RBA, 1867-78.

DICKSEE, Sir Francis Bernard PRA RI HRSA   **1853-1928**
Painter and illustrator. He was born in London in 1853, the son of T.F. Dicksee, the portrait painter. He was trained at the RA Schools, 1870-75, and was influenced by Leighton and Millais. He became a very competent book illustrator in the best black and white tradition of the 1870s, illustrated Longfellow's *Evangeline* in 1882 and *The Four Georges*, W.M. Thackeray, 1894. But his success as a society portrait painter enabled him to abandon this side of his art. He was elected ARA, 1881; RA, 1891, and PRA, 1924. He died in London 28 October 1928.
Exhib: G; GG; L; M; RA; RHA; RI; ROI; RSA.
Colls: BM; Manchester; V & AM.
Bibl: E.R. Dibdin, *FD*, 1905.
See illustration.

DICKSEE, Margaret Isabel   **1858-1903**
Landscape and figure painter and illustrator. She was born in 1858, the daughter of T.F. Dicksee, the portrait painter and sister of Sir Frank Dicksee (q.v.). She drew ink illustrations for a number of magazines including *The Quiver*, 1890, and *The Girls' Own Paper*. She was also a good decorative artist and designed borders for some of Woolner's poems. She died in London 6 June 1903.
Exhib: L; RA; RBA; RWS.
Colls: V & AM; Witt Photo.

DIGHTON, Denis   **1792-1827**
Military painter and draughtsman. He was born in London in 1792, second son of Robert Dighton (q.v.), and studied at the RA Schools. His wife was Fruit and Flower Painter to Queen Adelaide. He was patronised by the Prince of Wales and became Military Draughtsman to him from 1815, sometimes travelling abroad. He died at St. Servan, Brittany in 1827.
Illus: *Sketches [1821, 15 liths., AL. 121]*.
Exhib: BI; RA.

DIGHTON, Joshua   **fl.1820-1840**
Caricaturist. A son of Robert Dighton and a brother of Richard Dighton (qq.v.). Like his brother, he drew small full-length watercolour portraits in profile, concentrating on sporting celebrities.
Colls: Witt Photo.

DIGHTON, Richard   **1795-1880**
Caricaturist. Son of Robert Dighton (q.v.) whose successor he was.

He was born in London in 1795, and on his father's death, in 1814, he continued the series of portrait etchings, 1815-28. These were all in the 'Dighton style' of small full-length portraits in profile, coloured by hand, usually of sporting celebrities but also of politicians. The whole series of originals by father and son were purchased by King George IV. Dighton also etched some Anti-Radical caricatures between 1819-21 and died on 13 April 1880. His portrait drawings are still occasionally seen on the market, they are often in pencil and watercolour and well-handled. Work by other members of the family is stiffer and less convincing.
Colls: NPG; V & AM.
See illustrations.

Mr HOBHOUSE.

RICHARD DIGHTON 1795-1880. Mr. Hobhouse. 1819. Etching

ROBERT DIGHTON 1752-1814. 'A Lesson Westward'. Pen and ink
with watercolour, 1782

DIGHTON, Robert   **1752-1814**
Painter, caricaturist and actor. He was the founder of the dynasty of
Dightons that flourished in English caricature for a hundred years.
Dighton began exhibiting as a watercolourist and etcher in 1769 at
the Free Society of Artists and was an occasional exhibitor at the RA,
1775-1799. He worked for Carrington Bowles on humorous
mezzotints or 'postures' between 1774 and 1794. In 1793, he brought
out a *Collection of Portraits of Public Characters* which were an
immediate public success and from this date he concentrated wholly
on caricature. The series was something new in England as it was
more natural than exaggerated and spelled the way for Regency and
Early Victorian work. Dighton continued to do ordinary political
caricaturing which Williams found coarse compared with the
portraits. Dighton appears to have been a fairly reprobate personality
and was discovered in 1806 to have removed prints out of the British
Museum and replaced them with copies! He died in London in 1814.
A reassessment of Dighton's work was made possible when a
substantial collection of original watercolours was offered for sale by
Sotheby's on 23 February 1978.
Colls: Ashmolean; BM; Fitzwilliam; Manchester; V & AM.
Bibl: H.M. Hake, *Print Collectors Quarterly*, XIII, pp.136ff, 242ff;
Dennis Rose, *Life, Times and Recorded Works of RD (1752-1814)
Actor, Artist and Printseller and Three of his Artist Sons*, 1981.
See illustration.

DIGHTON, Robert Junior   **1786-1865**
Military portraitist. He was the son of Robert Dighton (q.v.) and
became an ensign in the West Norfolk Militia in 1808. He served in
India and the Peninsular and published an engraving of the Duke of
Wellington. He retired from the army in 1834.
Coll: Windsor.
Bibl: Dennis Rose, *Life, Times and Recorded Works of RD
(1752-1814) Actor, Artist and Printseller and Three of his Artist
Sons*, 1981.

DINKEL, Joseph   **fl.1833-1861**
Architectural and botanical illustrator. He was born in Munich and
travelled widely in Europe for The Linnaen Society, the Royal
Geological and Palaeontological Societies. Chatto records that he
was 'a very accurate draughtsman of subjects of Natural History,
especially of Fossil remains; but though he has most practice in this
department, he also undertakes Architectural and Engineering
drawings.'
Illus: *Poissons Fossiles [Agassiz, 1833-43]*.
Exhib: RA, 1840.
Colls: Neufchâtel.
Bibl: Chatto & Jackson, *Treatise on Wood Engraving*, 1861, p.593.

DINSDALE, George   **fl.1808-1829**
Landscape painter and topographer. He was working in Chelsea,
1818, and Bloomsbury, 1828-29, and contributed illustrations to
Griffith's *Cheltenham*, 1826.
Exhib: BI, 1808-29; RA.

DINSDALE, John
Figure artist working in Camden Town, 1884-90. He contributed
humorous and sporting drawings to *The Illustrated London News*,
1883 and *Fun*, 1890. Exhibited at the RI.

DISTON, A.
Topographer. Illustrated *Costumes of the Canary Islands*, 1829, AT
75 (liths).

DIXON, Charles Edward RI   **1872-1934**
Marine painter and illustrator. He was born at Goring in 1872 and
after exhibiting at the RA from the age of sixteen, he became a
prolific illustrator in *The Graphic*, 1900-10. He was a member of the
Langham Sketching Club and was elected RI in 1900. His work is
always very accurate, but he was able to create the atmosphere and
mood of the great shipping lanes by skilful washes, careful uses of
colour and sombre skies. He died at Itchenor, 12 September 1934.
Illus: *Britannia's Bulwarks [C.N. Robinson, 1901]*.
Exhib: FAS, 1916, G; L; M; RA; RI; ROI.
Colls: Greenwich; V & AM.

DIXON, Capt. Clive
Military artist, Captain, 16th Lancers and ADC to General Sir
George White, he provided the colour illustrations for *The Leaguer
of Ladysmith*, dated Ladysmith 3 March 1900.

DIXON, May
Amateur illustrator. Hon. Mention in *The Studio* book illustration
competition, Vol. 8, 1896, p.184, illus.

DIXON, O. Murray
Contributed colour illustrations of animals to *The Illustrated London
News*, 1909.

DOBELL, Clarence M   **fl.1857-1866**
Figure painter and illustrator. He contributed to *Good Words*, 1860,
and *Once a Week*, 1865, and illustrated *One Year*, 1862, for Messrs.
Macmillan. He was working in London, 1857-65, and then at
Cheltenham.
Exhib: BI, 1858-66; RA; RBA, 1857-66.

DOBSON, William Thomas Charles   **RA RWS**   **1817-1898**
Scriptural painter and illustrator. He was born at Hamburg in 1817 and
entered the RA Schools in 1836, becoming a teacher in the
Government School of Design in 1843. He left this work in 1845 and
travelled abroad, mostly in Italy and Germany. He was elected an ARA
in 1860 and RA in 1871 and RWS, 1875. Many of his pictures were
engraved by Graves & Co. He died at Ventnor on 30 January 1898.
Illus: *Legends and Lyrics [A.A. Proctor 1865]*.
Exhib: OWS; RA; RBA.
Colls: Sheffield; V & AM.

DODD, A.W.
Illustrator. Made illustrations of 'The Four Elements', *The Studio*,
Vol. 34, 1905, p.350, illus.

DODDS, Will L.   **fl.1881-1910**
Watercolourist and illustrator working at Galashiels, Scotland. He contributed small comic cuts and silhouettes to *Pick Me Up*, 1888-89.
Exhib: G; RBA; ROI; RSA; RSW.

DODGSON, Charles Lutwidge 'Lewis Carroll'   **1832-1898**
Writer and creator of 'Alice'. He was born at Daresbury, Cheshire, on the 17 January 1832 and after being educated at Rugby, gained a Fellowship at Christchurch, Oxford, where he remained for the rest of his life. Carroll, as he was known from 1856, produced his own small sketches to illustrate the first manuscript of *Alice in Wonderland*, January 1863, but because of their weakness he approached Sir John Tenniel (q.v.) in February 1864 to undertake the work. Carroll remained a scrupulous critic of his illustrators till his death.
Bibl: G. Ovenden, *The Illustrators of Alice*, 1972.

DODGSON, George Haydock   **1811-1880**
Topographer, landscape painter and illustrator. He was born at Liverpool on 16 August 1811 and was apprenticed to George Stephenson, the railway engineer, from 1827 to 1835. He left this employment due to the pressure of the work and began to paint, moving to London in 1836 and drawing its architecture. He did a great deal of illustration in the 1850s before turning his attention to landscapes. He then drew extensively on the Thames and made visits to Whitby and Wales. He was an ARWS from 1842-47 when he resigned and became OWS in 1848. He died on June 4 1880 at 28 Clifton Hill, St. John's Wood.
Illus: *Illustrations of the Scenery on the Line of the Whitby and Pickering Railway [1836]*.
Contrib: *The Illustrated London News [1853-6]; The Cambridge Almanack; Lays of the Holy Land [1858]; The Home Affections [C. Mackay, 1858]*.
Exhib: BI; OWS; RA; RBA, 1835-39; RWS.
Colls: BM; V & AM.
Bibl: Chatto & Jackson, *Treatise on Wood Engraving*, 1861, p.598.

DODWELL, Edward   **FSA**   **1767-1832**
Topographer and draughtsman. He was born in Dublin in 1767 and after being educated at Trinity College, Carnbridge, travelled in Greece, 1801 and 1805-6. He died at Rome in 1832.
Illus: *Alcuni Bassi rilievi della Grecia [1812]; A Classical and Topographical Tour of Greece [1819]; Views in Greece [1819-21, AT 130]; Views and Descriptions of Cyclonian or Pelasgic Remains...[1834]*.

DOLBY, Edwin Thomas   **fl.1849-1870**
Landscape and architectural illustrator. He specialised in views of churches and was a candidate for the NWS between 1850 and 1864.
Illus: *Great Britain as it is [E.H. Nolan, 1859]; A Series of Views... during the Russian War [1854]; D's Sketches in the Baltic [1854]*.
Contrib: *Recollections of the Great Exhibition of 1851 [1851]; ILN [1854, Denmark]; The Illustrated Times [1855, Crimea]; The Graphic [1870]*.
Exhib: RA, 1849-65.

DOLBY, Joshua Edward Adolphus   **fl.1837-1875**
Landscape painter. He specialised in picturesque buildings and drew for *Prague Illustrated*, 1845, AT 74 (liths.). He exhibited at RA and RBA, 1840-46.

DOLLMAN, Francis Thomas   **1812-1899**
Architectural draughtsman. Illustrated his own *Examples of Ancient Pulpits Existing in England*, 1849. Exhibited at the RA, 1840-78.
Colls: V & AM.

DOLLMAN, John Charles   **RI**   **1851-1934**
Painter and illustrator of animals. He was born at Hove, 6 May 1851, the son of a bookseller and after being educated at Shoreham, studied art at South Kensington and the RA Schools, where he won prizes for drawing from the living model. He practised black and white drawing for the magazines until 1901 when he began to paint in watercolours, specialising in historical genre subjects. He was

GUSTAVE DORÉ 1832-1883. 'Warehousing'. Illustration for *London, a Pilgrimage*, by Douglas Jerrold, 1872. Signed
Victoria and Albert Museum

elected RI, 1886; ROI, 1887; ARWS, 1906, and RWS, 1913. He died at Bedford Park 11 December 1934.
Illus: *In the days when we went Hog-Hunting [J.M. Brown, 1891]; Curly [John Coleman, 1897]; Told by the Northmen [E.M. Wilmott Buxton, 1908]*.
Contrib: *The Graphic [1880-88 (stories and theat.)]*.
Exhib: B; FAS, 1906; G; L; M; Paris, 1900; RA; RHA; RI; ROI; RSA.
Colls: G; M; Nottingham.
Bibl: *English Influences on Vincent Van Gogh*, Arts Council, 1974-75.

DONNELLY, W.A.
Contributed illustrations to *The Sporting and Dramatic News*, 1890 and *The Illustrated London News*, 1894.

DONNISON, T.E.
Illustrator, working at Rock Ferry, Cheshire, and contributing to *The Boys' Own Paper* in the 1890s. Exhibited at Liverpool, 1882.

DORÉ, Paul Gustave Louis Christophe   **1832-1883**
Painter, illustrator and sculptor. He was born at Strasbourg on 6 January 1832 and took up lithography at the age of eleven while living at Bourg-en-Bresse. He then went to Paris and in 1848 attached himself to Philippon's *Journal Pour Rire*, where he contributed a weekly page. He showed pen and ink drawings at the Salon of 1848 and a painting in 1851 but really made his reputation in 1854 with his illustrated *Rabelais*, followed by a whole series of classic titles in English and French editions. He became known to the British public with his contributions to *The Illustrated London News* from 1853, and with Crimean sketches from 1855-56 and in 1858. Vizetelly employed him even more extensively on *The Illustrated*

GUSTAVE DORÉ 1832-1883. 'The Pool of London'

Times, 1855-60, and there is no mistaking his crowded and wildly dramatic battle scenes. His great projected work on London with a text by Douglas Jerrold was prepared in the late 1860s but only came out in a shortened version in 1872 as *London: A Pilgrimage*. A similar scheme for Paris never materialised. Doré's success in England enabled him to open his own gallery here for a number of years, but his obsessive ambition to be recognised as a great painter rather than a great illustrator clouded his later years.

Doré's earlier work tends to be linear and his later work tonal. By the end of his career he was treating the page like a canvas and his dominance of the illustrated book here and in France was not very beneficial. His greatest works like the *Inferno* and *Don Quixote*, 1863, are extremely dramatic; Doré plays on the horror of emptiness and height very cleverly, but sometimes loses his hold with a super-abundance of detail. His later books, where tone was all important, did not have the drawings carefully inked out for the wood engraver but were simply supplied as wash drawings. These are occasionally seen on the market.

A further side to Doré's genius is provided by his caricature sketches, many of these were published as *Two Hundred Sketches, Humorous and Grotesque* in 1867; they show him as a brisk satirist of society, the drawing is rather harsh and there is a tendency to adopt the old tradition of caricature in enormous heads and skeletal bodies.
Illus: *The Wandering Jew [Sue, 1856]; Jaufry the Knight and the Fair Brunissende [A. Elwes, 1856]; The Adventures of St. George [W.F. Peacock, 1858]; Boldheart the Warrior [G.F. Pardon, 1858]; The History of Don Quixote [Cervantes, 1863]; The Ancient Mariner [S.T. Coleridge, 1865]; Days of Chivalry [L'Epine, 1866]; The Adventures of Baron Munchausen [1866]; Fables of La Fontaine [1867]; Elaine, Guinevere, Vivien, Enid and Idylls of the King, [Tennyson, 1867-68]; The Bible [1867]; Popular Fairy Tales [1871]; Poems of Thomas Hood [1872]; London: A Pilgrimage [1872].*
Contrib: *Cassell's Illustrated Family Paper [1857].*
Colls: V & AM.

Bibl: Blanchard Jerrold, *Life of Gustave Doré*, 1891, (complete bibliography); Millicent Rose, *G. Doré*, 1946; David Bland, *A History of Book Illustration*, 1958, pp.289-295; *Gustave Doré, 1832-1883*, Hazlitt, Gooden & Fox cat., 1983.
See illustrations.

DORING, Adolph G.
German landscape painter and etcher, working at Bernbourg and Ostsee, Germany. He contributed illustrations of animals to *The Strand Magazine*, 1894.
Exhib: RA, 1897.

DOUGLAS, Edwin   1848-1914
Sporting and animal painter. He was born at Edinburgh in 1848 and studied at the RA Schools, and the RSA. He spent most of his life working in the south of England, in Surrey, 1880-90, and then in Sussex until his death. His paintings are in the style of Edwin Landseer.
Contrib: *Poems and Songs of Robert Burns [1875].*
Exhib: B; G; L; M; RA; ROI.

DOWD, James H.   1884-1956
Painter, etcher and black and white artist. He was a regular contributor to *Punch* from about 1906, specialising in the humours of childhood and later in the illustrations for film criticism; R.G.G. Price calls him 'the Baumer of the nursery'. He was working at Sheffield in 1912 and in London from 1918. He must not be confused with L. Dowd, another *Punch* artist.
Contrib: *The Graphic [1915].*
Exhib: G; L; P; RA; RMS; RSA.
Bibl: R.G.G. Price, *A History of Punch*, 1957, p.210.

DOWNARD, Ebenezer Newman   fl.1849-1892
History painter, engraver and illustrator. He specialised in genre subjects and contributed work to *The Illustrated London News*, 1873-79.
Exhib: BI, 1861-66; G; RA; RBA; RHA; ROI.

DOWNEY, Thomas   fl.1890-1935
Figure painter and illustrator, caricaturist. He was a pupil of Alfred Bryan (q.v.) and worked for numerous magazines in the 1890s.
Illus: *Patsy [H. de V. Stacpoole, 1908 (frontis.)].*
Contrib: *Daily Graphic [1890]; Moonshine [1890]; The Sketch [1894-95]; Judy [1898]; The Idler; Chums; The Boys' Own Paper.*
Exhib: Arlington Gall., 1935.

DOWNING, Henry Philip Burke   FRIBA   1865-
Architect, etcher and illustrator. He was born in 1865 and after studying at the RA Schools and at the Architectural Association, he was articled to Hessell Tiltman, FRIBA. He then became Chief Assistant to Joseph Clarke FSA, Canterbury Diocesan architect, and started in private practice in 1888. He served on the RIBA Council and was a member of the London Topographical Society. His pen and ink drawings of buildings are in the style of Herbert Railton and Holland Tringham (qq.v.).
Illus: *Architectural Relics in Cornwall [1888]; Monumental Brasses.*
Contrib: *St. Paul's [1894]; Black & White; Lady's Pictorial.*
Exhib: RA; RSA, 1904-32.
Bibl: *Who's Who in Architecture*, 1914.

DOYLE, Charles Altamont   1832-1893
Humorous and fairy illustrator. He was the fourth son of John Doyle (q.v.) and was born in London in 1832. He was a professional civil servant for most of his life but worked as an illustrator in an amateur capacity. His sketches of imaginary subjects often have a rather sinister quality somewhat akin to those of his brother Richard Doyle (q.v.). He was the father of Sir Arthur Conan Doyle and died at Dumfries in 1893.
Illus: *Our Trip to Blunderland [Jean Jambon, 1877 (60 illus.)].*
Contrib: *The Illustrated Times [1859-60]; Good Words [1860]; London Society [1863-64]; The Graphic [1877].*
Exhib: RSA.
Colls: Witt Photo.
Bibl: Michael Baker, *The Doyle Diary*, 1978.

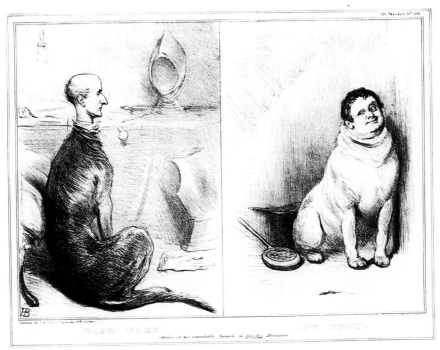

JOHN DOYLE 'HB' 1797-1868. 'High Bred – Low Bred'. No. 419 in *HB's Sketches*, published by McLean, 11th December 1835

DOYLE, Henry Edward RHA   **1827-1892**
Portrait and religious painter and caricaturist. He was born in Dublin in 1827, the third son of John Doyle (q.v.). He was trained in Dublin and on coming to London worked as a wood engraver and draughtsman for satirical journals. He made a number of small cuts for *Punch* in 1844, and was a contributor of caricatures to *The Great Gun*, 1845, and was cartoonist of *Fun*, 1867-69. His brother James Doyle (q.v.) rather dismisses this work as 'the merest child's play' but as Spielmann says, 'the spirit of humour was strong within him'. Doyle's public image was certainly very different (his illustrations to Telemachus were admired by Prince Albert) and in 1869 he became Director of the National Gallery of Ireland, formed an important collection there and carried out the decorations of a Roman Catholic chapel. He became ARHA in 1872 and RHA in 1874 and was awarded the CB in 1880. He died in Dublin, 17 February 1892.

Doyle's caricatures, which are occasionally to be found, are usually diminutive full-length portraits in watercolour with large heads; he frequently signed with a hen or 'Fusbos'.
Bibl: M.H. Spielmann, *The History of Punch*, 1895, p.459.

DOYLE, James William Edmund   **1822-1892**
Heraldic artist and illustrator. He was the eldest son of John Doyle (q.v.) and born in London in 1822. He studied under his father but soon turned all his attention to historical research, although he made a few designs in pen, ink and watercolour. He wrote and illustrated *A Chronicle of England*, 1864, which has colour plates printed by Edmund Evans; some authorities consider it finer work than Baxter's. He was the author of the *Historical Baronage of England*, 1886, and died in London in 1892.
Colls: V & AM.
Bibl: M. Hardie, *English Coloured Books*, 1906; Ruari McLean, *Victorian Book Design and Colour Printing*, 1972, p.184.

DOYLE, John   **'HB'**   **1797-1868**
Lithographer, portraitist and caricaturist. He was born at Dublin in 1797 and studied there under an Italian landscape painter, Gabrielli, and under the miniaturist, W. Comerford. He attended the Dublin Society's Drawing Academy and in about 1822 travelled to London to work as a portrait painter. This proving unsuccessful, he set himself up as a portrait lithographer, publishing portraits of well-known people such as Wellington, George IV at Ascot, and the

Princess Victoria in her pony phaeton. All of these were signed 'JD'. Doyle took to political caricature in 1827, publishing anonymous lithographs in that year and the next, and beginning in 1829 his famous series of *Political Sketches* signed 'HB'. The monogram was made up of two conjoined 'JD's, intended to hide the identity of the artist and excite curiosity, which it did! The series with its characteristically weightless but well observed figures, ran from 1829 to 1849 with a further plate in 1851, an astonishing output of nearly one thousand prints.

Doyle was fortunate to work during a period of reform and change ideally suited to his talents. Although there was intense political activity, the public desired it to be treated with a gentler wit than the savage satire of the Gillray and Cruikshank era. Doyle therefore is less of a caricaturist than a political illustrator. The plates were issued by McLean in volume form, 1841 and 1844, with an *Illustrative Key*. Many of the pencil studies are in the British Museum. John Doyle died in London 2 January 1868.
Exhib: RA, 1825-35.
Colls: BM; Windsor.
Bibl: G. Everitt, *English Caricaturists*, pp.235-276; M.D. George, *English Political Caricare*, 1959; G.M. Trevelyan, *The Seven Years of William IV, a reign cartooned by John Doyle*, 1952.
See illustrations.

DOYLE, Richard   **'Dick Kitcat'**   **1824-1883**
Humorous artist, cartoonist and fairy illustrator. He was born in London, September 1824, the second son of John Doyle (q.v.). He was the most gifted artist in a very gifted family and began from an early age to illustrate juvenilia, *Home for the Holidays*, a book for family circulation in 1836 (first published 1887) and *Dick Doyle's Journal*, 1840 (first published 1885). His first published work was the comic medieval book *The Eglinton Tournament*, 1840, which was widely acclaimed and the same year he collaborated with John Leech (q.v.) on the novel *Hector O'Halloran* by W.H. Maxwell; other book illustrating commissions followed from Dickens and Thackeray, Doyle working in wood and steel and sometimes signing 'Dick Kitcat'.

In 1843, Doyle was introduced to *Punch* and soon became a very regular contributor of decorations and initial letters, but did not graduate to cartooning until March 1844, eventually sharing about a third of the work with Leech. In January of the same year, Doyle

PRINCE ALBERT'S BEE-HIVES.

"These Hives are so constructed, that the HONEY may be removed without DESTROYING THE BEES."—*Morning Paper*

RICHARD DOYLE 1824-1883. 'Prince Albert's Bee Hives'

designed *Punch*'s sixth cover which remained in use until 1954, a spirited procession of tiny figures based on Titian's 'Bacchus and Ariadne'. By the middle 1850s, Doyle was almost a household name through his popular series 'Manners and Customs of Ye Englishe' and the later 'Bird's Eye Views of Society', and he had become a very proficient wood engraver after taking lessons from Swain. The source for much of Doyle's comedy remained the books of his childhood, the legends and the chivalry which gave him ideas but also an open-hearted naïveté in the drawing. It was probably this romance and freshness, the lack of shadow, that recommended his work to an artist like Holman Hunt and a critic like Ruskin, whose work he illustrated. Doyle's break with *Punch* came in 1850, when its attacks on the Papacy were more than Doyle, a devout Catholic, could tolerate. He devoted the rest of his life to the illustration of books and in particular children's stories and fairy tales where his delight in the grotesque is given full rein and he reveals himself as a vivid and magical colourist. Perhaps his masterpiece was *In Fairyland* by William Allingham, 1870, a folio with colour wood engravings by Edmund Evans. Doyle continued to paint landscapes and died after a visit to the Athenaeum on 11 December 1883. He signed his work with: ✠

Illus: his own work: *Mr. Pip's Diary: Manners and Customs of Ye Englishe [1849]; An Overland Journey to The Great Exhibition [1851]; Bird's Eye Views of Society [1864]; The Foreign Tour of Brown, Jones and Robinson [1854]; The Doyle Fairy Book [1890]. Grimm's Fairy King [1846]; A Jar of Honey From Mount Hylba [Hunt, 1847]; Fairy Tales [Montalba, 1849]; The Enchanted Doll [M. Lemon, 1849]; Rebecca and Rowena [W.M. Thackeray, 1850]; The King of the Golden River [J. Ruskin, 1851]; The Story of Jack and The Giants [1851]; the Newcomens [W.M. Thackeray, 1845-55]; A Juvenile Calendar and Zodiac of Flowers [1855], The Scouring of the White Horse [Hughes, 1859]; A Selection From the Works of Frederick Locker [1865]; An Old Fairy Tale [Planché, 1865]; Irish Biddy, The Visiting Judges, The Troublesome Priest [1868]; Lemon's Fairy Tales*

[1868]; In Fairy Land [W. Allingham, 1870]; Piccadilly [Oliphant, 1870]; The Enchanted Crow [1870]; The Feast of the Dwarfs [1871]; Fortune's Favourite [1871]; Snow White and Rose Red [1871]; Princess Nobody [A Lang, 1884]; The Family Joe Miller.
Contrib: *The Fortunes of Hector O'Halloran [W.H. Maxwell, 1842]; Punch [1843-51]; The Chimes [Charles Dickens, 1845]; The Battle of Life [Charles Dickens, 1846]; The Cricket on the Hearth [Charles Dickens, 1846]; ILN [1847]; L'Allegro and Il Penseroso [Milton, 1848]; Life of Oliver Goldsmith [J. Forster, 1848]; Gautier Ballads [1849]; Merry Pictures by The Comic Hands of H.K Browne and Richard Doyle [1857]; Puck on Pegasus [C. Pennell, 1862]; Disraeli in Cartoon [1878]; Cornhill Magazine [1861-62]; Pall Mall Gazette [1885-87].*
Exhib: GG; L; RA, 1868-83.
Colls: Ashmolean; BM; Fitzwilliam; V & AM.
Bibl: G. Everitt, *English Caricaturists*, 1883, pp.381-394; Chatto & Jackson, *Treatise on Wood Engraving*, 1861, pp. 578-579; F.G. Kitton, *Dickens and His Illustrators*, 1899; Daria Hambourg, *RD*, English Masters of Black and White, n.d.; B. Peppin, *Fantasy Book Illustration*, 1975, pp.9, 11, 20, illus.; R. Engen, *Richard Doyle and His Family*, V & A catalogue, 1983.
See illustrations.

D'OYLY, Sir Charles, 7th Bt.   **1781-1845**
Amateur artist and illustrator. He was born in Calcutta in 1781 and served for the whole of his life in India, first as assistant to the Registrar, Calcutta Court of Appeal, 1798, and then as Collector of Dacca and Resident at Patna, 1831. He studied drawings under George Chinnery in Dacca and made sketches of Anglo-Indian life and society. He returned to Europe in 1838 and died at Livorno in 1845.
Illus: *The European in India [1813]; Antiquities of Dacca [1814-15]; Behar Amateur Lithographic Scrap Book [1828, AT 446]; Indian Sports [1828, AT 447]; Tom Raw The Griffin [1828, AT 450]; The Feathered Game of Hindoostan [1828, AT 451]; Extra Behar Lithographic Scrap Book [1829, AT 452]; Oriental Ornithology [1829, AT 453]; Sketches of The New Road [1830, AT 455]; Views of Calcutta [1848, AT 497].*
Exhib: RA, 1815.
Bibl: *The Connoisseur*, Vol.CLXXV, 1970.

DRAKE, William Henry   **1856-**
American illustrator. He was born in New York on 4 June 1856 and studied in Paris at the Académie Julian. He is included here as the illustrator of *Stories of Child Life*, and *The Jungle Book*, by Rudyard Kipling, 1894. He was a noted still-life illustrator, specialising in black and white drawings of gold and silver antiquities and old armour.
Bibl: J. Pennell, *Pen Drawing and Pen Draughtsmen*, 1894, pp.242-243 illus.

DRAPER, Herbert James   **1864-1920**
Portrait, subject painter and illustrator. He was born in London in 1864, and studied at the St. John's Wood School, RA Schools and in Paris at Julian's, 1890 and Rome 1891. His painting 'The Lament for Icarus' was bought by the Chantrey Bequest in 1898. He died in Hampstead on 22 September 1920.
Illus: *St. Bartholomew's Eve [G.A. Henty, 1894]; A Young Traveller's Tales [Hope, 1894].*
Contrib: *The Yellow Book [1895].*
Exhib: G; L; M; New Gall.; Paris, 1900; RA; RBA; RHA.

DRAW   see WARD, Leslie

DRUMMOND, James   RSA   **1816-1877**
History painter. He was born in Edinburgh in 1816 and worked as a draughtsman for ornithological works. He then entered the Trustees Academy, Edinburgh, and studied with Sir William Allan, exhibiting at the RSA from 1835 and becoming ARSA in 1846 and Member in 1852. Drummond made a close study of archaeology and is noted for his historical accuracy in his large canvases of Scottish history.
Illus: *Ancient Scottish Weapons [J. Andersen, 1881].*
Contrib: *Good Words [1860].*
Exhib: RBA; RI.
Colls: Blackburn; Edinburgh; V & AM.

DUANE, William
Principal cartoonist of *Fun*, 1900.

DUBUISSON, Miss E.
Illustrated *Sketches of Character By E.D. The Mufflechop Family*, published by T. Pentress, 67 Newington Causeway & R. Ackermann. Lithographs coloured by hand c.1835. The only copy seen was inscribed as by 'The Misses Dubuisson…French refugees who were artists'.

DUDLEY, Ambrose   **fl.1890-1919**
Portrait painter and illustrator. He worked in London and exhibited at the RA, 1890-1919. A pleasant ink and wash drawing of a pedlar, probably intended for illustration, was in a London collection in 1976.

DUDLEY, Robert   **fl.1858-1893**
Painter, lithographer and illustrator. He specialised in English and continental views and seascapes, but outside his landscape work was an interesting minor figure in illustration. He first appears contributing the topography of Birmingham to *The Illustrated London News* in 1858 and seven years later, in 1865, the same paper sent him as correspondent on The Great Eastern when the Trans-Atlantic Cable was laid. The result of this was a handsome book of lithographs *The Atlantic Telegraph*, 1866, with text by W.H. Russell of *The Times*. A watercolour worked up from one of these subjects was shown by Dudley at the RBA in 1866. He was also well-known as a book decorator and drew designs for brass cut publishers' bindings, many of them signed. He worked in Kensington, 1865-75, and at Notting Hill from 1875 and died there about 1893.
Illus: *A Memorial of the Marriage of H.R.H. Albert Edward, Prince of Wales and H.R.H. Alexandra, Princess of Denmark [W.H. Russell, 1863].*
Contrib: *ILN [1858-73]; The Illustrated Times [1861]; The Boys' Own Magazine [1863]; London Society [1864-71]; Nature and Art [1866]; The Graphic [1869].*
Exhib: B; G; L; M; RA; RI.
Bibl: Ruari McLean, *Victorian Book Design and Colour Printing*, 1973, pp.139, 220, 221.

RICHARD DOYLE 1824-1883. From *Punch's Almanack*, 1846

DUFF, Sir C.G.   **'G C D' or 'Cloister'**
Contributing cartoons to *Vanity Fair*, 1899-1900 and 1903. Nobody of this name can be traced.

DUGDALE, Thomas Cantrell   RA   **1880-1952**
Painter and illustrator. He was born at Blackburn, Lancs. on 2 June 1880, and was educated at Manchester Grammar School. He studied at The Royal College of Art and Julian's, Paris. A fine subject painter and landscapist, he concentrated increasingly on portraits, became ROI in 1910, ARA 1936 and RA in 1944. Besides illustrations for magazines, the Witt Library has a collection of political cartoons for an unidentified publication, probably post-1914. He served throughout the First World War, mostly in the Middle East and the Balkans, being mentioned in despatches, 1915. In his student days, Dugdale designed some book decorations in a woodcut style and was an occasional illustrator in ink and watercolour. He later abandoned this for oil painting. He held a one man show at the Leicester Galleries in 1919.
Illus: *The Gateway to Shakespeare [Mrs. Andrew Lang, 1908].*
Contrib: *The Strand Magazine [1909]; The Graphic [1910].*
Exhib: G; GG; L; M; NEA, 1910-13; P; Paris, 1921; RA; RHA; ROI; RSA.
Bibl: *The Studio*, Vol.12, 1897-98 p.137 illus.

DULAC, Edmund   **1882-1953**
Artist and illustrator. He was born at Toulouse on 22 October 1882 and after attending the university there, he studied law and took up art, joining the drawing and painting classes of the Toulouse School of Art. He then went to Paris and studied at the Académie Julian for three weeks, concentrating from then onwards on work as a book illustrator, portrait painter, designer of costumes and stage sets and modeller. Dulac settled in London in 1906, and by the outbreak of war had established himself as one of the leading artists in the field. He became a naturalised British subject in 1912 and really cemented a popularity with his adopted country which has remained to the present day. Dulac was immensely versatile and had more sense of colour and design than most of his English contemporaries, excepting Rackham. He looked to the Middle and Far East for inspiration, his watercolours of legendary subjects have a gemlike brilliance found only in Mogul miniatures, their flat, stylised and sleepy beauty sometimes comes

RICHARD DOYLE 1824-1883. Decorative frontispiece to a Christmas number of *Punch*

EDMUND DULAC 1882-1953. Caricature of Arnold Bennett, novelist and man of letters. An illustration for *The Evening Standard*, c.1922. Pen and ink. 5in x 5½in (12.7cm x 14cm)

from the Japanese print, sometimes from the Pre-Raphaelites and even occasionally from the Renaissance. There are clearly a few borrowings from Rackham mannerisms but when he is depicting a tale like *Beauty and the Beast*, the repertoire is his own, the paper parchment, the colour vivid and thick and the design dominating the story. Dulac's early work is a precursor of Art Deco and in fact his middle period fell right into the 1920s when such highly-coloured and self-conscious work was in vogue The artist played his own part in this, designing a smoking room for one of the great luxury liners, *The Empress of Britain*.

Dulac was also a remarkable caricaturist, a disciplined artist in black and white who could capture a personality or situation in very few lines, but remain sympathetic. He also brought to this country the very French tradition of caricature sculpture, many examples of this were in his studio at his death.

Illus: *The Arabian Nights [1907]; Lyrics Pathetic and Humours [1908]: The Tempest [1908]; The Rubaiyat of Omar Khayyam [1909]: Fairies I have Met [1910]; Studies from Hans Andersen [1911]; The Sleeping Beauty and Other Tales [1912]; Princess Badoura [1913]; Sinbad the Sailor [1914]; Edmund Dulac's Book For The French Red Cross [1915]; Edmund Dulac's Fairy Book [1916]; Tanglewood Tales [1918], The Kingdom of the Pearl [1920]; The Green Lacquer Pavilion [1926]; Treasure Island [1927]; The Fairy Garland [1928]; Gods and Mortals in Love [1936]; The Golden Cockerel [1950].*
Contrib: *The Graphic [1906]; ILN [1911]; Princess Mary's Gift Book [1915]; The Outlook [1919].*
Exhib: L; Leicester Gall., from 1907; Paris, 1904-5; RI.
Colls: Author; BM; Fitzwilliam; V & AM.
Bibl: F. Rutter, *The Drawings of ED*; *The Studio*, Vol.45, 1908-9, pp.103-113 illus; *Modern Book Illustrators and Their Work*, Studio, 1914; D Larkin, *Dulac*, Coronet Books, 1975; *Times Literary Supplement*, 29 October 1976; Colin White, *ED*, Studio Vista, 1976; *ED 1882-1953*, A Centenary Exhibition, catalogue, Sheffield, Nov. 1982.
See illustrations.

DU MAURIER, George Louis Palmella Busson   1834-1896
Black and white artist, illustrator and novelist. He was born in Paris and came to London as a student to read chemistry at University College, 1851. He returned to Paris as an art student in 1856-57 to work under Gleyre and there made the acquaintance of J. McNeill Whistler and E.J. Poynter (qq.v.), a period of his life which was afterwards featured in his novel *Trilby*. Du Maurier moved on to

Antwerp from 1857-60 to study under De Keyser and Van Lerius, but the loss of an eye precluded him from following the career of a painter, and he decided to concentrate on black and white work which was at a new peak at the beginning of the 1860s. A naturally lazy man, although a very talented one, du Maurier returned to London in 1860 and gradually broke into book and magazine illustrating, developing as a fine figure draughtsman and the greatest social satirist of the period. An occasional contributor to *Punch* from 1860, du Maurier became a regular part of the magazine from 1864 when he succeeded John Leech (q.v.) as the chief observer and caricaturist of fashion and high life. His accuracy in depicting the houses and habits of the rich bourgeoisie was astonishing and his ink drawings remain a very complete chronicle of Victorian life. It is the situations that are humorous in du Maurier's work rather than the drawings, he satirises certain traits of the Victorians admirably, their artiness and aestheticism in 'Mrs Cimabue Brown', a culture-loving hostess, and their snobbery in the social-climbing 'Mrs Ponsonby de Tompkyns'. It was only late in life that du Maurier emerged as an important novelist with his three books, *Peter Ibbetson*, 1891, *Trilby*, 1894; and *The Martian*, 1896, all illustrated by himself. He died in Hampstead, 8 October 1896.

Du Maurier's pen drawings for *Punch* in black or brown ink are among the most delightful of the Victorian era, they are usually very finished, carefully hatched with little shadow on the faces but a concentration of black in hair and clothes. They are more usually signed than dated. There is a definite falling off of quality after 1880 and his compositions are sometimes awkward after this date.

Illus: *The Story of a Feather [Douglas Jerrold, 1866]; Frozen Deep [Wilkie Collins, 1875]; Poor Miss Finch [Wilkie Collins, 1872]; The New Magdalen [Wilkie Collins, 1873]; Misunderstood [F. Montgomery, 1874]; Pegasus Re-saddled [H.C. Pennell, 1877].*
Contrib: *The Welcome Guest [1860]; ILN [1860 (decor)]; Once a Week [1860-68]; Punch [1860-96]; Good Words [1861]; The Illustrated Times [1862]; London Society [1862-68]; The Sunday At Home [1863]: The Cornhill Magazine [1864, 1870, 1875-80]; English Sacred Poetry of The Olden Time [1864]; Our Life Illustrated in Pen and Pencil [1865], Divine and Moral Songs [1866]; Legends and Lyrics [1866]; Foxe's Book of Martyrs [1866]; Touches of Nature by Eminent Artists [1867]; The Savage Club Papers [1867]; Lucile [1868]; Pictures From English Literature [1870]; The Graphic [1871, 1888]; Thornbury's Legendary Ballads [1876]; Sons of Many Seasons [1876]; Harper's Magazine [1889-94]; Black & White [1891].*
Exhib: FAS, 1884, 1887, 1895 1897; OWS, 1870-93; RA.

EDMUND DULAC 1882-1953. 'The Entomologist's Dream'. Pen and ink and watercolour. Signed and dated 1909. 10⅜in x 11⅜in (26.3cm x 28.9cm)

GEORGE DU MAURIER 1834-1896. 'Appreciative Sympathy: Herr Bogoluboffski plays a lovely Nocturne, which he has just composed. To him as he softly touches the final note, Fair Admirer, "Oh Thanks! I am so fond of that Dear Old Tune!"'. Illustration for *Punch*, 20 November 1880. Pen and ink. 5in x 8in (12.7cm x 20.3cm)

Author's Collection

Colls: Ashmolean; Bradford; BM; Fitzwilliam; Manchester; V & AM.
Bibl: T. Martin Wood, *G du M*, 1913; D.P. Whiteley, *G du M*, English Masters of Black and White, 1948; Leonee Ormond, *G du M*, 1969; M.H. Spielmann, *The History of Punch*, 1895, pp.503-516; Daphne Du Maurier, *The Young George Du Maurier*, 1951.
See illustration.

DU MOND, Frank Vincent 1865-
Painter of genre subjects, landscapes and illustrator. He was born in Rochester, USA, in 1865 and became a pupil of Boulanger and Constant in Paris. He illustrated the English edition of *Personal Recollections of Joan of Arc*, Mark Twain, 1897.

DUNCAN, A.
Figure painter. He was working at London from 1853 to 1862 and illustrated *The Ancient Mariner*, 1856.
Exhib: BI, 1855-62; RBA, 1853-62.

DUNCAN, D.M.
Figure painter. He contributed illustrations to *Good Words*, 1880, and exhibited in Glasgow, 1880-82.

DUNCAN, Edward RWS 1803-1882
Marine and coastal painter and illustrator. He was born in London in 1803 and, showing artistic ability, was articled to Robert Havell and his son, the aquatint engravers. He then worked for Fores, the printsellers before giving up all engraving in favour of watercolours, becoming a member of the NWS in 1834. He became interested in marine subjects after making the acquaintance of William Huggins, the marine artist, and subsequently married his daughter; it was this side of his work that made him celebrated. He was a brilliantly clear colourist and showed life at the water-front and in the harbours of southern England with vividness and clarity. Duncan was specially

good at representing old jetties, nets drying and baskets piled with fish and the general impedimenta of fisher life. These watercolour studies for the exhibited pictures survive in abundance as do leaves from his sketch-books showing boats, gear and busy figures, drawn in careful pencil line. The artist resigned from the NWS and joined the OWS in 1847 and throughout the next twenty years made long sketching tours in England, Scotland and Wales, once visiting Holland and once travelling to Italy. Duncan was an accomplished illustrator of marine subjects and his output was extensive. He died at his home in Haverstock Hill, Hampstead, on 11 April 1882.

Duncan's watercolours and drawings are usually signed 'E. Duncan', and many of the sketches have the red stamp of the artist's studio sale at Christie's, March 11, 1885.
Publ: *Advanced Studies in Marine Painting [1889]; British Landscape and Coast Scenery [1889].*
Illus: *Southey's Life of Nelson.*
Contrib: *Poems and Pictures [1846]; ILN [1847-58 and 1868]; Willmott's Poets of the Nineteenth Century [1857]; The Home Affections [Charles MacKay, 1858]; Lays of the Holy Land [1858]; Favourite English Poems 1859]; Book of Favourite Modern Ballads [1860]; Montgomery's Poems [1860]; Early English Poems: Chaucer to Pope [1863]; Once a Week [1866]; Book of Rhymes and Roundelayes; Moore's Poems; The Soldier's Dream.*
Exhib: BI, 1833-57; NWS; RA; RBA, 1830-82; RWS.
Bibl: Chatto & Jackson, *Treatise on Wood Engraving*, 1861, p.583; M. Hardie, *Watercolour Paint. in Brit.*, Vol.III, 1968, pp.75-77 illus; F.L. Emanuel, *Walker's Quarterly*, xiii, 1923.
Colls: Bradford; BM; Glasgow; V & AM.

DUNCAN, James Allen fl.1895-1910
Illustrator, decorator and type-face designer. He worked at Glasgow, 1895-97 and at Milngorie, 1902, and was a regular contributor to magazines, an illustrator of children's stories and the designer of two alphabets for the Chiswick Press, c.1899.

Illus: *Children's Rhymes [1899].*
Contrib: *The Daily Graphic [1895]; The English Illustrated Magazine [1897]; Fun [1900]; The Graphic [1901-6]; The Connoisseur [1910 (decor.)].*
Exhib: G and RSA, 1895-1901.
Bibl: *The Studio,* Vol.15, 1899, pp.184-189, illus.

DUNCAN, John   RSA   **1866-1945**
Painter of legend and history and illustrator. He was born at Dundee in 1866 and studied art there and in London and Düsseldorf before settling in Edinburgh and working in Edinburgh and Glasgow, where for a time he was on the staff of *The Glasgow Herald.* He drew for both magazines and books, his earlier work showing a strong influence from Japanese art and particularly Japanese prints. As a decorative artist, his main work was the scheme for the University Hall, Edinburgh. As a teacher, his main contribution was as Professor at Chicago University, 1902-4. He was elected ARSA in 1910 and RSA in 1923. RSW, 1930.
Contrib: *The Evergreen [1895].*
Colls: Dundee; NG of Scotland; Edinburgh Art Centre, RSA.
Bibl: *The Artist,* 1898, pp.146-152 illus.; *The Last Romantics,* Barbican Gallery catalogue, 1989, pp.176-177.

DUNCAN, T.J.
A series of illustrations for *National Humour* and *Thistledown,* 1912-14, watercolour and pen and wash, were sold at Sotheby's in July, 1978.

DUNLOP, Marion Wallace   **fl.1871-1905**
Portrait painter, figure artist and illustrator. She was working in London from 1871 and in Ealing 1897-1903. Her black and white work is extremely competent and heavily art nouveau.
Illus: *Fairies, Elves and Flower Babies [1899]; The Magic Fruit Garden [1899].*
Exhib: G, NEA; RA; SWA.
Bibl: *The Studio,* Vol.10, 1897, illus. (competitions); Vol.12, 1897, illus. (competitions); R.E.D. Sketchley, *English Book Illus.,* 1902, pp.106, 165.

DUNN, Edith (Mrs T.O. Hume)   **fl.1862-1906**
Domestic painter and illustrator. She was working at Worcester, 1863, and in London, 1864, and exhibited at the RBA, 1862-67, and at the BI, 1864-67. She married the landscape painter Thomas O. Hume and lived after her marriage at South Harting, Petersfield, Hants.
Contrib: *The Quiver [1866].*

DURAND, Godefroy   **1832-**
Illustrator. He was born in 1832 at Düsseldorf but was of French extraction. After studying with Leon Cogniet, he settled in London in 1870 probably as a result of the French defeat of that year. He exhibited pictures of the Siege of Paris at the RBA in 1873. Durand joined the permanent staff of *The Graphic* in 1870 and remained on it for many years supplying the paper with military and horse subjects and foreign views. He was still there in 1890, when Hartrick joined the staff and he described him as 'an elderly Frenchman… permanently on the paper to do hackwork'.
Illus: *La Guerre au Maroc [Yriarte, n.d,]; The Life of Christ [Ernest Renan, n.d.].*
Exhib: M. 1882; RA; RBA, 1873.
Coll: Royal Library, Windsor.

DURDEN, James   ROI   **1878-1964**
Landscape and portrait painter. He was born in Manchester in 1878 and studied at Manchester School of Art and the Royal College of Art. He worked at Claygate, Surrey, 1909, London 1910 and 1927, finally settling at Keswick, Cumberland. He was elected ROI in 1927.
Illus: *The Five Macleods [C. G. Whyte, 1908].*
Contrib: *The Quartier Latin [1898]; The Graphic [1911-12].*
Exhib: G; L; M; P; Paris, 1927; RA; RI; ROI; RWA.

DURHAM, C.J.   **-1889**
Figure painter and illustrator. He was a teacher at the Slade School and contributed drawings of industry to *The Illustrated London News,* very regularly, 1861-74.
Exhib: RA, 1859; RBA, 1872-80.

DUTTON, Thomas G.
Marine watercolourist. He worked in London and contributed drawings of shipping to *The Illustrated London News,* 1877.
Exhib: RBA, 1858-79.

DUVAL, Marie   see ROSS, C.H.

DYCE, William   **1806-1864**
Painter, draughtsman and occasional illustrator. He was born at Aberdeen and educated at the Marischal College. He was trained at the RA Schools and spent two periods in Rome between 1825 and 1828 and came under the influence of the Nazarene painters. This was an unfashionable style in Britain and Dyce resorted to portrait painting in Edinburgh, becoming ARSA in 1835. He prepared a report for the Government School of Design and was involved in art education as Professor of Fine Arts, King's College, London. ARA, 1844 and RA, 1848.
  Dyce prepared six illustrations for *Poems and Pictures,* 1846, an influential gift-book which was the precursor of the famous art books of the 1850s and 1860s. His linear, Germanic but highly decorative work in this volume can be compared to the illustrations of Maclise (q.v.). He died at Streatham in 1864.
Illus: *Sir T.T. Lauder, The Morayshire Floods [1830]; Highland Rambles [1837].*
Exhib: BI, RA.
Colls: Aberdeen; Ashmolean; BM; Fitzwilliam; Manchester; NG of Scotland; Tate; V & AM; Windsor.
Bibl: *Centenary Exhibition of the Work of William Dyce,* Aberdeen and Agnew's, August – October 1964; Pointon, M. *William Dyce 1806-1864,* 1979.

DYSON, William Henry   **1883-1938**
Cartoonist. He was born at Ballarat, Australia, in 1883 and was educated in Melbourne and came to England in 1909. He was chief cartoonist to the *Daily Herald,* 1913-25, and again in 1931-38, noted for his extreme radical outlook and as an ardent supporter of socialist change. Dyson was a talented etcher, but his drawings, scratchy penwork over pencil and dark shading, are more reminiscent of Daumier than of English caricature. Veth considered that Dyson in his 'wild extravagance' often overshot the mark. He died 21 January 1938.
Illus: *Collected Drawings; Kultur Cartoons [(foreword by H.G. Wells) 1915].*
Exhib: Leicester Gall.; RHA; RSA.
Colls: V & AM.
Bibl: John Jensen, *WD: 20th Century Studies,* 1976.

EARLE, Augustus   **1793-1838**
The son of Ralph Earle, the American painter. He studied at the RA,
1813, and began to travel, visiting the Mediterranean, Africa, Tristan
da Cunha, the United States, New South Wales and New Zealand. He
worked as a portrait painter in Madras before returning to England
by way of France. His most famous voyage was made about 1833
when he acted as draughtsman to Charles Darwin on the expedition
of *HMS Beagle*. Earle was a skilled topographer but also drew
caricatures and genre subjects.
Illus: *Journal of a Voyage to Brazil [M. Graham, 1824, AT 708];*
Journal of a Residence in Chile [M. Graham, 1824, AT 714];
Sketches Illustrative of the Native Inhabitants and Islanders of New
Zealand [1832, AT 587].
Exhib: RA, 1806-38.s
Colls: BM.

EARLE, Percy
Contributed cartoons of horse subjects to *Vanity Fair*, 1909-10.

EARNSHAW, Harold   **fl.1908-1926**
Watercolour painter and illustrator. Husband of Mabel Lucie Atwell
(q.v.). He specialised in the illustrating of boys' novels and exhibited
at the RI.
Illus: *The Rebel Cadets [Charles Gleig, 1908]; Princess Mary's Gift*
Book [1915].
Contrib: *The Graphic [1912].*

EAST, Sir Alfred   RA FRS   **1849-1913**
Landscape painter and watercolourist. He was born at Kettering,
Northants, 15 December 1849, and began life in business at Glasgow
before attending the Glasgow School of Art, studying under Robert
Greenlees. He then went to Paris and was strongly influenced by the
Barbizon School. East was an etcher as well as a painter and was an
early member of the Royal Society of Etchers, Painters and
Engravers, President of the RBA in 1906, ARA, 1899, and RA, 1913.
He visited Japan in 1909 and was knighted in 1910. He died in
London 28 September 1913 and was buried at Kettering.

East is included here by virtue of the fact that his etchings and
paintings were sometimes used for books, for example in *Cassell's*
Picturesque Mediterranean, 1891. His *Brush and Pencil Works in*
Landscape was published posthumously, 1914.
Exhib: RA, 1883-1913.
Colls: Ashmolean; BM; Leeds; V & AM; Wakefield.
Bibl: F. Newbolt, 'The Etchings of Alfred East', *The Studio*, Vol. 34,
1905, pp.124-137; A. East, 'Art of the Painter Etcher', *The Studio*,
Vol. 40, 1907, pp.278-282.

EBBUTT, Phil
Figure and humorous illustrator. Working for magazines 1886-1903.
Contrib: *Fun [1886-87]; The Daily Graphic [1890]; The Quiver*
[1892]; Lady's Pictorial [1895]; The Graphic [1901-03].

ECKHARDT, Oscar   RBA   **fl.1893-1902**
Painter and illustrator, working in Kensington. He worked for
numerous magazines in thin pen and ink, 1893-1900. He was elected
RBA, 1896. He signs his work Eckhardt.
Contrib: *The Butterfly [1893]; Black & White [1894]; St. Paul's*

KATE EDWARDS fl.1865-1879. 'Five Minutes Late!' Illustration to
London Society, Vol.8, No.45, Wood engraving

[1894]; Daily Graphic [1895]; The Unicorn [1895]; The Windsor
Magazine [1895]; The Sketch [1895]; Eureka [1897]; The St.
James's Budget [1898]; Illustrated Bits [1900]; Pick-Me-Up; The
Ludgate Monthly; The Idler; The Strand Magazine.
Exhib: L; RBA; ROI.
Colls: V & AM.

EDMONSTON, Samuel   **1825-**
Landscape and marine painter, occasional illustrator. He was a pupil
of Sir William Allen and the RSA Schools and worked in Edinburgh,
painting in watercolour and drawing in chalks.
Contrib: *Pen and Pencil Pictures from the Poets [Edinburgh,*
1866]; Burns Poems [n.d.].
Exhib: RA, 1856-57; RSA.
Colls: N.G. Scot.; Witt Photo.
Bibl: Chatto & Jackson, *Treatise on Wood Engraving*, 1861, p.599.

EDWARDS, Amelia B.
Illustrator and contributor to *The Girls' Own Paper*, c. 1890.

EDWARDS, D   **fl.1850-1857**
Illustrator of poetry in a rather weak and sentimental manner. He
contributed two drawings to *Willmott's Poets of the Nineteenth*
Century, 1857.
Colls: Witt Photo.

KATE EDWARDS fl.1865-1879. 'June Dream'.

EDWARDS, The Rev. E.   1766-1849
Amateur topographer. He was a Norfolk vicar and antiquary and founded the Kings Lynn Museum in 1844. He was a competent pen and wash artist and contributed views to *Britton's Beauties of England & Wales*, 1810.

EDWARDS, George Henry
Figure and landscape painter and illustrator. He worked in London for juvenile magazines and novels and specialised in fairy and romantic subjects.
Illus: *The Temple of Death [E. Mitchell, 1894]; The Crimson Sign [Keightley, 1894]*,
Contrib: *ILN [1900]; The Boys' Own Paper; The Girls' Own Paper; The Royal Magazine.*
Exhib: L; RA; RBA, 1883-93; RI; ROI.

EDWARDS, Henry Sutherland   1828-
Author and minor illustrator. He was for some time Editor of the comic paper *Pasquin* and was engaged as a writer for *Punch*, 1848. He published *The Russians at Home*, 1858, *A History of the Opera*, 1862, *Malvina*, 1871. In 1867 he contributed some illustrations to magazines.
Colls: Witt Photo.

EDWARDS, Kate   fl.1865-1879
Illustrator. Nothing is known of this outstanding figure artist who worked in the middle 1860s. Her drawings of women can only be compared to those by M. Ellen Edwards (q.v.) and George Pinwell

(q.v.) by whom she was clearly influenced.
Contrib: *London Society [1865-66]; Once a Week [1867].*
Exhib: RBA, 1879.
See illustrations.

EDWARDS, Lionel Dalhousie Robertson   RI   1878-1966
Painter, illustrator and writer on sporting subjects. He was born 9 November 1878, the son of Dr. James Edwards of Chester. He studied art under A. Cope and Frank Calderon (q.v.) at the School of Animal Painting, Kensington. Edwards worked extensively for the press, specialising in hunting subjects, first for *The Graphic* in about 1910, where he reported the Lisbon Revolution. He was the successor of Alken and Leech in his love of country pursuits, and eventually of G.D. Armour (q.v.), but his drawings lacked their humour. He worked for *Punch* before the First World War and regularly in the 1920s, but his black and white work is more scratchy than Armour's, although his figures and landscapes are very authentic. Edwards was most at home in straight hunting sketches, ink and watercolour sometimes varied with colour chalk, or skilful smudges of bodycolour. The whole hunting field vividly realised, springing over fences or drawing a wood. In the inter-war years he made portraits of hunting celebrities, and there were few clubs or pubs at the time that did not possess a print of at least one of them. He was working in Wales, 1901-6, and Abingdon, 1909. He finally settled at Salisbury, Wiltshire, in 1923 and died there in 1966. He was elected RI in 1927.

Edwards' work has always been popular with the hunting fraternity and both paintings and drawings have risen in demand.
Illus: *Hunting and Stalking Deer [1927]; Huntsmen Past and Present [1929]; My Hunting Sketch Book [1928 and 1930, 2 vols.]; Famous Fox Hunters [1932]; A Leicestershire Sketch Book [1935]; Seen From the Saddle [1936]; The Maltese Cat [Kipling, 1936]; My Irish Sketch Book [1938]; Horses and Ponies [1938]; Scarlet and Corduroy [1941]; Royal Newmarket [1944]; Getting to Know Your Pony [1947].*
Contrib: *The Graphic [1910-16]; Punch.*
Exhib: L; RA; RCA; RI.
Bibl: *Mr. Punch with Horse and Hound*, New Punch Library, c.1930; *Autobiog. Reminiscences of a Sporting Artist*, 1948.
See **Horne**

EDWARDS, Louis
Illustrator of military subjects. Contributed to *The Illustrated London News*, 1889.

EDWARDS, Mary Ellen   1839-c.1910
    (Mrs. Freer 1866-69; Mrs. Staples 1872)
Book illustrator and figure artist. She was born 6 November 1839 at Kingston-upon-Thames and became one of the most prolific secondary illustrators of the third quarter of the 19th century. Her drawings of domestic life never advanced much beyond the competent and pretty, but she did illustrate Anthony Trollope's *The Claverings* and the novels of Mrs. Henry Wood in serial and book form. She was particularly good at child studies and in handling groups of children in a natural way. She was also associated with *The Argosy*, a magazine run by Mrs. Henry Wood's son. She used her maiden name until 1869, then Mrs. Freer until 1872 and finally her second husband's name, Mrs. Staples, from 1872. She lived at Chelsea, 1865-66, and at Hedingham, Essex. 1875-76, finally settling at Shere, Surrey, 1892. She died about 1910.
Illus: *The New House that Jack Built [Mrs. W. Luxton, 1883]; The Boys and I [Mrs. Molesworth, 1883]; A World of Girls [L.T. Meade, 1887].*
Contrib: *Puck on Pegasus [1862]; Churchman's Family Magazine [1863-64]; Parables From Nature [1861 and 1867]: London Society [1864-69]; Family Fairy Tales [1864]; The Quiver [1864]; Once a Week [1865-68]; Watts Divine and Moral Songs [1865]; Legends and Lyrics [1865]; The Sunday Magazine [1865]; Good Words [1866]; Aunt Judy's Magazine [1867]; Cassell's Magazine [1867-70]; The Churchman's Shilling Magazine [1867]; The Broadway [1867-70]; Golden Hours; The Illustrated Times; Idyllic Pictures [1867]; The Illustrated Book of Sacred Poems [1867]; Argosy [1868]; Dark Blue [1871-73]; Graphic [1869-80]; Mother's Last Words; ILN [1880-]; The Quiver [1890]; The Girls' Own Paper.*
Bibl: Gleeson White, 'Children's Books and Their Illustrators',

Studio Special No., 1897-98; F. Reid, *Illustrators of The Sixties*, 1928, pp.261-262; *English Influences On Van Gogh*, Arts Council, 1974-75, p.51.

EGAN, Pierce Junior
Presumably the son of the author Egan Pierce, he illustrated his father's *Capt. Macheath*, 1842.

EGERTON, Daniel Thomas
Amateur artist, murdered in Mexico in 1842. He illustrated *Man of Fashion* [1823, AL 286, aquatints] and *Fashionable Bores* [1824, AL 287].

EGERTON, Lord Francis
Illustrated *Journal of a Tour in the Holy Land by Lady Francis Egerton, 1840*, 1841.

EGERTON, M.   **fl.1824-1827**
Social caricaturist. He worked in London in the 1820s in the manner of George Cruikshank.
Illus: *Humorous Designs [1824, AL 288]; Sponge [1824, AL 289]; Airy Nothings [1825, AL 290]; Collinso Furioso [1825, AL 291]; Matrimonial Ladder [1825, AL 292]; Cross Readings [1826, AL 293]; Olla Padeida [1827, AL 294].*

EGLEY, William Maw   **1826-1916**
History painter and miniaturist who undertook some illustrations. He was born in 1826, the son of William E. Egley, 1798-1870, the miniaturist. Egley worked as a book illustrator from 1843 to 1855, but thereafter concentrated on scenes of contemporary life and period subjects under the influence of W.P. Frith. A design for a frontispiece in the Victoria and Albert Museum, dated 1843, is in pencil, heightened with white, a charming mock Gothic drawing, the handling reminiscent of 'Phiz' or G. Cruikshank. The same museum has a manuscript catalogue of the artist's work in its library.
Exhib: B; L; M; RA; RBA; RI; ROI, 1843-98.
Colls: BM; Fitzwilliam; V & AM.

EHNINGER, John W.   **1827-1889**
American landscape painter and illustrator. He was born in New York in 1827 and travelled to Paris in 1847 where he became a pupil of Thomas Couture, 1815-1879. He visited many European countries and, returning to the United States, became a member of the National Academy in 1860. He later published many engravings of his English drawings. He died in 1889.
Contrib: *Good Words [1864].*
Exhib: RA and RI, 1864.

ELAND, John S. ARCA   **fl.1905-1925**
Artist, working at Brook Street, Grosvenor Square. He illustrated *Willy Wind & Jack and The Cheeses* by the Duchess of Buckingham, 1905.

ELCOCK, Howard K.   **fl. 1910-1923**
Figure artist and illustrator. He contributed sporting subjects to *Punch* and designed dust jackets, notably that for the 1923 edition of *The Prisoner of Zenda* by Anthony Hope.

ELGOOD, George Samuel RI   **1851-1943**
Painter and illustrator of gardens. He was born in Leicester, 26 February 1851, and was educated privately and at Bloxham. He studied art at South Kensington and specialised in very finished watercolours of formal gardens, parterres and country house views, often peopled by figures in historic costume. Elgood became an authority on Renaissance gardens in England, Italy and Spain and generally spent five months of every year abroad, painting them. He worked in London, 1872-77, and afterwards in his two houses at Tenterden in Kent and at Markfield in Leicestershire. He was brother-in-law of J. Fulleylove RI (q.v.). RI 1882, ROI 1883.
Illus: *Some English Gardens [Gertrude Jekyll, 1904]; The Garden That I Love [Alfred Austin, 1905]; Lamia's Winter Quarters [Alfred Austin, 1905]; Italian Gardens [1907].*
Exhib: FAS, 1891, 1893, 1895, 1898, 1900, 1904, 1906, 1908, 1910, 1912, 1914, 1918, 1923; L; M; RBA, 1871-78; RI; ROI.

Colls: Brighton; Wakefield.
Bibl: 'The Garden And Its Art with Special Reference to the Paintings of G.S. Elgood'; *The Studio*, Vol.V, 1895, p.51, illus.; 'George S. Elgood's Watercolour Drawings of Gardens', *The Studio*, Vol.31, 1904, pp.209-215, illus.
See illustration (colour).

ELIZABETH, HRH, The Princess   **1770-1840**
Amateur illustrator. She was the daughter of King George III and the wife of Frederick Joseph Louis, Landgrave and Prince of Hesse-Homburg. She illustrated two books, *The Birth and Triumph of Cupid*, 1795 and *A Series of Etchings Representing the Power and Progress of Genius*, 1806. The second book was re-issued in 1834 to benefit the poor of Hanover.

ELLESMERE, Francis, 1st Earl of
    see GOWER, F. Leveson

ELLETT
Illustrator working c.1903. The Victoria and Albert Museum has one example by this rather weak artist in watercolours and body colour.

ELLIOTT, Alma
Black and white artist, probably for illustration. She is recorded as working in Leicester in 1926 and was a working member of the Design and Industries Association. She made drawings of period subjects with thin angular pen lines.
Illus: *Delight and Other Poems by Eden Phillpotts [1916].*

ELLIOTT, E.G.
Topographer. Draughtsman for *Travels in the Three Great Empires of Austria, Russia and Turkey*, by Charles Boileau Elliott, 1838, AT 31.

ELLIS, Maj.-General Sir Arthur GCVO   **1837-1907**
Amateur caricaturist. He was born at Gibraltar on 13 December 1837 and became Comptroller of the Lord Chamberlain's Dept., Extra Equerry to King Edward VII and died on 11 June 1907. His watercolours of court characters, animals and stamps are in the Royal Library, Windsor.

ELLIS, Edwin John   **1841-1895**
Landscape and marine painter and illustrator. He was born in Nottingham in 1841 and worked in a lace factory before studying art with Henry Dawson. He settled in London after completing his art studies in France and became a popular landscape painter, concentrating on the Welsh and Yorkshire coasts. He was a gifted poet and a champion of the poetry of William Blake (q.v.) and a friend of W.B. Yeats. RBA, 1875.
Publ: *The Real Blake, A Portrait Biography [1907].*
Illus: *Fate in Arcadia [E.J. Ellis, 1868-69].*
Contrib: *Punch [1867]; London Society [1868-69]; Cassell's Magazine [1870].*
Exhib: RA; RBA, 1868-91.
Colls: Manchester; Nottingham.
Bibl: M.H. Spielmann, *The History of Punch*, 1895.

ELLIS, Tristram James ARPE   **1844-1922**
Artist. He was born at Great Malvern in 1844 and was educated at Queenswood College and King's College, London. He was articled to an engineer and worked on the District and Metropolitan Railways until 1868. He then went to Paris to study painting under Bonnat, 1874, travelling to Cyprus, 1878, to Syria, Asia Minor and Mesopotamia, 1879-80, Egypt, 1881-82, Portugal, 1883-84 and Greece and Turkey, 1885-86. He made later tours to Spitzbergen, 1894, and Russia, 1898. He became ARE in 1887 and at about that time undertook some competent but not exciting book illustrations. Phil May (q.v.) shared his studio in London for some months. He died 25 July 1922.
Publ: *On a Raft and through the Desert [1881].*
Illus: *Fairy Tales of a Parrot [A.C Stephen, CB, CMG, 1873].*
Exhib: GG; New Gall.; RA; RBA.

ELLWOOD, George Montagu SGA   **1875-1955**
Artist and writer. He was born at Eton in 1875 and studied at South Kensington, Camden School of Art and in Paris, Vienna, Berlin and

FRANK LEWIS EMANUAL 1865-1948. 'The Merry Month of May'. Unidentified illustration. Pen and ink. 7½in x 6⅜in (19.1cm x 16.2cm)
Victoria and Albert Museum

Dresden. He was Designer of Applied Art at Holloway School of Art and Design Master at Camden School of Art. He was also a member of the Architectural Association, the Art Workers' Guild and the Society of Graphic Art, and was Joint Editor of Drawing and Design, 1916-24. Ellwood's interests were catholic and his work wide ranging from interior schemes for houses and churches to posters, books and pottery. He published handbooks for artists and died at Boscombe in 1955.
Publ: *English Furniture 1680-1800; Some London Churches, Figure Studies for Artists; The Human Form; Pen Drawing; Art in Advertising; English Domestic Art; Human Sculpture.*
Contrib: *The Dome [1899].*
Bibl: *The Studio,* Vol. 11, 1897, p.210, illus; Winter No.1900-01, p.69, illus.

ELMORE, Alfred   RA   **1815-1881**
History and genre painter. He was born at Clonakelty, County Cork, on 18 June 1815, the son of an army doctor, and moved to London with his family while still young. Showing an aptitude for art, he began drawing from the antique at the British Museum, entering the RA Schools in 1834 and exhibiting regularly there from the following year. He made an extensive tour to Paris, Munich, Venice and Florence, finally settling in Rome for two years and returning to England in 1844. He was elected ARA in 1846, and RA in 1857, and RHA 1878. He died in Kensington on 24 January 1881.

Elmore contributed one illustration, the frontispiece to *The Home Affections* by Charles Mackay, 1858; it is well drawn and decorative in the medieval idiom of the period and it is a pity the artist did not produce more work of this type.
Contrib: *Midsummer Eve [Mrs. S.C. Hall, 1842].*
Exhib: BI, 1835-47; RA; RBA, 1836-79.
Colls: Ashmolean; BM; Edinburgh; V & AM.
Bibl: S.C. Hall, *Retrospect of a Long Life,* 1883, pp.219-220; J. Maas, *Victorian Painters,* 1870, pp.239-240.

ELTZE, Fritz   **-1870**
The son of Mr. Eltze, private secretary to Sir Richard Mayne, Chief Commissioner of Police. He spent his early life at Ramsgate but was unable to live actively due to progressive consumption. He was

introduced to *Punch* in May 1864 when he submitted some sketches to Mark Lemon. In the same year he took over the production of the social illustrations that had been the responsibility of the recently deceased John Leech (q.v.). Eltze was best when allowed to mirror the follies of fashion, or the *bons mots* of childhood; his drawing was slightly amateurish and very distinctive for its broad outline. In *Once a Week,* 1869, Eltze perpetuates the vignette humour of the 1820s, 'Alteration in the Court Costume', 'A Siamese Twinge', etc.
Contrib: *Good Words [1864]; Punch [1864-70 (post.: 1872 and 1875)]; Sunday Magazine [1865]; Once a Week [1866-67]; A New Table Book [Mark Lemon, 1866]; ILN [1867]; Legendary Ballads [1876].*
Colls: Witt Photo.

ELVERY, Beatrice Moss (Lady Glenavy) RHA   1883-1970
Painter, stained-glass artist and illustrator. She was born in 1883, the elder daughter of William Elvery of Foxrock, Dublin, and married in 1912, 2nd Baron Glenavy. She studied at the Dublin School of Art and the Slade School where she won the Taylor scholarship and then became teacher at the Dublin Metropolitan School of Art. She was elected ARHA, 1932, and RHA, 1934. She illustrated *Heroes of the Dawn,* Violet Russell, c.1914, in a rather nationalistic Celtic style.
Exhib: RA; RCA; RHA; SWA.

ELWES, Alfred Thomas   **fl.1872-1884**
Illustrator of animals and birds. He was working in London, 1872-77, and was chief draughtsman of natural history subjects for *The Illustrated London News* during those years.
Illus: *The Pleasant History of Reynard the Fox [Sampson Lowe, 1872].*
Contrib: *Cassell's Illustrated Readings [1867]; The Graphic [1875]; The Cornhill Magazine.*

ELWES, Robert   **fl.1854-1871**
Landscape artist. He worked at Congham, near Lynn, 1861-71, and illustrated *A Sketcher's Tour Round The World,* 1854, AT 9 (liths.).
Exhib: BI, 1861; RBA, 1872.

EMANUEL, Frank Lewis   **1865-1948**
Topographer, etcher and illustrator. He was born in Bayswater in 1865 and was educated at University College School, University College and studied art at the Slade School. He worked in Paris at the Académie Julian and first exhibited at the Salon in 1886. After travelling to South Africa and Ceylon, he worked as a town planner and taught etching at the Central School of Arts and Crafts; he was also President of the Society of Graphic Art and a member of the Art Workers' Guild. He acted as special artist for *The Manchester Guardian* and was art critic of *The Architectural Review* for many years.

Emanuel was a copious writer, historian and polemicist for the arts; he wrote monographs on W.R. Beverley, Edward Duncan, William Callow and Charles Keene and his picture 'A Kensington Interior' was bought by the Chantrey Bequest in 1912. He was most at home with drawings of old buildings, principally those of London and the northern cities, which he drew very effectively in chalk or pencil, the contours of the houses built up with close hatching. He also reveals himself as a very good figure artist, capturing the spirit of cockney humour and the bustle of city life and produced one or two humorous sketches in the style of the Beggarstaff Brothers. He died at St. John's Wood, 1948. His work is signed 'Frank L. Emanuel' or 'F.L. Emanuel' or monogram €
Illus: *Manchester Sketches; The Illustrators of Montmartre.*
Contrib: *The Graphic; The Dome [1899]; The Butterfly [1899]; The Studio [1899]; The Bystander [1904]; The Manchester Guardian [1906-].*
Exhib: G; L; M; NEA; P; RA; RE; RI; ROI; RSA.
Colls: Author; London Museum; V & AM.
See illustration.

EMSLIE, Alfred Edward   **1848-1918**
Watercolourist, painter of genre and illustrator. He was born in 1848 and exhibited in London from 1867. He contributed many illustrations of social realism and industry to *The Illustrated London News* and *The Graphic,* 1880-85, and these were admired by Van

Gogh during his London years. He was elected ARWS in 1888 and won a medal at the Paris Exhibition of 1887.
Exhib: B; G; GG; L; M; RA; RBA; RWS; FAS, 1896.
Colls: Manchester; V & AM.
Bibl: *English Influences On Vincent Van Gogh,* 1974-75, Arts Council, p.51.

EPINAY, Prosper Comte d'   **1836-**
French sculptor and caricaturist who exhibited at the Salon des Humoristes in 1909. He contributed one cartoon to *Vanity Fair,* 1873.

ERICHSEN, Nelly   **fl.1883-1901**
Figure painter and illustrator. She specialised in figures in landscape and did some architectural illustration. Signs with monogram NE⌐
Illus: *The Novels of Susan Edmonstone Ferrier [1894]; The Promised Land [1896]; Emanuel or Children of the Soil [1896]; Mediaeval Towns [Dent, 1898-1901],*
Contrib: *The English Illustrated Magazine [1886 (North of England), 1896-97 (figs.)].*
Exhib: L; RBA; RA; ROI; SWA, 1883-97.

EVANS, H.
Black and white artist, contributing to *The Rambler,* 1897.

EVANS, William   **fl. 1797-1822**
Engraver and draughtsman. He worked from Newman Street, London, and illustrated Boydell's publications and drew for Cadell's *Gallery of Contemporary Portraits,* 1822, and engraved plates for the Dilettanti Society's *Specimens of Ancient Sculpture,* 1799-1807, published 1808.
Exhib: BI and RA, 1797-1808.

EVANS, William, of Bristol   **AOWS**   **1809-1858**
Landscape painter. He was born in Bristol in 1809 and spent his earlier years living in a remote area of North Wales, studying mountain scenery. He was elected AOWS in 1845 and lived in Italy from 1852. He illustrated an edition of Scott's works in 1834.
Exhib: OWS; RBA, 1844-59.
Colls: BM; Bristol.

EVERETT, Ethel Fanny   **fl.1900-1939**
Portrait painter and illustrator of children's books. She studied at the RA Schools and worked in Wimbledon, 1900, and Kensington 1915-25. She specialised in goblin drawings with vigorous compact pen lines and in a very decorative style. She signs her work E F E.
Exhib: L; RA; SWA.

EVISON, G. Henry   **fl. 1890-1925**
Illustrator. He was working at Bootle, 1890, and in London, 1896-1925. He is a particularly good figure artist and uses pen and ink with heavy bodycolour, often in conjunction with a spray giving a speckled effect to the ftnished drawing. He signs 'G. Henry Evison', or 'G. Henry Evison/oo'.
Contrib: *Judy [1896]: The English Illustrated Magazine [1900].*
Exhib: L; RA.
Colls: Author; V & AM.
See illustration (above).

EWAN, Frances   **fl.1897-1929**
Figure painter. She was working at Cricklewood, London, in 1907 and at St. Ives, Cornwall, in 1929. She contributed illustrations to *The English Illustrated Magazine* in 1897.
Exhib: RA, 1906; SWA.

G. HENRY EVISON fl.1890-1925. Illustration for a story. Pen heightened with white. 8½in x 6in (21.6cm x 15.2cm).
Author's Collection

EYRE, J.
Topographer. He illustrated Mann's *Picture of New South Wales,* 1811, AT 566.

EYRE, John   **RI ARCA**   **-1927**
Watercolourist and book illustrator. Born in Staffordshire and studied art at the South Kensington Schools. After designing for pottery he became a painter in watercolours and enamels and worked as a book illustrator. RBA, 1896, RI, 1917. He died at Cranleigh, 13 September 1927.
Illus: *English Poets.*
Exhib: G; L; M; RA; RBA; RHA; RI; RWS.

EYRE, Colonel Vincent   **CB**
Colonel in the Bengal Artillery, 1858. Contributed illustrations of India to *The Illustrated London News,* 1857.

FABIAN, J.   fl.c.1900
Illustrator, specialising in figure subjects, usually in pencil.
Colls: V & AM.

FAED, John RSA   1820-1902
Historical and genre painter and occasional illustrator. He began his
career as a miniaturist, later becoming an oil painter and
watercolourist after his move to Edinburgh in 1841. He became
ARSA in 1847 and RSA in 1851. His style is very much based on the
work of Wilkie.
Illus: *The Cottar's Saturday Night [1853]; The Legend of St.
Swithin, A Rhyme for Rainy Weather [1861 (slightly caricatured)].*
Colls: Bradford, G; Stratford Theatre.

FAHEY, Edward Henry   RI   1844-1907
Oil and watercolour artist and illustrator. Born in London in 1844
and studied at South Kensington Schools, RA Schools and in Italy,
1866-69. ARI 1870, RI 1876, ROI 1883. He held a one-man show
entitled 'English and Foreign Landscape', 1905. Died at Notting
Hill, 13 March 1907.
Contrib: *The Graphic [1870 and 1877 (architecture)].*
Exhib: GG; New Gall.; NWS; RA; RBA; RHA; RI; ROI.

FAIRBAIRN, Hilda   fl. 1893-1925
Figure painter and illustrator. She was born at Henley-on-Thames
and studied art at the Herkomer School, Bushey, and in Paris. She
made a speciality of portraits of children in watercolour or pastel.
ASWA, 1902.
Illus: *The Saga of the Sea Swallow [1896, with J.D. Batten (q.v.)].*
Exhib: L; New Gall; RA; ROI; SWA.

FAIRFIELD, A.R.
Amateur illustrator and clerk to the Board of Trade. He was born into
an artistic family and had only three months training at South
Kensington in 1857 before he began drawing on wood for *Fun*, 1861.
He started to draw for *Punch* and appeared regularly in 1864-65 and
again in 1887, contributing both drawings and initial letters. He was
a talented caricature portraitist, and a sketch of Austin Dobson dated
1874, is in the National Portrait Gallery. He signs his work with the
symbol 🖋
Contrib: *The Leisure Hour; Once a Week [1860-65]; Thornbury's
Legendary Ballads [1876].*
Colls: NPG; Witt Photo.
Bibl: M.H. Spielmann, *The History of Punch*, 1895, pp.522-523.

FAIRHOLT, Frederick William   FSA   1814-1866
Illustrator and engraver. He was born in London in 1814, the son of
German immigrants, and won a Society of Arts medal at an early age.
After working as a scene painter, he became assistant to S. Sly, the
wood engraver, in 1835. He soon established himself as an authority on
medieval heraldry and design and, as Chatto says, became
'distinguished for his knowledge of Costume and Medieval art, which
he has exemplified in a considerable number of shaded outlines,
mostly drawn and engraved by himself'. He was patronised by the Earl
of Londesborough and accompanied him or his son to Italy and Egypt

after 1856. Much of his work first appeared in *The Art Journal*, of
which he was assistant editor. He died in London in 1866.
Illus: *Lord Mayor's Pageants [1841]; Robin Hood [Gutch, 1847];
The Home of Shakespeare [1847]; Costume in England [1856];
Tobacco its History and Association [1859]; Gog and Magog
[1860]; A Walk From London to Fulham [T.C. Croker, 1860];
History of Domestic Manners and Sentiments [T. Wright, 1860]; Up
the Nile [1862]; Rambles of an Artist [FWF, c.1870]; History of
Richborough [C.R. Smith]; Roman London [C.R. Smith].*
Contrib: *London [Charles Knight, 1841]; Archaeological Album
[1845]; The Book of the Thames [S.C. Hall, 1859]; Book of British
Ballads; Arts of the Middle Ages [Labarte].*
Colls: BM; V & AM.
Bibl: Chatto and Jackson, *Treatise on Wood Engraving*, 1861, p.592;
S.C. Hall, *Retrospect of a Long Life*, 1883, pp. 360-362.

FAIRHURST, Enoch   1874-
Portrait and miniature painter, etcher and illustrator. Elected ARMS,
1918. He was working in London until 1918 and then at Bolton, 1924.
A talented delineator of architecture in pen and ink. Fairhurst
contributed a number of drawings to *The Ludgate Monthly* in the 1890s.
Contrib: *Punch [1902-03].*
Exhib: L.; M; RA; RCA; RMS; RSA; RWA.
Colls: V & AM.

FANE, Brigadier-General Walter   1828-1885
Amateur artist and illustrator. He was born 6 January 1828, the third
son of the Rev. E. Fane of Fulbeck, and served for most of his career
in India. His best works are of Indian landscape and architecture,
with brilliant colouring and creamy impasto. He contributed sketches
of Afghanistan to *The Illustrated London News*, 1880, which were
completed by Caton Woodville (q.v.) and he was a friend of W.
Simpson (q.v.). Died 17 June 1885.
Exhib: Dudley Gall.; OWS; RBA; RI.

FARMILOE, Edith
Children's book illustrator. She was the second daughter of Colonel
the Hon. Arthur Parnell and second cousin of C.S. Parnell, and
married the Rev. William D. Farmiloe, Vicar of St. Peter, Soho. Her
fanciful sketches of a make-believe world were partly influenced by
Caldecott and partly by Kate Greenaway. She was elected ASWA,
1905, and SWA, 1907.
Illus: *All the World Over [1898]; Rag, Tag and Bobtail [1899].*
Contrib: *Little Folks [1895]; The Child's Pictorial [1896];
Piccalilli [1908].*
Exhib: SWA.
Bibl: *The Studio*, Vol.18, 1895 pp.172-179 illus.; Winter No. 1900-
01, p.22.

FARREN, Robert
Etcher and illustrator. He was working in Cambridge in 1880 and at
Scarborough in 1889 and contributed 26 etched plates to *The
Graphic* and *The Cam*, Cambridge, 1880-81.
Exhib: L; M; RA; RE.

FARWIG, Robert
Contributing golf subjects to *Punch*, 1907.

FATIO, Morel   fl.1843-1859
Italian illustrator, contributing topographical works of France to *The
Illustrated London News*, 1843, and of Italy to *The Illustrated Times*,
1859.

FAU, Fernand
French caricaturist. He contributed comic genre subjects to *Fun*, 1900.

FAUCONNET, Guy Pierre   1882-1920
Painter, etcher, designer for the theatre and book illustrator. Became
a pupil of J.P. Laurens and Benjamin Constant. He worked in
London as a miniaturist and book illustrator during the First World
War, his style being influenced by Beardsley; his friendship with
Poiret is also reflected in his work.
Illus: *Form and Substance [Charles Marriott, 1917].*
Contrib: *La Gazette du bon ton [1914-20].*

FAULDS, James
Painter and illustrator. He was working in Glasgow, 1896-1938, and contributed to *The Graphic*, 1903.
Exhib: G; RSA; RSW.

FAULKNER, A.M.
Illustrator contributing to *The Lady's Pictorial*, 1895.

FAUX, F.W.
Illustrator contributing to *The Quest*, 1894-96.

FAWKES, Francis Hawksworth   **1797-1871**
Amateur caricaturist. He was born in 1797, the eldest son of Walter Fawkes of Farnley Hall, Yorkshire, Turner's friend and patron. He was also a friend of Turner and did spirited caricatures in wash.

FAWKES, L.G.
Irish artist and contributor to *Punch*, 1875.

FEARON, P.H.   'Poy'
Political cartoons. A series of ink drawings by this artist for *Judy*, signed and dated 1898, were sold at Sotheby's 2 May 1980.

FELL, Herbert Granville   **1872-1951**
Artist, illustrator, journalist and Editor of *The Connoisseur*, 1935-51. He was born in 1872 and married the daughter of Sir J.D. Linton, PRI (q.v.). Fell was educated at King's College, London and studied art at Heatherley's, in Paris, Brussels and in Germany before joining the firm of George Newnes Ltd. as editor of its Art Library. In 1907 he became Art Editor of *The Ladies Field*, holding the post until 1919, and in 1910-12 he was Art Editor of *The Strand Magazine*. He was Editor of *The Queen* from 1924-28 and Director of Drawing, Painting and Design at the Royal Albert Memorial College, Exeter. Fell was a well-known art journalist but his name as an artist deserves more recognition. He was a prolific book illustrator before 1910, drawing competent black and white figure studies for biblical and allegorical books, all strongly influenced by the late Burne-Jones; his pencil studies of *The Song of Solomon*, reproduced in half-tone, have more of the quality of Alphonse Mucha and international art nouveau.
Illus: *Our Lady's Tumbler [1894]; Wagner's Heroes [1895]; Cinderella [1895]; Ali-Baba [1895]; The Fairy Gifts [1895]; The Book of Job [1895]; Poems [W.B. Yeats, 1895]; The Song of Solomon [1897]; Wonder Stories from Herodotus [1900]; Tanglewood Tales [Nathaniel Hawthorne]; Stories of Siegfried [1908].*
Contrib: *The Ludgate Monthly [1892]; The Pall Mall Magazine; The Windmill [1899]; The Ladies Field.*
Exhib: New Gall.; RA.
Colls: Witt Photo.
Bibl: *The Artist*, 1897, pp.97-105 illus.; *The Studio*, Winter No. 1900-01, p.70, illus.; R.E.D. Sketchley, *English Book Illus.*, 1902 pp.27, 126.

FELLER, F.   **1848-1908**
Painter and illustrator. He was born at Bumpliz, Switzerland, on 28 October 1848 and studied in Geneva under the enamellist Albert Feller and then at Munich, Paris and in London, where he settled. He specialised in book and magazine illustration, in comic genre subjects and depicting the humours of mountaineering. He died in London, 6 March 1908.
Contrib: *ILN [1880-84]; Black & White [1891]; Strand [1891-94]; St. Pauls [1894]; Good Cheer [1894]; Chums.*
Exhib: RA and RBA, 1878-95.

FELLOES, Frank
Illus: *In A North Country Village [M.E. Francis, 1897].*

FELLOWES, William Dorset
Draughtsman and engineer. He illustrated *Antiquities of Westminster*, J.T. Smith, 1800 and *Historical Drawings*, 1828 by the same author and *A Visit to the Monastery of La Trappe*, 1818, AT 86.

FELLOWS, Henry
Amateur etcher who published privately *Etchings by H.E.*, 1866.

FENNELL, John G.   **1807-1885**
Landscape watercolourist and caricaturist. He studied with Henry Sass in London and became an intimate friend of H.K. Browne 'Phiz' (q.v.) and also of Dickens and Thackeray. His best works in art are landscape studies and caricatures. He was a noted angler.

FENNING, Wilson
Figure artist. He contributed an illustration to *Punch*, 1914.

FERGUSON, James   **fl.1817-1866**
Landscape painter and illustrator. He worked in London, Edinburgh, Darlington and Keswick and was an unsuccessful candidate for the NWS in 1850. He made vignette illustrations for an edition of Scott's *Gertrude of Wyoming* and was probably the illustrator of *Army Equipment*, 1865-66.
Exhib: BI, 1821-57; RA; RBA, 1827, 1849 and 1856.
Colls: Witt Photo.

FERGUSSON, James   **1808-1886**
Architectural writer. He was born in 1808 and started an indigo factory in India, at the same time devoting himself to the study of Indian art and architecture. He was elected a Fellow of the Royal Asiatic Society in 1840 and was awarded the Gold Medal of the RIBA in 1871. He published *An Historical Enquiry into the Five Principles of Beauty in Art*, 1844, *A History of Architecture in All Countries*, 1865-67, and *Fire and Serpent Worship*, 1868.
Illus: *Ancient Architecture in Hindoostan [1852, AT 480].*
Exhib: RA, 1850 and 1864.

FESCH, C.A.
Contributor to *Cassell's Illustrated Readings*, 1867.

FFOULKES, Charles John   FSA   **1868-1947**
Curator and draughtsman. He was born on 26 June 1868, the son of the Rev. E.S. ffoulkes and great-grandson of Sir Robert Strange, the eighteenth century engraver. He was educated at Radley, Shrewsbury and St. John's College, Oxford, before becoming a student of Doucet and Duran in Paris. He was appointed lecturer on Armour and Medieval Subjects to Oxford University, became Master of the Armouries, Tower of London, 1912-38, the first curator of The Imperial War Museum, London, 1917-33. ffoulkes wrote numerous books on armour and a study of Sir Robert Strange. He was given the OBE in 1925.
Illus: *The Happy Wanderer [Percy Hemingway, 1895-96].*
Exhib: L; Paris, 1900; RA; RBA.

FICHOT, Michel-Charles   **1817-1903**
Architectural draughtsman, painter and illustrator. Born at Troyes in 1817 and exhibited at the Salon regularly, 1841-75, being awarded the Chevalier of the Legion of Honour, he contributed to *The Illustrated London News*, 1867.
Colls: Troyes.

FIDDIAN, Emmil
Figure artist, contributing colour illustration to *The Graphic*, Christmas, 1889.

FIDLER, Gideon M.   **fl.1883-1910**
Figure painter and illustrator. He worked at Telfont-Magna in Wiltshire and contributed drawings for a story to *The English Illustrated Magazine*, 1893-94.
Exhib: B; L; RA; RBA; RI; ROI.

FIELD, G.C.
A very fine pen and wash drawing by this artist for an illustration to *The Ancient Mariner* appears in *The Studio*, 1911.

FILDES, Sir Samuel Luke   KCVO RA   **1844-1927**
Painter of genre and English and Venetian subjects, illustrator. He was born in Liverpool on 18 October 1843 and studied at the Liverpool Mechanics Institute, the Warrington School of Art, the South Kensington Schools and the RA Schools. At the outset of his London career in 1866, Fildes entered the world of black and white art and magazine illustration, remaining an outstanding figure in it

until 1872. During these years he concentrated primarily on social realism, images of the poor and destitute that came across very powerfully on the printed page. Many of them, especially those done for *The Graphic*, became famous and some, like 'Applicants For Admission To a Casual Ward' were afterwards turned into large oil paintings. In spite of this, Fildes' genius as an observer of social need is much more satisfactory in black and white and his decision to concentrate on painting after 1872 was a loss to this side of book illustration. In 1869, he was chosen by Charles Dickens to illustrate his novel *Edwin Drood*, which was left uncompleted at the author's death in 1870. Fildes' reputation was increased by this work and by the drawing of Dickens' study at Gads Hill Place entitled 'The Empty Chair', done the day after the novelist's death. Published in *The Graphic*, it was much admired by Van Gogh. Practically the whole of Fildes' archive of drawings, preparatory studies and proofs of wood engravings was presented to the Victoria and Albert Museum by his son, Sir Paul Fildes, in 1971.

Fildes continued in his career as one of the foremost subject and portrait painters of the Edwardian era. He painted state portraits of King Edward VII, Queen Alexandra and King George V, was elected ARA in 1879 and RA in 1887. He was married in 1887 to the sister of H. Woods, RA (q.v.) and was knighted in 1906. He died 27 February 1927.

Illus: *Peg Woffington [Charles Reade, 1868]; Griffith Grant [Charles Reade, 1869]; Edwin Drood [Charles Dickens, 1870]; The Law and The Lady [Wilkie Collins, 1870]; Miss or Mrs. [Wilkie Collins, 1885]; Catherine [W.M. Thackeray, Cheap Illustrated Edition, 1894].*

Contrib: *Once a Week [1866-69]; Foxe's Book of Martyrs [1866]; Illustrated Readings [1867-68]; Good Words [1867-68]; The Sunday Magazine [1868]; Cassell's Magazine [1868-70]; The Quiver [1868-69]; The Sunday At Home [1868]; The Gentleman's Magazine [1869-70]; The Graphic [1869-74 and 1880]; The Cornhill Magazine [1870-73]; The Leisure Hour [1870]; Pictures From English Literature [1870]; ILN [1880]; Time [1880 (cover)].*

Exhib: B; G; L; M; RA, 1872-1927.

Colls: Glasgow; Holloway College; V & AM.

Bibl: L.V. Fildes, *LF, RA, A Victorian Painter*, 1968; *English Influences on Vincent Van Gogh*, Arts Council 1974-75 p.51. See illustrations.

SIR LUKE FILDES RA 1844-1927. Study of a female figure for 'The Duet', an illustration in *Once a Week*, 30 January 1869. Pencil

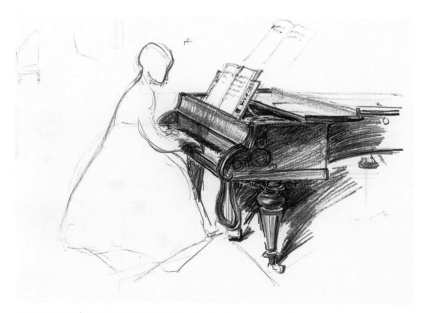

SIR LUKE FILDES RA 1844-1927. Study of a piano for 'The Duet', an illustration in *Once a Week*, 30 January 1869. Pencil

SIR LUKE FILDES RA 1844-1927. Detail of a dress from studies for 'The Duet', an illustration in *Once a Week*, 30 January 1869. Pencil

SIR LUKE FILDES RA 1844-1927. Study of the whole group for 'The Duet', an illustration in *Once a Week*, 30 January 1869. Pencil and wash

SIR LUKE FILDES RA 1844-1927. Illustration for 'The Duet', *Once a Week*, 30 January 1869. Wood engraving   Victoria and Albert Museum

SIR LUKE FILDES RA 1844-1927. 'Houseless and Hungry'. An illustration to *The Graphic*, 4th December 1869

FINBERG, Alexander Joseph   **1866-1939**
Art historian and illustrator. He was born in London in 1866 and after being educated at the City of London College and King's College, studied art at the Lambeth School and in Paris. In his early career Finberg alternated black and white illustration for the leading magazines with work as a journalist. For some years he was the art critic of the *Morning Leader, The Star, The Manchester Guardian* and *The Saturday Review*, and became a well known historian of the English romantic school. In 1905 he re-organised the Turner Collection at the National Gallery and made important discoveries among the paintings in the Turner Bequest, resulting in the building of the Turner Gallery. Finberg became the recognised Turner authority between the wars, and was Editor of the Walpole Society volumes, 1911-22 and lecturer in the history of painting at the London University. He died 15 March 1939.
    Finberg's drawings in pen and ink or wash are quite common; he handles figure subjects well, if not with great sparkle. Signs: AJF.
Publ: *English Watercolour Painters [1906]; The Drawings of David Cox; Ingres; The Watercolours of JMW Turner; Inventory of Turner's Drawings in the National Gallery [1909]; Turner's Sketches [1910]; The History of Turner's Liber Studiorum [1924].*
Contrib: *Pick Me Up [1889]; Fun [1890]; Lady's Pictorial [1890]; Puck and Ariel [1890]; The Ludgate Monthly [1892]; The Idler [1892]; The Sketch; Penny Illustrated Paper.*
Exhib: L; NEA; NWS; RA; RI.
Colls: V & A M.

FINCHETT, T.
Figure artist contributing to *The Illustrated London News*, 1896. Perhaps a relation of D.R. Finchett, artist working in Manchester, 1885.

FINNEMORE, Joseph   RI RCA   **1860-1939**
Painter and illustrator. Born in Birmingham 1860 and studied at the Birmingham Art School and in Antwerp with Charles Verlat. He returned to England in 1881 and then went on an extended tour of Malta, Greece, Turkey, South Russia and Bessarabia. He settled in London in 1884 and specialised in book and magazine illustration and black and white work. Finnemore was later to concentrate on colour work for English and Continental colour printers in the 1900s. He was elected RBA, 1893; RI, 1898. He died 18 December 1939.
Illus: *When London Burned [G.A. Henty, 1894].*
Contrib: *The Graphic [1886-1910]; English Illustrated Magazine [1887-88]; Black and White [1891]; The Strand Magazine [1891]; Chums [1892]; The Wide World Magazine [1898]; Cassell's Saturday Journal; Cassell's Family Magazine; The Boys' Own Paper; The Girls' Own Paper; The Windsor Magazine.*
Exhib: B; G; L; RA; RBA; RCA; RHA; RI; ROI; RWA.

FISH, Anne Harriet (Mrs. Sefton)   **-1964**
Black and white artist and magazine illustrator. She was born at Bristol and after being educated at home, studied under C.M.Q. Orchardson and John Hassall (q.v.), and at the London School and at Paris. Her very individual style of drawing, which typifies the period of Art Deco, is partly influenced by poster design and partly by fashion drawing. Fish's art is the art of reduction, mouths, eyes or ears are omitted in the pursuit of a harsh satire and the whole of society becomes a symbol in a few black lines. Her greatest vogue was in the inter-war years when her work appeared regularly in all the principal magazines. She also designed textiles and worked in London from 1913 and then at East Grinstead, 1934, and latterly at St. Ives where she died in 1964. Her drawings are not uncommon.
Illus: *The Rubaiyat of Omar Khayyam [1922].*
Contrib: *Eve; Punch; Tatler; Vanity Fair; Vogue; Harper's Bazaar; Cosmopolitan.*
Exhib: FAS, 1916; RA.
Bibl: Harry Furniss, *Paradise in Piccadilly*, 1925; *Caricature of Today*, Studio 1928 illus.; C. Veth, *Comic Art in England*, 1930 pp.196-197 illus.
See Horne

FISHER, Alfred Hugh　　　　　　　　　　　**1867-1945**
Painter, etcher, illustrator and writer. He was born in London on 8 February 1867 and was educated at the City of London and University College Schools before going into business for nine years. He then turned to art and studied at Lambeth School and South Kensington before going to Paris to work under Laurens and Constant. He travelled widely in Europe and the Near East for the Visual Instruction Committee of the Colonial Office before settling at Amberley, Sussex. ARE, 1898.
Publ: *The Cathedral Church of Hereford [1898]; Poems [1913]; The Marriage of Ilario [1919]; The Ruined Barn and Other Poems [1921].*
Illus: *Through India and Burmah with Pen and Brush [1911].*
Contrib: *The Idler, The Dome [1899-1900]; The Windmill [1899].*
Exhib: L; NEA; New Gall.; RA; RBA; RE; RI; ROI; RWA.
Colls: Witt Photo.
Bibl: F. Emanuel, 'Exhib. of Works by Mr. A.H.F.', *The Artist*, Jan. 1901.

FISHER, Harrison　　　　　　　　　　　**fl.1899-1906**
Figure artist and illustrator working until about 1906. He illustrated *The Market Place* by H. Frederics, 1899.

FISHER, Henry Conway 'Bud'
Contributor of strip cartoons to various children's comics, c.1917.
Colls: V & AM.

FISHER, Joshua Brewster　　　　　　　　　　　**1859-**
Landscape and figure painter and illustrator. He studied at Liverpool School of Art and spent the whole of his working life in the city.
Illus: *The Tyrants of Kool Sim [J. McLaren Cobban, 1896].*
Exhib: L; RCA, 1884-1933.

FISK, William Henry　　　　　　　　　　　**fl.1846-1873**
Landscape illustrator, working in Pimlico, London. He specialised in poetic and modern life subjects as well as in still life.
Contrib: *Cassell's Illustrated Readings [1867].*
Exhib: BI; RA; SS.

FITCH, Walter Hood　　　　　　　　　　　**fl.1827-1892**
Botanical illustrator. He made numerous illustrations for Sir W.J. Hooker's works on plants, mostly after 1835.
Illus: *Icones Plantarum [W.J. Hooker, 1827-54]; Illustrations of the Nueva Quinologia of Pavon [J.E. Howard, 1859]; The Forest Flora of N.W. and Central India [J.L. Stewart, 1874].*
Contrib: *The Botanical Magazine [W.J. Hooker, 1827-65].*
Exhib: London, 1848.
Colls: BM; Kew, Woburn Abbey.
Bibl: Mallalieu; Jan Lewis, *WHF A Celebration*, Royal Botanic Gardens, 1992.
See illustration (colour).

FITCHEW, Dorothy
Landscape and figure painter and illustrator. She worked at Bromley, Kent and made large and elaborate watercolours of Shakespearean and legendary subjects, particularly from 1911-15.
Exhib: L; RA; RI; SWA.

FITCHEW, E.H.
Portraitist and illustrator. Contributed studies of heads to *The English Illustrated Magazine*, 1886.

FITT, J. Nevill
Sporting writer, 'HH' of the *Sporting Gazette* and the *Field*. Lived at Hockliffe and made the frontispiece for his own *Covert-Side Sketches*, 1879.

FITTON, Hedley　RE　　　　　　　　　　　**1859-1929**
Editor and illustrator. He was born in Manchester in 1859 and worked for *The Daily Chronicle*, specialising in etchings of architectural subjects. Practising in Runcorn, Cheshire until 1890 he settled at Haslemere, Surrey in 1902 and remained there until his death, winning in 1907 the Gold Medal of the Société des Artistes Français. He was elected ARE in 1903 and RE in 1908. Besides his book illustrations, Fitton produced a long series of etchings of

London, Florence, Edinburgh and Paris. He died on 19 July 1929.
Illus: *English Cathedral Scenes [Isbister, 1899-1901]; Aeschylos [1901].*
Contrib: *The English Illustrated Magazine [1887]; The Quiver [1894]; Daily Chronicle [1895]; Good Words [1898].*
Bibl: R.E.D. Sketchley, *English Book Illus.*, 1902 pp.46, 133.

FITZCLARENCE, George Augustus Frederick, 1st Earl of Munster　　　　　　　　　　　**1794-1842**
Amateur artist. He was born on 29 January 1794, the natural son of King William IV by Mrs. Jordan. A professional soldier, he was the Lieutenant of the Tower of London and Governor of Windsor Castle, becoming a Major-General and ADC to Queen Victoria. He died 20 March 1842.
Illus: *Journal of a Route Across India [1819, AT 519].*

FITZCOCK, Henry　　　　　　　　　　　**1824-**
History painter and illustrator. He was born at Pentonville in 1824 and studied at the RA Schools and with Benjamin Robert Haydon. Fitzcock was a regular exhibitor in London from 1853, taking his subjects from literature and chiefly from the works of Longfellow and Cowper. He may have travelled to Sweden to make studies in about 1856.
Illus: *The Holy War [John Bunyan, 1864]; All About Shakespeare.*
Contrib: *ILN [1856-60 (Sweden)]; The Churchmen's Family Magazine [1864]; The Diverting History of John Gilpin [W. Cowper, c.1865].*
Exhib: BI, 1853-64; RA; RBA, 1853-72.

FITZGERALD, Lord Gerald　　　　　　　　　　　**1821-1886**
Amateur draughtsman and watercolourist. He was born in 1821, the second son of the 3rd Duke of Leinster. A professional soldier who served in the Scots Fusilier Guards, Lord Gerald became a member of the Etching Club of Dublin, and engraved ten scenes to illustrate the poems of Tom Hood.
Contrib: *Passages From Modern English Poets [1862].*

FITZGERALD, J. St. M.
Contributor to *The Idler*, c.1890.

FITZGERALD, John Anster　　　　　　　　　　　**1833-1906**
Figure and fairy illustrator. He was born on 25 November 1832 and exhibited regularly at London exhibitions, 1845-1903 from Newington. He contributed fairy subjects to the Christmas numbers of *The Illustrated London News*, 1863, 1876-77.
Contrib: *Cassell's Illustrated Readings [1867].*
Exhib: B; G; L; RA; RBA; RI; ROI.
Colls: Cardiff; Liverpool.
Bibl: J. Maas, *Victorian Painters*, 1969, pp.143-144 illus.

FITZGERALD, Michael　　　　　　　　　　　**fl.1871-1891**
Figure painter and illustrator. He was working in London from 1875 and contributed Irish peasant subjects and middle class subjects to various magazines. Van Gogh admired the former and considered his prison illustrations as fine as Régamey (q.v.).
Illus: *The Irish Sketchbook Ballads; The Roundabout Papers [W.M. Thackeray, Cheap Illustrated Edition, 1874].*
Contrib: *Dark Blue [1871-73]; ILN [1872-86, 1891]; The Pictorial World [1874-75]; The Cornhill Magazine [1885].*
Exhib: D; L; RA; RBA; RHA.
Bibl: *English Influences on Vincent Van Gogh*, Arts Council, 1974-75.

FITZMAURICE, Major The Hon. William Edward　　**1805-1889**
Amateur artist. He was born 21 March 1805, the second son of the Countess of Orkney and after serving as Major in the Life Guards he was MP for Buckingham, 1842-47. Died 18 June 1889.
Contrib: *ILN [1860 (Messina)].*

FITZPATRICK, Edmond ARHA　　　　　　　　　　　**fl.1848-1872**
Figure artist and illustrator specialising in Irish genre subjects. He contributed a series of drawings of the Irish Famine to *The Illustrated London News* in 1848 and further genre subjects, 1853-59. He was drawing for *London Society* in 1872. ARHA 1856.
Contrib: *Cassell's Illustrated Readings [1867].*
Exhib: BI, 1867; RBA, 1856-70.

HANSLIP FLETCHER 1874-1955. Charing Cross Hospital. Illustration for unidentified book. Ink and sepia wash. Signed and dated June 1914. 8¾in x 12in (22.2cm x 30.5cm)

Author's Collection

FITZPATRICK, Thomas   **1860-1912**
Draughtsman and cartoonist. He was born at Cork in 1860 and after working as an apprentice to a printing and publishing firm there left for Dublin where he became a lithographer and cartoonist for the *Weekly Freeman* and the *Weekly National Press*. He started his own monthly *The Leprechaun* in 1905 and drew the cartoons for it.

FLAGG, E.
Contributor of cartoons to *Vanity Fair*, 1899 and 1902.
Bibl: Roy T. Matthews & Peter Mellini, *In Vanity Fair*, 1982.

FLAXMAN, Maria Denman   **1776-1861**
Illustrator and sculptor. She was the sister-in-law and adopted daughter of John Flaxman RA. She received a Silver Medal from the Society of Arts in 1807 and presented the Flaxman models to University College, London.
Illus: *Flora's Dance*, Printed for J. Harris Successor to R. Newby At The Original Juvenile Library, The Corner of St. Paul's Church Yard.
Exhib: BI, 1812.

FLEMING-WILLIAMS, C.R.   **fl.1899-1925**
Black and white artist and watercolourist. He was cartoonist of *Judy*, 1899, his drawings showing strongly the American influence of C. Dana Gibson (q.v.). He was working at Letchworth, Herts, 1920-25.
Contrib: *Punch [1902-06 (sport)]; Sketchy Bits; The Graphic [1905-06]; ILN [1908]*.
Exhib: RA, 1920.

FLÈRE, Herbert H.   **fl.1893-1903**
Painter of genre. He was working in London in 1893. He contributed to *The Graphic*, 1902-3; *The Illustrated London News*, 1903.

FLETCHER, Hanslip   **1874-1955**
Architectural draughtsman and etcher. He was born in London in 1874, the son of G. Rutter Fletcher, FSA, and was educated at the Merchant Taylors School and at the Birkbeck College, University of London. Fletcher concentrated his efforts on depicting vanishing corners of London and other old cities, drawing every detail of their architecture and street scenes with meticulous pen work. For many years he was artist for *The Sunday Times* and his weekly drawings were a feature of the paper, later being gathered together in book form as *Changing London*, 1925-28 and 1933. Fletcher was a close friend of many artists and writers including F.L. Emanuel (q.v.), James Bone, Sir Albert Richardson and Sir Muirhead Bone (q.v.). He was a member of the Art Workers Guild and served on the Committee for the Protection of Ancient Buildings. A large collection of his drawings of London was purchased by the Guildhall Library. He died at Northampton in 1955 after a long illness.
Contrib: *The Pall Mall Magazine; The Dome [1900]; The Architect and Builders Journal*.
Illus: *The Path to Paris [Frank Rutter, 1908]; London Passed and Passing [1908]; Oxford and Cambridge Delineated [1909]; Edinburgh Revisited [James Bone, 1911]; Bombed London [1947]*.
Exhib: G; L; NEA; RA; RI; RSA.
Colls: Ashmolean; Author; Nat. Mus., Wales; V & AM.
Bibl: S.R. Houfe, 'Delineator of Change', *Country Life*, Jan. 18, 1973. See illustration.

FLETCHER, S.P.
Illustrator. He illustrated *Rowland Bradshaw, His Struggles and Adventures on The Way to Fame By The Author of The Raby Rattler* 1848. Fletcher's style is a clear derivative of the work of 'Phiz'(q.v.).

FLINT, Sir William Russell   RA PRWS   1880-1969
Draughtsman, watercolourist and illustrator. He was born at
Edinburgh, 4 April 1880 and was educated at David Stewart's College
and the Royal Institute of Art, Edinburgh. He settled in London in 1900
and after studying at Heatherley's, he was on the staff of *The
Illustrated London News*, 1903-07. From this period onwards, Flint
turned increasingly to watercolour, particularly for the illustration of
colour books. He was influenced strongly by the illustrations of *Rip
Van Winkle* by Arthur Rackham (q.v.) and between about 1905 and
1924 produced a whole series of brilliant luxury editions for the
Riccardi Press of the Medici Society. His figures are finely modelled
and contain elements of a Burne-Jones influence by way of Byam
Shaw. From the 1920s Flint became the unquestioned master of the
watercolour nude and these, and the prints from them, made his
reputation, even if they were less original than his illustrative work.

Flint served in the First World War with the RNVR Airship section
and made the first Atlantic crossing by airship in the R34, 1918-19.
He was elected ARWS in 1914, RWS, 1917 and was President of the
RWS from 1936. He became ARA, 1924 and RA, 1933 and was
knighted in 1947. He died in London in 1969.
Illus: *The Duel [Joseph Conrad]; King Solomon's Mines [Rider
Haggard, 1905]; The Imitation of Christ [1908]; The Song of
Solomon [1909]; Marcus Aurelius [1909]; The Savoy Operas [1909-
10]; The Scholar Gypsy [1910, 2 vols.]; Morte d'Arthur [1910-11];
The Heroes [C. Kingsley, 1912]; The Canterbury Tales [1913];
Theocritus [1922]; Odyssey [1924]; Judith [1928]; Airmen or
Noahs [1928]; The Book of Tobit [1929].*
Contrib: *The Studio [1899]; Opthalmological Society's Journal
[1901]; The Pall Mall Magazine [1903]; Pearson's Magazine
[1903]; Nash's Magazine [1903]; The Sketch [1903]; The Tatler
[1903]; The Bystander [1903]; The Quiver [1903]; The English
Illustrated Magazine [1903]; Black & White [1903]; The Idler
[1903]; Illustrated Sporting and Dramatic News [1903], Sunday at
Home [1903]; The Sphere [1903]; The World and his Wife [1903];
The Graphic [1904].*
Exhib. FAS, 1909, 1911, 1914, 1919, 1922, 1923, 1925, 1932, 1937,
1950, 1975; G; L; M; RA; RE; RHA; RI; ROI; RSA; RSW.
Colls: BM; Glasgow; Leeds; V & AM.
Bibl: *Modern Illustrators and Their Work*, Studio, 1914; Arnold
Palmer, *More Than Shadows – A Biography of WRF*, 1943; W.R. Flint,
Drawings, 1950 (with prologue, descriptive notes and bibliography).
See illustration.

FLORENCE, Mary Sargant   1857-1954
Decorative mural painter in tempera. She was born in London on 21
July 1857, and studied art at the Slade School under Legros and in
Paris at the Studio Merson. She carried out the mural decoration of
Chelsea Old Town Hall. In 1896, she illustrated *The Crystal Ball*,
designs which Walter Crane found full of 'power and decorative
feeling'. She became a Member of the NEA in 1911. Two of her
pictures were purchased for the Chantrey Bequest in 1932 and 1949.
She worked latterly at Marlow, Bucks.
Exhib: L; NEA; RA; SWA.
Bibl: *Studio*, 1894, Vol. 4 p.x.; K. Spence, 'A Country Refuge from
Bloomsbury', *Country Life*, November 15, 1973.

FLOWER, Clement   fl.1899-1908
Portrait and figure painter. He was working at Bushey, Herts., 1899-
1908 and contributed illustrations of social realism to *The Graphic*
in 1901.
Exhib: RA, 1899-1908.

FOLKARD, Charles James   1878-1963
Artist, illustrator and author of children's books. He was born in
1878 and after being educated at Lewisham, was apprenticed to a
firm of designers but left them to become a professional conjuror. He
later joined the *Daily Mail* staff as an artist, and invented the cartoon
character 'Teddy Tail', but abandoned this career to follow that of
book illustrator. He died 25 February, 1963.
Illus: *Flint Heart [1910]; Swiss Family Robinson [1910]; Pinnochio
[1911]; Grimms Fairy Tales [1911]; Aesop's Fables [1912];
Arabian Nights [1913]; Jackdaw of Rheims [1913]; Ottoman
Wonder Tales [1915]; Mother Goose Nursery Rhymes [1919];
British Fairy and Folk Tales [1920]; Songs From Alice in*

SIR WILLIAM RUSSELL FLINT RA PRWS 1880-1969. 'Then he
blew three deadly notes…' Illustration to *Morte d'Arthur*, Riccardi
Press. Watercolour, signed and dated 1910. 11⅛in x 8¾in (28.2cm x
22.2cm)   Victoria and Albert Museum

*Wonderland [1921]; Magic Egg [1922]; Granny's Wonderful Chair
[1925]; The Troubles of a Gnome [1928]; Land of Nursery Rhyme
[1932]; Tales of the Taunus Mountains [1937]; The Princess and the
Goblin [1949]; The Princess and Curdie [1949].*

FOLKARD, W.A.
Artist, contributing comic illustrations to Tom Hood's *Comic
Annual*, 1834.

**FORBES, Elizabeth Adela (née Armstrong, Mrs. Stanhope
Forbes)   1859-1912**
Landscape painter, etcher and illustrator. She was born in Canada on
29 December, 1859 and studied at the Art Students' League, New
York. She married in 1889, Stanhope Forbes, RA, and with him
founded the Newlyn School of Art, 1899. As an illustrator Elizabeth
Stanhope Forbes worked in pen and ink, or in watercolour in a very
broad and atmospheric way, reflecting her oil style. She became
NEA in 1886 and RE, 1885-89, ARWS, 1899. She died at Newlyn,
22 March 1912. Signs early work: Elizabeth A. Armstrong, or with
monogram: A
Illus: *King Arthur's Wood [written and illus. by ESF, 1905]; Robert
Herrick [Golden Poets, 1908].*
Contrib: *Black & White [1891]; The Yellow Book [1895].*
Exhib: B; FAS, 1900; G; L; M; NEA; RA; RBA; RI; ROI; SWA.
Colls: BM; V & AM.
Bibl: L. Birch, *SA Forbes and EF*, 1906; R. Pearsall, 'SF and the
Newlyn School of Painting', *The Antique Collector*, Vol.44, August
1973, pp.213-216.

FORBES, Professor James David   1809-1868
Scientist and draughtsman. He was elected FRSE at the age of
nineteen and was one of the joint founders of the British Association
in 1831 and FRS 1832. In 1833 he became Professor of Natural
Philosophy at Edinburgh and Principal of St. Andrews in 1859.
Illus: *Travels Through The Alps of Savoy [1843]; Norway And Its
Glaciers [1853, AT 257].*

HENRY JUSTICE FORD 1860-1941. 'Bensurdatu Attacks the Seven-Headed Serpent'. Illustration to *The Grey Fairy Book*, Andrew Lang, 1900

FORBES, J.
Topographical artist. Contributed to Griffith's *Cheltenham*, 1826.

FORBES, Margaret   **fl.1900-1914**
Painter and illustrator working in Chelsea. Made large figure drawings for magazines entitled 'Our Girls'.
Exhib: L.

FORD, Henry Justice   **1860-1941**
Artist and illustrator. He was born in London in February 1860 and was educated at Repton and Clare College, Cambridge; 1st Class Classical Tripos, 1882. He studied art under Alphonse Legros at the Slade and under Herkomer (q.v.) at Bushey. Ford was a friend of Edward Burne-Jones (q.v.) and was strongly influenced by the latter's iconography, if not directly by his style of drawing. Ford concentrated on legend and folklore as subjects to illustrate and mixed carefully observed objects from the real world with fantasy creatures from an imagined world in a very convincing way. His penwork is assured and clear and placed on the page with great decorative effect; he often supplied borders and vignettes to his published work. A whole generation of Edwardians grew up on Ford's illustrations to Andrew Lang's fairy tales, the long series of little books appearing between 1889 and 1913. The black and white work owes something to Walter Crane and a great deal to *Moxon's Tennyson*, but it is really in the later colour picture books that Ford's debt to the Pre-Raphaelites emerges; their minute detail and brilliant colours show that they are his real source. He died in 1941. Ford's pen drawings are sometimes seen on the market.
Illus. for Andrew Lang: *The Blue Fairy Book [1889]; The Red Fairy Book [1890]; The Blue Poetry Book [1891]; The Green Fairy Book [1892]; The True Story Book [1893]; The Yellow Fairy Book [1894]; The Animal Story Book [1896]; The Blue True Story Book [1896]; The Red True Story Book [1897]; The Pink Fairy Book [1897]; The Arabian Nights Entertainment [1898]; The Red Book of Animal Stories [1899]; The Grey Fairy Book [1900]; The Violet Fairy Book [1901]; The Disentanglers [1902]; The Red Romance Book [1905]; Tales of King Arthur [1905]; Tales of Troy [1907]; The Marvellous Musicians [1909].*
Illus: *Aesop's Fables [1888]; When Mother Was Little [1890]; A Lost God [1891]; Early Italian Love Stories [Vera Taylor, 1899]; The Luck Flower [G. Walker, 1907]; The Book of Princes and Princesses [L.B. Lang, 1911]; The Book of Saints [L.B. Lang, 1912]; The Strange Story Book [L.B. Lang, 1913]; Old Testament Legends [M.R. James, 1913]; Pilot [H.P. Greene, 1916]; The Happy Warrior [H. Newbolt, 1917]; David Blaize and The Blue Door [E.F. Benson, 1918]; The Pilgrim's Progress [1921].*
Contrib: *Punch [1902].*
Exhib: FAS, 1895; G; L; M; New Gall.; RA; ROI.
Colls: V & AM.
Bibl: R.E.D. Sketchley, *English Book Illus.*, 1902, pp.109, 110, 165; B. Peppin, *Fantasy Book Illus.*, 1975, p.l87, illus.
See illustrations.

FOREST, Eugène Hippolyte   **1808-**
French painter and lithographer. He was born at Strasbourg, 24 October 1808 and studied under Roqueplan and exhibited at the Salon from 1847. He contributed to *The Illustrated London News*, 1848.

FORESTIER, Amedée   **1854-1930**
Special artist and illustrator. He was probably born in Belgium but came to England to work for *The Illustrated London News* in 1882. He acted as Special Artist for that paper regularly until 1899, attending mostly royal occasions and ceremonial functions at home and abroad. He visited Morocco, Russia, Germany, Belgium, Italy and Scandinavia, attended the coronation of Nicholas II in Russia, 1896, and the Quebec Tercentenary of 1908. Forestier was a very good portraitist in chalk and drew several members of the Royal

HENRY JUSTICE FORD 1860-1941. 'Udea Found Lifeless'.
Illustration to *The Grey Fairy Book*, Andrew Lang, 1900

HENRY JUSTICE FORD 1860-1941. Fantastic bird. Pen and ink.
Signed. 8in x 7⅜in (20.3cm x 18.7cm)   Victoria and Albert Museum

Contrib: *Judy [1894]; St. Paul [1895]; Black and White [1899]; Moonshine [1900]; Illustrated Bits; The Idler.*
Exhib: L; RBA, 1893-1909.
Colls: Witt Photo.
See Horne

FORREST, Isabelle
Illustrator. Contributed a frontispiece to *Twelve Moons* by Frances A. Bardswell, 1912.
Illus: *Twelve Moons [Frances A. Bardswell]; The Herb Garden [Frances A. Bardswell].*
See Horne

FORRESTIER, Alfred Henry   see CROWQUILL, Alfred

FORSYTH, Adam
Landscape painter working at Harlesden, London, 1889-92. He contributed a topographical illustration to *The Illustrated London News* in 1891 and exhibited at the RA and RI.

FOSTER, Marcia Lane (Mrs. Jarrett)   **1897-**
Wood engraver and illustrator. She was born at Bonn and studied at the St. John's Wood School of Art and at the Central School of Arts and Crafts. She specialised in figure painting and exhibited with the NEA in 1924.
Illus: *Canadian Fairy Tales [Cyrus Macmillan, 1922].*

FOSTER, Myles Birket   **1825-1899**
Pastoral painter and illustrator. He was born into a Quaker family at North Shields on 4 February 1825. His grandfather was an acquaintance of Thomas Bewick, the wood engraver, and from a very early age he was set on being an artist himself. He went to Quaker Schools in Tottenham and Hitchin after the family had moved to London and at the age of sixteen he was apprenticed to an engraver named Stone, who unfortunately committed suicide on the day the indentures were completed. Foster was then moved to Ebenezer Landells, 1806-60, who had been a pupil of Bewick. He left Landells in 1846 at the age of twenty-one and began a career of his own in book illustration. This very productive period of his life lasted until 1859, when success enabled him to abandon this kind of work. He made his name with the public through the vignettes to Longfellow's *Evangeline*, 1850, and thereafter followed commissions for most of the classics and many books of modern poetry. Foster supplied initial letters to *Punch* in 1841-43, but his work for the magazines was very

Family from life. In later life he devoted himself entirely to the study and illustration of archaeology. He died 14 November 1930.
Illus: *One Dinner A Week [1884]; Blind Love [Wilkie Collins, 1890]; Barker's Luck [Bret Harte, 1896]; The World Went Well Then, For Faith and Freedom, In Deacon's Orders [Walter Besant, 1897]; Pablo The Priest [Baring Gould, 1899]; Belgium [G.W.T Ormond]; Bruges and West Flanders, Brabant and East Flanders [1908]; Liège and the Ardennnes.*
Contrib: *ILN [1882-99]; The Girls' Own Paper [1890-1900]; The Strand Magazine [1891]; The English Illustrated Magazine [1895-96]; Pearson's Magazine [1896]; The Quartier Latin [1898]; The Sporting and Dramatic News [1899]; The Lady's Pictorial; The Windsor Magazine.*
Exhib: RBA, 1882-83.
Colls: V & AM.
Bibl: W. Simpson, *Autobiography*, 1903.

FORREST, Archibald Stevenson   **1869-**
Landscape painter and illustrator. He was born at Greenwich in 1869 and was educated at Roan School, Greenwich, and in Edinburgh. He studied art at the Westminster School, the City and Guilds College and Edinburgh School of Art. He worked in Blackheath, 1908, and at Lymington, Hants, 1926, specialising in black and white work in the 1890s, colour work in the 1900s, and pure landscape painting from about 1910. He designed a poster for *The Idler*.
Illus: *South America [W.H. Koebel]; Morocco [S.L. Bensusan]; The West Indies [John Henderson, 1905].*

limited in comparison with his output on books. The latter were much more suitable vehicles for his gentle and subtle art, much of it in a small scale and low key, tiny detailed landscapes with pretty vegetation, herds of sheep and cows and cottagers at their doors. He was elected ARWS in 1860 and RWS in 1862. He died at Weybridge, 27 March 1899. He was brother-in-law of J.D. Watson (q.v.).

Foster designed book covers as well as illustrations and was one of the first artists to have his work reproduced by colour block in *The Illustrated London News* of 1857. He was on friendly terms with the Pre-Raphaelites and travelled abroad with Fred Walker (q.v.) whose figure work his own landscapes complement. His watercolours are very sentimental but have always attracted a large following among collectors.

Illus: *Burns Poems and Songs [1846]; Longfellow's Evangeline [1850]; Gray's Elegy [1853]; Longfellow's Poems [1854]; Proverbial Philosophy [1854]; Cowper's The Task [1855]; Adam's Sacred Allegories [1856]; Herbert's Poetical Works [1856]; Rhymes and Roundelays [1856]; Ministering Children [1856]; The Ancient Mariner [1856]; Bloomfield's Farmer's Boy [1857]; Course of Time [1857]; Poets of the Nineteenth Century [1857]; Kavanagh 1857]; Moore's Poetry [1857]; Gertrude of Wyoming [1857]; Choice Series [1857-64]; Poe's Poetical Works [1858]; Lays of the Holy Land [1858]; Home Affections [1858]; Favourite English Poems [1859]; Odes and Sonnets [1859]; The Seasons [1859]; Montgomery's Poems [1860]; The Book of South Wales [1861]; Household Song [1861]; Merrie Days of England [n.d.]; Early English Poems [1863]; Poetry of the Elizabethan Age [n.d.]; Christmas with the Poets [n.d.], Legends and Lyrics [1866]; Moore's Irish Melodies [1867]; Beauties of Landscape [1873]; The Trail of Sir Jasper [n.d.]; Pictures of English Landscape [1881]; Picturesque Mediterranean [1891].*
Contrib: *Punch [1841-43]; ILN [1847-57]; The Illustrated London Almanac For 1853; The Illustrated Times [c.1855].*
Exhib: G; L; M; RA; RE; RWS.
Colls: Aberdeen; Ashmolean; BM; Blackburn; Greenwich; Hitchin; Newcastle; Sydney; V & AM.
Bibl: Chatto & Jackson, *Treatise on Wood Engraving*, 1861, p.558; H.M. Cundall, *BF*, 1906; Jan Reynolds, *BF*, 1984.

FOSTER, William   **1853-1924**
Landscape watercolourist and black and white and animal illustrator. He was born in 1853, the son of Myles Birket Foster (q.v.). He lived near his father at Witley, Surrey, and later with him at Weybridge, 1899. He specialised in ink and wash illustrations to children's stories, including sketches of comic animals. He was a Fellow of the Zoological Society.
Exhib: L; M; RA; RBA; RI; RSA.
Colls: V & AM.

FOTHERGILL, George Algernon   **1868-1965**
Watercolourist and illustrator. He was born in 1868 and although trained as a doctor, he gave up the profession in order to become an artist. He was Medical Officer in charge of 1st Cavalry Brigade, 1918-19 and lived and worked principally in the north of England or in Scotland.
Illus: *Notes From The Diary of a Doctor, Sketch Artist and Sportsman…220 Illustrations…[York, 1901].*
Exhib: L; RSA; Walker's Gall.

'FOUGASSE'   **Cyril Kenneth Bird**   **1887-1965**
Black and white artist. He was born 17 December 1887 and was educated at Cheltenham College and King's College, London. He became Art Editor of *Punch* in 1937, succeeding George Morrow (q.v.), and had a great deal to do with modernising the paper's rather old fashioned image. He was Editor from 1949-52 and successfully steered the humour and drawing into the post-war world. Fougasse's own style was pithy and diagrammatic, due perhaps to the fact that he was trained as an engineer. His favourite form was the strip cartoon in which small outline figures, full of movement, but consisting of only the barest essentials for the story, raced along over the simplest of captions. He achieved great fame during the Second World War as a poster artist with his series 'Careless Talk Costs Lives'.
Illus: *A Gallery of Games [1920]; Drawn at a Venture [l922]; P.T.O. [1926]; E. and O.E. [1928]; Fun Fair [1934]; The Luck of the Draw [1930]; You Have Been Warned [1935]; Drawing the Line Somewhere*

[1937]; *Stop or Go [1938]; Jotsam [1939]; The Changing Face of Britain [1940]; and the Gatepost [1940]; Running Commentary [1941]; Sorry No Rubber [1941]; Just a Few Lines [1943]; Family Group [1944]; Home Circle [1945]; A School of Purposes [1946]; You and Me [1948]; Us [1951]; The Neighbours [1954]; The Good-tempered Pencil [1956]; Between the Lines [1958].*
Exhib: FAS, 1966; RSA.
Bibl: R.G.G. Price, *A History of Punch*, 1957, pp.285-286, 300-301, illus.

FOX, Mrs. Sarah Hustler
Amateur artist in the Pre-Raphaelite tradition with engravings printed in sepia. She illustrated *Poems Original and Translated*, 1863.

FOXLEY, C.
Flower illustrator. Contributed decorative pages of the seasons to the *English Illustrated Magazine*, 1896-97.

FOX-PITT, Douglas   **RBA**   **1864-1922**
Watercolourist and illustrator. He was born in London in 1864, the fifth son of General Pitt-Rivers, FRS. He studied art at the Slade and became a member of the London Group and a friend of Walter Sickert (q.v.). He made extensive tours abroad to Canada, Poland, Greece and the Ionian Isles and Ceylon. He visited Morocco in 1905-06 for Count Sternberg. He lived at Brighton from 1911 to 1918 and died at Chertsey, 19 September 1922. RBA, 1906.
Illus: *The Barbarians of Morocco [Count Sternberg, 1908].*
Exhib: GG; Leicester Gall.; M; NEA; RBA; RI.
Colls: Brighton; Fitzwilliam; Imperial War.
Bibl: *The Studio*, Vol.64, 1914, pp.56-57, illus.

FRAMPTON, Edward Reginald ROI   **1870-1923**
Painter and illustrator. He was born in 1870, the son of Edward Frampton, stained-glass artist. He was educated at Brighton and Westminster School and studied art in France and Italy. He was a member of the RBA, 1894, the Tempera Society, 1907, and the Art Workers Guild, 1910. Elected ROI, 1904. Frampton was for many years on the staff of the L.C.C. Higher Education Art Committee and published numerous papers on art. He is best known as a mural artist, he executed a number of designs for public buildings and most notably those in All Saints Church, Hastings, as well as designing stained glass and carrying out sculpture. His illustrated works were not extensive, they are in the black and white woodcutty manner which originates with Morris. Some of his drawings are very akin to those of Burne-Jones.
Illus: *The Poems of William Morris [n.d.].*
Exhib: B; FAS, 1924; G; L; M; New Gall.; P; Paris, 1910, 1920; RA; RBA; RI; ROI.
Colls: Bradford; V & AM.
Bibl. *The Studio*, Vol.58, 1913, p.21, illus.; *Who Was Who*, 1916-28.
See illustration.

FRANKLIN, John   **fl.1800-1861**
Landscape, historical and architectural painter and illustrator. He was born in Ireland and studied at the RDS Schools before working in Dublin. He exhibited at the RHA from its foundation in 1826 but settled in London in 1828. S.C. Hall calls him 'an artist of prodigious capability, who never gave himself fair play, frittering away his marvellous talent in comparatively small things, and avoiding the great works in which he would undoubtedly have excelled'. He was a fairly regular book illustrator in the 1850s, and his work was much admired by the young Walter Crane.
Illus: *Midsummer Eve [Mrs. S.C. Hall, 1842]; Seven Champions of Christendom; Poets of the West; Ireland Its Scenes and Character [S.C. Hall, 1841]; Parables of Our Lord [1851 Folio, 1855 Octavo]; The Irish Peasantry [Carleton, 1852]; The Psalms of David [1862].*
Contrib: *The Book of British Ballads.*
Exhib: BI, 1830-68; RA; RBA.
Bibl: Chatto & Jackson, *Treatise on Wood Engraving*, 1861, p.599; S.C. Hall, *Retrospect of a Long Life*, 1883, Vol.l p.332.

FRASER, Claud Lovat   **1890-1921**
Artist, book illustrator and decorator, theatre designer. He was born in London in May 1890 and was educated at Charterhouse, and afterwards studied with Walter Sickert (q.v.) for six months. He did

EDWARD REGINALD FRAMPTON ROI 1870-1923. St. Brandon. Illustration for unidentified book. Pencil on card. signed. 7in x 8¾in (17.8cm x 22.2cm)

some illustrating before the First World War but joined up in 1914 with the Durham Light Infantry and was severely shell-shocked and gassed at Loos, subsequently being invalided out of the army. He worked for two years in the Record Office but entered his most productive period after 1918, when he made a name as a theatrical designer, designing sets and costumes for *As You Like It* and *The Beggars Opera*, 1920. He developed a style of drawing and of illustration in the tradition of the chapbook with black outlines and flat areas of bright colour. There are hints of Crawhall in his work but also, perversely, echoes of Nielsen. Fraser was an excellent decorator of pamphlets and among his most striking works are the rhyme sheets he drew for Harold Monro's Poetry Bookshop. Their self-conscious simplicity and unaffected charm make them very much a part of art deco mannerism. Fraser's active service had so damaged his health that he died after this short-lived success at Sandgate on 18 June 1921.

Illus: *Flying Fame Broadsides*, [1st Series, 1913]: *A Song [R. Hodgson]; February [R. Hodgson]; The Robin's Song [Lovat Fraser under name Honeywood]; A Parable [Lovat Fraser]; Captain Macheath; The Lonely House [Lovat Fraser]. Flying Fame Chapbooks* [1st series, 1913]: *Eve and Other Poems [R. Hodgson]; Town: An Essay [H. Jackson]; The Two Wizards and Other Poems [Honeywood]; Six Essays in the XVIII Century [Honeywood]; The Almondsbury Garland [Honeywood]. Flying Fame Broadsides* [2nd series, 1913]: *The Old Men [Walter de la Mare]; Summer [Lovat Fraser]; The Gypsy Girl [R. Hodgson]; Staffordshire [O. Davies]; The Beggar [R. Hodgson]; The Wind [Lovat Fraser]; Playmates [R. Hodgson]; The Late, Last Book [R. Hodgson]; The Birdcatcher [R.*

Hodgson]; The Blind Fiddler's Dog. Flying Fame Chapbooks [2nd Series, 1913: *The Bull [R. Hodgson]; Song of Honour [R. Hodgson]; The Mystery and Other Poems [R. Hodgson]; Five New Poems [James Stephens]; A Garland of New Songs [Lovat Fraser]; A Garland of Portraitures. Eve and Other Poems [Ralph Hodgson, 1913]; Nursery Rhymes [1919]; The Chapbook; Poems from the Works of Charles Cotton Newly Decorated by Claud Lovat Fraser [1922]; The Luck of the Bean-Rows [C. Nodier, 1921]; Peacock Pie [Walter de la Mare, 1924].*
Contrib: *Methuen's Annual, 1914 (cover).*
Exhib: International Soc., NEA, 1917; Memorial Exhibition, 1921.
Colls: Tate (Curwen Press Gift); V & AM.
Bibl: E. Craig and De La Mare, *Catalogue of the Lovat Fraser Memorial Exhibition*, 1921; D. Bland, *A History of Book Illustration*, 1958, p.374; Joy Grant, *Harold Monro and The Poetry Bookshop*, 1967, pp.113-114.
See illustration (colour).
See Horne

FRASER, Eric George   **1902-1983**
Painter and etcher. He worked in Westminster and exhibited at the RA in 1924.
See Horne

FRASER, Francis Arthur   **fl.1865-1898**
Figure painter and illustrator. He was working in London from 1867 and at Dorking and Shere, Surrey, from 1881-82. He was a very prolific artist, especially in the late 1860s and his work which is

pleasantly ordinary, was considered decadent by Gleeson White. He was employed on *Fun* from 1878 and became cartoonist in 1898. His brother G.G. Fraser (q.v.) was also an illustrator.
Illus: *Great Expectations [Dickens Household Edition, 1871]; The Innocents at Home [Mark Twain, 1897].*
Contrib: *Once a Week [1867]; Cassell's Magazine [1867-70]; The Sunday Magazine [1868-70]; Good Words [1868-78]; St. Pauls [1869-73]; Good Words For The Young [1869-72]; London Society [1870]; Fun [1870-98]; ILN [1874]; The Chandos Poets; Judy [1894].*
Exhib: RA; RBA.

FRASER, G.G. fl.1880-1895
Humorous illustrator. He was the brother of F.A. Fraser (q.v.) and specialised in comic figure subjects and strip cartoons. He was a regular contributor to *Judy* and died in 1895.
Illus: *Diary of a Pilgrimage [Jerome K. Jerome, 1891].*
Contrib: *The Art Journal [1881]; Fun [1889-95]; The Ludgate Monthly [1892]; The Idler [1892]; The Strand Magazine [1894]; Judy [1894].*
Exhib: G; L; RA; RI.

FRASER, James Baillie 1783-1856
Traveller, writer and artist. With his brother W. Fraser, he explored Nepal and the sources of the Ganges and the Jumna in 1815. In 1821 he made the journey from Persia to Tabriz and rode through Asia Minor, 1833-34. He published a *Memoir of Lt-Colonel James Skinner*, 1851.
Illus: *Views of Calcutta [1824-26, AT 494]; Views in the Himala Mountains [AT 498].*
Exhib: BI and RBA, 1827-31.

FRASER, P.
Illustrator of genre. He contributed drawings of urchins to *Punch*, 1914.

FRASER, Robert Winchester fl.1874-1904
Watercolourist and landscape illustrator. He was the son of Dr. Robert Winchester Fraser of Bedford and was educated at Bedford School, where he studied drawing under Bradford Rudge (q.v.). His pictures are mostly of the Ouse in Bedfordshire and Huntingdonshire. He lived at Bedford, Hemingford Grey, Hemingford Abbots, but also at Islington 1878-80 and Highbury, 1881-85. His brothers Gordon Fraser and W. Garden Fraser, were also artists.
Contrib: *Good Words [1874-76, 1880].*
Exhib: L; M; RA; RBA; RHA; RI; RSA.
Colls: Darlington; Cecil Higgins Gall., Bedford.
Bibl: 'The Fraser Brothers Artists of Bedford', *Beds. Magazine*, 1978, Vol.16, pp.273-276; Mallalieu.

FRASER-TYTLER, M.
Contributed figure subjects to *Good Words For The Young*, 1872.

FREDERICS, A. fl.1877-1889
Illustrator. He worked chiefly for *Harper's Magazine* in what Pennell considered the English tradition. He illustrated *Three Men in a Boat* by Jerome K. Jerome, 1889, and exhibited at the RBA in 1877.

FREER, Mary Ellen see EDWARDS, Mary Ellen

FRENCH, Annie (Mrs. G.W. Rhead) fl.1900-1925
Painter, etcher and illustrator. She was probably trained at the Glasgow School and made many watercolours and pen drawings to illustrate children's books. Her style is influenced by the Pre-Raphaelites with its vivid colours, languid figures and garlands, but also present is a Beardsley influence, particularly in the use of massed dots giving the drawings a speckled appearance. In 1914 she married the etcher and stained-glass artist, George Wooliscroft Rhead (q.v.). Her work has had a great upsurge of popularity in recent years.
Illus: *Narcissus A Poem [Margaret Macewan, 1914].*
Contrib: *ILN [1913].*
Exhib: B; G; GG; L; M; RA; RHA; RI; RSA; RWA.
Colls: V & AM; Witt Photo.
Bibl: *The Last Romantics*, Barbican Gallery catalogue, 1989, p.202.
See illustration (colour).

FRENCH, Henry fl.1868-1875
Domestic painter and illustrator. He was working at Kentish Town in 1872-75, and exhibited at the RBA.
Contrib: *London Socicty [1868]; The Sunday Magazine [1869]; Good Words For The Young [1869]; Our Mutual Friend [Dickens Household Edition, 1871]; The Chandos Poets; The Quiver [1880].*

FRERE, P.H.
Botanical illustrator, contributing to *Nature and Art*, 1866-67.

FRENZENY, Paul fl.1887-1889
Illustrator. He appears to have acted as a Special Artist for *The Illustrated London News* in the Spanish American War of 1898 and had worked for the paper since 1887. He also specialised in theatrical studies, his work usually being in grey wash.
Illus: *Fifty Years on the Trail [H. O'Reilly, 1889]; The Jungle Book [Rudyard Kipling, 1894 (with others)].*
Exhib: RI, 1898.

FRIEDENSON, Joseph T. fl.1899-1909
Landscape painter and illustrator. He worked in London and contributed some ink drawings of rural life to the magazines. He signs his work J.T F.
Exhib: NEA; RA.
Colls: V & AM.

FRIPP, Charles Edward ARWS 1854-1906
Watercolourist, Special Artist and illustrator. He was born in London in 1854, the son of G.A. Fripp, RWS, the landscape painter. Fripp was a war correspondent on *The Graphic* from 1878, and in that capacity covered a great number of Queen Victoria's 'little wars'. He was special artist in the Transvaal, 1881, Ceylon, 1881, South Africa. 1885 and China, 1895-1903. He visited Japan, but died at Montreal in 1906 as a result of the hardships endured during the Manchurian campaign of the Sino-Japanese War of 1905. Hartrick describes him as 'a little terrier of a man'. He was elected ARWS in 1891.
Illus: *Fairy Tales [B. Field, 1898]; Gray's Elegy [Lane, 1907].*
Contrib: *Black and White [1893]; The Pall Mall Magazine.*
Colls: V & AM.
Bibl: A.S. Hartrick, *Painters Pilgrimage...1939*, p.71.
Exhib: L; M; RA; RHA; RWS.

FRISTON, David Henry fl.1853-1878
Figure painter and illustrator. He was working in Regent's Park in 1854 and in Kensington in 1863. Friston seems to have specialised in theatrical scenes and portraits in black and white.
Contrib: *The Churchman's Family Magazine [1863]; Tinsley's Magazine [1867]; ILN [1869-78 (theatrical)]; Dark Blue [1871-73].*
Exhib: BI, 1854-67; RA; RBA, 1863.

FRITH, William Powell RA CVO 1819-1909
Domestic and genre painter. He was born on 9 January 1819 and was educated at Knaresborough and Dover, before studying art under Sass and at the RA Schools. He began to exhibit at the RA in 1840 and from that period became the doyen of English subject pictures, including 'Ramsgate Sands', 1853, 'Derby Day', 1858, and 'The Railway Station', 1862. Frith tried unsuccessfully to be a moral painter in the manner of Hogarth and although he illustrates Victorian society in a very finished and photographic way, he did not penetrate its skin and remained a prosperous popular painter. He made one excursion into book illustration by contributing to S.C. Hall's *Book of British Ballads* in 1842, and there is a wash drawing in the Victoria and Albert Museum which may be a study for illustration. He became ARA in 1845, and RA in 1853, and was created CVO in 1908 in recognition of his long connection with the Royal Family as a painter of ceremonial events. He died at St. John's Wood, 2 November 1909.
Bibl: W.P.F. *My Autobiography...Further Reminiscences*, 1887-88; J. Laver and J. Mayne, *Cat. of...Paintings by WPF, RA, at Harrogate Art Gallery*, 1951.

FROHAWK, F.W.
Ornithological draughtsman who contributed illustrations to *British Birds Their Nests and Eggs*, 1891.

FRÖHLICH, Lorens   **1820-1908**

Painter, engraver and illustrator. He was born in Copenhagen on 25 October 1820, and studied in Denmark and at Munich, Dresden and Rome. In 1877, he was appointed professor of the Academy of Fine Art in Copenhagen but established his reputation more as an illustrator than a painter. He illustrated numerous Danish books of legend and contributed to English children's stories. He died at Copenhagen on 25 October 1908.

Illus: *What Makes Me Grow? [1875].*

Contrib: *Mrs. Gatty's Parables From Nature [1861]; Legends and Lyrics [A.A. Proctor, 1865]; ILN [1872].*

Exhib: FAS, 1883.

FROST, Arthur Burdett   **1851-1928**

Painter and draughtsman. He was born at Philadelphia on 17 January 1851 and was associated from an early date with *Harper's* for which he did many drawings serious and humorous. Pennell considered him to be the finest comic artist in the United States, but was even more impressed by his accuracy as a domestic illustrator. 'Mr. Frost's drawings of the farmer in the Middle States will later be as valuable records as Menzel's uniforms of Frederick the Great.' Frost was an exhibitor at the Paris Exhibition of 1900 and died in 1928.

Illus: *American Notes [Dickens Household Edition, 1871]; Phantasmagoria [Lewis Carroll, 1911].*

Contrib: *The Quiver [1882].*

Bibl: J. Pennell, *Pen Drawing and Pen Draughtsmen*, 1894.

FRY, Roger Elliott   **1866-1934**

Art critic and artist. He was born in 1866, the son of the Rt. Hon. Sir Edward Fry, one of the distinguished Quaker family. After being educated at Clifton and King's College, Cambridge, where he read science, Fry devoted himself to art and studied under Francis Bate and in Paris. After visiting Italy, he turned his attention to connoisseurship and writing and became the director of the Metropolitan Museum of Art, New York, 1905-10. He sponsored the first French Post-Impressionist exhibitions at the Grafton Gallery, 1910 and 1912, and founded the Omega Workshop in 1913. He wrote many books and articles, championing modern art and became Slade Professor of Fine Art at Cambridge in 1933. He died on 9 September 1934. Member of NEA, 1893.

Illus: *In a Garden [Rev. H.C. Beeching, 1896 (title)]; Polyphemus & Other Poems [1901].*

Exhib: G; L; M; NEA; RSA.

FRY, Windsor

Contributor of domestic illustrations to *The English Illustrated Magazine*, 1897.

FULLEYLOVE, John   RI   **1845-1908**

Landscape painter, watercolourist and illustrator. He was born at Leicester on 18 August 1845, and was at first apprenticed to an architect, Flint and Shenton of Leicester, before taking to painting as a profession. Fulleylove travelled abroad widely and painted architecture and gardens in Versailles, Florence, Rome and Athens and visited the Near East and the Holy Land. His work was published in a long series of late Victorian and Edwardian colour plate books and although attractive is often a too rich diet for today's taste. He was elected RI in 1879 and died in London on 22 May 1908. His brother-in-law was George S. Elgood RI (q.v.).

Illus: *Henry Irving [1883]; Oxford [Edward Thomas, 1889]; Pictures and Sketches of Greek Landscape [1897]; The Stones of Paris [1900]; The Holy Land [Rev. John Kelman MA, 1905]; Middlesex [Hope Moncrieff]; Edinburgh [Rosaline Masson]; In the Footsteps of Charles Lamb [c.1905]; Greece [A & C Black]; The Tower of London [A & C Black]; Westminster [A & C Black].*

Contrib: *The English Illustrated Magazine [1886]; The Picturesque Mediterranean [1891]; Good Words [1891]; ILN [1894]; Pastorals of France [F. Wedmore, 1894 (title)].*

Exhib: B; FAS, 1886, 1888, 1890, 1894, 1896, 1899, 1902, 1906; G; Leicester Gall.; RA; RHA; RI; ROI.

Colls: Cardiff; Leicester; Liverpool; V & AM.

Bibl: 'Mr. Fulleylove's Drawings of Greek Architecture and Landscape', *The Studio*, Vol.7, 1896, pp.77-82, illus.; R.E.D. Sketchley, *English Book Illus.*, 1902, pp.31, 39, 134.

HARRY FURNISS 1854-1925. Caricature of Lord Brampton. Pen and ink. 3½in x 2¾in (8.9cm x 7cm)   Author's Collection

FURNISS, Harry   **1854-1925**

Black and white artist, caricaturist and author. He was born at Wexford, Ireland, in 1854, the son of an English engineer. Furniss drew from an early age and first submitted work to A.M. Sullivan's Irish version of *Punch* and then to *Punch* itself, after he had settled in London in 1873. His sketches were rejected by *Punch*'s editor, Tom Taylor, and only accepted after Burnand had taken over the editorship; he joined the staff in 1880, but was never on the salaried staff. Furniss was well-travelled, visited America, Canada and Australia, and was sent to the Chicago World Fair as Special Artist by *The Illustrated London News*. For the same paper he also tried his hand at social realism, but it is as a humorous illustrator that he is most widely remembered.

There is little doubt that Furniss was one of the most talented black and white artists of his time, certainly one of the quickest in executing work. His pen line, which looks effortlessly precise, was often worked up from pencil, but when he introduces washes, the effect is far less successful. A master of political caricature, of the silhouette caricature and of the inspired doodle, he lacked the consistency to become a great illustrator. He was notoriously argumentative and egotistical, as is shown by obsessive use of self-portraits and his famous break with *Punch* in 1894 when he founded *Lika Joko* and *The New Budget*. He was at his most brilliant, however, in metamorphic caricatures such as 'Getting Mr. Gladstone's Collar Up' and subtly imitating the works of famous artists. His Parliamentary sketches are occasionally seen on the market. He died at Hastings, 14 January 1925 and signs his work

Illus: *Happy Thoughts; Incompleat Angler; The Comic Blackstone; Sylvie and Bruno [Lewis Carroll, 1889]; Thackeray's Ballads [Cheap Illustrated Edition, 1894]; All in a Garden Fair [W. Besant, 1897]; 'The Wallypug of Why [G.E. Farrow, 1900]; The Works of Charles Dickens [1910]; The Works of W.M. Thackeray [1911].*

Publ: *Royal Academy Antics [1890]; America in a Hurry [1900]; Peace with Humour; P and O Sketches [1898]; Confessions of a Caricaturist [1901]; Harry Furniss At Home [1903]; How To Draw in Pen and Ink [1905]; Friends without Faces [1905]; Our Lady Cinema [1914]; More about How to Draw in Pen and Ink [1915]; Peace in War [1917]; Deceit a reply to Defeat [1917]; My Bohemian*

HARRY FURNISS 1854-1925. 'The Race for the Country, Waiting for the Signal by our Americanised Artist'. Illustration for *Punch*, 18 June 1892. Pen and ink

Woburn Abbey Collection

Days; The Byways and Queer Ways of Boxing [1919]; Stiggins, Some Victorian Women [1923]; Some Victorian Men [1924].
Contrib: *ILN [1876-86]; Punch [1880-94]; Vanity Fair [1881]; Cornhill Magazine [1883-85]; The English Illustrated Magazine [1883, 1890-91]; The Graphic [1889]; Good Words [1890]; Black & White [1891]; The Pall Mall Budget; The Sketch; The Windsor Magazine; Cassell's Family Magazine; Illustrated Sporting and Dramatic News.*
Exhib: FAS, 1894, 1898, 1925; RA; RHA.
Colls: V & AM.
Bibl: H.F., *Confessions of a Caricaturist*, 1901; *HF*, NPG exhibition catalogue, Sept. 1983.
See illustrations.
See **Horne**

FURSE, Charles Wellington   ARA   1868-1904
Portrait painter. He was born in 1868, the son of the Ven. C.W. Furse, Archdeacon of Westminster. He was educated at Haileybury College and studied at the Slade School under Legros, winning a Slade

Scholarship and then working in Paris. He was a member of the NEA in 1892 and was elected ARA in 1904. He died 17 October 1904.
Contrib: *The Yellow Book; The Autobiography of a Boy [G.S. Street, 1894 (title)].*

FUSSELL, Joseph   fl.1821-1845
Landscape painter. He was probably the brother of A. and F.R. Fussell, and painted from addresses in Sadlers Wells and Bloomsbury, 1821-45. He contributed illustrations to Virtue's *Views of Kent*, 1829, and to Knight's *London*, 1841.
Exhib: BI, 1822-45; RBA, 1821-45.

FYFE, William Baxter Collier   1836-1882
Figure painter and illustrator. He was born at Dundee in 1836 and studied art at the RSA in Edinburgh. He specialised in Scottish genre subjects, exhibited his first picture in 1861, and settled in London in 1863, working latterly at St. John's Wood.
Contrib: *Good Words [1861].*
Exhib: G; RA; RI; RBA.

GAILDRAU, Jules   **1816-1898**
Figure artist and illustrator. He was born in Paris 18 September 1816, and worked for numerous French papers, principally for *L'Illustration*, and contributed to *The Illustrated London News* (Vizetelly). He exhibited at the Salon, 1848-57, and died in Paris in January 1898.

GAILLIARD, François   **1861-**
Painter of genre and illustrator. He was born at Brussels on 30 November 1861 and exhibited at Berlin in 1886. He worked for *L'Illustration* and contributed to *The Illustrated London News*, 1900.

GALE, William   **1823-1909**
Painter of history and religious themes. He was born in London in 1823 and studied at the RA Schools before travelling to the Continent, the Middle East and North Africa for study. He was a frequent exhibitor at London exhibitions, 1844-1892.
Contrib: *Passages From The Modern English Poets [1862]*.
Exhib: B; BI, 1844-67; G; L; M; RA; RBA, 1844-92; RI; ROI; RSA.
Colls: Glasgow.

GALLAGHER, F. O'Neill   **fl.1901-1910**
Landscape painter and illustrator. Working at Corbeil, France, in 1910 and exhibiting at the NEA the same year.
Contrib: *The Dome, [1899-1900]*.
Bibl: *The Studio*, Winter No.1900-01, p.62, illus.

GALPIN, Will Dixon   **fl.1882-1891**
Figure painter and illustrator. He was working at Roehampton, 1882-85, and at Bushey in 1884. In 1891 he contributed illustrations to Cassell's *The Picturesque Mediterranean*.
Exhib: B; G; L; RA; RBA.

GAMMON, Reginald   **1894-**
Watercolour artist, landscape painter and illustrator. He was born at Petersfield in 1894 and contributed black and white drawings to *Punch*, mostly of country subjects.
Exhib: NEA; RA; RBA; RI, 1938-40.
Bibl: *Mr. Punch With Horses and Hound*, New Punch Library, c.1930.
See Horne

GANDY, Herbert   **fl.1881-1911**
Figure and domestic painter. He exhibited regularly from 1881-1911 and contributed fairy illustrations to *The Illustrated London News*, Christmas, 1903.
Exhib: B; G; L; M; RA; RHA; RI; ROI.

GARDEN, G.M.
Book decorator, contributing endpieces to *The English Illustrated Magazine*, 1896.

GARDNER, W. Biscombe   **c.1849-1919**
Landscape painter, wood engraver and etcher. He was born in about 1849 and painted in both watercolour and oil, but was best known as an engraver. He engraved work for *The Illustrated London News* and

The Graphic, but specialised in work after such artists as Alma Tadema, Lord Leighton and G.F. Watts. He was working in London in 1880 and 1897, in Surrey, 1893 and 1883 and 1891, finally settling in Tunbridge Wells, 1906.
Illus: *Kent* and *Derbyshire [A & C Black]*.
Contrib: *The Pall Mall Magazine; The English Illustrated Magazine [1887-88 and 1891-92]*.
Exhib: G; L; New Gall.; RA: RI: ROI; RSW.
Colls: Margate; V & AM.

GARLAND, Charles Trevor   **fl.1874-1907**
Landscape, portrait and child painter and illustrator. He was working in London from 1874 and exhibiting regularly. He was living in Rome in 1880 and on his return to this country the following year, worked first in London and then in Penzance, 1892-1903. He was living in Colchester in 1907.
Contrib: *The Graphic [1874]; ILN [Christmas, 1882-86 (genre) and Christmas, 1892-93 (genre)]*.
Exhib: B; G; L; M; RA; RBA; RI; ROI.

GARLAND, Henry   **fl 1854-1892**
Painter of landscape, genre and animals. He was born at Winchester and worked in North London from 1854 and in Leatherhead, Surrey from 1887, exhibiting regularly at the major exhibitions.
Contrib: *ILN [1868]*.
Exhib: B; L; M; RA; RBA; ROI.
Colls: Leicester; Sunderland.

GARLAND, Robert   **c.1808-**
Draughtsman. He entered the RA Schools in December 1827 and drew views of London and its vicinity. He made the drawings for Winkle's *Cathedral Churches of England and Wales*, 1838.
Exhib: RA, 1826-31.

GARRATT, Arthur Paine   **1873-**
Portrait painter and illustrator. He was born in London on 17 July 1873 and was educated at the City of London School. He probably taught drawing at the Leys School, Cambridge and after some years portrait painting in America, returned to this country and settled in Chelsea. As a young man, Garratt was a prolific illustrator, and as a Londoner specialised in scenes of London life, crowded figure subjects such as the music hall and the riverside. A large pen and wash drawing of the Great Hall at Chelsea Hospital was recently on the market, the figures heavily built up in bodycolour.
Illus: *Lucian's Wonderland [St. J.B. Wynne Willson, 1899]*.
Contrib: *The Graphic [1899-1910]; Black & White [1899-1900]; The Quiver [1900]; The Pall Mall Magazine [1900]; Pearson's Magazine; The Royal Magazine; Punch; The Sphere*.
Exhib: FAS, 1911; L; P; RA; Salon, 1903.
Bibl: *Who's Who in Art 1927*.

GARRETT, Edmund Henry   **1853-**
Painter, illustrator and engraver. Although an American artist, born in Albany on 19 October 1853 and working in Boston, after studying in Paris, he is included here as the illustrator of English editions of Ouida's novels.

GASCOIGNE, John
Figure artist. Contributed illustrations to *London Society*, 1865.

GASKIN, Arthur Joseph   **1862-1928**
Painter, illustrator, portraitist, designer. He was born at Birmingham in 1862 and married in 1894 Georgie Evelyn Cave France, (Mrs. Arthur Gaskin, q.v.). He was educated at Wolverhampton Grammar School and then studied at the Birmingham School of Art, eventually teaching there. Gaskin became increasingly interested in the crafts after contact with William Morris (q.v.) and the influence of the Kelmscott Press, for which he designed, is discernible in his own work and that of his students. He became the Director of the Jewellers and Silversmiths School at Victoria Street, Birmingham and was a member of the Royal Birmingham Society of Artists, he died on 4 June 1928.
Illus: *Stories and Fairy Tales [Hans Andersen, 1893]; Good King Wenceslas [Dr. Neale, 1895-96]; The Shepheardes Calender [Spenser, Kelmscott Press, 1896]*.

GAVARNI (H.G.S. Chevalier) 1804-1866. 'Thieves'. An illustration for *Gavarni in London*, 1850. Tinted lithograph

Contrib: *The English Illustrated Magazine [1893-94]; A Book of Pictured Carols [Birmingham School, 1893]; A Book of Fairy Tales [Baring Gould, Birmingham School, 1894]; The Yellow Book [1896]; The Quarto [1897].*
Exhib: B; G; L.; M; New Gall; RA; RBA; RE.
Bibl: R.D. Sketchley, *English Book Illus.*, 1902, pp.10 and 126; Joseph B. Southall, *The Drawings of AG*; The Studio, Vol. 64, 1914; *Arthur & Georgie Gaskin*, Birmingham Art Gallery, Feb-March 1982, catalogue, *The Last Romantics*, Barbican Gallery catalogue, 1989.

GASKIN, Mrs. Arthur (née Georgie Evelyn Cave France)
Illustrator of children's books. She married Arthur J. Gaskin (q.v.), in 1894, helped him to design jewellery and exhibited 1896-1930.
Illus: *An ABC Book Pictured and Rhymed by...[1895-96]; Watts Divine and Moral Songs for Children [1896]; Horn-book Jingles [1896-97]; Little Girls and Little Boys [1898]; The Travellers and Other Stories [1898].*
Exhib: B; L; New Gall.; RMS.
Bibl: R.E.D. Sketchley, *English Book Illus.*, 1902, pp.l01, 166.

GASTINEAU, Henry G.   OWS   **1791-1876**
Landscape watercolourist and topographer. He was born in 1791 and studied at the RA Schools after being trained as an engraver. He travelled widely in Great Britain, painting picturesque scenery and was elected AOWS in 1821 and OWS in 1823. He worked as a drawing-master in Camberwell from 1827. He died there on 17 January 1876.
Publ: *Wales Illustrated [1829].*
Contrib: *The Surrey Tourist or Excursions Through Surrey [1821].*
Exhib: BI; OWS; RA.
Colls: BM; V & AM.

GATCOMBE, George   **fl. 1887-1897**
Black and white figure artist, specialising in theatrical illustrations.
Contrib: *Fun [1887-92]; Ally Sloper's Half Holiday [1890]; The Rambler [1897].*

GATTY, Margaret (Mrs. Alfred Gatty)   **1807-1873**
Writer of children's tales and amateur illustrator. She was born in 1807 the daughter of A.J. Scott and married Dr. Alfred Gatty in 1839. She was a tireless producer of children's literature such as *Parables From Nature*, 1855-71 and founded *Aunt Judy's Magazine*, 1866. She wrote *Aunt Judy's Tales*, 1859 and *Aunt Judy's Letters, 1862*. She was the sister of the equally prolific children's author Juliana Horatia Ewing. Her *Parables From Nature - Fourth Series - Light of Life*, 1864, have four sepia wood engravings. The contents page in this volume states 'The illustrations are by Mrs. Gatty and her daughters.' The inscribed copy in the present writer's collection is dated 'Dec. 1863.'
Illus: *Parables From Nature [1858].*

GAUDIER-BREZESKA, Henri   **1891-1915**
Painter, sculptor and designer. He was born in France and came to England in about 1909. He lived in grinding poverty in the Fulham Road and was a founder member of the London Group in 1913. He joined the French army in 1914 and was killed the following year. He is represented here as an illustrator by his contributions to *The Splendid Wayfaring* by Haldane Macfall, 1913.
Bibl: Ede, H.S., *Savage Messiah*, 1931; Cole, R., *Burning to Speak*, 1978; Cork, R., *Vorticism and abstract art in the first machine age*, 1976; *Gaudier-Brezeska Drawings*, Waddington catalogue, 1966.

GAUGNIET
French contributor to *The Illustrated London News*, 1848.

GAVARNI   H.G.S. Chevalier   **1804-1866**
Caricaturist and lithographer. He was born in Paris at 5 Rue des Vieilles-Haudriettes on 13 January 1804, his father having been an active revolutionary and his mother a member of a theatrical and painting family. In 1818 he went to study at the Pension Butet and then at the Conservatoire des Arts et Métiers, concentrating on

GAVARNI (H.G.S. Chevalier) 1804-1866. 'The Queen's State Coachman'. An unpublished study for *Gavarni in London*, 1850. Pencil and chinese white   Victoria and Albert Museum

machinery design. The artist had a few plates issued in Paris about 1825 signed 'HC' or 'H. Chevalier' but his main work was as an architectural etcher for Jean Adam and later surveying in the Haute Pyrénées. He settled in Paris again in June 1828.

From 1829 'Gavarni', as Chevalier now called himself, began to develop as a designer; his early productions were costumes and fashion plates and in 1830, during the Revolution of that year, he produced two satirical prints of the departing Bourbons. Gavarni's interests were always the study of humanity, faces, figures, groups on the Paris streets. A series of lithographs was published in the *Artiste* on the 'Physionomies de la Population de Paris' and followed by 'Travestissements' in a similar vein, both attracting enormous attention. He joined the staff of *Charivari* and from this time onwards, his work appeared there and in *Le Musée des Familles, Le Caricature, Le Figaro, La Renaissance, Le Bulletin de L'Amis Des Arts* and *La Sylphide*. He also contributed to *La Revue et Gazette Musicale, L'Illustration, Le Bossu, The Puppet Show* and *Paris*.

On November 21 1847, Gavarni left for England and spent the next four years there, travelling widely, making a journey to Scotland and meeting English artists. This resulted in *Studies: Rustic Groups of Figures*, published by Rowney. In 1850 he published a series of tinted wood engravings, *Gavarni in London* and on his return to Paris in 1851, *Les Anglais peints par aux-mêmes*. Gavarni profited by his visit to England by developing a much wetter and broader technique in watercolours. His work fell out of favour in the late 1850s and he died of consumption on 24 November 1866. Gavarni admired the work of his great contemporary Daumier, but unlike him was more of a humorist than a caricaturist.

Illus: *The Wandering Jew [Sue, 1845]; Dames Aux Camélias; Petits bonheurs de la Ville; Mille et Une Nuits; Symphonies de L'Hiver; Gil Blas [1863].*
Contrib: *ILN [1848-55]; Cassell's Illustrated Family Paper [1857].*
Colls: V & AM.
Bibl: Edmond and Jules de Goncourt, *Gavarni*, Paris 1924; Franzt and Uzanne, *Daumier and Gavarni*, Studio, 1904.
See illustrations.

GAVIN, Miss Jessie   **fl.1903-1914**
Illustrator. She was working at Oxton, Cheshire from 1903-14 and contributed frontispieces to some of Messrs. Jack's publications. She was a good portraitist in solid outline and was clearly influenced by the Beggarstaff Brothers. She signs G
Illus: *Stories of Hoffmann, Stories of Poe; Stories of Gautier [1908].*
Exhib: L, 1903-12.

GEAR, J.W.   **fl.1851-1852**
Painter of portraits and engraver. He specialised in family groups in watercolours, in theatrical personalities and paintings on porcelain. Contributed to *The Illustrated London News*, 1848.
Exhib: RA; RBA, 1821-52.

GEIKIE, Walter   RSA   **1795-1837**
Genre painter and etcher. He was born at Edinburgh on 9 November 1795 and was deaf and dumb from an early age. He studied under Patrick Gibson and at the Trustees Academy where he was patronised by Andrew Wilson. Some of his genre subjects were in the collection of Hopetoun House, but as he was no colourist, he preferred to work as an etcher. He became ARSA in 1831 and RSA in 1834. Geikie was strongly influenced by Wilkie and to some extent by the sort of etchings of street-folk carried out by J.T. Smith (q.v.). 'His collection of sketches of figures and of groups was immense. Many of these were disposed of by a private sale after his death, when part of them were purchased by Mr. James Gibson-Craig, and the greater number by Mr. Bindon Blood...' [*Etchings Illustrative of Scottish Character*, p.x].
Illus: *Etchings Illustrative of Scottish Character and Scenery Executed After His Own Designs by the late Walter Geikie, RSA [1841].*
Exhib: RA.
Colls: BM; NG of Scotland.
Bibl: *Print Collectors' Quarterly*, Vol.22, No.4, 1935, pp.304-324.

GELL, Sir William   **1774-1836**
Topographical draughtsman and traveller. He was born in 1774 and after studying at the RA Schools and practising as an architect, he

settled in Italy in 1820 and became Chamberlain to the exiled Caroline, Princess of Wales. He is best remembered by his series of illustrated books and he died at Naples in 1836.
Illus: *The Topography of Troy [1804, AT 399]; Geography and Antiquities of Ithaca [1807]; The Itinerary of Greece [1810, AT 129]; Views in Barbary [1815, AT 297]; Attica [1817]; Itinerary of the Moreo [1818]; Pompeiana [1817-19]; The Walls of Rome [1820]; Narrative of a Journey to the Morea [1823]; Topography of Rome [1834]; A Tour in the Lakes [1797 (edited by W. Rollinson, 1968)].*
Colls: Barrow-in-Furness; BM.

GENDALL, John   **1790-1865**
Topographical artist. He was born in 1790 on Exe Island, Exeter and after showing early talent was noticed by Sir John Soane and introduced by him to Rudolph Ackermann. He worked with him for many years as draughtsman, lithographer and manager, travelling all over Britain and to Normandy to make drawings. He settled at Exeter again in 1830 and taught drawing at Cole's School, dying in the city in 1865.
Illus: *Picturesque Tour of the Seine [1821, AT 90 (with A. Pugin)]; Westall's Country Seats [1823-28].*
Contrib: *Ackermann's Repository [1823-25].*
Exhib: BI, 1818-63; RA.

GÉNIOLE, Alfred André   **1813-1861**
Painter of genre and portraits. He was born at Nancy, France on 1 January 1813 and became a pupil of Baron Gros, exhibiting in the Salon from 1839. He contributed illustrations to *The Illustrated London News*, 1853. Died at Bicêtre on 12 January 1861.

GERE, Charles March   RA ARWS   **1869-1957**
Portrait painter and watercolourist, illustrator, decorator and designer of stained glass. He was born at Gloucester in 1869 and was educated at Birmingham and in Italy, training as an artist with the Birmingham School of Art, remaining for many years as a teacher. He was associated, like his colleague Arthur Gaskin (q.v.), with William Morris at the Kelmscott Press and later with C.H. St. John Hornby at the Ashendene Press. He was an accomplished decorative artist and designed for embroidery, but after settling at Painswick, Gloucestershire in 1902, began to specialise in landscapes of the Cotswolds and North Italy. He became a member of the NEA in 1911, ARWS, 1921, RWS, 1927 and was elected ARA in 1933 and RA in 1939.

Gere's illustrations in black and white have the rather mannered angularity of the Birmingham School and his topographical work is very close in feeling to that of E.H. New (q.v.).
Contrib: *News From Nowhere [William Morris, Kelmscott Press, 1893 (frontis.)]; Russian Fairy Tales [1893]; A Book of Pictured Carols [The Birmingham School [1893]; The Imitation of Christ [1894]; The Quest [1894-96]; The Yellow Book [1896].*
Exhib: B; G; L; M; NEA, 1910-24; New Gall.; RA 1890-1956; RHA; RWS.
Bibl: R.E.D. Sketchley, *English Book Illus.*, 1902, pp.12, 50, 126.

GERMAN, Dick
Figure artist. He contributed to *Punch*, 1914.

GIACOMELLI, Hector   **1822-1904**
Genre painter and illustrator of insects and birds. He was born in Paris on 1 April 1822 and established himself early as a lithographer and illustrator. He illustrated numerous French books, his masterpiece being *Nos Oiseaux*, 1886, but is not known to have worked specifically for British publishers. he died at Menton, 1 December 1904.
Contrib: *ILN [1879-80 (page decor)].*
Bibl: Ray, G.N., *The Art of the French Illustrated Book*, Morgan Library, 1982, pp.385-6.

GIBBS, Percy W.   **fl.1894-1937**
Portrait and landscape painter and illustrator. He studied at the RA Schools and won the Creswick prize in 1895. Worked at East Molesey. Contributed to *The Graphic*, 1906.
Exhib: G; L; RA.

CHARLES DANA GIBSON 1867-1944. 'His Sister'. Illustration to *Pictures of People*, 1897

GIBERNE, Edgar   **fl.1872-1890**
Sporting artist and illustrator. He worked from Epsom and drew
Highland and Indian sporting subjects for magazines and illustrated
children's books.
Illus: *Binko's Blue [H C Merivale, 1884].*
Contrib: *ILN [1889-90].*
Exhib: RA; RBA, 1872-88.

GIBSON, Charles Dana   **1867-1944**
Black and white artist and illustrator. He was born at Roxbury,
Massachusetts, USA on 14 September 1867 and was educated at
Flushing High School, followed by training at the Art Students'
League, New York. Gibson studied with Augustus Saint Gaudens and
attended Julian's in Paris. Within a year or so of his first drawing from
life in 1888, Gibson had become an international figure and recognised
on both sides of the Atlantic. He was the chronicler in visual terms of
American high society, the world of luxury-laden and zestful New
York and Boston where East Coast aristocrats hunted as a group and
rigorously excluded all newcomers. Gibson did more than create a
beautiful type of American girl 'the Gibson Girl', he created a fashion.
As Pennell remarks, 'Not only has he countless artless imitators on
both sides of the Atlantic, but Fifth Avenue today is like an endless
procession of Gibsons.' Although his subjects were mostly American,
he made visits to Europe and drew society in Paris and London. *The
Studio*, in 1897, considered that they were unsuccessful, Gibson
remaining a foreigner who could not capture a cockney or a society
figure. His sister-in-law was Lady Astor.
   His penwork was done on a very large scale which was greatly
reduced, giving an incredible fineness and finish to the printed page.
The execution is brilliant, but the compositions are often repetitive

and a nauseating sentimentality creeps in from time to time. Gibson
remains very much an American collecting field.
Illus: *Drawings by C.D. Gibson; Pictures of People [1897]; London
As Seen By C. Dana Gibson [1897]; People of Dickens [1897];
Sketches and Cartoons; The Education of Mr. Pipp; Americans; A
Widow and Her Friends; The Social Ladder; The Weaker Sex;
Everyday People; Our Neighbours; Other People [1911].*
Contrib: *Life.*
Exhib: FAS, 1896.
Bibl: Joseph Pennell, *Pen Drawing and Pen Draughtsmen*, 1894,
pp.244-245; Fairfax Davis Downey, *Portrait of an Era as drawn by
C.D. Gibson; A Biography*, NY Scribner's 1936; Simon Houfe, *Fin
de Siècle*, 1992, pp.55-59.
See illustration.

GILBERT, Frederick   **fl.1862-1877**
Painter. watercolourist and illustrator. He was the brother of Sir John
Gilbert (q.v.), and lived with him at Blackheath. He specialised in
genre and history subjects and illustrations from Tennyson's works.
Illus: *Rosa Lambert [George W.M. Reynolds, 1854].*
Contrib: *Cassell's Magazine [1866]; Aunt Judy's Magazine [1866];
London Society [1870].*
Exhib: RBA.

GILBERT, Sir John   **1817-1897**
Historical painter and illustrator. He was born at Blackheath in 1817
and after being apprenticed to an estate agent, he studied with
George Lance and taught himself to draw on the block, engrave, etch
and model. He was the first major figure to emerge alongside Harvey
(q.v.) in the revival of wood engraving. Chatto & Jackson date his

JOHN GILBERT 1817-1897. *Northampton Agricultural Meeting, July 1847*

success from the publication of *Hall's English Ballads* in 1843, 'the first work of any consequence that presented a combination of the best artists of the time. Indeed it was the leader in what may be called the Illustrated Christmas Books of the present day. Since this period Mr. Gilbert has probably produced more drawings on wood than any other artist…' Gilbert was the first serious artist to tackle news illustrating for *The Illustrated London News*, 1843 and remained as a major contributor until late in life. He made a reputation, however,

out of elaborate semi-allegorical pages, festive Christmas scenes and representations of the seasons for special issues of magazines, for which he was paid enormous sums of money. The acclaim with which Gilbert's work was met seems almost incredible, the Victorians considering his rather dull historical set-pieces as equal to the work of Doré! He became President of the Royal Society of Painters in Watercolours in 1871, was knighted in the following year and elected ARA in 1872 and RA in 1876. He died on 5 October

JAMES GILLRAY 1757-1815. 'The Table's Turn'd'. Published 4th March 1797. Engraving coloured by hand. 14in x 10½in (35.6cm x 26.7cm)

1897, having given a large collection of his works to various provincial art galleries in 1892.

Illus: *City Scenes [1845]; Children of the New Forest [Capt. Marryat, 1847]; The Pleasures of the Country, Stories For Young People [Mrs. Myrtle, 1851]; The Salamandrine [1853]; Hide and Seek [Wilkie Collins, 1854], Basil [Wilkie Collins, 1862]; Fairy Tales [Countess D'Aulnoy, 1881]; Shakespeare's Works [1856-58]; Adele [J. Kavanagh, 1862].*

Contrib: *Punch [1842 (frontis.)-1882]; ILN [1843-79]; Sunday at Home [1852]; The Illustrated London Magazine [1853]; Proverbial Philosophy [M. Tupper, 1854]; Longfellow's Poems [1855]; Scott's Lady of The Lake [1856]; The Illustrated Times [1856]; Poets of the Nineteenth Century [Willmott, 1857]; The Book of Job [1857]; The Proverbs of Solomon [1858]; Lays of the Holy Land [1858]; The Home Affections [Charles Mackay, 1858]; Montgomery's Poems [1858]; Poetry of the Elizabethan Age [1860]; Songs and Sonnets of Shakespeare [1860]; The Welcome Guest [1860]; Eliza Cook's Poems [1861]; The Leisure Hour [1861-63]; The British Workman [1862]; The Band of Hope Review [1862]: English Sacred Poetry [Willmott 1862]; Boys' Book of Ballads [1862]; Early English Poems [1863]; The Months Illustrated [1864]; Wordsworth's Poems [1865]; Legends and Lyrics [Proctor, 1866]; Foxe's Book of Martyrs [1866]; Once a Week [1866-67]; Cassell's History of England [1867]; London Society [1868-69]; Cassell's Family Paper [n.d.]; Choice Series [1857-64]; The Standard Poets and Standard Library; The Graphic [1877].*

Exhib: B; L; M; RA, 1838-51 and 1867-97; RBA, 1836-1892; RWS.
Colls: Ashmolean; BM; Manchester; Nat. Gall., Scotland; V & AM.
Bibl: F. Reid, *Illustrators of The Sixties*, 1928, pp.20-23; *Who Was Who 1897-1916*; M. Hardie, *Watercol. Paint. in Brit.*, Vol. III, 1968, pp.94-96, illus.
See illustration.

GILBERT, Sir William Schwenck   'BAB'   1836-1911
Journalist, playright and amateur illustrator. He was born at Southampton Street, Strand on 18 November 1836 and was educated at Ealing and London University. He was called to the Bar in 1864 and served as Clerk to the Privy Council, 1857-1902. From his first introduction to Sir Arthur Sullivan in 1869 developed the fertile production of Savoy operas up to the year 1896. Gilbert's earlier career and reputation was made as 'Bab', the contributor of humorous verse to *Fun* illustrated by the author's own grotesque thumbnail sketches. There were really two sides to his artistic productions. the monstrous and savage creatures of the *Bab Ballads*, very much in the tradition of Lear, and rather pretty fairy sketches and drawings of young girls. Although the sketches were slight, they won the admiration of that fastidious critic Max Beerbohm. Gilbert died at Harrow Weald 29 May 1911. He was knighted, 1907.
Contrib: *Juvenile Verse Picture Book [1848]; Fun [1861]; Magic Mirror [1867-68]; London Society [1868]; Good Words for The Young [1869]; The Graphic [1876].*
Colls: BM.
Bibl: Leslie Baily, *The Gilbert and Sullivan Book*, 1952, p.44; Philip James, *Introduction to Selected Bab Ballads*, 1955.

GILES, Alice B.   fl.1896-1924
Illustrator. She was a student at the New Cross Art School in 1896-97 and was working at Surbiton, Surrey in 1924 and was a member of the Design and Industries Association. She specialised in the illustration of child's stories where animals were included.
Exhib: RA, 1903.
Bibl: *The Studio*, Vol.8, 1896, p.229, illus.; 1897.

GILES, Godfrey Douglas   **1857-1923**
Painter of horses and military scenes and illustrator. He was born in India in 1857 and served as a professional soldier there, and in Afghanistan and Egypt. He studied in Paris and was a regular exhibitor in London, 1882-1904. He was also a caricaturist.
Contrib: *The Graphic [1885 (horses)]; Black & White [1891 (sport)]; Vanity Fair [1899-1909, 1903].*
Exhib: G; GG; L; M; RA; RBA; ROI; RSA.

GILKS, Thomas   **fl.1840-1876**
Wood engraver, writer and illustrator. His bill head describes him as 'Draughtsman, Engraver, Ornamental Printer'. He was active from about 1840, engraved the plates for John Leech's *The Comic English Grammar*, and H. Fitzcock's *All About Shakespeare*. He illustrated his own *Study of the Art and Progress of Wood Engraving.*
Contrib: *ILN [1858, (Australia)]; London Society [1870].*
Exhib: RBA, 1870.

GILL, Arthur J.P.
Contributor to *Judy*, 1889 and *Punch*, 1902-05.

GILLETT, (Edward) Frank   **RI**   **1874-1927**
Sporting artist and illustrator of equestrian subjects. He was born at Worlingham, Suffolk on 23 July 1874, son of the Rev. Jesse Gillett of Aldeby and was educated at Gresham's. He left school at sixteen and after six years as a Lloyds' clerk, joined the staff of the *Daily Graphic*, 1898, remaining on the paper until 1908. He was subsequently with *Black & White*, 1908-11 and with *The Illustrated Sporting and Dramatic News*, 1910-23. Gillett, who was elected RI in 1909, was working at St. Albans that year, in London 1911 and in Aldeby, Norfolk from 1918. His pen drawings of horses are always convincing but they can be stiff.
Contrib: *Fun [1895]; Judy [1898]; The Ludgate Monthly; The Idler.*
Exhib: G; L; RA; RI.

JAMES GILLRAY 1757-1815. 'Pulpit Eloquence', 1795. Engraving

JAMES GILLRAY 1757-1815. 'Billingsgate Eloquence', 1795. Engraving

GILLRAY, James   **1757-1815**
Caricaturist and engraver. He was born at Chelsea in 1757 and after being educated by the Moravians at Bedford was apprenticed to a letter engraver and worked under classical engravers such as Ryland and Bartolozzi in stipple. He trained at the R.A. Schools and did some book illustrations for Macklin's *Tom Jones* before turning to caricature in about 1780. His earlier works were published by the printseller Robert Wilkinson of Cornhill, forsaking him for Fores in about 1787. Gillray finally came to rest as chief caricaturist to Mrs. Humphrey at New and Old Bond Street, where he lodged till his death. Gillray was the first professional caricaturist in this country, he simplified the art of the amateurs by replacing archaic symbols with forceful design and his art training enabled him to work on a more heroic scale than his predecessors. His work hit very hard and as the artist was something of a political maverick, he was assiduously courted by all parties. His frequent satires on Royal extravagance such as 'A Voluptuary under the horrors of Digestion' 1792 and the caricatures of Napoleon and Charles James Fox, created in their realism and savagery a whole new field for the caricaturist. Although much of his work dates from before 1800, a group of marvellous caricatures appeared in the early 1800s including 'Tiddy-Doll, the great French-Gingerbread Baker', 1806, 'Uncorking Old Sherry', 1805, 'The Plum-pudding in danger', 1805 and, most famous of all, 'The King of Brobdingnag and Gulliver', 1803. Gillray's last work was engraved in 1811 shortly before he became insane; his position was taken by the young George Cruikshank (q.v.). Original drawings by this artist are very rare, they show a very free pen line and strong influence of the Old Masters. He died on 1 June 1815 and was buried at St. James's Church, Piccadilly.
Colls: Ashmolean; BM; New York Pub. Library; V & AM.
Bibl: T. Wright, *The Caricatures of JG*, 1851; Joseph Grego, *The Works of JG*, 1873; Draper Hill, *Mr. G The Caricaturist*, 1965; Draper Hill, *Fashionable Contrasts: Caricatures by JG*, 1966; *Country Life*, 12 January 1967.
See illustrations.

GLADWIN, May
Illustrator of children's books in a bright poster style.
Illus: *The Grey Rabbit [1903].*

GLAZIER, Louise M. fl.1900-1912
Wood engraver and illustrator. She was working at Mitcham in 1902 and at Bruges in 1906. Her domestic and village scenes recall the Newlyn School. She designed book plates and examples of her work occasionally come on the market.
Illus: *The Field Flowers Lore [1912].*
Contrib: *The Dome [1900]; The Venture [1903].*
Exhib: Baillie Gall.; L.

GLENNIE, J.D. 1796-1874
Painter, etcher and amateur lithographer. He was born in 1796 and illustrated Maria Graham's *Letters On India* and *Views on the Continent* and contributed to *The Antiquarian and Topographical Cabinet*, 1811.
Exhib: RA, 1810-19.

GLICK
Contributor of cartoons to *Vanity Fair*, 1897. This has been identified as Count Gleichen, 1833-1891, who died in London, or his daughter, Countess Feodora Gleichen, who worked there as a sculptor.
Bibl: Roy T. Matthews & Peter Mellini, *In Vanity Fair*, 1982.

GLIDDON, Charles fl.1865-1870
Illustrator. He apparently drew for an edition of Walter Scott's novels, studies for *Red Gauntlet* and *The Fortunes of Nigel* in pencil, brown ink and brown wash are in the Ashmolean Museum, Oxford.

GLOAG, Isobel Lilian ROI 1865-1917
Painter of romantic subjects, portraits and illustrator. She was born of Scottish parents in London in 1865 and studied at the St. John's Wood School, South Kensington and Paris and worked with M.W. Ridley (q.v.). She undertook poster design, flower paintings and stained glass work and was elected ROI in 1909. She died on 5 January 1917.
Illus: projected editions of: *William Tell* and *Loves Labour Lost.*
Contrib: *The Graphic [1910].*
Exhib: B; G; L; RA; RBA; RI; ROI; SWA.

GLOVER, G.C.
Figure artist. He contributed illustrations to *Fun*, 1890-92, *Chums* and *Cassell's Saturday Journal.*

GOBLE, Warwick 1862-1943
Watercolour painter and illustrator. After being educated at the City of London School, he joined the staff of *The Pall Mall Gazette* and later *The Westminster Gazette* as artist. Goble was strongly influenced by Japanese art and by Chinese paintings, his colour washes are extremely subtle and stroked on with the brush, his compositions consciously oriental. He worked almost entirely for publishers like Messrs. Black and Messrs. Macmillan who were specialising in colour plate books. He made a tour of the French battlefields in 1919. He died 22 January 1943.
Illus: *Constantinople [A. Van Milligen, 1905]; The Water Babies [C. Kingsley, 1909]; The Green Willow and Other Japanese Fairy Tales [Grace James, 1910]; Folk Tales of Bengal; The Fairy Book [Mrs. Craik, 1914]; The Modern Readers Chaucer; Treasure Island; Kidnapped [1924]; The Alhamhra; The Greater Abbeys of England; The Book of Fairy Poetry.*
Contrib: *The Minister [1895]; ILN [1897-98, 1912]; The World Wide Magazine [1898]; The Pall Mall Budget; The Windsor Magazine.*
Exhib: FAS, 1910, 1911; L; RA.
See Horne

GODDARD, George Bouverie 1832-1886
Animal painter and illustrator. He was born at Salisbury in 1832 and after recognition as an infant prodigy, travelled to London in 1849 and spent two years studying at the Zoological Gardens. After this he returned to Wiltshire for a period and finally settled in London in 1857. Goddard made drawings for many magazines and contributed some humorous and sporting subjects. He died at Brook Green, London in 1886.

Contrib: *ILN [1865-84]; Punch [1865]; Once a Week [1866]; London Society 1868]; The Graphic [1880-84].*
Exhib: B; G; L; RA; RBA, 1864-72.
Colls: Liverpool.

GODDARD, Louis Charles fl.1904-1921
Portrait painter. He worked at Stockport, Manchester and Wallasey, Cheshire. He contributed social subjects to *Punch*, 1904.
Exhib: B; FAS; G; L.

GODEFROY
French illustrator contributing comic genre strips to *Fun*, 1900, in the style of Caran D'Ache (q.v.).
Contrib: *Pick Me Up [1889].*
Bibl: J. Pennell, *Pen Drawing and Pen Draughtsmen*, 1894, p.129, illus.

GODWIN, James -1876
Painter of genre, draughtsman and illustrator. Working in Kensington from 1846, having studied at the RA Schools. Godwin's draughtsmanship was very influenced by the German School and although his pencil work is extremely exact and delicate, it lacks real power. He was a regular exhibitor at London exhibitions and died there in 1876.
Illus: *The Dream Chintz [1851 (child's book)].*
Contrib: *ILN [1853-67 (Christmas and decor)]; The Poetical Works of E.A. Poe [1853]; Poets of the Nineteenth Century [Willmott, 1857]; The Home Affections [Charles Mackay, 1858]; The Poetical Works of Goldsmith [1859]; London Society [1863].*
Exhib: BI, 1846, 1850; RA; RBA, 1846-51.
Colls: V & AM.

GOEDECKER, F.
Contributor to *Vanity Fair*, 1884-85, signing 'GD' or 'FG' in monogram.

GOFF, Colonel Robert RE 1837-1922
Illustrated *Assisi*, 1908.

GOLDIE, R. Cyril 1872-1942
Painter and illustrator, working in Liverpool. He contributed a headpiece and full page illustration to *The Quarto*, 1896, in a grotesque art nouveau style. Designed cover for the *Artist*, 1901.
Exhib: L; NEA, 1910-22.
Bibl: *The Last Romantics*, Barbican Gallery catalogue, 1989, p.201.

GOLDSMITH, J.
Amateur draughtsman. He contributed an illustration to Britton's *Beauties of England and Wales*, 1814.

GOODALL, Edward Angelo RWS 1819-1908
Landscape painter and illustrator. He was born on 8 June 1819, the son of E. Goodall, the engraver, and brother of F. and W. Goodall (qq.v.). He was educated at University College School, London and at the age of seventeen, won a Society of Arts silver medal for watercolour, 1836-37. In 1841 he was appointed artist to the British Guiana Boundary Expedition and travelled there with Sir Robert Schomburgh, remaining in South America for three years. In 1854-55, Goodall was artist correspondent to *The Illustrated London News* in the Crimea, and in succeeding years made study trips to France, Italy, Spain, Egypt, Tangiers, Turkey and Greece. He was elected ARWS, 1858 and RWS, 1864. He died on 16 April 1908 and was buried at Highgate.
Illus: *Twelve Views in the Interior of Guiana [Bentley and Schomburgh, 1840-41, AT 720].*
Contrib: *ILN [1855]; Poets of the Nineteenth Century [Willmott, 1857]; Rhymes and Roundelayes.*
Exhib: BI, 1841; L; M; RA; RBA, 1841-60; RWS.
Colls: Ashmolean, BM, Dublin; Liverpool; Manchester; Sydney; V & AM.
Bibl: Chatto & Jackson, *Treatise on Wood Engraving*, 1861, p.598; M. Hardie, *Watercolour Paint. in Brit.*, Vol.III, 1968, pp.163-164 illus.

GOODALL, Frederick RA HRI 1822-1904
Landscape, genre and biblical painter and illustrator. He was born on 17 September 1822, the son of Edward Goodall, the engraver and

brother of E.A. and W. Goodall (qq.v.). Studied engraving with his father and brother, encouraged by Ruskin and in 1837 won a Society of Arts silver medal. He travelled to Normandy in 1838, 1839 and 1840, to Brittany in 1841, 1842 and 1845 and to Ireland with F.W. Topham (q.v.) in 1843. He went to Egypt for eight months in 1858-59 and this to some extent changed his style; his earlier works followed the genre subjects of Wilkie, his later ones took the Nile and the Pyramids as their centre piece. He returned to Egypt again in 1870 with his brother E.A. Goodall. Goodall was elected RI, 1867, ARA, 1853 and RA, 1863 and became an Honorary Retired Academician in 1902. He died at Harrow, in the house designed for him by Norman Shaw, on 28 July 1904.

Contrib: *The Traveller [Goldsmith, Art Union, 1851]; Passages From The Poets [Junior Etching Club, 1862]; Rhymes and Roundelayes; Ministering Children.*
Exhib: B; FAS, 1894; G; GG; L; M; RA; RI; ROI.
Colls: BM; Leicester; Liverpool; Manchester; V & AM.
Bibl: *Reminiscences of FG*, 1902; Chatto & Jackson, *Treatise on Wood Engraving*, 1861, p.599; M. Hardie, *Watercol. Paint In Brit*, Vol.III, 1868, pp.163-164, illus.

GOODALL, Walter   RWS   1830-1889
Painter and watercolourist. He was born in London in 1830, the son of Edward Goodall, the engraver and brother of E.A. and F. Goodall (qq.v.). He studied art at the Clipstone St. Academy, the Government School of Design and at the RA Schools. He was elected RWS in 1853 and spent the winter of 1868 in Rome making Venetian studies. He died at Clapham, Bedfordshire in 1889.
Contrib: *Recollections of the Great Exhibition of 1851 [1851].*
Exhib: RA; RWS.
Bibl: M. Hardie, *Watercol. Paint in Brit.*, Vol.III, 1968, p.164.

GOODMAN, Arthur Jule   fl.1890-1913
Illustrator and special artist. He was born at Hartford, Connecticut, USA and studied as an architect at the Institute of Technology, Boston. He worked as a lithographer with Matt Morgan (q.v.) and then left for Europe to study at Julian's in Paris and under Bouguereau. His first published work was for *Harper's* in 1889 and on arrival in London, he became Special for *The Pall Mall Gazette* and contributed 'War Notes', making a considerable reputation as an illustrator of military subjects. He was working at Gedling, Nottinghamshire, from 1902 to 1913.
Illus: *Clarence [Bret Harte, 1897].*
Contrib: *The Girls' Own Paper [1890-1900]; The Pall Mall Magazine; The Pall Mall Budget [1893]; ILN [1893]; St. Pauls [1894]; Good Words [1894]; Good Cheer [1894]; The Minister [1895]; Pearson's Magazine [1896]; The English Illustrated Magazine [1895-96]; Madame; The Idler.*
Exhib: Nottingham; P.
Colls: V & AM.
Bibl: *The Idler*, Vol.9, pp.803-816, illus.

GOODMAN, Walter   1838-
Painter of portraits, genre and illustrator. He was born in London, 11 May 1838, the son of Julia Goodman, née Salaman, the domestic painter. He studied at Leigh's and travelled in Europe and in Cuba, 1864-69 and to North America. He exhibited regularly in London from 1859, including a portrait of Wilkie Collins. He was living at Brighton in 1889 and latterly at Henfield, Sussex in 1906.
Publ: *The Pearl of The Antilles or an Artist in Cuba.*
Contrib: *ILN [1877].*
Exhib: BI, 1859-61; RA; RBA, 1859-90; RSA.

GOODWIN, Ernest   'GEE'   fl.1894-1903
Black and white artist in the style of Phil May. He was working at 20 St. Bride St., London E.C., 1902-03.
Contrib: *St. Pauls [1894]; Pick-Me-Up, [1895]; The Sketch; The Idler.*

GORDON, G.A.
Contributed illustration to *The Parade*, 1897.

GORDON, Godfrey Jervis (Jan)   1882-1944
Painter, etcher, lithographer and illustrator. He was born at

Finchampstead, 11 March 1882 and was educated at Marlborough College and Truro School of Mines. He was art critic of *The New Witness*, 1916-19, of *The Observer* and *Athenaeum*, 1919 and of *Land and Water*, 1920. He collaborated with his wife on illustrated travel books. RBA, 1935. He signs his work 'J.G.' or 'Gordon'.
Illus: *Poor Folk in Spain [1922]; Misadventures with a Donkey in Spain [1924]; Two Vagabonds in the Balkans [1925]; Two Vagabonds in Languedoc [1925]; Two Vagabonds in Sweden and Lapland [1926]; Two Vagabonds in Albania [1927].*
Exhib: L; NEA; RA; RBA; RI.

GORDON, J.
Contributed to *Cassell's Illustrated Readings*, 1867.

GOSSE, Philip Henry   1810-1888
Zoologist and artist. He farmed in the United States and Canada before returning to England to devote himself to the study of insects in 1839. He illustrated many of his own books and was elected FRS in 1856; he was the father of Sir Edmund Gosse.
Publ: *The Canadian Naturalist [1840]; Introduction to Zoology [1843]; Birds of Jamaica [1847]; A Naturalist's Sojourn in Jamaica [1851, AT 688]; Rambles on the Devonshire Coast [1853]; The Aquarium [1854]; Manual of Marine Zoology [1855-56]; Actinologia Britannica [1858-60]; Romance of Natural History [1860].*
Bibl: E. Gosse, *Father and Son*, 1907.

GOSSOP, Robert Percy   fl.1901-1925
Black and white artist, sometimes working in wash. He was a contributor to *Fun*, 1901, and was working at Henrietta St., Covent Garden, London in 1925.
Colls: V & AM.

GOUGH, Arthur J.   fl.1897-1914
Landscape painter and illustrator. He was working at West Hampstead, 1903-14 and contributed black and white drawings to *The Rambler*, 1897.
Exhib: RA; RI.

GOULD, Elizabeth (née Coxon)   1804-1841
Ornithological painter. She was born at Ramsgate, the daughter of a sea captain and in 1829 married John Gould FRS, 1804-1881, the author and publisher of *Gould's Birds*. She worked with the young Edward Lear in producing watercolours as guides to the finished illustrated works. She helped with *The Birds of Europe*, and *A Century of Birds from The Himalayan Mountains* and accompanied her husband to Australia, for his *Birds of Australia*, 1838-40. Her husband frequently took the credit for her work.
Bibl: *Country Life*, June 25 1964.

GOULD, Sir Francis Carruthers   1844-1925
Political cartoonist and caricaturist. He was born at Barnstaple on 2 December 1844, the son of an architect, and after being educated in private schools, joined the London Stock Exchange. While working as a broker and jobber, he began to draw caricatures for his own amusement, eventually endowing them with his own brand of radicalism and publishing them. Gould illustrated for the Christmas numbers of *Truth*, became a member of the staff of *The Pall Mall Gazette* in 1890 and of *The Westminster Gazette*, 1893-1914, acting as assistant editor in 1896. He founded his own paper, *Picture Politics*, which ran from 1894-1914 and published numerous illustrated books. His reputation in the Edwardian period was considerable and Lord Rosebery was reported to have called him 'the greatest asset of the Liberal Party'. Gould was not a great artist, but he was a very political animal and had the talent to catch a likeness and develop a theme. His sketches of the sharp face of Joseph Chamberlain are amongst his best works and he introduced silhouette work into political satire. He was knighted in 1906 and died on 1 January 1925.

His cartoons are among the more attractive ephemera of the 1890s still obtainable.
Illus: *Michael's Crag [Grant Allen, 1893]; Who Killed Cock Robin? [1897]; Tales Told in the Zoo [1900]; Froissart's Modern Chronicles; The Struwwelpeter Alphabet [H. Begbie, 1900];*

Birds of a Feather.

Oom Paul (to the Duke): "Ah, Mr Duke, I wish you had had charge of the business; it would have saved a lot of trouble. I always heard you were easily Boered."

SIR FRANCIS CARRUTHERS GOULD 1844-1925. 'Birds of a Feather'. caricatures of Kruger and the Duke of Bedford. Pen and ink. Signed with initials   Woburn Abbey Collection

Political Caricature [1903]; Cartoons in Rhyme and Line [Sir W Lawson, 1905].
Contrib: *Vanity Fair [1879, 1890, 1897-99]; The Strand Magazine [1891]; Cassell's Family Magazine; Fun [1901].*
Exhib: Brook St. and Walker's Galleries, 1907-24.
Colls: BM; V & AM.
Bibl: *The Studio*, Winter No., 1900-01, p.40, illus.
See illustration.

GOURSAT, George See 'SEM'

GOW, Mary L. (Mrs. Hall)   RI   1851-1929
Figure artist and illustrator. She was born in London in 1851 and studied at the Queens Square School of Art and at Heatherley's. She married Sydney P. Hall, MVO, the painter and illustrator (q.v.) and was elected NWS in 1875 and RI in the same year.
Contrib: *The Quiver [1890]; The Graphic [1892]; Cassell's Family Magazine.*
Exhib: B; G; GG; M; New Gall; RA; RI.

GOWER, Charlotte
Botanical illustrator. She provided the illustrations in colour and tailpieces for *The Wild Flowers of Great Britain*, by R. Hogg and George W. Johnson, 1863-64.

GOWER, Francis LEVESON-, 1st Earl of Ellesmere KG
**   1800-1857**
Amateur artist. He was born 1 January 1800 and is only known to have illustrated one work, his wife's *Journal of a Tour in the Holy Land* 1841, AT 384. He died 18 February 1857.

GOWER, S.J.
Contributor to *The Illustrated London News*, 1860.

GRAHAM, J.   fl.1810-1840
Contributor to *Bell's British Theatre* and *Cookes British Theatre*.

GRAHAM, Peter   RA ARSA   1836-1921
Landscape painter. He was born in Edinburgh and studied under R.S. Lauder at the Trustees Academy and with John Ballantyne. He settled in London in 1866, being elected ARA in 1877 and RA in 1881. He made a considerable reputation as a painter of Scottish

scenery and was elected ARSA in 1860. He died at St. Andrews on 19 October 1921.
Contrib: *London Society [1878].*
Exhib: B; G; L; M; RA; RSA.
Coll: Worcester.

GRAHAM, Thomas Alexander Ferguson   1840-1906
Figure and portrait painter. He was born at Kirkwall in 1840 and studied at the Trustees Academy, 1855 alongside Orchardson, J. Pettie, P. Graham and J. MacWhirter (qq.v.) under R.S. Lauder. On moving to London, he set up house with Pettie and Orchardson and exhibited there from 1863. He was elected HRSA in 1883 and received a commendation at the Paris Exhibition, 1900. He died in Hampstead, 24 December 1906.
Contrib: *Good Words [1861-63].*
Exhib: B; G; GG; L; M; New Gall.; RA; RBA; RI; ROI; RSA.

GRAHAM, Winifred   (Mrs. Green)
Illustrator of children's books. She was described in *The Studio*, Vol.18, 1899-1900, as an artist of 'poke-bonnetted and short waisted maidens...made familiar to us by Miss Greenaway'.
Illus: *Lamb's Poetry for Children [1898]; Mrs Leicester's School [C. & M. Lamb, 1899].*
Bibl: R.E.D. Sketchley, *English Book Illustration*, 1902, pp.101, 166.

GRANBY, The Marchioness of
**   See RUTLAND, Violet, Duchess of**

GRANDVILLE, Jean-Ignace Isidore Gérard   1803-1847
Draughtsman, watercolourist, caricaturist and lithographer. He was born at Nancy on 15 September 1803 and went to Paris in 1823, where he had considerable success as a lithographer and produced a series of cartoons on domestic and political matters. He made many drawings for *La Caricature*, specialising in metamorphosed objects and animals, wildly fantastic and offering a nineteenth century foretaste of surrealism. His books were widely bought in England and many English versions appeared. He died insane on 17 March 1847.
Illus: *The Flowers Personified [1855]; Comical People [c.1860]; Vie Privée et Publique des Animaux [1867].*
Colls: Nancy; Rochefort; Tours.
Bibl: C. Baudelaire, *The Painter of Modern Life*, edited by J. Mayne, 1964, pp.181-182.

GRANT, Charles Jameson   'CJG'   fl.1831-1846
Draughtsman, wood engraver and caricaturist. He was the leading artist of the penny Radical papers during the Chartist agitation, producing spirited if rather coarse work. He does not appear to be the same as Charles Grant, portrait painter, exhibiting at RA, 1825-39.
Colls: Witt Photo.
Bibl: M.D. George, *English Political Caricature*, Vol.II, 1959, pp.237-238, 245, 250, illus.

GRANT, William James   1829-1866
History painter, wood engraver and illustrator. He was born at Hackney in 1829 and attended the RA Schools in 1845. He concentrated on scriptural subjects, occasionally borrowing themes from modern poetry. He died at Hackney in 1866.
Illus: *Favourite Modern Ballads; Bloomfield's Farmers Boy.*
Exhib : BI, 1849-63 ; RA.
Bibl: Chatto and Jackson, *Treatise on Wood Engraving*, 1861, p.598.

GRAVE, Charles   1886-
Black and white artist, illustrator and watercolourist. He was born at Barrow-in-Furness in 1886 and was educated at Tottenham Grammar School. He began to draw for *Punch* in 1912 and was then successively on the staff of *Sporting Life*, *The Daily Chronicle*, and *The Daily Graphic*, serving in the First War with the Middlesex Regiment. Grave was at his best with low life characters, especially those of dockland and was a good draughtsman of shipping and boats although the situations are usually less funny than the sketches. For a time in the 1930s he was relief cartoonist of *Punch*. His work is not uncommon. He signs his work Chas Grave.
Contrib: *Lest We Forget, Illustrated Sporting and Dramatic News.*
Bibl: R.G.G. Price, *A History of Punch*, 1957, p.248.

GRAVES, The Hon. Henry Richard   **1818-1882**
Amateur caricaturist and portrait painter. He was the second son of
the 2nd Baron Graves and was born on 9 October 1818. On marrying
in October 1843 Henrietta Wellesley, Graves formed links with the
Paget and Wellesley families whose members frequently feature in
his sepia caricatures. They are very amateur works, but delightfully
fanciful, the characters dramatised and cigars and other objects
flying about with wings. An album of society portraits in pencil was
sold at Sotheby's on 1 January 1976.
Exhib: RA, 1846-1881.

GRAY, Alfred
Contributor of comic strips and caricatures to *Judy*, 1887-89.

GRAY, D.B.
Black and white artist. He specialised in animal drawings,
particularly horses and humanised dogs.
Contrib: *The English Illustrated Magazine [1895]; Punch [1902]*.

GRAY, George Kruger   **fl.1915-1940**
Painter, poster artist and sculptor, working in London. The Victoria
and Albert Museum has a series of process engravings by him for
book illustration.
Exhib: RA, 1919-40.

GRAY, Millicent Ethelreda   **1873-**
Figure and portrait painter and illustrator. She was born in London,
12 September 1873, and studied at the Cope and Nicols School of
Art and at the RA Schools.
Illus: *A Book of Children's Verse; Little Women [Alcott]*.
Contrib: *The Queen's Gift Book [c.1915]; Princess Mary's Gift
Book [c.1915]*.
Exhib: G; L; Leicester Gall; P; RA; ROI; SWA.

GRAY, Paul Mary   **1842-1866**
Illustrator. He was born in Dublin on 17 May 1842 and after
attending a convent, worked in Dublin as an artist. He taught
drawing at the Tullabeg School and worked for Dillon, the Dublin
printseller, at the same time exhibiting at the RHA, 1861-63. He
worked in London from 1863, getting his earliest commissions from
Punch, for whom he drew initials and socials which were thought
very attractive. By the middle 1860s he was quite successful, but was
struck down by consumption and died in London on 14 November
1866. Spielmann considered that Gray's drawings lacked 'backbone'
and Reid considered them rather overrated, but they are among the
most gentle pastoral studies of the great black and white period.
Illus: *Medwyns of Wykeham; Kenneth and Hugh*.
Contrib: *Punch [1863-65]; Once a Week; Good Words; London
Society; Shilling Magazine; The Argosy; The Quiver; The
Broadway; Jingles and Jokes for Little Folks [1865]; A Round of
Days [1866]; Idyllic Pictures [1867]; Ghosts Wives [1867]; The
Spirit of Praise [1867]; The Savage Club Papers [1867];
Longfellow [The Chandos]; Fun (political cartoons)*.
Exhib: RBA, 1867.
Colls: BM; V & AM.
Bibl: M.H. Spielmann, *The History of Punch*, 1895, p.517; Forrest
Reid, *Illustrators of The Sixties*, 1928, p.262.
See illustration.

GRAY, Mrs. Robert
Amateur artist. She was the wife of Bishop R. Gray and is believed
to have designed churches in her husband's South African diocese
She illustrated *Three Months Visitation*, 1856, AT 346.

GRAY, Ronald   RWS   **1868-1951**
Figure and landscape painter and illustrator. He was born in 1868
and studied at Westminster School of Art under Fred Brown and at
Julian's. One of his oil paintings, 1908, was bought by the Chantrey
Bequest in 1925. He was elected NEA, 1923, ARWS, 1934 and
RWS, 1941.
Contrib: *Cassell's Family Magazine [1898-99]; The Pall Mall
Budget; The Idler*.
Exhib: G; GG; L; M; NEA; P; RA; RHA; RI; RSA.
Colls: BM; Imperial War; Tate; V & AM.

PAUL MARY GRAY 1842-1866. Woman and child. Illustration
study for *The Quiver*. Pencil. 6⅜in x 4¾in (16.2cm x 12.1cm)
Victoria and Albert Museum

GRAY, Tom
Subject painter, working from Howland Street, London in 1866. He
exhibited at the BI that year and contributed illustrations to *London
Society*, 1860, 1868; *Belgravia*, 1868; *The Graphic*, 1872 (rural).

GREAVES, R.B. Brook
Caricaturist in watercolours, working in art deco style, c.1920.

GRECO, J.
Wood engraver, who contributed illustrations to *The Book of the
Sword*, Sir Richard Burton, 1884.

GREEN, Charles   RI   **1840-1898**
Painter and illustrator. He was born in 1840 and studied at
Heatherley's and with J.W. Whymper (q.v.), thereby establishing
himself as a master of figure and genre subjects and an accomplished
draughtsman on the block. He was elected ARI in 1864 and RI in
1867, quickly establishing himself in the forefront of book
illustrating, particularly in novels with a period setting. One of his
major achievements was in illustrating *The Old Curiosity Shop* for
Dickens *Household Edition*, in 1871, bringing a delicacy to the pen
work and softness to the washes that made a great contrast with the
earlier interpretations. Green was also involved in the early numbers
of *The Graphic*, and his work was admired by Van Gogh there; this
was yet another side of his character, the social realist, with sketches
of street folk and factory workers. He exhibited oils at the RA from
1862-83. He died at Hampstead 4 May 1898.
   The finest of Green's drawings date from the 1860s and 1870s and
are rare. He signs his work CG.
Illus: *Playroom Stories [Craik, 1863]; Our Untitled Nobility
[Tillotson, 1863]; Tinykins' Transformation [M. Lemon, 1869]; The
Doom of St. Querec [Burnand, 1875]; The Old Curiosity Shop
[1876]; Dorothy Forster [Walter Besant, 1897]*.
Contrib: *Once A Week [1860]; Churchman's Family Magazine*

CHARLES GREEN RI 1848-1898. Illustration for *Once a Week*, 24th November 1860

[1863-64]; ILN [1866]; Cassell's Magazine [1867]; The Graphic [1869-86]; London Society; Sunday Magazine; Good Words For The Young; Sunday at Home; English Sacred Poetry of the Olden Times [1864]; Life and Lessons of Our Lord [1864]; Choice Series [1864]; Watts Divine and Moral Songs [1865]; The Nobility of Life [L. Valentine, 1869]; Episodes of Fiction [1870]; Thornbury's Legendary Ballads [1876].
Exhib: B; G; L; M; RA; RI; ROI.
Colls: BM; Cardiff; Leicester; V & AM.
Bibl: J. Pennell, *Pen Drawing and Pen Draughtsmen*, 1894, pp.279-300, 304, illus.; *English Influences on Vincent Van Gogh*, Arts Council, 1974-75.
See illustrations.

GREEN, Henry Towneley RI   1836-1899
Illustrator. He was born in 1836 and was the brother of Charles Green (q.v.). After a career in banking, he took up art and followed his brother into illustrating and watercolour work, though never with the same success. He was elected ARI in 1875, RI in 1879 and ROI in 1883.
Contrib: *Once A Week [1867]; The Sunday Magazine [1869]; Cassell's Magazine [1870]; Golden Hours [1869]; Good Words For The Young [1870]; Thornbury's Legendary Ballads [1876]; ILN [1872 and 1887]; The Quiver [1880]; The Cornhill Magazine [1885].*
Exhib: B; L; M; RA; RBA, 1865-67; RI.
Colls: V & AM.
Bibl: *English Influences On Vincent Van Gogh*, Arts Council, 1974-75.

GREEN, Percy E.
Contributor of rustic figures to *Punch*, 1908.

GREEN, William Curtis   RA ARIBA   1875-1960
Architect. He was born on 16 July 1875 and was educated at Newton College, South Devon, and studied at the RA Schools. He is best remembered as the architect of the Dorchester Hotel, Park Lane, London. He was elected ARA in 1923 and RA in 1933. He won the RIBA Gold Medal in 1922.
Illus: *Old Cottages and Farmhouses in Surrey [1908].*
Exhib: G; RA; RSA.
Bibl: *The Drawings of W. Curtis Green*, Foreword by A.E. Richardson, 1949.

GREENAWAY, Kate   RI   1846-1901
Watercolourist and illustrator. She was born in London, the daughter of J. Greenaway, engraver to *The Illustrated London News* and was a cousin of Richard and Frank Dadd (qq.v.). She studied art at the Islington School, Heatherley's and at the Slade under Legros and began to exhibit at the RA in 1877. The same year, she began to work for Edmund Evans, the printer and publisher, who recognised her unusual talent for capturing an enchanted Regency world, and used it in the illustration of numerous children's books. Her style was loosely based on designs by artists such as Stothard, whom she admired, but endowed with a child-like innocence and charm which greatly appealed to the Victorians. Ruskin liked her work and encouraged her although he would have liked her to study directly from nature, which she never did. Her popular books were being produced in editions of over ten thousand copies in the 1880s and beginning to sell widely in the United States. From 1883-95 she produced a yearly almanack and at other times designed bookplates and painted portraits in oil. She was elected RI in 1889. She died in Hampstead in 1901.

Kate Greenaway's style had its effects on clothing and other accessories as well as on book illustration where it spawned a great number of copyists. Her meticulous pen drawings in outline, with no shadow, are charming if rather static studies; her watercolours are really the pen drawings lightly washed over with muted colours. Miss Greenaway's work was never very difficult to copy or imitate, and fakes abound.
Illus: *Aunt Louisa's London Toy Books: Diamonds and Toads [1871]; Madam D'Aulnoy's Fairy Tales [c.1871]; Fairy Gifts [Kathleen Knox, 1874]; The Quiver of Love [1876]; Poor Nelly [Mrs. Bonavia Hunt, 1878]; Topo [G.E. Brunefille (Lady C. Campbell), 1878]; Under The Window [K. Greenaway, 1878]; The Heir of Redclyffe [C.M. Yonge, 1879]; Amateur Theatricals [W.H. Pollock, 1879]; Heartsease [C.M Yonge, 1879]; The Little Folks Painting Book [1879]; Kate Greenaway's Birthday Book [1880]; The Library [Andrew Lang, 1881]; A Day in a Child's Life [1881]; Mother Goose [1881]; Little Anne [1882]; Almanack [1883-95]; Fors Clavigera [John Ruskin, 1883-84]; A Painting Book [1884]; Language of Flowers [1884]; The English Spelling Book [W. Mavor, 1884]; Dame Wiggins of Lee [1885]; Marigold Garden [1885]; Kate Greenaway's Alphabet [1885]; An Apple Pie, The Queen of the Pirate Isle [Bret Harte, 1886]; Queen Victoria's Jubilee Garland [1887]; Rhymes For The Young Folk [William Allingham, 1887]; Orient Line Guide [1888]; The Pied Piper of Hamelin [R. Browning, 1888]; Kate Greenaway's Book of Games [1889]; The Royal Progress of King Pepito [B.F Creswell, 1889]; The April Baby's Book of Tunes [1900].*
Contrib: *The People's Magazine [1868]; Little Folks [1873-80]; Cassell's Magazines [1874-]; ILN [1874-82]; St. Nicholas; The Graphic; The American Queen; Every Girl's Annual [1882]; The Girls' Own Paper [1879-90].*
Exhib: FAS, 1894, 1898, 1902; RA; RBA, 1870-75; RI.
Colls: Ashmolean; BM; Manchester; V & AM.
Bibl: M.H. Spielmann, *KG*, 1905; H.M. Cundall, *KG Pictures From Originals Presented by Her to John Ruskin...*, 1921; A.C. Moore, *A Century of KG*, 1946; Ruth Hill Viguers, *The KG Treasury*, 1967; M. Hardie, *Watercol. Paint. in Brit.*, Vol.III, 1968, p.143, illus.; Susan Ruth Thomson, *KG A Catalogue of the KG Collection*, Rare Book Room, Detroit Public Library, 1977.
See illustration.

GREGORY, Charles   RWS   1849-1920
Historical and genre painter and illustrator. He was born at Milford, Surrey and was working in London, 1880 and at Godalming, 1894, finally settling at Marlow, Bucks, where he died on 21 October 1920. He was elected ARWS in 1882 and RWS in 1884.
Contrib: *ILN [1876, 1877, 1879].*
Exhib: B; G; L; M; RA; RBA; RWS.
Colls: Bristol; Liverpool.

GREGORY, Edward John   RA PRI   1850-1909
Painter and illustrator. He was born at Southampton on 19 April 1850, grandson of John Gregory, engineer to Sir John Franklin's Expedition. He was educated in Southampton and worked for some time in the P & O Company's drawing office, 1865, and with Hubert Von Herkomer (q.v.). On the latter's advice he went to London in

CHARLES GREEN RI 1848-1898. 'The Caledonian Market'. Pen and ink with chinese white. 12in x 20in (30.5cm x 50.8cm)
Victoria and Albert Museum

CHARLES GREEN RI 1848-1898. 'Quilp in a Wherry'. Illustration for *The Old Curiosity Shop*, by Charles Dickens, 1871. Pen and wash with chinese white 3⅞in x 5½in (9.9cm x 14cm)
Victoria and Albert Museum

MAURICE GREIFFENHAGEN RA 1862-1931. 'The Holy Flower'. Illustration to a book of the same name, by Sir H. Rider Haggard, 1915. Watercolour and chinese white. 19in x 13in (48.3cm x 33cm)

Author's Collection

1869 and studied at the South Kensington Schools and at the RA Schools, 1871-75. Gregory was employed on the decorations of the new Victoria and Albert Museum and was employed by *The Graphic* to draw on the wood, often finishing the work of S.P. Hall (q.v.). He was elected RI in 1876 and became PRI in 1898. He was elected ARA in 1879 and RA in 1898. He settled at Great Marlow, Buckinghamshire and died there on 22 June 1909.

Gregory specialised in scenes of life aboard ship and did some illustrations of the Battle of Hastings for an unidentified edition. The former genre subjects were admired by Vincent Van Gogh.
Contrib: *The Graphic [1870-83]*.
Exhib: B; G; L; M; RA; RI; ROI; RSA.
Colls: Ashmolean; Tate.
Bibl: *The English Influences on Vincent Van Gogh*, Arts Council, 1974-75.

GREGORY, Margaret
Irish illustrator and daughter of Lady Gregory of Coole Park. She contributed woodcut illustrations to *The Kiltartan Wonder Book* by Lady Gregory, c.1918, and is associated with the Cuala Press, Churchtown, Dundrum, County Dublin. Her brother, Robert Gregory, contributed two designs for the Press including one for this book, before being killed in action, January 1918. She signs her work ⌐G⌐
Bibl: Liam Miller, *The Dun Elmer Press, Later The Cuala Press*, with a Preface by Michael B. Yeats. Dolmen Press, Dublin, 1973.

GREIFFENHAGEN, Maurice   RA RWS   1862-1931
Painter and illustrator. He was born in 1862 and studied at the RA Schools, where he won the Armitage Prize. He became Headmaster

of the Life School, Glasgow School of Art, in 1906, was elected ARA in 1916 and RA in 1922. His painting 'Women By A Lake' was purchased by the Chantrey Bequest in 1914 and 'Dawn' in 1926. The earlier part of Greiffenhagen's career was devoted almost exclusively to illustrative work for books and magazines. Throughout the 1890s he was producing high quality black and white work, some of it in its economy of line and free handling, clearly influenced by Phil May. He is particularly associated with the illustrations to Sir Henry Rider Haggard's novels and somewhat oddly appears to have been D.H. Lawrence's favourite artist. He died at St. John's Wood, 26 December 1931.
Illus: *Vain Fortune [George Moore, 1894]; Omar Khayyam [1913]*.
Contrib: *Pictorial World [1881]; Judy [1887-90]; Black and White [1891-96]; Fun [1892]; ILN [1892-98]; The Butterfly [1893 & 1899]; The Pall Mall Budget [1894]; Daily Chronicle [1895]; Pick-Me-Up [1895]; The Unicorn [1895]; Ally Sloper's Half Holiday; The Sketch; The Lady's Pictorial; The Windsor Magazine*.
Exhib: B; G; L; M; NEA; RA; RBA; ROI; RSA.
Colls: Author; V & AM.
Bibl: J. Stanley Little, *Maurice Greiffenhagen and his Work*, The Studio, Vol 9, 1897, pp.235-245, illus.
See illustration.

GREIG, James   RBA   1861-1941
Painter and illustrator in black and white. He was born at Arbroath in 1861 and went to London to study art in 1891 and to Paris in 1895, settling in London in 1896. Greig became art critic of *The Morning Post* and a noted historian, publishing a monograph on Raeburn and editing *The Farington Diaries*, 1922-28. RBA, 1898. His domestic and rustic figure drawings in *Punch* and elsewhere are attractive, if a little weak.
Contrib: *Black & White [1892]; The English Illustrated Magazine [1893-96]; St. Pauls [1894]; The Sketch [1895-96]; The Temple [1896]; Good Words [1898-99]; Punch [1902-3]; Cassell's Family Magazine; The Ludgate Monthly, The Idler; The Pall Mall Magazine; The Windsor Magazine, The Quiver*.
Exhib: RBA, 1897-1907.
Coll: V & AM.

GREIG, John   fl.1807-1824
Landscape painter. A draughtsman, engraver and lithographer, he was associated with J.S. Storer in publishing *The Antiquarian Cabinet*, and supplying many antiquarian drawings.
Illus: *Promenades Across London [D. Hughson, 1817]; Views of London [J. Hakewill]; Tours in Cornwall [F. W. L. Stockdale, 1824]*.
Contrib: *Britton's Beauties of England & Wales; Border Antiquities of England and Wales [1817]*.

GRIFFITHS, Tom   fl.1880-1904
Landscape painter and illustrator. He was working for *The Graphic* from 1880-87, mostly military subjects. He may have acted as a Special in Africa in 1881, but it is more likely that he was an understudy to T.W. Wilson and worked up his sketches at home. He was living at Amberley from 1893 and at Bideford from 1901.
Exhib: B; G; L; M; RA; RBA; RHA; RI.

GRIGGS, Frederick Landseer Maur   RA   1876-1938
Draughtsman, etcher and book illustrator. He was born at Hitchin, Hertfordshire in 1876 and was educated privately. Griggs was one of the younger group of artists who, influenced by Morris, brought to their art a great exactitude and a reverence for the work of past craftsmen. He had established himself by the early 1900s as the most sensitive of architectural illustrators, chiefly through his drawings to Messrs. Macmillan's 'Highways and Byways' series, which appeared between 1902 and 1906 and then at longer intervals till 1928. Griggs removed to Chipping Campden, Gloucestershire before the First World War, and remained there till his death, strongly identifying himself with its Guild. 'Though his sympathies extended to Georgian and later architecture' ran *The Times* obituary, 'it can be said of Griggs, who was a Roman Catholic, that his spiritual home was in the Middle Ages and his works were full of a nostalgia for that period.' His meticulous work shows a direct sympathy for stone buildings, carving and the clean structure of regional styles from which a craftsman would be able to work stone by stone; his

landscapes are akin to those of Samuel Palmer (q.v.). Griggs' range included the designing of two sets of Roman letters, known as Littleworth and Leysbourne, in 1933 and 1934. He bacame ARA in 1922 and RA in 1931. He was made Hon. ARIBA in 1926. He died on 7 June 1938 after being taken ill on a visit to London. A centenary exhibition was held at the Ashmolean Museum, March-May, 1976.

Illus: *The Collected Works of William Morris; The Life of G.F. Watts; Seven Gardens and a Palace [EVB, 1900]; Stray Leaves From a Border Garden [1901]; The Chronicle of a Cornish Garden [1901]; Highways and Byways in Hertfordshire [1901]; Memorials of Edward Burne-Jones [1904]; Highways and Byways in London; Highways and Byways in Berkshire [1906]; A Book of Cottages and Little Houses [C.R. Ashbee, 1906]; Highways and Byways in Buckinghamshire [1908]; Old Colleges of Oxford [1912]; Highways and Byways in Lincolnshire [1912]; Highways and Byways in Northamptonshire [1914]; Highways and Byways in Leicestershire [1918]; Highways and Byways in Nottinghamshire [1928]; Highways and Byways in Sussex; Highways and Byways in Oxford and The Cotswolds, Highways and Byways in South Wales; Highways and Byways in Cambridge and Ely; Essex.*

Contrib: *The Oxford Almanack [1922-23].*
Exhib: G; L; RA; RE; RSA.
Colls: Ashmolean; BM; V & AM.
Bibl: *The Studio*, Winter No., 1900-01, p.63, illus.; R.E.D. Sketchley, *English Book Illus*, 1902, pp.54, 134; *Print Collectors' Quarterly*, Vol.11, No.1, 1924, pp.95-124; Vol.20, No.4, 1933, pp.320-345; H. Knight, *The Work of FLG*, Print Collectors Club, No. 20, 1941; F.A. Comstock, *A Gothic Vision: FLG*, Ashmolean, 1966.

GRIMM, Constantine von   'Nemo' or 'C de Grimm'
German painter and illustrator. He contributed six cartoons to *Vanity Fair*, 1884.

GRIP pseudonym of Alfred BRICE   fl.c.1895-1896
Cartoonist for *The Sketch*, c.1895-96. Brice specialised in grey wash figures with large and detailed heads, highlighted with white on cheeks and hair. His range is usually political and literary, although the Victoria and Albert Museum has an admirable caricature of Aubrey Beardsley. He signs his work GRIP (with toucan), thus
Contrib: *The Ludgate Monthly [1893-94].*
Colls: V & AM.

GRISET, Ernest Henry   1844-1907
Illustrator and comic draughtsman of animals. He was born at Boulogne-sur-Mer in 1844, and studied under Louis Gallait, presumably in Brussels. The latter had strong links with England and

it may have been through him that Griset came to London in the mid-60s. Although intending to become a serious watercolourist, he was spiritually akin to Grandville (q.v.) in his delight in drawing animals and people and showing their basic similarities, not in caricature, but in behaviour. His mournful beasts and gangling half-savage hunters in pursuit of them, occupy a world of half legend, critical and comic. His work was exhibited first in a bookshop in Leicester Square and after attracting the notice of the Dalziel Brothers and Tom Hood, he was invited to join *Fun* and eventually *Punch*. Griset's style, delicate pen drawings, beautifully tinted with soft colours, are more French than English in their subtlety; one would not guess from the economic use of line and the precision of hand that the artist was a very rapid and hard worker, dashing off hundreds of such for *Griset's Grotesques*, 1867. Griset died on 22 March 1907, having outlived his popularity, but his sketches have a charm that has gained them a special place among collectors.

Illus: *The Hatchet Throwers [James Greenwood, 1867]; Legends of Savage Life [James Greenwood, 1867]; Among The Squirrels [Mrs. Deniston, 1867]; Vikram and The Vampire [1869]; Robinson Crusoe [1869]; The Rare Romance of Reynard The Fox [1869]; The Hunchback of Notre Dame [Hugo, 1879].*

Contrib: *Fun; Punch [1867]; Once a Week [1867]; The Broadway [1867]; Good Words For The Young [1870-71]; The Graphic [1870-71]; Hood's Comic Annual [1878].*
Exhib: RBA, 1871-72 (animals).
Colls: Author; BM; V & AM.
Bibl: Hesketh Hubbard, 'A Forgotten Illustrator', *The Connoisseur*, 1945; L. Lambourne, *Country Life*, January, 1977.
See illustration.

GROB, Conrad   1828-1904
Painter of history and genre, lithographer, engraver and illustrator. He was born at Andelfingen, Switzerland on 3 September 1828 and did not begin his artistic career until he was thirty-eight, when he joined the Munich Academy and studied under Ramberg. He died at Munich 4 January 1904.
Contrib: *The Illustrated Times [1860 (Italian War)].*
Exhib: Paris, 1900.
Colls: Basle; Berne.

GROOME, William Henry Charles   RBA   fl.1881-1914
Landscape painter and illustrator. He was working at Ealing from 1881-1914 and became RBA in 1901. Prepared drawings for an edition of *David Copperfield*.
Illus: *East London [Henry Walker, 1896].*
Contrib: *ILN [1889-92 (rustic)]; Chums.*
Exhib: GG; RA; RBA; RI; ROI.

ERNEST HENRY GRISET 1844-1907. 'Two Ragamuffins'. Pen and washes.
4½in x 6in (11.4cm x 15.2cm)
Author's Collection

JAMES JOSHUA GUTHRIE 1874-1952. 'Dreamland'. Wood engraving. 9in x 7⅝in (22.9cm x 19.4cm) Victoria and Albert Museum

GROSSMITH, Walter Weedon   **1854-1919**
Painter and actor. He was born in 1854, the brother of George Grossmith, and was educated at Simpson's School, Hampstead, before being trained at the Slade and RA Schools. He was the author of the Victorian classic, *Diary of a Nobody*, which first appeared in *Punch* in 1888. Grossmith was a talented black and white artist and landscape painter, but this increasingly gave way to his success as a comedy actor and later to his management of the Vaudeville Theatre, 1894-96 and the Avenue Theatre, 1901. He died 14 June 1919. The thirty-two drawings for *Diary of a Nobody* were purchased by the V & A Museum in 1987.
Exhib: B; GG; L; M; RA; RBA; RHA; ROI.
Colls: V & AM.
Bibl: WG, *From Studio to Stage*, 1912.

GROVES, S.J.
Draughtsman. Contributed illustrations to *Pen and Pencil Pictures From The Poets*, Edinburgh, 1866.

GUERARD, Eugène Charles François   **1821-1866**
Painter and lithographer. He was born at Nancy 6 July 1821 and died there 6 July 1866. He studied with Paul Delaroche and exhibited at the Salon in 1842, 1848, and 1852. He contributed to *The Illustrated London News*, 1855.

GUILLAUME, Albert   **1873-1942**
Figure painter and humorous draughtsman. He was born in Paris on 14 February 1873 and studied in the Atelier Gérome and illustrated numerous French books. He died at Faux in the Dordogne in 1942.
Contrib: *The Graphic [1901-03].*
Exhib: L, 1910-24.

GULICH, John Percival RI   **1865-1898**
Illustrator, engraver and caricaturist. He was born at Wimbledon in 1864 and worked for many of the leading magazines in the 1890s, having begun with *The Graphic*, 1887 and *Harper's Magazine*. He was elected RI, 1897 and was a member of the Langham Sketch Club. He died of typhoid fever in 1898.

Illus: *Three Partners [Bret Harte, 1897]; John Ingerfield [Jerome K. Jerome, 1897].*
Contrib: *The Graphic [1887-97]; The Strand Magazine [1891]; Black & White [1892]; The Idler [1892]; Chums [1892]; The Quiver [1895]; Cassell's Family Magazine; The Pall Mall Magazine.*
Exhib: GG; L; Paris, 1900; RA; RBA; RI.
Colls: V & AM.

GUNNIS, Louis J.   **fl.1887-1897**
Painter and illustrator. He worked in London 1887-97 and specialised in domestic scenes.
Contrib: *ILN [1889]; Judy [1889]; The Sphere [1894]; The Sketch [1895 (dramatic ports)]; The English Illustrated Magazine [1895-96]; The Ludgate Monthly; Chums; The Idler; The Royal Magazine.*
Exhib: L; RA, 1887-97.
Colls: V & AM.

GURNEY, Ernest T.
Landscape painter. He was working at Ampthill Square, Hampstead Road in 1900-02. He contributed to *The Idler* and exhibited at the RA in 1900.

GUTH, Jean Baptiste   **fl.1883-1921**
French painter and caricaturist. He was a regular contributor to *Vanity Fair*, 1889-1908. He signs his work GUTH or JB GUTH.

GUTHRIE, James Joshua   **1874-1952**
Painter and illustrator and designer of bookplates. He was born in 1874 and although he had no formal training, studied as assistant to Reginald Hallward (q.v.). Guthrie was a talented hand printer and founded the Pear Tree Press at South Harting, Hampshire in May 1905. Guthrie was one of the leading wood engravers associated with the development of the private presses and the return to romanticism. His range extended from the illustrations to children's books to those of poets, living and dead. His mood was a direct inheritance from the work of Blake, Palmer and Calvert (qq.v.) with his own idiosyncracies of curly trees, eddying water and wild sky, ideal for the brooding quality of Poe. The poet Gordon Bottomley has left an amusing description of his method of work. 'So far as I have seen he takes a piece of granulated cardboard and washes it over with a few brushfuls of a thin mixture of plaster of Paris. Then he digs into that with a pen and Indian ink. Then he puts on a film of Chinese White (Paris, India, China) what riches all at once.' This was in a letter to John Nash with whom some comparison might be found. Guthrie founded and illustrated a magazine called *The Elf* in 1895 and decorated rhymesheets for Harold Monro's Poetry Bookshop.
Illus: *Wedding Bells [1895]; The Elf [1895-1904]; The Little Man in Scarlet [1896]; An Album of Drawings [1900]; Virgil's Alexis [1905]; The Beatitudes [1905]; Midsummer Eve [Gordon Bottomley, 1905]; In Summer Time [Dorothy Radford, 1906]; A Second Book of Drawings [1908]; Echoes of Poetry [1908]; The Poems of E.A. Poe [1908]; The Riding of Lithend [Gordon Bottomley, 1909]; The Paradise of Tintoretto [1910]; The Blessed Damozel [1911 (decor)]; Art & Nature Sonnets [F.B. Osmaston, 1911]; Six Poems [Edward Eastaway]; Trees [Harold Monro, 1916], Root and Branch [1916]; Space and Man; The Castle of Indolence.*
Contrib: *The Yellow Book [1896]; The Quartier Latin [1896]; The Dome [1897]; The Windmill [1899]; The Page [1899]; The Idler.*
Colls: V & AM.
Bibl: *The Artist*, May-Aug., 1898, pp.238-241, illus; Sept., 1900, pp.197-202, illus.; *The Private Library*, Second Series, Vol.9, 1, Spring 1976, with check list.
See illustration.
See **Horne**

GUYS, Constantin Ernest Adolphe Hyacinthe   **1802-1892**
Figure artist in pen and watercolour. The known facts about this great French draughtsman are scarce. He was born at Flushing, Holland of French parentage in 1802 and died in Paris in poverty at the advanced age of ninety in 1892. He is believed to have gone to Greece to fight in the War of Independence alongside Byron, action of any kind and particularly that of soldiers and horses always

inspiring him. By the 1840s he was in England, acting as French tutor to the family of Dr. T.C. Girtin, son of Girtin the watercolourist. Guys gained employment with the newly-founded *Illustrated London News* in 1843 and appears to have worked for them until as late as 1860. He covered the Crimean War for the magazine in 1854-56, although his work is often unsigned though very recognisable, in the journal. He also went to Spain, Italy, Germany, Turkey and Egypt as their special correspondent. He seems to have been particularly associated with the English press, even by the French – the Goncourts mention him in their journal in April 1858 as "the draughtsman of the ILLUSTRATED LONDON". Baudelaire brilliantly analysed Guys' style in his celebrated essay 'The Painter of Modern Life' (*Figaro*, 1863). Guys, characteristically mercurial and elusive, is referred to by his initials only. This and much else about his work, his casual attitude to completed drawings, his sketching from memory not life, his dismissal of the conventions, place him squarely in the literary bohemia associated with Balzac.

With little else to go on the drawings speak for themselves about the originality and verve of Guys the artist. Baudelaire describes him as 'the painter of the passing moment' and links him to the vision of the moralist and the novelist. These rapid pen and ink sketches with light colour washes radiate their own period in a way that the finished illustrators could not attain. For Guys they are statements about society and leaves from the notebook of a reporter, in which the symbols of crowd or event matter more than their delineation. For Baudelaire they were living history, the documents on which the age would be judged, for him, a very valid role for a minor master. The drawings have remained timeless with the sparkle of life so vividly apparent, the tawdry mock heroic *demi-monde*, the glitter of soldiery in the Park, the vibrant rapidity of the Brighton coach. In later years Guys used less colour and his sketches became more synthesised, but he had left actual illustrative work far behind. Although he was not widely known in his own time (Thackeray mentions him, Gavarni copied him) he had a growing following by the early twentieth century when many of his values, freedom of expression and immediacy came to be recognised. He is now a much sought-after artist and his drawings are among the highest priced of illustrators work.

Colls: BM; Paris (Petit Palais); V & AM.
Bibl: Charles Baudelaire, 'Un peintre de la vie moderne', *Figaro*, 3 December 1863; Armand Dayot, *Catalogue de l'Exposition de l'oeuvre de Constantin Guys*, 1904; Henri Frantz, 'A Forgotten Artist', *The Studio*, Vol.34, 1905, pp.107-112; Gustave Geffroy, *CG, l'historien du Second Empire*, 1904-20; *CG, Collection Des Maîtres*, 1949; *The Painter of Modern Life and Other Essays By Charles Baudelaire*, edited by Jonathan Mayne, 1964.
See illustration.

GWENNETT, W. Gunn   **fl.1903-1940**
Landscape painter and illustrator. He worked in Richmond. Surrey, 1903 and London.
Contrib: *Punch [1909]*.
Exhib: L; RA; RI; RSA

GYFFORD, Edward   **1772-1834**
Architect, draughtsman and illustrator. He was born in 1772 and studied at the RA Schools, winning the Gold Medal in 1792. He published *Designs For Small Picturesque Cottages and Hunting-Boxes*, 1807 and contributed illustrations to *The Beauties of England and Wales*, 1810.
Exhib: RA, 1791-1801.
Bibl: H.M. Colvin, *Biog. Dict. of English Architects*, 1954, p.256.

GYLES, Althea   **1868-1949**
Celtic illustrator, working in symbolist style. She was a friend of A.J. Symons and Ernest Dowson, later becoming the mistress of the publisher Leonard Smithers in 1899. W.B. Yeats wrote about her.
Illus: *The Harlot's House [Oscar Wilde, 1910]*.
Contrib: *The Dome [1898]*.
Bibl: Muddiman, *The Men of the Nineties*, 1920, pp.120-121.

CONSTANTIN GUYS 1802-1892. 'The Purple Roans'.

HAAG, Carl   **1820-1915**
Watercolourist and illustrator. He was born at Erlangen in Bavaria on 20 April 1820, the son of an amateur artist. He studied art at Nuremberg, 1834, and Munich, 1844-46 while working as a miniaturist and book illustrator. He worked in Brussels and then came to London in 1847 to study watercolour and attend the RA Schools. He visited Italy in 1847, travelled to Cairo with F. Goodall (q.v.) in 1858 and to Egypt in 1860, where he lived with the desert tribes. He ran studios in both London and Oberwesel, finally retiring to the latter in 1903 and dying there on 24 January 1915. He was elected AOWS in 1850 and OWS in 1853.
Contrib: *ILN [Christmas, 1869].*
Exhib: FAS, 1882; L; M; RA; RBA, RWS.
Colls: BM; Leeds; V & AM.
Bibl: M. Hardie, *Watercol. Paint. in Brit.*, Vol.III, 1968, p.67.

HACKER, Arthur RA   **1858-1919**
Portrait and genre painter and occasional illustrator. He was born in London on 25 September 1858, the son of Edward Hacker, the line engraver. He was educated in London and Paris and studied art at the RA Schools, 1876, and under Bonnat in Paris, 1880-81. He became a popular portrait painter and travelled widely in Italy and North Africa collecting material for classical and religious subjects. He was elected ARA in 1894 and RA in 1910. He died in London 12 November 1919.
Contrib: *The Graphic [1903 (story illus.)].*
Exhib: B; G; L; M; RA; RI; ROI.

HADDON, Arthur Trevor   **1864-1941**
Portrait and genre painter. He was born in 1864 and studied at the Slade School under Legros from 1883-86, winning the painting medal in 1885. He worked in Spain, 1887 and at the Herkomer School, Bushey, 1888-90, becoming a Fellow of it in 1891. He then studied in Rome from 1896-97 and was elected RBA in 1896.
Publ: *The Old Venetian Palaces; Southern Spain.*
Illus: *The Snow Garden [Elizabeth Wordsworth, 1897].*
Exhib: FAS; L; M; New Gall.; P; RA; RBA; RHA; RI; ROI.

HADGE
Contributor of a cartoon to *Vanity Fair*, 1899.

HAGHE, Louis   RI   **1806-1885**
Painter and illustrator of architecture with figures. He was born at Tournai, Belgium, in 1806 and studied lithography under de la Barrière and J.P. de Jonghe, afterwards coming to London where he went into partnership with William Day, the publisher. From the 1830s onwards, Haghe issued collections of lithographs of his travels and frequently lithographed the works of other artists, particularly David Roberts's *Holy Land*. He was President of the RI from 1873-1884 having been a member since 1835. Haghe's work is extremely accurate, if lacking in imagination. He died in London in 1885.
Illus: *Sketches in Belgium and Germany [1840-50, AT 35 and 37]; Portfolio of Sketches [1850, AT 41].*
Contrib: *Bold's Travels Through Sicily [1827, AT 265]; Dickinson's Comprehensive Picture of The Great Exhibition of 1851.*
Exhib: NWS, 1835-
Colls: BM; G; Manchester, V & AM.
Bibl: M. Hardie, *Watercol. Paint. in Brit.*, Vol.III, 1968, p.93, illus.

HAITÉ, George Charles RI   **1855-1924**
Landscape painter and illustrator. He was born at Bexley in 1855, the son of a designer. After being educated at Mitcham College, he taught himself to draw and began work as a designer at the age of sixteen. He exhibited at the RA from 1883 and worked in black and white for a number of magazines, designing the covers of *The Strand Magazine* and *The Strand Musical Magazine*, 1891. He was the President of the Langham Sketching Club, 1883-87 and 1908. He was elected RI in 1901, and died at Bedford Park, 31 March 1924.
Illus: *Haité's Plant Studies.*
Colls: BM, Leeds, Manchester.
Bibl: *Who Was Who 1916-28.*

HAKEWILL, James   **1778-1843**
Architect, draughtsman and illustrator. He was born in 1778, the son of John Hakewill, painter and decorator, and trained as an architect and exhibited designs at the RA from 1800. He was however more of an antiquary than a practical designer and turned increasingly to the publications of tours undertaken by him and his wife, also a talented artist. Hakewill had some association with J.M.W. Turner (q.v.) who made finished drawings from his Italian sketches. He died on 28 May 1843.
Illus: *The History of Windsor and Its Neighbourhood [1813]; A Picturesque Tour of Italy [1818-20, AT 683]; Picturesque Tour in the Island of Jamaica [1825]; Plans, Sections and Elevations of Abattoirs of Paris [1828]; An Attempt to Determine the Exact Character of Elizabethan Architecture [1835]; Antiquarian and Picturesque Tour [1849].*
Bibl: H.M. Colvin, *Biog. Dict. of English Architects*, 1954, p.259.

HALCOMBE, Will   **fl.1897-**
Black and white artist specialising in comic history subjects. He contributed pen and watercolour drawings to *The Sketch*, 1897. mostly signed and dated.
Colls: V & AM.

HALE, Edward Matthew ROI   **1852-1924**
Painter and illustrator. He was born at Hastings in 1852 and studied art in Paris under Cabanel and Carolus Duran. He was Special Artist for *The Illustrated London News* in the Russo-Turkish War, 1877-78 and in Afghanistan. He was a Colonel in the Middlesex Rifle Volunteers. Elected ROI in 1898 and died at Godalming, 24 January 1924.
Exhib: B; G; L; M; RA; RBA; RI; ROI.
Colls: Leeds.

HALKETT, George Roland   **1855-1918**
Artist, illustrator and writer on art. He was born at Edinburgh on 11 March 1855 and studied art in Paris. He later returned to Edinburgh and concentrated on making caricatures for the press and producing book illustrations. He was art critic of the Edinburgh Evening News, 1876, joined the *Pall Mall Gazette* as political cartoonist in 1892 and was successively art editor of *The Pall Mall Magazine*, 1897, and Editor, 1900-05. He was most celebrated for his caricatures of Mr. Gladstone which he issued in *New Gleanings From Gladstone* and a *Gladstone Almanack* and for *The Irish Green Book* produced during the Home Rule debates of 1887. His style is of the *portrait chargée* type adopted by 'Ape', but in the 1900s there is a definite Beggarstaff influence, chalky black lines on toned paper. He travelled extensively in the colonies and died in London, December 1918.
Contrib: *Edinburgh University Liberal Association [booklet 1883 (frontis.)]; St. Stephen's Review [1885]; Pall Mall Budget [1893]; Pall Mall Magazine [1897]; Punch [1897-1903]; The Butterfly.*
Illus: *The Elves and The Shoemaker [child's book, n.d.].*
Exhib: G; RSA.
Colls: V & AM.

HALL, Basil   **fl.1886-1888**
Black and white artist specialising in military subjects. He contributed story illustrations to *The Graphic* in 1886-87 and events in 1888.

HALL, E.
Black and white artist contributing genre and social subjects to *The Illustrated Times*, 1856-59. Also contributed to *Cassell's Illustrated Readings*, 1867.

HALL, Frederick　　　　　　　　　　　　　　**1860-1948**
Figure and landscape painter. He was born at Stillington, Yorks, in 1860 and studied at Lincoln Art School and under Verlat at Antwerp. He worked for fifteen years at Newlyn, Cornwall and drew for *The Graphic* in 1902, and caricatured for *Black & White*, 1891, *The Sketch*, 1894.

HALL, Harry　　　　　　　　　　　　　　**fl.1838-1886**
Equestrian artist and illustrator. Hall worked first as a horse painter at Tattersall's in London, later moving to Newmarket where he became friendly with Mark Lemon, the Editor of *Punch*. He became chief artist on *The Field* and contributed only one drawing to *Punch*. He was the father of Sydney Hall (q.v.).
Contrib: *Tattersall's British Race Horses; Sporting Review [1842-46 (engs. and title)]; ILN [1857-58, 1866-67].*
Exhib: BI, 1847-66; RA, 1838-86; RBA, 1839-75.

HALL, L. Bernard　　　　　　　　　　　　**1859-1935**
Portrait and figure painter. He was born in Liverpool, 28 December 1859 and was educated at Cheltenham College before studying art at South Kensington, Antwerp and Munich. He began his professional career in 1882, exhibiting at the RA from that year. In 1892, he was appointed Director of the National Gallery of Victoria at Melbourne, a post he held until his death on 14 February 1935.
Contrib: *The Graphic [1887]; Black & White.*
Exhib: L; M; NEA; RA; RBA; ROI.

HALL, Sydney Prior　　　**MVO**　　　　**1842-1922**
Painter, draughtsman and illustrator. He was born at Newmarket in 1842 and studied with his father Harry Hall (q.v.), with Arthur Hughes (q.v.) and at the RA Schools. Hall was a popular painter of military subjects and illustrated many stories, his most famous collaboration being on *Tom Browne's School Days*, 1869, with his teacher, Arthur Hughes. He was a favourite painter of the Royal Family and accompanied Lord Lorne to Canada in 1881. He was a *Graphic* contributor from its first year, 1870, and a Special Artist in the Franco-Prussian War. See E.J. Gregory.
Illus: *The Law and The Lady [Wilkie Collins, 1876].*
Contrib: *The Quiver [1869]; The Graphic [1870-1906]; Dark Blue [1871-73]; The Sketch.*
Exhib: G; L; M; New Gall.; RA; RHA; RI.

HALLIDAY, Michael Frederick　　　　　　**1822-1869**
Amateur artist and illustrator. He exhibited at the RA from 1853-56 and at the RBA in 1853. The National Portrait Gallery has his portrait of Joseph Priestley; he died at Thurlow Place, London in 1869.
Contrib: *Passages From the Poems of Tom Hood [Junior Etching Club, 1858].*

HALLS, Robert　　　　　　　　　　　　　**fl.1892-1909**
Miniature painter. He worked in London and Birkenhead and contributed to *The Yellow Book*, 1895.
Exhib: NEA; P; RA; RMS.

HALLTHORPE
Comic artist contributing to *Fun*, 1901.

HALLWARD, Cyril R.　　　　　　　　　　**fl.1886-1890**
Comic artist in pen and ink specialising in figure subjects. His drawings are poor and the penline rather scratchy.
Contrib: *Judy [1886-89]; ILN [1889]; Lady's Pictorial [1890]; Puck and Ariel [1890].*

HALLWARD, Ella F.G.　　　　　　　　　　**fl.1896-98**
Illustrator. Perhaps the daughter of Reginald and Adelaide Hallward (qq.v.). She exhibited at the Arts and Crafts Exhibition Society in 1896 an illustration for an untraced book issued by Messrs. H.S. Nicholls. *The Studio* said: 'One can scarce recall any other attempt to work in white upon black which has mastered the problem so easily.'
Exhib: New Gall., 1898.
Bibl: *The Studio*, Vol. 9, 1897, p.283, illus.

HALLWARD, Reginald　　　　　　　　　　**1858-1948**
Painter, stained glass artist, illustrator and designer. He was born 18 October 1858 and studied art at the Slade and at the Royal College

of Art. He had J.J. Guthrie (q.v.) as an assistant for some time. Hallward ran The Woodlands Press at Shore near Gravesend from about 1895 to about 1913, printing various books of verse by Michael and Faith Hallward illustrated by his own chalk drawings. His wife, Adelaide (q.v.) was also an artist and illustrator.
Illus: *Vox Humana; Apotheosis; Wild Oats; Flowers of Paradise; The Babies Quest [1913, all Woodlands Press]; Rule Britannia; Quick March; The Religion of Art; The Next Step; Stories From The Bible [E.L. Farrar, 1897].*
Contrib: *Punch [1876]; Root and Branch [No. 4, 1916].*
Exhib: G; L; NEA; New Gall.; RA; RBA.
Bibl: *RH*, Christopher Wood Gallery, 1984; *The Last Romantics*, Barbican Gallery catalogue, 1989.

HALLWARD, Mrs. Reginald (née Adelaide Bloxam) fl.1888-1922
Artist and illustrator. She was married to Reginald Hallward (q.v.) and helped him with his various ventures. She illustrated *The Child's Pictorial* for The SPCK and exhibited five works at the RA between 1888 and 1890. She was still painting though not exhibiting in 1922.

HALSWELLE, Keeley　　　**ARSA**　　　　**1832-1891**
Landscape painter and illustrator. He was born at Richmond, Surrey, of Scottish parents on 23 April 1832. After studying at the British Museum and in Edinburgh, Halswelle started a career in book illustration from 1860 onwards, working for a number of leading magazines. Gleeson White comments that 'in these you find those water-lilies in blossom which in after years became a mannerism in his landscape foregrounds.' From 1869 he lived in Italy for some years, painting peasant subjects, and he also worked in Paris. A new dimension to his art as an illustrator was revealed in November 1975, when Sotheby's Belgravia offered a remarkable ink drawing of 1858, entitled 'A Child's Dream of Christmas'. Centred on a sleeping child surrounded by many small fairy figures, it places him firmly in the tradition of Richard Doyle (q.v.). He was elected ARSA in 1865 and RI in 1882.
Illus: *The Princess Florella and the Knight of the Silver Shield [1860]; Six Years in a House-boat.*
Contrib: *ILN [1860]; Good Words [1860]; Pen and Pencil Pictures From the Poets [1866]; Scott's Poems [c.1866].*
Exhib: RA, 1862-91; RBA, 1875-79.
Colls: Dublin; Glasgow; Leeds; Tate.
Bibl: *The Art Journal*, 'The Works of KH', 1879, p.49.

HAMERTON, Robert Jacob　　　**RBA**
Illustrator and lithographer. Born in Ireland, he was teaching drawing in a school in County Longford by the age of fourteen and then travelled to London to study lithography under Charles Hullmandel. He contributed to *Punch*, 1843-48 a number of cartoons of an Irish flavour, signing himself first 'Shallaballa' and then with a 'Hammer on the side of a Tun'. He continued to work on stone as a book illustrator until 1891 'when the drawings on the huge stones became too much for my old back' (Spielmann, pp.452-453). He was a close friend of H.G. Hine (q.v.). RBA, 1843.
Illus: *Comic Blackstone [G. a'Beckett]; Life of Goldsmith [Forster].*
Exhib: BI, 1831-47; RA and RBA, 1831-58.

HAMILTON, Lady Anne　　　　　　　　　　**1766-1846**
Amateur artist. She was born in 1766, daughter of the 9th Duke of Hamilton and died unmarried in 1846. She contributed a drawing of Ashton Hall to *The Beauties of England and Wales*, 1807.

HAMILTON, James　　　　　　　　　　　　**1819-1878**
American illustrator. He was born in Ireland in 1819 but went to America when young. He returned to England during the years 1854-56 and later became an art master in Philadelphia, where he died in 1878. He was most celebrated for illustrating an edition of the *Arabian Nights*.

HAMLEY, General Sir Edward Bruce　　　　**1824-1893**
Amateur illustrator. He was born in 1824 and after entering the Royal Horse Artillery in 1843, became Colonel in 1855 and served in the Crimean War. He contributed articles to *Blackwood's* and *Fraser's* magazines in 1858 and was Professor of Military History at Sandhurst, 1859-64. He was Commandant of the Staff College, 1870-77 and KCB, 1882, serving as MP for Birkenhead, 1885-92.
Illus: *The Campaign of Sebastopol [1855, AT236].*

CHRISTINE HAMMOND fl.1886-1910. 'Lor! Ain't I glad!'
Drawing for illustration in *The English Illustrated Magazine*. Pen
and ink. Signed   Victoria and Albert Museum

HAMMERSLEY, James Astbury   **1815-1869**
Headmaster of the Manchester School of Design, 1849-1862. He
illustrated The *Shipwreck of the Premier*, G.R. Dartnell, 1845.

HAMMOND, Christine E. Demain 'Chris'   **1861-1900**
Painter and illustrator. Sister of Gertrude E. Demain Hammond
(q.v.). She lived with her sister in London, 1886-90 and with her was
the principal illustrator to *St. Paul's*, 1894. Her penwork is rather free
and she excels in costume subjects in a style not unlike that of the
Brocks eighteenth century pastiches.
Illus: *Goldsmith's Comedies [1894-96]; Sir Charles Grandison;
Castle Rackrent* and *Popular Tales; The Absentee [Maria
Edgeworth, 1895]; Belinda* and *Helen [Edgeworth, 1896]; The
Parents Assistant [Edgeworth, 1897]; The Charm [W. Besant];
Henry Esmond [W.M. Thackeray, 1897]; Emma; Sense and
Sensibility [Jane Austen]; John Halifax Gentleman [Mrs. Craik,
1898]; Stories From Shakespeare [T. Carter, 1910].*
Contrib: *The Pall Mall Budget [1891-92]; The Ludgate Monthly
[1891 and 1895]; The Idler [1892]; The English Illustrated
Magazine [1893-96]; St. Paul's [1894]; The Quiver [1894-95];
Madame [1895]; The Temple [1896], Pearson's Magazine [1896];
Cassell's Family Magazine [1898]; Pick-Me-Up.*
Exhib: RA, 1886-93; RBA, 1886-90; RI; ROI.
Colls: V & AM.
See illustration.

HAMMOND, Gertrude E. Demain   RI   **1862-1952**
Painter and illustrator. She was born in Brixton in 1862 and studied
art at the Lambeth School, 1879 and at the RA Schools, 1885,
gaining sketch and decorative design prizes there. From about 1892
she was engaged in illustrative work, becoming a very accomplished
pen draughtsman, particularly of female figures. She worked in oil
and watercolour as well as in black and white and after her marriage
in 1898, painted from West Kensington, 1902-14 and from Stow-on-
the Wold, 1925.
Illus: *The Clever Miss Foillett [J.K.H. Denny, 1894]; frontis. to
novels by Robert Barr [1897]; The Virginians IW.M. Thackeray,
1902]; Martin Chuzzlewhit; Our Mutual Friend [Dickens, 1903];
The Beautiful Birthday Book [1905]; George Eliot [American
edition, 1907]; Arethusa [Marion Crawford, 1907]; Fairies of Sorts
[Mrs. Molesworth, 1908].* Colour illus. to *Shakespeare [1902-03];
The Pilgrims Progress [1904]; Faerie Queen [1909]; Stories from
Shakespeare [1910].*
Contrib: *A Book of Poems and Pastorals [c.1885]; The Quiver
[1890]; The Ludgate Monthly [1891]; The Queen; The Idler [1892];
St Paul's [1894]; Madame [1895]; The Yellow Book [1895]; The
Minister [1895]; Lady's Pictorial; Pick-Me-Up.*
Exhib: L; M; RA; RBA, 1887-89; RHA; RI.
Colls: Gateshead; Shipley; V & AM.

HAMNETT, Nina   **1890-1956**
Portrait and landscape painter and illustrator. She was born in Tenby,
South Wales in 1890 and studied at the London School of Art and
became a member of the London Group, 1917. She contributed
lively and linear figure sketches to *The Gypsy*, 1915.
Exhib: L; NEA, 1913-17.

HANCOCK, Charles   **fl.1819-1868**
Sporting artist, illustrator and drawing master. He was teaching at
Marlborough in 1819, Reading, 1827-28, Wycombe, 1829,
Aylesbury, 1830, Knightsbridge, 1831-49 and Highbury, 1849-67.
He was a very prolific artist, illustrated an edition of *Nimrod* and
contributed to *Tattersall's English Race Horses* and *The Sporting
Review*, 1842-46.
Exhib: BI, 1827-67; NWS; RA, 1819-47

HANCOCK, John   **1896-1918**
Poet, illustrator and mystic. Born in England, he was taken to
Canada by his parents at an early age and returned to live in the
Midlands in his teenage years. He studied at St. John's Wood Art
School from the age of fifteen and then lived with his parents,
developing into an introspective, solitary and visionary young man.
His greatest debts were to Beardsley and Blake, he drew and painted
in the mornings and read and wrote at night. His early works are in
black and white, later he graduated to watercolours using imagery
that he believed had been given to him in a vision. After being
diagnosed as having Bright's disease, he drowned himself in the
Regents Park Canal in 1918.
During his brief career he designed calendars, book illustrations
and book covers and a retrospective exhibition was held at the
Birmingham Repertory Theatre shortly after his death. An important
collection of work from his studio was sold at Christie's on 16
December, 1994.
Illus: *Come unto these Yellow Sands [Margaret L. Wood, 1915].*
Contrib: (Book covers) *Roses Pearls and Tears [Raymond
Heywood, 1918]; Escape and Fantasy [George Rostrevor, 1918].*
Lit: *The Weekly Westminster Gazette*, 18 November, 1922; *The
Bookman*, Christmas No., 1922, pp.147-149.
Coll: Cardiff.

HANKEY, William Lee   **1869-1952**
Landscape painter in oil. He was born at Chester on 28 March 1869
and educated at King Edward's School, Chester; he served in the
First World War, 1914-18 and was a member of the RI from 1898-
1906 and 1918-1924. He died in 1952.
Illus: *The Deserted Village [Goldsmith]; The Compleat Angler
[Walton].*
Publ: *An Old Garden; At the Well.*
Exhib: Paris; RA; RBA; RI.

HANSCOM, Adelaide   (later LEESON)
Illustrator. She contributed drawings to an edition of *Omar Khayyam* published by Messrs. Harrap in 1908.
Illus: *Sonnets from the Portuguese [Browning, c.1910].*

HARDING, Emily J.   **fl.1877-1902**
Miniaturist and illustrator of children's books. She was married to the painter Edward William Andrews, worked closely with T.H. Robinson (q.v.) and was a translator as well as artist.
Illus: *An Affair of Honour [Alice Weber, 1892]; The Disagreeable Duke [E.D. Adams, 1894]; Fairy Tales of the Slav Peasants and Herdsmen; Hymn on the Morning of Christ's Nativity [1896]; Lullabies of Many Lands [A. Strettell, 1896].*
Exhib: RA, 1877, 1897-98;RMS.
Bibl: R.E.D. Sketchley, *English Bk. Illus.*, 1903, pp. 112, 166.

HARDING, James Duffield   **1797-1863**
Watercolourist, topographer, lithographer and teacher. He was born at Deptford in 1797 and studied with Samuel Prout and Charles Pye, the engraver. Preferring drawing to engraving, he worked from an early age as a landscape artist, exhibiting at the RA from 1810. He was an excellent lithographer and worked for Hullmandel producing folios from the works of Bonington, Roberts and Stanfield. He visited the Rhine, Italy and Normandy in the 1820s, 1830s and 1840s, producing books of his travels and at the same time issuing copy-books for amateur artists. He was highly regarded by John Ruskin, whose drawing-master he had been. Finished watercolours and studies are seen with some frequency on the market, those prepared for the books, in pencil with slight highlighting.
Publ: *Lithographic Drawing Book [1832]; Art, or the Use of The Lead Pencil [1834]; Principles and Practices of Art [1845]; Lessons on Trees [1852].*
Contrib: *Scotland Delineated [J.P. Lawson, 1858].*
Illus: *Views in Spain [E.H. Locker, 1824, AT 147]; Britton's Cathedrals [1832-36 (figures)]; Sketches At Home and Abroad [1836, AT 29]; The Book of South Wales [S.C. Hall, 1861].*
Exhib: BI; OWS; RA; RBA.
Colls: Ashmolean; BM; Fitzwilliam; Glasgow; Manchester; Nottingham; V & AM.
Bibl: M. Hardie, *Watercol. Paint. in Brit.*, Vol. III, 1968, pp.24-27; Peter Bicknell, *Gilpin to Ruskin*, Fitzwilliam Museum, 1987-88, pp.111-115.

HARDWICK, J. Jessop   ARWS   **1831-1917**
Watercolourist and illustrator. He was born in Beverley, Yorks. and apprenticed to Henry Vizetelly who helped to found the *Illustrated London News*. Hardwick joined the staff of that paper in 1858 but continued to work as a watercolourist, exhibiting under the name of 'Hunt'. He became ARWS in 1882 and died at Thames Ditton in 1917.
Contrib: *Good Words [1874].*
Coll: Reading.

HARDWICKE, Elizabeth Yorke, Countess of   **-1858**
Amateur artist. She was the daughter of 5th Earl of Balcarres and married Philip, 3rd Earl of Hardwicke in 1782. She died on 26 May 1858.
Publ. and Illus: *The Court of Oberon or The Three Wishes [1831, AL 421 lith.].*

HARDY, Dorothy   **fl.1908-1925**
Illustrator of children's books. Contributed drawings to *In Nature's School* by Lillian Gask, 1908. Working at Long Eaton, Derby in 1925.

HARDY, Dudley   RBA RI   **1867-1922**
Artist and illustrator. He was born at Sheffield, 15 January 1867, the son of T.B. Hardy, the marine painter. He was educated at Boulogne School and at University College School, London, and studied art at Düsseldorf, at Antwerp with Verlat, 1884-85 and in Paris. It was his period in Paris and his contact with French chalk drawings and poster art that had the most lasting influence on his style. On his return to England, he was able to give a panache to his illustrative work which was only surpassed by Phil May (q.v.), using his black lines economically and mastering the black and white spaces of the page. He is at his best when most dashing, the more careful sketches can sometimes verge on the pretty. A prolific magazine artist, he drew many theatrical posters, including most of the Gilbert and Sullivan operettas and other Savoy Theatre productions. His oil paintings, colourful and with strong impasto are often of oriental and biblical subjects He became RBA, 1889 and RI, 1897.
Illus: *The Humour of Holland [Werner, 1894]; The Bell Ringer of Angels [Bret Harte, 1897]; Sensations of Paris [R. Strong, 1912].*
Contrib: *ILN [1889-94]; Illustrated Bits; Puck and Ariel [1890]; The Idler [1892]; The English Illustrated Magazine [1893-97]; The Pall Mall Budget [1894]; The Ludgate Monthly [1895]; Eureka [1897]; The Longbow [1898]; The Gentlewoman; The Sketch; The Minister; Punch [1900-02]; The Graphic [1902, 1910].*
Exhib: G; L; M; New Gall.; RA; RBA; RI; ROI.
Colls: Author; Leeds; Newport.
Bibl: E. Spence, 'Some Leaves From Mr. Dudley Hardy's Sketch Book', *The Studio*, Vol.8, 1896, pp.33-38; A.E. Johnson, edited by, *DH, RI, RMS*, Brush, Pen and Pencil Series, c.1920; P.V. Bradshaw, *The Art of the Illustrator*, 1918.
See illustration.

DUDLEY HARDY RBA RI 1867-1922. 'Their College Boys'. Illustration for *London Opinion*, 1894. Pen and ink and wash. 9½in x 15in (24.1cm x 38.1cm)   Author's Collection

HARDY, Evelyn
Contributed small military drawing to *The Illustrated London News*, 1889.

HARDY, F.C.
Brother of Dudley Hardy (q.v.). He contributed to *The Longbow*, 1898.

HARDY, Flo
Figure illustrator in *Pick Me Up*, 1888.

HARDY, Heywood RWA   **1842-1933**
Animal painter, etcher and illustrator, decorator. He came from Bristol but settled in London in about 1870 having exhibited landscapes and animal paintings from 1861. He was elected RE, 1880, ROI, 1883 and ARWS, 1885. He contributed illustrations to *The Illustrated London News*, 1876 (Christmas) and *The Graphic*, 1880 (Christmas colour). He worked in North London and latterly at Littlehampton.

HARDY, M.D.
Animal illustrator. Contributed to *The Strand Magazine*, 1891.

HARDY, Norman H.   **fl.1864-1914**
Illustrator, etcher. He worked for most of his life in London, but in 1896 was attached to the Sydney Herald, New South Wales. He specialised in archaeological drawings for *The Illustrated London News*, 1889-90.
Illus: *The Savage South Seas [A & C Black]*.
Exhib: Dudley Gall.; RA, 1891.

HARDY, Paul   **fl.1886-1899**
Historical painter and illustrator. Hardy worked at Bexleyheath, Kent and married the artist Ida Wilson Clarke. He is seen at his best in costume romances and adolescent series, like Jarrald's 'Books For Manly Boys', 1894. A prolific, competent but unexciting purveyor of adventure.
Illus: *Little Peter [L. Malet, 1888]; Children of the New Forest [1892]; A Jacobite Exile [G.A. Henty]; The Whispering Wilds [Debenham]; Afloat in a Gypsy Van [Thompson]; That Bother of a Boy [Stebbing]; Sayings and Doings in Fairyland; Lord Lynton's Ward [1892]; Barker's Luck [Bret Harte, 1897].*
Contrib: *The English Illustrated Magazine [1886]; Sporting and Dramatic News; The Quiver; The Boys' Own Paper [1890]; Black & White [1891]; Strand Magazine [1891]; Chums [1892]; St. Pauls [1894]; The Rambler [1897]; The St. James's Budget [1898]; Cassell's Family Magazine; Cassell's Saturday Journal; The Gentlewoman; The Ludgate Monthly; The Girls' Own Paper; The Wide World Magazine.*
Exhib: L; RA.

HARDY, Ruth   **fl.1895-1898**
Portrait and figure painter. Contributed social illustrations to *The English Illustrated Magazine*, 1895.
Exhib: P.

HARDY, T.D.
An illustration by this untraced artist appears in Willmott's *Poets of the Nineteenth Century*, 1857. It seems unlikely to be an error for Thomas Bush Hardy 1842-1897.

HARE, Augustus John Cuthbert   **1834-1903**
Writer of guide-books, illustrator and topographer. He was born in Rome in 1834 and, left an orphan, was adopted by his aunt and uncle. After an unhappy childhood, he was educated at Harrow and University College, Oxford. He travelled abroad in the 1860s and began to publish guide-books of the places he had visited. On his own admission he had visited every town and almost every village in Italy and France. He settled in England at St. Leonards, and died there in 1903.
Publ: *Epitaphs From Country Churchyards; Murray's Handbooks for Berks, Bucks, Oxfordshire, Durham and Northumberland; Memorials of a Quiet Life [1872-76]; Walks in Rome [1871]; Days Near Rome; Cities of Northern Italy; Cities of Central Italy; Cities of Southern Italy; Venice; Wanderings in Spain; Sketches of Holland and Scandinavia; Walks in London.*
Exhib: Leicester Gall., 1902.
Colls: Dundee; Leeds.

HARE, St. George RI   **1857-1933**
Portrait and subject painter and illustrator. He was born in Limerick in 1857 and studied with N.A. Brophy and then at the South Kensington Schools, 1875. RI, 1892. Died 30 January 1933.
Illus: *The Dead Gallant [Tristram, 1894 (with Hugh Thomson)]*.
Contrib: *The Graphic [1893, 1899 and 1912]*.
Exhib: G; L; M; RA; RBA; RHA; RI; RWA.
Colls: V & AM.

HARE, Thomas M.
Scientific illustrator to *The Illustrated London News*, 1847-49.

HARGRAVE, John Gordon   **1894-**
Artist and writer. He was born in 1894, the son of Gordon Hargrave, landscape painter. Educated at the Wordsworth School, Hawkshead, Hargrave produced illustrations tor *Gulliver's Travels* and *The Rose and The Ring*, 1909 and was chief cartoonist of the *London Evening Times* in 1911 at the age of seventeen. He joined the staff of C. Arthur Pearson in 1914.
Bibl: *Modern Book Illustrators and their Work*, Studio, 1914.

HARKER, E.
Contributed illustration to *The Illustrated London News*, 1860.

HARMSWORTH, Alfred Charles William   **1865-1922**
Viscount Northcliffe
Millionaire newspaper proprietor and founder of *The Daily Mail*, 1896. Harmsworth apparently contributed sketches of the Arctic to *The English Illustrated Magazine*, 1895, perhaps in connection with exploration schemes that he was financing.

HARPER, Charles G.   **1863-1943**
Artist, illustrator and author. He was born in 1863 and from the late 1880s was producing a steady stream of books on the English countryside, illustrated by himself. He specialised in coaching scenes and represented another nostalgic look backwards at the 18th century, a favourite Edwardian pastime. He died in Surrey on 8 December 1943.
Illus: *Royal Winchester [1889]; The Brighton Road [1892]; From Paddington to Penzance [1893]; The Marches of Wales [1894]; The Dover Road [1895]; The Portsmouth Road [1895]; Some English Sketching Grounds [1897]; Stories of the Streets of London [1899]; The Exeter Road [1899]; The Bath Road [1899]; The Great North Road [1900].*
Contrib: *The Pall Mall Budget [1891-92]*.
Exhib: L, 1886.
Bibl: R.E.D. Sketchley, *English Book. Illus.*, 1903, pp.47, 134.

HARPER, Henry Andrew   **1835-1900**
Author and painter. He was born at Blunham, Bedfordshire in 1835 and specialised in landscapes of the Holy Land. He accompanied the Earl of Dudley to the Near East, but in 1874, failed to be elected to the NWS. He died at Westerham in 1900.
Contrib: *ILN [1872 (Christmas)]*.
Exhib: L; RA; RBA; RI.

HARPER, H.G.   'G G'   **1851-**
Sporting journalist and artist. He was born in Cheshire in 1851 and lived for most of his life at Epsom, where he trained and rode his own race-horses. He hunted with the Surrey foxhounds and wrote several sporting novels and books.
Illus: *Romance of the Brighton Road [c.1892]*.

HARPER, T.   **fl.1817-1843**
Portrait painter and miniaturist. He exhibited at the RA from 1817-1843 and contributed illustrations to *Heath's Gallery* 1836.

HARRIS, Major Sir William Cornwallis   **1807-1848**
Artist and Big Game Hunter. He was born at Wittersham, Kent on 2 April 1807. He had a military education and was commissioned at the age of sixteen, serving in the Bombay Engineers. He travelled to South Africa in 1836 and made an expedition to the Tropic of Capricorn. He reached the Orange River and the Limpopo. Harris worked on his animal watercolours for three years 1837-40, published as *Portraits of the Game and Wild Animals of Southern*

Africa, 1840. He mounted a mission to Ethiopia resulting in his illustrated *The Highlands of Aethiopia*, 1844. He was knighted in 1844 and died of fever at Poona on 9 October 1848.
Bibl: Alexander Maitland, 'Up the Great Limpopo', *CL*, 27 August 1987.

HARRISON, Charles   **d.1943**
Black and white artist and cartoonist. A very prolific contributor to *Punch* in the period 1896-1914, Harrison brought a rather more modern and jokey style into the paper during its formal years. His drawings are not carefully hatched black and white work, but vigorous and imaginative cartooning with the flatness of the Japanese print and the outline of French caricaturists such as Mars (q.v.). He was one of a number of artists who used comic ancients for his jokes. He was later cartoonist on *The Daily Express* and contributed work to American magazines. He sometimes signs his work Harry's Son.
Contrib: *The Strand Magazine [1891]; Chums; The St. James's Budget; Funny Folks; Cassell's Saturday Journal; Punch [1896-1914].*
See Horne

HARRISON, Emma Florence   **fl.1887-1918**
Figure painter and illustrator. She was working in London from 1887 and specialised in illustrating poetry and children's books in a later Pre-Raphaelite style deriving something as well from William Morris.
Illus: *In The Fairy Ring [1908]; Poems of Christina Rossetti [1910]; Guinevere [Tennyson, 1912]; Elfin Song [1912]; Early Poems of William Morris [1914]; The Pixy Book [1918].*
Exhib: RA, 1887-91.
See Horne

HARRISON, George L.   **fl.1881-1904**
Figure and domestic painter, working in West Kensington. He contributed hunting subjects to *The Illustrated London News*, 1884-86.
Exhib: RA; RBA, 1881-1904.

HARRISON, Thomas Erat   **1853-1917**
Sculptor, painter, illustrator and engraver. Although not a very prolific illustrator, Harrison drew for books at various times and designed bookplates. Two examples of the latter, dated 1887 and 1907, are in the Victoria and Albert Museum.

HART, Dorothy
Possibly a member of the Birmingham School, clearly influenced by it. She was working at Heathdale, Harborne, Birmingham in 1897, when she won a *Studio* competition.
Bibl: *The Studio*, Vol.II, 1897, p.71, illus.

HART, Frank   **1878-1959**
Black and white figure artist. He was born at Brighton on 1 November 1878 and was drawing for magazines from the age of twenty. He was a regular contributor to *Punch*, most frequently in the 1920s, where his work is notable for fine penmanship and a carefully observed view of country life and ways. Hart was a lecturer on black and white art and gave many talks throughout the country, drawing directly on to the blackboard. He died in 1959.
Publ: *Dolly's Society Book [1902]; How The Animals Did Their Bit [1914-18]; Andrew, Bogie and Jack; One Long Holiday.*
Illus: *Master Toby's Hunt; Little Lass; Peter and Co.*
Contrib *The Temple Magazine [1896-97]; The Graphic; Punch [1914].*
Exhib: RA; RI.
Colls: Brighton; Eastbourne.

HART, William Matthew   **1830-1908**
Landscape painter. He was born at Paisley, 31 March 1830 and emigrated to the United States. He worked first as a coach painter, then as a portrait painter, finally setting up a studio in New York in 1853. He became a member of the National Academy in 1858 and President of the Brooklyn Academy of Design. He made a number of illustrations for the books of John Gould. A very important series of watercolour illustrations by Hart for Gould's *The Birds of Great Britain*, 1862-73 was sold from the Godman Collection at Christie's on 4 October 1994.
Lit: T*he Godman Collection of Watercolours for John Gould's 'The Birds of Great Britain'*, Christie catalogue with an introduction by Maureen Lambourne, 1994.

ARCHIBALD STANDISH HARTRICK RWS 1864-1950. 'Pulling Down the Strand'. Drawing for illustration, unpublished. Pen and ink. 16¼in x 11⅜in (41.3cm x 28.9cm)   Victoria and Albert Museum

HARTE, George C.   **fl.1885-1893**
Genre painter. He was working at Bedford Park, 1885-86 and contributed boating subjects to *The Illustrated London News* in 1893.
Exhib: L.

HARTRICK, Archibald Standish   **RWS**   **1864-1950**
Painter, black and white artist and illustrator. He was born at Bangalore on 7 August 1864, the son of an army officer and was educated at Fettes College and Edinburgh University. He studied art at the Slade School under Alphonse Legros, 1884-85, in Paris under Boulanger and Cormon, 1886-87 and joined the staff of *The Daily Graphic* in 1890. Although Hartrick was very prolific as a magazine artist and often worked as a special for *The Graphic*, his style remained consistently high and he was almost unsurpassed in chalk by any other British artist. It was perhaps typical of the man that he did not think of himself as an illustrator and went on to become an excellent watercolourist and a significant lithographer. He was at his best when depicting rural characters and many of them have an uncanny affinity with the rustic illustrators of the 60s. A whole set of these drawings called Cotswold types was acquired for the British Museum. He was a member of the NEA from 1893 and became ARWS in 1910 and RWS in 1920. He died in 1950.
Illus: *Soldiers Tales [Rudyard Kipling, 1896], The Body Snatcher [R L Stevenson].*
Contrib: *The Graphic [1889-95]; Daily Graphic [1890]; The Pall Mall Budget [1893]; Daily Chronicle; The Quiver; The New Budget [1895]; Black and White [1899-1900]; The Butterfly [1899]; Cassell's Family Magazine [1899]; Fun [1901]; The Yellow Book; The Ludgate Monthly; The Strand Magazine; Pearson's Magazine; The Pall Mall Magazine.*
Exhib: B; G; L; M; NEA; RA; RBA; RHA; RSA; RWS.

JOHN HASSALL RI 1868-1948. 'Drunken Man and Teetotaler'. Pen and watercolour. 5in x 3½in (12.7cm x 8.9cm)　　Author's Collection

JOHN HASSALL RI 1868-1948. 'Diner and Waiter'. Pen and watercolour. 5in x 3½in (12.7cm x 8.9cm)　　Author's Collection

Colls: Aberdeen; BM; Liverpool; Manchester; Melbourne; Sydney; V & AM.
Bibl: *The Studio* Winter No., 1900-01, p.72, illus.; *Apollo*, XXIV, 1936; A.S. Hartrick, *Painter's Pilgrimage Through Fifty Years*, 1939.
See illustration.

HARVEY, Mrs. A
Amateur illustrator of Ickwell Bury, Bedfordshire. She made drawings for *Our Cruise in the Claymore With a Visit to Damascus & The Lebanon*, 1861, Chapman & Hall, tinted lithographs.

HARVEY, Sydney　　　　　　　　　　　　　　**fl. 1897-1907**
Cartoonist for *Moonshine*, about 1901. He worked at Muswell Hill and contributed drawings to *Punch*, 1897-1902.

HARVEY, William　　　　　　　　　　　　　　**1796-1866**
Wood engraver and illustrator. He was born at Newcastle-upon-Tyne on 13 July 1796 and was apprenticed to Thomas Bewick (q.v.) who employed him on the woodcuts for the famous edition of *Aesop's Fables*, published in 1823. Harvey left Bewick in 1817, retained contact with the engraver till his death, but became a pupil of B.R. Haydon in London. He studied anatomy under Sir Charles Bell and became associated with Charles Knight, the popular journalist and educator for whom he undertook work. Harvey did little wood engraving after his success in engraving Haydon's 'Dentatus' in the manner of a copper plate. This heralded a new style and expertise in wood engraving which was to result in elaborate Victorian compositions. Harvey gradually became the most popular illustrator of the 1840s, taking on work of such a scale, hundreds of vignettes in *The Arabian Nights* and three thousand illustrations in the decade 1828 to 1838, that it almost revolutionised the market. Harvey was one of the first to use numerous outside engravers on his work, thus opening the way for a less personal approach but also for speed. His shortcomings were his lack of success with modern subjects and his

total lack of humour in drawing. He designed the third cover of *Punch* in July 1842 but it was considered too serious and his initial letters were thought too graceful! By the 1860s his decorative pages, elegant figures and balanced foilage, were considered 'too mannered' but his influence on Gilbert and early Fred Walker was considerable. He died at Richmond on 13 January 1866.
Illus: *History of Wines [Henderson, 1824]; The Tower Menagerie [1828]; Northcote's Fables [1828]; The Garden and Menagerie of the Zoological Society [1830]; Children in the Wood [1831]; The Blind Beggar of Bethnal Green [1832]; Story Without An End; Pictorial Prayer Book; Thousand and One Nights [Lane, 1840]; London [Knight, 1841]; Metrical Tales [Samuel Lover, 1849]; The Pilgrim's Progress and the Holy War [1850]; Oriental Fairy Tales [1854]; The Fables of John Gray [1854]; Tales From Shakespeare [C. and M. Lamb, 1856]; The Queen of Hearts [Wilkie Collins, 1859]; Eugene Aram [T. Hood], Natural History [J.G. Wood].*
Contrib: *The Observer [1828]; Bell's Life; Punch [1841-42]; ILN [1843-59 (decor and political)]; The Illustrated London Magazine [1854].*
Colls: BM; Fitzwilliam; V & AM.
Bibl: M.H. Spielmann, *The History of Punch*, 1895, pp.42-44, The Brothers Dalziel, *A Record of Work, 1840-1890*, 1901, pp.12-21; P. Muir, *Victorian Illustrated Books*, 1971, pp.28-33, illus.

HARWOOD, John　　　　　　　　　　　　　　**fl.1818-1829**
Architectural and landscape painter. He worked in London and contributed to *Lancashire Illustrated*, 1829.

HASELDEN, William Kerridge　　　　　　　　**1872-1953**
Cartoonist and caricaturist. He was born at Seville in 1872 and began drawing professionally in 1903. He joined the staff of the *Daily Mirror* in 1904 and began to contribute to *Punch* in 1906, concentrating on theatrical caricatures. In the 1920s and 1930s he was well-known for his 'art deco' caricatures of Edith Evans, Gertrude Lawrence, Shaw, Ivor Novello etc.

JOHN HASSALL RI 1868-1948. Gunfight. Illustration for a boys' magazine. Watercolour. 10in x 12in
(25.4cm x 30.5cm)
Author's Collection

HASSALL, John   RI   **1868-1948**
Watercolourist, poster-designer and illustrator. He was born at
Walmer in 1868 and educated at Newtown Abbot College, Devon
and Neuenheim College, Heidelberg. He began life as a farmer in
Manitoba, abandoning this for art and studying at Antwerp and Paris,
1891-94, in the former under P. Van Havermaet and in the latter with
Bougereau. Hassall was an original and versatile designer of
illustrations from 1895 onwards, contributing cartoons to many
leading magazines, designing theatre posters, commercial posters for
Messrs. David Allen and greetings cards, boys' books and nursery
rhymes. His chief influence would seem to be the flat colours and
two-dimensional decorative quality of Japanese prints, which he
adapts to his own work with thick outline and careful patterning. He
also executed fine watercolours for boys' adventure stories, the scene
drawn in with the brush and the washes applied dryly and carefully.
Hassall's work is synonymous with colour except for his First War
booklets in line. He was elected RI in 1901, and RMS, the same year.
A Centenary Exhibition was held at Leighton House 1-11 April 1968.
He signs his work Hassall or JH
Illus: *Two Well Worn Shoes [1899]; The Princess and The Dragon;
John Hassall's New Picture Book [1908]; Ye Berlyn Tapestrie
Wilhelm's Invasion of Flanders [1916]; Keep Smiling [c.1916].*
Contrib: *The Daily Graphic [1890]; The Sketch [1894], Judy;
Moonshine; Pick-Me-Up; The New Budget [1895]; The West End
Review [1898]; The Graphic [1899-1911]; Illustrated Bits; The
Idler; Eureka; ILN [1900, 1908 (Christmas)]; The Sphere.*
Exhib: B; G; L; RA; RI; RMS; RSW.
Colls: Author; V & AM.
Bibl: 'The London Sketch Club' *The Magazine of Art*, March 1899,
p.229; 'The Poster Paintings and Illustrations of John Hassall RI', *The
Studio*, Vol. 36, 1906, illus.; *The Studio*, Winter No., 1900-01, pp.44-
47, illus; A.E Johnson (editor), *JH, RI*, Pen and Pencil Series, c.1920.
See illustrations.

HASSELL, Edward   **-1852**
Topographical artist and lithographer. He was the son of John
Hassall 1767-1825, the engraver and drawing master, and was
awarded premiums by the Society of Arts, 1828-29. He was a

member of the RBA from 1841 and held the office of Secretary. He
died at Lancaster in 1852.
Illus: *Historical Account of the Parish of St. Marylebone [Thomas
Smith, 1833].*
Exhib: BI; RA; RBA.

HASSELL, John   **1767-1825**
An engraver and drawing master and close friend of George
Morland. He produced numerous guide-books with aquatints after
his own drawings.
Publ: *Tour of the Isle of Wight [1790]; Picturesque Guide to Bath
[1793]; Life of George Morland [1806]; Speculum or the art of
Drawing in Watercolours [1808]; Aqua Pictura [1813]; Picturesque
Rides and Walks [1817]; The Tour of the Grand Junction Canal
[1819]; Camera or the Art of Watercolour [1823]; Excursions of
Pleasure and Sports on the Thames [1823].*
Contrib: *The Antiquarian Itinerary [1816].*
Exhib: RA, 1789.
Colls: BM; Guildford; Manchester.

HASWELL
Landscape artist and designer of initial letters in the style of Richard
Doyle. He contributed to *The Illustrated London Magazine*, 1853-54.

HATHERELL, William   RI RWA   **1855-1928**
Landscape and figure painter and illustrator. He was born at
Westbury-on-Trym on 18 October 1855 and was educated at private
schools before entering the RA Schools in 1877. He was a regular
contributor to magazines from about 1889, having done his first
illustrative work for Cassell's. Hatherell was at his best with stories,
where his moody wash drawings and his care to reflect accurately a
town, country or historical period could be shown to the full. Thorp
says that his flowing wash style was influential on younger men, it is
certainly typical of the 1890s. He was one of the few artists to
produce illustrations in oil on board, grey monochrome studies
which often have a rather French appearance. He was elected RI in
1888, ROI, 1898 and RWA in 1903. He died 7 December 1928.
Illus: *Annals of Westminster Abbey [E.J. Bradley, 1895]; Tantalon*

Castle [E.R. Pennell, 1895]; Sentimental Tommy [J.M. Barrie, 1897]; Romeo and Juliet [1912]; Island Night's Entertainments [R.L. Stevenson, 1913]; The Prince and the Pauper [S.L. Clemens, 1923].
Contrib: *The Graphic [1889-1912]; The Quiver [1890]; Black and White [1891]; The Picturesque Mediterranean [Cassell, 1891]; The English Illustrated Magazine [1891-92]; The Pall Mall Budget [1892]; Cassell's Family Magazine; Chums; Cassell's Saturday Journal; Harper's Magazine; Scribner's Magazine.*
Exhib: B; G; L; M; NEA; RA; RBA; RI; ROI.
Colls: V & AM.

HATTON, Brian   **1887-1916**
A promising young black and white artist who was killed in the First World War. He gained a Bronze Medal from the Royal Drawing Society at the age of eight and later studied at Oxford, 1905-06 and at South Kensington and Julian's in Paris. An extremely strong draughtsman of the country and its people, in thick ink lines.
Contrib: *The Graphic [11 Dec. 1915].*
Exhib: P; RA; ROI.
Colls: Witt Photo.
Bibl: W. Shaw Sparrow, 'BH', *Walker's Quarterly*, Feb.1926; Celia Davies, *BH A Biography of the Artist 1887-1916*, Lavenham, 1978.

HATTON, Helen Howard (Mrs. W.H. Margetson)   **1860-**
Watercolourist and pastellist. She was born in Bristol in 1860 and studied art at the RA Schools and at Colarossi's in Paris. She married the painter W.H. Margetson 1861-1940 (q.v.), and worked mainly in Berkshire.
Contrib: *The English Illustrated Magazine [1886 (architecture)].*
Exhib: B; G; L; M; RA; RI; ROI.

HAUGHTON, Matthew   **1768-1821**
Liverpool artist and caricaturist. He specialised in weird mythological creatures, strongly influenced by Fuseli. Six drawings were on the London art market in 1980, the caricature close to Gillray, the handling to J.H. Mortimer.

HAVELL, William   **1782-1857**
Topographical painter and draughtsman. He was born at Reading on 9 February 1782, the son of Luke Havell, a painter and glazier but also a drawing master. Probably aided by an artist uncle in London, he was already making a sketching tour to Wales in 1802 with Joshua Cristall and the Varley brothers. He came under the influence of Turner and in 1803-04 joined Cotman's Sketching Society. He was a founder member of the Society of Painters in Watercolours. In 1816 he sailed with Lord Amherst's embassy to China via South America, visiting Calcutta in 1817, Ceylon in 1819 and Madras in 1820. He was resident at Calcutta in 1821, Hydrabad 1822 and returned to England in 1826. He visited Italy for his health in 1828-29 and died on 24 May 1857.
Illus: *Picturesque Views of the River Thames [1812]; Architectural Antiquities of Great Britain [J. Britten, 1814]; A Series of Picturesque Views of Noblemens and Gentlemens Seats [1814-1823]; Peacock's Polite Repository [1813-17, 1829-44].*
Bibl: *WH 1782-1857*, Reading Museum & Art Gallery, Jan-Feb 1982, illus. catalogue.

HAVELOCK, Helen
Amateur topographer and daughter of W. Havelock of Ingress Park. She contributed an illustration to *Britton's Beauties of England and Wales*, 1808.

HAVERS, Alice (Mrs. Frederick Morgan)   **1850-1890**
Watercolourist and illustrator. She was born in Norfolk in 1850, the daughter of the manager of the Falkland Islands, where she was brought up. She returned to England in 1870 to study at South Kensington and in 1872, married the artist Frederick Morgan. She exhibited at the Salon, receiving a special mention in 1888 and was patronised by Queen Victoria.
Illus: *Cape Town Dicky; The White Swans [1890]; Odatis [c.1890]; A Book of Old Ballads [c.1890]; A Book of Modern Ballads [1890].*
Contrib: *Cassell's Family Magazine; A Book of Poems and Pastorals [c.1885].*
Exhib: G; L; M; RA; RBA; RHA; SWA.
Colls: Cardiff; Liverpool; Norwich; Sheffield.

HAWEIS, Mrs. H.R. (née Mary Eliza Joy)   **d.1898**
The daughter of the artist T.M. Joy, she married the Rev. Hugh Reginald Haweis, incumbent of St. James's, Marylebone. She was very much involved in interior decoration and the arts and wrote and illustrated *Chaucer For Children, A Golden Key*, 1877 and *Beautiful Homes*, 1882.

HAWKER, J.   **fl.1804-1812**
Topographer and landscape painter. He exhibited at the RA 1804-09 and contributed to *Britton's Beauties of England and Wales*, 1812.

HAWKER, Peter   **1786-1853**
Artist, soldier and author. He served in the Peninsular War with the 14th Light Dragoons and afterwards patented improvements to the pianoforte and wrote a sporting journal. He died in 1853.
Illus: *Instructions to Young Sportsmen [1824, AL 389].*

HAWKSWORTH, John
Topographer, working in London about 1820. He contributed to *The History and Antiquities of Islington*, 1823.

'HAY'
Pseudonym of caricaturist contributing to *Vanity Fair*, 1886, 1888-89 and 1893. His style is close to that of Pellegrini.

HAY, George   RSA   **1831-1913**
History and subject painter and illustrator. He was born in Edinburgh in 1831 and studied in the RSA School and at the Trustees Gallery, entering the architectural profession at the age of seventeen. He later abandoned this for painting, specialising in pictures of Scottish life and history. He was elected ARSA in 1869, RSA in 1876 and Secretary, 1881-1907. He died 31 August 1913.
Illus: *Pen and Pencil Pictures from the Poets [1866]; Poems and Songs by Robert Burns [1875]; Red Gauntlet [Walter Scott, 1894].*
Exhib: G; RSA.

HAY, Helen   **fl.1895-1940**
Black and white artist. She was probably associated with the Glasgow School and contributed to *The Evergreen*, 1895-96. She was working in Paisley in 1933 and at Egglesham, 1937.
Exhib: G; RSA.

HAYDON, G.H.   **fl.1860-1892**
Barrister, traveller and amateur artist. According to G.S. Layard, Haydon went to Australia as a youth to seek his fortune and made a number of sketches of the interior, later reproduced in the *Australian Illustrated* in about 1876. He was back in England by 1860 and became steward of Bridewell and Bethlem Hospitals. Haydon was a member of the Langham Sketch Club, became a friend of Charles Keene and John Leech, and was used by the latter as a model in some of his sporting drawings. He himself drew for *Punch*, 1860-62.
Bibl: C.S. Layard, *Charles Keene*, 1892, p.247.

HAYES, Frederick William   ARCA FRGS   **1848-1918**
Landscape painter, illustrator and author. He was born at New Ferry, Cheshire on 18 July 1848 and was educated at Liverpool College and privately. He trained as an architect with a firm in Ipswich, but turned to painting and studied with H. Dawson. Returning to the North-West, Hayes helped to found the Liverpool Watercolour Society; he remained in the city until about 1880 when he moved to London. A socialist and historian, Hayes specialised in the scenery of North Wales and illustrated his own books. He died 7 September 1918.
Illus: *The Story of the Phalanx [1894], A Kent Squire [1900]; Gwynett of Thornhaugh [1900]; The Shadow of a Throne [1904]; A Prima Donna's Romance [1905]; Captain Kirk Webbe [1907]; The United Kingdom Limited [1910].*
Exhib: B; L; M; RA; RBA; RCA; RI; ROI.
Colls: BM; Glasgow; V & AM.

HEAPS, Chris
Black and white artist. Contributor to *The Graphic*, 1915.

HEATH, Charles   **1785-1848**
Engraver and illustrator. He executed plates for popular works and engraved the pictures of Benjamin West. He is best remembered as the publisher of illustrated 'Annuals' during the 1830s.
Exhib: RA and RBA, 1801-25.

HEATH, Ernest Dudley   **fl.1886-1927**
Painter and illustrator. He was the son of Henry Charles Heath, Miniature Painter to Queen Victoria. He studied at the RA Schools and became lecturer on art, University of London Extension, 1903-08, Principal of the Hampstead Garden Suburbs School of Arts and Crafts, 1914-26, and lecturer on Principles of Art Teaching, Royal College of Art, 1927.
Contrib: *The English Illustrated Magazine [1893-94 (cockney figures)].*
Exhib: L; M; RA; RBA; RMS; ROI.

HEATH, Henry   **fl.1824-1850**
Probably the brother of William Heath (q.v.). He was a versatile and imitative artist, working in the loose and coarse Heath manner between the years 1824-30. He did imitation caricatures in the style of John Doyle 'HB' signed 'HH' for Messrs. Fores, 1831 and etched vignettes in the style of Cruikshank and lithographs in the style of Seymour from 1834. He was employed to make political caricatures by Spooner, the publisher and his work was collected and published by Charles Tilt. Heath undertook one cartoon for *Punch* in 1843 and his sets include *London Characters*, 12 pls., 1834 and *Domestic Miseries, Domestic Blisses*, 12 liths., 1850. He is believed to have emigrated to Australia.

HEATH, Thomas Hastead of Cardiff   **fl.1879-1905**
Portrait and figure painter. He specialised in seascapes but did fine figure studies in sepia ink, reminiscent of Wilkie. He also designed a fixture card for the 'Cardiff Harlequins'.
Exhib: L; RA; RBA.

HEATH, William   'Paul Pry'   **1795-1840**
Watercolourist and caricaturist who worked mostly under the pseudonym of Paul Pry. He called himself 'Portrait and Military painter' and was reputed to be an 'ex-captain of dragoons' but is not recorded in the Army List. Heath began life as a draughtsman and his main claim to fame rests on his having produced the first caricature magazine in Europe, *The Glasgow* later *Northern Looking-Glass*, 1825-26. Although this was a provincial work and without much text, it does pre-date Charles Philipon's similar publication. The height of his popularity fell between the years 1809-34, after which his humour was displaced by that of Robert Seymour and John Doyle (qq.v.). After this period he concentrated on topography and straight illustration.
Publ: *Rustic sketches [1824, AL 143]; Marine studies [1824, AL 144].*
Illus: *The Wars of Wellington A Narrative Poem [W. Coombe, AL 357 & 358]; Studies From The Stage [1823, AL 415]; The Life of a Soldier [1823]; Common-place Book [1825, AL 302]; Illustrations of Heraldry [1828, AL 303]; The Looking-Glass [1830]; Sayings of the Ancients [1831, AL 304]; Minor Morals [Bowring, 1834-39]; The Martial Achievements of Great Britain and Her Allies and Historical Military and Naval Anecdotes.*
Colls: V & AM.
See illustration (colour).

HEAVISIDE, John Smith   **1812-1864**
Engraver. He was born at Stockton on-Tees in 1812 and worked in London and Oxford. He illustrated Parker's archaeological books and died at Kentish Town on 3 October 1864.

HEAVISIDE, T.
Brother of John Smith Heaviside (q.v.). He engraved portraits of Thomas Bewick and John Owen and contributed to *The Illustrated London News*, 1849-51.

HEBBLETHWAITE, H. Sydney
Black and white artist. Thorpe describes him as an artist of promise and invention who died young. He contributed drawings to *Pick-Me-Up* in 1899 and another drawing, perhaps posthumous, appeared in *The Graphic*, 1908.

HEFFER, Edward A. of Liverpool   **fl.1860-1885**
Decorative designer, architect and illustrator. He contributed work to *The Illustrated London News*, 1860-61.
Exhib: L; RA.

HEIGHWAY, Richard   **fl.1894-1898**
Illustrator of children's books. He illustrated *Aesop's Fables*, 1894 (Macmillan) and *Blue Beard*, 1895, for the Banbury Cross series (Dent).
Bibl: White, Gleeson, 'Children's Books and Their Illustrators', *Studio* Special No., 1897-98.

HELLÉ, André
French theatrical designer and illustrator. He was closely associated with the Opera Comique at Paris and did a great deal of work for children's books.
Contrib: *The Graphic [1910].*

HELLEU, Paul César   **1859-1927**
Painter and etcher. He was born at Vannes on 17 December 1859 and became a pupil of Gérôme at the École Nationale des Beaux-Arts. Helleu was a talented painter of churches and of architecture but was best known in this country during the Edwardian period for his sensitive and charming etchings of society beauties. Among his subjects were Queen Alexandra, the Princess of Connaught and the Duchess of Marlborough. He became ARE, 1892, and RE, 1897. He died at Paris, 23 March 1927.
Contrib: *The Graphic [1901].*
Exhib: L; P; RE.

HELMICK, Howard   **1845-1907**
American figure painter and illustrator. He was born at Zanesville, Ohio, in 1845 and studied in Paris under Cabanel. He lived in London for some years and on returning to the United States became Professor of the History of Art at Georgetown University. He died on 18 April 1907. RBA, 1879, and RE, 1881.
Contrib: *The Graphic [1880].*
Exhib: B; G; L; M; RA; RBA; RE.

HEMING, Matilda (Miss Lowry)   **fl.1808-1855**
Portrait painter. She was the daughter of the engraver Willson Lowry and exhibited at the RA, 1808-09 and 1847-55. She contributed an illustration to *Britton's Beauties of England and Wales*, 1807.

HEMY, Charles Napier   RA RWS   **1841-1917**
Marine, landscape and still-life painter. He was born at Newcastle-upon-Tyne on 24 May 1841 and studied with William Bell Scott (q.v.). From 1850 to 1852, he sailed round the world developing a great knowledge of and interest in shipping, but on his return entered the Dominican order and studied for three years in monasteries at Newcastle and Lyons. He finally abandoned this life in 1862 and went to Antwerp to study art under Henri Leys, settling in London in 1870 and finally moving to Falmouth. Hemy's reputation is principally as a marine artist and he made many studies from his own yacht, the *Van der Meer*, which he kept at Falmouth. He was elected ARA in 1898 and RA in 1910, and RWS in 1897. He died on 30 September 1917.
Contrib: *The English Illustrated Magazine [1883-87].*
Exhib: B; G; L; M; New Gall.; RA; RI; RSA; RWS.
Colls: Birmingham; Bristol; Leeds; Newcastle.

HENDERSON, Keith   OBE RWS   **1883-1982**
Writer and illustrator. He was born in 1883 and after being educated at Marlborough, studied art at the Slade School and in Paris. He served in the First World War and was War Artist to the Royal Air Force in 1940.
Publ: *Letters to Helen; Palmgroves and Hummingbirds; Prehistoric Man; Burns by Himself; Romaunt of the Rose [1911]; No Second Spring; Christina Strang.*
Illus: *Conquest of Mexico [Prescott, 1922]; Green Mansions [W.H. Hudson, 1931]; Buckaroo [E . Cunningham, 1934].*
Exhib: B; FAS, 1914, 1917; G; L; NEA; RA; ROI; RSA; RWS.
Colls: V & AM.
Bibl: *Modern Book Illustrators and their Work*, Studio, 1914.

HENDRY, Sydney
Black and white artist specialising in children. He contributed to *Punch* in 1903.

HENFREY, Charles
Contributed illustrations to *Public Works of Great Britain*, 1838, AL 410.

HENLEY, A.W.   **fl.1880-1908**
Landscape artist working in West London. He contributed illustrations to R.L. Stevenson's *Fontainebleau*.
Exhib: GG; RHA; RSA.

HENLEY, Lionel Charles RBA   **1843-c.1893**
Genre painter. He was born in London in 1843 and studied art at Düsseldorf, making his début at exhibitions in Magdebourg. He returned to England and exhibited regularly from 1862, becoming RBA in 1879.
Contrib: *London Society [1865]; Fun [1865]; Foxe's Book of Martyrs [1867]; Cassell's Illustrated Readings [1867]; The Graphic [1870].*
Exhib: B; L; RA; RBA; ROI.

HENNESSY, William John   ROI   **1839-1917**
Landscape and genre painter and illustrator. He was born at Thomastown, Ireland, in 1839 and emigrated with his family to America when very young, remaining there till 1870. He attended the National Academy in New York in 1856 and became a member in 1863, but in 1870 settled in England, alternating his residence from time to time between Normandy and Sussex. Hennessy was something of an expert on American art and his own drawing style, very finished and slick, owes a good deal to that school. Amongst his best work is probably the series of illustrations to Jean Ingelow's 'Sarah de Berenger' in *Good Words*, 1880. He became ROI in 1901.
Illus: *Broken Wings [Avery Macalpine, 1897]; Marriage [Susan Ferrier, 1895]; The Suicide Club; The Rajah's Diamond [R.L. Stevenson, 1913].*
Contrib: *ILN; Dark Blue [1871-73]; The Graphic [1872-76, 1880]; Punch [1873-75]; The English Illustrated Magazine [1884-92]; Black & White [1891]; The Girls' Own Paper.*
Exhib: B; G; GG; L; M; NEA; RA; RHA; ROI.

HENNING, Archibald Samuel   **-1864**
Comic illustrator. He was the third son of the sculptor John Henning and the brother-in-law of Kenny Meadows (q.v.). A rather slap-dash artist and bohemian character, he designed *Punch's* first wrapper and was rated 'a fair and prolific draughtsman on wood' by W.J. Linton. He may have undertaken medical and natural history illustrations in the 1850s.
Contrib: *Punch [1841-42]; The Squib; The Great Gun; Joe Miller the Younger; The Man in The Moon; The Comic Times; The Illustrated London Magazine [1854].*
Illus: *The Natural History of 'Stuck-up' People [Albert Smith, 1847]; The Natural History of the Ballet-Girl [Albert Smith, 1847]; The Bal Masqué [Albert Smith (with Cham), 1848]; A Bowl of Punch [Albert Smith, n.d.].*

HENRY, Paul   RHA   **1876-**
Landscape painter. He worked in Liverpool, Belfast, Dublin and County Wicklow, and was elected ARHA in 1926 and RHA, 1929. He contributed illustrations of children to *The Graphic*, 1910.

HENRY, Thomas   **fl.1891-1914**
Painter and illustrator. He contributed to *Punch*, 1914.
Exhib: Dowdeswell Gall.

HENTY, George Alfred   **1832-1902**
Author, journalist and amateur artist. He was born at Trumpington, Cambridge, on 8 December 1832 and educated at Westminster and at Caius College, Cambridge. Henty went out to the Crimea in the Purveyors' Department of the Army and after being invalided home, served with the Italian Legion. From 1866, he was special correspondent for *The Standard* in the Austro-Italian, Franco-Prussian and Turco-Serbian Wars and the Abyssinian and Ashanti Expeditions. His illustrated reports attracted considerable attention,

but for their writing rather than their drawing! Henty went on to use these experiences in numerous adventure books for boys. He died 16 November 1902.
Contrib: *ILN [1868].*
Bibl: G.M. Fenn, *GAH The Story of an Active Life*, 1907, p.27.

HERALD, James Watterson   **1859-1914**
A landscape and coastal painter. He was born at Forfar in 1859 and studied under Herkomer (q.v.). His style is closely associated with the Glasgow School, he died at Arbroath in 1914. Some prints by this artist, dating from about 1900, may have been intended as book illustrations.

HERBERT, John Rogers RA RHI   **1810-1890**
Portrait, romantic and religious painter. He was born at Maldon, Essex, in 1810 and studied at the RA Schools, 1826. He was an early teacher of art at the Government School of Design at Somerset House, Herbert was a regular book illustrator in the early part of his career, but after his conversion to Roman Catholicism, he gave this up to concentrate on large religious paintings. He was elected ARA in 1841 and RA in 1846, retiring in 1886.
Illus: *Legends of Venice [Edited by Roscoe, 1840].*
Contrib: *The Keepsake [1836]; Heath's Gallery [1838].*
Exhib: BI; NWS; RA; RBA.
Colls: BM; L; V & AM.

HERDMAN, Robert   RSA   **1829-1888**
Portrait and history painter. He was born at Rattray on 17 September 1829 and after studying at St. Andrews University, became a pupil of R.S. Lauder at the Edinburgh Trustees Academy. He travelled to Italy, 1855-56 and established himself from 1861, when he became ARSA, as a leading portrait painter and painter of Scottish history. He left his large collection of artists' portraits to Aberdeen. He died at Edinburgh on 10 January 1888.
Contrib: *Poems and Songs by Rohert Burns [1875].*
Exhib: RA; RSA.
Colls: Edinburgh; Glasgow.

HERING, George Edwards   **1805-1879**
Painter and illustrator. Born in London in 1805, the son of a bookbinder of German extraction. He studied art and worked in Munich and then travelled in Italy and Turkey, Hungary and Transylvania, which were the most usual subjects for his pictures. He settled in London, but frequently travelled on painting expeditions.
Illus: *Sketches On The Danube, in Hungary and Transylvania, [1838]; The Mountains and Lakes of Switzerland, The Tyrol and Italy [1847, AT 63].*
Exhib: BI; RA, 1836; RBA, 1838-
Colls: V & AM.

HERKOMER, Sir Hubert von RA   **1849-1914**
Painter and illustrator. He was born at Waal, Bavaria, on 26 May 1849, the son of Lorenz Herkomer, who settled in England in 1857. He studied art at South Kensington from 1866, founded the Herkomer School of Art at Bushey in 1883 and was Slade Professor at Oxford, 1885-94. Herkomer was one of the grandees of Victorian painting in the 1880s and 1890s, receiving many honours both at home and abroad. He became ARA in 1879, RA in 1890 and was knighted in 1907.

Herkomer's greatest strength was as a composer of pictures and as a figure painter. His principal achievement in book illustration was the series of social realistic subjects that he drew for *The Graphic*, 1870-79. These included his famous 'Heads of the People', 1875, and such famous images of Victorian society as 'Christmas in a Workhouse'. Herkomer's talent for expressing the plight of the under-privileged was again used when he illustrated Hardy's *Tess of the D'Urbervilles* for the same magazine in 1891. Herkomer died at Budleigh Salterton on 31 March 1914.
Contrib: *The Quiver [1868]; The Sunday Magazine [1870]; Good Words for The Young [1870]; The Graphic [1870-79]; ILN [1871-73]; London Society [1872]; The Cornhill Magazine [1872]; Fun; Black & White [title].*
Exhib: B; G; GG; L; M; New Gall; P; RA; RBA; RE; RHA; ROI; RSA; RWS.
Colls: BM; Leeds; Manchester.
Bibl: *Autobiography*, 1890; *English Influences On Vincent Van*

Gogh, Arts Council 1974-75, p.52; Nicholas Usherwood, 'Quiet Contradictions', *CL*, 5 Feb. 1982; *A Passion For Work*, Watford Art Gallery catalogue, Feb. 1982.

HÉROND, L.J.
French artist, contributing illustrations of Paris to *Cassell's Illustrated Family Paper*, 1857.

HERRING, Benjamin   **-1871**
Sporting artist. He was the son of J.F. Herring (q.v.) who looked upon him as his real successor in equestrian art. He was, however, a, rather mediocre painter but contributed to *The Illustrated London News*, 1850-60 and 1864.
Exhib: BI; RBA, 1861-63.

HERRING, John Frederick   **1795-1865**
Sporting artist and illustrator. He was born in Surrey in 1795, the son of an American, and was inspired at an early age to draw horses. He worked as a coach painter and even for some time as a coach driver, later residing in Doncaster and setting up as a horse portraitist. He worked also at Newmarket, London and at Tunbridge Wells, where he died in 1865; he became a member of the SBA, later RBA, in 1841.
Contrib: *The Sporting Review [1842-46]; ILN [1844-45, 1864]; The Illustrated Times [1859]; Bell's Life in London.*
Exhib: BI; RA; RBA.
Bibl: W. Shaw Sparrow, *British Sporting Artists*, 1922, pp.215-227.

HERRING, John Frederick, Jnr.   **1815-1907**
Sporting artist. He was born in 1815, the eldest son of J.F. Herring (q.v.) and the brother of the B. Herring (q.v.). He made a speciality of farmyard scenes but was a less inspired painter than his father whom he mercilessly imitated. He died at Cambridge in 1907.
Contrib: *Old Sporting Magazine.*
Exhib: B; BI; RA; RBA.

HERVIEU, Auguste   **fl.1815-1858**
Portrait painter and figure illustrator. The son of a colonel in Napoleon's army, killed on the retreat from Moscow, Hervieu was involved in underground activities against Louis XVIII and went on an anti-monarchist expedition to Spain. Unable to return to France, he fled to England in 1827 and was adopted as part of the family of Mrs. Fanny Trollope, the novelist and travel writer, at her farm, Julian's near Harrow. He travelled to America with Mrs. Trollope 1827-31 and lived with her at Cincinnati, where he had some success with his historical painting 'The Landing of Lafayette'. Hervieu travelled with Mrs. Trollope as her illustrator to Belgium, 1833; Paris, 1835; Austria, 1836, after which he left her retinue. He was in Brittany in 1840 and married a Swiss wife in 1848. Everitt calls him 'an artist of considerable ability'.
Illus: (all for Mrs. Trollope) *Domestic Manners of the Americans [1832]; The Mother's Manual; or Illustrations of Matrimonial Economy. An Essay in Verse [1833]; Paris and the Parisians in 1835 [1836]; The Life and Adventures of Jonathan Jefferson Whitlaw [1836* (reissued 1857 as *Lynch Law); The Vicar of Wrexhill [1837]; Vienna and the Austrians [1838]; The Life and Adventures of Michael Armstrong, the Factory Boy [1840* (with R.W. Buss and T.W. Onwhyn). *The Clockmaker [Samuel Slick, 1840-41 (frontis. and one pl. dated 1838, subsequently succeeded by Leech, 1840)].*
Contrib: *Bentley's Miscellany.*
Exhib: BI; RA; RBA.
Coll: NPG.
Bibl: Johnston, Johanna, *The Life, Manners and Travels of Fanny Trollope*, 1979.
See illustration.

HESTER, R. Wallace   **fl.1897-1913**
Engraver and caricaturist. He worked at Tooting, 1897, and at Purley, 1901, and contributed to *Vanity Fair*, 1910-13.
Exhib: RA, 1897-1904.

HEWERDINE, Matthew Bede   **1871-1909**
Cartoonist and book illustrator. He worked in Hull and Oxford and illustrated *Lest We Forget Them*, Lady Glover, 1900, and *Cloister and the Hearth*, C. Reade, 1904.

AUGUSTE HERVIEU fl.1815-1858. 'Pro Patria', 1835

HEWETSON, Edward
Architectural draughtsman. He contributed illustrations to *Ackermann's Repository*, 1825.

HEWITT, John
Contributed illustrations to *Public Works of Great Britain*, 1838, AL 410.

HICKLING, P.B.   **fl.1895-1914**
Illustrator. A very competent but unrecorded pen artist who worked for magazines. Contributed to *Fun*, 1895; *The Boys' Own Paper* and *The Graphic*, 1902-06; *Punch*, 1914. He also illustrated a novel, *The Three Clerks*, John Long, c.1908.

HICKS, George Elger   **1824-1914**
Genre and portrait painter and illustrator. He was born at Lymington in Hampshire in 1824 and trained as a doctor, abandoning this career for one of a painter and training at the Bloomsbury and RA Schools. Hicks was one of the most lush painters of Victorian life, such busy subjects as 'The General Post Office – One Minute to Six', 1860 and elaborate wedding pieces with every present shown in glittering oil, are his. He was also a very competent illustrator of figures and did a fair amount of this work in early life. He died in London in 1914. RBA, 1889.
Publ: *A Guide to Figure Painting*, 1853.
Contrib: *Campbell's Gertrude of Wyoming [Art Union of London, 1846]; Sacred Allegories [1856]; The Farmer's Boy [Robert Bloomfield, 1847]; Favourite Modern Ballads [1859].*
Exhib: B; GG; L; M; RA, RBA, RSA.
Colls: Ulster Museum.
Bibl: Chatto & Jackson, *Treatise on Wood Engraving*, 1861, p.598; J. Maas, *Victorian Painters*, 1969, p. 117; Rosamond Allwood, *GEH*, Geffrye Museum catalogue, 1982-83.

EVELYN B. HOLDEN 1877-1968. Illustration to *The House That Jack Built And Other Nursery Rhymes*, 1895, illustrated with Violet M. Holden

HIGHAM, Bernard   fl.1895-1925
Landscape painter and illustrator. He was working at Wallington, Surrey, 1917-25. Contributed drawings to *The Idler*, c.1895; *The English Illustrated Magazine*, 1897.
Exhib: RA, 1917-19.

HIGHAM, Sydney   fl.1890-1905
Comic artist in black and white. His drawings are amusing but rather coarse in execution, he worked for a number of magazines and may have emigrated to Canada in about 1905.
Contrib: *Daily Graphic [1890]; Penny Illustrated Paper; The Graphic [1901 and 1903-05]*.
Colls: Author.

HIGHAM, Thomas   1796-1844
Topographer and engraver. Contributed to *The Antiquarian Itinerary*, 1817. Exhibited at RA, 1824-30.

HILL, David Octavius   RSA   1802-1870
Landscape painter, illustrator and photographer. He was born at Perth in 1802 and studied with Andrew Wilson at Edinburgh, making his debut in exhibitions in 1823. Hill specialised in Scottish life and landscape pictures, but he was always an experimenter and worked also in lithography. He was the first Secretary of the Royal Scottish Academy, 1830-69, and ARSA in 1826 and RSA three years later. He was one of the first artists to appreciate the potential of photography when he used calotypes made by the Adamsons for his celebrated painting 'The Disruption', commemorating a religious furore of the

1840s. From about 1843, he concentrated on photography and died in Edinburgh 17 May 1870.
Illus: *Sketches of Scenery in Perthshire [liths]; The Abbot, Red Gauntlet, The Fair Maid of Perth [Scott]; Poems and Songs by Robert Burns [1875]; The Land of Burns; Views of the Opening of the Glasgow and Garnkirk Railway [1832 AL 403]*.
Exhib: BI; RA; RBA; RSA.
Colls: Birkenhead; Edinburgh; Glasgow.
Bibl: D. Bruce, *Sun Pictures*, Studio Vista, 1973.

HILL, Leonard RAVEN-   see RAVEN-HILL, Leonard

HILL, Rowland   see 'RIP'

HILL, Vernon   1887-1953
Illustrator, lithographer and sculptor. He was born in Halifax in 1887, apprenticed to a trade lithographer at thirteen and was a student teacher at seventeen. In 1908 he was working under John Hassall RI (q.v.) and published his first illustrations the year following. Hill is strongest as a figure draughtsman and his swirling bodies and large wave and plant shapes, make him a classical equivalent of the Beardsley eroticism. In November 1909, *The Bodleian*, referred to him as 'a youth only just past his teens, his inventions have the eternal quality of beauty, his imagination is so rich so astonishing in its originality, and he is beside so gifted with rare humour, that his work defies comparison with anything known to us …'
Illus: *The Arcadian Calendar for 1910 [1909]; The New Inferno [Stephen Phillips Jnr, 1911]; Ballads Weird and Wonderful [Richard Chope, 1912]; Tramping with a Poet in the Rockies [Stephen Graham, 1922]*.
Exhib: Leicester Gall.; NEA; RA; RSA; 1908-27.
Colls: V & AM.
Bibl: *The Studio*, Vol.57, 1912-13; *Modern Book Illustrators and Their Work*, Studio, 1914, illus.; B. Peppin, *Fantasy Book Illustration*, 1975, pp 155-163, illus.

HILLS, Robert   1769-1844
Watercolourist. He was born in Islington on 26 June 1769 and received drawing lessons from John Gresse. He is principally remembered as a painter and etcher of animals and as a founder of the OWS in 1804 and its first Secretary and Treasurer. He died in London on 14 May 1844. Hills is included here for his book *Sketches in Flanders and Holland*, 1816, AT 186.
Exhib: OWS, RA.
Colls: Ashmolean; BM; Fitzwilliam; Leeds; V & AM.
Bibl: M. Hardie, *Watercol. Paint. In Brit.*, Vol.II, 1967, pp.139-141, illus.

HILLS, W. Noel   fl.1889-1924
Landscape painter and illustrator. He was working at Leyton, London in 1920-24 and contributed comic genre subjects to *Judy*, 1889.
Exhib: RA.

HILTON, Robert   fl.1881-1907
Architectural illustrator. He worked in Cricklewood in 1886 and in Chester, 1902-07.
Exhib: RA; RBA, 1886.

HINDLEY, Godfrey C.   fl.1880-1910
Figure and flower painter and illustrator. He became a Member of the ROI in 1898. Specialised in boys' books.
Illus: *In the Heart of the Rockies [1894]*.

HINE, Henry George   VPRI   1811-1895
Watercolourist and illustrator. He was born in Brighton in 1811, the son of a coachman and was largely self-taught. He was apprenticed in London to Henry Meyer, the stipple engraver and after completing indentures, worked for two years in Rouen, France, before joining the Landell's firm as a wood engraver. During the 1840s and early 1850s, Hine was a considerable illustrator, working in particular for *Punch* and drawing for one of Wilkie Collins' earliest stories in part works, 1843-44. Hine was like 'Phiz', a competent but not inspired humorous artist. In later life, Hine became a serious landscape watercolourist,

concentrating on views of the Downs and coastal subjects showing the influence of Copley Fielding. He became RI in 1864 and Vice-President, 1888-95. He died in London on 16 March 1895.
Illus: *The Natural History of Bores [A.B. Reach, 1847]; Change for a Shilling [H. Mayhew, 1848]; Acting Charades – Deeds Not Words [Mayhew, c.1850, Col.]; Comical People Illustrated With Sixteen Pictures Taken from the Embroidered Tapestry Contributed By Maria Fusinata, of Belluno, to the Great Exhibition,* grouped from J.J. Grandville [W.G. Mason, 1852 (folding pls.)]; *The Cracker Bon Bon for Christmas Parties [Bough, 1852, Col.].*
Contrib: *Punch [1841-44]; The Illuminated Magazine [1843-45]; ILN [1847-55]; Illustrated London Magazine [1853-54]; The Welcome Guest [1860].*
Exhib: L; M; RA; RBA; RI.
Colls: BM; Fitzwilliam; Leeds; V & AM.

HIPSLEY, John Henry   fl.1882-1910
Flower painter. He was working at Liverpool, 1882, and Hemel Hempstead, 1891, and at Birmingham in 1899. He contributed to *The Strand Magazine,* 1891.
Exhib: B; L; RBA; RI.

HITCHCOCK, Arthur   fl. 1884-1898
Watercolourist and illustrator. He illustrated *Hero and Heroine* by A.R. Hope, 1898 and exhibited at the RBA in 1884.

HODGSON, Edward S.   fl.1906-1925
Landscape painter. He worked at Bushey, Herts., and exhibited at RA 1922. He illustrated *A Middy in Command,* Harry Collingwood, 1908.
Contrib: *Strand Magazine [1906].*
See Horne

HODGSON, George   d.1921
Landscape and allegorical painter and cartoonist. A leading member of the Nottingham Society of Artists, Hon. Sec., 1892 and Vice-President, 1908-17. He illustrated Edith W. Robinson's *The Lay of Saint Lucundus,* 1887 in the style of E.M. Jessop (q.v.). He was living in Nottingham in 1886 and at West Bridgford from 1887 to 1892, and Ruddington in 1897.
Exhib: B; N; RA; RBA.

HODGSON, John Evan   RA   1831-1895
Landscape and historical painter. He was born in London 1 March 1831 but spent the early part of his life in Russia. returning at the age of twenty-two to study at the RA Schools. He was a good military painter and specialised in oriental scenes after travelling in North Africa. He was elected ARA in 1873 and RA in 1880, becoming Librarian and Professor of Painting in 1882 until his death.
  The Victoria and Albert Museum has a series of drawings by Hodgson for unidentified illustrations, one dated 1855. They are large figure drawings rather loosely handled in pencil, sepia, ink and watercolour.
Contrib: *The Graphic [1876].*
Exhib: B; G; L; M; RA; RE; ROI.
Colls: Cardiff; V & AM.

HODGSON, William J.   fl.1878-1903
Black and white sporting artist. He was working at Scarborough in 1878 and at Clovelly, Devon in 1891. His book illustrations for children are in the style of Caldecott and his *Punch* work, contributed most regularly from 1892-97 is in the best tradition of pen draughtsmanship.
Illus: *The Men of Ware [F.E. Weatherley, c.1884]; The Maids of Lee [F.E. Weatherley, c.1884]; There's Many A Slip Twixt Cup and Lip [F.E. Weatherley, n.d.].*
Contrib: *Punch [1892-97,1900, 1902-03].*
Exhib: L; RA, 1891-93.

HOFFLER
Artist who supplied illustrations of Cuba to *The Illustrated London News,* 1869. Possibly the same as Adolph HOEFFLER of Frankfurt who travelled to North America in 1848.

HOGG, H. Arthur
Black and white artist, specialising in horses. Contributed to *Fun,* 1901, and *Punch,* 1906-07.

EVELYN B. HOLDEN 1877-1968. 'Binnorie O Binnorie' for *The Yellow Book,* 1896

HOGGARTH, Arthur Henry Graham   1882-1964
Black and white artist and watercolourist. He was born at Kendal in 1882 and was educated at Kendal School and Keble, Oxford. He was Headmaster of Churcher's College, Petersfield, Hants., from 1911.
Contrib: *Punch [1904-06].*
Exhib: L; RA; RI.

HOLDEN, Edith Blackwell   Mrs. Smith   1871-1920
Illustrator and artist. Attended Birmingham Municipal School of Art 1885-1901 and was in the studio of Joseph Denovan Adam, Carigmill, Stirlingshire, 1891-92.
Illus: *Woodland Whisperings [1911]; Animals Around Us [1913]; Daily Bread; Three Billy Goats Gruff; Birds, Beasts and Fishes; Country Diary of An Edwardian Lady.*
Exhib: B; L; RA; SWA.
See Horne

HOLDEN, Evelyn B.   1877-1968
Illustrator. Attended the Birmingham Municipal School 1895-99. She was strongly influenced by the work of Walter Crane (q.v.) and was quite different in style from her sister Edith B. Holden (q.v.). She worked closely with her sister Violet Holden.
Illus. with V.M. Holden: *The Real Princess [B. Atkinson, 1894]; The House That Jack Built [1895].*
Contrib: *The Quest [1894-96]; The Yellow Book [1896].*
Exhib: B.
Bibl: *The Studio,* Vol.6, 1895, p.193; Vol. 13, 1898, p.195; R.E.D. Sketchley, *English Book Illus.,* 1903, pp.102, 167.
See illustrations.

HENRY JAMES HOLIDAY 1839-1927. 'The Beaver'. Illustration for *The Hunting of The Snark* by Lewis Carroll, 1876. Wood engraving

HOLDEN, Violet Mary   **1875-1960**
Illustrator. Attended the Birmingham Municipal School 1890 onwards. From 1904 she was on the teaching staff of the School for Writing and Illumination. See Evelyn Holden (q.v.).
Contrib: *A Book of Christmas Carols [1893 (Birmingham School with Arthur Gaskin)].*
Exhib: FAS.
Bibl: *The Studio*, Vol.2, 1893, pp.110, 172; Vol.6, 1895, p.193.

HOLDING, Frederick   **1817-1874**
Watercolourist. He was born in Manchester in 1817 and was the brother of H.J. Holding, landscape painter. There are two illustrations of Shakespearean subjects in the Victoria and Albert Museum collection.

HOLE, William   **ARSA**   **1846-1917**
Painter and illustrator. He was born at Salisbury on 7 November 1846 and after being educated at the Edinburgh Academy, served an apprenticeship as a civil engineer. He abandoned this career for art in 1870 and travelled in Italy, studied at the RSA and took up etching and mural painting. He is best known as an illustrator of Scottish subjects. He was elected ARSA in 1878, RSA, 1889, and died 22 October 1917.
Illus: *The Master of Ballantrae [R.L. Stevenson, 1891]; A Widow in Thrums [Barrie, 1892]; The Heart of Mid-Lothian [Scott, 1893]; The Little Minister [Barrie, 1893]; Auld Licht Idylls [Barrie, 1895]; Kidnapped [R.L. Stevenson, 1895]; Catriona [R.L. Stevenson, 1895]; Beside the Bonnie Brier Bush [1896]; Poetry of Robert Burns [1896].*
Contrib: *The Quiver [1882].*
Exhib: B; G; L; M; RA; RE; RHA; RSA; RSW.
Bibl: R.E.D. Sketchley, *English Book Illus.*, 1903 pp.92, 151; *Who Was Who 1916-28.*

HOLIDAY, Gilbert   **1879-1937**
Black and white artist. He was born in 1879 and studied at the RA Schools and served in the First War with the RFA. He worked in London and at East Molesey, Surrey.
Contrib: *The Graphic [1900-02 (military)]; Punch.*
Exhib: M; RA; RI; ROI; RSA.

HOLIDAY, Henry James   **1839-1927**
Painter, sculptor, illustrator and stained glass artist. He was born in London on 17 June 1839 of an English father but French mother. He went to Leigh's Academy, 1854, and RA Schools the same year, becoming deeply interested in the work of the Pre-Raphaelites and forming friendships with Holman Hunt and Burne-Jones (qq.v.). While at the RA he formed his own sketching club with Albert Moore, Marcus Stone (q.v.) and Simeon Solomon (q.v.). Holiday's chief importance lies in his work as a glass designer (he started his own glass-works in 1890) and as a decorative artist in murals and mosaics. He wrote extensively on techniques and invented a new form of enamel on metal in relief. He died on 15 April 1927.
As an illustrator, Holiday's fame rests on the drawings for Lewis Carroll's *The Hunting of the Snark*, 1876, which show a weird intensity of detail which is among the most disturbing aspects of Victorian literature. The source of this drawing is Pre-Raphaelite and an even more astonishing example of the artist's work was on the London market in 1977, 'Beethoven at the First Performance of His Ninth Symphony', dating from about 1860.
Illus: *The Hunting of The Snark [L. Carroll, 1876]; The Mermaid [Hans Andersen, n.d.].*
Exhib: GG; L; M; RA.
Colls: Liverpool.
Bibl: *Reminiscences*, 1914; A.L. Baldry, 'HH', *Walker's Quarterly*, 1930, No.31-32.
See illustration.

HOLL, Francis Montague 'Frank'   **RA ARWS**   **1845-1888**
Portrait painter in oils, chalk draughtsman and illustrator. He was born in London, 4 July 1845, the son of Francis Holl, RA, the engraver. He studied at the RA Schools in 1861 and won a travelling scholarship which was not useful to him and which he never completed. He worked as an illustrator in the middle 1870s, chiefly on *The Graphic*, where he gained a great reputation for social realistic subjects, such as 'Sketches in London' which were admired by Van Gogh. Some of these compositions were taken from his oil paintings and others were developed into oil paintings, Queen Victoria bought 'Home From The Sea' in 1870 and Holloway 'Newgate – Committed For Trial', 1878. Holl worked almost entirely as a portrait painter from 1878, when he was elected ARA, becoming an academician in 1883. He died from heart disease on 31 July 1888.
Illus: *Phineas Redux [A. Trollope, 1874].*
Contrib: *The Graphic [1872-83]; ILN [1881, 1884].*
Exhib: B; GG; L; M; RA; RE; RHA; RI; RSA.
Colls: Birmingham; Bristol; Leeds; Royal Collection; Royal Holloway College.
Bibl: A.M. Reynolds, *Life and Work of FH*, 1912; A.L. Baldry, *FH*; *English Influences on Vincent Van Gogh*, Arts Council, 1974-75, p.52.

HOLLAND, Frank
Contributed strip cartoons to *Fun*, 1900-01.

HOLLAND, Henry T.   **fl.1879-1906**
Figure painter and illustrator. He contributed humorous figure subjects to *Judy*, 1879-87, and to *Punch*, 1906. He worked in Bloomsbury and exhibited at the RI in 1887-90.

HOLLANDS, S.D.
Still-life and fruit painter. He made drawings and a tailpiece for *The English Illustrated Magazine*, 1888.

HOLLIDAY, F.
Figure artist, contributing to *Punch*, 1907.

HOLLOWAY, Herbert
An unrecorded artist who illustrated *Fairy Tales From South Africa*, 1908.

GEORGE PERCY JACOMB-HOOD 1857-1929. 'The Heir'. An illustration to *The Graphic*, 6 January 1906. Chalk and wash. Signed with monogram

Victoria and Albert Museum

HOLME, C. Geoffrey   **fl.1906-1914**
Artist and illustrator working at Fleet, Hants., 1911-14. He was elected RBA, 1912, and illustrated *The Old Man Book*, R.P. Stone, 1906.
Exhib: L; RBA.

HOLMES, George
Irish topographer and illustrator. He studied art in Dublin and worked as a landscape painter and engraver. He made a tour of Southern Ireland with J. Harden in 1797 and settled in London in 1799.
Illus: *Sketches of Some of the Southern Counties of Ireland...[1801].*
Contrib: *Sentimental and Masonic Magazines; Copper Plate Magazine; Antiquities of Ireland [Ledwich]; Beauties of Ireland [Brewer, 1825-26].*
Exhib: RA; RHA.
Bibl: D. Foskett, *John Harden of Brathay Hall 1772-1847*, 1974.

HOLMES, George Augustus   **RBA**   **-1911**
Genre painter. He worked at Chelsea and was elected RBA in 1869.
Contrib: *ILN [1882].*
Exhib: BI; RA; RBA.

HOLMES, R.   **fl.1870**
Caricatures in *The Household Scrapbook*, Royal Library, Windsor.

HOLT, W.G.
Figure artist. Contributed to *Punch*, 1878.

HOMERE, Stavros
Engraver and illustrator. He studied at Paris with Jules Lefebvre and

Robert Fleury. He was working at Bridgnorth, 1897, and at Étaples and Wallingford in 1907 and 1913.
Exhib: L; RA.
Bibl: *The Studio*, Vol.11, 1897, p.211, illus.

HOMEWOOD, Florence M.
Black and white artist.
Bibl: *The Studio*, Vol.8, 1896, p.227, illus.

HOOD, George Percy JACOMB-   **MVO**   **1857-1929**
Painter, etcher and illustrator. He was born at Redhill, 6 July 1857, the son of an engineer. He was educated at Tonbridge School and studied art at the Slade School and under J.P. Laurens in Paris. For most of his career Hood worked in Chelsea and followed the calling of an illustrator while continuing to paint portraits. He was attached to *The Graphic* for many years and was sent by them to Greece in 1896 and to India for the Prince of Wales's tour, 1905-06. He was a founder member of the NEA, of the Society of Portrait Painters and a member of the ROI. A very dependable and accurate artist for the story or the event, his work lacks fire. He was created MVO in 1912 and died 11 December 1929. He signs his work 〔HH〕
Illus: *Odatis, An Old Love Tale [Lewis Morris, 1888]; Lysbeth A Tale of The Dutch [H. Rider Haggard, 1900].*
Contrib: *ILN [1889-94]; Black & White [1891]; Daily Chronicle [1895]; The Graphic [1896-1911]; The Quarto [1896].*
Exhib: B; G; L; M; NEA; RA; RBA; RE; ROI.
Colls: V & AM.
Bibl: *With Brush and Pencil*, 1925.
See illustration.

Worth Knowing

E 378 - 194

EVERARD HOPKINS 1860-1928. 'Worth Knowing'. Pen and ink. Signed with initials. 9⅜in x 5¾in (23.8cm x 14.6cm)

Victoria and Albert Museum

HOOD, Sybil Eleanor JACOMB-   1870-
A sketchbook of designs for illustrations by the above artist is in the Victoria and Albert Museum collection and dated 1897 'Slade School'.

HOOD, Thomas   1799-1845
Poet and humorous draughtsman. He was born in London in 1799 and while living at Dundee during his adolescence, contributed sketches to local papers. Returning to London, he was apprenticed to an engraver called Harris, then to his uncle Robert Sands and finally to the Le Keux brothers. Hood worked on comic illustrations until his literary efforts such as 'The Song of The Shirt' made that unnecessary. He drew for *The Comic Annual*, 1830, 1834, 1837 and 1838, his humour and line being that of the punster, his drawing reflecting the savage, brutal and callous wit of the 18th century. Most biographies or notices of him neglect his work as an illustrator and even the 1869 edition of *The Works* with notes by his family, does not refer to it.
Publ: *Whims and Oddities [1826-27]; Comic Annual [1830-38]; Hood's Own [1838]; Up The Rhine [1840]; Hood's Magazine [1844]; Whimsicalities [1844]; Collected Works [1882-84].*
Colls: BM.
Bibl: Douglas Jerrold, *TH His Life and Times*, 1907; J.C. Reid, *TH*, 1963.

HOOK, Bryan   fl.1880-1923
Landscape painter and etcher. He was the son of James Clarke Hook RA (q.v.) and travelled widely in Africa. He was working at Churt, Surrey, in 1880 and at Brixham in 1923.
Contrib: *The English Illustrated Magazine [1887 (animals)].*
Exhib: L; M; RA; RI; ROI.

HOOK, James Clarke   RA   1819-1907
Landscape and portrait painter. He was born in London in 1819 and after being educated at the North London Grammar School, studied art at the RA Schools in 1836. He travelled in France and Italy between 1845 and 1848 and worked in Cornwall and the Scilly Isles. Hook specialised in his early career in history and poetic subjects and his only illustrations date from this period. He was elected ARA in 1850 and RA in 1860, dying in Churt on 14 April 1907.
Contrib: *Songs and Ballads of Shakespeare Illustrated by The Etching Club [1853]; A Selection of Etchings...Etching Club [1865, 1872, 1879].*
Exhib: B; G; L; M; RA; RE; RSA.

HOOKER, Sir Joseph Dalton   OM FRS   1817-1911
Botanist, artist and author. He was born at Halesworth, Suffolk, on 30 June 1817 and was educated at the High School and the University, Glasgow. He was surgeon and naturalist on Ross's Antarctic Expedition, 1839-43, travelled in the Himalayas, 1847-51, Syria, 1860, Morocco, 1871, and the Rocky Mountains, 1877. Director of the Royal Gardens, Kew, 1865-85 and President of the Royal Society, 1872-77. He was made KCSI in 1877 and OM in 1907. He died 10 December 1911.
Publ: *Flora of Tasmania [1860]; Genera Plantarum [1862-83]; Handbook of The New Zealand Flora [1867]; Flora of British India [1883-97].*
Illus: *The Rhododendrons of Sikkim – Himalaya [1849].*

HOOPER, William Harcourt   1834-1912
Designer and engraver. He was born in London on 22 February 1834 and was a pupil of Bolton. He worked principally for magazines, but towards the end of his life was associated with William Morris (q.v.) at the Kelmscott Press and in particular with the production of *The Golden Legend of Master William Caxton*, 1892, and the *Kelmscott Chaucer*, 1896. Hooper was afterwards employed at the Essex House Press, 1902, and was engraving from the designs of C.M. Gere (q.v.) at the Ashendene Press in 1909 for *Tutte le opera di Dante Alighieri*. He died at Hammersmith, 24 February 1912.

HOPE, Mrs. Adrian C. (née Laura Trowbridge)   -1929
Portrait and figure painter, illustrator. She specialised in children's books and worked in Chelsea 1893-1929.
Illus: *The Sparrow with One White Feather [Lady Ridley, 1908].*
Contrib: *The English Illustrated Magazine [1891-92 (fairies)].*
Exhib: L; New Gall.; P; SWA.

HOPKINS, Arthur   RWS   1848-1930
Watercolourist and illustrator. He was born in London in 1848, the brother of Gerard Manley Hopkins, poet and of Everard Hopkins (q.v.). He was educated at Lancing College and spent some years in the city before becoming an artist and entering the RA Schools in 1872. He painted in watercolour but was chiefly known by his social subjects contributed to the leading magazines. Hopkins' figure drawing is rather stiff and he has a very fussy pen line which works against him when he appears in *Punch* alongside Du Maurier. He died at Hampstead, 16 September 1930.
Illus: *Sketches and Skits [1900]; The Haunted Hotel [W. Collins].*
Contrib: *ILN [1872-98]; The Cornhill Magazine [1875, 1884]; The Graphic [1874-86]; The Quiver [1890]; Cassell's Family Magazine; Punch [1893-1902].*
Exhib: B; G; L; M; RA; ROI; RSW; FAS, 1900.
Colls: Ashmolean; BM; Exeter; V & AM.

HOPKINS, Everard   1860-1928
Watercolourist and illustrator. He was born in London in 1860, the brother of Gerard Manley Hopkins, the poet, and of Arthur Hopkins (q.v.). He worked extensively for the magazines and was a much more accomplished black and white artist than his more celebrated brother. He studied at the Slade School and was a Slade scholar in 1878 and Assistant Editor of *The Pilot*. He died on 17 October 1928. He signs his work ℰH
Illus: *A Costly Freak [Maxwell Gray, 1894]; Sentimental Journey [1910].*
Contrib: *The Graphic [1883-85]; ILN [1887-92]; The Quiver*

[1890]; Punch [1891-1904]; Black & White [1891]; Cassell's Family Magazine.
Exhib: G; M; RA; RI.
See illustration.

HOPKINS, Fritz
Contributor to *Fun*, 1900.

HORNE, Adam Edmund Maule 1883-
Figure artist. He contributed to *The Graphic*, 1908 and to *Punch*, 1913.
Colls: V & AM.

HORNE, Herbert P. 1864-1916
Architect, writer, designer and connoisseur. He was born in London on 18 February 1864. He designed a number of buildings including the Church of the Redeemer, Bayswater Road, Brewhouse Court at Eton College and part of St. Luke's, Camberwell. Horne retired to Florence in 1892 and became a writer, producing a number of notable books on the Rennaissance, among them, *Life of Leonardo da Vinci*, 1903 and of *Sandro Botticelli*, 1903. He devoted his time to collecting fine paintings and sculptures in the Palazzo Alberti, Florence, which he left to the Italian State as the Horne Museum on his death on 14 April 1916.
Publ: *Diversi Colores: Poems [1891].*
Contrib: *The Hobby Horse [1886-93].*
Exhib: RA, 1875.
Colls: BM.
Bibl: Carlo Gamba, *Il Museo Horne a Fireze*, 1961.

HORNEL, Edward Atkinson 1864-1933
Genre painter of the Scottish School. He was born in Australia in July 1864 and studied at Antwerp under Professor Verlat. He visited Japan, 1892-94, and Ceylon and Australia, 1907. He died July 1933.
Contrib: *The Evergreen [1895-96].*
Exhib: B; G; L; M; NEA; RA; ROI; RSA.

HORWITZ, Herbert A. 1892-1925
Portrait painter. He studied at the RA Schools and was working in North London until 1925. He contributed to *The English Illustrated Magazine*, 1896 (decor).
Exhib: G; L; New Gall.; RI; RBA.

HORSLEY, John Callcott RA 1817-1903
Painter and etcher. He was born on 29 January 1817, the great-nephew of Sir Augustus Callcott RA. A prolific artist, he studied at the RA Schools and concentrated on book illustration in the earlier part of his career, favouring in both oil and black and white, subjects from history or from Shakespeare. He was elected RA in 1864, became Treasurer in 1882 and was Professor of Drawing. He died at Cranbrook, 19 October 1903.
Illus: *The Beauty and The Beast, The King was in the Counting House, Puck Reports to Oberon, The Home Treasury series [Felix Summerly, 1843]; The Little Princess [1843]; Poems and Pictures [1846].*
Contrib: *The Deserted Village [1841]; Etch'd Thoughts [1844]; Gray's Elegy [1847]; L'Allegro [1849]; Songs and Ballads of Shakespeare [1853]; Etching Club; Etchings for Art Union [1857, 1865, 1872, 1879]; Moxon's Tennyson [1857]; Poems and Songs of R. Burns [1858]; A Book of Favourite Modern Ballads [1859]; The Churchman's Family Magazine [1863]; Adam's Sacred Allegories; The Poetry of Thomas Moore.*
Exhib: B; BI; G; M; RA.
Colls: Sheffield, V & AM.

HORSLEY, Walter Charles 1867-1934
Figure and landscape painter. He was the son of J.C. Horsley RA (q.v.) and worked in London. He contributed to *The Graphic*, 1880.
Exhib: B; G; M; RA; RBA; RI; ROI.

HORTON, Alice M. fl.1897-1911
Illustrator. Studied at Mount Street School of Art and contributed to *The Studio*. Working in Birkenhead, 1911.
Exhib: L.
Bibl: *The Studio*, Vol.13, 1897, pp.192-193, illus.

ARTHUR BOYD HOUGHTON 1836-1875. 'The Meeting of the Prince and Badoura'. Illustration for *Dalziel's Arabian Nights*, 1865. Pencil. 6⅞in x 5⅛in (17.4cm x 13cm)

HORTON, William Thomas 1864-1919
Black and white artist and illustrator. Born in Brussels in 1864 and was educated there and at Brighton Grammar School where he was a schoolmate of Aubrey Beardsley (q.v.). Studied architecture at the RA Schools, 1887, but abandoned architecture in 1894 for novel writing, drawing and mysticism. He was a member of 'The Brotherhood of New Life'. It is on record that Beardsley considered Horton to have some 'kind of talent' and he was clearly influenced by the younger man. His drawings are mannered, sharp and with strong contrasts of black and white, but miss the subtle nuances of Beardsley. Some of his drawings and their sources are influenced by William Blake's work.
Illus: *A Book of Images [Introduced by W B. Yeats, 1898]; The Raven, The Pit and The Pendulum [Poe, 1899]; The Way of the Soul [1910].*
Contrib: *The Savoy [1896]; Pick-Me-Up [1897]; The Dome [1898-99].*
Exhib: RA, 1890.
Bibl: *The Studio*, Vol.35, 1905-06, p.335; *Modern Book Illustrators and their Work*, Studio, 1914; Roger Ingpen, *WTH*, London, 1929.

HORWOOD, Arthur M.
Contributed comic strip illustrations to *The Graphic*, 1904.

HOSKINSON, E.
Contributed genre and figure subjects to *Punch*, 1903

HOUGHTON Arthur Boyd 1836-1875
Painter and illustrator. He was born at Kotagiri, Madras, in 1836. He studied at Leigh's and entered the RA Schools in 1854 and through Charles Keene (q.v.) was probably introduced to J.W. Whymper (q.v.) and soon afterwards began work for the Dalziels. Financial circumstances forced Houghton to concentrate on book illustrations rather than on oil paintings and ironically drove into the field of black and white one of the most original geniuses of

THE MEETING OF THE PRINCE AND BADOURA.

ARTHUR BOYD HOUGHTON 1836-1875. 'The Meeting of The Prince and Badoura'. Completed illustration for *Dalziel's Arabian Nights*, 1865. Wood engraving. 6⅞in x 5⅛in (17.4cm x 13cm)

Victoria and Albert Museum

mid-Victorian England. He was a very powerful draughtsman and as an illustrator of romance, the *Arabian Nights* for example, was the only artist on this side of the Channel to rival Doré (q.v.) in visual effects. He brought many aspects into his drawing, the composition of the Japanese print, the domestic humour of Leech and the imagination and accuracy of Rossetti and Holman Hunt. The founding of *The Graphic* in December 1869, gave Houghton a unique opportunity. He was sent to the United States for several months to draw the Americans and their way of life. The results are among his best work and perhaps the finest piece of pictorial journalism carried out by a Special Artist in the whole period. Houghton was elected ARWS in 1871 and died of progressive alcholism on 25 November 1875.

Houghton's drawings and oil paintings are tinged with Pre-Raphaelitism and often follow similar themes. A comprehensive exhibition of the artist's work was held at the Victoria and Albert Museum in May 1975.

Illus: *Dalziel's Arabian Nights, Victorian History of England [1864]; Home Thoughts and Home Scenes, Don Quixote [1865]; Ernie Elton, The Lazy Boy, Patient Henry, Stories Told to a Child, The Boy Pilgrims [1866-67]; Ballad Stories of the Affections, Foxe's Book of Martyrs, Touches of Nature [1866]; Jean Ingelow's Poems, Idyllic Pictures, Spirit of Praise, Longfellow's Poems, Golden Thoughts From Golden Fountains, A Round of Days, Savage Club Papers [1867]; Christian Lyrics, North Coast [1868]; The Nobility of Life [1869]; Novellos National Nursery Rhymes [1871]; Thornbury's Legendary Ballads [1876]; Dalziel's Bible Gallery [1880].*

Contrib: *Good Words [1862-68]; Churchman's Family Magazine [1864]; ILN [1865-66]; The Sunday Magazine [1865-71]; The Argosy, The Quiver, Every Boy's Magazine [1866]; Fun [1866-67]; Tinsley's Magazine, The Broadway [1867]; Golden Hours [1868]; The Graphic [1869-75].*

Exhib: BI; OWS; RA; RBA.

Colls: Ashmolean; BM; Fitzwilliam; V & AM; Witt Photo.

Bibl: Laurence Housman, introduction to *ABH A Selection from His Work in Black and White*, 1896; *Print Collectors' Quarterly*, Vol.10, No.1, 1923, pp.94-122; Vol.10, No.2, 1923, pp.125-148; P. Hogarth, *ABH*, V & AM, 1975; P. Hogarth, *ABH*, Gordon Fraser, 1981.

See illustrations.

FOR THE KING!

ARTHUR BOYD HOUGHTON 1836-1875. 'For The King!' Illustration to a story in *Tinsley's Magazine*, 1868. Wood engraving

HOUGHTON, Elizabeth Ellen
1853-1922

Illustrator. She worked at Warrington, Lancashire, between 1886 and 1910 specialising in children's books. Her style owed a great deal to the influence of Randolph Caldecott both in line and tinting. She signs her work E.E.H.

Illus: *Abroad for Marcus Ward (with T. Crane) [c.1881]; The Adventures of Little Man-Chester [1887].*
Contrib: *The Dome [1899].*
Exhib: L; M.
Colls: V & AM.
See illustration.

HOUGHTON, J.H.
fl .1886-1900

Cartoonist for *Judy*, 1897. He also contributed to *Fun*, 1886-92 and 1900.

HOURY, J.J.

Amateur illustrator. Contributed to *The Studio* competitions, 1896, Vol.8, p.253, illus., from Bristol.

HOUSMAN, Clemence
1861-1955

Woodcut artist. Sister of Laurence Housman (q.v.) Engraved many blocks after her brother's designs, including illustrations to *The Field of Clover, The Imitation of Christ*, 1898; *The Little Land with Songs from its Four Rivers*, 1899; *The Blue Moon*, 1904; *Maud*, 1905; *Prunella*, 1907, etc.
Exhib: Baillie Gall.
Bibl: *Print Collectors' Quarterly*, Vol.11, No.2, 1924, pp.191-204.

HOUSMAN, Laurence
1865-1959

Painter, illustrator and author. He was born on 18 July 1865 and during the 1890s established himself as a leading book illustrator, basing his style on the traditional wood engraving of the 60s. He has been described as the last of the 'facsimile' engraver-illustrators and his wish to be in this line of succession gives his work a marvellous purity of style and a freedom from *fin de siècle* mannerism. Housman was a great admirer of A.B. Houghton (q.v.) and published and edited his work in 1896. But it is not so much to this great black and white artist that Housman is in debt as to the Pre-Raphaelites and to artists such as Leighton. Housman paraphrases some of their best illustrative work, but with sufficient inventiveness and good manners to set himself well apart from the copyists. Like Rossetti, whose

LAURENCE HOUSMAN 1865-1959. 'King Bugdemagus Daughter'. Pen and ink. Signed L.H. 7⅝in x 4⅛in (19.4cm x 10.5cm)
Victoria and Albert Museum

ELIZABETH ELLEN HOUGHTON 1853-1922. Illustration to *The Adventures of Little-Man-Chester*, 1887. Pen and ink, and watercolour. 8½in x 8⅞in (21.6cm x 22.5cm)
Victoria and Albert Museum

figures he imitated, Housman was a literary man as well as an artist and his books have a pleasant cohesion in design and text which was praised by contemporaries. He remained a rather isolated and nineteenth century figure and died at Street, Somerset, at a great age in 1959. Signs:

Illus: *Jump to Glory Jane [George Meredith, 1892]; Goblin Market [Rossetti, 1893]; Weird Tales From Nothern States [1893]; The End of Elfintown [J. Barlow]; A Random Itinerary [John Davidson]; Poems [Francis Thompson]; Cuckoo Songs [Katharine Tynan, 1894]; A Farm in Fairyland [1894]; The House of Joy [1895]; A Pomander of Verses [E. Nesbit]; Sister Songs [Francis Thompson]; Green Arras: Poems by Laurence Housman [1895]; The Were Wolf, All Fellows, The Viol of Love [C.N. Robinson, 1896]; The Sensitive Plant [P.B. Shelley]; The Little Flowers of St. Francis, Of The Imitation of Christ [1898]; The Little Land [1899]; At the Back of the North Wind [Macdonald, 1900]; The Princess and the Goblin [Macdonald, 1900]; The Blue Moon [1904]; Prunella or Love in a Dutch Garden [1907]; A Doorway in Fairyland [1923 etc.].*
Contrib: *The English Illustrated Magazine [1893-94]; The Pall Mall Magazine [1893]; The Yellow Book [1896]; The Pageant [1896]; The Parade [1897]; The Dome [1897-99]; The Quarto [1898]; The Venture [1903].*
Exhib: Baillie Gall.; FAS, 1901; NEA, 1894-1901.
Colls: V & AM.
Bibl: *The Studio*, Vol.19, 1897, p.220; *The Artist*, Feb. 1898, pp.99-103, illus; *The Studio*, Winter No., 1900-01, p.19 illus; R.E.D. Sketchley, *English Book Illus.*, 1903, pp.15, 127; R. Engen, *LH, Artist and Critic series*, 1982.
See illustration.

SAMUEL HOWITT 1832-1915. 'Dooreahs of Dog Keepers Leading out dogs, Plate XXXVII'. Illustration to *Oriental Field Sports*

HOUSTON, Mary G.

Painter and decorative artist. She contributed to *The Studio* competitions (Vol,8, 1896, p.184, illus.). She was working at Chelsea, 1901-04 and exhibited at the RA.

HOWARD, Francis   1874-1954

Painter and writer. He was born 1 January 1874, great-great-grandson of Benjamin Franklin. He studied art in Paris and London and was for many years art critic of *The Sun*, and a contributor on the arts to many periodicals. He founded the International Society of Sculptors, Painters and Engravers in 1898, and the National Portrait Society, 1910. He was Managing Director of the Grafton and the Grosvenor Gallery and arranged many exhibitions at home and abroad. He contributed a series of portrait drawings entitled 'Bodley Heads' to *The Yellow Book*, 1896. He died in 1954.
Exhib: G; L; New Gall.; P.

HOWARD, George 9th Earl of Carlisle HRWS   1843-1911

Watercolourist and illustrator. He was born on 12 August 1843, a grandson of the 6th Earl of Carlisle. He studied at South Kensington and was a patron of William Morris, Edward Burne-Jones, H.J. Ford and J.D. Batten (qq.v.). He was M.P. for East Cumberland, 1879-80 and 1881-85, but was more notable for the artists and radicals that he gathered round him at Naworth Castle, Cumberland. He travelled widely in Europe and Africa and was chairman of the Trustees of the National Gallery. He died 16 April 1911.
Illus: *A Picture Song Book by the Earl of Carlisle [1910]*.
Contrib: *The English Illustrated Magazine [1895]*.
Exhib: G; L; M; New Gall.; RA; RHA; RWS.
Bibl: Virginia Surtees, *The Artist and the Autocrat*, 1988.

HOWARD, Captain Henry R.   -1895

Black and white artist. He was born at Watford, the son of a country gentleman and studied art under Ramburg in Hanover before being taught by John Leech (q.v.) to draw on the block. According to Spielmann he had the unusual practice of buying wood blocks from Messrs. Swain instead of having them supplied in his contract. He specialised in humanised beasts and birds and signed first with a manx emblem and then with a trident. He contributed to *Punch*, 1853-67 and died on 31 August 1895.

HOWARTH, F.M.   -1908

American illustrator, who died at Philadelphia on 22 September 1908. He contributed to *Pick-Me-Up*, 1889.

HOWELL, Charles A.

Amateur illustrator working in Upper Tooting. Contributed to *The Studio* competitions, Vol.15, 1899, p.144 , illus.

HOWITT, Samuel   1756-1822

Sporting artist and illustrator. He was born in 1756, the son of an old Nottinghamshire family who were squires at Chigwell in Essex. Howitt was an amateur artist who turned professional after experiencing financial troubles. He worked as a drawing-master at a private academy in Ealing and began to exhibit at the Incorporated Society of Artists in 1783. He acquired great skill as an animal draughtsman, his studies usually taken from life at the Tower of London Menagerie. He married the sister of Thomas Rowlandson, whose penwork Howitt's sometimes resembles. He died at Somers Town, London in 1822.
Illus: *Miscellaneous Etchings of Animals [1803]; Oriental Field Sports [1805-07 and 1808, AT 427]; Fables of Aesop, Gay and Phaedras [1809-11]; The British Sportsman [1812]*.
Contrib: *Ackermann's Repository [1809-10]*.
Exhib: RA, 1784-
Colls: BM: Fitzwilliam; Mellon; V & AM.
Bibl: M. Hardie, *Watercolour Paint. in Brit.*, Vol.1, 1966, p.225, illus.; J. Ford, *Ackermann 1783-1983*, 1983.
See illustration.

ARTHUR HUGHES 1832-1915. Illustration for Tennyson's *Enoch Arden*, Moxon Edition, 1866. Pen and ink. Signed with monogram
Victoria and Albert Museum

HOYNCK, C. van Papendrecht   **1858-**
Dutch history and military painter and illustrator. He was born at Rotterdam on 18 September 1858 and exhibited in Munich and Berlin from 1888 and in Paris in 1900. He contributed to *The Graphic*, 1901-04.
Colls: V & AM (prints).

HUARD, Louis   **-1874**
Illustrator of genre. He was born at Aix-en-Provence and studied art at Antwerp. He worked in London for more than twenty years and contributed regularly to magazines. Gleeson White had a low opinion of this artist because he worked for the penny journals, his drawings are not inspired but he was thought good enough to succeed Sir John Gilbert on *The London Journal* in about 1859.
Contrib: *The British Workman [1855]; The London Journal [1859]; ILN [1861-63, 1875-76 and 1881]; London Society [1863]; Churchman's Family Magazine [1863]; Cassell's Magazine [1865]; The Band of Hope Review; Belgravia [1868].*
Exhib: BI, 1857-72.
Coll: Sydney.

HUDSON, Gwynedd M.   **fl.1912-1925**
Painter and illustrator of fairy tales. She studied at the Municipal School of Art, Brighton, and worked in Hove, Sussex.
Illus: *Peter Pan and Wendy [J.M. Barrie, c.1925].*
Exhib: RA, 1912.
See Horne

HUGHES, Arthur   **1832-1915**
Painter and illustrator of genre and history, decorator and illustrator of children's books. He was born in London on 27 January 1832 and was educated at Archbishop Tenison's Grammar School, showing such ability in drawing that he was allowed to attend the Government School of Design at Somerset House at the age of fourteen and work under Alfred Stevens. Entering the RA Schools in 1847, he won the silver medal for antique drawing in 1849. Shortly afterwards he came into contact with the Pre-Raphaelite Brotherhood, who particularly admired his paintings exhibited at the RA in 1851, 1854 and 1856. He posed for Millais in 1853 as 'The Proscribed Royalist' and was much admired as an artist by John Ruskin. He worked on the Oxford Union

murals and painted a number of famous pictures including 'Home From Sea' in the Ashmolean Museum and 'The Long Engagement' in the Birmingham City Art Gallery. Hughes lived a rather withdrawn life at Kew Green and died there on 22 December 1915.

Hughes was alone among the Pre-Raphaelites in recognising that book illustration was more than the illustration itself. All his designs are conceived as part of the text and the ornament of the book and perhaps his classical study under Stevens, gave him this greater discipline. He is fond of placing his figures in a circle or a semi-

ARTHUR HUGHES 1832-1915. 'Fairies', 1855

185

ARTHUR HUGHES 1832-1915. 'The Vision of Serena'. Illustration to *The Poets of the Nineteenth Century* by the Rev. R.A. Willmott, 1857

circle, often gives them the arched neck of the Pre-Raphaelites and in his fairy drawings, the delicacy of Doyle. Although he is best-known for his black and white work, Hughes was a most brilliant colourist. He signs his work with gothic monogram Ƥ₂

Illus: *The Music Master* [W. Allingham, 1855 (with others)]; *My Beautiful Lady* [T. Woolner, n.d.]; *Enoch Arden* [Tennyson, 1866]; *Dealings with the Fairies* [George Macdonald, 1867]; *Five Days Entertainment at Wentworth Grange* [F.T. Palgrave, 1868]; *Tom Brown's Schooldays* [T. Hughes, 1869]; *Mother Goose* [1870 (with others)]; *At the Back of the North Wind* [George Macdonald, 1871]; *Ranald Bannerman's Boyhood* [George Macdonald, 1871]; *The Princess and the Goblin* [George Macdonald, 1872]; *Parables and Tales* [T. Gordon Hake, 1872]; *Story of Elizabeth* [Anne Thackeray, 1872]; *Sing Song* [Christina Rossetti, 1872]; *Gutta-Percha Willie* [George Macdonald, 1873]; *Sinbad the Sailor* [1873]; *Speaking Likenesses* [Christina Rossetti, 1873]; *Old Kensington* [Anne Thackeray, 1874-76]; *Four Winds Farm* [1887]; *Babies Classic* [1904]; *The Magic Crook* [Greville Macdonald, 1911]; *Trystie's Quest* [Greville Macdonald, 1912]; *Jack and Jill* [Greville Macdonald, 1913].

Contrib: *Poets of the Nineteenth Century* [Willmott, 1857]; *The Welcome Guest* [1858]; *The Queen* [1861]; *The Cornhill Magazine* [1863]; *Good Words* [1864-72]; *London Society* [1865-70]; *Good Cheer* [1868]; *Sunday Magazine* [1869-72], *Good Words For The Young* [1870-73]; *Novello's National Nursery Rhymes* [1870]; *The Graphic* [1887, 1889]; *London Home Monthly* [1895]; *The Girls' Own Paper.*

Exhib: B; G; GG; L; M; New Gall.; RA; RI; ROI.
Colls: Ashmolean; BM; Manchester; V & AM.
Bibl: Forrest Reid, *Illustrators of The Sixties*, 1928, pp 83-95.
See illustrations.

HUGHES, Arthur Ford   **1856-1914**
Landscape painter and painter of windmills. He was born in 1856 and studied at Heatherley's and at the Slade and RA Schools. He was working at Wallington, Surrey in 1880 and in London in 1890. He contributed headpieces to *The English Illustrated Magazine*, 1886-87.
Exhib: G; L; RA; RBA; RI; ROI.

HUGHES, Edward   **1832-1908**
Portrait and genre painter and illustrator. He worked in Kensington,

Chelsea and Notting Hill and contributed literary and historical subjects to the magazines.
Illus: *Poor Miss Finch* [Wilkie Collins, 1872 (with Du Maurier)].
Contrib: *Once a Week* [1864-66]; *The Shilling Magazine* [1865-66]; *The Sunday Magazine* [1866, 1869]; *Cassell's Magazine* [1870]; *The Argosy* [1866]; *Hurst and Blackett's Standard Library*, etc.; *ILN* [1870-75]; *The Graphic* [1871].
Exhib: BI; GG; RA; RBA.

HULL, Edward   **1823-1905**
Watercolourist and illustrator. He was born at Keysoe, Bedfordshire, the son of a farmer and was encouraged to draw by his brother, William. He illustrated a comic book *The Compliments of The Season* by Piers Shafton (pseudonym of Herbert Trevelyan), 1849, in the style of Phiz (q.v.). He contributed to *The Illustrated Times* 1849-61 and probably to *The Illustrated London News*. Between 1888 and 1891, Frederick William Cosens of Melbury Road, Kensington and "The Shelleys" Lewes, commissioned Hull to make illustrations after William Cowper. He died at Sharnbrook in 1905.
Exhib: RA from 1849; RBA.
Bibl: *The William Cowper Album by Edward Hull*, published at Southill House, Beds., 15 November 1981.

HULLMANDEL, Charles-Joseph   **1789-1850**
Artist and lithographer. He was born in London on 15 June 1789 and studied under Faraday. He travelled widely, experimented with lithography and perfected the litho-tint. He died in November 1850.
Illus: *Views of Italy* [1818, AT 167]; *The Art of Drawing on Stone* [1824]; *Ancient Castellated Mansions In Scotland* [1833].

HULME, Frederick J. or E.   **fl.1880-1940**
Flower painter and illustrator. He illustrated his own book *Flower Painting in Watercolours*, 1886, and a children's book, *The Little Flower Seekers*, c.1880.
Exhib: NEA; RA.

HULME, Frederick William   **1816-1884**
Landscape painter and illustrator. He was born at Swinton on 22 October 1816 and studied under a Yorkshire artist before going to London in 1844 to work for engravers. He died in London 14 November 1884.
Contrib: *The Illustrated London Magazine* [1853]; *The Poetical*

Works of E.A. Poe [1853]; The Book of South Wales [Mr. and Mrs. S.C. Hall, 1861]; Rhymes and Roundelayes.
Exhib: B; BI; L; RA; RBA; ROI.
Colls: Leicester; Liverpool; Montreal.

HULME, Robert C.   **fl.1862-1876**
Still-life painter and illustrator. He contributed drawings of ceremonies to *The Illustrated London News*, 1864-69 and 1873.
Exhib: RA; RBA, 1862-76.

HULSTROP, T.
Illustrator. A very competent pen draughtsman, inclined to spoil his work with heavy washes. He illustrated *The Refugees, A Tale of Two Continents*, by Conan Doyle, on its first appearance in 1891 and when reissued in 1912.
Contrib: *The Graphic [1889]; ILN [1895].*

HUMPHREY, Miss K. Maude   **fl.1883-1894**
Portrait and figure painter. She worked in London and illustrated *The Light Princess* by George Macdonald, 1894.
Exhib: B; M; RA; RBA; SWA.

HUMPHREYS, H. Noel   **1810-1879**
Numismatist, naturalist and illustrator. He was born in Birmingham on 4 January 1810 and after working for some time in Italy, returned to England in 1843 to work as an illustrator. Humphreys was a very original designer in all the fields of art that he tackled, especially in that of illustration. A master of Chromo-lithography, he produced the finest illuminated gift-books of the Victorian age under the inspiration of Italian and Flemish illumination of the Middle Ages. He died intestate on 10 June 1879.
Illus: *The Illuminated Calendar [1845]; The Coins of England [1846]; Parables of Our Lord, The Poets Pleasuance, Insect Changes [1847]; The Good Shunamite [Longman, 1847]; The Miracles of Our Lord, Maxims and Precepts of The Saviour [1848]; A Record of the Black Prince, The Art of Illumination and Missal Painting [1849]; The Book of Ruth [1850]; Sentiments and Similes of William Shakespeare [1851]; Two Centuries of Art [1852]; The History of Writing [1853]; Proverbial Philosophy [1854]; Coinage of the British Empire [1855]; Roman Anthology [1856]; Stories by an Archaeologist [1856]; River Gardens [1857]; Ocean Gardens [1857]; Rhymes and Roundelayes in Praise of Country Life [1857]; The Butterfly Vivarium [1858]; The Shipwreck [Falconer, 1858]; The Genera and Species of British Butterflies [1859]; Goldsmith's Poems [1859]; Thomson's Seasons [1859]; The White Doe of Rylstone [1858-59]; The Penitential Psalms [1861]; A Little Girl's Visit to a Flower Garden [Routledge Toy Books].*
Contrib: *The Illustrated Times [1855 (decor.)].*
Bibl: Chatto and Jackson, *Treatise on Wood Engraving*, 1861, p.599; R. McLean, *Victorian Book Design…*, 1972, pp.99-113; R. McLean, *Victorian Publishers Bookbinding in Paper*, 1983.

HUMPHRIES, A.
Illustrator. Contributing half tone work to *Punch*, 1905, in a poster style.

HUMPHRIS, William H.   **fl.1881-1916**
Figure painter and illustrator of social realism. He worked in London, Wales and Cornwall and exhibited regularly.
Contrib: *The Graphic [1905-10].*
Exhib: B; L; RA; RI; ROI.

HUNT, Alfred   **fl.1860-1884**
Painter and illustrator. He was a student of the RA Schools and practised as a painter in Yorkshire until about 1860 when he returned to London and joined the staff of *The Illustrated London News*. He contributed large comic genre subjects to the paper, mainly for Christmas numbers at first and then more regularly. His double pagers present crowds of figures, usually rather wooden but interesting for their period details.
Illus: *Life and Lessons of Our Lord [Cummings, 1864].*

HUNT, William   **fl.1864-1880**
Illustrator. He was apparently the brother of Alfred Hunt (q.v.) and worked in a very similar style, possibly for *The Illustrated London News* and *The Graphic*. A large collection of their drawings was sold at Sotheby's on 27 July 1984 and displayed at Maas Galleries. These were mostly crowded figure subjects, showing how difficult it is to tell the brothers apart.

HUNT, William Holman OM   **1827-1910**
Painter and illustrator. He was born in Wood Street, Cheapside, London, on 2 April 1827, the son of a warehouse manager. He worked for some years as a clerk to an estate agent, but received lessons from the portrait painter, H. Rogers. He also studied at the British Museum, the National Gallery and after 1844 at the RA Schools. He began to exhibit at the Academy in 1846 and in 1848-49, he joined Millais and Rossetti in founding the Pre-Raphaelite

AT NIGHT.

WILLIAM HOLMAN HUNT 1827-1910. 'At Night'. Illustration to *Once a Week*, Vol.3, 1860. Wood engraving

WILLIAM HYDE 1858-. 'An Imaged World'. Illustration for *The Yellow Book*, 1895

Brotherhood. Thereafter followed a whole series of visits abroad, first to the Continent with Rossetti in 1849 and then as his ideas became more eastern and mystical, Egypt and Syria in 1854, a long stay in the Holy Land, 1869-71, and return visits to Palestine, 1875-78 and 1892. Hunt's greatest contribution was in portraying religious truth in terms of aesthetic truth as seen by the Pre-Raphaelites. His 'Light of The World' was to become a Victorian favourite and for his 'Finding of Christ in the Temple' he was paid the handsome sum of 5,500 guineas.

Hunt was not a prolific illustrator of books, but the work that he did was outstanding and highly inventive. His 'Lady of Shalott' in the *Moxon Tennyson*, 1857, set a seal on black and white drawing for a decade and his other contributions to magazines have a directness and mystery which makes them very compelling. He was awarded the OM in 1905 and died 7 September 1910.
Contrib: *Moxon's Tennyson [1857]; Once a Week [1860]; Parables from Nature [1861]; Willmott's Sacred Poetry [1862]; Good Words [1862]; Watt's Divine and Moral Songs [1865]; Macmillan's Golden Treasury Series; Studies From Life [Hurst and Blackett's Standard Library].*
Exhib: B; FAS, 1885-86; G; GG; L; M; NEA; New Gall.; RBA; RHA; RSA; RWS.
Colls: Ashmolean; BM; Manchester; V & AM.
Bibl: W.H. Hunt, *Pre-Raphaelitsm and the Pre-Raphaelite Brotherhood*, 1905; F.W. Farrar, *WHH*, 1893; Diana Holman Hunt, *My Grandmothers and I*; Mary Bennett, *WHH*, Walker Art Gallery catalogue, 1969; Jeremy Maas, *HH & The Light Of The World*, 1984. See illustration.

HUNTER, John Young   **1874-1955**
Figure and portrait painter. He was born in Glasgow in 1874 and studied at the RA Schools. He married Mary Y. Hunter (q.v.), and became RBA in 1914.
Illus: *The Clyde [1908].*
Exhib: B; FAS, 1903, 1907; G; L; M; P; RA; RBA; RI; ROI; RWA.
Colls: Liverpool.

HUNTER, (George) Leslie   **1879-1931**
Landscape and portrait painter, illustrator. He was born at Rothesay in 1879 and studied art in San Francisco and Paris. He worked in Scotland from 1906 and contributed to *The Graphic*, 1910.
Exhib: G; L; RSA.

HUNTER, Mary Young   **fl.1900-1925**
Landscape and figure painter and illustrator. The wife of John Y. Hunter (q.v.), elected ASWA, 1901. She was working in Kensington 1902-14 and at Helensburgh, 1925.
Illus: *The Clyde [1908 (with JYH)].*
Contrib: *The Graphic [1912].*
Exhib: FAS, 1903, 1907; G; L; New Gall.; P; RA; ROI; SWA.

HURST, Hal   **1865-c.1938**
Painter, watercolourist, miniaturist and illustrator. He was born in London on 26 August 1865, the son of Henry Hurst, the African traveller. He began as an artist by drawing scenes of the Irish evictions and had work published at the age of twenty-three. He then went to America and worked as a special artist on the *Philadelphia Press* and several New York newspapers, covering the Atlantic City flood and other major events. He studied in the Art League in the United States before returning to Europe to train under Bouveret and Constant in Paris. His drawing line is strongly American and influenced by the studies of Dana Gibson (q.v.). He claimed to be the 'Artist of the man and woman about town'. RBA, 1896 and ROI, 1900.
Illus: *The Sikh War [G.A. Henty, 1894]; Sou'Wester and Sword [St. Leger, 1894]; The American Claimant [Mark Twain, 1897]*; various novels by Robert Barr, 1897.
Contrib: *Pick-Me-Up [1889-94]; Fun [1890-1901]; The Idler [1892]; St. Paul's [1894]; The Minister [1895]; Vanity Fair [1896]; The Gentlewoman; Illustrated Bits; The Pall Mall Magazine; ILN [1912-13].*
Exhib: L; New Gall.; RA; RBA; RHA; RI; RMS; RWS.
Bibl: *The Idler*, Vol. 9, pp.657-670, illus.

HUSKISSON, Robert   **1820-1861**
Fairy painter and illustrator. A totally uneducated man who made a reputation in this genre and was taken up by Lord Northwick. He produced a fairy frontispiece for *Midsummer Eve* by Mrs. S.C. Hall in 1848.
Exhib: RA.
Bibl: Beatrice Phillpotts, *Fairy Painting*, Ash & Grant, 1978.

HUTCHINSON, George W.C.   **fl.1881-1892**
Figure and domestic painter. He worked in London, 1881, and in Bristol, 1889, and contributed the illustrations to Stevenson's 'Treasure Island' in *Chums*, 1892.
Contrib: *ILN [1889]; The Ludgate Monthly [1891]; Black & White [1892]; The Idler [1892]; Chums [1892]; The Pall Mall Budget; Puck and Ariel.*
Exhib: RA; RBA; RHA.

HUTTULA, Richard C   **fl.1866-1888**
Domestic painter. He contributed to *The Broadway*, c.1867-74.
Illus: *Hurricane Harry [W.H.C. Kingstone, 1874].*
Exhib: B; L; RBA; RI.

HYDE, Edgar
Artist working in Limerick, Ireland. He contributed drawings to *The Illustrated Times*, 1859.

HYDE, William Henry   **1858-**
Portrait painter and illustrator. He was born in New York on 29 January 1858 and studied under Boulanger in Paris and exhibited at the Paris Exhibition of 1900. Hyde was a mainstay of *Harper's Magazine*, producing fine ink studies in a gently humorous vein. He appears to have lived and worked in England for some considerable time and kept close contacts with British publishers.
Illus: *An Imaged World [E. Garnett, 1894]; L'Allegro & Il Penseroso [1896]; Beyond the Dreams of Avarice [Walter Besant, 1897]; The Nature Poems Of George Meredith [1897]; London Impressions [Alice Meynell, 1898]; London in Song [Whitten, 1898 (cover and end papers)]; The Cinque Ports [Blackwood, 1901]; The Victoria County Histories: Hampshire and Norfolk [1901]; The Poetical Works of John Milton [Astolat Press, 1904].*
Contrib: *The Yellow Book [1894-95], The Pall Mall Magazine.*
Bibl: *The Studio*, June, 1894; *The Artist*, January, 1898, pp.1-6;.R.E.D. Sketchley. *English Book Illus.*, 1903. pp.39, 135.
See illustration.

HYLAND, Fred
Illustrator working in London, 1894. He contributed a drawing in the Beardsley idiom to *The Yellow Book*, 1895.
Contrib: *The Savoy [1896].*
Exhib: RBA, 1894.

ILLINGWORTH, F.W.
Figure artist. He contributed to *Punch*, 1914.

ILLINGWORTH, S.E.
Illustrator, contributing to *London Society*, 1868.

IMAGE, Selwyn   **1849-1930**
Watercolourist, illustrator and poet. Born at Bodiam, Sussex in 1849, the son of the Rev. J. Image. He was educated at Marlborough and New College, Oxford and then at the Slade School, Oxford under John Ruskin. He took Holy Orders in 1872, becoming curate at various London churches from 1875-80. He designed stained glass windows for the Paris Exhibition in 1900 and for St. Luke's, Camberwell and Morthoe Church, Devon. He was elected Master of the Art Workers' Guild in 1900 and was Professor of Fine Art at Oxford, 1910-16. He was an occasional illustrator, a designer of ex-libris, and died 21 August 1930.
Illus: *Lyric Poems [Laurence Binyon, 1894]; A London Rose and Other Rhymes [Ernest Rhys, 1894], A Little Child's Wreath [E.R. Chapman, 1895-96]; Stephania [Michael Field, 1895-96]; Poems [Vincent O'Sullivan, 1895-96]* (in each case, title and cover).
Contrib: *The Century Guild Hobby Horse [1884-91].*
Exhib: FAS.
Colls: BM; V & AM.
See illustration.

IMARGIASSI, Mario
Contributor to *The Illustrated London News*, 1889.

IMMANNEY, J.D.
A small illustration in pencil by this artist for Virgil's *Aeneid*, Book 6 and dated 1829, was sold by Sotheby's 2 May 1980.

INCE, Charles   **1875-**
Landscape painter and illustrator. He was educated at the Cowper School and at King's College, London, and studied art with Henry George Moon, the landscape painter. Ince was an accountant and a director of a family printing firm as well as an artist. He was for some years the auditor of the RBA, after being elected to it in 1912. He contributed to *Punch*, 1905-06, favouring chalk drawings reminiscent of Belcher's work.
Exhib: G; L; M; RA; RBA; RI; ROI; RWS.

INCE, Joseph Murray   **1806-1859**
Watercolourist and topographer. He was born at Presteign, Radnorshire in 1806 and became a pupil of David Cox in 1823, remaining with him for three years. Ince then lived in London and later lived in Cambridge, returning finally to Presteign in about 1835 on inheriting property there. He died 24 September 1859.
Illus: *Views Illustrating the County of Radnor [1832]; The Cambridge Portfolio [Rev. J.J. Smith, 1838-40].*
Exhib: RA; RBA.
Colls: BM; Fitzwilliam; V & AM.
Bibl: M. Hardie, *Watercolour Paint. in Brit.*, Vol.III, p.l9, illus.

SELWYN IMAGE 1849-1930. Book illustration for *The Century Guild Hobby Horse*, 1884

INGELOW, George
Brother of the poet, Jean Ingelow. He was a school friend of Charles Keene (q.v.) and at the latter's instigation, his West Indian sketches were reproduced in *The Illustrated London News*.
Bibl: Layard, *Life and Letters of Charles Keene*, 1893, p.15n.

INGLIS, Archie
Figure artist. Contributed a 'portrait' of Mr. Punch to *Punch*, 1904.

INGLIS, G.
Illustrator and book decorator. He illustrated *Ditties of the Olden Time*, c.1840, the ornamental work of a high quality, the figures less successful.

INGLIS, Lionel
Humorous figure artist. He illustrated with R.A. Sterndale *The Lays of Ind* by Aliph Cheem, Calcutta, 1883, a satire of the British Raj.

INGRAM, Master H.   **-1860**
Amateur artist. He was the son of Herbert Ingram, founder of *The Illustrated London News* and contributed illustrations to the paper in 1859 and 1860. He perished with his father in a steamer accident on Lake Michigan in 1860.

JACK, Richard   **RA**   **1866-1952**
Portrait, figure and landscape painter. He was born in Sunderland in 1866 and studied at the York School of Art, winning a National Scholarship to South Kensington in 1886. He studied at the Académie Julian in Paris, 1890-91 and won medals at the Academy Colarossi and exhibited a prize-winning portrait at the Paris Exhibition, 1900. Jack was elected an ARA in 1914 and an RA in 1920, having become RP in 1900 and RI, 1917. He was working in Montreal, Canada in 1932.
Contrib: *The Windsor Magazine; The Idler [1892].*
Exhib: G; GG; L; M; New Gall.; P; RA; RI.

JACKSON, Francis Ernest   **ARA**   **1872-1945**
Portrait painter, lithographer. He studied in Paris and was for some time drawing instructor at the RA Schools. Jackson was very influential in bringing the art of lithography back into notice by serious artists and taught it at London County Council Schools in the 1900s. He ran his own lithography class in Camberwell and with Spenser Pryse (q.v.) he ran *The Neolith*, 1907-08, a magazine with both text and illustrations lithographed. His early work is clearly influenced by Beardsley and Mucha and with its candles and ironwork and 'coquettish' delicacy, looks forward to art deco. Jackson also carried out posters for the Underground Railway. ARA, 1944.
Exhib: G, L, M; NEA; P; RA; RHA; RSA.
Bibl: *The Studio*, competition, Vol.5, 1895, illus.; Vol.18, 1899-1900, pp.282-285.

JACKSON, Frederick Hamilton   **1848-1923**
Painter, illustrator and designer. He was born in 1848 and entered his father's wholesale book business, but gave this up to follow art. He studied at the RA Schools, later becoming master in the Antique School of the Slade under Poynter and Legros (qq.v.). He founded with E.S. Burchett the Chiswick School of Art in 1880, was lecturer on perspective at South Kensington and a member of the Art Workers' Guild from 1887. He also worked on schemes for ecclesiastical decoration and designed for mosaics. He was elected RBA in 1889 and died 13 October 1923.
Illus: *The Stories of the Condottieri; A Little Guide to Sicily [1904]; The Shores of the Adriatic [1906]; The Italian Side and the Austrian Side; Rambles in the Pyrenees [1912].*
Exhib: B; G; GG; L; M; New Gall.; RA; RBA; RHA; RI; ROI.

JACKSON, J.
Illustrator, contributing drawings of Spain to *The Illustrated London News*, 1875.

JACKSON, James Grey
Artist. He wrote and illustrated *An Account of the Empire of Morocco*, 1809, AT 296.

JACKSON, Mason   **1819-1903**
Wood engraver and illustrator. He was the son of John Jackson, the wood engraver, who with W.A. Chatto published *A Treatise on Wood Engraving*, 1838. He was a pupil of his brother John Jackson 1801-48 and became Art Editor of *The Illustrated London News* in 1860 and Editor in about 1875. He was the first historian of illustrated journalism. He died in West London in 1903.
Illus: *Walton's Compleat Angler [Bohn]; Ministering Children.*

Contrib: *Cassell's Illustrated Family Paper [1857]; ILN [1876-78].*
Exhib: RA.
Bibl: M. Jackson, *The Pictorial Press*, 1885.

JACKSON, Sir Thomas Graham, Bt   **1835-1924**
Architect and draughtsman. He was born at Hampstead 21 December 1835 and was educated at Brighton College and Wadham College, Oxford. He was a pupil with Sir Gilbert Scott, 1858-61 and in 1864 became a Fellow of Wadham College, remaining at Oxford until 1880. He was a notable architect of collegiate buildings, mostly in Oxford and carried out many restorations of Tudor and Jacobean houses. He was elected ARA in 1892 and RA in 1896. He was created a Baronet in 1913 and died on 7 November 1924.
Illus: *Wadham College: Its History and Buildings [1893].*
Exhib: RA.
Colls: Ashmolean (book-plates).
Bibl: *Recollections of TGJ*, 1950.

JACOBS, Louise R.   **fl.1910-1938**
Landscape and flower painter and illustrator. She was working in London in 1910 and in Hull, 1923-25.
Contrib: *The Graphic [1915 (allegory)].*
Exhib: L; RA; RBA; RCA; RHA; RSA; SWA.

JACOMB-HOOD, Percy   See HOOD, Percy JACOMB-

JACQUE, G.H.
French figure artist. He contributed drawings to *The Illustrated London News*, 1851.

JALLAND, G.H   **fl.1888-1908**
Black and white artist specialising in equestrian subjects. He was a regular contributor to *Punch* from 1888 and was considered by M.H. Spielmann to be a natural successor to Leech with his humours of the hunting field and of sport. He did small free pencil sketches which are very lively. He signs his work ⟨monogram⟩
Illus: *The Sporting Adventures of Mr. Popple [c.1890].*
Contrib: *Punch [1888-1905]; ILN [1891-98]; The Sporting and Dramatic News [1892]; The Pall Mall Magazine; The Graphic [1908].*
Exhib: FAS, 1901.
Bibl: *Mr. Punch with Horse and Hound*, New Punch Library, c.1930.

JAMES, Gilbert   **fl.1895-1926**
Figure and still-life painter and illustrator. He was born at Liverpool and after working in commerce, turned to art and on moving to London began to contribute black and white drawings to the leading magazines. James worked mostly in a heavy art nouveau style, strong contrasts and very mannered and symbolic subjects often with an Eastern setting. His work is very variable in quality.
Illus: *Contes de Grimm [1908]; Contes de Anderson [1908]; The Rubaiyat of Omar Khayyam [1910].*
Contrib: *The Ludgate Monthly [1891]; The English Illustrated Magazine [1895-97]; The Sketch [1897]; Pick-Me-Up [1897]; The Quartier Latin [1898]; The Butterfly [1899].*
Exhib: L; NEA.
Colls: V & AM.

JAMES, The Rt. Rev. J.T. Bishop of Calcutta   **1786-1828**
Author and artist. He was born in 1786 and educated at Rugby, Charterhouse and Christ Church, Oxford. MA, 1810. He lived at Barnet, 1810-16, was Vicar of Flitton-cum-Silsoe, Bedfordshire, 1816-27, and Bishop of Calcutta, 1827-28. He published two books on art, *The Italian Schools of Painting*, 1820 and *The Flemish School* a year or so later. He learned lithography under C.J. Hullmandel (q.v.). He died of fever only six months after taking up his bishopric in Calcutta. There is a portrait of him at Christchurch, Oxford.
Illus: *Journal of a Tour in Germany, Sweden and Russia, Poland [1816, AT 16]; The Semi-Sceptic [1825]; Views in Russia, Sweden, Poland and Germany [1826-27 (liths.) AT 23].*
Exhib: RA, 1810-16.
Bibl: Houfe, Simon, 'Flitton's Artist Bishop', *Bedfordshire Magazine*, Summer 1993, pp.3-8.

JAMES, Lionel
Special Artist for *The Graphic* in Russia, 1904, and during the Russian political outrages, 1905-10. This artist is not further recorded.

JAMESON, Margaret   fl.1909-1920

Flower and portrait painter and illustrator. She worked in London and illustrated *The Vicar of Wakefield*, for Chapman and Hall in 1910 with lucid ink and watercolour drawings.
Exhib: L; RA; SWA.

JANE, Fred T.   1870-1916

Naval artist and author and originator of *Jane's The World's Warships*, 1915. He was born at Upottery, Devon, on 6 August 1870 and was educated at Exeter School. Jane was the inventor of the Naval War Game and a successful naval journalist, being correspondent for *The Engineer*, *The Scientifc American* and *The Standard*. He contested Portsmouth as Navy Interest Candidate in the General Election of 1906. Lived at Havant, Hants and died 8 March 1916.
Publ: *The Imperial Russian Navy [1900]; The Imperial Japanese Navy [1904]; All The World's Aircraft [1910]; The British Battle Fleet [1912].*
Contrib: *ILN [1892-96]; The English Illustrated Magazine [1893-95]; The Penny Illustrated Paper.*
Exhib: RA, 1894.

JANET, Gustave   1829-

Draughtsman, lithographer and illustrator. He was born in Paris in 1829 and was the brother of Janet Lange (q.v.). He worked for most of the leading French magazines, particularly *Monde Illustrée* and *Revue de la Mode*. He did a certain amount of fashion illustration and was employed by Henry Vizetelly on English publications. The latter writes of him that he 'excelled in depicting such scenes as a ball or reception at the Tuileries, his women always being very gracefully drawn although they were remarkably alike in face being in fact so many portraits of the artist's handsome wife.'
Publ: *Caricatures Politiques [1849]; Souvenirs de L'Opéra; La Mode artistique.*
Contrib: *Cassell's Illustrated Family Paper [1853]; The Illustrated Times [1855-66]; ILN [1867-71].*

JANOWSKI, C.

Illustrator of genre. A series of designs of French markets by this artist are in the Victoria and Albert Museum collection, signed and dated 1904. The book for which they were intended has not been identified.

JEHNE, Linton

Political cartoonist. He illustrated *Alice in Blunderland* by Louis Carllew, 1910.

JELLICOE, A.

Contributor to *Cassell's Illustrated Readings*, 1867.

JELLICOE, John F.   fl.1865-1903

Figure painter and illustrator. He drew mainly domestic scenes for novels and popular magazine stories.
Illus: *Queen of Beauty [Mrs. Henry, 1894]; Cherry and Violet [Miss Manning, 1897].*
Contrib: *ILN [1889]; The Sporting and Dramatic News [1890]; Good Words [1891]; St. Paul's [1894]; The Lady's Pictorial; The Windsor Magazine.*
Exhib: RBA, 1887-88.

JENKINS, Joseph John   RSA   1811-1885

Genre painter, watercolourist and engraver. He was born in London in 1811, the son and pupil of the painter D. Jenkins. He became a member of the NWS in 1842 and an Associate of the OWS in 1849 and Secretary, 1854-64. He was a considerable historian of the progress of watercolour in this country, Roget basing his *History* on Jenkins' notes. He was also the first artist to introduce the idea of private press views of exhibitions in this country. He died on 8 March 1885.
Contrib: *The Chaplet [c.1840].*
Exhib: BI; NWS; OWS; RA; RBA.
Colls: V & AM.

JENKINS, Will

Book decorator. He contributed borders and ornament to *The Connoisseur*, 1914.

JENNER, Stephen   fl.1820-1830

Amateur caricaturist. He was a great-nephew of Dr. Jenner and drew portrait figures in pencil, usually signed 'S. Jenner del.'

JENNINGS, Edward   fl.1865-1888

Landscape painter in watercolour and illustrator. He contributed to *Good Words*, 1880.
Exhib: NWS; RA; RBA; RI.

JENNINGS, Reginald George   1872-1930

Figure, portrait and landscape painter and illustrator. He studied at the National Art Training School and at the Westminster School of Art, becoming Instructor at King's College for Women and Instructor in Painting and Design to Middlesex County Council.
Contrib: *Fun [1900].*
Exhib: L; New Gall.; RA; RI.

JENNIS, Gurnell Charles   1874-1943

Black and white artist and etcher. He specialised in country and horse subjects in an individual scratchy style which he contributed to *Punch* and other magazines. He worked in London and was elected ARE in 1914.
Contrib: *Pick-Me-Up [1896]: Punch [1913-22]; The Graphic [1916].*
Exhib: L; NEA; RA; RE.
Colls: V & AM.
Bibl: *Mr. Punch with Horse and Hound*, New Punch Library, c.1930.

JESSOP, Ernest Maurice   fl.1883-1907

Painter, etcher and illustrator. He worked in London and specialised in domestic subjects and children's books.
Illus: *The Knight and The Lady [Thomas Ingoldsby, c.1880]; The Lays of St. Aloys A Legend of Blois [Thomas Ingoldsby, 1884]; The Knight and The Dragon [Tom Hood, 1885]; Misadventures at Margate, A Tale of Jarvis's Jetty [Thomas Ingoldsby, 1887]; Netley Abbey [Thomas Ingoldsby, 1889].*
Contrib: *The Girls' Own Paper [1890-1900]; The Idler [1892].*

'JEST'

Cartoonist contributing one caricature to *Vanity Fair*, 1903.

JEWITT, Llewellyn Frederick William   1816-1886

Illustrator, designer and wood engraver. He was born at Kimberworth, Yorks, on 24 November 1816, the son of T.O.S. Jewitt (q.v.). He worked on blocks for the *Pictorial Times*, *The Illustrated London News* and *Punch* and on various books with his father. He died at Duffield on 5 June 1886.
Contrib: *Good Words*, 1873 [architecture].

JEWITT, Thomas Orlando Sheldon   1799-1869

Architectural draughtsman and illustrator, engraver on wood. He was born in 1799, the son of Arthur Jewitt and worked with his father on the latter's newspaper, *The Northern Star*. He established himself at Oxford in 1838 and later moved to London where he became well-known as an illustrator of Gothic architecture and ornament. According to Chatto he was 'one of the very few who continue to combine designing and drawing with engraving'. He died in London on 30 May 1869.
Illus: *Bloxham's Gothic Architecture [1829]; Bohn's Glossary of Ecclesiastical Ornament [1846]; Glossary of Architecture [J.H. Parker, 1849]; Brick and Marble Architecture of Italy [G.E. Street, 1855]; Murray's English Cathedrals [1861-69, 7 vols.]; Baptismal Fonts [Van Voorst]; Westminster Abbey [Scott].*
Bibl: Chatto & Jackson, *Treatise on Wood Engraving*, 1861, pp.584-585.

JOBLING, Robert   1841-1923

River painter and illustrator of panoramic views. He was born in Newcastle in 1841 and trained there as a glass-maker. He attended evening classes in art and after acting as the foreman painter at a shipyard, he became a full-time artist in 1899. He was married to a painter, Isa Thompson, and died at Whitley Bay in 1923.
Illus: *Tales of the Borders [Wilson].*
Contrib: *Illustrated London Magazine [1885]; The Graphic [1889].*
Exhib: B; L; RA; RBA.

JOHANNOT, Tony   1803-1852

French illustrator. He was born at Offenbach on 9 November 1803 and was the foremost illustrator of the 1840s in France, following the romantic tradition and introducing vignette work into his books. His popularity in England was not widespread although some English editions of his illustrated volumes did appear. He died in Paris, 4 August 1852.

Illus: *Don Quixote [1836-37, English edition 1842]; The Works of Molière [1835-36]; Sentimental Journey [Sterne, 1851]; Summer at Baden Baden [Guinot, 1853].*

Contrib: *ILN [1851].*

Bibl: Percy Muir, *Victorian Illustrated Books*, 1971, pp.221-222.

JOHNSON, Alfred J.   fl.1874-1905

Figure and domestic painter and illustrator. Johnson was a Vice-President of the Camden School of Art. According to a group of letters that were on the market in 1995, he was chiefly employed by *The Illustrated London News* in drawing and engraving after Royal Academy works and many academicians gave him sittings and interviews. Worked in North London and was a very regular contributor to the magazines. He signs his work.

Illus: *Seven Little Australians [Ethel S. Turner, 1894].*

Contrib: *ILN [1874-93]; The Quiver [1890]; The Strand Magazine [1891-1905]; The Wide World Magazine.*

Exhib: L; RA; RBA; RI.

JOHNSON, C.K.

Contributor of comic genre subjects to *The Graphic*, 1887.

JOHNSON, Cyrus RI   1848-1925

Genre painter and illustrator. He was born at Cambridge on 1 January 1848 and after studying at the Perse School, worked in London as a domestic and portrait painter. He was elected RI in 1887 and died at Baron's Court, 27 February 1925.

Contrib: *The Strand Magazine [1891].*

Exhib: RA; RBA; RWS.

JOHNSON, Edward Killingworth RWS   1825-1896

Rustic artist and illustrator. He was born at Stratford-le-Bow in 1825 and taught himself to paint, taking up the career of a painter in 1863. He attended some classes at the Langham Life School but preferred to study from nature in the countryside and moved to Essex in 1871, remaining there for the rest of his life. He was a popular contributor to *The Graphic* and, in 1887, was described by that magazine as 'Our Country Artist'. In 1855, Johnson was employed to draw illustrations on the wood for the Cundall Edition of Goldsmith's *The Deserted Village*. He was elected AOWS in 1866 and a full member in 1876. He died at Halstead in 1896.

Contrib: *The Welcome Guest [1860]; London Society [1863]; The Churchman's Family Magazine; The Graphic [1874-89].*

Exhib: OWS; RA; RBA.

JOHNSON, Ernest Borough RBA ROI RI   1867-1949

Lead pencil artist and illustrator, painter, etcher, lithographer. He was born in Shifnal, Salop in 1867 and studied at the Slade School under Legros and at the Herkomer School, Bushey. Johnson was Professor of Fine Arts at Bedford College, University of London and Headmaster of the Art Department at Chelsea Polytechnic. He also taught at the London School of Art, the Byam Shaw School and the Vicat Cole School. He was a writer, a collector of antiques and porcelain and his drawings of 'Blitzed London' were acquired by the Guildhall Museum in 1945. He collaborated with Sir H. Von Herkomer (q.v.) in illustrating Thomas Hardy's *Tess* for *The Graphic* in 1891. He was elected RBA in 1896; RMS, 1897; ROI, 1903 and RI, 1906.

Publ: *The Drawings of Michelangelo; The Woodcuts of Frederick Sandys; The Techniques of the Lead Pencil; Chalk and Charcoal; A Portfolio of Rapid Studies From the Nude; The Art of the Pencil.*

Contrib: *The Graphic [1889-91]; Black & White [1891].*

Exhib: B; G; L; M; New Gall.; P; RA; RBA; RI; RSA; ROI.

Colls: V & AM.

JOHNSON, Herbert   1848-1906

Figure and landscape painter and illustrator. He worked mostly at Clapham, London, but was sent by *The Graphic* as Special Artist on the Royal Tour of India, 1875 and to Egypt in 1882. He specialised in military and ceremonial subjects.

Contrib: *The Graphic [1870-89]; The English Illustrated Magazine*

[1888]; The Daily Graphic [1890]; The Girls' Own Paper; The Windsor Magazine.

Exhib: G; L; M; RA; RBA; ROI.

Colls: Witt Photo.

JOHNSON, Patty née Townsend   fl.1880-1907

Landscape and figure painter and illustrator. She worked from Nuneaton, Warwicks and was a member of the Society of Women Artists from 1893.

Illus: *Punch and Judy [F.W. Weatherley, 1885].*

Exhib: G; L; M; RA; RBA; RI; SWA.

Bibl: White, Gleeson, 'Children's Books and Their Illustrators', *Studio Special No.*, 1897-98.

JOHNSTON, Sir Harry Hamilton FRGS   1858-1927

Painter and explorer. He was born at Kennington on 12 June 1858 and was educated at Stockwell Grammar School and King's College, London. He studied at the RA Schools, 1876-80 and was a medallist at South Kensington Schools, 1876. Johnston travelled in North Africa, 1879-80, West Africa and the River Congo, 1882-83, and led the Royal Society's expedition to Kilimanjaro in 1884. He became British Vice-Consul in the Cameroons in 1885, Consul General of The British Central African Protectorate, 1891 and Consul General at Tunis, 1897-99. He was created KCB, 1896 and GCMG in 1901, and died in Sussex on 31 July 1927.

He was a very talented painter of African scenery and animals in watercolours, which he contributed to various publications and magazines.

Contrib: *The Graphic [1889-1906].*

Exhib: L; M; RA; RWS.

Bibl: *The Story of My Life*, 1923.

JOHNSTONE, Alexander   1815-1891

Genre painter and illustrator. He was born in Scotland in 1815 and studied at the Edinburgh Academy and at the RA Schools, principally painting history subjects. He died in March 1891.

Contrib: *The Home Affections [Charles Mackay, 1858].*

Exhib: BI; RA; RBA.

JONES

Various engravings to *The Illustrated London News*, 1843 are signed 'Jones del'.

JONES, Adrian   1845-1938

Sculptor. He was born on 9 February 1845, the son of James Brookholding Jones of Ludlow and was educated at Ludlow Grammar School. He served for twenty-three years as a veterinary officer in the regular Army before devoting his time entirely to sculpture. He executed a large number of military statues and the Victoria and Albert Museum has a drawing by him for illustration. MVO, 1907. He died 24 January 1938.

Exhib: G; GG; L; RA; ROI.

Bibl: *Memoirs of a Soldier Artist*, 1933.

JONES, Alfred Garth

Landscape painter, illustrator and poster artist. He studied first in Manchester and then at the Westminster School of Art and the Slade, followed by working under Laurens and Constant in Paris, 1893 and a period at South Kensington. He was influenced by the works of Dürer and his pen drawings have a strong woodcut style that was sometimes criticised. A very versatile artist, he was as much at home in imaginative work as in political cartooning or pure decoration. He was better known in France in the early part of his career, working for *Revue Illustrée*, later establishing himself in this country as design master at the Lambeth and Manchester schools.

Illus: *The Tournament of Love [Brentano 1894]; The Minor Poems of Milton [1898]; Contes de Haute Lisse [Doucet, 1900]; Contes de la Fileuse [Doucet, 1900]; The Essays of Elia [Charles Lamb, 1902]; A Real Queen's Fairy Book; In Memoriam [Tennyson, 1903]; Goldsmith's Works; Poems and Dramatic Works of Coleridge; Journal to Stella [J. Swift]; Keats' Poems; The Voyage of Marco Polo.*

Contrib: *The Quartier Latin [1896]; The Quarto [1896-97]; The Parade [1897]; Fun [1901]; The Graphic [1910]; Strand Magazine [1910].*

Exhib: NEA; RA.

Bibl: *The Studio*, Winter No, 1900-01, p.82, illus; Vol.25, 1901-02, p.131; R.E.D. Sketchley, *Eng. Bk. Illus.*, 1903, pp.14-15, 128; *Modern Book Illustrators and their Work*, Studio, 1914.

JONES, E.A.T.
Illustrator. Four coloured ink drawings for a book, signed by this artist and dated 1871-85, were on the art market in 1976.

JONES, F.
Contributed drawings to *Small Arms*, published by the War Office in about 1900.
Coll: V & AM

JONES, George   RA   1786-1869
Military painter, Librarian and Keeper of the RA. He was born in London and became a pupil of John Jones, proceeding to the RA Schools in 1801. ARA, 1822; RA, 1824. Although not known as an illustrator, an important album of pencil drawings for Byron's *Corsair*, signed and dated 1817, was sold at Sotheby's on 14 July 1978.

JONES, George Kingston   fl.1890-1925
Illustrator. He worked in London and according to A.S. Hartrick (q.v.) was on the staff of *The Graphic*, 'established as toucher-up of photographs and general utility man'.
Contrib: *The Daily Graphic [1890]; The Windsor Magazine; The Graphic [1890-1910].*
Exhib: RA, 1896-99.
Bibl: A.S. Hartrick, *A Painter's Pilgrimage*, 1939, p.67.

JONES, G. Smetham   fl.1888-1894
Black and white artist, specialising in horses. Worked in North London and exhibited at the RA and RBA, 1888-1893.
Contrib: *Pick-Me-Up [c.1890]; Judy; St. Pauls [1894].*
Coll: Witt Photo.

JONES, Maud Raphael   fl.1889-1902
Landscape and rustic painter. She worked at Bradford and exhibited in London, 1889-93.
Colls: Witt Photo (illus.).

JONES, Owen Carter   1809-1874
Architect, designer and topographer. He was of Welsh descent and born in Thames Street, London on 15 February 1809. For six years he was a pupil of Lewis Vulliamy, the architect, and attended the RA Schools, 1830. Jones made extensive visits to France, Italy, Egypt and Spain in 1836, beginning a book on the Alhambra which was not completed for nine years and cost £24 a copy! He had also become interested by Sir Henry Cole's attempts to improve industrial design and contributed many illustrations to the latter's *Journal of Design and Manufactures*, 1849. He supervised the decoration of the Great Exhibition in 1851 and of the Crystal Palace at Sydenham, 1852. Jones was influential in opening up new possibilities for lithography and for applying new styles to wall-papers and textiles. He died on 19 April 1874.
Illus: *Alhambra [1836-42]; Ancient Spanish Ballads [J.G. Lockhart, 1841, AL 325]; Book of Common Prayer [1845, AL 226]; Gray's Elegy [1846, AL 227]; Flowers and their Kindred Thoughts [1848]; Song of Songs [1849, AL 229]; One Thousand and One Initial Letters [1862].*
Exhib: RA, 1831-61.
Colls: BM.
Bibl: Chatto & Jackson, *Treatise on Wood Engraving*, 1861, p.599; Ruari McLean, *Victorian Book Design*, 1972, pp.73-98, illus.; P. Muir, *Victorian Illustrated Books*, 1971, pp.154-155.

JONES, Sydney Robert   1881-1966
Painter, etcher and illustrator. He was born on 27 February 1881 and studied art at the Birmingham School. A very accomplished pen artist, he made tours of England, France, Belgium and Holland and published the results in a series of travel books. He worked for *The Studio* in 1912-13, designing for their special numbers, and was associated with Messrs. J. Connell, publishers. He died at Wallingford in 1966.
Illus: *Old English Country Cottages [1906]; The Charm of the English Village [P.H. Ditchfield, 1908]; The Manor Houses of England [1910]; Old Houses in Holland; Cottage Interiors and Decoration; On Designing Small Houses and Cottages; The Village Homes of England [1912]; England in France [C. Vince, 1919]; Posters and Their Designers; Art and Publicity; Touring England; Old English*

Household Life; London Triumphant; Thames Triumphant.
Contrib: *The Sphere.*
Exhib: L; RA; RI.
Colls: V & AM.
Bibl: *Modern Book Illustrators and their Work*, Studio, 1914.

JONES, T.W.
Figure artist. Contributed drawings to *Punch*, 1904.

JONES, Thomas   fl.1836-1848
Caricaturist. He was active in the early Victorian period, drawing very much in the style of Bunbury.
Colls: Witt Photo.

JONES, V.
Contributor to *The Illustrated London News*, 1858.

JONES, W.L.
He contributed genre subjects to *Good Words*, 1873. He may be identified with the sculptor, 'W.L. Jones' exhibiting at the RA in 1852-55.

JOPLING, Joseph Middleton   1831-1884
Painter, portraitist and caricaturist. He was self-taught and was elected ARI, 1859. He married Louisa Goode, the first woman to be elected RBA, 1902. He contributed two cartoons to *Vanity Fair*, 1883.

JOSEPH, George Francis ARA   1764-1846
Portrait and miniature painter. He entered the RA Schools in 1784 and won the gold medal, 1792. He was elected ARA in 1813 and died in Cambridge in 1846. He designed some illustrations for historical books.
Colls: BM.

JOUQMART, W.
Contributor of social subjects to *Punch*, 1900.

JOY, Thomas Musgrove   1812-1866
Historical painter and book illustrator. He was born at Boughton Monchelsea, Kent, in 1812 and studied art with Samuel Drummond ARA. He moved to London and became the teacher of John Philip RA, and was patronised by Queen Victoria, 1841-43. His illustrative work makes use of vignettes and elaborate borders. He died in London, 7 April 1866.
Exhib: RA; RBA, 1832-
Colls: York.

JUNGMAN, Nico W.   RBA   1873-1935
Dutch artist who became a British subject, painter and illustrator. He was born in Amsterdam in 1873 and was apprenticed at the age of twelve to a church decorator. He then attended the Academy of Plastic Art in Amsterdam and won a scholarship to London to study its life. He settled in London but continued to paint Dutch scenes, much of the illustrative work being in large chalk drawings with pastel colours and very sculptural in effect. He is much influenced by the Japanese colour print, but also by Millet and his sympathy for the peasant at work. He was a close friend of the artist Charles W. Bartlett with whom he worked.
Illus: *Holland [Beatrix Jungman, c.1905]; Norway [Beatrix Jungman, c.1905]; Normandy [G.E. Mitton, c.1905]; The People of Holland [c.1905].*
Contrib: *The Parade [1897].*
Exhib: B; L; M; RA; RBA; RHA.
Bibl: *Some Drawings by Mr. NJ*, Studio, Vol.13, 1898, pp.25-32, illus.

JUSTYNE, Percy William   1812-1883
Landscape painter and book illustrator. He was born at Rochester, Kent in 1812 and was principally a contributor to the magazines. Justyne specialised in architectural illustration and particularly church architecture, gothic buildings and the monuments of the East and Spain, where he lived from 1841-48.
Illus: *History of Greece [Smith]; Biblical Dictionary [Fergusson]; Handbook of Architecture [C. Kingsley]; Christmas in the Tropics.*
Contrib: *Cassell's Illustrated Family Paper [1857]; Churchman's Family Magazine [1863]; The Graphic [1873]; ILN; Floral World.*
Exhib: RA; RBA.
Colls: Nottingham.

KAPP, Edmond Xavier   1890-1978

Painter, draughtsman and caricaturist. He was born in London on 5 November 1890, and was educated at Owen's School and Christ's College, Cambridge before studying art in Paris and Rome. Although Kapp's training dates from before the First World War, in which he served with the BEF, his popularity as a caricaturist stemmed from his first one man show in London, 1919. He became one of the leading artists of the 1920s in this field, drawing most of the writers, musicians, artists and actors of the decade and publishing a number of books. He subsequently turned his attention to more serious painting and particularly abstract work. He died on 31 October 1978.

Illus: *Personalities, Twenty-Four Drawings [1919]; Reflections, Twenty-Four Drawings [1922]; Ten Great Lawyers [1924]; Minims, Twenty-Eight Drawings [1925]; Pastiche, A Music Room Book [1926 (with his wife)]; publications of original lithographs from 1932; The Nations at Geneva [1934-35, twenty-five portraits on stone].*

EDMOND XAVIER KAPP 1890-1978. Caricature of Wyndham Lewis at the Café Royal, 1914. Ink and watercolours, chalk. 10¾in x 8in (27.4cm x 20.5cm)   Victoria and Albert Museum

Contrib: *The Sketch; Trimblerigg [L. Housman, 1924]; The Law Journal [1924-25].*
Exhib: Leicester Gall.; Wildenstein.
Colls: Ashmolean; B; BM; Manchester; V & AM.
Bibl: *Strand Magazine,* 1914, p.567; Charles Spencer, 'From Caricature to Abstraction', *Studio,* June, 1961.
See illustration.

KAUFFER, Edward McKnight   1890-1954

Artist, poster-designer and illustrator. He was born at Great Falls, Montana, USA and educated at American public schools. He began his career as a theatrical scene painter, attending evening classes at the Art Institute, Chicago and then studying at Munich. He spent two years in Paris before settling in London in 1914, making his name there with his poster work for the Underground Railways. He was the first poster-artist in Britain to design advertisements where the visual and the verbal were totally integrated. He worked extensively for the private presses but his book illustration is less well-known. He became a member of the London Group, 1916.

Illus: *Anatomy of Melancholy [Robert Burton, Nonesuch, 1925]; Benito Cereno [Herman Melville, Nonesuch, 1926]; Elsie And The Child [Arnold Bennett, Curwen Press, 1929]; Don Quixote [Cervantes, Nonesuch, 1930]; Marina [T.S. Eliot, Ariel, 1930]; The World in 2030 A.D. [The Earl of Birkenhead, 1930].*
Contrib: *The Broadside [Harold Monro, Poetry Bookshop].*
Exhib: NEA.
Colls: V & AM.
Bibl: EMcKK, *The Art of the Poster,* 1924.
See Horne

KAY, J. Illingworth   fl.1894-1918

Designer of covers and title-pages. He worked for Lane's Bodley Head and exhibited at the RA, 1917-18.
Illus: *Orchard Songs [Norman Gale, 1894]; Poems [Richard Garnett, 1894]; Romantic Professions [1894]; The Lower Slopes [Grant Allen, 1895].*
Contrib: *The Yellow Book [1896 (cover)].*

KAY, John   1742-1826

Caricaturist and miniaturist. He was born in Dalkeith in 1742 and apprenticed to a barber and print-seller at Edinburgh. In 1782, a customer left him a legacy which enabled him to live independently as an artist. From that time until his death he produced nine hundred portrait caricatures and some political squibs. His drawings are in profile and spindly, rather like the work of Robert Sayer, but they were considered good likenesses and cover the whole of Edinburgh Society. *Kay's Edinburgh Portraits* were issued in 1837-38 and a further *Series of Original Portraits by John Kay, Edinburgh,* followed in 1877.
Colls: Witt Photo.
Bibl: Hilary & Mary Evans, *John Kay of Edinburgh,* 1977.

KEARNAN, Thomas   fl.1821-1850

Watercolourist and draughtsman. He worked in London and contributed to *Public Works of Great Britain,* 1838, AL 410. NWS, 1837.
Exhib: NWS; RA; RBA.

KEELING, William Knight   RI   1807-1886

Portrait painter and watercolourist. He was born at Manchester in 1807 and was apprenticed to a wood-engraver there before moving to London to work under the portrait painter, W. Bradley. He returned to Manchester in 1835 and helped to found the Manchester Academy of Fine Arts of which he was President, 1864-77. He was elected AWS in 1840 and NWS the following year. Keeling made a voyage to Spain in middle life and died at Manchester 21 February 1886.
Contrib: *The Chaplet [1840].*
Exhib: BI; M; RA.
Colls: V & AM.

KEENE, Charles Samuel   1823-1891

Black and white artist, illustrator and etcher. He was born at Hornsea, London in 1823 and when a child moved with his family to Ipswich, where he remained until his father's death in 1838. He was articled first to a solicitor and then to Pilkington, the architect, finally being articled to Charles Whymper, the wood-engraver. After leaving

CHARLES SAMUEL KEENE 1823-1891. 'A Soft Answer'. Illustration for *Punch*, 1879. Pen and ink. Signed with initials. 5in x 7½in (12.7cm x 19.1cm)

Whymper in 1852, he set up on his own in the Strand and worked for various publishers, especially for the nearby office of *The Illustrated London News*. Keene began to draw for *Punch* in 1852, a connection that was to last until the day of his death and bring him great celebrity. A rather withdrawn and slightly bohemian man, he relied principally on urban social life for his subjects, often taking his characters from the alley-way and the market where Du Maurier's folk would not be seen! He relied heavily on his friends for amusing situations and was supplied with many by his friend Joseph Crawhall (q.v.).

Keene's career as a draughtsman runs through several phases. His earlier works for Thomas Barrett's *Book of Beauty*, 1846, show an almost Georgian burlesque and caricature. By the 1850s he was under the influence of Menzel and develops a rather hard and Germanic drawing line, which gradually softens during the 1860s. In his last drawing, 'Arry on the Boulevard', published in *Punch* in 1891, his economy of line is such that he might almost be compared to the French draughtsmanship of a master like Lautrec. A memorial exhibition of the artist was held at the Fine Art Society in March 1891. He signs his early work: ⊂K and his later work: ⫝̸

Illus: *Robinson Crusoe [1847]; Green's Nursery Annual [1847]; The Wooden Walls of Old England [1847]; The De Cliffords [Mrs. Sherwood, 1847]; The White Slave [1852]; A Story with a Vengeance [1852]; Marie Louise [1853]; The Giants of Patagonia [1853]; The Book of German Songs [W.H. Dulcken, 1856]; A Narrative of the Indian Revolt [Sir Colin Campbell, 1858]; The Boy Tar [Mayne Reid, 1860]; The Voyage of the Constance [1860]; Jack Buntline [W.H. Kingston, 1861]; Sea Kings and Naval Heroes [1861]; The Cambridge Grisette [H. Vaughan, 1862]; Tracks for Tourists [F.C. Burnand, 1864]; Mrs. Caudle's Curtain Lectures [1866]; Roundabout Papers [W.M. Thackeray, 1879]; The Cloister and The Hearth [Reade, 1890].*

Contrib: *Willmott's Sacred Poetry [1862]; Ballads and Songs of Brittany [1865]; Legends and Lyrics [A.A. Proctor, 1866]; Touches of Nature [1867]; Thornbury's Legendary Ballads [1876]; Passages From Modern English Poets [1876]; ILN [1850-56]; Punch [1852-*

CHARLES SAMUEL KEENE 1823-1891. 'The Struggle'. Pen and ink. Signed with initials. 5½in x 4½in (14cm x 11.4cm)

91]; Once a Week [1859-65 & 1867]; Good Words [1862]; The Cornhill Magazine [1864]; London Society [1866-70].
Exhib: FAS.
Colls: Ashmolean; BM; Fitzwilliam; Newcastle; V & AM.
Bibl: G.S. Layard, *The Life and Letters of CSK*, 1892; G.S. Layard, *The Work of CK*, 1897; F.L. Emanuel, *CK*, Print Collectors' Club, 1935; D. Hudson, *CK*, 1947; Simon Houfe, 'Extracting the Honey', *ABMR*, Feb. 1984, pp.44-49; Simon Houfe, *Charles Keene*, Christie's exhibition, 1991.
See illustrations.

KEENE, Thomas
Relation or follower of Charles Keene (q.v.). There are some prints of his work in the Witt Photo Library.

KELLER, Arthur L.
Illustrator of Winston S. Churchill's only novel *Mr. Crewe's Career*, 1908.

KELLY, A.D.
Figure artist. He contributed Irish subjects such as the Land League unrest and the detention of Parnell to the *Illustrated London News*, 1881-83.

KELLY, Robert George Talbot   RBA RI   1861-1934
Landscape painter and illustrator. He was born at Birkenhead on 18 January 1861, the son of R.C. Kelly, the landscape painter. He was educated at Birkenhead School before studying art with his father. He specialised in oriental scenery and from 1882 onwards travelled abroad in Morocco, Egypt and Burma, undertaking the illustrations of travel books for Messrs. Black in the 1900s. He became RI in 1907, RBA, 1893 and died on 30 December 1934.
Illus: *Fire and Sword in the Sudan [Sir R.C. Slatin, 1896]; Egypt Painted and Described [1902]; Burma [1905]; Peeps at Many Lands [1908].*
Exhib: B; FAS, 1902, 1904, 1916, 1924; G; L; M; RA; RBA; RHA; RI; RSA.

KELLY, Tom   fl.1887-1901
Landscape painter, topographer and flower illustrator. He was working in Newmarket, 1888, Bedford in 1892 and London in 1901. He travelled to South Africa in 1890-91 and exhibited at the New Gallery.
Contrib: *The English Illustrated Magazine [1887-91, 1896].*

KEMBLE, Edward Windsor   1861-
American magazine illustrator. He was born at Sacramento on 18 January 1861 and is associated with pen drawings of the Deep South, a similar sort of realism to that of F. Remington (q.v.). He is included here as the illustrator of *Mark Twain's Library of Humour, The Adventures of Huckleberry Finn*, etc., Chatto, 1897. Pennell considers him a fine but uneven draughtsman, tending to carelessness.
Bibl: J. Pennell, *Pen Drawing and Pen Draughtsmen*, 1894, pp.236-240.

KEMP, Percy E.   fl.1889-1895
Black and white artist showing the strong influence of Phil May.
Contrib: *Pick-Me-Up [1889]; Daily Chronicle [1895].*

KEMP-WELCH, Lucy Elizabeth   RI   1869-1958
Horse and animal painter. She was born at Bournemouth in 1869 and studied at the Herkomer School, Bushey, Herts. She was Principal of the Kemp-Welch School of Painting at Bushey, was elected RBA, 1902 and RI, 1907. She was President of the Society of Animal Painters in 1914 and had paintings purchased by the Chantrey Bequest in 1897 and 1917. A one man exhibition of her work was held in London in 1938.
Illus: *Round About A Brighton Coach Office [M.E. King, 1896]; The Making of Mathias [1897].*
Exhib: B; FAS, 1905; G; L; M; RA; RBA; RCA; RHA; RI; ROI; RSA; RWA; SWA.
Bibl: *The Studio*, Winter No., 1900-01, p.67. illus.; *LK-W*, Antique Collectors' Club, 1976, 1996.
See illustration.

KENNARD, Edward   fl.1883-1888
Sports illustrator. He contributed illustrations of Highland sports to *The Illustrated London News*, 1883-86 and to *The Graphic*, 1888.
Contrib: *ILN [1883-86].*

KENNEDY, Theodosia   'Theo'
Amateur caricaturist. She illustrated the amusing album book *Visit of a London Exquisite To His Maiden Aunts in the Country*, published by Wm. Kent & Co., London, 1859. She is mentioned in the unpublished diary of Dawson Watson of Settle.

KENNION, Edward   FSA   1744-1809
Landscape painter and drawing-master. He was born in Liverpool in 1744 and travelled to Jamaica and Cuba as a young man from 1762 to 1769. He returned to England and worked in Bath, London and Malvern, making frequent visits to the North-West and the Lakes. He was a member of the Society of Artists and died in London in 1809.
Publ: *Elements of Landscape and Picturesque Beauty [1790]; An Essay on Trees in Landscape [1815, AL 147].*
Exhib: RA; SA.

KEPPEL, William Coutts, Viscount Bury and 7th Earl of Albermarle   1832-1894
Artist and politician. He was born on 15 April 1832, the only son of the 6th Earl of Albermarle whom he succeeded in 1876. He exhibited in London from 1878-83 while living in Nuremburg. He died 28 August 1894.
Contrib: *Passages from Modern English Poets [1862].*

KERR, Charles Henry Malcolm   RBA   1858-1907
Portrait and landscape painter. He worked in London and was elected RBA in 1890. He died at Campden Hill, Kensington on 27 December 1907.
Illus: *The Curse of Carne's Hold [G.A. Henty, 1890].*
Exhib: L; M; NEA; RA; RBA; RHA; RI; ROI.

KERR, Henry Wright   RSA RSW   1857-1936
Genre and landscape painter, and character painter. He was born at Edinburgh in 1857 and studied in Dundee and at the RSA Schools. He travelled in Ireland in 1888 and was elected ARSA in 1893 and RSA in 1909. He died on 17 February 1936.
Illus: *Reminiscences of Scottish Life and Character [Dean Ramsay]; Annals of the Parish [M.R. Mitford, 1911]; The Lighter Side of Irish Life [G.A. Birmingham, 1911]; The Last of the Lairds [J. Galt, 1926].*
Exhib: G; L; RA; RI; RSA; RSW.
Colls: Dundee.

KERR-LAWSON, James   1864-1939
Figure and landscape painter, mural painter and lithographer. He was born at Anstruther, 28 October 1865, and was taken to Canada in early childhood. He was educated in Rome and Paris and studied art with Lefevbre and Boulanger, before returning to live in Chelsea. According to Hartrick he was one of the early experimenters in the revival of lithography in the 1900s. He contributed to F.E. Jackson's *The Neo-Lith*, 1907-08. He carried out the decorations to the Senate in Ottawa and in later life retired to Italy.
Exhib: B; G; L; M; RBA; ROI.

KEYL, Frederick Wilhelm   1823-1871
Engraver and animal illustrator. He was born at Frankfurt on 17 August 1823, coming to London in 1845. He studied under Landseer and Verboeckhoven and began exhibiting in 1847. Several of his works were bought for the Royal Collection. He died 5 December 1871.
Illus: *Echoes of An Old Bell [The Hon. Augusta Bethell, 1865]; Homes Without Hands [Rev. J.G. Wood]; Featherland: Or How The Birds Lived at Greenlawn [G.M. Fenn, 1877].*
Contrib: *ILN [1864-69]; Churchman's Family Magazine [1864]; Beaton's Annual [1866]; Nature and Art [1866-67]; Gatty's Parables From Nature [1867].*
Exhib: BI; RA.

KIDD, John Bartholomew   fl.1807-1858
Contributor to *The Antiquarian and Topographical Cabinet*, 1808.

LUCY KEMP-WELCH 1869-1958. Original drawing for an illustration

KIDD, Joseph Bartholomew   RSA   1808-1889
Genre and landscape painter. He was born in Edinburgh in 1808 and
studied with Thomson of Duddingston. He was a founder member of
RSA in 1829, resigning from the institution when he settled in
London in 1836. He practised as a drawing master at Greenwich, and
died in May 1889.
Illus: *The Miscellany of Natural History [Sir T.D. Lauder, 1833];
West Indian Scenery [1838-40, AT 686].*
Exhib: BI; RSA.

KILBURNE, George Goodwin   RI ROI   1839-1924
Painter, watercolourist, engraver and illustrator. He was born in
Norfolk on 24 July 1839 and was apprenticed to the Brothers Dalziel
whose niece he married. He turned from engraving to painting and
specialised in hunting scenes and genre subjects set in the 18th
century. A very talented draughtsman, Dalziel records of his
apprentice work that it was 'so perfect, that it was published with the
set to which it belonged'. He died in London in September 1924. RI,
1868 and ROI, 1883.
Illus: *Thackeray's Ballads [Cheap Illus. Edit., 1894].*
Contrib: *ILN [1873]; The Graphic [1873-77 (domestic &
theatrical)]; The Cornhill Magazine [1884].*
Exhib: B; G; L; M; RA; RBA; RI; ROI.

KIMBALL, Katherine   ARE   1866-1949
Painter and illustrator. She was born in New England and educated
at Jersey Ladies' College and at the National Academy of Design,
New York, 1897. She specialised in pen illustrations of towns and
cities for travel books. She was elected ARE, 1909.
Illus: *Paris [Okey, 1904]; Brussels [Gilliatt Smith, 1906];
Canterbury [Sterling Taylor, 1912]; Rochester [1912].*
Contrib: *The Century; The Studio; The Artist; Gazette Des Beaux
Arts, The Queen.*
Exhib: L; RA; RE.
Colls: BM; Congress Library; V & AM.

KING, Edward R.   fl.1883-1924
Genre painter and illustrator. He was probably the brother of
Gunning King (q.v.) and began contributing to *The Illustrated
London News* in 1883. He was one of the group of artists who treated
both rural and metropolitan subjects in a new and realistic way,

giving through sensitive drawing and minute hatching, a sympathetic
view of poor Londoners and country folk. He was one of the artists
much admired by Van Gogh. He was still working at East Molesey,
Surrey in 1924. He became NEA in 1888.
Contrib: *ILN [1883-87]; The Pall Mall Magazine; Punch [1905].*
Exhib: B; G; L; M; NEA; RA; RBA; ROI.
Colls: Witt Photo.
Bibl: *English Influences on Vincent Van Gogh,* Arts Council, 1974-75.

KING, Gunning   1859-1940
Painter, etcher and illustrator. He studied art at the South Kensington
and the RA Schools and became a member of the NEA in 1887. King
was one of the most vigorous illustrators of rural life to emerge
during the eighties, combining great human interest with fine
quality penwork. He was an early advocate of chalk drawings and
in his figure subjects owes something to the freedom of
Charles Keene (q.v.). He worked for most of his life at Petersfield,
Hants.
Contrib: *ILN [1882-99]; The Graphic [1883]; The Windsor
Magazine; Punch; The Sketch; The Sporting and Dramatic News
[1896]; The English Illustrated Magazine [1896]; Pick Me-Up
[1897]; The Quiver [1897].*
Exhib: B; G; GG; L; M; NEA; RA; RBA; RI; ROI.
Colls: V & AM; Witt Photo.
Bibl: R.G.G. Price, *A History of Punch,* 1955, p.158.

KING, H.W.
Illustrator. Contributed drawings of animals to *The Graphic,* 1871.

KING, Henry John Yeend   RBA RI   1855-1924
Landscape painter and illustrator. He was born in London on 25
August 1855 and was apprenticed to Messrs. O'Connors, glass
painters of Berners St. He left after three years and studied painting
with William Bromley, RBA, later going to Paris and working with
Bonnat and Cormon. He began to exhibit at the RA in 1876 and was
elected RBA in 1879, RI in 1887 and VPRI in 1901. King's work for
the magazines is usually rural or domestic in character. He died on
10 June 1924.
Contrib: *The Graphic [1880-82]; ILN [1887-94].*
Exhib: B; G; GG; L; M; RA; RBA; RHA; RI.
Colls: Liverpool; Reading; Witt Photo.

KING, JESSIE MARION (MRS E.A. TAYLOR) 1876-1949. 'Percival and the Damsel',
original drawing for the illustration in *The High History of the Holy Graal*, 1906

KING, Jessie Marion (Mrs E.A. Taylor)　　　　　**1876-1949**

Painter and illustrator. She was born in 1876 and studied at the Glasgow School of Art, where she won a travelling scholarship to France and Italy, in the latter coming under the influence of Botticelli's paintings. She was considered unsuccessful as a student because of her individuality, 'language of line' and imaginative sense, *The Studio*, Vol. 26, p.177. Her style is inseparable from the angular *art nouveau* concepts of the Glasgow School and her decorative work in books is often the counterpart of C.R. Mackintosh's applied art. A great deal of her work was done on parchment, built up with carefully drawn thin pen lines and delicately coloured and tinted. Most of her designs have elaborate borders of stylised birds or foliage, suggesting metal-work rather than the printed page. It is not surprising to discover that she was in fact a jewellery designer and a painter of murals. Miss King lived in

Paris from 1911 to 1913 and then at Kirkcudbright after her marriage to the artist E.A. Taylor. She died in 1949.

The drawings have become extremely popular in recent years and are among the more sought after illustrations. Sotheby's held an important sale of her work at the Charles Rennie Mackintosh Society in Glasgow on 21 June 1977, when the contents of her studio were auctioned by request of her daughter.

Illus: *The Light of Asia [Arnold, 1898]; Jephtha [G. Buchanan, 1902]; The High History of The Holy Graal [trans. by S. Evans, 1903]; The Defence of Guenevere [William Morris, 1904]; Comus [John Milton, 1906]; Poems of Spenser [intro. by W.B. Yeats, n.d.]; Budding Life [1906]; Poems of Shelley [1907]; The Legend of Flowers [P. Mantegazza, 1908]; Dwellings of An Old World Town [1909]; The Grey City of the North [1910]; The City of the West [1911]; The Book of Bridges [E. Ancambeau, 1911]; Ponts de Paris*

RUDYARD KIPLING 1865-1936. Initial letter for *The Just So Stories For Little Children*, 1902

[E. Ancambeau, 1912]; Songs of the Ettrick Shepherd [James Hogg, 1912]; Isabella and The Pot of Basil [John Keats, 1914]; A House of Pomegranates [Oscar Wilde, 1915]; The Little White Town of Never-Weary [1917]; Good King Wenceslas [1919]; L'Habitation Forcée [Rudyard Kipling, 1921]; How Cinderella Was Able To Go To The Ball [1924]; Mummy's Bedtime Story Book [1929]; Whose London [c.1930]; Our Lady's Garland [Arthur Corder, 1934]; Kirkcudbright [1934]; The Fringes of Paradise [Florence Drummond, 1935]; The Enchanted Capital of Scotland [I. Steele, 1945]; The Parish of New Kilpatrick [J. McCardel, 1949].
Contrib. (covers): International Library Editions, *The Marriage Ring [Jeremy Taylor, 1906]; Everyman [1906].*
Exhib: G; L; RHA; RSA; RSW; SWA.
Colls: V & AM.
Bibl: *The Studio*, Vol. 26, 1901-02, p.177, illus; Vol. 36, 1906, pp.241-246, illus; Vol. 46, 1909, pp. 148-150, illus.; *The Studio Yearbook*, 1909, 1911, 1912, 1913, 1919; *Modern Book Illustrators and their Work*, Studio, 1914; *JMK*, Scottish Arts Council Exhibition Cat., 1971; The Last Romantics, Barbican Gallery cat., 1989, p.202. See illustration.

KING, W.H. fl.1808-1836
Topographical illustrator. He worked at Edmonton and contributed to *Brittons Beauties of England and Wales*, 1808.
Exhib: RBA, 1836.

KINGSFORD, Florence fl.1899-1903
Figure and domestic painter. She worked in West London from 1899 and 1902 and designed initial letters for the Essex House Press.
Decor: *Tam O'Shanter [Essex House, 1902]; Rime of The Ancient Mariner [Essex House, 1903].*
Exhib: RA.

KINGSLEY, Charles 1819-1875
Author and amateur artist. After leaving Cambridge in 1842, young Kingsley worked on a life of St. Elizabeth of Hungary, illustrated by his own pen and ink drawings. This was not intended for publication but as a present for his wife. He continued to sketch on holidays after

his marriage and, as a lecturer, illustrated all his points with chalk on a blackboard. In 1855 he tried to establish drawing classes for artisans at Bideford and later on was consulted by C.H. Bennett and Frederick Shields (qq.v.) over their editions of Bunyan. He died in 1875.
Illus: *The Heroes [1856 (eight illus. by the author)].*
Bibl: *CK His Letters and Memories,* Edited by His Wife, 1877.

KIPLING, John Lockwood 1837-1911
Architect, sculptor and illustrator. He was born at Pickering, Yorks, in 1837 and was educated at Woodhouse Grove and South Kensington. He taught at the Bombay School of Art and was Principal of the Mayo School of Art, Lahore, 1865-75, and became Curator of the Central Museum, Lahore from 1875-93. He was related by marriage to Sir E.J. Poynter and Sir E. Burne-Jones (qq.v.) and was the father of Rudyard Kipling (q.v.). He died 26 January 1911.
Illus: *Beast and Man in India [1891].*
Contrib: *The Jungle Book; The Second Jungle Book [1894 (with R.K.)].*
Colls: India Office Lib.

KIPLING, Rudyard 1865-1936
Author and occasional illustrator. He was born in Bombay in 1865 and clearly influenced by the study of Indian art and culture made by his father, J. Lockwood Kipling (q.v.). He was educated in England, living in the vacations with the family of his uncle Sir E. Burne-Jones (q.v.). He returned to India as a journalist from 1882-89 and after early success, travelled to the United States and settled at Bateman's in Sussex. Kipling's black and white illustrations to *Just So Stories*, 1902, show a good decorative sense, if not a very developed manner of execution.
See illustrations.

RUDYARD KIPLING 1865-1936. 'The Elephant'. An illustration to *The Just So Stories For Little Children*, 1902

KITTON, Frederick George   **1856-1903**
Author, artist and illustrator. He was born in Norwich on 5 May 1856 and was educated there before training as an engraver and draughtsman on wood with W.L. Thomas of *The Graphic*. From 1882, Kitton began to write on both illustration and English literature, eventually having a dozen works to his credit. He was a prolific if not very dazzling pen draughtsman and died at St. Albans on 10 September 1903.
Publ: *Phiz – A Memoir [1882]; John Leech, Artist and Humorist [1883]; Dickensiana [1886]; Charles Dickens by Pen and Pencil [1889-90]; The Novels of Charles Dickens [1897]; Dickens and His Illustrators [1898-99]; Zechariah Buck [1899]; The Minor Writings of Dickens [1900]; Charles Dickens, His Life, Writings and Personality [1902]; Autograph Edition of Dickens [Editor].*
Illus: *Hertfordshire County Homes [1892]; St. Albans Historical and Picturesque [1893]; St. Albans Abbey [1897]; The Romany Rye [1900].*
Contrib: *Thc Graphic [1874-85]; ILN [1889-90]; The English Illustrated Magazine [1891-92]; Black & White [1892]; The Sunday Magazine [1894].*
Exhib: Norwich, 1886-87; RBA, 1880.
Bibl: R.E.D. Sketchley, *Eng. Bk. Illus.*, 1902, pp.48,135.

KITTON, R.   **fl.1832-1847**
Draughtsman at Norwich. He contributed illustrations to *Brittons Cathedrals*, 1832-36.
Exhib: RA, 1847.

KLEMPNER, E.G.
Contributor of military figure subjects to *Punch*, 1905.

KLINGENDER, Martin
Illustrator and wood engraver of Shortlands, Kent. He illustrated and printed *The Tulip*, Summer and Winter 1900 engintled 'A Little Book of Music, Poetry and Woodcuts'. The style is similar to that of Nicholson and Craig (qq.v.) but cruder.

KNIGHT, Captain Charles Raleigh
Amateur illustrator. He illustrated his own *Scenery on the Rhine*, 1850, AT 220.

KNIGHT, Henry Gally   **1786-1846**
Writer, traveller and amateur artist. He was born in 1786 and educated at Eton and Trinity College, Cambridge. He had independent means and an estate in Langold, Yorkshire, enabling him to travel throughout Europe and Palestine, writing about his journeys. He was a friend of J.M.W. Turner (q.v.) and illustrated his own books.
Illus: *An Architectural Tour of Normandy [1836]; The Normans in Sicily [1838]; Saracenic and Norman Remains to illustrate the 'Normans in Sicily' [1840]; The Ecclesiastical Architecture of Italy [1842-44].*

KNIGHT, J. Louis
Contributed scenes of Dockland to *The Illustrated London News*, 1889.

KNIGHT, John William Buxton   **1843-1908**
Landscape painter, watercolourist, occasional illustrator. He was

born at Sevenoaks in 1843 and studied with J. Holland in Kent before attending the RA Schools, 1860. He was elected RBA in 1875 and RE in 1881.
Contrib: *The English Illustrated Magazine [1887 (figs. and lands.)].*
Exhib: B; G; GG; L; M; RA; RBA; RE; RI.

KNOWLES, Davidson   **fl.1879-1902**
Landscape painter, figure painter and illustrator. He worked in London and was elected RBA in 1890, specialising in country genre subjects and animals.
Illus: *Songs and Lyrics For Little Lips [W.D. Cummings, n.d.].*
Contrib: *The Graphic [1880]; ILN [1883-96]; The English Illustrated Magazine [1893-94].*
Exhib: B; G; L; M; NEA; RA; RBA.

KNOWLES, George Sheridan   **RI**   **1863-1931**
Genre painter and illustrator. He was born in Manchester on 25 November 1863, and studied at the Manchester School of Art and the RA Schools, 1884. He was elected RI in 1892 and became Treasurer. He died on 15 March 1931.
Contrib: *The Quiver [1890]; ILN [1894-99 (short stories)].*
Exhib: B; G; L; M; NEA; P; RA; RBA; ROI.

KNOWLES, Horace J.   **1884-1954**
Decorator of books. Worked with his brother Reginald L. Knowles (q.v.).
See Horne

KNOWLES, Reginald Lionel   **1879-1950**
Illustrator. A talented Edwardian artist of whom very little is known. He worked in the manner of Arthur Rackham, muted watercolours with highly decorative penwork and borders. He also designed book covers and book plates, and was responsible for Dent's *Everyman Library*.
Illus: *Legends From Fairyland [Holme Lee, 1908]; Norse Fairy Tales [P.C. Asbjornsen and J.I. Moe, 1910]; Marie de France – Old World Love Stories [1913]; The Months [Leigh Hunt, 1936].*
Bibl: *The Art of The Book*, Studio Year Book, 1914, illus; B. Peppin, *Fantasy Book Illustration*, 1975, pp.17, 188, illus.
See Horne

KOEKKOEK, H.W.
Illustrator. Presumably one of the large family of Dutch painters of this name. He illustrated *Barclay of the Guides*, Herbert Strang, 1908.

KRETSCHNER, Albert   **1825-1891**
Genre painter and illustrator. He was born at Burghof, Germany on 27 February 1825, and studied at the Berlin Academy. He died in the same city on 11 July 1891.
Contrib: *The Illustrated Times [1859].*
Exhib: RA, 1852.

KRIEGHOFF, Cornelius   **1812-1872**
Painter of Canadian scenery and life. This very popular artist was active in the 1850s and 1860s. He illustrated *Construction of the Great Victoria Bridge*, 1860, AT 631.

'KYD'   **See CLARKE, Joseph Clayton**

L, E.H late 19th century

A watercolour for illustration by this artist is in the Victoria and Albert Museum.

L.R.

Illustrator, contributing to *The Illustrated London News*, 1872.
Colls: V & AM.

LABY, Alexander fl.1840-1879

History painter and illustrator. He was working in Paris and exhibiting there, 1840-44. He contributed drawings of Flemish industry to *The Illustrated London News*, 1879.
Exhib: RBA, 1864-66.

LADER, A.S.

Contributor to *The Illustrated London News*, 1889 topography.

LAMB, Henry fl.1826-1861

Landscape painter. He worked at Malvern, Worcestershire, for most of his life and contributed illustrations to *Griffith's Cheltenham*, 1826.
Exhib: BI; NWS, 1834-61.

LAMBERT, George ARA **1873-1930**

Portrait painter and illustrator. He was born in Russia in 1873 and came to England in 1878. He went to Australia in 1891 and studied at the Sydney School of Art, where he won a scholarship to Paris. He taught at the London School of Art in 1910 and returned to Australia in 1928, having been elected A.R.A. in 1922. He died on 29 May 1930.
Contrib: *The Graphic [1887-88]; The Strand Magazine [1891]; The English Illustrated Magazine [1893-94]*.

LAMBERT, John fl.1806-1814

Topographer and traveller. He visited N. America to study the cultivation of hemp in 1806 and travelled widely 1806-08. He illustrated *Travels Through Canada and the United States*, 1814, AT 613.

LAMI, Eugène **1800-1890**

Genre painter, watercolourist, lithographer and illustrator. He was born in Paris on 12 January 1800 and studied under Baron Gros, H. Vernet and at the École des Beaux-Arts. Lami was an important lithographer and watercolourist during the reigns of Louis-Philippe and Napoleon III. His elegant ink drawings with watercolour washes of courtly interiors and scenes of high life were popular both in England and in France, typifying the artificial life of mid-19th century France. Lami produced a series of prints of *Uniforms of the French Army, 1791-1814*, in 1822 and *Uniformes français 1814-1824*, in 1825. His output was considerable, he produced 344 lithographs as well as numerous illustrations for books. He exhibited regularly at the Salon from 1824 to 1878 and as well as becoming a Chevalier de la Légion d'honneur in 1837, founded the French Society of Watercolourists. He died in Paris, 19 December 1890.
Illus: *Voyage en Angleterre [1829-30 (with Monnier)]; L'Hiver et L'Été [Janin]; Les Œuvres de Alfred de Musset*.
Contrib: *The Keepsake [1841]; ILN [1852]*.
Exhib: RA, 1850.
Colls: Author; Louvre; Royal Coll.; V & AM; Versailles; Wallace Coll.
Bibl: P.A Lemoisne, *L'Œuvre de EL; Print Collectors' Quarterly*, Vol.17, No.1, 1930, pp.72-91.
See illustration.

EUGÈNE LAMI 1800-1890. 'Le Repos'

LAMONT or LA MONTE, Elish **1800-1870**
Miniature painter. She was born in Belfast in about 1800 and worked
in Belfast and Dublin. She contributed portraits to *The Court Album*,
1857 and did some illustrations for Swain in the 1860s.
Exhib: RA, 1856-69; RHA, 1842-57.

LAMONT, Thomas Reynolds   **ARWS**   **1826-1898**
Landscape painter and illustrator. He was born in Scotland in 1826
and studied art in Paris with George Du Maurier (q.v.) who
immortalised him as 'the Laird' in his novel *Trilby*. He was elected
ARWS in 1866 but did little work after 1880.
Contrib: *London Society [1865]; The Shilling Magazine [1865-66].*
Exhib: GG; OWS: RA.
Colls: V & AM.

LANCELOT, Dieudonné Auguste   **1822-1894**
Lithographer and illustrator. He was born at Sezanne in 1822 and
became a pupil of J.F. Arnaud de Troyes. He exhibited at the Salon
from 1853 to 1876 and illustrated landscapes and views in books. He
died in Paris in 1894.
Illus: *Le Tour du Monde; Le Magasin pittoresque; Jardins [1887].*
Contrib: *ILN [1857, Paris].*

LANCON, Auguste André   **1836-1887**
Painter, engraver and sculptor. He was born at Saint-Claude in 1836
and studied art in Lyons and Paris, specialising in the painting and
sculpting of animals. Lancon was implicated in the Commune of
1871 and imprisoned, but with the new regime he became a Special
Artist for *L'Illustration* and went to the Balkans for them in 1877.
Contrib: *ILN [1870].*

LANDELLS, Ebenezer   **1808-1860**
Engraver and illustrator. He was born at Newcastle-upon-Tyne in
1808 and worked as a pupil to Thomas Bewick (q.v.) and for a short
time to Isaac Nicholson. He went to London in 1829 and became the
right-hand man of John Jackson and William Harvey (q.v.)
superintending the fine art department of the firm of Branston &
Vizetelly. Landells was inventive and original as a projector of
newspapers, but lacked business acumen. He was intimately
concerned with the founding of *Punch*, but left it in 1842 to become
Editor of the less successful *Illuminated Magazine*, 1843. He started
The Lady's Newspaper in 1847, which was incorporated in *The
Queen* and had M.B. Foster, the Dalziels and Edmund Evans (qq.v.)
as his pupils. Landells was not a very strong artist, but acted as *The
Illustrated London News* Special on Queen Victoria's first tour of
Scotland. The Queen later bought the drawings, the first of their kind
to be made for a newspaper on the spot. Landells died at Brompton
on 1 September 1860.
Contrib: *The Sporting Review [1842-46]; ILN [1844-56].*
Exhib: RBA,1833 & 1837 (engravings).
Bibl: M.H. Spielmann, *The History of Punch*, 1895, pp.15-19; *The
Brothers Dalziel, A Record of Work, 1840-1890*, 1901, pp.4-10.

LANDELLS, Robert Thomas   **1833-1877**
Illustrator and War artist. He was born 1 August 1833, the eldest son
of Ebenezer Landells (q.v.). He was educated in France but studied
drawing and painting in London, specialising in battles and military
subjects. He was Special War Artist for *The Illustrated London News*
from 1855 to 1871, covering the Crimea, Schleswig-Holstein, 1864,
Austro-Prussia, 1866, and the Franco-Prussian campaign of 1870-
71. He was awarded the Prussian Iron Cross on this occasion.
Landells also acted for *The Illustrated London Magazine*, 1853-55.
He died in London in 1877.
Exhib: RBA, 1863-76.

LANDER, Edgar   **1883-**
Black and white artist. He was born in 1883 and worked in North
London. He regularly exhibited watercolours and etchings and
married Hilda Cowham (q.v.)
Contrib: *Punch [1902, 1904-05 (social)].*
Exhib: G: L: RA: RSA.

LANDSEER, Charles   **RA**   **1799-1878**
History painter and illustrator. He was the second son of John

Landseer, ARA, and brother of Sir E.H. and T. Landseer (qq.v.). He
was a pupil of B.R. Haydon and studied at the RA Schools in 1816,
afterwards travelling to South America. He became RA in 1845.
Illus: *Days of Deerstalking [W. Scrope, 1838].*
Contrib: *Finden's Illustrations ... To the Life and Works of Lord
Byron [1833-34].*

LANDSEER, Sir Edwin Henry   **RA**   **1802-1873**
Animal painter and caricaturist. He was born in 1802, the youngest
son of John Landseer, ARA, and became the most popular painter of
animals in Victorian England, his work widely engraved and
admired from the Queen downwards. He is included here for his
brown ink and wash caricatures which he often made while staying
in country houses.
Illus: *Days of Deerstalking [W. Scrope, 1838, with C. Landseer].*
Colls: BM; Fitzwilliam; V & AM.

LANDSEER, George   **1834-1878**
Painter, watercolourist and illustrator. Son of Thomas Landseer
(q.v.). Worked in India from 1864-1870, painting the rajas and their
courts and landscapes.
Contrib: *ILN [1847].*
Exhib: BI; RA; RBA.

LANDSEER, Thomas   **ARA**   **1795-1880**
Engraver and illustrator. He was the eldest son of John Landseer,
ARA, and brother of Sir E.L. and C. Landseer (qq.v.). He was a pupil
and assistant to his father and studied with B.R. Haydon, but became
best known for his engravings from his famous brother's works.
Early in his career, Thomas Landseer indulged in some humorous
engraved caprices which are his most delightful works. They
consisted of vigorous prints of animals, often in flight or fighting
with men, mostly published by Moon, Boys & Graves in the 1820s
or 1830s. Linton describes him as 'a short, broad-shouldered deaf
man... evincing more originality and vigour of drawing than is to be
seen in the excellently painted pictures of the more famous Sir
Edwin'. He was elected ARA in 1868.
Illus: *Monkeyana or Men in Miniatures [1827-28]; Tam O'Shanter
& Souther Johny [R. Burns, 1830]; The Devil's Walk [S.T. Coleridge,
1831]; Characteristic Sketches of Animals [1832]; The Boy and The
Birds [Emily Taylor, 1840]; Stories about Dogs [Thomas Bingley,
n.d.].*
Contrib: *The People's Journal [1846]; ILN [1844].*
Exhib: BI; NWS; RA; RBA.
Colls: BM; Witt Photo.

LANE, Richard James   **ARA**   **1800-1872**
Engraver. He was born in 1800 and was a great-nephew of Thomas
Gainsborough. Lane's career was mainly in making engravings after
the work of Landseer, Leslie, Lawrence and Gainsborough and in
teaching at the engraving school at South Kensington. He became
ARA in 1827 and was made lithographer to the Queen in 1837. The
Victoria and Albert Museum has three drawings for illustration by
this artist, two of them of Shakespearean subjects.

LANE, Theodore   **1800-1828**
Painter and caricaturist. He was born at Isleworth in 1800 and was
apprenticed to J.C. Barrow at Battle Bridge. Shortly after completing
his time, he produced *The Life of an Actor*, 1822, six pls., which had
some popular success. After meeting Pierce Egan, he issued with him
as author, *Life of an Actor Peregrine Proteus*, 1825 with 27 colour
plates, and many woodcuts. During the Queen Caroline scandals,
Lane worked for the printseller Humphrey, 1820-21, and did several
satirical prints probably in collaboration with Theodore Hook. He
died tragically on 21 February 1828 by falling through a skylight,
being so badly mutilated that he was only recognisable by his card
case. The RA ran a subscription for his widow.
Illus: *The Show Folks [Pierce Egan, 1831]; To Which Is Added
A Biographical Sketch of the Life of Mr Theodore Lane [Small
12 mo].*
Exhib: RA, 1819-20, 1826.
Colls: BM.
Bibl: G. Everitt, *English Caricaturists*, 1893, pp.84-88, illus; D.
George, *English Political Caricature*, Vol.II, 1959, pp.197-198.

LANGE, Janet fl.1855-1860
French illustrator. He was the brother of Gustave Janet (q.v.) and according to Vizetelly an artist 'whose reputation stood high as a delineator of military episodes, Court pageants, and the like...'
Contrib: *Cassell's Illustrated Family Paper [1855]; The Illustrated Times [1860]; ILN.*

LANOS, Henri fl.1886-1905
French genre painter and watercolourist. He contributed drawings of the Simplon Tunnel to *The Graphic*, 1902-03 and 1905. He was a member of the Artistes Français.

LARSEN, Carl Christian 1853-1910
Painter and illustrator. He was born at Viborg, Denmark on 16 March 1853 and studied at the Copenhagen School of Art. He was Special Artist for *The Illustrated London News* in Siberia in 1882. He died at Vienna on 6 June 1910.

LARUM, Oscar
Contributed drawings of comic animals to *Punch*, 1909.

LATHBURY, Mrs (née Miss M.A. Mills) fl. 1807-1815
Amateur artist. She contributed topographical drawings of the West Country and Wales to *Britton's Beauties of England and Wales* 1812-15 and to *The Antiquarian and Topographical Cabinet*, 1807.

LAUDER, Sir Thomas Dick, Bt. 1784-1848
Amateur landscape artist. He was born in 1784 and succeeded his father as 7th Baronet of Fountainhall, County Haddington in 1820. He died 29 May 1848.
Illus: *A Voyage Round the Coasts of Scotland and the Isles [James Wilson, FRSE, 1842. Engraved by Charles H. Wilson].*

LAUGHLIN, J.E.
Illustrated *Three Boys in The Wild North Land* by E.R. Young, 1897.

LAURENS, Jules Joseph Augustin 1825-1901
Draughtsman and watercolourist. He was born at Carpentras, France, on 26 July 1825 and became a pupil of his brother J.J.B. Laurens. He exhibited regularly at the Salon and died at St. Didier 5 May 1901.
Contrib: *The Illustrated Times [1856 (Persia)].*
Colls: Angoulême; Avignon; Bagnères; Carpentras; Metz; Montpellier; Narbonne; Orléans; Paris; Rouen.

LAVEROCK, Florence fl.1900-1915
Black and white artist working at Warrington. She did several pretty 'crinoline story-book' type illustrations in about 1900 which may have been published.
Exhib: L.

LAWLESS, Matthew James 1837-1864
Illustrator and etcher. He was born in 1837, the son of Barry Lawless, a Dublin solicitor. As a Catholic he was educated at the Prior Park School, Bath and then at the Langham, Cary's and Leigh's Art Schools in London. He was for some time a pupil of Henry O'Neill, RA and was influenced by the Pre-Raphaelites and by the Dutch masters of the 17th century. Although often unequal in his compositions and his handling of figures, sometimes very large and sometimes very small, Lawless at his best ranks very high among the artists on the wood. He worked briefly for *Punch* but made his name in the more serious or poetic areas of illustration, particularly in *Good Words* and *Once a Week*. He was one of a number of the 1860's illustrators who had tragically short working lives. He was ill from 1860 onwards and died at Bayswater in 1864.
Contrib: *Once a Week [1859-64]; Punch [1860-61]; Lyra Germanica [1861]; Life of St. Patrick [1862]; Good Words [1862-64]; London Society [1862-70]; Passages from Modern English Poets [1862]; Churchman's Family Magazine [1863]; Pictures of Society [1866]; Touches of Nature [1867]; Thornbury's Legendary Ballads [1876].*
Exhib: RA; RBA, 1857-63.
Colls: BM.
Bibl: Chatto & Jackson, *Treatise on English Wood Engraving*, 1861, p.599; G. White, *English Illustration The Sixties*, 1895; F. Reid,

MATTHEW JAMES LAWLESS 1837-1864. 'The Headmaster's Sister'. Illustration to *Once A Week*, 28 April 1860. Wood engraving

Illustrators of the Sixties, 1928; Gleeson White, 'MJL In Memoriam', *The Quarto*, 1898, pp.45-59.
See illustration.

LAWSON, Cecil Gordon 1851-1882
Landscape painter in oil and illustrator. He was born at Wellington, Salop, in 1851, the son of William Lawson, the Scottish portrait painter. He came to London with his father in 1861 and in 1870 began to draw on the wood for the engravers. In some ways Lawson was a proto-impressionist and his oils of the Thames and the countryside of Kent and Yorkshire are having a revival among collectors. Lawson suffered from acute ill health and after travelling to the South of France in 1881, returned to London and died on 10 June 1882. He was the younger brother of F.W. Lawson (q.v.).
Contrib: *The Quiver; Good Words; The Sunday Magazine; Dark Blue [1871-72]; Poems and Songs by Robert Burns [1875].*
Exhib: GG; RA; RBA.
Colls: Birmingham; BM; Edinburgh; V & AM.
Bibl: F. Reid, *Illustrators of The Sixties*, 1928, pp.266.

LAWSON, Francis Wilfrid 1842-1935
Painter and illustrator. He was born in 1842, the elder brother of Cecil G. Lawson (q.v.) whom he taught. He was a very versatile artist, specialising not only in the figure but in landscape work as well. Reid considers his best work to be that for *The Cornhill Magazine* and Foxe's *Book of Martyrs*. Charles Keene (q.v.) had a studio in Lawson's house.
Illus: *Poetical Works of Henry W. Longfellow [c.1870, Moxon]; The Law and The Lady [Wilkie Collins, 1876 (with Fildes and Hall)].*
Contrib: *Once a Week; London Society; The Cornhill Magazine [1867-69]; Book of Martyrs [Foxe, 1866]; Heber's Hymns [1867]; Belgravia [1868 (figures)]; The Shilling Magazine; The Sunday Magazine; Cassell's Magazine; The Broadway; Dark Blue; Aunt Judy's Magazine; Fun; The Graphic [1869-76]; Punch [1876].*
Exhib: B; G; GG; L; M; NEA; RA; RBA; ROI; RI; RSA.
Colls: Liverpool; V & AM; Witt Photo.

LAWSON, G.
Illustrator. The British Museum has drawings by this artist of Reading Room personalities, published in *Atlanta*, 1888.

LAWSON, John fl.1865-1909
Landscape painter and illustrator, working mostly in Scotland, but at Sheffield, 1892-93. He is rated by Reid and White as a very competent draughtsman of the second rank, producing excellent figure work for the magazines of the 1860s.
Contrib: *Once a Week [1865-67]; The Sunday Magazine; Cassell's Magazine; The Quiver [1865]; The Children's Hour [1865]; The*

EDWARD LEAR 1812-1888. 'Collepardo'. Illustration to *Views in Rome,* 1841. Tinted lithograph

EDWARD LEAR 1812-1888. 'Frascati'. Illustration in *Rome and its Environs,* 1841. Tinted lithograph

Shilling Magazine [1866]; The Argosy [1866]; British Workman [1866]; Pen and Pencil Pictures from the Poets [1866]; Ballad Stories [1866]; Golden Thoughts from Golden Fountains [1867]; Roses and Holly [1867]; Ballads, Scottish and English [1867]; Nursery Time [1867]; Early Start in Life [1867]; The Children of Blessing [1867]; The Golden Gift [1868]; Original Poems [1868]; Tales of the White Cockade [1870]; The Runaway [1872]; The Childrens Garland [1873]; The Fiery Cross [1875]; The World Well Lost [1877]; Clever Hans [1883]; There Was Once [1888]; Childhood Valley [1889].

Exhib: G; L; M; RI; RSA.

Colls: Witt Photo.

Bibl: F. Reid, *Illustrators of the Sixties,* 1928, pp.228-229, illus.

LAWSON, Lizzie (Mrs R. Mack)   **fl.1884-1902**

Figure painter and illustrator. She worked at Hurlingham Lane, Fulham and drew colour illustrations for *Old Proverbs,* Cassells, n.d.

Contrib: *Little Folks.*

Exhib: RA; RSA.

Bibl: White, Gleeson, 'Children's Books and Their Illustrators', *Studio Special No.,* 1897-98.

LAYARD, Major Arthur   **fl.1894-1911**

Watercolourist and illustrator. He worked in Hammersmith and at Pangbourne, 1902-03. He was principally a figure artist.

Illus: *The People of The Mist [H.R. Haggard, 1894]; The Winged Wolf [Ha Sheen Kaf, 1894]; Billy Mouse [(child's book) c.1906].*

Contrib: *The Pall Mall Magazine; Fun [1901].*

Exhib: Bruton Gall.; NEA

LEAR, Edward   **1812-1888**

Topographical artist, ornithological and comic illustrator. He was born at Holloway on 12 May 1812 and by the age of fifteen was already making his living by bird drawings. In 1831 he became a draughtsman at the Zoological Society's Gardens and in 1832 published his first book of coloured plates of parrots. From 1832 to 1836, Lear was employed as drawing-master to the children of the Earl of Derby at Knowsley, where he continued to paint and drew and wrote *The Book of Nonsense* for the Earl's children. The result of his Knowsley years was the privately printed book *Knowsley Menagerie,* 1856 and an introduction to Queen Victoria to whom he gave lessons in 1846.

From 1831 onwards, Lear made extensive tours abroad, publishing the resulting drawings in albums of lithographs. His chief excursions were to Rome in 1837, where he remained and taught until 1848, to Greece, Albania and Malta in 1848 and Egypt in 1849. At this point Lear returned to England and studied at the RA Schools, meeting W. Holman Hunt (q.v.) before commencing another period abroad from 1853 to 1857, visiting Greece, Egypt and the Holy Land. From about 1860, he was living entirely abroad, based at Cannes, Corfu and finally at San Remo. He visited India and Ceylon in 1872-74 and returned to England for the last time in 1880 before settling in San Remo where he died in January 1888. Lear's sketches are unusual among the art of the Victorians for being principally pen and ink works with wash, rather than drawn in watercolours. Many of them have lengthy inscriptions about their locations and the date and time of day that they were done.

Illus: *The Family of Psittacidae, or Parrots [1832]; The Naturalists Magazine [n.d.]; Views in Rome [1841, AT 183]; Excursions in Italy [1846, AT 172 (two parts)]; A Book of Nonsense [1846 and 1861]; The Knowsley Menagerie [1846]; Journal of a Landscape Painter in Albania and Illyria [1851]; Journal of a Landscape Painter in Southern Calabria [1852, AT 175]; Views of the Seven Ionian Islands [1863]; Journal of a Landscape Painter in Corsica [1870]; Nonsense Songs, Stories, Botany and Alphabets [1871]; More Nonsense, Pictures, Rhymes, Botany Etc. [1872]; Tortoises, Terrapins and Turtles [1872]; Indian Pheasants [n.d.]; Laughable Lyrics, A Fourth Book [1877]; Nonsense Songs and Stories [1895].*

Exhib: FAS, 1938; RA; RBA.

Colls: Ashmolean; BM; Glasgow; Greenwich; Mellon; V & AM; Witt Photo.

Bibl: Vivien Noakes, *EL, The Life of a Wanderer,* 1968; Vivien Noakes, *EL 1812-1888,* RA exhibition catalogue, 1985; Ruth Pitman, *Edward Lear's Tennyson,* 1988.

See illustrations.

GILBERT LEDWARD RA 1888-1960. 'An aged enchanter'. Illustration to *The Story of Princess Carena.* Signed with monogram. 9⅛in x 6in (23.2cm x 15.2cm)   Victoria and Albert Museum

LE BRETON, Miss Rosa

Domestic painter, exhibiting in 1865. She contributed similar subjects to *Cassell's Illustrated Family Paper,* 1857.

LEDWARD, Gilbert   **RA**   **1888-1960**

Sculptor. He was born in 1888, the son of the sculptor R.A. Ledward. He studied at the RCA and the RA Schools and was awarded the first sculpture scholarship at the British School of Rome in 1913, and the RA travelling scholarship. He was Professor of Sculpture at the RCA, 1926-29 and was elected ARA in 1932 and RA in 1937. He died in 1960.

Illus: *The Story of Princess Carena [n.d].*

Exhib: G; GG; L; RA; RSA.

Colls: V & AM.

See illustration.

LEE, Arthur

Humorous artist, working in Coventry and exhibiting at Birmingham 1910. He may have worked for *The Pall Mall Magazine.*

LEE, J.

Perhaps John Ingle Lee, a figure artist who exhibited at the RA and RBA, 1868-91.

Contrib: *Book of Martyrs [Foxe, 1866].*

LEE, Joseph Johnson   **1876-**

Artist and author. He was born in Dundee in 1876 and studied at the Slade School and at Heatherley's. He served in the First World War 1914-18 in the Black Watch.

JOHN LEECH 1817-1864. 'A Leetle Contre-temps'. Illustration to *Ask Mamma*, by R.S. Surtees, 1858. Engraving coloured by hand

JOHN LEECH 1817-1864. 'Imperial John's attempt to show the way'. Illustration to *Ask Mamma*, by R.S. Surtees, 1858. Engraving coloured by hand

206

The Gypsey Prophecy.

JOHN LEECH 1817-1864. 'The Gypsy's Prophecy'. Wood engraving

Publ: *Tales of Our Town [1910]; Fra Lippo Lippi [1914]; Ballads of Bartle [1916]; Work-a-day Warriors [1917]; A Captive at Carlsruhe [1920].*
Contrib: *Punch.*
Colls: Witt Photo.

LEE, Sydney   RA   1866-1949
Painter, etcher and wood engraver. He was born at Manchester and studied in Manchester and Paris. He was working in Manchester in 1886 and London by 1893. He was a member of the NEA, 1906; ARA, 1922 and RA, 1930. He was also RBA, 1904, RE, 1915 and a member of the Society of 25 Artists. His work was purchased by the Chantrey Bequest, 1924.
Contrib: *The Venture [1903 (topog. woodcut)].*
Exhib: B; G; L; M; NEA; RA; RBA; RE; RHA; RSA.

LEE, William   NWS   1810-1865
Watercolourist. He was born in 1810 and was a member and secretary of the Langham Sketch Club and elected NWS in 1848. He died in London on 22 January 1865.
Contrib: *London [Knight, 1841].*
Exhib: NWS; RA; RBA.
Colls: V & AM.

LEECH, John   1817-1864
Artist and illustrator. He was born in London on 23 August 1817, the son of a vintner and showed a remarkable aptitude for drawing from an early age. After being educated at Charterhouse and then entering St. Bartholomew's Hospital to study medicine, Leech abandoned it for the

career of an artist. At Charterhouse he had become a friend of W.M. Thackeray (q.v.) and at St. Bartholomew's he had made the acquaintance of Albert Smith and Percival Leigh, the writers, all of whom were to further him in his profession. He spent some time in Paris in 1836 and worked under a French caricaturist. He produced his first book *Etchings and Sketchings,* caricatures of Londoners, in 1835 and followed this with a series of satirical and political lithographs. Leech was taught to draw on the wood by Orrin Smith and it was in this field of black and white work that he was to make his name. His humour was like his talent, gentle, warm-hearted and positive, his world, the ups and downs of middle class life, the sports of the squirearchy, and the peccadilloes of army officers and undergraduates. He became really established in 1840 when he joined the staff of *Bentley's Miscellany,* contributing over 140 etchings to the magazine. In August 1841 he contributed his first block to the newly-established satirical journal *Punch;* Leech's art was ripe for this type of pictorial satire and within a few months he had made it his own, establishing a convention of social humour that was to last until the 1920s. From 1843, Leech shared the cartoons with Tenniel, completing no less than 720 before 1864. But his strength was in the drawings of the hunting field and London fashion, epitomised in the characters of Tom Noddy and Mr Briggs. Extravagantly praised by Ruskin, Leech's often careless but never crude drawings have survived in charm and humour to give us a refreshing glimpse of mid-Victorian society. He died after a short illness in 1864.

Leech prepared sketches in oil of some of his illustrations and exhibited them in the Egyptian Hall, Piccadilly, in June 1862. The pencil sketches for the *Punch* cartoons are more generally available, though often slight.

JOHN LEECH 1817-1864. Frontispiece and title page to *Punch's Pocket Book For 1851*. Wood engravings coloured by hand

ALFRED CHEW LEETE 1882-1933. Black and white illustration for humorous magazine, c.1914. Pen and ink   Jeffrey Gordon Collection

Illus: *Etchings and Sketchings [A. Pen, 1835]; The Human Face Divine and De Vino [1835]; Bell's Life in London [1836]; Jack Brag [T. Hook, 1837]; Droll Doings [1837-38]; Funny Characters [1837-38]; American Broad Grins [1838]; Local Legends and Rambling Rhymes [John Dix, 1839]; Pencillings By The Way [N.P. Willis, 1839]; The Comic English Grammar [Paul Prendergast, 1840]; The Comic Latin Grammar [G. à Beckett, 1840]; The Fiddle-Faddle Fashion Book [Percival Leigh, 1840]; The Ingoldsby Legends [1840]; The Clockmaker [T.C. Haliburton, 1840]; The Bachelors Walk in a Fog [Peter Styles, 1840]; The Children of the Mobility [1841]; Written Caricatures [C.C. Pepper, 1841]; Stanley Thorn [Henry Cockton, 1841]; The Porcelain Tower [1841]; Merrie England in the Olden Time [Daniel, 1842]; The Barnabys in America [Mrs Trollope, 1843]; The Wassail Bowl [A.R. Smith, 1843]; Jack The Giant Killer [1843]; A Christmas Carol [Charles Dickens, 1843-44]; Jessie Phillips [Mrs*

Trollope, 1844]; Nursery Ditties [1844]; The Adventures of Mr Ledbury [Albert Smith, 1844]; The Comic Arithmetic [1844]; Sketches of Life and Character [George Hodder, 1845]; The Fortunes of the Scattergood Family [Albert Smith, 1845]; Hints on Life [1845]; The Quizzology of the British Drama [G. à Beckett, 1846]; The Battle of Life [Charles Dickens, 1846]; Mrs. Caudle's Curtain Lectures [D. Jerrold, 1846]; The Comic History of England [G. à Beckett, 1847]; The Silver Swan [de Chatelain, 1847]; The Handbook of Joking [1847]; Hillside and Border Sketches [W.H. Maxwell, 1847]; The Haunted Man [Charles Dickens, 1847-48]; Life and Adventures of Oliver Goldsmith [Forester, 1848]; The Rising Generation [1848]; The Struggle and Adventures of Christopher Tadpole [Albert Smith, 1848]; Ballads of Bon Gaultier [1849]; A Man Made of Money [D. Jerrold, 1849]; The Natural History of Evening Parties [Albert Smith, 1849]; Toil and Trial [Mrs. Crosland, 1849]; The Crock of Gold [M.F. Tupper, 1849]; Fun, Poetry and Pathos [W. Y. Browne, 1850]; Dashes of American Humour [Howard Paul, 1852]; The Comic History of Rome [G. à Beckett, 1852]; Picturesque Sketches of London [Thomas Millet, 1852]; Uncle Tom's Cabin [H.B. Stowe, 1852]; The Fortunes of Hector O'Halloran [W.H. Maxwell, 1853]; Mr. Sponge's Sporting Tour [R.S. Surtees, 1853]; The Great Highway [S.W. Fullom, 1854]; Handley Cross [R.S Surtees, 1854]; Reminiscences of a Huntsman [The Hon. G. Berkeley, 1854]; The Paragreens [Ruffini, 1856]; The Militia Man At Home and Abroad [1857]; A Month in the Forests of France [The Hon. G. Berkeley, 1857]; The Encyclopaedia of Rural Sports [1858]; Ask Mama [R.S Surtees, 1858]; The Cyclopaedia of Wit and Humour [1858]; The Path of Roses [F. Greenwood, 1858]; The Fliers of the Hunt [John Mills, 1859]; A Little Tour in Ireland [Reynolds Hole, 1859]; Newton Dogvane [J. Francis, 1859]; Soapey Sponge [1859]; Paul Prendergast [1859]; Mr. Briggs and His Doings [1860]; Plain or Ringlets [R.S. Surtees, 1860]; Life of a Foxhound [John Mills, 1861]; The Follies of the Year [1864]; Mr. Facey-Romford's Hounds [R.S. Surtees, 1864], Carols of Cockayne [1869].

Contrib: *The London Magazine [1840]; Bentley's Miscellany [1840-49]; Colin Clink [Hooton, 1841]; Punch [1841-64]; New Monthly Magazine [1842-43]; The Sporting Review [1842-46]; Hoods Comic Annual [1844-46]; The Illuminated Magazine [1843-45]; The Cricket on the Hearth [Charles Dickens, 1845-46]; Jerrold's Shilling Magazine [1845-48]; ILN [1845-57]; The Month [1851]; Illustrated London Magazine [1854]; Merry Pictures [1857]; Once A Week [1859-64]; Puck on Pegasus [Pennell, 1861]; The Gardeners Annual [1863].*

Colls: BM; Dickens House, Doughty Street, London; Fitzwilliam; Royal Collection; V & AM.

Bibl: John Brown, 'JL' *North British Review,* March 1865, pp.213-244; Russell Sturgis, 'JL' *Scribners,* Feb. 1879, pp.553-565; 'JL and Other Papers', *North British Review* Edinburgh, 1882; F.G. Kitton, *JL Artist and Humourist,* 1883; F.G. Kitton, *Charles Dickens by Pen*

FREDERIC LORD LEIGHTON PRA 1830-1896. 'Moses views the Promised Land'. Drawing for the illustration in *Dalziel's Bible Gallery*, 1881, Indian ink and black chalk, 8¼in x 5in (21cm x 12.7cm)
Victoria and Albert Museum

FREDERIC LORD LEIGHTON PRA 1830-1896. 'Coming Home'

and Pencil, 1890; Harry Thornber, *JL* 1890; W.P. Frith, *JL, his Life and Works,* 2 vols, 1891; C.L. Chambers, *A List of Works containing Illustrations by JL,* 1892; Graham Everitt, *English Caricaturists...,* 1893; Frederick Dolman,'JL and His Method', *The Strand,* March 1903, pp.158-164; H. Saint-Gaudens, *JL, The Critic,* Oct. 1905, pp.358-367; Stanley Kidder Wilson, *Cat. of...Exhibition of Works by JL,* Grolier Club, New York, 1914; H. Silver, 'The Art of JL' *Magazine of Art, Vol. XVI;* Rev. G. Tidy, *A Little About Leech,* 1931; Thomas Bodkin, *The Noble Science, JL in the Hunting Field,* 1948; R.G.G. Price, *A History of Punch,* 1957, pp.62-65; J.N.P. Watson 'JL in the Hunting Field' *Country Life,* 20 Jan. 1977; Simon Houfe, *JL and the Victorian Scene,* Antique Collectors' Club, 1984; Simon Houfe, 'Down From The City', *Country Life,* 5 Oct. 1989.
See illustrations.

LEETE, Alfred Chew   **1882-1933**
Black and white artist and cartoonist. He was born at Thorpe Achurch, Northamptonshire in 1882 and educated at Weston-super-Mare Grammar School before starting work in printing at the age of fifteen. From 1905 to 1933, Leete was a regular contributor to *Punch,* specialising in figure drawings in ink and some political cartoons and caricatures. His surviving drawings tend to be on a rather large scale. He died on 17 June 1933.
Contrib: *Strand Magazine [1912-23]; The Pall Mall Gazette; London Opinion [1913].*

Bibl: *The Studio,* Vol. 18, 1900, p.72; *AL,* Woodspring Museum, exhibition catalogue, Weston-super-Mare, 1982.
See illustration.
See Horne

LE FANU, G. Brinsley   **fl.1878-1925**
Landscape painter and illustrator. He worked in London and exhibited regularly at the RA and RBA.
Illus: *Nursery Rhymes [1897-98 (with Gertrude Bradley)].*
Contrib: *Pick Me Up [1888]; The Ludgate Monthly [1891].*

LEIGHTON, Edmund Blair   ROI   **1853-1922**
Painter of genre. He was born in London on 21 September 1853, the son of Charles Blair Leighton, the artist. He was educated at University College School and studied art at the RA, exhibiting there from 1887. He became ROI in 1887. Leighton amassed a large collection of historical musical instruments, arms and furniture at his house in Bedford Park, where he died on 1 September 1922.
Contrib: *The Quiver [1887].*
Exhib: B; G; L; M; RA; RBA; ROI.
Colls: V & AM.

LEIGHTON, Frederic, Lord Leighton of Stretton PRA
                                                          1830-1896
Painter. He was born at Scarborough in 1830, the son of a doctor, and received a very wide visual education, travelling with his father on the Continent. He learnt drawing from F. Meli at Rome and attended the Florence Academy and studied under J.E. Steinle at Frankfurt after 1849. He set up his own studio in 1852 and spent three years working in Rome, settling in London in 1859. Leighton had great success with his 'Cimabue's Madonna' exhibited at the RA in 1855 and

FREDERIC LORD LEIGHTON PRA 1830-1896. 'The Painted Record'. An illustration for *Romola* by George Eliot, published in *The Cornhill Magazine*, Vol.6, July to December 1862. Wood engraving

very quickly became one of the grandees of the Victorian art world. He was elected ARA in 1864, RA in 1868 and became PRA, 1878; this was followed by his creation as a baronet in 1886 and a peer in 1896, the only artist to be so honoured. He died on 25 January 1896.

Leighton was a very strong black and white artist and made contributions to *The Cornhill Magazine* which rank among the best work of the 1860s. Forrest Reid refers to them as having 'a kind of cold, formal dignity' rather underrating the power of the draughtsmanship in George Eliot's medieval story of *Romola*, ideally suited to the artist. These plates were brought together in a special limited edition in 1880.
Illus: *A Week in a French Country House [A. Sartoris, 1867].*
Contrib: *The Cornhill Magazine [1860-63]; Dalziel's Bible Gallery [1881]; Black and White [1891].*
Exhib: B; FAS, 1896-97; G; GG; L; M; RA; RHA; RSA.
Colls: Ashmolean; BM; V & AM.
Bibl: Mrs. Barrington-Ward, *The Life, Letters and Work of FL,* 1906; R. and L. Ormond, *Lord L,* 1975; *FL,* cat. of exhibition at RA, 1996, contribs. from R. Ormond, L. Ormond, C. Newall, S. Jones and B. Reed.
See illustrations.

LEIGHTON, John FSA 'Luke Limner'   1822-1912
Artist, illustrator, book decorator and designer of ex-libris. He was born in London on 22 September 1822 and studied under Henry Howard RA. Leighton was a lecturer and polemicist on behalf of the arts and in pushing forward technical innovations, an early friend of the camera. He joined with Roger Fenton to found the Photographic Society in 1853, now the Royal Photographic Society of Great

Britain. Leighton was best known for his designs for frontispieces and decorative borders, what Gleeson White refers to as 'a pioneer of better things' in their simplicity. He was a founder proprietor *of The Graphic* in 1869 and designed their title page which remained in use until 1930! Leighton designed bookbindings from about 1845 and also turned his hands to Christmas cards. He wrote extensively under the name of 'Luke Limner' and died at Harrow on 15 September 1912.
Illus: *Contrasts and Conceits [c.1850, 20 liths]; London Out of Town [c.1850, 16 liths.]; Life of Man Symbolised [1866]; The Poems of William Leighton [1894].*
Contrib: *Lyra Germanica [1861 and 1868]; Moral Emblems [1862]; Good Words [1864]; Once a Week [1866]; London Society [(cover) 1868]; The Graphic [1869 (title)]; The Sunday Magazine [1871]; Dalziel's Bible Pictures [1881]; Puck and Ariel [1890]; Fun [1890-92]; Strand Magazine [1891, 1914-16]; Punch [1900-02].*
Exhib: L, 1898.
Bibl: Chatto and Jackson, *Treatise on Wood Engraving,* 1861, p.582; R. McLean, *Victorian Book Design,* 1972, pp 218-219.

LEIST, Fred   RBA   fl.1901-1930
Portrait and figure painter and illustrator. He was elected RBA in 1913 and ROI in 1916. Working in Australia, 1901-02.
Illus: *The Gold-Marked Charm [B. Marchant, 1919].*
Contrib: *The Graphic [1901-10 (realism)]; Strand Magazine [1914-16].*
Exhib: L; P; RA; RBA; ROI.

LEITCH, Richard Principal   fl.1840-1875
Drawing-master and illustrator. He was the brother of W. L. Leitch (q.v.) and painted landscapes and wrote instructional books. He was sent by *The Illustrated London News* to Italy in 1859 to cover the Franco-Italian War.
Contrib: *ILN [1847-61]; Poets of the Nineteenth Century [1857]; Good Words [1864]; The Sunday Mazazine [1865]; Idyllic Pictures [1867]; Belgravia [1868]; The Quiver.*
Exhib: RA, 1844-60; RBA, till 1862.
Colls: BM; Maidstone; V & AM.

LEITCH, William Leighton   RI   1804-1883
Landscape painter. He was born in Glasgow on 22 November 1804, the son of a manufacturer, and brother of R.P. Leitch (q.v.). He was apprenticed to a lawyer after being educated at the Highland Society School and later studied art with D. Macnee. After working for a sign painter, he became scene painter at Glasgow's Theatre Royal in 1824, later moving to London to work at the Pavilion Theatre where he became a friend of D. Roberts and C. Stanfield (qq.v.). Leitch went to Italy in 1833 and did not return for five years, having used his time in extensive travel, teaching and sketching. He then set up in London as a fashionable watercolourist and teacher being patronised by Queen Victoria. He died 25 April 1883.
Contrib: *ILN [1859].*
Exhib: BI; NWS; RA; RBA.
Colls: BM; V & AM.
Bibl: A MacGregor, *Memoir of WL,* 1884

LE JEUNE, Henry L.   ARA   1819-1904
Painter of genre. He was born in London on 12 December 1819 and studied at the RA Schools, becoming Drawing-master there in 1845 and curator in 1848. He was elected ARA in 1863 and died at Hampstead 5 September 1904.
Contrib: *Ministering Children [1856]; Lays of the Holy Land [1858]; The Poetry of Thomas More.*
Exhib: BI; RA; RBA.
Colls: Witt Photo.

LELONG, René   fl.1895-1912
Painter. Born at Arrou, France, and exhibited at The Salon, 1895, becoming a medallist, 1898. Contributed to *The Graphic,* 1912.

LE MAIR, H. Willebeek   1889-1966
Baroness H. van Tuyll van Serooskerken
Dutch designer and illustrator. She was born in Rotterdam on 23 April 1889, the daughter of a wealthy family who were artists and patrons of

the arts. At an early age she was influenced by the French illustrator Maurice Boutet de Monvel whom she met at her father's and was advised by him to attend the Rotterdam Academy, 1909-11. From 1911 she had growing contacts with London publishers and was to remain very popular as an illustrator of children's books for the British public throughout the 1920s and 1930s. Her style is rather flat in the drawing with muted colours and decorative borders. A sideline of her artistic life was making designs for children's breakfast sets for the Gouda pottery, dating from about 1923. She lived the whole of her married life in the Hague and died there on 15 March 1966.

An exhibition of books and drawings by H. Willebeek Le Mair was held at the Bethnal Green Museum, London, in October 1975.

Illus: *Premières Rondes Enfantines [1904]; Our Old Nursery Rhymes [1911]; Little Songs of Long Ago [1912]; Schumann Album of Children's Pieces [1913]; Grannie's Little Rhyme Book; Mother's Little Rhyme Book, Auntie's Little Rhyme Book; Nursie's Little Rhyme Book; Daddy's Little Rhyme Book [c.1913]; The Children's Corner [1914]; What the Children Sing [1915]; Old Dutch Nursery Rhymes [1917]; A Gallery of Children [A.A. Milne, c.1925]; A Child's Garden of Verses [1926]; Twenty Jatka Tales [1939]; Christmas Carols; The Births of the Founders of Religion [1950-53].*

LEMANN, Miss E.A.   **fl.1878-1889**
Landscape painter and illustrator. She worked at Bath and specialised in children's books.
Illus: *The Cold of Farnilee [Andrew Lang]; King Diddle [H.C. Davidson]; Under the Water [Maurice Noel, c.1889].*
Exhib: RBA; SWA.

LENFESTEY, Gifford Hocart   RBA   **1872-1943**
Landscape painter and illustrator of architectural subjects. He was born at Faversham on 6 September 1872 and studied art at the RCA and in Florence and Paris under Raphael Collin. He was elected RBA in 1898 and served on the Council. He died on 22 December 1943.
Exhib: M, RA; RBA; RI; ROI.
Bibl: *The Studio*, Vol.8, 1896, pp.142-148, illus.

LE QUESNE, Rose   **fl.1886-1895**
Painter, sculptor and illustrator, working in London, but at Jersey in 1890. She contributed drawings of social realism, child workers etc. to *The Strand Magazine,* 1891.
Exhib: L; NEA; RA; RBA.

LESLIE, Charles Robert RA   **1794-1859**
Historical and portrait painter. He was born of American parents at Clerkenwell in 1794 and left with them for America in 1799 where he was brought up. He returned to England in 1811 to study art under Benjamin West and Washington Allston, becoming a student of the RA in 1813 and exhibiting for the first time in that year. He was elected ARA in 1821 and RA in 1826 and returned to the States in 1833 to become Drawing-Master at West Point. He settled in London finally the following year, becoming Professor of Painting at the RA, 1847-52 and as a painter specialised in very finished oil paintings of subjects from 17th and 18th century literature. He is included here for his series of illustrations for the novels of Washington Irving. Leslie, who became a notable art historian, died at St. John's Wood on 5 May 1859.
Pub: *Life of Constable [1845]; Life of Sir Joshua Reynolds.*
Exhib: BI; OWS; RA.
Colls: BM; V & AM.
Bibl: *Autobiographical Recollections,* Edited by Tom Taylor, 1865.

LESLIE, George Dunlop   **1835-1921**
Landscape and figure painter. He was born on 2 July 1835, younger son and pupil of C.R. Leslie, RA (q.v.). He was educated at the Mercer's School, before becoming a student at the RA in 1856. He was elected ARA in 1868 and RA in 1876. He specialised in views of the Home Counties and Thames Valley and White described his book illustrations as 'pretty half mediaeval, half modern…' He died at Lingfield, Sussex, on 21 February 1921.
Contrib: *Two Centuries of Song [1867]; ILN [1878].*
Pub: *Our River [1881]; Letters to Marco [1894]; Riverside Letters [1896]; The Inner Life of the Royal Academy.*

L'ESTRANGE, Roland 'Armadillo'   **1869-1919**
Amateur caricaturist. A member of the family of L'Estrange of Hunstanton Hall, Norfolk. He contributed cartoons to *Vanity Fair,* 1903-04 and 1907. He signs his work Ao for Armadillo.

LEVESON, Major A.H.
Amateur draughtsman. He contributed drawings to *The Illustrated London News* during the Abyssinian Expedition of 1868.

LEVETUS, Celia   **fl.1896-1901**
Illustrator. She was born in Birmingham, the sister of Edward, Lewis and Amelia Levetus, writers and critics. She studied at the Birmingham School and published black and white work in the Morris manner but as Sketchley comments 'in a more flexible style'.
Illus: *Turkish Fairy Tales [1896]; Verse Fancies [1898]; Songs of Innocence [1899].*
Contrib: *The Yellow Book [1896]; English Illustrated Magazine [1896].*
Bibl: *The Artist,* May 1896; R.E.D. Sketchley, *English Book Illustration,* 1903, pp.12, 128.

LEVIS, Max   **1863-**
Portrait and figure painter. He was born in Hamburg, on 27 January 1863 and after studying at the Karlsruhe Academy and at Munich, worked in Vienna from 1888. He contributed an illustration to *The Illustrated London News,* 1892 (Christmas).

LEWIN, Frederic George   **fl.1902-1930**
Humorous illustrator in black and white and colour. He worked throughout his life at Redland, Bristol, and specialised in rural figure subjects and children's books in the chap-book style.
Illus: *Rhymes of Ye Olde Sign Boards [c.1910].*
Contrib: *Punch [1902-08].*
Bibl: *Mr. Punch With Horse and Hound,* New Punch Library, c.1930.

LEWIS, Arthur James   **1825-1901**
Landscape and portrait painter, working in London. He contributed illustrations to *Passages From Modern English Poets,* 1862.
Exhib: BI; GG; New Gall; RA.

LEWIS, F.
Animal artist, contributing illustrations to *The Graphic,* 1886 from Dublin.

LEWIS, Frederick Christian   **1779-1856**
Engraver and painter. He was born in London on 14 March 1779 and apprenticed to J.C. Stadler, the German engraver. He attended the RA Schools and was later appointed as engraver to Princess Charlotte of Wales then successively to Leopold I, George IV, William IV and Queen Victoria. He aquatinted Plate 43 of Turner's *Liber Studiorum.* He died at Enfield on 18 December 1856.
Illus: *Scenery of The River Dart [1821]; The Scenery of The Rivers Tamar and Tavy [1823].*
Exhib: BI; OWS; RBA.

LEWIS, George Robert   **1782-1871**
Genre painter, landscape painter and illustrator. He was born in London in 1782, the younger brother of F.C. Lewis (q.v.). He was a pupil of Fuseli at the RA Schools and after working with his brother for Chamberlain and Ottley, made an extensive tour on the Continent in 1818. This journey, made with the eccentric bibliophile Thomas Frognall Dibdin, was the start of a partnership which lasted some years, Dibdin writing reminiscenses and Lewis illustrating them. He died at Hampstead in 1871.
Illus: *The Bibliographical Decameron [T.F. Dibdin, 1817]; Muscles of The Human Frame [1820]; The Bibliographical Tour [T.F. Dibdin, 1821 & 1829, 3 vols.]; Illustrations of Kilpeck Church [1842]; Banks of The Loire Illustrated; Early Fonts of England [1843]; British Forest Trees; Description of Shobdon Church [1856].*
Exhib : RA, 1820-59.
Colls: BM; Leeds.
Bibl: E.J. O'Dwyer, *Thomas Frognall Dibdin,* Private Libraries Association, 1967.

LEWIS, John Frederick   RA   **1805-1876**
Painter of figures and Eastern scenes. He was born in 1805, the
eldest son of F.C. Lewis (q.v.) and began work as an animal painter
in oils, exhibiting at the RA from the age of sixteen. His precocious
talent attracted the notice of Sir Thomas Lawrence, who employed
him as his assistant for a year. He published six mezzotints after his
own work in 1825, which gained him a commission from George IV
to paint sporting scenes at Windsor. His first visit to Spain in 1832
was of major significance to his work, his style became more
assured, his colours brighter and he developed an interest in the
peninsular and the Middle East that soon became his hall-mark.
Lewis lived abroad, first at Rome and then in the East from 1840 to
1851, basing himself at Cairo but visiting Greece and Albania. He
was President of the OWS in 1855, having been elected in 1829, was
elected ARA in 1859 and RA in 1865. Lewis's watercolours, which
are much sought after today, are among the most brilliant Victorian
achievements in the medium, brilliantly coloured and finely drawn.
He died at Walton-on-Thames in 1876.
Illus: *Sketches and Drawings of the Alhambra [1835, AT 148];
Sketches of Spain and Spanish Character [1836, AT 149]; Sketches
of Spain [1836, AT 150]; Illustrations of Constantinople [1838, AT
394].*
Exhib: BI; OWS; RA; RBA.
Colls: Birmingham; Blackburn; Fitzwilliam; V & AM.
Bibl: *Walker's Quarterly,* XXVIII, 1929; M. Hardie, *Watercol.
Paint. in Brit.,* Vol.III, 1969, pp.48-55, illus.; *JFL RA,* Maj.-Gen.
Michael Lewis, pub. F. Lewis, Leigh-on-Sea, 1978.

'LIB' (Liberio Prosperi)
Italian caricaturist. He contributed to *Vanity Fair,* 1886-94 and 1902-
03.

LIGHT, Kate
Black and white artist. Contributed illustration and decor to a poem
in *The Studio,* Vol.6, 1896.

LILLIE, Charles T.   **fl.1881-1882**
Comic draughtsman. He trained as an engineer and travelled widely
to Africa and America before settling at Haverstock Hill, London, as
an author and artist. He contributed to *Punch* in 1881 and exhibited
flower paintings at the RBA in 1882.

LINDSAY, G.
Contributed drawings of comic fashions to *Punch,* 1906

LINDSAY, Norman Alfred William   **1879-**
Black and white artist. He was born at Creswick, Victoria, Australia,
on 23 February 1879 and joined the art staff of *The Sydney Bulletin*
in 1901. He was chief cartoonist of the paper for many years,
developing a pungent satirical style and a virtuosity of pen line that
makes him the greatest black and white artist Australia has produced.
He illustrated a number of books in addition to his cartooning, most
of his work being left-wing, pacifist and anti-clerical in subject.
Illus: *Theocritus; Boccaccio; Casanova; Petronius; Satyrs and
Sunlight [Hugh McCrae]; Songs of a Campaign [Colombine and
Geelert]; Norman Lindsay's Book No.1 [1912]; No.2 [1915].*
Colls: V & AM.
Bibl: *Pen Drawings of NL,* Sydney, 1918.

LINDSELL, Leonard   **fl.1890-1907**
Illustrator. He was working in Bedford Park, London, during the
1890s and 1900s, contributing to the leading magazines.
Contrib: *The Girls' Own Paper [1890-1900]; The Lady's Pictorial
[1895]; The Idler; The Royal Magazine.*
Colls: V & AM.

LINNEY, W.
Contributed a drawing to *Good Words,* 1861.

LINSDALE, J.
Contributed figure subjects to *Fun,* 1892.

LINTON, Sir James Dromgole   PRI   **1840-1916**
Historical painter and illustrator. He was born in London on 26

December 1840 and educated at Clevedon House, Barnes, before
studying art at Leigh's in Newman Street. He exhibited at the Dudley
Gallery and the RI from 1863, was elected RI in 1870 and became the
first President, 1883-97. He was knighted in 1885. Linton worked in
black and white during the early part of his career, his best work being
done for *The Graphic.* He died in London on 3 October 1916.
Illus: *The Pilgrim's Progress.*
Contrib: *Good Words [1870]; Cassell's Magazine [1870]; The
Graphic [1871-74].*
Exhib: B; G; GG; L; M; New Gall.; P; RA; RI; ROI.
Colls: Ashmolean; V & AM.
Bibl: *English Influences on Vincent Van Gogh,* Arts Council, 1974-
75, p.52.

LINTON, William   **1791-1876**
Landscape painter. He was born at Liverpool in 1791 and after being
educated at Rochdale, entered a merchant's office in Liverpool. He
spent much of his time in sketching the scenery of North Wales and
studied the work of Claude and the Richard Wilson paintings at Ince
Blundell Hall. He made extensive tours of Italy, Sicily and Greece in
1840, gathering information on classical antiquities which he
incorporated in his pictures. Died in London in 1876.
Illus: *Ancient and Modern Colours [1852]; The Scenery of Greece
[1856]; Colossall Vestiges of the Older Nations [1862].*
Exhib: BI; RA; RBA.
Colls: BM; Fitzwilliam; Woburn; V & AM.

LINTON, William James   **1812-1898**
Engraver, poet and socialist. He was born in London on 7 December
1812 and was apprenticed to G.W. Bonner, the engraver, before
entering partnership with Orrin Smith in 1842. He established *The
National* in 1839, which reprinted pieces from other papers for the
benefit of the working man; in 1845 he became editor of *The
Illuminated Magazine* and founded *The English Republic,* 1850-55.
In 1857 he was responsible for engraving the blocks to the historic
Moxon Tennyson and was brought into contact with the Pre-
Raephalites, in the 1860s he engraved for many books and was
influential on a great many black and white artists who were his
pupils, particularly Walter Crane (q.v.). He emigrated to the United
States in 1866 and was elected a member of the Academy in 1882.
He died at Newhaven, Conn., 1 January 1898.
Contrib: *Poems and Pictures [1846]; Good Words [1866]; The
Lake Country [1864]; Wise's Shakespeare; Book of British Ballads
[1842].*
Exhib: RA; RBA.
Bibl: *A History of Wood Engraving in America,* 1882; *Masters Of
Wood Engraving,* 1890; *Memories,* 1895.

LINTOTT, Edward Barnard   **1875-1951**
Portrait and landscape painter. He was born in London in 1875 and
studied at Julian's, the Sorbonne and the École des Beaux-Arts,
Paris. He won a Carnegie Prize for work exhibited at The Salon and
in the 1900s did a certain amount of illustrative work. He may have
visited Russia in 1918 during the Revolution, was based in Chelsea
after the First World War and died there in 1951.
Illus: *The Philharmonic-Symphony Orchestra of New York [W.G.
King, 1940].*
Exhib: G; GG; L; M; NEA; P; RA.
Colls: V & AM.

LINVECKER, J.B.
Animal illustrator, contributing to *The Graphic,* 1872.

LIOTROWSKI
Russian artist, contributing drawings of the Revolution of 1905 to
The Graphic.

LIVETT, Berte
Comic black and white artist. He contributed illustrations to *Judy,*
1899 and *Fun,* 1900.

LIVINGSTON-BULL, Charles
Illustrator of children's books. Drew for C. Lee Bryson's *Tan and
Teckle,* 1908.

LIX, Frédéric Théodore   1830-1897
Genre painter. He was born in December 1830 and began to exhibit at the Paris Salon in 1859. He contributed equestrian subjects to *The Illustrated London News,* 1862-63 and died in Paris in 1897.

LLOYD, Arthur Wynel   1883-
Cartoonist and illustrator. He was born at Hartley Wintney in 1883 and after being educated at Rugby and Queen's College, Oxford, he served in the 25th Royal Fusiliers, 1916-17 and won the MC. He was chief cartoonist for the Essence of Parliament in *Punch* from 1914 and cartoonist of *The News of the World.* Signs
Exhib: Cooling Gall., 1934.

LLOYD, W.W.
Illustrated *P & O Pencillings,* c.1880, a landscape album of lithographs.

LLUELLYN, Mrs Y.A.D.
Black and white artist, working for *The Longbow* and *The Ludgate Monthly* in the 1890s.
Exhib: ROI, 1889.

LOCK, Agnes   fl.1905-1925
Black and white artist working at Frensham, Surrey, from 1918 to 1925. She illustrated *Haunts of Ancient Peace* by Alfred Austin, c.1905.
Exhib: RI, 1918-19.

LOCKE, William
Genre painter and etcher. He was a pupil and friend of Henry Fuseli and worked in Paris and Rome. An undated drawing for Pope's *The Rape of the Lock,* possibly intended for illustration, is in an American private collection.
Bibl: Robert Halsband, *The Rape of the Lock and Its Illustrators 1714-1896,* 1980, p.56.

LOCKHART, Lena   **Mrs Norman Ault**   -1904
Illustrator of children's books, Christmas cards and bookplates. She married the illustrator Normal Ault (q.v.) in 1902. Together they worked on the Dumpy books for Grant Richards and Lena Ault worked on publications for Dean, 1903-04. A collection of her work was sold at Sotheby's 12 December 1980. Signs: 'LL'.

LOCKWOOD, Sir Frank (Francis)   1847-1897
Amateur caricaturist. He was born in 1847 and was educated at Manchester Grammar School, St. Paul's, London and afterwards at Caius College, Cambridge. He was called to the Bar at Lincolns Inn and became Recorder of Sheffield in 1884, MP for York and Solicitor-General, 1894-95. He specialised in legal caricatures and contributed them to *Punch* for many years. R.G.G. Price says that they were 'worked up' by E.T. Reed (q.v.). He died 19 December 1897.
Contrib: *Punch, The Sketch; ILN [25 Dec. 1897].*
Bibl: A. Birrell, *Sir FL,* 1898; R.G.G. Price, A *History of Punch,* 1955, p.168.

LODGE, George Edward   fl.1881-1925
Figure and landscape painter. He specialised in natural history subjects and continental views, which he illustrated with great accuracy. He was working in London to 1917 and then at Camberley.
Contrib: *The English Illustrated Magazine [1886, 1893-94]; The Pall Mall Magazine.*
Exhib: B; L; M; RA; RBA; ROI.

LOEB, Louis   1866-1909
American illustrator. He was born at Cleveland in 1866 and became a member of the National Academy in 1906, dying at Canterbury, New Hampshire in 1909. He is included here as the illustrator of the English edition of *Pudd'nhead Wilson* by Mark Twain, 1897.

LOEFFLER, Ludwig   1819-1876
History painter and lithographer. He was born at Frankfurt-sur-Oder in 1819 and studied under Hensel and attended the Berlin Academy. He died at Berlin in 1876.
Contrib: *ILN [1868-74].*

LOGSDAIL, William   1859-1944
Portrait, architectural and landscape artist. He was born at Lincoln in 1859 and was educated at the Grammar School and School of Art at Lincoln. He won Gold Medals in the National Competition, 1875-76 and began to exhibit at the RA in 1877. He made further studies at the Académie des Beaux-Arts in Antwerp and worked as a painter in Venice, Cairo and Sicily. He was elected to the NEA in 1886.
Contrib: *The Graphic [1889 (topog.)].*
Exhib: G; GG; L; M; New Gall; RA; RBA; ROI.

LONGMIRE, R.O.   fl.1904-1923
Black and white artist working in Liverpool. He contributed illustrations to *Punch,* 1904.
Exhib: L.

LORAINE, Nevison Arthur   RBA   fl. 1889-1908
Figure and landscape painter. He was elected RBA in 1893 and contributed to *The Illustrated London News,* 1895.
Exhib: L; RA; RBA; ROI.

LORIOU, Felix
French illustrator. Contributed colour plates to *The Illustrated London News,* Christmas 1916, in the style of Poiret.

LORNE, The Marquess of   1845-1914
PC KG afterwards 9th Duke of Argyll.
Amateur artist. Born 6 August 1845, eldest son of George, 8th Duke of Argyll. He was educated at Eton and Trinity College, Cambridge and was MP for Argyllshire in 1868. In 1871, he married HRH Princess Louise (q.v.), fourth daughter of Queen Victoria, becoming successively Governor-General of Canada, 1878-83 and MP for South Manchester, 1895. Lord Lorne published numerous books including *Canadian Pictures,* 1885 and died 2 May 1914.
Illus: *Guido & Lita, A Tale of the Riviera [1873 (4 illus.)].*
Contrib: *The Graphic [1883].*

LORON, G.A.   fl.1895-1914
Illustrator. The Victoria and Albert Museum has illustrations by this artist for *The Heptameron* by Margaret of Navarre, in pen, ink, black chalk and wash on primed canvas.

LORSAY or LORSA, Louis Alexandre Eustache   1822-
Portrait painter and draughtsman. He was born at Paris on 23 June 1822 and studied with Paris and Monvoisin, exhibiting at the Salon in 1847 and 1859. He contributed figure subjects to *The Illustrated Times* in 1855.

LOUDAN, William Mouat   1868-1925
Genre and portrait painter. He was born in London of Scottish parents in 1868 and educated at Dulwich College before attending the RA Schools for four years, and winning the travelling scholarship. He then worked in Paris under Bouguereau and returned to England where he was elected NEA in 1886 and RP in 1891. He later devoted himself entirely to portraiture and died in London on 26 December 1925.
Contrib: *ILN [1889-94].*
Exhib: B; G; GG; L; M; NEA; New Gall.; P; RA; RBA.
Colls: Leeds; Liverpool; V & AM.
Bibl: *The Artist,* 1899, pp.57-63, illus.

LOUGHRIDGE, E.G.
Amateur. Contributed some portrait into caricature subjects to *Punch* in 1903.
Contrib: *Punch [1903-07].*

LOUISE, HRH   1848-1939
The Princess Louise Caroline Alberta, Marchioness of Lorne.
Artist, sculptress and writer. She was born at Windsor Castle on 8 March 1848, the sixth child and fourth daughter of HM Queen Victoria. She was married at Windsor on 21 March 1871 to the Marquess of Lorne, later 9th Duke of Argyll (q.v.). Princess Louise studied sculpture under Sir E. Boehm and was elected HRE, 1897, and RSW, 1884. She died at Kensington Palace in 1939.
Illus: *Auld Robin and The Farmer [Walter Douglas Campbell, 1894].*
Exhib: G; GG; L; M; RMS; RWS.

LOUTHERBOURG, Philippe Jacques de RA   **1740-1812**

Landscape painter, illustrator and inventor. He was born, according to the inscription on his tomb, on 1 November 1740 at Strasbourg, the son of a painter of Polish extraction. He studied at Strasbourg University and under F.G. Casanova and Carlo Vanloo in Paris, becoming a member of the Académie Royale in 1767. He settled in England in 1771, painting battle pieces and scenery for David Garrick at Drury Lane. An incurable romantic, Loutherbourg invented in 1781 the Eidophusicon for Spring Gardens, a machine that gave the illusion of changing light and movement on a stage set. He began to exhibit at the RA in 1782, was elected ARA in 1780 and RA in 1781. He died at Hammersmith Terrace, Chiswick on 11 March 1812.

Between 1775 and 1780, Loutherbourg developed an interest in caricature based on a study of P.L. Ghezzi and a knowledge of Hogarth. In 1775 he published *Caricatures of the English* from the shop of G.M. Torre. From this period many of the subsidiary groups in his landscapes develop a slightly caricatured form like those of Rowlandson. Loutherbourg gathered together his topographical paintings to form *The Picturesque Scenery of Great Britain*, 1801, and *The Picturesque and Romantic Scenery of England and Wales*, 1805. In 1789, Loutherbourg agreed to contribute plates to Thomas Macklin's edition of *The Holy Bible*. He provided twenty-two out of the seventy-one plates, plus one hundred and twenty-five vignettes. The project lasted from 1789 to 1800 and was based on subscription, Macklin holding annual exhibitions in his Poets' Gallery.

Illus: *Hume's England [Bowyer's Edition]; Nelson's Victories [frontis.]*.

Colls: BM; Derby; Dulwich; Glasgow; Louvre; Stockholm; V & AM.

Bibl: Rudiger Joppien, *PJ de L, RA, 1740-1812*, Catalogue of exhibition at Iveagh Bequest, GLC, 1973.

LOVER, Samuel   **1797-1868**

Song-writer, novelist and miniature artist. He was Secretary of the Royal Hibernian Academy in 1830 and founded the *Dublin University Magazine* in 1833, working in London from 1835. There he was associated with Dickens in founding *Bentley's Magazine* which gave work to many important illustrators. Lover illustrated his own *Legends and Stories of Ireland*, 1831 and *Handy Andy A Tale of Irish Life*, 1842 with good figure subjects in the style of Phiz.

Exhib: RA.

LOVERING, Ida

Illustrated *A Modern Man* by Ella McMahon, 1895.

LOW, Sir David   **1891-1963**

Cartoonist and caricaturist. He was born in Dunedin, New Zealand on 7 April 1891 and educated at the Boys' High School, Christchurch. He became Political Cartoonist of *The Spectator*, Christchurch, in 1902 and joined *The Sydney Bulletin* in 1911. He became cartoonist of *The Star*, London, 1919, and from 1927 worked for *The Evening Standard*, where much of his finest work appeared, and on *The Daily Herald* from 1930.

Publ: *Low's Annual [1908]; Caricatures [1915]; Man [1921]; Lloyd George & Co. [1922]; Low & I [1923]; Low & I Holiday Book [1925]; Lions and Lambs [1928]; The Best of Low [1930]; Low's Russian Sketch Book [1932]; Portfolio of Caricatures [1933]; Low and Terry [1934]; The New Rake's Progress [1934]; Ye Madde Designer [1935]; Politcal Parade [1936]; Low Again [1938]; A Cartoon History of Our Time [1939]; Europe Since Versailles [1939]; Europe at War [1940]; Low's War Cartoons [1941]; Low on the War [1941]; British Cartoonists [1942]; The World at War [1942]; C'est La Guerre [1943]; Valka Zacala Mnichovem [1945]; Dreizehn Jahre Weltgeschehnen [1945]; Kleine Weltgeschichte [1949]; Years of Wrath [1949]*.

Bibl: *Low's Autobiography*, 1956.

See Horne

LOW, Harry (Henry Charles)   **fl.1914-1939**

Landscape painter and black and white artist. He was working at Wimborne, 1939-40 and contributed figure subjects to *Punch*, 1914.

LOW, K

Illustrator and designer. He supplied illustrations and initials to an edition of Oscar Wilde's *A House of Pomegranates*, c.1900-10. He signs his work 'KL'.

Colls: V & AM.

LOWELL, Orson

Illustrator. Contributed drawings to *The Choir Invisible* by James Lane Allen, c.1908.

LOWINSKY, Thomas Esmond   **1892-1947**

Painter and illustrator. He was born in London on 2 March 1892 and was educated at Eton and Trinity College, Oxford. He studied art at the Slade School and enlisted in August 1914, serving throughout the War and on active service in France. Lowinsky was closely associated with the private presses in the 1920s and worked as illustrator for The Nonesuch Press, the Fleuron Press and The Shakespeare Head Press at various times. He specialised in coloured wood cuts, rather linear in style with strong art deco mannerism. He worked in Sunninghill, Berks., until 1914 and then at Kensington Square. London and Aldbourne, Wilts., where he died on 24 April 1947. He became a member of the NEA, 1926. He signs his work:

Illus: *Sidonia the Sorceress [William Meinhold, 1923]; Elegy on Dead Fashion [Edith Sitwell]; Paradise Regained [John Milton, 1924]; Dr Donne and Gargantua [Sacheverell Sitwell]; Exalt the Eglantine [Sacheverell Sitwell]; The Princess of Babylon [1927]; Plutarch's Lives [1928]; The School For Scandal [1929]; Modern Nymphs [Raymond Mortimer, 1930]*.

Exhib: G; L; NEA; RA.

Colls: Fitzwilliam.

Bibl: Monica Bohum Duche, *TL*, Tate Gallery catalogue, 1990.

See Horne

LUARD, John Dalbiac   **1830-1860**

Genre painter and illustrator. He was born in 1830 at Blyborough and followed a military career, serving in the Crimean War. Luard then joined the Langham Sketching Club and studied under John Philip RA. White had little regard for his work which he felt 'shows ...pre-Raphaelite manner and promise which later years did not fulfill'. He died at the early age of thirty, at Winterslow.

Contrib: *Once A Week*.

Exhib: RA, 1855-58.

Bibl: Stacy Marks, *Pen & Pencil Sketches*, p 59.

LUCAS, Horatio Joseph   **1839-1873**

Amateur etcher. He was born on 27 May 1839 and exhibited at the RA, 1870-73. Died 18 December 1873.

Contrib: *Good Words [1863]*.

LUCAS, John Seymour RA RI   **1849-1923**

Historical and portrait painter and illustrator. He was born in London on 21 December 1849, the nephew of John Lucas, the portrait painter. He studied at the St Martin's School of Art and at the RA Schools, specialising in sculpture but later turning to painting. He began to exhibit at the RA, in 1872, was elected NWS and RI in 1877 and ARA and RA in 1886 and 1898 respectively; visitor at the RA 1886. Lucas did a considerable amount of illustrating in the 1890s, mostly of historical stories for magazines, the sketches for these are in grey washes with heavy bodycolour. He died at Blythborough, Suffolk on 8 May 1923.

Illus: *The Cruise of the River [1882]; The Grey Man [S.R. Crockett, 1896]*.

Contrib: *The Graphic [1893, 1901-06]*.

Exhib: B; G; L; M; RA; RBA; RCA; RHA; RI; ROI; RSA.

Colls: Birmingham; Leicester; Sydney; V & AM; Witt Photo.

LUCAS, John Templeton   **1836-1880**

Portrait painter and author. He was born in 1836, the son of John Lucas, the portrait painter and cousin of J. Seymour Lucas (q.v.). He wrote a farce and published some fairy tales in 1871, but is included here for the contributions he made to *The Illustrated London News* in 1865 and 1879 (genre subjects) and in 1876 (Christmas subjects). He died at Whitby in 1880.

Exhib: BI, 1859-76; G; RA; RBA.

LUCAS, Sydney Seymour RA RI   **fl.1904-1940**
Portrait painter and illustrator. The son of J. Seymour Lucas, RI (q.v.)
with whom he collaborated in illustrations. He worked in Bushey,
Herts., in 1909 and at London and Blythborough, Suffolk in 1934
and 1936.
Contrib: *The Graphic [1904, 1905 (military)]; Strand Magazine
[1910-32].*
Exhib: P; RA; RSA.

LUCAS-LUCAS, Henry Frederick   **1848-1943**
Portrait and horse painter. Born at Louth, Lincs., the nephew of Sir
J. Bazalgette. For many years he had a studio in Rugby. Signs with
monogram.
Illus: *The Fox Hunting Alphabet [c.1900 (long octavo album)].*
Exhib: B.
Bibl: *Who's Who, 1926;* Walker, Stella A., *British Sporting Art in
The Twentieth Century,* 1989, pp.26-27.

LUDLOW, Henry Stephen 'Hal'   **1861-**
Portrait and domestic painter and illustrator. He was born in 1861
and studied at Heatherley's and Highgate College and worked in
London from 1880. Ludlow was a very competent all round
magazine illustrator, his subjects ranging from theatrical sketches to
Parliamentary reporting, stories and cattle shows. He was chief
cartoonist to *Judy,* 1889-90. He worked at Hanwell, 1902-25.
Contrib: *Fun [1879-87]; ILN [1882-89]; Judy [1889-90]; The
Queen [1892]; The Rambler [1897]; The Sketch; Ally Sloper's Half
Holiday; Illustrated Bits; Cassell's Family Magazine; Chums; The
Strand Magazine.*
Exhib: B; G; L; RA; RI.
Colls: V & AM.
See illustration.

LUDLOW, S.
Contributed illustrations of birds to *The Graphic,* 1870.

LUDOVICO or LUDOVICI, Albert, Junior   **1852-1932**
Figure and landscape painter and illustrator. He was born at Prague
on 10 July 1852, the son of Albert Ludovici Senior, the artist. He
painted genre subjects and worked in London and Paris after
studying in Geneva. He was elected RBA in 1881 and NEA in 1891.
His Parisian years brought him into contact with many famous artists
and he was influenced by J.M. Whistler (q.v.). He died in London in
1932.
Contrib: *The Strand Magazine [1891 (legal)].*
Exhib: BI; G; GG; L; M; NEA; RA; RBA; RHA; RI.
Colls: Sheffield.
Bibl: *An Artist's Life In London and Paris,* 1926.

LUKER, William   RBA   **1867-**
Animal and figure painter, painter of portraits and illustrator. He
was born in Kensington in 1867, the son of William Luker, the
portrait, genre and animal painter. He was educated at private
schools in London and Oxford before studying art at the South
Kensington Schools. He worked for most of his life in London, but
at Stanford-le-Hope, Essex, 1893 to 1903, and a studio at Amberley,
Sussex from 1915. He was elected RBA in 1895 and retired to
Amberley in 1936.
Illus: *Kensington Picturesque and Historical; London City Suburbs;
Textile London; The Children's London [1902]; Souvenir of the
Indian Peace Contingents Visit.*
Contrib: *Souvenir of Indian Peace Contingent.*
Exhib: B; L; M; NEA; RA; RBA; RHA; RI; ROI.

LUMLEY, Arthur   **1837-1912**
American illustrator. He was born in Dublin in 1837 but emigrated
to the United States where he worked as a painter in New York. He
died there 27 September 1912.
Contrib: *ILN [1875-76, 1881].*
Exhib: RA, 1876.

LUMLEY, Augustus Savile   **fl.1855-1899**
Genre and portrait painter. He exhibited at the RA, RBA and BI as
well as at Liverpool, and contributed illustrations to *Sketchy Bits.*

HENRY STEPHEN LUDLOW 'HAL' 1861-. 'Scenes at Smithfield
Cattle Show'. Signed and dated

LUNEL, Ferdinand   **b.1857**
Born in Paris, he was a pupil of Gérôme and a friend of Caran D'Ache.
Contrib: *Pick Me Up [1889 (large figures)].*

LUNT, Wilmot
Illustrator. He was born at Warrington, Lancs. and was educated at
the Boteler Grammar School and studied art at the Beaux Arts and
Julian's in Paris. Lunt was principally a figure artist in black and
white and contributed to many magazines. He worked at Elstree,
Hertfordshire from 1914.
Contrib: *Punch [1908-09]; The Graphic [1915-16]; The Bystander;
The Tatler.*
Exhib: L; RA; RI.
Bibl: *Who's Who in Art,* 1927.

LUTYENS, Sir Edwin Landseer PRA   **1869-1944**
Architect and caricaturist. He was born in 1869 and studied at South
Kensington under Sir Ernest George. He began to practice in 1888
and built country houses and later the brilliant New Delhi complex,
1913-30. Throughout his life, Lutyens was a talented and compulsive
caricaturist and many of his letters and drawings are decorated in the
margins with his humorous inspirations. He was elected PRA in
1938 and died in office in 1944; he had been knighted in 1918 and
received the OM in 1942.
Colls: RIBA.
Bibl: A.S.G. Butler, *The Architecture of Sir EL;* C. Hussey, *The Life of
Sir EL,* 1950; Clayre Percy & Jane Ridley, *The Letters of EL,* 1965.

LYDON, A.F.   **1836-1917**
Engraver and illustrator. He worked at Great Driffield, Yorkshire,
and specialised in ornithological and natural history illustration.
Illus: *Gems From The Poets [c.1860]; Houghton's British Fresh-
water Fishes [1879].*
Contrib: *ILN [1890]; The English Illustrated Magazine [1891-92].*
Exhib: RA, 1861.
Colls: Witt Photo.

LYNCH, Albert 1851-
Portrait and genre painter, he was born at Lima, Peru and studied in Paris at the École des Beaux-Arts and with Gabriel Ferrier. Gold medal at the Paris Exhibition, 1900. Chevalier of the Legion of Honour, 1901.
Illus: *La Parisienne [Henri Becque, c.1900].*

LYNCH, F.
Caricaturist, contributing portraits chargés to *Fun,* 1901.

LYNCH, Ilbery fl.1905-1925
Black and white artist. Very little is known about this talented follower of Aubrey Beardsley. He illustrated *The Transmutation of Ling* by Ernest Bramah and designed a cover for *The Wallet of Kai Lung.* The Victoria and Albert Museum has an extremely fine pen drawing in pastiche of Beardsley, signed and dated 1909.
Exhib: FAS, 1913.
Colls: V & AM.
Bibl: Grant Richards, *Author Hunting,* 1960.
See illustration.

LYNCH, J.F.A.
Topographical artist. He contributed to *The Illustrated London News* and *The Illustrated Times* in 1860.

LYNCH, J.G. Bohun 1884-
Author and caricaturist. He was born in London on 21 May 1884 and was educated at Haileybury and University College, Oxford. Lynch was a popular caricaturist in the early 1920s, usually working in chalk and drawing large heads. He wrote a perceptive study of Max Beerbohm (q.v.).
Publ: *Glamour [1912]; Cake [1913]; Unofficial [1915]; The Complete Gentleman [1916]; The Tender Conscience [1919]; Forgotten Realms [1920]; A Perfect Day [1923]; Menace From The Moon; Max Beerbohm in Perspective [1921]; A Muster of Ghosts [1924]; Decorations and Absurdities.*
Bibl: *Caricature of Today,* Studio, 1928, pl.89.

LYON, Captain George Francis 1795-1832
Naval officer and traveller. He was born in 1795 and entered the Navy in 1808. He travelled to Africa in 1818-20 and published a narrative account of this in 1821. He formed part of Parry's Arctic Expedition in 1821-23 and after visiting Mexico and South America died at sea in 1832.
Illus: *The Private Journal of Captain GFL of HMS Hecla [1824].*

ILBERY LYNCH fl.1905-1925. 'Just Published'. An illustration in the style of Aubrey Beardsley. Pen and ink. Signed and dated 1909, and inscribed to Robert Ross. 8¼in x 11¼in (21cm x 28.6cm)

Victoria and Albert Museum

MACBETH, Ann fl.1902-1925
Watercolour artist. She may have been trained at the Glasgow School and was working in the city, 1902-07 and again in 1925. Her style of drawing in pen and ink heightened with bodycolour and stippled, is close to that of Jessie M. King and Annie French (qq.v.) who offer an interesting comparison. Her drawing of 'Sleeping Beauty' sold by Sotheby's on 15 November 1977, may be for illustration.
Exhib: G; L.

MACBETH, James 1847-1891
Landscape painter and illustrator. He was born in Glasgow in 1847, the son of Norman Macbeth, RSA and brother of R.W. Macbeth, RA (q.v.). He worked in London and at Churt, Surrey and died in 1890.
Contrib: *ILN [1872-73]; The Graphic [1872-74].*
Exhib: G; GG; L; M; RA; RBA; RI; ROI; RSA.
Colls: Norwich.

MACBETH, Robert Walker RA 1848-1910
Painter and illustrator. He was born in Glasgow on 30 September 1848, the son of Norman Macbeth, RSA, and was educated at Edinburgh and at Friedrichsdorf, Germany. He studied art at the RSA Schools and on coming to London in 1870, began to work as an illustrator for *The Graphic*, then in its first year. Macbeth drew a wide variety of subjects for the paper, including sketches of the Commune but became well-known for his rustic scenes and his etchings. As an etcher he was much influenced by Velazquez and Titian and was elected RE on the foundation of the Society. Macbeth, who gave his recreation in *Who's Who* as 'sleeping when too dark to work', became ARA in 1883 and RA in 1903. He died in London on 1 November 1910.
Illus: *A Thousand Days in the Arctic [F.G. Jackson, 1899].*
Contrib: *The Graphic [1870-71, 1901-03]; Once a Week [1870]; The Sunday Magazine [1871]; The English Illustrated Magazine [1883-85].*
Exhib: G; GG; L; M; New Gall.; P; RA; RBA; RE; RI; ROI; RSA; RWS.
Colls: Aberdeen; V & AM; Witt Photo.

MACBETH-RAEBURN, Henry Raeburn RA 1860-1947
Artist and engraver. He was born in Glasgow on 24 September 1860, the son of Norman Macbeth, RSA and brother of R.W. and J. Macbeth (qq.v.). He was educated at the Edinburgh Academy and University and studied art at the RSA and at Julian's in Paris. He began his career as a portrait painter in London in 1884 and turned to engraving in 1890. In 1889, he made a visit to Spain and in 1896-97 etched a series of frontispieces for Osgood & Co.'s edition of *The Wessex Novels* by Thomas Hardy. Macbeth-Raeburn was best known in the 1920s for his engravings after the works of old masters, especially Raeburn. He was elected RE in 1899, ARA in 1921 and RA in 1933. He died in 1947.
Contrib: *ILN [1894-96].*
Exhib: G; L; M; P; RA; RBA; RE; RI; ROI; RSA.
Colls: V & AM.

McCLURE, Griselda M.
Illustrator, contributing drawings to *The Dawn at Shanty Bay*, a boy's story by R.E. Knowles, 1908.

McCONNELL, William fl.1850-1865
Cartoonist and comic artist. He was the son of a tailor of Irish extraction, learnt wood engraving from Swain and was a popular contributor to illustrated papers in the 1850s. He had two official appointments, that of cartoonist to *Punch*, 1852 and cartoonist of *The Illustrated Times*, 1855-56. His style is always exaggerated and grotesque with slight similarities to 'Phiz' or John Leech but never so well drawn. Spielmann says that he was a friend of G.A. Sala (q.v.) and was much commended by Mark Lemon for his *Punch* work which had included fierce attacks on Prince Louis Napoleon. According to Spielmann he 'revelled in beggars', 'swells' and 'backgrounds' and died of consumption soon after 1852. This must be incorrect information as he was still contributing to other periodicals in the 1860s.
Illus: *Boys & Their Rulers [1854];* Blackwood's Books for Everybody advertised the following titles in 1856: *George Wrackett's Monkey The Mischief He Made and the Pranks he Played Cut out by George Wrackett designed and drawn by W. McConnell [n.d.]; Sayings & Doings of The Celebrated Mrs Partington [illus. by W. McC, n.d.]; Houses with the Fronts Off [J.H. Friswell, n.d.]; Love Affairs! Or caught In His Own Trap by Mrs Caustic [n.d.]; Twelve Insides By One Out [J.H. Friswell, n.d.]; Mrs Partington's Tea Party with Strawberries and Cream [n.d.]; Twice Round The Clock [G.A. Sala, 1859]; The Adventures of Mr. Wilderspin [1860]; Upside Down Or Turnabout Traits [1868, col.].*
Contrib: *Punch [1850-52]; ILN [1851-58, 1860]; The Illustrated London Magazine [1855]; The Illustrated Times [1855-61]; The Welcome Guest [1858 & 1860]; London Society [1864]; The Churchman's Family Magazine [1864]; The Sunday Magazine [1865].*
Bibl: M.H. Spielmann, *The History of Punch*, 1895, pp.460-461; Dalziel, *A Record of Work*, 1901, p.190.

McCORMICK, Arthur David RBA FRGS 1860-1943
Artist and illustrator. He was born at Coleraine on 14 October 1860 and was educated at Coleraine and Belfast, studying art at South Kensington, 1883-86. He accompanied Sir Martin Conway's expedition to Karakoram, Himalayas, as artist in 1892-93 and Clinton Dent to the Caucasus in 1895. He was elected RBA in 1897 and ROI and RI in 1905 and 1906 respectively. He was FRGS from 1895 and died at St John's Wood in 1943. An exhibition of his work was held at the Alpine Gallery in 1904.
Illus: *Climbing and Exploring in the Karakoram Himalayas [W.M. Conway, 1894]; Silent Gods and Sun-Steeped Lands [R.W. Frazer, 1895]; Climbs in the New Zealand Alps [E.A. Fitzgerald, 1896]; The Kahirs of the Hindu-Kush [Sir G.S. Robertson, 1896]; New Climbs in Norway [E.C. Openheim, 1898]; Prince Patrick [A. Graves, 1898]; From the Cape to Cairo [E.S. Grogan, 1900]; Wanderings in Three Continents [Sir R. F. Burton, 1901]; The Alps [Sir W.M. Conway, 1904]; The Netherlands [M. Macgregory, 1907]; New Zealand [R. Horsley, 1908]; India [V. Surridge, 1909].*
Contrib: *The English Illustrated Magazine [1885-88]; ILN [1886-97]; Good Words [1898]; Arabian Nights [1899]; Strand Magazine [1906].*
Exhib: B; G; L; RA; RBA; RHA; RI; ROI; RWA.
Bibl: *An Artist in the Himalayas*, 1895.

McCORMICK, Fred
Artist. Contributed sketches of China to *The Graphic*, 1902-03.

McCULLOCH, Horatio RSA 1805-1867
Landscape painter. He was born in Glasgow on 9 November 1805, the son of a weaver and studied art with W.L. Leitch and Daniel Macnee. He first worked with the latter, painting snuff boxes and then moved to Edinburgh where he became an engraver. He began to exhibit at the RA in 1829 and was elected ARSA in 1834 and RSA in 1838. He specialised in Highland scenery and was influential on the younger generation of Scottish painters. He died at Edinburgh on 24 June 1867.
Contrib: *Scotland Illustrated [1838].*
Exhib: BI; RA; RSA.
Colls: Edinburgh; Glasgow.
Bibl: A. Frazer, *H. McC*, 1872.

WILLIAM BROWN MACDOUGALL d.1936. 'The Mother and the Dead Child'. An illustration to *The Eerie Book* by Margaret Armour, 1898

MACDONALD, A.K.   **fl.1898-1947**
Illustrator. Contributed to *The Longbow,* 1898 and was working in London, 1914-25.
See Horne

MACDONALD, Margaret   **1865-1933**
Designer. She set up a studio with her sister in Glasgow in 1894 and married the architect Charles Rennie Mackintosh in 1900. One of the Glasgow 'Four', she was a highly original designer in the fields of textiles, brassware, leather, illumination and posters. Her only contribution to illustration was a geometric design which appeared in *The Yellow Book,* July 1896.
Bibl: *Charles Rennie Mackintosh, 1868-1928, Architecture, Design and Painting,* Scottish Arts Council Catalogue, 1968.

MACDOUGALL, William Brown   **-1936**
Painter, etcher, wood engraver and illustrator. He was born in Glasgow and educated at the Glasgow Academy. He studied art in Paris at Julian's and under Bouguereau, J.M. Laurens and R. Fleury. Macdougall was a regular exhibitor at the Salon and became a member of the NEA in 1890. His style changes distinctly after his appearance in *The Yellow Book* in 1894 and contact with Aubrey Beardsley (q.v.). From this point his illustrative work is symbolic and sombre with a great emphasis on black and white contrasts, but he lacks the wit of his great predecessor. He died at Loughton, Essex, 20 April 1936.
Illus: *Chronicles of Streatham [1896]; The Book of Ruth [1896];*

The Fall of the Nibelungs [Margaret Armour, 1897]; Thames Sonnets and Semblances [1897]; Isabella...[1898]; The Shadow of Love and Other Poems [Margaret Armour, 1898]; The Eerie Book [Margaret Armour, 1898]; The Blessed Damozel [D.G. Rossetti, 1898]; Omar Khayyam [1898]; Fields of France; St. Paul [F. W. Myers].
Contrib: *The Yellow Book [1894]; The Evergreen [1894]; The Savoy.*
Exhib: G; L; M; NEA; RA; RSA.
Bibl: *The Studio,* Vol.10, 1897, p.141; Vol.15, 1898, p.210; R.E.D. Sketchley, *Eng. Bk. Illus.,*1902, pp.26, 128.
See illustration.

McEVOY, Arthur Ambrose   **ARA ARWS**   **1878-1927**
Landscape and portrait painter, born at Crudwell, Wiltshire in 1878 and studied at the Slade School. He was strongly influenced by J McNeil Whistler (q.v.) worked with Augustus John and Walter Sickert, and developed a free style of watercolour portraits for which he is best known. He was commissioned to paint portraits of the naval VCs in the First World War and was elected ARA in 1924 and ARWS in 1926, having been a member of the NEA, 1902. An exhibition of his watercolours was held at the Leicester Galleries in 1927 and memorial exhibitions at the RA and Manchester in 1928 and 1933. He died in London on 4 January 1927 of pneumonia.
Contrib: *The Quarto [1896].*
Exhib: G; GG; L; M; NEA; RA; RHA; RSA; RSW; RWS.
Colls: Bradford; Leeds; Manchester; Paris.
Bibl: C. Johnson, *The Works of AM,* 1919; R.M Y. Gleadowe, *AM,* 1924; OWS Club, VII, 1931.

McEWEN, D.H.
Illustrator. Contributed to *The Book of South Wales* by Mr and Mrs S.C. Hall, 1861.

MACFALL, Major C. Haldane   **1860-1928**
Artist and writer. He was born on 24 July 1860 and was educated at the Royal Military Academy, Sandhurst. Civil list pension for literature, 1914. He wrote numerous books on eighteenth century painting and a *History of Art* in eight volumes, 1910. He died in London, 25 July 1928.
Contrib: *The Graphic [1891];* his own *The Splendid Wayfaring [1913].*
Exhib: RA; RWA.
See Horne

MacFARLANE, T.D.   **fl.1894-1908**
Illustrator of children's books. He was working in Glasgow, 1894-97 and illustrated *Minstrelsy of the Scottish Border,* Noyes, 1908 and *Days That Speak,* 1908, both in colour.
Exhib: G.

MACGILLIVRAY, James Pittendrigh RSA   **1856-1938**
Sculptor. He was born at Inverurie, Aberdeenshire, in 1856 and studied art under William Brodie, RSA and John Mossman, HRSA. He became RSA in 1901, LLD, Aberdeen, 1909 and Kings Sculptor for Scotland, 1921. Macgillivray was a fine black and white draughtsman and some prints in the Witt Photo Library appear to be for book illustration. He died at Edinburgh, 29 April 1938.
Publ: *Verse Pro Patria [1915]; Bog Myrtle and Peat Reek [1922].*
Exhib: G; GG; L; M; NEA; RA; RSA.

MACGREGOR, Archie G.
Sculptor and illustrator. Working in London, 1884 to 1907 and exhibiting regularly.
Illus: *Katawampas [Judge Parry, 1895]; Butterscotia [Judge Parry, 1896]; The First Book of Klab [Judge Parry, 1897]; The World Wonderful [Charles Squire, 1898].*
Exhib: L; M; New Gall; NWS; RA; RHA; RI; ROI.
Bibl: R.E.D. Sketchley, *Eng. Bk. Illus.,* 1903, pp.107, 167.

MACGREGOR, G.
Probably G.S. Macgregor, working in Glasgow, 1891 and exhibiting at the RSA.
Contrib: *ILN [1887 (figures)].*

MacGREGOR, Jessie   **-1919**
Portrait, genre and historical painter and illustrator. She was working in Liverpool from 1872 and in London from 1886 and was elected ASWA in 1886 and SWA in 1887.
Illus: *Christmas Eve at Romney Hall [1901].*
Exhib: B; G; L; M; RA; ROI; SWA.

McHUTCHON, F.
Humorous animal artist. Contributed illustrations to *Punch*, 1904-05.

McIAN, Robert Ronald   ARSA   **1803-1856**
Genre painter and illustrator. He was born in 1803 and worked as a professional actor as well as being a painter. He specialised in scenes of the Highlands and after 1840 abandoned the theatre for the life of a painter, having exhibited at the RA from 1836. He was elected ARSA and died at Hampstead in 1856.
Illus: *The Clans of the Scottish Highlands, Illustrated by Appropriate Figures [James Logan, 1845-47 (2 vols.)]; The London Art Union Prize Annual [1845].*
Exhib: BI; RA; RBA; RSA.

MacINTOSH, John MacIntosh   **1847-1913**
Landscape and view painter. He was born at Inverness in 1847 and studied at Heatherley's, the West London School of Art and in Versailles. He worked at Woolhampton near Reading, and died at Shanklin in 1913. He illustrated E.G. Hayden's *Islands of the Vale*, 1908.
Colls: Reading; V & AM.

MACKAY, Wallis 'WV'   **fl.1870-1893**
Black and white artist and caricaturist. He was a social cartoonist for *Punch*, 1870-74 but offended Tom Taylor, the Editor and was dismissed, although work by him was still appearing in 1877. He became cartoonist of *Fun* in 1893.
Contrib: *Judy; ILN [1880].*
Bibl: M.H. Spielmann, *The History of Punch*, 1894, pp.540-541.

MACKENZIE, Frederick OWS   **1787-1854**
Topographical draughtsman. He was born in 1787 and became a pupil of John A. Repton and began a career as an architectural draughtsman for leading publishers such as Britton, Ackermann and Le Keux. He became an Associate of the OWS in 1822, and a Member in 1823, holding the post of Treasurer from 1831 till his death. Mackenzie was a very accurate delineator of gothic buildings at a time when clarity was all important. His drawings in grey washes are small and feathery and beautiful and have the definition that seems to be lost in the prints after his works. In later life his work was superceded by early photography. He died in London on 25 April 1854.
Illus: *Etchings of landscapes for the use of students [1812]; History of the Abbey Church of St. Peter, Westminster [1812]; Britton's Salisbury Cathedral [1813]; History of the University of Oxford [1814]; History of the University of Cambridge [1815]; Illustrations of the Principal Antiquities of Oxfordshire [1823]; Graphic Illustrations of Warwickshire [1829]; Memorials of Architectural Antiquities of St Stephen's Chapel, Westminster [n.d.].*
Contrib: *Britton's Beauties of England and Wales [1810-15]; The Oxford Almanack [1822, 1827, 1838, 1848, 1850, 1851, 1853].*
Exhib: OWS; RA; RBA.
Colls: Ashmolean; BM; Fitzwilliam; Lincoln; Manchester; V & AM; Witt Photo.
Bibl: M. Hardie, *Watercol. Paint. in Brit.*, Vol.3, 1968, pp.17-18 illus; Petter, *Oxford Almanacks*, 1974.

MACKENZIE, John D.   **fl.1886-1896**
Painter, black and white artist and illustrator. He was working in London from 1886 and at Newlyn, Penzance from 1889. He supplied a cover and title page to *The Yellow Book* in October 1895, and exhibited at the RA and RBA.
Illus: *Sonnets and Songs [May Bateman, 1895-96 (title etc.)].*

MACKEWAN, Arthur
Amateur contributor to *Punch*, 1907.

MACKIE, Charles Hodge RSA RSW   **1862-1920**
Genre and landscape painter. He was born at Aldershot of Scottish parents in 1862 and was educated at Edinburgh University before studying at the RSA Schools. He travelled in Spain, Italy and France, where he met Gauguin and Vuillard and settled at Murrayfield. Mackie was a prolific and diverse artist and engaged in etching, mural decoration, sculpture and colour printing as well as painting. He was elected ARSA in 1902 and RSA in 1912, RSW, 1902. He died on 12 July 1920.
Contrib: *The Evergreen [1895].*
Exhib: G; L; M; NEA; RA; RHA; RSA; RSW.
Colls: BM; Edinburgh; Leeds; Liverpool; V & AM; Witt Photo.
Bibl: *The Studio*, Winter No., 1900-01, p.48 illus.; Vol.58, 1913, pp. 66,137, 295; Vol.68, 1913, pp.61, 122, 125; Vol.70, 1913, pp.107; *A.J.* 1900, p.287; *The Connoisseur*, Vol.37, 1912, p.53.

McKIE, Helen Madeleine   **fl.1915-1936**
Illustrator. She studied at the Lambeth School of Art and was for a time on the staff of *The Bystander*. She contributed to *The Graphic*, Christmas number, 1915.
Exhib: RHA; SWA.

MACKLIN, Thomas Eyre   **1867-1943**
Painter and sculptor. He was born at Newcastle-upon-Tyne in 1867, the son of a journalist, and was educated privately before studying art at the RA Schools and in Paris. Macklin became Special Artist to *The Pall Mall Budget* from 1882 to 1892 and made many designs for books, magazines and posters. He travelled in Italy and lived for some time in France but also painted in his native Newcastle. He died in 1943. He was elected RBA, 1902.
Illus: *The Works of Nathaniel Hawthorne [1894].*
Exhib: L; RA; RBA; RSA.
Colls: Gateshead.

McLEISH, Annie
Illustrator. Pupil of the Mount Street School of Art and contributed illustration to *The Studio*, Vol. 13, 1897, pp.192-193.

MACLEOD, Jessie   **fl.1845-1875**
Historical painter and illustrator, working in Chelsea and Marylebone. She illustrated *Fifteen Designs Illustrating Tears* for Ackermann & Co., 1851.
Exhib: BI; RA; SS.

McLEOD, Lyons
Artist. Illustrated *Travels in Eastern Africa and Mozambique*, 1860. AT 277.

MACLISE, Daniel RA   **1806-1870**
Historical and portrait painter. He was born at Cork in 1806, the son of a former Scottish soldier and while attending the Cork Art School was brought to public notice by a sketch he made of Sir Walter Scott, 1825. He travelled to London in July 1827 and attended the RA Schools, winning the silver and gold medals in 1828. He exhibited at the RA from 1829 and after a brief spell in Ireland that year, returned in 1830 to make a career in book illustration. Maclise contributed eighty caricatures to *Fraser's Magazine* between then and 1836. Most of them were drawn with a lithographic pen and suited his linear style and meticulous rendering. The caricatures were accompanied by biting literary sketches from the pen of William Maginn and relied more for their effect on their stylization than on their grotesqueness. Thomas Carlyle, sitting for his caricature, described Maclise as 'a quiet shy man with much brogue'. *Fraser's Illustrations*, the originals of which are now in the BM, made the artist's name and he illustrated many books of legend in the 1840s. Always concerned as an illustrator in fantasy rather than reality, Maclise found his sources in contemporary German illustration. He had been elected ARA in 1835 and RA in 1840 and became an immensely popular painter, declining a knighthood and the Presidency of the RA in 1866. But by the time his illustrations for *Moxon's Tennyson* were appearing in 1857 and 1861, these and his *Norman Conquest* for The Art Union, 1866, were already in an outmoded style. He died at 4 Cheyne Walk, Chelsea on 25 April 1870.
Illus: *Fairy Legends [Crofton Croker, 1826]; Tour Round Ireland*

DANIEL MACLISE RA 1806-1870. 'Lesbia'. Illustration to *Irish Melodies* by Tom Moore, London 1846

[John Barrow, 1826]; Ireland its Scenery and Character [1841]; The Chimes: A Goblin Story...[Charles Dickens, 1844]; The Cricket on The Hearth, A Fairy Tale...[Charles Dickens, 1845]; Thomas Moore's Irish Melodies [1845]; Leonora [Gottfried Burger, 1847]; Moxon's Tennyson [1857, 1861]; The Princess [Tennyson, 1860]; Idylls of The King [Tennyson]; Story of the Norman Conquest [Art Union, 1866].
Contrib: *Fraser's Magazine [1830-36]; The Keepsake [1835]; Heath's Gallery [1836, 1838]; The Old Curiosity Shop [Charles Dickens (Chap.55), 1841].*
Exhib: BI; RA; RBA.
Colls: Ashmolean; BM; Ireland; Nat. Gall; NPG; V & AM; Witt Photo.
Bibl: Chatto & Jackson, *Treatise on Wood Engraving*, 1861, p.569; R. Ormond, *DM 1806-1870*, NPG, 1972.
See illustration.

MACLURE, Andrew   fl.1857-1881
Landscape painter and lithographer. This artist illustrated *Queen Victoria in Scotland*, 1842 and *Highlands and Islands of The Adriatic*, 1849, AT 44.
Illus: *Flowers and Their Poetry [J. Stevenson Bushman, c.1845].*
Exhib: G; RA, 1857-81.
Colls: Witt Photo.

McMANUS, Henry ARHA   c.1810-1878
Painter. He was elected an associate of the RHA in 1857 and Professor of the RHA. He died at Dalkey, Dublin on 22 March 1878.
Illus: *Bob Norbery or Sketches from the Note Book of An Irish Reporter [1846].*
Colls: Dublin; NG; V & AM.

MACMICHAEL, William   1784-1839
Amateur artist, physician and writer. He was educated at Christ Church, Oxford, MA, 1807 and became Radcliffe Travelling Fellow in 1811, MD in 1816 and FRCP in 1818. He was appointed physician to William IV in 1831.
Pub: *The Gold-headed Cane [1827].*
Illus: *Journey from Moscow to Constantinople [1819, AT 20].*

MACNAB, Peter   RBA   -1900
Genre painter and illustrator. Working in London and Woking, Surrey and exhibiting from 1864. He was elected RBA in 1879.
Contrib: *ILN [1882-83]; The Cornhill Magazine [1884]; The English Illustrated Magazine [1885].*
Exhib: B; BI; FAS; G; L; M; RA; RBA; RI; ROI.

MACNEIL, H.
Illustrator. Contributed military subjects to *The English Illustrated Magazine*, 1896.

MACPHERSON, Douglas   1871-
Illustrator. He was born in Essex on 8 October 1871 the son of John Macpherson, artist. After being educated at a private school, he studied art at Westminster School of Art and became a member of the original staff of *The Daily Graphic*, 1890-1913. He served as Special Artist at home and abroad for *The Daily Graphic* and *The Graphic* until he joined *The Sphere* in 1913 attending, among other events, The Spanish-American War, 1898, The St Petersburg Revolt, 1905 and the Assassination of Don Carlos in 1908. He served with the RNVR 1914-18 and was present for *The Sphere* at Tutankhamun's Tomb, 1923-24. Drew the Coronation of King George VI for *The Daily Mail*, 1937 and sketches of the Second World War for *The Sphere, Daily Telegraph* and *Daily Mail*, 1939-45.
Contrib: *The Daily Graphic [1890-1913]; St Pauls [1894]; The Ludgate Monthly; The Graphic [1901-10]; Punch [1906-09].*
Exhib: L; RA.

MACQUOID, Percy T.   RI   1852-1925
Artist, illustrator, designer and historian of English furniture. He was born in 1852, the son of T.R. Macquoid (q.v.) and was educated at Marlborough and studied art at Heatherley's, at the RA Schools and in France. He worked for *The Graphic* from 1871, at first concentrating on animal subjects but later painting historical and genre pictures. He was elected RI, 1882 and ROI, 1883. He was a designer of theatrical costumes but in his later years concentrated wholly on the study of English furniture, publishing his four volumes *History of English Furniture*, 1905. He died on 20 March 1925.
Illus: *The Bridal of Triermain [Walter Scott, Art Union, 1886].*
Contrib: *The Graphic [1871-90]; ILN [1874-82]; The Quiver [1880].*
Exhib: B; FAS; G; L, M, RA; RI; ROI.
Bibl: *English Influences on Vincent Van Gogh*, Arts Council, 1974-75, p.52.

MACQUOID, Thomas Robert   RI   1820-1912
Painter, illustrator and ornamental designer for books. He was born in Chelsea on 24 January 1820 and after being educated in Brompton, studied art at the RA Schools and specialised in book illustration. He is specifically mentioned by Chatto for his work on 'ornamental Letters and Borders' and supplied much decoration of this kind to the early volumes of *The Illustrated London News*, all showing great architectural accuracy and delicacy of execution. He collaborated with his wife, Mrs K.S. Macquoid on a number of travel books. RI, 1882 and ROI, 1883, he died on 6 April 1912. A memorial exhibition of his work was held at the New Dudley Gallery, London in 1912.
Illus: *Little Bird Red and Little Bird Blue [M.B. Edwards, 1861]; The Primrose Pilgrimage [M.B. Edwards, 1865]; Through Normandy [K.S. Macquoid. 1874]; Pictures and Legends of Normandy and Brittany [K.S. Macquoid, 187]; Pictures in Umbria [K.S. Macquoid, 1905]; The Paris Sketchbook [W.M. Thackeray, 1894].*
Contrib: *Examples of Architectural Art in Italy and Spain [1850]; ILN [1851-61, 1863-69]; Favourite English Poems [1857]; The Welcome Guest [1860]; The Churchman's Family Magazine [1863]; The Graphic [1873]; Rhymes and Roundelayes; Burns Poems; Thornbury's Legendary Ballads [1876]; Good Words [1880]; The English Illustrated Magazine [1886-87 (architecture)]; The Pall Mall Magazine.*
Exhib: G; L; M; RA; RBA; RI; ROI; RSW.
Bibl: Chatto & Jackson, *Treatise on Wood Engraving*, 1861, p 599.

McTAGGART, William   RSA RSW   **1835-1910**
Painter and Scottish impressionist. He was born at Aros, near
Campbeltown, and began by painting portraits of the inhabitants of
this Scottish burgh in his spare time. He attended the Trustees
Academy at Edinburgh for seven years from 1852, studying
alongside Sir W.Q. Orchardson (q.v.) and J. MacWhirter (q.v.). He
became ARSA in 1859 and RSA in 1870. He was Vice-President of
the RSW in 1878 and died at Broomieknowe on 2 April 1910.
Contrib: *Good Words [1861].*
Exhib: G; L; NEA; RA; RHA; RSA; RSW.
Colls: Aberdeen; Glasgow; Nat. Gall., Scotland.

MacWHlRTER, John   RA   **1839-1911**
Landscape painter and illustrator. He was born at Slateford near
Edinburgh in 1839, the son of a papermaker and was educated at
Peebles School, the Edinburgh School of Design and the Trustees
Academy. He was elected ARSA in 1867 and moved to London in
1869, where he attracted the notice of Ruskin and became a popular
painter of Highland and Continental landscapes. He made extensive
tours in France, Switzerland, Italy, Austria, Turkey and Norway and
visited the United States. He was a strong advocate of drawing direct
from nature and published a book on technique. Most of his book
illustrations date from his early career in Scotland. He was elected
ARA in 1879 and RA in 1893 and died at St John's Wood on 28
January 1911.
Illus: *Landscape Painting in Watercolours [1901]; The MacWhirter
Sketchbook [1906]; Sketches from Nature [1913].*
Contrib: *Good Words [1861]; The Golden Thread [1861];
Wordsworth's Poems for the Young [1863]; The Sunday Magazine
[1869]; Pen and Pencil Pictures from the Poets [1866]; Poems and
Songs of Robert Burns [1875]; The Picturesque Mediterranean [1891].*
Exhib: B; FAS; G; GG; L; M; New Gall; RA; RE; RHA; RI; RMS;
ROI; RSA; RSW.
Colls: BM; Dundee; Glasgow; Manchester; Nat. Gall, Scotland; V &
AM.
Bibl: M.H. Spielmann, *The Art of JMcW,* 1904.

McWILSON, J.
Contributing comic animal illustrations to *Punch,* 1908.

MADOT, Adolphus M.   **-1864**
Figure artist and illustrator. He was a pupil of the RA Schools and
studied at Julian's in Paris. He exhibited figure subjects in London,
1852-64, but died young.
Contrib: *The Home Affections [Charles Mackay, 1858]; The
Poetical Works of E.A. Poe [1858].*
Exhib: BI; RA; RBA.

MAHONEY, J.   **fl.1865-1876**
Illustrator and engraver. He was practically uneducated and spent
some years as errand boy for the firm of Vincent, Son and Brooks,
lithographic printers. He was said to be a natural artist and his
drawings came to the notice of J.W. Whymper, to whom he had to
deliver proofs. Whymper took him into his employ and he made
quick progress as a draughtsman, being given small illustrations to
do after a comparatively short time. He was later with the Dalziel
Brothers, but in both cases had to leave because of drunkenness and
disorderly behaviour, finally dying in a latrine in London in the same
unhappy condition. He undertook some important commissions such
as *Oliver Twist, Little Dorrit* and *Our Mutual Friend,* 1871, for
Dickens 'Household Edition' and did a great deal of magazine work.
Reid is however critical of his uneven style – 'A curious tendency to
dwarf his figures is carried, one might fancy, into the very shape of
many of Mahoney's designs, and into the square squat monogram
with which they are signed.'
Illus: *Scrambles on the Alps [Whymper, 1870]; Oliver Twist, Little
Dorrit, Our Mutual Friend [Dickens 'Household Edition', 1871];
Three Clerks [A. Trollope (frontis.)]; Little Wonder-Horn [Jean
Ingelow, 1872]; Frozen Deep [Wilkie Collins, 1875 (with Du
Maurier)].*
Contrib: *Leisure Hour [1865-66]; Sunday Magazine [1866-70];
The Argosy [1866]; Cassell's Magazine [1867]; Touches of Nature
[1867]; Cassell's Illustrated Readings [1867]; The Peoples
Magazine [1867]; The Quiver [1868]; The Nobility of Life [1869];*

*Good Words For The Young [1869]; National Nursery Rhymes
[1870]; Little Folks [1870]; Judy; Fun; The Day of Rest.*
Colls: V & AM.
Bibl: Forrest Reid, *Illustrators of The Sixties,* 1928, pp.255-256,
illus.

MAHONEY, James   **1816-1879**
Watercolourist and engraver on wood. He was born at Cork in about
1816 and studied in Rome and other European centres, before
returning to work in London, where he died on 29 May, 1879. He
was a member of the NWS.
Contrib: *ILN [1847].*
Exhib: RA, 1866-77.

MAJENDIE, Aline
Caricatures by her in the Royal Household Scrapbook, Royal
Library, Windsor, c.1870.

MALCOLM, James Peller   **1767-1815**
Draughtsman and engraver. He was born in Philadelphia in 1767 and
came to England in 1788-89, attending the RA Schools for three
years. He was acquainted with Benjamin West and J. Wright of
Derby, who patronised him, but he never made a success of painting
and turned to engraving for a living. Malcolm was also a writer, a
Fellow of the Society of Antiquaries and one of the first artists to
write a treatise on caricature. He died in London in 1815.
Illus: *Twenty Views Within Ten Miles of London [1800]; Excursions
in the County of Kent [1802]; The History of Leicestershire
[Nichols]; Biographical Dictionary of England [Granger];
Londinium Redivivium [1902-07]; Manners and Customs of London
during the XVIII Century [1808, 50 views]; Excursions in the
Counties of Kent, Gloucester, Hereford, Monmouth and Somerset
[1813]; An Historical Sketch of The Art of Caricaturing with
Graphic Illustrations [1813].*
Contrib: *The Gentleman's Magazine; Lyson's Environs of
London [1797-1800]; The Beauties of England and Wales
[1801-05].*
Exhib: RA, 1791.
Colls: V & AM; Witt Photo.

MALLETT, R.W.
Artist. Contributing illustrations of industry to *The Illustrated
London News,* 1875.

MALTON, Thomas the Younger   **1748-1804**
Architectural draughtsman and illustrator. Although the bulk of his
work falls outside the period of this book, he produced three major
works in these years: *Designs for Rural Retreats...chiefly in the
Gothic and Castle Styles,* 34 plates, 1802; *Picturesque Tour
through...London and Westminster,* 1792-1801 and *Views of Oxford,*
1810.

MANN, Harrington   **1864-1937**
Portrait painter and illustrator. He was born at Glasgow in 1864 and
studied art at the Slade School and in Paris and Rome. He was a
member of the Royal Society of Portrait Painters and of the
International Society of Sculptors, Painters and Gravers. He was an
important member of the Glasgow School of painters and an
accomplished decorative artist, working as an illustrator for both *The
Daily Graphic* and *The Scottish Art Review.* He is represented in
most British galleries and died on a visit to New York, 28 February
1937.
Publ: *The Technique of Portrait Painting [1933].*
Exhib: B; G; GG; L; M; NEA; New Gall; P; RA; RBA; RE; RI;
ROI; RSA.
Bibl: *The Artist,* August 1897, pp.363-369, illus.

MANSEL, Miss   afterwards Mrs Bull
Amateur artist. She contributed one drawing to *Punch* in 1863,
which was touched up by John Leech!

MANTON, G. Grenville   RBA   **1855-1932**
Portrait painter and illustrator. He was born in London in 1855, the
son of Gildon Manton, gunmaker. He was educated in London and

The Sleepy Porter

Knock, knock: Never at quiet! (Porter).

HENRY STACY MARKS RA 1829-1898. 'The Sleepy Porter'. An illustration for Shakespeare's *Macbeth*. Pen and ink, signed with monogram and dated 1859. 10½in x 7½in (26.7cm x 19.1cm)
Author's Collection

Paris and was an RA medallist, but left England for America in 1890 and worked there for some years as a portrait painter, exhibiting at The National Academy. On returning to London, he became a staff artist on *Black and White*. He was working at Bushey, Hertfordshire from 1895 till his death on 13 May 1932. He was elected RBA in 1899.
Illus: *True to The Core [Jarrold's Books for Manly Boys, 1894].*
Contrib: *Black & White [1892]; The Quiver [1892]; Pearson's Magazine [1896]; The Ludgate Monthly: The Pall Mall Magazine; The Sphere.*
Exhib: B; L; P; RA; RBA; ROI

MANUEL, J. Wright T. -1899
Illustrator. He worked in London from about 1894 and specialised in comic sporting subjects in black and white but also in chalk and watercolour. He became RBA in 1896 and died in 1899.
Contrib: *Pick-Me-Up [1894]; The Unicorn [1895]; ILN [1896]; Eureka [1897]; The Butterfly [1899]; The Idler; The Minister.*
Exhib: RBA; ROI.
Colls: V&AM.

MARGETSON, William Henry RI 1861-1940
Landscape and genre painter in oil and watercolour, illustrator. He was born at Denmark Hill, London, in December 1861 and after being educated at Dulwich College, studied art at South Kensington and at the RA Schools. He lived and worked in Berkshire from 1914, first at Blewbury and then at Wallingford and was elected RI in 1909. Margetson had a pleasing eye for colour and was most popular as an illustrator of adventure stories. He died 2 January 1940.

Illus: *The King's Pardon [Overton, 1894]; The Village of Youth [B. Hatton, 1895]; With Cochrane The Dauntless [G.A. Henty, 1897]; A Missing Witness [Frank Barrett, 1897]; Aglyaine and Selysette [Sutro, 1898]; The Wild Geese [S.J Weyman, 1908]; Humphrey Bold [H. Strang, 1908].*
Contrib: *The English Illustrated Magazine [1885, 1891-92]; The Quiver [1890]; Black & White [1891]; Cassell's Family Magazine; The Idler; The Pall Mall Magazine; The Graphic [1904-06].*
Exhib: B; G; GG; L; M; RA; RBA; RI; ROI.

MARIE, Adrien-Emmanuel 1848-1891
Painter and illustrator. He was born at Neuilly-sur-Seine on 20 October 1848, and was a pupil of Bayard, Camino and Pils. He was a regular exhibitor at the Salon from 1866 to 1881 and won a bronze medal at the 1889 Exhibition. His connection with England began in 1873, when he started to contribute French genre and social realistic subjects to *The Graphic*. A bold figure draughtsman, he was most prolific in the pages of the magazine from 1885-89, supplementing a rather weak period for English illustrators. He died at Cadiz in April 1891.
Exhib: FAS, M.
Colls: Calais, Tourcoing; Sydney.

MARKLEN, H.
Contributed illustrations to *Griffith's Cheltenham*, 1826.

MARKS, A.J.
Amateur caricaturist. Contributed cartoons to *Vanity Fair*, 1889. Signs his work AJM.

MARKS, Henry Stacy RA 1829-1898
Painter and illustrator. He was born in London on 13 September 1829 and studied art at Leigh's School, Newman Street and at the RA Schools, 1851. He spent some months in Paris with Calderon in 1852 and began exhibiting at the RA in 1853. Marks was very clearly influenced by the Pre-Raphaelites at this time and became a very brilliant pen and ink draughtsman and a masterly painter of animals. Marks seems to have been a very lazy artist and his drawings fall away dramatically after the 1860s into thick outline and clumsy handling. He was obsessed by the Middle Ages and painted many ludicrous subjects of them including 'Toothache in the Olden Time'. His best work is in his bird paintings and his stained glass design. He was elected ARA in 1871 and RA in 1878, and RSW in 1883.
Illus: *Sketching From Nature [T.J. Ellis, 1876]; The Good Old Days [E. Stuart, 1876].*
Contrib: *Home Circle [1855]; Legends of the the Cavaliers and the Roundheads [Thornbury, 1857]; Punch [1861 and 1882]; Willmott's Sacred Poetry [1862]; Passages from Modern English Poets [1862]; Once a Week [1863]; The Churchman's Family Magazine [1863]; Two Centuries of Song [1867]; Ridiculous Rhymes [1869]; London Society [1870]; National Nursery Rhymes [1871]; The Quiver [1873]; The Child's History of England [1873]; ILN [1876 and 1879]; The Graphic.*
Exhib: B; BI; FAS, 1889, 1890, 1895; G; L; M; RA; RCA; ROI; RWS.
Colls: Ashmolean; Exeter; Liverpool; V & AM.
Bibl: H.S. Marks, *Pen and Pencil; Sketches*, 2 vols. 1894; Forrest Reid, *Illustrators of The Sixties*, 1928, pp.254-255; J. Maas, *Victorian Painters*, 1970, p.82, illus.
See illustration.

MARKS, Lewis fl.1814-1815
Amateur caricaturist, specialising in well-drawn figures of Napoleon and Paul Pry.
Colls: Witt Photo.

MARRYAT, Captain Frederick CB FRS 1792-1848
Novelist, draughtsman and caricaturist. He was born in Great George Street, Westminster on 10 July 1792, the son of an MP, and went to sea in 1806, serving throughout the Napoleonic Wars. He served in St Helena, 1820-21, and in North America, 1837-38. On his retirement he became celebrated as a novelist and writer of books for children and died at Langham, Norfolk on 9 August 1848.

JOHN MARTIN 1789-1854. 'The Flight Into Egypt'

Publ: *The Children of the New Forest; The Naval Officer [1829]: Peter Simple [1834]; Midshipman Easy [1836], The Metropolitan Magazine [Editor, 1832-35].*
Colls: V & AM.

'MARS' Maurice BONVOISIN　　　　　　　　**1849-1912**
Draughtsman, engraver and cartoonist of the Belgian School. He was born at Verviers on 26 May 1849 and became a regular illustrator in the French papers *Journal amusant* and *Charivari*. He was the only continental artist to be used consistently for cartoon work by British periodicals, his sketchy crayon style, based on the poster and anticipating May, being rather avant-garde here. He was a master of the purely visual joke without text and his books seem to have been popular in this country, some of his subjects being British ones. He died in 1912.
Illus: *Nos Cheris [Plon, Paris, 1886].*
Contrib: *The Graphic [1880-91]; ILN [1882-92]; The Daily Graphic [1890]; The Sketch [1894]; Illustrated Bits.*
Colls: V & AM.

MARSHALL, Benjamin Marshall　　　　　　**1768-1835**
Sporting artist. He was born in Leicestershire on the 8 November 1768 and went to London in 1791 to follow the career of a painter. He exhibited at the RA from 1801 and between 1812 and 1825 had his studio near Newmarket. He died in London on 24 July 1835. He is included here for the illustrations of his work that appeared in *The Sporting Review,* after his death, 1842-46.

MARSHALL, C.A.　　　　　　　　　　　**fl.1889-1890**
Amateur artist and solicitor at Retford in Nottinghamshire. Contributed two drawings to *Punch,* 1889 and one to *Judy,* 1890.

MARSHMAN, J.
Artist working at Bangor, N. Wales. He contributed sporting subjects to *The Graphic,* 1876 and exhibited in the same year.

MARTEN, John II　　　　　　　　　　　**fl.1808-1834**
Topographical artist and son of John Marten of Canterbury, the landscape painter. He contributed drawings to Britton's *Beauties of England and Wales,* 1808 and exhibited at the RA and NWS, 1822-34.
Colls: V & AM.

MARTENS, Henry　　　　　　　　　　　**fl.1828-1854**
Battle painter in oil and watercolour. He worked in London and improved drawings by serving officers for engravings and published his own work.
Illus: *Yeomanry Costumes [1844-47, AT 369]; Costumes of the Indian Army [1846]; Costumes of the British Army in 1855 [1858, both for Ackerman].*
Exhib: BI; RBA.
Colls: Witt Photo.

MARTIN, Charles
Watercolourist and caricaturist. He was the son of John Martin, (q.v.) but according to Spielmann was too indolent to succeed as a painter. He contributed illustrations to *Punch,* in 1853.

MARTIN, John　　　　　　　　　　　　**1789-1854**
Historical and biblical painter and illustrator. He was born at Eastlands End, Haydon Bridge, near Hexham on 19 July 1789 and was apprenticed to a coach painter in Newcastle before running away and studying with an Italian artist, Boniface Musso. He reached London in 1806 and began to exhibit regularly, winning a prize at the BI in 1816 and a premium of 200 guineas for his 'Belshazzar's Feast' in 1821. Martin achieved great popular acclaim from this period onwards for his huge canvases of classical or biblical subjects, most of them featuring dramatic effects of earthquake, destruction and flight. S.C. Hall, the sober editor of *The Art Journal,* considered that Martin 'possessed the genius that to madness nearly is allied', two of the artist's brothers were deranged. Martin's imagery was drawn partly from the mystical and partly from the

PHILIP WILLIAM MAY RI 1864-1903. 'Fair Women'

industrial, while being an incurable romantic he was also a child of the Industrial Revolution and his vast palaces, gorges and subterranean caverns have a quality of fact and experimental engineering about them. His work was exhibited abroad and he was made a member of the Belgian Academy and St Luke's Academy, Rome. Although much of his work was prepared in small scale brown and black ink and wash sketches for album books, a great deal was for straight mezzotint and not book form at all. Martin's most lasting achievements were probably the *Last Judgement* series, on which he was still working, when he died in the Isle of Man on 17 February 1854.

Illus: *Characters of Trees [1817]; Imposing Edifice in the Indian Style [1817]; Paradise Lost [1823-27]; Illustrations of The Bible [1831-35]; The Poetical Works of John Milton [1836]; The Wonders of Theology [1838]; The Wars of Jehovah [1844]; The Imperial Family Bible [1844]; The Holy Bible [1861-65]; Art and Song [1867].*
Contrib: *The Amulet; Forget-Me-Not, Friendship's Offering; The Gem; The Keepsake, The Literary Souvenir [1826-37]; The Wonders of Geology [G. Mantell, 1838, (frontis.)]; The Book of the Great Sea Dragons [Thomas Hawkins, 1840 (frontis.)]; The Traveller [1840, Art Union].*
Exhib: BI; RA; RBA.
Colls: Glasgow; Liverpool; Manchester; Newcastle; Nottingham; V & AM.
Bibl: W Martin, *A Short Outline of the Philosopher's Life... and an Account of Four Brothers and a Sister,* 1833; W. Feaver, *The Art of JM,* 1975.
See illustrations.

MARTIN, Jonathan   'Mad'   1782-1838
Artist and fanatic. He was born at Hexham in 1782, the brother of John Martin (q.v.). He was unbalanced and was responsible for setting York Minster on fire in 1829, for which offence he was confined in St Luke's Hospital, London as insane. He was responsible for producing numerous strange caricature drawings.

MASON, Abraham John   1794-
Illustrator and wood engraver. He was born in London on 4 April 1794 and became a pupil of Robert Branston. He engraved the plates

for George Cruikshank's *Tales of Humour,* 1824, exhibited at the RBA in 1829 and emigrated to New York the same year. He became a member of the National Academy in the United States.
Contrib: *ILN [1851].*

MASON, Ernold E.   fl.1883-1902
Figure painter working in London. He contributed to *The Illustrated London News* in 1889, a series of comic sketches. Exhibited at the RA in 1883 and was living at Tilford, Surrey in 1902.

MASON, Frank Henry   1876-1965
Marine painter, etcher, illustrator and poster designer. He was born at Seaton Carew, County Durham in 1876 and was educated at private schools and on H.M.S. Conway. Worked at sea and later became an engineer in Leeds and Hartlepool and was Lieutenant RNVR, 1914-18. He became RBA in 1904 and RI in 1929.
Illus: *The Book of British Ships.*
Contrib: *The Graphic [1910].*
Exhib: B; G; L; M; RA; RBA; RHA; RI.
See Horne

MASON, Fred   fl.1893-1897
Black and white artist and illustrator. He belonged to the Birmingham School and illustrated a number of books in the 1890s, leaning heavily on the Morris style.
Illus: *The Story of Alexander, retold by Robert Steele [1894]; Huon of Bordeaux, retold by Robert Steele [1895]; Renaud of Montaubon, retold by Robert Steele [1897].*
Contrib: *A Book of Pictured Carols [Birmingham School, 1893].*
Bibl: R.E.D Sketchley, *Eng. Bk. Illus.,* 1903, p.12,128.

MASON, George Finch   1850-1915
Sporting painter and illustrator, caricaturist. He was the son of an Eton master and attended the school from 1860-64, painting a set of caricatures of Eton life, entitled 'Eton in The Sixties'. He died in July, 1915.
Publ: *Sporting Recollections [by F.M., 1885]; The Run of the Season [1902]; Sporting Nonsense Rhymes [1906].*
Contrib: *Punch [1881-83].*
Exhib: London. 1874-76.
Colls: V & AM.

MASON, W.G.
Contributor to *The Illustrated London News,* 1850.

MASTERS
Illustrator, contributing to *London,* edited by Charles Knight, 1841.

MASTERSON, H.I.
Contributor of figure subjects to *Fun,* 1900.

MATANIA, Professor Eduardo   1847-
Painter and illustrator. The father of F. Matania (q.v.), he was born in Naples on 30 August 1847 and was an occasional contributor to *The Sphere.*

MATANIA, Fortunino   RI   1881-1963
Historical and battle painter. He was born in Naples in 1881, the son of Professor Eduardo Matania (q.v.) and was trained in his father's studio, illustrating his first book at fourteen. He worked in Milan as Special Artist for *Illustrazione Italiana,* followed by work in Paris for *L'Illustration Française* and in London for *The Graphic.* He returned to Italy at the age of twenty-two in 1903 to do military service with the Bersaglieri and then settled in London where he joined the staff of *The Sphere,* becoming Special Artist in 1914 and seeing action on all fronts. He was elected RI in 1917. Matania's style of drawing was heroic rather than realist and his work has gone completely out of fashion. The greatest attention paid to the shape of a bridle or the cut of a uniform is useless when the picture itself is lifeless.
Contrib: *Illustrazione Italiana [1895-1902]; The Graphic [1902-05]; The Sphere [1904-26]; Britannia and Eve [1929-30].*
Exhib: L, RA; RI.
Bibl: Percy V. Bradshaw, *FM and His Work,* The Art of The Illustrator, 1916-17.

MATANIA, Ugo   'M. Ugo'   **1888-**
Figure painter. He was born at Naples 1 December 1888 and was the nephew of Professor Eduardo Matania (q.v.) and cousin of F. Matania (q.v). He trained with his uncle and contributed drawings to *The Sphere.*
Exhib: L; RA, 1909-18.

MATHES, Louis
Decorator of books. Contributing ornamental headpieces to *The English Illustrated Magazine,* 1883.

MATHEWS, Minnie   **fl. 1886-1896**
Flower and landscape painter. She drew the title and cover for *Pansies* by May Probyn, 1895-96.
Exhib: RA, 1886-87.

MATTHEWS, Winifred   **-1896**
Painter and illustrator. She specialised in drawing children and some of her work was published by Cassell & Co.
Exhib: NEA, 1894.
Bibl: Prof. Fred Brown, 'WM' *The Quarto,* 1896, pp.9-14, illus.

MATTHISON, William   **fl.1885-1923**
Landscape and coastal painter. He was living in Banbury, 1885 to 1902, and in Oxford, from 1905. He illustrated *Cambridge* by M.A.R. Tuker 1905.
Exhib: B; FAS; G; L; M; RA; RBA; RI.

MAUD, W.T.   **1865-1903**
Portrait painter and war artist for *The Graphic.* He was born in 1865 and became a pupil of the RA Schools, winning the Landseer Scholarship in 1893. He was appointed to *The Daily Graphic* the same year and succeeded A.S. Hartick on *The Graphic,* 1895. His campaigns as Special Artist for the magazine were considerable. He rode through Armenia from the Mediterranean to the Black Sea, 1895, was with the insurgents in Cuba, 1896, with the Greek Army in Thessaly, 1897; the Sudan, 1897, the North-West Frontier, 1897-98; he was at the Siege of Ladysmith and volunteered as A.D.C. to Sir Ian Hamilton, but was invalided home with enteric fever. He died during the Somali War on 12 May 1903. The *Graphic* obituary on 16 May 1903 referred to him as 'A Vigorous, capable artist, he had not only an eye for a good subject but the ability to transfer that sketch rapidly to his notebook.'
Illus: *Facey Romford's Hounds, Hawbuck Grange [R.S. Surtees]; Wagner's Heroines [Miss C. Maud, 1896].*
Contrib: *Punch.*
Exhib: RA; ROI.

MAUND, Miss S.   **fl.1840-1873**
Flower painter and illustrator. She illustrated *Flowering Plants,* 1873, and contributed to *The Botanist,* c.1840.

MAXWELL, Donald   **1877-1936**
Painter, illustrator and writer. He was born in London in 1877 and after being educated at Manor House School, Clapham, studied art at South Kensington, 1896, Slade School, 1897, and at Clapham Art School. From about 1910, Maxwell was Naval Artist to *The Graphic,* travelling widely and being appointed official artist by the Admiralty during the First World War, 1914-18. He accompanied the Prince of Wales on his Indian Tour and made numerous illustrations for travel books. He was working at Rochester, 1914-25, and afterwards at Harrietsham, Kent, where he died on 25 July 1936.
Illus: *The Enchanted Road; The Log of the Griffin [1905]; Adventures with a Sketchbook [1914]; The Prince of Wales' Eastern Book,* etc.
Exhib: L; M; RA.
Bibl: *The Studio,* Vol.34, 1905, pp.113-117; *Modern Book Illustrators and their Work,* Studio, 1914.
See Horne

MAY, Charles   **1847-1932**
Artist and decorator. He was the elder brother of Phil May (q.v.) and contributed to magazines as well as designing wall-papers.
Contrib: *Fun, Frolic and Fancy [1894]; Madame [1895]; The English Illustrated Magazine [1895-97]; Pearson's Magazine.*
Exhib: New Gall, 1896.

PHILIP WILLIAM MAY RI 1864-1903. The cover for the Christmas number of *The Graphic,* 1893

MAY, E.M.
Decorative designer for *The Connoisseur,* 1914.

MAY, Philip William   'Phil' RI   **1864-1903**
Black and white artist, caricaturist and illustrator. He was born on 22 April 1864, the son of a Leeds engineer whose family had been landowners. He was educated at St George's School, Leeds, and became assistant scene painter at the Grand Theatre there, gaining a reputation for caricatures of members of the company. He left for London in about 1883 and joined *Society* and *St Stephen's Review* as artist, before leaving for Australia for the years 1885 to 1888. There he worked for *The Sydney Bulletin* and on returning to Europe studied art in Paris for a time. He made a major success of the highly popular *Parson and Painter,* series of drawings, published in 1891 and continued it by issuing *Annuals* from 1892 to 1904. He was on *The Graphic* staff until 1903 and joined *Punch* in 1895 making an instant mark with the readership that had enjoyed the drawings of the recently deceased Charles Keene (q.v.). He lived a raffish bohemian life, squandered his money and died of cirrhosis of the liver and tuberculosis at the age of thirty-nine, on 5 August 1903.

May was the most important black and white artist to emerge in the 1890s in the British tradition. In many ways he was the reverse of the Beardsley coin, the discovery of line which was easy to print and which was used with great economy. His *dramatis personae* were the same as Keene's, urchins, costers, cabbies and drunks, but he reduced the fine pen of the latter to a simplified language of strokes. His drawings are always lively but vary a great deal in execution, some include self-portraits and some are tinted with watercolour. He was elected RI in 1897 and his remaining drawings were exhibited at a memorial show in the Leicester Galleries in 1903.
Illus: *The Parson and the Painter, their Wanderings and Excursions among Men and Women [Rev. Joseph Slapkins (Alfred Allison) and*

PHILIP WILLIAM MAY RI 1864-1903. 'Overheard near the Zoo –
"Nuts for the Monkeys Sir!"' Pen and ink. Signed and dated 1899.
11in x 9in (27.9cm x 22.9cm)   Author's Collection

*illus. by Charlie Summers (Phil May), 1891]; Phil May's Winter and
Summer Annuals [1892-1904]; The Comet Coach [H.H. Pearse,
1894]; Fun, Frolic and Fancy [1894]; Guttersnipes, Fifty Original
Sketches [1896]; Zig-Zag Guide [F.C. Burnand, 1897]; Songs and
Their Singers [1902]; East London [Walter Besant, 1902]; Littledom
Castle [Mrs. H.M. Spielmann, 1903].*
Contrib: *The Yorkshire Gossip; The Busy Bee [Leeds, 1878]; St.
Stephen's Review [1883-85 and 1890-91]; The Penny Illustrated
Paper [1883]; The Pictorial World [1883]; Society [1885]; The
Sydney Bulletin [1886-94]; Puck and Ariel [1889]; The Daily
Graphic [1890-96]; The Graphic [1891-92]; Black & White [1891];
Pick-Me-Up [1891-93]; ILN [1892-97, with advertisements]; The
Sketch [1893-1903]; The Pall Mall Budget [1893-94]; The English
Illustrated Magazine [1893-94]; Punch [1893-1903]; Daily
Chronicle [1895]; The Unicorn [1895]; Eureka; The Savoy [1896];
The Mascot [1897]; The Century Magazine [1900]; The Tatler
[1901]; The Jewish Chronicle [1903].*
Exhib: FAS; G; RA.
Colls: BM; Bradford; Glasgow; Leeds; V & AM.
Bibl: J. Thorpe, *PM,* 1932; *The Studio,* Vol.29, 1903, pp.280-286
'Life and Genius of Late PM'; *The Graphic,* Dec. 19, 1903, pp.840-
841; D. Cuppleditch, *PM The Artist & His Wit,* 1981.
See illustrations.

MAY, Captain Walter William   RI   **1831-1896**
Marine artist and illustrator. He served in the Royal Navy from 1850
to 1870, retiring with the rank of Captain. He did rather accurate and
traditional work in the style of Clarkson Stanfield (q.v.) and
illustrated many books. He was elected ANWS in 1871 and NWS in
1874 and died in 1896.
Publ: *Marine Painting [1888].*
Illus: *Fourteen Sketches Made During the Voyage Up Wellington
Channel [1855, AT 646]; Quedah [Osborn, 1857, AT 520]; Will
Weatherhelm [W.H.G. Kingston, 1879]; Sea Fishing [J. Bickerdyke,
1895]; In The Queen's Navee [C.N. Robinson and J. Leyland, 1902].*

Contrib: *The Book of South Wales [Mr and Mrs S. C. Hall, 1861];
ILN [1875 Discovery expedition]; The Graphic [1869-75].*
Exhib: BI; L; M; NWS; RA; RBA; RI; ROI.
Colls: Greenwich.

MAYBANK, Thomas   **fl. 1898-1925**
Fairy illustrator and genre painter. He practised in Beckenham,
Croydon and Esher, contributing a number of startling fairy designs
to *Punch* between 1902 and 1904. These include 'A Bank Holiday in
Goblin Land', 'Coronation of Titania' and 'New Years Eve', all
taking their inspiration from Doyle's work, pages of meticulous little
figures drawn with pen and ink.
Contrib: *Punch [1902-09]; Pick-Me-Up [1899].*
Exhib: RA; RBA; RHA; ROI.
Colls: V & AM.

MAYE, H.
Contributed illustrations to Wyatt's *Industrial Arts of the 19th Century.*
Colls: V &: AM.

MAYER, Henry   **1868-**
Caricaturist and illustrator. He was born at Worms in Germany in
1868 and worked in New York.
Contrib: *Illustrated Bits; Punch [1906].*

MAYER, Luigi   **fl.1776-1804**
Watercolourist and draughtsman. He was of Italian origin and
worked as view painter to Sir Robert Ainslie, British ambassador at
Constantinople, 1776 to 1792. He was later employed in making
watercolours for aquatints, some of which were from sketches by the
Countess of Harrington. Mayer was the most accurate delineator of
the Near East before David Roberts (q.v.), most of the finished
watercolours are identified by inscriptions in classical lettering
running along the bottom; it is believed that he was assisted in some
of them by his wife Clara.
Illus: *Lyric Airs [Edward Jones, 1804, AL 417 (etched by
Rowlandson)].*
Colls: Searight Coll. at V & AM.

MAYSON, S.   **fl.1850-1856**
Illustrator. An oil over pencil on millboard, presumably for a book,
is in the Ashmolean Collection.

MEADOWS, Joseph Kenny   **1790-1874**
Illustrator and caricaturist. He was born at Cardigan on 1 November
1790, the son of a retired naval officer. He was making a reputation
in London by the 1830s and was one of the first illustrators to
recommend wood engraving to publishers. In 1832, he collaborated
with Isaac and Robert Cruikshank in *The Devil in London,* and in
1840 illustrated *Portraits of the English,* published by Robert Tyas,
which achieved some success. In 1843, the same publisher issued his
Shakespeare, which was specially well received in Germany;
Meadows worked for *The Illustrated London News,* among his best
work being designs for its Christmas numbers. He also appears in the
first seven volumes of *Punch,* before being superceded by the
stronger draughtsmanship of Leech and Doyle (qq.v.).

Meadows was an unoriginal but competent hand whose designs
suffered most in mechanical figures with puffy faces and straight
arms. He was a kindly but temperamental artist and this shows
clearly in his uneven work. He was the brother-in-law of Archibald
S. Henning (q.v.). He died in London in August 1874.
Illus: *Costume of Shakespeare's Historical Tragedy of King John
[1823]; Shakespeare's Works [1839-42]; Autobiography of Jack
Ketch [1835]; Lalla Rookh [Moore, 1842]; Palfrey, A Love Story of
Old Times [Leigh Hunt, 1842]; Whist, Its History and Practice;
Backgammon, Its History and Practice; Leila; Calderon [E. Lytoon
Bulwer, 1847]; The Family Joe Miller [1848]; Sketches from Life
[Laman Blanchard, 1849]; Metrical Poems and Tales [Samuel
Lover, 1849]; The Magic of Kindness [The Brothers Mayhew];
Midsummer Eve [Mrs S.C. Hall].*
Contrib: *Bell's Life in London; London [Charles Knight, 1841];
Punch [1841]; Book of British Ballads [S.C. Hall, 1842-44]; The
Illuminated Magazine [1843-45]; The Pictorial Times [1843-47];
The Illustrated Musical Annual [F.W.N. Bailey]; The Man in the*

Moon; Cassell's Illustrated Family Paper [1853]; The Book of Celebrated Poems; The Illustrated London Magazine [1854-55]; The Illustrated Times [1855-59]; The Welcome Guest [1860].
Exhib: RA; RBA, 1830-38.
Colls: V & AM; Witt Photo.
Bibl: G. Everitt, *English Caricaturists*, 1893, pp.355-363; M.H. Spielmann, *The History of Punch*, 1895, pp.446-449; The Dalziel Brothers, A *Record of Work, 1840-1890*, 1901, pp.38-41.

MEASOR, W.   **fl.1837-1870**
Painter of scriptural and marine subjects, working at Exeter. He exhibited at the BI, RA and RBA between 1837 and 1864 and contributed to *The Illustrated London News*, 1848, and *The Graphic*, 1870.

MEIN, W. Gordon 'Will Mein'   **fl.1886-1925**
Figure painter and illustrator. He was working in Edinburgh, 1894, and afterwards in London. Specialised in boys' stories.
Illus: *Hidden Witchery [Nigel Tourneur, 1898]; My Two Edinburghs [S.R. Crockett, 1913].*
Contrib: *The Dome [1899-1900].*

MELLOR, Sir John Paget, Bt. 'Quiz' KCB   **1862-1929**
Amateur artist and caricaturist. He was called to the Bar at the Inner Temple, 1886, and served as a barrister and assistant solicitor to the Treasury, 1894-1909, and as solicitor, 1909-23. He was created CB in 1905 and KCB, 1911, and died on 4 February 1929. Mellor's cartoons are usually *portraits chargés* and signed 'Quiz'.
Contrib: *Punch [1886-88]; Vanity Fair [1890, 1893, 1898].*
Bibl: M.H Spielmann, *The History of Punch*, 1895, pp.558-559.

MELVILLE, Arthur   **ARWS, HRSA**   **1858-1904**
Painter and watercolourist. He was born at the Loanhead of Guthrie, East Linton, Scotland on 10 April 1858 and was apprenticed to a grocer. He studied at the RSA and with J. Campbell Noble, before working his way round France and studying in Paris. He returned to Edinburgh, but left again in 1881 to tour in Egypt, Persia, Turkey and Asia, riding from Baghdad to the Black Sea. He made a special study of oriental subjects, became a friend of Frank Brangwyn (q.v.) and visited Spain with him in 1892. He died in London 29 August 1904.
Contrib: *The Graphic [1882].*
Exhib: B; BM; G; GG; L; M; New Gall; P; RA; RI; RSA; RWS.
Colls: Edinburgh; Glasgow; Liverpool; V & AM.

MELVILLE, Harden Sidney   **fl.1837-1882**
Painter of landscapes, animals and sport. He worked in London for most of his life, but may have made tours abroad, possibly to Australia.
Illus: *Sketches in Australia [1849, AT 581]; The War Tiger [W. Dalton, 1859]; Wild Sports of the World [J. Greenwood, 1862]; Curiosities of Savage Life [J. Greenwood, 1864]; The Adventures of a Griffin [1867].*
Contrib: *London [Charles Knight, 1841]; ILN [1848 and 1865-66]; The Illustrated Times [1865]; The Welcome Guest [1860]; The Field [c.1863].*
Exhib: B; BI; RA; RBA.
Colls: BM.

MENPES, Mortimer   **FRGS**   **1860-1938**
Painter, etcher, raconteur and rifle shot. He was born in Australia in 1860 and educated at a grammar school in Port Adelaide, but came to England in the early 1880s and was working with J.M. Whistler as a studio assistant by 1884. He became one of those disciples of the American master who scouted out streets and corners and alleys for him to paint and, working alongside him, absorbed much of his style in their etchings and oil paintings. Menpes travelled extensively and was particularly influenced by the arts of Japan, but also by those of India, Mexico, Spain, Morocco and Venice. He was instrumental in holding an exhibition of coloured etchings, an attempt to revive this art. He was Special Artist for *Black & White* in South Africa, 1900. He was elected RE, 1881, RBA, 1885, NEA, 1886 and RI, 1897, and died at Pangbourne, Berks, 1 April 1938.
Illus: *Paris [1900]; War Impressions [1901]; Japan [1901]; World Pictures [1902]; Worlds Children [1903]; The Durbar [1903];*

Venice [1904]; Brittany [1905]; India [1905]; Thames [1906].
Publ: *Whistler as I Knew Him [1904].*
Exhib: FAS, 1901, 1902, 1908, 1911; G; GG; L; M; New Gall; RA; RE; RI; ROI .
Colls: V & AM.
Bibl: *The Studio*, Winter No., 1900-01, p.61, illus.

MERRITT, F.R.
Contributor to *The Graphic*, 1884.

MERRY, Tom   **1852-1902**
Caricaturist and cartoonist. Merry was for many years the chief cartoonist of *St. Stephen's Review*, being most prolific in the period 1885-90. He became cartoonist of *Puck and Ariel* in that year. His style is rather wooden, although he has a good eye for portraiture and making his political points on a large scale. All his work appeared as two-pager coloured lithographs, often wittily taken from famous paintings of the day by Seymour Lucas, Stanley Berkeley, or parodies of Hogarth. He died in 1902.

METCALFE, Gerald Fenwick   **fl.1894-1929**
Portrait painter, miniaturist, illustrator and modeller. He was born at Landour, India and studied art at South Kensington, St John's Wood School and the RA Schools. He was working in Chelsea. 1902-03 and at Albury, Surrey, 1914-25.
Illus: *The Wrecker [R.L. Stevenson].*
Contrib: *Punch [1906].*
Bibl: *Modern Book Illustrators and Their Work*, Studio, 1914.

METEYARD, Sidney Harold   **1868-1947**
Artist, stained-glass designer and illustrator. He was born in Stourbridge in 1868 and is associated with the Birmingham School, where he studied under E.R. Taylor. His paintings and drawings are strongly influenced by Burne-Jones; he was elected a member of the R.S.B.A., 1908.
Illus: *The Golden Legend [H.W. Longfellow, 1910].*
Contrib: *The Quest [1894-96]; The Yellow Book [1896].*
Exhib: B; L; New Gall; RA.

METEYARD, Tom B.   **1865-**
Painter and illustrator. He was born at Rock Island, U.S.A. on 12 November 1865 and worked as an artist at Fernhurst, Sussex.
Illus: *Songs From Vagabondia [Bliss Carmen and Richard Hovey, 1895-96].*
Exhib: FAS, 1922.

METTAIS, Charles-Joseph   **fl.1846-1857**
French portrait painter and illustrator. He exhibited at the Salon from 1846-48 and contributed to *Cassell's Illustrated Family Paper*, 1857.

MICHAEL, C.A.   **fl.1903-1916**
Painter and etcher, working in Bedford Park, London. He was artist for *The Morning Star* and illustrated books.
Illus: *The Ghost King [H. Rider Haggard, 1908]; King Solomon's Mines [H. Rider Haggard, 1912].*
Contrib: *The Graphic [1903]; The Illustrated London News [1915-16].*
Exhib: RA; RI.
Bibl: CAM, *An Artist in Spain*, 1914.

MICHAEL, J.B.
Architectural illustrator on *The Illustrated London News,* 1873.

MICHAEL, L.H   **fl.1845-1874**
Architectural illustrator. He contributed drawings to Wyatt's *Industrial Arts of the Nineteenth Century, The Welcome Guest*, 1860 and *The Illustrated London News*, 1865-66.
Exhib: RA; RBA.
Colls: V & AM.

MILES, Marie   **fl.1897-1914**
Black and white artist, specialising in children.
Contrib: *The Parade [1897]; Cassell's Family Magazine [1898]; The Royal Magazine; Punch [1914].*

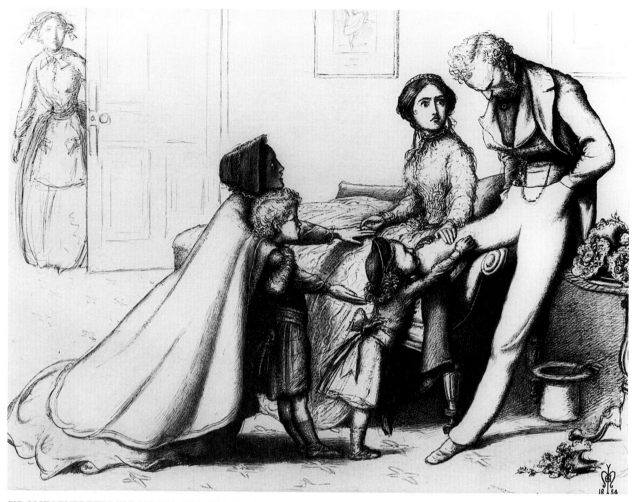

SIR JOHN EVERETT MILLAIS PRA 1829-1896. 'Retribution'. Pen and ink. Signed with monogram and dated 1854   Maas Gallery

MILLAIS, Sir John Everett, Bt. PRA   1829-1896

Painter, illustrator and President of the Royal Academy. He was born in Southampton in 1829 and was brought up in Jersey and Brittany, coming to London in 1838 to study at Henry Sass's Academy and at the RA Schools, 1840. With Holman Hunt (q.v.) and D.G. Rossetti (q.v.) founded the Pre-Raphaelite Brotherhood, 1848. From the first, Millais was a masterly draughtsman and excelled in line drawings, preparing some for *The Germ,* the magazine of the Pre-Raphaelites in 1850. His most powerful black and white work was done in the period 1851-55 when he was concerned with modern moral subjects, but these remained unpublished. His most influential work was published in Moxon's edition of *Tennyson,* 1857, where he showed two styles of drawing developing, a highly finished manner for the romantic subjects and a more sketchy modern style for the contemporary illustration. The latter is best seen in his fine series of drawings prepared for the novels of Anthony Trollope, which appeared in *The Cornhill Magazine,* 1860. Millais' brilliant groups grasp perfectly the underlying tensions and complexities of Victorian society and are arguably the best of their kind done for a novelist in the entire 19th century.

Millais ceased to do illustration after the 1860s, although he undertook some for his son, and his falling away in expression dates from the same time. Marriage with Effie Ruskin in 1855 was followed by election as RA in 1863 and increasing popularity as a portrait painter of the great. He was created a baronet in 1885 and was elected PRA in 1896, serving only six months before dying of cancer of the throat on August 13 that year.

The drawings prepared by Millais for his famous book illustrations were mostly lost in the cutting, but his Pre-Raphaelite sketches and finished drawings sometimes emerge on the market. A

group 'Married For Money', 'Married For Love' and 'Married For Rank' appeared in the London galleries in 1972.

Illus: *Framley Parsonage [Anthony Trollope, 1860-62]; Orley Farm [Anthony Trollope, 1861-62]; Small House at Allington [Anthony Trollope, 1862]; Phineas Finn [Anthony Trollope, 1869]; Kept in the Dark [Anthony Trollope, 1882].*

Contrib: *The Germ [No. 5, 1850 (not used)]; Mr. Wray's Cashbox... A Christmas Sketch [Wilkie Collins, 1852]; The Music Master [W. Allingham, 1855]; Poems [by Tom Hood, 1858]; Moxon's Tennyson [1857]; The Poets of the Nineteenth Century [Rev. R.A. Willmott, 1857]; Lays of the Holy Land [1858]; The Home Affections [Charles Mackay, 1858]; Once a Week [1859-63 and 1868]; The Cornhill Magazine [1860-63]; Good Words [1861-64, 1878, 1882]; London Society [1862-64]; The Illustrated London News [1862]; Cornhill Gallery [1864]; The Churchman's Family Magazine [1863]; Papers For Thoughtful Girls [Sarah Tytler, 1862]; Puck on Pegasus [Pennell, 1862]; Parables of Our Lord [1863]; Punch [1863 and 1865]; Lilliput Levee [1864]; Little Songs For Me To Sing, Touches of Nature By Eminent Artists [1866]; Ballads and Songs of Brittany from the French of Hersant de la Villemarque [Tom Taylor, 1866]; St Pauls [1867]; Gems of Poetry [Mackay, 1867]; Leslie's Musical Annual [1870]; Passages From Modern English Poets [1876]; The Memoirs of Barry Lyndon Esq. [W.M. Thackeray (Complete Works, Vol.XIX), 1879]; Game Birds and Shooting Sketches [J. G. Millais, 1892 (frontis)].*

Colls: Ashmolean; BM; Bedford; Glasgow; Manchester: V & AM.

Exhib: BI; GG; G; L; M; New Gall; RA; RHA; RSA.

Bibl: J.G. Millais, *Life and Letters of JEM,* 1899. M. Lutyens, *M and the Ruskins,* 1967. M. Bennett, *M,* RA Exhibition Cat., Jan-April, 1967. Michael Mason, 'The way we look now: Millais illustrations of Trollope', *Art History,* Vol. 1, No.3, 1978, pp.309-340; Malcolm

SIR JOHN EVERETT MILLAIS PRA 1829-1896. 'Married for Rank'. Pen and ink drawing. Signed with monogram and dated 1853.
9¾in x 7in (24.8cm x 17.8cm)

Mrs Nicolette Wernick Collection

"I wish to regard you as a dear friend,—both of my own and of my husband."

SIR JOHN EVERETT MILLAIS PRA 1829-1896. 'And I ain't in a hurry either'. Illustration to *Phineas Finn* by Anthony Trollope, 1869. Wood engraving

SIR JOHN EVERETT MILLAIS PRA 1829-1896. 'I wish to regard you as a dear friend'. Illustration to *Phineas Finn* by Anthony Trollope, 1869. Wood engraving

Warner, *The Drawings of JEM*, Fitzwilliam catalogue, 1979; N. John Hall, *Trollope and His Illustrators*, 1980; *The Pre-Raphaelites*, Tate Gallery, 1984.
See illustrations.

MILLAIS, John Guille   FZS   **1865-1931**
Animal painter and illustrator. He was born on 24 March 1865, the fourth and youngest son of Sir John E. Millais (q.v.). He was educated at Marlborough and Trinity College, Cambridge and after serving with the Somerset Light Infantry, 1883-86, travelled in Africa, Canada, America and the Arctic as a big game hunter. Millais published numerous books on these subjects, many illustrated from his own drawings. He became FZS and died on 24 March 1931.
Illus: *A Fauna of Sutherland [1887]; A Fauna of the Outer Hebrides [1888]; A Fauna of the Orkney Islands [1891]; Game Birds and Shooting Sketches [1892]; A Breath From the Veldt [1895]; British Deer and Their Horns [1897]; The Wild Fowler in Scotland [1901]; Surface-Feeding Ducks [1902]; The Mammals of Great Britain [1904-06]; [Newfoundland 1907]; British Game Birds [1909]; British Diving Ducks [1913]; Deer and Deer Stalking [1913]; European Big Game [1914]; American Big Game [1915]; Rhododendrons ond Their Hybrids [1917]; Wanderings and Memories [1919]; Far Away up the Nile [1924]; Magnolias [1927].*
Contrib: *The Graphic [1886]; Pearson's Magazine.*
Exhib: FAS, 1901, 1919, 1923.
Bibl: R.E.D. Sketchley, *Eng. Bk. Illus.* 1903, pp.54, 135.

MILLAIS, William Henry   **1828-1899**
Painter, watercolourist and illustrator. He was the elder brother of Sir

John E. Millais (q.v.) and was born in 1828. He worked at Farnham and specialised in landscapes.
Publ: *The Princess of Parmesan [1897].*
Contrib: *Parables From Nature [Mrs. Gatty, 1861, 1867]; Legends and Lyrics [A.A. Proctor, 1865]; Strand Magazine [1891-1916].*
Exhib: FAS; M; RA; RI.
Colls: Ashmolean; BM; V & AM.

MILLAR, Harold R.   **fl.1891-1935**
Painter and illustrator. He was born at Dumfries and intended to study engineering, but abandoned this for art and became a student of the Birmingham School. His earliest work was for Birmingham magazines such as *Scraps* and *Comus*, and he derived a very strong and free ink style based on the work of Vierge and Gigoux. A collector of ancient weapons and eastern works of art, Millar became known for his authenticity in illustrating eastern stories in the 1900s.
Illus: *The Golden Fairy Book [George Sand, 1894]; The Humour of Spain [1894]; Fairy Tales From Far and Near [1895]; The Adventures of Haji Baba [Morier, 1895]; The Silver Fairy Book [Bernhardt, 1895]; Headlong Hall, Nightmare Abbey [Peacock, 1896]; The Phantom Ship [Marryat, 1896]; The Diamond Fairy Book [Bellerby, 1897]; Untold Tales of the Past [B. Harraden, 1897]; Frank Mildmay [Marryat, 1897]; Snarleyow [1897]; Phroso [Anthony Hope, 1897]; Eothen [A.W. Kinglake, 1898]; The Book of Dragons [E. Nesbitt, 1900]; Nine Unlikely Tales For Children [E. Nesbitt, 1901]; The Story of the Bold Pecopin [Hugo, 1902]; Queen Mab's Realm [1902]; The Phoenix and the Carpet [E. Nesbitt, 1904]; The New World Fairy Book [1904]; Oswald Bastable and Others [E. Nesbitt, 1905]; Kingdom Curious [Myra Hamilton,*

SIR JOHN EVERETT MILLAIS PRA 1829-1896. 'The Sower'.
Illustration for *The Parables of Our Lord*, 1863. Wood engraving by
the Brothers Dalziel

SIR JOHN EVERETT MILLAIS PRA 1829-1896. 'The Finding of
Moses'. Illustration to *The Lays of the Holy Land*, 1858. Wood
engraving

HAROLD R. MILLAR fl.1891-1935. 'The Amulet'. Drawing for
illustration in *The Strand Magazine*, Vol.21, 1905. Pen. Signed and
dated 1905. 7¾in x 6⅞in (19.7cm x 17.4cm)

SIR JOHN EVERETT MILLAIS PRA 1829-1896. 'A Dream of Fair
Women'. Illustration for Moxon's *Tennyson*, 1857. Wood engraving

1905]; Puck of Pook's Hill [Rudyard Kipling, 1906]; The Enchanted Castle [E. Nesbitt, 1917];The Magic City [1910]; The Wonderful Garden [E. Nesbitt, 1911]; Wet Magic [E. Nesbitt, 1913]; The Dreamland Express [1927]; Hakluyt's Voyages [1929].
Contrib: *Judy [1890]; The Girl's Own Paper [1890-1900]; Fun [1891-92]; The Strand Magazine [1891, 1905]; The English Illustrated Magazine [1891-92]; Chums [1892]; Good Words [1893]; Good Cheer [1894]; The Sketch [1898]; Black & White [1899]; The Quiver [1900]; Punch [1906-09]; The Ludgate Monthly; Pick-Me-Up; Cassell's Family Magazine; The Idler; The Minister; Eureka.*
Exhib: RA.
Colls: V & AM.
Bibl: *The Idler,* Vol. 8, pp.228-236; R.E.D. Sketchley, *Eng. Bk. Illus.,* 1903, pp.109, 112, 167; Brigid Peppin, *Fantasy Book Illustration,* 1975, pp.188-189, illus.
See illustration.

MILLER, F.
Book decorator. Contributed tail-pieces to *The English Illustrated Magazine* 1895.

MILLER, J.H.   fl.1803-1829
Landscape painter and topographer. He contributed to Britton's *Beauties of England and Wales,* 1805 and exhibited at the RA, RBA and OWS from 1803 to 1829.

MILLER, William Edwards   fl.1873-1929
Portrait painter. Worked in London and contributed one cartoon to *Vanity Fair,* 1896.
Exhib: B; G; L; New Gall; RA; RSA.

MILLER, William Frederick   1834-1918
Architectural draughtsman. He undertook some illustrative work for Messrs. T. Nelson & Sons, 1853-54.
Colls: V & AM.

MILLS, A. Wallis   1878-1940
Black and white artist. He was born in 1878, the son of the rector of Long Bennington, Lincolnshire, and trained at the South Kensington Schools, becoming a friend of F.H. Townsend, G.L. Stampa and G.K. Haseldon (qq.v.). He was working for illustrated magazines from about 1898, specialising in drawings of old country characters, many of them modelled on those he had known in Lincolnshire or who lived near him at Little Gransden, Hunts., in the 1920s. He served in the Royal Artillery in the First World War and made official war sketches. He died at his club in St. James's in April 1940.
Illus: *Novels of Jane Austen [n.d.].*
Contrib: *Judy [1898]; The Strand Magazine [1906]; Punch [1907-14]; The Humourist; The Ludgate Monthly; The Royal Magazine; The Graphic [1915].*
Exhib: Nottingham; RA.
Bibl: R.G.G. Price, A *History of Punch,* 1957, p.205.

MILLS, Charles A. ARHA   -1922
Painter and illustrator. He worked in Dublin and contributed figure drawings to *Fun,* 1901 and to *The Graphic,* 1903-05. He was elected ARHA in 1913 and died in 1922.
Exhib: RHA.

MILLS, Walter   fl.1880-1903
Painter and illustrator working in Dublin. He acted as *The Graphic* Special in Ireland, 1903.
Exhib: RHA.

MINNS, B.E.   fl.1895-1913
Illustrator. He worked at Hendon, London and contributed to magazines in the 1890s.
Contrib: *The Strand Magazine [1907-15]; The Idler; The Minister; Pearson's Magazine; Punch [1914].*
Exhib: G; L; RA; RI.

MITCHELL, Hutton   fl.1892-1925
Illustrator and the original creator in line of Billy Bunter. He is recorded as being an able but dilatory artist who was replaced after

thirty-nine issues of *The Magnet* by Arthur Clarke (q.v.). He was working at Paignton, S. Devon, 1920-25.
Contrib: *Fun [1892]; Daily Graphic [1893]; The Longbow [1898]; The Gem.*
Exhib: L.
Bibl: W.O. Lofts and D.J. Adley, The *World of Frank Richards,* 1975.

MOIRA, Gerald Edward RWS   1867-1959
Landscape, flower and decorative painter. He was born in London in 1867 as Giraldo de Moura, the son of a Portuguese miniaturist and anglicized his name. He was elected ARWS in 1917 and RWS in 1932, serving as Vice President from 1953. He died at Northwood in 1959.
Illus: *Shakespeare's True Life [J. Walter, 1890].*
Colls: BM.
Bibl: J.H. Watkins, *The Art of GEM,* 1922.

MOLINARI, Aleksander Ludwig or Lukwik   1795-1868
Painter, caricaturist and lithographer. He was born at Blonie near Warsaw in 1795 and became a pupil at the Warsaw Academy and then in Munich and Paris. He was a history painter but interested himself in caricature in the style of Cruikshank or Alken.
Illus: *The March of Machinery,* 'Sketched and drawn by A.L. Molinari – Pub. by Charles Tilt, Fleet Street. Printed from Zinc by J.Grieve', c.1825. These are lithographs coloured by hand.

MONCRIEFF, Robert SCOTT-
Amateur caricaturist. His drawings of Scottish lawyers of the years 1816-20 were published as *Scottish Bar,* 1871.
Colls: Witt Photo.

MONNIER, G.
French artist contributing to *The Illustrated London News,* 1870.

MONRO, A.
Illustrator of boys' stories. He contributed to *Chums,* c.1890 in a style like that of Gordon Browne (q.v.).

MONSELL, Elinor May   Mrs. Darwin   -1954
Figure artist and illustrator, painter on silk and fans and woodcut artist. She was born at Limerick, Ireland, the daughter of W.T. Monsell and won a scholarship to the Slade School in 1896. In 1906 she married Bernard Darwin, the grandson of Charles Darwin, and lived in London, Cambridge and later at Downe, Kent.
Contrib: *The Venture [1903 (allegory)].*
Exhib: M; NEA; RA; RHA.
See **Horne**

MONSELL, J.R.   1877-
Illustrator, who drew for *Grimms Fairy Tales,* 1908 and *The Buccaneers,* 1908, published by Cassells.
See **Horne**

MONSON, Frederick John   5th Baron Monson   1809-1841
Amateur artist. He illustrated *Views in the Department of The Isère and The High Alps,* 1840. Lithographs by L. Haghe from Monson's drawings.

MONTAGU, H. Irving   fl. 1873-1893
Figure painter, illustrator and war artist. He was Special Artist for *The Illustrated London News* from 1874, when he was present during the Carlist uprising in Spain and later served in Hungary, Turkey and Russia.
Contrib: *The Sunday Magazine [1881].*
Exhib: B; RA; RBA.
Bibl: H.I.M., *Wanderings of a War Artist,* 1889; H.I.M, 'Anecdotes of the War Path', *The Strand Magazine,* Vol. 1, 1891, pp.576-585.

MONTBARD, G.   Charles Auguste Loyes   1841-1905
Landscape painter, illustrator and caricaturist. He was born at Montbard on 2 August 1841 and took his professional name from the town. He worked first with O'Shea on *Chronique Illustrée* and had his introduction to the English public when he illustrated scenes at Compiègne for *The Illustrated London News* in 1868. Montbard was strongly political and after taking the side of the Commune in 1871,

was proscribed from France and resided in England until his death. He very soon became a regular contributor to *The Illustrated*, making a series of drawings of country houses, usually devoid of figures at which he was very weak. He also undertook some flower paintings and died in London on 5 August 1905.
Illus: *The Land of the Sphinx [GM, 1894].*
Contrib: *ILN [1868-99]; The Graphic [1871-73]; Judy [1871]; Vanity Fair [1872]; Good Words [1880-99]; The English Illustrated Magazine [1895]; St James's Budget; The Windsor Magazine; The Pall Mall Magazine.*
Exhib: L; M; RA; RBA; RI; ROI.
Colls: V & AM.

MONTEFIORE, Edward Brice Stanley   fl.1872-1909
Landscape and genre painter, working in London and Newnham, Glos., 1909.
Contrib: *Sporting & Dramatic News [1894].*
Exhib: M; RA; ROI.

MOODY, Fannie   (Mrs. Gilbert King)   1861-
Animal painter and illustrator. She was born in London on 10 May 1861, the daughter of T.W. Moody 1824-1886, master at the South Kensington Schools. She studied under J.T. Nettleship and became well known for her sentimental dog subjects, beloved of the Victorians. She drew for advertisements and was still working in Battersea 1920. SWA, 1887.
Contrib: *ILN [1892-99].*
Exhib: B; L; M; RA; RBA; RMS; ROI; SWA.
Bibl: 'The Animal Sketches of Miss Fannie Moody', *The Artist*, 1899, pp.121-130.

MOODY, John   1884-
Painter, etcher and black and white artist. He was born 21 June 1884 and studied at the Regent St. Polytechnic and then in Paris and in Italy. He became a member of the Society of Graphic Art in 1920 and worked at Hampstead and Highgate from 1914 to 1925 and then at Burpham, Sussex. Principal of Hornsey School of Art, 1927. ARE, 1921; RE, 1946; RI, 1931.
Exhib: G; L; RA; RE; RI; ROI.
Bibl: *The Studio*, Vol. 38,1906, p.317, illus.

MOORE, Albert Joseph   1841-1893
Figure painter and illustrator. He was born at York in 1841, the son of the portrait painter William Moore. On his mother's widowhood in 1855, he settled in London, travelling to Scotland and to France and visiting Rome in 1862. Moore was often employed by architects and worked as a mural painter. He was a frequent exhibitor at the RA from 1857 and developed a reputation for classical Greek studies which are the forerunners of Alma Tadema (q.v.). He died in London in 1893. RWS, 1884.
Contrib: *Specimens of Medieval Architecture [W. Eden Nesfield, 1862].*
Exhib: B; FAS; G; L; M; NEA; New Gall; RA; RI; RWS.

MOORE, Alexander Poole   1777-1806
Topographer. He was born about 1777 and entered the RA Schools in 1792, winning the silver medal in 1794. He was a pupil of James Lewis, the architect, and was described as 'a young man of very eccentric habits but a clever Artist'.
Contrib: *Beauties of England & Wales [Britton, 1802].*
Exhib: RA, 1793-1806.
Colls: Witt Photo.
Bibl: H.M. Colvin, *Biog. Dict. of Eng. Architects*, 1954.

MOORE, C. Aubrey
Illustrator of the child's book *Adventures in Noah's Ark*, 1908.

MOORE, Henry   1776-1848
Topographer and drawing master at Derby. He was born in 1776 and won a Society of Arts medal for his process of etching on marble.
Illus: *Excursions from Derby to Matlock, Bath and its Vicinity [1818].*
Contrib: *Beauties of England & Wales [Britton, 1802-13]; Antiquarian and Topographical Cabinet [Britton, 1806].*
Colls: Derby; Witt Photo.

MOORE, Henry   RA RWS   1831-1895
Marine painter and engraver. He was born at York on 7 March 1831, the son and pupil of the portrait painter William Moore and brother of Albert Joseph Moore (q.v.). He studied at the York School of Design and at the RA Schools, 1853, and after settling in London made a series of tours abroad to France, Switzerland and Ireland. He was principally a marine painter but did landscapes, the earlier works being influenced by the Pre-Raphaelites. He was elected ARA in 1885 and RA in 1893, RWS, 1880. He died at Margate, 22 June 1895.
Contrib: *ILN [1856]; Poems [Tom Hood]; Passages From Modern English Poets [1862, Junior Etching Club].*
Exhib: B; BI; FAS, 1887; G; GG; L; M: New Gall; RA; RBA; RHA; ROI; RSA; RWS.
Colls: Birmingham; Tate; V & AM.

MOORE, R.H.   fl.1875-1890
Animal and bird illustrator. He was a sculptor and black and white artist and worked extensively for *The Illustrated London News*, 1875-90.
Contrib: *Lady's Pictorial; Sporting & Dramatic News [1890].*
Exhib: NWS; RBA.

MOORE, Thomas Sturge   1870-1944
Illustrator, wood engraver, designer of bookplates and poet. He was born on 4 March 1870 and studied wood engraving at the Lambeth School of Art under Charles Roberts. Moore had strong connections with the private presses and particularly with the Essex House and Eragny Presses and was a member of the Society of Twelve. Moore's designs were not so consciously archaic as Morris's and extremely well balanced in light and shade. He was also engaged in decorations for the rhyme sheets produced by Harold Monro's Poetry Bookshop.
Publ: *The Vine Dressers and Other Poems [1899]; Aphrodite Against Artemis [1901]; Absalom [1903]; Danae [1903]; The Little School [1905]; Poems Marianne [1911]; The Sicilian Idyll and Judith [1911]; The Sea is Kind [1914]; The Little School Enlarged [1917]; The Powers of the Air [1920]; Tragic Mothers [1920]; Judas [1923].*
Illus: *The Centaur and The Bacchante [Maurice de Guerin, Vale Press, 1899]; Some Fruits of Solitude [W. Penn, 1901]; Poems from Wordsworth [Vale Press, 1902]; Histoire de Peau d'Ane [Perrault, Eragny Press, 1902].*
Contrib: *The Dial [1895]; The Venture [1903].*
Exhib: RSA.
Colls: BM; Carlisle, V & AM; Witt Photo.
Bibl: R.E.D. Sketchley, *Eng. Bk. Illus.* 1903, pp.18, 24, 129; *The Artist Engraver*, 1904; *The Studio*, Vol. 66, 1916, p.28 and Winter, 1923-24, pp.34 and 105; *The Connoisseur*, Vol. 55, 1919, p.187; *Print Coll. Quarterly*, Vol. 18, No.3, 1931, p.203-219; Frederick L. Gwyn, *Sturge Moore and the Life of Art*, Univ. of Kansas, 1951; Simon Houfe, *Fin de Siècle*, 1992, pp.29-30.

MORCHEN, Horace   fl.1880-1890
Humorous illustrator and caricaturist. He studied under Alfred Bryan (q.v.) and specialised in theatrical subjects.
Contrib: *ILN [1880-83]; Moonshine [1890]; Sporting & Dramatic News; Cassell's Saturday Journal.*

MOREL, Charles   1861-1908
French draughtsman and illustrator. He was born in 1861 and became a pupil of Detaille. He contributed to *The Graphic*, 1904, and died in Paris, 27 July, 1908.

MORELAND, A.
A cartoonist of *The Morning Leader*, c.1895. A book of 160 of these designs in colour was issued at the same date entitled *Humours of History*.

MORGAN, Charles W.   fl.1867-1879
Figure artist, working at Evesham. He contributed to *Cassell's Illustrated Readings*, 1867.

MORGAN, Frederick   ROI   1856-1927
Painter of genre and children. He was born in 1856 and married the

MATT SOMERVILLE MORGAN 1836-1890. 'The Unemployed at the East End of London'. Wood engraving in *The Illustrated London News*, 1886

painter, Alice Mary Havers. He worked in Aylesbury in early life and later in London and at Broadstairs, 1914-25. He became ROI in 1883.
Contrib: *The Sunday Magazine [1894].*
Exhib: B; BI; FAS; G; L; M; RA; RBA; RI; ROI.
Colls: Leeds; Liverpool; Sheffield.

MORGAN, Matt Somerville   **1836-1890**
Painter of social realism, lithographer and caricaturist. He was born in London in 1836 and from the late 1850s gained a high reputation as a figure artist and decorator in the magazines. He went to Italy in 1859-61 and covered the campaigns there for both *The Illustrated London News* and *The Illustrated Times* as a Special, later travelling in Algeria. From about 1866, he became interested in social questions and drew powerful studies of reform demonstrations and the poor in London. On becoming cartoonist to *The Tomahawk*, a radical paper, in 1867, his talents for figure drawing and brilliant political images were brought together on the page. His sharp satire established for him a greater freedom than any other Victorian cartoonist and his work was marked by its individuality in being printed from tinted wood blocks. Morgan emigrated to the United States and painted panoramas of the Civil War, he died in New York in 1890.
Illus: *Miles Standish.*
Contrib: *The Illustrated Times [1859-66]; The ILN [1859-86]; London Society [1863]; The Broadway [1867-74]; The Tomahawk [1867]; Judy; Britannia [1869]; Arrow; Will o' the Wisp.*
Bibl: Chatto & Jackson, *Treatise on Wood Engraving*, 1861, p.599; Clement & Hutton, *Art of the 19th Cent*, 1893; Fielding, *Dict of American Painters*, 1926; *Victorian Studies*, Vol. XIX, No. 1, Sept. 1975.
See illustrations.

MORGAN, Walter Jenks RBA   **1847-1924**
Genre painter and illustrator. He was born in 1847 and studied at the Birmingham School and at South Kensington. He worked for the magazines and Messrs. Cassell's, chiefly on domestic and children's subjects. He died at Birmingham on 31 October 1924. RBA, 1884.
Illus: *Spenser For Children [1897].*
Contrib: *The Graphic [1875-76]; ILN [1877-81].*
Exhib: B; L; RA; RBA; RI.

MORIN, Edward   **1824-1882**
Watercolourist, lithographer and illustrator. He was born at Le Havre on 26 March 1824 and became a pupil of Gleyre, exhibiting at the Salon from 1857. He came to London to work for the illustrated magazines and was taught wood engraving by Sir John Gilbert (q.v.) and was described by Vizetelly as 'a spirited French artist'. Although Benezet says that he returned to Paris in 1851, his work was still appearing in English journals until 1861. He died at Sceaux on 18 August 1882.
Contrib: *Cassell's Illustrated Family Paper [1853-55]; The Illustrated Times [1855-61]; ILN [1856-57].*
Bibl: Vizetelly, *Memoirs*, 1893.

MORLEY, Frances, Countess of   **-1857**
Amateur caricaturist. She was the daughter of Thomas Talbot of Gonville and married the 1st Earl of Morley on 23 August 1809. She worked closely with the Revd. Walter Sneyd (q.v.).
Illus: *The Flying Burgomaster, A Legend of the Black Forest* 'F. Morley invent et sculp 1832'.

MORNER, C.H.
An important genre artist of whom nothing is known. He illustrated

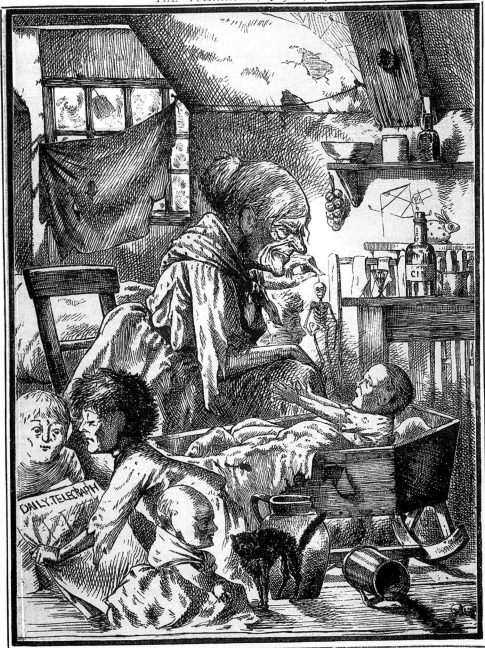

THE DEVIL'S TRADE!

(DEDICATED TO THE SUPPORTERS OF BABY-FARMERS.)

MATT SOMERVILLE MORGAN 1836-1890. 'The Devil's Trade'. July, 1870

Humorous Sketches Drawn by C.H. Morner, 1832, lithographs of street incidents with short titles.

MORRELL, G.F.
Draughtsman, contributed scientific drawings to *The Graphic*, 1910.

MORRIS, William   **1834-1896**
Poet, designer and polemicist. He was born at Walthamstow in 1834 and after studying at Oxford was converted to craft design and socialism, founding manufactures for the production of textiles and tapestries, stained-glass and furniture, having a profound influence on Victorian design. Morris developed an interest in the decoration of books over many years, culminating in his illumination of some works by hand in the early 1870s. He supervised the production of *The House of Wolfings* at the Chiswick Press, 1888, and founded the renowned Kelmscott Press in 1890. During the last six years of his life, Morris concentrated most of his energies on book production, upwards of fifty books being produced at Kelmscott for which he had designed borders and initial letters. He believed that 'ornament must form as much a part of the page as the type itself' and in many of the books the decoration, based on early printed motifs, seems rather to impinge on the text than otherwise. Morris employed Sir E.

235

WILLIAM MORRIS 1834-1896. Initial letters and page decoration for *Maud! A Monodrama* by Alfred, Lord Tennyson, Kelmscott Press, 1894

Burne Jones, Walter Crane and C.M. Gere as illustrators, the most famous production being the former's Kelmscott *Chaucer*, 8 May 1896. Morris died at Hammersmith in 1896.
Colls: BM; V & AM; Walthamstow; Wightwick, Nat. Trust.
Bibl: Aymer Vallance, *WM His Art His Writings & Public Life*, 1897; D. Robinson & S. Wildman, *Morris & Co. in Cambridge*, Fitzwilliam, 1980; Fiona McCarthy, *WM A Life For Our Time*, 1994. See illustration.

MORRISON, Douglas   fl.1842-1845
Lithographer. He illustrated his own *Views of Haddon Hall*, 1842 and *Views of Saxe-Coburg and Gotha*, 1846, AT 121.

MORROW, Albert George   1863-1927
Black and white and poster artist. He was born in 1863 at Comber, County Down, Ireland, the son of a decorator. He studied in Belfast and at South Kensington and began illustrating for magazines in 1884. He was the brother of George and Edwin Morrow (q.v.). He died at West Heathly, Sussex in October 1927.
Contrib: *The English Illustrated Magazine [1884]; Illustrated Bits [1890]; Good Words [1890]; Punch.*
Exhib: RA; RBA.
Colls: V & AM.

MORROW, Edwin A.   fl.1903-1914
Landscape painter and illustrator. Brother of George and Albert Morrow (qq.v.).
Contrib: *Punch [1914].*
Exhib: RA.

MORROW, George   1869-1955
Comic artist and illustrator. He was born in Belfast in 1869, the brother of Albert and Edwin Morrow (qq.v.), and studied in Paris in

the 1890s, being greatly influenced by the work of Caran d'Ache (q.v.). He began to contribute to *Punch* in 1906 and soon became known for his humorous historical episodes, in which history was treated in light-hearted manner in subject and in line. He joined the staff of *Punch* in 1924 and was Art Editor from 1932-37 and continued to draw for the paper until a month before his death on 18 January 1955. *The Times* wrote of him on that occasion as 'probably the most consistently comic artist of his day'.
Illus: *Country Stories [Mary Russell Mitford, 1896].*
Contrib: *Pick-Me-Up [1896]; The Idler: The Windsor Magazine; Punch [1906-54]; Strand Magazine [1909-30].*
Exhib: RA; RBA.
See Horne

MORROW, Norman   fl.1911-1916
Irish illustrator. He contributed drawings to *The Graphic*, 1911-16.

MORTEN, Thomas   1836-1866
Illustrator and occasional painter. He was born at Uxbridge in 1836 and studied at Leigh's of Newman Street from an early age, specialising in drawing on wood. He worked for most of the leading magazines of the 1860s and his finest illustrations were for *Gulliver's Travels*, 1866, where he brought to the subject a new wit and vision. In other works, Reid considered him to be rather a plagiarist, borrowing ideas from Doré, Sandys and J.D. Watson (qq.v.) among others. He died in the autumn of 1866, probably by committing suicide due to pecuniary difficulties.
Illus: *Gulliver's Travels [1866].*
Contrib: *Good Words [1861-63]; Once a Week [1861-66]; Entertaining Things [1861-62]; The Laird's Return [1861]; London Society [1862-69]; Every Boy's Magazine [1862-63]; Churchman's Family Magazine [1863-64]; Dalziel's Arabian Nights [1863]; A Round of Days [1865]; Watts Divine and Moral Songs [1865]; Legends and Lyrics [1865]; Jingles and Jokes For Little Folks [1865]; The Quiver [1865-66]; Aunt Judy's Magazine [1866]; Beeton's Annuals [1866]; Cassell's Family Paper [1866]; Idyllic Pictures [1867]; Two Centuries of Song [1867]; Young Gentlemen's Magazine [1867]; Foxe's Book of Martyres [1867]; Belgravia [1871]; Thornbury's Legendary Ballads [1876]; Cassell's History of England.*
Exhib: BI; RA.
Colls: V & AM.
Bibl: Forrest Reid, *Illustrators of The Sixties*, 1928, pp.211-216.

MORTON, Juliana S.   Mrs. Harvey Morton   1829-1918
Amateur artist. She was the wife of an Indian Army officer, whom she divorced, returning to live at Clevedon, Somerset with six children. She illustrated *The Indian Alps and How We Crossed Them By a Lady Pioneer*, 1876.

MOSER, Oswald RI   1874-1953
Painter and illustrator. He studied at St John's Wood Art School and worked in London until 1925 and afterwards at Rye. He exhibited at the Salon in 1907 and was elected RI, 1909 and ROI, 1908. He died 31 March 1953.
Illus: *John Halifax, Gentleman [Mrs Craik, Black, 1905].*
Exhib: G; L; RA; RI; RSA.

MOSES, Henry   1782-1870
Draughtsman and engraver. He was born in London in 1782 and became the foremost outline engraver of his generation, specialising in antiquities and closely associated with the Greek Revival. He was engraver to the British Museum and died at Cowley, Middlesex on 28 February, 1870.
Illus: *The Gallery of Pictures Painted by Benjamin West [1811]; The Mausoleum at Castle Howard [1812]; A Collection of Vases [1814]; Picturesque Views of Ramsgate [1817]; Select Greek and Roman Antiquities from Vases...Gems...[1817]; Vases From the Collection of Sir Henry Englefield [1819-20]; Modern Costume [1823]; Sketches of Shipping [1824]; The Marine Sketchbook [1825-26]; The Works of Canova [1824-28]; Selection of Ornamental Sculptures From the Museum of the Louvre [1828]; Visit of William IV to Portsmouth [1840].*
Exhib: RBA.
Colls: Witt Photo.

MOULIN   fl.1859-1860

French figure artist and illustrator. Vizetelly records that Moulin had access to the palaces of the Second Empire because he was related to Napoleon III's chef but in fact he was an informer of the secret police!
Contrib: *The Illustrated Times [1859-60]; ILN [1860].*

'MOUSE'

Contributed one cartoon to *Vanity Fair,* 1913.

MUCKLEY, Louis Fairfax   fl.1889-1914

Painter, etcher and illustrator. He was born at Stourbridge and studied at Birmingham School of Art, contributing to various lavish books in a late Pre-Raphaelite style with Morris decoration. He was associated with the Birmingham School of Handicraft and designed for *The Quest;* he may have been a relation of W.J. Muckley, Art Director at Manchester and Wolverhampton.
Illus: *Fringilla [R.D. Blackmore, 1895-96]; Spenser's Faerie Queen [1897].*
Contrib: *Rivers of Great Britain [1889]; The Graphic [1889]; The Quiver [1890]; Strand Magazine [1892]; ILN [1893-96]; Cassell's Family Magazine.*
Exhib: B; New Gall; RA.
Bibl: R.E.D. Sketchley, *Eng. Bk. Illus,* 1903, pp.12, 129.

MULREADY, Augustus Edward   -1886

Genre painter. He worked with F.D. Hardy, G.B. O'Neill and T. Webster as a member of the Cranbrook 'Colony'. He concentrated on domestic subjects and died in London in 1886.
Contrib: *ILN [1886].*
Exhib: RA; ROI.
Bibl: *Cat. of Works of Art, Corp. of London,* 1910.

MULREADY, William   RA   1786-1863

Genre painter and illustrator. He was born at Ennis, County Clare in 1786 and brought to London as a child where he early showed a talent for drawing. He received instruction from Thomas Banks, the sculptor, and entered the RA Schools in 1800. He formed a friendship with John Varley, whose sister he married in 1803, but the marriage ended after a few years. Mulready concentrated on oil paintings in the Wilkie style, but was also a very prolific illustrator, producing huge numbers of vignette designs in the period around 1810. He was elected ARA in 1815 and RA a few months later, but continued his illustrative work into late middle age, appearing under the same covers as the Pre-Raphaelites. Mulready is a charming but never a strong illustrator of fiction and his delicate drawings were best suited to the age before the wood engraving. He designed the first Penny Postage envelope for Sir Rowland Hill in 1840 and died at Bayswater on 7 July 1863.
Illus: *The Vicar of Wakefield [Goldsmith, 1843]; The Mother's Primer [1844]; Peveril of the Peak [Walter Scott 1846]; Frontispiece to Moore's Irish Melodies [1856]; Tennyson [Moxon, 1857].*
Exhib: BI; RA; RBA.
Colls: BM; Burnley; Glasgow; V & AM.
Bibl: F.G. Stephens, *Memorials of WM,* 1867; Chatto & Jackson, *Treatise on Wood Engraving,* 1861, p.598; Anne Rorimer, *Drawings of WM,* V & AM Cat., 1972; K.M. Heleniak, *WM,* 1980; Marcia Pointon, *M,* V & AM catalogue, July-Oct. 1986; R. De Beaumont, 'The Vicar of Wakefield', *Private Library,* Fourth series, Vol. 51, Spring 1992, pp.4-19.

MUNN, George Frederick   RBA   1852-1907

American genre and flower painter. He was born at Utica in 1852 and studied under Charles Calverley at the National Academy and at South Kensington. He was elected RBA in 1884 and died in New York on 10 February 1907.
Contrib: *ILN [1891].*
Exhib: RA; RBA; ROI.

MUNNINGS, Sir Alfred   PRA   1878-1959

Painter, sculptor and poet. He was born at Mendham, Suffolk on 8 October 1878 and studied at Framlingham School and Norwich School of Art. Munnings' great love of his native county and his knowledge of its life, made him one of the finest painters of the horse since George Stubbs. Although never strictly an illustrator, he began life in poster work at Norwich, designing wrappers for Caley's Chocolates and calendars for Bullard's Brewery. In later life he illustrated his own *An Artist's Life,* 1950. Elected RA in 1925, he was President of the RA from 1944 to 1949.
Coll: Castle House, Dedham.

MURCH, Arthur   fl.1871-1881

Black and white artist. He was apparently working in Italy, 1871-73, and Walter Crane says that he was a meticulous man who produced little. His wife was a frequent exhibitor at the Grosvenor Gallery 1880-90.
Contrib: *Dalziel's Bible Gallery [1881].*

MURDOCH, W.G. Burn   fl.1882-1919

Painter, lithographer and etcher. He studied at the Antwerp Academy and under Carolus Duran in Paris, then in Madrid, Florence and Naples. He worked in Edinburgh and contributed to *The Evergreen.*
Exhib: G; L; New Gall; RA; RSA.

MURRAY, Charles Oliver   RPE   1842-1924

Painter and etcher. He was born at Denholm in 1842 and was educated at Minto School and at the Edinburgh School of Design and the RSA. He gained medals there for his anatomical studies and drawings from the antique and the National Medallions Queens Prize. He worked as engraver and illustrator for the magazines but later devoted himself entirely to etching and worked on pictures after famous artists. He became RPE on its foundation in 1881 and was a member of the Art Workers Guild. He died 11 December 1924.
Illus: *Spindle Stories [Ascot R. Hope, 1880].*
Contrib: *Golden Hours [1869]; Good Words [1880]; The English Illustrated Magazine [1891-92].*
Exhib: FAS; L; M; RA; RE; RSA.
Colls: BM.

MURRAY, Sir David   RA ARSA PRI   1849-1933

Landscape painter. He was born at Glasgow in 1849 and after studying at the Art School, moved to London and became a very fashionable painter in the tradition of Constable. He was elected ARA in 1891 and RA in 1905 and was President of the RI, 1916-17. He is included here for the illustrations he drew for *The English Illustrated Magazine* in 1887.
Colls: Birkenhead; Glasgow.

MURRAY, George   fl.1883-1922

Painter and decorative designer. He was working in Glasgow in 1883, in London 1899 and 1903 and in Blairgowrie, 1902. A title page design by this artist appears in *The Studio,* Vol.14, 1898, p.71.
Exhib: G; L; RA; RI; RSA.

MURRAY, W. Bazett   fl.1871-1890

Illustrator. This artist specialised in social realism and drawings of an industrial nature which are fine studies of the Victorian working class. His work was admired by Vincent Van Gogh during his English years.
Contrib: *The Graphic [1874-76]; ILN [1874-90].*
Exhib: RA, 1871-75.

MURRAY, Mrs. Wolfe

Illustrated *The Arab's Ride to Calais,* by G. J. Whyte-Melville, c.1860.

MURRELL, Claire

Contributing decoration to *The Studio,* Vol. 12, 1871, illus.

Twelve views of the Antiquities of London [1805-10]; Picturesque views of the City of Paris and its Environs [1819-23].
Contrib: Howlett's Views in the County of Lincoln [1802]; Britton's Beauties of England and Wales [1801-15]; Ackermann's Oxford [1814]; Antiquarian and Topographical Cabinet [1809].
Exhib: BI; RA; RBA, OWS.
Colls: Bradford; Nottingham; V & AM.
Bibl: Martin Hardie, Watercol. Paint, in Brit., Vol.3, 1968 pp.16-17; H. Mallalieu, Dictionary of British Watercolour Artists - 1920, 1976.

NASH, John RA   **1893-1977**

Artist, flower painter and illustrator. He was born in Kensington in 1893, the brother of Paul Nash (q.v.). He was educated at Wellington College and on the advice of his brother took no formal art training and thus developed a very personal style in his interpretation of nature, both innocent and observant. He served in the Artists Rifles 1916-18 and was appointed an official War Artist in 1918. During the 1920s both brothers were very successful artists, notably in landscape, where they led a school that sought out a more abstract direction, based on its colour, structure and massing. Nash's talent as a comic artist and writer led him to the field of book illustration, which was having a revival at the time with the Cresset and Golden Cockerell presses. Although most of his work post-dates our period, he is included here as an artist active before 1914. He was elected ARA in 1940 and RA in 1951; he was a member of the London Group and was an assistant teacher of Design at the RCA, 1934. A one man exhibition of his work was held at the RA in 1967.

Illus: Dressing Gowns and Glue [1919]; Drawings in the Theatre [1919]; The Nouveau Poor [1921]; Directions to Servants [1925]; Ovid's Elegies and Epigrams [Sir John Davies, 1925]; Bats in the Belfry [1926]; Catalogue of Alpine and Herbaceous Plants [1926]; Poisonous Plants [1927]; Celeste [1930]; The Shepherds Calendar [1930]; Cobbett's Rural Rides [1930]; When Thou Wast Naked [T.F. Powys, 1931]; The New Flora and Sylva [1931]; One Hundred and One Ballades [1931]; The Curious Gardener [Jason Hill, 1931]; Flowers and Faces [1935]; Wild Flowers in Britain [1938]; Plants with Personality [1938]; The Contemplative Gardener [1940]; The Almanack of Hope [1946]; English Garden Flowers [1948]; The Natural History of Selborne [1951]; Parnassian Molehill [1953]; The Tranquil Gardener [1958]; The Guinness Year Book [1959]; Thorntree Meadows [1960]; The Native Garden [1961]; B.B.C. Book of the Countryside [1963]; The Art of Angling [1965].

Contrib: The Broadside; Rhyme Sheets [Poetry Bookshop]; The Listener [1933-34 (plant illus.)].

Bibl: JN, RA cat., 1967.

See Horne

NASH, Joseph   **1808-1878**

Draughtsman and illustrator. He was born at Great Marlow on 17 December 1808 and worked as an assistant to Pugin, who took him to Paris in 1829 to prepare topographical sketches for Paris and its Environs, 1830. Nash is best remembered however for his large lithographed books of picturesque architecture which appeared in the 1830s and 1840s and are still regarded as the most accurate views of medieval houses and castles. Nash's figures, in the style of Cattermole, brought the buildings to life, without detracting from the serious antiquarianism of the book. He was elected AOWS in 1834 and OWS in 1842, but his work declined in later years possibly due to illness. He died at Bayswater on 19 December 1878.

Illus: Architecture of the Middle Ages [1838]; Mansions of England in the Olden Time [1839-49]; Views of Windsor Castle [1848]; Scotia Delineata [Lawson, 1847]; Merrie Days of England [E.A. MacDermott]; Dickenson's Comprehensive Picture of the Great Exhibition of 1851; Old English Ballads [1864].

Exhib: BI; NWS; OWS; RA.

Colls: Fitzwilliam; Glasgow; Greenwich; Maidstone; V & AM; Witt Photo.

NASH, Joseph, Jnr.   **RI**   **-1922**

Marine and landscape painter and illustrator. He was the son of Joseph Nash (q.v.) and worked in London from 1859, latterly at Bedford Park. He undertook some magazine work, mostly shipping subjects and is the artist of the amusing plate in The Graphic 1874, showing Ruskin's navvies mending the Oxford Road! He was

NAFTEL, Maud   **ARWS**   **1856-1890**

Flower painter and illustrator. She was born in 1856, the daughter of the artist Paul Naftel, a family of Guernsey origin. She studied at the Slade School, then in Paris with Carolus Duran, and became a member of the SWA in 1886 and was elected ARWS in 1887. She died in London in 1890.

Publ: Flowers and How to Paint Them [1886].

Exhib: B; FAS; GG; G; L; M; New Gall; RA; RI; RWS; SWA. Colls: Liverpool.

NAIRN, Mr.

Illustrator contributing drawings of the New Zealand Gold Rush to The Illustrated London News, 1863. He may be identified as the father of J.M. Nairn, the New Zealand artist who died at Wellington on 2 February 1904.

NANCE, Robert Morton   **fl.1895-1909**

Illustrator, painter and ship modeller. He probably studied at the Herkomer School at Bushey in 1895 and then lived in South Wales, 1903 and at Penzance, 1909 where he was associated with the St. Ives artists.

Exhib: L; New Gall; RA.

Bibl: The Studio, Bk. Illus. competition, 1897; Vol.14, 1898 pp.257-262 illus.

NANKIVELL, Frank Arthur   **1869-**

Painter, etcher and comic artist. He was born in Australia in 1869 and studied in New York, London, Japan and China.

Contrib: Punch [1903 (figures)].

Exhib: FAS, 1930.

NASCHEN, Donia Esther   **fl.1910-1935**

Born in Russia, studied at the Slade School. Figure artist and illustrator, working at Stamford Hill, London.

Exhib: RA; ROI.

See Horne

NASH, Frederick   **OWS**   **1782-1856**

Painter, watercolourist, lithographer and architectural illustrator. He was born at Lambeth in 1782 and learned drawing with T. Malton, Junior, and studied at the RA Schools. He exhibited at the RA from 1800 and began by working as an architectural draughtsman, occasionally being employed by Sir R. Smirke RA. He contributed to numerous publications and was one of a number of artists who gained success by satisfying the early 19th century craving for extreme accuracy. It was this which won him the post as artist to the Society of Antiquaries in 1807, made Turner commend him and Ackermann employ him. Nash was elected a member of the OWS in 1811 and five years later began a series of foreign sketching tours to Switzerland, France and Germany, some of the results of which were published. He made tours in Great Britain, from 1827-41 and was accompanied on some of them by Peter de Wint. His work becomes more moody in his later years when he had almost ceased illustration and concentrated on views of Windsor and Brighton, where he settled and died in 1856.

Illus: The Collegiate Chapel of St. George at Windsor [1805];

elected RI in 1886 and died in 1922.
Illus: *The Dash For Khartoum [G.A. Henty, 1892].*
Contrib: *The Graphic [1872-1902].*
Exhib: B; G; L; M; RA; RHA; RI; ROI.
Bibl: *The Studio,* Winter No., 1923-24, p.27; *Apollo,* 1925, p.126; *The Connoisseur,* Vol.71, 1925, p.112.

NASH, Paul   **1889-1946**
Painter, wood engraver, illustrator and theatrical designer. He was born in London on 11 May 1889, the elder brother of John Nash (q.v.). He was educated at St. Pauls and studied at Chelsea Polytechnic and the Slade School, 1909-10. He held his first exhibition of drawings at the Carfax Gallery in 1911 and followed this with an exhibition of work jointly with his brother at the Dorien Leigh Gallery, 1913. Nash enlisted with the Artists Rifles in 1914 and after being transferred to the Hampshire Regiment was wounded at Ypres, 1917 and the same year appointed official War Artist on the Western Front. The war drawings, grey wash studies of tortured landscapes and crabbed humanity, were the most significant contribution that Nash made to twentieth century art. The shapes and symbols from this time recur again and again in his later landscape paintings and drawings. An exhibition of the war work was held at the Leicester Galleries in 1918 and another was held in 1924. Nash was a member of the London Group, the Modern English Watercolour Society and the Society of Wood Engravers and founded a group of imaginative painters called 'Unit One'. He was author of *Room and Book,* a series of essays on decoration, published in 1932 and he died in July 1946.
Illus: *Loyalties [John Drinkwater, 1918]; Images of War [Richard Aldington, 1919]; Places, Prose Poems and Wood-Engravings [1922]; Genesis [12 engravings on wood 1924]; Urn Burial [Sir Thomas Browne]; Abd-er-Rahman [Jules Tellier, 1928]; The Seven Pillars of Wisdom [T.E. Lawrence].*
Contrib: *The Graphic [1918]; The Broadside; Rhymesheets [The Poetry Bookshop].*
Exhib: FAS; L; M; NEA; P; RSA; RSW.
Bibl: *Poet and Painter,* Oxford, 1955, edited by Abbott and Bertram.
See Horne

NASH, Thomas
Illustrator working for *The Broadway,* 1867-74.

NASMYTH, Alexander   **1758-1840**
Portrait and landscape painter. He was born at Edinburgh on 9 September 1758 and after becoming a pupil of Allan Ramsay, he worked in London and studied at Rome 1782-84. On his return to Edinburgh, he established a wide reputation for soft and sensitive oil landscapes in the manner of Claude. Nasmyth ran art classes in his house and five of his daughters and one son became distinguished artists. He died at Edinburgh on 10 April 1840.
Illus: *The Border Antiquities of England and Scotland [Walter Scott, 1817].*
Exhib: BI; RA; RBA.
Colls: Bristol, Edinburgh, Glasgow; Mellon, Nottingham.
Bibl: Peter Johnson, *The N Family of Painters; AN,* Balcarres Gallery, St Andrew's University, Feb.–Mar. 1979.

NAST, J.   **1840-1902**
American caricaturist. He was born at Landau on 27 September 1840 of American parentage, but left with his parents for the United States and settled with them in New York. He began his career as an artist for various American magazines but came to England in 1860 for *The New York Illustrated Newspaper* to cover the boxers Heenan and Sayers. A man who clearly preferred action to the newspaper office, Nast enlisted with Garibaldi and became a Special Artist to English, French and American magazines during the Italian campaign. On his return to the United States in 1861, he fought in the American Civil War with distinction and became the leading cartoonist of his generation, noted for the power of his images and his draughtsmanship. He died at Guayaquil on 7 December 1902.
Contrib: *The Illustrated Times [1860]; The Illustrated London News [1860-61]; Vanity Fair [1872].*
Bibl: A.B. Paine, *N His Period and His Pictures,* 1905; *American Art Journal,* Vol.4, 1903 p.143; T. Nast St Hill, *N Cartoons and Illustrations,* Dover, 1974.

NATTES, John Claude   **c.1765-1822**
Topographer and drawing master. He was born in England in about 1765 and studied under Hugh P. Dean and was a founder member of the OWS in 1804, but was expelled in 1807 for exhibiting other artists' works under his own name. He travelled to Italy and the South of France in 1820-22 and specialised in Italian landscapes and topographical views. He died in London in 1822.
Illus: *Scotia Depicta [1801-04]; Hibernia Depicta [1802]; Bath and its Environs Illustrated [1804-05]; Versailles, Paris and Saint Denis [1810, AT 103]; Select Views of Bath, Bristol [1805].*
Exhib: RA, 1782-1814.
Colls: Barnsley; BM; Leeds; Lincoln: V & AM.
Bibl: Hardie, *Watercol. Paint. in Brit.,* 1967, Vol.2, pp.133-134 illus.; Gowing & Clarke, *Drawings of Stowe by John Claude Nattes in The Buckinghamshire County Museum,* 1983.

NEALE, Adam
Amateur artist who illustrated his own *Travels Through Germany, Poland, Moldavia and Turkey,* 1818, AT 19.

NEALE, Edward   **fl.1880-1899**
Animal and bird artist and illustrator. Worked in London and contributed to *The Illustrated London News,* 1899.
Exhib: B; L; RA.

NEALE, John Preston   **1780-1847**
Architectural and topographical illustrator. He was born in 1780 and after working in the Post Office, turned to draughtsmanship and became one of the leading topographers of the gothic revival. His pen drawings, which were exceptional for their accuracy, were often in monochrome washes and were used for numerous books as well as those published under his own name. He died at Tattingstone on 14 November 1847.
Illus: *The History and Antiquities of the Abbey Church of Westminster [1818]; The Seats of Noblemen and Gentlemen [1818-29]; Views of the Most Interesting Collegiate and Parochial Churches of Great Britain [1824-25].*
Contrib: *Britton's Beauties of England and Wales [1808-16]; London and Middlesex [Brayley]; Jones's Views [1829-31].*
Exhib: BI; OWS; RA; RBA.
Colls: Ashmolean; BM; Nottingham; V & AM.
Bibl: Iolo Williams, *Early English Watercols.,* 1952, p.225, illus.

NEIL, H.   **See O'NEILL, Hugh**

NEILSON, Harry B.   **fl.1895-1901**
Illustrator of comic animal subjects. He worked at Claughton, Cheshire and published books for children which *The Studio* called 'wild and domesticated beasts disporting themselves in human garb', Vol.12.
Illus: *Micky Magee's Menagerie [1897]; Droll Days [1901]; Tiny Tots [1911].*
Contrib: *The Sketch; Cassell's Family Magazine.*
Exhib: L.

NELSON, Harold Edward Hughes   **1871-**
Artist, illustrator and designer of bookplates. He was born at Dorchester on 22 May 1871 and studied at the Lambeth School of Art and the Central School of Arts and Crafts, London. Nelson made a speciality of medieval illustrations with elaborate borders and was particularly accomplished as a decorator of books. He was influenced by the books of Morris and by the Pre-Raphaelites, but made his mark as a designer of bookplates. He was also an early designer of Cadbury's advertisements.
Publ: *25 Designs by HN [Edinburgh, 1904].*
Illus: *Undine and Aslauga's Knight [F.H.C. de la Motte Fouqué, 1901]; Early English Prose Romances [W.J. Thomas, 1904].*
Contrib: *The Graphic [1915]; The Sphere; The Queen; Ladies Field; Royal Academy Pictures [cover, 1908]; Old Colleges of Oxford [Aymer Vallance, 1912 (frontis.)].*
Exhib: L; RA; RI; RMS.
Bibl: H.W. Fincham, *Art of the Bookplate,* 1897; C.P. Horning, *Bookplates by HN,* New York, 1929; B. Peppin, *Fantasy Book Illustration 1860-1920,* 1975, p.189; *The Studio.* Vol.7, 1896, p.93; Vol.8 1896, p.226; Vol.24, 1902, p.63; Vol.63, 1915, p.148; Vol.73, 1918, p.67; Vol.81, 1921, p.19; Vol.83, 1922, p.96.

EDMUND HORT NEW 1871-1931. 'Stanstead Abbots'. Illustration for *The Yellow Book*, 1896

NESBIT, Charlton   **1775-1838**
Illustrator and wood engraver. He was born at Swalewell in 1775 and became a pupil for four years of Beilby and Thomas Bewick (q.v.), working on his *British Birds*. He began painting in about 1795 and established himself in London in 1799, where he gained a reputation for book illustrations. He died there in 1838.
Illus: *Shakespeare's Works; The Works of Sir Egerton Bridges; Hudibras; Ackermann's Religious Emblems [1809]; Northcote's Fables [1828-33].*
Colls: BM; Witt Photo.

NESBITT, Frances E.   **fl.1864-1934**
Landscape, figure and marine painter. She was elected ASWA in 1899 and illustrated her own *Algeria and Tunis* for Messrs. Black in 1906.
Exhib: L; New Gall; RA; RBA; RHA; RI; ROI; SWA.

NESFIELD, William Eden   **1835-1888**
Architect and artist. He was the son of the artist William Andrews Nesfield and was closely associated with Richard Norman Shaw in the development of the romantic Victorian country house. He illustrated his own *Specimens of Medieval Architecture Chiefly Selected From Examples of the 12th and 13th Centuries in France and Italy,* 1862.

NETTLESHIP, John Trivett   **1847-1902**
Animal painter, illustrator and author. He was born at Kettering on 11 February 1841 and was educated at Durham School before joining the staff of his father's law firm. He abandoned this career for art and studied at Heatherley's and the Slade School, working as an illustrator in pen and ink and making drawings in the Zoological Gardens. He visited India in 1880-81, but made his reputation from expressive paintings of animals in the style of Delacroix. He died in London on 31 August 1902, having been elected ROI in 1894.
Publ: *Robert Browning Essays and Thoughts [1890]; George Morland [1898].*

Illus: *An Epic of Women [A.W.E. O'Shaughnessy, 1870]; Emblems [Mrs. A. Cholomondeley, 1875]; Natural History Sketches Among the Carnivora [1885]; Ice-bound on Kolguev [A.R. Battye, 1895].*
Contrib: *The Boys' Own Paper.*
Exhib: G; L; M; New Gall; RA; RHA; RI; ROI.
Colls: Ashmolean.
Bibl: *The Magazine of Art,* 1903, pp.75, 79; *The AJ,* 1907, p. 251.

NEW, Edmund Hort   **1871-1931**
Landscape painter, architect and illustrator. He was born in Evesham in 1871, the son of a solicitor and was educated at Prince Henry's School, Evesham and at the Birmingham Municipal School of Art under E.R. Taylor and A.J. Gaskin (q.v.) 1886-95. New taught at a branch school of the School of Art and became well-known in the Midlands, spending much of his working life in Oxford. His black and white illustrations are characteristic of Birmingham, cleanly drawn in the woodcut style with large foregrounds and meticulous care in the delineation of each building and its materials. New was a member of the Art Workers Guild, was elected Hon. ARIBA, and died at Oxford on 3 February 1931.
Illus: *The Gypsy Road [Cole, 1894]; In the Garden of Peace [1896]; The Compleat Angler [1896]; The Vale of Arden [Alfred Hayes, 1896 (title and cover)]; White Wampum [Pauline Johnson, 1896 (title and cover)]; Oxford and Its Colleges [1897]; Cambridge and Its Colleges [1898]; Shakespeare's Country [1899]; Pickwick Papers [1899]; The Life of William Morris [1899]; The Natural History of Selborne [1900]; Westminster Abbey [1900]; Oliver Twist [1900]; Outside the Garden [1900]; Sussex [1900]; The Malvern Country [Windle, 1901]; The Wessex of Thomas Hardy; Some Impressions of Oxford [1901]; Haunts of Ancient Peace [1902]; Wren's Parentalia [1903]; Chester [1903]; Evesham [1904]; Temple Topographies series, College Monographs series; The Last Records of a Cotswold Community [C.R. Ashbee, 1905]; The Scholar Gypsy and Thyrsis [1906]; Twenty Drawings of Sir Christopher Wren's Churches [1906]; Poems of Wordsworth [1907]; Berkshire [1911]; Coleridge and Wordsworth in the West Country [Professor Knight 1913]; Highways and Byways in Shakespeare's Country [1914]; Cranford [1914]; The New Loggan Guides to Oxford Colleges [1907-25, issued together 1932]; Prints issued of: The Towers of Oxford [1908]; High Street Oxford [1912]; Firenze [1914]; The City and Port of London [1920].*
Contrib: *The English Illustrated Magazine [1891-92]; The Quest [1894-96]; Daily Chronicle [1895]; The Yellow Book [1896]; The Pall Mall Magazine.*
Exhib: B, FAS; RA.
Colls: Birmingham; V & AM.
Bibl: R.E.D. Sketchley, *Eng. Bk. Illus.* 1903, pp.10, 38, 50, 136; *Modern Book Illustrators and Their Work,* Studio, 1914.
See illustration.

NEWCOMBE, Bertha   **fl.1880-1908**
Landscape, figure and flower painter and illustrator. She worked in London and at Croydon and was elected NEA in 1888. She contributed illustrations of church and village life to *The English Illustrated Magazine,* 1895-97.
Exhib: FAS; L; M; NEA; RA; RBA; RI; ROI; SWA.

NEWELL, Rev. Robert Hassell   **1778-1852**
Amateur artist and illustrator. He was born in Essex in 1778 and after being educated at Colchester and St. John's College, Cambridge where he was admitted Fellow in 1800, he became Rector of Little Hormead, Hertfordshire in 1813. He studied with W.H. Payne (q.v.) and illustrated his own works.

NEWHOUSE, C.B.   **fl.1834-1845**
Artist and traveller. He illustrated his own *Scenes On The Road,* 1834-35, 18 aquatints, AL 406, and *Roadster's Album,* 1845, 17 aquatints, AL 407.

NEWILL, Mary J.   **fl.1884-1925**
Black and white artist, illustrator and embroiderer. She studied at the Birmingham School of Art and worked in Edgbaston, basing many of her designs on the Morris style. She was particularly imaginative in her renderings of wood and foilage and *The Studio* in 1897

referred to her trees having 'the strength of those by a little master of Germany'.

Illus: *A Book of Nursery Songs and Rhymes [1895].*
Contrib: *The Quest [1894-96]; The Yellow Book [1896].*
Exhib: B; FAS.
Bibl: *The Studio*, Vol.5, 1895, p.56, illus; Vol. 10, 1897, p.232.

NEWMAN, William   **fl.1842-1865**
Comic artist. A friend of Ebenezer Landells (q.v.), he was much employed on *Punch* in the period, 1846-50. A talented humorist, he was most versatile in small comic cuts in the manner of Tom Hood, but was rather despised for his coarse manners by the *Punch* Table and was poorly paid. He is believed to have emigrated to the United States in the early 60s.
Illus: *Moveable shadows by William Newman (of Punch) [Dean & Son, c.1865 (col. liths.)]; Zoological Oddities by William Newman [c.1865]; Moveable Shadows For The People, Drawn on Stone by W. Newman [c.1865 (col. liths.)].*
Contrib: *The Squib [1842]; Puppet Show; Diogenes; Comic News [1864].*
Bibl: M.H. Spielmann, *The History of Punch*, 1894, pp.413-414.

NEWTON, Gilbert Stuart   RA   **1795-1835**
Painter and illustrator. He was born at Halifax, Nova Scotia in 1795 and began studies with his maternal uncle Gilbert Stuart, the American portrait painter, at an early age. He visited Italy in 1817, and after spending some time in Paris settled in London and studied at the RA Schools, concentrating on painting in the style of Watteau. Newton had some success in painting genre and historical subjects and was patronised by the 6th Duke of Bedford. He was a friend of Washington Irving and died on 5 August 1835, having been insane since 1833. He was elected ARA in 1828 and RA in 1832.
Contrib: *The Literary Souvenir [1826].*
Exhib: BI; RA.
Colls: V & AM.

NEWTON, Richard   **1777-1798**
Caricaturist and miniaturist working in the manner of Gillray.
Illus: *Sentimental Journey [Sterne, 1795, AL 250].*
Colls: BM.

NIBBS, Richard Henry   **1816-1893**
Musician and painter. He was born in London in 1816 and worked principally in London with a studio in Brighton, settling permanently there after 1841. He travelled on the Continent and illustrated his own publications.
Publ: *Marine Sketch Book of Shipping Craft and Coast Scenes [1850]; The Churches of Sussex [1851]; Antiquities of Sussex [1874].*
Exhib: BI; L; RA; RBA.
Colls: BM; Brighton; Greenwich; V & AM.

NIBLETT, F.D.   'NIBBS'   **fl.1882-1913**
A talented illustrator and caricaturist, working first in Edinburgh and then from Charles Street, Knightsbridge. He made large scale caricatures in colour on the mottoes of peers for the shortlived magazine *Crown*, 1906-07.
Illus: *Dulcima's Doom and Other Tales [Willis, c.1880].*
Contrib: *Vanity Fair [1913 (22 ports.)].*
Exhib: RA.

NICHOLL, Andrew
Natural history illustrator of fish, contributing to *Nature and Art*, 1866-67.

NICHOLL, Andrew   RHA   **1804-1886**
Landscape painter. He was born in Belfast in 1804 and trained with a printer on the newspaper *The Northern Whig*. He was self-taught as an artist and worked in London, Dublin and Belfast, being elected ARHA in 1832 and RHA in 1837; he taught art in Ceylon during 1846, having previously illustrated S.C. Hall's *Ireland its Scenery and Character* 1841. He died in London in 1886.
Contrib: *The Illustrated London News [1851].*
Colls: BM; V & AM.

NICHOLSON, George   **c.1795-c.1839**
Topographer, working in Liverpool with his elder brother Samuel Nicholson. He published *Twenty-six Lithographic Drawings in the Vicinity Of Liverpool*, 1821; *Plas Newydd and Vale Crucis Abbey*, 1824. He exhibited at Liverpool, 1827-38.

NICHOLSON, J.B.R.   **fl.c.1815**
Illustrator. A series of watercolour drawings of soldiers and bandsmen, one showing Edinburgh Castle, signed and dated by this artist 1815, were sold at Sotheby's in November 1976.

NICHOLSON, Thomas Henry   **-1870**
Draughtsman, illustrator, engraver and sculptor. Nicholson worked in London and excelled in equestrian subjects, some of which he modelled in plaster, teaching the technique to Count Alfred d'Orsay. He was the principal artist for *Cassell's Illustrated Family Paper* 1853-57 and worked for other magazines. Much of his work is busy and mannered in the style of H.K. Browne (q.v.). He died at Portland in 1870.
Illus: *Faces in the Fire [1850]; Works of Shakespeare [n.d.].*
Contrib: *ILN [1848]; The Illustrated Times [1855-59].*

NICHOLSON, William   RSA   **1781-1844**
Portrait painter and etcher. He was born at Ovingham-on-Tyne in 1781 and after working in Newcastle, moved from there to Edinburgh in 1814. He was a Founder Member of the RSA and was its Secretary from 1826 to 1830. He published *Portraits of Distinguished Living Characters*, 1818.
Colls: Edinburgh; Newcastle.

NICHOLSON, Sir William Newzam Prior   **1872-1949**
Painter and illustrator. He was born at Newark-on-Trent in 1872, the son of W.N. Nicholson MP. He studied at Julian's, Paris, and from about 1894, collaborated with his brother-in-law James Pryde (q.v.) on a series of posters and illustrated books. Their style was based on the French poster which they admired in the hands of Toulouse Lautrec and others and the designs were most different from contemporary work in their careful lettering and effects gained by massing of the shadows and bold outlines. The artists became known as 'The Beggarstaff Brothers' and their work, which was mostly in woodcut coloured by hand and then lithographed, became widely influential. The books, as opposed to posters, were the sole

SIR WILLIAM NICHOLSON 1872-1949. 'December'. Illustration from *An Almanac of Twelve Sports*, 1898, with words by Rudyard Kipling. Lithograph after woodcut

Mr Vanslyperken.

SIR WILLIAM NICHOLSON 1872-1949. 'Mr. Vanslyperken'

production of Nicholson. His books were designed as a whole and have very little text, the lay-out and the squared illustrations give them the freedom and charm of the early chapbooks which both 'Brothers' had come to admire. After 1900, Nicholson's contributions to illustrations were spasmodic although he carried out a certain amount of it in the 1920s. His later career was almost entirely devoted to portrait painting. Nicholson was elected RP in 1909 and was knighted in 1936. He died in 1949.

Illus: *Tony Drum [1898]; An Alphabet [1898]; An Almanac of Twelve Sports [R. Kipling, 1898]; London Types [W.E. Henley, 1898]; The Square Book of Animals [Arthur Waugh, 1899]; Twelve Portraits [1899]; Characters of Romance [1900]; Twelve Portraits: Second Series [1902]; Oxford [1905]; Selected Poems of Thomas Hardy [1921]; The Velveteen Rabbit [M. Williams, 1922]; The Hour of Magic [W.H. Davies, 1922]; Polly [John Gay, 1923]; True Travellers [W.H. Davies, 1923]; Moss and Feather [W.H. Davies, 1928]; The Pirate Twins [W. Nicholson, 1929]; Memoirs of a Fox-Hunting Man [S. Sassoon, 1929]; The Book of Blokes [1929]; Time Remembered [Lady Horner, 1934];* and numerous covers for

Heinemann and other publishers, 1898-1927.

Contrib: *L'Estampe Originale [1894]; The New Review [1897-98]; Studio [1897]; The Dome [1897]; L'Estampe Moderne [1898]; The World of Dress [1899]; Black and White [1899]; The Athenaeum [1900]; Harper's Weekly [1900]; The Artist Engraver [No. 4, 1904]; Outlook [1905]; Britain's Efforts and Ideals in the Great War [1918]; The Owl [1919]; Form [1921]; The Legion Book [1929]; The Winter Owl [1923].*

Exhib: FAS; GG; G; L; M; NEA; P; RHA; ROI; RSA; RSW.

Colls: Fitzwilliam; Tate; V & AM.

Bibl: *The Idler,* Vol.8, pp.519-528, illus; *The Studio,* Vol.12, 1898, pp.177-183; Marguerite Steen, *WN*; Colin Campbell, *The Beggarstaff Posters,* 1990; Colin Campbell, *WN - The Graphic Work,* 1992.

See illustrations.

NICKSON, Fred J. fl.1902-1903

Black and white figure artist contributing social subjects to *Punch,* 1902-03.

KAY NIELSEN 1886-1957. 'The Czarina's Violet'. Head piece for *In Powder and Crinoline* by Sir Arthur Quiller-Couch, 1913. Pen and ink. 2¾in x 6⅝in (7cm x 16.8cm)

NICOL, Erskine   ARA RSA   **1825-1904**
Painter of Irish genre subjects. He was born at Leith in 1825 and trained at the Trustees Academy at the age of twelve after being apprenticed to a house-painter. He worked as a drawing-master at Leith before moving to Dublin in 1846, where he began to gain a reputation for Irish peasant scenes. Although settling in London, he continued to make visits to Ireland; he was elected RSA in 1859 and ARA in 1868. He died at Feltham on 8 March 1904.
Illus: *Tales of Irish Life and Character [A.M. Hall, 1909]; Irish Life and Humour [W. Harvey, 1909].*
Contrib: *Good Words [1860].*
Exhib: G, RA, RSA.
Colls: BM; Edinburgh; Sheffield; Tate; V & AM.

NICOL, John Watson   ROI   **1856-1926**
Genre painter and illustrator. He was born in 1856, the son of Erskine Nicol ARA (q.v.). He worked in Scotland and France as well as in London and was elected ROI in 1888.
Contrib: *Good Words [1890]; Black & White [1896].*
Exhib: B; G; L; M; RA; ROI; RSA.

NIELSEN, Kay   **1886-1957**
Illustrator and designer for the theatre. He was born at Copenhagen on 12 March 1886 and was a pupil of L. Find, before studying at Julian's in Paris and at Colarossi's, 1904-11. Nielsen worked in London from 1911 until 1916 which accounts for his inclusion here, it was an intensive period of work and he was strongly influenced by Aubrey Beardsley. In general Nielsen is a brilliant colourist and a highly decorative illustrator, his works formed into frieze-like patterns, are closest to Persian or Middle Eastern designs and therefore akin to Leon Bakst or Edmund Dulac (q.v.). He uses stippling effects and elaborate rococo motifs which are reminiscent of Beardsley, but also the swirling lines of Vernon Hill (q.v.) and the more sculptural lines of incipient art deco. Nielsen held a big exhibition in New York in 1917 and after acting as stage designer to the Theatre Royal, Copenhagen, 1918-22, he emigrated to the United States, living in California from 1939 and designing for the Hollywood companies. He died there in 1957.
Illus: *In Powder and Crinoline [A. Quiller Couch, 1912]; East of the Sun, West of the Moon [Asbjornsen and Moe, 1914]; Old Tales From The North [1919]; Fairy Tales by Hans Andersen [1924]; Hansel and Gretel [1925]; Red Magic [Romer Wilson, 1930].*
Contrib: *ILN [1912-13 (Christmas)].*
Exhib: Dowdeswell Gall., 1912; Leicester Gall., 1914.
Colls: V & AM.
Bibl: Marion Hepworth Dixon, 'The Drawings of KN', *The Studio,* Vol. 60, 1914; B. Peppin, *Fantasy Book Illustration 1860-1920,* 1975, p.189 illus.; Keith Nicholson, *Introduction to KN,* Coronet Books, 1975. See illustration.

NINHAM, Henry   **1793-1874**
Watercolourist and engraver. He was born at Norwich in 1793, the son of an heraldic artist and engraver. He was a topographical artist, specialising in street scenes and was a member of the Norwich School and friendly with J.S. Cotman. He died in the city in 1874.
Publ: *8 Original Etchings of Picturesque Antiquities of Norwich [1842]; Views of the Gates of Norwich made in 1792-93 by the late John Ninham [1861]; 23 Views of the Ancient City Gates of Norwich [1864]; Remnants of Antiquity in Norwich, Views of Norwich and Norfolk [1875]; Norwich Corporation Pageantry.*
Illus: *Castle Acre [Blome]; Eastern Arboretum [Grigor, 1841].*
Colls: BM; Norwich; V & AM.

NISBET, Hume   **1849-1923**
Painter and author, illustrator. He was born in Stirling on 8 August

SIR WILLIAM NICHOLSON 1872-1949. 'Queen Victoria'. One from the series of *Twelve Portraits,* 1899. Lithograph

1849 and studied art under Sam Bough RSA. At the age of sixteen he began to travel and spent seven years exploring Australia, being appointed on his return, Art Master at the Watt College and Old Schools of Art, Edinburgh. He resigned the post in 1885, when he was sent by Cassell & Co. to Australia and New Guinea, 1886; visited China and Japan, 1905-06. He concentrated on his work as novelist in the latter part of his life and died at Eastbourne in 1923.
Illus: *Her Loving Slave [1894]; A Sappho of Green Springs [Brett Harte, 1897]; The Fossicker [Ernest Glanville, 1897].*
Contrib: *The English Illustrated Magazine [1890-91 (ornament)].*
Exhib: G; RA; RBA; RHA; RSA.

NIXON, J. Forbes   **fl.1864-1867**
Still-life painter working at Tonbridge. He designed the cover for *The Young Gentleman's Magazine,* 1867.
Exhib: RBA.

NIXON, James Henry   **fl.1830-1847**
History painter and expert on heraldry. He was born in about 1808 and became a pupil of John Martin (q.v.).
Illus: *The Eglinton Tournament [Rev. J. Richardson, 1843, AL 388].*
Contrib: *Scott's Works [1834].*
Exhib: BI; RA; RBA.
Colls: Witt Photo.

NIXON, John   **c.1750-1818**
Landscape painter and amateur caricaturist. He was born about 1750 and carried on the business of merchant in Basinghall Street, befriending many artists and going on sketching tours with some of them. Nixon had business connections with Ireland and visited the island frequently in the 1780s and 1790s, once in 1791 in company with Captain Grose, the antiquary. Some of his drawings were used in *Watt's Seats,* 1779-1786 and he visited the Continent in 1783-84 and in 1802 and 1804, when he was at Paris. Nixon was at Bath with Thomas Rowlandson (q.v.) in 1792 and a drawing of the Abbey by him, sold at Christie's in March 1974, shows strong similarities to this artist in pen outlines. Although Nixon remained a coarse draughtsman compared with Rowlandson, he has something of his bravura and sense of the grotesque and his best works are datable from this contact to the period after 1800. Nixon was Secretary to The Beefsteak Club and a member of the Margravine of Anspach's circle at Brandenburg House in Hammersmith. He died in 1818.
Contrib: *European Magazine; Journey from London to The Isle of Wight [Thomas Pennant, 1801]; Guide to The Watering Places [1803].*
Exhib: RA, 1781-1815.
Colls: BM; V & AM; Witt Photo.
Bibl: H. Angelo, *Reminiscences,* 1830.

NOBLE, John Edwin   **RBA FZS**   **1876-**
Animal painter and illustrator. He was born in 1876, the son of John Noble RBA 1848-1896 and studied at the Slade, Lambeth and RA Schools. He worked in London and Surrey and at Milford on Sea, Hants from 1922; he was elected RBA in 1907 and FZS in 1908.
Bibl: *The Studio,* Vol.14, 1898, p.145, illus.

NORBURY, Edwin Arthur   **RCA**   **1849-1918**
Painter and illustrator. He was born in Liverpool in 1849, the son of Richard Norbury, RCA. He was educated at Dr. Wand's School, Liverpool and at the age of fifteen began sending contributions to *The Illustrated London News* and *Illustrated Times,* later joining *The Graphic* as artist correspondent. He lived in North Wales 1875-90 and went to Siam in 1892 to teach at the Royal School of Arts and while there acted as *Graphic* Special Artist during the Franco-Siamese War, 1893. He was a Founder Member of the Royal Cambrian Academy and ran his own Norbury Sketching School and St James' Life School in Chelsea. He was Principal of the Henry Blackburn Studio and died in London, 16 October 1918.
Illus: *The Kingdom of the Yellow Robe [Ernest Young, 1898]; The Arabian Nights Entertainments [1899]; Animal Arts and Crafts.*
Exhib: L; M; RA; RCA; RHA; RI; ROI.

NORIE, Orlando   **1832-1901**
Military artist and illustrator. He belonged to a celebrated family of Edinburgh artists but worked in London and Aldershot where he kept a studio. He is notable for his great accuracy in depicting uniforms and military customs, but is not a particularly imaginative painter.
Illus: *The Memoirs of the 10th Royal Hussars [R.S. Liddell, 1891].*
Exhib: NWS; RA.
Colls: India Office Lib.; Nat. Army Mus.; V & AM; Royal Coll.

NORMAN, Philip   **FSA**   **c.1843-1931**
Draughtsman and antiquary. He was born at Bromley Common in about 1843, the son of a Director of the Bank of England and was educated at Eton and studied at the Slade School. Norman devoted his life to the study of old London buildings and made many hundreds of pencil drawings of its old courts and alleys during the last quarter of the 19th century. They are reliable records of vanished architecture, but not strong drawings, he was a rather weak figure draughtsman. A collection of these was presented to the Victoria and Albert Museum by the artist and an *Annotated Catalogue of Drawings of Old London* by the artist, was issued by the museum in 1900. He died in London 17 May 1931.
Publ: *The Inns of Old Southwark [1888 (with W. Rendle)]; Cromwell House, Highgate [1917].*
Illus: *London Signs and Inscriptions [1893]; Modern History of The City of London [C. Welch, 1903].*
Contrib: *The English Illustrated Magazine [1890-92 (taverns)].*
Exhib: L; M; NEA; New Gall; RA; RBA; RI; ROI.
Colls: V & AM.

NORMAND, B.
Artist contributing illustrations of Italy to *The Illustrated London News,* 1847.

NORRIS, Arthur   **1888-**
Landscape painter and teacher. He was born in 1888, the son of William Foxley Norris, Dean of Westminster, and studied at the Slade School, 1907-10. He contributed figure subjects to *Punch* in 1909 and 1914.
Exhib: FAS; NEA; P; RA.

NORRIS, Charles   **1779-1858**
Architectural draughtsman and amateur engraver. He was born at Marylebone in 1779, and though from a wealthy family became an orphan at an early age. He was educated at Eton and Christ Church, Oxford, before serving in the Army. After his marriage, Norris concentrated on the arts and made ambitious plans to publish antiquarian and picturesque views, teaching himself engraving in the process. He settled at Tenby in 1810 and died there in 1858.
Illus: *The Architectural Antiquities of Wales [1810]; Saint David's in a Series of Engravings [1811]; Etchings of Tenby [1812]; An Historical Account of Tenby [1818].*
Bibl: A.L. Leach, *CN,* 1949.

NORTH, Lady Georgina   **1798-1835**
Amateur figure artist and illustrator. She was born in 1798, the third daughter of the 3rd Earl of Guilford and his second wife, Susannah Coutts. Since the appearance of one of this artist's watercolours on the market in 1973, she has emerged as one of the most accomplished amateurs, working in the style of Fuseli. An illustration to *The Rape of The Lock,* dated 1831, was published and this together with a drawing of 'The Infancy of Wellington' are in an American private collection. She died unmarried on 25 August 1835.
Bibl: H. Mallalieu, *Dictionary of British Watercolour Artists – 1920,* 1976; R. Halsband, *The Rape of the Lock and Its Illustrators,* 1980, pp.58, 60, 63.

NORTH, John William   **ARA RWS**   **1842-1924**
Landscape painter, watercolourist and illustrator. He was born on the outskirts of London in 1842 and was apprenticed to J.W. Whymper's wood engraving workshop where he came into contact with Fred Walker and G.J. Pinwell (qq.v.). From 1862-66, North did a great deal of work for the Dalziel Brothers, and illustrated their *Wayside Poesies* 1867 and other books. North was a close friend of Fred Walker and they went on sketching tours together, Walker finding his

subjects in the country folk and North in the landscapes. His work represents the best landscape work of the 1860s, a broad treatment of the countryside, superb detail showing up in the foreground, but as Reid has pointed out 'in his own day his work never attained popularity, and was underrated even by his fellow-artists'. North moved to Somerset in 1868 and the Halsway and Withycombe areas were to provide frequent subjects for his drawings. He was elected AOWS in 1871, RWS in 1883 and ARA in 1893. The later years of his life were spent in patenting and marketing a special watercolour paper, which greatly impoverished him. He died at Washford on 20 December 1924.

Illus: *English Sacred Poetry of the Olden Time [1864]; Our Life Illustrated by Pen and Pencil [1864]; A Round of Days [1865]; The Sunday Magazine [1865-67]; Good Words [1866]; Once a Week [1866-67]; Touches of Nature by Eminent Artists [1866]; Longfellow's Poems [1866]; Poems by Jean Ingelow [1867]; Wayside Poesies [1867]; The Spirit of Praise [1867]; The Months Illustrated with Pen and Pencil [n.d.]; The Illustrated Book of Sacred Poems.*

Contrib: *The English Illustrated Magazine [1887].*
Exhib: B; FAS; GG; G; L; M; New Gall; RA; RHA; RSW; RWS.
Colls: Ashmolean; BM; Bristol; V & AM.
Bibl: Gleeson White, *English Illustration The Sixties* 1906; Forrest Reid, *Illustrators of the Sixties*, 1928, pp.163-165; Martin Hardie, *Watercol. Paint. in Brit.* Vol.3, 1968, pp.137-138; *Country Life,* 18 August 1977, 'A Somerset Draw For Painters' by R.M. Billingham.

NORTHCOTE, James   RA   1746-1831
Painter and author. He was born in Plymouth in 1746, and was apprenticed to a watchmaker, before going to London in 1771 and being patronised by Sir Joshua Reynolds, whose assistant he became. He studied at the RA Schools and, after a brief return to Plymouth, left for Italy in 1777 where he copied the old masters and particularly the works of Michelangelo, Raphael and Titian. He returned to London in 1780 and became a successful portrait painter, contributing illustrations to various works. He was elected ARA in 1786 and RA in 1787. At the end of his career, Northcote devoted himself to animal painting and to writing, he published a standard life of Sir Joshua Reynolds in 1813 and his *Conversations* were published by William Hazlitt in 1830. In 1828, he produced an edition of *One Hundred Fables,* illustrated by himself, which includes 280 wood engravings of animal and landscape subjects which have almost the charm and romance of Bewick about them.
Contrib: *Boydell's Shakespeare [1792].*
Exhib: BI; RA; RBA.
Colls: Witt Photo; NPG; V & AM.
See illustration.

NORTON, Eardley B.   fl.1895-1902
Caricaturist. He was working in London and contributed two cartoons to *Vanity Fair,* 1895 and 1902. Signs: E.B.N.

NORTON, Val
Contributor of figure subjects to *Punch,* 1902-05.

NYE, Herbert   fl.1885-1927
Painter and sculptor. He was working at Walton on Thames, 1895-1902 and at Pulborough, 1923. He made nine etchings for Garnett's edition of *Vathek* by William Beckford, 1893.
Exhib: L; RA; RI; ROI.

JAMES NORTHCOTE RA 1746-1831. Vignette illustration for *One Hundred Fables*, 1828. Wood engraving

OAKES, John Wright   **ARA HRSA**   **1820-1887**
Landscape painter. He was born at Sproston House, Middlewich, Cheshire on 9 July 1820 and was educated at Liverpool College and at the Mechanics Institute under W.J. Bishop. Oakes concentrated on fruit paintings in the early part of his career but after 1843, worked with landscapes, especially the scenery of Wales, Scotland and Devon. He moved to London in 1859 and was elected ARA in 1876 and Hon. RSA in 1883. He was Secretary of the Liverpool Academy from 1839, and died in London on 8 July 1887.
Contrib: *Passages From The Modern English Poets [Junior Etching Club, 1862 and 1876]; Cassell's Illustrated Readings [1867].*
Exhib: BI; L; NWS; RA; RBA.
Colls: Birkenhead; V & AM.

OAKLEY, William Harold   **fl.1887-1925**
Architect and illustrator. He practised in Maiden Lane, Strand, 1881-88 and was still active in 1925. He contributed architectural drawings to *The English Illustrated Magazine,* 1887-92 and to *The Strand Magazine,* 1891.

ODLE, Alan Elsden   **1888-1948**
Illustrator, black and white artist and caricaturist. He was born in 1888 and studied at the Sidney Cooper School of Art, Canterbury and at the St John's Wood Art School. Odle specialised in Black Comedy subjects and in the grotesque, his drawings are often in chalk or black ink and show crowded and tortured scenes of revelry, with a strong sinister element derived from Beardsley. He apparently sold few of his drawings in his lifetime and illustrated few books for an artist with so powerful and individual a vision. Two sales of his work, much of it unused, at Sotheby's in April and November 1976 have helped to put his art into perspective. He was married to the novelist Dorothy Richardson, and died in 1948.
Illus: *Candide [Voltaire, 1925]; The Mimiambs of Herondas [trans. by Jack Lindsay, Fanfrolico Press, 1926].*
Contrib: *The Gypsy [1915]; The Golden Hind.*
Exhib: RSA.
Colls: Author; V & AM.
Bibl: John Rosenberg, *The Genius They Forgot,* 1973; *Drawing and Design,* Vol.5, July 1925, p.40; *The Studio,* Vols. 89, 95.
See illustration (colour).

OFFORD, John James   **fl.1860-1886**
Figure painter and illustrator. He contributed drawings to *The Illustrated London News,* 1860.
Exhib: RA, 1886.

OGDEN, H.A.   **1856-**
American illustrator. He was born at Philadelphia on 17 July 1856 and was a pupil of the Art Students League of New York. He specialised in military and historical subjects and contributed to *The Illustrated London News,* 1885.

O'KELLY, Aloysius   **1853-**
Painter and illustrator. Born in Ireland into a fiercely nationalist family, his brother James J. O'Kelly was MP for Roscommon and imprisoned with Parnell in 1881. He may have trained with his uncle, the sculptor, John Lawlor, going on to study at the École des Beaux Arts, Paris in 1874, where he worked under Gérôme and Bonnat. He travelled in the Middle East. He appears to have been working extensively for the *Illustrated London News* in 1881, contributing many truthful and pro-Irish illustrations of the Land League and

other political events. He was resident in London in 1880 and 1886, lived in Galway in 1881 when his Irish subjects were executed and then at Yalding, Kent, 1885.
Exhib: L; M; RA; RBA; RHA; RI; ROI.

OLIPHANT, Laurence   **1829-1888**
Artist and war correspondent, traveller. He was born at Cape Town in 1829 and travelled with his parents throughout Europe, 1846-48. He practised as a barrister in Ceylon and was secretary to Lord Elgin at Washington and in Canada, 1853-54. He represented *The Times* in Circassia, accompanied Lord Elgin to China, 1857-59 and worked with Garibaldi in Italy, 1860-61. He was *Times* correspondent again in the Franco-Prussian War of 1870 and was MP for Stirling, 1865-67. Oliphant was a contributor to *The Owl* and was associated with the spiritual teachings of T.L. Harris. He died in 1888.
Publ: *Journey to Khatmandhu [1852].*
Illus: *The Russian Shores of The Black Sea [1853, liths., AT 233].*
Contrib: *ILN [1855].*

OLIPHANT, W.M.
Figure artist, contributing to *Pick Me Up,* 1888-89.

OLIVER, Lieutenant Samuel P.
Amateur artist and Royal Artillery officer. He contributed to *The Illustrated London News,* 1867.

O'NEILL, Harry   **fl.1902-1915**
Painter and illustrator. He contributed figure and social subjects to *Punch,* 1902-03.
Exhib: RHA.

O'NEILL, Henry   **1798-1880**
Artist and antiquary. He was born at Clonmel in 1798 and in 1815 entered the RDS Schools and worked for a Dublin printseller. He worked as an illustrator before settling in London for some time, but making little success, he returned to Dublin where he became known for his publications. He was elected ARHA in 1837 but resigned in 1844. He died in Dublin in 1880.
Illus: *Picturesque Sketches of some of the Finest Landscapes and Coast Scenery of Ireland [1835 (with Nicholl and Petrie)]; Fourteen Views in the County of Wicklow [1835 (with Nicholl)]; Ireland its Scenery and Character [Hall, 1841]; Descriptive Catalogue of Illustrations of the Fine Arts of Ancient Ireland [1855]; Illustrations of the most interesting of the Sculptured Crosses of Ancient Ireland [1863]; The Round Towers of Ireland Part 1 [1877].*
Colls: Belfast.

O'NEILL, Hugh   **1784-1824**
Topographer and illustrator. He was born in Lascelles Place, Bloomsbury on 26 April 1784, the son of an architect and was patronised by Dr Thomas Monro. He won a Society of Arts silver palette in 1803 and in 1806 applied for the drawing-mastership at the RMC, Great Marlow. He eventually became a drawing-master in Oxford, Edinburgh, Bath and Bristol and died in the latter city on 7 April 1824.
Publ: *Bristol Antiquities [1826, etched by Skelton].*
Contrib: *Britton's Beauties of England and Wales [1801-13]; Antiquarian and Topographical Cabinet [1807]; The Oxford Almanac [1809, 1810, 1811, 1812, 1814].*
Exhib: RA, 1800-04.
Colls: Ashmolean; BM; Manchester; Reading; V & AM.
Bibl: Martin Hardie, *Watercol. Paint. in Brit.,* Vol.3, 1968, p.219.

ONIONS, G. Oliver   **1873-1961**
Author and illustrator. He was born in Bradford in 1873 and after studying art, worked as a draughtsman for the Harmsworth Press. He married Bertha Ruck, the novelist and artist. Onions devoted himself entirely to novels from about 1910, winning the Tait Black Memorial Prize in 1947. He died on 9 April 1961.
Contrib: *Lady's Pictorial [1895]; The Quartier Latin [1896]; The Quarto [1897].*

ONSLOW, A.G.
Amateur artist contributing illustration to *Punch,* 1903.

ONWHYN, Thomas   **-1886**
Illustrator. He was born in London, the youngest son of Joseph Onwhyn a bookseller and publisher of the magazine *The Owl,* 1864. Young Onwhyn produced 21 illegitimate drawings to an edition of *Pickwick Papers,* published by E. Grattan in 1837 and signed 'Sam

Weller'. Further pirated examples followed, 40 for *Nicholas Nickleby* issued by Grattan in 1838 and another Pickwick set was begun but not published till 1893 by Albert Jackson. Onwhyn carried Dickens imitation to its logical conclusion by drawing in the manner of H.K. Browne and George Cruikshank (qq.v.). He never adapted to wood engraving and his best work is etched, but even that is rather wooden though he has an eye for the comic. He sometimes etched other people's work as in *Oakleigh* by W.H. Holmes, 1843 and drew for guidebooks and letterheads. He did no illustration for the last thirty years of his life and died on 5 January 1886.
Illus: *Memoirs of Davy Dreamy [1839]; Maxims and Specimens of William Muggins [Selby, 1841]; George St George Julian [H. Cockton, 1841]; The Mysteries of Paris [Eugene Sue, 1844]; The Life and Adventures of Valentine Vox [Henry Cockton, 1849]; Etiquette Illustrated by an XMP [1849]; Marriage à la Mode, Mr and Mrs Brown's Visit to the Exhibition [1851]; What I Saw At The World's Fair...by Mr Comic Eye [1851]; Visitor's Souvenir of the Sea Shore [a pull-out book, Rock Bros., Dec. 23 1853]; Peter Palette's Tales and Pictures in Short Words for Young Folks [1856]; Cupid's Crinoline [a pull-out book, Rock Bros., Oct. 20 1858]; Marriage à La Mode [a col. pull-out book, Rock Bros., May 1 1859]; 300L a Year Or Single and Married Life [1859]; Mrs Caudle's Crinoline [a pull-out book, n.d.].*
Contrib: *Punch [1847-48].*

OPPENHEIM, E. Phillips   1866-1946
Illustrator. He began to work in 1887 and supplied ink drawings for *A Monk of Cruta*, c. 1900.

ORCHARDSON, Sir William Quiller   1836-1910
Painter of subject pictures and portraits. He was born in Edinburgh in 1836 and entered the Trustees Academy there in 1850 where he was a fellow student with John Pettie (q.v.). He moved to London in 1863 and exhibited Shakespearean subjects at the RA, but he became increasingly known for his High Life paintings in the 1880s, where great play is made of dramatic figures in a large pictorial space. As a young artist he had undertaken a small amount of illustration for magazines in a competent unremarkable style. He became ARA in 1868, RA in 1877, and was knighted in 1907. He died on 13 April 1910. An exhibition was held at the RA in 1911 and at FAS, 1972.
Contrib: *Good Words [1860-61, 1878]; Touches of Nature [1866].*
Exhib: B; GG; G; L; New Gall; P; RA; RHA; RSA.
Bibl: J. Maas, *Victorian Painters* 1970, p.244, illus.

ORD, G.W.
Illustrator of children's books, illustrated *Tommy Smith's Animals*, Edmund Selous, 1899.

O'REILLY, Rear-Admiral Montague Frederick   1822-1888
Amateur artist and illustrator. He was born in 1822 and as a professional naval officer, he served in North Australia and Hong-Kong and took part in the Chinese war of 1841. From 1845 he served on the West coast of Africa and in the Mediterranean and between 1851 and 1852 was on the South African station. He joined H.M.S. *Retribution* at Sebastopol and during this time made numerous sketches and diagrams of the Fleet in action in the Crimea. In 1856 he was appointed commander and from 1862 was commander of *Lapwing* in the Mediterranean and was promoted rear-admiral in 1878. O'Reilly sent many sketches to *The Illustrated London News*, in the years 1854-56 and in the issue of October 21, 1854 appears a self-portrait of him explaining his sketches.
Illus: *Twelve Views in the Black Sea and Bosphorus [1856 AT 241].*
Contrib: *Cust's Naval Prints [1911]; Moore's Sailing Ships [1926].*
Colls: Greenwich.
Bibl: *ILN,* June 7, 1888.

ORFORD, H.W.
Amateur illustrator contributing to *Fun*, 1900.

ORME, Edward   1774-
Publisher, engraver and architectural draughtsman. He was the brother of Ernest and William Orme (qq.v.) and studied at the RA Schools in 1793. He published numerous books on drawing from his address at 59 Bond Street and was still active in 1820.
Publ: *A Brief History of Ancient and Modern India [1805]; Orme's Graphic History of... Horatio Nelson [1806]; Essay on Transparent Prints [1807]; An Historical Memento [1814]; Bartolozzi Prints [1816 (a re-issue)]; Historic Military and Naval Anecdotes [1819].*
Colls: V & AM.

ORME, Ernest   fl.1801-1808
Architectural draughtsman and illustrator. He was a brother of Edward and William Orme (qq.v) and shared the latter's London address when he exhibited portraits at the RA, 1801-03. He published a drawing-book and illustrated a *Collection of British Field Sports,* 1807-08.
Colls: V & AM (sketchbook); Witt Photo.

ORME, William
Landscape artist and illustrator. He was born in Manchester, the brother of Ernest and Edward Orme (qq.v.) and worked there as a drawing-master from about 1794 to 1797. He had been awarded a silver palette by the Society of Arts in 1791-92. From 1797 when he moved to London he exhibited regularly at the RA and worked closely with his publisher brother.
Illus: *The Old Man, his Son and the Ass [c.1800]; Costume of Hindustan [1800]; Twenty-Four Views of Hindustan [1805].*
Contrib: *The Copperplate Magazine.*
Colls: Greenwich; V & AM.

ORMEROD, George   fl.1801-1827
Amateur artist. Possibly George Ormerod of Charlton Hall, Cheshire, listed in *Patterson's Roads,* 1824.
Contrib: *Britton's Beauties of England and Wales [1801].*

ORPEN, Sir William   RA RI   1878-1931
Landscape painter and occasional caricaturist. He was born at Stillorgan in Ireland on 27 November 1878 and studied at the Dublin Metropolitan School of Art and at the Slade School, 1897-99. Although Orpen established his reputation in portrait painting and is remembered for very competent and slick studies of famous Edwardians in a lavish manner derived from Sargent, he made an impressive contribution as War Artist, 1917-18. These drawings, which were exhibited as War Pictures in 1918, were later published as a book and many of them were presented to Government collections. Orpen was knighted in 1918, elected RA in 1919 and was President of the International Society of Sculptors, Painters and Gravers from 1921. He was elected ARHA in 1904, RHA 1907 and RI in 1919, having been a member of the NEA since 1900. He died on 29 September 1931.
    The Ashmolean collection has two caricatures by this artist, one of which is a self-portrait.
Illus: *An Onlooker in France [1921]; Stories of Old Ireland and Myself [1924].*
Exhib: B; FAS; GG; G; L; M; NEA; P; RA.
Colls: Ashmolean; Imperial War Mus.

ORR, Monro Scott   1874-
Painter, etcher and illustrator. He was born at Irvine on 7 October 1874, the brother of Stewart Orr (q.v.) and studied at the Glasgow School of Art under Newbery. Orr's work is bold and rather posterish and is comparable in style to that of John Hassall (q.v.). He was also much influenced by William Nicholson as is clear from the thick border line to his drawings and his direct imitation of that artist in *Twelve Drawings Of Familar Characters...* 1903. A contemporary criticism was that his drawings seemed to be cramped into a space too small for them.
Illus: *Twelve Drawings of Familar Characters in Fiction and Romance [1903]; Ye Twelve Months; The Old Ayrshire of Robert Burns; Poems of Robert Fergusson; The Arabian Nights; Grimms Fairy Tales; Mother Goose; Jane Eyre;* Book covers for: *The Unchanging East; Our Naval Heroes; Towards Pretoria; The Blessings of Esau; Kidnapped.*
Exhib: G; L; RSA; RSW.
Colls: Witt Photo.
Bibl: *Art Journal, 1900, p.310; The Studio, Vol.29, 1903, p.215-217; Modern Illustrators and Their Work,* Studio, 1914.

ORR, Stewart   RSW   1872-1944
Watercolourist and book illustrator. He was born in Glasgow on 21 January 1872, the brother of Monro S. Orr (q.v.). He studied at the Glasgow School of Art and Glasgow University and after working in Essex in about 1902, lived chiefly in Glasgow or the Isle of Arran. He died in 1944, having been elected RSW in 1925.
Contrib: *Rob Roy Macgregor; The Feuds of the Clans; The Romance of Poaching in the Highlands [W. McCombie Smith]; The Scottish Abbeys and Scottish Martyrs [John Jamieson].*
Exhib: G; L; RA; RI; RSA; RSW.
Bibl: *Modern Book Illustrators and Their Work,* Studio, 1914.

ANDREA DEL SARTO

But do not let us quarrel any more,

HENRY OSPOVAT 1877-1909. 'Andrea del Sarto'. Illustration for Browning's *Men and Women*. Pen, 14in x 10in (35.6cm x 25.4cm)
Victoria and Albert Museum

ORROCK, James   RI   **1829-1913**
Landscape painter, collector and lecturer. He was born in Edinburgh in 1829 and was educated at Irvine, Ayrshire and at Edinburgh University where he read surgery and dentistry. He then studied art with James Fergusson and J. Burgess in Leicester and with Stewart Smith at the Nottingham School of Design until 1866 when he moved to London. He took lessons from W.L. Leitch (q.v.) in London and was elected ANWS in 1871 and NWS in 1875.

   Orrock was however best known for the books that he published on the arts and for his fine collections of Chippendale furniture and Nankin china which he had in his home at Bedford Square, Bloomsbury. He presented watercolours and drawings to both the Victoria and Albert Museum and the Glasgow City Art Gallery, 1899. He died on 10 May 1913, at Shepperton, Middlesex.
Illus: *In the Border Country [W.S.Crockett, 1906]; Mary Queen of Scots [W.S. Sparrow, 1906]; Old England [1908].*
Exhib: B; G; L; M; New Gall; RA; RI; ROI.
Colls: Bradford; Maidstone; Nottingham; V & AM.
Bibl: B. Webber, *JO*, 1903.

OSBORNE, Walter Frederick   RHA   **1859-1903**
Portrait painter. He was born in Dublin in 1859 and studied at the RDS Schools, 1876 and then at Antwerp, 1881 to 1883. He made extensive painting tours in England, France and Spain, was elected ARHA in 1883 and RHA in 1886. Osborne was an accomplished painter of animals and of town and country life; he died in London in 1903.
Contrib: *Black & White [1891].*
Colls: BM; Nat. Gall. Ireland.
Bibl: T. Bodkin, *Four Irish Landscape Painters,* 1920.

OSPOVAT, Henry   **1877-1909**
Painter, draughtsman and illustrator. He was born in Russia in 1877 and migrated with his family to Manchester where they settled. Ospovat was trained at the Manchester School of Art in 1897 and was perhaps encouraged by Walter Crane (q.v.) whose bookplate he designed. He

then attended the South Kensington School and received some important commissions at a very early age and was much influenced by the Pre-Raphaelites and the work of C.S. Ricketts (q.v.). His drawing style might be compared to that of Laurence Housman, another Rossetti devotee, but his line is much broader and his effects altogether more powerful and sensuous. He was also a brilliant caricaturist, particularly of the London music-hall and his death in London on 2 January 1909 removed a significant figure from English illustration. A memorial exhibition was held at the Baillie Gallery in 1909.
Illus: *Shakespeare's Sonnets [1899]; The Poems of Matthew Arnold [1900]; Shakespeare's Songs [1901]; Heroines of Poetry [Maud, 1903]; Men and Women [Browning, 1903]; The Song of Songs [1906]; Browning's Poems [projected but not issued].*
Contrib: *The Idler.*
Exhib: NEA.
Colls: V & AM.
Bibl: *The Studio* Vol.10, 1897, p.111, illus; Vol.43, 1908, p.235; Winter No., 1923-24, pp.37, 133; R.E.D. Sketchley, *Eng Bk. Illus.,* 1903, pp.13-14, 129; Oliver Onions, *The Works of HO With An Appreciation By...,* 1911; Arnold Bennett, *Books and Persons,* 1917. See illustration.

OVEREND, William Heysman   **1851-1898**
Marine painter and illustrator. He was born at Coatham in Yorkshire in 1851 and was educated at Charterhouse. He began principally as a marine artist but increasingly, from about 1872, undertook work for *The Illustrated London News* and for book illustration. During the next three decades his output was extensive and nearly every issue of the magazine has pages of his coastal realism, fishermen and trawlermen fighting the sea and anxious women waiting on shore. He was elected ROI in 1886 and died in the USA 1898.
Illus: *The Fate of the Black Swan [F.F. Moore, 1865]; On board the Esmerelda [J.C. Hutcheson, 1885]; One of the 28th [G.A. Henty, 1889]; Benin the City of Blood [R.H.S. Bacon, 1897]; Devils Ford [Bret Harte, 1897].*
Contrib: *ILN [1872-96]; The English Illustrated Magazine [1891-94]; Good Words [1894]; The Rambler [1897]; The Boys' Own Paper; Chums; The Pall Mall Magazine.*
Exhib: G; L; RA; R0I.
Colls: V & AM.
Bibl: Joseph Pennell, *Modern Illustration,* 1895, p.108.

OVERNELL, T.J.
Illustrator and designer and student of RCA working in an art nouveau style and contributing programme covers and book plates to the National Competition, South Kensington, 1897.
Bibl: *The Studio,* Vol.8, 1896, p.224, illus.

OWEN, Rev. Edward Pryce   **1788-1863**
Amateur artist and topographer. He was born in 1788 and was educated at St John's College, Cambridge before becoming Vicar of Wellington and Rector of Eyton-upon-the-Wildmoors, Shropshire in 1823. He made extensive tours to the Continent, making sketches that he used for watercolours and etchings. He died at Cheltenham in 1863.
Illus: *Etchings of Ancient Buildings in Shrewsbury [1820-21]; Etchings [1826]; The Book of Etchings [1842-55].*
Exhib: RBA, 1837-40.
Colls: Shrewsbury Lib.

OWEN, Samuel   **1768-1857**
Marine painter. He was born in 1768 and is associated with watercolour sketches of the south coast and the Thames estuary. He published with W. Westall (q.v.) *Picturesque Tour of the River Thames,* 1828 and illustrated W.B. Cooke's *The Thames,* 1811.
Exhib: RA, 1794-1807.

OWEN, Will   RCA   **1869-1957**
Artist, caricaturist and lecturer. He was born in Malta in 1869 and educated in Rochester and at the Lambeth School of Art. Owen worked in a humorous poster style and did much commercial work, his chief contribution to books was as illustrator of W W Jacobs' novels.
Publ: *Old London Town [n.d.].*
Contrib: *Pick-Me-Up [1895]; The Windsor Magazine; The Temple Magazine; Punch [1904-07]; Strand Magazine [1901-16 and 1924 and 1939].*

OWL
Unidentified artist. He produced twenty-two cartoons for *Vanity Fair* in 1913 with well handled watercolour.
Bibl: Roy T. Matthews and Peter Mellini, *In Vanity Fair,* 1982.

'PAL' Jean de Paleologu 1855-. 'Sir John Millais PRA'. Ink and watercolour

PADDAY, Charles Murray RI   fl.1889-1937
Marine and landscape painter and illustrator. He was a leading illustrator of shipping for *The Illustrated London News* from 1896 until about 1916. He worked in London from 1889-93 and then at Bosham, 1902, Hayling Island, 1914 and Hythe, 1925. He also travelled on sketching tours to Brittany. He was elected ROI in 1906 and RI in 1929.
Illus: *Gun Boat and Gun Runner [T.T. Jeans, 1915].*
Contrib: *Black & White [1899].*
Exhib: L; RA; RBA; RI; ROI.
Bibl: *A.J.*, 1906, p.168.

PADGETT, William   1851-1904
Landscape painter. He worked in Twickenham, 1881 and Campden Hill, London from 1882. He contributed one illustration to *Punch* in 1882.
Exhib: GG; G; L; M; New Gall; RA; RBA; ROI.

PAGE, P.N.
Architectural draughtsman contributing to *The Illustrated London News*, 1858 (col. block).

PAGE, William   1794-1872
Landscape painter and topographer. He studied at the RA Schools, 1812-13 and travelled in Asia Minor and Greece in the period 1818 to 1824. He was an accurate depictor of buildings and a competent figure artist and contributed drawings to *Finden's Landscape and Portrait Illustrations To The Life and Works of Lord Byron*, 1833-34 and to *Finden's Landscape Illustrations of the Bible*, 1836.
Exhib: RA, 1816-60.
Colls: BM; Coventry; Searight Coll. at V & AM.
Bibl: *Country Life*, September 26, 1968.

PAGET, Henry Marriott   1856-1936
Artist and illustrator. He was born in London on 31 December 1856, brother of Sidney and Walter Stanley Paget (qq.v.). He was educated at Atherstone Grammar School, the City Foundation Schools and entered the RA Schools in 1874. He made a series of foreign tours beginning in 1879 to Italy, Greece and Crete and was in Western Canada, 1909. He was sent as Special Artist by *The Sphere* to Constantinople to cover the Balkan War, 1912-13 and served with the BEF in the First World War, 1916. He was elected RBA, 1889 and died in London, 27 March 1936.
Illus: *The Bravest of the Brave [G.A. Henty, 1887]; The Talisman, Kenilworth [Walter Scott, 1893]; Quentin Durward [Walter Scott, 1894]; Pictures From Dickens [1895]; Annals of Westminster Abbey [Bradley, 1895]; The Vicar of Wakefield [Goldsmith, 1898]; The Black Arrow [R.L. Stevenson, c.1913].*
Contrib: *The Graphic [1877-1906]; The Quiver [1890]; The Illustrated London News [1890]; The Windsor Magazine.*
Exhib: B; FAS; GG; G; L; M; RA; RBA; ROI.
Colls: Bodleian.

PAGET, Sidney E.   1860-1908
Artist and illustrator. He was born in London on 4 October 1860, the brother of Henry Marriott and Walter Stanley Paget (qq.v.). He was educated privately and studied art at the BM and at Heatherley's and

the RA Schools, where he was a bronze and gold medallist, 1884. Paget was a very prolific illustrator and was the first artist to draw Sherlock Holmes for Conan Doyle's short stories in *The Strand Magazine* 1892-94. He was on the staff of *The Illustrated London News* and *The Sphere* and died in London on 28 January 1908.
Illus: *The Adventures of Sherlock Holmes [1892]; The Memoirs of Sherlock Holmes [1892-94]; Rodney Stone [1896]; The Tragedy of Korosko [1898]; Old Mortality [Walter Scott, 1898]; Terence [1898]; The Sanctuary Club [1900].*
Contrib: *ILN [1884]; The Quiver [1890]; The Strand Magazine [1891-1904]; Cassell's Family Magazine; The Graphic.*
Exhib: L; M; New Gall; RA; RBA; RI.
Colls: Bristol.
Bibl: R.E.D. Sketchley, *Eng. Bk. Illus.*, 1903, pp.68,152; *The Times*, 27 November 1976, Correspondence.

PAGET, Walter Stanley 'Wal'   1863-1935
Artist and illustrator. He was born in 1863, the brother of Henry Marriott and Sidney E. Paget (qq.v.).
Illus: *The Black Dwarf, Castle Dangerous, The Talisman, A Legend of Montrose [Walter Scott, 1893-95]; Out of Fashion [Mrs L.T. Meade, 1894]; Robinson Crusoe [1896]; At Agincourt [G.A. Henty, 1897]; Treasure Island [1899]; Lamb's Tales From Shakespeare [1901].*

And let us not remember Italy the less regardfully, because, in every fragment of her fallen Temples, and every stone of her deserted palaces and prisons, she helps to inculcate the lesson that the wheel of Time is rolling for an end, and that the world is, in all great essentials, better, gentler, more forbearing, and more hopeful, as it rolls !

THE END.

London : Bradbury & Evans, Printers, Whitefriars.

SAMUEL PALMER, RWS, 1805-1881. Vignette illustration and ornament for Charles Dickens' *Picture of Italy*, 1846

Contrib: *The English Illustrated Magazine [1891-92]; ILN [1892-98]; The Queen [1894]; The Quiver; Cassell's Family Magazine.*
Exhib: G; L; M; New Gall; RA; RBA; ROI.
Bibl: R.E.D.Sketchley, *Eng. Bk. Illus.*, 1903, pp.92, 152.

PAILLET, Fernand   1850-1918
French portrait, watercolour and enamel painter. He exhibited at the Salon from 1873 and illustrated *Persian Lustre Ware* by Henry Wallis 1899.
Colls: V & AM.

PAILTHORPE, F.W.   fl.c.1880-c.1899
Illustrator. A number of watercolours by this artist for an edition of Dickens are in the Victoria and Albert Museum. They are very Georgian in spirit and reminiscent of the work of H.K. Browne.
Illus: *Posthumous Papers of the Pickwick Club [1882]; Great Expectations [1885]; Oliver Twist [1886 (all issued by Robson & Kerslake)].*

PAINE, Henry A.
Black and white artist of the Birmingham School, contributed to *The Quest*, 1894-96.

PALEOLOGU, Jean de   'PAL'   1855-
Figure artist and caricaturist of Romanian origin. He was a contributor to *Vanity Fair,* 1889-90 and to *The Strand Magazine,* 1892-94. Signs: PAL.

PALMER, John   fl.1856-1887
Genre painter and illustrator. He specialised in industrial and theatrical scenes as well as in domestic subjects and contributed to *The Illustrated Times,* 1856-61 and *The Illustrated London News,* 1864-66.
Exhib: RA; RBA.

PALMER, Samuel   RWS   1805-1881
Visionary landscape painter and watercolourist. He was born at Newington on 27 January 1805, the son of a bookseller and began painting at the age of thirteen. He started exhibiting at the RA in 1819 at the age of fourteen and soon after came under the influences of Varley, Stothard and Linnell, and that of William Blake (q.v), whom he met first in 1824. Fired by Blake and forming one of his mystical circle of 'Ancients' at Shoreham, Palmer produced a series of watercolours of the area, outstanding for their poetic beauty and innocence. He married Linnell's daughter in 1837 and travelled in Italy for two years, returning to live near his father-in-law and to teach drawing. His later work is usually considered to have lost the intensity of his early vision of landscape. He was elected OWS in 1856 and died at Redhill in 1881.

Palmer's work as a book illustrator is very small. It was Blake's small wood engravings that first inspired him, but in his long life, only Charles Dickens' *Pictures from Italy,* 1846, has four tiny vignettes from his hand. Two important posthumous works were Virgil's *Eclogues,* 1883, and Milton's *Minor Poems,* 1888, issued by his son and filled with fine etchings. The Ashmolean has a print for an edition of *The Pilgrim's Progress,* 1848.
Exhib: BI; OWS; RA; RBA.
Colls: Birkenhead; Birmingham; Blackburn; BM; Manchester; V & AM.
Bibl: A.H. Palmer, *SP: A Memoir,* 1882; A.H. Palmer, *Life and Letters of SP,* 1892; R.L. Binyon, *The Followers of W. Blake,* 1926; G. Grigson, *The Visionary Years,* 1947; E. Malins, *SP's Italian Honeymoon,* 1968; David Cecil, *Visionary and Dreamer* 1969; R. Lister, *SP,* 1974; *SP A Vision Recaptured The Complete Etchings for Milton & Virgil,* 1978.
See illustration.

PALMER, Sutton   1854-1933
Landscape painter and illustrator. He was born at Plymouth in 1854 and was educated at Camden Town High School before studying at the South Kensington School. He changed from being primarily a still-life painter to a landscape painter and illustrated a number of colour plate books. He was elected RBA in 1892 and RI in 1920. He died on 8 May 1933.
Illus: *Rivers and Streams of England [A.G. Bradley]; Bonnie Scotland [Hope Moncreiff]; Surrey [Hope Moncreiff]; The Heart of Scotland [Hope Moncreiff, 1905]; The Wye; Berks and Bucks.; California; Devon.*
Exhib: FAS; G; L; M; RA; RBA; RI.
Colls: V & AM.

PANNET, R.   fl. 1895-1925
Figure artist and illustrator working in London.
Contrib: *The Lady's Pictorial [1895]; St. Pauls [1899]; Illustrated Bits [1900]; The Temple Magazine; The Royal Magazine; The Graphic [1908].*

PAPÉ, Frank Cheyne   1878-1972
Black and white artist and illustrator. He was a very prolific illustrator of books although the majority of his work falls outside our period. He was married to the illustrator, Agnes Stringer (q.v). A remarkable series of watercolours mounted together, depicting the Legend of Siegfried, was sold at Christie's on 6 November 1995. They were dated 1904 and demonstrate that Papé was already a mature illustrator at this date, four years before his first illustrated book.
Illus: *Children of the Dawn [E.F. Buckley, 1908]; Pilgrim's Progress [J. Bunyan, 1910]; Hans Andersen's Fairy Tales [1910]; At The*

Back of The North Wind [G. Macdonald, 1911]; The Wings of Courage [G. Sand, 1911]; The Story Without An End [F.W. Carové, 1912]; As It Is In Heaven [A. Clark, 1912]; The Fairy of Old Spain [M.M. Staweil, 1912]; The Gateway to Spenser [1912]; Siegfried & Kriemhild [1912]; Stories from Spenser [1912]; The Book of Psalms [1913]; The Indian Story Book [1914].
See Horne.

PAPWORTH, John Buonarotti　　　　　**1775-1847**
Architect and topographical illustrator. He was born in London on 24 January 1775 and studied architecture on the advice of Sir William Chambers, learning drawing from John Deare and working under the architect John Plaw. He entered the RA Schools in 1798 and by that date had already exhibited drawings there and designed his first house, in Essex, for Sir James Wright, 1793-99. Papworth was well established as an architect by the age of twenty-five and had a large practice in country houses and villas and designed such Regency landmarks as the Cheltenham Pump Room, 1825-26. As a draughtsman, Papworth was much employed by R. Ackermann and on his own books, many of them issued by Ackermann. He had public appointments as Architect to the King of Württemberg, 1820 and was Secretary of the Associated Artists, 1808-10. He died at Little Paxton, Huntingdonshire on June 16 1847.
Illus: *The Social Day [Peter Coxe, 1823]; Select Views in London [1816]; Designs For Rural Residences consisting of a series of Designs for Cottages, small villas, and other Buildings [1818, 2nd Ed. 1832]; Hints on Ornamental Gardening [1823]; Forget-Me-Not Annual [1825-30 (covers)].*
Contrib: *Ackermann's Repository [1809-28].*
Exhib: RA.
Colls: RIBA; V & AM.
Bibl: W.A. Papworth, *JBP 1879; Arch Review,* Vol.79, 1936; H.M. Colvin, *Biog. Dict. of Eng. Arch.,* 1954, pp.436-443.
See illustration (colour).

'PAQUE'　　　　　**see PIKE, W.H.**

PARK, Carton Moore　　　　　**1877-1956**
Portrait, decorative and animal painter and illustrator. He was born in 1877 and studied at the Glasgow School of Art under Francis Newbery and his first efforts at illustration were published in *The Glasgow Weekly Citizen* and *St. Mungo*. Park was a talented book decorator and caricaturist, but concentrated on animal illustration which he was able to treat in a strong and unsentimental way derived from Japanese prints. In 1899 he was elected RBA, resigning in 1905, and he continued to exhibit in the UK before emigrating to America in about 1910. He was editor and illustrator for Messrs. George Allen's *Child's Library*. He died in New York on 23 January 1956.
Illus: *An Alphabet of Animals [1899]; A Book of Buds [1900]; A Book of Elfin Rhymes [1900]; A Book of Dogs; A Child's London [1900]; The Child's Pictorial Natural History [1901]; La Fontaine's Fables for Children; The King of the Beasts;* Mural panels – *The Zoo; The Farmyard;* Lithographs – *Uncle Remus; Tales of the Old Plantation; Breer Rabbit;* For Allen's Child's Library – *A Countryside Chronicle [S.L. Bensusan]; The Bee; Biffel; The Story of a Trek-Ox.*
Contrib: *The Butterfly [1899]; The Idler.*
Exhib: G; L; NEA; RA. RBA.
Bibl: *The Studio,* Winter No. 1900-01, pp.16-17, illus.; R.E.D. Sketchley, *Eng. Bk. Illus,* 1903 pp.118, 168; *Modern Book Illustrators and Their Work,* Studio, 1914.
See illustration.

PARKES, David　　　　　**1763-1833**
Amateur artist and schoolmaster. He was born at Cakemore, Salop in 1763 and ran a school at Shrewsbury. He died there on 8 May 1833.
Contrib: *Britton's Beauties of England & Wales [1813-14]; The Gentleman's Magazine.*

PARKINSON, William　　　　　**fl.1883-1895**
Figure artist and cartoonist of *Judy,* 1890. He worked in London and contributed to various magazines including *Ally Sloper's Half Holiday,* 1890 and *Black and White,* 1891.
Exhib: RA.
Colls: V & AM.

CARTON MOORE PARK 1877-1956. 'Panthers'. Illustration for *The Studio*, 1900

PARNELL, R.
Illustrator of children's books. He was the brother of Mrs. E. Farmiloe (q.v.) and worked for *The New Budget, Lika Joko* and *Little Folks.* He made a speciality of comic animals.
Bibl: *The Studio,* Vol.21, 1900-01, pp.51-54.

PARRIS, Edmund Thomas　　　　　**1793-1873**
Portrait painter. He was born in London on 3 June 1793 and entered the RA Schools in 1816, exhibiting there from that year. He worked at Horner's Colosseum in Regents Park from 1824 to 1829 and became Historical Painter to Queen Adelaide in 1838. His restorations to the Thornhill paintings in the cupola of St. Paul's cathedral, 1853-56 were unsympathetic and his sentimental style and pretty washes were best suited to album illustration. He died in London on 17 November 1873.
Illus: *Flowers of Loveliness [Lady Blessington, 1836]; Confessions of an Elderly Gentleman [Lady Blessington, 1836]; Confessions of an Elderly Lady [Lady Blessington, 1838].*
Contrib: *The Keepsake [1833, 1836-37].*
Exhib: BI; NWS; RA; RBA.
Colls: BM; Doncaster; V & AM.

PARRISH, Maxwell　　　　　**1870-1966**
Painter and illustrator. He was born in Philadelphia on 25 July 1870 and studied at the Boston Academy of Fine Arts under Howard Pyle (q.v.). Although principally an American illustrator, he made the designs for *Dream Days* by Kenneth Grahame, 1906. He died 30 March 1966.
Bibl: *The Studio,* Vol.38, 1906, pp.35-43 (Herkomer on his illus.).

PARRY, James　　　　　**c.1805-1871**
Landscape and figure artist at Manchester. He drew and engraved some illustrations of topography for Corry's *History of Lancashire.*
Exhib: M, 1827-56.

PARRY, John　　　　　**1812-c.1865**
Caricaturist. He was probably an amateur and the Victoria and Albert Museum has two sheets of his work, one inscribed 'Whims' and dated '1850'. He seems to have specialised in silhouette caricatures of men, women and animals, often done on visiting cards.

PARSONS, Alfred　RA PRWS　　　　　**1847-1920**
Landscape painter, watercolourist and illustrator. He was born at Beckingham, Somerset on 2 December 1847 and started his life as a Post Office clerk before studying at South Kensington. Parsons made

ALFRED PARSONS RA PRWS 1847-1920. The Old Mosque at Rustchuk, Bulgaria. Illustration for *Harper's Monthly Magazine*, July 1892. Pencil. Signed with monogram. 7⅞in x 6¼in (20cm x 15.9cm)

Victoria and Albert Museum

a speciality of garden and plant drawings and was a masterly book decorator in designs for initial letters. He did a great deal of magazine work before turning his attention to books and was elected ARA in 1897 and RA in 1911. He became RWS in 1905 and was President in 1913. His meticulous pen landscapes have a slight similarity to Joseph Pennell (q.v.), but his pencil drawing is quite special in its toned softness. He died at Broadway on 16 January 1920. Signs ⒜

Illus: *God's Acre Beautiful [W. Robinson, 1880]; Poetry of Robert Herrick [1887]; Springham [R.D. Blackmore, 1888]; Old Songs [1889]; The Quiet Life [1890 with J.R. Abbey]; Sonnets Of William Wordsworth [1891]; The Warwickshire Avon [Quiller Couch, 1892]; The Danube [F.D. Miller, 1892]; The Wild Garden [Robinson 1895]; The Bamboo Garden [Freeman-Mitford, 1896]; Notes in Japan [1896]; Wordsworth [Andrew Lang, 1897].*
Contrib: *The English Illustrated Magazine [1883-86, 1891-92]; Harper's Monthly Magazine [1891-92]; The Daily Chronicle [1895].*
Exhib: B; FAS, 1885, 1891, 1893, 1894; GG; G; L; M; NEA; New Gall; RA; RHA; RI; ROI; RSW; RWS.
Colls: V & AM.
Bibl: *The Studio,* Winter No., 1900-01, p.73, illus.; R.E.D. Sketchley, *Eng Bk. Illus.,* 1903, pp.31, 35, 137; Martin Hardie, *Watercol. Paint. in Brit.,* Vol.3, 1968, p.96, illus.
See illustration.

PARTRIDGE, Sir J. Bernard   **RI**   **1861-1945**
Black and white artist and principal cartoonist of *Punch*. He was born in London on 11 October 1861, the son of Professor Richard Partridge, Professor of Anatomy to the RA and nephew of John Partridge, Portrait Painter Extraordinary to Queen Victoria. Partridge

was educated at Stonyhurst College and then trained with a firm of stained-glass artists, studying the design of drapery, 1880-84. He was extremely interested in the theatre and acted for some time under the name of 'Bernard Gould', appearing in the first production of Shaw's *Arms and The Man.* Many of his early drawings are of theatrical subjects or personalities and some of his finest caricatures in later life were still drawn from the world of the stage. He was introduced to *Punch* by F. Anstey and G. Du Maurier (q.v.) and joined the staff in 1891, becoming successively second cartoonist, 1901 and principal cartoonist, 1909-45. An artist who was well suited to theatrical sketches and book illustrations, he found himself having to do most of the 'heavy' work of the magazine. Although he was trained with the woodblock, he adapted his pen line to process quite easily, but some of his cartoons are overworked and lack contrast. By the close of his working life, the statuesque figures of symbol looked slightly out of place on the magazine's pages, even when accompanied by excellent portraits of Churchill, Hitler and Mussolini. Partridge also painted in oil, watercolour and pastel, was elected a member of the NEA in 1893 and RI in 1896. He died in 1945.
Illus: *Stageland [Jerome K. Jerome, 1889]; Voces Populi [F. Anstey, 1890]; The Travelling Companions [F. Anstey, 1892]; My Flirtations [Margaret Wynman, 1892]; The Man From Blankley's [F. Anstey, 1893]; Proverbs in Porcelain [Austin Dobson, 1893]; Mr Punch's Pocket Ibsen [F. Anstey, 1893]; Under the Rose [F. Anstey, 1894]; Lyre and Lancet [F. Anstey, 1895]; Barrie's Works [1896]; Puppets at Large [1897]; Baboo Jabberjee B.A. [1897]; Lyceum Souvenirs; The Crusade of the Excelsior [Bret Harte, 1897]; The Tinted Venus [1898]; Wee Folk [1899]; A Bayard From Bengal [F. Anstey, 1902].*
Contrib: *ILN [1885-89 (theat.)]; Judy [1886]; The Quiver [1890]; Punch [1891-1945]; Black & White [1892]; The Idler [1892]; New Budget [1895]; Vanity Fair [1896]; Sporting and Dramatic News [1899]; Lady's Pictorial; The Sketch; Lika Joko; Pick-Me-Up; Illustrated Bits.*
Exhib: FAS, 1902, 1946; G; L; NEA; RA; RI.
Colls: BM (Millar Bequest); V & AM; Mus. of London.
Bibl: Joseph Pennell, *Pen Drawing and Pen Draughtsmen*, 1894, pp.332-333; M.H. Spielmann, *The History of Punch*, 1895, pp.564-565; *The Studio*, Winter No., 1900-01, pp.11-13, illus.; R.E.D. Sketchley, *Eng. Bk. Illus.*, 1903, pp.58, 86, 153; R.G.G. Price, A *History of Punch*, 1957, pp.160-163, illus.; Martin Hardie, *Watercol. Paint. in Brit.*, Vol.3, 1968, p.96.
See illustrations.

PASQUIER, C.A.
Decorative illustrator contributing to *The Graphic*, 1911 (Christmas).

PASQUIER, J. Abbott   **fl.1851-1872**
Genre painter, watercolourist and illustrator. Although very little is known about him, Dalziel credits him with being 'a clever artist in black and white, and a skilful painter in watercolours'. His drawings for illustration have a very soft line with nice washes and slight caricature reminiscent of Leech. His favourite subjects were London ones, crossing sweepers, rainy days etc.
Contrib: *The Home Affections [Charles Mackay, 1858]; ILN [1856, 1866]; The Illustrated Times [1860]; London Society [1865-68]; Foxe's Book of Martyrs [1865]; Aunt Judy's Magazine [1866]; Beeton's Annuals [1866]; The Broadway [1867]; The Sunday Magazine [1868]; The Quiver [1868].*
Bibl: Dalziel, *A Record of Work 1840-1890*, 1901, p.190.

PATERSON, Frank
Illustrated landscape for the magazine *Cycling* c.1910 and ran the Paterson School of Sketching.

PATON, Frank   **1856-1909**
Figure painter and illustrator. He worked in London and Gravesend and contributed one cartoon of an equestrian subject to *Vanity Fair*, 1910.
Colls: BM.

PATON, Sir Joseph Noël   **1821-1901**
Religious and fairy painter and illustrator. He was born at Dunfermline on 13 December 1821 and educated there before entering the RA

SIR BERNARD PARTRIDGE RI 1861-1945. 'The Comic Lovers'.
A design for a music title cover, about 1895. Pen and ink. Signed.
9½in x 7¼in (21.4cm x 18.4cm)   Author's Collection

Schools in 1843. He was awarded a premium in the Westminster Hall
Competition, 1845 and again in 1847, becoming ARSA in 1847 and
RSA in 1850. He was a very versatile man, working as poet and
sculptor as well as painter; he had close connections with the Pre-
Raphaelites in his early days and retained their colouring, he
remained a lifelong friend of J.E. Millais (q.v.). His most famous
illustrated book was Kingsley's *Water Babies,* 1863 and though he
was approached by Dodgson to illustrate the second volume of *Alice,*
he declined. Paton was most at home in the realm of fairyland where
Celtic romance and myth mixed together in his powerful
imagination. Such paintings as the 'Reconciliation of Oberon and
Titania' in the National Gallery of Scotland are among the best works
in this field. Some of this spills over into his books for The Art
Unions. An immensely successful public figure, Paton was made Her
Majesty's Limner for Scotland in 1866 and knighted in 1867. He
died at Edinburgh on 26 December 1901.
Illus: *Compositions from Shakespeare's Tempest [1845];
Compositions from Shelley's Prometheus Unbound [1845]; Silent
Love [James Wilson, 1845]; Coleridge's Life of the Ancient Mariner
[1863]; Lays of the Scottish Cavaliers [W.E. Aytoun, 1863]; The
Water Babies [Charles Kingsley, 1863]; Gems of Literature [1866];
The Story of Wandering Willie [1870]; The Princess of Silverland
and other Tales [E. Strivelyne, 1874]; Rab and his Friends [John
Brown, 1878].*
Contrib: *A Book of British Ballads [1842]; Puck on Pegasus
[Pennell 1861]; The Cornhill Magazine [1864].*
Exhib: GG; G; L; RSA.
Colls: BM; Glasgow; Nat. Gall, Scotland.
Bibl: J.Maas, *Victorian Painters,* 1970, pp.152-153, illus.; M.H.
Noël Paton & J.R. Campbell, *NP,* 1990.

PATON, Walter Hugh   RSA   1828-1895
Landscape painter and illustrator. He was born at Dunfermline on 27

July 1828, the brother of Sir J.N. Paton (q.v.). He began his career as
an industrial designer in the textile industry until 1848 and then
became a pupil of J.A. Houston. He was elected ARSA in 1866 and
RSA in 1868. He died in Edinburgh on 8 March 1895.
Illus: *Lays of the Scottish Cavaliers [W.E. Aytoun, 1863 (with J.N.
Paton)]; Poems and Songs by Robert Burns [1875].*
Exhib: G; L; M; New Gall; RA; RHA; RI; RSA; RSW.
Colls: Dundee; Glasgow.
Bibl: *Art Journal,* 1895.

PATTEN, Leonard   fl.1889-1914
Painter. He contributed one humorous drawing in the style of
Meryon to *Punch,* 1914.
Exhib: RA, 1889.

PATTEN, William
Topographer. He contributed illustrations to *Westminster* by Walter
Besant, 1897.

PATTERSON, J. Malcolm   fl.1898-1925
Black and white artist, etcher and illustrator. He was born at
Twickenham in 1873 and educated at Clifton. He worked at St.
Andrews, Scotland where he was art master at St. Leonard's School,
and specialised in rustic genre subjects with finely detailed cottage
interiors.
Contrib: *Fun [1896]; The Dome [1898]; The Quiver [1900]; Punch
[1900-07]; Illustrated Bits; Sketchy Bits; The Idler; The Windsor
Magazine; The Royal Magazine.*
Exhib: L; RSA.

SIR BERNARD PARTRIDGE RI 1861-1945. 'The Wings of
Victory'. A preliminary sketch for the cartoon that appeared in
Punch on 14 May 1912, marking the inauguration of the Royal
Flying Corps. Pencil, pen and ink. 14⅛in x 11½in (35.9cm x 29.2cm)
Victoria and Albert Museum

PAUL, Evelyn   fl.1906-1911

Illustrator. She studied at South Kensington in about 1906 and exhibited in the National Competition that year.

Illus: *Cranford [Mrs. Gaskell, 1910]; Stories From Dante [Susan Cunnington, 1911]; Claire de Lune [1918].*

Bibl: *The Studio,* Vol.38, 1906, p.316.

See Horne

PAUL, Sir John Dean, Bt.   1802-1868

Amateur illustrator. He was born on 27 October 1802 and was educated at Westminster and Eton before joining the family bank of Snow, Paul and Paul, from 1828. He succeeded his father as second baronet in 1852 and in 1855 the bank stopped payment and its partners were tried for fraud and sentenced to transportation. He died at St. Albans in 1868.

Publ: *A.B.C. of Foxhunting [1871].*

Illus: *The Country Doctor's Horse [Sir J.D. Paul, 1847].*

PAUQUETTE, Hippolyte Louis Emile   1797-

French illustrator. He was the brother-in-law of Gustave Janet (q.v.) and was an occasional contributor to *The Illustrated London News* in about 1869. He exhibited at the Salon, 1821-49.

PAXTON, Robert B.M.   fl.1895-1925

Portrait painter and illustrator. In his early years he shared a studio with A.S. Hartrick (q.v.) and later worked in Fulham and Putney.

Contrib: *The Daily Graphic [1895]; The Windsor Magazine; The Graphic [1902-07]; The Strand Magazine [1906].*

Exhib: G; RA.

PAYNE, C.N.

Contributed motoring sketches to *Punch,* 1906.

PAYNE, Charles Johnson 'SNAFFLES'   1884-1967

Caricaturist. Born at Leamington Spa, the son of a shopkeeper. He served in the Leicestershire Yeomanry in the First World War, becoming a War Artist for the *Sporting and Dramatic News,* then served with the Royal Naval Air Service and Norman Wilkinson's camouflage team.

Bibl: *Snaffles – Charles Johnson Payne,* Court Gallery Limited Edition, 1983; J.N.P. Watson, 'The Right Man on the Right "Oss"', *CL,* 8 Dec. 1983.

See Horne

PAYNE, Dorothy M.   fl.1910-1914

Illustrator. She was a student of the Lambeth School and shows a strong influence of Walter Crane in her work. She exhibited at South Kensington, 1910-11.

Bibl: *The Studio,* Vol.53, 1911, p.299; *Pen, Pencil & Chalk,* Studio, 1911; *Modern Book Illustrators and Their Work,* Studio, 1914.

PAYNE, Henry Albert   **RWS**   1868-1940

Portrait and landscape painter, stained-glass artist and illustrator. He was born at Kings Heath, Birmingham in 1868 and studied art under E.R. Taylor at the Birmingham School and taught at it for eighteen years. He learned the craft of stained glass and made many windows and painted frescoes for the chapel of Lord Beauchamp and for the House of Lords. He married the flower painter Edith Gere in 1903 and was elected ARWS in 1912 and RWS in 1920. He lived at Amberley, Gloucestershire from about 1912 and died on 4 July 1940.

Contrib: *The Strand Magazine [1891]; A Book of Carols [1893]; The Dome [1898].*

Exhib: B; FAS; G; L; M; New Gall; P; RA; RSW; RWS.

Bibl: *The Last Romantics,* Barbican Gallery cat., 1989, pp.107-108.

PEACOCK, Mildred A.

Illustrator working at West Bromwich and possibly a student of the Birmingham School.

Bibl: *The Studio,* 1897, p.273, illus.

PEACOCK, Ralph   1868-1946

Portrait and landscape painter and illustrator. He was born in 1868 and studied at the Lambeth School of Art, 1882, the St. John's Wood School and the RA Schools, 1887, where he won the gold medal and Creswick prize. He was a teacher at the St. John's Wood School for many years and died on 17 January 1946.

Illus: *Wulf The Saxon [G.A. Henty, 1894]; Both Sides The Border [G.A. Henty, 1897].*

Contrib: *The English Illustrated Magazine [1896]; The Graphic [1899].*

Exhib: B; G; GG; L; M; New Gall; P; RA; RBA; RCA; ROI.

Colls: Birmingham; Liverpool; Tate.

Bibl: 'Ralph P and His Work', *The Studio,* Vol. 21, 1900, pp.3-15, illus.

PEAKE, Richard Brinsley   fl.1816-1819

Figure and domestic painter. He illustrated *The Characteristic Costume of France,* 1819, AT 87.

Exhib: RA.

PEARS, Charles   **ROI**   1873-1958

Marine painter, illustrator, lithographer and poster artist. He was born at Pontefract 9 September 1873 and was educated at Hardwick College. He served in the RM in the First World War and was Official War Artist to the Admiralty, 1915-18 and again in 1940. He was a regular magazine illustrator in the 1890s and 1900s and was elected ROI in 1913. He wrote extensively on sailing and yachting and died in 1958.

Illus: *Two Years Before The Mast; Saltwater Ballads [John Masefield]; Dickens Works; The Pedlars Pack [Mrs Alfred Baldwin, 1904-05].*

Contrib: *The Yellow Book [1896-97]; Judy [1896]; The Quartier Latin [1896]; The Dome [1897-99]; Punch [1897-1914]; The Longbow [1898]; The Windsor Magazine; The Ludgate Monthly; The Sketch; Fun [1901]; The Strand Magazine [1905-19 & 1930]; The Graphic [1910].*

Exhib: FAS; L; NEA; RA; RI; ROI; RWA.

Colls: V & AM.

PEARSE, Alfred   1856-1933

Painter, black and white artist and illustrator of boys' books. He worked in London from about 1877 and died in 1933.

Illus: *By England's Aid [G.A. Henty, 1890]; Westward with Columbus [Gordon Stables, 1894].*

Contrib: *ILN [1882]; Boys' Own Paper [1890]; The Girls' Own Paper [1890-1900]; The Strand Magazine [1891-1909]; The Wide World Magazine [1898]; Cassell's Family Magazine [1898]; Punch [1906].*

Exhib: RA; RBA.

PEARSE, Susan B.   1878-1980

Watercolour painter. She studied at the New Cross Art School and exhibited book illustrations at the National Competition, South Kensington in 1898.

Exhib: RA; RI; SWA.

See Horne

PEARSON, Mathew

Black and white artist. He drew 189 drawings for *An Inventory of the Church Plate of Leicestershire,* by the Rev. Andrew Trollope, 1890.

Colls: V & AM.

PEARSON, William   fl.1798-1813

Landscape painter and topographer. He was a friend of the watercolour artist F.L.T. Francia and probably illustrated *Select Views of the Antiquities of Shropshire,* 1807. Contributed to Britton's *Beauties of England and Wales,* 1812-14.

Exhib: RA.

Colls: BM; V & AM (sketchbook); Witt Photo.

PEGRAM, Frederick   **RI**   1870-1937

Black and white artist and illustrator. He was born in London on 19 December 1870 and was first cousin of H., C.E., and R. Brock (qq.v.). He joined the staff of *The Queen* and then *The Pall Mall Gazette* in 1886, having studied under Fred Brown and spent some time in Paris. From then onwards he became one of the most prolific and consistent of magazine illustrators, his pen work is always of a high standard and his own preference was for drawing subjects with a Georgian setting. He was also an etcher and did occasional advertisements for the papers. Elected RI, 1925, he died in London on 23 August 1937.

Illus: *Macmillans Illustrated Standard Novels – Midshipman Easy [1896]; Masterman Ready [1897]; Poor Jack [1897]; The Last of the Barons [Bulwer Lytton, 1897]; The Arabian Nights Entertainments [1898]; The Bride of Lammermoor [1898]; The Orange Girl [Besant, 1899]; Ormond [Maria Edgeworth, 1900]; Concerning Isobel Carnaby [1900].*

Contrib: *Pall Mall Gazette [1886]; Pictorial World [1888]; ILN [1889-1916]; Judy [1889-90]; Lady's Pictorial [1893]; Punch [1894-1917]; The New Budget [1895]; The Quiver [1895]; Daily Chronicle [1895]; The Rambler [1897]; Black & White [1897]; Pall Mall Budget; The Gentlewoman; The Idler; The Pall Mall Magazine; The Minister; Cassell's Family Magazine.*

Exhib: FAS, 1938; G; L; P; RA; RI.

Colls: V & AM.

Bibl: *The Idler* Vol.11, pp. 673-683, illus.; J. Pennell, *Pen Drawing and Pen Draughtsmen*, 1894, p.370, illus.

PELCOQ, Jules   **fl.1866-1877**

French artist and illustrator. He was born in Belgium of an old family and studied art at the Antwerp School and then went to Paris to work as a caricaturist. He worked for *Charivari* and *Journal Amusant* and illustrated some of Dumas' novels and specialised in subjects from Parisian life. He was employed by *The Illustrated London News* in figure drawing and was their chief artist in Paris during the Siege of 1870, his work being despatched by balloon. He visited Vienna for the magazine in 1873 to cover the International Exhibition.

Bibl: H. Vizetelly, *Glances Back Over Seventy Years,* 1893, pp.340-342.

PELLEGRINI, Carlo   'APE'   **1836-1889**

Caricaturist, draughtsman and lithographer. He was born in Capua in 1838, the son of landed aristocrats, and made a considerable name in Neapolitan Society for his caricatures, which were directly inspired by the *portraits chargés* of Baron Melchiorre Delfico. The young Pellegrini was politically minded and before leaving Italy was associated with Garibaldi's liberation struggle to free Italy from foreign oppression. He moved to London in November 1864, where he soon became a central figure in the Prince of Wales' Marlborough House Set. He joined Thomas Gibson Bowles' *Vanity Fair* in 1865 and virtually made its name for the publisher, each issue having caricatures by the artist done in *portraits chargés* manner, quite new to an English public. He was later succeeded to some extent by James Tissot (q.v.) and then by his understudy Sir Leslie Ward (q.v.). Pellegrini had ambitions to be a serious portrait painter but his eccentricity and dilettante lifestyle were against this; he exhibited some portraits at the RA and Grosvenor Gallery. He was very influential on Max Beerbohm (q.v.), who considered him his master and dedicated his first book to him in 1896. Pellegrini died in London on 22 January 1889.

Colls: NPG; Royal Coll., Windsor; V & AM.

Bibl: Eileen Harris, 'Ape or Man', *Apollo,* Jan. 1976, pp.53-57; *Vanity Fair,* NPG Exhibition Cat., July-August, 1976; Roy T. Matthews & Peter Mellini, *In Vanity Fair,* 1982.

See illustration.

PELLEGRINI, Professor Ricardo   **1866-**

Genre painter and illustrator. He was born at Milan in 1866 and illustrated an edition of *Gil Blas.* He acted as Special Artist for *The Graphic,* 1905.

PENGUILLY L'HARIDON, Octave   **1811-1870**

French illustrator, watercolourist and engraver. He was born on 4 April 1811 and after serving as a professional soldier studied under Charlet. He was curator of the Artillery Museum in Paris and exhibited at the Salon, 1835-70.

Illus: *The Works of Scarron.*

Contrib: *ILN [1853].*

PENLEY, Aaron Edwin   **1807-1870**

Miniaturist, landscape watercolouist and teacher. He was working in

CARLO PELLEGRINI 'APE' 1838-1889. Sir Charles John Forbes, Bt., of Newe. Original drawing for the illustration in *Vanity Fair*, 14 August 1880. Watercolour and bodycolour on grey paper. Signed. 12in x 7in (30.4cm x 17.8cm)   Author's Collection

Manchester in 1834 and exhibited regularly at the RA from that year. He was assistant teacher at the Addiscombe Military Academy from 1851 and then Professor of Drawing, moving to Woolwich. He was appointed Watercolour Painter to King William and Queen Adelaide. He resided in London but painted all over the country and in Scotland. He died at Lewisham in 1870.

Publ. and illus: *A System of Watercolour Painting [1850]; Elements of Perspective [1851]; English School of Painting in Watercolours [1861]; Sketching From Nature In Watercolours [1869].*

Contrib: *Nature and Art [1866-67].*

Colls: BM; V & AM; Fitzwilliam; Leeds; Manchester; NG, Scotland.

PENNELL, Joseph   **1860-1926**

Artist, illustrator and author. He was born in Philadelphia in 1860 and educated at the School of Industrial Art there and at the Pennsylvania Academy of Fine Arts. He married Elizabeth Robins Pennell, the authoress, and they settled in England in the 1880s, swiftly becoming members of the circle surrounding James McNeil Whistler (q.v.). Pennell was an extremely competent topographer in black and white and with his wife illustrated numerous travel books which she wrote. He is perhaps most significant, however, as the chronicler of late Victorian illustration in a number of books which

JOSEPH PENNELL 1860-1926. 'Old Shops in Gray'. Original drawing for illustration in *The Saône* by P.G. Hamerton, 1887. Pen. 7⅛in x 7¼in (18.1cm x 18.4cm) Victoria and Albert Museum

not only brought new names to the fore, but were powerful advocates for the new processes of mechanisation. He was Art Editor of *The Daily Chronicle*, 1895, and was elected RE in 1882 and was a member of the American Academy of Arts. He returned to New York about 1914 and died there on 23 April 1926.
Publ: *Pen Drawing and Pen Draughtsmen [1889]; Modern Illustration [1895]; The Illustration of Books [1896]; The Work of Charles Keene [1897]; Lithography and Lithographers [1900]; The Life of James McNeil Whistler [1907]; Etchers and Etching [1919]; The Whistler Journal [1921]; The Graphic Arts [1922]; Adventures of an Illustrator [1925].*
Illus: *A Canterbury Pilgrimage [1885]; An Italian Pilgrimage [1886]; Two Pilgrims Progress [1887]; Our Sentimental Journey Through France and Italy [1888]; Our Journey to The Hebrides [1889]; The Stream of Pleasure [1891]; The Jew At Home [1892]; Play in Provence [1892]; To Gipsyland [1893]; A London Garland [W.E. Henley, 1895]; The Alhambra [1896]; Highways and Byways Series, Devon and Cornwall [1897]; N. Wales [1898]; Yorkshire [1899]; Normandy [1900]; A Little Tour in France [Henry James, 1900]; Gleanings From Venetian History [1908]; Pictures of The Panama Canal, [1912]; Pictures of War Work in England [1917].*
Contrib: *The English Illustrated Magazine [1884]; The Graphic [1888]; ILN [1891]; The Pall Mall Budget [1893]; The Yellow Book; The Savoy [1896]; The Pall Mall Magazine; The Quarto [1896-97]; The Butterfly; The Neolith [1907-08].*
Exhib: FAS, 1896,1912, 1917, 1922; G; GG; L; NEA; RSA.
Colls: V & AM.
Bibl: *Print Collectors' Quarterly*, Vol.14, No.1, 1927, pp.47-68; E.R. Pennell, *Journal of JP*, 1931; Simon Houfe, *Fin de Siècle*, 1992.
See illustration.

PENNINGTON, Harper   1854-
American illustrator. He was born at Newport in 1854 and while in Europe, 1874-86, was a pupil of Gérôme, Carolus Duran and J.M. Whistler (q.v.). He contributed to *Punch* in 1886.

PETERS, C.W.
Contributor of railway sketches to *The English Illustrated Magazine*, 1896.

PETHERICK, Horace William   1839-1919
Painter and illustrator. He was working at Addiscombe in 1891 and at Croydon from 1919 and specialised in children's stories and particularly those with costume subjects. He did some work for the Kronheim 'Toy Book' series.
Illus: *Home For the Holidays [1880]; Among the Woblins [S. Hodges]; Among the Gibjigs [S. Hodges, 1883]; Cornet of Horse [G.A. Henty, 1892].*
Contrib: *ILN [1870-77, 1887, 1890].*
Exhib: L; RA; RBA.
Colls: V & AM.

PETHERICK, Rosa C.   fl.1896-1903
Illustrator. She was probably the daughter of Horace William Petherick (q.v.) and competed in book illustration competitions run by *The Studio*, Vol. 8, 1896, p.!84. She later illustrated *Mother Hubbard's Cupboard of Nursery Rhymes*, 1903.
See Horne

PETHYBRIDGE, J. Ley   fl.1885-1897
Figure and landscape painter and occasional illustrator. He was working at Lyndhurst, 1885 and at Launceston, 1889 and was described by Thorpe as 'a too infrequent contributor to magazines'.
Contrib: *The Ludgate Monthly; The Temple Magazine [1896-97].*
Exhib: L; RA; RBA.

PETIT, The Rev. John Louis   1801-1868
Amateur topographer. He was born at Ashton-under-Lyne in 1801 and educated at Trinity College, Cambridge, and was for many years curate of Bradfield, Essex. He moved to Shropshire in 1846 and died at Lichfield in 1868.
Publ: *Remarks on Church Architecture [1841]; The Abbey Church of Tewkesbury [1848]; Architectural Studies in France [1854].*
Colls: Lichfield; V & AM.

PETO, Gladys Emma   1891-1977
Black and white artist and illustrator. She was born in 1891 at Maidenhead and studied at the Maidenhead School of Art and the London School of Art. Her style was strongly influenced by the work of Aubrey Beardsley, and she worked for *The Sketch* from 1915-26. She married Col. C.L. Emmerson and died in Northern Ireland in 1977.
Illus: *The Works of Louisa M. Alcott [1914]; Malta, Egypt, Cyprus [1928].*
See Horne

PETRIE, George   PRHA   1789-1866
Landscape painter and topographer. He was born in Dublin in 1789 and studied at the RDS Schools and with his father, a miniature painter, before turning wholly to landscape. He made extensive tours in Ireland and Wales with fellow artists such as F. Danby and J.A. O'Connor in the years 1808-19. He was elected ARHA in 1826 and RHA in 1828, becoming Librarian in 1829 and President in 1856-59. He wrote antiquarian articles for the *Dublin Penny Journal*, 1832-33, and was Editor of the *Irish Penny Journal*, 1842. His ink drawings are reckoned to be more attractive than his watercolour drawings, which are rather formal in composition. He died in Dublin on 17 January 1866.
Publ: *Ancient Music of Ireland [1855].*
Illus: *Excursions Through Ireland [Cromwell, 1819]; New Picture of Dublin [J.J. McGregor, 1821]; Historical Guide to Ancient and Modern Dublin [C.N. Wright, 1821]; Beauties of Ireland [Brewer, 1825-26].*
Contrib: *Guide to the County of Wicklow [CN. Wright].*
Exhib: RHA.
Colls: BM; Nat. Gall., Ireland; V & AM.
Bibl: A. Stokes, *Life of G.P.*, 1868.

PETRIE, Henry   FSA   1768-1842
Topographer and antiquary. He was born at Stockwell, Surrey in 1768 and was patronised by Thomas Frognall Dibdin and Earl Spencer. In 1818 Petrie began editing the *Monumenta Historica*

Britannica of which one volume appeared by Sir T.D. Hardy, 1848. He was also involved in making a survey of Southern English Churches from about 1800 which was not completed and not published. His watercolours for this work are clear and accurate, if somewhat dead through lack of figures and anything but architectural interest. He died at Stockwell in 1842, having been Keeper of the Records at The Tower since 1819.

PETT, Norman
Amateur illustrator, contributed one rustic subject to *Punch*, 1914.

PETTIE, John   RA   1839-1893
Painter and illustrator. He was born at East Linton, Scotland, on 17 March 1839 and showed early promise as a figure draughtsman. He studied with his uncle Robert Frier in Edinburgh and then at the Trustees Academy, 1856, under R.S. Lauder, where his fellow students were Orchardson, MacWhirter and McTaggart (qq.v.). In 1862 he moved to London with Orchardson and shared a studio with him, becoming an ARA in 1866 and an RA in 1873. He died at Hastings on 23 February 1893. Although Pettie's output in illustration is small it is among his most charming work; he excelled in costume pieces and produced figures of incomparable strength with subtle grey washes.
Illus: *The Postman's Bag [J. de Liefde, 1865]; The Boys of Axelford [L.G. Seguin, 1869]; Rural England [1881].*
Contrib: *Good Words [1861-63]; Wordsworth's Poetry for the Young [1863]; Pen and Pencil Pictures from the Poets [1866]; Touches of Nature by Eminent Artists [1866]; The Sunday Magazine [1868-69]; Good Words For the Young [1869].*
Exhib: B; G; GG; L; M; P; RA; RHA; ROI; RSA.
Colls: Ashmolean; Glasgow; V & AM.
Bibl: M. Hardie, *JP*, 1908.
See illustration.

PEYTON, A.
Illustrator of comic strips of sporting subjects to *The Graphic*, 1904.

PHILIPS, John   fl.1828-1838
Illustrator. He worked in Soho and was an early contributor to *Punch* and collaborated with Alfred Crowquill (q.v.) in the illustrations of Reynolds' *Pickwick Abroad: or a Tour in France*, 1838. Also illustrated with his own etchings *Much Ado About Nothing Or Illustrations of Old Sayings*, R. Ackermann, May 1828.
Exhib: NWS; RBA.

PHILIPS, Nathaniel George   1795-1831
Landscape painter and topographer. He was born in Manchester in 1795 and was educated at Manchester Grammar School and Edinburgh University. He travelled in Ireland and the Lake District and visited Italy in 1824-25, where he was elected to the Academy of St. Luke in place of Henry Fuseli. He died at Liverpool in 1831, having published etchings in 1822-24.
Illus: *Lancashire and Cheshire [1893].*

PHILLIPS, John   FRS   1800-1874
Lithographer and geologist. He was Keeper of the York Museum, 1825-40 and Professor of Geology at Trinity College, Dublin, 1844-53. He was Keeper of the Ashmolean Museum, Oxford, 1854-70, having been elected FRS in 1834. He published *The Geology of Yorkshire* and illustrated *The Rivers, Mountains and Sea Coast of Yorkshire*, 1853.

PHILLIPS, Paul
Fashion illustrator, contributing to *The Graphic*, 1871.

PHILLIPS, T.W.   fl.1808-1826
Landscape artist and topographer. He contributed drawings to *Britton's Beauties of England and Wales*, 1808.
Exhib: BI; RA; RBA.

PHILLIPS, W. Alison
Illustrator of rustic genre subjects. Contributed to *Punch*, 1896-97.

PHILLIPS, Watts   1825-1874
Artist, illustrator and dramatist. He was born in 1825 and became the

JOHN PETTIE, RA, 1839-1893. 'Macleod of Dare'

only pupil of George Cruikshank (q.v.). He was an early contributor to *Punch*, the founder of a short-lived periodical *Journal for Laughter* and was on the fringe of the arts and the stage in Paris and then in London where he settled in 1853-54. He brought out plays at the Adelphi, 1857-59 and published novels in the *Family Herald*.
Illus: *M.P. Drawn and Etched by Watts Phillips [c.1840, AL 313]; The Model Republic or Cato Pope's Paris by Watts Phillips [1848, Bogue, pull-out book]; Great Exhibition – Wot is to be [G.A. Sala, 1850, pull-out book]; The Young Ladies Oracle A Fireside Amusement [1850]; The Palace of Glass by Watts Phillips and Percy Cruikshank [1851]; Adventures of Five Americans Entirely On Their Own Resources And Without Any Aid From Their Government [Blackwood's list, 1856].*
Contrib: *Punch [1844-46]; Puck; Diogenes; ILN [1852].*
Colls: Witt Photo.
Bibl: E. Watts Phillips, *Watts Phillips Artist & Playwright*, 1891 (illus.); M.H. Spielmann, *The History of Punch*, 1895, pp.458-459.

'PHIZ'   see BROWNE, H. K.

PHOENIX, George   fl.1886-1935
Figure and landscape painter. He worked at Wolverhampton, 1889 to 1925 and contributed spirited black and white drawings of rustic and cockney genre subjects to *Punch*, 1902-03.
Exhib: B; L; New Gall; RA.

FREDERICK RICHARD PICKERSGILL RA 1820-1900. 'Familiar Love'. Illustration for *The Home Affections* by Charles Mackay, 1858

PICKEN, Andrew   **1815-1845**
Lithographer and illustrator. He was born in 1815, the son of the author, Andrew Picken, and studied with Louis Haghe (q.v.). Due to poor health, Picken settled in Madeira in 1837 and lived in London again from 1840 until his death in 1845. He lithographed Dillon's *Sketches in the Island of Madeira*, 1850, AT 193.
Illus: *Madeira Illustrated [1840, AT 191]*.
Exhib: RA.

PICKERING, George   **1794-1857**
Landscape painter and illustrator. He was born in Yorkshire in 1794 and became a pupil and close follower of John Glover. He began as a drawing-master at Chester, taking over the practice of George Cuitt (q.v.) and opening a studio at Liverpool in 1836. He taught drawing at Birkenhead, where he died in 1857, having been for many years a non-resident member of the Liverpool Academy.
Illus: *History of Cheshire [G. Ormerod, 1819]; History of the County Palatine of Lancaster [E. Baines]; Traditions of Lancashire [J. Roby, 1829 and 1831]*.
Contrib: *Fisher's Scrapbook [1834]*.
Exhib: L; OWS; RBA.
Colls: V & AM; Witt Photo.

PICKERSGILL, Frederick Richard   RA   **1820-1900**
Historical painter and illustrator. He was born in London in 1820, nephew of H.W. Pickersgill, RA, and W.F. Witherington, under whom he studied. He entered the RA Schools and exhibited there from 1839, being elected ARA in 1847 and RA in 1857; he was Keeper from 1873-87. Pickersgill was a beautiful colourist and much influenced by William Etty, his illustrative work is full of fine figure drawing even if with a characteristic German hardness in places. The finest collection of his drawings of this sort of work is at the Barber Institute, Birmingham. He died on the Isle of Wight on 20 December 1900.
Illus: *Virgin Martyr [P. Massinger, 1844]; Illustrated Life of Christ*

[1850]; Comus [Milton, 1858]; Poetical Works of E.A. Poe [1858].
Contrib: *Book of British Ballads [1842]; Tupper's Proverbial Philosophy [1854]; Poets of the Nineteenth Century [Willmott, 1857]; The Home Affections [Charles Mackay, 1858]; Lays of the Holy Land [1858]; The Seasons [James Thomson, 1859]; Montgomery's Poems [1860]; Sacred Poetry [1862]; The Lord's Prayer [1870]; Dalziel's Bible Gallery [1880]; Art Pictures From The Old Testament [1897]*.
Exhib: BI; RA.
Colls: Barber; V & AM.
Bibl: Chatto & Jackson, *Treatise on Wood Eng.*, 1861, p.598.
See illustration.

PIDGEON, Henry Clark   **1807-1880**
Landscape watercolourist, etcher and illustrator. He was a teacher of drawing in London until 1847, when he moved to Liverpool to become Professor of Drawing at the Institute and successively a member and Secretary of the Liverpool Academy, 1850. He was a founder of the Historic Society of Lancashire and Cheshire and is notable for the antiquarian details in his drawings and prints. In London, where he taught again from 1851, he was a member of the Clipstone St. Academy. He died there in 1880.
Contrib: *Recollections of the Great Exhibition of 1851; Wyatt's Industrial Arts of the Nineteenth Century*.
Exhib: BI; RA; RBA.

PIFFARD, Harold H.   **fl.1894-1903**
Military painter and illustrator. He worked in Bedford Park, London, and was a prolific illustrator in the style of Caran d'Ache (q.v.).
Contrib: *Strand Magazine [1894-98]; Cassell's Family Magazine [1899]; The Quiver [1900]; The Windsor Magazine; Pearson's Magazine; Illustrated Bits*.
Exhib: B; L; RA.

PIKE, W.H. 'Oliver Paque' RBA   **1846-1908**
Landscape painter and illustrator. He was born at Plymouth in 1846 and painted in Devon and Cornwall until 1881 when he settled in London. He was elected RBA in 1889.
Contrib: *The Daily Graphic [1890]; The Sketch [1894]; The Graphic [1902]*.
Exhib: L; RA; RBA; RHA; RI; ROI.

PILKINGTON, Major-General Robert W.   **1765-1834**
Landscape painter and soldier. He trained at the RMA, Woolwich and saw service in Canada and North America and was appointed Major-General in 1825 and Inspector-General of Fortifications in 1832. He painted in the manner of Richard Wilson and contributed a drawing to Britton's *Beauties of England and Wales*, 1814.
Exhib: RA, 1808-27.

PILOTELLE, Georges
Fashion illustrator to the *Lady's Pictorial*, c.1890.

PIMLOTT, E. Philip   **fl.1893-1940**
Painter and etcher. He worked at Aylesbury and London and was ARE, 1901-11. He supplied an ink drawing for *The Yellow Book*, 1897 and illustrated *The Happy Exile*, H.D. Lowry, 1898.
Exhib: NEA; RA; RE.

PINWELL, George John   **1842-1875**
Painter and illustrator of rural life. He was born at Wycombe on 26 December 1842, the son of a builder and had his first employment as a designer for embroiderers. He entered the St. Martin's Lane Academy and in 1862 studied at Heatherley's, earning money to support himself by supplying drawings to *Fun* and designs to Elkingtons, silversmiths. He began to work for the Dalziel Brothers in 1864 and there met J.W. North and Fred Walker (qq.v.), the three of them becoming the outstanding rustic and landscape illustrators of the 1860s. He was elected AOWS in 1869 and OWS in 1870 and received important commissions such as the *Illustrated Goldsmith*, 1864, for which he made one hundred drawings, completed in six months. Pinwell's health began to fail in 1873 and he went to Tangiers in 1875 to recover but died in London on his return, 8 September 1875.
Pinwell was closely allied in style to Fred Walker but he was more of

GEORGE JOHN PINWELL 1842-1875. 'The Dovecote'. 1865

a figure artist and less of a landscape artist than the other. He was a brilliant colourist and Reid considered him to have greater decorative sense than Walker and to be at his best in contemporary subjects.

Illus: *Dalziel's Illustrated Goldsmith [1864]; The Happy Home [H. Lushington, 1864]; Hacco the Dwarf [H. Lushington, 1864]; The Adventures of Gil Blas [1866]; Jean Ingelow's Poems [1867]; The Uncommercial Traveller [C. Dickens, 1868]; It Is Never Too Late To Mend [Reade, 1868].*

Contrib: *Punch [1863]; Once a Week [1863-69]; Good Words [1863-75]; The Churchman's Family Magazine [1863-64]; The Sunday at Home [1863-64]; London Society [1863-67]; Lilliput Levee [1864]; The Cornhill Magazine [1864, 1870]; The Sunday Magazine [1865-77]; The Leisure Hour [1865]; Our Life Illustrated*

by Pen and Pencil [1865]; Dalziel's Arabian Nights [1865]; The Quiver [1866-68]; The Argosy [1866]; The Spirit of Praise [1866]; Ballad Stories of the Affections [1866]; A Round of Days [1866]; Wayside Poesies [R.W. Buchanan, 1867]; Golden Thoughts From Golden Fountains [1867]; Cassells Magazine [1868]; Good Words For the Young [1869]; Leslie's Musical Annual [1870]; Novellos National Nursery Rhymes [1870]; The Graphic [1870-73]; Fun [1871]; Judy [1872]; Sunlight of Song [1875]; Dalziel's Bible Gallery [1894].

Exhib: Deschamps Gall., Bond St., Feb. 1876; FAS, 1895.

Colls: Aberdeen; Bedford; BM; Nottingham; V & AM; Witt Photo.

Bibl: Harry Quilter, *A Catalogue of Pictures and Sketches...*Royal Society of Arts, Birmingham, 1895; G.C. Williamson, *G.P and His*

GEORGE JOHN PINWELL 1842-1875. 'Stray Thoughts and Parables For the Winter'. Illustration to *Good Words*, January 1868

Work, 1900; *Print Collectors' Quarterly*, Vol.11, No.2, 1924, pp.163-189; F. Reid, *Illustrators of the Sixties*, 1928, pp.152-163; 'English Influences on Vincent Van Gogh', Arts Council, 1974; Paul Goldman, *Victorian Illustrated Books, The Heyday of Wood-Engraving*, 1994. See illustrations.

PIOTROWSKI, Antoine   **1853-1924**
Painter and illustrator. He was born at Kunow on 7 September 1853 and studied at Warsaw and Munich. In 1877 he became a pupil at the Mateiko School in Krakow and worked there until his death in Warsaw on 12 September 1924. He was *The Graphic* Special Artist in the Servo-Bulgarian War of 1885-86.

PIRKIS
Figure artist contributing drawings in the manner of John Hassall to *Punch*, 1905.

PISSARRO, Lucien   **1863-1944**
Artist, landscape painter, wood engraver, designer and printer of books. He was born in Paris on 20 February 1863, the eldest son of the French painter Camille Pissarro. He was educated in France and studied with his father and the wood engraver Lepere, before coming to England to work in 1883. Here he met Charles Ricketts and C.H. Shannon (qq.v.) and came into contact with the revived interest in wood engravings and the new ideas in book design formulated by Kelmscott and other private presses. He contributed designs to *The Dial* and started the Eragny Press in 1894, producing a whole series of French classics in the next twenty years, most of them slightly illustrated but beautifully ornamented and designed. Pissarro stayed close to the Morris tradition in books, but his wood engravings do

have a naturalism and flow that is not always present in Morris. Pissarro broke most new ground in his use of colour woodcuts and brought them to new heights in his *Livre de Jade,* 1911 and *La Charrue d'Erable,* 1912. Both his wife and Sturge Moore (q.v.) collaborated on these books. He designed the Brook typeface for use in his books after 1902. As a landscape painter he provided an important bridge between English art and impressionism; he was also a talented caricaturist. He was a member of the NEA from 1906.
Illus: *The Queen of the Fishes [1896]; Moralités légendaires [Laforgue, 1897]; Choix de sonnets [Ronsard, 1902]; Peau d'Ane [Perrault, 1902]; Areopagitica [1904]; Livre de Jade [Gautier, 1911]; La Charrue d'Erable [1912].*
Contrib: *The Venture [1903]; Série Londinienne [1895-95]; The Torch [1895-96].*
Exhib: G; L; NEA; RA; RHA; RSA.
Colls: Ashmolean; Birmingham; Manchester.
Bibl: Colin Franklin, *The Private Presses,* 1969 (full bibliog.); *LP His Influence on English Art,* Canterbury Museum, 1986; Anne Thorold, *Letters of LP,* 1993.

PITCHFORD, D.W.
Illustrator c.1910 specialising in medieval subjects.

PITMAN, Rosie M.M.   **fl.1883-1907**
Illustrator of children's books. She worked in Manchester, 1883, London, 1894-1902 and at Ledbury, 1907.
Illus: *Maurice or The Red Jar [Lady Jersey, 1894]; Undine [Fouqué, 1897]; The Magic Nuts [Mrs. Molesworth, 1898].*
Contrib: *The Quarto [1896].*
Exhib: G; L; M; RA; RSA.
Bibl: R.E.D. Sketchley, *Eng. Bk. Illus.,* 1903, pp.117, 168.

PITTMAN, Oswald ROI   **1874-1958**
Landscape painter. He was born in London on 14 December 1874, the son of Robert Pittman, ACA, and was educated at Palace School, Enfield and at the RA Schools. He took part in a number of *The Studio* book illustration competitions. He was elected ROI, 1916, and died on 25 October 1958.
Exhib: G; L; RA; RI; ROI.
Bibl: *The Studio,* Vol.13, 1897, p.64 illus.; Vol.14, 1898, p.71 illus.

PIXELL, Maria   **fl.1793-1811**
Landscape painter. She may have been a pupil of S. Gilpin and she exhibited at the RA and BI, 1793-1811. She contributed a drawing to Britton's *Beauties of England and Wales,* 1813.

PLANK, George
Black and white artist who illustrated *The Freaks of Mayfair* by E.F. Benson, 1916, in the style of Aubrey Beardsley.

POCOCK, E.
Architectural illustrator, contributing to *The Illustrated London News,* 1875.

POGANY, William Andrew   'Willy'   **1882-1955**
Painter, etcher and illustrator. He was born at Szeged in Hungary on 24 August 1882 and educated at the Budapest Technical University and at the Art Schools of Budapest, Munich and Paris. Pogany settled in the United States where he designed many stage-sets and illustrated more than one hundred books. His art was very strongly decorative in character and has begun to return to favour with the advent of the cult of Art Deco. He is included here for the many books that he illustrated for the English market during the Edwardian years.
Illus: *The Adventures of a Dodo [G.E. Farrow, 1907]; The Welsh Fairy Book [W. Jenkyn Thomas, 1907]; Milly & Olly [Mary Augusta Ward [1907]; Faust [Goethe, 1908]; The Rubaiyat of Omar Khayyam [E. Fitzgerald, 1909]; Tanglewood Tales [Nathaniel Hawthorne, 1909]; Norse Wonder Tales [G.W. Darent, 1910]; The Witch's Kitchen [Gerald Young, 1910]; The Rime of the Ancient Mariner [S.T. Coleridge, 1910]; Tannhauser [1911]; Parsifal [1912]; The Hungarian Fairy Book [Nandor Pogany, 1913]; The Tale of Lohengrin [1913]; Forty-Four Turkish Fairy Tales [Egnacz Kunow, 1913]; Atta Troll [Heinrich Heine, 1913].*
Contrib: *ILN [1913].*

POIRSON, V.A.
French artist and illustrator of comic genre subjects. He contributed to *The Graphic*, 1888-89.

PONSONBY, Sir Frederick Edward Grey, 1st Baron Sysonby
1867-1935
Amateur caricaturist. He was the son of Sir Frederick Ponsonby, PC and was assistant private secretary and equerry to Queen Victoria, 1895-1901 and to King Edward VII, 1901-10, Keeper of the Privy Purse. His drawings from 1898-1913 appear in the Household Scrapbook in the Royal Library, Windsor.

PONT, J.
Topographer. He contributed drawings to Britton's *Beauties of England and Wales*, 1813.

POOLE, G.T.
Amateur artist. He acted as Special Artist for *The Graphic* in Russia in 1904.

POOLE, William   **fl.1826-1840**
Portrait painter. He worked in London, 1826 to 1838, and contributed to *The Chaplet*, c.1840.
Exhib: RBA.

'POPINI'
Name or pseudonym of artist contributing to *Illustrated Bits*, c.1890.

PORTCH, Julian   **-1865**
Illustrator and Special Artist. He came from a very poor background and was self-taught as an artist. He was a pupil of Henry Vizetelly (q.v.) who gave him a lot of work and sent him as Special Artist for *The Illustrated Times* to the Crimea in 1855. Portch caught rheumatic fever in the camps of the Crimea and was afterwards paralysed, although he continued to do theatrical illustrations, comic animals and decoration for the *Punch Pocket Books*. He died in September 1865.
Illus: *The Illustrated Book of French Songs [John Oxenford, 1855].*
Contrib: *The Illustrated Times [1855-61]; Punch [1858-61, 1870]; The Welcome Guest [1860]; Puck on Pegasus [C. Pennell, 1861]; London Society [1862]; Poetry of the Elizabethan Age [1862]; Uncle Tom's Cabin; Boswell's Life of Johnson.*

PORTER, J.L.
This is likely to be John Porter, the historical and landscape painter who worked in London and Folkestone and exhibited at the BI, RA and RBA, 1826-70.
Contrib: *Good Words [1861].*

PORTER, Sir Robert Ker   **1777-1842**
Historical painter and illustrator. He was born at Durham in 1777, the son of an army officer and spent his boyhood at Edinburgh, becoming a student in the RA Schools in 1790 through the influence of Benjamin West. He won a Society of Arts silver palette in 1792 and joined the Sketching Club in 1799. In 1800, Porter was engaged in scene painting at the Lyceum Theatre and in producing panoramas and battle subjects. In 1804 he went to Russia and was appointed Historical Painter to the Czar and married the Princess Marie Schertakoff. He was knighted in 1813 and then went on extensive tours that took him to Sweden, Spain and Persia and he acted as British Consul in Venezuela from 1826 to 1841 before returning to St. Petersburgh where he died in 1842. His important collections were sold at Christie's on 30 March 1843.
Publ: *Narrative of the Campaign in Russia [1812, 1813]; Travels in Georgia, Persia, Armenia and Ancient Babylonia [1821-22, AT 359].*
Illus: *Travelling Sketches in Russia and Sweden, 1805-1808 [1809, AT 13]; Letters From Portugal and Spain [1809, AT 130].*
Exhib: RA; RBA.
Colls: BM; V & AM.

POTT, Charles L.   **fl.1886-1907**
Landscape painter and illustrator. He specialised in military and sporting subjects and worked at St. John's Wood, London. He was a regular contributor to many magazines but particularly to the pages of *Punch*, 1900-07.

Contrib: *Cassell's Saturday Journal [1890]; The Sporting and Dramatic News [1891]; Chums [1892]; Illustrated Bits [1900]; The Graphic [1902-03].*
Exhib: RBA; ROI.

POTTER, Helen Beatrix (Mrs. Heelis)   **1866-1943**
Illustrator of children's books. She was born in London in 1866, the daughter of a wealthy family who had connections in the arts and knew contemporary artists, among them J.E. Millais (q.v.). Beatrix Potter had a repressed girlhood, however, and found her chief solace in sketching fungi, fossils and animals on her Scottish holidays and in keeping a secret journal. She wrote illustrated letters to children and it was this that led to the creation of *Peter Rabbit,* a masterpiece that was quietly and privately printed in 1900. It was accepted by Warne & Co. and published in 1902, gaining instant success for its brilliant watercolours and interplay of text and pictures. Many books followed, which gave her independence from her family and eventually the opportunity to buy her own farm in the Lake District and marry William Heelis, a solicitor. She claimed to have been influenced by the Pre-Raphaelites and by Randolph Caldecott (q.v.) and is known to have admired the drawings of Mrs. Blackburn (q.v.) and the woodcuts of Thomas Bewick (q.v.). But she was essentially an amateur artist who loved children and wished to enliven their books with animals that were still recognisably animalish. She died at Sawrey in 1943 and left her home and farm to the National Trust. An exhibition was held at the V & A Museum in December 1972.
Illus: *Peter Rabbit [1902]; Squirrel Nutkin [1903]; The Tailor of Gloucester [1903]; Benjamin Bunny [1904]; Two Bad Mice [1904]; Mrs. Tiggy-Winkle [1905]; The Pie and the Patty Pan [1905]; Mr. Jeremy Fisher [1906]; A Fierce Bad Rabbit [1906]; Miss Moppet [1906]; Tom Kitten [1907]; Jemima Puddleduck [1908]; The Roly-Poly Pudding [1908]; The Flopsy Bunnies [1909]; Ginger and Pickles [1909]; Mrs. Tittlemouse [1910]; Timmy Tiptoes Rhymes [1922]; Little Pig Robinson [1930]; A Happy Pair [F.E. Weatherly, n.d.];* and posthumously *The Fairy Caravan [1952]; The Sly Old Cat [1971].*
Colls: BM; Nat. Bk. League; Tate.
Bibl: M. Lane, *The Tale of BP*, 1947; Anne Carroll Moore, *The Art of Beatrix Potter With An Appreciation*, 1955; *The Journal of BP*, 1966.

POTTER, Raymond   **fl.1893-1898**
Illustrator. He specialised in theatrical subjects, current events and may have visited India in 1898.
Contrib: *The Ludgate Monthly [1892]; The English Illustrated Magazine [1893-97]; ILN [1897]; The Sketch; The Penny Illustrated Paper; The Windsor Magazine; Pearson's Magazine; The Royal Magazine.*
Colls: V & AM.

POWELL, Sir Francis   PRSW   **1833-1914**
Marine and landscape artist. He was born at Pendleton, Manchester, in 1833 and studied at the Manchester School of Art, becoming OWS in 1876. He was first President of the RSW in 1878 and was knighted in 1893. He died at Dunoon on 27 October 1914.
Contrib: *Passages from Modern English Poets [1862].*
Colls: Dundee; Glasgow; V & AM.

POWELL, Joseph PNWS   **1780-1834**
Landscape painter and topographer. He was a drawing-master and specialised in views of the South Coast, Wales and the Lakes. He was first President of the NWS in 1832 and made etchings and lithographs as well as drawings.
Contrib: *The Antiquarian and Topographical Cabinet [1809].*
Colls: BM; V & AM.

POYNTER, Ambrose   **1796-1886**
Architect, still-life and landscape painter and illustrator. He was born in London in 1796 and became a pupil of T.S. Boys (q.v.), and of John Nash. He travelled in Italy during the years 1819-21 and on his return set up as an architect designing government schools and London churches and becoming a founder member of the RIBA in 1834. He retired from practice in 1858 due to failing eyesight and died at Dover on 20 November 1886; he was the father of Sir E.J.

Poynter (q.v.). Poynter did a considerable amount of illustrative work for Charles Knight who referred to 'the most beautiful architectural drawings, which imparted a character of truthfulness to many scenes' in his *Pictorial Shakespeare.*
Publ: *An Essay on the History and Antiquities of Windsor Castle [1841].*
Illus: *Genealogical History of England [Sandford].*
Contrib: *Knight's London [1841-42].*
Exhib: RA.
Colls: BM; Fitzwilliam; V & AM.
Bibl: H.M. Poynter, *The Drawings of AP*, 1931.

POYNTER, Sir Edward John, Bt. PRA   **1836-1919**
Painter and illustrator. He was born in Paris on 20 March 1836, the son of Ambrose Poynter (q.v.). He studied art in Paris under Gleyre, 1856-59, at the same time as Alma Tadema, Du Maurier and Whistler (qq.v.), having previously attended the RA Schools. He was elected ARA in 1868 and RA in 1877, having become the first Slade Professor of University College, 1871-75, and Principal of the South Kensington School, 1875-81. He was Director of the National Gallery, 1894-1904, and President of the Royal Academy from 1896 to 1918. He was knighted in 1896 and created a baronet in 1902. He died in London on 26 July 1919.

Poynter was very influential as a teacher in late Victorian Britain and especially through holding so many public appointments. His illustrations were all confined to the early part of his career but show a great aptitude for figure work and even a flare for handling modern subjects.
Contrib: *Once a Week [1862-67]; London Society [1862, 1864]; The Churchman's Family Magazine [1863]; Poems by Jean Ingelow [1867]; The Nobility of Life [1869]; ILN [1870]; Dalziel's Bible Gallery [1880].*
Exhib: B; FAS, 1903; G; GG; L; M; New Gall; RA; RE; RHA; RSA; RWS.
Colls: BM; Bradford; Manchester; V & AM.
Bibl: A. Margaux, *The Art of EJP*, 1905; M Bell, *Drawings of EJP*, 1906; J. Maas, *Victorian Painters,* 1969, pp.183-184.
See illustrations.

PRATER, Ernest   **fl.1897-1914**
Black and white artist and illustrator. He worked at London and Westcliffe-on-Sea and was on the staff of *Black & White, The Sphere* and *The Graphic,* acting as Special Artist for the first in the Sino-Japanese War of 1894.
Illus: *The Castle of the White Flag [E.E. Green, 1904].*
Contrib: *The St. James's Budget; The Boys' Own Paper; The Ludgate Monthly; The Idler; Chums; Pearson's Magazine; The Graphic [1905-10].*
Exhib: RA.
Bibl: A.C.R. Carter, *The Work of War Artists in South Africa,* Art Journal, 1900.

PRATER, S.W.
Illustrator of industrial and Cornish subjects for the *Illustrated London News,* 1880-84 and 1893.

PRATT, Edward   **fl.1810-1812**
Topographer. He contributed to Britton's *Beauties of England and Wales,* 1812.

PREHN, William   **fl.1862-1890**
Sculptor. He was working in London in the last quarter of the nineteenth century and contributed to *Punch* in 1865.
Exhib: G; GG; L; RA.

PRENTIS, Edward   **1797-1854**
Genre painter and illustrator. He was born at Monmouth in 1797 and was an early member of the Society of British Artists. He specialised in domestic scenes of a humorous nature, many of which were engraved and he died in London in December 1854.
Contrib: *Layard's Monuments of Nineveh [1849, AL 29].*
Exhib: BI, RA; RBA.
Colls: Glasgow.

PRESCOTT-DAVIES, Norman RBA   **1862-1915**
Portrait, flower and miniature painter and illustrator. He was born at Isleworth in 1862 and educated at the London International College

SIR EDWARD JOHN POYNTER Bt. PRA 1836-1919. 'The Painter's Glory'. Illustration to a story in *The Churchman's Family Magazine,* 1862. Wood engraving

SIR EDWARD JOHN POYNTER Bt. PRA 1836-1919. 'Joseph distributing corn'. Original drawing for illustration to *Dalziel's Bible Gallery*, 1881. Pen and ink. Signed with initials and dated 1864. 8¾in x 10¼in (22.2cm x 26cm)　　Victoria and Albert Museum

and at South Kensington, City Guilds and Heatherley's Art Schools. He worked in London and at Radway, Warwickshire, and was elected RBA in 1893 and ARCA in 1891. He died on 15 June 1915.
Illus: *Gray's Elegy [De Luxe Edition].*
Contrib: *The Strand Magazine [1891].*
Exhib: B; G; L; M; New Gall; RA; RBA; RCA; RHA; RI; ROI.

PRICE, Edward
Topographer. The son of the Vicar of Needwood, he was a pupil of John Glover and accompanied him on tours of North Wales and Dovedale. He corresponded with John Constable, RA, and was patronised by the Duke of Sutherland. He helped organise some exhibitions of Glover's work in London, 1820-24, and was living in Nottinghamshire in 1856.
Illus: *Norway Views of Wild Scenery [1834]; Dovedale, 12 Views in Dovedale and Ilam [1845]; Views in Dovedale [1868].*
Exhib: BI; RA; RBA.
Bibl: *John Constable's Correspondence,* Vol.4, 1966, pp.312-313.

PRICE, Julius Mendes　　　　　　　　　　　　　　**-1924**
Illustrator and Special Artist. He was born in London, the son of a merchant and was educated at University College School and in Brussels, before studying at the École des Beaux-Arts in Paris. He joined the staff of *The Illustrated London News* in about 1884, and was

described as 'Travelling Special Artist' although his chief function was as war correspondent. He took part in the Bechuanaland Campaign of 1884-85, enlisting as a trooper in Methuen's Horse, visited Siberia, Mongolia and the Gobi Desert, 1890-91, and the Western Australian Goldfields in 1895. He represented the magazine at the Graeco-Turkish War, 1897, Klondike, 1898, at the Russo-Japanese War, 1904-05, and on the French front throughout the First World War. He was appointed a lecturer in the British Army of Occupation in Germany in 1919. He died on 29 September 1924.
Publ: *From the Arctic Ocean to the Yellow Sea [1892]; The Land of Gold [1896]; From Euston to Klondike [1898]; Dame Fashion [1913]; My Bohemian Days in Paris [1913]; My Bohemian Days in London [1914]; Six Months on the Italian Front [1917]; On the Path of Adventure [1919].*
Contrib: *ILN [1884-1919]; The Sporting and Dramatic News [1890]; The English Illustrated Magazine [1893-94].*
Exhib: Paris; RA; RBA; RHA; ROI.

PRICE, Norman M.
Figure artist, possibly working for the press with an address in Fleet Street. His published work is in the style of Eleanor Fortescue Brickdale (q.v.).
Illus: *Tales From Shakespeare [Charles and Mary Lamb, 1905].*
Exhib: RA, 1905.

PRIMROSE, Priscilla
Amateur artist. She contributed drawings of Rome to *The Illustrated Times*, 1859.

PRINCE, Val R.   fl.1890-1893
Painter and illustrator. He was working in Kensington in 1890 and contributed to *The Pall Mall Budget* in 1893.

PRINSEP, James   1799-1840
Architect, orientalist and draughtsman. He was born in 1799, the brother of Charles Robert Prinsep, the economist. He acted as Assistant Assay Master at the Calcutta Mint, 1819, was appointed Assay-Master in 1832 and carried out some architectural works there including the completion of the Hooghly Canal.
Illus: *Benares Illustrated in a Series of Drawings [1831].*
Colls: Witt Photo.

PRINSEP, Val C.   RA   1838-1904
Printer and author. He was born at Calcutta on 14 February 1838 and educated at home. He studied art at the RA Schools and with Gleyre in Paris before spending some time in Rome. He was elected ARA in 1879 and RA in 1894, and was Professor of Painting from 1900 to 1903. He died on 11 November 1904.
Publ: *Imperial India, An Artist's Journal [1879].*
Contrib: *Once A Week [1869].*
Exhib: B; G; GG; L; M; New Gall; RA; RHA.
Colls: Hamburg; Sheffield, Tate.

PRIOLO, Paolo
Historical and biblical painter and illustrator. He worked in Stockwell, London, 1857-90 and contributed an illustration to *The Churchman's Family Magazine*, 1863.

PRIOR, Melton   1845-1910
Special Artist and illustrator. He was born in London in 1845, the son of W.H. Prior (q.v.) and studied under his father in Camden Town. From about 1873 he was war correspondent of *The Illustrated London News* and served in numerous campaigns. He followed the Ashanti War in 1873, the Carlist Rising, 1874, the Servian, Turkish, Kaffir, Zulu and first Boer Wars, the Egyptian Campaign, 1882, the Cretan Insurrection, the Siege of Ladysmith, 1900. He also went on a number of Royal Tours including the Prince of Wales' visit to Athens, 1875, the King of Denmark's visit to Iceland and the Marquess and Marchioness of Lorne's (qq.v.) visit to Canada. He was present at the Berlin Conference and drew for the magazine at the marriage of Tsar Nicholas II and later travelled with Prince George of Wales through Canada, 1901. He attended the Delhi Durbar of 1902, was on the Somaliland Expedition of 1903 and reported on the Russo-Japanese War of 1904. He died in London on 2 November 1910.
Contrib: *The Sketch; The English Illustrated Magazine [1893-94].*
Colls: V & AM.
Bibl: *The Idler,* Vol. 8, pp.337-346; A.C.R. Carter, *The Work of War Artists in South Africa*, Art Journal, 1900; S.L. Bensusan (Editor), *Campaigns of a War Correspondent*, 1912.

PRIOR, William Henry   1812-1882
Landscape paintre and illustrator. He was born in 1812 and worked in London and painted views in the South of England and on the Rhine. He was the father of Melton Prior (q.v.).
Illus: *Lyrics of a Life-Time [S. Smith, 1873].*
Contrib: *Knight's London [1841]; The Illuminated Magazine [1845]; ILN [1850]; Cassell's Illustrated Family Paper [1853]; The Illustrated London Magazine [1854]; The Illustrated Times [1866].*
Exhib: BI; RA; RBA.

PRITCHETT, Robert Taylor   **FSA**   1828-1907
Illustrator and gunsmith. He was born at Enfield in 1828, the son of a gun manufacturer, and was educated at King's College School. He became a partner in the family business and was the originator of the Enfield rifle and invented with W.E. Metford the 'Pritchett bullet' in 1853, and the three grooved rifle in 1854. As an artist he specialised in black and white work and watercolours of the sea and ships, accompanying Lord and Lady Brassey on their tours of 1883 and 1885 on the *Sunbeam*. He was an intimate friend of John Leech, Charles Keene and Birket Foster (qq.v.). He died on 16 June 1907.
Illus: *Belgravia [1868]; Brush Notes in Holland [1871]; Gamle Norge [1878]; Smokiana [1890]; Pen and Pencil Sketches of Shipping [1899].*
Contrib: *Punch [1863-69]; Once a Week; Good Words [1864-80]; The Sunday Magazine [1865]; Cassell's Magazine [1867]; The Leisure Hour [1867]; The Graphic [1887].*
Exhib: RA; RBA.
Colls: Glasgow; V & AM.
Bibl: M.H. Spielmann, *The History of Punch*, 1894, pp.520-521.

PROCTOR, J. James
Black and white artist and illustrator. He illustrated *Yarns On The Beach,* by G.A. Henty, 1885, and contributed to *Illustrated Bits.*

PROCTOR, John   fl.1866-1898
Cartoonist. Although little is known about his background or training, Proctor developed as one of the best political cartoonists of the end of the Victorian period, characterised by invention and strong drawing of animals. He was chief cartoonist for *Judy* 1867-68, following this with a period on *Will o' The Wisp* and *Moonshine*, 1868-85 and as chief cartoonist on *The Sketch*, 1893 and *Fun*, 1894-98. He was apparently employed by *The Illustrated London News* to act as Special Artist in St. Petersburg in 1874 and he also worked for *Cassell's Saturday Journal.*
Illus: *Dame Dingle's Fairy Tales [1866-67].*
Exhib: RBA.
Colls: Witt Photo.
See illustration.

PROSSER, George Frederick   fl.1828-1868
Artist and topographical illustrator. He worked at Winchester and Eton and published a number of books.
Illus: *Select Illustrations of the County of Surrey [1828]; Select Illustrations of Hampshire [1833]; Scenic and Antiquarian Features...of Guildford [1840]; The Antiquities of Hampshire [1842].*

PROUT, John Skinner   NWS   1806-1876
Architectural painter and illustrator. He was born at Plymouth in 1806, the nephew of Samuel Prout (q.v.) and was virtually self-taught but specialised in subjects similar to his uncle. As a young man he made a lengthy visit to Australia and lived in both Sydney and Hobart, forfeiting by his absence the membership of the NWS, which he had gained in 1838. He was re-elected on his return in 1849 and settled at Bristol where he became a close friend of the artist W.J. Muller. He died at Camden Town 29 August 1876.
Illus: *Sydney Illustrated [1842-44, AT 576]; Antiquities of Bristol [n.d.].*
Exhib: NWS; RI.
Bibl: M. Hardie, *Watercol. Paint. in Brit.* Vol.3, 1968, pp.11-12.
Colls: BM; Fitzwilliam; V & AM.

PROUT, Samuel   1783-1852
Watercolourist, topographical illustrator and drawing-master. He was born at Diss, Norfolk on 17 September 1783 and was taught by J. Bidlake, master of the Plymouth Grammar School. He was friendly with B.R. Haydon, the historical painter, and with him made sketching tours in Devonshire. In 1796, John Britton (q.v.) employed him to tour Cornwall for his *Beauties of England and Wales,* but his work proved unsatisfactory. By 1802 his work had improved and on sending fresh drawings to Britton, he was re-employed by him and lived with him at Clerkenwell for two years. Prout was continually dogged by ill health, but managed to finish work for Britton in Cambridgeshire, Essex and Wiltshire, 1804, and in Devon and Cornwall, 1805. From 1819 onwards, when he made his first visit to France, Prout became a frequent traveller on the Continent, visiting Belgium, the Rhine and Bavaria and Italy in 1824. He made his last tour to Normandy in 1846 by which time he was a sick man and unable to do much work between then and his death.

Prout's sympathy in rendering Gothic architecture with great accuracy and yet giving it mood and atmosphere was exactly suited to the romanticism of the 1820s and 1830s. His effects of light on crumbling masonry and flecks of colour on figures contrasting with

WHERE IS JOHN BRIGHT NOW?

WELL, PEACE PROFESSIONS HAVING PLUNGED US INTO ALMOST UNIVERSAL WAR, JOHN BRIGHT IS—HIDING.

JOHN PROCTER fl.1866-1898. 'Where is John Bright Now?' A cartoon for *Moonshine*, 25 August 1885

the whites and greys of the buildings was widely copied for a generation. Perhaps this was partly due to the championship of John Ruskin who calls him in *Modern Painters* 'among our most sunny and substantial colourists'. He became a member of the OWS in 1819 and was Painter in Watercolours to George IV and Queen Victoria. He died at Denmark Hill on 10 February 1852.

Illus: *Rudiments of Landscape in Progressive Studies [1813, AL 170]; Rudiments [1814, AL 171]; New Drawing Book [1819, AL 172]; Series of Easy Lessons in Landscape Drawing [1819, AL 173]; Views of Cottages [1819, AL 174]; Illustrations of the Rhine [1824]; Facsimiles of Sketches made in Flanders and Germany [1833]; Hints [1834, AL 176]; Sketches in France, Switzerland and Italy [1839, AL 34].*

Contrib: *Beauties of England and Wales [1803-14]; Antiquarian and Topographical Cabinet [1809]; Jennings Landscape Annual [1831]; The Continental Annual [1832]; Microcosm [1841]; Sketches At Home and Abroad [1844]; Rhymes and Roundelayes; ILN [1850].*

Exhib: BI, OWS, RA.

Colls: Aberdeen; Ashmolean; BM; Birkenhead; Blackburn; Derby; Exeter; Fitzwilliam; Leeds; Manchester; V & AM.

Bibl: J. Ruskin, *Notes on SP and Hunt*, 1879; *The Studio*, Special No., 1914; J. Quigley, *Prout and Roberts*, 1926; A. Neumeyer, *Collection of Eng. Watercols. at Mills Coll.*, 1941; C.E. Hughes, *O.W.S.* Vol.6; M. Hardie, *Watercol. Paint. in Brit.*, Vol.3, 1968, pp.4-11; Peter Bicknell, *Gilpin to Ruskin, Drawing Masters and Their Manuals 1800-1860*, Fitzwilliam Museum 1987-88, pp.41-46.

PROUT, Victor   **fl. 1888-1903**

Watercolour painter. He contributed an angling subject to *The Graphic*, 1903.

Exhib: Goupil Gall., 1888.

PROVOST, W.

French illustrator. He contributed views of Paris to *Cassells Illustrated Family Paper*, 1857.

PRY, Paul   see HEATH, William

PRYDE, James Ferrier   **1866-1941**

Painter and illustrator. He was born at St. Andrews on 30 March 1866 and was educated at George Watson's College, the RSA Schools and in Paris at Julians under Bouguereau. He married Mabel Nicholson, sister of William Nicholson (q.v.) and with his brother-in-law began to design and produce posters and illustrations as the Beggarstaff Brothers. Pryde claimed to be part of the Glasgow School but his work is closer to the French poster art of Toulouse Lautrec and of Phil May. Both artists experimented with woodcuts and produced a periodical, *The Page*, 1898, based on archaic chapbook printing. Pryde was less of a book illustrator than a designer and his later career was devoted to stage design and dramatic paintings of shadowy interiors. Pryde was elected HROI, 1934 and died in London, 24 February 1941.

Illus: *The Little Glass Man [Wilhelm Hauff, 1893].*

Contrib: *Tony Drum [1898]; The Page [1898-99].*

Exhib: G; GG; L; NEA; RHA; RSA.

Colls: V & AM; Witt Photo.

Bibl: Derek Hudson, *JP, 1866-1941*, catalogue, 1949; Colin Campbell, *The Beggarstaff Posters, The Work of JP and William Nicholson*, 1990.

PRYSE, Gerald Spencer   **1882-1956**

Painter and illustrator. He was born in 1882 at Ashton and was educated privately, studying art in London and Paris. He served in the First World War and won both the MC and the Croix de Guerre. Pryse was a member of the International Society and exhibited at Venice from 1907. He was working at Hammersmith from 1914 to 1925 but lived in Morocco after 1950. He died in 1956.

Publ: *Through the Lines to Abd el Karim's Stronghold in the Riffs; Four Days.*

Illus: *Salome and the Head, a Modern Melodrama [E. Nesbitt, 1909]; The Book of the Pageant [Wembley Exhibition, 1924].*

AUGUSTUS NORTHMORE WELBY PUGIN 1812-1852. Title page to *Designs for Gold & Silversmiths*, 1836. Etching

Contrib: *Punch [1903-04 (children) 1905]; The Neolith [1907-08]; The Strand Magazine [1910]; The Graphic [1910].*
Colls: V & AM.

PUGIN, Augustus Charles   **1762-1832**
Architect, antiquary and architectural illustrator. He was born in France in 1762 into an old family, and fled to England in about 1798 where he was befriended by John Nash, the architect. Pugin was extensively employed by Nash as a Gothic draughtsman and his accuracy and knowledge of it was influential in establishing a purer appreciation of the style. He had lessons in aquatinting from Merigot in London and attended the RA Schools, at the same time carrying out a great deal of work for Ackermann, the publisher. At about the same time he set up a school of architectural drawing and published his own works, visiting Normandy in 1825 and Paris in 1830. His drawings reflect the current fashion in architectural work, meticulous tinted penwork, the figures frequently added by other artists such as Rowlandson and Stephanoff (qq.v.). His son was A.W.N. Pugin (q.v.). He died in Bloomsbury on 19 December 1832.
Illus: *Ackermann's Microcosm of London [1808]; Specimens of Gothic Architecture From Oxford; Specimens of Gothic Architecture [1821-22]; Views of Islington and Pentonville [1823]; Illustrations of Public Buildings in London [1825-28]; Specimens of Architectural Antiquities of Normandy [1826]; Examples of Gothic*

Architecture [1828-31]; Views of Paris and Environs [1828-31]; Gothic Ornaments from Ancient Buildings in England and France [1831]; Ornamental Gables [1831]; Cassiobury Park [Britton, 1838].

Contrib: *Ackermann's Repository of the Arts [1810-27].*
Exhib: BI; OWS; RA.
Colls: BM; Lincoln; Nat. Gall. of Scotland; RIBA: V & AM; Witt Photo.
Bibl: B. Ferrey, *Recollections of Welby and his Father ACP,* 1861.

PUGIN, Augustus Northmore Welby   **1812-1852**
Architect, designer, draughtsman and polemicist. He was born in London in 1812, the son of A.C. Pugin (q.v.). He was educated at Christ's Hospital and studied architecture with his father, before being discovered by Rundell's the silversmiths and being employed by them and Jeffery Wyattville as a designer. He was received into the Roman Catholic church in 1835 and from then onwards had an extensive practice among wealthy co-religionists, notably the Earl of Shrewsbury and Ambrose March Phillips. He continued to design ecclesiastical buildings and ornaments until his death, his best work in illustration being the etchings for Ackermann which express in their fine lines an almost medieval mysticism. Pugin's large practice and obsessive pamphleteering caused him to lose his reason in 1851 and he died at Ramsgate in 1852.
Illus: *Gothic Furniture consisting of twenty-seven coloured engravings...[1828]; Gothic Furniture in the style of the 15th century [1835]; Ornaments of the 15th and 16th centuries [1835-37]; Contrasts [1836]; Details of ancient timber houses of the 16th and 17th cent....[1836]; Designs for Gold and Silversmiths [1836]; Designs for Iron and Brass work in the style of the XV and XVI centuries [1836]; The True Principles of Pointed or Christian Architecture [1841], An Apology For the Revival of Christian Architecture in England [1843]; Glossary of Ecclesiastical Ornament and Costume [1844]; Floriated Ornament, a series of thirty-one designs [1849]; Modèles d'orfèvrerie, argenterie, etc....[1850]; A Treatise on Chancel Screens and Fonts [1851]; A series of Ornamental Timber Gables, from existing examples in England and France [1854].*
Exhib: RA.
Colls: BM; Maidstone; RIBA; V & AM.
Bibl: B. Ferrey, *Recollections of Welby and his Father A.C.P,* 1861; *Victorian Church Art,* V & A Museum Cat., 1971-72; *AP,* V & AM cat., 1994.
See illustration.

PURSER, William   **c.1790-1852**
Architect and topographical draughtsman. He was born about 1790, the son of an architect at Christ Church, Surrey. He entered the RA Schools in 1807 and travelled in Italy and Greece in 1817-20 with John Sanders, undertaking major archaeological work. He may have visited India.
Illus: *Syria [J. Carne, 1836].*
Contrib: *Finden's Landscape and Portrait Illustrations To The Life And Works of Lord Byron [1833-34]; Fisher's Scrapbook [1834].*
Exhib: RA; RBA.
Colls: BM; V & AM; Witt Photo.
Bibl: H.M. Colvin, *Biog. Dict. of Eng. Architects, 1660-1840,* 1954, p.481.

PYLE, Howard   **1853-1911**
Author and illustrator. He was born at Wilmington, Delaware, USA in 1853 and after being privately educated, studied at the Art Students League, New York. Pyle was among the most assured black and white draughtsmen of the American School, excelling in 18th century subjects and in drawings in the manner of Dürer whom he studied closely. Pennell considered that his early works suffer from having no direct contact with Europe, which he did not visit until his early middle age. He was a prolific illustrator of books for English as well as American publishers and died in Florence on 9 November 1911.
Illus: *The Merry Adventures of Robin Hood [1883]; Pepper and Salt [1885]; Rose of Paradise [1887]; The Wonder Clock [1887]; A Modern Aladdin [1891]; Poems [O.W. Holmes, 1892]; Twilight Land [1895]; The Garden Behind the Moon [1895]; Rejected of Men*

[1903]; The Story of King Arthur and His Knights [1902]; The Story of the Champions of the Round Table; The Story of Sir Lancelot and His Companions; The Ruby of Kishmoor [1908]; The Story of the Grail [1910].
Contrib: *ILN [1880]; The Graphic [1883].*
Colls: V & AM.
Bibl: J. Pennell, *Pen Drawing and Pen Draughtsmen*, 1894, pp.232-234; J. Pennell, *Modern Illustration*, 1895, pp.124-125 .

PYM, T.
Illustrator of children's books. Contributed illustrations to *Victoria Bess; The Ups and Downs of a Doll's Life*, c.1880.
Illus: *The Angel of Love [L.T. Meade, 1885].*

PYNE, Charles Claude   **1802-1878**
Landscape and genre painter. He was the second son of W.H. Pyne, (q.v.) and brother of G. Pyne (q.v.). He travelled on the Continent and practised as a drawing master at Guildford, where he died in 1878.
Contrib: *Lancashire Illustrated [W.H. Pyne, 1829].*
Exhib: BI; NWS; RA.
Colls: Nottingham; V & AM.

PYNE, George   **1800-1884**
Topographical watercolourist. He was born in 1800, the elder son of W.H. Pyne (q.v.) and brother of C.C. Pyne (q.v.). He was an excellent architectural artist and specialised in views of the Oxford and Cambridge Colleges and Eton, but was a less competent hand than his father. He was elected AOWS in 1827 and married the daughter of John Varley but later separated from her.
Publ: *A Rudimentary and Practical Treatise on Perspective for Beginners [1848]; Practical Rules on Drawing for the Operative Builder and Young Student in Architecture [1854].*
Contrib: *Lancashire Illustrated [W.H. Pyne, 1829].*
Colls: BM; Coventry; V & AM; York.

PYNE, William Henry   **1769-1843**
Landscape and genre painter in watercolours, illustrator, etcher, caricaturist and author. He was born in London in 1769 and studied with H. Pars, before beginning a career in book illustration. He was a founder member of the OWS in 1804 and remained a member until 1809 when he resigned. His greatest successes were in his collaborations with the publisher Rudolph Ackermann, when they were jointly engaged in issuing colour plate books from about 1803 to 1819. Pyne produced several drawing books for amateurs which are notable for their fine groups of figures and it is probably this aspect of his contribution to the romantic school that is most significant. He was an assiduous art critic, catalogued Benjamin West's collection in 1829 and Watson Taylor's in 1832 and was editor *of The Somerset House Gazette* under the pseudonym of Ephraim Hardcastle and author of *Wine and Walnuts,* an anthology of the former, in 1823. *The Microcosm*, 1803-05 is his largest undertaking and many of the original drawings for the illustrations are in the Leeds City Art Gallery. He was a poor businessman and spent the last years of his life in the King's Bench Debtors' Prison, before dying at Pickering Place, Paddington on 29 May 1843.
Illus: *Microcosm or a Picturesque Delineation of the Arts, Agriculture and Manufactures of Gt. Britain [1803-08, AT 177]; Nattes Practical Geometry [1805 (title and vignettes)]; The Costume of Great Britain [1808]; Rudiments of Landscape Drawing [1812, AT 178]; Rustic Figures [1815, AT 179]; The History of the Royal Residences [1819]; Microcosm [1822-24, AT 80]; Lancashire Illustrated [1831].*
Contrib: *Knight's London [1841].*
Exhib: OWS; RA; Witt Photo.
Colls: BM; Leeds.
Bibl: M. Hardie, *Watercol. Paint. in Brit.,* 1968, Vol.3, pp.280-281; A Bury, *O.W.S.,* Vol.XXVIII, 1950; G. Jackson-Stops, 'A Noble Simplicity', Pyne's Views of Buckingham House, *Apollo,* August 1993.

QUENNELL, Charles Henry Bourne   **1872-1935**
Architect, author and illustrator. He was born on 5 June 1872 and was educated at South Kensington, beginning practice in Westminster in 1896. Quennell worked as a church architect as well as carrying out numerous houses in the arts and crafts style before 1914. In later life he devoted himself principally to books on social history, most of them illustrated by himself and his wife Marjorie Courtney whom he married in 1904. He held many posts at the RIBA and died on 5 December 1935.
Publ: *Norwich Cathedral [1900]; Modern Suburban Houses [1906]; A History of Everyday Things in England [1918-34]; Everyday Life in the Old Stone Age [1921]; New Stone, Bronze and Early Iron Age [1922]; Roman Britain [1924]; Anglo-Saxon, Viking and Norman Times [1926]; Everyday Things in Homeric Greece [1929]; Everyday Things in Archaic Greece [1931]; Everyday Things in Classical Greece [1932]; The Good New Days [1935].*
Bibl: Peter Quennell, *The Marble Foot*, 1976.

QUESTED, George R.   **fl.1895-1901**
Illustrator and book plate designer. He was working at St. John's Wood, 1895 and Edgbaston, 1897. He won prizes in *The Studio* book illustration competition, 1895.
Exhib: RA.
Bibl: *The Studio,* Winter No., 1900-01, p.59, illus.

QUINTON, Alfred Robert   **1853-**
Landscape and watercolour painter. He was born in 1853 and studied at Heatherley's and contributed to *The Illustrated London News,* 1884-86, 1894 and to *The Sporting & Dramatic News* 1890.
Illus: *Cycling in the Alps [C.L. Freeston, 1900]; The Historic Thames [J.H.P. Belloc, 1907]; The Avon and Shakespeare's Country [A.G. Bradley, 1910]; A Book of the Wye [L: Hutton, 1911]; The Cottages of Rural England [P.H. Ditchfield, 1912].*
Exhib: B; GG; G; L; M; RA; RBA; RHA; ROI.
Contrib: *ILN [1884-1919]; The Sporting and Dramatic News [1890]; The English Illustrated Magazine [1893-94].*
Exhib: Paris; RA; RBA; RHA; ROI.

'QUIZ'   **see MELLOR**

R, N.
Unidentified illustrator of landscape subjects, dating from about 1900.
Colls: V & AM.

RACKHAM, Arthur   **RWS**   **1867-1939**
Illustrator and watercolourist. He was born at Lewisham on 19 September 1867 and after being educated at the City of London School, studied art at Lambeth School where he was influenced by his fellow student Charles Ricketts (q.v.). Rackham joined the staff of *The Westminster Budget* in 1892 and from that time forward concentrated on the illustration of books and particularly those of a mystical, magic or legendary background. He very soon established himself as one of the foremost Edwardian illustrators and was triumphant in the early 1900s when colour printing first enabled him to use subtle tints and muted tones to represent age and timelessness. Rackham's imaginative eye saw all forms with the eyes of childhood and created a world that was half reassuring and half frightening. His sources were primarily Victorian and among them are evidently the works of Cruikshank, Doyle, Houghton and Beardsley (qq.v.) but also the prints of Dürer and Altdorfer. He was elected RWS in 1902 and after 1922 he undertook oil painting and some stage designing. He was a member of the Langham Sketch Club, exhibited widely at home and abroad and died on 6 September 1939.
Illus: *The Dolly Dialogues [1894]; Sketchbook, Tales of a Traveller [Washington Irving, 1895]; Bracebridge Hall [1896]; The Money Spinner [1896]; The Grey Lady [Seton Merriman, 1897]; Two Old Ladies etc. [M. Browne, 1897]; Evelina [Fanny Burney, 1898]; The Ingoldsby Legends [1898]; Gulliver's Travels [1899]; Tales from Shakespeare [Lamb, 1899]; Grimm's Fairy Tales [1900]; The Argonauts of the Amazon [C.R. Kenyon, 1901]; Rip Van Winkle [1905]; Peter Pan in Kensington Gardens [J.M. Barrie, 1906]; Alice's Adventures in Wonderland [Lewis Carroll, 1907]; A Midsummer Night's Dream [Shakespeare, 1908]; Undine [Fouqué, 1909]; The Book of Betty Barber [M. Browne, 1910]; The Rhinegold and The Valkyrie [Wagner, 1910]; Siegfried and the Twilight of the Gods [Wagner, 1911]; Aesop's Fables [1912]; The Old Nursery Rhymes [1913]; Arthur Rackham's Book of Pictures [1913]; A Christmas Carol [Charles Dickens, 1915]; The Allies Fairy Book [1916]; Little Brother and Little Sister [1917]; The Romance of King Arthur and his Knights of the Round Table [1917]; English Fairy Tales Retold [Flora Annie Steel, 1918]; The Springtide of Life [A.C. Swinburne, 1918]; Cinderella [1919]; Snickerty Nick, Rhymes by Whitter Bynner [J.E. Ford, 1919]; Some British Ballads [1919]; The Sleeping Beauty [1920]; Irish Fairy Tales [James Stephens, 1920]; A Dish of Apples [Eden Philpotts, 1921]; Comus [Milton, 1921]; A Wonder Book [Nathaniel Hawthorne, 1922]; Where the Blue Begins [Christopher Morley, 1925]; Poor Cecco [M.W. Bianco, 1925]; The Tempest [Shakespeare, 1926]; The Legend of Sleepy Hollow [Washington Irving, 1928]; The Vicar of Wakefield [Goldsmith, 1929]; The Compleat Angler [Izaak Walton, 1931]; The Night Before Christmas [C.C. Moore, 1931]; The King of the Golden River [J. Ruskin, 1932]; Fairy Tales [Andersen, 1932]; Goblin Market [Christina Rossetti, 1933]; The Pied Piper of Hamelin [Robert Browning, 1934]; Tales of Mystery and Imagination [E.A. Poe, 1935]; Peer Gynt [H. Ibsen, 1936]; A Midsummer Night's*

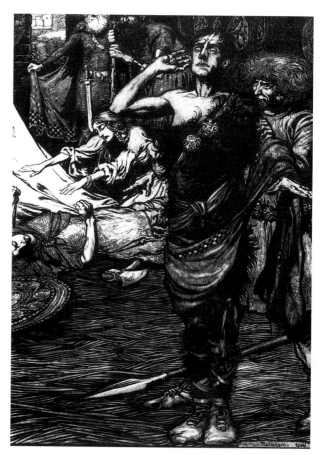

ARTHUR RACKHAM 1867-1939. 'The Death of Balder'. Original illustration in pen and ink. Signed and dated 1904. 15in x 11⅛in (38.1cm x 28.2 cm)

Dream [Shakespeare, 1939]; The Wind in the Willows [K. Grahame, 1940].
Contrib: *Pall Mall Budget [1891-92]; Westminster Budget, The Graphic [1901]; Punch [1905-06]; The Sketch; Black & White; The Gentlewoman; Cassell's Magazine; Cassell's Family Magazine; Chums.*
Exhib: B; FAS, 1917; G; L; RA; RBA; RI; ROI; RSA; RSW; RWS.
Colls: Bradford; Fitzwilliam; Tate; V & AM.
Bibl: *The Studio*, Vol.34, 1906 pp.189-201, illus.; F. Coykendall, *A Bibliography*, 1922; *O.W.S. Club*, XVIII, 1940; D. Hudson, *AR, Life and Work*, 1960; F. Gettings, *AR*, 1975; B. Peppin, *Fantasy Book Illustration*, 1975; Gordon N. Ray, *The Illustrator and the Book in England*, 1976, pp. 203-206.
See illustrations.

RADCLIFFE, Revd. C. Delmé   **1806-1865**
He illustrated *The Noble Science of Fox Hunting* by F.P. Delmé Radcliffe, 1839.

RADCLYFFE, Charles Walter   **1817-1903**
Landscape painter, watercolourist, lithographer. He was born at Birmingham in 1817 and worked there throughout his life, specialising in views of old buildings in tinted lithographs and especially illustrations of the public schools. He came from a distinguished family of engravers and died at Birmingham in 1903.
Illus: *The Palace of Blenheim [1842]; Memorials of Shrewsbury School [1843]; Memorials of Charterhouse [1844]; Memorials of Eton College [1844]; Memorials of Westminster School [1845]; Memorials of Winchester College [1847].*
Exhib: B; RA; RI; ROI.
Colls: B; V & AM.

ARTHUR RACKHAM 1867-1939. 'A Girl By A Pool'. Pen and ink. Signed and dated 1909. 3½in x 5⅜in (8.8cm x 13.6cm)

RAEMAKERS, Louis   1869-1956

Cartoonist. He was born at Roermond, Holland on 6 April 1869 and educated there and in Amsterdam and Brussels and received many diplomas for drawing. He was Director of a drawing school at Wageningen in Gelderland and about 1908 began to produce political cartoons and posters. Raemakers first attracted the attention of the British public during the First World War with his powerful chalk cartoons of the European situation, 1914-18. His bold and unsparing criticism of German atrocities was something new and his style has been compared to that of Steinlen. He later worked for French newspapers and died in 1956. Elected HRMS, 1916.

Illus: *The Great War in 1916; The Great War in 1917; Devant L'Histoire [1918]; Cartoon History of the War [1919].*
Exhib: FAS, 1915, 1916, 1917, 1918,1920.
Colls: V & AM.

RAFFET, Denis Auguste Marie   1804-1860

Battle painter, illustrator, engraver and lithographer. He was born in Paris on 2 March 1804 and after being apprenticed to a wood turner he went to Cabanel as a decorator of porcelain. In 1824 he worked for Charlet who taught him lithography and on leaving in 1829 he became a pupil of Gros. He failed to win the Prix de Rome in 1831 and from then concentrated entirely on lithography and illustration, publishing a number of albums. Raffet followed the French army to Italy in 1849 and attended the siege of Rome. He was patronised by Prince Demidoff and visited England and Scotland with him during his later years. He died at Gênes on 11 February 1860.

Illus: *Musée de la Revolution; Histoire de France; La Revolution; Le Consulat et L'Empire; History of Napoleon; Voyage en Crimée.*
Contrib: *The Illustrated Times [1855].*

RAFTER, H.

Illustrator and sporting artist. He was working in Coventry in 1856 and contributed to *Wyatt's Industrial Arts of the 19th Century.*
Colls: V & AM.

RAILTON, Fanny (Mrs. Herbert Railton)   fl.1894-1902

Illustrator of children's books. Wife of the black and white artist Herbert Railton (q.v.).
Illus: *Lily and Lift [Seeley, 1894]; A Midsummer Night's Dream [1902].*

RAILTON, Herbert   1857-1911

Black and white artist and illustrator. He was born at Pleasington, Lancashire on 21 November 1857 and educated at Mechlin, Belgium and at Ampleforth. Railton's picturesque pen drawings of old buildings set a fashion in topographical draughtsmanship that lasted for many years, concentrating on the atmosphere and maturity of stone and brick. His drawings are characterised by an individual wriggly line and a strong decorative sense of the book page. Pennell considered him very influential, this is best seen in his follower Holland Tringham (q.v.). He died on 15 March 1911.

Illus: *Windsor Castle [1886]; Pickwick Papers [Charles Dickens Jubilee Edition, 1887]; Coaching Days and Coaching Ways [1888 (with Hugh Thomson)]; Westminster Abbey [1889]; Select Essays of Dr. Johnson [1889]; Poems and Plays of Goldsmith [1889]; Pericles and Aspasia [W.S. Landor, 1890]; Dreamland in History [1891]; The Citizen of the World [Goldsmith, 1891]; Beddoes Poetical Works [1891]; Collected Works of T.L. Peacock [1891]; Essays and Poems of Leigh Hunt [1891]; The Peak of Derbyshire [Leyland, 1891]; Ripon Millenary [1892]; The Inns of Court [Loftie, 1893]; Living English Poets [1894 (frontis)]; H. Kingsley's Novels [1894]; The Household of Sir Thomas More [1896]; The Haunted House [Hood, 1896]; Hampton Court [1897]; Cherry and Violet [Miss Manning, 1897]; English Cathedral Series [1897-99]; Travels in England [Le Gallienne, 1900]; Natural History of Selborne [White, 1900]; The Story of Bruges [1901]; Life of Johnson [1901].*
Contrib: *The English Illustrated Magazine [1884-96]; The Graphic [1887]; ILN [1889-99]; The Sporting & Dramatic News [1890]; Good Words [1890-94]; The Pall Mall Budget [1891-92]; Daily Chronicle [1895]; The Sketch; The Idler, The Windsor Magazine; The Temple Magazine.*
Colls: Blackburn; V & AM.

HERBERT RAILTON 1857-1911. 'Crane Bridge, Salisbury'. Illustration for *Coaching Days and Coaching Ways* by W. Outram Tristram, 1888

HERBERT RAILTON 1857-1911. 'Old Tabard Inn'

W. RAINEY RBA RI 1852-1936. 'A Regency skating party'. Original drawing for illustration. Grey wash and bodycolour. Signed and dated 1891

Bibl: J. Pennell, *Pen Drawing and Pen Draughtsmen*, 1895, p.360, illus.; R.E.D. Sketchley, *Eng. Bk. Illus.*, 1903 pp.31, 38, 45, 74, 139.
See illustrations.

RAIMBACH, Abraham   1776-1843

Miniature painter and engraver. He was born in London in 1776 of Swiss extraction and after being educated at Archbishop Tenison's Library School, he attended the RA Schools. He was then employed by J. Hall, the engraver and worked on Smirke and Forster's edition of the *Arabian Nights, Macklin's Bible, Hume's History of England, Woodmason's Shakespeare* and *Bell's British Theatre*...He engraved a number of plates after Wilkie's works and died at Greenwich in 1843. Although not principally an illustrator, Raimbach's *Memoirs and Recollections*, 1843, remain an important source for the history of the art.
Colls: BM.

RAINEY, William   RBA RI   1852-1936

Artist and illustrator. He was born in London on 21 July 1852 and studied art at South Kensington and at the RA Schools before starting his career in book illustration. Rainey was much influenced by the 18th century revivalism of Thomson and others, was an assured pen artist and a fine wash artist. Much of his best work was done for the magazines but he illustrated a number of boys' stories. He was elected RI in 1891 and ROI, 1892, becoming HROI in 1930. He lived for the latter part of his life in Eastbourne and died on 24 January 1936.
Publ: *All the Fun of the Fair [1888]; Abdulla [1928]; The Last Voyage of the 'Jane Ann' [1929]; Admiral Rodney's Bantam Cock [1938]; Who's on My Side [1938].*
Illus: *Sweet Content [Mrs. Molesworth, 1891]; At Aboukir and Acre [G.A. Henty, 1898]; The Rebel of the School [L.T. Meade, 1902]; The Giant of the Treasure Caves [1908]; The Court Harman Girls [Meade, 1908].*
Contrib: *ILN [1884-94]; The Graphic [1884-1901]; The Quiver [1890]; Good Words [1891]; Black & White [1891-92]; The Strand Magazine [1891, 1906]; The Ludgate Monthly [1896]; The Temple Magazine [1896]; Cassell's Family Magazine; Chums.*
Exhib: G; L; M; RA; RBA; RI; ROI.
Colls: Leeds.
Bibl: J. Pennell, *Pen Drawing and Pen Draughtsmen*, 1894, p.352.
See illustration.

RALSTON, John McL.   fl.1872-1880

Figure artist, illustrator and watercolourist. According to Dalziel this artist came from Scotland to work in London in about 1873. He worked for magazines and contributed to books.
Illus: *A Child's History of England [Charles Dickens, The Household Edition, 1873]; The Pilgrim's Progress [1880].*
Contrib: *ILN [1872-73, 1880-81].*
Exhib: Dowdeswell Galleries.
Bibl: The Brothers Dalziel, *A Record of Work, 1840-1890*, 1901.

RALSTON, William   1848-1911

Comic artist. He was born in Dumbarton in 1848 and probably studied under his younger brother after abandoning a career as a photographer. He contributed a great many drawings to *Punch* from 1870 to 1886, specialising in genre and military subjects. He later became a master of the episodic illustration and strip cartoon, making up in humour for a certain deficiency in his drawings. He died at Glasgow in October 1911.
Illus: *Barry Lyndon [W.M. Thackeray, 1894].*
Contrib: *Punch [1870-86]; ILN [1870-73]; The Graphic [1870-1911]; The Quiver [1880]; The Cornhill Magazine [1883-84]; The Daily Graphic; The Sporting and Dramatic News [1895].*
Exhib: G.
Bibl: M.H. Spielmann, *The History of Punch*, 1895 p.543.

RAMBERG, Johann Heinrich   1763-1840

Painter, engraver and caricaturist. He was born in Hanover in 1763 and came to England in 1781 to study at the RA Schools. He was a

pupil of Sir Joshua Reynolds and Bartolozzi and after travelling to Italy and Dresden was appointed Court Painter at Hanover in 1792. His caricatures are mostly political ones dating from the later 1780s. He died at Hanover on July 6, 1840.
Exhib: RA.
Colls: BM; Hanover; Nottingham.
Bibl: M.D. George, *English Political Caricature*, Vol.l, 1959, p.194.

RAMBLE, Fred
Illustrator. Contributed to *Public Works of Great Britain*, 1838 AL 410.

RANKIN, Andrew Scott   **1862-1942**
Animal painter. He was born at Aberfeldy in 1862 and studied at the Manufacturers School, Royal Institute and Life School, Edinburgh. He was on the staff of *Today* and was caricaturist of *The Idler*, c.1893. He worked at Strathtay, 1902-14 and at Pitlochry, 1925.
Exhib: G; L; M; RA; RCA; RSA; RSW.

RANKIN, Arabella Louisa   **1871-c.1935**
Painter and colour woodcut artist. She was born at Muthill, Perthshire in 1871 and worked at Edinburgh, 1903, Crieff, 1914 and in London 1922-35.
Bibl: *The Studio*, Vol.8, 1896, p.252, illus.

RAVEN-HILL, Leonard   RWA   **1867-1942**
Black and white artist and cartoonist. He was born at Bath on 10 March 1867 and was educated at Bristol Grammar School and Devon County School before entering the Lambeth School of Art where he met Charles Ricketts and Charles H. Shannon (qq.v.). He then went to Paris and studied with Bouguereau and Aimé Morot and exhibited at the Salon from 1887. Raven-Hill's connection with *Punch* began in 1896, but he had had a varied career on the magazines before this. He was appointed Art Editor of *Pick-Me-Up* in about 1890 and in 1895 founded his own illustrated publication *The Unicorn*, which had a short run. Other notable successes included his drawings for Rudyard Kipling's *Stalky & Co.* which first appeared in *The Windsor Magazine*.

Raven-Hill was one of the most versatile of the Edwardian *Punch* artists. He was strongly influenced by Ricketts, admired Japanese art and studied closely the work of Charles Keene (q.v.) with whose delicate pencil line and superb washes his own work has the closest affinities. He was second cartoonist and understudy to Partridge until 1935, but he was more at home in the domestic and genre subjects which he handled simply and brilliantly.

LEONARD RAVEN-HILL 1867-1942. 'Edwin and Angelina find the only place they can meet in London!' Original drawing, probably intended as an illustration for *Punch*. Pen and ink. Signed and dated 1891. 8in x 9½in (20.3cm x 24.1cm)   Victoria and Albert Museum

Illus: *The Promenaders [1894]; Stalky & Co. [Rudyard Kipling, 1899]; Raven-Hill's Indian Sketchbook [1903].*
Contrib: *Judy [1889]; Pick-Me-Up [1890]; Daily Graphic [1890]; Black & White [1891]; The Butterfly [1893-94, 1899-1900]; The Pall Mall Budget [1893]; ILN [1893]; The Unicorn [1895]; Punch [1896-1935]; The Minister [1895]; The Rambler [1897]; The Sketch [1897]; Fun [1901]; The Graphic [1906]; St Paul's; Pearson's Magazine; The Pall Mall Magazine; The Nutshell.*
Exhib: FAS, 1899; GG; G; L; NEA; RA; RBA; RI; ROI; RSA.
Colls: Author; Birmingham; V & AM; Witt Photo.
Bibl: J. Pennell, *Pen Drawing and Pen Draughtsmen*, 1895, pp.340-341; *The Idler*, Vol.8, pp.124-132, illus; *The Studio*, Winter No., 1900-01, p.25, illus.; R.G.G. Price, *A History of Punch*, 1957, pp.217-218.
See illustrations.

RAVERAT, Gwen   **1885-1957**
Wood engraver. She was born at Cambridge in 1885, the daughter of Sir George Darwin, Plumian Professor at Cambridge. She studied at the Slade School and worked mostly in Cambridgeshire but also in France, her style influenced by Eric Gill. ARE, 1920, RE, 1934. An exhibition of her work was held at the Fitzwilliam Museum in November 1977.
Illus: *The Bird Talisman, An Eastern Tale [H.A. Wedgwood].*
Exhib: G; L; NEA; RE; RHA; RSA.
Bibl: G. Raverat, *Period Piece*, 1952; Reynolds Stone, *The Wood Engravings of GR*, 1989.
See Horne

RAWLE, Samuel   **1771-1860**
Landscape painter in oil and watercolours. He drew a number of illustrations for *The Gentleman's Magazine* and for J. Britton's publications. He illustrated *The Arabian Antiquities of Spain* by Murphy and died in London in 1860.
Colls: V & AM.

RAWLINGS, Alfred   **1855-1939**
Landscape and flower painter and illustrator. He was born in London in 1855 and became an art master at Leighton Park School, Reading and a member of the Berkshire Art Society where he exhibited.
Publ: *Anthology of Sea and Flowers [1910, 1913]; Book of Old Sundials [1915].*
Illus: Our *Village [M.R. Mitford, 1910].*
Exhib: B; RA.
Colls: Manchester; Northampton; Reading.

RAWLINS, Thomas J.   **fl.1837-1860**
Topographer and illustrator. Rawlins specialised in sporting subjects and was employed to illustrate works by Nimrod, Charles James Apperley, with H.T. Alken (q.v.). It seems that the artist visited India either in 1837 or in 1858-60.
Illus: *Gamonia or The Art of Preserving Game [L. Rawstorne, AL 392]; Elementary Drawing as Taught at St. Mark's College, Chelsea [1848].*
Contrib: *ILN [1858-60].*
Exhib: RA.

RAYNER, Samuel A.   **-1874**
Architectural and historical painter and illustrator. Rayner began exhibiting in London in 1821, most of his work being in the style of George Cattermole (q.v.). He was a successful artist and prints were made after his drawings and he was elected AOWS in 1845. He was however struck off in 1851 after being convicted of fraud. He had five daughters who painted architecture in his style and he died at Brighton in 1874.
Illus: *Sketches of Derbyshire Scenery [1830]; The History and Antiquities of Haddon Hall [1836]; The History...of Derby [1838].*
Contrib: *Britton's Cathedrals [1832-36].*
Exhib: BI; OWS; RA; RBA.
Colls: Birkenhead; Coventry; Derby; Ulster.

READ, Blackwood Moutray   **1820-1865**
Caricaturist. An important group of works by this artist was

LEONARD RAVEN-HILL 1867-1942. Customer: 'Quite a Fancy Article. But what can it be used for?' Salesman: 'Well I really couldn't say, Madam, but I think its intended for a Christmas present'. Original drawing for illustration in *Humorists of the Pencil*, 1903. Pen and ink. Signed and dated 1899. 7in x 11¼in (17.8cm x 28.6cm)
Author's Collection

exhibited in London in 1980. The caricatures of fashionable and military life are usually in watercolour heightened with bodycolour and occasionally signed 'B.M. Read'. Many refer to the 15th Hussars or Indian scenes and the inscription 'Copies available' suggests that he had more than amateur status. Most date from the 1840s.
Coll: Stanford University.

READ, Edward Henry Handley   **1870-**
Portrait and landscape painter and illustrator. He studied at South Kensington, at the Westminster School of Art and at the RA Schools wherc he won the Creswick prize. He was elected RBA in 1895 and was an Official War Artist for the Army, 1918.
Contrib: *The English Illustrated Magazine [1897]; The Graphic [1902].*
Exhib: FAS; G; L; M; RA; RBA; RI, ROI.
Coll: Bedford.

READ, H. Hope   **fl.1906-1928**
Figure painter. He was working in London from 1908 and contributed subjects to *Punch*, 1905-07.
Exhib: M; NEA; RA.

READ, Samuel   **RWS**   **1815-1883**
Landscape and architectural painter and illustrator. He was born at Needham Market, Suffolk in 1815 and was placed in a lawyer's office at Ipswich and then as an assistant to an architect. Neither professions suiting him, he went to London and learnt drawing on wood under J.W. Whymper (q.v.). He also studied with W.C. Smith and became an accomplished watercolour painter, sending many works to exhibitions. In 1844 he began to work as an illustrator for *The Illustrated London News,* a connection which lasted until his death. In 1853; just before the outbreak of the Crimean War, Read was despatched to Constantinople, the first occasion that the paper

had sent an artist abroad on an assignment. He also travelled to Germany and North Italy and Spain as well as visiting and recording nearly every well-known ecclesiastical or manorial landmark in Great Britain. Over the years his pictures became an institution in *The 'News* and he was unofficially retained as Art Editor. His drawings of cathedrals, ruins and mysterious castles are delightfully dank and gloomy, always covered in thick undergrowth and with the appearance of having been painted in partly melted candle wax. He died at Sidmouth on 6 May 1883, having been elected OWS in 1880.
Illus: *Zoological Studies [S.P.C.K., 1844].*
Contrib: *The Home Affections by the Poets [Charles Mackay, 1858]; Willmott's Sacred Poetry of the 16th, 17th and 18th Centuries [1862]; Rhymes and Roundelayes.*
Exhib: OWS; RA; RBA.
Colls: Newcastle; Reading; V & AM.
Bibl: *Leaves From a Sketch-Book,* 1875; John Blatchly, *SR.*

REASON, Florence   **fl.1896-1914**
Genre and flower painter. She studied at the Queen's Square School of Art and won a National Silver Medal and Gilchrist Scholarship. She contributed figures to *The English Illustrated Magazine,* 1896.
Exhib: B; L; M; RA; RBA; RI; SWA.

REDFARN, William Beales   **fl.1870-1916**
Topographical artist. He made drawings of old buildings at Cambridge which were published as *Old Cambridge, 1876* and he illustrated J.W. Clark's *Ancient Wood and Ironwork in Cambridge,* 1881.
Coll: Fitzwilliam.

REDGRAVE, Richard   **RA**   **1804-1888**
Genre painter and illustrator. He was born in Pimlico on 30 April 1804, the son of a wire fence manufacturer, and worked with his

RÉGAMEY, FÉLIX ELIE, 1844-1907. Régamey's impression of German shells bursting at the Porte d'Auteuil during the Siege of Paris, 1871. Régamey worked for *The Illustrated London News* throughout the sieges and his sketches were sent out by balloon

father before studying at the RA Schools. Redgrave became a drawing master in 1830 and was always heavily committed to art education and art history. He was associated with the Government School of Design from 1847, was on the Paris Exhibition Committee in 1855 and was Director of the Art Division, South Kensington, until 1875. He was Surveyor of the Queen's Pictures from 1857 to 1880 and was made CB in that year. Redgrave returned to the Bible and the English poets for much of his inspiration and this was also true of the small body of illustrative work he undertook. He was elected ARA in 1840, RA in 1851 and died in London on 14 December 1888.

Publ: *An Elementary Manual of Colour [1853]; A Century of Painters of the British School [1866].*
Contrib: *The Deserted Village [Etching Club, 1841]; Book of British Ballads [1842]; Songs of Shakespeare [Etching Club, 1843]; The Song of the Shirt [Etching Club]; Favourite English Poems [1859]; Early English Poems, Chaucer to Pope [1863].*
Exhib: BI; RA; RBA.
Colls: BM; V & AM; Witt Photo.
Bibl: F.M. Redgrave, *RR, a Memoir,* 1891; S.P. Casteras & Ron Parkinson, *RR RA,* Yale, 1988.

REDON, Georges   **1869-1943**
Painter, lithographer, humorous illustrator. He was born at Paris on 16 November 1869 and exhibited at the Salon. He died in 1943.
Contrib: *The Graphic [1901].*

REED, C.W.
Illustrator of *Jack the Fisherman,* E. Stuart Phelps, 1897.

REED, Edward Tennyson   **1860-1933**
Cartoonist and illustrator. He was born on 27 March 1860, the son of Sir Edward James Reed, the naval architect and MP. He was educated at Harrow and then travelled to Egypt, China and Japan in 1880, before being appointed to the *Punch* staff in 1890 by Sir F. Burnand. He very soon became an established part of the paper, introducing his 'Prehistoric Peeps' series in 1893 and following Furness (q.v.) as parliamentary caricaturist in 1894, a post he held till 1912. He was also a talented lecturer and published a number of books.

Reed introduced the grotesque into *Punch* art once again after a long absence, he was also unusual in drawing principally in pencil with careful hatching and shading. A good portraitist and very inventive, his drawings are nevertheless rather angular and somewhat bizarre in quality. He died 12 July 1933.
Illus: *Mr Punch's Prehistoric Peeps [1896]; Tales With a Twist [1898]; Unrecorded History Mr Punch's Animal Land [1898]; Mr Punch's Book of Arms [1899]; The Tablets of Azit-Tigleth-Miphansi; The Scribe [1900]; The Unlucky Family [Mrs De La Pasture, 1908].*
Contrib: *Punch [1889-1933]; The Sketch [1894]; The Graphic; The Bystander.*
Exhib: FAS, 1899; G; New Gall; ROI.
Colls: V & AM.
Bibl: M.H. Spielmann, *The History of Punch,* 1895, pp.560-563; *The Idler,* Vol.9, pp.493-508; *The Studio,* Winter No., 1900-01, p.23, illus.; Shane Leslie, *ETR,* 1957.

REED, Ethel   **1876-**
American illustrator. She was born at Newburyport in 1876 and

specialised in babies' and children's books which were published in the United Kingdom.
Illus: *Arabella and Araminta Stories; Verses [Mrs. L.C. Moulton].*
Contrib: *The Yellow Book [1897 (cover and illus.)].*
Bibl: 'The Work of Miss ER', *The Studio*, Vol.10, 1897, pp.230-236.

REES, F.
Amateur artist contributing to *Punch*, 1908.

REEVE, A.
Illustrator of comic genre subjects for *The Graphic*, 1886.

RÉGAMEY, Félix Elie　　　　**1844-1907**
Portrait and history painter, engraver and illustrator. He was born in Paris on 7 August 1844, the son and pupil of the artist L.P.G. Régamey. He started his career as a caricaturist on *Journal Amusant, la Vie Parisienne, au Monde Illustré, l'Illustration, l'Éclipse, La Lune, Paris Caprice, Monde Comique* and *La Guêpe.* He founded his own journal *Salut Public* in 1870. Régamey remained at Paris during the Siege and acted as reporter and Special Artist for *The Illustrated London News,* producing very strong and rugged work. He left France in 1873 and travelled to England and then to Japan and the United States where he made powerful sketches of American prisons. He became an inspector of drawings at the Paris Schools in 1881 and died there on 7 May 1907.
Exhib: London, 1872.
Bibl: *English Influences on Vincent Van Gogh,* Arts Council, 1974-75.
See illustration.

REGNAULT, Henri Alexandre Georges　　　　**1843-1871**
Genre and history painter. He was born in Paris on 30 October 1843 and entered the École des Beaux Arts in 1860, winning the Prix de Rome in 1866 and studying in Italy until 1868. He travelled in Spain and Morocco but was killed with the l9th Infantry Regiment after enlisting in 1870.
Contrib: *The Graphic [1871 (carnival)].*
Colls: Bolton; Chicago; Marseilles; Louvre.

REID, Sir George　RSA HRHA　　　　**1841-1913**
Black and white artist and illustrator. He was born at Aberdeen on 31 October 1841 and was educated at Aberdeen Grammar School. He studied art in Edinburgh, Utrecht and Paris and returning to this country became the leading landscape pen draughtsman of his time. Pennell regarded his powers very highly – 'he can, in a pen drawing, give the whole character of northern landscape…while his portraits contain all the subtlety and refinement of a most elaborate etching by Rajon.' Reid exhibited his work very widely, received many honours, was knighted in 1891 and was President of the RSA, 1891 to 1902. He died in Somerset on 9 February 1913.
Illus: *The Selected Writings of John Ramsay [1871]; Life of a Scotch Naturalist [Smiles, 1876]; George Paul Chalmers [1879]; Johnny Gibb [W. Alexander, 1880]; Twelve Sketches of Scenery [1882]; Natural History and Sport in Norway [1882]; The River Tweed [1884]; The River Clyde [1886]; Salmon Fishing on the Ristigouche [1888]; Lacunar Basilicae [1888]; St. Giles' Edinburgh [1889]; Royal Edinburgh [Mrs Oliphant, 1890]; Familiar Letters of Sir Walter Scott [1894].*
Contrib: *The English Illustrated Magazine [1890-91].*
Exhib: B; G; L; M; New Gall; P, RA; RHA; ROI; RSA.
Bibl: J. Pennell, *Pen Drawing and Pen Draughtsmen,* 1904, pp.277-279 illus; R.E.D. Sketchley, *Eng. Bk. Illus.,* 1903, pp.31, 141.

REID, John Robertson　RI　　　　**1851-1926**
Genre, history and landscape painter. He was born in Edinburgh on 6 August 1851 and studied at the RSA Schools under Chalmers and McTaggert. He specialised in marine and coastal paintings, many of them of Cornwall and distinguished for their clarity and colour. He was elected RI in 1897 and died at Hampstead on 10 February 1926.
Contrib: *The Graphic [1892 (birds)]; The Sketch [1894].*
Exhib: B; FAS, 1899; G; GG; L; M; NEA; New Gall; RA; RBA; RHA; RI; ROI; RSA.
Colls: Leicester; Liverpool; V & AM.

REID, Stephen　　　　**1873-1948**
Painter and illustrator. He was born at Aberdeen in 1873 and studied at the Grays School of Art, Aberdeen and at the RSA Schools. In his early years he was strongly influenced by the work of E.A. Abbey (q.v.) and favoured Georgian settings and costume pieces for his work, he was also a competent topographer in pen and ink. He was elected RBA in 1906 and died at Hampstead on 7 December 1948.
Illus: *The Magic Casement [Alfred Noyes, 1908].*
Contrib: *The Windsor Magazine; The Temple Magazine [1896-97]; The Idler; The Strand Magazine [1906]; The Deserted Village [Goldsmith, 1907]; The Connoisseur [1910 (decor)].*
Exhib: L; M; RA; RBA; RI; RSA.

REID, W.E.
Illustrator. Contributed drawings to *Embassy to the Court of Ava* by J. Crawford 1829, AT 405.

REINAGLE, George Philip　　　　**1802-1835**
Marine painter. He was born in 1802 and was the younger son of R.R. Reinagle and began his career by copying Dutch masters. He was present with the Fleet at the Battle of Navarino in 1827, the last battle under sail, and with the Fleet off Portugal in 1833.
Illus: *Illustrations of the Battle of Navarino [1829]; Illustrations of the Occurrences at the Entrance of the Bay of Patras... [1828].*
Colls: BM.

REINAGLE, Philip　RA　　　　**1749-1833**
Sporting artist and animal painter. He was born in Scotland in 1749 and entered the RA Schools in 1769 after which he studied with Allan Ramsay. He made botanical and anatomical drawings for book illustrations and was elected ARA in 1787 and RA in 1812. He died in London in 1833.
Illus: *Sportsman's Cabinet [Taplin, 1803]; Sexual System of Linnaeus [1799-1807]; Philosophy of Botany [1809-10].*
Exhib: BI; RA; RBA.
Colls: BM; V & AM.
Bibl: *AJ*, 1898.

REINHART, Charles Stanley　　　　**1844-1896**
American painter and illustrator. He was born at Pittsburg in 1844 and studied art at Paris and in Munich with Strahuber and Karl Otto. He worked principally in New York but contributed to British publications. These included the illustrations to Thomas Hardy's 'Romantic Adventures of a Milk-Maid' in *The Graphic*, 1883. He died in 1896.
Exhib: L; RI.

REJCHAN, Stanislas
Polish artist and illustrator. He worked in Paris and contributed Belgian scenes to *The Graphic*, 1902.

RÉNAUD, G.
Humorous artist. Contributed to *Judy*, 1886-89.

RENÉ
Decorative artist contributing to *The English Illustrated Magazine,* 1895.

RENNELL, Joseph
Draughtsman. He contributed illustrations to *Public Works of Great Britain*, 1838, AT 410.

RENOUARD, Charles Paul　　　　**1845-1924**
Painter, engraver and illustrator. He was born at Cour Cheverny on 5 November 1845 and studied at the École des Beaux Arts after which he worked as a mural painter. Renouard worked for the Parisian papers *l'Illustration* and *Paris Illustré* before starting work for *The Graphic* in 1884. Renouard's forte was in pencil and chalk drawings which had a power and expressiveness quite new in the pages of English magazines. For a decade he was the giant among illustrators and his flamboyant full page sketches of social realism, London life and Parisian fashion burst on the British public. For some reason this masterly artist, who must have been widely influential on such Paris trained Englishmen as Dudley Hardy (q.v.), has been almost

CHARLES PAUL RENOUARD 1845-1924. 'A Shower of Words and a Shower of Rain'. Drawing for illustration about 1896. Black chalk. 14in x 10½in (35.6cm x 26.7cm)   Author's Collection

CHARLES PAUL RENOUARD 1845-1924. 'Recruiting the Sandwich Men'. Illustration for *The Graphic*, 1894

forgotten. He exhibited at the Salon from 1877 and died in Paris on 2 January 1924. Elected RE, 1881.
Contrib: *The Graphic [1884-1910]; ILN [1886-89]; The Butterfly [1893]; The English Illustrated Magazine [1893-94]; Daily Graphic.*
Exhib: L; NEA; P; RE.
Bibl: *Print Collector's Quarterly,* Vol.9, No.2, 1922, pp.128-148; Simon Houfe, 'Genius in Chalk', *CL*, 23 July 1983.
See illustrations.

RENTON, John   **1774-c.1841**
Figure and landscape painter. He lived in London and worked in the Thames Valley and Lake District. Contributed illustrations to *The Border Antiquities of England and Scotland,* Walter Scott, 1817.
Colls: BM.

REPTON, Humphry   **1752-1818**
Landscape gardener and watercolourist. He was born at Bury St Edmunds in 1752 and educated at Bury, Norwich and on the Continent. He became interested in botany and landscape design and from the 1780s developed a large practice in the new 'picturesque' style of gardening. Repton developed a habit of presenting elaborate Red Books to his clients in which projected improvements were set out in 'before and after' scenes in brilliant watercolours. He was not strictly an illustrator at all, but drew for some of his own works. He died at Romford on 14 March 1818.
Publ: *Sketches and Hints on Landscape Gardening [1794]; Observations on the Theory and Practice of Landscape Gardening [1803]; Odd Whims and Miscellanies [1804]; Fragments on the Theory and Practice of Landscape Gardening [1816].*
Exhib: RA.
Colls: BM, V & AM.
Bibl: J.C. Loudon, *The Landscape Gardening...of HR,* 1840; D. Stroud, *HR,* 1962; *HR Landscape Gardener,* V & AM, 1982-83.

REPTON, John Adey   **FSA**   **1775-1860**
Architect. He was the eldest son of H. Repton (q.v.) and was born in Norwich on 29 March 1775. He became a pupil of the architect William Wilkins and made drawings of Norwich cathedral. Although he went into practice with his father, he was stone deaf and could only lead a retired life, but was the teacher of F. Mackenzie (q.v.). He was elected FSA in 1803 and died at Springfield, Essex on 26 November 1860.
Publ: *A Trewe...Hystorie of the...Prince Radapanthus [1820]; Some Account of the Beard and Moustachio [1839].*
Contrib: *Britton's Cathedrals [1832-36.]*
Exhib: RA.
Colls: RIBA; Soc. of Antiquaries.
Bibl: H.M. Colvin, *Biog Dict. of Eng. Architects,* 1954, p.491.

REYNOLDS, Ernest G.
Humorous artist. Contributed to *Judy,* 1886 and *Fun,* 1887.

REYNOLDS, Frank   **RI**   **1876-1953**
Black and white artist and illustrator. He was born in London on 13 February 1876 and studied at Heatherley's before working for *The Illustrated London News* and *The Sketch.* He joined the staff of *Punch* in 1919 and was Art Editor from 1920-32, having been a contributor from 1906. Reynolds was most successful in urban genre subjects, interiors, street corners and where groups of people were included. His characters, portly policemen, charladies and drunks were not as individual as Belcher's, but Fougasse later considered that his fluid pen line had done a lot to alter the image of *Punch.* He was elected RI in 1903 and died in April 1953.
Illus: *Pictures of Paris and Some Parisians [Raphael, 1908]; The F.R. Golf Book [1932]; Hamish McDuff [1937]; Off to the Pictures [1937]; Humorous Drawings [1947].*
Contrib: *Pick-Me-Up [1896]; The Longbow [1898]; Judy [1899]; Sketchy Bits; Punch [1906-53]; ILN [1909-11]; The Sketch.*

Exhib: L; RI; Walker's.
Colls: Author; Fitzwilliam.
Bibl: *FR, RI*, Ed. by A.E. Johnson, Brush, Pen, Pencil series, c.1910; *Modern Book Illustrators and their Work,* Studio, 1914.
See Horne
See illustration.

REYNOLDS, H.   **fl.1882-1896**
Artist and illustrator. He worked at Birmingham and contributed decoration to *The English Illustrated Magazine,* 1896.
Exhib: B.

REYNOLDS, J.H.
Humorous artist. Contributed illustrations to *Hood's Comic Annual,* 1830.

REYNOLDS, Percy T.   **fl.1890-1914**
Humorous artist. He worked in London at Muswell Hill and contributed to *Fun,* 1890-92 and *Punch,* 1914.
Exhib: RA.

REYNOLDS, Warwick   **fl.1871-1879**
Black and white artist. He contributed comic heads to *Judy,* 1871-79. He was a member of the NWS from 1864-65.

REYNOLDS, Warwick   **1880-1926**
Black and white artist and illustrator. He was born in Islington in 1880, the son of Warwick Reynolds (q v.). He was educated at Stroud Green and studied at the Grosvenor Studio, St. John's Wood Art School and at Julians in Paris, 1908. He made a particular study of animals in the collection of the Zoological Society, 1895-1901, and began to work for the magazines in 1895. He died in Glasgow on 15 December 1926.
Illus: *Babes of the Wild [1912].*
Contrib: *The Strand Magazine [1913-18]; Pearson's Magazine; Royal Windsor Magazine; The Quiver; Thc Idler; Ally Sloper's Half Holiday.*
Exhib: G; L; RA; RSA; RSW.
Colls: Glasgow; Witt Photo.
See Horne

RHEAD, F.A.
Humorous figure artist. Contributed to *Punch,* 1914.

RHEAD, George Wooliscroft   **RE**   **1855-1920**
Painter, etcher and illustrator. He was born in 1855 and won a National Art Scholarship and silver medals before studying with Alphonse Legros and Ford Madox Brown. Rhead designed for stained glass, wrote on ecclesiastical art and was a member of the Art Workers Guild and Hon. ARCA. He was elected RE in 1883 and in 1914 married the illustrator Annie French (q.v.). He died on 30 April 1920.
Publ. his own etchings: *The Foundation of Manchester by the Romans; The Dream of Sardanapalus.*
Illus: *Bunyan's Pilgrim's Progress; Life of Mr Badman; Idylls of the King [Tennyson]; Modern Practical Design [1912].*
Exhib: G; L; New Gall; RA; RBA; RE; RI.
Bibl: *The Studio,* Vol.9, 1897, p.282 illus.

RICE
Illustrator contributing to *London Society,* 1868.

RICH, Anthony   **fl.1854-1914**
Landscape painter and illustrator working at Croydon and Hassocks. He contributed to *Thornbury's Legendary Ballads,* 1876.

RICH, E.
Topographer. He was a pupil of J. Hawksworth and illustrated *The History and Antiquities of Islington,* 1823.

RICHARDS, Frank   **fl.1883-1925**
Landscape and figure painter. He was probably born in Birmingham where he worked early in his career before settling in Dorset and the West Country from 1887. He was elected RBA in 1921.

FRANK REYNOLDS 1876-1953. 'Sir Henry Irving and companion'. Pen and ink. Signed with initials. 9½in x 5½in (24.1cm x 14cm)   Author's Collection

Contrib: *Pick-Me-Up [1894]; The Graphic [1898]; The Queen; The Sketch; The Windsor Magazine.*
Exhib: B; L; M; RA; RBA.

RICHARDS, G.E.
Figure artist specialising in children. He contributed to *Punch* 1903 and may be the George Richards exhibiting at Liverpool in 1900.

RICHARDSON, Charles   **1829-1908**
Landscape and marine painter. He was born in 1829, the son of T.M. Richardson (q.v.) by his second marriage. He assisted his brother H.B. Richardson but moved to London in 1873, finally settling in Hampshire. He died in 1908.
Illus: *The Conquest of Camborne [Sir W. Lawson, 1903].*
Exhib: L; RA; RI.

RICHARDSON, Charles
Animal and bird illustrator. He contributed comic sketches to *Punch,* 1905.

RICHARDSON, Charles James   **1806-1871**
Architect and draughtsman. He was born in 1806 and became a pupil of Sir John Soane and a specialist on Tudor and Jacobean buildings and ornament. He was Master of the Architectural Class at Somerset House, 1848-52.
Illus: *Architectural Remains of the Reigns of Elizabeth and James I [1838-40]; Studies from Old Mansions, their Furniture, Gold and Silver Plate...[1841]; Studies of Ornamental Design [1848]; Picturesque Designs for Mansions, Villas, Lodges...[1870].*
Exhib: RA.
Colls: Soane Museum; V & AM (Lib.).

CHARLES DE SOUSY RICKETTS RA 1866-1931. 'Venus Bird Messenger'. Original drawing for wood engraving in *The Marriage of Cupid and Psyche*, Vale Press, 1899. Circular pen and wash, touched with white. Diameter 3in (7.6cm)   Victoria and Albert Museum

RICHARDSON, Henry Burdon   **1811-1874**
Landscape artist and topographer. He was born at Warkworth in about 1811, the son of T.M. Richardson (q.v.). He travelled widely before settling down as a drawing-master at Newcastle-upon-Tyne and undertaking the series of large views of the Roman Wall, illustrated in Sir Gainsford Bruce's *History of the Wall*. He died at Newcastle in 1874.
Exhib: RA; RBA.
Colls: Newcastle.

RICHARDSON, Ralph J.   **fl.1896-1925**
Painter and illustrator. He specialised in comic genre subjects in black and white mostly associated with horsemanship.
Contrib: *Punch [1896-1907]; The Graphic [1901]*.
Exhib: RA, 1900.

RICHARDSON, S.T.
Amateur artist at Darlington. He illustrated *Splutterings of a Sporting Pen*, published by Bailey, Darlington and Simpkin Marshall, London, n.d. Advertised in the same book were *Friends in Council*, 1874 and *The World's First Railway Jubilee*, 1875.

RICHARDSON, Thomas Miles   **1784-1848**
Landscape painter and watercolourist. He was born at Newcastle-upon-Tyne on 15 May 1784 and after being apprenticed to an engraver, became a drawing-master and devoted his time entirely to painting from 1813. He travelled widely and his work is chiefly associated with the more picturesque areas of Italy, Switzerland and France. Richardson was a fine colourist and by far the most distinguished watercolourist of the North East, founding the Newcastle Watercolour Society in 1831. He was ANWS from 1840 for three years and exhibited regularly. He began to publish a work on Newcastle in 1816 and in 1833 began to issue *The Castles of The English and Scottish Borders*. He died in Newcastle on 7 March 1848.
Contrib: *Howitt's Visits to Remarkable Places [1841]*.
Exhib: BI; NWS; OWS; RA, 1814-45; RBA.
Colls: BM; Bradford; Derby; Leeds; Manchester; Newcastle; V & AM.
Bibl: *Memorials of Old Newcastle on Tyne...with a sketch of the artist's life*, 1880.

RICHARDSON, Thomas Miles, Jnr.   RWS   **1813-1890**
Landscape painter and watercolourist. He was born at Newcastle-upon-Tyne in 1813, the son of T.M. Richardson (q.v.). He worked closely with his father, but moved to London in 1846 after being

elected AOWS in 1843; he became a full OWS in 1851. Richardson made tours of the Continent and chose many of the same localities as his father for his exhibition works. These are always brightly coloured and highly finished, tending towards an over elaboration and a too great size for the medium. His smaller studies are often charming with an effective use of chinese white. He died at Newcastle on 5 January 1890.
Illus: *Sketches in Italy, Switzerland, France etc, [1837]; Sketches at Shotley Bridge Spa and on The Derwent [1839]*.
Contrib: *Howitt's Visits to Remarkable Places [1841]*.
Exhib: BI; L; M; RA; RBA; RWS.
Colls: Blackburn; BM; Cardiff; Manchester; V & AM.

RICHTER, Henry Constantine   **1821-1902**
Ornithological illustrator. He was born at Brompton on 7 June 1821 from an artistic family of German extraction, his father being the historical painter H.J. Richter. Probably trained as a natural history draughtsman before coming to the notice of John Gould. He worked for Gould on the latter's *Birds of Australia*, acting as both painter and lithographer. He worked from living specimens at London Zoo for Gould's *Mammals of Australia*, 1845-63. He made about 280 watercolours for *The Birds of Great Britain* and was the first artist to depict them in their natural environment.
Illus: *Gray's Genera of Birds [1844-49]*.
Lit: *The Godman Collection of Watercolours for John Gould's 'The Birds of Great Britain'*, Christie's catalogue, 1994 with an introduction by Maureen Lambourne.

RICHTER, Willibald   **fl.1840-1856**
Watercolourist and illustrator. He worked at Vienna and travelled to England, Italy and Poland, exhibiting views of these countries at the Vienna Academy 1840-50.
Contrib: *ILN [1855-56 (Turkey)]*.

RICKARDS, Edwin A.   **1872-1920**
Architect, draughtsman and caricaturist. He was born in Chelsea in 1872 and spent some time in the RA Schools and at the Architectural Association but chiefly taught himself from study in the museums. He entered the office of Richard J. Lovell in 1887 as an architectural assistant and later joined the firms of Howard Ince and George Sherrin. Toured Italy and made himself familiar with the baroque before returning to England to do competition work and enter partnership with H.V. Lanchester in 1897. He died as a result of war disabilities in 1920.
Illus: *Parisian Nights and Other Impressions of Places and People [Arnold Bennett, 1913]*.
Bibl: *The Art of EA with a Personal Sketch by Arnold Bennett, an Appreciation by H. V. Lanchester and Technical Notes by Amor Fenn*, 1920.

RICKETTS, Charles de Sousy   RA   **1866-1931**
Painter, printer, stage designer, writer and collector. He was born in Geneva in 1866, the son of the marine painter C.R. Ricketts (q.v.). He was brought up in France and Italy and studied at the Lambeth School of Art where he met his lifelong friend C.H. Shannon (q.v.). With him he owned and edited *The Dial*, 1889-97 and ran the Vale Press, 1896-1904, producing eighty-three volumes, many with type, bindings or illustrations by him. Among them were *Daphne and Chloe*, the first book of the new woodcut revival. Ricketts concentrated in later life on stage designing and sculpture, was elected ARA in 1922 and RA in 1928 and died in London on 7 October 1931 .
Illus: *A House of Pomegranates [Wilde, 1891]; Poems Dramatic and Lyrical [de Tabley, 1893]; Daphne and Chloe [1894]; Hero and Leander [1894]; In the Key of Blue [J.A. Symonds, 1894 (cover)]; The Sphinx [Wilde, 1894]; The Incomparable and Ingenious History of Mr W.H. [Wilde, 1894]; Dramatic Works of Oscar Wilde [1894]; Nymphidia [1896]; Spiritual Poems [T. Gray]; The Early Poems of John Milton [1896]; The Poems of Sir John Suckling; Fifty Songs of Thomas Campion; Empedocles on Etna [Matthew Arnold]; Songs of Innocence [Blake, 1897]; Sacred Poems of Henry Vaughan [1897]; Cupide and Psyche 118971; The Book of Thel [Blake, 1897]; Blake's Poetical Sketches [899]; The Rowley Poems of Thomas Chatterton [1898]; Julia Domna [Michael Field, 1903]; Oscar Wilde as I Knew Him [1932]*.

Contrib: *Black and White [1891]; The Venture [1903].*
Exhib: FAS; G; GG; L; M; RA; RBA; RI; ROI; RSA.
Colls: Ashmolean, BM; Fitzwilliam; Leeds; Manchester; Reading; V & AM.
Bibl: *Print Collector's Quarterly*, Vol.14, No.3, 1927, pp.195-217; T.S. Moore, *CR*, 1933; R.E.D. Sketchley, *Eng. Bk. Illus.*, 1903, pp.18, 129; C. Franklin, *The Private Presses*, 1969; Stephen Calloway, *CR, Subtle & Fantastic Decorator*, 1979; J. Darracott, *CR*, 1980, J.G.P. Delaney, *The World of CR*, 1989. For full bibliography of Vale Press see Franklin, C.
See illustration.

RICKETTS, Charles Robert   fl.1868-1879
Marine painter. He worked in London and contributed to *The Graphic* 1871 .
Exhib: RA; RBA.

RIDCOCKS, E.F.
Black and white artist in New Zealand. Contributed to *Punch,* 1902.

RIDDELL, Robert Andrew   fl.1790-1807
Landscape painter and topographer who illustrated A *History of Mountains,* J. Wilson, 1807.

RIDLEY, B.
Black and white artist. He contributed to *London Society,* 1869.

RIDLEY, Mathew White   1837-1888
Landscape painter, illustrator and engraver. He was born at Newcastle-upon-Tyne in 1837 and studied at the RA Schools under Smirke and Dobson. Ridley became the earliest pupil of James McNeil Whistler (q.v.) and a friend of Fantin Latour. He developed a very direct reportage in his illustrations of social realism in the 1870s and these were admired by Van Gogh. He contributed to numerous magazines and died on 2 June 1888.
Contrib: *Cassell's Family Magazine [1867]; The Quiver [1867]; Every Boy's Magazine [1867]; The Graphic [1869-77]; ILN [1872-81].*
Exhib: G; GG; RA; RI.
Bibl: *English Influences on Vincent Van Gogh,* Arts Council, 1974-75; 'Artists Fruitful Friendship', V. Gatty, *Country Life,* 7 March 1974.

RIMER, William   fl.1845-1888
Historical and subject painter and illustrator. His drawings are usually in pencil, very meticulous in execution and showing strong German influence. He worked in Westminster and London and illustrated *Thomson's Castle of Indolence* for the Art Union of London, 1845.
Exhib: BI; RA; RBA.
Colls: Witt Photo; V & AM.

RIMMER, Alfred   1829-1893
Black and white artist, woodcut artist and antiquary. He was born at Liverpool on 9 August 1829 and worked for some years as an architect, spent a period of time in Canada, finally settling at Chester as an artist and writer. He died there on 27 October 1893.
Illus: *Ancient Streets and Homesteads of England; Pleasant Spots About Oxford; Rambles About Eton and Harrow; About England with Dickens.*
Contrib: *The English Illustrated Magazine [1885].*
Exhib: L; M.
Colls: BM.

RIOU, Edouard   1833-1900
Landscape painter, designer and illustrator. Born at Saint-Servan on 2 December 1833 and exhibited at the Salon from 1859. He specialised in book illustration including the works of Jules Verne and the poetry of A. Riou. He died in Paris on 27 January 1900.
Contrib: *The Illustrated Times [1859]; ILN [1894].*
Colls: Witt Photo.

'RIP' Rowland HILL   1873-p.1925
Cartoonist. He was born at Halifax in 1873 and worked at Halifax before studying at Bradford School of Art and at the Herkomer

School, Bushey. Travelled on the Continent and settled at Hinderwell, Yorks, 1908.
Contrib: *Black & White; Truth; The Sketch.*
Exhib: L; RA.
Colls: Leeds.

RISCHGITZ, Edward   1828-1909
Landscape painter. He was born at Geneva on 28 July 1828 and became a pupil of Diday and worked in Paris. He settled in London before 1878 and was elected RE in 1881. He died at the home of his daughter, the artist Mary Rischgitz on 3 November 1909.
Contrib: *Good Words [1880].*
Exhib: GG; RE.

RITCHIE, Alick P.F   fl.1892-1913
Caricaturist and illustrator.
Contrib: *The Ludgate Monthly [1892]; St Pauls [1894]; The Pall Mall Budget [1894]; Sketchy Bits [1895]; Eureka [1897]; Penny Illustrated Paper; Vanity Fair [1911-13].*

RIVERS, A. Montague   fl.1910-1915
Painter and illustrator. He worked in Hornsey, London and contributed to *The Illustrated London News*, 1915.
Exhib: M; RA; RI.

RIVIERE, Briton   RA   1840-1920
Genre, landscape and animal painter. He was born in London on 14 August 1840, the son of William Riviere, drawing-master at Cheltenham College. He was educated at Cheltenham and St Mary Hall, Oxford, where he began making humorous pen drawings. These came to the notice of Mark Lemon of *Punch*, who gave him work and he then undertook drawing for American magazines. Riviere maintained that one of his eyes was permanently damaged by the strain of this drawing and he only painted after 1870. He became very well-known for his animal subjects and was elected ARA in 1878 and RA in 1881. He died in London on 20 April 1920.
Contrib: *Punch [1868-69]; Good Words [1868]; Good Words For The Young [1869]; ILN [1870].*
Exhib: B; FAS; G; GG; L; M; RA; RCA; RHA; RSA.
Colls: BM; Blackburn; Manchester; V & AM.
Bibl: *AJ*, 1878, 1891.

RIVIERE, Hugh Goldwin   1869-1956
Portrait painter. He was born at Bromley, Kent on 1 January 1869, the son of Briton Riviere (q.v.). He was educated at St Andrews and studied at the RA Schools, being elected RP in 1900 and ROI in 1907. He died in 1956.
Illus: *John Halifax Gentleman [Mrs Craik, 1897].*
Exhib: B; FAS; G; L; M; New Gall; P; RA; RHA; ROI; RSA.

RIVINGTON, Reginald   fl.1908
Illustrator of children's books. He illustrated *The Snow King* and *Buffs and Boys,* Amy Sims, 1908.

ROBERTS, Charles J. Cramer   1834-1895
Landscape painter and illustrator. He was a professional soldier who joined the Army in 1853 and served in India and the Crimea retiring in 1887. He contributed portraits, social and military illustrations to *The Graphic*, 1872-77.
Colls: India Office Lib.

ROBERTS, David   RA   1796-1864
Landscape and architectural painter. He was born at Stockbridge, Edinburgh on 2 October 1796, the son of a shoemaker and was apprenticed for seven years to a house painter, before working as scene painter at theatres in Carlisle, Glasgow and Edinburgh. In 1822 he went to London and while scene painting at Drury Lane formed his lifelong friendship with Clarkson Stanfield (q.v.). Roberts was very successful in what he undertook, became Vice-President of the SBA on its foundation in 1823-24 and President in 1830. He began travelling on the Continent in the 1820s and on Wilkie's recommendation visited Spain and Tangier in 1832-33, following this with trips to Egypt and Palestine in 1838 and Italy in 1851 and 1853. Roberts' great accuracy as a draughtsman, his strong sense of

country and place, combined with his love of architecture, made his Middle Eastern views the touchstone of a fashion among the early Victorians. The temples and monuments brought to life for the first time were drawn on the stone by J.D. Harding and Louis Haghe (qq.v.) and issued in amazingly lavish form to subscribers. Roberts was elected ARA in 1838 and RA in 1841 and acted as a Commissioner for the Great Exhibition. He died in London on 25 November 1864, still at work on a series of Thames views.

Illus: *Picturesque Sketches in Spain during the years 1832 and 1833 [AT 152]; Views in the Holy Land, Syria, Idumea, Egypt, Nubia [1842-49].*
Contrib: *Jennings Landscape Annual [1835-38]; The Chaplet [c.1840]; Scotland Delineated [Lawson, c.1845]; Lockhart's Spanish Ballads.*
Exhib: BI; RA; RBA.
Colls: Aberdeen; BM; Fitzwilliam; Glasgow; Leeds; Manchester; Nat. Gall, Scotland; V & AM.
Bibl: J. Ballantine, *The Life of DR*, 1866; J. Quigley, DR, *Walker's Quarterly*, X, 1922; M. Hardie, 'DR' *O.W.S.*, 1947; M. Hardie, *Watercol. Paint. In Brit.*, Vol.III, 1968, pp.179-183 illus.; *DR*, Barbican Art Gallery cat., 1986.

ROBERTS, Edwin   fl.1862-1890
Genre and rustic painter. He worked in Chelsea and contributed figure illustrations to *Judy*, 1889.
Exhib: RA; RBA.

ROBERTS, Henry Benjamin   1832-1915
Genre painter and watercolourist. He was born in Liverpool in 1832, the son of a landscape painter and studied with his father. He closely followed the work of W.H. Hunt, was elected a member of the Liverpool Academy in 1855, of the NWS in 1867 and the RBA in 1878. He was living in Leyton, Essex from 1883 except for a period in North Wales. He died in 1915.
Contrib: *ILN [1871-75].*
Exhib: B; L; RI.
Colls: Birkenhead; V & AM.

ROBERTS, I.
Contributed a social illustration to *The Graphic*, 1870.

ROBERTS, J.H.
Black and white artist. He was an architect who had become a caricaturist, journalist and political versifier. He contributed to *Punch*, 1892-97; *Fun*, 1893; *Chums*.

ROBERTSON, George Edward   1864-
Portrait painter and illustrator. The son of a painter, he studied at St Martin's School of Art and worked in London.
Contrib: *The Graphic [1905].*
Exhib: G; L; M; RA; RBA; ROI.

ROBERTSON, Henry Robert   1839-1921
Landscape, genre and figure painter and engraver. He was born at Windsor in 1839 and studied at the RA Schools. He worked in Hampstead and was elected RE, 1881 and RMS, 1896. He died on 6 June 1921.
Illus: *The Trial of Sir Jasper [S.C. Hall, 1870]; Life on The Upper Thames [1875]; The Art of Etching Explained and Illustrated [1883]; The Art of Painting on China [1884]; The Art of Pen and Ink Drawing [1886]; Plants we Play With [1915]; More Plants we Play With [1920].*
Contrib: *ILN [1874,1881]; The English Illustrated Magazine [1886].*
Exhib: B; G; L; M; New Gall; RA; RBA; RE; RI; RMS; ROI.
Colls: Sheffield.

ROBERTSON, James   of Constantinople
Amateur artist and photographer. He contributed an illustration of the Crimea to *The Illustrated London News* in 1855 and produced daguerrotype pictures of the War after Roger Fenton the photographer left the front. After the War he worked with Felice Beato and became an official British photographer. Drawings based on his photographs appeared in *The Illustrated Times*, 1856.
Bibl: *The Camera Goes to War*, Scottish Arts Council, 1974-75, p.58.

ROBERTSON, Walford Graham   RBA ROI   1867-1948
Portrait and landscape painter, illustrator and designer. He was born in 1867 and educated at Slough and Eton. He studied art at South Kensington with Albert Moore and became a member of the NEA, 1891, the RBA in 1896 and the ROI in 1910. Robertson was part of the talented group of artists and illustrators who flourished in London in the 1890s, his portrait was painted by Sargent and he claimed to have been influenced by W. Crane and the Glasgow School and must have admired W. Nicholson (q.v.).
Illus: *Old English Songs and Dances [1903]; A Masque of May Morning [1904]; The Napoleon of Notting Hill [G.K. Chesterton, 1904]; Chansons de L'Ancienne France [Bibliophiles Indépendants Chez H.Fleury, Paris, 1905, limited edn.]; Gold, Frankinsense and Myrhh and other Pageants for a Baby Girl [1906]; A Year of Songs; The Baby's Day Book; Wind in the Willows [Kenneth Grahame, 1908 (frontis)]; Old Fashioned Fairy Tales [n.d.].*
Contrib: *The English Illustrated Magazine [1896].*
Exhib: B; G; GG; L; M; NEA; New Gall; RA; RBA; ROI.
Bibl: 'The Illustrated Books and Paintings of WGR', by T.M. Wood, *The Studio*, Vol.36, pp.99-107 illus; *Modern Book Illustrators and Their Work*, Studio, 1914; *Time Was*, a book of Memories, WGR, n.d.; *The Last Romantics*, Barbican Gallery cat., 1989, pp.97-98; Simon Houfe, *Fin de Siècle*, 1992, pp.123, 124.
See illustration.

ROBINSON, C.   -1881
Illustrator and engraver. He was born in London, the son of a wood engraver and book binder and was apprenticed to the firm of Maclure, Macdonald and Macgregor, lithographers before joining *The Illustrated London News* in about 1862. He had attended Finsbury School of Art in about 1857, winning a silver medal in the National Competition. He contributed regular and rather wooden work to *The 'News* until his death and also to *The Illustrated Times* in 1865. He was the uncle of Charles, T.H. and W. Heath Robinson (qq.v.).
Bibl: L. de Freitas, *Charles Robinson*, Academy Edit, 1976.

ROBINSON, Charles   RI   1870-1937
Painter in watercolours, illustrator and decorator. He was born in London on 22 October 1870, the son of Thomas Robinson, wood engraver, and nephew of C. Robinson (q.v.). He was educated at Islington High School and Highbury School of Art, but spells at the RA Schools were abandoned for lack of finance, 1892. He was then apprenticed to Waterlow & Sons as a lithographic artist but came to the fore in 1895 when his drawings were published in *The Studio* and he was asked to design for R.L. Stevenson's A *Child's Garden of Verses*. Robinson, in company with his brothers T.H. and W. Heath Robinson (qq.v.), became one of the most popular Edwardian black and white artists. His style was very decorative, flowing and imaginative scenes were surrounded by elaborate borders and in the faces and forms of his children he recaptured something of the innocence of childhood. His drawings were partly inspired by the prints of Dürer, partly by the Pre-Raphaelites, their space often suggestive of Japanese prints. But he was no copyist and his colouring and fantasy are often highly original, perhaps based on his lack of formal training. He was elected President of the London Sketch Club, and was elected RI in 1932. He died in Buckinghamshire on 13 June 1937.
Illus: *Come Ye Apart [Sunday School Union, 1894]; Aesops Fables; A Child's Garden of Verses [R.L. Stevenson]; The Infant Reader; The First Primer; The Second Primer [1895]; Animals in the Wrong Places [E. Carrington]; The Child World [G. Setoun]; Christmas Dreams [Awfly Weirdly]; Make Believe [H.D. Lowry]; Minstrel Dick [C.R. Coleridge, 1896]; Dobbie's Little Master [Mrs. A. Bell]; Lullaby Land [E. Field]; Cranford [Mrs Gaskell, 1897]; King Longbeard [B. MacGregor]; Lilliput Lyrics [W.D. Rands]; Richard Wagner and The Ring [1898]; Fairy Tales From Hans Christian Andersen [With T.H. and W.H.]; The New Noah's Ark [J.J. Bell]; Pierrette [H. de V. Stacpoole]; The Suitors of Aprille [N. Garstin, 1899]; The Adventures of Odysseus [Homer]; Child Voices [W.E. Cule]; Jack of All Trades [J.J. Bell]; The Little Lives of the Saints [P. Dearmer]; The Master Mosaic Workers [G. Sand]; Sintram and His Companions [de la Motte Fouqué]; Tales of Passed Times [C. Perrault]; The True Annals of Fairyland [Ed. W. Canton, 1900]; A*

Book of Days For Little Ones [C. Bridgman]; The Farm Book [W. Copeland]; The Mother's Book of Song [J.H. Burn]; Nonsense! Nonsense! [W. Jerrold]; The Shopping Day [C. Bridgman]; Stories For Children [Charles and Mary Lamb]; The True Annals of Fairyland [J.M. Gibbon, 1901]; The Bairns Coronation Book [C. Bridgman]; The Book of the Zoo [W. Copeland]; The Coronation Autograph Book [1902]; The Big Book of Nursery Rhymes [W. Jerrold]; Fireside Saints [D. Jerrold]; The New Testament of Our Lord...[1903]; Siegfried [Baring Gould, 1904]; The Black Cat Book [W. Copeland]; A Bookful of Fun; The Book of Ducks and Dutchies [W. Copeland]; A Book of The Dutch Dolls [W. Copeland]; The Book of the Fan [W. Copeland]; The Book of the Little Dutch Dots [W. Copeland]; The Book of the Little J.Ds [W. Copeland]; The Book of the Mandarinfants [W. Copeland]; The Cloud Kingdom [I.H. Wallis]; The Ten Little Babies [1905]; Awful Airship [W. Copeland]; Baby Town Ballads [Netta]; The Books of Dolly's Doings [W. Copeland]; The Book of Dolly's House [W. Copeland]; The Book of Dollyland [W. Copeland]; Bouncing Babies [W. Copeland]; The Child's Christmas [E. Sharp]; Fanciful Fowls; A Little Book of Courtesies [K. Tynan]; Mad Motor [W. Copeland]; Peculiar Piggies; Road, Rail & Sea [C. Jerrold]; The Silly Submarine [W. Copeland, 1906]; Alice's Adventures in Wonderland [L. Carroll]; Black Bunnies; Black Doggies; Black Sambos; The Cake Shop [W. Copeland]; Prince Babillon [Netta]; Songs of Love and Praise [A. Matheson]; The Story of the Weathercock [E. Sharp]; The Sweet Shop [W. Copeland]; The Toy Shop [W. Copeland, 1907]; Babes and Blossoms [W. Copeland]; The Book of Other People [W. Copeland]; The Book of Sailors [W. Copeland]; The Book of Soldiers [W. Copeland]; A Child's Garden of Verses [R.L. Stevenson]; The Fairies Fountain [Countess Cesaresco]; Songs of Happy Childhood [I. Maunder, 1908]; Babes and Birds [J. Pope]; The Vanishing Princess [N. Syrett, 1909]; Brownikins and Other Fancies [R. Arkwright]; Grimm's Fairy Tales; In The Beginning [S.B. Macy, 1910]; The Baby Scouts [J. Pope]; The Big Book of Fairy Tales [W. Jerrold]; The Secret Garden [F. Hodgson Burnett]; The Sensitive Plant [P.B. Shelly, 1911]; Babes and Beasts [J. Pope]; Bee: The Princess of the Dwarfs [A. France]; The Big Book of Fables [W. Jerrold]; The Four Gardens [Handasyde]; Longfellow [M. MacLeod]; Old Time Tales [Ed. L. Marsh]; Songs of Innocence [W. Blake, 1912]; A Child's Book of Empire [A.T. Morris]; Fairy Tales [C. Perrault]; The Happy Prince [O. Wilde]; Margaret's Book [Fielding-Hall]; The Open Window [E. T. Thurston]; Rainbows [M. Dykes Spicer]; Topsy Turvy [W.J. Minnion, 1913]; Our Sentimental Garden [A. & E. Castle, 1914]; Arabian Nights; The Open Window [E.T. Thurston]; Rip Van Winkle [W. Irving]; Robert Herrick; The Songs and Sonnets of Shakespeare; What Happened At Christmas [E. Sharp. 1915]; Bridget's Fairies [Mrs. S. Stevenson, 1919]; Songs of Happy Childhood [I. Maunder]; Teddy's Year With the Fairies [M.E. Gullick, 1920]; The Children's Garland of Verses [G. Rhys]; Father Time Stories [J.G. Stevenson, 1921]; Doris and David All Alone [E. Marc]; The Goldfish Bowl [P. Austin, 1922]; Wee Men [B. Girvin & M. Cosens, 1923]; Once On A Time [A.A. Milne, 1925]; The Saint's Garden [W. Radcliffe, 1927]; Mother Goose Nursery Rhymes; The Rubaiyat of Omar Khayyam [1928]; Granny's Book of Fairy Stories [1930]; Young Hopeful [1932].

Contrib: *Black & White [1895]; The Yellow Book [1896]; ILN [1912]; The Graphic [1915]; The Queen.*
Exhib: G; L; RA; RI.
Colls: V & AM.
Bibl: *The Studio,* Vol.63, pp.150-151, illus; R.E.D. Sketchley, *Eng. Bk. Illus.,* 1903, pp.102, 114, 169; *Modern Book Illustrators and Their Work,* Studio, 1914; L. de Freitas, *CR,* Academy Edit., 1976.
See illustration (colour).

ROBINSON, Frederick Cayley ARA   **1862-1927**
Painter, illustrator and poster artist. He was born at Brentford on Thames on 18 August 1862 and after being educated at the Lycée de Pau, studied art at the St Johns Wood and RA Schools. He lived on a yacht, 1888-90 and studied at Julian's 1890-92, later studying in Italy. He became Professor of figure composition and decoration at Glasgow, 1914-24 and was elected ARA in 1921. He had been RBA since 1890 and NEA since 1912. Robinson's style of work was based on Italian quattrocento sources and was not best adapted to the book. He did however, illustrate *The Book of Genesis* for the Riccardi Press in 1914. He died in London on 4 January 1927.

Exhib: G; L; M; NEA; New Gall; RA; RBA; ROI; RSA; RSW, RWS.
Colls: BM; Fitzwilliam; Manchester.
Bibl: *FCR,* FAS Cat.,1969, 1977; *The Studio,* Vol.31, 1904, pp.235-241 illus.
See illustration (colour).
See Horne

ROBINSON, Gordon   **fl.1905-1913**
Illustrator of children's books. He illustrated *Puss in Boots* in about 1905 and contributed to *The Illustrated London News,* 1908-13 in the style of J. Hassall (q.v.).

ROBINSON, H.R.
Contributor of cartoon to *Punch,* 1864.

ROBINSON, Joseph   **fl.1882-1885**
Landscape painter working in London. He contributed a view of Thanet to *The Illustrated London News,* 1885.
Exhib: RI.

ROBINSON, Ruth H.
Amateur illustrator. *The Studio* book illustration competition 1897 shows her work.

WALFORD GRAHAM ROBERTSON RBA ROI 1867-1948. 'The Man Whom The Trees Loved'. Illustration in *The Studio,* 1914

ROBINSON, Miss S.A.H.   **fl.1890-1902**
Illustrator. She contributed to the *Daily Graphic*, c.1890 and to *The Graphic*, 1902.

ROBINSON, Thomas
Wood engraver and illustrator, probably the father of C., T.H. and W. Heath Robinson (qq.v.). Worked chiefly for *The Penny Illustrated Paper*, contributed to *Dark Blue*, 1871-73.

ROBINSON, Thomas Heath   **fl.1890-1902**
Black and white artist and illustrator. He was the son of Thomas Robinson (q.v.) and elder brother of C. and W. Heath Robinson (qq.v.). He studied with his father and by 1896 had an extensive output among the magazines and was developing as a designer of bookplates.
Illus: *Old World Japan [1895]; Legends From River and Mountain [1896]; Cranford [Mrs Gaskell, 1896]; Henry Esmond [W.M. Thackeray, 1896]; The Scarlet Letter [Hawthorne, 1897]; A Sentimental Journey [Sterne, 1897]; Hymn on the Morning of Christ's Nativity [1897]; A Child's Book of Saints [1898]; The Heroes [Kingsley, 1899]; Fairy Tales From The Arabian Nights [1899]; Fairy Tales from Hans Andersen [1899]; A Book of French Songs For The Young [1899]; Lichtenstein [1900]; The Scottish Chiefs [1900].*
Contrib: *Cassell's Family Magazine [1898-99]; The Windmill [1899]; The Quiver [1900]; The Idler; The Pall Mall Magazine.*
Bibl: R.E.D. Sketchley, *Eng. Bk. Illus.*, 1903, pp.114, 170.
See Horne

ROBINSON, Will B.   **fl.1892-1902**
Architectural draughtsman and illustrator. He was working in Lincoln's Inn, London in 1902 and specialised in industrial subjects, views of international exhibitions and decorations.
Contrib: *ILN [1892-1900]; The English Illustrated Magazine [1895-97].*

ROBINSON, William Heath   **1872-1944**
Black and white artist and illustrator, the only British illustrator to become a 'household name'. He was born in London on 31 May 1872, the son of Thomas Robinson (q.v.) and younger brother of C. and T.H. Robinson (qq.v.). He was educated in Islington and studied at the RA Schools before beginning to draw for the publishers. His earliest work was conventional book illustration very much in the idiom of his brother Charles and it was only with the approach of the First World War that the Robinson fantasy developed in him as a passion for mad machinery. His pen and ink drawings of inventions and contraptions were ideally suited to the industrial age and were in some ways the visual counterparts to Lewis Carroll's prose, having as their base a kind of perverse logic. With his success, Robinson was imitated and taken into the language as the arch-priest of scatter-brained improvisation. He expanded into stage design and had a large following abroad.
Illus: *The Pilgrim's Progress [1897]; Don Quixote [1897]; The Giant Crab [1897]; Danish Fairy Tales [1897]; Arabian Nights [1899]; The Talking Thrush [Rouse, 1899]; Tales For Toby [1900]; Uncle Lubin [1902]; Bill the Minder [1912]; Rabelais; Twelfth Night; A Song of the English [Rudyard Kipling]; Kipling's Collected Verse; A Midsummer Night's Dream [1914]; The Water Babies; Perrault's Tales; Peacock Pie [Walter de la Mare].*
Contrib: *The Sketch; The Bystander; The Graphic [1910-]; The Illustrated Sporting & Dramatic News; London Opinion; Puck; The Strand Magazine; The Quiver, The Sportsman and Humorist [1931].*
Exhib: FAS, 1924; RA (Memorial Exhib, FAS 1945).
Colls: BM; V & AM.
Bibl: A E. Johnson, *WHR*, Brush, Pen and Pencil series, 1913; *My Line of Life by WHR*, 1938; Langton Day, *The Art and Life of WHR*, 1947; Beare, Geoffrey, *The Illustrations of WH*, 1983; Simon Houfe, 'Journeys, Oracles & Strange Herbs', Heath Robinson's Rabelais, *CL*, 22 Oct. 1984.
See Horne
See illustration.

ROBLEY, Major-General Horatio Gordon   **1840-1930**
Amateur black and white artist. He was born at Funchal, Madeira on

28 June 1840 the son of Capt. J.H. Robley and served as a professional soldier in Burma, 1859-63, the Maori War, 1864-66, in Zululand, 1884 and Ceylon, 1886-87. He was one of a number of artists who sent suggestions to Charles Keene (q.v.) and some of his drawings were improved by Keene for *Punch*. Robley was well-known for his collection of preserved and tattooed Maori heads! He died on 29 October 1930.
Contrib: *Punch [1873 78]; The Graphic; ILN.*
Bibl: G.S. Layard, *Charles Keene*, 1892, p.179.

ROE, Fred   **RI**   **1864-1947**
Genre painter and illustrator. He was born in 1864, the son of Robert Henry Roe, landscape and miniature painter and studied at Heatherley's and with J. Seymour Lucas (q.v.). He was elected RBA in 1895 and RI in 1909. Roe, who became a leading expert and collector of antique furniture, wrote many articles for art magazines and died in Londonin 1947.
Illus: *Ancient Coffers and Cupboards [1902]; Vanishing England [1910]; Old Oak Furniture; A History of Oak Furniture [1920].*
Contrib: *Fun [1892]; Judy [1895].*
Exhib: B; L; M; RA; RBA; RI; ROI; RWA.
Colls: Greenwich; V & AM.

ROE, John, of Warwick
Landscape painter and topographer in watercolours. He worked chiefly in the Midlands and drew ruins, exhibiting at the RA and the Society of Artists. He was still active in 1812.
Illus: *Warwick Castle, a Poem [1812].*
Contrib: *Antiquarian and Topographical Cabinet [1811].*
Colls: BM; Coventry; V & AM.

ROFFE, F.
Illustrator. Contributed drawings of modern sculpture to *The Art Journal*, 1862-71 and 1891.
Colls: V & AM.

ROGERS, James Edward   **RHA**   **1838-1896**
Architectural and marine painter. He was born in Dublin in 1838 and practised as an architect before giving this up to become a watercolourist. He was elected ARHA in 1871, RHA in 1872 and moved to London in 1876. He died on 18 February 1896.
Illus: *More's Ridicula; Ridicula Rediviva; The Fairy Book [Miss Mulock, c.1870].*
Contrib: *The English Illustrated Magazine [1893-94].*
Exhib: L; RA; RE; RHA; RI; ROI.
Colls: Nat. Gall., Dublin.

ROGERS, W.A.
Genre illustrator. Illustrated *City Legends* by Will Carleton, 1889 and contributed to *The Graphic*, 1887.

ROGERS, William Harry   **1825-1873**
Illustrator and designer. He was the son of W.G. Rogers and specialised in ornament, emblems and designs based on German books of the 16th century. He worked at Wimbledon and died there in 1873.
Illus: *Poems and Songs [Robert Burns, 1858]; Quarle's Emblems [c.1861]; Spiritual Conceits [c.1862]; Poe's Poetical Works [1858]; The Merchant of Venice [1860].*
Bibl: Chatto & Jackson, *Treatise on Wood Eng.*, 1861, p.600; Ruari McLean, *Victorian Book Design*, 1972, pp.145-146, illus.

ROLLER, George R.   **RPE**   **1858-**
Domestic and portrait painter and illustrator. He was born in 1858 and studied at Lambeth School of Art and in Paris under Bouguereau and Fleury. He was the designer of advertisements for Burberry's for thirty years and also picture restorer at the RA. He worked at Basingstoke, 1889 to 1914 and in London from 1925. He was elected RE, 1885.
Contrib: *Black & White [1894]; Pick-Me-Up; The Pall Mall Magazine; Fun [1901].*
Exhib: FAS; L; RA; RBA; RE; ROI.

ROLLESTON, D.
Marine illustrator. Contributed to *The English Illustrated Magazine*, 1895.

WILLIAM HEATH ROBINSON 1872-1944. 'Inspecting Stockings on Christmas Eve'. Original drawing for illustration in *The Sketch*. Pen and ink and wash. Signed in full. 15¾in x 11¼in (40cm x 28.6cm)

Victoria and Albert Museum

ROLLINSON, Sunderland   **1872-**
Painter, etcher and lithographer. He was born at Knaresborough in 1872 and studied at Scarborough School of Art and at the RCA. In his student years he contributed a number of landscape illustrations with enormous foregrounds to the National Competitions and *The Studio* book illustration competitions. He was working at Fulham, 1902 and at Cottingham, Yorks, 1914 to 1925, he married the artist Beatrice Malam.
Exhib: G; L; RA; RBA; RI; RSA.
Bibl: *The Studio*, Vol.11, 1897, p.261 illus.; Vol.14, 1898, p.144 illus.; Winter No., 1900-01, p.60 illus.

ROLT, Charles   **fl.1845-1867**
Figure artist working at Merton and in Bloomsbury. He illustrated *The Sermon on The Mount*, 1861 (chromo-liths).
Exhib: BI; RA; RBA.

ROOKE, Noel   **1881-1953**
Painter, engraver and book illustrator and decorator. He was born in 1881, the son of T.M. Rooke, portrait painter. He studied at the Slade School and at the Central School of Arts and Crafts, becoming the Head of the School of Book Production there. He was elected ARE in 1920 and died in 1953.

Illus: An Inland Voyage [R.L. Stevenson, 1913]; Travels with a Donkey [R.L. Stevenson, 1913].
Exhib: NEA; RA; RE.
See Horne

ROOS, Eva   **1872-**
Portrait and figure painter, black and white illustrator of children's books. She was born in London and studied at Colarossi's and Delecluse's in Paris. Married to the distinguished animal painter S.H. Vedder (q.v.). She illustrated *Lullabies & Baby Songs* for J.M. Dent, 1900.
Contrib: *The Graphic [1910].*
Exhib: B; L; M; RA; ROI.

ROPE, George Thomas   **1845-1929**
Landscape and animal painter. He was born at Blaxhall, Suffolk in 1845 and became a pupil of the landscape painter W.J. Webbe, visiting the Continent in 1882. He worked for most of his life at Wickham Market and excelled as a pencil artist. He died in 1929.
Illus: *Sketches of Farm Favourites [1881]; Country Sights and Sounds [1915].*
Exhib: L; RA.

ROSE, Robert Traill   **1863-1942**
Painter, designer and lithographer. He was born at Newcastle-upon-Tyne in 1863 and studied at the Edinburgh School of Art. He worked chiefly in Edinburgh and Tweedsmuir and produced a series of fine symbolic illustrations to *The Book of Job*, c.1912. He died at Edinburgh 3 December 1942.
Illus: *Rubaiyat of Omar Khayyam [Jack edition, c.1909].*
Exhib: G; L; RSA; RSW.
Bibl: The *Studio*, Vol.55, 1912, p.312 illus.; *Modern Book Illustrators and Their Work*, Studio, 1914.

ROSS, Charles H.   **fl.1867-1883**
Dramatist, novelist and illustrator. He was employed in the Civil Service at Somerset House and began to write and draw in his free time. He was brought to the notice of William Tinsley, the publisher, who gave him two Christmas annuals to edit describing him as a 'very clever, but very nervous young man'. Ross's facility with writing and drawing won him the Editorship of *Judy* where many of his quips and drawings were published in the years 1867-78. Dalziel mentions that they were 'generally signed "Marie Duval", his wife's maiden name and the subjects often savoured somewhat of a French origin'. His small lively figures were full of humour but not great satiric art although they had in them the makings of real satire. One such was a large-headed man who became Ally Sloper and was taken to great heights by the artist W.G. Baxter (q.v.). Ross was also the proprietor of *C.H. Ross's Variety Paper*.
Illus: *Queens and Kings and Other Things; The Boy Crusoe; Merry Conceits and Whimsical Rhymes written and drawn by CHR [1st edition, 1866, reprinted 1883].*
Contrib: *Every Boy's Magazine.*
Bibl: W. Tinsley, *Random Recollections*, 1900, pp.267-268; The Brothers Dalziel, *A Record of Work, 1840-1890*, 1901, p.320.

ROSS, Sir John   **1777-1856**
Arctic explorer. He was born at Inch, Wigtonshire in 1777 and joined the East India Company in 1794 and the Royal Navy in 1805. He was commander in the Baltic and North Sea in 1812-17 and made his famous expeditions in search of the North-West Passage in 1818 and 1829-33. He was consul at Stockholm, 1839-46 and Rear-Admiral, 1834. He died in London in 1856.
Illus: *A Voyage of Discovery [1819, AT 634]; Narrative of a Second Voyage in Search of a North-West Passage [1835, AT 636].*
Colls: BM; Greenwich.

ROSS, Robert Thorburn ARSA   **1816-1876**
Painter of genre subjects and portraits. He was born at Edinburgh and was a pupil of Sir William Allan. He was elected ARSA in 1852 and RSA is 1869.
Illus: *The History of a Pin [E.M.S., 1862]* (Nimmo, the illus. in sepia print).
Exhib: RA; RSA; SS.

ROSSETTI, Dante Gabriel   **1828-1882**
Painter, poet and occasional illustrator. He was born in London on 12 May 1828, the son of Gabriel Rossetti, an Italian refugee and Professor of Italian at King's College. He was educated at King's College, studied drawing under J.S. Cotman (q.v.) and in 1845 entered the RA Schools, going in 1848 into the studio of Ford Madox Brown (q.v.). It was this meeting and later those with Millais and Holman Hunt (qq.v.) that caused the foundation of the Pre-Raphaelite Brotherhood of which Rossetti was the mainstay. The movement, which lasted from 1848 until 1853, was to have repercussions right through the Victorian age, although it was first met with hostility. From 1857-58, vhen Edward Burne-Jones helped him with the decoration of the Oxford Union, Rossetti was much involved with the younger Pre-Raphaelite followers and poets and craftsman like William Morris (q.v.). His model, Elizabeth Siddal, whom he married in 1860, was the source of much of his inspiration in both painting and poetry, most of his important illustration was done prior to her death in 1862.

Rossetti can be seen as a larger than life influence on the later illustrators although his own contribution was small. He provided much of the hot imagery and passion in the decade following which made the 1860s memorable in book art. Rossetti lived for some time at 16 Cheyne Walk, Chelsea with W.M. Rossetti, A.C. Swinburne and George Meredith. He died at Birchington, Sussex on 9 April 1882 and was buried there.
Illus: The *Music Master [William Allingham, 1855]; Tennyson's Poems [Moxon Edition, 1857]; The Goblin Market [Christina Rossetti, 1862]; The Prince's Progress and other Poems [Christina Rossetti, 1866]; Flower Pieces [1888]; Early Italian Poets [n.d (unused frontis)]: The Risen Life [R.C. Jackson, 1884 (cov. & frontis.)*
Exhib: London, 1849-50.
Colls: BM, Birmingham; V & M.
Bibl: W.M. Rossetti, *DGR his Family Letters*, 1895; F.M. Hueffer, *R, A Critical Essay*, 1902; H.C. Marillier, *R*, 1904; Surtees, *DGR*, 1971; *DGR, Painter and Poet*, RA Cat., Jan.-March, 1973; Gordon N. Ray, *The Illustrator and The Book in England*, 1976, pp.101-103 illus.; *The Pre-Raphaelites*, Tate Gallery, 1984; *Pre-Raphaelite Papers*, 1984, pp.170-183.
See illustrations.

ROSSITER, Charles   **1827-c.1890**
Genre painter. He was born in 1827 and taught painting. He married in 1860 Miss Frances Fripp Seares, the artist.
Contrib: *Passages From Modern English Poets [Junior Etching Club, 1862].*
Exhib: L; M; RA; RBA.

ROTHENSTEIN, Sir William   **1872-1945**
Painter and portrait artist. He was born at Bradford, Yorks in 1872 and educated at Bradford Grammar School and studied at the Slade School and at Julians, Paris, 1889-93. He made his debut as a draughtsman at Oxford in 1893, when he drew its celebrities. His portrait drawings are very French in treatment and some have a decidedly Whistlerish feel to them. Rothenstein travelled to India in 1910 and was Official War Artist, 1917-18 and to the Canadian Occupation, 1919. From 1917 to 1926 he was Professor of Civic Art at Sheffield University and Principal of the RCA, 1920-35. He was elected NEA, 1894, RP, 1897 and was knighted in 1931. He died in 1945.
Illus: *Oxford Characters, A Series of Lithographed Portraits by Will Rothenstein [1894]; English Portraits [1898]; Manchester Portraits [1899]; Liber Juniorum [1899]; The French Set and Portraits of Verlaine [1898]; Six Portraits of Sir Rabindranath Tagore [1915]; Twenty-Four Portraits [1920]; Twenty-Four Portraits, 2nd Series [1923].*
Contrib: *The Yellow Book; The Savoy [1896]; The Quarto [1898]; The Page [1899]; The Dome [1899].*
Exhib: B; FAS; G; GG; L; M; NEA; P; RA; RHA; RSA; RSW.
Colls: Liverpool; Tate.
Bibl: Robert Speaight, *WR, The Portrait of an Artist in His Time*, 1962.

ROUNTREE, Harry   **1878-1950**
Illustrator in black and white and colour. He was born in Auckland,

DANTE GABRIEL ROSSETTI 1828-1882. Design for frontispiece to *The Early Italian Poets*, 1861, unused. Pen and ink over pencil. 6in x 4⅞in (15.2cm x 12.4cm)   Marshall Collection

New Zealand in 1878 and was educated at Queen's College, Auckland. He came to London in 1901 and studied with Percival Gaskell at the Regent Street Polytechnic before getting commissions through the Editor of *Little Folks*. Rountree's métier was always comic animals and books for children although he undertook a certain amount of poster work. His drawings are characterised by subtle colours and fluid washes with a great accuracy of natural background.
Illus: *The Magic Wand [1908]; The Wonderful Isles [1908]; Peep in the World [F.E. Crichton, 1908]; Alice's Adventures in Wonderland [1908].*
Contrib: *Little Folks; The Strand Magazine; Punch [1905-09, 1914]; The Graphic [1906, 1911]; ILN [1911].*
Bibl: *Modern Book Illustrators and Their Work*, Studio, 1914; *HR and His Work, The Art of the Illustrator*, P.V. Bradshaw, 1916.
See Horne

ROUSE, Robert William Arthur RBA   **fl.1883-1927**
Landscape painter, etcher. He worked in Surrey, Buckinghamshire and Oxfordshire and was elected RBA in 1889. He illustrated a series of articles by W. Raymond in *The Idler* called 'The Idler out-of-doors' and contributed to *The Windsor Magazine.*
Exhib: G; L; M; RA; RBA; RHA; RI; ROI; RSA.

ROWLAND, Ralph
Humorous illustrator. Contributed golf sketches to *Punch*, 1905.

ROWLANDSON, George Derville   **1861-**
Sporting illustrator. He was born in India in 1861 and studied art in Gloucester, Westminster and Paris. He worked in Bedford Park and the majority of his contributions are military or equestrian. He signs

his work GDR.
Contrib: *ILN [1897-1900]; The English Illustrated Magazine [1899-1900].*
Exhib: RI.

ROWLANDSON, Thomas   **1756-1827**
Watercolour painter, illustrator and social caricaturist. He was born in London in 1756, the son of a bankrupt merchant and was educated at Dr Barrow's School and at the RA Schools, which he entered in 1772. He made visits to Paris in 1774 and 1777 to visit relatives and the rococo delicacy of his pen and wash drawings probably owes something to this French connection. Rowlandson hereafter made extensive journeys on the Continent to France, Italy, Germany and Holland and in Great Britain, filling notebooks with a mixture of grotesque humanity and sylvan ideal landscapes. He often travelled with other caricaturists, notably, H. Wigstead and J. Nixon (q.v.). His work is always tinted pen drawing rather than full-scale watercolour, but he changed his humorous style to do drawings after the Old Masters and figures reminiscent of Thomas Gainsborough. He was one of the major caricaturists to become an extensive book illustrator, particularly in his work for Ackermann from 1798 in *The Tours of Dr. Syntax* and *The Microcosm of London,* 1808. In later life, Rowlandson's quality of work tailed off, a not surprising feature of someone who was a gambler, dissolute and naturally lazy. The later drawings often show a sloppiness and lack of interest in the subject and as countless versions of one subject exist this is not wholly surprising. The artist was extensively faked, but these copies tend to be wooden ; although the signature is often convincing. He died in London in 1827.
Illus: *Poems of Peter Pindar [1786-92]; Tom Jones [Fielding, Edinburgh, 1791 and 1805]; Joseph Andrews [Fielding, 1793]; Siebald [Smollett, 1793]; Humphrey Clinker [Smolett, 1793]; The Beauties of Sterne [1800]; Remarks On a Tour to North and South Wales in the Year 1797 [1800]; Matrimonial Comforts [1800]; Country Characters [1800]; Jones's Bardic Museum [1802]; A Compendious Treatise On Modern Education [1802]; Pleasures of Human Life [1807]; The Microcosm of London [1808]; Smollett's Miscellaneous Works [1809]; Poetical Magazine [1808-11];*

DANTE GABRIEL ROSSETTI 1828-1882. 'The Lady of Shalott'. An illustration for *Moxon's Tennyson*, 1857. Wood engraving

Beauties of Tom Brown [1809]; Gambado [1809]; Baron Munchausen's Surprising Adventures [1809]; Antidote to The Miseries of Human Life [Beresford, 1809]; Advice to Sportsmen [1809]; Rowlandson's Sketches From Nature [1809]; Views in Cornwall, Devon...; The Art of Ingeniously Tormenting [1809]; Annals of Sporting [1809]; The Trial of the Duke of York [1809]; Chesterfield Burlesqued [1811]; The Tour of Dr Syntax in Search of the Picturesque [1812]; Petticoat Loose [1812]; Poetical Sketches of Scarborough [1813]; Letters From Italy [Engelbach, 1813]; The Military Adventures of Johnny Newcome [1815]; Naples and the Campagna [Engelbach, 1815]; The Dance of Death [1815]; The Grand Master [1816]; Figure Subjects For Landscapes [1816]; Relics of a Saint [1816]; Vicar of Wakefield [Goldsmith, 1817]; The Dance of Life [1817]; Grotesque Drawing Book; World in Miniature [1817]; Thc Second Tour of Dr Syntax [1820]; Rowlandson's Characteristic Sketches of the Lower Orders [1820]; Voyage du Docteur Syntaxe [1821]; Journal of Sentimental Travels in the Southern Provinces of France [1821]; The History of Johnny Quae Genus [1822]; The Third Tour of Dr Syntax: In Search of a Wife [1822]; Die Reise des Doktor Syntax [1822]; Crimes of the Clergy [1822]; The Spirit of the Public Journals [1823-25]; Bernard Blackmantle, English Spy [18251; The Humorist [1831].

Exhib: RA; Soc. of Artists.
Colls: Aberdeen; Ashmolean; Bedford; Birmingham; BM; Fitzwilliam; Leeds; Manchester; Mellon Coll; Wakefield; V & AM.
Bibl: Joseph Grego, *R, The Caricaturist*, 1880; A.P. Oppé, *TR, Drawings and Watercolours*, 1923; O. Sitwell, *TR*, 1929; F.G. Roe, *TR*, 1947; A.W. Heintzelman, *Watercolour Drawings of TR*, 1947; A. Bury, *R Drawings*, 1949; B. Falk, *TR, Life and Art*, 1949; J. Hayes, *R*, 1972; R. Paulson, *R, A New Interpretation*, 1972.
See illustration (colour).

ROWLEY, The Hon. Hugh   1833-1908

Flower painter and amateur illustrator. He was born in 1833, the son of the 2nd Baron Langford. He was educated at Eton and Sandhurst, taking a commission in 10th Lancers, 1852 and retiring in 1854. He lived at Westfield House, Brighton and was the author of various humorous publications and Editor of a shortlived magazine, *Puniana*. He died on 12 May 1908.
Illus: *Gamosagamnon or Hints on Hymen [1870].*
Contrib: *London Society [1867].*
Exhib: RA, 1866.
Bibl: James Edward Holroyd, 'Victorian Punster at Play', *CL*, 9 Dec. 1982.

ROYLE, C.   RN

Amateur illustrator. He contributed a drawing to *The Illustrated London News*, 1859.

RUDGE, Bradford   1805-1885

Landscape painter and teacher. He was the son of Edward Rudge, a competent Midlands artist who taught at Rugby School. He settled at Bedford in 1837, having been an unsuccessful candidate for the NWS that year, and became the first drawing-master on the staff of the Harpur Schools. His early work is more in the tradition of the romantics, his later work very flowery. He painted mostly on the Ouse, in Surrey and in North Wales and retired in 1875, dying at Bedford in 1885.
Illus: *A Short Account of Buckden Palace [1839].*
Exhib: L; RBA; RSA.
Colls: Author; Bedford, Coventry.
Bibl: *Bedfordshire Magazine*, Vol.7, 1960-61, pp. 247-250.

RUSDEN, Athelstan

Cartoonist at Manchester. He worked for *Moonshine* and for *Punch*, 1879.

RUSKIN, John   1819-1900

Poet, painter and critic. He was born in London on 8 February 1819, the son of a Scottish wine importer with artistic inclinations. He studied at King's College, London and learned drawing under Copley Fielding and J.D. Harding (q.v.). He went up to Christ Church, Oxford in 1836 and won the Newdigate Prize three years later, then travelling in Europe, 1840-41. He had become acquainted

with Turner in 1840 and paid his first visit to Venice in 1841, two events which were crucial to his writing career, his championship of Turner and his love of Venetian architecture. He published his first volume of *Modern Painters* in 1843 and the series continued until 1860, by which time he was the leading art critic in the country and a stout defender of the Pre-Raphaelites. In 1869 he was elected Slade Professor of Art at Oxford, where he gave regular lectures until 1884. Ruskin's reforming zeal was demonstrated by his founding of the Guild of St George in 1871 for the 'workmen and labourers of Great Britain'. He went to live at Coniston in 1871 and became more and more a recluse from recurring attacks of brain fever. He died there of pneumonia in 1900.

In spite of his vast literary output, Ruskin did not neglect his own considerable talents as a watercolourist. His pencil drawings of buildings are accurate and delicate, owing something to the work of Harding and Prout, his watercolours very much in the style of Turner, his still-life pictures having a Pre-Raphaelite detail. He was elected HRWS, 1873.

An important collection is being formed at the Ruskin Centre, University of Lancaster.
Illus: *The Seven Lamps of Architecture [14 etched pls., 1849]; The Stones of Venice [1853]; The Poems of John Ruskin [Ed. W.G. Collingwood, 1891]; Poetry of Architecture [1893].*
Exhib: FAS, 1878,1907; RHA; RWS.
Colls: Ashmolean; Birkenhead; Birmingham; BM; Brantwood; Fitzwilliam; Glasgow; Sheffield; V & AM.
Bibl: T.J. Wise and J.P. Smart, *Biography*, 1893; W.G. Collingwood, *The Art Teaching of JR*, 1891; J.H. Whitehouse, *The Painter and His Work at Bembridge*, 1938; P. Quennell, *JR*, 1949; J. Evans, *JR*, 1954; K. Clark, *Ruskin Today*, 1964; Mary Lutyens, *Effie in Venice*, 1965; *Brantwood* Ruskin catalogue (Assoc. of Liberal Education), n.d.; M. Lutyens, *Millais and the Ruskins*, 1967; P.H. Walton, *The Drawings of JR*, 1972; Mary Lutyens, *The Ruskins and The Grays*, 1972; Tim Hilton, *JR The Early Years*, 1985; *Ruskin and the English Watercolour*, Whitworth Art Gallery, 1989.

RUSSELL, Sir Walter Westley   RA RWS   1867-1949

Painter, teacher and illustrator. He was born at Epping in 1867 and studied at the Westminster School of Art under Fred Brown. He was Drawing Teacher at the Slade School from 1895 to 1927 and served with the Camouflage Corps in the First War, 1916-19. Russell was elected ARA in 1920 and RA in 1926. He was Keeper of the RA, 1927-42 and was influential in altering the teaching arrangements of the Schools and in bringing them up to date. He was an important link between the Academy and outsiders like P. Wilson Steer and Henry Tonks who were his friends. He was made CVO in 1931, knighted in 1935 and died on 16 April 1949.
Contrib: *Pick Me Up [1889]; ILN [1892-94]; Daily Chronicle [1895]; The Graphic [1895]; The Yellow Book [1895]; The Quarto [1898]; Lady's Pictorial; The Pall Mall Magazine.*
Exhib: G; GG; L; M; NEA; P; RA; RHA; RSW; RWS.
Colls: V & AM.
See illustration.

RUTHERSTON, Albert Daniel   1881-1953

Artist, stage designer and illustrator. He was born in Bradford on 5 December 1881, the son of M. Rothenstein and brother of Sir W. Rothenstein (q.v.). He was educated at Bradford Grammar School and studied at the Slade School, 1898-1902 and became Visiting Teacher at Camberwell School of Arts and Crafts and Ruskin Master of Drawing at Oxford from 1929. He served in the First War with the Northants Regiment in Palestine, 1916-19. Rutherston did a considerable amount of designing for private presses in the 1920s and was responsible for some wrappers, all in the current craze for linear naïvety in startling colours. He was a member of the NEA, 1905 and RWS, 1941.
Publ: *Decoration in the Art of the Theatre; A Memoir of Claude Lovat Fraser [with John Drinkwater]; Sixteen Designs For The Theatre.*
Illus: *The Children's Blue Bird [G. LeBlanc, 1913]; Cymbeline [1923]; The Cresset Herrick; The Soncino Haggadah; A Box of Paints [Geoffrey Scott, 1923]; Sons & Lovers (D.H Lawrence, 1924 (wrappers)]; Yuletide in a Younger World [Thomas Hardy, 1927]; The Passionate Fools [1927 (wrappers)].*

SIR WALTER WESTLEY RUSSELL RA RWS 1867-1949. Mr and Mrs Gladstone at Gorebridge, 4 July 1892. Original drawing for illustration in *The Illustrated London News*, Vol.101, 1892. Black crayon. 8¼in x 7¼in (21cm x 18.4cm)   Victoria and Albert Museum

Contrib: *The Gypsy [1915]; The Broadside; The Chapbook [1921].*
Exhib: Carfax Gall; FAS; G; L; M; NEA; RSA; RWS.
Colls: Ashmolean; V & AM.
See Horne

RUTLAND, Elizabeth   Duchess of   -1825
Amateur artist. She was the daughter of the 5th Earl of Carlisle KG and married the 7th Duke of Rutland in 1799 and became a leader of taste and fashion, extensively altering her husband's home Belvoir Castle. She died on 29 November 1825.
Illus: *Journal of a Short Trip to Paris, 1814, 1815 [AT 106, privately printed].*

RUTLAND, Florence M.
Illustrator. Student of the Birmingham School who contributed to *The Yellow Book,* April 1896.

RUTLAND, Violet Duchess of   1856-1937
Amateur artist. She was born at Wigan, Lancs in 1856, the daughter of Col. the Hon. C.H. Lindsay. She married the 8th Duke of Rutland.
She concentrated on portrait drawings in pencil and chalks but also did sculpture. She died on 27 December 1937. Elected SWA, 1932.
Illus: *Portraits of Men and Women [1899].*
Exhib: FAS; G; GG; L; New Gall; P; RA; RMS; SWA.

RYLAND, Henry RI   1856-1924
Painter and illustrator. He was born at Biggleswade, Bedfordshire in 1856 and became a pupil of Benjamin Constant, Boulanger, Lefebvre and Cormon in Paris. Ryland was a versatile artist and after being strongly influenced by Pre-Raphaelite art, turned his attention to stained glass, decorating and book illustrations as well as to the painting of subject and legend. He was elected RI in 1898 and died in Bedford Park, London on 23 November 1924.
Contrib: *The English Illustrated Magazine.*
Exhib: B; G; GG; L; M; New Gall; RA; RBA; RHA; RI; ROI; RSW.
Colls: Manchester.
Bibl: *Cassells Mag.,* CXCIV; *The Artist,* September 1898, pp.1-9; Simon Houfe, 'A Bedfordshire Pre-Raphaelite', *Beds. Magazine,* No.18, Spring 1982, pp.135-139.

S., C.L.
Unidentified illustrator working about 1900.
Colls: V & AM.

S., M.H.
Unidentified illustrator working in the second half of the 19th century. Contributed to *The Gentleman's Journal and Youth's Miscellany*.
Colls: V & AM.

SABAITIER, Louis Rémy   **fl.1894-1910**
French portrait painter. He was born at Annonay and studied with Gérôme and de Boulanger, exhibiting at the Salon from 1890.
Contrib: *The Graphic [1910]*.

SACHS, William J.
Topographical illustrator. He contributed to *The Illustrated Times*, 1866.

ST CYR   **fl.1912**
Fashion illustrator working in pen and ink and watercolour for magazines, about 1912.
Colls: V & AM.

SANITON, Charles Prosper   RI   1861-1914
Portrait, figure and landscape painter and silver point artist. He was born in London on 23 June 1861 and educated at Hastings, before studying at the Slade School and in Florence and Paris. He held a one man show of silverpoints at the Burlington Gallery in 1892 and exhibited at the Salon from 1889. He was elected RI 1897 and RMS, 1904. Died on 7 December 1914, possibly at New York.
Contrib: *The English Illustrated Magazine [1893-94 (portraits)]*.
Exhib: B; FAS; G; GG; L; M; RA; RI; RMS; ROI.
Colls: V & AM.

SALA, George Augustus Henry   **1828-1896**
Journalist, author and illustrator. He was born in 1828 and educated in Paris before studying drawing in London. He worked as a clerk and a scene painter at the Princess's and Lyceum Theatres before becoming a book illustrator and the Editor of *Chat*. Sala was sent by Dickens to cover the Crimean War on the Russian side in 1856 and contributed artides to *All The Year Round*, 1858. He founded and edited *Temple Bar*, 1860-66 and was a correspondent of *The Illustrated London News*, 1860-86 and of *The Daily Telegraph* in the American Civil War, 1863. In his early days he was a strong opponent of the youthful *Punch*.
Illus: *A Word With Punch [Bunn]; The House That Paxton Built [1851, pull-out book]*.
Contrib: *The Cornhill Magazine [1860]*.
Bibl: *The Life and Adventures of GS*, 2 vols., 1895; Ralph Straus, *GAS*, 1942.

SALMON, J.M. Balliol   **1868-1953**
Artist and illustrator. He was born on 1 June 1868, the son of a surgeon and barrister. He was educated privately and studied art under Fred Brown at the Westminster School and afterwards at

EDWARD LINLEY SAMBOURNE 1844-1910. Initial letter for *Water Babies*.

Julian's in Paris. He was a teacher of drawing for a short time before becoming a full-time illustrator on *The Graphic* in about 1901. He was working in Glasgow in 1914 and at Bedford Park at the time of his death on 3 January 1953. He was one of the best pencil and chalk artists to work for the press in the Edwardian period.
Contrib: *The Quiver [1890]; The Pall Mall Budget [1893]; The New Budget [1895]; The Graphic [1899-1930]; The Sporting and Dramatic News [1900]; Cassell's Family Magazine; The Ludgate Monthly; The Pall Mall Magazine*.

SALT, Henry   **1780-1827**
Topographer. He was born at Lichfield in 1780 and took lessons from J. Glover, J. Farrington and J. Hoppner. He accompanied Lord Mountnorris to India in 1802 as secretary and draughtsman and returned via Egypt and Ethiopia in 1806. He was sent on a diplomatic mission to Ethiopia in 1811 and became Consul-General in Egypt in 1815. He died at Alexandria in 1827.
Illus: *Voyages and Travels to India [Lord Valentia, 1809]; Twenty-Four Views in St Helena [1809]; A Voyage to Abyssinia [1814]*.
Colls: BM; India Office Lib.
Bibl: J.J. Halls, *Life of S*, 1834.

SAMBOURNE, Edward Linley   **1844-1910**
Black and white artist, cartoonist and designer. He was born in London on 4 January 1845 and was educated at the City of London School and Chester College. In 1860 he was apprenticed to a firm of marine engineers and continued in that career until his drawings began to be received by *Punch* in 1867. He under-studied Sir John Tenniel as cartoonist and succeeded him as first cartoonist of the magazine when he retired in January 1901. Sambourne was well-known for the great accuracy of his drawings and the care he took over details of dress and construction. He was an inventive artist who appreciated page design and fantasy although his ink sketches can show a Germanic hardness of line. He was considered by Du

EDWARD LINLEY SAMBOURNE 1844-1910. 'The New Tale of a Tub'. Political cartoon for *Punch*, 20th June 1891. Pen and ink. Signed and dated 1891. 10in x 8in (25.4cm x 20.3cm)

Maurier to be the only artist in London who could draw a top hat correctly! He died in Kensington on 3 August 1910.

Illus: *The Modern Arabian Nights [c.1870]; The New Sandford and Merton [1872]; Our Autumn Holidays on French Rivers [1874]; The Royal Umbrella [1880]; The Water Babies [Charles Kingsley, 1885]; Buz or The Life and Adventures of a Honey Bee [Maurice Nod, 1889]; The Four Georges [W.M. Thackeray, 1894]; The Real Adventures of Robinson Crusoe [1893].*

EDWARD LINLEY SAMBOURNE 1844-1910. 'Falstaff drinking from a tankard with Doll Tearsheet beside him'. Original drawing for illustration. Pen and ink. Signed and dated 1886. 5⅝in x 9¼in (14.3cm x 23.5cm)   Author's Collection

Contrib: *London Society [1868]; ILN [1876]; Good Words [1890]; Black & White [1891]; The Sketch [1893]; The Pall Mall Magazine [1893]; Daily Chronicle [1895]; The Minister [1895].*
Exhib: FAS, 1893; G; L; RA.
Colls: V & AM.
Bibl: M.H. Spielmann, *The History of Punch*, 1895, pp.531-537; *The Studio,* Winter No., 1900-1, p.85 illus.; Shirley Nicholson, *A Victorian Household*, based on the diaries of Marion Sambourne, 1988.
See illustrations.

SAMBOURNE, Maud   **fl.1892-1895**
Illustrator. She was the daughter of Linley Sambourne (q.v.) and contributed occasional drawings to *Punch*, 1892-94.
Contrib: *The Pall Mall Magazine; The Minister.*

SANDERCOCK, Henry Ardmore   **fl.1865-1907**
Marine and landscape painter in watercolour, illustrator. He worked at Bideford, Devon and illustrated for children's stories. He signs his work ⌇
Exhib: L; RA; RBA; RI; RWS.
Colls: Montreal.

SANDERSON, H.   **fl.1862-1865**
Figure artist. He illustrated *Legends from Fairyland,* Holmeden, 1862 and contributed to *London Society,* 1862-63, *The Churchman's Family Magazine,* 1863, *Fun,* 1865.

SANDHEIM, May or Amy   **fl.1908-1929**
Artist and illustrator. She illustrated *The Prince's Progress* by Christina Rossetti in 1908.

SANDS, J.   **fl.1862-1888**
Minor Scottish poet and amateur draughtsman. He was a close friend of Charles Keene (q.v.) whom he first met in 1862. He subsequently went on expeditions in Scotland with Keene in 1869, 1871 and later in the 1870s. Although trained as a solicitor, Sands fancied himself

as an artist and at one time drew for a newspaper in Buenos Aires. He began to contribute to *Punch* in 1870 and continued to do so for a decade, also supplying Keene with material for his jokes. Keene illustrated his *King James Wedding and Other Rhymes*, 1888. He finally broke with *Punch* because he considered that they were more interested in printing the work of Keene's nephew, A. Corbould (q.v.), than his. He became a recluse at Walls, Shetland for the remainder of his life. Signs with an hourglass device.
Publ: *Out of this World or Life in St Kilda [1876].*
Colls: V & AM (album).
Bibl: G.S. Layard, *The Life and Letters of Charles Samuel Keene,* 1892, pp.123-128.

SANDY, A.C.
Illustrator. Contributed to *The Rambler,* 1897; *Moonshine,* 1898; *Fun,* 1899-1901; *Illustrated Bits,* 1900 and *The Sketch* and *Sketchy Bits.*

SANDYS, Frederick Augustus   **1832-1904**
Portrait-draughtsman and illustrator. He was born at Norwich in 1832, the son of a journeyman dyer who had set up as an artist. He showed promise at an early age and was noticed by the Rev. Bulwer and was enabled to attend Norwich Grammar School. He studied also in the newly established Government School of Design there and by the time that he arrived in London in about 1851, had already contributed illustrations to *The Birds of Norfolk* and *The Antiquities of Norwich.* He worked for wood engravers but showed his first picture, a portrait at the RA, that year. After 1857, Sandys became part of Rossetti's circle at a time when the artists surrounding him were embarking on the production of illustrated books. Sandys was to join them in this and it is on these superbly finished designs that his reputation really rests. His influences were Rossetti himself, but also the prints of Dürer (he copied his own monogram freely from Dürer) and the work of Alfred Rethel, 1816-59. From the late 1860s, Sandys concentrated mostly on chalk drawings of women on toned paper, a surer medium for his exquisitely fine draughtsmanship than oils had ever given him. Despite some success, the artist remained largely unrecognised, partly due to his lack of business sense and

FREDERICK AUGUSTUS SANDYS 1832-1904. 'The Little Mourner'. Illustration to *Willmott's Sacred Poetry*, 1862

pecuniary troubles. He died at 5 Hogarth Road, London on 25 June 1904.
Contrib: *Once a Week [1861-67]; The Cornhill Magazine [1860, 1866]; Good Words [1862-63]; Willmott's Sacred Poetry [1862]; The Churchmans Family Magazine [1863]; The Shilling Magazine [1865]; The Quiver [1866]; The Argosy [1866]; The Shaving of Shagpat [Meredith, 1865]; Christian's Mistake [Mrs Craik, 1866]; Touches of Nature by Eminent Artists [1866]; Idyllic Pictures [1867]; Thornbury's Legendary Ballads [1876]; The British Architect [1879]; Cassell's Family Magazine [1881]; Dalziel's Bible Gallery [1881]; Pan [1881]; The Century Guild Hobby Horse [1888]; The English Illustrated Magazine [1891]; The Quarto [1896].*
Exhib: FAS; L; New Gall; P; RA.
Colls: Ashmolean; BM; Bradford; Fitzwilliam; Leeds; V & AM.
Bibl: *Woodcuts by FS,* Pub. by Hentchel, c.1904; *The Artist,* Dec. 1897, pp.7-63 illus.; Gleeson White, *English Illustration 'The Sixties',* 1906, pp.172-175; Forrest Reid, *English Illustrators of the Sixties,* 1928, pp.59-64; B. O'Looney, *FS,* Brighton Art Gallery cat., 1974; Gordon N. Ray, *The Illustrator and The Book in England,* 1976, pp.107-108 illus.
See illustrations.

SANSOM, Nellie   **fl.1894-1936**
Portrait painter and illustrator. She studied at the RCA and was elected RMS in 1896.
Contrib: *ILN [1903].*
Exhib: B; G; L; M; RA; RBA; RCA; RI; RMS; SWA.

SARG, Tony   **1882-1942**
American painter, illustrator and caricaturist. He was born in Guatemala in 1880, worked for many magazines and executed mural paintings in New York hotels. He became a member of the London Sketch Club in 1914 and illustrated a number of English books.
Illus: *Children For Ever [J.F. Macpherson, 1908]; Molly's Book [1908].*
Contrib: *Punch [1907-12]; The Graphic [1908-10].*

SARGENT, G.F.   **fl.1840-1860**
Illustrator. Lived in London and was a prolific illustrator of topographical and antiquarian works. He was considered too poor an artist to be seconded for the NWS in 1854.
Illus: *Polite Repository [T.L. Peacock].*
Contrib: *Knight's London [1841-42]; Shakespeare Illustrated [1842]; The Pilgrim's Progress and the Holy War Illuminated [c.1850]; Cassell's Illustrated Family Paper [1853]; The Illustrated London Magazine [1853-55]; The Seasons and The Castle of Indolence [1857]; The Welcome Guest [1860]; ILN [1860].*
Colls: Nottingham.

SARGENT, John Singer   **1856-1925**
Portrait and landscape painter and watercolourist. He was born in Florence in 1856, the son of an American doctor and travelled widely in Europe and America, before studying in Rome, Florence and Paris, under Carolus Duran. Although principally known as a portrait painter of exceptional dexterity and sparkle in the Edwardian years, he was also a fluid watercolourist, making great effects with rapid washes and brilliant colours, particularly those undertaken during the First World War. He received many honours, the Légion d'Honneur, was elected ARA in 1894 and RA in 1897. He died in Chelsea on 15 April 1925 and his studio was sold at Christie's on July 24 and 27, 1925.
Illus: *Five Songs From a Book of Verses [W.E. Henley (title page)].*
Exhib: B; FAS; G; GG; L; M; NEA; New Gall; RA; RHA; ROI; RSA; RSW; RWS.
Colls: Ashmolean; BM; Bradford; Fitzwilliam; Imperial War; Manchester; Tate.
Bibl: The Hon. E. Charteris, *JSS,* 1927; M. Hardie, *JSS,* 1930; R. Ormond, Cat. of Exhibition, Birmingham, *JSS,* Sept-Oct 1964; R. Ormond, *JSS,* 1970.

FREDERICK AUGUSTUS SANDYS 1832-1904. 'Life's Journey'. Illustration for *English Sacred Poetry* by Rev. A. Willmott, 1862. Wood engraving

JOHANN NEPOMUK SCHONBERG 1844-. 'Crossing the Citrol'.
Original drawing for illustration, perhaps for *The Illustrated London
News*. Pen, grey wash and bodycolour. 20½in x 14in (52.1cm x
35.5cm)   Author's Collection

SARGENT, Waldo
Illustrator, contributing to *London Society,* 1863.

SARGISSON, Ralph M.   **fl.1906-1937**
Artist and illustrator. He worked in Birmingham and contributed
good ink drawings of interiors with figures to *Punch,* 1906. He was
elected RBSA, 1935.
Contrib: *Punch [1906-08].*
Exhib: B.

SATCHWELL, R. William   **1732-1811**
Miniaturist and portrait painter. He designed frames and border
ornament for an edition of *The Rambler,* c.1795.
Illus: *Cooke's Sacred Classics [1793]; Devout Meditations [1793];
Shakespeare's Plays [1798-1800].*
Colls: V & AM.
Bibl: Hammelmann & Boase, *Book Illustrators in Eighteenth
Century England,* Yale, 1975.

SAUBER, Robert   RBA   **1868-1936**
Painter and illustrator. He was born in London on 12 February 1868,
the grandson of Charles Hancock, the animal painter. He studied at
Julian's, Paris and in Munich and was an exhibitor in both places.
From about 1890, Sauber was living in London and working for
most of the leading weekly and monthly magazines. He claimed to
be most influenced by French 18th century art in his drawings, a
particular mannerism of his work being heavy washes with busy pen
work on top of them. He became RBA in 1891 and RMS in 1896,
acting as Vice-President of the RMS, 1896-98. He lived at Hartwell
near Northampton from about 1925 and died on 10 September 1936.

Illus: *Mrs Tregaskis [Mrs Praed, c.1894].*
Contrib: *The English Illustrated Magazine [1893-96]; The Sketch
[1894]; St Pauls [1894]; The Sporting & Dramatic News [1895];
The Minister [1895]; Pearson's Magazine [1896]; ILN [1897-99
(theat.)]; The St James's Budget; The Queen; The Windsor
Magazine; The Idler; The Pall Mall Magazine; Fun [1901].*
Exhib: B; L; New Gall; RA; RBA; RMS; ROI.
Colls: V & AM.
Bibl: 'An Illustrator of Note', *The Artist,* June 1897, pp.241-248
illus.

SAVAGE, Reginald   **fl.1886-1933**
Painter, illustrator and wood engraver, associated with Charles Ricketts
in the 1890s. He was a talented and imaginative designer and woodcut
artist and worked for C.R. Ashbee's Essex House Press. He taught at
Camberwell School of Art from 1910, where one of his pupils was
David Jones. His subjects are usually from history and poetry and he
was commended by Walter Crane (q.v.) for his 'weird designs'.
Illus: *Der Ring des Nibelungen [described by R. Farquharson
Sharp, 1898]; Pilgrim's Progress [1899]; The Poems of William
Shakespeare [1899]; Venus and Adonis [1900-01]; The Eve of St
Agnes [1900-01]; The Journal of John Woolman [1900-01]; The
Epithalmion of Spenser [1901]; A Book of Romantic Ballads [1901];
Alexander's Feast [John Dryden, 1904]* (All Essex House Press).
Contrib: *Black & White [1891]; The Dial [1892]; The Butterfly
[1893]; St Pauls [1894]; Madame [1895]; The Ludgate Monthly;
The Pageant [1896]; Fun [1901]; The Venture [1903].*
Exhib: New Gall; RA; RBA; RI; ROI.
Colls: V & AM.
Bibl: *The Art of The Book,* Studio, 1914; R.E.D. Sketchley, *Eng. Bk.
Illus.,* 1903, pp.18, 24, 130; *The Last Romantics,* Barbican Gallery
cat., 1989, pp.167-8.

SAWYER, Amy   **1887-1909**
Figure and decorative artist. She worked at Bushey, 1887 where she
probably attended the Herkomer School. She later worked from
Ditchling, Sussex and was elected ASWA, 1901.
Contrib: *Black & White [1891].*
Exhib: B; FAS; L; M; RA; ROI; SWA.

SCANNELL, Edith S.
Illustrator of children's books. She illustrated *The Child of the
Caravan,* E.M. Green, c.1888.

SCHARF, George   **1788-1860**
Miniature painter, drawing-master and illustrator. He was born at
Mainburg, Bavaria in 1788 and studied at Munich before travelling
in Flanders and France. During the Empire, he was in the Low
Countries and escaped from Antwerp during the siege of 1814. He
studied in Paris at the Musée Napoleon after 1815 and came to
England in 1816, where he learnt lithography and became an
employee of Moser and Hullmandel. He was employed for many
years to draw on stone for the illustrations of the Geological
Society's *Transactions* and made topographical drawings of
London. He was a member of the NWS from 1833 to 1836 and he
died in London in 1860. He was the father of Sir G. Scharf (q.v.).

SCHARF, Sir George   **1820-1895**
Draughtsman and illustrator. He was born in London in 1820, the son
of G. Scharf (q.v.) and was educated at University College School and
studied at the RA Schools, 1838. In 1840 he accompanied Sir Charles
Fellowes to Asia Minor as draughtsman, visiting Italy on the way and
returning to Asia Minor again in 1843. He assisted Charles Keene in
the scenery and costumes of his Shakespearean revivals, 1851-57 and
became celebrated for his work as an art historian and cataloguer. He
was made as a result of this the first Secretary and then Director of the
National Portrait Gallery, 1857 and 1882. He was knighted in 1895.
Publ: *Catalogue of the Collection of Pictures at Knowsley Hall
[1875]; Descriptive and Historical Catalogue of the Collection of
Pictures at Woburn Abbey [1890].*
Illus: *Recollection of Scenic Effects [1839]; Smiths Classical
Dictionaries; Keats Poems [1866-67].*
Exhib: RA; BI.
Colls: BM; Witt Photo.

Christian enters the Valley of the Shadow of Death.

DAVID SCOTT RSA 1806-1849. 'Christian enters the Valley of the Shadow of Death'. Illustration engraved by W. Bell Scott for *The Pilgrim's Progress*, 1860. Wood engraving

SCHETKY, John Christian   **1778-1874**
Draughtsman and drawing-master. He was born in Edinburgh in 1778, the son of a Hungarian musician and Maria Reinagle. He took lessons from Alexander Nasmyth and from an early age taught drawing to support his family. He worked as a scene painter and in 1801 walked to Rome, returning through France. He was then drawing-master at Oxford, at the Military College at Marlow and after 1810 was appointed master at the Portsmouth Naval Academy where he remained until 1836. Schetky's official appointments included being Watercolour Painter to the Duke of Clarence and Marine Painter in Ordinary to George IV and Queen Victoria. He died in London in 1874.
Illus: *Sketches and Notes of a Cruise in South Waters [Duke of Rutland, 1850]; Court Martial [Hon. H.S. Rous, AL 343].*
Exhib: BI; OWS; RA; RBA.
Colls: BM; Greenwich.
Bibl: S.F.L. Schetky, *Life of JCS*, 1877; Winifred Greenaway, 'Artistic Passion for Sea and Ships', *CL*, 10 April 1980.

SCHLOESSER, Carl Bernhard   **1832-1914**
Portrait painter and etcher. He was born in Darmstadt in 1832 and studied under Couture and at the École des Beaux Arts, exhibiting at the Salon from 1861. He was living in London by 1890 and died there in 1914.
Illus: *Ormond [Maria Edgeworth, c.1895].*
Exhib: B; FAS; G; GG; L; M; RA; RHA.

SCHNEBBLIE, Robert Blemmel   **-1849**
Topographical draughtsman. He was the son of the celebrated topographer J.C. Schnebblie, 1760-92. He worked in his father's style and illustrated for *The Gentleman's Magazine* and Wilkinson's *Londina Illustrata*, 1808. He died of starvation in 1849.
Exhib: RA.
Colls: BM; V & AM.

SCHONBERG, Johann Nepomuk   **1844-**
Figure artist and illustrator. He was born in Austria in 1844, the son of the lithographer Adolf Schonberg, 1813-1868. He studied at the Vienna Academy and then went to France where he worked for *Monde Illustré* and *Journal Illustré.* He was appointed Special Artist to *The Illustrated London News* in Romania in 1877 and worked for the magazine until 1895, often improving drawings sent in by other artists. His style is characterised by heavy use of bodycolour with grey washes.
Illus: *History of the Popes [Patuzzi]; Universal History [Alvensleben]; The Young Buglers [G.A. Henty, 1880]; The Dash For Khartoum [G.A. Henty, 1892].*
Exhib: RA, 1895.
See illustration.

SCHWABE, Randolph   **RWS**   **1885-1948**
Watercolourist and illustrator. He was born in Manchester in 1885 and after being educated privately, studied at the Slade School and then at Julian's in Paris, 1906. Schwabe was a member of the NEA from 1917 and of the London Group from 1915, being elected ARWS in 1938 and RWS in 1942. In 1930 he was appointed Slade Professor of Fine Arts in the University of London. Schwabe was a fluid draughtsman with pen and ink and his views of cities in this medium are among his best works. He carried out some book illustration in the 1920s and died in 1948.
Illus: *Historic Costume, 1490-1790 [1929, with F.M. Kelly]; A Short History of Costume and Armour, 1066-1800 [1931, with F.M. Kelly]; Summer's Fancy [Edmund Blunden, Beaumont Press, 1930]; Costume in Ballet [Cyril W. Beaumont].*
Contrib: *Oxford Almanac [1940].*
Exhib: FAS; G; GG; L; M; NEA; RSA; RWS.
Colls: Ashmolean; V & AM.
Bibl: *RS*, FAS catalogue, Nov 1982.
See Horne

SCOTSON-CLARK, G.F.   **1872-1927**
Illustrator, writer and businessman. He was educated at Brighton Grammar School where he was a contemporary and friend of Aubrey Beardsley (q.v.). he was later a correspondent of Beardsley. After working in the city of London, he emigrated to the United States in 1892. He wrote *Eating Without Fears*, 1924. He illustrated *The Halls*, 1899 (Fisher Unwin), portraits of Dan Leno, Robey, Randall, Marie Lloyd and Vesta Tilley in a Beggarstaff style.

SCOTT, David   **RSA**   **1806-1849**
Painter and illustrator. He was born at Edinburgh in 1806, the son of the engraver Robert Scott and elder brother of W.B. Scott (q.v.). He worked as an engraver before turning to painting, studied at the Trustees Academy and was one of the founders of the Edinburgh Life Academy Association in 1827. He worked for a short time in Italy in 1832-34 where he made anatomical studies in the Hospital for Incurables. His paintings are heroic in concept and his illustrations have considerable interest, deriving as they do in both symbol and style from William Blake (q.v.). He died at Edinburgh in 1849.
Illus: *The Ancient Mariner [S. T. Coleridge, 1837]; Architecture of the Heavens [Prof. Nichol, 1851]; The Ancient Mariner; Pilgrim's Progress [1860].*
Exhib: RA; RSA.
Colls: BM.
Bibl: W.B. Scott, *Memoir of DS,* 1850; W.B Scott, *Autobiographical Notes of the Life of,* Vol.2, 1892, pp.216-219 and 259-268.
See illustration.

SCOTT, Georges   **1873-c.1948**
French portrait painter. He was born in 1873 and worked in Paris, contributing illustrations of events to *The Graphic*, 1901-11. He painted a portrait of King George V now in the Bristol City Art Gallery.
Exhib: L; RA, 1909-12.

SCOTT, J.
Figure artist. Contributed comic illustrations to *Thomas Hood's Comic Annual*, 1837-38.

SCOTT, Septimus Edwin   **1879-**
Landscape painter and poster artist. He was born at Sunderland on 19

March 1879 and studied at the RCA. He was elected ARBA in 1919, RI in 1927 and ROI in 1920.
Contrib: *The Graphic [1910].*
Exhib: B; L; RA; RBA; RI; ROI.

SCOTT, Stuart H.
Topographer. Contributed to *The Illustrated London News,* 1896.

SCOTT, Thomas D.   **fl.1850-1893**
Portrait illustrator and miniaturist. He worked at Peckham and was described by White as 'a well-known portrait engraver' and by Chatto as an 'able reducer and copyist of pictures on wood'.
Illus: *The Gold of Fairnilee [Andrew Lang, c.1889 (frontis)].*
Contrib: *The Book of British Ballads [S.C. Hall, 1842]; The Illustrated London News [1850]; Examples of Ornament [Bell & Daldy 1855]; Heber's Hymns [1867]; Once a Week [1867].*
Exhib: RA.
Bibl: Chatto & Jackson, *Treatise on Wood Engraving,* 1861, p.600.

SCOTT, William   **fl.1880-1905**
Painter and etcher. He was elected RE in 1881 and lived much of his life in Italy, at Rome, 1882, Venice, 1884 and Bodighera 1896.
Illus: *Lamia's Winter Quarters [Alfred Austin, c.1905 (head and tail pieces)]; The Riviera [A & C Black, 1907].*
Exhib: B; G; M; RA; RBA; RE; ROI.

SCOTT, William Bell   **1811-1890**
Painter, illustrator, critic and poet. He was born at Edinburgh on 12 September 1811, the son of Robert Scott, the engraver and younger brother of David Scott (q.v.). He studied art with his father and then attended the Trustees Academy in Edinburgh in 1831. He assisted his father in the engraving business and then in 1837 left for London where he hoped to earn a livelihood as an illustrator. This proved not to be a success and he turned to painting, making friends with W.P. Frith and Augustus Egg. In 1842 he entered an unsuccessful design for the Houses of Parliament Cartoon Competition and the next year was appointed master of the School of Design at Newcastle-upon-Tyne, where he remained till 1863. Scott developed a considerable facility as a mural painter and did major works at Wallington Hall, Northumberland for the Trevelyan family and at Penkill Castle, Ayrshire for his patron Mr. Boyd. A friend of Rossetti and the Pre-Raphaelites, Scott was often inspired in his compositions and clumsy in his executions, giving a slightly provincial echo of the Brotherhood. His watercolours are generally conceived on too large a scale, their symbolism often borrowed from Dürer or Blake. He died at Penkill Castle in 1890.
Publ: *Antiquarian Gleanings in the North of England [1851]; Half-hour Lectures...of the Fine and Ornamental Arts [1861]; Our British Landscape Painters [1872]; William Blake [1878].*
Illus: *The Ornamentist or Artisan's Manual [1845]; The Year of the World [1846]; Landon's Poetical Works; Pilgrim's Progress [1860, with D. Scott]; Poems [1875]; The Nursery Rhymes of England [1886]; Illustrations to the King's Quair of James I [1887].*
Contrib: *Landscape Lyrics [c.1837]; The Observer [1842]; The Family Bible [1867].*
Exhib: BI; RA; RBA; RSA.
Colls: Author, Newcastle.
Bibl: *Autobiographical Notes on The Life of WBS,* 1892; M.D.E. Clayton-Stamm, 'Observer of the Industrial Revolution', *Apollo,* May 1969, pp.386-390; R. Trevelyan, *WBS, Apollo,* September 1977.
See illustration.

SEARLE, A.A.
Equestrian draughtsman. Contributed to *Punch,* 1907.

SEARLE, Henry   **fl.1840-1850**
Illustrator of contemporary and historical characters in ink and watercolour. An album of his work was sold at Sotheby's on 27 July 1984. It was inscribed 'Sketches for Punch, Man-in-the-Moon etc. by Hy Searle (Pupil of Leech)'. T.J. Serle was a literary contributor to *Punch* in the 1840s.

SEARS, M.V.
He illustrated *The Yorkshire Hunt* by William Cowper, 1830, 'After the Manner of Cruikshank'.

SECCOMBE, Colonel Thomas S.   **fl.1865-1885**
Military painter and illustrator. He joined the Royal Artillery in 1856 and retired with the rank of Colonel. He illustrated a considerable number of children's books and some period novels, his style of drawing being lively and humorous but often very wooden.
Illus: *The Poetical Works of Thomas Moore; The Poetical Works of William Cowper; The Poetical Works of James Thomson [c.1870 (all Moxon's Popular Poets)]; The Poetical Works of John Keats [n.d.]; Miss Kilmansegg [T. Hood, 1870 (2 edits.)]; The Rape of the Lock [1873]; Army and Navy Drolleries [c.1875]; The Story of Prince Hildebrand and the Princess Ida – Related in Rhyme [1880]; Comic Sketches from English History [n.d.]; Military Misreadings of Shakespeare [n.d.].*
Contrib: *Punch [1864-66, 1882]; London Society [1865]; Belgravia [1868]; Fun; The Illustrated Times.*
Exhib: RBA.
Colls: Witt Photo.

SEDDING, A.E.
Designer of ornaments. This must be an error for the architect J.D. Sedding, 1838-91, contributing two geometric initial letters to *The English Illustrated Magazine,* 1887. Sedding was a member of the RIBA from 1874 and attempted to start a school of carvers and gilders.

SEELEY, Miss E.L.   **fl.1873-1880**
Figure painter and illustrator. She worked in Camden Town and illustrated a child's book *Eva's Mulberry Tree,* c.1880.
Exhib: RA; SWA.

SELBY, Prideaux John   **1788-1867**
Botanical and ornithological illustrator. He was born at Alnwick, Northumberland in 1788 and after studying at University College, Oxford, he lived entirely in Northumberland and devoted himself to natural history. He became a member of the Royal Society of Edinburgh and of the Linnaean Society. He died at Twizell in 1867.
Illus: *Illustrations of British Ornithology [1821-34]; Illustrations of Ornithology [1825-43, with Sir W. Jardine]; British Forest Trees [1842].*

SELOUS, Henry Courtney   **1803-1890**
Portrait and landscape painter and illustrator. He was born at Deptford in 1803, the son of George Selous, the miniature painter. He became a pupil of John Martin (q.v.) and was admitted a student at the RA Schools in about 1818. Selous entered the Westminster Hall Competition in 1843, having previously worked for a panorama painter and specialised in mural treatments. This background was to continue to influence his work, which though powerful, was always rather flatly conceived. He excelled in rather Germanic outline book illustrations and was an author of children's books under the names of 'Aunt Cae' and 'Kay Spen'. He died at Beaworthy in North Devon on 24 September 1890.
Illus: *The Pilgrim's Progress [Art Union, 1844]; The Life of Robert The Bruce; Hereward the Wake [1870].*
Contrib: *The Book of British Ballads [S.C. Hall, 1842]; Sintram and His Companions [Fouqué, c.1844]; Poems and Pictures [1846]; The Churchman's Family Magazine [1863]; Cassell's History of England; Our Life Illustrated by Pen and Pencil [1865]; Cassell's Shakespeare [1865]; Heber's Hymns [1867]; The Illustrated Book of Sacred Poems [1867]; Cassell's Illustrated Readings [1867]; The Man-Eaters of Tsaro [J.H. Patterson (1908 Edit.)].*
Exhib: BI; RA.
Colls: BM; Fitzwilliam; V & AM.
Bibl: Chatto & Jackson, *Treatise on Wood Engraving,* 1861, p.599.

'SEM'   George GOURSAT   **1863-1934**
French portrait painter and caricaturist. He was born at Périgueux, Dordogne on 23 November 1863 and from the first had a talent for rapid sketching, giving the feel of his subjects' faces rather than direct portraits of them. He epitomised the Paris of the Entente

WILLIAM BELL SCOTT 1811-1890. 'The Rending of the Veil in the Temple'. Original drawing for illustration in *The Family Bible*, 1867. Ink. This version signed with initials and dated 1869. 10⅜in x 12¾in (26.3cm x 32.4cm) Author's Collection

Cordiale and drew fashionable scenes in the style of poster art. He was a frequent visitor to England in the years 1905-10 when he sketched the celebrities of Newmarket and Cowes and left indelible images of Edward VII. He had an exhibition at the Baillie Gallery in 1907, and died in Paris in 1934.
Illus: *Messieurs les Ronds-de-cuir [G. Courteline].*

SETON, Ernest Thompson   **1860-**
Animal illustrator in black and white. He was born at South Shields on 14 August 1860 and emigrated with his family to Canada. He studied in Paris under Gérôme, Bouguereau, Ferrier and Mosler 1878-81. He returned to America and worked as a writer and naturalist at Santa Fe. His drawings are notable for their accuracy and also for their strong decorative sense in the context of the book.
Illus: *Wild Animals I Have Known; Art Anatomy of Animals; Birds of Manitoba; Mammals of Manitoba; Trail of the Sandhill Stage; Biography of a Grizzly; Lives of the Hunted Containing a True Account of The Doings of Five Quadrupeds and Three Birds [1901]; Two Little Savages; Pictures of Wild Animals; Monarch, The Big Bear; Woodmyth and Fable; Animal Heroes; Birch Bark Roll of the Woodcraft Indians; Natural History of the Ten Commandments; Biography of a Silver-Fox [1909]; Life Histories of Northern Animals [1910]; Manual of Scouting [1910]; Rolf in the Woods [1911]; The Arctic Prairies [1911]; The Forester's Manual [1911]; The Book of Woodcraft and Indian Lore [1912]; Wild Animals At Home [1913]; Wild Animal Ways [1916]; The Sign Language*

[1918]; The Preacher of Cedar Mountain [1917]; Sign Talk Dictionary [1918]; Woodland Tales [1921]; Bannertail [1922]; Lives of Game Animals [1925].

SEVERN, Joseph Arthur Palliser   RI   1848-1931
Watercolourist. He was born in Rome in 1848, the son of Joseph Severn, artist and consul. He studied in Rome and Paris and in 1872 accompanied John Ruskin (q.v.) to Italy and nine years later married his niece Joan Ruskin. He was responsible for Ruskin during the latter's derangement and lived with him at Brantwood, painting Lake District views. In later middle age, Marie Corelli, the novelist, developed an embarrassing passion for Severn and he illustrated her book *The Devil's Motor* in 1910. RI, 1882.
Exhib: FAS; G; L; M; RA; RI; ROI.
Colls: BM.

SEVERN, Walter   RCA   1830-1904
Landscape and marine painter. He was born at Rome in 1830, the son of Joseph Severn, the artist and the brother of Arthur Severn. He was educated at Westminster and entered the Civil Service for a time before devoting himself to painting. He was interested in the applied arts, fostered needlework and embroidery designing and collaborated as a designer with Sir Charles Eastlake. He became President of the Dudley Art Society and RCA. He died in London on 22 September 1904.
Illus: *Good Night and Good Morning [Lord Houghton, 1859];*

JOHN BYAM LISTON SHAW ARWS 1872-1919. Original drawing for an illustration in Reade's *The Cloister and The Hearth*, 1909. Pen and ink. Signed. 7¾in x 5¾in (19.7cm x 14.6cm)   Author's Collection

Golden Calendar; Deer and Forest Scenery; Morning and Evening Service.
Contrib: *Passages From Modern English Poets [1862].*
Exhib: G; L; RBA; RCA.
Colls: V & AM.

SEWELL, Ellen Mary   **1813-1905**
Drawing and school mistress, amateur artist. She was born at Newport, Isle of Wight and lived most of her life on the island where she ran a school, from 1851 to 1891.
Publ: *Sailors' Hymns [1883].*
Illus: *Sacred Thoughts in Verse [W. Sewell, 1885]* .

SEYMOUR, George L.   **fl.1876-1916**
Genre and animal painter and illustrator. He worked in London and illustrated architecture and topography for many of the magazines.
Illus: *Songs and Lyrics For Little Lips [W.D. Cummings, n.d].*
Contrib: *Good Words [1880, 1890-95]; The Graphic [1886]; ILN [1887-92]; The English Illustrated Magazine [1888,1897]; The Pall Mall Magazine.*
Exhib: FAS; L; M; RBA; RI; ROI.
Colls: Witt Photo.

SEYMOUR, Robert   **1798-1836**
Humorous illustrator and caricaturist. He was born in Somerset in 1798 and apprenticed to a London pattern designer, where he slowly developed an interest in history painting. He had little success with

this and turned his hand to caricature and comic illustration, where his talent for the grotesque and the absurd could be given full range. Seymour was a somewhat inadequate draughtsman, but modelled himself on the far stronger repertoire of George Cruikshank (q.v.) and even aped the latter's signature by signing himself 'Short Shanks'. Seymour learnt the art of copper engraving in about 1827 and used lithography in the 1830s, much of his work was in the form of folios of prints with little or no text. His greatest contribution was in creating the routine of comic sportsmen from London having adventures in the country, a theme that established itself for a hundred years. It was his fame in this field that led the publishers, Chapman and Hall, to commission the text of *Pickwick Papers* from young Charles Dickens as an accompaniment to Seymour's sketches. Only two issues were produced before the sensitive Seymour committed suicide in London on 20 April 1836.
Illus: *Vagaries in Quest of the Wild and Wonderful [1827]; The Heiress [1830, AL 319]; New Readings [1830-35, AL 320]; Journal of a Landsman From Portsmouth to Lisbon [1831, AL 346]; Humorous Sketches [1834, 1836]; Pickwick Papers [1836].*
Contrib: *Friendship's Offering [1824-36]; The Looking Glass [1830-32]; The Comic Offering [1831-35]; Figaro in London [1831-36]; The Comic Magazine; Hood's Comic Almanack [1836]; The Squib Annual [1836]; Sayings Worth Hearing; Terrific Penny Magazine; Book of Christmas [Hervey].*
Exhib: RA, 1822.
Colls: Dickens House, Doughty Street, London; V & AM; Witt Photo.
Bibl: Graham Everitt, *English Caricaturists,* 1893, pp.208-234 illus.; M. Dorothy George, *English Political Caricature,* 1959, illus.

SHACKLETON, William   **1872-1933**
Landscape, figure and portrait painter. He was born at Bradford on 14 January 1872 and educated at Bradford Grammar School and Technical College before studying at the RCA, 1893. He won a travelling scholarship to Paris and Italy in 1896 and worked in London from 1905 undertaking sketching tours with W.E. Stott. He was a dramatic colourist in the Turner tradition and was successful enough to have one man shows in London in 1910 and 1922. He became NEA in 1909 and died on 9 January 1933.
Contrib: *The Quartier Latin [1896]; The Parade [1897].*
Exhib: B; G; GG; L; M; NEA; New Gall; RA; RBA; RHA; RI.
Colls: Bradford; Manchester.

SHANNON, Charles Hazelwood RA   **1863-1937**
Portrait and subject painter. He was born at Sleaford, Lincolnshire in 1863 and studied wood engraving at the Lambeth School of Art in 1882, where he met his lifelong friend Charles Ricketts (q.v.). They joined together with Sturge Moore (q.v.) to form *The Vale Press,* 1894-1904, which produced forty-eight books conspicious for their fine design and unassuming quality. Shannon was principally an artist and Ricketts was the guiding hand in design and production. He was a member of the Society of Twelve, was elected an ARA in 1911 and an RA in 1921. He died in London on 18 March 1937.
Illus: *House of Pomegranates [1891]; Daphnis and Chloe [1893]; Hero and Leander [1894];* etc.
Contrib: *Judy [1887]; Black & White [1891]; The Savoy [1896]; The Venture [1903].*
Exhib: FAS; G; GG; L; M; NEA; New Gall; RA; RBA; RE; RHA; RI; ROI; RSA.
Colls: BM; V & AM; Witt Photo.
Bibl: *Catalogue of Mr S's Lithographs.* Vale Press, 1900; E.B. George, *CS,* Benn Contemp. British Artists, 1924; Colin Franklin, *The Private Presses,* 1969.

SHARPE, Charles Kirkpatrick   **1781-1851**
Portrait painter, caricaturist and antiquary. He was born at Hoddam Castle, Dumfriesshire on 15 May 1781 and was educated at Edinburgh University and Christ Church, Oxford. Although destined for the church, he became interested in painting and antiquarian research, spending most of his life in Edinburgh engaged in these pursuits. He also practised etching. He died in March 1851.
Contrib: *Witch of Fife [Hogg, 1820]; Fugitive Scottish Poetry [1823]; The Romances of Otuel, Roland and Vernagu [Abbotsford Club, 1836]; Flora's Fete.*
Colls: BM; Nat. Gall., Scot.

Bibl: A. Allardyce, *CKS's Letters*, 1868; *The Etchings of CKS*, 1869; R. Halsband, *The Rape of the Lock & Its Illustrators*, 1980, pp.63-67.

SHAW, A.   **fl.1826-1839**
Architectural draughtsman. He was a friend of R.P. Bonington and illustrated for Pugin's *Paris,* 1831.
Exhib: BI; RA; RBA.
Colls: Witt Photo.

SHAW, Henry   **FSA**   **1800-1873**
Architectural draughtsman, illuminator and antiquary. He was born in London on 4 July 1800 and concentrated on the research, decoration and production of a number of lavish Victorian heraldic books. Shaw was a perfectionist whose skills coincided with the beginning of the high Gothic revival culminating in the works of A.W. Pugin (q.v.). The books were usually published by William Pickering, printed by the Chiswick Press, and as McLean says 'are among the finest achievements of Victorian book design and illustration'. He was elected FSA in 1833 and died at Broxbourne, Herts on 12 June 1873.
Illus: *The History and Antiquities of the Chapel at Luton Park [1829]; Illuminated Ornaments [1833, AL 234]; Examples of Ornamental Metalwork [1836]; Specimens of Ancient Furniture [1836]; The Encyclopaedia of Ornament [1842]; Dresses and Decorations of the Middle Ages [1843]; Alphabets, Numerals and Devices of the Middle Ages [1845, AL 235]; The Arms of The Colleges of Oxford [1855]; The Art of Illumination [1866].*
Contrib: *Britton's Cathedrals [1832-36]; New Testament [Longman, 1864].*
Bibl: Ruari McLean, *Victorian Book Design,* 1972, pp.65-71 illus.

SHAW, James   **fl.1883-1902**
Illustrator. He worked in Edinburgh and contributed to *Punch.*
Exhib: G; L; RSA.
Colls: V & AM.

SHAW, John Byam Liston   **ARWS**   **1872-1919**
Painter, designer and illustrator. He was born at Madras on 13 November 1872 and came to England in 1878 and to London in 1879. He was educated privately and studied at the St John's Wood Art School, entering the RA Schools in 1889. Shaw was strongly influenced by the work of the Pre-Raphaelite painters and by the illustrators of the 1860s. His black and white drawings are more successful than his colour, his organisation of the page is usually good but his imagination weaker. He went into partnership with Rex Vicat Cole to found a School of Art at Campden Hill, which still continues today. He was elected RI in 1898 and ARWS, 1913. He died in London on 26 January 1919.
Illus: *Browning's Poems [1897]; Tales From Boccaccio [1899]; Chiswick Shakespeare [1899]; Old King Cole's Book of Nursery Rhymes [1901]; Pilgrim's Progress [1904]; Coronation Book [1902]; Ballads and Lyrics of Love [1908]; The Cloister and The Hearth [1909]; Tales of Mystery and Imagination [E.A. Poe, 1909]; The Garden of Kama [Laurence Hope, 1914].*
Contrib: *The Dome [1898]; Cassell's Family Magazine [1898]; The Graphic [1899-1905]; The Connoisseur [1902, decor]; Punch [1905-07]; Strand Magazine [1913].*
Exhib: B; G; L; M; New Gall; RA; RI; ROI; RSA; RWS.
Colls: Ashmolean; V & AM.
Bibl: *The Studio,* Vol.12, pp.173-176; Vol.13, p.129; Winter No., 1900-01, p.75 illus.; R.E.D. Sketchley, *Eng. Bk. Illus.,* 1903, pp.13, 130; *Modern Book Illustrators and Their Work,* Studio, 1914; Rex Vicat Cole, *The Art and Life of BS,* 1933.
See illustration.

SHEERES, C.W.   **fl.1855-1859**
Illustrator. He contributed views of industrial subjects to *The Illustrated London News,* 1855-59.

SHEIL, Edward   **1834-1869**
Figure painter. He was born at Coleraine in 1834 and worked in Cork where he died on 11 March 1869.
Contrib: *Once a Week [1867].*
Exhib: RA; RBA.

SHELDON, Charles M.   **fl.1891-1910**
Figure artist and illustrator. He was, according to A.S. Hartrick, born in the United States and came to England to work as Special Artist for *Black & White.* He was sent by that magazine to the Sudan in 1897-98.
Illus: *Won By The Sword [G.A. Henty, 1900].*
Contrib: *The Pall Mall Budget [1891-92]; Black & White [1897-98]; The Ludgate Monthly [1895]; The Strand Magazine [1900-1910]; Chums; The Wide World Magazine.*

SHEPARD, Ernest Howard   **1879-1976**
Black and white artist and cartoonist. He was born in St John's Wood, London on 10 December 1879, the son of an architect. He was educated at St Paul's School and then studied art at Heatherley's and the RA Schools, 1897-1902. He worked in Glebe Place, Chelsea, from 1901-3 and in 1904 moved to Shamley Green, Guildford. Shepard began drawing for *Punch* in 1907 and was elected to the *Punch* table in 1921, becoming chief cartoonist in 1945. His delicate caressing pen and ink style was more suited to episodes of childhood than political cartooning, but he managed to produce some striking subjects connected with the Second World War. His great success and chief celebrity came when he undertook the splendidly imaginative drawings for A.A. Milne's *Pooh* series, 1926. He died in 1976, when his last picture was exhibited at the RA, his first having been shown there seventy-five years previously.
Illus: *When We Were Very Young [1924]; Playtime and Company [1925]; Holly Tree [1925]; Winnie-the-Pooh [1926]; Everybody's Pepys [1926]; Jeremy [1927]; Little Ones Log [1927]; Let's Pretend [1927]; Now We Are Six [1927]; Fun and Fantasy [1927]; The House at Pooh Corner [1928]; The Golden Age [1928]; Everybody's Boswell [1930]; Dreamy Days [1930]; Wind in the Willows [1931]; Christmas Poems [1931]; Bevis [1931]; Sycamore Square [1932]; Everybody's Lamb [1933]; The Cricket in the Cage [1933]; Victoria Regina [Housman, 1934]; Modern Strewelpeter [1936]; Golden Sovereign [Housman, 1937]; Cheddar Gorge [1937]; As The Bee Sucks [E. V. Lucas, 1937]; The Reluctant Dragon [1939]; Gracious Majesty [Housman, 1941]; Golden Age and Dream Days [1948-49]; Bertie's Escapade [Grahame, 1948-49].*
Contrib: *The Graphic [1906-07].*
Exhib: B; G; L; M; RA.
Colls: BM; V & AM; Witt Photo.
Bibl: R.G.G. Price, *A History of Punch,* 1957, pp.210-212; Rawle Knox, *The Work of EHS,* 1979.
See Horne

SHEPHEARD, George   **1770-1842**
Landscape painter and caricaturist. He was born in Herefordshire in 1770 and studied at the RA Schools before working chiefly in Surrey and Sussex. He visited France in 1816 and Wales in 1825, his caricature drawings are spirited and in the manner of Hogarth.
Illus: *Vignette Designs [1814-15].*
Colls: BM; Leeds; Witt Photo.

SHEPHERD, E.
Topographer. Contributed Herefordshire view to *Britton's Beauties of England and Wales,* 1808.

SHEPHERD, F.H. Newton   **fl.1898-1902**
Figure artist and illustrator. He contributed to *The St. James's Budget,* 1898; *The Longbow,* 1898; *The Graphic,* 1902.

SHEPHERD, G.E.
Figure artist. He illustrated *Bubbles in Birdland* by H. Simpson, 1908.

SHEPHERD, George   **c.1782-c.1830**
Architectural draughtsman and topographer. He had great success in the first decade of the 19th century and won the Society of Arts silver palettes in 1803-04 for draughtsmanship. He was principally an illustrator but did some landscape work.
Illus: *Londina Illustrata [Wilkinson, 1808]; The History of the Abbey Church of St Peter's, Westminster [1812]; History of the County of Kent [1829-30].*

CLAUDE ALLIN SHEPPERSON ARA ARWS 1867-1921.
Original drawing for unidentified book illustration. Pen and ink.
Signed. 10¾in x 6in (27.3cm x 15.2cm)   Author's Collection

Contrib: *Beauties of England and Wales; Knight's London [1841].*
Exhib: BI; RA.
Colls: BM; Chester; Greenwich; Manchester; Nottingham; V & AM.
Bibl: M. Hardie, *Watercol. Paint. in Brit.,* Vol.3, 1968, pp.14-15.

SHEPHERD, James Affleck   1867-c.1931
Comic animal draughtsman. He was born in London on 29
November 1867 and was educated at various private schools. He had
no formal training, but worked with Alfred Bryan (q.v.) the
cartoonist of *Moonshine* for two years on that magazine.
Shepherd was a master draughtsman of animals and birds in pen and ink and
this enabled him to do humorous drawings in which the creatures
wore human attire and had human personalities. This became his
speciality and he invented a series of caricatures called 'Zig-Zags'
for *The Strand Magazine,* of which this was the main attraction. He
was invited to join *Punch* in 1893 and contributed many drawings
over the years, living latterly at Charlwood, Surrey.
Illus: *Zig-Zag Fables [1897]; Illustrated Uncle Remus [1901];
Wonders in Monsterland [1901]; Nights With Uncle Remus [1903];
The Three Jovial Puppies [1907]; The Life of a Foxhound [1910]; The
Story of Chanticleer [1913]; The Bodley Head Natural History [1913].*
Contrib: *Judy [1886-89]; Moonshine [1890-93]; The Sporting &
Dramatic News [1892]; Chums [1892]; The Strand Magazine*
*[1894]; Punch [1894]; Good Words [1894]; Black & White [1896];
Cassell's Family Magazine; The Boy's Own Paper.*
Exhib: G.
Colls: Witt Photo.
Bibl: M.H. Spielmann, *The History of Punch,* 1894, p.567; *The
Studio,* Vol.12, 1898; Winter No., 1900-01, p.77 illus.

SHEPHERD, Thomas Hosmer   c.1817-c.1842
Topographical illustrator. He was the son of George Shepherd (q.v.)
and he was employed by Frederick Crace to make drawings of
London which were outstanding for their skill and beauty.
Illus: *Metropolitan Improvements [1827]; London and Its Environs
in the Nineteenth Century [1829]; Modern Athens Displayed or
Edinburgh in the Nineteenth Century [1829]; Bath and Bristol
[1829-30]; London Interiors [1841].*
Exhib: RBA.
Colls: BM; Newcastle.
Bibl: M. Hardie, *Watercol. Paint. in Brit.,* Vol.3, 1968, p.15.

SHEPPARD, Raymond
Illustrator of bird subjects in about 1890.

SHEPPARD, W.   fl.1801-1814
Topographer. He contributed illustrations to *Britton's Beauties of
England and Wales,* 1801-14.

SHEPPERSON, Claude Allin   ARA ARWS   1867-1921
Painter and illustrator. He was born at Beckenham, Kent on 25 October
1867 and was intended for the law, which he studied. He studied art at
Heatherley's in 1891 and then at Paris, taking up principally
illustration and lithography but also some watercolour. He is a graceful
artist whose work is at its best when children and pretty young women
are involved, he was a regular contributor of this sort of drawing to
Punch from about 1905. He was elected RI in 1900 and ARWS in
1920, but was exceptional among illustrators in being elected ARA in
1919. He died in Chelsea on 30 December 1921.
Illus: *Shrewsbury [Weyman, 1898]; Merchant of Venice [1899]; The
Heart of Mid-Lothian [1900]; Lavengro [Borrow, 1900]; Coningsby
[Disraeli, 1900]; As You Like It [1900]; Magic Dominions [Arthur
F. Wallis, 1912]; The Open Road [E.V. Lucas, 1913].*
Contrib: *The English Illustrated Magazine [1893-96]; St Pauls
[1894]; The Graphic [1895-1910]; The Idler; Pick-Me-Up; The
Sketch; Illustrated Bits; Cassell's Family Magazine; The Queen; The
Pall Mall Magazine; The Wide World Magazine [1898]; The Strand
Magazine [1906]; The Windsor Magazine; ILN [1912-13].*
Exhib: FAS; G; GG; L; M; RA; RI; RMS; RSA; RWS.
Colls: Birmingham; Leeds; V & AM; Witt Photo.
Bibl: R.E.D. Sketchley, *Eng. Bk. Illus,* 1903, pp.68, 74, 154; *Cat. of
CS Memorial Exhibition,* Leicester Gall., March-April 1922; *Print
Collectors Quarterly,* Vol.10, No.4, 1923, pp.444-471.
See illustration.

SHÉRIE, Ernest F.
Military illustrator. He worked for *The Royal Magazine* and *The
Illustrated London News,* 1899-1900, supplying South African War
drawings.

SHERINGHAM, George   1884-1937
Decorative designer, theatrical designer and illustrator. He was born
in London in 1884 and was educated at the King's School,
Gloucester before studying at the Slade School and in Paris.
Sheringham's work is decidedly art deco in form, he uses primary
colours and a rather sculptural line like that of Gill. He painted fans
in the tradition of Conder (q.v.) and made studies for book covers
and magazines and posters. A one man show of his work was held at
the Brook Street Art Gallery in 1908. He died on 11 November 1937.
Illus: *The Happy Hypocrite [Max Beerbohm, 1918]; Canadian
Wonder Tales [Cyrus Macmillan]; La Princesse Lointaine [Edmund
Rostand]; The Duenna [R.B. Shendan, 1925].*
Contrib: *The Sketch [1933].*
Exhib: FAS, 1937; L; M; RA; RMS; ROI; RSA.
Colls: BM; Fitzwilliam; Manchester; V & AM.
Bibl: *The Studio,* Vol.53, 1911, pp.136-139 illus; Special Spring No.,
1922, 'Pen and Pencil Drawings'.

FREDERICK JAMES SHIELDS ARWS 1833-1911. Study for scrambling figure. Original drawing for illustration in *The Pilgrim's Progress*, 1864. Pen and ink with chalk and bodycolour

Victoria and Albert Museum

SHERLOCK, William P.   c.1780-c.1820
Landscape painter and topographer. He was the son of William Sherlock, the portrait painter and worked in London producing Wilson-like ideal landscapes. He was also an etcher and made prints after his own work and that of Cox, Prout and Girtin.
Illus: *Dickinson's Antiquities of Nottinghamshire [1801-06].*
Contrib: *Howitt's Views in the County of Lincoln [1800]; Britton's Beauties of England and Wales [1808-14].*
Exhib: RA.
Colls: BM; Birkenhead; Leeds; V & AM; Witt Photo.

SHERWILL, Captain George   fl.1848-1856
Amateur artist. He was an officer in the Royal Marines from 1848 and contributed views of India to *The Illustrated London News*, 1856.

SHETKEY   See SCHETKY, J.C.

SHIELDS, Frederick James   ARWS   1833-1911
Landscape artist, mural painter and illustrator. He was born of poor parents at Hartlepool in 1833 and was educated at a charity school before beginning work for a commercial lithographer at Manchester from the age of fourteen. Shields was influenced by the Pre-Raphaelites from an early date and carried out a considerable number of frescoes which show their marked effect on him, among them the Chapel of the Ascension, Hyde Park Place and Eaton Hall. He was a very strong illustrator, his powerful drawings and fine washes only losing a little of their crispness in wood engraving. He was elected ARWS in 1865 and died at Merton in Surrey on 26 March 1911.
Illus: *History of the Plague of London [Defoe, 1862]; The Pilgrim's Progress [1864].*
Contrib: *The Grey Eggshibishun [Manchester, 1851]; Touches of Nature By Eminent Artists [1866]; The Sunday Magazine [1866]; Once a Week [1867]; Punch [1867-70].*

FREDERICK JAMES SHIELDS ARWS 1833-1911. Initial letter C. Original drawing for decoration in *The Pilgrim's Progress*, 1864. Pen and pencil   Victoria and Albert Museum

FREDERICK JAMES SHIELDS ARWS 1833-1911. Initial letter C. Completed wood engraving for decoration in *The Pilgrim's Progress*, 1864   Victoria and Albert Museum

Exhib: L; M; New Gall; RWS.
Colls: BM; Fitzwilliam; Hartlepool; Manchester; V & AM.
Bibl: E. Mills, *Life and Letters of FJS,* 1912; *The Chapel of the Ascension,* 1912; Ball, *The Eng. Pre-Raphaelite Painters,* 1901; M. Hardie, *Watercol. Paint. in Brit.,* Vol.3, 1968, pp.128-129; J. Maas, *Victorian Painters,* 1970, p.146.
See illustrations.

SHINDLER, H.   **fl.1900-1908**
Illustrator of children's books. Worked in London and contributed rather weak drawings to *Fun,* 1900.
Illus: *Hullabulloos at Hucksters [W.A. Clark, 1908].*

SHIRLAW, Walter   **1838-1910**
Landscape painter. He was born at Paisley and became the first President of the Society of American Artists. He died at Madrid in 1910. He designed initial letters for books.
Exhib: RA.

SHOUBRIDGE, W.   **fl.1831-1853**
Topographical artist. He worked in Clapham, London and contributed to *The Cambridge Portfolio,* 1840.
Exhib: BI; NWS; RA; RBA.

SHURY, J.
Topographer. He contributed drawings of Oxfordshire to *Britton's Beauties of England and Wales,* 1813.

SHUTE, Mrs. E.L.   **fl.1883-1907**
Portrait painter. She worked in London and illustrated a child's book, *The Kelpie's Fiddle-Bow,* in 1892.
Exhib: G; L; RHA; RI; SWA.

SIBSON, Thomas   **1817-1844**
Painter, etcher and illustrator. He was born at Cross Canonby, Cumberland in 1817 and worked in Edinburgh before coming to London in 1838. According to W.J. Linton his first effort in illustration was a series of drawings to Dickens's *Old Curiosity Shop* and *Barnaby Rudge* which were not a success. He was then paid for by subscription to study under Kaulbach in Munich, 1842-44, but returned with consumption and lived with Linton. He died at Malta in 1844.
Illus: *Anatomy of Happiness [Ackermann, 1838]; Sibson's Racy Sketches of Expeditions From The Pickwick Club [1838, reissued 1885]; A Pinch of Snuff by Dean Snift of Brasen Nose [1840]; The Old Curiosity Shop [Dickens, 1841 (frontis)]; Hall's British Ballads; The History of England.*
Colls: BM; V & AM (sketchbook).
Bibl: W.J. Linton, *Memoirs,* 1895, p.70.

SICKERT, Bernard   1862-1932

Landscape painter, architectural painter and engraver. He was born at Munich in 1862, the brother of W.R. Sickert (q.v.). He became a member of the NEA in 1888 and died at Jordans on 2 August 1932.
Contrib: *The Yellow Book [1894 (portrait)].*
Exhib: G; GG; L; M; NEA; New Gall; RA; RBA; ROI.

SICKERT, Walter Richard   1860-1942

Street, interior and genre painter, etcher and illustrator. He was born in Munich in 1860, the brother of B. Sickert (q.v.). He studied at the Slade School in 1881 and then with Whistler from 1882, who took him on etching expeditions in London and taught him discipline in colouring. Sickert's best period was that following the death of his master, 1905 to 1920. During this time he made the drab areas of North London and particularly Camden Town his very own haunt, inspiring young painters with his French technique and contemptuous of fashion. He also painted in Dieppe and in Venice but never flattered these places or the sitters who came to his house for portraits. Sickert was a highly individual and bohemian figure who had the strength as artist and man to carry with him a circle of friends including critics like Roger Fry and artists such as Henry Tonks, Wilson Steer and Matthew Smith. He was a member of the London Group, 1916, was elected to the NEA in 1888, RE, 1887-92 and ARA, 1924 and RA, 1934. He resigned from the RA in 1935. He died at Bath in 1942.
Contrib: *The Idler; Cambridge Gazette; The Yellow Book; The Savoy; The Pall Mall Budget; Whirlwind; Vanity Fair;* all 1887-97, mostly portraits.
Exhib: FAS, 1973; G; GG; L; M; NEA; RA; RBA; RE; RHA; RI; ROI; RSA.
Colls: B; Manchester; Tate.
Bibl: *Print Collectors' Quarterly,* Vol.10, No.1, 1923, pp.31-60; Osbert Sitwell, *Noble Essences,* 1950, pp.163-206; Marjorie Lilly, *S The Painter and his Circle,* 1971; Wendy Barron, *S,* 1973; Denys Sutton, *WS,* 1976.

SIME, Sydney Herbert   1867-1941

Draughtsman and caricaturist. He was born in Manchester of a poor family and went down the mines as a boy to work as a scoop pusher. He then worked for a linen draper and a barber, before turning to sign-writing and entering the Liverpool School of Art. He moved to London and began to work for *Pick-Me-Up* and various halfpenny papers, his style being influenced by Aubrey Beardsley and Raven-Hill (qq.v.). He was Editor of a paper called *Eureka,* and became Joint Editor of *The Idler* from Volume 15.

Sime was a master of the macabre and the sinister finished with a beautiful cold pen line. Thorp saw in him the influence of Doré as well as Beardsley and considered that 'Pattern and colour were introduced not as a cover but as an aid to capable draughtsmanship...'. Sime claimed to be influenced by the Japanese print and many of his more startling compositions have a distinctly eastern composition and penmanship. The quality of brooding menace had its admirers and he was extensively employed for Lord Dunsany's stories and much patronised by Desmond Coke and Lord Howard de Walden. He held a one man show at the St George's Gallery in 1927 and died at Worplesdon, Surrey in 1941.
Illus: *The Sword of Welleran [Lord Dunsany, 1908; A Dreamer's Tale [Lord Dunsany, 1910]; Tales of Wonder [Lord Dunsany, 1917]; The Gods of Pegana [Lord Dunsany, 1919]; Time and the Gods [1923]; The King of Elfland's Daughter [Lord Dunsany, 1924]; Bogey Beasts [1930].*
Contrib: *The Ludgate Monthly [1891]; The Boy's Own Paper [1891-93]; The Sporting & Dramatic News [1893]; The Minister; The Windsor Magazine; The Pall Mall Magazine; The Idler; The Unicorn [1895]; Pick-Me-Up [1895]; Eureka [1897]; The Butterfly [1899]; Black & White [1899]; The Tatler [1901]; The Sketch [1904].*
Exhib: L; RBA.
Colls: V & AM; Worplesdon Hall.
Bibl: *'Apotheosis of the Grotesque',* The Idler, Vol.12, pp.755-766 illus; *The Studio,* Winter No., 1900-01, p.79, illus; Desmond Coke, *Confessions of an Incurable Collector,* 1928, pp.222-225; B. Peppin, *Fantasy Book Illustration,* 1975, pp.7, 18 illus.; Simon Heneage and Henry Ford, *SS Master of the Mysterious,* 1980.
See illustration.

SYDNEY HERBERT SIME 1867-1941. 'Midnight Oil'. Original drawing perhaps for illustration. Signed. 8¼in x 6¼in (32cm x 15.9cm)
Victoria and Albert Museum

SIMKIN, Richard   1840-1926

Military painter and illustrator. He worked at Aldershot and specialised in watercolours of uniforms and in designing posters for military recruitment. He died at Herne Bay in 1926.
Illus: *The Boys' Book of British Battles [1889]; Our Armies [1891]; Where Glory Calls [1893].*
Contrib: *Army and Navy Gazette; Chums [1892].*
Colls: India Office Lib.

SIMMONS, Graham C.   fl.1913-1919

Illustrator of comic genre subjects with bold hatching. He worked in London and contributed to *London Opinion,* 1913 and *Punch,* 1914.
Exhib: Inter Soc., 1916-19.

SIMMONS, W. St Clair   fl.1878-1917

Portrait, landscape and genre painter. He worked mostly in London, but at Hemel Hempstead, 1883.
Contrib: *The Pall Mall Budget [1893]; The English Illustrated Magazine [1893-95]; The Temple Magazine [1896]; The Windsor Magazine.*
Exhib: B; G; L; M; NEA; New Gall; P; RA; RBA; RI; ROI.

SIMONSEN, Niels   1807-1885

Painter, sculptor and lithographer. He was born in Copenhagen on 10 December 1807 and became a pupil of J.L. Lund, later visiting Italy and Algeria. He is described as 'Our Danish Artist' in *The Illustrated London News,* 1864.

SIMPSON, Joseph W.   RBA   1879-1939

Illustrator and caricaturist. He was born at Carlisle in 1879 and educated at Carlisle, studying art in Edinburgh. He became a close friend of D.Y. Cameron (q.v.) and was elected RBA in 1909. Simpson designed covers for Edinburgh publishers and was a prolific designer of bookplates, many of which were exhibited abroad. He died on 30 January 1939.

Publ: *Twelve Masters of Prose and Verse [1912]; God Save The King in La Grande Guerre [1915]; War Poems From The Times [1915].*

Illus: *Simpson His Book [1903]; The Book of Book Plates [1903]; Ibsen [1907]; Lions [1908]; Literary Lions [1910]; Edinburgh in 1911.*

Contrib: *Strand Magazine [1910-12, 1934, 1938]; The Student [Edinburgh]; London Opinion.*

Exhib: G; L; RBA; RSA; RSW.

Bibl: Haldane Macfall, '*JS Caricaturist'*, The Studio, 1905-06., pp.21-25; *Print Collectors' Quarterly,* Vol.19, No.3, 1932, pp.212-233.

SIMPSON, William   RI FRGS   1823-1899

Artist, special artist and illustrator. He was born at Glasgow on 28 October 1823. He was educated in Perth and Glasgow and after starting in an architect's office, was apprenticed to Glasgow lithographers and moved to Day & Sons of London in 1851. His first major commission was to prepare drawings for a lithographic folio of the Crimean War published by Colnaghi's, and he was sent to the Baltic and the Crimea itself. He can claim to be the first Special Artist to be in action. This was the beginning of a long series of tours, many of them for *The Illustrated London News* whose permanent staff he joined in 1866. He was in India for three years, visited Kashmir and Tibet, was on the Abyssinian campaign of 1868, at the Franco-German War of 1870 and witnessed the Paris Commune, 1871. He accompanied the Prince of Wales to India in 1875-76 and illustrated Dr Schliemann's excavations in 1877 and the work of the Afghan Boundary Commission in 1884-85. Simpson was not a great artist, but an able recorder in pencil, wash and watercolours. Many of his sketches are in pencil only with detailed colour notes and instructions added and usually accurately dated. He died in London on 17 April 1899. RI, 1879.

Illus: *Illustrations of the War in the East [1855-56]; Meeting the Sun, a Journey Round the World [1873]; Picturesque People or Groups from all Quarters of the Globe [1876]; Shikar and Tamasha [1876]; The Buddhist Praying Wheel [1896]; The Jonah Legend [1899]; Glasgow in the Forties [1899].*

Contrib: *Nature and Art [1867]; The Quiver [1890]; The Picturesque Mediterranean [1891]; The English Illustrated Magazine [1893-96].*

Exhib: G; L; RI; ROI.

Colls: Glasgow; V & AM; Witt Photo.

Bibl: *WS, RI,* Autobiography, 1903.

See illustration.

SIMSON, William RSA   1800-1847

Portrait and marine painter. He was born at Dundee in 1800 and studied at the Trustees Academy and visited the Low Countries in 1827. He was elected RSA in 1830 and travelled to Italy to study in the 1830s. He died on 29 August 1847, in London.

Illus: *Sinbad the Sailor [n.d]; Lockart's Ancient Spanish Ballads, 1841.*

Exhib: BI; RA; RBA; RSA.

Colls: Birkenhead; V & AM.

SINCLAIR, Helen Mok   fl.1912-1917

Miniature painter, black and white artist and illustrator. She illustrated children's books and worked in London.

Exhib: L; RA.

Colls: V & AM.

Bibl: *Modern Book Illustrators and Their Work,* Studio, 1914 illus.

SINGLEHURST, Mary

Student at Liverpool School of Art, 1906. A book illustration by her appears in *The Studio,* Vol. 38, 1906, p.77.

SINGLETON, Henry   1766-1839

Historical painter. He was born in London in 1766 and after studying at the RA Schools, he became a very prolific and successful painter, but failed to be elected to the RA. He undertook a great many book illustrations, his later work verging on the sentimental. He died in London in 1839.

Exhib: BI; RA; RBA.

Colls: BM; V & AM.

SKELTON, Joseph   FSA   1785-c.1850

Topographer and antiquary. He worked in London and Paris and ilustrated Robert Montgomery's poem *Oxford* in 1831.

Illus: *The Antiquities of Bristol; Cantabrigia Depicta [1809]; Oxonia Antiqua Restaurata [1823]; Antiquities of Oxfordshire [1823]; Pietas Oxoniensis [1828]; Meyrick's Arms and Armour [1830].*

SKELTON, Joseph Ratcliffe   RWA   fl.1888-1927

Figure painter and illustrator. He was born at Newcastle-upon-Tyne and was working in Bristol in 1893 and in London in 1925. Skelton's drawings are rather 1890s in style but the figures and drapery are North Country and solid. He was elected RWA.

Illus: *Our Empire Story [Black, 1908].*

Contrib: *The Graphic [1885-1912]; The Sketch [1897]; The Bystander [1904]; ILN [1907].*

Exhib: M; P; RA; RI; ROI.

Colls: V & AM.

SKELTON, Percival   fl.1849-1887

Landscape painter and illustrator. He was a relation of the 18th century engraver Joseph Skelton (q.v.) and a prolific illustrator of books. He was an unsuccessful candidate for the NWS from 1852 to 1861 and specialised in Scottish and coastal scenes in a detailed and sentimental mid-Victorian manner.

Illus: *The Tommiebeg Shootings [T. Jeans, 1860]; Harry's Big Boots [S.E. Gay, 1873].*

Contrib: *Metrical Tales [Samuel Lover, 1849]; The Poetical Works of Edgar Allan Poe [1858]; Childe Harold [1858-59]; ILN [1860]; The Illustrated Times [1860]; The Welcome Guest [1860]; The Churchman's Family Magazine [1863]; The Water Babies [Kingsley, 1863 (with Paton)]; Life and Lessons of Our Lord [1864]; Once a Week [1866]; Heber's Hymns [1867]; Episodes of Fiction [1870]; The Graphic [1870-76]; Thornbury's Legendary Ballads [1876].*

Exhib: RA; RBA.

Bibl: Chatto & Jackson, *Treatise on Wood Engraving,* 1861, p.569.

SKILL, Frederick John   RI   1824-1881

Landscape and portrait painter and illustrator. He was born in 1824 and trained as a steel engraver, working as a portrait artist on *The London Journal.* He lived in Venice for several years and acted as a Special Artist for *The Illustrated London News* during the Schleswig-Holstein affair. He may have been sent to China, but had little success with his work and committed suicide as a result of depression in London on 8 March 1881. He had been elected NWS in 1876.

Illus: *Holidays among the Mountains [M.B. Edwards, 1861].*

Contrib: *Metrical Tales [Samuel Lover, 1849]; ILN [1854-67]; The Illustrated Times [1860-65]; Cassell's Family Paper [1860-61]; The Welcome Guest [1860]; London Society [1862]; Foxe's Book of Martyrs [1866]; Beeton's Annual [1866]; The Graphic [1870-71].*

Exhib: NWS; RA; RBA.

Colls: BM; V & AM; Wallace; Witt Photo.

Bibl: *Art Journal,* 1881.

SKINNER, Edward F.   fl.1888-1925

Portrait and landscape painter and illustrator. He worked in London, 1888, Lewes, 1891 and St Ives, Cornwall, 1925. He contributed to *The Royal Magazine* and *Black & White,* 1891.

Exhib: L; RA; RBA; RWA.

SKINNER, Captain H.F.C.   fl.1904-1915

Figure artist. He worked in London and contributed to *Punch,* 1904 and 1914.

Exhib: RA; RI.

SLADER, Alfred   fl.1856-1866

Landscape painter. He contributed to *The Illustrated Times,* 1856-66 and especially to its Christmas issues.

SLEIGH, Bernard   1872-1954

Watercolourist, wood engraver, illustrator and decorator. He was born at Birmingham in 1872 and studied there, becoming associated with the Birmingham Guild of Handicraft. He was also connected with the Campden Guild of Handicraft and with the Essex House Press, for which he carried out work and cut blocks from the designs

WILLIAM SIMPSON 1823-1899. 'The Mont Cenis Railway – Ascent from Lanslebourg'. Original drawing for *The Illustrated London News*, 1869. Watercolour and wash. Signed and dated 1869. 8⅝in x 9⅛in (21.9cm x 23.2cm)

Victoria and Albert Museum

of William Strang (q.v.). His illustrations are characterised by a certain naïve charm combined with strength of design. He was elected RBSA in 1928.

Illus: *The Sea-King's Daughter [A. Mark, 1895]; The Faery Calendar [1920]; The Chapel, Madresfield Court [1923]; A Faery Pageant [1924].*

Contrib: *A Book of Pictured Carols [Birmingham School, 1893]; The Yellow Book [1896]; The Dome [1899-1900]; The Venture [1903].*

Exhib: B; FAS; G; L; New Gall; RA.

Colls: BM; V & AM; Witt Photo.

Bibl: *'The Future of Wood Engraving',* The Studio, Vol.14, 1898, pp.10-16, illus.; R.E.D. Sketchley, *Eng. Bk. Illus.,* 1903, pp.12, 130; C. Franklin, *The Private Presses,* 1969, pp.78, 153; *The Last Romantics,* Barbican Gallery cat., 1989, pp.112-113.

See Horne

SLEIGH, Henry

Book decorator. He contributed ornament to *Odes and Sonnets,* 1859 illustrated by Birket Foster (q.v.).

SLEIGH, John   **fl.1841-1872**

Landscape painter and illustrator. He worked in London and was a close friend of Charles Keene (q.v.) with whom he went on a sketching tour of Brittany. A record of this is preserved in twenty-four drawings by Keene, contributed to *Punch* on 6, 13 and 20 September 1856.

Contrib: *The Home Affections [Charles Mackay, 1858]; Passages From Modern English Poets [1862]; Sacred Poetry of the 16th, 17th and 18th Centuries [c.1862].*

Exhib: RA; RBA.

Bibl: G.S. Layard, *C.K.,* 1892, p.59.

SLINGER, F.J.   **fl.1858-1871**

Genre painter and illustrator. He worked in London and was assistant at the Slade School to Alphonse Legros.

Contrib: *Once A Week; The Graphic [1871].*

Exhib: BI, RA.

Bibl: W. Shaw Sparrow, *Memories of Life and Art,* 1925.

SLOCOMBE, Alfred   **fl.1865-1886**

Flower painter, etcher and watercolourist. He was a member of the RCA and did decorations for *The Illustrated London News,* 1866.

Exhib: BI; OWS; RA; RBA.

SLOCOMBE, Edward C.   **-1915**

Painter and etcher. He was the brother of Alfred Slocombe (q.v.) and worked at Watford, Hertfordshire from 1883. He contributed social and military subjects to *The Graphic,* 1873.

Exhib: FAS; L; New Gall; RA; RE; RHA.

SLY, B.

Topographer. He contributed drawings to *Knight's London,* 1841.

WILLIAM SMALL RI 1843-1929. Illustration to *Amelia*. Ink and wash with bodycolour. Signed and dated 1882. 4¼in x 7in (10.8cm x 17.8cm)

Author's Collection

SMALL, William   RI   **1843-1929**
Artist and illustrator. He was born in Edinburgh on 27 May 1843 and studied at the RSA Schools before coming to London in 1865. He had worked at Edinburgh in the art department of Messrs. Nelson, the publishers, and was already a highly competent black and white artist when he began to work for the leading magazines. Small was a very quick worker, very powerful in conception and very prolific. His genre subjects are drawn with a brilliance of detail and truth to line which is among the best work of the 1860s, but it is this early period up to 1870 which contains his most attractive work. Afterwards, Small begins to innovate and lose his way. He experiments with wash effects and these gradually supersede the beautiful line work and because of his reputation are copied by a whole generation of artists. He has therefore been quite rightly condemned by both White and Reid. His power was still expressed in the double pages that he was given in *The Graphic* until about 1900, vast areas for which he was paid sixty guineas, making him the most highly paid illustrator of his time. Small's life span stretches amazingly from the early numbers of *Once a Week* right up to the avant-garde *Gypsy* of 1915. For the last few years of his life he lived at Worcester, having been elected RI in 1883 and HRSA in 1917. He died on 23 December 1929.
Illus: *Words for the Wise; Miracles of Heavenly Love; Marion's Sundays [all 1864]; Washerwoman's Foundling [1867]; A Protégée of Jack Hamilton's [Bret Harte, 1894].*
Contrib: *Shilling Magazine [1865-66]; Once a Week [1866]; Good Words [1866-68]; The Sunday Magazine [1866-68, 1871]; Cassell's Family Paper [1866, 1870]; Sunday At Home [1866]; Pen and Pencil Pictures From the Poets [1866]; Touches of Nature by Eminent Artists [1866]; Ballad Stories of the Affections [1866]; London Society [1867-69]; The Argosy [1867]; The Quiver [1867]; Poems by Jean Ingelow [1867]; Idyllic Pictures [1867]; Two Centuries of Song [1867]; Foxe's Book of Martyrs [1867]; Heber's Hymns [1867]; The Spirit of Praise [1867]; Illustrated Book of Sacred Poems [1867]; Golden Thoughts From Golden Fountains*

[1867]; Ode on the Morning of Christ's Nativity [1867]; North Coast and Other Poems [1868]; The Graphic [1869-1900]; Pictures From English Literature [1870]; Good Words For The Young [1871]; Novello's National Nursery Rhymes [1871]; Judy's Almanac [1872]; Thornbury's Legendary Ballads [1876]; Dalziel's Bible Gallery [1880]; Chums [1892]; Fun; The Gypsy [1915].
Exhib: B; FAS; G; L; M; RA; RHA: RI; ROI; RSA.
Colls: Birmingham (St George's Soc.); V & AM.
Bibl: Forrest Reid, *Illustrators of the Sixties,* 1928, pp.216-227 illus. See illustration.

SMALLFIELD, Frederick   ARWS   **1829-1915**
Genre and portrait painter and illustrator. He was born at Homerton in 1829 and studied at the RA Schools and was elected ARWS in 1860. He was a prolific watercolourist, worked in London and died there on 10 September 1915.
Contrib: *Willmott's Sacred Poetry [1862]; Passages From Modern English Poets [1862].*
Exhib: B; BI; G; GG; L; M; RA; RI; ROI; RWS.

SMALLWOOD, William Frome   **1806-1834**
Architect and draughtsman. He was born in London on 24 June 1806 and became a pupil of the architect D.N. Cottingham. He travelled to the Continent to make drawings of churches for *The Penny Magazine* and exhibited landscapes. He died in London on 22 April 1834.
Contrib: *Knight's London [1842].*
Exhib: RA; RBA.
Bibl: *Architectural Magazine*, Vol.I, 1834, p.184.

SMIRKE, Robert   RA   **1752-1845**
Artist and illustrator. He was born at Wigton near Carlisle in 1752 and came to London in 1766, studying at the RA Schools in 1771. Smirke was one of the most prolific book illustrators of the early 19th century, working for all the leading publishers and specialising in the 'conversation piece' drawing within decorative borders which

augmented so many three volume novels. His drawings are usually very fine in execution, the pen line clear, the shadows and modelling in washes sometimes with a trace of blue. He was elected an ARA in 1791 and an RA in 1793. He died in London in 1845.
Illus: *Bowyer's History of England; The Adventure of Hunchback [1814, AT 366]; Don Quixote [1818].*
Exhib: BI; RA; RBA; Soc. of Artists.
Colls: BM; V & AM.
Bibl: Hammelmann & Boase, *Book Illustrators in Eighteenth Century England*, Yale, 1975.

SMITH, A.T.   fl.1899-1914
Humorous figure artist. He contributed wooden doll subjects to *Punch*, 1902-14 and to *Fun*, 1899.
Colls: Witt Photo.

SMITH, Arthur Reginald RWS RSW   1872-1934
Landscape and figure painter. He was born at Skipton-in-Craven in 1872 and studied and taught at the Keighley School of Art and then at South Kensington. He travelled in Italy and had a one man show at Leighton House in 1907-08. He was elected ARWS in 1917 and RWS in 1925 and RSW in 1925. He died at Bolton Abbey in 1934.
Illus: *The Lake Counties [W.G. Collingwood, 1932].*
Exhib: B; FAS; G; L; M; RA; RI; RSW; RWS.
Colls: Bradford; Bristol; V & AM.

SMITH, Lieutenant-Colonel Charles Hamilton   1776-1859
Topographical draughtsman and antiquary. He was born in East Flanders in 1776 and was educated at Richmond, Surrey before training as an officer in the Austrian military academy at Malines and Louvain. He joined the British Army in 1797 as a volunteer and served in the West Indies and Holland before becoming quartermaster on the Walcheren Expedition. After a visit to the United States he retired in 1820 and settled at Plymouth where he formed an artists' club. For most of his life, Smith made watercolours of costume and natural history which he used to illustrate his books. He died at Plymouth in 1859.
Publ: *Selections of Ancient Costume of Great Britain and Ireland, 7th to 16th Century [with S.R. Meyrick, 1814]; Costume of the Original Inhabitants of the British Isles to the 6th Century [1815]: Natural History of the Human Species [1848].*
Colls: BM; Greenwich.

SMITH, Charles John   1803-1838
Engraver and antiquary. He was born in Chelsea in 1803 and became a pupil of Charles Pye, the engraver. He painted views of London buildings, illustrated antiquarian works and was elected FSA in 1837. He died in London on 23 November 1838.
Colls: BM.

SMITH, Edwin Dalton   1800-
Miniaturist and painter of flowers. He was the son and pupil of Anker Smith and was born in London on 23 October 1800. He made drawings for *The Botanic Garden*, B. Maund, 1825-35.
Exhib: NWS; RA; RBA.

SMITH, J.
Contributor of genre subjects to *The Illustrated London News*, 1873.

SMITH, J. Moyr   fl.1885-1920
Decorative designer and occasional illustrator. After starting as an architect, he began to produce illustrations for *Fun* and other magazines in the 1870s. He was Editor of *Decoration*, 1880-89 and drew in a flat Etruscan style derived from his study of ancient art. The drawings are very often as flat as the jokes; there was one example of this artist in the Handley-Read collection.
Illus: *Tales of Old Thule Collected and Illustrated by J. Moyr Smith [1879]; Shakespeare For Children: Lamb's Tales [c.1897].*
Contrib: *Fun; Doré's Thomas Hood [1870, decor]; Punch [1872- 78].*
Exhib: B; G; L; RA; RBA; RSA; RSW.
Colls: Witt Photo.

SMITH, James Burrell   1822-1897
Landscape painter. He was born in 1822 and between 1843 and 1854, lived at Alnwick and studied under T.M. Richardson (q.v.) during his

JOHN THOMAS SMITH 1766-1833. 'Black Joe'. Illustration in *Vagabondiana* or *Anecdotes of Mendicant Wanderers*, 1817. Etching

first years. He set up as a drawing-master in London in 1854 and made sketches in the manner of Richardson, particularly of waterfalls. He died in London in 1897.
Contrib: *ILN [1883-87].*
Exhib: RBA.
Colls: Alnwick Castle; Fitzwilliam; Newcastle; V & AM.

SMITH, Jessie Wilcox   -1935
Artist and illustrator. She was born in Philadelphia and worked in New York, many of her books being published in this country. She studied with Howard Pyle (q.v.) at the Philadelphia Fine Art Institute and specialised in children's books. She died in New York on 4 May 1935.
Illus: *A Child's Garden of Verses [R.L. Stevenson, 1905].*

SMITH, John Thomas   1766-1833
Draughtsman and antiquary. He was born in London in 1766, the son of Nathaniel Smith, the sculptor and printseller. He studied art with Joseph Nollekens and J.K. Sherwin and then set up for himself as a portrait and topographical engraver. He worked at Edmonton from 1788 and was made Keeper of Prints and Drawings at the British Museum from 1816. Smith is better remembered as a writer on the arts than as an artist, he produced a number of books of memoirs which form important links between the 18th and 19th century schools and are valuable sources of facts. His own work as an etcher is incisive and reminiscent of Callot and sometimes even of Rembrandt. He died in London in 1833.
Publ: *Nollekens and his Times [1828]; A Book for a Rainy Day [1845, re-issued 1905].*
Illus: *Remarks on Rural Scenery [1797]; Antiquities of London*

SNEYD, REV. WALTER 1809-1888. Illustration to the *Spruggins Gallery*. Lithograph

[1800]; *Antiquities of Westminster [1807]; The Ancient Topography of London [1815]; Vagabondiana [1817]; The Cries of London [1839]*.
Contrib: *Knight's London [1842]*.
Exhib: RA.
Colls: BM; Fitzwilliam.
See illustration.

SMITH, Joseph Clarendon　　　　　　　　　**1778-1810**
Topographical draughtsman. He worked in the Thames Valley and the Home Counties, touring in Warwickshire in 1805 and Cornwall in 1806. He died after a visit to Madeira which he had visited as a cure for consumption, 1810.
Contrib: *The Beauties of England and Wales [1803, 1814-15]; Topographical Cabinet [1811]; The Antiquarian Itinerary [1817]*.
Exhib: BI; RA.
Colls: BM; V & AM; Witt Photo.

SMITH, Percy John Delf　　　　　　　　　**1882-1948**
Painter, etcher and illustrator. He was born in London on 11 March 1882 and was mainly self-taught although he studied at the Camberwell School of Art. After service in the First War, he worked in the US, 1927, and in Palestine, 1932. Smith specialised in fine lettering and the illumination of books but also designed alphabets and worked for private presses. There is a bookplate by this artist in the Victoria and Albert Museum.
Illus: *Quality in Life [1919]; The Dance of Death [1914-18]; Twelve Drypoints of the War, 1914-18; The Bible in Spain [1925]; The Metamorphosis of Aiax [Sir J. Harrington, Fanfrolico, 1927]*.
Exhib: L; RI.
Colls: V & AM; Witt Photo.

SMITH, Robert Catterson　　　　　　　　　**fl.1880-1892**
Landscape and figure painter. He worked in London and contributed figure subjects and architecture to *The English Illustrated Magazine,* 1890-92.
Exhib: L; M; RA; RBA; RHA; RI.

SMITH, Sydney　　　　　　　　　**fl.1852-1867**
Illustrator of rural figure subjects. He contributed to *Cassell's Illustrated Readings,* 1867.
Exhib: RA; SS.

SMITH, Thomas C.
Figure artist. Contributed to *Punch,* 1903.

SMITH, W.G.　　　　　　　　　**fl.1866-1880**
Botanical illustrator. He contributed drawings to *The Wild Flowers of Great Britain,* R. Hogg and George W. Johnson, 1866-80 and drew an initial letter for *Punch* in 1878.

SMITH, W. Thomas　　　　　　　　　**1862-**
Portrait, figure and historical painter. He was working in London in 1890, but may have emigrated to Canada before 1925.
Illus: *The Wilds of the West Coast [Oxley, 1894]*.
Contrib: *The Quiver [1890]; Good Cheer [1894]; The Boy's Own Paper*.
Exhib: L; M; P; RA; RBA; RI.

SMITH, Winifred　　　　　　　　　**fl.1890-1896**
Illustrator of children's books. She won commendations at the Nat. Competition, South Kensington in 1896 and was described by *The Bookman,* in August 1894, as an artist 'whose designs in black and white are witty, pretty and effective'.
Illus: *Childrens Singing Games [1894]*.
Bibl: *The Studio,* Vol.8, 1896, p.228 illus.

SMYTH, Dorothy Carleton　　　　　　　　　**fl.1901-1925**
Painter and illustrator. She studied at the Glasgow School, c.1901 and worked in Glasgow, 1907 and at Cambuslang, 1925.
Exhib: G; L; RSA; RA.
Bibl: *The Studio,* Winter No., 1900-01, p.55 illus; Vol.25, 1901-02, pp.281-286.

SMYTHE, Ernest　　　　　　　　　**fl.1896-1899**
Illustrator and watercolourist. He specialised in hunting subjects and contributed to *The Sketch,* 1896 and *The Illustrated London News,* 1899.
Colls: V & AM.

SMYTHE, Lionel Percy   RA　　　　　　　　　**1839-1918**
Figure and landscape painter in watercolours. He was born in London on 4 September 1839 and was educated at Kings College School and studied art at Heatherley's. Smythe worked in the warm colours and genre subjects popularised by Fred Walker (q.v.) and worked chiefly at the Château de Honvault, Wimereux, Pas-de-Calais. He was elected ARA in 1898 and RA in 1911, having been RWS from 1894. He died on 10 July 1918.
Contrib: *ILN [1874, 1879, 1880]*.
Exhib: B; FAS; G; L; M; RA; RBA; RI; ROI; RWS.
Colls: Greenwich; V & AM.
Bibl: R.M. Whitlaw and W.L. Wyllie, *LPS, RA,* 1923; M. Hardie, *Watercol. Paint. in Brit.,* Vol.3, 1968, p.140-141.

SNARK, The
Pseudonym of sports illustrator in the *Winning Post, Winter Annual,* 1906-07.

SNEYD, Rev. John　　　　　　　　　**1766-1835**
Amateur caricaturist. He was born in 1766, the son of Ralph Sneyd of Keele Hall, Staffs, (now Keele University) and was Rector of Elford for over forty years. He was a friend and patron of Gillray and died unmarried on 2 July 1835. His nephew was the Rev. W. Sneyd (q.v.).
Bibl: M.D. George, *English Political Caricature,* Vol.2, 1959, p.263.

SNEYD, Rev. Walter　　FSA　　　　　　　　　**1809-1888**
Amateur caricaturist. He was born in 1809, the son of Walter Sneyd of Keele Hall and his wife the Hon. Louisa Bagot, and nephew of the Rev. John Sneyd (q.v.). He was educated at Westminster and Christ Church, Oxford, taking his BA in 1831. He succeeded his brother at Keele Hall in 1870 and died there on 2 July 1888.

Illus: *Portraits of the Spruggins Family [1829, privately printed].*
Bibl: *Walford's County Families; Alumni Oxoniensis;* Simon Houfe, 'Caricaturist of the Country House', *CL,* 3 April 1980.
See illustration.

SNOW, J.W.   **fl.1832-1848**
Horse painter. He worked in London and contributed illustrations to *Tattersalls British Race Horses,* 1838 and *The Illustrated London News,* 1848.
Exhib: RBA, 1832.
Colls: BM.

SNOWMAN, Isaac   **1874-**
Genre and portrait painter. He was born in London in 1874 and studied at the RA Schools before becoming a pupil of Bouguereau and Constant in Paris. He painted state portraits of Edward VII and George V and eventually emigrated to Israel.
Contrib: *ILN [1897-98].*
Exhib: B; L; RA; ROI.

SOLOMON, Abraham   **1824-1862**
Painter and illustrator. He was born in London in May 1824 and studied at Sass's Bloomsbury Art School in 1838, entering the RA Schools in 1839. Solomon painted a great number of subjects from literature but scored instant success with his railway carriage dramas of 1854, 'First Class – The Meeting' and 'Second Class – The Parting'. His work was well-known to the public through its popularisation in prints and he was a regular RA exhibitor. He died at Biarritz on 19 December 1862. He was the brother of Simeon and Rebecca Solomon (qq.v.).
Contrib: *ILN [1857]; Favourite Modern Ballads; Household Song [1861].*
Exhib: BI; RA.
Bibl: Chatto & Jackson, *Treatise on Wood Engraving,* 1861, p.599; J. Maas, *Victorian Painters,* 1970, p.238.

SOLOMON, Rebecca
Portrait and history painter. She was the sister of Abraham and Simeon Solomon (qq.v.) and exhibited regularly between 1852 and 1869. She contributed illustrations to *The Churchman's Family Magazine,* 1864 and *London Society.*
Exhib: RA.
Colls: Witt Photo.

SOLOMON, Simeon   **1840-1905**
Painter, draughtsman and illustrator. He was born in London in 1840, the brother of Abraham and Rebecca Solomon (qq.v.). He was a pupil of Cary's Academy in Bloomsbury and then entered the RA Schools, exhibiting at the exhibitions from 1858. Solomon became part of the Rossetti circle, was a friend of Burne-Jones (q.v.) and A.C. Swinburne and these contacts had a strong influence on his work. He travelled to Florence in 1866 and to Rome in 1869, but gradually sunk into a life of idleness and dissipation. His most vivid works are those featuring contemporary Jewish life such as the illustrations to *Jewish Customs* and they have an almost Rembrandtesque intensity. He was capable of evoking an air of eastern mystery in his drawings and fortunately his best work is his earliest and it was at this time that he was working for the book. He died in penury in 1905.
Publ: *A Vision of Love Revealed in Sleep [1871].*
Contrib: *Once A Week [1862]; Good Words [1862]; The Leisure Hour [1866]; Dark Blue [1871-73]; Dalziel's Bible Gallery [1880]; Art Pictures From The Old Testament [1897]; Lives of the Minor Saints [Mrs. Jameson, c.1860].*
Exhib: RA.
Colls: V & AM.
Bibl: A.C. Swinburne, SS, The Bibelot, XIV, 1908; B. Falk, *Five Years Dead,* 1937; Forrest Reid, *Illustrators of the Sixties,* 1928, pp.103-104; J.E. Ford, SS, 1964; J. Maas, *Victorian Painters,* 1970, p.146; L. Lambourne, *A SS Sketch-Book,* Apollo, Vol.85, 1967, pp.59-61.
See illustration.

SOLOMON, Solomon Joseph   **1860-1927**
Portrait and figure painter and illustrator. He was born in London on

SIMEON SOLOMON 1840-1905. 'Jepthah and his daughter'. Original drawing for illustration, probably intended for *Dalziel's Bible Gallery,* 1881, not used. Pen and ink. Signed. 6¼in x 4¼in (15.9cm x 10.8cm)   Victoria and Albert Museum

16 September 1860 and studied at Heatherley's and the RA Schools before going to the Munich Academy and the École des Beaux Arts in Paris, 1879. He travelled and worked in Italy, Spain and Morocco and became Vice-President of the Maccabeans Society and President of the RBA, 1918. He had been elected ARA in 1896 and RA in 1906, having been a member of the NEA since 1886. He was the first artist to initiate camouflage for the British Army in the First World War. He died in London on 27 July 1927.
Illus: *For The Temple [G.A. Henty, 1887].*
Contrib: *Black & White [1891]; The Graphic [1897-1904].*
Exhib: B; G; GG; L; M; NEA; New Gall; P; RA; RBA; RHA; ROI.
Bibl: J. Maas, *Victorian Painters,* 1970, p.232.

SOLON, Leon Victor   **1872-**
Artist, sculptor and decorator. He was born at Stoke-on-Trent in 1872, the son of Louis M. Solon, artist and author. He was educated privately and then studied at the RCA where he was a scholar and medallist. Solon's connection with the Staffordshire potteries provides an interesting relationship between illustration and ceramics, many of his designs for Mintons for example, reflect the Symbolists and the work of Aubrey Beardsley (q.v.). Solon was the designer of one of the early posters for *The Studio,* but he emigrated to the United States early in the century and worked in Lakeland, Florida.
Contrib: *The Parade [1897]; Les Trophées [De Herdia, 1904].*
Bibl: *The Studio,* Winter No., 1900-01, p.65, illus.

SOMERVILLE, Edith Anna Œnone   **1858-1949**
Author and illustrator. She was born at Drishane, Ireland in 1858, the daughter of Lt.-Colonel Somerville of a leading Anglo-Irish family. After being educated at home, she studied art in Paris under

Colarossi and Delecluse and attended the Westminster School of Art. Edith Somerville returned to Ireland and set up house with her cousin Violet Martin, collaborating with her on a number of books on Irish life and character. Her knowledge of the country and particularly its sport, gained from two spells as Master of the West Carbery Foxhounds, made her books both individual and popular. Most of them were illustrated by black and white sketches which typify the shabby genteel life of the Irish landowner before 1914. Edith Somerville continued to write after the death of Violet Martin and became a vociferous and ardent feminist, dying at her old childhood home of Drishane in 1949. She had one man shows at Goupil and Walker's Galleries in 1920 and 1923.

Illus: *The Real Charlotte [1894]; Clear As The Noon Day [E. Penrose, 1894]; The Silver Fox; Some Experiences of an Irish R.M. [1899]; Further Experiences of an Irish R.M. [1908]; Dan Russel the Fox [1911]; In Mr Knox's Country [1915].*
Contrib: *Black & White [1893].*
Exhib: FAS; L; RHA; SWA.
Bibl: M. Collis, *Somerville & Ross A Biography*, 1958.

SOMERVILLE, Howard   **1873-c.1940**
Figure painter, illustrator and etcher. He was born at Dundee in 1873 and after being privately educated, studied science and engineering at Dundee but abandoned this for art. He settled in London in 1899 and began to contribute to *Punch* and other magazines. Somerville, who also specialised in interiors and still-life, worked for some time in New York and Glasgow and was elected RPE in 1917. His ink drawings of women are rather highly finished and mannered.
Contrib: *Moonshine [1900]; Punch [1903-06]; ILN [1911].*
Exhib: B; G; GG; L; NEA; P; RA; RSA.
Colls: Liverpool; Witt Photo.

SONNTAG, W. Louis   **1870-**
American illustrator. Born in New York in 1870. Contributor of railway drawings to *The English Illustrated Magazine,* 1896.

SOPER, George   **RE**   **1870-1942**
Watercolourist, etcher, wood engraver and illustrator. He was born in London in 1870 and studied with the etcher Sir Frank Short. He worked at Harmer Green, Welwyn, Hertfordshire from about 1911 and was still exhibiting in 1930.
Illus: *The Water Babies [Charles Kingsley, 1908].*
Contrib: *ILN [1897 (S. Africa)]; Cassell's Magazine [1898]; The Boys' Own Paper; Chums; The Graphic [1901-04]; Strand Magazine [1911].*
Exhib: FAS; G; L; NEA; RA; RBA; RE; RHA; RI; RSA.
See Horne

SOUTHALL, Joseph Edward   **1861-1944**
Painter, designer and engraver. He was born at Nottingham in 1861 and educated at York and Scarborough before serving an apprenticeship to an architect, 1878-82. In 1883 he came to realize that all fine art was architectural and that the architect must study art and therefore he spent some time in Italy studying tempera painting. He was also much influenced by John Ruskin and studied drawing and carving and interested himself in furniture design and embroidery. He painted frescoes at the Birmingham Art Gallery and was examiner at the Birmingham School of Art. He was elected RBSA in 1902, NEA in 1926 and RWS in 1931. Southall's work is often anaemic in colouring and lifeless in content but it had some popularity at the time. He died in 1944.
Illus: *The Story of Bluebeard [1895]; The Ghosts of the Slain: A Vision of the Future [1915]; Fables and Illustrations – The Obliterator [1918].*
Contrib: *The Quest [1894-96]; The Yellow Book [1896];* political pamphlets during the First World War, n.d.
Exhib: B; FAS; G; GG; L; M; NEA; New Gall; RA; RWS.
Colls: Birmingham; Witt Photo.
Bibl: *Modern Book Illustrators and Their Work*, Studio, 1914; *JES*, FAS catalogue, 1980.

SOWERBY, Amy Millicent   **1878-1967**
Watercolourist and illustrator. She was the daughter of John G.

Sowerby (q.v.) and was working at Colchester, 1900 and Abingdon, 1904. She illustrated *A Child's Garden of Verses,* R.L. Stevenson, 1913.
Illus: *Childhood [1907]; Yesterday's Children [1908]; Cinderella [1915]; The Joyous Book; The Bonnie Book; The Dainty Book [1915-22].*
See Horne

SOWERBY, James   **1757-1822**
Botanical illustrator. He was born in London in 1757 and studied at the RA Schools. He set up in practice as a portrait and flower painter in London but finally abandoned this for the study of botany. He issued and illustrated *English Botany,* 1790-1814; *English Fungi,* 1797-1815; *English Botany or Coloured Figures of British Plants,* 1832-40. He died in London in 1822, leaving a large family, many of whom became botanical artists.
Publ: *An Easy Introduction to Drawing Flowers [1778]; A New Evidence of Colours...[1809].*
Exhib: RA; Soc. of Artists.
Colls: BM; Nat. Hist.
Bibl: Peter Bicknell, *Gilpin to Ruskin, Drawing Masters & Their Manuals 1800-1860*, Fitzwilliam Museum, 1988.

SOWERBY, John G.   **fl.1876-1925**
Landscape and flower painter. He worked in Newcastle-upon-Tyne, Gateshead and Ross-on-Wye and contributed a number of illustrations to children's books, all showing the marked influence of Kate Greenaway (q.v.). Father of Millicent Sowerby (q.v.).
Illus: *Afternoon Tea – Rhymes for Children [c.1880]; At Home [1881].*
Exhib: B; G; L; M; RA; RI; RSA.

SPARE, Austin Osman   **1888-1956**
Painter, engraver, imaginary artist and illustrator. He was born at Snowhill on 31 December 1888 and studied at the Lambeth School and the RCA, exhibiting in the National Competition of 1903. Spare was a mystic and poetic draughtsman who was strongly influenced by Aubrey Beardsley's work in his early years. He was Editor of *Form,* 1916-17 and *The Golden Hind,* 1922-24 and illustrated in pen and ink as well as in chalk and watercolour and designed bookplates. He became unbalanced in later life and died in 1956.
Illus: *Earth Inferno [1905]; A Book of Satyrs [1907]; The Book of Pleasure; The Psychology of Ecstasy [1913]; Anathema of Zos; The Sermon of Hypocrites.*
Contrib: *Form [1916-17].*
Exhib: RA.
Colls: Ashmolean; Leeds; V & AM; Witt Photo.
Bibl: K. Grant, *Oracles of AOS*, 1975; *The Left Hand Path*, 1976.

SPECHTER, Otto or SPEKTER   **1807-1871**
German illustrator of children's books. Born and died in Hamburg. He was extremely popular in Britain in the mid-19th century. He contributed to *Parables From Nature* by Mrs Gatty, 1867.

SPEED, Harold   **1872-1957**
Landscape and portrait painter. He was born in London in 1872, the son of Edward Speed, the architect and was educated privately before studying at the RCA, 1887, at the RA Schools, 1890, and in Paris, Vienna and Rome, on a travelling scholarship, 1893. He was elected RP in 1897 and was Master of the Art Workers Guild in 1916.
Publ: *The Science and Practice of Drawing [1913]; The Science and Practice of Oil Painting [1924].*
Contrib: *The Graphic [1899-1902].*
Exhib: B; FAS, 1914, 1922, 1938; G; L; M; NEA; New Gall; P; RA; RBA; RCA; RHA; ROI; RSA.
Colls: Belfast; Birmingham; Bristol; Liverpool; Manchester.

SPEED, Lancelot   **1860-1931**
Coastal painter and black and white illustrator. He was born in London in 1860, the son of a barrister and was educated at Rugby and Clare College, Cambridge. Speed worked principally as a book illustrator from about 1890, concentrating on shipping subjects. He worked in Barnet and Southend-on-Sea and died there on 21 December 1931.
Illus: *The Red Fairy Book [c.1890]; The Limbersnigs [1896]; The Last Days of Pompeii [Lytton, 1897]; Hypatia [C. Kingsley, 1897];*

Novels of Robert Barr [1897]; The Romance of Early British Life [1908].
Contrib: *ILN [1887-94]; The Sporting & Dramatic News [1892]; The English Illustrated Magazine [1895-97]; Good Words [1898]; The Sphere; Punch; The Windsor Magazine.*

SPENCE, Percy F.S.   **1868-1933**
Painter and illustrator. He was born at Sydney, NSW, in 1868 and spent his early career in Australia and Fiji, exhibiting his work with the Art Society at New South Wales. He came to London in 1895 and resided there for the rest of his life, working from Kensington and contributing to many magazines. Spence was a fine figure draughtsman, his pen work frequently used with colour washes. He was acquainted with R.L. Stevenson in the South Seas and drew portraits of him. He died in London in September 1933.
Contrib: *The Graphic [1900-06]; Punch [1903]; ILN [1905]; The Ludgate Monthly; The Pall Mall Magazine; The Windsor Magazine.*
Exhib: B; L; New Gall; RA.
Colls: V & AM.

SPENCE, Robert   RE   **1870-**
Painter, etcher and illustrator. He was a cousin of Birket Foster (q.v.). He was born at Tynemouth on 6 October 1870 and studied at the Newcastle School of Art, at the Slade School, 1892-95 and in Paris with Cormon. Spence is an important and original figure because of his use of the etched plate for both illustrations and text in the book, thus continuing the visionary tradition of William Blake (q.v.). His most notable achievement in this medium is the *George Fox His Journal.* He also etched scenes from Wagner and illustrated for magazines. His work was particularly commended by Walter Crane for its romantic feeling and dramatic force. He was elected ARE in 1897 and RE in 1902.
Contrib: *The Quarto [1896].*
Exhib: FAS; L; NEA; RA; RE; RWA.
Bibl: *British Book Illustrators Yesterday and Today,* Studio, 1923.

SPILSBURY, Francis B.   **fl.1799-1805**
Amateur artist and draughtsman. He was a naval doctor and made drawings on his voyages, some of which were used in publications. Some of these were published by Daniel Orme as *Picturesque Scenes in the Holy Land and Syria,* 1803, AT 381.
Colls: Searight Coll. at V & AM; Witt Photo.

SPOONER, Mrs Minnie Dibdin (née Davison)   **fl.1893-1927**
Portrait painter and etcher. She drew for children's books and married the artist C.S. Spooner. She was elected RMS in 1901.
Illus: *The Gold Staircase [Wordsworth, 1906].*
Exhib: L; New Gall; RA; RHA; RMS.

SPOTTISWOODE, William
Amateur artist. He published *Journey Through Eastern Russia,* 1857, AT 232, illustrated by lithos from his own drawings.

SPREAT, William   **fl.1841-1848**
Landscape painter working in the Exeter area. He published *Picturesque Sketches of the Churches of Devon,* 1842.
Colls: Exeter.

SPURRIER, Steven   RA RBA   **1878-1961**
Painter, black and white and poster artist. He was born in London in 1878 and studied art at Lambeth School and Heatherley's, being elected ROI in 1912, RBA in 1934 and ARA in 1943 and RA in 1952. In his early days he specialised in genre and social realistic subjects for the magazines, later undertaking theatre illustration. He died in 1961.
Contrib: *The Graphic [1910]; Strand Magazine [1910-19, 1931-49]; Radio Times [1936].*
Exhib: G; GG; L; M; RA; RBA; RHA; RI; ROI; RSA.
Colls: RA; V & AM; Witt Photo.
See Horne

SPURRIER, W.R.   **fl.1896-1905**
Figure artist specialising in cockney children. He contributed to *Fun,* 1896-1900 and to *Punch,* 1902-05.

STACEY, Walter S.   **1846-1929**
Landscape and genre painter and illustrator. He was born in London in 1846 and studied at the RA Schools and was elected RBA in 1881 and ROI in 1883. He worked in Hampstead, 1890 to 1902 and then in the West Country at New Milton, Tiverton and Newton Abbot. His largest output of illustrations was for boys' books of adventure. He died at Newton Abbot in September 1929.
Illus: *Follow My Leader [T.B. Read, 1885]; Bible Pictures [1890]; In Greek Waters [G.A. Henty, 1893]; The White Conquerors of Mexico [Kirk Munroe, 1894]; In Press Gang Days [Pickering, 1894]; Bible Stories [L.L. Weedon, 1911].*
Contrib: *The Cornhill Magazine [1883-84]; The Quiver [1891-95]; The Strand Magazine [1891-1906]; Good Words [1891]; Chums [1892]; The Temple Magazine [1896]; The Wide World Magazine [1898]; Cassell's Family Magazine; The Boys' Own Paper; The Girls' Own Paper; Black & White.*
Exhib: L; M; NEA; RA; RBA; RI; ROI.

STAFFORD, John Phillips   **1851-1899**
Painter and humorous artist. He was born in 1851 and acted as cartoonist for *Funny Folks* for a number of years and was also a contributor to *Punch,* 1894. He made stage designs for the theatre and died in March 1899.
Exhib: RA, 1871-86.

STAMP, Winifred L.   **fl.1899-1925**
Figure and miniature painter. She worked in Stepney, London and was trained at the Regent Street Polytechnic. She exhibited some book illustrations in the National Competition, South Kensington in 1905-06.
Exhib: RA; RMS.

STAMPA, George Loraine   **1875-1951**
Black and white artist. He was born in London on 29 November 1875, the son of an architect, and was educated at Bedford Modern School. He studied art at Heatherley's, c.1892 and at the RA Schools, 1895-1900. Stampa was a raffish bohemian who was the spiritual successor of Charles Keene and Phil May (qq.v.), preferring the London streets for his drawings to the salons of Mayfair. It was not surprising therefore to find him adopted as a *Punch* artist from 1895, contributing bushels of urchins, street arabs, cockney servant gals and drunken cabbies. He gave a touch of realism to *Punch* which was much needed, but his pen work was very traditional. He undertook some decorative work such as covers and initial letters and also made portraits.
Illus: *Easy French Exercises; Ragamuffins [1916]; Anthology In Praise of Dogs.*
Contrib: *Punch [1895-1950]; Moonshine [1898]; Strand Magazine [1909-33]; The Graphic [1910].*
Exhib: RA; Walker's Gall.
Bibl: R.G.G. Price, A *History of Punch,* p.249; Flavia Stampa Gruss, *The Last Bohemian,* 1991.
See Horne

STANDFUST, G.B.
Draughtsman and illustrator. He illustrated *Shelley's Poetical Works,* 1844 and drew humorous subjects. There is a delightful study of Count D'Orsay by this artist in the Witt Photo Library.
Exhib: RA,1844.

STANFIELD, William Clarkson   **1793-1867**
Marine and landscape painter and illustrator. He was born at Sunderland in 1793, the son of J.F. Stanfield, an Irish actor and anti-slavery writer. He was apprenticed to an Edinburgh heraldic painter but went to sea in 1808 and was pressed into the Navy in 1812. He made voyages on an East Indian ship to China, but left the service in 1818 to devote all his time to theatrical scene painting. He met and became a close friend of David Roberts (q.v.) and went to London with him in 1820, where they were employed on the stage work at Drury Lane Theatre. Stanfield soon had great success, became part of Charles Dickens's circle and an intimate with Douglas Jerrold and Captain Marryat whose books he illustrated. He was a founder member of the SBA in 1823 and was elected ARA in 1832 and RA in 1835. He made tours to Italy, France and Holland and visited Scotland on a number of occasions in later life, settling from 1847 in Hampstead. Stanfield's seascapes are remarkable for their accuracy

WILLIAM CLARKSON STANFIELD 1793-1867. Charles Dickens in the character of 'Bobadil'. Watercolour and wash   The Garrick Club

and his Continental views were much used in the Annuals of the 1830s. He died at Hampstead on 18 May 1867.

Illus: *The Pirate and The Three Cutters [Capt. Marryat, 1835]; Poor Jack [Capt. Marryat, 1840 (20 engrs.)]; Coast Scenery [1847]; American Notes [C. Dickens, 1850 (frontis)].*

Contrib: *Heath's Picturesque Album [1832-34]; Heath's Gallery [1836-38]; Finden's Life and Poems of the Rev. G. Crabbe [1834]; Sketches on the Moselle, The Rhine and the Meuse [1838, AT 32]; The Chimes, A Goblin Story [C. Dickens, 1845]; The Cricket on The Hearth [C. Dickens, 1846]; The Haunted Man and The Ghost's Bargain [C. Dickens, 1848]; Moxon's Tennyson [1857].*

Exhib: BI; RA; RBA.

Colls: Aberdeen; BM; Fitzwilliam; Greenwich; Leeds; Manchester; V & AM; Garrick Club; Witt Photo.

Bibl: *Gentleman's Magazine,* IV, July 1867; J. Dafforne, *CS Short Biographical Sketch,* 1873; C. Dickens, *The Story of a Great Friendship,* 1918; M. Hardie, *Watercol. Paint. in Brit.,* Vol.3, 1968, pp.68-70 illus.

See illustrations.

STANIFORTH, J.M.   **fl.1895-1906**

Cartoonist and humorous artist. He was chief cartoonist of the *Evening Express,* Cardiff and of *The Western Mail.* He contributed comic animals and figures to *Punch,* 1906.

Illus: *The General Election 1895, Evening Express Political Cartoons; Cartoons of the Welsh Coal Strike [1898].*

STANILAND, Charles Joseph   **1838-1916**

Marine painter and illustrator. He was born at Kingston-upon-Hull on 19 June 1838 and studied at the Birmingham School of Art, Heatherley's, South Kensington and the RA Schools, 1861. He was elected ARI in 1875 and RI in 1879, becoming ROI in 1883. Staniland's strength was in marine illustrations where the ships and tackle were seen at close quarters and the working seaman was observed in large scale. His many contributions to *The Illustrated London News* and *The Graphic* were a mainstay of those periodicals in the 1870s and 1880s, readers had practically to wipe the brine from their faces as they turned the pages. He was also an excellent portrait artist and painted still-life and bird subjects in watercolour. He was among the most prolific artists of the period and was much admired by Van Gogh during his English years. Staniland died in London in 1916.

Illus: *The Gentleman Cadet [A.W. Drayson, 1875]; The Dragon and The River [G.A. Henty, 1886]; Traitor or Patriot [M.C. Rowsell]; Britannia's Bulwarks [C.N. Robinson, 1901].*

Contrib: *The Leisure Hour [1866]; Cassell's Family Magazine [1867]; Idyllic Pictures [1867]; The Quiver [1868]; Episodes of Fiction [1870]; ILN [1870-87]; The Graphic [1880-90]; The English Illustrated Magazine [1886-92]; The Boys' Own Paper [1892-93]; Chums [1892]; Cassell's Family Magazine [1895-96]; The Pall Mall Magazine [1896-97]; The Wide World Magazine [1898].*

Exhib: B; FAS; G; L; M; RA, RI.

Colls: Greenwich; Sunderland; V & AM; Witt Photo.

Bibl: *English Influences on Vincent Van Gogh,* Arts Council, 1974-75.

STANLAWS, Penrhyn

Figure artist. He contributed drawings to *Punch*, 1903-04 in a spirited but scratchy style.

STANLEY, Lady   See TENNANT, Dorothy

STANLEY, G.   **fl.1800-1817**

Topographical artist. He may be the same artist who exhibited a landscape at the RA in 1800.
Contrib: *The Antiquarian Itinerary [1817 (Yorkshire)].*
Colls: Witt Photo.

STANLEY, Harold J.   **1817-1867**

Painter and illustrator. He was born at Lincoln in 1817 and went to Munich to work under Kaulbach. He travelled to Italy but returned to Munich to work and died there in 1867.
Exhib: BI; RA; RBA.

STANLEY, Sir Henry Morton   **1841-1904**

African explorer and amateur artist. He was born at Denbigh on 29 June 1841 with the name of John Rowlands, but being left an orphan was brought up in the St Asaph workhouse, 1847-56. As a boy he shipped to America and was adopted by Henry Stanley, a New Orleans cottonbroker whose name he took. Stanley served in the Confederate army, 1861-62 and in the United States navy, 1864-65, afterwards adopting the life of a roving journalist in Asia Minor, Abyssinia and Africa. In October 1869, he was ordered by the *New York Herald* to mount an expedition to find Dr Livingstone in central Africa. He found Dr Livingstone at Ujiji on 10 November 1871 and published his account of the journey in *How I Found Livingstone,* 1872. He was Governor of the Congo and knighted in 1899, he served as MP for Lambeth, 1895-1900 and married on 12 July 1890 Dorothy Tennant (q.v.) the artist and illustrator. He died on 10 May 1904.
Contrib: *ILN [1878].*

STANLEY, L.

Topographer. He contributed illustrations of Palermo to *The Illustrated Times,* 1860.

STANNARD, Henry John   **1844-1920**

Landscape and sporting artist and illustrator. He was born at Woburn, Bedfordshire in 1844, the son of John Stannard, 1795-1881. He studied at the South Kensington Schools and established his own Academy of Arts at Bedford in 1887, specialising in bird studies and publishing a number of country books illustrated by himself. He was elected RBA in 1894, was a member of the Dudley Art Society and died at Bedford on 15 November 1920.
Contrib: *ILN [1897-99 (decor and birds)]; Encyclopaedia of Sport; Bailey's Magazine; The Sporting & Dramatic News.*
Exhib: B; L; M; RA; RBA; RCA; RI.
Bibl: Anthony J. Lester, *The Stannards*, 1980.

STANNARD, Lilian (Mrs Silas)   **1884-1944**

Flower painter. She was born at Woburn, Bedfordshire in 1884, the daughter of Henry John Stannard (q.v.). She lived at Blackheath and specialised in flower and garden pictures, having one man shows at the Mendoza Gallery, 1906, 1907 and 1927. She died in 1944.
Illus: *Popular Garden Flowers [W.P. Wright, 1912].*
Exhib: B; L; RA; RBA; RCA; RI; SWA.
Colls: Newport.

STANNUS, Anthony Carey   **fl.1862-1909**

Genre, landscape and marine painter. He drew views of Cornwall but also visited Ireland and Belgium for subjects and may have made a trip to Mexico in about 1867. He is probably the brother of the architect and writer H.H. Stannus, 1840-1908.
Illus: *The King of the Cats [1903].*
Contrib: *ILN [1867].*
Exhib: BI; L; RA; RBA; RHA.
Colls: V & AM.

STANTON, G. Clark   RSA   **1832-1894**

Sculptor, painter and illustrator. He was born at Birmingham in 1832 and studied as a designer for a commercial firm and attended the

WILLIAM CLARKSON STANFIELD 1793-1867. Title page of Heath's Picturesque Annual for 1832

Birmingham School of Art. He visited Italy for some years and returned in 1855 to settle permanently in Edinburgh. He was a prolific painter of genre subjects with an 18th century tinge to them, popular in the third quarter of the century, but also designed stained glass windows and sculpted. He was elected ARSA in 1862 and RSA in 1883 and was also Curator of the RSA Life School. He died at Edinburgh on 8 January 1894.
Contrib: *Good Words [1860]; Poems and Songs by Robert Burns [1875].*
Exhib: B; G; L; M; RSA; RSW.
Colls: Dundee; Glasgow.

STANTON, Horace Hughes   **1843-1914**

Landscape painter. He was born in 1843 and worked in Chelsea and Kensington until 1913 when he went to America. He died in New York on September 13, 1914.
Contrib: *London Society [1869].*
Exhib: B; G; GG; L; M; RA; RHA.

STAPLES, Sir Robert Ponsonby   12th Baronet   **1853-1943**

Painter and illustrator. He was born on 30 June 1853, the third son of Sir Nathaniel A. Staples Bt. He was educated at home, and studied at the Louvain Academy of Fine Arts, 1865-70, with Portaels in Brussels, 1872-74 and in Dresden, 1867. Staples visited Paris in 1869 and made tours to Australia, 1879-80 and was elected RBA in 1898. He was art

master at the People's Palace, Mile End Road in 1897 and was a member of the International Union. He did a considerable amount of figurative work for magazines and died on 18 October 1943.
Contrib: *ILN [1893-96]; The Sketch [1894].*
Exhib: B; G; GG; L; M; NEA; P; RA; RBA; RHA; ROI.
Colls: Witt Photo.

STARR, Sydney   **1857-1925**
Landscape and decorative artist and illustrator. He was born at Kingston-upon-Hull in 1857 and worked in St John's Wood until 1890 when he emigrated to the United States. He was a friend of Walter Sickert (q.v.) and worked up paintings after the latter's drawings. His black and white work is characterised by very pronounced vertical hatching, and some of it appeared in *The Whirlwind.* He was elected NEA and RBA in 1886 and died in New York on 3 October 1925.
Exhib: G; GG; L; M; NEA; RA; RBA; RI; ROI.
Colls: V & AM; Witt Photo.

STAYNES, Percy Angelo ROI   **1875-**
Painter, designer and illustrator. He was born in 1875 and studied at the Manchester School of Art, at the Royal College of Art and at Julian's in Paris. He worked in Bedford Park, London, 1914-48 and was elected ROI in 1916 and RI in 1935.
Illus: *Roundabout Ways [Ffrida Wolfe, 1912]; Gulliver's Voyages [1912].*
Exhib: G; RI; ROI.

STEAVENSON, C. Herbert   **fl.1900-1917**
Landscape painter at Gateshead. He published *Colliery Workmen Sketched at Work,* 1912.

STEELL, Gourlay RSA   **1819-1894**
Animal painter. He was born in 1819 and studied at the Trustees Academy in Edinburgh under R.S. Lauder. He was appointed painter to the Highland and Agricultural Society and Animal Painter for Scotland to Queen Victoria. He became Curator of the National Gallery of Scotland and was elected ARSA in 1846 and RSA in 1859. He died at Edinburgh on 31 January 1894.
Contrib: *Poems and Songs by Robert Burns [1875].*
Exhib: L; M; RA; RSA.
Colls: Edinburgh; Witt Photo.

STEEPLE, John   **-1887**
Landscape and coastal painter. He worked in Birmingham and London and specialised in subjects of Welsh, Midlands and Sussex scenery. He was an unsuccessful candidate for the NWS in 1868 and in subsequent years.
Illus: *Through Norway With a Knapsack [Williams, 1859, AT 258].*
Exhib: B; FAS; RA; RBA; RI; RSA.
Colls: Birmingham; Manchester; V & AM.

STEER, Philip Wilson   **1860-1942**
Landscape, portrait and genre painter in oil and watercolour. He was born at Birkenhead in 1860 and studied at Gloucester School of Art and at Julian's in Paris. He was teacher of painting at the Slade School from 1895 and a member of the NEA from 1886. Steer was very impressionistic in his treatment of landscape and although it was usually the English countryside that he was painting, the feeling remains French. Most of his illustrative work is landscape although he contributed chalk drawings to the *Pall Mall.*
Contrib: *The Whirlwind [1890]; The Pall Mall Budget [1893]; The Yellow Book [1894-95]; Albermarle; Prose Fancies [Le Gallienne].*
Exhib: FAS; G; GG; L; M; NEA; P; RA; RBA; RHA; ROI; RSA; RSW.
Colls: BM; Bedford; Bradford; Exeter; Fitzwilliam; Gloucester; Leeds; Manchester; Tate; V & AM.
Bibl: R. Ironsode, *PWS,* 1943; D.S. Macoll, *PWS,* 1945.

STEPHANOFF, Francis Phillip   **1788-1860**
Painter and illustrator. He was born in London in 1788, the younger brother of James Stephanoff (q.v.). He exhibited with the AA from 1809 and with the OWS from 1813. He remained less well known than his brother with whom he is often confused. He contributed

designs to Heath's Gallery, 1836-38 and died after suffering from poor health at West Hanham, near Bristol in 1860.
Exhib: BI; OWS; RA; RBA.
Colls: BM; Exeter; Nottingham; V & AM; Witt Photo.

STEPHANOFF, James   RA OWS   **c.1786-1874**
Historical painter and topographer. He was born in Brompton, London in about 1786, the elder brother of F.P. Stephanoff (q.v.). He studied for a short time from 1801 at the RA Schools and was a frequent exhibitor in London from about 1810. He concentrated principally on scriptural, poetic and legendary subjects which he treated realistically and with attention to costume and detail. He was made Historical Painter in Watercolours to King William IV in 1831 and was elected OWS in 1819. He retired from the society due to ill health in 1861, having moved to Bristol in 1850; he died there at Frederick Place, Clifton, in 1874.
Contrib: *Pyne's Royal Residences [1819]; Finden's Tableaux [1841].*
Exhib: BI; RA.
Colls: BM; Bradford; Nat. Gall.; Edinburgh; V & AM.

STEPHENSON, James   **1828-1886**
Engraver and lithographer. He was born in Manchester on 26 November 1828 and was described by Chatto as 'a skilful engraver on steel'. He engraved all the illustrations for *Manchester As It Is,* 1839 and contributed to *Clever Boys* and *Wide Wide World.* He died on 28 May 1886.
Bibl: Chatto & Jackson, *Treatise on Wood Engraving,* 1861, p.600.

STERNER, Albert Edward   **1863-1946**
Genre and portrait painter, etcher and illustrator. He was born in London on 8 March 1863, the son of American parents and worked chiefly in New York. He studied at Julian's in Paris with Boulanger, Lefevbre and Gerôme, returning to the United States in 1879 and founding his own atelier in 1885. Sterner's pen drawing which was mostly done for *Harper's Magazine* is very typical of the American school, bold lines with concentration on the figures and little background detail. Sterner exhibited at the Paris Exhibition of 1900 and won a bronze medal.
Illus: *L'ennui Madame [D. Meunier].*
Contrib: *Harper's Magazine; The Quiver [1895]; Pick-Me-Up; The English Illustrated Magazine [1896]; The Savoy [1896]; Black & White [1896].*
Exhib: FAS.
Colls: V & AM.
Bibl: Joseph Pennell, *Pen Drawing and Pen Draughtsmen,* 1894, p.259.
See illustration.

STEVENSON, Robert Louis   **1850-1894**
Author and amateur woodcut artist. He was born in Edinburgh in 1850 and studied engineering at the university there and was admitted an advocate in 1875. Stevenson's adolescent talent for writing developed in the 1870s and he published a series of best-sellers which rapidly became classics. They included *An Inland Voyage,* 1878, *Travels with a Donkey on the Cevennes,* 1879, *Treasure Island,* 1882, *Kidnapped* and *Dr Jekyll and Mr Hyde,* 1886. He travelled to America in 1887 to recover his health and after visiting Australia, settled at Samoa in 1890 where he died in 1894. None of his illustrations was ever published during his life time.
Bibl: J. Pennell, *RLS, Illustrator,* The Studio, Vol.9, 1897, pp.17-24 illus.

STEWART, Allan   **1865-1951**
Military and historical painter and illustrator. He was born in Edinburgh on 11 February 1865, and educated at the Edinburgh Institution, studying art at the RSA Schools. He worked for *The Illustrated London News* from about 1895 and acted as their Special Artist in South Africa. He later accompanied King Edward VII on his Mediterranean tours for the same magazine and contributed fairy illustrations to its Christmas numbers. He worked at Kenley, Surrey till about 1925 and then at Castle Douglas, Kircudbright. He died on 29 January 1951.
Illus: *Red-Cap Adventures [S.R. Crockett, 1908].*
Contrib: *ILN [1895-1908].*
Exhib: FAS; G; L; M; RA; RSA; RSW.

ALBERT EDWARD STERNER 1863-1946. 'My Unwilling Neighbour'. Original drawing for illustration in *The English Illustrated Magazine*, 1896. Signed with initials and dated 1896

Victoria and Albert Museum

STEYERT, Auguste   **1830-1904**
French draughtsman and designer of book plates. He was born at Lyons in 1830 and died there in 1904.
Contrib: *The Illustrated Times [1856]*.

STICKNEY, S.
Amateur artist of humorous subjects in line. His *Contrasts, A Series of Twenty Drawings...* was published by Ackermann, 1832.

STOCK, Henry John   RI   **1853-1930**
Portrait, genre and imaginary painter and illustrator. He was born in Greek St, Soho on 6 December 1853 and studied at the RA Schools. He worked in Fulham until 1910 and then at Felpham, Sussex, being elected RI in 1880. He died on 4 November 1930.
Illus: *West Indian Fairy Tales [Gertrude Shaw, 1912]*.
Exhib: FAS; L; M; RA; RI; ROI.
Colls: Witt Photo.

STOCKDALE, Frederick Wilton Litchfield   **fl.1803-1848**
Topographer. He was assistant to the Military Secretary of the East India Company until forced to resign through ill-health. He was a prolific contributor to travel works.

Illus: *Etchings...of Antiquities in...Kent [1810]; A Concise...Sketch of Hastings, Winchelsea and Rye [1817]; Excursions in...Cornwall [1824]; The Cornish Tourist [1834]*.
Contrib: *The Beauties of England and Wales [1801-13]; Antiquarian Itinerary [1818]; Ackermann's Repository [1825-28]*.
Exhib: RA.
Colls: BM; Fitzwilliam; Nat. Mus., Wales; V & AM; Witt Photo.

STOCKDALE, W. Colebrooke   **fl.1852-1867**
Draughtsman. He specialised in buildings and sporting subjects and contributed to *The Illustrated London News* in 1852.
Exhib: RA, 1860-67.

STOCKS, Lumb   RA   **1812-1892**
Portrait draughtsman, miniaturist, illustrator and engraver. He was born at Lightcliffe on 30 November 1812 and became a pupil of Charles Cope. He settled in London in 1827 and learnt the art of engraving with Rolls for six years, becoming one of the most competent of Victorian engravers. Chatto mentions that 'Mr Stocks has considerable reputation as an engraver on steel'. He was one of the few engravers to be elected on that art to the RA, becoming ARA in 1853 and RA in 1872. Many of his works are crayon portraits and

313

he was an assiduous engraver after Stothard's works. He died in London on 28 April 1892. He was the father of the artists, Arthur, Bernard, Katherine and Walter Fryer Stocks.
Contrib: *Ministering Children; Ministry of Life; English Yeoman.*
Exhib: RA; RBA.
Bibl: Chatto & Jackson, *Treatise on Wood Engraving,* 1861, p.600.

STOKER, Matilda   **fl.1880-1888**
Book decorator. She worked in Dublin and London and contributed Celtic ornament to *The English Illustrated Magazine,* 1886-88.
Exhib: RHA, 1880-84.

STOKES, Adrian Scott   RA ARWS   **1854-1935**
Landscape painter in oil and watercolour and tempera, occasional illustrator. He was born at Southport in 1854 and was educated at the Liverpool Institute and studied at the RA Schools, 1872-75 and in Paris under Dagnan Bouveret, 1885-86. Stokes travelled widely in Europe and wrote extensively on Renaissance art, he exhibited work at the major exhibitions of Paris, 1889 and Chicago and two of his paintings were acquired by the Chantrey Bequest, 1888 and 1903. He was elected ROI, 1888, ARA, 1910 and RA, 1919, his talent as a watercolourist being recognised by his election as RWS in 1926 and VPRWS in 1933. He died in London on 30 November 1935.

His wife, Marianne Stokes (q.v.), née Preindlsberger, 1855-1927 was also an artist. A joint exhibition of their work was held at the FAS in 1900.
Publ: *Landscape Painting [1925]; Pansy's Flour-Bin [1880]; Hungary [1909].*
Illus: *The Three Brides [Charlotte M. Yonge]; The Clever Woman Of The Family [Charlotte M. Yonge]; Tyrol and its People [C. Holland, 1909].*
Exhib: B; FAS; G; GG; L; M; NEA; New Gall; RA; RBA; RHA; RI; ROI; RSA; RSW; RWS.
Colls: V & AM.
See illustration.

STOKES, George Vernon   **1873-1954**
Landscape and animal painter and etcher. He was born in London on 1 January 1873 and after a private education specialised in black and white illustration and was elected ARBA in 1923 and RBA in 1929. He worked at Carlisle, 1911-14 and latterly at Deal, dying there in 1954.
Publ: *Colour Etchings in Two Printings; How to Draw and Paint Dogs.*
Illus: *British Dogs At Work.*
Contrib: *The Gentlewoman [c.1890]; Punch [1905 (dogs)]; ILN [1915]; The Graphic; The Sphere.*
Exhib: FAS; New Gall; RA; RBA; RI; RMS.
Colls: Carlisle.

STOKES, Marianne (née Preindlsberger)   **1855-1927**
Portrait and biblical painter. She was born in Southern Austria in 1855 and studied under Lindenschmidt in Munich and worked at Graz. She married Adrian Stokes, RWS (q.v.) and died in London in 1927. She was elected NEA in 1887 and ASWA the same year, becoming ARWS in 1923.
Contrib: *The Graphic [1886].*
Exhib: B; FAS; G; GG; L; M; NEA; New Gall; RA; RBA; ROI; RWS; SWA.

STONE, Frank   ARA   **1800-1859**
Figure painter and illustrator. He was born in Manchester in 1800 and began life as a cotton spinner before setting up for himself as a painter. He settled in London in 1831 and began to make illustrations for the albums and watercolours for the dealer Roberts. He was elected OWS in 1842 but resigned in 1846 in order to be elected an ARA in 1851. He was a close friend of Charles Dickens and his circle and acted with him. Stone's son Marcus (q.v.) was more successful than his father, who died in London in 1859.
Illus: The *Haunted Man [Charles Dickens, 1848].*
Contrib: *Heath's Gallery [1836].*
Exhib: BI; OWS; RA; RBA.
Colls: Manchester; NPG; V & AM; Witt Photo.
Bibl: *The Connoisseur,* Vol.62, 1922.

STONE, Marcus   RA   **1840-1921**
Genre painter and illustrator. He was born in London on 4 July 1840, the second son of Frank Stone, ARA (q.v.). He studied art under his father and began exhibiting at the RA in 1858, specialising in figure subjects in interiors. He was elected ARA in 1877 and RA in 1887. He died in London on 24 March 1921.
Illus: *Great Expectations [Charles Dickens, 1860-61]; Our Mutual Friend [Charles Dickens, 1865].*
Contrib: *London Society [1863-64]; The Sunday Magazine [1865]; Touches of Nature by Eminent Artists [1866]; The Graphic [1872]; The Cornhill Magazine [1873]; ILN [1873].*
Exhib: B; FAS; G; L; M; RA.
Colls: BM, Manchester; V & AM; Witt Photo.
Bibl: *Art Annual,* 1896.

STONEY, Thomas Butler   **fl.1899-1912**
Coastal painter and illustrator. He worked in London in 1899 and 1912 and at Portland, Co. Tipperary in 1910. With John Hassall (q.v.) he illustrated *The Princess and The Dragon,* 1908.
Exhib: B; L; NEA; P; RA; RHA.

STONHOUSE, Charles   **fl.1833-1865**
Painter and engraver. He specialised in genre and literary subjects and worked in Bloomsbury from 1833 to 1865. He contributed to *The Deserted Village,* Etching Club, 1841.
Exhib: BI; RA.

STOPFORD, Robert Lowe   **1813-1898**
Marine and view painter and lithographer. He was born at Dublin in 1813 and became a drawing-master in Cork where he worked as Special Artist for *The Illustrated London News.* His son was W.H. Stopford, 1842-90. He died at Cork on 2 February 1898.
Contrib: *The Illustrated Times [1859 (Ireland)].*

STORER, Henry Sargant   **1797-1837**
Topographer, draughtsman and engraver. He was born in 1797, the son of James Sargant Storer (q.v.) with whom he collaborated on many books. He worked at Cambridge with his father but moved to London and died there on 8 January 1837.
Exhib: RA.

STORER, James Sargant   **1771-1853**
Topographer, draughtsman and engraver. He was born in Cambridge in 1771 and practised there, his chief works being illustrative surveys of the medieval buildings and the cathedrals of England. 'The Messrs Storer had not the artistic skill of the artists employed by Ackermann, and moreover their drawings are on a very small scale. On the other hand, the general accuracy of their representations of existing buildings induces us to conclude that those which have been destroyed were delineated with equal accuracy.' (Willis & Clark, *Arch. Hist. of Univ. of Cambridge,* Vol.1, p.128.) The elder Storer died in London in 1853.
Illus: *Cathedrals of Great Britain [1823-24]; Illustrations of Cambridge [1827-32]; Britton's Cathedrals [1832-36]; The Cambridge Almanac [1832]; Cantabrigia Illustrata [1835]; Collegiorum portae apud Cantabrigium [1837]; Delineations of Fountains Abbey; Delineations of the Chapel of Kings College; Delineations of Trinity College.*

STOREY, George Adolphus   RA   **1834-1919**
Genre and portrait painter and illustrator. He was born in London on 7 January 1834 and educated in Paris, where he studied paintings and mathematics under Professor M. Morand. He returned to London and spent some time with an architect before entering J.M. Leigh's Art School in Newman Street. He subsequently became a student at the RA Schools in 1854 and came strongly under the influence of the Pre-Raphaelites. He worked in Hampstead and St John's Wood where he was a founder-member of the Clique. He was elected ARA in 1876 and RA in 1914, having been Professor of Perspective from 1900 to 1919. He died on 29 July 1919.
Publ: *Sketches from Memory [1899]; Theory and Practice of Perspective [1910].*
Illus: *Homely Ballads and Old-Fashioned Poems [1880].*

ADRIAN SCOTT STOKES RA ARWS 1854-1935. 'Mackerel Lane'. Original drawing for illustration to *The Clever Woman of the Family* by Charlotte M. Yonge. Indian ink. 3½in x 4⅞in (8.9cm x 12.4cm)

Victoria and Albert Museum

Contrib: *Punch [1882]; The Ludgate Monthly [1892]; ILN [1893].*
Exhib: B; G; L; M; RA; RI; ROI; RBA.
Bibl: *AJ,* 1875; A.M. Eyre, *Saint Johns Wood,* 1913, pp.181-199; *Apollo,* June, 1964; J. Maas, *Victorian Painters,* 1970, p.13.

STOTHARD, Charles Alfred   **1786-1821**
Painter and illustrator. He was born in London on 5 July 1786, the son of Thomas Stothard, RA (q.v.) and attended the RA Schools in 1807. He made a tour of Northern England in 1815, gathering material for illustrating Lyson's *Magna Britannia.* Having some skill as a classical draughtsman, he was made Draughtsman to the Society of Antiquaries and in 1816 visited Bayeux to draw the tapestry. He married the novelist Anna Eliza Bray who wrote biographies of both him and his father. He died at Beerferris, Devonshire on 27 May 1821 as the result of an accident in France.
Illus: *Monumental Effigies of Great Britain [1817]; Letters Written During a Tour Through Normandy, Brittany and Other Parts of France, 1820 [by Mrs CAS, AT 88]; Painted Chamber [J.G. Rokewode, 1842, AL 69].*
Contrib: *Lyson's Devonshire [1822].*
Exhib: RA.
Colls: BM.
Bibl: Mrs A.E. Bray, *Memoirs of CAS,* 1823; Mrs A.E. Bray, *Autobiography,* 1889.

STOTHARD, Robert T.   FSA   **fl.1821-1857**
Miniature painter. He worked in London and there is an undated illustration in the V & A Museum for Scott's *Lady of the Lake* by this artist.
Exhib: BI.

STOTHARD, Thomas   RA   **1755-1834**
Illustrator. He was born in London in 1755 but on being left an orphan he was brought up in Yorkshire and educated in Tadcaster. He began his career as a silk pattern designer, but went to London and entered the RA Schools in 1777, where he attracted the notice of John Flaxman (q.v.). He had already begun to design book illustrations by 1779, doing work for *The Town and Country Magazine,* on Bell's *British Poets* and Harrison's *Novelists Magazines.* In the period 1780-83, Stothard was engaged on shop-cards, pocket-books and other ephemera at the same time studying Dürer prints and becoming a friend of William Blake (q.v.). He was elected ARA in 1785 and RA in 1794, following this with an important mural commission at Burghley House for Lord Exeter. Stothard was by far the most successful and distinguished illustrator of his day, his total contributions are estimated to be over five thousand, most of them figure subjects which the artist took from nature. His work is usually well finished, generally in monochrome wash but sometimes in full watercolours. He died on 27 April 1834.
Illus: *Peregrine Pickle [1781]; Clarissa [1784]; Robinson Crusoe [1790]; Pilgrims Progress [1789]; Young's Night Thoughts [1802]; Shakespeare's Works [1802]; The Spectator [1803]; Poems of Burns [1809]; Tales From Landlord [1820]; Cupid and Psyche [1820]; The Songs of Burns [1824]; Walton's Angler [1825]; Dramatic Works of Shakespeare [1826]; The Surprising Adventures of Baron Munchausen [1826];* etc.
Contrib: *The Novelists Magazine [1780-83]; The Poetical Magazine; Macklin's Bible [1791]; Boydell's Shakespeare; Bell's British Theatre; The Bijou [1828]; The Keepsake [1828-30];* etc.
Exhib: BI; RA; RBA.
Colls: Ashmolean; Birkenhead; BM; Fitzwilliam; Manchester; Nottingham; Tate; V & AM, Witt Photo.

WILLIAM STRANG RA 1859-1921. 'The Crucifixion'. Etching. Signed

WILLIAM STRANG RA 1859-1921. Original drawing for illustration to *The Surprising Adventures of Baron Muchausen*, 1895. Ink and bodycolour. Signed with initials. 8⅜in x 6⅛in (21.3cm x 15.5cm)

Victoria and Albert Museum

Bibl: Mrs A.E. Bray, *Life of TS*, 1851; *Memorial to TS*, 1867-68; V & AM MSS; A. Dobson, *Eighteenth Century Vignettes*, 1897; A.C. Coxhead, *TS*, 1906; I. Williams, *Early Eng. Watercolours*, 1952, pp.129-133; M. Hardie, *Watercol Paint. in Brit.*, Vol.I, 1966, pp. 138-141 illus.

STOTT, William R.S.   **fl.1905-1937**
Portrait and landscape painter and illustrator. He worked in Chelsea for most of his life, but worked at Aberdeen in 1909. He was employed by *The Graphic* from 1903 to 1923 to illustrate royal and public events.

Illus: *Kidnapped [R.L. Stevenson, c.1913].*
Contrib: *Strand Magazine [1908-37].*
Exhib: G; L; RA; RHA.
Colls: Witt Photo.

STOWERS, Thomas   **1778-1814**
Illustrator. He may have been a friend of Rowlandson, but his figure work is more like that of J.H. Mortimer. He exhibited at the BI, RA and OWS.

STOWERS, T. Gordon   **fl.1880-1894**
Portrait painter. He worked in London and contributed to *Punch*, 1880.
Exhib: B; RA; RBA.

STRANG, Ian   **RE**   **1886-1952**
Painter and etcher. He was born in 1886, the eldest son of William Strang, RA (q.v.) and was educated at Merchant Taylors' School before studying art at the Slade School, 1902-06 and at Julian's, Paris 1906-08. He travelled in France, Belgium, Sicily, Spain and Italy, where he became a member of the Faculty of the British School at Rome. He was elected ARE in 1926 and RE in 1930. He died at Wavendon, Bucks in 1952.
Publ: *The Students Book of Etching [1937]; Town and Country in Southern France [Frances Strang, 1937].*
Exhib: FAS; G; L; M; NEA; RA; RE; RHA; RSA.
Colls: Bedford; V & AM.
Bibl: R.A. Walker, 'The Etchings of I.S.', *Print Collectors Quarterly*, 18, 1934, pp.129-149.

STRANG, William   **RA**   **1859-1921**
Painter and etcher. He was born at Dumbarton on 13 February 1859 and was educated at Dumbarton Academy and studied at the Slade School. He worked in London from 1875, carrying out some book illustrations but issuing a series of etchings notable for their imaginative power and insight and their concern with a wide range of subjects from poetry to social realism. He was elected RE in 1881 and ARA and RA in 1906 and 1921. He was President of the International Society of Sculptors, Painters and Gravers from 1918 to 1921, was LL.D. of Glasgow University, 1909 and a medallist of the Paris Exhibition of 1897. Strang's artistic debt is to the master engravers like Rembrandt, Forain and Daumier, but also to Alphonse Legros with whom he studied. He died on 12 April 1921.
Illus: *The Earth Friend [1892]; Death and the Ploughman's Wife [1894]; Nathan the Wise [1894]; The Ballad of Hadji [Ian Hamilton 1894]; Baron Munchausen [1895]; Pilgrim's Progress [1895]; Christ Upon the Hill [1895]; Sinbad the Sailor and Ali Baba [1896, with J.B. Clark]; Milton's Paradise Lost [1896]; A Book of Ballads*

WILLIAM STRANG RA 1859-1921. 'The Fair Ground', 1892

[Alice Sargant, 1898]; A Book of Giants [1898]; Western Flanders [Laurence Binyon, 1899]; Etchings From Rudyard Kipling [1901]; The Praise of Folie [1901]; Walton's The Compleat Angler [1902]; Tam O'Shanter [Burns, 1902]; The Rime of the Ancient Mariner [Coleridge, 1902]; Thirty Etchings of Don Quixote [1903].
Contrib: *The English Illustrated Magazine [1890-91]; The Yellow Book [1895]; The Dome [1898-1900].*
Exhib: FAS; G; GG; L; M; NEA; P; RA; RE; RHA; RSA.
Colls: Ashmolean; Leeds; V & AM; Witt Photo.
Bibl: F. Sedmore, *Frank Short & WS*, English Illustrated Magazine, Vo1.8, 1890-91, pp.457-466; R.E.D. Sketchley, *Eng. Bk. Illus*, 1903, pp.58,154; *Print Collector's Quarterly,* Vol.8, No.4, 1921, pp.249-376; *WS*, NPG, 1980-81.
See illustration.

STRASYNSKI, Leonard Ludwik   **1828-1889**
Artist and lithographer. He was born on 11 January 1828 at Tokarowka, Poland and studied art at the St Petersburg Academy, 1847-55. He then travelled to Berlin, Paris, Brussels and Rome and was a member of the Academies of both Rome and St Petersburg. He appears to have been in London in 1867-68 when he designed initial letters for *London Society*. He died at Shitomir on 4 February 1889.
Contrib: *Punch [1867-68]; Once A Week [1867].*

STRATTON, Helen   **fl.1892-1925**
Portrait and figure painter and illustrator. She worked in Kensington and Chelsea and specialised in children's stories and fairy tales.
Illus: *Songs For Little People [1896]; Tales From Hans Andersen [1896]; Beyond the Border [W.D. Campbell, 1898]; The Fairy Tales of Hans Christian Andersen [1899]; The Lily of Life [c.1915].*
Contrib: *Arabian Nights [1899].*
Exhib: L; RA; RBA; RHA; RI; SWA.
Colls: Witt Photo.
Bibl: R.E.D. Sketchley, *Eng. Bk. Illus.*, 1903, pp.116,172.

STREATFIELD, Rev. Thomas   FSA   **1777-1848**
Topographer and heraldic artist and illustrator. He was born in London in 1777 and educated at Oriel College, Oxford, becoming curate of Long Ditton and Tatsfield, Surrey and Chaplain to the Duke of Kent. He lived at Westerham from 1822 and collected material for a history of Kent, he died there in 1848.
Illus: *The Bridal of Armagnac [1823]; Excerpta Cantiana [1836]; Lympsfield and its Environs [1839]; Hasted's History of Kent, corrected and enlarged [1886].*
Contrib: *The Copper Plate Magazine [1792-1802]; Britton's Beauties of England and Wales [1813].*
Exhib: RA, 1800.
Colls: BM; Greenwich.

STRETCH, Matt   **fl.1880-1896**
Figure and humorous artist. He worked for *The Gentlewoman* and for *Fun*, 1886-96 and *Moonshine*, 1891.
Exhib: RHA, 1880.

STRINGER, Agnes   **fl.1900-1908**
Illustrator. She worked at Sunbury and Putney and illustrated with D. Andrewes (q.v.) *The Little Maid Who Danced To Every Mood*, 1908.
Exhib: RBA; SWA.

STRONG, Joseph D.   **1852-1900**
American illustrator. He was born at Bridgeport, Connecticut in 1852 and studied in California and Munich under Piloty before travelling in the South Seas. He died in San Francisco on 5 April 1900.
Illus: *The Silverardo Squatters [R.L. Stevenson, 1897].*

STRUBE, Sidney   **1891-1956**
Artist. There is a pencil and watercolour caricature by this artist in the V & A Museum, signed and dated 1916.
See Horne

EDMUND JOSEPH SULLIVAN RWS 1869-1933. Original pen illustration for Airy Fairy Lillian in Tennyson's *Dreams of Fair Women*, 1900
Author's Collection

EDMUND JOSEPH SULLIVAN RWS 1869-1933. Study for an illustration of Sarah Bernhardt
Private Collection

STRUTT, Alfred William RE FRGS   1856-1924
Animal, figure and landscape painter and illustrator. He was born at Tarahaki, New Zealand in 1856, the son of William Strutt, the genre painter, (q.v.) under whom he studied. He studied at South Kensington and exhibited in Paris and in Colonial exhibitions. He accompanied King Edward VII as official artist on a hunting trip to Scandinavia and was an occasional magazine illustrator. He was elected RBA in 1888 and ARE in 1889. He died at Wadhurst, Sussex on 2 March 1924.
Contrib: *ILN [1894 (rustic)]*.
Exhib: FAS; L; M; RA; RBA; RCA; RE; RHA; RI; ROI; RSA; RWS.

STRUTT, Jacob George   1790-1864
Painter of portraits and forests, etcher. He was born in 1790 and worked in London until 1831 when he moved to Lausanne and Rome. He died in Rome in 1864.
Illus: *Bury St Edmunds illustrated [1821]; Sylva Britannica [1822]; Deliciae Sylvarum [1828]*.

STRUTT, William   1827-1915
Animal and genre painter. He was born at Teignmouth, Devon in 1827, the grandson of Joseph Strutt, the antiquary and artist. He studied in Paris and went to Australia in 1850 where he founded the *Australian Journal* and *The Illustrated Australian Magazine*. He worked in New Zealand from 1856 and returned to England in 1862 and died at Wadhurst, Sussex in 1915. His son was A.W. Strutt (q.v.). He was elected RBA in 1891.
Exhib: L; M; RA; RBA; ROI.

STUDDY, G.E.   1878-1948
Illustrator. He was born in Devonshire in 1878 and after studying at Heatherley's, specialised in drawings of children and contributed to *Punch* in 1902 and to *The Graphic* in 1910 and 1912.
Colls: Witt Photo.
See Horne

'STUFF'   See WRIGHT, H.C. Seppings

STURGESS, John   fl.1875-1903
Sporting painter and illustrator. He worked in London and was the principal hunting and racing artist for *The Illustrated London News* for about ten years from 1875. His drawings are accurate though somewhat wooden and he was among the first black and white artists to go wholeheartedly into advertising with his hunting sketches for Ellerman's Embrocation.
Illus: *Sketches In The Hunting Field [A.E.T. Watson, 1895]; The Magic Jacket [Nat Gould, 1896]*.
Contrib: *ILN [1875-97]; The English Illustrated Magazine [1884]; The Sporting & Dramatic News [1890]*.
Exhib: RBA; RHA.
Colls: V & AM; Witt Photo.

STYCHE, Frank   fl.1913-1925
Black and white figure artist. He worked at Hendon and Golders Green and contributed to *London Opinion*, 1913.

SULLIVAN, Edmund Joseph   RWS   1869-1933
Painter, watercolourist and illustrator. He was born in London in 1869, the son and pupil of M. Sullivan, an artist working at Hastings. He studied under his father and was, in 1889, one of the new recruits along with Dean and Hartrick (qq.v.) for Thomas's new venture *The Daily Graphic*. From then onwards Sullivan established himself as one of the foremost illustrators of his time, although eclipsed by his contemporaries Rackham and Dulac. He was a superb figure draughtsman, especially in chalks, and had a strong and inventive imagination. Hartrick later said of his colleague 'he could do

EDMUND JOSEPH SULLIVAN RWS 1869-1933. 'Night and Morning'. Original drawing for unidentified magazine illustration. Chalk and wash. Indistinctly signed and dated 1 Jan 1903. 14in x 10in (35.6cm x 25.4cm)   Author's Collection

EDMUND JOSEPH SULLIVAN RWS 1869-1933. 'Margaret'. Illustration to *Dreams of Fair Women* by Alfred Tennyson, 1900

anything with a pen and do it with distinction' (*Sullivan*, by Thorpe, p.14). Sullivan was a careful textual illustrator, his work on such books as *Sartor Resartus* are very accurately thought out, the decorative element in the design beautifully balanced. His preliminary sketches are very vivid and dramatic and sometimes they lose their greatest impact when completed as a finished drawing, but they never lack virtuosity. Sullivan had two main drawing styles, a very clear black and white one, used with most consistency about 1900 for books and a more atmospheric treatment with washes and swirling chalk lines, closer to the rough working notes. Less well known is his character study work, among the best of these being a series of Gloucestershire portraits which were purchased by the National Art Collections Fund for the BM.

Sullivan's lasting influence was probably not so strong in his books as in his teaching. He was lecturer in Book Illustration and Lithography at Goldsmiths College for a number of years and was examiner in art for the Board of Education. He wrote two important text books on his subject. He was elected ARWS in 1903 and ARE in 1925. He died in London on 17 April 1933. His brother was J.F. Sullivan (q.v.).

Publ: *Line, an Art Study [1921]; The Art of Illustration [1922].*
Illus: *Lavengro [Borrow, 1896]; Tom Brown's Schooldays [1896]; The Compleat Angler [1896]; The Pirate and Three Cutters [Marryat, 1897]; Sartor Resartus [Carlyle, 1898]; Maud [Tennyson, 1900]; A Dream of Fair Women [1900]; The Pilgrim's Progress [1901]; Poems by R. Burns [1901]; A Citizen of the World [1904]; A Modern Utopia [H.G. Wells, 1905]; Sintram and His Companions [1908]; The French Revolution [1910]; The Rubaiyat of Omar Khayyam [1913]; The Vicar of Wakefield [1914]; The Kaiser's Garland [1915]; Legal and other Lyrics [G. Outram, 1916].*

EDMUND JOSEPH SULLIVAN RWS 1869-1933. 'Herr Diogenes'. Illustration for *Sartor Resartus* by Thomas Carlyle, 1898

He had that sense of delicacy! His corn hurt him dreadfully, till he said "I will cut it". Then it flashed upon him that it would involve looking upon his toe in a state of nudity! He crimsoned to the roots of his hair (an asterisk shows position of corn)

For a while he contemplates cutting the corn from the outside

With a strong effort against the innate delicacy inseparable from the pure-minded, he forced himself to remove the slipper

Then – but with what mental torture! the sock. But the sense of impropriety was fearful

But he steeled himself, Ah, how easy it is to lose all shame once we have overstepped the bounds! And as he was about to operate HIS LANDLADY CAME IN!

JAMES FRANK SULLIVAN 1853-1936. 'The Artist As He Should Be'. Original drawings for illustration to *Fun*, 10 June 1885. Pen and ink. One signed with monogram. 4in x 10in (10.2cm x 25.4cm)

Author's Collection

GEORGE HEYWOOD MAUNOIR SUMNER 1853-1940. Head piece for The English Illustrated Magazine, 1883. Wood engraving

Contrib: *The Graphic [1889]; The Daily Graphic [1890]; The English Illustrated Magazine [1891-94]; The Pall Mall Budget [1893]; The Yellow Book [1894]; The Daily Chronicle [1895]; The New Budget [1895]; A London Garland [W.E. Henley, 1895]; Good Words [1896]; The Lady's Pictorial [1898]; The Pall Mall Gazette [1899]; Black & White [1900]; Natural History of Selborne [Gilbert White, 1900-01]; The Old Court Suburbs [Leigh Hunt, 1902]; Strand Magazine [1903, 1910-11]; The Penny Illustrated Paper; The Pall Mall Magazine; The Gentlewoman; The Ludgate Monthly; The Windsor Magazine; Pearson's Magazine; Punch [c.1920].*
Exhib: FAS; G; L; NEA; RA; RE; RHA; RSA; RSW.
Colls: Ashmolean; BM; Bradford; V & AM; Witt Photo.
Bibl: *The Studio*, Winter No., 1900-01, pp.28-29 illus.; R.E.D. Sketchley, *Eng. Bk. Illus.*, 1903, pp.15, 74, 77, 155; *Modern Book Illustrators and Their Work*, Studio, 1914; J. Thorpe, *EJS*, 1948; B. Peppin, *Fantasy Book Illustration*, 1975, pp.98-99 illus.; Gordon N. Ray, *The Illustrator and The Book in England*, 1976, pp.186-193 illus.; Simon Houfe, 'An Artists Artist', *CL*, 25 May 1985.
See illustrations.

SULLIVAN, G.M.
Contributor of humorous figure subjects to *Punch,* 1908.

SULLIVAN, James Frank   **1853-1936**
Draughtsman, illustrator and author. He was born in 1853, the son of M. Sullivan, an artist working at Hastings, and elder brother of E.J. Sullivan (q v.). He went to the South Kensington Schools and began to work for the leading periodicals from about 1878. His greatest success was through the pages of *Fun,* where he was resident illustrator for about twenty-four years. Sullivan favoured the strip story cartoon and created a popular character 'The British Working Man' who features in issue after issue of his magazines. The main character is conceived in traditional cartoon idiom of small body and large head but is always very well drawn. Sullivan died in London on 5 May 1936.
Contrib: *Fun [1878-1901]; Black & White [1891]; Strand Magazine [1891-95]; The Idler [1892]; The Butterfly [1893]; Lady's Pictorial [1893]; Punch [1893-94, 1905]; The Sketch [1893]; St Pauls [1894]; The Minister [1895]; The New Budget [1895]; Pearson's Magazine [1896]; Lika Joko: Pick-Me-Up; Cassell's Saturday Journal; Cassell's Family Magazine.*
Exhib: FAS; RBA.
Colls: Author; V & AM.
Bibl: *The Studio*, Winter No., 1900-01, p.76 illus.
See illustrations.

SULMAN, T.   **fl.1855-1890**
Architectural illustrator. This artist specialised in topographical views and panoramas and was architectural illustrator for *The Illustrated London News* from 1859 to 1888. His work was still appearing in 1890. He was described by Chatto as expert in

'Ornamental Borders and Vignettes'.
Illus: *Kalidasa-Sakoontala [Indian Drama, Monier Williams, 1855].*
Contrib: *Churchman's Family Magazine [1863]; The Illustrated Times [1860-65]; Once A Week [1867]; Good Words For The Young [1869]; The Boy's Own Paper [1882]; Lalla Rookh.*
Bibl: Chatto & Jackson, *Eng. Book Illus*, 1861, p.600.

SUMMERS, W.
Caricaturist. He published a series of illustrations entitled *Black Jokes,* 1834, AL 322.

SUMNER, George Heywood Maunoir   **1853-1940**
Etcher and archaeologist. He was born in 1853 and was a leading figure in the revival of wood engraving in the 1880s and 1890s. His work, which is associated with the countryside, has a lyrical quality about it owing something to Blake and Palmer, his decorative illustration is somewhat akin to Morris. He died in 1940.
Illus: *The Itchen Valley [1881]; The Avon From Naxby to Tewkesbury [1882]; Epping Forest [1884]; Sintram and His Companions [1883]; Undine [1888]; The Besom Maker [1888]; Jacob and the Raven [1896].*
Contrib: *The English Illustrated Magazine [1883-86].*
Exhib: G; RA; RE.
Bibl: *The Studio*, Winter No., 1900-01, p.50 illus.; R.E.D. Sketchley, *Eng Bk Illus.*, 1903, pp.6, 130; Richard Bassett, C.L. 28 Sept. 1978.
See illustration.

SUMNER, Margaret L.   **fl.1882-1914**
Landscape painter and illustrator. She was working at Grasmere in 1898 and contributed to *The Yellow Book* in 1895.
Exhib: L.

SUTCLIFFE, John E.   **-1923**
Figure painter and illustrator. He worked in London, Bushey and Richmond and was married to the domestic painter E. Earnshaw. He contributed to *The Illustrated London News,* Christmas Number, 1916. He was elected ROI in 1920 and died in 1923.
Exhib: RA; RBA; RI; ROI.

SUTHERLAND, Elizabeth   **Duchess of**   **1765-1839**
Amateur artist. She was born in 1765, the daughter and heir of the 18th Earl of Sutherland and married in 1785 the 1st Duke of Sutherland. Her claim to the title of Countess was allowed by the House of Lords. She was a pupil of Girtin and many of her watercolours of Continental scenes were engraved. Her *Etchings of the Orkney Isles* and *Views on the Northern and Western Coasts of Sutherland,* were privately printed in 1807.

SWAINSON, William   **1789-1855**
Zoological illustrator. He travelled widely in Europe and formed a natural history collection. He lived in Brazil from 1816 to 1818 and

GODFREY SYKES 1824-1866. Original drawing for the first cover of *The Cornhill Magazine*, 1860. Pen. 7½in x 4⅝in (19.1cm x 11.7cm)
Victoria and Albert Museum

after returning to England in 1819, he finally emigrated to New Zealand in 1837, dying at Hutt Valley in 1855. He illustrated many of his own works.
Illus: *Zoological Illustrations [1820-23]; Ornithological Drawings, Birds of Brazil [1834-35]; Birds of Western Africa [Sir J. Richardson, 1837].*

SWAN, Mary E.   1889-1898
Fruit and flower painter. She worked in Bromley and London and drew the title page for *Poems by Emily H. Hickey,* 1895-96.
Exhib: B; FAS; L; New Gall; RA; ROI.

SWEETING, John   fl.1867-1880
Figure artist at Worthing, Sussex. He contributed figure subjects to the *London Magazine,* 1867.
Exhib: RBA, 1879; RHA, 1880.

SWETE, Rev. John   c.1752-1821
Topographer. He was educated at University College, Oxford and became Prebendary of Exeter in 1781, the majority of his drawings being of Devonshire. He settled at Oxton House near Exeter, but made sketching tours to Scotland and Cumberland as well as to Switzerland and Italy, 1816. An important group of his drawings of country houses was sold at Christie's on 15 July 1976.
Contrib: *Antiquarian and Topographical Cabinet [1808]; Britton's Beauties of England and Wales [1813].*
Colls: Exeter.

SYDDALL, Joseph   fl.1898-1910
Portrait and genre painter. He was trained at the Herkomer School, Bushey and worked from 1898 to 1910 at Chesterfield. He contributed illustrations with Sir H. von Herkomer (q.v.) to *Tess of the D'Urbevilles* when serialised in *The Graphic,* 1891.

SYKES, Charles   'Rilette'   1875-1950
Sculptor and illustrator. He was born in 1875 and worked in London as a poster designer and magazine illustrator, contributing to *The Sunday Dispatch* and *Woman* under the name of 'Rilette'. He also designed De Reske cigarette advertisements, fashion plates and in 1911 the mascot for the Rolls Royce car that is still in use. He was responsible for designing the Ascot race cups from 1926.
Exhib: G; L; RA: RI.
Colls: V & AM.

SYKES, Godfrey   1824-1866
Landscape and interior painter and designer. He was born at Malton in 1824 and studied at the Government School of Design at Sheffield, while serving his apprenticeship to an engraver. He subsequently became a teacher in the School under Young Mitchell and painted scenes of mills and forges. He worked with Alfred Stevens on coming to London and then with Captain Fowke on the decoration of the South Kensington Museum and the Horticultural Gardens. Linton, who much admired his work, says that he 'was starved on a low salary' and in consequence died of consumption in 1866. A memorial exhibition was held at South Kensington in the summer of 1866.
Contrib: *Cornhill Magazine [1860 (first cover design)].*
Exhib: RA.
Colls: Manchester; V & AM.
Bibl: W.J. Linton, *Memoirs,* 1895, p.182.
See illustration.

SYMES, Ivor I. J.   fl.1899-1937
Genre painter and illustrator. He studied at the Herkomer School, Bushey and married Mabel Gear, RI. He worked at Tadley, Hants.
Contrib: *The Graphic [1906].*
Exhib: RA; ROI.

SYMINGTON, J. Ayton   fl.1890-1908
Illustrator. He specialised in adventure stories and contributed to numerous magazines.
Illus: *Tom Cringle's Log [Michael Scott, 1895]; Peter Simple [Captain Marryat, 1895]; The Wonderful Wapentake [J.S. Fletcher, 1896]; The Enchanting North [J.S. Fletcher, 1908].*
Contrib: *The Sporting & Dramatic News [1890]; Good Words [1893]; Chums; The Windsor Magazine.*

SYMONS, William Christian   1845-1911
Portrait, genre, landscape and still-life painter and illustrator. He was born in London in 1845 and studied at the Lambeth School of Art and the RA Schools. He worked as a stained-glass designer and produced the controversial mosaics for the new Westminster Cathedral. He was elected RBA but resigned with Whistler in 1888 and later worked in Newlyn and Battle, dying in London in 1911. A memorial exhibition was held by the Goupil Gallery in 1912.
Contrib: *The Graphic [1885]; Strand Magazine 1891-1903]; Good Words [1898]; The Wide World Magazine [1898].*
Exhib: B; G; L; M; NEA; RA; RBA; RHA; RI; ROI.
Colls: BM.

SYNGE, Edward Millington   1860-1913
Painter and etcher. He was born at Great Malvern in 1860 and educated at Norwich Grammar School and Trinity College, Cambridge. He became a land agent and practised etching in his spare time, being elected ARE in 1898. He devoted himself entirely to art from 1901 and travelled in Italy and Spain. He died in 1913.
Illus: *Romantic Cities of Provence [A.M. Caird, 1906].*
Exhib: G; L; RA; RE; RHA.

SYRETT, Nellie or Netta
Illustrator. Artist drawing in the black and white style of L. Housman (q.v.). She contributed to *The Yellow Book* and *The Quarto,* 1896.
Exhib: SWA.

TABER, I.W.
Illustrator. He supplied the drawings for *Captains Courageous* by Rudyard Kipling, 1896.

TADEMA   See Sir L. ALMA- and Lady L.T. ALMA-

TAFFS, Charles H.   fl.1894-1911
Black and white artist. He worked in Clapham, London and illustrated for the leading magazines.
Contrib: *St Pauls [1894]; Lady's Pictorial [1895-98]; The Quiver [1895]; The New Budget [1895]; Pick-Me-Up [1897]; Sketchy Bits; The Royal Magazine; The English Illustrated Magazine [1897]; ILN [1899, 1908]; The Graphic [1910-11].*
Exhib: RA.

TARLING, G.T.   fl.1894-1907
Artist and illustrator. He was a member of the Birmingham Guild of Handicraft in 1907.
Contrib: *The Quest [1894-96].*

TARLTON, J.   fl.1872-1875
Wood engraver and illustrator. He worked in London and contributed to *The Illustrated London News*, 1874-75.

TARRANT, Margaret Winifred   fl.1888-1959
Illustrator and postcard artist. She was the daugher of Percy Tarrant (q.v.). Most of her work falls outside the scope of this book, but she illustrated *The Water Babies* by Charles Kingsley in 1908.
Coll: Gertler
See Horne

TARRANT, Percy   fl.1881-1930
Landscape, coastal and figure painter and illustrator. He worked in South London and then at Leatherhead and Gomshall, Surrey.
Illus: *Tom's Boy [Chambers, 1901].*
Contrib: *ILN [1884-89]; The Quiver [1890]; Black & White [1891]; Cassell's Family Magazine; The Girls' Own Paper; The Graphic [1911].*
Exhib: B; L; RA; RBA; RI; ROI.
See Horne

TATHAM, Helen S.   fl.1878-1891
Landscape painter and illustrator. She worked at Shanklin, Isle of Wight and illustrated a children's book *Little Margaret's Ride*, 1878.
Exhib: B; L; M; RA; RBA; SWA.

TATTERSALL, George   1817-1852
Architectural and sporting illustrator. He contributed to *Tattersall's English Race Horses*, c.1841, under the name of 'Wildrake'.
Exhib: RA, 1840-48.
Colls: Witt Photo.

TAVERNER, J.
Illustrator. Contributed railway scenes to *The Graphic*, 1870.

TAYLER, John Frederick RWS   1802-1889
Landscape and figure painter, etcher and illustrator. He was born at

Boreham Wood, Hertfordshire in 1802, the son of an impoverished squire and was educated at Eton and Harrow. He was intended for the Church but instead attended art classes at Sass's and the RA Schools and studied in Paris under Horace Vernet, sharing rooms with R.P. Bonington. He worked with Samuel Prout (q.v.) and then lived in Rome before returning to London and achieving considerable fame as a watercolourist. He was elected AOWS in 1831 and OWS in 1834 becoming President from 1858 to 1871. Tayler was most fond of painting country scenes involving hunting and hawking and based on the landscapes of Scotland where he was a frequent visitor; these were also the most frequent subjects for his book illustrations. He died at West Hampstead in 1889.
Contrib: *The Deserted Village [Goldsmith, Etching Club, 1841]; The Traveller Art Union, 1851].*
Exhib: BI; L; RA; RCA; RWS.
Bibl: M. Hardie, *Watercol. Paint. in Brit.,* Vol.III, 1968, pp.91-92.

TAYLOR, Edwin   fl.1858-1884
Landscape painter. He worked in Birmingham and published *Pictures of English Lakes and Mountains*, 1874.

TAYLOR, Horace Christopher   RBA   1881-1934
Painter, illustrator and poster artist. He was born in London on 10 January 1881 and was educated at Islington High School and studied at the Camden School of Art, 1898 and the RA Schools, 1902. He then worked in Munich, 1905 and was lecturer in commercial art at Chelsea School, 1931-34. Taylor worked as a caricaturist and cartoonist for *Pan* in about 1920 and also for *The Manchester Guardian*. He was one of the very few humorous artists to paint caricatures in oil. He died at Hampstead on 7 February 1934. He was elected ARBA in 1919 and RBA, 1921.
Illus: *Prehistoric Parables; The Second Show – Atta Troll.*
Exhib: RA; RBA; ROI.
Colls: Witt Photo.
Bibl: *The Studio*, Vol.48, 1909.

TAYLOR, Leonard Campbell   RA   1874-1963
Portrait painter and illustrator. He was born at Oxford on 12 December 1874, the son of Dr. J. Taylor, Organist to the University. He was educated at Cheltenham College and studied at the Ruskin School, Oxford, the St. Johns Wood School and the RA Schools. He was working at Hindhead, Surrey in 1905 and at Odiham, Basingstoke in 1921. He was elected ARA in 1928 and RA in 1931. He died in 1963.
Contrib: *The English Illustrated Magazine [1900-01].*
Exhib: B; L; M; New Gall; RA; RHA; RI; ROI; RSA; RWA.
Bibl: Herbert Furst, *LCT, RA His Place in Art*, 1945; G.E. Bunt, *LCT, RA*, 1949.

TAYLOR, Thomas   c.1770-1826
Topographer. He entered the RA Schools in 1791 and practised as an architect in the Leeds area, designing a number of churches. He illustrated Whitaker's *Loidis and Elmete* and his edition of Thoresby's *Ducatus Leodiensis*, both published in 1816. He died in March 1826.
Colls: BM.
Bibl: F. Beckwith, 'TT, Regency Architect', *Thoresby Society*, 1949.

TAYLOR, Tom   fl.1883-1911
Figure and domestic painter and illustrator. He worked in Camden, London from 1883 and contributed to *The Illustrated London News*, Christmas number, 1895-96.
Exhib: B; L; M; RA; RBA; RHA; RI; ROI.

TAYLOR, Weld
Amateur artist. He belonged to the family of Mitford and contributed illustrations to *Howitt's Visits to Remarkable Places*, 1841.

TAYLOR, Zillah
Amateur illustrator. She lived in Nottingham and won a *Studio* book illustration competition, 1895-96.

TAWSE, Sybil   fl.1908-1940
Portrait painter, poster artist and illustrator. She studied at the Lambeth School of Art and worked in London and Hythe, Kent. Most of her work falls out of the scope of this book, but she

SIR JOHN TENNIEL 1820-1914. Original drawing for the title page to *Punch*, Vol.CXIII, 1897. Pencil. 8in x 6¼in (20.3cm x 15.9cm)

SIR JOHN TENNIEL 1820-1914. 'The Press as Scare Monger'

illustrated Lamb's *The Essays of Elia*, 1910; *The Fairchild Family* [M.M. Butt, 1913]; *Cranford* by Mrs Gaskell, 1914; *The Heroes* [Kingsley, 1915]; *Tales From The Poets*, 1915; *Count of Monte Cristo* [Dumas, 1920]; *Mr Midshipman Easy* [Marryat, 1921]; *Miss Esperance and Mr Wycherly* [L.A. Hawker, 1936]; *Mother Goose*, 1932 and *Anne of Green Gables* [Montgomery, 1933].
Coll: Gertler.
Bibl: Peppin & Micklethwait; Mahony, Latimer & Folmsbee, *Illustrators of Children's Books 1744-1945*.
See Horne

TEALL, Gardner C.
American ornamental artist. He designed the Contents page for *The Quartier Latin,* Vol.3, September 1897.

TEBBY, Arthur Kemp   **fl.1883-1928**
Landscape, figure and flower painter and illustrator. He was working in Bloomsbury in 1883 and later moved to Heybridge, Essex; he acted as *The Graphic* naval artist for some time.
Contrib: *Daily Graphic [1890]; The Graphic [1903-05]; The Windsor Magazine; Pearson's Magazine.*
Exhib: RA; RBA; ROI.

TECK, His Royal Highness Francis, Duke of   **1837-1900**
Amateur caricaturist and father of H.M. Queen Mary. There is a fine ink caricature of Maria, Marchioness of Ailesbury and other court officials, 1866, in the Royal Library, Windsor. Signs: Teck fecit.

TEIGNMOUTH, Commander Henry Noel Shore
5th Baron   **1847- 1926**
Painter of oriental subjects. He was born in 1847 and joined the Navy in 1868, becoming Lieutenant in 1872 and Commander in 1891. He died on 25 February 1926 at Clevedon, Somerset.
Publ: *The Flight of the Lapwing [1881]; Smuggling Days and Smuggling Ways [1892]; Three Pleasant Springs in Portugal*

[1899]; The Diary of a Girl in France in 1821 [1905]; The Smugglers [1923 (with C.G. Harper)].
Exhib: RI.

TEL, S.
Contributed one cartoon to *Vanity Fair,* 1891.

TENISON, Nell Marion (Mrs Cyrus Cuneo)   **fl.1893-1940**
Figure painter and illustrator. She studied at the Cope and Nicholl School, London, 1879 and afterwards in Paris. She married Cyrus Cuneo (q.v.) and was elected SWA in 1918.
Contrib: *The Graphic [1904].*
Exhib: L; RA; RBA; RHA; ROI; SWA.
See Horne

TENNANT, C. Dudley   **fl. 1898-1931**
Marine and sporting painter and illustrator. He worked in Liverpool, 1898 and Surrey, 1913 and contributed to *Punch,* 1907-8 and *The Graphic,* 1910.
Contrib: *Strand Magazine [1913-31].*
Exhib: L; RA.
See Horne

TENNANT, Dorothy   Lady Stanley   -1926
Genre painter, illustrator and writer. She was the daughter of C. Tennant of Cadoxton Lodge, Glamorgan and studied at the Slade School and with Henner in Paris. She made a study of domestic subjects and children and in 1890 she married Sir H.M. Stanley (q.v.) the African explorer. She was RE from 1881 and died on 5 October 1926. Signs: ⟁
Publ: *Autobiography of H.M Stanley [1909].*
Illus: *London Street Arabs [1890].*
Contrib: *The English Illustrated Magazine [1885].*
Exhib: FAS; G; L; M; New Gall; RA; RE; RHA; ROI.
Colls: Tate; Witt Photo.

TENNANT, N.
Topographer. He was producing illustrations of Scotland for books in about 1849.

TENNIEL, Sir John   **1820-1914**

Cartoonist and illustrator. He was born in London in 1820 and studied at the RA Schools and the Clipstone Street Life Academy, rising to notice through his animal drawings in the 1840s. It was his edition of *Aesop's Fables*, 1848 that brought him to the attention of Mark Lemon of *Punch* and he joined the magazine as second cartoonist in 1851, graduating to principal cartoonist in 1864. Tenniel drew during his half century of association with the paper over 2,000 cartoons. They represented not only the essence of Victorian *Punch*, but of Victorian society, imperial, dignified and Olympian. Tenniel's superb draughtsmanship, meticulous silvery grey pencil strokes made with a special 6H pencil produced some of the household images of the period – 'The British Lion Attacking The Bengal Tiger' and 'Dropping the Pilot'. Despite a serious vein in his work, Tenniel was a fine illustrator of fantasy and his greatest opportunity for really humorous drawing came with his work for Lewis Carroll's *Alice in Wonderland,* 1865, a singular example of painstaking professionalism for both artist and author. *Through The Looking Glass* followed in 1872. Tenniel was elected ANWS in 1874 and a full member the same year. He was knighted in 1893 and died in London in early 1914. *Punch* issued a special Tenniel Supplement on March 4, 1914 to mark his death.

Contrib: *Undine [1845]; The Juvenile Verse and Picture Book [1848]; Aesop's Fables [1848]; Pollok's Course of Time [1857]; Poets of the Nineteenth Century [1858]; The Poetical Works of E.A. Poe [1857]; ILN [1857, 1868]; The Home Affections [Charles Mackay, 1858]; Blair's Grave [1858-59]; Once a Week [1859-67]; Lalla Rookh [1861]; Parables From Nature [1861]; Good Words [1862-64]; Puck on Pegasus [Pennell, 1862]; Passages From Modern English Poets [1862]; Arabian Nights [1863]; The Ingoldsby Legends [1864]; English Sacred Poetry [1864]; Legends and Lyrics [18651]; The Mirage of Life [1867-68]; A Noble Life [c.1870].* (For full bibl. see Sarzano, F.).

Exhib: FAS, 1895, 1900; NWS; RA; RBA.

Colls: BM; V & AM; Witt Photo.

Bibl: M.H. Spielmann, *The History of Punch*, 1895, pp.461-474; Frances Sarzano, *Sir JT*, English Masters of Black and White, 1948; R.G.G. Price, *A History of Punch*, 1957, pp.70-74; Rodney Engen, *Sir JT Alice's White Knight*, 1991.

See illustrations.

TERRY, George W.   **fl.1854-1858**

Ornamental artist. He contributed decorative work to *The Illustrated London News* in 1854 and initial letters to *Punch,* 1856-58.

TERRY, Herbert Stanley   **1890-**

Illustrator of comic genre subjects. He was born in Birmingham on 13 March 1890 and was educated at Bede College, Northumberland and at the Wolverhampton School of Art. He specialised in comic genre subjects and contributed to the major magazines from about 1914.

Contrib: *Punch [1914]; The Bystander; The Tatler; The Sketch; Illustrated Sporting and Dramatic News; London Opinion; Humorist; Passing Show; Windsor Magazine.*

THACKERAY, Lance   **RBA**   **-1916**

Painter, illustrator and writer. He worked in Notting Hill Gate, London and specialised in sporting subjects, often with a humorous side to them. He travelled extensively in the Middle East and had one man exhibitions at the Leicester Galleries, 1908, the FAS, 1910 and at Walker's Galleries, 1913. He was elected RBA in 1899 and died at Brighton on 11 August 1916.

Illus: *The Light Side of Egypt [1908]; The People of Egypt [1910].*

Contrib: *The Sphere [1894]; Sketchy Bits [1895]; The Graphic [1904-11]; Punch [1905-08].*

Exhib: FAS; RA; RBA; RI.

THACKERAY, William Makepeace   **1811-1863**

Novelist, illustrator and caricaturist. He was born in Calcutta in 1811 and after the family fortune was lost he turned to his aptitude for drawing for a living before his aptitude for writing. His pen drawing with light washes was always free and in the spirit of the amateur caricaturists of the 18th century and with undoubted borrowings from Hogarth. Despite a rather wooden appearance, Thackeray's figures have great value as being the only illustrations by a major writer for his own works. These began with the slight lithographs in

WILLIAM MAKEPEACE THACKERAY 1811-1863. Frontispiece of *The Paris Sketch Book*

Flore et Zephyr, 1836, made at a time when he was studying art in Paris and lead on to the more sustained work of *The Book of Snobs* and *Vanity Fair,* 1847-48. Thackeray was an able critic of caricature and humorous art both at home and on the Continent and his interest in artists was continued by his connection with *Punch,* 1842-54. His own attempts to illustrate his novel *Phillip* in the early numbers of *The Cornhill Magazine,* which he was editing, resulted in the young artist Fred Walker (q.v.) being employed. He died in London in 1863.

Illus: *Flore et Zephyr [1836]; The Paris Sketchbook [1840]; Comic Tales and Sketches [1841]; The Irish Sketchbook [1843]; Christmas Books [1846-50]; Vanity Fair [1847-48]; The History of Pendennis [1849-50]; Etchings by the late WMT while at Cambridge [1878]; The Orphan of Pimlico [1883].*

Contrib: *Figaro in London [1836]; Punch [1842-54]; The Cornhill Magazine [1860-61].*

Colls: BM; Fitzwilliam; V & AM; Witt Photo.

Bibl: Graham Everitt, *English Caricaturists,* 1893, pp.375-380; M.H.Spielmann, *WMT,* 1899; Melville, *T. As Artist,* The Connoisseur, March 1904; Gleeson White, *English Illustration,* 1906, p.18; *American Magazine,* Vol.28, 9 September 1935, p.555; Gordon N. Ray, *The Illustrator and the Book in England,* Morgan Library, 1976.

See illustration.

THIEDE, Edwin Adolf   **fl.1882-1908**

Miniature portrait painter and illustrator. He worked in Lewisham and London and worked for the leading magazines.

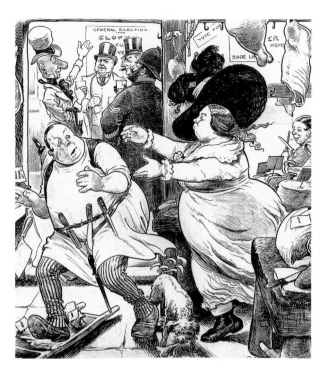

WILLIAM F. THOMAS fl.1890-1907. 'Ally Sloper canvassing for votes'. Original drawing for illustration in *Ally Sloper's Half Holiday*, 1906. Pen and ink. 10¾in x 9¾in (27.3cm x 24.8cm)

Author's Collection

Contrib: *The Queen [1892]; ILN [1893, 1900]; The Ludgate Monthly; The Windsor Magazine; The Temple Magazine.*
Exhib: RA; ROI.

THIELE, Reinhold
Illustrator. He illustrated *After School,* Robert Overton and *Lights Out,* by the same author in Jarrold's series 'Books For Manly Boys', 1894.

THIRTLE, John   **fl.1896-1902**
Painter and illustrator. He worked at Ewell, Surrey and drew pen and ink illustrations in the style of the Birmingham School for *The Studio* competitions, 1896-97.
Exhib: RA; RI.
Bibl: *The Studio,* Vol.8, 1896, p.184 illus.; Vol.10, 1897; Vol.12, 1897.

THOMAS, Bert   **1883-1966**
Black and white artist and illustrator. He was born at Newport, Montgomery in 1883, the son of the sculptor Job Thomas and was educated at Swansea. He worked in London for many of the leading magazines, taking as his subjects a raffish metropolitan world of policeman, waitresses, soldiers and sailors, set down with a spontaneous broken line. He drew a number of posters and died in 1966.
Contrib: *Fun [1901]; Punch [1905-35]; Strand Magazine [1906-43]; The Graphic [1910]; London Opinion [1913-].*
Exhib: London Salon, 1909.
Colls: BM; V & AM.
Bibl: *Mr Punch with Horse and Hound,* New Punch Library, c.1930; R.G.G. Price, A *History of Punch,* 1957, p.221 illus.
See Horne

THOMAS, George Housman   **1824-1868**
Wood engraver and illustrator. He was born in London in 1824, the brother of W.L. Thomas (q.v.). He worked from the age of fourteen with the wood engraver Bonner, and won a Society of Arts silver palette at the age of fifteen. He began his career as a book illustrator in Paris where he worked with Henry Harrison and had a small workshop with half a dozen assistants. During this period he was employed by an American journal and to engrave U.S. bank notes

and went to New York in 1846, where he and his brother founded a magazine which was unsuccessful. On his return in 1848, Thomas went to Rome and was present at Garibaldi's defence of the city, illustrations of it being accepted by *The Illustrated London News.* His work for books and magazines was quite extensive after this date, but his drawing lacks the fire to make him a great illustrator, although his work was much admired by Queen Victoria. He died at Boulogne in 1868 after falling from his horse; a memorial exhibition was held at the German Gallery the following year.
Illus: *Uncle Tom's Cabin [1852]; Hiawatha [1855-56]; Vicar of Wakefield [1857]; Pilgrim's Progress [1857]; Rohinson Crusoe [1865]; Armadale [Wilkie Collins, 1866]; The Last Chronicle of Barset [Anthony Trollope, 1867].*
Contrib: *ILN [1848-67]; Punch [1851-52]; Merrie Days of England [1858-59]; The Home Affections [Mackay, 1858]; Thomson's Seasons [1859]; Household Songs [1861]; Early English Poems [1862]; London Society [1863]; The Churchman's Family Magazine [1863]; The Cornhill Magazine [1864-65]; Legends and Lyrics [1865]; Aunt Sally's Life [1866-67]; Foxe's Book of Martyrs [1866]; Cassell's Magazine [1867]; The Quiver [1867]; The Broadway [1867]; Idyllic Pictures [1867].*
Exhib: BI; RA.
Colls: Fitzwilliam; V & AM; Windsor, Royal Collection (Napoleon III's visit).
Bibl: *In Memoriam GHT,* n.d., Cassell; Gleeson White, *English Illustration,* 1906, pp.155-156; Forrest Reid, *Illustrators of the Sixties,* 1928, p.248.

THOMAS, Inigo   **fl.1891-1903**
Architectural illustrator. He contributed to *The English Illustrated Magazine,* 1891-92 and illustrated Reginald Blomfield's *The Formal Garden,* 1892.
Bibl: R.E.D. Sketchley, *Eng. Bk. Illus.,* 1903, pp.50, 142.

THOMAS, Margaret   **-1929**
Artist, illustrator, sculptor and author. She was born at Croydon and emigrated with her parents to Australia. There she studied with Charles Summers and returned to Europe to study in the RA Schools and in Paris and Rome. She lived in Melbourne and London and made extensive tours of the Mediterranean coasts, her researches being published in a number of books. She died on 24 December 1929.
Illus: *A Hero of the Workshop [1880]; A Scamper Through Spain and Tangier [1892]; Two Years in Palestine and Syria [1899]; Denmark Past and Present [1901]; From Damascus to Palmyra [1905].*
Exhib: RBA; RHA; ROI; SWA.
Bibl: *Who Was Who,* 1929-40.

THOMAS, William F.   **fl.1890-1907**
Landscape painter and cartoonist. He followed W.G. Baxter (q.v.) as chief cartoonist on *Ally Sloper's Half Holiday* in 1890 and produced meticulous and detailed pen drawings of this character until at least 1906. He lived from about 1901 at Lydstepp House, Southwold, Suffolk.
Contrib: *Judy [1886-90]; Lika Joko [1894]; Punch [1895]; The New Budget [1895].*
Exhib: RA.
See illustration.

THOMAS, William Luson   **RI**   **1830-1900**
Wood engraver and newspaper proprietor. He was born in 1830, the brother of G.H. Thomas (q.v.), and in 1846 left with him for the United States where they founded the unsuccessful journals, *The Republic* and *The Picture Gallery.* They returned to Europe in 1848 and lived in Paris and Rome and in 1855, W.L. Thomas married the daughter of the watercolourist and illustrator J.W. Carmichael (q.v.). Thomas's work for *The Illustrated London News* from about 1850 gave him the idea of another illustrated periodical and *The Graphic* was founded in December 1869. Mainly due to Thomas's dynamism and first hand knowledge of the work, the new paper flourished in the 1870s and attracted a remarkable group of young social realistic artists who published their best work in its pages. In 1890, he became the first promoter of a daily illustrated paper *The Daily Graphic.* Although principally a businessman, Thomas was an able watercolourist and was elected ANWS in 1864 and NWS in 1875. He died

at Chertsey in 1900. His son, W. Carmichael Thomas, b.1856, was a wood engraver on *The Graphic* and managing director from 1900-17.
Exhib: L; M; RI; ROI.

THOMPSON, Alfred   -1895
Amateur painter, draughtsman and caricaturist. He was a cavalry officer, who took the advice of Mark Lemon of *Punch* to abandon the army and study art in Paris. He contributed to many periodicals, his caricatures reflecting the delicate portraits chargés of Tissot (q.v.). He finally became manager of the Theatre Royal at Manchester and designed costumes and scenery and edited the magazine *Mask*. He died in New York in September 1895.
Contrib: *Journal Amusant [Paris]; Diogenes [1854]; Punch [1856-58]; Vanity Fair [1862-76]; Comic News [1865]; The Arrow [1865]; The Broadway [1867-74]; Cassell's Illustrated Readings [1867]; ILN [1867]; Belgravia [1868]; Fun [1870].*

THOMPSON, George   fl.1892-1894
Portrait painter. He worked in London and contributed to *The Yellow Book*, 1894.
Exhib: London, 1892.

THOMPSON, J.G.
Contributor to *Cassell's Illustrated Readings*, 1867.

THOMPSON, Margaret   fl.1883-1923
Figure and flower painter and illustrator. She was a student at the New Cross School of Art and won a gold medal at South Kensington in 1898. She won a *Studio* competition in 1899 and worked in Hitchin and Hereford.
Exhib: B; RA; RBA; RI; RSA; SWA.
Bibl: *The Studio*, Vol.15, p.294 illus.

THOMSON, Emily Gertrude   RMS   -1932
Portrait painter, miniaturist, sculptor and illustrator. She was born in Glasgow and studied at the Manchester School of Art and was elected ARMS in 1911 and RMS in 1912. She worked at Brook Green, London from 1908 and died in 1932.
Illus: *A Soldier's Children [1897 (with E. Stuart Hardy)]; Three Sunsets and Other Poems with Twelve Fairy Fancies by EGT [1898].*
Exhib: G; L; M; RMS.
Colls: V & AM.

THOMSON, George   1860-1939
Townscape painter and illustrator. He was born at Towie, Aberdeenshire in 1860 and studied at the RA Schools and was a lecturer at the Slade 1895 to 1914. He settled at Château Letoquoi at Samer in the Pas-de-Calais in 1914 and died at Boulogne on 22 March 1939. He was elected NEA in 1891.
Contrib: *The Pall Mall Budget [1891-92].*
Exhib: B; G; GG; L; M; NEA; RA; RBA; RHA; RI; ROI.

THOMSON, Gordon   fl.1864-1886
Figure artist and illustrator. He was originally a civil servant and then cartoonist for *Fun*, 1870-78, having made his name with double page illustrations of the Franco-Prussian War for *The Graphic*. Dalziel refers to the 'large pictures for Christmas and other Holiday Numbers…remarkable for the varied topical events he crowded into them, and those who remember his "Academy Skits" will know what quaint burlesques they were'. He signed his work ℱ
Illus: *Pictures From Italy [C. Dickens, 1870].*
Contrib: *Punch [1864]; London Society; The Graphic [1869-86]; Fun [1870-78, 1890-93].*
Exhib: RA, 1878.

THOMSON, Henry   RA   1773-1843
Painter of history and allegory. He was born at Portsea on 31 July 1773 and studied in Paris before the Revolution, returning to this country to become a pupil of John Opie. He travelled to Italy and Germany, his main illustrative work being for Boydell's *Shakespeare* and portraits for *The Theatrical Recorder*, 1805. He was elected ARA in 1801 and RA in 1804, serving as Keeper from 1825-27. He died at Portsea on 6 April 1843.

HUGH THOMSON 1860-1920. 'The warm west-looking window seat'. Illustration to *The Ballad of Beau Brocade*, 1892

THOMSON, Hugh   1860-1920
Watercolour artist and illustrator. He was born at Coleraine, Co. Londonderry in 1860 and first came to prominence with his series of drawings of 18th century ballads and stories in *The English Illustrated Magazine*, 1883. Thomson was an instinctive artist with little formal training. He had left Coleraine for Belfast in 1877 and started work in the factory of Messrs Marcus Ward, engaged in Christmas card colour printing. He attended a few classes at the Belfast School of Art, but his real teacher was the artist and designer John Vinycomb (q.v.). His contact with Carr of *The English Illustrated* gave him the opportunity for figurative work and the partnership with W. Outram Tristram, the author, provided him with an ideal text. His name was made with *Coaching Days and Coaching Ways,* by the latter, 1888 and in such delightful examples of nostalgia as *Days with Sir Roger de Coverley*, 1886. Influenced by Randolph Caldecott and the novels of Thackeray (qq.v.), Thomson created an idyllic world of stage coaches, sedan chairs, feasts and port wine, which was a little more convincing than the earlier artists but very pretty. From the late 1880s he was continuously in demand for the novels of Jane Austen, Fanny Burney, Mrs Gaskell, Charles Reade and others as well as for contemporaries like J.M. Barrie and Austin Dobson. His studies of London life and the cockney poor are a notable achievement and show the diversity of this talented artist. Thomson was most prolific in the years 1900 to 1914 when his watercolour work was put to good use in the colour gift books, page plates of period scenes, their colour washed into a gentle ink drawing, usually pastellish and muted. He was elected RI in 1897 and retired in 1907. He died at Wandsworth on 7 May 1920. The artist was influential on the following generation, especially on the work of C.E. and H.M. Brock (qq.v.).
Illus: *Days with Sir Roger de Coverley [1886]; Coaching Days and Coaching Ways [Outram Tristram, 1888]; The Vicar of Wakefield*

HUGH THOMSON 1860-1920. 'The Gods – The Vaudeville Gallery'.
Original drawing for *The Graphic*. Pen, pencil and watercolour.
Signed and dated 1899. 11⅞in x 9¾in (30.1cm x 24.8cm)
Victoria and Albert Museum

HUGH THOMSON 1860-1920. Illustration for *Evelina* by Fanny
Burney, 1903

*[1891]; Cranford [Mrs. Gaskell, 1891]; The Antiquary [1891]; The
Bride of Lammermoor [1891]; The Ballad of Beau Brocade [1892];
Our Village [Miss Mitford, 1893]; The Piper of Hamelin [1893];
Pride and Prejudice [Jane Austen, 1894]; Coridon's Song [1894];
The Dead Gallant [Outram Tristram, 1894]; St. Ronan's Well
[1894]; The Story of Rosina [1895]; Sense and Sensibility [1896];
Emma [1896]; The Chase [1896]; Highways and Byways in Devon
and Cornwall [1897]; Mansfield Park [1897]; Northanger Abbey
[1897]; Persuasion [1897]; Riding Recollections [1898]; Highways
and Byways in North Wales [1898]; Jack the Giant Killer [1898];
Peg Woffington [Reade, 1899]; Highways and Byways, Donegal and
Antrim [1899]; Yorkshire [1899]; This and That [1899]; Ray Farley
[1901]; The History of Samuel Titmarsh [1902]; Evelina [1903];
Scenes of Clerical Life [George Eliot, 1906]; Highways and Byways
in Kent [Jerrold, 1907]; As You Like It [1909]; The Merry Wives of
Windsor [1910]; The School for Scandal [1911]; She Stoops to
Conquer [1912]; Quality Street [J.M. Barrie, 1913]; The Chimes
[1913]; The Admirable Crichton [J.M. Barrie, 1914]; Tom Brown's
School Days [1918]; The Scarlet Letter [Hawthorne, 1920].*
Contrib: *The English Illustrated Magazine [1883-92]; Pall Mall
Budget [1890]; The Graphic [1890-1905]; Black & White [1891];
The New Budget [1895]; The Ludgate Monthly [1895].* (See
Spielmann and Jerrold for complete bibl.)
Exhib: FAS, 1887, 1893; Leicester Galls; Walker's Galls.
Colls: BM; Ulster Mus; V & AM.
Bibl: *The Studio,* Winter No., 1900-01, p.30 illus.; R E.D Sketchley,
Eng. Bk. Illus., 1903, pp.68, 79, 156; M.H. Spielmann and W. Jerrold,
HT, 1931; Simon Houfe, 'Colouring the Past', *CL,* 5 Jan. 1989.
See illustrations.

THOMSON, James William　　　　　c.1775-c.1825
Architectural draughtsman. He entered the RA Schools in 1798 and
contributed illustrations to *The History of the Abbey Church of St.
Peter's Westminster,* 1812 and *Ackermann's Repository,* 1825.
Exhib: RA, 1795.

THORBURN, Archibald　　　　　1860-1935
Painter of birds. He was born on 31 May 1860, the son of Robert
Thorburn, RA, the miniature painter. He was educated at Dalkeith
and Edinburgh and married the daughter of C.E. Mudie, the
proprietor of Mudie's Libraries. Thorburn was a very scientific
painter whose renderings of colour and texture in his ornithological
books cannot be faulted, at the same time the works can be dull. He
had a wide following among the sporting fraternity and lived latterly
at Godalming, Surrey. He died on 9 October 1935.
Illus: *British Birds [1915-18]; A Naturalists Sketchbook [1919];
Bntish Mammals [1920]; Game Birds and Wild Fowl of Great
Britain and Ireland [1923].*
Contrib: *The Sporting and Dramatic News [l896]; The Pall Mall
Magazine; ILN [1896-98]; The English Illustrated Magazine
[1897]; British Diving Ducks [1913].*
Exhib: FAS; L; RA; RBA.
Colls: BM; V & AM; Woburn.
Bibl: *The Studio,* Vol.91, 1926; Maureen Lambourne, *The Art of Bird
Illustration,* 1991, pp.176-179.
See Horne
See illustration.

THORIGNY, Felix　　　　　1824-1870
Landscape painter and draughtsman. He was born at Caen on 14 March
1824 and studied with Julian at Caen. He then went to Paris to work for
Monde Illustré; Magazin Pittoresque; Musée des Familles and
Calvados Pittoresque. He died in Paris on 27 March 1870.
Contrib: *ILN [1859-68]; Illustrated Times [1859].*

THORNELY, H.
Equestrian illustrator. He contributed drawings to *The Penny
Illustrated Paper.*

THORNTON, Alfred Henry Robinson　　　　　1863-1939
Landscape painter. He was born in Delhi on 25 August 1863 and was

ARCHIBALD THORBURN 1860-1935. Original drawing for illustration to *British Diving Ducks*, 1913. Watercolour. Signed

educated at Harrow and Trinity College, Cambridge, then studying at the Slade and the Westminster School of Art. He was a member of the NEA from 1895 and Hon. Secretary from 1928 to 1939. He lived at Bath until 1914 and then at Painswick, Gloucestershire. He died on 20 February 1939.

Publ: *Fifty Years of the NEAC [1935]; The Diary of an Art Student of the Nineties [1938].*
Contrib: *The Yellow Book [1894-95].*
Exhib: FAS; L; M; NEA; RA; RBA; RSA.
Colls: BM; Cheltenham.

THORNTON, Robert John   1768-1837

Botanist, medical writer and occasional artist. He was the son of Bennell Thornton and was educated at Trinity College, Cambridge and Guy's Hospital, London. He travelled extensively abroad before settling down as a doctor in London in 1797. Thornton's most important scientific treatise was his *New Illustrations of the Sexual System of Linnaeus*, 1797-1807. Thornton enlisted such artists as Beechey, Opie, Reinagle, Russell and Burney to contribute portraits to this. From our point of view his crowning achievement was *The Temple of British Flora or Garden of Nature*, 1799, less scientific but more visually interesting. In his own superbly painted illustrations, Thornton set plants in an elaborate landscape background and made them part of the decorative arts. It was such a personal work and so lavishly produced that its bibliography is extremely complicated, no two examples being exactly alike. He published a *British Flora* in 1812 for which he organised a lottery at the European Museum in King Street. Tickets were taken for three sections of his master work, *The Temple of Flora*, five volumes, *British Flora* and *Elements of Botany*. The venture was not a success.

Bibl: David M. Knight, *Natural Science Books in English 1600-1900*, 1972, pp.163-164.
See illustration (colour).

THORPE, James H.   1876-1949

Painter and illustrator. He was born on 13 March 1876 and after being educated at Bancrofts School studied at Heatherley's. He served in the

First World War, 1915-19 and was the first designer of advertisements to the London Press Exchange, 1902-22. Thorpe's posterish style with heavy outline owes something to Hassall but is less competent in execution; his main contribution was as the historian of 1890s illustration and of monographs of two famous illustrators. He died in 1949.

Publ: *A Cricket Bag [1929]; Phil May [1932]; Jane Hollybrand [1932]; Happy Days [1933]; English Illustration The Nineties [1935]; Edmund J. Sullivan [1947].*
Illus: *The Compleat Angler [Izaak Walton, 1911]; Over [de Selincourt, 1932].*
Contrib: *Punch [1909-38]; The Graphic [1908-15]; Windsor Magazine; Strand Magazine [1916-28].*
Exhib: RI.
Colls: Author; V & AM.

THRUPP, Frederick   1812-1895

Sculptor. He was born at Paddington, London on 20 June 1812 and studied at Sass's Academy before working in Rome 1837-42. Thrupp won a Society of Arts silver medal in 1829 and designed statues for Westminster Hall. He died at Torquay on 21 May 1895.

Illus: *Paradise Lost [n.d.].*
Exhib: BI; RA; RBA.
Colls: BM, Winchester.
Bibl: R. Gunnis, *Dict. of Brit. Sculp.*, 1954, pp.394-395.

THURSTON, John   1774-1822

Watercolourist, illustrator and wood engraver. He was born at Scarborough in 1774 and specialised in copper plate and wood engraved book illustrations to stories. He was elected AOWS in 1805 and died in London in 1822.

Illus: *A Lecture on Heads [G.A. Stevens, 1802]; Rural Tales [R. Bloomfield, 1807]; Thomson's Seasons [1805]; Religious Emblems [1808]; Shakespeare's Works [1814]; Falconer's Shipwreck [1817]; Somerville's Rural Sports [1818].*
Contrib: *Hood's Comic Annual [1830].*
Exhib: OWS; RA.
Colls: BM; Greenwich; Nottingham.

TIDMARSH, H.E.   **fl .1880-1925**
Landscape and figure painter. He worked in North London and at Barnet from 1914, specialising in architectural subjects.
Contrib: *The Graphic [1886-87]; ILN [1889-91].*
Exhib: B; M; RA; RBA; RI.

TIFFIN, Henry   **fl.1845-1874**
Landscape painter. He worked in London and contributed to *Knight's London,* 1841.
Exhib: BI; RA; RBA.

TIMBRELL, James Christopher   **1807-1850**
Marine and genre painter. He was born at Dublin in 1807 and specialised in studies of sailors and shipping, contributing to *Knight's London,* 1841. He died at Portsmouth on 5 January 1850.
Exhib: BI; RA; RBA.

TISSOT, Joseph James Jacques   **1836-1902**
Painter of social genre, illustrator and caricaturist. He was born at Nantes on 15 October 1836 and studied art with Lamotte and Flandrin, exhibiting at the Salon from 1851. Tissot took an active part in the Franco-German War of 1870-71 and afterwards came to England and studied etching with Seymour Haden. In the 1870s he became the supreme genre painter of high life, the portrayer of balls and receptions, fashionable marriages and galas, transformed into luscious paint and correct in every detail. It was perhaps his observation that enabled him to be a good caricaturist for Vanity Fair, 1869-77, although Leslie Ward (q.v.) felt that the subjects in portraits chargés were too soft for caricature. In later life, Tissot became a convinced Christian and devoted all his time to religious painting, some of this work is foreshadowed in his book illustrations of 1865. He died at Buillon on 8 August 1902. He was elected RE in 1880.
Illus: *Ballads and Songs of Brittany [1865]; The Life of Our Lord Jesus Christ [1897, 2 Vols.].*
Exhib: B; FAS; G; L; M; RA; RE
Colls: V & AM.
Bibl: *JT,* Barbican Gallery catalogue, 1984.

TITCOMB, William Holt Yates RBA   **1858-1930**
Landscape, figure and flower painter. He was born at Cambridge in 1858 and studied at South Kensington and at Antwerp under Verlat and in Paris with Boulanger and Lefebvre. He also attended the Herkomer School at Bushey and was elected RBA in 1894. Titcomb worked at St. Ives, Cornwall and at Bristol and died in 1930.
Contrib: *The Graphic [1886 (story)].*
Exhib: FAS; G; L; M; NEA; New Gall; RA; RBA; RHA; RI; ROI.

TOD, Colonel James   **1782-1835**
Army officer and artist. He was sent to India in 1800 and carried out surveys, later acting as political agent at Rajput until 1822. He published and illustrated *Annals and Antiquities of Rajasthan,* 1829-32 and *Travels in Western India,* 1839. He died in London in 1835.

TOFT, Albert   **1862-1949**
Sculptor, modeller and designer. He was born in Birmingham in 1862 and studied at the Hanley and Newcastle-under-Lyme Schools of Art. He was at the RCA under Professor Lanteri for two years before being apprenticed to Messrs Wedgwood as a modeller. Toft undoubtedly designed Christmas cards and may have done some book illustration. He died in 1949. FRBS, 1923.
Publ: *Modelling and Sculpture.*
Exhib: B; G; L; RA.
Colls: Birmingham; Glasgow; Liverpool.

TOMKINS, Charles   **c.1750-1810**
Landscape painter and engraver. He was born about 1750, the son of William Tomkins, a landscape painter.
Contrib: *Britton's Beauties of England and Wales [1801-08].*
Exhib: RA.

TOMKINS. Charles F.   **1798-1844**
Landscape painter and caricaturist. He worked with David Roberts and Clarkson Stanfield (qq.v.) and was elected SBA in 1838. He

contributed drawings for the early numbers of *Punch,* and died in 1844.
Exhib: RBA.
Colls: V & AM.

TOMKINS, Peltro William   **1759-1840**
Engraver and illustrator. He was born in London in 1759 and studied with F. Bartolozzi before working on *Sharpes's British Poets* and *The British Theatre.* He acted as a printseller in Bond Street and produced *The British Gallery of Art* by Tresham and Ottley and *The Gallery of the Marquess of Stafford.* He died in London in 1840.
Colls: BM; Manchester.

TONKS, Henry   **1862-1936**
Painter of interiors and caricaturist. He was born at Solihull in 1862 and educated at Clifton before training at the London Hospital and becoming Senior Medical Officer at the Royal Free Hospital and FRCS. He left medicine for art and studied under Fred Brown at the Westminster School, becoming his assistant at the Slade School, 1894. Tonks was Slade Professor of Fine Art at University College, London from 1917-30 and Emeritus Professor from 1930. He was elected NEA in 1895 and died in London on 8 January 1937.
Contrib: *The Quarto [1896].*
Exhib: G; L; M; NEA; RA; RHA, RSA.
Colls: Ashmolean; Manchester.
Bibl: Lynda Morris, *HT and the Pure Art of Drawing,* Norwich School of Art, 1985.

TOPHAM, Edward   **1751-1820**
Caricaturist. He was a Captain and Adjutant in the First Life Guards and was also a journalist and playwright. He made some Cambridge caricatures in 1771 and worked for W. Darly of the Strand in 1771-72, his most celebrated print 'The Macaroni Shop' appearing under his imprint on 14 July 1772. He was later caricatured by Rowlandson and Gillray. He died in 1820.
Colls: BM; Witt Photo.

TOPHAM, Francis William   **1808-1877**
Painter of genre subjects, illustrator and engraver. He was born in Leeds on 15 April 1808 and apprenticed to an uncle who was an engraver. He came to London in 1830 and became an heraldic engraver and then a line engraver, illustrating Moore's and Burns's works. He studied with the Clipstone Street Academy and gradually abandoned engraving for watercolour at which he was very proficient. He made a speciality of peasant scenes and figures and particularly those of Ireland, which he visited in 1844 and Spain where he travelled in 1852-53 and 1864. Topham was elected ANWS in 1842 and NWS in 1843, followed by OWS in 1848. He revisited Spain in 1876 and died there at Cordova on 31 March 1877.
Contrib: *Book of Gems; Fisher's Drawing Room Scrapbook; History of London [Fearnside and Harrall]; Midsummer Eve [Mrs S.C. Hall]; Book of British Ballads [S.C. Hall, 1842]; The Sporting Review [1842-46]; ILN [1852]; Child's History of England [Dickens, 1852-54]; The Home Affections [Charles Mackay, 1858].*
Exhib: BI; NWS; OWS; RA; RBA.
Colls: BM; Reading; V & AM.
Bibl: Chatto & Jacxson, *Treatise on Wood Engraving,* 1861, p.600; F.G. Kitton, *Dickens and His Illustrators,* 1899; J. Maas, *Victorian Painters,* 1970, p.240; Tom Pocock, 'The Quest for FWT', *CL,* 26 Nov. 1981, pp.1860-61.

TOPPI, W.
Amateur figure artist. He contributed to *Punch,* 1902.

TORRANCE, James   **1859-1916**
Painter and illustrator. He was born at Glasgow in 1859 and specialised in fairy books for children. He died in Helensburgh in 1916.
Illus: *Scottish Fairy Tales & Folk Tales [1893]; Irish Folk & Fairy Tales [selected by W.B. Yeats, 1893]; The Works of Nathaniel Hawthorne [1894].*
Exhib: G.
Colls: V & AM.

TORRY, John T.　　　　　　　　　　　　**fl.1886**
Landscape painter. He contributed social realism subjects to *The Illustrated London News,* 1886.
Exhib: RBA; RI.

TOVEY, John　　　　　　　　　　　　**fl.1826-1843**
Topographer. He contributed to *Griffith's Cheltenham,* 1826.
Exhib: BI, 1843.

TOWNSEND, Frederick Henry Linton Jehne　　　**1868-1920**
Illustrator, black and white artist and etcher. He was born in London on 25 February 1868 and studied at the Lambeth School of Art. He was contributing figure drawings to *Punch* from 1903 and became the magazine's first Art Editor in 1905. Townsend's pen line is always assured and his compositions are good, but the subjects themselves lack humour and have little individuality in the *Punch* œuvre. Before his connection with the magazine in the 1890s, Townsend was a prolific illustrator of books, having some claim to be influenced by Abbey (q.v.) and the draughtsmen of the 1860s. He died in London on 11 December 1920. His early work is sometimes signed 'Fin de ville'.
Illus: *A Social Departure [S.J. Duncan, 1890]; An American Girl in London [S.J. Duncan, 1891]; The Simple Adventures of a Memsahib [S.J. Duncan, 1893]; The Jones's and the Asterisks [Campbell, 1895]; Maid Marian and Crotchet Castle [T.L. Peacock, 1895]; Melincourt [1896]; Gryll Grange [1896]; Jane Eyre [1896]; The Misfortunes of Elfin; Rhododaphne [1897]; Shirley [1897]; Rob Roy [1897]; The Scarlet Letter [1897]; The House of the Seven Gables [1897]; Bladys of the Stewponey [1897]; The Blithedale Romance [1898]; The King's Own [Marryat, 1898]; For Peggy's Sake [1898]; The Cardinal's Snuff Box [1900].*
Contrib: *ILN [1889-99]; The Gentlewoman; Judy [1892]; The Pall Mall Budget [1893-94]; Good Words [1894]; The Unicorn [1895]; The New Budget [1895]; Daily Chronicle [1895]; The Quiver [1897]; Pick-Me-Up [1897]; Black & White [1897]; The Longbow [1898]; St. James's Budget [1898]; The Graphic [1899-1901]; Penny Illustrated Paper; The Lady's Pictorial; The Queen; The Idler; The Pall Mall Magazine; The Royal Magazine; Cassell's Family Magazine; The Windsor Magazine; Fun [1901]; The Sphere; The Tatler.*
Exhib: FAS, 1921; NEA; New Gall; RA; RBA; RE; RSA.
Colls: Author; BM; V & AM.
Bibl *The Studio,* Winter No., 1900-01, p.52 illus.; R.E.D Sketchley, *Eng. Bk. Illus.,* 1903, pp.68, 69, 72, 157; P.V. Bradshaw, *The Art of the Illustrator FHT,* 1918; R.G.G. Price, *A History of Punch,* 1957, pp.156-157.

TOWNSEND, G.
Ornamental artist. He supplied decoration for *The Illustrated London News* in 1860 and was then working in Exeter.

TOWNSEND, Henry James　　　　　　　　　**1810-1890**
Surgeon, painter and etcher. He was born at Taunton in 1810 and between 1839 and 1866 taught art at the Government School of Design, Somerset House. He died in 1890.
Illus: *The Book of Ballads [Mrs. S.C. Hall, 1847].*
Contrib: *The Deserted Village [Etching Club, 1841]; Gray's Elegy [Etching Club, 1847]; Milton's Allegro [Etching Club]; The Illustrated Times [1855].*
Exhib: BI; RA; RBA.
Colls: V & AM.

TOWNSEND, Pattie or Patty　　　　　**see JOHNSON**

TOWNSHEND, George　1st Marquess　　　**1724-1807**
Soldier, politician and amateur caricaturist. He was born in 1724, the son of the 3rd Viscount Townshend and was educated at St. John's College, Cambridge, joining the 7th Dragoons in 1745, he fought at the Battle of Culloden. 1746. He had a distinguished career in the Army, acting as aide-de-camp to George II and as general under Wolfe at Quebec. He succeeded his father in 1764 and was made Lord-Lieutenant of Ireland in 1767 and created a marquis in 1786. Concurrently with this career, Townshend developed a superb hand for caricature and was the first amateur artist to publish his work in the country and the first caricaturist to apply caricature to political satires. He worked closely with Darly, the printseller from 1756, and

may have learnt the art from Darly's wife, Mary. His drawings created many enemies and irritated both William Hogarth and Horace Walpole. He died on 14 September 1807.
Bibl: Eileen Harris, *The Townshend Album,* National Portrait Gallery, 1974.

TOY, W.H.
Amateur figure artist. He contributed to *Punch,* 1909.

TOZER, Henry E.　　　　　　　　　　　**fl.1873-1907**
Marine painter and illustrator. He worked at Penzance and was a very extensive contributor of shipping scenes to *The Illustrated London News,* 1873-80.
Exhib: B; RA.
Colls: Cape Town.

TREGLOWN, Ernest G.　　　　　　　　　　　**-1922**
Artist and illustrator. He was a student of the Birmingham School and contributed black and white work to *The Yellow Book,* 1896 in a strong Beardsley idiom, and to *The Quest,* 1894-96.
Exhib: B; L, 1891-1916.

TRESIDDER, Charles
Illustrator. He drew for *The Old Miller and His Mill* by M.G. Pearse, a child's story of 1881.

TRINGHAM, Holland　RBA　　　　　　　　　**-1909**
Painter and architectural illustrator. He was a pupil of Herbert Railton (q.v.) whose work his much resembles. He lived in Streatham and did a great deal of magazine work up to the time of his death, he was elected RBA in 1894.
Contrib: *The Quiver [1891]; Black & White [1891]; ILN [1892-1908]; The Gentlewoman; The Sketch; Cassell's Famlly Magazine; Chums; The English Illustrated Magazine [1894].*
Exhib: B; RA; RBA.
Colls: V & AM.

TROTMAN, Samuel H.　　　　　　　　　　**fl.1866-1870**
Amateur illustrator and painter of sea pieces. He lived at 2 Lansdown Villas, Lillie Road, Fulham and privately published, in about 1870, *Photographic Illustrations of The Pilgrim's Progress Being Ten Photographs By Vernon Heath From The Original Pen and Ink Sketches By Samuel Trotman.*
Exhib: RBA.

TRUE, Will
Poster designer and illustrator. He contributed to *Fun,* 1892.

TUCK, Harry　　　　　　　　　　　　**fl.1870-1907**
Landscape and genre painter and illustrator. He was on the permanent staff of *Fun,* 1878-1900 and worked at Haverstock Hill, London.
Contrib: *The Strand Magazine [1891].*
Exhib: B; G; L; M; RA; RBA; RI; ROI.

TUCKER, Alfred Robert, Bishop of Uganda　　　**1860-1914**
Amateur artist. He was educated at Oxford and was curate at Bristol and Durham before entering the Colonial Episcopate as Bishop of Uganda from 1890 to 1911. He died after retiring to Durham in 1914.
Publ: *African Sketches [1892]; Toro [1899]; Eighteen Years in Uganda [1908].*
Bibl: J. Silvester, *ART,* 1926.

TUCKET, Elizabeth Fox
Black and white artist. She illustrated *Zigzagging Amongst the Dolomites* for Longmans in 1871.
Colls: V & AM.

TURBAYNE, Albert Angus　　　　　　　　　**1866-1940**
Designer and book decorator. He was born at Boston, United States in 1866 of Scottish parents and was educated there and at Coburg, Canada. From about 1900, Turbayne concentrated on the design of books, winning bronze medals in the Paris Exhibition of that year for his tool bindings for Oxford University Press. He was for many years Demonstrator in Design at the LCC School of Photo-engraving and

JOSEPH MALLORD WILLIAM TURNER, RA 1775-1851.
Illustration for Moore's *Lalla Rookh*. Watercolour. Signed

Lithography. He lived at Bedford Park, London and died on 29 April 1940.
Designed: *The Beautiful Birthday Book [Black, 1905 (borders)]; Prose Works of Rudyard Kipling [1908 (cover)].*
Publ: *Alphabet and Numerals; Monograms and Ciphers.*

TURNER, Joseph Mallord William   RA   1775-1851
Landscape painter in oils and watercolours. He was born in London on 23 April 1775, the son of a barber and wig maker in Covent Garden. He entered the RA Schools in 1789, becoming a pupil of T. Malton and in 1791 and 1792 went on sketching tours in the Bristol and South Wales areas. He joined Dr. Monro's evening study classes in 1794 and in the following years visited the 'picturesque' landscapes of the Lake District and Wales and worked for William Beckford at Fonthill Abbey. He was elected ARA in 1799 and RA in 1802, making his first Continental trip to France and Switzerland that year. Turner's tours increased after the Napoleonic Wars to include visits to Italy in 1819, Paris and Normandy in 1821, Holland, Belgium and the Rhine in 1825, the French rivers in 1826, France and Italy in 1828 and Northern France in 1829. These visits were interspersed with tours of England and stays with patrons like the Fawkes of Farnley Hall and Lord Egremont of Petworth. In the 1830s he was touring in the Baltic, Germany and Austria and paid his first visit to Venice in 1833 and made trips to the Rhine and Germany in 1840 and to Switzerland in 1841 and 1842 and again in 1844. He was in Normandy for the last time in 1845.

Turner's first move towards engraved work was in 1806 when W.F. Wells suggested that his paintings would reach a wider public if published. The result was the *Liber Studiorum,* a series of studies which were intended to classify his ideas about landscape. Turner etched the plates before they were mezzotinted and carefully superintended every stage under skilled engravers such as Lupton, Charles Turner and William Say. As Hardie has put it 'He trained a whole school of engravers and personally superintended their work'. In

these inspired and harmonious productions the complete effect of a Turner drawing remains supreme. The fashion for the picturesque and for landscape annuals grew in the 1820s and the artist continued to work for these publications which were not so much books as plates between covers with a text. In many cases Turner, not principally a figure painter, had to crowd his foregrounds with interest to satisfy the public and his accuracy as a topographer was never a strong point. An extremely literary artist, Turner's pictures were full of allusions but he was too big an artist to sit comfortably in an ordinary volume and the *Liber* was never really surpassed. Turner acted as Professor of Perspective at the RA from 1807 to 1837 and died in London in 1851.
Contrib: *The Copper Plate Magazine; The Pocket Magazine [c.1798]; Cooke's Picturesque Views of the Southern Coast of England [1814-26]; Views in Sussex [1816-20]; The Rivers of Devon [1815-23]; Hakewill's Picturesque Tour of Italy [1818-20]; Whitaker's History of Richmondshire [1818-23]; Provincial Antiquities of Scotland [1819-26]; Picturesque Views in England and Wales [1827-38]; Roger's Poems [1834]; Byron's Life and Works [1832-34]; Rivers of France [1833-35]; Scott's Poetical and Prose Works [1834-37].*
Exhib: BI, RA, RBA.
Colls: Aberdeen; Ashmolean; Bedford; Birkenhead; BM; Derby; Exeter; Fitzwilliam, Glasgow; Leeds; Lincoln; Manchester; Nottingham; Tate; V & AM.
Bibl: W. Thornbury, *Life of JMWT,* 1862; A.J. Finberg, *T's Sketches and Drawings,* 1910; A.J. Finberg, *T's Watercolours at Farnley Hall,* 1912; A.P. Oppe, *Watercolours of T,* 1925; A.J. Finberg, *Life of JMWT,* 1939; J. Rothenstein, *T,* 1962; M. Butlin, *T Watercolours,* 1962; L. Hermann, *JMWT,* 1963, J. Gage, *Colour in Turner,* 1969; Agnew *exhib. cat.,* Nov-Dec. 1967; RA *exhib. cat.,* Nov. 1974-March 1975. See illustration.

TURNER, William   1792-1867
Diplomat and amateur topographer. He was attached to the embassy at Constantinople and was envoy to Columbia 1829-38. He illustrated his own *Journal of a Tour in the Levant,* 1820, AT 375.

TWIDLE, Arthur   1865-1936
Painter and illustrator. He worked at Sidcup, Kent from 1902-13 and then at Godstone, Surrey. He died in 1936.
Contrib: *The Quiver [1890]; The English Illustrated Magazine [1893-94]; The Temple Magazine [1896]; The Strand Magazine [1906 (Conan Doyle)].*
Exhib: RA.

TWINING, Louisa   1820-1900
Artist and writer. She was born on 16 November 1820 and published a number of books on art and social matters illustrated by herself. She was made a Lady of Grace of St. John of Jerusalem and died on 25 September 1911.
Publ: *Recollections of Life and Work [1893]; Workhouses and Pauperism [1898].*
Colls: BM.

TYNDALE, Walter Frederick Roofe   RI   1856-1943
Architectural painter. He was born at Bruges in 1856 and came to England in 1871, later studying art at Antwerp and Paris. He began as an oil painter but after contact with Helen Allingham (q.v) turned entirely to watercolour. He made tours of Morocco, Egypt, Lebanon, Syria and Japan and lived in Venice. During the First World War he acted as Head Censor for the Army at Boulogne. He died in 1943. He was elected RI in 1911, and one man shows were held at the FAS in 1920 and 1924.
Publ. or Illus: *The New Forest [1904]; Wessex [1906]; Below the Cataracts [1907]; Japan and the Japanese [1910]; Japanese Gardens [1912]; An Artist in Egypt [1912]; An Artist in Italy [1913]; An Artist on the Riviera [1916]; The Dalmatian Coast [1925]; Somerset [1927].*
Exhib: B; FAS; G; GG; L; M; New Gall; RA; RBA; RHA; RI; ROI.
Colls: BM; Bradford; V & AM.

TYRER, Mary S.
Amateur illustrator. She was living at Cheltenham in 1896 and at Willesden in 1897 and won *The Studio* illustration competitions, Vol. 8, p.252 and Vol. 11, p.210 illus.

UBSDELL, Richard Henry Clements   fl.1828-1856
History painter, miniaturist, illustrator and photographer. He worked in Portsmouth and drew watercolours of churches. He contributed to *The Illustrated Times,* 1856 (marine).
Exhib: RA; RBA.
Colls: Portsmouth.

UNDERWOOD, Edgar Sefton   FRIBA   fl.1898-1914
Architect and humorous draughtsman. He was a Fellow of the RIBA and practised at Queen Street, Cheapside.
Contrib: *Fun [1901].*
Exhib: RA.

UPTON, Florence K.   1873-1922
Portrait painter and illustrator. She was working in Paris from 1905-07 and produced a whole series of children's books called the 'Golliwog Books' in the years 1899-1905. Her drawings of figures and toys are imaginative if rather stiff. She died in 1922.
Illus: *The Adventures of Two Dutch Dolls [1895]; The Adventures of Borbee and The Wisp [1908]; The Golliwog's Fox Hunt; The Golliwog's Air Ship; The Golliwog's Polar Adventures.*
Contrib: *Strand Magazine [1894-1903 (French ports)]; The Idler [1895].*
Exhib: FAS; L; P; RA.

URQUHART, Annie Mackenzie   fl.1904-1928
Watercolour painter and illustrator. She studied at the Glasgow School of Art under F.H. Newbury and in Paris with M. Delville. She worked in Glasgow and specialised in drawings of children and foliage, often on vegetable parchment with the colour stippled on to an outline drawing.
Exhib: L; RA; RSA.
Bibl: *The Studio,* Vol.47, 1909, pp.60-63 illus.

URQUHART, William J.   -1905
Cartoonist and illustrator. He was a native of Leicester and for many years drew for the *Leicester Guardian* and the *Wyvern.* He then moved to London in 1899 and worked for *Punch* and other periodicals. Some drawings exhibited in London in 1990 show him to have been a talented portraitist and character draughtsman and to have included such celebrities as Yvette Guilbert and Derwent Wood among his subjects. He also used the same model as Phil May (q.v.). He travelled to Holland in 1901 and settled in Davos, Switzerland in an effort to overcome tuberculosis. He died there in November 1905.
Illus: *The Davos Sketchbook; Davos Doings [c.1904-05].*
Exhib: RA, 1895, 1899-1901.
Colls: Leicester, drawings, watercolours and sketchbooks.

UWINS, Thomas RA   1782-1857
Painter and illustrator. He was born at Pentonville on 24 February 1782, the son of a Bank of England official and was apprenticed to the engraver Benjamin Smith in 1797. He left this employ after a

THOMAS UWINS RA 1782-1857. 'Henry Seventh's Chapel'. An illustration to *The History of the Abbey Church of St Peter's, Westminster,* 1812. Engraving coloured by hand

year to study at a Finsbury drawing school and at the RA Schools, making his living by book frontispieces and vignette illustrations. He was elected AOWS in 1809 and OWS in 1810, acting as Secretary from 1813-11. He resigned from this due to poor health in 1818 but money difficulties caused him to undertake another intensive round of book illustrating, 1818-24. He was employed as a topographer and visited France in 1817, and lived in Italy from 1824 to 1831. A commission to illustrate *Scott's Works* resulted in him living in Edinburgh for a time, but it was the copying of miniature portraits that was supposed to have ruined his eyesight and cost him his career. He later turned to oil painting and was elected ARA in 1833, RA in 1838 and served as Librarian to the Academy 1844 and Surveyor to the Queen's Pictures from 1845. He died at Staines on 25 August 1857.
Illus: *Nourjahad [Mrs Sheridan]; Histoire de Charles XII [Voltaire]; Don Quixote.*
Contrib: *Ackermann's Repository [fashion pls.]; The History of the Abbey Church of St. Peter's, Westminster [1812]; History of the University of Oxford [1813-14]; History of the University of Cambridge; Britton's Cathedrals [1832-36].*
Exhib: BI, NWS; OWS; RA; RBA.
Colls: BM, Birkenhead; Fitzwilliam; V & AM.
Bibl: Mrs. T. Uwins, *Memoir,* 1858; M. Hardie, *Watercol. Paint. in Brit,* Vol.1, 1966, p.157 illus.
See illustration.

UZANNE, Octave   1852-1931
Essayist and writer. He was born at Auxerre on 14 September 1852 and was editor and proprietor of *Le Livre, Revue mensuelle,* 1880-90 and *L'Art et L'Idée.* His books on fans and fashions were published in England with some drawings by himself. He was an early contributor to the *Studio.*

VALENTIN, Henry   **1820-1855**
Painter and illustrator. He was born at Allarmoint in the Vosges in 1820 and worked for *l'Illustration*, drawing figures in the style of Gavarni (q.v.). He was French correspondent of a number of British papers and died in Paris in 1855.
Contrib: *ILN [1848-56]; Cassell's Illustrated Family Paper [1855]; The Illustrated Times [1859].*

VALERIO, Theodore   **1819-1879**
Painter, engraver, etcher and lithographer. He was born at Herserange on 18 February 1819 and became a pupil of Charlet, exhibiting at the Salon from 1838. He travelled widely and visited Italy, Switzerland, Hungary and England and made studies of the Crimea. He died at Vichy on 14 September 1879.
Contrib: *The Illustrated Times [1856, 1860 (Arabia and Austria)].*

VALLANCE, Aymer   **-1943**
Flower painter, illustrator and designer. He worked in London and designed initial letters, endpapers and ornament for his own books and made playing card designs. He died in 1943.
Publ: *William Morris His Art, Writings and Public Life [1897]; Old Colleges of Oxford [1912]; Old Crosses and Lychgates [1919].*
Contrib: *The Yellow Book [1894].*
Exhib: RBA.

VALLENCE, William Fleming RSA   **1827-1904**
Marine and landscape painter. He was born at Paisley on 13 February 1827 and apprenticed to a gilder in 1841 after which he studied at the Paisley School of Design and the Trustees Academy, Edinburgh. He was a full time artist from 1857 and was elected ARSA in 1875 and RSA in 1881. He died at Edinburgh on 31 August 1904.
Contrib: *Pen and Pencil Pictures From The Poets [1866].*
Exhib: RA; RSA.

VAN ASSEN, Benedictus Antonio   **-1817**
Watercolour painter and engraver. He worked in England during the last decade of the 18th century and in the early 19th century. He engraved a portrait of Belzoni, 1804, J.H. Mortimer RA in 1810 and died in London in 1817.
Illus: *Emblematic Devices [1810].*
Exhib: RA, 1788-1804.
Colls: BM.

VANDERLYN, Nathan   **fl.1897-1937**
Watercolourist, etcher, engraver and illustrator. He studied at the Slade School and at the RCA. He was Painting Instructor at the LCC Central School of Arts and Crafts and was elected RI in 1916 although his name was removed in 1937.
Contrib: *The English Illustrated Magazine [1897].*
Exhib: L; RA; RRA; RI; RMS.

VEAL, Oliver
Illustrator. Contributed drawings to *Sketchy Bits*, 1895.

VEDDER, Simon Harmon   **1866-**
Painter, sculptor and illustrator. He was born in New York on 9 October 1866 and studied at the Metropolitan Museum School, N.Y. He studied in Paris at Julian's under Bouguereau and Robert Fleury and at the École des Beaux Arts. He settled in London by 1896 and married the painter Eva Roos.

Contrib: *Black & White [1900]; The Strand Magazine [1906]; Cassells Family Magazine; The Idler; The Pall Mall Magazine.*
Exhib: B; FAS; L; RA; ROI.

VENNER, Victor L.   **fl.1904-1924**
Humorous illustrator. He contributed to *Punch*, 1904.
Exhib: L.

VERHAEGE, L.
Silhouette illustrator. He contributed scenes of Paris to *The English Illustrated Magazine*, 1896.
Colls: V & AM.

VERHEYDEN, François   **1806-1890**
Genre painter and caricaturist. He was born at Louvain 18 March 1806 and studied in Paris before working at Antwerp. He contributed six cartoons to *Vanity Fair* in 1883 and died in Brussels about 1890.

VERNER, Captain Willoughby
Amateur artist. He was an officer in the Rifle Brigade, taking part in the Nile Expeditionary Force, 1884-85.
Illus: *Sketches in the Soudan [1885 (col. liths.)].*

VERNEY, Lady Frances Parthenope   **-1890**
Illustrator of natural history. She was the elder daugher of William Edward Nightingale of Embly and sister of Florence Nightingale. She married in 1858, Sir Harry Verney, Bt., of Claydon.
Contrib: *Good Words for The Young [1872].*

VERNON, R. Warren   **fl.1882-1908**
Painter, etcher and illustrator. He worked mostly in the South of England but in Dresden in 1903. He contributed a drawing to *Punch* in 1903.
Exhib: B; G; L; RA; RBA; RCA; RHA; RI; ROI.

VERPILLIEUX, Emile   **1888-1964**
Portrait and landscape painter, engraver and illustrator. He was born of Belgian parents in London on 3 March 1888 and studied in London and at the Académie des Beaux Arts, Antwerp. He produced coloured wood engravings and views of London and was elected RBA 1914. He died in 1964.
Contrib: *Strand Magazine [1912-24]; The Graphic [1915].*
Exhib: L; NEA; RA; RBA; RSA.

VICKERS, Alfred Gomersal   **1810-1837**
Landscape painter and illustrator. He was the son of the artist A. Vickers and was sent by Charles Heath to St. Petersburg to record the city for *The Picturesque Annual*, 1836 and *Heath's Gallery*, 1838. He died at Pentonville in 1837.
Exhib: BI; NWS; RA; RBA.
Colls: BM; V & AM; Witt Photo.

VICKERS, Vincent Cartwright   **1879-**
Black and white artist. He was born in 1879 and was a member of the armament and shipbuilding family. He lived and worked at Royston.
Illus: *The Google Book [1913].*
Exhib: Arlington Gall; RA.
Bibl: *Strand Magazine*, Dec. 1926.

VICTORIA, HM Queen   **1819-1901**
Artist and etcher. She was taught drawing at an early age and developed a greater interest in the arts after her marriage to the Prince Consort (q.v.) in 1841. The Queen's prints were made for her own amusement and were sometimes sent to friends. Her innocent hobby made legal history in 1849 when plates, sent to a Windsor printer for new impressions, were appropriated by a Mr Strange. Mr Strange attempted to put the prints on exhibition and charge for admission. The Prince Consort went to law, inaugurating the case of Albert v Strange on behalf of the Queen. The case made legal history and established a precedent of the misuse of confidence, which is an appropriate tool for computer hacking!
Illus: *Leaves from the Journal of Our Life in the Highlands [1867 and 1868].*
Coll: Royal Library, Windsor.
Bibl: Marina Warner, *Queen Victoria's Sketchbook*, 1979; *The Times*, 18 February, 1985; 'Royal Flushes', *Law Society Gazette*, March 1993.

VIERGE, M. Daniel 'Vierge Urrabieta Ortiz'   **1851-1904**
Genre painter, draughtsman and illustrator. He was born at Madrid on 5 March 1851, the son of a leading Spanish illustrator and studied

at the Madrid Academy. In 1867 he was working for the *Madrid la nuit* and in 1869 left for Paris to find an opening in illustrated journalism but his plans were prevented by the Franco-Prussian War. After returning to Madrid he was recognised by Yriarte, editor of *Monde Illustré* and worked for the paper from that time. Vierge illustrated an important edition of Victor Hugo's works, 1874 to 1882 and Quevedo's *Don Pablo*, 1882 and *Cervantes*, 1893. The artist was severely crippled by a stroke in 1881 but recovered sufficiently to do much good work subsequently.

Pennell points out that Vierge's influence on illustration in France, Spain and the United States was very considerable. His pen line was very pure, there was little cross hatching and yet a great suggestion of colour without colour at all. Several of the Edwardian artists such as H.R. Millar (q.v.) owe a debt to him and Ludovici records that Vierge was interested in his English public and wished to exhibit in London. Vierge won many honours including the Legion of Honour and died at Boulogne-sur-Seine on 4 May 1904.

Contrib: *ILN [1897].*
Exhib: International, 1904.
Bibl: *The Century Magazine,* June 1893; J. Pennell, *Pen Drawing and Pen Draughtsmen*, 1889; A. Ludovici, *An Artist's Life In London and Paris*, 1926.

VIGNE, Godfrey Thomas   **1801-1863**
Amateur artist and illustrator. He worked at Woodford and specialised in figure subjects. He travelled overland to India, 1833-39.
Illus: *A Personal Narrative of a Visit to Ghuzni, Kabul and Afghanistan [1840, AT 505].*
Contrib: *ILN [1849].*
Exhib: RA.
Colls: Searight Coll. at V & AM.

VILLIERS, Fred   **1851-1922**
Special Artist and illustrator of military subjects. He was born in London on 23 April 1851 and was educated at Guines in the Pas-de-Calais. He studied art at the BM and at South Kensington, 1869-70 and was a student at the RA Schools in 1871. He became Special Artist for *The Graphic* in 1876, being sent first to Servia and then to Turkey in 1877. He went on a world tour for the paper and was afterwards at Tel-el-Kebir, 1882, attended the Russian coronation in 1883 and saw action in Eastern Soudan, 1884, Khartoum, 1884, Bulgaria, 1886, Burma, 1887 and in the Graeco-Turkish War of 1897. Villiers was the earliest correspondent to be equipped with a cinematograph camera in the 1900s. He was present at the Siege of Port Arthur in 1904 and worked during the Great War, 1914-18. He was awarded twelve service medals. He died on 3 April 1922.
Publ: *Pictures of Many Wars [1902]; Port Arthur [1905]; Peaceful Personalities and Warriors Bold [1907]; Villiers, His Five Decades of Adventure [1921].*
Contrib: *The English Illustrated Magazine [1883-84]; Black & White [1891]; The Idler; ILN [1900].*
Exhib: M; RA; ROI.

VILLIERS, H.
Architectural draughtsman. He contributed to *The History of the Abbey Church of St. Peter's Westminster*, Ackermann, 1812.

VILLIERS, Jean Francois Marie Huet   **1772-1813**
Miniature painter and draughtsman. He was born in Paris in 1772, the son of J.B. Huet and settled in London in 1801. He painted portraits and landscapes in oil and watercolours and was a member of the Sketching Society. He was appointed Miniature Painter to the Duke and Duchess of York and styled himself 'Miniature Painter to the King of France'. He died in London in 1813.
Illus: *Rudiments of Cattle [1805]; Rudiments and Characters of Trees [1806].*
Contrib: *The History of the Abbey Church of St. Peter's Westminster [1812].*
Exhib: BI; OWS; RA.
Colls: BM.

VINE, W.
Caricaturist. He contributed two cartoons to *Vanity Fair*, 1873. He signs 'WV' in monogram.

VINYCOMB, John Knox LRIBA   **fl.1894-1914**
Architect, heraldic draughtsman and illustrator. He was probably born in Belfast and became a member of the Royal Irish Academy and a Fellow of the Royal Society of Antiquaries of Ireland. He was an authority on and a designer of bookplates and became Vice-President of the Ex Libris Society.
Publ: *On the Processes For the Production of Ex Libris [1894]; Fictitious and Symbolic Creatures in Art [1906].*
Colls: Newcastle.

VIVIAN, George   **1798-1873**
Amateur artist. He was born in 1798, one of the family of Vivian of Claverton Manor near Bath. He went to Eton and Christ Church, Oxford, before travelling on the Continent and in the Near East where he met Lord Byron in 1824. He lived in Italy from 1844 to 1846 but contracted malaria from which he never fully recovered. He was a friend of J.D. Harding with whom his landscapes have some similarity. He died in 1873.
Illus: *Spanish Scenery [1838]; Scenery of Portugal and Spain; The Gardens of Rome [1848].*

VIZETELLY, Frank   **1830-1883**
Special Artist and illustrator. He was born in London, the younger brother of Henry Vizetelly (q.v.). He was trained as a wood engraver and worked with his brother on *The Pictorial Times* and was Editor of *Monde Illustré* in Paris, 1857-59. In 1859 he was sent by *The Illustrated Times* to cover the Italian Campaign as Special Artist and was subsequently engaged by *The Illustrated London News* as their permanent War Artist. He was with Garibaldi in Sicily in 1860 and saw action on both sides in the American Civil War, 1861 and was present during the Prusso-Austrian War of 1866. He founded a society periodical called *Echoes of the Clubs* and in 1883 was sent by *The Graphic,* to accompany Hicks Pasha to the Sudan. He never returned and was believed to have been killed at El Obeid.
Colls: Witt Photo.
Bibl: H. Vizetelly, *Glances Back Through Seventy Years,* 1893.

VIZETELLY, Henry   **1820-1894**
Wood engraver, illustrator and editor. He was born in London on 30 July 1820, the elder brother of F. Vizetelly (q.v.). He was an engraver for *The Illustrated London News,* which he helped to found in 1842 and later established his own illustrated journals *The Pictorial Times,* 1843 and *The Illustrated Times,* 1855-65. In 1865 he became Paris correspondent of *The Illustrated London News* and lived there till 1872 when he settled in Berlin. He returned to London and worked on translations of Russian and French novels, dying at Fareham in 1894.
Publ: *Glances Back Through Seventy Years [1893].*

VOIGHT, Hans Henning 'Alastair'   **1887-1969**
Imaginative draughtsman and illustrator. He was born about 1889 of English, Spanish and Russian extraction. He was a self-taught artist and worked most of his life in Germany, interesting himself in decadence and transvestism. His black and white work is very sensuous and derivative from the work of Beardsley (q.v.), his colour illustrations have more the feel of the contemporary Russian school of ballet designers.
Illus: *Count Fanny's Nuptials [G.G. Hope Johnstone, 1907]; The Sphinx [Oscar Wilde, 1920]; Sebastian Van Storck [Walter Pater, 1927]; Manon Lescaut [Abbé Prevost, 1928]; Dangerous Acquaintances [Laclos, 1933 (Paris ed., 1929-30)].*
Bibl: *Alastair: Forty-Four Drawings in Colour and Black and White With a Note of Exclamation by Robert Ross,* 1914; *Salome,* 1922; *Alastair: Fifty Drawings,* New York, 1925.

VON HOLST, Theodore M.   **1810-1844**
Genre painter. He was born in London on 3 September 1810, the son of a music teacher and after studying in the British Museum, attended the RA Schools under H. Fuseli. The latter's strong influence is seen in his work, which can be rather hard and Germanic in line. He died in London on 14 February 1844.
Illus: *The Rape of the Lock [c.1825].*
Exhib: BI; RA; RBA.
Bibl: Robert Halsband, *The Rape of The Lock And Its Illustrators,* 1980.

VOSPER, Sydney Carnow   **1866-1942**
Watercolour painter, etcher and dry-point artist. He was born at Plymouth in 1866 and studied at Colarossi's in Paris, being elected ARWS in 1906 and RWS in 1914. He was working at Morbihan, France in 1904 and at Oxford from 1928. He died in 1942.
Contrib: *Punch [1902].*
Exhib: B; L; M; RA; RI; RSW; RWS.

WADDY, Frederick   fl.1878-1897
Ornamental artist and illustrator. He contributed initial letters to *The Illustrated London News,* 1883-84 and exhibited pencil drawings in London from 1878. He was political cartoonist to *Once A Week* in the 1870s.
Illus: *Cartoon Portraits by Frederick Waddy [Tinsley, 1873]; For Faith and Freedom [Besant, 1897 (with Forestier)].*

WADE, Charles Paget   ARIBA   1883-1956
Architect, craftsman and illustrator. He was the son of a wealthy sugar planting family owning estates in the West Indies at St. Kitts and Nevis. He studied architecture and practised as an architect at Yoxford and Forest Gate, London before acquiring Snowshill Manor, Gloucestershire in 1925, which he totally restored and presented to the National Trust in 1951. He died in 1956.
Illus: *Bruges, A Record and Impression [Mary Stratton, 1914]; The Spirit of the House [G. Murray, 1915].*
Exhib: RA.
Colls: Nat. Trust, Snowshill Manor.
Bibl: *Modern Book Illustrators and Their Work,* Studio, 1914.

WADHAM, Percy   fl.1893-1907
Painter and illustrator. He was born at Adelaide, Australia and studied with T.S Cooper and James Chapman. He was ARE from 1902-10.
Contrib: *The Pall Mall Magazine [1897].*
Exhib: FAS; RA; RE.

WAGEMAN, Thomas Charles   NWS   c.1787-1863
Portrait and landscape painter and illustrator. He was born about 1787 and was a founder member of the NWS in 1831 and became Portrait Painter to the King of Holland. He specialised in portraits of famous actors. He died in 1863.
Contrib: *Annals of Sporting [1827].*
Exhib: BI; NWS; RA; RBA.

WAIBLER, F.
German illustrator. He contributed to *The Illustrated London News,* 1872.

WAIN, Louis William   1860-1939
Animal caricaturist and illustrator. He was born in London on 5 August 1860 of an English father and French mother. He was educated by the Christian Brothers and studied for a musical career until 1879. He then went to the West London School of Art, 1877-80 and was Assistant Master there, 1881-82. He joined the staff of *The Illustrated Sporting and Dramatic News* in 1882 and *The Illustrated London News,* 1886. From 1883, Wain began to draw cats as they had never been drawn before, cats in humorous guises in human situations but always beautifully handled. The titles speak for themselves, 'A Kittens Christmas Party', 'Nine Lives of a Cat' and 'Cats at Circus' although he was sometimes forced to draw dogs before he became well-known! His main success stemmed from his recognition by Sir William Ingram of *The 'News* who employed him regularly and included one picture of 150 cats that took him eleven days to draw. Wain became popular in

the United States and visited New York, 1907-10 where he was on the staff of the *New York America* for a time. He also turned his talents to the illustrating of short stories, published yearly gift books and was employed on postcards for Messrs Raphael Tuck. He was President of the National Cat Club and a member of many other committees connected with feline reform, but his obsession slowly turned to insanity and he died in poverty on 4 July 1939.
Illus: *Louis Wain's Annuals [1901-26]; Louis Wain's Summer Book [1906-07]; The Kitcats; 9 China Futurist Cats [1922]; Louis Wain Big Midget Book [1926-27].*
Contrib: *The Sporting & Dramatic News [1882]; ILN [1883-99]; The English Illustrated Magazine [1884-1900]; Moonshine [1893]; The Sketch; The Gentlewoman; Pall Mall Budget; The Boy's Own Paper; Judy [1898]; The Windsor Magazine; Lloyds Weekly News [1905].*
Exhib: RBA.
Colls: V & AM; Witt Photo.
Bibl: *The Idler,* Vol.8, pp.550-555; Rodney Dale, *LW The Man Who Drew Cats,* 1968, with bibliog. and chapter on Wain's illness by D.L. Davies.
See Horne
See illustration.

WAITE, Edward Wilkins   fl.1878-1920
Watercolourist and illustrator. He worked at Blackheath and then at Dorking, 1892, Fittleworth, 1919 and Haslemere, 1920. He was elected RBA in 1893.
Illus: *The Story of My Heart [Richard Jefferies, 1912]; The Roadmender, 1911].*
Exhib: B; G; L; M; New Gall; RA; RBA; RCA; RHA; ROI; RSA.
Colls: Bristol.

WAKE, Richard   1865-1888
Special Artist. He was born on 24 September 1865, the son of Hereward Crauford Wake, CB, Civil Magistrate of Arrah and a grandson of Sir George Sitwell. He was appointed artist for *The Graphic* at Suakim in 1888 and died there on 6 December after making his first drawings.

WAKEFIELD, T.H
Amateur illustrator. Contributed design to *The Studio* competition, Vol. 8, 1896, p.252.

WAKEMAN, William Frederick   1822-1900
Landscape and topographical artist. He was born at Dublin in 1822 and was attached to the Ordnance Survey through the influence of G. Petrie (q.v.). He later worked as a drawing master in Dublin and taught at St. Columba's College, Stackallan and at the Royal School, Portora. He died in Coleraine in 1900.
Illus: *Ecclesiastical Antiquities [Petrie]; Ireland Its Scenery and Character [S.C. Hall]; Catalogue of Antiquities in the Royal Irish Academy [Wilde]; Lives of the Insh Saints [O'Hanlon].*
Contrib: *The Irish Penny Journal; Dublin Saturday Magazine; Hibernian Magazine.*
Exhib: RHA.
Colls: RHA.

WALKER, Arthur George   RA   1861-1939
Sculptor, painter and designer in mosaics. He was born on 20 October 1861 and studied at the RA Schools and in Paris. He worked in Chelsea until 1914 and later at Parkstone, Dorset, he was elected ARA in 1925 and RA in 1936. He died on 13 September 1939.
Illus: *The Lost Princess [G. Macdonald, 1895]; Stories From The Faerie Queen [Mary Macleod, 1897]; The Book Of King Arthur [Mary Macleod, 1900]; The Wonder Book of Old Romance [F. Harvey Darton, 1907].*
Exhib: G; L, RA, RI; RMS; ROI; RSA.
Bibl: R.E.D. Sketchley, *Eng. Bk. Illus.,* 1903, pp.116, 172.

WALKER, E.J.   fl.1878-1886
Domestic painter. He worked at Liverpool, 1878-79 and then at Regents Park, London. He contributed to *The Illustrated London News,* 1886, Christmas Number.
Exhib: L.

LOUIS WILLIAM WAIN 1860-1939. 'A quiet game at Nap'. Original drawing for illustration. Grisaille, signed and dated 1st Dec '94. 17in x 22½in (43cm x 56.5cm)

WALKER, Francis S.   RHA   1848-1916
Landscape and genre painter, illustrator of social scenes and engraver. He was born in County Meath in 1848 and studied art at the Royal Dublin Society and at the RHA Schools. He obtained a scholarship there to study in London and came in 1868 to begin work with the Dalziel Brothers. He began to work for *The Graphic* in 1870 and *The Illustrated London News* in 1875. He was elected ARHA in 1878, RHA in 1879 and RE in 1897. He worked chiefly in North London and died at Mill Hill on 17 April 1916.
Illus: *Ireland [1905]; Westminster [Walter Besant, 1897 (with others)].*
Contrib: *Cassell's Family Magazine [1868]; Good Words [1869]; The Sunday Magazine [1869]; Good Words For The Young [1869-72]; The Nobility of Life [1869]; London Society [1870]; Dalziel's Bible Gallery [1880]; Fun.*
Exhib: B; G; L; M; RA; RE; RHA; RI; ROI.
Colls: Witt Photo.

WALKER, Frederick   ARA   1840-1875
Painter and illustrator. He was born in Marylebone on 24 May 1840 and began to study art at the British Museum before being apprenticed to an architect named Baker. He returned to the Museum after leaving the architect, sketched the Greek sculpture and attended Leigh's Life School in Newman Street. He attended the RA Schools and then went, in 1858, to work for J.W. Whymper (q.v.) who taught him to draw on the wood, where he met J.W. North (q.v.). He began to draw for the magazines in 1860 and that year, through the influence of Thackeray (q.v.), he started to work for *The Cornhill*

Magazine. It was the latter's admission of failure in illustrating his own story that gave Walker a wider public through its pages in 1862. In some ways Walker's art was an inheritance from Millais, but it was also an inheritance from his studies of sculpture and his studies of nature. All his illustrations, whether contemporary in subject or costume pieces, show a familiarity with the figure and with movement that is outstanding. Although his name is usually linked with George Pinwell (q.v.) their acquaintanceship was slight, and Walker is more of a narrative painter than either Pinwell or North with whom he went sketching, 1868. Walker visited Paris in 1867, Venice in 1868 and 1870 and visited the Highlands with Richard Ansdell, RA (q.v.).

From book illustration Walker stepped into watercolours, proving himself an exquisite colourist and with a superb eye for detail. Such paintings as 'The Harbour of Refuge' show the second mood of Pre-Raphaelitism in the 1870s with an increased naturalism. Walker's failing health caused him to winter in Algiers in 1873-74 but he returned to this country and died at St Fillan's, Perthshire on 5 June 1875. He was elected AOWS in 1864, OWS in 1866 and ARA in 1871.
Contrib: *Everybody's Journal [1860]; Leisure House [1860]; Tom Cringle's Log [1861]; The Twins and Their Stepmother [1861]; Hard Times, Reprinted Pieces [Charles Dickens, 1861]; Good Words [1861-64]; The Cornhill Magazine [1861-66]; London Society [1862]; Willmott's Sacred Poetry [1862]; The Cornhill Gallery [1864]; English Sacred Poetry [1864]; Punch [1865, 1869]; A Round of Days [1866]; Ingoldsby Legends [Barham, 1866]; Touches of Nature by Eminent Artists [1866]; Wayside Poesies [1867]; Story*

FREDERICK WALKER ARA 1840-1875. 'One Mouth More'. An illustration to *A Round of Days*, 1866. Wood engraving

FREDERICK WALKER ARA 1840-1875. 'In the November Night'

of Elizabeth [1867]; Village on the Cliff [1867]; The Graphic [1869]; A Daughter of Heth [1872]; ILN [1875]; Thornbury's Legendary Ballads [1876].
Exhib: OWS; RA.
Colls: Ashmolean; BM; Fitzwilliam; Manchester; V & AM; Witt Photo.
Bibl: J. Comyns Carr, *FW An Essay*, 1885; Claude Phillips, *The Portfolio*, June 1894; J.G. Marks, *Life and Letters of FW, RA*, 1896; The Brothers Dalziel, *A Record of Work*, 1840-90, 1901, pp.193-205; Gleeson White, *English Illustration*, 1906 pp.165-166; Forrest Reid, *Illustrators of the Sixties*, 1928, pp.134-152.
See illustrations.

WALKER, George   **fl.1803-1815**
Watercolourist and illustrator working in London. He drew forty illustrations for reproduction in aquatint for his own *Costume of Yorkshire*, engraved by R. Havell and published by Robinson & Son, Leeds in 1814.
Coll: V & AM.
See illustration.

WALKER, Jessica (Mrs Stephens)   **fl.1904-1932**
Painter, illustrator and writer. She was born in Arizona, USA and studied at the Liverpool School, winning the travelling scholarship to Italy and studying in Paris and Florence. She was for some years art critic of *The Studio*.
Contrib: *Women and Roses [Browning, 1905].*
Exhib: L; M; RCA.

WALKER, John
Topographer and illustrator. He is probably the same artist as the J. Walker exhibiting at the RA, 1796 to 1800.
Contrib: *The Copper Plate Magazine [1792~1802].*

WALKER, Marcella   **fl.1872-1917**
Flower painter and illustrator. She worked at Haverstock Hill and contributed genre subjects to the magazines.
Contrib: *ILN[1885-94, 1903]; The Girl's Own Paper.*
Exhib: L; M; RA; RHA.

WALKER, T. Dart
Marine artist. He contributed illustrations of ships to *The Illustrated London News*, 1899.

WALKER, W.H.   **fl.1906-1926**
Watercolourist and illustrator. He worked in pen with fresh colours in the style of Rackham and illustrated *Alice's Adventures in Wonderland* for Messrs Lane, in 1908. He was a member of the family who ran Walker's Galleries.
Exhib: L; RA.

WALL, A.J.   **fl.1889-1897**
Illustrator specialising in animals and birds. He worked at Stratford-upon-Avon, but probably visited Australia in 1889-90 when he worked for *The Illustrated London News*.
Contrib: *The Sporting and Dramatic News [1891]; The Boy's Own Paper; The English Illustrated Magazine [1896-97].*
Exhib: B.

WALL, Tony
Figure artist. He contributed to *Punch*, 1902.

WALLACE, Robert Bruce   **-1893**
Figure artist in watercolour and illustrator. He lived and worked in Manchester and assisted Ford Madox Brown (q.v.) with his Manchester frescoes. His illustrative work began with *Punch*, where he made contributions from 1875-78 after an introduction from Swain. He hoped to succeed Miss G. Bowers (q.v.) on the paper but when he failed to do so, he concentrated on serious illustration elsewhere. He was Secretary of the Manchester Academy of Fine Arts, a friend of Frederick Shields (q.v.) and died at Manchester in 1893.
Illus: *The Adventures of Phillip [W.M. Thackeray]; Catherine [W.M. Thackeray, Cheap Illustrated Edition, 1894].*
Contrib: *Punch [1875-78]; ILN [1898].*
Exhib: M; RBA.

GEORGE WALKER fl.1803-1815. 'Infantryman'. Illustration for *Costume of Yorkshire*, 1814

WALLACE-DUNLOP   **See DUNLOP, Marion W.**

WALLER, Pickford R.   **1873-1927**
Amateur illustrator and decorator. He worked in Pimlico, was a friend of J. McNeil Whistler (q.v.) and patronised many artists including S.H. Sime (q.v.). He practised the decoration of manuscript and extra illustrated books with his own initial letters. His sketchbooks, including some designs for Guthrie's Pear Tree Press, were sold at Sotheby's in April and November 1976.
Illus: *Songs and Verses by Edmund Waller [Pear Tree Press, 1902].*
Contrib: *The Studio [Vol.8, 1896 pp.252~253 illus.].*

WALLER, Samuel Edmund   **1850-1903**
Genre and animal painter and illustrator. He was born at Gloucester on 16 June 1850 and studied with the Gloucester artist John Kemp. He was educated at Cheltenham and went to the RA Schools in 1869, beginning regular work for the magazines from about 1874. Waller was a good painter of horses and developed a style of sentimental genre picture in which they were usually involved, but he also made zoological studies and painted landscapes. He married the portrait painter, Mary Lemon Waller, and was elected ROI in 1883. He died at Haverstock Hill on 9 June 1903.
Publ: *Six Weeks in the Saddle; Sebastian's Secret.*
Illus: *Strange Adventures of a Phaeton [William Black, 1874].*
Contrib: *The Graphic [1874-81]; ILN [1895]; The Sporting and Dramatic News [1899].*
Exhib: B; FAS; G; L; M; RA; ROI.
Colls: Tate; Witt Photo.

WALLIS, Henry   RWS   **1830-1916**
Landscape and history painter and writer. He was born in London on

21 February 1830 and studied at Cary's Academy and then in Paris and at the RA Schools. He came under the influence of the Pre-Raphaelites at an early date and painted 'The Death of Chatterton', 1856 and 'The Stone-breaker'. His first flush of youthful talent did not last and he is included here for the academic illustrations that he made for his own books on ceramics. He was elected ARWS in 1878 and RWS in 1880. He died at Sutton, Surrey in December 1916.
Illus: *Egyptian Ceramic Art [1898]; Persian Lustre Vases [1899]; Nicola da Urbino at the Correr Museum [1905]; The Oriental Influence on Italian Ceramic Art [1900].*
Exhib: BI; G; L; M; RA; RBA; New Gall; RWS.
Colls: Birmingham; Tate; V & AM.
Bibl: J. Maas, *Victorian Painters,* 1970, pp.l32-133 illus.

WALSH, Captain Thomas
Army officer and amateur artist. He illustrated *Journal of the Late Campaign in Egypt,* 1803, AT 266.

WALSHE, J.C.   fl.l889-1909
Genre painter and illustrator. He worked in Birmingham and contributed figure drawings to *Punch,* 1903-09, specialising in strong interiors.
Exhib: B.

WALTERS, Thomas   fl.1856-1875
Domestic painter and illustrator. He worked in London and contributed to *Punch,* 1867-75.
Exhib: BI; RA; RBA.

WALTON, Edward Arthur   RSA   1860-1922
Landscape painter and genre artist. He was born in Glanderstone, Renfrewshire on 15 April 1860 and studied at the Glasgow School of Art and in Düsseldorf. He lived in London after 1894 but returned to Edinburgh in 1904. He was elected ARSA in 1889, RSA in 1905 and was President of the Royal Scottish Society of Painters in Watercolours, 1915. He died in Edinburgh on 18 March 1922.
Contrib: *The Yellow Book [1895-97].*
Exhib: G; L; M; NEA; New Gall; P; RA; RI; RSA; RSW; RWS.
Colls: Dundee; Glasgow; Leeds.

WALTON, Elijah   1833-1880
Landscape and genre painter in watercolour and illustrator. He was born at Birmingham in 1833 and studied in Birmingham and at the RA Schools. He visited Switzerland and Egypt in 1860-62 and spent much of his time on the Continent or travelling in the Near East in the succeeding years. He is at his best when drawing mountainous landscape. He died at Bromsgrove in 1880. Fellow, Royal Geographical Society.
Publ: *The Camel its Anatomy, Proportions and Paces [1865]; Clouds and their Combinations [1869]; Peaks in Pen and Pencil [1872].*
Illus: *The Peaks and Valleys of the Alps [T.G. Bonney, 1867]; Flowers From the Upper Alps [T.G. Bonney, 1869]; The Coast of Norway [T.G. Bonney, 1871].*
Exhib: BI; RA; RBA.
Colls: BM; Birmingham.

WALTON, George
Topographer. He contributed a view of Lichfield to *The Copper Plate Magazine,* 1792-1802.

WALTON, T.
Contributor to *The Illustrated London News,* 1860.

WARD, Charles D.   1872-
Landscape and portrait painter and illustrator. He was born at Taunton on 19 June 1872 and studied at the RCA. He married the portrait painter Charlotte Blakenay Ward and was elected ROI in 1915.
Contrib: *The Temple Magazine [1896-97]; The English Illustrated Magazine [1900-01].*
Exhib: D; G; L; NEA; RA; RBA; RI; ROI; RWA.
Colls: V & AM.

WARD, Edward Matthew   RA   1816-1879
Historical painter. He was born in Pimlico in 1816 and studied at the RA Schools and in Rome. He carried out extensive decorations for the new Houses of Parliament and was elected ARA in 1847 and RA in 1855. He was the father of Sir Leslie Ward (q.v.) and died at Slough in 1879.
Contrib: *The Traveller [Goldsmith, Art Union of London, 1851].*
Exhib: BI; NWS; RA; RBA.
Colls: BM; Witt Photo.

WARD, Enoch   fl.1891-1921
Landscape and figure painter. He worked in the London area, was RBA 1898, and contributed genre subjects including social realism to the magazines.
Contrib: *ILN [1891]; Black & White [1891]; The Queen [1892]; The Ludgate Monthly [1897]; The Pall Mall Magazine.*
Exhib: RA; RBA; RI.

WARD, Colonel Francis Swain   c.1734-1805
Army officer and artist. He had two periods of service in India and retired as lieutenant-colonel in 1787. He died at Negapatam in 1805. Fellow of the Society of Antiquaries.
Contrib: *Twenty-Four Views in Hindustan [1805].*
Exhib: Society of Artists.

WARD, Sir Leslie Matthew   'Spy'   1851-1922
Portrait painter and caricaturist, He was born in London on 21 November 1851, the eldest son of E.M. Ward RA and the grandson of James Ward RA. He was educated at Eton and studied architecture with Sydney Smirke RA and at the RA Schools. He made caricature contributions to *The Graphic* from 1874, but is best remembered as the under-study and successor to Carlo Pellegrini (q.v.) on Vanity Fair, 1873-1909. Ward was the first English artist to develop the *portrait chargé,* but in a much gentler style than his predecessor. His likenesses are accurate and lively if lacking in insight, the watercolours are usually mixed with bodycolour and are often found on dove grey papers. Ward was a very popular artist and his range of characters from the turf, the army, the church, the stage and high life decorated the walls of many an Edwardian home. He was elected RP in 1891 and knighted in 1918. He died in London on 15 May 1922.
Signs:
Contrib: *Cassells Family Magazine.*
Exhib: G; P: RA; RE.
Colls: BM; Liverpool; NPG; V & AM; Garrick Club; Witt Photo.
Bibl: Leslie Ward, *Fifty Years of Spy,* c.1915; E. Harris & R.Ormond, *Vanity Fair,* NPG cat. 1976; Roy T. Matthews and Peter Mellini, *In Vanity Fair,* 1982.
See illustration.

WARD, Martin Theodore   1799-1874
Animal painter. He was born in London in 1799, the son of William Ward and a pupil of Landseer. He worked in London at first and then in about 1840, moved to Yorkshire, dying there in poverty in 1874.
Contrib: *The Annals of Sporting [1826].*
Exhib: BI; RA; RHA.
Colls: Witt Photo.

WARDLE, Arthur   1864-1949
Animal painter. He worked in London, where he was born and was elected RI in 1922. A painting of his was purchased by the Chantrey Bequest in 1904. He died in 1949.
Contrib: *The Queen.*
Exhib: B; FAS; G; L; M; RA; RBA; RHA; RI; ROI; RSA; RSW.

WARING, John Burley   1823-1875
Landscape painter, watercolourist and architect. He was born at Lyme Regis on 29 June 1823, the son of a naval officer and was apprenticed to an architect and studied with Samuel Jackson. He travelled to Italy and wrote his autobiography, he died at Hastings on 23 March 1875.
Illus: *Architectural Art in Italy and Spain [1850, AT 42]; Studies in Burgos [1852, AT 157].*
Exhib: RA.
Colls: V & AM.

WARREN, Henry PNWS   **1794-1879**

Landscape and genre painter and illustrator. He was born in London on 24 September 1794 and studied under Joseph Nollekens, the sculptor, and at the RA Schools, 1818. Warren began as an oil painter but gradually turned his attention exclusively to watercolour, being elected NWS in 1835. He made many illustrations for the albums and annuals, particularly those of a Spanish or Shakespearean flavour. He was also a musician and lithographer and was President of the NWS from 1839-73. He died in London in 1879.

Publ: *Hints upon Tints [1833]; On the Fine Arts [1849]; Artistic Anatomy [1852]; Painting in Watercolours [1856]; Warren's Drawing Book [1867]; A Text Book of Art Studies [1870]; A Treatise on Figure Drawing [1871]; Half-hour Lectures on Drawing and Painting [1874].*

Illus: *Sketches in Norway and Sweden [Rev. A. Smith, 1847].*

Contrib: *The Book of British Ballads [S.C. Hall, 18421; The Book of Common Prayer [1845]; ILN [1848]; Lays of the Holy Land [1858]; The Welcome Guest [1860]; A Winters Tale; Lockhart's Spanish Ballads; Wordsworth's Pastoral Poems; Moore's Paradise and the Peri; The Children's Picture Book of Scripture Parables [1861].*

Exhib: BI; NWS, RA; RBA.

Colls: BM; V & AM; Witt Photo.

WARRY, Daniel Robert   **fl.1855-1913**

Architect and illustrator. He worked at Lewisham and Eltham and specialised in architectural and antiquarian drawings.

Contrib: *The Graphic [1881-82, 1884].*

Exhib: RA.

WATERFORD, Louise, Marchioness of   **1818-1891**

Watercolourist and sculptress. She was born in Paris in 1818, the second daughter of Lord Stuart de Rothesay and inherited from him Highcliffe Castle in Hampshire. She married the 3rd Marquess of Waterford in 1841 and lived at Curraghmore in Ireland, becoming a friend and correspondent of John Ruskin (q.v.), Burne-Jones (q.v.) and G.F. Watts. Between 1862 and 1883 she decorated the School Room at Ford with religious murals. She died at Ford Castle, Northumberland on 12 May 1891.

Illus: *Life Songs [1884 with Lady Tankerville].*

Contrib: *Story of Two Noble Lives [Augustus J.C. Hare].*

Exhib: G; M; RHA; SWA.

Colls: Lady Waterford Hall, Ford; V & AM; Tate; Witt Photo.

Bibl: *Magazine of Art*, Vol. 5, 1882, pp.108-113; Michael Joicey, *Louisa Anne, Marchioness of Waterford*, 1991.

WATERLOW, Sir Ernest Albert   **RA**   **1850-1919**

Landscape and animal painter. He was born in London and studied in Heidelberg, Lausanne and at the Royal Academy Schools. ARA, 1890; RA, 1903; PRWS, 1897. Some works were produced for *The Graphic*.

Colls: V & AM; Witt Photo.

WATERS, David B.   **fl.1887-1910**

Marine painter. He acted as Special Artist to the Fleet for *The Graphic,* in 1910. He worked in Edinburgh and London.

Contrib: *The Graphic [1901-10]; Punch [1906-07].*

Exhib: RA; RSA.

WATERSON, David   **RE**   **1870-1954**

Painter, etcher and engraver. He was born in 1870 and was elected ARE in 1901 and RE in 1910. He worked in Brechin, Scotland and undertook some illustration. He died on 12 April 1954.

Exhib: L; RE; RSA; RWA.

Bibl: *The Studio,* Vol.34, 1905, pp.346-348 illus.

WATHEN, James   **c.1751-1828**

Traveller and topographer. He was born at Hereford in about 1751 where he was a glover. He became famous as a pedestrian traveller under the name of 'Jemmy Sketch', making tours of Britain and Ireland from 1787. Wathen travelled to Italy to visit Byron in 1816 and made a tour of the East in 1811; he visited Heligoland in 1827. He died in Hereford in 1828.

Illus: *Journal of a Voyage to Madras and China [1814, AT 517];*

SIR LESLIE WARD 'SPY' 1851-1922. Caricature portrait of the writer and traveller, A.G. Hales. Original drawing for *Vanity Fair*. Watercolour. Signed. 21¼in x 15in (54cm x 38.1cm)

Author's Collection

Views Illustrative of the Island of St Helena [1821, AT 314].

Contrib: *The Copper Plate Magazine [n.d.].*

Exhib: RA.

Colls: Witt Photo.

WATKINS, Frank   **fl.1859-1894**

Architectural illustrator. He was working at Feltham, 1875-76 and at Maida Hill, London, in 1890. He worked principally for *The Illustrated London News*, beginning in 1859, contributing in 1875, but featuring continuously from 1884-94.

Exhib: M; RHA.

WATSON, Edward Facon   **fl.1830-1864**

Topographical and landscape painter. He was probably a pupil of J. Barber and collaborated with Cox in illustrating *Wanderings in Wales* by Radclyffe.

Exhib: RBA.

WATSON, Harry   **1871-1936**

Landscape and figure painter. He was born in Scarborough on 13 June 1871 and was educated at Scarborough and in Winnipeg. He studied at the Scarborough School of Art, the RCA and at the Lambeth School of Art. He was Life master at the Regent Street Polytechnic Art School and was elected ARWS in 1915 and RWS in 1920. He became ROI in 1932 and died in London on 17 September 1936.

Publ: *Figure Drawing [1930].*

JOHN DAWSON WATSON 1832-1892. 'God's Minister'. A preparatory drawing for *Pilgrim's Progress*, 1861, p.37. 6in x 4in (15.2cm x 10.2cm)   Author's Collection

Contrib: *The Lady's Pictorial [1895]; The English Illustrated Magazine [1899].*
Exhib: B; G; GG; L; M; NEA; RA; RBA; RI; ROI; RSA; RSW; RWA; RWS.
Colls: Maidstone; Tate; V & AM.

WATSON, John Dawson   **1832-1892**
Figure painter in oils and watercolour and illustrator. He was born at Sedbergh on 20 May 1832 and entered the Manchester School of Art in 1847. He attended the RA Schools in 1851 and returned to Manchester in 1852 where he exhibited at the Institution and made friends with Ford Madox Brown, 1856. He eventually left the North-West for London in 1860 and at once succeeded in obtaining important commissions particularly the illustrating of *Pilgrim's Progress* for Messrs Routledge in 1861. Watson began to do work for the magazines and became one of the most popular of the 1860s illustrators with his dependable black and white figure work. He was clearly influenced by the Pre-Raphaelites and by the work of J.E. Millais (q.v.) in particular. His strongest subjects are those of rustic genre, where good penwork made up for his occasional lack of fire, his religious and historical drawings can be rather stiff. Watson's best work was done before 1865, after this he experimented more as a colourist and took up oil painting more vigorously. This move followed his election to the OWS in 1864 and full membership in 1869 and may be connected to his sister's marriage to Birket Foster (q.v.). He designed furniture and costumes for a production of Henry V at Manchester in 1872. He was elected RBA in 1882 and died at Conway, North Wales on 3 January 1892.

Watson's early illustrations and drawings are usually signed with one or other of his two monograms, the later work simply by his initials. A representative exhibition of his work was shown at Manchester in 1877. Signs 𝔍𝒲 𝔸𝒲 𝔍𝒟𝒲
Illus: *Pilgrim's Progress [1861]; Eliza Cook's Poems [1861]; The Golden Thread [Dr. Norman Macleod, 1861]; Bennetts Poems [1862]; The Golden Harp [1864]; Robinson Crusoe [1864]; Old Friends and New [1867]; Wild Cat Tower [1877]; Princess Althea [1883].*
Contrib: *Once a Week [1861]; Good Words [1861-63]; ILN [1861 1872]; London Society [1862-67]; Willmott's Sacred Poetry [1862]; The Churchman's Family Magazine [1863]; The British Workman [1863]; The Arabian Nights [1863]; English Sacred Poetry of the Olden Time [1864]; Our Life Illustrated by Pen and Pencil [1865]; The Shilling Magazine [1865]; A Round of Days [1866]; Legends and Lyrics [1866]; Ellen Montgomery's Bookshelf [1866]; Ballad Stories of the Affections [1866]; Foxe's Book of Martyrs [1866]; The Sunday Magazine [1867]; Touches of Nature by Eminent Artists [1867]; The Savage Club Papers [1867]; The Illustrated Book of Sacred Poems [1867]; Cassell's Illustrated Readings [1867]; Cassell's Magazine [1868-69]; Tinsley's Magazine [1868-69]; The Nobility of Life [1869]; Pictures From English Literature [1870]; The Graphic [1870-77]; Leslie's Musical Annual [1870]; The Quiver [1873]; People's Magazine [1873]; Thornbury's Legendary Ballads [1876].*
Exhib: BI; G; GG; L; M; RA; RBA; RCA; RWS.
Colls: Bedford; Manchester; Newcastle; V & AM; Worcester, Witt Photo.
Bibl: Chatto & Jackson, *Treatise on Wood Engraving,* 1861 p 600; The Brothers Dalziel, *A Record of Work 1840-1890,* pp.170-174; Forrest Reid, *Illustrators of the Sixties,* 1928, pp 166-171 illus.; Simon Houfe, 'An Artist of Country Manners', *CL,* 13 Sept. 1979. See illustration.

WATT, T.
Illustrator and decorator supplying the head-pieces and initials to *The Pilgrim's Progress and The Holy War, Illuminated,* Lumsden Edition, c. 1850.

WATTS, Arthur George   **1883-1935**
Artist and caricaturist. He was born in 1883 and was educated at Dulwich College and studied at Antwerp, Paris and the Slade School. He served in the First World War with the RNVR and won the DSO in 1918. He was a regular pen and ink contributor to the humorous magazines. He died on 20 July 1935. ARBA, 1923.
Contrib: *Punch; Life.*
Exhib: FAS; RA; RBA.
Colls: V & AM; Witt Photo.
See Horne

WATTS, C.M.
Book decorator in the Celtic style. He illustrated *The Wild Harp* by Katherine Tynan, 1913.

WATTS, Louisa Margaret   **fl.1890-d.1914**
(Mrs. J.T. Watts née Hughes)
Landscape painter. She worked in Liverpool and London and married James Thomas Watts, the Birmingham painter. She contributed an illustration to *The Quarto,* 1896, in a slight woodcut style.
Exhib: B; M; RA; RCA; RI; ROI; SWA.

WATTS, William   **1752-1851**
Topographer and engraver. He was born at Moorfields in 1752 and studied with Paul Sandby and Edward Rooker. He took over the publication of the latter's *Copper Plate Magazine* and during the years 1779 to 1788, issued one of the finest series of topographical views *Views of The Seats of the English Nobility and Gentry.* He lived in Camarthen, Bath and Bristol at various times and was in Paris during the Revolution. He eventually retired to Cobham and died there on 7 December 1851.
Contrib: *The Copper Plate Magazine [1792-1802]; Britton's Beauties of England and Wales [1802].*
Colls: Witt Photo.

WAUGH, F.J.   fl.1894-1906
Landscape painter. He worked in Sark, 1894 and London from 1899 and probably visited South Africa from 1901-04 where he contributed views of the Transvaal to *The Graphic.*
Exhib: L; RA.

WAUGH, Ida
Illustrator. She provided the drawings for *Twenty Little Maidens,* a child's book by Blanchard, 1894.

WAY, Thomas Robert   1861-1913
Landscape and portrait painter and lithographer. He worked in London and was a significant figure in the revival of lithography in Britain. He taught the medium to J. McNeil Whistler in 1878 and the artist became his intimate friend, working with Way on the printing of the Venice etchings for the Fine Art Society's exhibition in 1880. He was a regular exhibitor at London exhibitions and died there in 1913.
Publ: *The Art of James McNeil Whistler [1903].*
Illus: *Reliques of Old London [H.B. Wheatley FSA, 1896].*
Exhib: L; NEA; RA; RBA; RI; ROI.
Contrib: *The Savoy [1896].*
Bibl: *The Studio,* Vol.34, 1905, pp.317-323 illus; E.R. and J. Pennell, *The Life of James McNeil Whistler,* 1908, p.157.

WAYLETT, F.   fl.1895-1898
Painter and illustrator. He worked in Hampstead and contributed to *The Sketch,* 1898.
Exhib: NEA.

WEBB, Ernest   fl.1907-1940
Sculptor and illustrator. He was working at Nottingham in 1923 and in London from 1927.
Contrib: *Punch [1906-71].*
Exhib: G; L; RA.

WEBB, Harry George   1882-1914
Landscape painter, etcher and book decorator. He worked in London and specialised in architectural drawings and decorated *The Acorn,* 1905-06.
Exhib: L; M; RA; RBA; RI; ROI.

WEBB, John   fl.1805-1816
Topographer. He contributed a view of Herefordshire to *Britton's Beauties of England and Wales,* 1805.
Exhib: RA, 1816.

WEBB, William J.   fl.1853-1882
Animal and genre painter and illustrator. He studied in Düsseldorf and then worked at Niton, Isle of Wight, 1855-60, London 1861-64 and Manchester, 1882. His work for magazines was mainly topography and travel, some influenced by the Pre-Raphaelites.
Illus: *The Great Hoggarty Diamond [Cheap Illustrated Edition, 1894].*
Contrib: *ILN [1872-74].*
Exhib: BI; M; RA; RBA; Witt Photo.

WEBER, H.
Topographer. He contributed illustrations to *The Border Antiquities of England and Scotland,* Walter Scott, 1814-17. He may be synonymous with 'H. Webber' who exhibited scriptural subjects at the BI in 1830.

WEBSTER, George   fl.1797-1832
Marine painter. He was based in London but travelled to Holland before 1816 and to Tripoli and the Gold Coast.
Publ: *Views of Various Sea-Ports [1831].*
Exhib: BI; RA; RBA.
Colls: BM; V & AM.

WEBSTER, Thomas   RA   1800-1886
Genre painter. He was born in London on 20 March 1800 and was a chorister of St George's Chapel, Windsor. He entered the RA Schools in 1821 and made a speciality of children or as Chatto puts it

'Infantine Subjects'. The most famous of these is 'The Village Choir' and this and similar paintings were popularised by engravings. He was elected ARA in 1840 and RA in 1846. He died at Cranbrook on 23 September 1886.
Contrib: *The Deserted Village [Junior Etching Club, 1841]; Book of British Ballads [S.C. Hall, 1842]; Favourite English Poems [1859].*
Exhib: BI; RA; RBA.
Colls: Bury; Preston; V & AM; Witt Photo.
Bibl: Chatto & Jackson, *Treatise on Wood Engraving,* 1861, p.599.

WEBSTER, Tom   fl.1900-1930
Designer of music title covers, c.1900. Cartoonist for *The Daily Mail.*

WEEDON, E.   fl.1848-1872
Marine painter and illustrator. This artist, of whom nothing is known, was chief marine illustrator for *The Illustrated London News* from 1848-72. His work could be classified as ship portraiture and is usually accurate and spirited. He may be a relation of A.W. Weedon 1838-1908, the landscape painter.
Exhib: RA, 1850.

WEEDON, J.F.
Illustrator of sporting subjects. He contributed to *The Graphic,* 1888.

WEEKES, William   fl.1856-1909
Animal and genre painter. He was the son of Henry Weekes 1807-1877, the sculptor. He lived at Primrose Hill, London and was a regular exhibitor.
Contrib: *ILN [1883].*
Exhib: B; FAS; G; GG; L; M; RA; RBA; ROI.

WEGUELIN, John Reinhard   RWS   1849-1927
Painter and illustrator. He was born at South Stoke, Sussex on 23 June 1849, the son of a clergyman and was educated at Cardinal Newman's Oratory School, Edgbaston. He became a Lloyd's underwriter, 1870-73 and then entered the Slade School, where he studied under Poynter (q.v.) and Legros. He was a Victorian classicist and painted in the style of Alma-Tadema (q.v.), illustrating many books. He was elected ROI in 1888, ARWS in 1894 and RWS in 1897. He had worked in Sussex from 1900 and died at Hastings on 28 April 1927.
Illus: *Lays of Ancient Rome [Macaulay, 1881]; The Cat of Bubastes, A Tale of Ancient Egypt [G.A. Henty 1889]; Anacreon [1892]; The Little Mermaid [Hans Andersen, 1893]; Catullus [1893]; The Wooing of Malkatoon [1898].*
Contrib: *The Graphic [1888-1906].*
Exhib: B; FAS; G; GG; L; M; New Gall; RA; RBA; RHA; ROI; RWS.
Bibl: R.E.D. Sketchley, *Eng. Bk. Illus.,* 1903, pp.29 131; *The Connoisseur,* Vol.78, 1927.

WEHNERT, Edward Henry   1813-1868
Historical painter and illustrator. He was born in London in 1813, the son of a German tailor and was educated at Gottingen. He returned to England in 1837 after working in Paris and Jersey and settled in London where he made historical paintings and book illustrations. He was elected NWS in 1837 and was a competitor in the Westminster Hall Competition of 1845. Wehnert's art was strongly linear and Chatto describes it as 'essentially German'. He is known to have made one visit to Italy in 1858. He died at Kentish Town on 15 September 1868.
Illus: *History of the British Nation [Hutchinson, c.1835]; Grimm's Household Stories [1853]; Poe's Works [1853]; Longfellow's Poems [1854]; Eve of St Agnes [J. Keats, 1856]; Ancient Mariner [1856]; The Pilgrim's Progress [John Bunyan, 1858]; Grimm's Tales [1861]; Fairy Tales [Hans Andersen, 1861]; Robinson Crusoe [D. Defoe 1862].*
Contrib: *Art Union Annual [1845]; ILN [1848-49]; The Traveller [Art Union 1851]; The Churchman's Family Magazine [1863]; Aunt Judy's Magazine.*
Exhib: BI; NWS; RA; RBA.
Colls: V & AM; Witt Photo.
Bibl: Chatto & Jackson, *Treatise on Wood Engraving,* 1861, p.594.

WEHRSCHMIDT, Daniel Albert later Veresmith   1861-1932
Portrait painter, engraver and lithographer. He was born at Cleveland, Ohio, USA on 24 November 1861 and studied at the Herkomer School, Bushey, Herts. He was Art Master at the Herkomer for 12 years, 1884-96, and was elected RP in 1915. He later lived at Doneraile, Co. Cork, 1921 and North Curry, Somerset, from 1927. He died on 22 February 1932.
Contrib: *The Graphic [1891].* (Illustrations for Hardy's *Tess.)*
Exhib: B; FAS; G; L; M; New Gall; P; RA; RHA; RSA.

WEIGALL, Charles Harvey   NWS   1794-1877
Landscape and genre painter and illustrator. He was born in 1794 and was elected a member of the NWS in 1834 and was Treasurer of the Society from 1839-41. Weigall was interested in technique and wrote a number of exemplars, also modelling in wax and making intaglio gems. He was a proficient draughtsman of animals and birds. He died in 1877.
Publ: *The Art of Figure Drawing [1852]; A Manual of The First Pnnciples of Drawing, with Rudiments of Perspective [1853]; The Projection of Shadows [1856]; Guide to Animal Drawing [1862].*
Illus: *Juvenile Verse and Picture Book [1848].*
Contrib: *ILN [1844-50]; The Illustrated London Magazine; The Graphic [1873].*
Exhib: NWS; RA; RBA.
Colls: BM; Nat. Gall, Ireland; V & AM; Witt Photo.

WEIR, Harrison William   1824-1906
Animal painter and illustrator. He was born at Lewes, Sussex on 5 May 1824 and was educated at Camberwell before learning colour-printing under George Baxter. He preferred painting and from an early date devoted all his time to studies of birds and animals. Weir was an independent minded artist with an amazing capacity for work; he started to draw for *The Illustrated London News* in 1847 and was still working for them at the turn of the century, their longest serving artist. He was elected ANWS in 1849 and NWS in 1851, but retired in 1870 because he preferred working on commission. He numbered among his friends Charles Darwin and among his hobbies pigeon fancying and natural history; a further link with the animal painters was provided by his marriage to the daughter of J.F. Herring (q.v.). Weir is characterised by an extraordinary accuracy and life in his drawings, his poultry live in the farmyard and his birds in the wild, rare among Victorians. He designed some race cups for Messrs Garrard and among his less successful ventures were sentimental fancy pictures of cats and dogs which may have influenced Louis Wain. He died at Poplar Hall, Appledore, Kent on 3 January 1906.
Illus: *Domestic Pets [Mrs Loudon, 1851]; Cat and Dog Memories of Puss and Captain [1854]; The Farmer's Boy [Bloomfield, 1857]; Wild Sports of The World [J. Greenwood, 1862]; The History of the Robins [Mrs Trimmer, 1868]; Animals and Birds [1868]; The Tiny Natural Histories [1880]; 0ur Cats and All About Them [1889]; Sable and White [Stables, 1894]; Shireen [Stables, 1894]; Poultry and All About Them [1903]; Animal Stories Old and New; Bird Stories Old and New.*
Contrib: *ILN [1847-1900]; The Poetical Works of E.A. Poe [1853]; Punch [1854]; Poets of the Nineteenth Century [Willmott, 1857]; Gertrude of Wyoming [Scott, 1857]; Dramatic Scenes [Cornwall, 1857]; The Home Affections [Mackay 1858]; Comus [1858]; Montgomery's Poems [1860]; The Welcome Guest [1860]; The Illustrated Times [1860]; Sacred Poetry [1862]; Parables From Nature [1867]; Episodes of Fiction [1870]; The British Workman The Band of Hope Review; Chatterbox [1880]; Wood's Natural History; The Field; Black & White; The Poultry and Stock Keeper; The English Illustrated Magazine [1887].*
Exhib: BI; NWS; RA; RBA.
Colls: V & AM; Witt Photo.
Bibl: Chatto & Jackson, Treatise on Wood Engraving, 1861, p.553; *AJ*, 1906.

WEIRD, R. Jasper
Probably a pseudonym of a figure artist contributing comic groups and animals to *Punch*, 1906.

WEIRTER, Louis   1873-1932
Artist, lithographer and illustrator. He was born in Edinburgh in 1873, the son of a Professor of Music and was apprenticed to a lithographer

while studying at the RSA and the Board of Manufacturers Schools. He was elected RBA in 1902 and worked in London, 1907 and Baldock, 1914, specialising in pictures of current events, the Diamond Jubilee and the War in the Air, 1914-18. He died 12 January 1932. He signs his paintings 'Louis Weirter' and his etchings 'Louis Whirter'.
Illus: *The Story of Edinburgh Castle; Stories and Legends of the Danube.*
Contrib: *The Evergreen.*
Exhib: RA; RBA; RSA.
Colls: V & AM.

WELLS
Topographer. Contributed drawings for *Knight's London*, 1841.

WELLS, H.T.   1828-1903
Portrait painter. He was born in London on 14 December 1828 and trained as a miniature painter and became an ARA in 1866 and RA in 1870. He died on 16 January 1903.
Colls: Dublin; NG; Tate.

WELLS, Joseph Robert   fl.1872-1895
Marine artist. He was the principal marine artist of *The Illustrated London News* from 1873 to 1883, specialising in ship portraits. After this date he contributed occasional drawings till 1895, the figures usually by C.J. Staniland (q.v.).
Contrib: *The English Illustrated Magazine [1885].*
Exhib: B;G; L; M; RA; RBA; RI; ROI.

WELLS, Reginald Fairfax   1877-1951
Sculptor and potter. He was born in Brazil in 1877 and studied at the RCA and under E. Lantieri. He was employed in the Chelsea Manufactory and acted as designer for Messrs Coldrum & Sons Pottery. He died in 1951.
Contrib: *The Sketch [1898].*
Exhib: FAS; G; GG; L; RSA; RA.
Colls: V & AM.

WEST, J.B.   fl.1804-1828
Landscape painter and caricaturist. He published in 1804, *Design for Imperial Crown to be used at Coronation of the New Emperor.*

WEST, J.C.
Topographer. He contributed to *Griffiths' Cheltenham*, 1826.

WEST, Joseph Walter   RWS   1860-1933
Landscape and genre artist, illustrator and bookplate designer. He was born in Hull in 1860 and educated at Bootham School, York, by the Quakers and at the St Johns Wood and the RA Schools. He later studied in Paris and Italy and became proficient in many other media including tempera and lithography and practised mural painting. He used his Quaker background for many of his genre paintings, his illustrating is usually romantic. He was elected RBA in 1893, ANWS in 1901 and RWS in 1904. He worked at Northwood from 1902 and died there on 27 June 1933.
Illus: *Tryphena in Love [Walter Raymond, 1895]; Rosemary For Remembrance [Mary Brotherton, 1896 (title & cover)]; Ballads in Prose [Nora Hopper, 1896 (title & cover)]; Virgil's Georgics [frontis].*
Contrib: *The English Illustrated Magazine [1887]; The Pall Mall Magazine.*
Exhib: B; FAS; G; L; M; New Gall; RA; RBA; RHA; RSW; RWS.
Colls: Hull; Tate; V & AM.
Bibl: *The Studio,* Winter No. 1900-01 pp.87-100 illus; Vol.37 1906 pp.158-159 illus; Vol.40 1907 pp.87-100 illus; *Pearson's Magazine,* 1907.

WEST, Maud Astley   fl.1880-1916
Flower painter. She was a student of the Bloomsbury School of Art and worked in London and Tunbridge Wells. She illustrated *Through Woodland and Meadow,* 1891, with M. Low.
Exhib: B; RA; SWA.

WESTALL, Richard   RA   1765-1836
Historical and figure painter and illustrator. He was born at Hertford in 1765 and apprenticed to a silver engraver in Cheapside, attending

the RA Schools from 1785. He turned wholly to art on completing his apprenticeship in 1786 and became a popular and prolific book illustrator. He worked chiefly for publishers of poetry, decorating their pocket editions with vignettes and 'conversation piece' subjects within decorative borders. His drawings for these are firmly in the 18th century tradition, charming and delicate tinted drawings with highly finished faces. He collaborated with Alderman Boydell in painting five Milton subjects for his *Shakespeare Gallery* 1795-96 and illustrated the works of Crabbe, Moore and Gray. He was elected ARA in 1792 and RA in 1794 and gave lessons in drawing to the Princess Victoria. He died in London on 4 December 1836.

Publ: *A Day in Spring [1808].*
Illus: *Paradise Lost [Sharpe's Classics, 1822]; Boydell's Shakespeare [1802]; Elizabeth [Madame Cottin, 1817]; Illustrations from the Bible [1822]; Vicar of Wakefield [1828]; Illustrations of the Bible [1835-36]; Reflections on the Works of God.*
Contrib: *The Keepsake [1829]; Heath's Gallery [1836-38]; National Portrait Gallery of the 19th century.*
Exhib: BI; RA; RBA.
Colls: Ashmolean; BM; Eton College; Hertford; Nat. Gall. Scot; V & AM; Witt Photo.
Bibl: M. Hardie, *Watercol. Paint. in Brit.,* Vol.1, 1966, p.150 illus. Hammelmann & Boase, *Book Illustrators in Eighteenth Century England*, Yale, 1975.
See illustration (colour).

WESTALL, William   ARA   1781 -1850
Topographical illustrator. He was born at Hertford in 1785, the younger brother of Richard Westall (q.v.). He studied with his brother and at the RA Schools and was chosen by Benjamin West PRA to accompany the Flinders expedition to Australia as artist. On his return voyage he visited China and India, 1803-04 and was in Madeira and Jamaica in about 1808. He was elected AOWS in 1810 and resigned in 1812 when he was elected ARA. He spent the rest of his life painting English topography and died in London on 22 January 1850.
Illus: *Views of Scenery in Madeira, at the Cape, in China and India [1811]; Views of Australian Scenery [1814, AT 567]; Views of the Yorkshire Caves [1818]; Victories of the Duke of Wellington [1819, AL 381]; Britannia Delineata [1822]; Scenery, Costumes and Architecture of India [Grindlay, 1826-30, AT 422]; Picturesque Tour of the River Thames [1828].*
Contrib: *Ackerman's History of Rugby School [1816]; Ackermann's Repository [1825]; Illustrations of Warwickshire [1829]; Great Britain Illustrated [Thomas Moule, 1830]; Landscape Album [1832].*
Exhib: BI; OWS; RA; RBA.
Colls: Ashmolean, BM; Glasgow; Leeds; Manchester; Nottingham; Witt Photo.
Bibl: AJ, April 1850; Iolo Williams, *Early English Watercolours*, 1952, p.59 illus.

WESTRUP, E. Kate   fl.1908-1927
Sporting artist. She worked at New Milton, Hants, 1910 and in Cornwall, 1911-27. She was elected ASWA in 1923.
Illus: *The Rosebud Annual [1908].*
Contrib: *Punch [1914 (hunting)].*
Exhib: L; NEA; RA; SWA.

WHARTON, S.   fl.1810-1816
Architect. He was an honorary exhibitor at the RA, 1810-14 and showed drawings of London improvements. He published and illustrated *Waterloo*, 1816, AL 382.

WHATLEY, Henry   1842-1901
Landscape and genre painter. He was born in Bristol in 1842 and worked as a drawing-master there, teaching at Clifton College and other schools. He died at Clifton in 1901.
Illus: *Quiet War Scenes [J. Baker, 1879]; Pictures of Bohemia [J. Baker, 1894].*
Contrib: *ILN.*
Colls: Bristol.

WHEELER, Dorothy Muriel   1891-1966
Watercolour painter and illustrator. She worked in Plumstead, Kent

and Esher, Surrey, in the 1900s and 1920s, producing pretty figure studies in a late Greenaway style with shepherdesses and architectural ornament.
Exhib: RA; SWA.
See Horne

WHEELER, Edward J.   fl.1872-1902
Domestic painter and black and white artist. He began to work for *Punch* in 1880 and contributed figures for the theatrical pages, for the editorial and provided initial letters. He used an unusual sign-manual of a 'four-wheeler'.
Illus: *Tristram Shandy [Smollett, 1894]; Mother Goose [Routledge, 1895]; The Captains Room [W. Besant, 1897].*
Contrib: *Punch [1880-1902]; The Cornhill Magazine [1883].*
Exhib: London, 1872.
Bibl: M.H. Spielmann, *The History of Punch*, 1895, p.549.

WHEELHOUSE, Mary V.   fl.1895-1933
Painter and illustrator. She was probably a student at Scarborough School of Art, 1895 and lived in Chelsea from 1900.
Illus: *Cousin Phillis [Mrs Gaskell, Bells Queens Treasures Series, 1908]; Six to Sixteen [Mrs Ewing, 1908].*
Exhib: M; New Gall; RA; SWA.
See Horne

WHICHELO, C. John M.   AOWS   1784-1865
Watercolourist and topographer of marine and river subjects. He was born in 1784 and became a pupil successively of John Varley and J. Cristall. He became Marine and Landscape Painter to the Prince Regent in about 1812 and was elected AOWS in 1823. Whichelo drew mainly British subjects but travelled in the Low Countries, Germany and Switzerland.
Contrib: *Antiquarian and Topographical Cabinet [1806]; Britton's Beauties of England and Wales [1815].*
Exhib: BI; OWS; RA.
Colls: BM; Greenwich; V & AM; Witt Photo.

WHISTLER, James Abbot McNeil   1834-1903
Painter, etcher, lithographer and caricaturist. He was born at Lowell, Massachusetts on 11 July 1834, the son of an army officer. He was brought up in Russia and England before entering West Point Military Academy, to begin an army career. He was later moved to the Navy as a cartographer, where he learned etching, but abandoned this for art and went to Paris in 1855 to study under Gleyre, where he met G. Du Maurier (q.v.), E.J. Poynter (q.v.) and was influenced by the work of Manet and Courbet. Whistler settled in London in 1859, remaining a leading figure in its art world but arrogant, temperamental and fiercely independent. His early years, particularly 1862, are the ones in which he undertook his few but very striking book illustrations for the magazines. They are very powerfully conceived and have a freedom of line which is unusual among the wood engravings of the 1860s, the finest is 'The Morning Before The Massacre of St Bartholomew', for *Once a Week*.

Whistler's libel action with Ruskin in 1879 and his subsequent bankruptcy divides a spectacular career into two. His return to London in 1880 resulted in a triumphant exhibition of Venetian etchings and a series of fine lithographs. As Gleeson White commented 'one might as well praise June sunshine as Mr Whistler's etchings' and the whole force of his genius appears in the plates. His later polemical books have some decoration in their pages, but otherwise his contribution in this direction was small. His caricatures are witty and sharp, those of his adversary F.R. Leyland executed with an almost pathological savagery. Whistler was President of the SBA from 1886-88 but resigned due to controversy. He died in London in July 1903.
Contrib: *Once a Week [1862]; Good Words [1862]; Passages From Modern English Poets [1862]; Thornbury's Legendary Ballads [1876]; Scribner's Monthly and St Nicholas [1880-81].*
Exhib: FAS; G; GG; L; M; NEA; P; RA; RBA; RSA; RSW.
Colls: Ashmolean; Fitzwilliam; Glasgow; Manchester; V & AM.
Bibl: T.R. Way and G.R. Dennis, *The Art of JMcN W*, 1903; H.W. Singer, *JAMcN W*, 1904; J and E.R. Pennell, *The Life of JAMcN W*, 1908; B. Sickert, *W*, 1908; J. and E.R. Pennell, *The W Journal*, 1921; J. Laver, *W*, 1930; H. Pearson, *The Man W*, 1952; D. Sutton,

JAMES McNEILL WHISTLER 1834-1903. 'Rotherhithe'. Etching and drypoint, 1860. 10⅞in x 7⅞in (27.6cm x 19.9cm)

Nocturne, 1963; D. Sutton, *JMcN W,* 1966; R. McMullen, *Victorian Outsider,* 1973; S. Weintraub, *W,* 1974; *W The Graphic Work,* Walker Art Gall. Cat. 1976; R. Dorment & M. F. Macdonald, *Whistler,* Tate Gallery cat., 1994-95.
See illustration.

WHITE, Edmund Richard   fl.1864-1908
Landscape and genre painter in watercolour and illustrator. He worked in London and at Walham Green from 1880, and contributed comic genre subjects to *The Illustrated London News,* 1871.
Exhib: B; L; RA; RBA; RI; RSW.

WHITE, George Francis   1808-1898
Professional soldier and watercolourist. He was born at Chatham in 1808 and served in India with the 31st Regiment until 1846 and sketched the landscape of the Himalayas. He was later a Chief Constable and DL of County Durham and died there in 1898.
Illus: *Views in India Chiefly Among The Himalaya Mountains... 1829-31-32,* Publ. in 2 pts. 1837.

WHITE, Gleeson   1851-1898
Book decorator and editor. He was born at Christchurch on 8 March 1851 and was educated at Christchurch School before entering journalism. He was deeply involved with the arts and crafts movement and worked as Associate Editor on the New York magazine *Art-Amateur* from 1891-92. He then became first Editor of *The Studio,* 1893-94, and was largely responsible for its international reputation and its encouragement of book illustration. Walter Crane recalled of White that his 'quick sympathy and recognition ... extended to all young and promising designers in black and white.' He was himself a talented designer of book covers and the foremost historian of the art of the book of his period. He died in London on 19 October 1898.
Publ: *Ballads and Rondeaus, Canterbury Poets [1887]; Practical Designing [1893]; Salisbury Cathedral [1896]; English Illustration*

[1897]; Master Painters of Britain [4 Vols, 1897-98].
Designed: *Hake, A Selection From His Poems [1894 (cover)]; Out of Egypt [P. Hemingway 1895-96 (cover)].*
Bibl: *The Studio,* Vol. 15 1899 p.141 (obit.); *The Artist,* Nov. 1898; *Apollo,* Vol. 108, Oct. 1978, pp.256-261.

WHITE, William Johnstone   fl.1804-1812
Illustrator. He worked in London and contributed drawings to Ackermann's *The History of the Abbey Church of St Peter's, Westminster,* 1812.
Exhib: RA.
Colls: BM; Nottingham.

WHITEFORD, Sydney Trefusis   fl.1860-1881
Still life, bird and flower painter, working in Plymouth and London.
Contrib: *Cassell's Illustrated Readings,* 1867.
Exhib: RA; RBA.

WHITEHEAD, Frances M.   fl.1887-1929
Landscape painter and etcher. She worked in the Birmingham area and illustrated a child's book, *The Withy Wood,* Skeffington, 1903.
Exhib: B; RA; RI; SWA.

WHITELAW, George   fl.1907-1930
Artist and illustrator. He worked in Glasgow, 1912 and London, 1920 and contributed cockney figure subjects to *Punch,* 1907.
Exhib: G; L.
See Horne

WHITING, Frederic or Fred   1873-1962
Portrait and figure painter and Special Artist. He was born at Hampstead in 1873 and was educated at Deal and St Mark's College, Chelsea and studied at the St John's Wood and RA Schools. He attended Julians, Paris, and was appointed artist on *The Daily Graphic,* 1890. He became Special Artist and War Correspondent on *The Graphic* in China, 1900-01 and during the Russo-Japanese War of 1904-5, he excelled in action subjects and equestrian scenes. He was elected RBA in 1911, ROI, 1915, RI, 1918 and RSW, 1921. Whiting was President of the Artists Society, 1919 and died on 1 August 1962.
Exhib: G; GG; L; P; RA; RBA; RHA; RI; ROI; RSA; RSW.
Colls: Brighton; Liverpool.

WHITTOCK, Nathaniel   fl.1828-1851
Draughtsman and lithographer. He worked principally in London and Oxford and published drawing-books.
Illus: *The British Drawing Book [nd]; The Oxford Drawing-Book [1825]; History of the County of Yorks [Allan, 1828]; The Art of Drawing and Colouring From Nature [1829]; A Topographical and Historical Description of Oxford [1829]; The Microcosm of Oxford [1830]; The Decorative Painter and Glaziers Guide [1837]; The Miniature Painters Manual [1844].*
Contrib: *Tallis's Illustrated London [1851 (frontis)].*
Colls: BM; Witt Photo.

WHYMPER, Charles H. RI   1853-1941
Landscape and animal painter and illustrator. He was born in London on 31 August 1853, the son of J.W. Whymper (q.v.) and studied at the RA Schools. He spent the whole of his working life illustrating books on travel, natural history and sport and had a one man show at the Walker Galleries in 1923. He was elected RI in 1909. He worked in London and then at Houghton, Hunts. from 1915 and died on 25 April 1941.
Illus: *Wild Sports in the Highlands [1878]; The Game-Keeper at Home [Jefferies, 1880]; Siberia in Europe [Seebohm, 1880]; Matabele Land [Oates, 1881]; The Fowler in Ireland [Gallwey, 1882]; A Highland Gathering [Lennox Peel, 1885]; Our Rarer Birds [Dixon, 1888]; Story of the Rear-Guard of Emin Relief Expedition [Jameson, 1890]; Travel and Adventure in South Africa [F.C. Selous, 1893]; Sporting Days in Southern India [Pollock, 1894]; Birds of Waye and Woodland [P. Robinson, 1894]; Big Game Shooting [1895]; The Pilgrim Fathers of New England [1895]; Icebound on Kolguev [Trevor-Battye, 1895]; The Hare [Macpherson, 1896]; The World's Roof [Oxley, 1896]; In Haunts of Wild Game [Kirby, 1896];*

In and Beyond The Himalayas [Stone, 1896]; Sunshine and Storm in Rhodesia [F.C.Selous, 1896]; Letters to Young Shooters [Gallwey 1896 (with J.G. Millais)]; The Art of Wildfowling [Chapman, 1896]; Wild Norway [Chapman, 1896]; Travel and Big Game [Selous and Bryden]; Lost and Vanishing Birds [Dixon, 1898]; The Rabbit [Harting, 1898]; Exploration and Hunting in Central Africa [Gibbons, 1898]; The Salmon [A.E. Gathorne-Hardy, 1898]; Off to Klondyke [1898]; Bird Life in a Southern County [C. Dixon, 1899]; Homes and Haunts of the Pilgrim Fathers [Mackennal, 1899]; Among the Birds in Northern Shires [Dixon, 1900]; Birdlife in a Southern County [Dixon, 1900]; Shooting [Lord Walsingham and Payne-Gallwey, 1900]; Egyptian Birds [1909].
Contrib: *ILN [1887-89]; Good Words [1891-]; The English Illustrated Magazine [1883-].*
Exhib: B; FAS; L; M; New Gall; RA; RBA; RI.
Colls: Witt Photo.
Bibl: R.E.D. Sketchley, *Eng. Bk. Illus.,* 1903, pp.142-144.

WHYMPER, Edward J.   **1840-1911**
Alpinist and illustrator. He was born on 27 April 1840, the second son of J.W. Whymper (q.v.) and brother of Charles Whymper (q.v.). He joined the family wood engraving business and was responsible for engraving and illustrating many books in the 1860s, but his fame really rests on his pioneer work as an alpinist. He wrote *Peaks, Passes and Glaciers,* 1862 and was a medallist of the RGS. He died on 16 September 1911.
Illus: *Scrambles Among the Alps [1870]; Travels Among the Great Andes of the Equator [1892]; Chamonix and Mont Blanc [1896]; Zermatt and the Matterhorn [1897].*
Contrib: *The Sunday Magazine [1865]; The Leisure Hour [1867]; The Graphic [1870].*

WHYMPER, F.   **fl.1857-1869**
Landscape painter. He was working in London, 1857-61 and contributed illustrations of Russian America to *The Illustrated London News,* 1868-69.
Exhib: RA; RBA.

WHYMPER, Josiah Wood   RI   **1813-1903**
Landscape painter and engraver. He was born at Ipswich in 1813 and after being apprenticed to a stone mason, taught himself to draw. He settled in London in 1829 and studied with W.C. Smith, establishing himself as an illustrator after publishing an etching of London Bridge, 1831. Whymper's wood engraving business became one of the most thriving in London and did most of the work for Murrays, the publishers, and for the Religious Tract Society and the S.P.C.K., both at that time employing good artists. He had at various times Frederick Walker, Charles Keene, J.W. North, Charles Green, and G.J. Pinwell as pupils. He was elected ANWS in 1854 and NWS in 1857, and lived at Haslemere, where he died on 7 April 1903.
Illus: *The Child's History of Jerusalem [C.R. Conder, 1874]; Field Paths and Green Lanes [L.J. Jennings, 1877]; Tent Work in Palestine [C.R. Conder, 1878].*
Contrib: *Missionary Travels [David Livingstone, 1857].*
Exhib: L; M; RI; ROI.
Colls: V & AM.

WIDGERY, Frederick John   **1861-1942**
Landscape and marine painter. He was born in 1861, the son of William Widgery, the Exeter painter, and studied at the Exeter School of Art and at South Kensington and Antwerp.
Illus: *A Perambulation of Dartmoor [S. Rowe, 1896]; Fair Devon Album [S. Rowe, 1902]; Devon [Lady R. Northcote, 1914]; Torquay [J. Presland, 1920].*
Exhib: L; RA; RI; ROI.
Colls: Exeter.

WIEGAND, W.J.   **fl.1869-1882**
Figure artist. He worked in London and illustrated *Elliott's Nursery Rhymes* for Novello, 1870, and contributed to *Good Words For The Young,* 1869-73 and *The Sunday Magazine,* 1870.

WIGHTWICK, George   **1802-1872**
Architect and draughtsman. He was born at Mold, Flintshire on 26

August 1802 and was educated at Wolverhampton Grammar School. He failed to gain entrance to the RA Schools in 1818 but was given £100 by his stepfather to visit Italy, a tour he undertook from 1825-26. On his return he became an assistant to Sir John Soane and began illustrating and publishing, but success eluded him in London and he finally moved to Plymouth in 1829 and set up an architectural practice. He retired to Clifton in 1851 and to Portishead in 1855 and died there on 9 July 1872.
Illus: *Select Views of Roman Antiquities [1827]; Remarks on Theatres [1832]; Sketches of a Practising Architect [1837]; The Palace of Architecture [1840]; Hints to Young Architects [1846].*
Contrib: *Public Buildings of London [Britton]; Union of Architecture [Britton, 1827, AL 7].*
Exhib: RA.
Bibl: *Bentley's Miscellany,* Vol. 1852-54, pp.31-35; Vol. 1857-68 pp. 42-43.

WIGRAM, Sir Edgar Thomas Ainger, 6th Bart   **1864-1935**
Amateur artist and illustrator. He was born on 23 November 1864, and succeeded his cousin in the title 1920. He was educated at Kings School, Canterbury and Trinity Hall, Cambridge and was Mayor of St. Albans, 1926-27. He died on 15 March 1935.
Illus: *Northern Spain [1906]; The Cradle of Mankind [1914]; Spain [J. Lomas, 1925].*
Colls: Hertford.

WILD, Charles   OWS   **1781-1835**
Architectural and topographical illustrator. He was born in London in 1781 and was articled to the younger Thomas Malton. Wild was a careful delineator of Gothic cathedrals and colleges and was very influential through the engravings after his work in spreading the enthusiasm for Gothic art. He concentrated mainly on Britain but travelled abroad in the 1820s. He was elected AOWS in 1809 and OWS in 1812 and was Treasurer and Secretary in 1833. Increasing blindness caused his resignation in that year and he died in London on 4 August 1835.
Illus: *Twelve Views of Canterbury Cathedral [1807]; Twelve Views of York [1809]; An Illustration of Chester [1813]; An Illustration of Lichfield [1813]; An Illustration of Lincoln [1819]; An Illustration of Worcester [1823]; Foreign Cathedrals [1826, AT 93]; Select Examples... of Architecture... in England [1832]; Twelve Outlines... [1833]; Selected Examples of Architectural Grandeur [1837].*
Contrib: *History of the Western Division of the County of Sussex [Rev J. Dallaway, 1815-30]; Royal Residences [W.H. Pyne, 1819]; Oxford Almanac [1815, 1818, 1819, 1829, 1831, 1845].*
Exhib: BI; RA; OWS.
Colls: Ashmolean; BM; Chester; V & AM.
Bibl: M Hardie, *Watercol. Paint. in Brit.,* Vol.3 1968, pp.15-16 illus.

'WILDRAKE' see TATTERSALL, G.

WILES, Frank E.   **fl.1899-1925**
Portrait painter. He was working in Cambridge, 1899, when he entered for the South Kensington Competitions and in London, 1914-25.
Exhib: RA.
Bibl: *Modern Book Illustrators and Their Work,* Studio 1914.

WILEY, H.W.
Probably a student of the Birmingham School. Watercolour illustrations for a child's book in a Dutch whimsy style appear in *The Studio,* Vol.29, 1903 pp.69-70.

WILKIE, Sir David   RA   **1785-1841**
Genre and portrait painter and caricaturist. He was born at Cult, Fifeshire on 18 November 1785, the son of a Scottish minister. He studied at the Trustees Academy and at the RA Schools from 1805. Wilkie exhibited at the RA from 1806 and caused considerable interest with his domestic genre subjects which were based on Dutch genre paintings but had an obstinate Scottishness of their own. He was elected ARA in 1809 and RA in 1811, later being appointed King's Limner for Scotland, 1823, and Painter in Ordinary to the King, 1830. He travelled to Paris in 1814, to Scotland in 1817 and

1822 and ventured further afield for his health after 1825. He went on an extensive tour of the East in 1840, but died at sea on his return, 1 June 1840. He had been knighted in 1836.

Illus: *Old Mortality [Scott, 1830]; Sketches in Turkey, Syria and Egypt [1843, AT 379]; Sketches Spanish and Oriental [1846, AT 39].*

Contrib: *The Keepsake [1830]; Heath's Gallery [1836].*

Exhib: BI; RA.

Colls: Aberdeen; Bedford; BM; Fitzwilliam; V & AM; Witt Photo.

Bibl: D. Cunningham, *Life of DW*, 1843; A.L. Simpson, *The Story of Sir DW*, 1879; Lord G. Gower, *Sir DW*, 1902; W. Bayne, *Sir DW*, 1903; RA Exhibition Cat., 1958.

WILKINS, Frank W.   **c.1800-1842**

Portrait painter, miniaturist and engraver. He was born in about 1800 and was a pupil of Charles Wilkins. He died in London in 1842.

Contrib: *British Gallery of Contemporary Portraits [1822]; National Portrait Gallery of the Nineteenth Century [c.1830]; Burke's Female Portraits [1833].*

Exhib: BI; RA.

Colls: Witt Photo.

WILKINSON, Charles A.   **fl.1881-1925**

Painter of landscapes and ships. He worked in London from 1881 and at Farnborough, 1916.

Contrib: *Black & White [1891].*

Exhib: G; L; M; RA; RBA; RHA; RI; ROI; RSA.

WILKINSON, G. Welby   **fl.1900-1925**

Decorative artist. He worked at Haverstock Hill, London and contributed to *Fun*, 1900.

Exhib: London Sal.

WILKINSON, Rev. Joseph   **1764-1831**

Amateur landscape painter and illustrator. He was born at Carlisle in 1764 and educated at Corpus Christi, Cambridge, where he became a Fellow of the College. He became Rector of Wretham, Norfolk in 1803, having been a minor canon of Carlisle. He died at Thetford in 1831.

Illus: *Select Views in Cumberland [Wordsworth, 1810]; The Architectural Remains of Thetford [1822].*

Colls: V & AM.

WILKINSON, Norman   PRI   **1878-1971**

Marine painter and etcher. He was born in Cambridge on 24 November 1878 and was educated at Berkhamsted School and St. Paul's Cathedral Choir School. Wilkinson worked as an artist and illustrator on the magazines until 1914 when he entered the RNVR and invented camouflage for the shipping of the Allies, 1914-18, known as Dazzle painting. He was made OBE for this work in 1918. Wilkinson became Marine Painter to the Royal Yacht Squadron and was elected RBA in 1902 and ROI in 1908; he was RI from 1906 and President, 1937. He died in London in 1971.

Publ: *Virginibus Puerisque and other Papers [1913]; The Dardanelles: Colour Sketches from Gallipoli.*

Illus: *The Royal Navy [1909].*

Contrib: *ILN [1898-99]; The Graphic [1902-03]; The Idler.*

Exhib: FAS, 1907, 1915, 1953, 1958; G; GG; L; New Gall; RA; RBA; RI; ROI; RWA.

WILKINSON, Tom   **fl.1895-1925**

Black and white artist. He lived at Ipswich, 1914 to 1925, and drew figures in the style of Phil May (q.v.).

Contrib: *Judy [1895]; Fun [1895]; Punch [1897, 1903]; Illustrated Bits [1900].*

WILKINSON, Tony

Illustrator of children. He contributed to *Punch*, 1897-1902.

WILLES, William   **-1851**

Landscape painter. He was born in Cork and studied at the RA Schools, becoming Master at the Cork School of Design, 1849. He died there in 1851.

Contrib: *Ireland [S.C. Hall, 1841].*

Exhib: BI; RA.

WILLIAMS, Captain   RA

Army officer and amateur artist. He contributed illustrations of Canada to *The Illustrated London News,* 1860.

WILLIAMS, Alexander   RHA   **1846-1930**

Landscape painter in oil and watercolour. He was born in County Monaghan in 1846 and educated at Drogheda Grammar School and was in the choir of Trinity College, Dublin. He studied art at the RDS and was elected ARHA in 1883 and RHA in 1891. He wrote many articles on ornithology. He died in Dublin on 15 November 1930.

Illus: *Beautiful Ireland [S. Gwynn, 1911].*

Exhib: B; RHA.

WILLIAMS, Alfred SHELDON-   **fl.1871-1875**

Farmer and illustrator. He lived and worked at Winchfield and specialised in equestrian subjects. He was the father of Inglis Sheldon-Williams (q.v.).

Illus: *The Book of The Horse [Cassell, 1875].*

Contrib: *The Graphic [1871]; ILN [1874-75].*

Exhib: RA; RBA.

WILLIAMS, Alice Meredith see WILLIAMS, (Gertrude) Alice Meredith

WILLIAMS, Ann Mary

Genre painter and illustrator. She was the sister and collaborator of Samuel Williams (q.v.).

WILLIAMS, Charles   **fl.1797-1830**

Illustrator and caricaturist. He was the chief caricaturist for Fores, the printseller and was a follower and copyist of James Gillray. His early work is published under the name 'Ansell' but the later is usually anonymous.

Illus: *Dr Syntax in Paris [1820, AT 109].*

Colls: BM; Witt Photo.

Bibl: M.D. George, *Eng. Pol. Caricat.*, Vol.2, 1959.

WILLIAMS, Mrs Crawshay   **fl.1890-1912**

Artist and illustrator. She was working in London in 1890 under her maiden name of Miss C. Crawshay.

Illus: *Oddle and Iddle [Lily Collier, 1912].*

Exhib: L.

WILLIAMS, F.A.

Illustrator of comic animals. He contributed to *Punch*, 1903-07.

WILLIAMS, (Gertrude) Alice Meredith   **-1934**

Decorative painter and sculptor, stained glass artist. She was born at Liverpool and studied at the Liverpool School of Architecture and Applied Art, before going to Paris, 1904-07. She exhibited book illustrations at the Walker Art Gallery in 1900. She married the painter Morris Meredith Williams (q.v.) and died in 1934.

Exhib: G; L; RA; RSA; RSW.

Bibl: *The Studio*, Vo1.20, 1900, p. l96 illus.

WILLIAMS, Hamilton

Figure artist. He was working at Buckhurst Hill, Essex, 1913-14.

Contrib: *Punch [1909]; London Opinion [1913].*

Exhib: RA; RSA.

WILLIAMS, Hugh William   'Grecian'   **1773-1829**

Landscape painter. He was born in 1773, the son of a sea captain and soon orphaned, being brought up at Edinburgh. He was a founder of the Associated Artists in 1808 and published engravings of Highland views. He made his reputation and eamed his name from a Mediterranean tour he undertook through Italy and Greece in 1818. He retired to Edinburgh and died there on 23 June 1829.

Illus: *Travels in Italy, Greece and the Ionian Islands [1820]; Select Views in Greece [1827-29].*

Contrib: *Scots Magazine; Britton's Beauties of England and Wales [1812].*

Exhib: Edinburgh, 1808-09.

Colls: Aberdeen; BM; V & AM.

INGLIS SHELDON-WILLIAMS 1870-1939. 'The Coronation Durbar in Delhi, 1903'. Original drawing for illustration. Ink and watercolour. Signed and dated

WILLIAMS, Inglis SHELDON-   **1870-1939**
Painter and Special Artist. He was born in 1870, the son of Alfred Sheldon-Williams (q.v.) and after the death of his father he emigrated to Canada where he farmed from 1887 to 1891. He returned to Europe and studied at the Slade, at the École des Beaux-Arts, Paris and with Sir Thomas Brock. He returned to Canada, 1895-96 and in 1899 after settling in London was appointed Special Artist to *The Sphere* to cover the Boer War in South Africa. The magazine sent him to cover the Russo-Japanese War in 1903 and the Fine Art Society commissioned him to make watercolours of the Delhi Durbar, 1902-03. He married in 1904, Ida Maud Thomson, the flower painter, who had been a Slade student. Sheldon-Williams worked at Stroud, Gloucestershire in 1908 and later at Sharnbrook, Bedfordshire, 1934. A one man show was held at the Regina Art Gallery, in Canada in October 1969.
Illus: *After Pretoria, The Guerilla War [1902]; The Canadian Front; A Dawdle in France [1926]; A Dawdle in Lombardy and Venice [1928].*
Contrib: *The Quest [1894-96].*
Exhib: B; FAS, 1903; G; L; NEA; RA; RI; ROI.
Colls: BM.
Bibl: *The Studio*, Vol.41, 1907, pp.111-115; *Country Life*, 15 May l975; *Bedfordshire Magazine*, Autumn 1992, pp.223-228.
See illustration.

WILLIAMS, J. Scott   **fl.1909-1921**
Painter and illustrator. He worked in London, 1921 and contributed story illustrations to *The Illustrated London News,* 1909, with A.H. Buckland (q.v.).
Exhib: RA.

WILLIAMS, Joseph Lionel   **c.1815-1877**
Painter, watercolourist and engraver. He worked in London and drew architectural subjects and machinery for the magazines. He was an unsuccessful NWS candidate, and died in London in 1877.
Contrib: *ILN [1848-51]; The Art Journal.*
Exhib: BI, RA; RBA.
Colls: Sheffield.

WILLIAMS, Morris Meredith   **1881-**
Painter, illustrator and stained glass artist. He was born at Cowbridge, Glamorgan, in 1881 and studied at the Slade School and in Paris and Italy. He worked in Edinburgh, 1914-25 and afterwards at North Tawton, Devon. He married the decorative artist (Gertrude) Alice Meredith Williams (q.v.).
Contrib: *Punch [1906-07 (rustic)].*
Exhib: G, L; P; RA; RSA; RSW.
Colls: Liverpool.

WILLIAMS, Penry   **1798-1885**
Landscape and view painter. He was born at Merthyr Tydfil in 1798 and studied at the RA Schools and won a Society of Arts silver medal in 1821. He settled in Rome in 1826 and remained there until his death, painting pictures of the city for the tourist market. He was AOWS from 1828-33.
Publ: *Recollections of Malta, Sicily and the Continent [1847].*
Contrib: *Britton's Union of Architecture [1827, AL 7].*
Exhib: BI; OWS; RA; RBA.
Colls: BM; Fitzwilliam; V & AM.

WILLIAMS, Richard James   **1876-**
Painter and illustrator of children's books. He was born at Hereford in 1876 and studied at Cardiff University College, Birmingham and London, becoming Headmaster of the Worcester School of Arts and Crafts. He also worked as a wood engraver. ARCA.
Exhib: RCA; RI.

WILLIAMS, Samuel **1788-1853**
Draughtsman, wood engraver and natural history illustrator. He was born on 23 February 1788 at Colchester and was apprenticed to a house-painter before learning the art of wood engraving. He settled in London in 1819 and became a popular and prolific illustrator, engraving much of his own work. He was assisted by his sister Ann Mary Williams (q.v.) and died in London in 1853.
Illus: *Robinson Crusoe [Daniel Defoe, 1822]; Natural History [Mrs Trimmer, 1823-24]; Hone's Everyday Book [1825]; British Forest Trees [Selby, 1842]; Pictures of Country Life [Miller, 1847]; The Poetical Works of John Milton [1854]; Wit Bought [Peter Parley, c.1868].*
Contrib: *Thomson's Seasons, The Castle of Indolence [1851].*
Exhib: BI; RA.
Colls: BM.
Bibl: Chatto and Jackson, *Treatise on Wood Engraving,* 1861, p.572.

WILLIAMS, Thomas H.
Illustrator and engraver. He worked in Plymouth and Exeter and made topographical views of West Country subjects.
Illus: *Picturesque Tours in Devon and Cornwall [1801]; The Environs of Exeter [1815]; A Tour in the Isle of Wight [n.d.]; A Walk on the Coast of Devonshire [1828].*
Exhib: NWS; RA; RBA.
Colls: Fitzwilliam.

WILLIAMSON, F.M.
Illustrator. He contributed comic animal drawings to *Punch,* 1903-06.

WILLIAMSON, Isobel B.
Illustrator. She may have been a Liverpool student and contributed drawings for *The Studio* competitions in 1897.
Bibl: *The Studio,* Vols. 11 and 12, 1897 illus.

WILLIAMSON, John **fl.1885-1896**
Portrait and figure painter and illustrator. He was working in Edinburgh, 1885-90 and in London from 1893, specialising in costume subjects.
Illus: *Kilgorman [Reed, 1894].*
Contrib: *The English Illustrated Magazine [1895-96 (social)].*
Exhib: RA; RBA; RSA.

WILLIAMSON, Captain Thomas George **c.1758-1817**
Amateur artist. He contributed drawings which Howitt engraved for *Oriental Field Sports,* 1807.
Colls: Witt Photo.

WILLIS, J.B.
Amateur artist. He contributed figure subjects to *Punch,* 1908.

WILLOUGHBY, Mrs. Vera **1870-1939**
Watercolour painter, poster artist, book illustrator and decorator. She worked at Slindon, Sussex until 1913 and then in London. Her work is inspired by 18th century decoration, transformed by incipient art deco into pretty but stiff fantasies. Some of her soft pencil work dating from the 1920s is pleasantly cubist in feeling.
Illus: *The Humours of History [c.1914]; The Memoirs of a Lady of Quality, being Lady Vane's Memoirs [1925]; A Vision of Greece [1925]; Horati Carminum [1926]; The Recruiting Officer [G. Farquhar, 1926]; A Sentimental Journey [L. Sterne, 1927]; Four Gospels [1927]; Sappho Revocata [1928]; Pride and Prejudice [J. Austen, 1929]; Lovely Laughter [1932].*
Exhib: L; P; RI.
Colls: V & AM.
See Horne

WILLSON, Beckles
Domestic painter. He contributed to *The Strand Magazine,* 1894.

WILLSON, Harry **fl.1813-1852**
Townscape painter. He worked in the style of Samuel Prout (q.v.).
Publ: *The Use of a Box of Colours [1842].*
Illus: *Willson's Fugitive Sketches in Rome, Venice etc. [1838].*
Colls: BM.

WILLSON, John J. **fl.1875-1902**
Landscape and sporting painter. He worked at Headingley, Leeds, and was married to the painter E. Dorothy Willson.
Contrib: *The Graphic [1875].*
Exhib: L; RA.

WILLYAMS, Rev. Cooper **1762-1816**
Artist and topographer. He was born in Essex in 1762 and entered Emmanuel College, Cambridge, 1780, being ordained in 1784. He held the living of Exning, near Newmarket, 1788 and St. Peter, West Lynn, 1793. He became chaplain to Admiral Earl Jervis in 1793 and accompanied him to the West Indies and with the Mediterranean Fleet, 1798-1800, being present at the Battle of the Nile. He later held livings at Kingston, Canterbury and Stourmouth. He died in London in 1816.
Illus: *A History of Sudeley Castle [1791]; An Account of the Campaign in the West Indies in 1794 [1796, AT 672]; Voyage up the Mediterranean [1802, AT 196]; A Selection of Views in Egypt, Palestine, Rhodes, Italy, Minorca and Gibraltar [1822, AT 198].*
Contrib: *The Topographer.*
Colls: Witt Photo.

WILMSHURST, George C. **fl.1897-1911**
Portrait painter and illustrator. He worked in London and contributed pen and ink drawings to magazines.
Illus: *The Cardinal's Snuff Box [Henry Havland, 1903].*
Contrib: *ILN [1905, 1908, 1911 (Christmas Nos)].*
Exhib: M; RA.

WILSON, Alexander **1766-1813**
Ornithologist and engraver. He was born at Paisley on 6 July 1766 and illustrated and engraved his own works, most notably *The American Ornithology,* 1808-14. He died at Philadelphia on 23 August 1813.
Colls: Witt Photo.

WILSON, Andrew **1780-1848**
Landscape painter. He was born at Edinburgh in 1780 and studied under Alexander Nasmyth (q.v.) and at the RA Schools. He made several extensive tours of Italy, and on the second in 1803-05, he acted as a dealer and brought a number of masterpieces back with him. He was Professor of Drawing at the RMA, Sandhurst for ten years until 1818 and in 1826 he returned to Italy and settled there for twenty years. He died in Edinburgh in 1848.
Contrib: *Britton's Beauties of England and Wales [1813-15 (Wales and Oxford)].*
Exhib: BI.
Colls: BM; V & AM.

WILSON, Charles Heath **1809-1882**
Landscape painter and illustrator. He was born in London in 1809, the son of the landscape painter Andrew Wilson (q.v.), with whom he toured Italy, 1825. He went to live in Edinburgh in 1834, was elected ARSA in 1835 and continued membership until 1858. He was Master of the Trustees Academy, 1843-48, and he finally settled in Florence in 1869. He died there in 1882.
Illus: *Viaggio Antiquario [P. Pifferi, 1832]; Voyage Round the Coasts of Scotland [1842].*
Exhib: BI; RA.
Colls: Nat. Gall., Scotland.

WILSON, David **fl.1895-1916**
Draughtsman and caricaturist. He worked for various magazines beginning with the *Daily Chronicle* in 1895. He was chief cartoonist to *The Graphic,* 1910-16, specialising in full page drawings in chalk, often strongly symbolic and fantastic.
Contrib: *Punch [1900-14]; Fun [1901]; The Graphic [1910-14]; The Sketch; The Temple Magazine.*

WILSON, Dower **fl.1875-1897**
Domestic illustrator. He may be the same as 'D.R. Wilson' exhibiting at the RA from Bushey, 1884-86.
Contrib: *ILN [1875]; Judy [1878-79]; Punch [1879, 1897]; Moonshine [1891].*

EDGAR W. WILSON 1898-1928. Headpiece for *The Butterfly*, Vol.1, 1899

WILSON, E.   fl.1792-1802
Landscape painter and topographer. He contributed to *The Copper Plate Magazine*, 1792-1802.
Exhib: RA.
Colls: Witt Photo.

WILSON, Edgar W.   1898-1928
Painter and illustrator. He worked in London from 1886 and specialised in the design of covers, initial letters and head and tail pieces for books. He usually works in pen and ink or pen and wash and is strongly influenced by Japanese art.
Contrib: *The Strand Magazine [1891]; Black & White [1891]; The Butterfly [1893, 1899 (covers)]; St. Pauls [1894]; Madame [1895]; The Sketch; Pick-Me-Up; Daily Chronicle [1895]; The English Illustrated Magazine [1896]; The Pall Mall Magazine [1897]; Pall Mall Gazette [1897]; The Windsor Magazine; The Unicorn.*
Exhib: RA; RI.
Colls: V & AM; Witt Photo.
Bibl: Simon Houfe, *Fin de Siècle*, 1992.
See illustration.

WILSON, Godfrey
Figure artist. He contributed to *Punch*, 1904.

WILSON, H.P.   fl.1890-1895
Figure painter in watercolour, illustrator. He worked in London and contributed to *The Sporting and Dramatic News*, 1890 and *Black and White*, 1891.
Exhib: RA.

WILSON, Helen Russell   RBA
Painter and etcher. She studied at the Slade School and at the London School under Frank Brangwyn (q.v.) and then went to Tokyo to learn Japanese painting. She was elected RBA in 1911, settled at Tangier in about 1913 and died there 22 October 1924.
Illus: *Angling and Art in Scotland [1908].*
Exhib: RA; RBA; RI.

WILSON, John
Amateur. He contributed illustrations of humorous insects to *Punch*, 1903.

WILSON, Leslie   fl.1893-1934
Figure artist. He worked in London and contributed extensively to magazines. Art Director of *Pick Me Up*, 1889.
Contrib: *Judy [1886-93]; The English Illustrated Magazine [1893-94]; St. Pauls [1894]; Madame [1895]; The Sketch; Pick-Me-Up; The Royal Magazine.*
Exhib: RBA.

WILSON, Oscar   1867-1930
Portrait painter and illustrator. He was born in London in 1867 and studied at South Kensington and Antwerp under Beaufaux and Verlat. He was elected RMS in 1896 and ARBA in 1926, he died on 13 July 1930.
Contrib: *St. Pauls [1894]; The Sketch [1894-95]; Madame [1895]; ILN [1897].*
Exhib. G; L; M; RABA; RCA; RI; RMS; ROI; RSA.

PATTEN WILSON 1868-1928. 'So the wind drove us on...' for *The Yellow Book,* 1896

WILSON, Patten   **1868-1928**

Black and white artist and illustrator. He was born at Cleobury Mortimer in 1868 and studied under Fred Brown. Wilson was a very competent and original illustrator of fantastic subjects and a talented decorator of books. His talents led him to be employed by Messrs. Lane on book covers and title pages, and he completed the Keynote series for the firm after Beardsley's dismissal and was technical adviser for the later numbers of *The Yellow Book,* 1895-96. His greatest failing was over-invention and his drawings, which are rich in imagery and finely executed, lack a degree of clarity essential to textual illustration. He worked principally in London and died in 1928.

Illus: *Miracle Plays [1895]; Life in Arcadia [J.S. Fletcher, 1896]; A Houseful of Rebels [1897]; God's Failures [J.S. Fletcher, 1897]; Selections From Coleridge [1898]; King John [1899]; The*

Tremendous Twins [Ernest Ames, 1900]; The Gospel Story of Jesus Christ [Hutchison, 1901]; A Child's History of England [1903].
Contrib: *The Pall Mall Magazine.*
Exhib: L; RA.
Colls: V & AM.
Bibl: *The Artist,* Jan. 1898, pp.17-24, illus; *The Studio.* Winter No, 1900-01 p.51, illus; R.E.D. Sketchley, *Eng. Bk. Illus.,* 1903, pp.28, 131.
See illustration.

WILSON, Thomas Harrington   **fl.1842-1886**
Landscape, genre and portrait painter and illustrator. He studied art at the National Gallery in company with Sir John Tenniel (q.v.) and Charles Martin, later specialising in theatrical portraiture and being introduced to *Punch* by Swain, the engraver. He also made drawings of military subjects and contributed to *The Punch Pocket Books,* 1854-57.
Contrib: *Punch [1853]; ILN [1854-61 (theatre, 1855-60, objects, 1876, 1890]; The Illustrated London Magazine [1855]; The Graphic [1871].*
Exhib: BI; RA; RI; ROI.
Colls: Witt Photo.

WILSON, Thomas Walter   RI   1851 -1912
Landscape painter and illustrator. He was born in London on 7 November 1851, the son of T. Harrington Wilson (q.v.) and was educated in Chelsea, before studying at South Kensington Schools, 1868 and winning their scholarship, 1869. He was sent by the Department of Science and Art to study at Bayeux and then worked in Belgium and Holland. Wilson undertook a great deal of magazine work and as a *Graphic* artist was one of the finishers of drawings sent in by Fred Villers (q.v.), the Special Artist. He was elected ARI in 1877 and RI in 1879 and ROI in 1883. He died in 1912.
Contrib: *The Graphic [1880-85]; ILN [1888-99]; The English Illustrated Magazine [1895]; Good Words [1898-99]; The Sketch; The Minister; The Idler.*
Exhib: L; M; RI; ROI.
Colls: V & AM.

WIMBUSH, Henry B.   **fl.1881-1908**
Landscape painter. He painted in Scotland and Wales and illustrated *The Channel Islands* (E.F. Carey, 1904).
Exhib: B; FAS; L; M; RA; RI.

WIMBUSH, John L.   **-1914**
Painter and illustrator. He was working in London from 1890 to 1902 and then at Dartmouth. He died in 1914.
Contrib: *The Strand Magazine [1891-]; The World Wide Magazine [1898]; The Idler; The Boy's Own Magazine.*
Exhib: B; L; M; RA; RBA.

WIMPERIS, Edmund Morrison VPRI   1835-1900
Landscape painter and illustrator. He was born at Chester on 6 February 1835 and after being put in a business there, he was apprenticed at the age of fourteen to Mason Jackson (q.v.), the London wood engraver. He studied with Birket Foster (q.v.) and did a great deal of work for *The Illustrated London News* and other publications before turning almost wholly to landscape watercolour. His best work is of Suffolk, Wales and the Home Counties, much of the work being drawn directly from nature. He was elected ANWS in 1873 and NWS in 1875, becoming Vice-President in 1895. He died on Christmas Day 1900.
Contrib: *The Book of South Wales [Mr. and Mrs. S.C. Hall, 1861]; Gray's Elegy [1869].*
Exhib: B; FAS; L; M; New Gall; RBA; RI; ROI.
Colls: BM, Bradford; Manchester; V & AM; Witt Photo.
Bibl: *Walker's Quarterly,* 4, 1921.

WINGFIELD, James Digman   **1800-1872**
Historical painter. He worked in London and specialised in costume subjects, often with Hampton Court Palace as their background. He made drawings of the 1851 Exhibition and was almost certainly an illustrator, two poetic works of his being engraved by Dalziel.
Colls: Nottingham;Witt Photo.

WINZER, Charles Freegrove   **1886-**
Painter and illustrator. He was born at Warsaw on 1 December 1886 and worked in Morocco, Spain and Britain. He later travelled to India, Nepal and Ceylon, where he became Inspector of Fine Art. He contributed illustrations to a number of books in the 1920s and decorated the rhymesheets of Harold Monro's Poetry Bookshop.
Illus: *Sixteen Poems [J.E. Flecker]; The Chinese Drama [Johnson].*
Exhib: Toothe Gall.
Colls: Cambridge; Cardiff.

WIRGMANN, Charles   **1832-1891**
Figure artist and caricaturist. He was born in 1860, the brother of T.B. Wirgmann (q.v.). He worked in London before settling in Yokohama, Japan in 1860 and painting Japanese life. He contributed drawings of Manila, 1857 and China, 1860, to *The Illustrated London News.* He died in 1891 and an exhibition of his work was held in London in 1921.
Colls: BM.

WIRGMANN, Theodore Blake   **1848-1925**
Portrait painter and illustrator. He was born at Louvain, Belgium on 29 April 1848 into a Swedish family and entered the RA Schools, winning a silver medal there in 1865. He went to Paris to study with Hebert and on his return, worked extensively for *The Graphic* and as an assistant to Sir John Millais (q.v.). Perhaps his most notable achievement is the series of brilliant chalk portraits that he carried out for the magazine in 1884 to 1889, including politicians, writers and royalty. Wirgmann worked in London where he had an extensive practice, was elected RP in 1891 and died there on l6 January 1925.
Contrib: *Cassell's Family Magazine [1868]; The Graphic [1875-1901]; Daily Chronicle [1895].*
Exhib: B; G; GG; L; M; New Gall; P; RA; RHA; RI; ROI.
Colls: Bradford; Middle Temple; NPG; Witt Photo.

WITHERBY, Arthur George   **fl.1894-1919**
Caricaturist. He was a painter, draughtsman and writer of Newton Grange, Newbury, who was a keen sportsman and for some time the proprietor of *Vanity Fair* to which he contributed illustrations, 1894-95 and 1899-1901.
Exhib: Walker's Gall.

WITHERINGTON, William Frederick RA   1785-1865
Landscape painter. He was born in Goswell Street, London on 26 May 1785 and studied at the RA Schools, 1805. Although he first exhibited landscapes, he gradually turned his attention to genre subjects and painted a scene from *The Rape of the Lock,* which may have been used for illustration, 1835. He was elected ARA in 1830 and RA in 1840. On account of ill health he spent many of his later years in the country, but died in London on 10 April 1865.
Exhib: BI; RA.
Colls: V & AM.
Bibl: Robert Halsband, *The Illustrators of the Rape of The Lock,* 1980.

WITHERS, Alfred ROI   **1856-1932**
Landscape painter, architectural painter and etcher. He was born on 15 October 1856 and worked in Kent and Surrey before settling in London in about 1903. He was elected ROI in 1897 and was a member of the Society of 25 Artists. He was also a member of the Pastel Society and received the Royal Order of Alfonso XII of Spain. He died on 8 August 1932.
Contrib: *ILN [1896].*
Exhib: B; FAS; G; GG; L; M; New Gall; RA; RBA; RE; ROI; RSA.

WITHERS, Augusta Innes   **fl.1829-1865**
Botanical illustrator. She was a member of the RBA and of the Society of Lady Artists and contributed to *The Botanist,* c.1840.
Exhib: NWS; RA; RBA.

WODDERSPOON, John   **fl.1812-1862**
Landscape painter. He worked at Norwich, where he was sub-editor of *The Mercury.*
Publ: *Historic Sites of Suffolk [1841]; A New Guide to Ipswich [1842]; Picturesque Antiquities of Ipswich [1845]; Notes on the*

Grey and White Friars, Ipswich [1848]; Memorials of the Ancient Town of Ipswich [1850].
Colls: Norwich.

WOLF, Joseph　　RI　　　　　　　　1820-1899
Animal and bird painter and illustrator. He was born at Mors, near Koblenz in 1820 and studied lithography at Darmstadt before entering the Antwerp Academy. He came to England in 1848 under the patronage of the Duke of Westminster and through the friendship of D.G. Rossetti and was employed at the BM on Gray's *The Genera of Birds*. He illustrated extensively for the Zoological Society and visited Norway in 1849 and again in 1856 with John Gould, the ornithologist and illustrator. He was elected RI in 1874 and died in London on 20 April 1899. A very important series of watercolour illustrations by Wolf for Gould's *The Birds of Great Britain*, 1862-73 was sold from the Godman Collection at Christie's on 4th October 1994. Wolf's illustration of a 'Snowy Owl' made £34,500.
Illus: *Life and Habits of Wild Animals [D.G. Elliott, 1873]*.
Contrib: *ILN [1853-57, 1872]; Eliza Cook's Poems [1856]; Wordsworth's Selected Poems [1859]; Montgomery's Poems [1860]; Band of Hope Review [1861]; Good Words [1861-64]; Wilmott's Sacred Poetry [1862]; Wood's Natural History [1862]; The Sunday Magazine [1866-68]; Once a Week [1866]; Nature and Art [1866]; Poems by Jean Ingelow [1867]; North Coast and Other Poems [Buchanan, 1868]; Gould's Birds of Great Britain*.
Lit: *The Godman Collection of Watercolours for John Gould's 'The Birds of Great Britain'*, Christie's catalogue with introduction by Maureen Lambourne, 1994.
Exhib: BI; RA; RI.
Colls: BM; V & AM; Sir John Witt.
Bibl: Chatto & Jackson, *Treatise on Wood Engraving*, 1861 p.573; *The Artist*, May 1899, pp.1-15 illus.; Maureen Lambourne, *The Art of Bird Illustration*, 1991, pp.166-167.

WOLFE, Major W.S.M.　　　　　　fl.1855-1862
Amateur illustrator. Royal Artillery officer, who was promoted Captain in 1856 and Major of Artillery Brigade at Aldershot, 1862. He held the Crimean War medal and contributed drawings of the War to *The Illustrated London News*, 1855.

WOLLEN, William Barnes　　RI　　　　1857-1936
Military painter and illustrator. He was born at Leipzig on 6 October 1857 and was educated at University College School and studied at the Slade. He was intended for an army career but took up painting as a professional and was sent as Special Artist for *The Graphic* to South Africa in 1900. He was elected RI in 1888, ROI in 1897 and HROI in 1934. He lived for most of his life in Bedford Park, West London and died there on 28 March 1936.
Illus: *Rex [L. Thompson 1894]*.
Contrib: *ILN [1882-99]; The Strand Magazine [1891-94]; Black & White [1891]; Chums [1892]; The Boy's Own Paper [1892-93]; Daily Chronicle [1895]; The Penny Illustrated Paper; Cassell's Family Magazine; The Wide World Magazine [1898]; The Graphic [1900-06]*.
Exhib: B; G; L; M; RA; RHA; RI; ROI; RSA.
Colls: Witt Photo.
Bibl: A.C.R. Carter, *The Work of War Artists in South Africa*, AJ, 1900.

WOMRATH, Andrew K.　　　　　　　1869-
Painter and illustrator. He was born at Frankfurt on 25 October 1869 and studied at the New York Academy and with L. O. Messon in Paris, before working at Mentone.
Contrib: *The Evergreen [1896]; The Savoy [1896]*.

WOOD, F.W.
Animal and bird illustrator. He contributed extensively to *The Illustrated London News*, 1855-58 and again in 1865-75.

WOOD, Fane
Figure artist. He contributed to *London Society*, 1868.

WOOD, John George　　　　　　　fl.1793-1838
Topographical illustrator. He contributed to Britton's *Beauties of England and Wales*, 1810.
Exhib: RA.

WOOD, Lawson　　　　　　　　　　1878-1957
Black and white artist and illustrator. He was born at Highgate in 1878, the grandson of L.J. Wood, the landscape painter. He studied at the Slade School and at Heatherley's and was for six years the chief artist on the staff of C.A. Pearson Ltd. He served in the RFC during the First World War. Wood's work is usually in ink and watercolour and most of it is humorous in drawing and content, his repertoire of characters including peppery army officers, namby-pamby men and dominating old dames. The figures are heavily caricatured and he was one of the group of artists who made capital out of imaginary prehistoric scenes. He died in 1957.
Contrib: *Pearson's Magazine; The Royal Magazine; ILN [1905, 1908, 1912]; The Graphic [1907-11]; London Opinion [1913]*.
Exhib: D; L; RA; RI.
Colls: V & AM; Witt Photo.
Bibl: *LW*, Brush, Pen and Pencil Series, Ed. by A.E. Johnson, c.1910. See illustration.
See Horne

WOOD, Margery
Amateur illustrator. She was a student at the Lambeth School and won a prize at the National Competition, 1904 for an illustration of Cranfordesque type.
Bibl: *The Studio*, Vol 32, p.327.

WOOD, Olive　　　　　　　　　　fl.1914-1933
Miniature painter and illustrator of children's books. She studied at the Clapham and Camberwell Schools of Art and worked in Dulwich Village.
Exhib: RA.

WOOD, Stanley L.　　　　　　　　1866-1928
Military painter and illustrator. He was born in 1866 and worked in London for the leading magazines and was employed almost continuously by Messrs Chatto's as an illustrator of boys' adventure stories. He died in 1928.
Illus: *The Arabian Nights Entertainments [1890]; A Waif of the Plains [1890]; Maid Marian and Robin Hood [1892]; Romances of the Old Seraglio [1894]; Mr Sadler's Daughters [H.C. Davidson, 1894]; Rujub the Juggler [G.A. Henty, 1894]; A Protegée of Jack Hamlin [Bret Harte, 1894]; A Fair Colonist [1894]; The King's Assegai [B. Mitford, 1894]; A Ramble Round the Globe [T.R. Dewar, 1894]; The Lost Middy [(G. Manville Fenn]; Rough Riders of the Pampas [Capt. F.S. Brereton, 1908]; In Empire's Cause [E. Protheroe, 1908]*.
Contrib: *ILN [1889-90]; The Sporting and Dramatic News [1890]; Black & White [1891]; The Graphic [1903]; The Strand Magazine [1906]; Cassells Family Magazine; The Idler; The Windsor Magazine; Pearson's Magazine; Wide World Magazine [1927]*.
Exhib: L; M; RA; ROI.
Colls: Witt Photo; V & AM.

WOOD, Starr　　　　　　　　　　1870-1944
Caricaturist and black and white artist. He was born in London on 1 February 1870 and was educated privately before being entered in a chartered accountant's office in 1887. He left in 1890 and began to draw for the magazines, having sufficient success to found his own magazine *The Windmill*, a quarterly, and later to run *Starr Wood's Magazine*, from 1910 until at least 1935. The latter is filled entirely with his illustrations, à la May, à la Belcher and à la everyone else! Wood's humour is seldom above that of the seaside postcard but he can be a funny draughtsman, many of his works appear under the name of The Snark. He died on 2 September 1944.
Illus: *Rhymes of the Regiments [1896]*.
Contrib: *Puck and Ariel [1890]; Fun [1892]; The Sketch [1893]; Judy [1895]; Pick-Me-Up [1895]; The Idler; Chums; The Parade [1897]; The English Illustrated Magazine [1898]; Punch [1900-02, 1908 , 1914]*.
Exhib: L.
Colls: V & AM; Witt Photo.

WOOD, T.W., Jnr.　　　　　　　　fl.1865-1880
Illustrator. He was the son of the animal artist Thomas W. Wood, and

LAWSON WOOD 1878-1957. 'Remarkable Escapes'. Original drawing for illustration. Wash. Signed and dated 1903. 7½in x 13in (19.1cm x 33cm)

Victoria and Albert Museum

he illustrated *The Common Moths of England* by Rev. J.G. Wood, c.1880.
Contrib: *Punch [1865]; Nature and Art [1866].*
Exhib: RA.

WOOD, William   **1774-1857**
Doctor and amateur topographer. He was born at Kendal in 1774 and practised in Calcutta. In 1833 he published *A Series of Twenty-eight Panoramic Views of Calcutta,* 1833.
Colls: BM.

WOODHOUSE, F.W.
Artist. He illustrated *Representation of the Brigade Field Day in Ware Park,* 1853, AL 383.

WOODROFFE, Paul Vincent   **1875-1954**
Painter, illustrator and stained glass artist. He was born in Madras, India in 1875 and was educated at Stonyhurst and studied at the Slade School. Woodroffe specialised in book decoration, covers and end-papers as well as in illustration, he was also a poster artist. He settled in Campden, Gloucestershire in about 1904 and was associated with the Arts and Crafts movement there and particularly in the design of stained glass. He was a member of the Art Workers Guild and of the Society of Master Glass Painters. He died in Eastbourne in 1954.
Illus: *Second Booke of Nursery Rhymes [Moorat, 1896]; Ye Booke of Nursery Rhymes [1897]; Herrick's Hesperides [1897; 1907]; Shakespeare's Songs [1898]; The Little Flowers of St. Francis [1899]; The Confessions of St. Augustine [1900]; The Little Flowers of St Benet [1901]; Aucussin & Nicolette [L. Housman, 1902]; Noel [L. Housman, 1903]; The World is Old Tonight [1903]; The Princess & Other Poems [Alfred Tennyson, 1904]; The Flight of the Duchess [Robert Browning, 1905]; Humpty Dumpty & Other Songs [Moorat, 1905]; A Little Child's Life of Jesus [Amy Steedman, 1906]; The Child's Life of Jesus [C.M. Steedman, 1906]; Thirty Old Time Nursery Songs [Moorat, 1907]; Stories from Roman History [Lena Dalkeith, 1907]; The Tempest [1908]; Alls Well [Robert Browning [1913 (cover)]; The Enchanted Doll [Mark Lemon, 1915]; Froissart's Cronycles [1927-28].*

Contrib: *The Quarto [1896]; The Parade [1897]; ILN [1909].*
Exhib: FAS; G; NEA; RA; RHA; RMS.
Colls: V & AM, Witt Photo.
Bibl: R.E.D. Sketchley, *Eng. Bk. Illus.,* 1903, pp.13, 14,131; Peter Cormack, *PW 1875-1954 Illustrator, Book Designer, Stained Glass Artist,* William Morris Gallery, 1982.
See Horne

WOODS, Henry   RA   **1846-1921**
Genre and landscape painter and illustrator. He was born at Warrington on 22 April 1846 and studied at Warrington School of Art, winning a travelling scholarship. He attended the South Kensington Schools and joined *The Graphic* as an illustrator in 1870 with his brother-in-law, Sir Luke Fildes (q.v.). He did a considerable amount of work for the paper, often in collaboration with S.P. Hall (q.v.). He became ARA in 1882 and RA in 1893 having settled in Venice since 1876. He died there on 27 October 1921.
Illus: *Miss or Mrs? [Wilkie Collins, 1885 (with Fildes)].*
Exhib: B; FAS; L; M; RA; ROI.
Colls: Liverpool; Tate; Warrington; Witt Photo.

WOODS, T.W.
Contributor to *Punch,* 1895.

WOODS, William
Military illustrator. He contributed drawings to *The Illustrated London News,* 1860.

WOODVILLE, Richard Caton, Snr.   **1825-1855**
Painter of battle scenes. He was born at Baltimore in 1825 and died in London in 1855. He contributed a drawing to *The Illustrated London News,* 1852.
Exhib: BI; RA.

WOODVILLE, Richard Caton, Jnr.   **1856-1927**
Painter of battle scenes, Special Artist and illustrator. He was born in London on 7 January 1856, the son of R.C. Woodville Senior (q.v.). He studied art in Düsseldorf under Kamphussen after being brought

up in St Petersburg, and lived in Paris before settling in London in 1875. He began to work almost at once for *The Illustrated London News* and went as artist to the Turkish War of 1878 and the Egyptian War of 1882, also serving in Albania and the Balkans. He turned increasingly to oil painting in the 1880s and finally abandoned black and white work altogether in 1897. Woodville's war drawings were always accurate and highly finished if somewhat lacking in the realities of action. The high gloss and glamour earned him comparisons with Meissonnier. He was elected RI in 1882 and ROI in 1883. He died in North London on 17 August 1927.
Illus: *Ravenstones [H. Kingsley 1894].*
Contrib: *ILN [1876-1911]; The Cornhill Magazine [1883]; The Sketch; The Boy's Own Paper; The Windsor Magazine; The English Illustrated Magazine [1895-97]; Pearson's Magazine [1896].*
Exhib: FAS; G; L; M; New Gall; RA; RHA; RI; ROI.
Colls: Royal Coll., Windsor; BM; V & AM.
Bibl: *The Illustrated London News* , 7 December 1895; *The Idler* 1897, Vol.10 pp.758-775; A.C.R. Carter, *The Work of War Artists in South Africa, AJ*, 1900; R.C.W., *Random Recollections,* 1913.

WOODWARD, Alice Bolingbroke   1862-1951
Illustrator of children's books. She was born on 3 October 1862, the fourth daughter of Dr Henry Woodward of the British Museum. She was encouraged to draw in the galleries and was given a drawing lesson by John Ruskin. She studied at South Kensington and at the Westminster Art School under Professor Fred Brown. She worked principally in pen and watercolours but also in pencil, her designs have something of Rackham about them but lack his atmospheric and sinister elements. Her work was greatly admired by *The Studio*. During the First World War she settled at her own cottage in Bushey, Herts. and worked for Naval Intelligence. She died at Barnet on 28 July 1951.
Illus: *Eric, Prince of Lorlonia [Lady Jersey , 1895]; Banbury Cross [1895]; To Tell The King The Sky is Falling [1896]; Bon Mots of the Eighteenth Century [1897]; Bon Mots of the Nineteenth Century [1897]; Brownie [1897]; Red Apple and Silver Bells [1897]; Adventures in Toyland [1897]; The Troubles of Tatters [1898]; Brownie [Alice Sargant, 1898]; The Elephant's Apology [A.T. Morris, 1899]; The Princess of Hearts [1899]; The Cat and the Mouse [1899]; The Golden Ship [1900]; The House That Grew [Mrs. Molesworth , 1900]; Jock and the Fairy Robin [1902]; Round The World To Whympland [E. Sharp, 1902]; To Fairyland on a Swing [E.K. Crawford, 1904]; Forty Fables for Fireside Reflection [W.B. Allen, 1905]; Bimbo A Little Real Story for Jill and Molly [Young, 1905]; Nebula to Man [H.R. Knipe, 1905]; The Peter Pan Picture Book [1907]; The Pinafore Picture Book [W.S. Gilbert, 1908]; The Water Babies [C. Kingsley, 1909]; Lob-Lie By-The-Fire [Mrs Ewing, 1909]; Parables From Nature [Mrs Gatty, 1909]; The Brownie and other Tales [Mrs Ewing, 1910]; More About Jack [1910]; Evolution In the Past [Henry R. Knipe, 1912]; The Story of Peter Pan [Daniel O'Connor, 1912]; The Story of HMS Pinafore [W.S. Gilbert, 1913]; The Three Pearls [The Hon. J.W. Fortescue, 1916]; Alice's Adventures in Wonderland [n.d]; Lost Legends of the Nursery Songs [M.S. Clark, 1920]; A Story of Santa Claus [Margaret I. Cole, 1920]; The Story of the Mikado [W.S. Gilbert, 1921]; A Fairytale of the Sea [Macleod Yearsley, 1923]; The History of Little Goody Two Shoes [1924]; Myths and Legends of the Australian Aborigines [1930].*
Contrib: *ILN [1895]; Daily Chronicle [1895]; The Quarto [1896]; Strand Magazine [1905].*
Exhib: G; L; M; NEA; RA; RBA; RI; RSW.
Bibl: *The Studio* Vol. 9, 1897 p.216; Vol.10, 1897 p.232; Vol.15, 1899 p.214; Winter No. 1900-01 p.31 illus.; R.E.D. Sketchley, *Eng. Bk. Illus.* 1903 pp.104, 172; Gerald Cinammon, *ABW*, The Private Library, Vol.2: 4: Winter 1989, pp.149-177.

WOODWARD, George Moutard   1760-1809
Amateur caricaturist. He was born in Derbyshire in 1760 and came to London about 1792. Between 1794 and 1800 he produced numerous political caricatures, some of them in strip form of his own innovation. His work is usually coarse and crude and was often etched by Rowlandson, Isaac Cruikshank, Roberts and Williams (qq.v.). He lived a dissolute life and died in a tavern in 1809.

Illus: *Elements of Bacchus [1792]; Familiar Verses from the Ghost of Willy Shakespeare to Sammy Ireland [1795]; The Olio of Good Breeding [1801]; The Musical Mania for 1802; The Bettyad [1805]; The Fugitive [1805]; Caricature Magazine [1807]; Eccentric Excursions [1807]; Chesterfield Travestie...[1808]; The Comic Works, in Prose and Poetry [1808].*
Colls: BM; Leeds; Witt Photo.

WOODWARD, Mary   fl.1890-1914
Miniaturist. She worked in London and designed invitation cards and may have illustrated books.
Exhib: B; G; L; RA; RBA; RHA; RI; RMS; RSA; SWA.

WOOLEY, Harry   fl.1912-1920
Figure artist. He worked in Bristol, 1912-13 and specialised in comic sketches in colour after the manner of Starr Wood (q.v.).
Exhib: L; RA; RMS.
Colls: Witt Photo.

WOOLF, M.
Illustrated *The Mott Street Poker Club* by William Parkinson, 1888.

WOOLNER, Thomas   1826-1892
Sculptor and draughtsman. He was born at Hadleigh, Suffolk on 17 December 1825 and after showing early promise he was apprenticed to the sculptor William Behnes. He entered the RA Schools in 1842 and won a silver medal of the Society of Arts in 1845, two years later meeting Rossetti and becoming a member of the Pre-Raphaelite Brotherhood. In the next few years Woolner concentrated on producing medallions, but in 1852, he set sail from Gravesend to try his fortune on the Australian goldfields, thus inspiring Ford Madox Brown's picture 'The Last of England'. He returned in 1854 and soon made a success of his portrait sculpture, being elected ARA in 1871 and RA in 1874. He died in London on 7 October 1892.
Contrib: *The Golden Treasury [1870]; Book of Praise [C. H. Seers].*
Exhib: M; RA.
Bibl: Amy Woolner, *TW, Life and Letters.*

WOOLNOTH, Thomas   1785-c.1836
Painter and engraver. He worked in London as a pupil of Charles Heath and contributed to *Heath's Gallery*, 1836. He illustrated c.1850? *The Juvenile Album* by Mrs R. Lee.
Exhib: BI; NWS; RA; RBA.
Colls: NPG.

WORMS, Jaspar von   1832-1924
Painter, etcher and illustrator. He was born in Paris on 16 December 1832 and studied at the École des Beaux-Arts from 1849, exhibiting at the Salon from 1859. He specialised in Spanish genre subjects and died in 1924.
Contrib: *Cassell's Illustrated Family Paper [1853-57 (Crimea)].*

WORTLEY, Mary Stuart (Countess of Lovelace)   -1941
Portrait painter and illustrator. She was the daughter of the Rt. Hon. J.A. Stuart Wortley and married 2nd Earl of Lovelace in December 1880. She died on 18 April 1941.
Illus: *Zelinda and The Monster [1896].*
Exhib: B; G; M; New Gall.

WRAY, A.W.   fl.1830-1840
Figure artist and illustrator. He was a follower of George Cruikshank and 'Phiz' and made illustrations in their style for an unidentified novel.
Colls: Witt Photo.

WRIGHT, Alan   fl.1889-1925
Painter, illustrator and poet. He was working in Kensington in 1890 and at Burghfield Common, Berkshire after 1914. Wright was an illustrator of children's books and a book decorator of talent. Much of his work is in the style of the woodcut with strong Celtic and Gothic emphasis, he also made designs for eastern subjects. His book, *Climbing in the British Isles* was illustrated by Ellis Carr (q.v.).
Illus: *Queen Victoria's Dolls [1894]; The Wallypug in London [G.E.*

Farrow, 1898]; Adventures in Wallypug Land [1898]; The Little Panjandrum's Dodo [1899]; The Mandarin's Kite [1900].
Contrib: *Pick Me Up [1889]; The Girl's Own Paper [1890-1900]; The Strand Magazine [1891-94, 1906]; The Pall Mall Magazine; The Parade [1897]; The Dome [1897-99]; The Windmill [1899]; Punch [1905].*
Exhib: L; NEA; RA; RBA; ROI.
Bibl: R.E.D. Sketchley, *Eng. Bk. Illus.,* 1903 pp.107, 173.
See Horne

WRIGHT, Anne B.
Illustrated *Sketches Round Bath By An Amateur, Twenty Lithographic Drawings From Original Sketches,* Holloway & Son, Bath, c.1835-40.

WRIGHT, Frank   **fl.1905-1911**
Landscape painter. He worked in London and contributed illustrations of rustic figures to *Punch,* 1905.
Exhib: RA.

WRIGHT, Gilbert S.   **fl.1900-1911**
Figure painter. He worked in Forest Hill, South London and contributed drawings to *The Graphic* 1910-11, Christmas numbers.
Exhib: RA.

WRIGHT, Henry Charles Seppings   **1850-1937**
Painter and Special Artist. He was born in Cornwall in 1850, where his father had a parish and after studying in Paris, worked for *The Pictorial World* from 1883. He joined the staff of *The Illustrated London News* in about 1888 and attended the Ashanti, Grecian, Spanish-American and Balkan wars on behalf of the paper. He was the representative of Armstrong-Whitworth in the Russo-Japanese War of 1904-05 and was on the Russian front in the First World War, 1915-16. He is believed to have contributed caricatures to *Vanity Fair* 1891-1900 under the name of 'Stuff'. He died on 7 February 1937.
Publ: *The Soudan [1896]; With Togo [1906]; Two Years under The Crescent.*
Contrib: *The Graphic [1887]; ILN [1888-1900]; Black & White [1891]; The Boy's Own Paper [1892-93]; The Idler; Chums [1892]; The Pall Mall Magazine; The Sketch; The English Illustrated Magazine [1893-94]; The Sporting and Dramatic News [1896].*
Exhib: L; M; RA; RBA; RI.
Colls: V & AM; Witt Photo.
Bibl: *The Idler,* Vol.11, pp.89-101.

WRIGHT, John Massey OWS   **1777-1866**
Historical painter in watercolours. He was born at Pentonville on 14 October 1777, the son of an organ builder and worked as a piano tuner for Broadwoods. He was acquainted with Thomas Stothard (q.v.) and on settling in London he was introduced to a number of artists and was commissioned to paint scenery for the Strand Panorama and for Covent Garden. He was elected AOWS and OWS in 1824 and set up a fashionable drawing-master's practice in London, also working for the Annuals. He died on 13 May 1866.
Contrib: *The Literary Souvenir [1825-26]; The Amulet [1826-27]; Heath's Gallery [1836].*
Exhib: BI; OWS; RA; RBA.
Colls: Leeds; Manchester; V & AM; Witt Photo.
Bibl: Martin Hardie, *Watercol. Paint. in Brit.* Vol.3, 1968 pp.87-88.

WRIGHT, John William OWS   **1802-1848**
Figure and portrait painter. He was born in London in 1802, the son of the miniature painter John Wright, and was apprenticed to Thomas Phillips, RA. His main work was in supplying historical portraits and scenes to the Annuals, he was elected AOWS in 1831 and OWS in 1841. He died in poor circumstances in 1848.
Contrib: *The National Gallery of Contemporary Portraits [1822]; Heath's Gallery [1836]; Finden's Gallery.*
Exhib: OWS; RA.
Colls: BM; Witt Photo.

WRIGHT, Louise Mrs John W. Wright   **1875-**
Fashion illustrator. She was born at Philadelphia, USA, in 1875 and

married the watercolourist and etcher John Wright, 1857-1933. She also painted portraits, landscapes and still-lifes.
Exhib: Beaux Arts Gall; RA.
Bibl: *LW, The Art of The Illustrator,* ed. P V. Bradshaw, 1916.
See illustrations (colour).

WRIGHTSON, J.   **-1865**
Engraver and illustrator. He worked at Boston and New York between 1854 and 1860 and drew three illustrations for Roscoe's *North Wales,* 1836.
Colls: Witt Photo.

WYATT, Henry   **1794-1840**
Portrait painter. He was born at Thickbroom, Lichfield, on 17 September 1794 and entered the RA Schools in 1812. He studied with Sir Thomas Lawrence before opening his own studio as a portrait painter in Birmingham, Manchester and finally London in 1825. He died at Prestwich on 27 February 1840.
Contrib: *Heath's Gallery [1836-38].*
Exhib: BI; RA; RBA.
Colls: V & AM; Witt Photo.

WYATT, Thomas Henry FSA   **1807-1880**
Architect. He was born in 1807, the brother of Sir Mathew Digby Wyatt. He was President of the RIBA, 1870-73 and Gold Medallist in 1873. He designed theatres and barracks and died in 1880.
Contrib: *Britton's Cathedrals [1832-36].*

WYBURD, Francis John   **1826-**
Genre painter. He was born in London in 1826 and was educated at Lille and studied with the lithographer, T. Fairland. He entered the RA Schools in 1848 and travelled in Italy in the 1850s. His only illustrations were the highly romantic and decorative ones for *The Poetry and Pictures of Thomas Moore* c.1845. He died after 1893. RBA, 1879.
Exhib: BI; L; RA; RBA; ROI.
Colls: Witt Photo.

WYLD, William RI   **1806-1889**
Landscape painter. He was born in London in 1806 and became Secretary to the British Consul at Calais, where he took lessons in watercolours from F.L.T. Francia. He was a friend of Horace Vernet and travelled with him to Italy, Spain and Algiers, and settled in Paris. He was elected ANWS in 1849 and NWS in 1879. He died in Paris in 1889.
Illus: *Voyages Pittoresque dans La Région d'Alger [1833].*
Colls: BM; Fitzwilliam; Searight Coll. at V & AM.

WYLLIE, Charles William or Charlie RBA   **1859-1923**
Marine painter and illustrator. He was born in London on 18 February 1859, the brother of W.L. Wyllie, RA (q.v.). He studied at Leigh's and the RA Schools and concentrated on coastal and genre subjects. He was elected RBA in 1886 and ROI in 1888. He worked in St John's Wood and died there on 28 July 1923.
Contrib: *The Graphic [1881-90]; The Picturesque Mediterranean [1891]; ILN [1893-96]; The Sunday Magazine [1894].*
Exhib: B; G; GG; L; M; New Gall; RA; RBA; ROI.
Colls: BM; V & AM; Witt Photo.

WYLLIE, William Lionel RA   **1851-1931**
Marine painter, illustrator and etcher. He was born in London in July 1851, the brother of C.W. Wyllie, RBA (q.v.) and half-brother of Lionel Percy Smythe (q.v.). He was brought up at Wimereux and studied at Heatherley's and the RA Schools and learnt the art of boat building. His pictures of the Thames Estuary and the shipping of Britain at the height of its Empire are among the most evocative and accurate existing. He was on the staff of *The Graphic* for some years as their marine illustrator and was sent to the United States by them in 1894. He was Marine Painter to the Royal Yacht Squadron, was elected NEA in 1887, ARA in 1889 and RA in 1907. He died on 6 April 1931.
Contrib: *The Graphic [1880-1904].*
Exhib: B; FAS, 1884, 1889, 1892, 1907; G; GG; L; M; NEA; RA; RBA; RE; RHA; RI; ROI.
Colls: BM; Fitzwilliam; Liverpool; Tate; Witt Photo.

YEATS, Jack Butler   RHA   **1871-1957**
Painter, illustrator and caricaturist. He was born in Ireland in 1871, the son of J.B. Yeats, RHA and the brother of W.B. Yeats. He was educated in County Sligo and studied art at South Kensington and at the West London and Westminster Schools of Art. He lived in England from about 1890 to 1898 and concentrated on figure drawing for illustrations. His work at this period is highly inventive and free and among the best of it is the social realism of the East End of London captured magnificently in chalk or ink. His drawing was often criticised at the time for its lack of precision but its ruggedness looks forward to the 1920s and the humour of his sketches for *Fun*, 1901, is very modern in quality. Yeats returned to Ireland in about 1902-03 and concentrated for the remainder of his life on oil paintings. He was elected ARHA in 1915 and RHA in 1916. He sometimes illustrated under the name 'W. Bird'.
Illus: *The Life and Adventures of Captain Singleton [Defoe, 1895]; Romance and Narratives [Defoe, 1900]; Life in the West of Ireland [1912].*
Contrib: *Puck and Ariel [1890]; Chums [1892]; ILN [1892]; The Sketch [1894]; Judy [1895]; The New Budget [1895]; Lika Joko; Punch [1896-1914]; Cassell's Saturday Journal; The Quartier Latin [1898]; The Longbow [1898]; Fun [1901]; The Broadsheet [1902-03]; The Manchester Guardian [1905]; The Broadside [1908-15].*
Exhib: G; L; RA; RHA; ROI.
Colls: Nat. Gall., Ireland; V & AM; Witt Photo.
Bibl: *Modern Book Illustrators and Their Work,* Studio, 1914; C. Neve, *JY; Rider to The Sea,* Country Life, July 30, 1970; *The Dun Emer Press Later The Cuala Press,* 1973; Catalogue of *JBY Early Drawings and Watercolours,* Victor Waddington Gallery, 26 Oct.-18 Nov. 1967.
See Horne
See illustration.

YENDIS, M.
Illustrator. He contributed to *Fun,* 1901.

YOHN, Edmond Charles or YON   **1836-1897**
French landscape painter. He was born in Paris on 2 February 1836 and became a pupil of Pouget and exhibited at the Salon from 1865. He was a talented wood engraver and worked on the illustrations for an edition of Victor Hugo. He died in Paris on 15 March 1897
Contrib: *The Graphic [1905-06].*
Exhib: G.

YORKE, Hon. Eliot Thomas   **1805-1885**
Landscape painter. He was the son of Admiral Sir J.S. Yorke and nephew of Elizabeth, Countess of Hardwicke (q.v.). He was taught watercolour by de Wint and sat as MP for Cambridgeshire, 1854-65.
Illus: *The Wanderer in Western France[G.T. Lowth, 1863].*

JACK BUTLER YEATS 1871-1957. Illustration to *Life in The West of Ireland*, 1912

'YORRICK'
Pseudonym of illustrator of children's books. He illustrated *A Knowing Dog,* Greening, 1908 and contributed to *The Minster* and *The Idler,* 1895.

YOUNG, Austin
Book decorator. He contributed the cover design and title page to *The Sonnet in England and Other Essays* by J.A. Noble for the Bodley Head, 1894.

YOUNG, John   **1755-1825**
Engraver, Mezzotint Engraver to George IV and Keeper of the British Institution. He was one of the founders of the Artists Benevolent Fund.
Illus: *A Series of Portraits of the Emperors of Turkey [Ackermann, 1815].*

YOUNG, William Weston   **fl.1797-1835**
Topographer. He was originally a corn-merchant who settled at Neath in 1797, moving to Newton Nottage in 1806. He was also a coal owner and associated with the Swansea porcelain works.
Illus: *Guide to the Scenery of Glyn Neath [1835].*
Bibl: *The Connoisseur,* Vol.96, 1935 No.407.

YRIARTE, Charles   **1832-1898**
Architectural painter and writer. He was born in Paris on 5 December 1832 and became a pupil of Constant-Dufeux. He died in 1898.

ZANGWILL, Mark **fl.1890-1896**
Rural and domestic illustrator. He may have been a relation of I. Zangwill, the Editor of *Puck and Ariel,* to which he contributed in 1890. He also made drawings for *The English Illustrated Magazine,* 1896.

ZORNLIN, Georgiana Margaretta **1800-1881**
Portrait painter. She was born in 1800 and became a pupil of Benjamin Robert Haydon.
Contrib: *Dennis's Landscape Gardener [1835, AL 13 (liths)].*
Exhib: RA; RBA.
Colls: NPG.

ZWECKER, Johann Baptist **1814-1876**
History painter, illustrator and etcher. He was born at Frankfurt on 18 September 1814 and became a student of the Institute Stadel and worked in Düsseldorf. He settled in London in about 1850 and made numerous illustrations for books and magazines, many of them of natural history subjects. He died in London on 10 January 1876.
Illus: *Wild Sports of the World [J. Greenwood, 1862]; Out on the Pampas [G.A. Henty, 1871; The Child's Zoological Garden [1880]; The Rifle and The Hound in Ceylon [S.W. Baker, 1892].*
Contrib: *ILN [1860-66, 1872 (animals)]; Good Words [1861, 1868]; Wood's Natural History [1862]; The Churchman's Family Magazine [1863]; London Society [1864]; Krilof and His Fables [1867]; North Coast and Other Poems [Buchanan, 1868]; Good Words For The Young [1869-72]; The Graphic [1875].*
Exhib: BI; RA; RBA.
Bibl: Chatto and Jackson, *Treatise on Wood Engraving,* 1861 p.600.

Monograms

BATEMAN, H.M.

BEERBOHM, Max

BRANGWYN, F.W.

BROCK, H.M.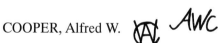

CADENHEAD, James

CLAXTON, Marshall C.

COODE, Miss Helen Hoppner

COOPER, Alfred W.

CORBOULD, Aster Chantrey

CROWQUILL, Alfred

DA COSTA, J.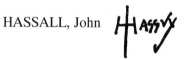

DOLLMAN, J.C.

DOYLE, Richard

EMANUEL, Frank Lewis

ERICHSEN, Nelly

FAIRFIELD, A.R.

FORBES, Elizabeth Adela, née
    Armstrong, Mrs. Stanhope Forbes

FURNISS, Harry

GAVIN, Miss Jessie

GERE, C.M.

GREGORY, Margaret

'GRIP', pseudonym of Alfred BRICE

HASSALL, John

HOOD, George Percy JACOMB-

HOPKINS, Everard

360

HUGHES, Arthur

HOUSMAN, Laurence

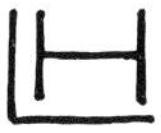

JALLAND, G.H.

JOHNSON, Alfred J.

KEENE, Charles Samuel

LLOYD, Arthur Wynell

LOW, D.

LOWINSKY, Thomas Esmond

LUDOVICI, A.

PARSONS, Alfred

PARTRIDGE, B.

PISSARRO, L.

PRIDE, J.

RUTLAND, V. Duchess of

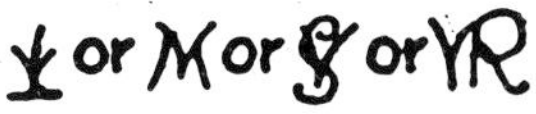

SANDERCOCK, Henry Ardmore

SEM

SOUTHALL, J.E.

STANNARD, H.J.S.

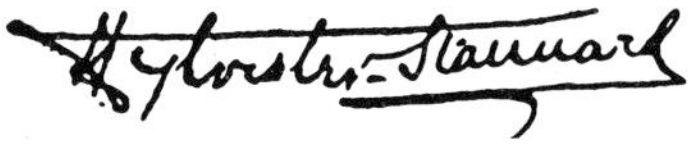

TENNANT, Dorothy, Lady Stanley

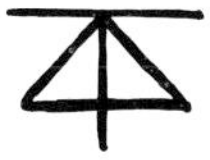

THOMSON, Gordon

WARD, Sir Leslie Matthew 'Spy'

WATSON, John Dawson

YEATS, J.B.

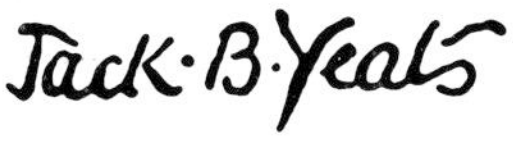

YEEND-KING, L.

Appendix A

*Schools of Illustration**

Birmingham

ARMOUR, Jessie Lamont
BATTEN, John Dixon
BRADLEY, Gertrude M.
BRISCOE, Arthur John Trevor
DAVIS, Louis
FAUX, F.W.
FRANCE, G. Cave (see A. Gaskin)
GASKIN, Arthur
GASKIN, Mrs Arthur
GERE, Charles March
HOLDEN, Evelyn B.
HOLDEN, Violet M.
JONES, S.R.
LEVETUS, Celia
MASON, Fred
METEYARD, Sidney H.
MILLAR, Harold R.
MUCKLEY, L.F.
NEWILL, Mary J.
PAYNE, Henry A.
PEACOCK, Mildred A.
ROBINSON, F. Cayley
RUTLAND, Florence M.
SLEIGH, Bernard
SMITH, Winifred
SOUTHALL, J.E.
TARLING, G.T.
TREGLOWN, E.G.

Glasgow

CAMERON, Katharine
CARTER, D.B.
CHAMBERLAIN, D.
DUNCAN, J.A.
FRENCH, Annie
HAY, Helen
HORNEL, E.A.
KING, Jessie M.
MACBETH, Ann
MACDOUGALL, W.B.
ORR, Monro S.
ORR, Stewart
PARK, Carton Moore
PRYDE, James
SMYTH, Dorothy C.
URQUHART, Annie

*Artists listed may have been influenced by the Schools rather than have attended them as students.

Arts influenced by Aubrey Beardsley

BRADLEY, W.H.
CARMICHAEL, Stewart
CLARKE, Harry
FRENCH, Annie
HYLAND, Fred
JACKSON, F.E.
JAMES, Gilbert
KETTLEWELL, John
MACDOUGALL, W.B.
NIELSEN, Kay
ODLE, A.E.
PLANK, George
SPARE, Austin O.
VOIGHT, H.H.

Artists influenced by Greenaway and Caldecott

ANDRÉ, R.
ANGUS, Christine
EMERSON, H.H.
FARMILOE, Edith
GRAHAM, Winifred
HODGSON, William J.
HOUGHTON, Elizabeth Ellen
SOWERBY, J.G.

Artists influenced by the Chap Book style

ADAMS, W. Dacres
COLMAN-SMITH, Pamela
CRAIG, E. Gordon
CRAWHALL, Joseph
GAVIN, Jessie
HALKETT, George R.
HARDY, Dudley
KAPP, E.X.
NICHOLSON, William
PRYDE, James
ROBERTSON, W. Graham
SIMPSON, Joseph

Appendix B

Specialist Illustration

Fairy Artists

ARMFIELD, Maxwell
BAUERLÉ, Amelia
BILLINGHURST, P.J.
BOYLE, The Hon. Mrs E.V.
BREWTNALL, Edward Frederick
BROCK, H.M.
BRUNTON, W.S.
BYAM SHAW, John
CALTHROP, Dion Clayton
COLLINGWOOD, W.G.
CRANE, Walter
CRUIKSHANK, George
DADD, Richard
DEARMER, Mrs Percy
DOYLE, Charles Altamont
DOYLE, Richard
DULAC, Edmund
EDWARDS, K. Ellen
FITZGERALD, J. Anster
FLAXMAN, Maria
FOLKARD, Charles
FORD, Henry Justice
GANDY, Herbert
GASKIN, Arthur J.
GERE, Charles March
GILBERT, William Schwenk
GOBLE, Warwick
GREENAWAY, Kate
HALSWELLE, Keeley
HARDING, Emily J.
HARRISON, Florence
HASSALL, John
HILL, Vernon
HOLLOWAY, W. Herbert
HOPE, Mrs Adrian C.
HUDSON, Gwynedd M.
HUSKISSON, Robert
JAMES, Gilbert
KNOWLES, H.J.
KNOWLES, R.J.
LANDSEER, Thomas
MAYBANK, Thomas
MILLAR, Harold R.
MONSELL, J.R.
PATON, Sir J. Noël
POGANY, William Andrew

RACKHAM, Arthur
RAILTON, Fanny
RIVINGTON, Reginald
ROBERTSON, W. Graham
ROBINSON, Charles
ROBINSON, Thomas
ROBINSON, W. Heath
ROUNTREE, Harry
SANDERSON, H.
SAVAGE, Reginald
SPEED, Lancelot
STEWART, Allan
STOCK, Henry John
STRATTON, Helen
TARRANT, Margaret Winifred
TORRANCE, James
UPTON, Florence K.
WOODWARD, Alice B.

Special Artists

ANDREWS, G.H.	*ILN*
BELL, Joseph	*ILN*
BULL, René	*Black and White*
CARMICHAEL, J.W.	*ILN*
CORBOULD, Chantrey	*ILN*
GOODMAN, A. Jules	*Pall Mall Gazette*
HALE, E.M.	*ILN*
HALL, Sidney	*Graphic*
HENTY, G.A.	*Standard*
HOUGHTON, A. Boyd	*Graphic*
LANDELLS, Ebenezer	*ILN*
LANDELLS, R.T.	*ILN*
LARSEN, C.C.	*ILN*
LARSON, Axel	*ILN*
MACPHERSON, Douglas	*Sphere*
MATANIA, F.	*Sphere*
MAUD, W.T.	*Graphic*
MAXWELL, Donald	*Graphic*
MENPES, Mortimer	*Black and White*
MONTAGU, Irving	*ILN*
MORGAN, Matt	*Illus. Times*
NAST, J.	Various
NORBURY, E.A.	*Graphic*
PAGET, H.M.	*Sphere*
PELCOQ, Jules	*ILN*
PELLEGRINI, Ricardo	*Graphic*
PORTCH, Julian	*Illus. Times*

PRATER, Ernest	*Black and White*	VIZETELLY, Frank	*ILN*
PRICE, Julius M.	*ILN*	VIZETELLY, Henry	*ILN*
PRIOR, Melton	*ILN*	WAKE, R.	*Graphic*
READ, Samuel	*ILN*	WATERS, D.B.	*Graphic*
RÉGAMEY, F.E.	*ILN*	WHITING, Fred	*Graphic*
SCHONBERG, John	*ILN*	WILLIAMS, I. Sheldon-	*Graphic* and *Sphere*
SHELDON, C.M.	*Black and White*	WILSON, T. Harrington	*ILN*
SIMPSON, William	*ILN*	WILSON, T.W.	*ILN*
SKILL, F.J.	*ILN*	WOLLEN, W.B.	*Graphic*
TEBBY, A.K.	*Graphic*	WOODVILLE, R.C.	*ILN*
VALENTIN, Henry	Various	WRIGHT, H.C. Seppings	*ILN*

Appendix C

Famous Books and Their Illustrators

Alice in Wonderland **by Lewis Carroll**

ATTWELL, Mabel Lucie
CARROLL, Lewis
FURNISS, Henry
MAYBANK, Thomas
POGANY, William Andrew
RACKHAM, Arthur
ROBINSON, Charles
ROBINSON, William Heath
ROUNTREE, Harry
SOWERBY, Millicent
TENNIEL, Sir John
WALKER, W.H.

Black Beauty **by Anna Sewell**

ALDIN, C.
KEMP-WELCH, Lucy
WOODWARD, A.B.

Sherlock Holmes Stories

PAGET, S.E.

Lorna Doone **by R. D. Blackmore**

AUSTIN, J.
BROCK, C.E.
BROWNE, Gordon
CLARK, Chris
SMALL, W.

Peter Pan **by J. M. Barrie**

BLAMPIED, E.
HUDSON, G.M.
RACKHAM, Arthur

The Pilgrim's Progress **by John Bunyan**

BARNARD, F.
BENNETT, C.H.
COPPING, H.
CRUIKSHANK, George
DALZIEL, T.
GILBERT, Sir John
HAMMOND, G.D.
HARVEY, W.
PAPE, Frank
RHEAD, G.W.
ROBINSON, Charles
SCOTT, David
SHIELDS, Frederick
STOTHARD, T.
STRANG, William
SULLIVAN, E.J.
WATSON, John Dawson
WEHNERT, E.

Robsinson Crusoe **by Daniel Defoe**

CRUIKSHANK, George
BROCK, H.M. and C.E.
BROWNE, Gordon

BROWNE, H.K.
DOYLE, R.
FINNEMORE, J.
GILBERT, Sir John
KEENE, Charles
MACQUOID, T.R.
MILLAIS, J.E.
PAGET, W.
THOMAS, George
WATSON, J.D.

The Water Babies by Charles Kingsley

GOBLE, W.
PATON, Sir J.N.
ROBINSON, W.H.
SAMBOURNE, L.

Winnie The Pooh by A.A. Milne

SHEPHERD, E.H.

Illustrators of Dickens

BARNARD, Frederick
BREWER, W.H.
BROCK, C.E.
BROWNE, H.K. 'Phiz'
CATTERMOLE, George
CLARKE, Joseph Clayton 'Kyd'
COOKE, W.C.
CRUIKSHANK, George
DALZIEL, Edward
DOYLE, Richard
FILDES, Luke
FROST, A.B.
FURNISS, H.
GREEN, Charles
GROOME, W.H.C.
LEECH, John
MACLISE, Daniel
MAHONEY, James

NEW, E.H.
PAILTHORPE, F.W.
PEARS, Charles
PINWELL, George
RACKHAM, A.
RAILTON, H.
RALSTON, J. McL.
SEYMOUR, Robert
SIBSON, T.
STANFIELD, William Clarkson
STONE, Frank
STONE, Marcus
TOPHAM, F.W.
WALKER, Fred

Illustrators of Trollope

BROWNE, H.K. 'Phiz'
CRANE, W.
EDWARDS, Mary Ellen
FRASER, F.A.
HOLL, Frank
MILLAIS, John Everett
STONE, Marcus
TAYLOR, E.
THOMAS, George Housman

Illustrators of Kipling

DETMOLD, E.J. & M.
DRAKE, W.H.
EDWARDS, Lionel
HARTRICK, A.S.
KIPLING, J.L.
MILLAR, H.R.
NICHOLSON, Sir W.
RAVEN HILL, L.
ROBINSON, W. Heath
TABER, I.W.
TOWNSEND, F.H.

Bibliography

GENERAL 1800-1850

Abbey, J.R.
Scenery of Great Britain and Ireland In Aquatint And Lithography 1770-1860... from the library of J.R. Abbey, 1952.
Life in England in Aquatint and Lithography 1770-1860... from the library of J.R. Abbey, 1953.
Travel in Aquatint and Lithography 1770-1860... from the library of J.R. Abbey, 2 vols., 1956-57.

Beck, Hilary
Victorian Engravings, Victoria and Albert Museum, 1973.

Darton, F.J. Harvey
Children's Books in England, 1932.

Faxon, F.W.
Literary Annuals and Gift Books, a Bibliography, edited by E. Jamieson and I. Bain, Private Libraries Assoc., 1973.

Hammelmann, Hans & Boase, T.S.R.
Book Illustrators in Eighteenth Century England, 1975.

Harvey, J.R.
Victorian Novelists and Their Illustrators, 1970.

Jerdan, W.
An Autobiography, 4 vols., 1853.

Kitton, F.G.
Dickens and his Illustrators, 1899.

Leslie, C.R.
Autobiographical Recollections, 2 vols., 1860.

Linton, W.J.
Memories, 1895.

Pye, John
Patronage of British Art – An Historical Sketch, 1845.

Raimbach, A.
Memoirs and Recollections... , 1843.

Spielmann, M.H.
The History of 'Punch', 1895.

Vizetelly, Henry
Glances Back Over Seventy Years, 2 vols., 1893.

GENERAL 1860-1875

Casteras, Susan P.
Editor. *Pocket Cathedrals, Pre-Raphaelite Book Illustrations,* Yale Center, 1991.

Dalziel Brothers
A Record of Work, 1840-1890, 1901.

Engen, Rodney
Dictionary of Victorian Wood Engravers, Cambridge, 1985.

Freedmann, W.E.
Pre-Raphaelitism A Bibliographical Study, 1965.

Goldman, Paul
Victorian Illustrated Books 1850-1870, The Heyday of Wood Engraving, 1994.
The Pre-Raphaelite Illustrators and The Idyllic School, A Survey and A Catalogue [to be published 1996].

Hall, N. John
Trollope and His Illustrators, 1980.

Hardie, Martin
Catalogue of Modern Wood-Engravings, Victoria and Albert Museum, 1919.

Houfe, Simon
The Dalziel Family, Engravers and Illustrators, Catalogue, Sotheby's Belgravia, 16th May, 1978.

Layard, G.S.
Tennyson and His Pre-Raphaelite Illustrators, 1894.

Reid, Forrest
Illustrators of the Sixties, 1928.

Sparrow, W.S.
Book Illustration of the Sixties, 1939.

Tinsley, W.
Random Recollections, 1900.

White, Gleeson
English Illustration 'The Sixties' 1857-70, 1897.

GENERAL 1890s

Franklin, Colin
Private Presses, A Bibliography, 1969.

Hartrick, A.S.
Painter's Pilgrimage Through Fifty Years, 1939.

Houfe, Simon
Fin de Siècle, The Illustrators of the Nineties, 1992.

Jackson, Holbrook
The Eighteen-Nineties, A Review of Art and Ideas At the Close of the Nineteenth Century, 1913.

Krishnamurti, G.
The Eighteen-Nineties – A Literary Exhibition, National Book League, 1973.

Ludovici, A.
An Artist's Life in London and Paris, 1926.

Pennell, Joseph
Pen Drawing and Pen Draughtsmen, 1889.
Modern Illustration, 1895.
The Illustration of Books, 1896.

Sketchley, R.E.D.
English Book Illustration of Today, 1903.

Taylor, John Russell
The Art Nouveau Book in Britain, 1966.

Thorpe, James
English Illustration of the Nineties, 1935.

CARICATURE

Ashbee, C.R.
Caricature, 1928.

Ashton, John
English Caricature and Satire on Napoleon I, 1888.

Brinton, Selwyn
The 18th Century in English Caricature, 1904.

Buss, R.W.
English Graphic Satire, 1874. Privately printed.

Davies, Randall
Editor. *Caricature of Today*, Studio, 1928.

Everitt, Graham
English Caricaturists and Graphic Humorists of the Nineteenth Century, 1893.

Feaver, William
Masters of Caricature from Hogarth and Gillray to Scarfe and Levine, 1981.

George, M. Dorothy
British Museum Catalogue of Political and Personal Satires, Vols. V-XI, 1935-1954.
English Political Caricature, 2 vols., 1959.

Hofmann, Werner
Caricature from Leonardo to Picasso, 1957.

Klingender, F.D.
Hogarth and English Caricature, 1944.

Low, David
British Cartoonists, Caricaturists and Comic Artists, 1942.

Lynch, Bohun
History of Caricature, 1927.

Malcolm, J.P.
Historical Sketch of the Art of Caricaturing, 1813.

Parton, James
Caricature and Other Comic Art, 1878.

Paston, George
Social Caricature in the 18th Century, 1905.

Veth, Cornelis
Comic Art in England, 1930.

Wright, Thomas
Caricature History of the Georges, 1867.

TECHNICAL

Dyson, Anthony
Pictures to Print, The Nineteenth Century Engraving Trade, 1984.

Hardie, Martin
English Coloured Books, 1906.

Lewis, C.T.C.
The Story of Picture Printing in England during the Nineteenth Century, 1928.

Lister, Raymond
Prints and Printmaking... A Handbook of The Art In The Nineteenth Century, 1984.

McLean, Ruari
Victorian Book Design and Colour Printing, 1963.
Joseph Cundall, A Victorian Publisher, 1976.
Victorian Publishers' Book-Bindings In Paper, 1983.

Sullivan, E.J.
Line An Art Study, 1921.
The Art of Illustration, 1922.

Wakeman, Geoffrey
Victorian Book Illustration – The Technical Revolution, 1973.

SURVEYS

Bland, David
A History of Book Illustration – The Illuminated Manuscript and The Printed Book, 1958.

Bliss, D.P.
A History of Wood Engraving, 1928.

Chatto, W.A. & Jackson
A Treatise On Wood Engraving, 1839, enlarged 1861.

Crane, Walter
Of The Decorative Illustration of Books Old and New, 1896.

Dyos, H.J. & Wolff
The Victorian City, 1973.

Du Maurier, G.
Social Pictorial Satire, 1898.

Hogarth, Paul
The Artist As Reporter, 1967.

Jackson, Mason
The Pictorial Press Its Origins and Progress, 1885.

James, Philip
English Book Illustration 1800-1900, 1947.

Mahony, B.E., Latimer, L.P., Folmsbee, B.
Illustrators of Children's Books 1744-1945, 1947 & 1970.

Muir, Percy
Victorian Illustrated Books, 1971.

Peppin, B.
Fantasy Book Illustration, 1975.

Peppin, Brigid & Mickelthwait
Dictionary of British Book Illustrators The Twentieth Century, 1983.

Price, R.G.G.
A History of 'Punch', 1957.

Ray, Gordon N.
The Illustrator And The Book in England From 1790 to 1914, Pierpont Morgan Library, 1976.

Slythe, R. Margaret
The Art of Illustration 1750-1900, Library Association, 1970.

*Bibliographies of individual artists will be found in their Dictionary entries.

THE COMIC ALMANACK

MAY JUNE JUL AUG
APRI
MAR SEP
FEB OCT
JAN NOV
DEC

EDITED BY HORACE MAYHEW & Illustrated BY George Cruikshank

1848. ONE SHILLING.

DAVID BOGUE, 86 FLEET STREET.

Vizetelly Brothers and Co Printers and Engravers, 135 Fleet Street.